MONTVALE PUBLIC LIBRARY   254

driksen, John C.
volutionary War
almanac.

ALMANACS OF AMERICAN WARS

REVOLUTIONARY WAR ALMANAC

John C. Fredriksen

Revolutionary War Almanac

Copyright © 2006 by John C. Fredriksen

All rights reserved. No part of this book may be reproduced or utilized in any form or by any means, electronic or mechanical, including photocopying, recording, or by any information storage or retrieval systems, without permission in writing from the publisher. For information contact:

Facts On File, Inc.
An imprint of Infobase Publishing
132 West 31st Street
New York NY 10001

Library of Congress Cataloging-in-Publication Data

Fredriksen, John C.
   Revolutionary War almanac / John C. Fredriksen. — 1st ed.
     p. cm.—(Almanacs of American wars)
   Includes bibliographical references and index.
   ISBN 0-8160-5997-7 (hardcover: alk. paper)
   1. United States—History—Revolution, 1775–1783. 2. United States—History—Revolution, 1775–1783—Miscellanea. 3. Almanacs, American. I. Title. II. Series.
   E208.F725 2006
   973.3'3—dc22   2005007333

Facts On File books are available at special discounts when purchased in bulk quantities for businesses, associations, institutions or sales promotions. Please call our Special Sales Department in New York at (212) 967-8800 or (800) 322-8755.

You can find Facts On File on the World Wide Web at http://www.factsonfile.com

Text design by Erika K. Arroyo
Cover design by Pehrsson Design
Maps by Jeremy Eagle

Printed in the United States of America

VB FOF 10 9 8 7 6 5 4 3 2 1

This book is printed on acid-free paper.

Contents

Introduction iv

Chronology 1

Historical Dictionary A–Z 241

Appendix 713
 Maps 713

Bibliography 734

Index 743

Introduction

The Revolutionary War, a seminal event in human history, forever altered the political, ideological, and philosophical outlook of national governance. What began as a protest against taxes in 1765 multiplied exponentially over the ensuing decade into full-scale rebellion against parliamentary missteps and misrule. Nor should it be understated that more than a year lapsed before the struggling American polity severed cherished economic, social, and emotional ties with Britain. It fell upon a brilliant clique of radicals in Philadelphia to finally declare, with an eloquence that still resonates, that they were no longer colonies but a sovereign people newly emergent among the community of nations. Hostilities ended eight years later with the birth of a new republic, founded for the first time upon both classical and Enlightenment precepts. This new entity, the United States of America, would gradually wield an indelible impact upon world affairs. Its intrinsic idealism, posited as self-evident in the Declaration of Independence, ultimately transcended the thunderous fields of Lexington and Yorktown to command a dominant place on the stage of human events. Historically speaking, the Revolution's genesis, course, and conclusion are well known and need no recounting here, yet they nonetheless remain an intriguing topic of scholarly research and wellsprings of enlightenment and inspiration.

The book you hold is designed to highlight the military facets surrounding this conflict, with extensive coverage granted to the leading players involved and several of the more significant battles. Many lesser lights, including militia leaders, individual soldiers and scouts, Loyalists, and Native Americans—figures usually on the periphery of military concerns—are also present, to lend added breadth to its content. But, as a reference work, I cast a large net intellectually and also extended coverage to select social, political, and diplomatic considerations, such as treaties, African Americans, and women. In this manner, the totality of the Revolutionary War, 1763–83, with its rich tapestry of causation, people, and events, can be investigated with questions answered and inquiries directed. But, more than anything else, I proffer it as an intellectual counterweight to the egregious misconceptions and contrived villainies depicted in movies such as *The Patriot* (2000). Thoroughly researched and painstakingly objective, the *Revolutionary War Almanac* portrays the military equations of both sides—all sides—in a more accurate and, hence, truthful light.

In essaying this task I chose a relatively conventional format of two distinct but integral parts. The first consists of a near-daily almanac of happenings. Subject content varies as to the events recorded, but where more than one occurrence is listed on a given day, the invariable order is politics/diplomacy, North, South, West,

Caribbean, and, finally, naval. The second part of this book contains an alphabetical listing of 368 topical essays, each ranging in length from 500 to 2,000 words. All entries are uniform in style and consist of a title, dates, position, text, and bibliography. Cross-references, where relevant, are indicated by small capital letters. Biographies are specifically written to provide useful background information such as birth and death dates, background and education, followed by discussion of wartime contributions and a summation of postwar activities. Historical events such as acts of Congress and Parliament, or military battles, present background information for greater context, a main descriptive body, and usually a brief summary of significance. As noted previously, this is a military almanac thematically, and the bulk of the contents addresses army and naval issues as they impacted events from 1775 to 1783. However, important legislation such as the Stamp Act, nonmilitary occurrences like the "battle" of Golden Hill, and major political activities such as committees of correspondence are also present.

Revolutionary War almanacs are abundant on library shelves, but most are out of date and usually lack bibliographical citations for further inquiry. Where references do exist they invariably consist of books and periodical articles that are themselves decidedly dated. In contrast, I feel it incumbent as a reference-book author to assist prospective users by citing only the very latest scholarship available—since older materials are usually listed in their bibliographies anyway. I achieved this through extensive topical searches of the Library of Congress and WorldCat Web sites, along with forays through numerous periodical databases available at any college library. Inquiring minds are thereby exposed to relevant books and articles, along with varied sources such as master's theses and doctoral dissertations. Readers thus have the fullest and most recent intellectual discourse on any given subject at their disposal. Furthermore, I append a detailed bibliography of the very latest Revolutionary War publications, 2000–05, with materials that would not logically fit elsewhere, to supplement literature already cited in the essays. These two compilations, mutually exclusive, very much render this tome a reference source for 21st-century scholars.

Another distinctive feature of this almanac is its emphasis on proper visuals. The library market is replete with reference titles that perennially utilize worn-out woodblock engravings (book illustrations) from the 19th century. These materials, while significant in their day, look dated and suggest a lack of earnestness on behalf of book designers. To counter such a pervasive malaise, no effort was spared in combing the great picture libraries of England, Scotland, Canada, and the United States to secure requisite portraits and paintings. The result is a stunning survey of contemporary military and naval uniforms, along with their intrinsic artistic technique. For devotees of British military history, this is also the first Revolutionary War book where portraits of important leaders such as Alexander Leslie, Hugh Percy, Francis Rawdon, and Alexander Stewart appear together in one volume. The same principle applies to traditionally neglected Revolutionary War portraiture, such as naval leaders, the French, and Native Americans, where possible. Simply perusing the pages treats even untutored eyes to splendid portraits by Gainsborough, Reynolds, Peale, Stuart, and other contemporary masters. Collectively, they render an otherwise dour reference source appealing and interesting simply by browsing through. This emphasis on military art is the facet of my work that I find most satisfying.

The *Revolutionary War Almanac* will go far in promoting comprehension of the numerous personalities and complex variables inherent in so wide-ranging a conflict. Great lengths were taken to afford users the most complete military coverage possible, combined with the latest scholarship and simply sumptuous illustrations. There has never been a military almanac like it on this conflict anywhere and, hence, it resides in a class by itself. I extend thanks to my editor, Owen Lancer, for suggesting the title to me. Arduous in conception and exacting in execution, this book proved both a challenge to compile and a learning experience to write; I am certainly a better historian because of it.

—John C. Fredriksen, Ph.D.

Chronology

1763

February 10
DIPLOMACY: The Treaty of Paris is signed in Paris, France, concluding the Seven Years' War and its New World corollary, the French and Indian War. Victorious Great Britain acquires all of Canada, in addition to Florida and the Caribbean islands of Tobago, Dominica, Grenada, and St. Vincent. Spain, under a separate arrangement, receives New Orleans and all lands west of the Mississippi River, in addition to Cuba and the Philippines. However, Britain's fiscal ability to garrison and administer such far-flung gains is compromised by national debts approaching £130,000,000. It falls upon Chancellor of the Exchequer George Grenville to seek previously untapped revenues and defray the cost of governing these newest acquisitions. Unknown at the time, removal of the French threat to North America also triggers a profound reevaluation of colonial perceptions toward Great Britain, from that of protector and benefactor to oppressor.

April 27
WEST: A gathering of disaffected Ottawa, Ojibway, and Pottawatomie chiefs confers near Detroit to protest English encroachment on their lands, and a loose military confederation is formed under the aegis of Ottawa chief Pontiac. The tribes eventually adopt his plan for a wide-ranging, simultaneous assault on British forts along the frontier.

May 7
WEST: Chief Pontiac leads a large-scale uprising against British-held Detroit but fails to capture the fort. A lengthy and costly siege ensues until relief forces arrive months later. This act also signals the beginning of what the English come to regard as "Pontiac's Conspiracy." The campaign is initially highly successful and comes close to eliminating Britain's presence in the Old Northwest.

June 2
WEST: A large throng of Indians stage a lacrosse game outside Fort Michilimackinac, Michigan, and entreat the British garrison to step outside and watch. At a given signal the warriors arm themselves with hidden weapons, rush the fort, and massacre the garrison.

August 4–6
WEST: Pontiac, having handily defeated a British force pressing for the relief of Fort Pitt, attacks another column commanded by Colonel Henry Bouquet at Bushy Run.

The Indians are driven off by a determined bayonet charge and the fort is successfully relieved. Pontiac's rebellion, which commenced with impressive coordination and devastating results, begins unraveling.

October 7
POLITICS: To circumvent future Indian hostility, King George III signs the Proclamation of 1763 forbidding colonial settlements west of a demarcation line drawn along the Appalachian Mountains. Moreover, future land grants and surveying activities are expressly outlawed. Settlers already established west of that line are supposed to withdraw back to British territory. These measures are evoked to placate Native Americans and preclude the outbreak of future hostility. But, as a sop to future colonial expansion, the new colonies of Quebec and East and West Florida are also organized. Many colonials nonetheless regard the act as an arbitrary obstacle to westward expansion and resent imperial interference.

October 30
WEST: Pontiac, abandoned by his Pottawatomie, Ojibway, and Wyandot allies, abandons the siege of Detroit and withdraws his Ottawa clansmen to the Miami River.

November 16
NORTH: General Thomas Gage, a distinguished veteran of the French and Indian War, is appointed commander in chief of British forces in North America, with headquarters at New York.

December 2
POLITICS: In a major shift of territorial policy, the British government instructs colonial governors to first acquire approval before designating land grants in or near Indian-held regions.

1764

April 5
POLITICS: Parliament passes the American Revenue Act, better known as the Sugar Act, the first measure intended to levy revenues from the colonies. Henceforth, duties are doubled on sugar, wine, coffee, textiles, and other imported commodities. This expedient is expected to raise £200,000 per year and help subsidize the maintenance of army garrisons on the western frontier. To better ensure enforcement of the Navigation Acts and suppression of widespread smuggling, the act also authorizes the dispatching of customs agents and collectors. This legislation marks a shift in relations with the homeland from strictly commercial to increasingly revenue-oriented. Worse, from colonial perspectives, the measure transfers legal matters from civil courts to the Vice-Admiralty courts in Halifax, Nova Scotia, thereby negating time-honored traditions of trial by jury.

April 19
POLITICS: Parliament authorizes the Currency Act, through which all colonies are forbidden from issuing paper money. This was enacted to control the inflationary tendencies associated with such tender, and it assuages British creditor fears of being

paid with depreciated script. Colonists, however, resent the destabilizing effect and arbitrary hardships it inflicts on domestic commercial activity.

May 24
NORTH: James Otis advances the concept of "taxation without representation" during a protest in a Boston town meeting and urges a united colonial response to denounce it.

June 12
NORTH: The Massachusetts General Court establishes a committee of correspondence to coordinate grievances over the Sugar Act with other colonies.

July 23
NORTH: James Otis publishes *The Rights of the British Colonies Asserted and Proved,* a polemic against the concept of taxation without representation, and urges local merchants to initiate boycotts of English goods.

November 17
WEST: Chief Pontiac concludes his rebellion by surrendering to British forces near the Muskingum River, Ohio.

1765

February 5
DIPLOMACY: Benjamin Franklin and other colonial agents meet in London to protest the impending stamp tax before Prime Minister George Grenville. They are cordially received but otherwise ignored.

March 22
POLITICS: The Stamp Act, whose provisions will be enacted as law on November 1, is authorized by King George III. This statute imposes fees on such widely varied items as legal documents, newspapers, and almanacs, along with gambling impedimenta like playing cards and dice. Said items are required to bear an official stamp signifying that the tax has been paid. Again, all revenues accrued will defray up to one-third the cost of garrisoning and protecting the colonies. It also authorizes violators of the act to appear before juryless Admiralty courts. Thus, for the first time in 150 years, Parliament imposes a direct levy upon its North American colonies. Moreover, said revenues will not be paid to local legislatures but directly to English coffers. Unforeseen at the time, this action will trigger unprecedented and unified resistance from a broad spectrum of merchants, lawyers, publishers, land owners, and shipbuilders throughout the colonies.

March 24
POLITICS: The Quartering Act, requested by General Thomas Gage to assist the garrisoning and provisioning of British troops, is approved by Parliament. The law mandates that, in the absence of barracks, the colonial legislatures must subsidize shelter and sustenance for British soldiers over a two-year period. Fixed prices are also stipulated for provisions and services provided to the troops.

May 29
SOUTH: Patrick Henry, in a fiery diatribe, strongly denounces British tax policy and introduces the Seven Virginia Resolves into the House of Burgesses. The fifth resolution unflinchingly demands that only colonial legislatures—not Parliament—have the right to impose taxes on their own citizens. When interrupted by cries of "treason!" Henry boldly declares to fellow delegates that "if this be treason, make the most of it." The house subsequently passes the Virginia Resolves to protest the Stamp Act and its implicit notion of taxation without representation. Henry and his supporters depart on May 30, whereupon the remaining members vote to rescind the fifth resolve. However, all motions are printed and circulated throughout the colonies.

June 6
NORTH: The General Court of Massachusetts, at the behest of James Otis, dispatches a circular letter throughout the colonies proposing an intercolonial congress to meet and formally protest the Stamp Act.

July 10
POLITICS: George Grenville resigns as chancellor of the Exchequer and prime minister. His replacement is Charles Watson-Wentworth, marquess of Rockingham, a figure far more sympathetic toward colonial sensibilities.

August 13
NORTH: The Boston office of stamp master (tax collector) Andrew Oliver is destroyed by rioters orchestrated by the Sons of Liberty. Furthermore, he is hung in effigy on a tree at the corner of Essex and Washington Streets, which subsequently becomes hailed as the Liberty Tree. When Lieutenant Governor Thomas Hutchinson arrives to calm the mob, he is stoned and beats a hasty retreat. Royal Governor Francis Bernard likewise seeks refuge in a fort within Boston Harbor.

August 15
NORTH: A deputation of citizens forcefully convinces Andrew Oliver to resign as stamp master.

August 26
NORTH: The home of Lieutenant Governor Thomas Hutchinson of Massachusetts is torched by a mob protesting the Stamp Act. The Sons of Liberty later sack the Vice-Admiralty court and burn the records.

September 16–17
NORTH: Violence against Stamp Tax officials spreads to Philadelphia.

October 7–25
NORTH: The Stamp Act Congress convenes at City Hall, New York, to protest Britain's arbitrary taxation of the colonies. Present are 28 delegates from nine colonies. They debate and pass 13 resolutions, insisting upon preserving their rights as Englishmen, especially trial by jury. John Dickinson also pens his *Declaration of Rights and Grievances,* while others directly petition the king for redress. The delegates subsequently demand the Stamp Act's repeal, reiterate their belief that only local legislatures have the right to impose taxes, and threaten nonimportation of British goods in retaliation. The congress establishes a historic precedent for collective action by

heretofore disjointed colonial assemblies. While the Stamp Act Congress in New York adjourns, the Massachusetts General Court passes its own resolutions reaffirming the rights of colonists.

October 28
NORTH: Merchants in New York City promulgate a nonimportation strategy to boycott British goods until the Stamp Act is revoked. Other port cities quickly follow suit as the protest gathers momentum.

November 1
NORTH: The Stamp Act officially goes into effect while mobs attack colonial courts and tax officials in New York. The unrest neatly coincides with Guy Fawkes day celebrations, memorializing the thwarting of an attempt in 1605 to destroy the House of Parliament with gunpowder.

December 9
NORTH: Some 250 Boston merchants participate in nonimportation, leading to steep declines in exports from Great Britain. A merchant's committee is subsequently established in Parliament to agitate for the Stamp Act's repeal.

December 13
NORTH: General Thomas Gage, as commander in chief, formally requests the New York assembly to raise the necessary revenues stipulated by the Quartering Act.

1766

January 17
POLITICS: London merchants, reeling from colonial nonimportation, petition Parliament to repeal the Stamp Act. They are joined in their opposition by William Pitt and other leading Whigs on the basis of no taxation without representation.

February 13
DIPLOMACY: Benjamin Franklin, as colonial agent for Pennsylvania, testifies before Parliament over the hardships incurred by the Stamp Act. Furthermore, he cautions that using the British military to enforce the tax might spark armed resistance.

February 22
POLITICS: The House of Commons, on a vote of 276 to 168, responds favorably to colonial unrest and repeals the Stamp Act. William Pitt lauds the colonies for opposing taxes levied by a body in which they lack representation.

March 17
POLITICS: The Stamp Act is rescinded by the House of Lords in a victory for colonial interests. The numerous petitions of British merchants, hurt by nonimportation, is another major factor in its repeal.

March 18
POLITICS: Parliament, at the behest of Prime Minister Charles Watson-Wentworth, marquess of Rockingham, reaffirms its authority over the colonies through the

Declaratory Act. More than a face-saving expedient, this extends that legislature's authority to influence colonial matters "in all cases whatsoever." It also declares that colonial legislation that questioned parliamentary prerogatives was "utterly null and void." The document diplomatically skirts the issue of taxation for the time being, but this issue will be raised again—backed by military force. The imperial government also uses this measure to further tighten existing trade laws through the new American Board of Customs Commissioners.

April 7
North: General Guy Carleton is appointed lieutenant governor-general of Canada.

April 26
North: News of the Stamp Act repeal triggers widespread celebration throughout the colonies, especially in Massachusetts, and the boycott of English goods wanes.

July 24
West: Chief Pontiac confers with British forces at Oswego, New York, and concludes a peace treaty with Indian superintendent Sir William Johnson.

November 1
Politics: In another political retreat, Parliament withdraws a duty on the import of foreign molasses. However, colonial products intended for northern Europe now have to be cleared through British ports in advance.

December 6
North: The Massachusetts assembly passes compensation for victims of Stamp Act violence, but the offenders also receive pardons.

December 15–19
North: The New York assembly refuses to provide revenues for the Quartering Act and is suspended by Governor Henry Moore.

1767

June 6
North: Governor Henry Moore reconvenes the New York assembly after a six-month impasse, having been assured that the Quartering Act will be approved and funding provided.

June 29
Politics: Chancellor of the Exchequer Charles Townshend prevails upon Parliament to pass the Revenue Act, more popularly known as the Townshend Duties. This imposes taxes on glass, lead, paint, paper, and tea imported by the colonies. Four additional Vice-Admiralty courts are then created with juryless jurisdiction over accused violators. Moreover, funds raised will be used to pay the salaries of colonial officials, rendering them independent of colonial legislatures. A Board of Customs Commissioners is also subsequently established in Boston to help eradicate widespread smuggling.

August 10
NORTH: While the New York assembly debates paying for the Quartering Act as requested by General Thomas Gage, the Sons of Liberty begin actively protesting in the street. This leads to the first of many violent clashes with British troops over the erection of a "Liberty Pole."

September 4
POLITICS: Lord Frederick North succeeds Charles Townshend as chancellor of the Exchequer.

October 1
POLITICS: Parliament passes the Suspending Act, which dissolves the New York colonial assembly for refusing to facilitate provisions of the Quartering Act.

October 28
NORTH: A Boston town meeting protests imposition of the Townshend Duties by drawing up a list of British luxuries to be boycotted. The resumption of nonimportation is subsequently adopted by merchants in Providence and Newport, Rhode Island, and in New York.

November 5
NORTH: The first American Board of Customs Commissioners arrives in Boston.

November 20
POLITICS: The Townshend Duties take effect although their author, Charles Townshend, never lives to see their implementation—or ramifications.

December 2
NORTH: John Dickinson anonymously pens 12 *Letters from a Farmer in Pennsylvania to the Inhabitants of the British Colonies* in the *Pennsylvania Chronicle* to protest the Townshend Duties. The author acknowledges Parliament's authority to regulate commerce but posits that levying external taxes is unconstitutional. He also warns that suspending the New York assembly is an implicit threat to all colonial liberties.

1768

February 11
DIPLOMACY: Benjamin Franklin receives appointment as colonial agent for Georgia in London.
NORTH: Samuel Adams and James Otis pen a circular letter addressed to colonial assemblies informing them of Massachusetts's resistance to the Townshend Duties and renewing calls for a unified colonial response. The letter acknowledges Parliament's authority over the colonies but reiterates dissent over its ability to tax them without representation. It further warns that governors and judges are growing increasingly independent from local legislatures.

April 22
Politics: Lord Hillsborough, secretary of state for the colonies, orders colonial governors to prevent circular letters from being drafted by their own assemblies. He also orders Massachusetts governor Francis Bernard to dissolve the general court if it refuses to retract its circular letter.

May 8
Politics: Benjamin Franklin, then in London, publishes a British edition of John Dickinson's *Letters from a Farmer in Pennsylvania*. It acquires a large readership and a further edition appears in French.

May 16
South: The Virginia House of Burgesses composes a circular letter advocating joint action with other colonies in the face of any British attempt to "enslave" them. It also mandates a "hearty union" among the colonies in the face of growing tyranny.

May 17
North: The 50-gun warship HMS *Romney* docks in Boston Harbor as a symbol of Britain's determination to protect customs officials and enforce parliamentary dictates.

June 6
North: The New York assembly finally complies with provisions of the Quartering Act and votes £3,000 to support the British army under General Thomas Gage.

June 10
North: John Hancock's sloop *Liberty* is seized by Comptroller Benjamin Hallowell and Collector Joseph Harrison for failing to pay duties on a cargo of Madeira wine. The vessel is subsequently towed from the wharf and anchored alongside the warship HMS *Romney*. A mob organized by the Sons of Liberty subsequently attacks customs officials on the dock. After much legal wrangling, the *Liberty* is eventually returned to Hancock on March 25, 1769.

June 21
North: Royal governor Francis Bernard, in fulfillment of Lord Hillsborough's instructions, demands that the Massachusetts General Court rescind its circular letter.

June 30
North: In an act of defiance, the Massachusetts General Court refuses to rescind its circular letter, on a vote of 92 to 17. An angry Governor Francis Bernard dissolves the legislature in consequence.

August 15
North: Boston merchants enact a new nonimportation policy against British goods while Samuel Adams and James Otis orchestrate noisy celebrations on the anniversary of riots against Andrew Oliver and the Stamp Act.

August 27
NORTH: New York merchants follow Boston's example and adopt strict nonimportation of British goods unless the Townshend Duties are canceled.

September 13
NORTH: Twenty-six Massachusetts towns dispatch delegates to attend a convention called in protest of the closing of the assembly and the Townshend Duties. Governor Francis Bernard refuses to discuss the pending arrival of additional British troops in Boston.

September 23–29
NORTH: A provincial convention, meeting as an extralegal body, convenes in Boston to discuss the closing of the assembly and the Townshend Duties, among other grievances. Present are 70 representatives from 66 towns and districts, and these petition Governor Francis Bernard to restore the legislature.

October 1
NORTH: Two British infantry regiments, the 14th West Yorks and the 29th Worcesters, transfer from the garrison at Halifax, Nova Scotia, ostensibly to help customs officials enforce the law. They are actually there to raise the military profile of imperial authority–it is anticipated that this show of strength will awe the opposition into compliance. The troops initially encamp on Boston Common but eventually settle in privately owned warehouses and facilities rented from citizens.

October 26
NORTH: General Guy Carleton arrives and assumes responsibilities as governor-general of Canada.

1769

March 10
NORTH: Philadelphia merchants agree to support the nonimportation movement until the Townshend Duties are revoked and also ban all British imports after April 1.

March 30
SOUTH: Baltimore merchants resort to nonimportation of British goods until the Townshend Duties are revoked.

May 7
SOUTH: A set of nonimportation resolutions, the Virginia Resolves, is drafted by George Mason and introduced into the House of Burgesses by George Washington. These reassert that the colony's legislature is the sole authority on the issue of imposing taxes and are unanimously adopted. A petition to the king, enunciating these same principles, is subsequently penned by Patrick Henry and Richard H. Lee.

May 17
SOUTH: The Virginia House of Burgesses is dissolved after rejecting Parliament's authority to tax the colonies without representation. Members subsequently convene at the Raleigh Tavern in Williamsburg as an extralegal body and promulgate

the Virginia Association to enforce the boycott of British goods, luxury items, and slaves. Other colonies follow suit with similar measures.

June 22
SOUTH: The nonimportation movement gathers additional steam when a convention held at Annapolis, Maryland, lends its support to the movement.

June 27
NORTH: King George III is petitioned by the Massachusetts House of Representatives to remove Governor Francis Bernard.

July 31
NORTH: Chief Justice Thomas Hutchinson is tapped to replace outgoing Francis Bernard as acting governor of Massachusetts. The former executive resigns from office and sails from Boston to England amid raucous celebrations.

September 5
NORTH: An altercation erupts between James Otis and Tory commissioner John Robinson over an alleged slight in a Boston coffeehouse. Otis sustains a head injury that effectively ends his public career.

October 12
NORTH: The New Jersey assembly adopts nonimportation agreements previously espoused by New York and Pennsylvania merchants.

October 28
NORTH: Boston printers John Mein and John Fleeming, whose ads impugned Samuel Adams and listed the names of merchants continuing to import British goods, are attacked by the Sons of Liberty on King Street.

December 16
NORTH: Alexander McDougall, head of the New York Sons of Liberty, anonymously publishes *A Son of Liberty to the Betrayed Inhabitants of the City and Colony of New York*. It is immediately condemned as an incendiary and seditious document.

1770

January 16
NORTH: British soldiers provocatively hew down the Liberty Pole in New York City and pile its remains in front of a tavern known to be frequented by the Sons of Liberty.

January 19–20
NORTH: The so-called Battle of Golden Hill erupts between British soldiers and the Sons of Liberty after the former cut down a new Liberty Pole in the Golden Hill section of Manhattan, New York. One man is killed and several injured.

January 22
NORTH: In light of escalating tensions on the streets of New York, British soldiers are confined to barracks unless accompanied by an officer.

January 31
POLITICS: Lord Frederick North formally assumes responsibilities as prime minister of England and lends his support to repealing the Townshend Duties.
NORTH: A proposed boycott of tea receives public support from 500 Boston women.

February 8
NORTH: Alexander McDougall, leading the Sons of Liberty in New York, is arrested for having published a broadside deemed hostile to the colonial assembly. He subsequently refuses to post bond and remains behind bars until his trial.

February 22
NORTH: When Loyalist Ebenezer Richardson is attacked by a mob of Bostonians, he fires a gun into the crowd, killing an 11-year-old boy. A Boston jury subsequently finds him guilty of murder.

March 5
NORTH: The Boston Massacre unfolds in a midnight confrontation when a mob begins lobbing stones at a British guard under Captain Thomas Preston, which returns fire. Five colonials are killed, including African-American Crispus Attucks, with a further eight wounded. This violent clash, effectively propagandized by Paul Revere, functions as a catalyst for mounting resistance to British rule.

April 12
POLITICS: In another victory for colonial intransigence, Parliament, bombarded by complaints from British merchants suffering under nonimportation, concedes that the Townshend Duties have failed and repeals them. The Quartering Act is also allowed to expire without renewal. Ironically, to underscore Parliament's intrinsic ability to tax the colonies without consent, Prime Minister Lord Frederick North preserves the existing levy on tea. Nonetheless, the nonimportation movement in the colonies begins to unravel.

July 7
NORTH: The New York assembly votes to suspend nonimportation of all British goods except tea.

July 25
NORTH: Alexander McDougall leads protests against the suspension of nonimportation by the New York assembly.

October 24–30
NORTH: Captain Thomas Preston, charged with deaths at the Boston Massacre, is successfully defended at his trial by John Adams and Josiah Quincy, Jr. He nevertheless receives personal threats and seeks refuge in Castle Williams, Boston Harbor.

November 27–December 5
NORTH: Of eight British soldiers tried for their involvement in the Boston Massacre, six are acquitted and two found guilty of manslaughter. Privates Matthew Kilroy and Hugh Montgomery are consequently branded on the thumb and released.

December 13
NORTH: Alexander McDougall is imprisoned for contempt by New York authorities.

1771

January 15
SOUTH: The North Carolina assembly passes the so-called Bloody Act, which equates riotous behavior with treason. It is aimed at lawless settlers supporting regulator activity on the western frontier.

March 14
NORTH: Thomas Hutchinson is appointed royal governor of Massachusetts. He will be the last civilian authority to head the unruly colony.

March 19
SOUTH: Governor William Tryon of North Carolina mobilizes the militia to protect judicial proceedings held at Hillsboro from attacks by backcountry "regulators."

May 9
SOUTH: A force of 243 North Carolina militia under General Hugh Waddell departs Salisbury to join Governor William Tryon at Hillsboro, but en route he encounters a much larger force of regulators and withdraws.

May 11
SOUTH: Governor William Tryon marches from New Bern toward Hillsboro, North Carolina, with 1,200 militia and several cannon.

May 16
SOUTH: Governor William Tryon and 1,200 militiamen crush a ragged force of 2,000 regulators at the Battle of Alamance, North Carolina. The rebels, poorly armed and disciplined, argue among themselves whether to fight or disband, but Tryon forces the issue by advancing upon them in force. After pelting his opponents with artillery for several minutes, the governor forms up his men into two lines and commences trading volleys. The regulators resist for nearly two hours before fleeing the scene in disorder. Tryon's losses are nine killed and 61 wounded in exchange for 20 killed and 50 injured. Of 12 prisoners taken, one is hung on the battlefield, six are executed on June 19, and the rest pardoned. Furthermore, 6,500 settlers in the region are required to sign oaths of allegiance to the Crown.

1772

February 28
NORTH: The Boston assembly threatens the British Empire with secession unless traditional rights of Englishmen are respected.

June 9
NORTH: The British revenue cutter HMS *Gaspée* under Lieutenant William Dudingston runs aground in Narragansett Bay, Rhode Island, while chasing suspected

smugglers. That night eight boats carrying armed citizens under Abraham Whipple capture the vessel and burn it to the waterline. Dudingston, wounded in the attack, is arrested for having illegally seized several colonial vessels and he remains incarcerated until the Admiralty agrees to pay his fine.

June 13
NORTH: Massachusetts governor Thomas Hutchinson summarily declares that his salary will accrue from tea tax revenues and not the General Court's coffers, decreasing that body's influence over him. Similar provisions are also adopted for Superior Court judges. This newfound independence of the executive and judiciary branches from the legislature is viewed as a threat to self-rule.

August 20
NORTH: A royal commission is established to investigate the *Gaspée* affair, with the power to suspend trial by jury. Moreover, the British Crown authorizes a large reward for information leading to the arrest of perpetrators, but no witnesses are forthcoming.

September 2
NORTH: The English government appoints a commission consisting of Governor Joseph Wanton of Rhode Island, the Boston Vice-Admiralty judge, and the chief justices of Massachusetts, New York, and New Jersey to investigate and arrest perpetrators behind the *Gaspée* affair. A large award is posted for information, but the threat of dispatching perpetrators directly to England for trial again undermines the concept of trial by jury.

November 2
NORTH: A 21-member committee of correspondence is founded in Boston, with James Otis, Samuel Adams, and Dr. Joseph Warren as chairmen. Their task is to communicate with town governments throughout Massachusetts and better coordinate resistance to official policies. The committee's proceedings are subsequently published as the *Boston Pamphlet,* which decries British attempts to enslave the colonies with taxes, troops, and suspension of trial by jury.

November 20
NORTH: Samuel Adams and Dr. Joseph Warren pen a declaration of rights and a list of grievances against the British government, which is summarily dispatched to towns throughout the colony. They also appeal to Governor Thomas Hutchinson to reconvene the General Court, but he refuses.

1773

January 6
NORTH: Governor Thomas Hutchinson presides over the new session of the Massachusetts General Court and sternly lectures members on the proper roles of Parliament and the colonies. A more alarming development to colonials is the threat to dispatch suspected felons directly to England for trial, eliminating traditional trial by jury.

March 12
South: The Virginia House of Burgesses authorizes a committee of correspondence under Thomas Jefferson, Patrick Henry, and Richard H. Lee to expand lines of communication with other colonial legislatures. They are protesting the *Gaspée* affair commission's ability to revoke trial by jury and send suspected malcontents to England for trial.

May 7
North: Rhode Island constitutes a committee of correspondence.

May 10
Politics: Parliament passes and King George III approves the Tea Act, an attempt by Lord Frederick North to rescue the cash-strapped British East India Company, forced into near-bankruptcy by colonial boycotts. Henceforth, the company enjoys a monopoly on the importation of tea to the colonies, which is sold more cheaply than smuggled tea and undercuts local merchants.

May 21
North: Connecticut forms its own committee of correspondence.

May 27
North: New Hampshire adopts a committee of correspondence.

June 2
North: Private correspondence written by Governor Thomas Hutchinson and Lieutenant Governor Andrew Oliver to British authorities calling for severe measures against dissent are surreptitiously obtained by members of the Massachusetts General Court and read aloud.

June 25
North: The Massachusetts assembly, incensed over Governor Thomas Hutchinson's letters to British officials demanding suppression of rebellious colonials, petitions the king for his removal.

July 7
North: Governor Thomas Hutchinson, informed that Postmaster Benjamin Franklin arranged for his letters to fall into the hands of the assembly, demands that he be prosecuted for treason.

July 8
South: South Carolina establishes its own committee of correspondence.

September 10
South: Georgia creates a committee of correspondence.

October 14
South: A cargo of British tea is torched by a mob in Annapolis, Maryland.

October 15
South: Maryland adopts a committee of correspondence.

October 16
NORTH: Pennsylvania creates its own committee of correspondence. A mass meeting then adopts resolutions declaring any individual who imports tea as an "enemy to his country" and also forces local tea agents to resign.

October 23
NORTH: Delaware adopts a committee of correspondence.

November 27
NORTH: Tensions in Boston increase following arrival of the East India tea ship *Dartmouth*. The government insists that all duties must be levied and paid by the colony on December 16.

November 29
NORTH: A mass meeting in Boston elects to defy the governor and orders the *Dartmouth* back to England without the requisite duties. Consequently, Governor Thomas Hutchinson orders harbor officials to retain all tea vessels of Boston Harbor until taxes have been levied.

December 8
SOUTH: North Carolina enacts a committee of correspondence.

December 16
NORTH: A meeting at Old South Church, Boston, draws 8,000 attendees and is harangued by Samuel Adams. Mounting colonial resentment culminates that evening in the Boston Tea Party. The Sons of Liberty, disguised as Indians, board the tea ships *Dartmouth, Eleanor,* and *Beaver* at Griffith's Wharf and dump 342 chests of tea, valued at £10,000, into Boston Harbor. This is the first violent act by colonials against royal authority; the wanton destruction of private property induces Parliament to weigh harsher measures for Massachusetts.

December 25
NORTH: The Massachusetts General Court again petitions King George III to remove Thomas Hutchinson as governor and also provincial secretary Andrew Oliver, based upon contents of the former's secret correspondence.

1774

January 20
NORTH: New York adopts a committee of correspondence.

January 25
NORTH: Customs official John Malcolm is publicly tarred and feathered in Boston.

January 27
POLITICS: Thomas Hutchinson's report of the Boston Tea Party reaches the government in London. Prime Minister Lord Frederick North decides that draconian measures are now necessary to preserve the hegemony of king and Parliament over the colonies.

January 30
POLITICS: Benjamin Franklin is dismissed as postmaster general by the Privy Council for Plantation Affairs after forwarding Governor Thomas Hutchinson's private correspondence to the Massachusetts assembly.

February 7
POLITICS: A petition from the Massachusetts General Court demanding the removal of Governor Thomas Hutchinson is received and ignored by the English government.

February 8
NORTH: New Jersey adopts a committee of correspondence.

March 18
POLITICS: Acting upon ministerial prerogatives, Lord Frederick North introduces the Boston Port Bill to the House of Commons; it mandates the closure of Boston to all trade until compensation is paid to the East India Company. This is regarded as the first of the Coercive Acts, more popularly regarded as the Intolerable Acts.

March 25
POLITICS: Parliament passes the Boston Port Bill as punishment for the Boston Tea Party. The bustling port of Boston is ordered closed until restitution is paid for the destroyed tea. But instead of intimidating the colonies, they begin sending food and other supplies in support of Massachusetts.

March 30
NORTH: Governor Thomas Hutchinson dissolves the Massachusetts General Court.

April 22
NORTH: Taking a leaf from associates in Boston, the New York Sons of Liberty board the British ship *London* dressed as Indians and dump British tea into New York Harbor.

April 30
WEST: A raiding party of frontiersmen attacks and kills a party of Indians at Logan's Camp, Virginia, including the entire family of Chief Logan of the Shawnee. Indian resentment culminates in the start of the so-called Dunmore's War.

May 3
NORTH: Effigies of Governor Thomas Hutchinson and Solicitor General Alexander Wedderburn are burned in Boston.

May 12
NORTH: The Boston committee of commerce calls for reinstating nonimportation of British goods until the Tea Act and Boston Port Bill are repealed. A circular letter is then carried to New York and Philadelphia by Paul Revere.

May 13
NORTH: General Thomas Gage arrives at Boston and replaces Thomas Hutchinson as the new royal governor of Massachusetts, backed by the bayonets of four addi-

tional infantry regiments. He also retains his usual duties as commander in chief of British forces.

May 17
NORTH: Citizens of Providence, Rhode Island, appeal for the first intercolonial body to resist the Coercive Acts.

May 20
POLITICS: King George III signs the next of the Coercive Acts, the Massachusetts Government Act, which annuls the colony charter, and the Administration of Justice Act, which tightens political and legal control. Henceforth all persons accused of a capital crime will be forced to stand trial in England or in a different colony from that in which the crime was committed. The government will also appoint all colonial officials, while town meetings are forbidden without prior consent of the royal governor.

May 26
SOUTH: Virginia governor John Murray, Lord Dunmore, dissolves the House of Burgesses for its overt political and religious sympathies toward Massachusetts.

May 27
SOUTH: Dismissed Virginia assemblymen reconvene at the Raleigh Tavern in Williamsburg to enunciate further support for Massachusetts, economic retaliation, and calls for an intercolonial congress.

June 1
NORTH: The Boston Port Bill becomes law and closes all harbor traffic until restitution is made to the East India Company.

June 2
POLITICS: Parliament revises the Quartering Act and expands its provisions to include all colonies. Moreover, each colony is required to pay for all expenditures related to maintaining their assigned garrison.

June 5
NORTH: Dr. Joseph Warren publishes the *Solemn League and Covenant,* an agreement by Boston merchants to support another round of nonimportation.

June 10
NORTH: The Massachusetts General Court, convening in Salem, approves a resolution calling for an intercolonial congress.
SOUTH: Governor John Murray, Lord Dunmore, calls out the militia in response to the Shawnee uprising along the frontier. The ensuing conflict becomes popularly known as Lord Dunmore's War.

June 14
NORTH: Rhode Island becomes the first colony to select delegates to the First Continental Congress; ultimately 11 other colonies follow suit.

June 17
North: General Thomas Gage suspends the Massachusetts General Court after convening use to choose delegates to the First Continental Congress. Meanwhile, Samuel Adams convenes a Boston town meeting, which defiantly votes not to pay for damages assessed from the Boston Tea Party.

June 22
Politics: King George III signs the Quebec Act, which establishes a formal government in Canada. It also enlarges the province of Quebec as far as the Mississippi and Ohio Rivers to thwart colonial land claims in the West. This eliminates territories long-claimed by Massachusetts, Connecticut, and Virginia, while granting religious freedom to the Roman Catholic Church in Quebec. This last feature raises fears of "popery" in the largely Protestant colonies.

June 26
North: At a large public gathering in New York City, Alexander Hamilton and Alexander McDougall condemn British tyranny and support nonimportation.

August 6
South: The Virginia Convention extends the Virginia Association and its boycott of English goods.

August 10
South: Georgia declines to send representatives to the First Continental Congress and instead opts for adopting a declaration of rights.

August 17
North: Philadelphia lawyer James Wilson publishes his *Considerations on the Nature and Extent of the Legislative Authority of the British Parliament*. This postulates the so-called dominion theory, which confirms allegiance to the king and rejects parliamentary hegemony over the colonies.

September 1
North: General Thomas Gage directs that the militia arsenal in Somerville, six miles from Boston, be seized. He then dispatches Lieutenant Colonel George Maddison of the 4th Regiment with 260 soldiers to fulfill the task. The British march unimpeded and seize 250 barrels of gunpowder before returning to base. This raid becomes subsequently known as the Powder Alarm and ominously portends events to come.

September 4
North: News of British activities in Somerville serve as a catalyst among the enraged populace. Several thousand armed citizens gather at Cambridge in a show of defiance.

September 5
Politics: The First Continental Congress convenes at Carpenter's Hall, Philadelphia, as an intercolonial forum to address grievances against the British Crown. The 55 delegates wrangle with defining their rights along with a means of defending them. Radicals under Samuel Adams seek and achieve protest against British

attempts to "enslave America," along with resolutions advising the colonies to raise and train their own militia. Virginian Peyton Randolph is elected its first president.
NORTH: General Thomas Gage, gauging the tenor of the times, orders fortifications built at Boston Neck to sever any direct connection to the mainland. Boston is unofficially under siege.

September 9
NORTH: The Massachusetts county convention in Suffolk adopts the so-called *Suffolk Resolves* as penned by Dr. Joseph Warren. This philippic strongly denounces changes in colonial government as imposed by the Coercive Acts. Moreover, it enunciates specific measures to counteract such Imperial inroads upon colonial governance, and urges adoption of widespread civil disobedience. This includes withholding taxes to the government, ignoring the rulings of appointed judges, and imposing another round of nonimportation. It also castigates Lord North for arbitrariness. More ominously, Warren entreats residents to make military preparations to defend the colony by force, if necessary. Rider Paul Revere is then dispatched to the First Continental Congress in Philadelphia with a copy of the resolves.

September 10
POLITICS: The fact that British imports have fallen by 90 percent over the previous year is stark testimony to colonial nonimportation's effectiveness.

September 17
POLITICS: In its first official action the Continental Congress adopts the *Suffolk Resolves* to encourage organized colonial resistance against the Coercive Acts and approves political resistance. This action marks the emergence of that body as a guiding entity for the colonies in their continuing struggle with the homeland.

September 28
POLITICS: Pennsylvania delegate and Loyalist Joseph Galloway proposes a pragmatic union of colonies with Great Britain to forestall the outbreak of hostilities. He proposes creation of a grand council drawn from the colonies under a governor-general appointed by the king. The plan narrowly fails on a vote of six to five, demonstrative proof of how divided colonial opinion is.

October 5
NORTH: Governor Thomas Gage again dissolves the Massachusetts General Court. Undeterred, the assembly reconvenes itself as the extralegal Provincial Congress at Salem. John Hancock serves as president and authorizes a committee of public safety, which votes to mobilize the militia and purchase weapons.

October 10
WEST: Virginia militia under Colonel Andrew Lewis engage and defeat Shawnee warriors under Chief Cornstalk at Point Pleasant near the mouth of the Kanawha River. The Indians, strongly ensconced across a river, repel two militia columns under Colonels Charles Lewis and William Fleming and then withdraw from the battlefield. Militia losses are 81 killed and 140 wounded; Indian casualties are unknown

but equally heavy. Cornstalk then accepts the inevitable and sues for peace. This is the concluding act of Dunmore's War.

October 14
POLITICS: The Continental Congress adopts the *Declaration of Rights and Grievances*, consisting of 14 resolutions, all carefully drawn from natural law and other Enlightenment precepts. It clearly enunciates the litany of grievances by colonies against their homeland and, moreover, reasserts that their rights as Englishmen have been violated. It specifically outlines and opposes the Coercive Acts, the Quebec Act, and all punitive measures adopted by England over the past decade. While skirting the issue of independence, it reaffirms colonial belief that Parliament has no jurisdiction over American affairs except for regulating commerce and imperial defense. This is the first such document submitted to Parliament by an aggregation of colonies and also denotes the gradual radicalization of such heretofore moderates as John Adams and John Dickinson. It also anticipates many precepts of the forthcoming Declaration of Independence.

October 19
SOUTH: The tea ship *Peggy Stewart* is burned at Annapolis, Maryland, by a mob.

October 20
POLITICS: The Continental Congress adopts the Continental Association, modeled after the Virginia Association, as a colony-wide enforcement of nonimportation of British goods. The slave trade is also abolished. Implicit is a December 1, 1774, deadline for Parliament's compliance lest a ban on exports to Great Britain be enacted the following spring.

October 21
POLITICS: A congressional address drafted by John Jay, Robert R. Livingston, and Richard H. Lee warns the British populace that if tyranny remains unchecked in America it will inevitably take root in England.

October 26
POLITICS: The First Continental Congress adjourns, having voted to convene again on May 10, 1775, if Great Britain fails to address American grievances.
NORTH: The Massachusetts Provincial Congress at Cambridge reorganizes the colonial militia into a rapid-response force, the minutemen.

November 17
NORTH: The Philadelphia Troop of Light Horse, filling 26 saddles, is organized as one of the first colonial military units.

November 30
NORTH: British political agitator Thomas Paine arrives at Philadelphia at the invitation of Benjamin Franklin.

December 9
NORTH: A cache of British ordnance is seized by colonials at Newport, Rhode Island, and sequestered at Providence.

December 13
POLITICS: Word of the *Suffolk Resolves* arrives at London and is denounced by the government as treason.

December 14
NORTH: In Boston, General Thomas Gage determines to raid another colonial supply dump, this time at Fort William and Mary in Portsmouth, New Hampshire, 50 miles distant. When the colonial intelligence network is alerted, Paul Revere gallops forth and warns the local militia of British intentions. A group of 400 militia under Major John Sullivan then storm the arsenal at Fort William and Mary, taking six soldiers prisoner and confiscating 100 barrels of powder. The commanding officer is wounded when the rebels lower the British flag and he draws his sword. Gage's force arrives the following day and finds the fort sacked and deserted.

1775

January 18
SOUTH: Georgia's First Provincial Congress, culled from five Patriot-oriented parishes, assembles in Savannah to express solidarity with the inhabitants of Massachusetts. However, seven Loyalist-dominated parishes refuse to send delegates to Philadelphia.

January 27
POLITICS: Secretary of State for the Colonies William Legge, Lord Dartmouth, instructs General Thomas Gage in Boston to take active measures and enforce the Crown's authority. Gage commands a garrison of nine infantry regiments and five Royal Artillery companies totaling 4,000 soldiers. Additionally, four large warships in the harbor contribute another 460 Royal Marines under Major John Pitcairn.

February 1
POLITICS: William Pitt, seconded by Edmund Burke, makes impassioned but unsuccessful pleas for Parliament to repeal the Coercive Acts, to remove troops from Boston, and to acknowledge colonial consent on the issue of taxation. The plan is overwhelmingly defeated.
NORTH: The Second Massachusetts Provincial Congress convenes in Cambridge, Massachusetts, under John Hancock and Dr. Joseph Warren, and initiates preparations for the military defense of that colony.

February 6
NORTH: John Adams publishes his *The Rule of Law and the Rule of Men in the Massachusetts Gazette,* insisting on the supreme authority of provincial legislatures over Parliament.

February 9
POLITICS: King George III declares the colony of Massachusetts to be in a state of rebellion.

February 20
NORTH: The Second Massachusetts Provincial Congress reconvenes in Concord and takes positive steps to enhance colonial defenses. Among measures taken are

establishment of a military commissary, the enlistment of the Stockbridge Indians, military rules of governance, and delegates to visit adjoining colonies with requests for reinforcements.

February 26

NORTH: General Thomas Gage orders the colonial supplies held in Salem, Massachusetts, seized. A detachment of the 64th Regiment under Colonel Alexander Leslie sails to Marblehead and marches inland toward its objective. Townspeople begin gathering at North Bridge to oppose them and raise the drawbridge. Leslie angrily demands to pass and violence threatens to break out until an agreement is reached: The British will be allowed to cross the bridge and proceed to the building where cannon are supposedly held. Leslie obliges and, when no ordnance is discovered, he turns around and marches back to Marblehead without incident. "Leslie's retreat," as it becomes known, is a public relations disaster for the government and further emboldens colonial resistance to British arms.

February 27

POLITICS: Parliament approves Lord North's Conciliatory Resolution, whereby new taxes upon the colonies are abolished once the latter assume fiscal responsibility for their own defense. However, it is addressed to individual colonies to avoid dealing with the Continental Congress directly, thereby denying that body political recognition.

March 10

WEST: Settlers under Daniel Boone depart Fort Chiswell, Virginia, and advance through the Cumberland Gap into Kentucky.

March 22

POLITICS: Edmund Burke rails against the New England Restraining Act in the House of Commons. This action would curtail that region from trading with any countries other than England, Ireland, and the West Indies. He also denounces taxation without representation and insists that only colonial legislatures are empowered to raise revenues.

March 23

SOUTH: Patrick Henry denounces Lord Dunmore's suspension of the Virginia assembly and thunders "Forbid it, Almighty God—I know not what course others may take; but as for me—give me liberty or give me death" at the Virginia Convention in Richmond. He then forcefully expounds the necessity for military preparedness against the Crown.

March 25

SOUTH: The Virginia Convention mandates that each county will raise a company of infantry and cavalry.

March 30

POLITICS: King George III approves of the New England Restraining Act, which restricts that region to trading only with England and bans it from the Atlantic fisheries. Moreover, it extends the action to include any colony partaking of the Continental Association.

North: General Thomas Gage, in a show of military strength, orders an entire brigade of soldiers under Colonel Hugh Percy paraded to Cambridge and back. The Massachusetts militia provocatively plants a cannon at Watertown bridge and removes the planks from another bridge at Concord, but otherwise Percy completes his mission without incident.

April 1

North: The New York assembly requires all males of military age to enlist in the militia.

April 5

North: The Massachusetts Provincial Congress adopts 53 articles of war, principally derived from the British Articles of War of 1765, in the event of hostilities. The preamble carefully enunciates Massachusetts's denial of rebellion or treason and reiterates a long list of grievances against the government.

April 8

South: Royal governor Josiah Martin of North Carolina, unable to gain compliance from the colonial assembly, peremptorily dissolves that body. Fearing the worst, he relocates his family to New York.

April 14

North: General Thomas Gage receives positive instructions from Secretary of the Colonies William Legge, Lord Dartmouth, authorizing him to use whatever force necessary to implement the Coercive Acts, including the arrest of colonial leaders. However, his request for an additional 20,000 troops has been refused.

Benjamin Franklin and Benjamin Rush organize The Society for the Relief of Free Negroes Unlawfully Held in Bondage at Philadelphia, America's first abolition society for the benefit of African Americans.

April 15

North: General Thomas Gage prepares for action by ordering the Boston garrison to glean men from all elite flank companies (light infantry and grenadiers) and concentrate them into a strike force of 700 picked soldiers. He also decides against arresting leaders of the Provincial Congress in favor of a preemptive strike upon colonial stores of ammunition and military supplies at Concord and Worcester. Despite great emphasis on secrecy, the American spy network quickly catches wind of the scheme.

April 16

North: Dr. Joseph Warren dispatches Paul Revere from Boston to Lexington to warn John Hancock and Samuel Adams of the army's possible approach. The warning eventually reaches militia forces at Concord, which relocate their supplies to Worcester and await the British. His mission completed, Revere arranges for lanterns from the steeple of Boston's Old North Church to signal the British approach: one lamp by land, two by sea.

April 18

NORTH: General Thomas Gage orders his elite flank-company force under Lieutenant Colonel Francis Smith to seize the colonial arms cache at Concord, Massachusetts. Smith is seconded by the formidable presence of Major John Pitcairn, Royal Marines. Smith is to embark and cross the Charles River to Lechmere Point under the cover of darkness to avoid detection. Forewarned, Dr. Joseph Warren again dispatches Paul Revere and William Dawes to Lexington to alert Samuel Adams and John Hancock. Revere is temporarily apprehended en route but Dawes makes his appointed rounds and the two men flee. Militia in the vicinity of Concord are contacted by a third individual, Dr. Samuel Prescott.

April 19

NORTH: A gathering of 70 minutemen under Captain John Parker confronts the advance forces of light infantry under Major John Pitcairn at Lexington. Parker parades his men on the green and does not obstruct the British march, but Pitcairn feels that he can not leave a potentially hostile force to his rear. Deploying his men on the green in front of the Americans, Pitcairn rides ahead and entreats the Americans to lay down their arms and disperse. Parker gives his nervous men permission to leave and, although they refuse to surrender their arms, the militia begins gingerly departing. Suddenly a shot rings out of nowhere—and the hungry, wet, and greatly fatigued British troops perceive themselves as under attack. Against Pitcairn's orders they fire two volleys into the milling militiamen, killing eight and wounding nine. It takes several minutes before British officers can restore order to the ranks—but a war has begun.

Within the hour the balance of Colonel Francis Smith's column arrives at Lexington and proceeds to its main objective at Concord. The grenadiers are then ordered to search the premises for stored weapons—long removed at this juncture—and they also set fire to a courthouse and several buildings. Meanwhile, a detachment of light infantry under Captain Walter Laurie, sent to guard the North Bridge, is engaged by colonial militia and driven back, losing three killed and eight wounded. His mission complete, Smith then turns his force around and tramps back to Boston. En route his march is continually intercepted by throngs of angry militiamen who rake the column with musket fire from behind rocks, trees, and all available cover. The British take fearful loses while Smith is wounded and Pitcairn unhorsed. They are almost overwhelmed when suddenly a column under Colonel Hugh Percy reinforces them at Lexington. Percy skillfully conducts a withdrawal under fire and at the last minute redirects his escape route toward Charlestown instead of Cambridge—a move that most likely saved the army. Of 1,800 British engaged they lose 73 killed and 201 wounded on this momentous day; of roughly 3,800 Americans present the toll reached 49 killed and 97 wounded. The incredible news quickly spreads throughout the colonies and a violent upheaval against continuing British rule finally congeals.

SOUTH: A secret committee in Charleston, South Carolina, removes mail from the British packet ship *Swallow* and finds instructions from the government intent upon driving the colonies into submission. The correspondence is then forwarded to the Second Continental Congress.

The first shots of the American Revolution are fired on April 19, 1775, in Lexington, Massachusetts. Painting by Don Troiani *(National Guard Bureau)*

April 20
NORTH: The Massachusetts Committee of Safety mobilizes 13,000 colonial militia for military service. Meanwhile, American militia men coalesce in large numbers outside Boston, initiating an informal siege. General Israel Putnam arrives in Boston from Connecticut, covering 100 miles in only 18 hours.

April 21
NORTH: New Hampshire militiamen deploy at Cambridge, Massachusetts, in the wake of Lexington and Concord.
SOUTH: Retaliating against a rebellious legislature, Virginia's royal governor John Murray, Lord Dunmore, preemptively orders Royal Marines to seize militia powder supplies at Williamsburg.

Colonial forces begin seizing powder supplies and arms in Charleston, South Carolina.

April 23
NORTH: The Massachusetts Provincial Congress, reconvened in Concord, calls for a New England "army of observation" so as not to appear excessively militant against the British Crown. This has an authorized strength of 30,000 volunteers, including

13,600 local militia under General Artemas Ward. It then appoints William Heath, John Thomas, Dr. Joseph Warren, and John Whitcomb as major generals under Ward's command. Nor is time wasted dispatching messengers to neighboring colonies with pleas for immediate reinforcements. The region responds by sending troops under Nathanael Greene of Rhode Island, John Stark of New Hampshire, and David Wooster of Connecticut.

Word of Lexington and Concord causes riots in New York City, and a mob under Lieutenant Colonel Marinus Willett storms the public arsenal and seizes weapons.

April 28
NORTH: Colonel Ethan Allen and a group of the Green Mountain Boys arrive at Castleton, Vermont, to debate the seizing of the stores and munitions at Fort Ticonderoga.

April 29
NORTH: The Massachusetts Provincial Congress dispatches the schooner *Quero* to England with word of Lexington and Concord. Major Benedict Arnold marches into Cambridge, Massachusetts, at the head of a Connecticut militia company.

May 2
SOUTH: Major Patrick Henry directs colonial forces to recapture powder and supplies taken from the militia at Williamsburg, while Governor John Murray, Lord Dunmore, is forced to compensate the colony for property confiscated.

May 3
POLITICS: Benjamin Franklin, residing in London as a colonial agent since 1757, drops his long-standing policy of reconciliation and arrives in Philadelphia, fully committed to the American cause. The following day he is appointed a member of the Second Continental Congress.

NORTH: Connecticut militia officer Benedict Arnold prevails upon the Committee of Safety in Cambridge to provide forces for a preemptive strike against Fort Ticonderoga, New York, for the valuable guns and supplies sequestered there. Arnold, who is commissioned a colonel in the Massachusetts militia, receives authority to raise 400 men for the expedition, which promises to net 50 cannon and 20 other brass pieces for the patriot cause.

May 5
NAVAL: The 16-gun British sloop HMS *Falcon* under Captain John Linzee captures an American sloop off Martha's Vineyard, Massachusetts. He then anchors at the town of Dartmouth to seize another sloop at dockside. His presence induces the townspeople to sail two sloops against him and the prizes are promptly recaptured in a sharp fight. The *Falcon* escapes but loses 15 prisoners.

May 8
NORTH: A force of 100 Green Mountain Boys under Colonel Ethan Allen departs Castleton, Vermont, intent upon seizing the cannon and stores held at Fort Ticonderoga, New York. Meeting Benedict Arnold en route, the two leaders grudgingly agree to coordinate their efforts.

South: News of the battles at Lexington and Concord prompts the South Carolina assembly to authorize two infantry regiments and a force of rangers.

May 10
Politics: The Second Continental Congress convenes at Independence Hall, Philadelphia. John Hancock is elected president and he begins orchestrating armed resistance to Great Britain. Members also continue exploring possible reconciliation with Great Britain. Georgia, which was absent at the first assembly, has dispatched Lyman Hall as its representative.
North: A colonial force of 83 men under Colonels Benedict Arnold and Ethan Allen crosses Lake Champlain in two barges under cover of a rainstorm and surprises the garrison at Fort Ticonderoga, New York. The Americans quickly clamber over the crumbling southern wall and overpower two sentries. When a British officer, Lieutenant Jocelyn Feltham, 26th Regiment, demands to know by what authority the Americans have entered His Majesty's fort, Allen bellowed "Come out of there, you British sons of whores, or I'll smoke you out!" The garrison commander, Captain William De La Place, is badly outnumbered and capitulates without resistance. The Americans seize 48 prisoners along with 78 cannon and a large cache of military supplies. Allen and Arnold successfully conclude America's first offensive operation of the war.

When a New York mob threatens Loyalist Dr. Myles Cooper, president of King's College (now Columbia University), he is rescued by Alexander Hamilton.
Naval: Captain Henry Mowat of the Royal Navy sloop HMS *Canceau* comes ashore to confer with the inhabitants of Falmouth (Portland, Maine), Massachusetts, and is taken prisoner. He escapes shortly after.

May 11
North: The fortified post at Crown Point, 10 miles north of Fort Ticonderoga, falls to 45 Green Mountain Boys under Lieutenant Colonel Seth Warner, who captures an additional 100 cannon for the Patriot cause. Nine soldiers and 10 women are also taken without a struggle. Canada is now open to invasion along the Richelieu River.
South: Colonial forces storm a royal magazine and confiscate powder supplies in Savannah, Georgia.

May 13
North: In a show of force, General Artemas Ward parades his ragtag "army of observation" from Cambridge to Charlestown, Massachusetts, passing within gunshot of British cannon, yet eliciting no response. General Israel Putnam then provocatively leads 3,000 men on to Charlestown Heights, astride Boston Harbor; when the British fail to react, he withdraws back to the mainland without incident.

May 15
Politics: In light of the present crisis, the Continental Congress urges New York and all other colonies to place themselves in a state of military preparedness.

May 16
North: The Massachusetts assembly drafts the first American constitution subject to popular will, although it is ultimately rejected by voters.

May 17
NORTH: Having disbanded the colonial assembly, the New York Provincial Congress is established to resume the functions of governance.

Colonel Benedict Arnold boards a captured schooner at Skeensboro, New York, and sails to Saint Johns, Quebec, with 50 soldiers. That post and its 15-man garrison quickly succumb, along with the 16-gun sloop HMS *George III* and four boats. Returning to Ticonderoga, Arnold encounters Colonel Ethan Allen with 60 men, now intent upon occupying the fort. Disregarding Arnold's warning, Allen approaches Fort St. John's only to find it hastily reoccupied by 200 British soldiers and six cannon from neighboring Chambly. The Americans are quickly driven off after losing three prisoners.

NAVAL: The American schooner *Franklin* under Captain James Mugford captures the British transport HMS *Hope* outside Boston Harbor. Its valuable cargo of 1,000 barrels of gunpowder and 1,000 muskets is quickly forwarded to the army outside the city.

May 18
POLITICS: The Continental Congress reelects Peyton Randolph of Virginia and Charles Thomson of Philadelphia as its president and secretary, respectively. The delegates are heartened by news of Fort Ticonderoga's capture, and many hope its fall will induce the inhabitants of Canada to join the rebellion.

SOUTH: Royal governor Josiah Martin of North Carolina notifies authorities in London that he is powerless to stop the population from joining the militia or starting a new government.

May 21
NORTH: To alleviate supply shortages, General Thomas Gage authorizes forage parties to land on various islands in Boston Harbor. However, when a party of troops ventures upon Grape Island, many inhabitants gather into three boats and land there to oppose them. The British draw off before violence flares.

May 24
POLITICS: Peyton Randolph resigns as president of the Second Continental Congress in order to return to the Virginia House of Burgesses and is replaced by John Hancock.

May 25
POLITICS: Congress resolves to begin fortifying Kingsbridge, the Hudson Highlands, and Lake George with no less than 3,000 men.

NORTH: British reinforcements arrive in Boston under Generals John Burgoyne, Henry Clinton, and William Howe. General Thomas Gage now commands a force of 6,500 trained and highly disciplined soldiers. However, the arrival of three generals is unmistakably indicative of the government's displeasure over his handling of affairs.

May 26
NORTH: General Artemas Ward orders 30 militiamen under Colonel John Nixon to confiscate livestock on Noddle's and Hog Island, in Boston Harbor.

May 27
NAVAL: Admiral Samuel Graves orders a contingent of 40 Royal Marines to Noddle's Island in Boston Harbor to attack the American detachment there. The schooner HMS *Diana* under Lieutenant Thomas Graves—the admiral's nephew—is also dispatched to cut off the American retreat. Generals Isaac Putnam and Dr. Joseph Warren counter the move by rushing in 1,000 reinforcements of their own and two cannon. Heavy skirmishing results in the destruction of the *Diana* after it runs aground and the British withdraw. The ensuing fracas is a rather noisy affair, but both sides suffer only four casualties apiece.

May 29
POLITICS: In Philadelphia, a declaration penned by John Jay invites the inhabitants of Canada to side with the Americans as the 14th colony. Eventually, the Catholic French-speaking population will ally itself with Great Britain rather than risk cultural assimilation as part of the United States.

May 31
POLITICS: The Continental Congress initially votes to abandon Forts Ticonderoga and Crown Point over the objections of delegates from New York and New England. Upon further reflection, members reverse themselves and order the forts held as conduits for a possible invasion of Canada.
SOUTH: A committee, meeting at Charlotte, Mecklenburg County, North Carolina, drafts 20 resolutions for its congressional delegates at Philadelphia. These include suspension of royal and parliamentary authority throughout the colony and reaffirmation of the supremacy of colonial legislatures—it falls just short of declaring independence. The so-called Mecklenburg Declaration is never presented to Congress itself.

Governor Josiah Martin of North Carolina flees New Berne and eventually boards the British sloop HMS *Cruzier* on the Cape Fear River.

June 2
NORTH: The Massachusetts Provincial Congress requests that the Continental Congress take command and responsibility for the New England army, it having been raised for the rights of all Americans. Congress dithers on the question but does authorize a pay department for the nascent Continental army.
NAVAL: The British armed cutter HMS *Margaretta* under Midshipman James Moore anchors off Machias, Massachusetts (Maine), escorting two timber sloops, *Polly* and *Unity*. Their mission is to obtain lumber for British forces in Boston.

June 3
NORTH: Ichabod Jones, a Loyalist merchant, rows ashore to Machias, Massachusetts (Maine), and offers to purchase lumber from the citizens in exchange for needed supplies. He assures the inhabitants that the wood is not going to be used to build fortifications in Boston, but they remain skeptical and uncooperative.

June 5
SOUTH: A mob ransacks the state arsenal in Williamsburg, Virginia, and makes off with 400 muskets.

June 6

North: A rancorous town meeting held at Machias, Massachusetts (Maine), votes to allow Loyalist Ichabod Jones to purchase lumber for the British in Boston. To further coax cooperation, Midshipman James Moore maneuvers his four-gun schooner HMS *Margaretta* within bombardment distance of the town.

The British begin evacuating New York and Lieutenant Colonel Marinus Willett, backed by the Sons of Liberty, seizes five wagons of arms from British soldiers attempting to smuggle them out of the city. Feeling this violates a previous agreement with the British, the New York Provincial Congress orders the arms returned but is ignored.

June 7

North: American militia capture a British magazine at Turtle Bay, New York, without authority from the Provincial Congress.

June 8

South: Governor John Murray, Lord Dunmore, seeks refuge onboard HMS *Fowey* at Yorktown, Virginia, as violence between Patriot and Loyalist forces escalates.

June 9

North: Governor-General Guy Carleton declares martial law in Canada, suspends all administrative provisions of the Quebec Act, and begins recruiting volunteers to augment his under-strength forces.

June 10

Politics: At Philadelphia, John Adams proposes creation of a new Continental army.

June 11

North: Ichabod Jones, Loyalist merchant, again comes ashore to purchase lumber for British troops in Boston. A heated debate ensues amongst the townspeople, who again vote to sell the lumber to Jones. However, when he is seized and imprisoned by the Patriots, Midshipman James Moore maneuvers the sloop HMS *Margaretta* into bombardment position and threatens to shell the town if Jones is hurt or his vessels attacked. A mob nonetheless seizes the transports *Unity* and *Polly* and demands that the British surrender. Moore hastily cuts his cable and slips downstream to safety.

June 12

North: General Thomas Gage proclaims martial law in Massachusetts and entreats rebel soldiers to lay down their arms and be pardoned. The amnesty does not apply to Samuel Adams and John Hancock, who are to stand trial for their outlandish sedition. But Gage's declaration, composed by General John Burgoyne, aspiring playwright, proves overly pompous in tenor and elicits contempt from the populace.

Naval: The first naval action of the Revolution occurs when 40 armed lumbermen under Jeremiah O'Brien sail the captured sloops *Unity* and *Polly* against the British sloop HMS *Margaretta* off Machias, Massachusetts (Maine). When adverse winds cripple *Margaretta's* sails, the Americans pull alongside and board it after a stiff fight.

Midshipman James Moore is fatally wounded in the struggle and the British suffer eight killed and five wounded to an American tally of three killed and two wounded. The *Margaretta* becomes the first Royal Navy vessel captured during the Revolution; its guns are transferred to the transport *Unity,* which is subsequently renamed *Machias Liberty.*

Rhode Island commissions two armed sloops, the first such vessels approved by public authority.

June 14
POLITICS: The Continental Congress authorizes six companies of riflemen to be raised in Pennsylvania, Maryland, and Virginia; this action marks the birth of the new Continental army. A committee is also appointed to draw up the rules and regulation for governing the embryonic force.
NORTH: General Thomas Gage falls under increasing pressure from subordinates William Howe, John Burgoyne, and Henry Clinton to take some kind of offensive action and secure greater "elbow room" for the Boston garrison. He reluctantly agrees to seize strategic Dorchester Heights, still vacant, before moving on to Roxbury and Charlestown Heights. With this accomplished, the British will be free to launch an overland assault against rebel headquarters in Cambridge.

June 15
POLITICS: Congress unanimously appoints George Washington general and commander in chief of the Continental army. A tall, imposing figure, resplendent in the bluff and buff uniform of the Fairfax County militia, he volunteers to serve without pay. Washington was nominated by John Adams of Massachusetts, who wished to shore up southern support for the rapidly unfolding revolution. The Continental Congress authorizes the commissioning of two major generals, five brigadier generals, and various other officers for administrative branches of the army.
NORTH: The Committee of Safety in Cambridge is informed by its extensive network of spies that General Thomas Gage intends to occupy the high ground surrounding Boston Harbor. It then instructs General Artemas Ward to occupy Bunker Hill on the Charlestown peninsula to preempt the British from deploying troops along Dorchester Heights. This strategic vantage point has been heretofore overlooked by the contending armies.
NAVAL: A squadron of two Rhode Island state vessels under Captain Abraham Whipple captures a British tender on the Providence River.

June 16
POLITICS: The Continental Congress commissions Charles Lee, Israel Putnam, Philip J. Schuyler, and Artemas Ward as major generals. Three more brigadier generals are also authorized to promote greater geographical balance.
NORTH: Throughout the night, Colonel Richard Gridley, the Continental army's first chief engineer, directs construction of fortifications upon Breed's Hill overlooking Boston Harbor. His men dig furiously, constructing a large redoubt on the hilltop before the British can react, and are subsequently reinforced by 1,200 men under Colonel William Prescott and General Israel Putnam. In the early morning hours they

are joined by small groups of men under Colonel Thomas Knowlton, Colonel John Stark, with Generals Seth Pomeroy and Dr. Joseph Warren, fighting as volunteers.

June 17
NORTH: At dawn General Thomas Gage is amazed to behold a complex series of earthworks that have miraculously appeared overnight at Charlestown. The danger these pose to the Boston garrison finally rouses him to fight. After further consultation, he resolves that a direct display of British military power is necessary to cow the rebels into submission. Gage then authorizes 2,200 soldiers under General William Howe to land on the peninsula and drive the rebels off by direct assault. Given the low regard that professional British officers hold for their rebellious kinsmen, no particular difficulties are anticipated. Howe's force then crosses the harbor in barges, and he draws up his men in full battle array and advances upon the American lines as if on parade. Exercising superb fire control discipline, Colonels John Stark and William Prescott allow the vaunted redcoats to advance to within 60 paces

Despite being driven from their positions, the American militia proves its prowess against the British in the Battle of Bunker Hill, June 17, 1775. *(National Guard Bureau)*

before unleashing a devastating point-blank volley. The attackers are staggered by heavy losses, especially among company grade officers, and flee back down the slopes. An attack on the American right under General Robert Pigot is likewise rebuffed with many casualties. Stunned by such resistance, Howe rallies the survivors and leads then back up the hill a second time. Once again, the precise, closely ordered British approach to within a few yards of American defenses before being cut down by sheets of accurate musketry.

Howe's entire staff has been shot down beside him, yet he miraculously emerges unscathed. He nonetheless resolves on a final assault to settle affairs with cold steel and orders his men to drop their 80-pound backpacks. He is also reinforced by 400 men under General Henry Clinton and a battalion of royal marines under Major John Pitcairn. Once again the British tramp up the steep slopes of Breed's Hill in perfect formation—no mean task considering the terrain and intense summer heat—and close with the defenders. By this time the Americans are rapidly running out of ammunition. Their next volley staggers the attackers but does not stop them. Howe, sword in hand, then leads them over the parapet and into the redoubt. A vicious hand-to hand struggle erupts along the line as the American defense collapses under the weight of vengeful bayonets. Clinton, against orders, also comes up and pitches the fray, and General Putnam orders a retreat back to the mainland. The fighting then dies down and the exhausted British decline to pursue. Howe has lost 226 killed and 828 wounded, an appalling 48 percent of forces engaged. American losses were noted as 140 killed (including Dr. Joseph Warren) and 271 wounded. An additional 30 prisoners, principally wounded, are also taken. General Clinton, appalled by such carnage, considers Bunker Hill "a dear bought victory, another such would have ruined us."

June 20
POLITICS: General George Washington is ordered north by the Continental Congress while Thomas Jefferson arrives in Philadelphia to replace Peyton Randolph as Virginia's delegate.

June 21
NORTH: Nathanael Greene is appointed brigadier general of Rhode Island forces.

June 22
POLITICS: The Continental Congress authorizes an issue of $2 million in paper money to raise arms and supplies for the army—this is the first Continental currency. The delegates pledge that all bills of credit will be redeemed, although the scrip, constantly devalued over the next six years, will occasion the derogatory phrase "Not worth a Continental."
SOUTH: After long delays Georgia finally establishes a committee of safety.

June 23
NORTH: General George Washington and his entourage, consisting of Generals Philip J. Schuyler, Charles Lee, and Thomas Mifflin, depart Philadelphia for New York.

June 25
POLITICS: The Continental Congress appoints General Philip J. Schuyler commander of the Northern Department in New York; two days later it grants him discretionary power to invade Canada, if practicable.

June 26
POLITICS: A congressional committee, tasked with composing *A Declaration on Taking up Arms* on June 23, delivers an unsatisfactory first draft. Thomas Jefferson and John Dickinson are subsequently added to the committee and work resumes.
NORTH: General George Washington, en route to Boston, declares it his intention, once the cause of liberty is achieved, to resign from the military and live as a private citizen.

June 30
POLITICS: Congress approves 69 articles of war as regulations for the Continental army, which more or less mirror the existing British Articles of War of 1765. Discipline is somewhat moderated, with courts-martial restricted to handing out 39 lashes, fines restricted to two months' pay, and prison terms limited to one month. The death penalty is retained only for severe crimes, but routine church attendance is encouraged to promote good behavior and proper morality among the rank and file.

July 3
NORTH: General George Washington arrives at Cambridge, Massachusetts, and in his first orders he hopes "that all distinctions of colonies will be laid aside so that one and the same spirit may animate the whole." Washington's first task is to replace Artemas Ward as commander of the Continental army, a force 14,000 strong but problematically armed, trained, and led. He first tries to impose a greater semblance of military and logistical order on his unruly mob by dividing the army into three wings under Ward, Israel Putnam, and Charles Lee. He then orders the line of fortifications surrounding the city extended between Dorchester and the Mystic River to further bottle up the British. Washington also takes remedial disciplinary action to transform these armed amateurs into a respectable force. General orders then harangue the men to promote discipline, improve hygiene, and refine combat effectiveness. But the greatest challenge confronting Washington is expiring enlistments at the end of the year. He will face the prospect of persuading this rather unruly lot to reenlist and submit to proper discipline.

July 5
POLITICS: Moderates in Congress under John Dickinson extend the *Olive Branch Petition* to King George III, which reiterates colonial grievances, yet entreats rapprochement with the government. This is a carefully crafted missive addressed to the monarch instead of Parliament, whose authority the Continental Congress refuses to recognize. The petition acknowledges all responsibilities to the Crown as loyal subjects and beseeches him to cease military hostilities in order to schedule further negotiations. To radicals present the petition seems like a waste of time, but Dickinson cleverly calculates that its rejection will serve to unify most disparate ele-

ments at Philadelphia. The document will be conveyed to London by Arthur Lee and Richard Penn, a noted Loyalist.

July 6
POLITICS: The Continental Congress adopts the *Declaration of the Causes and Necessities of Taking up Arms,* penned by Thomas Jefferson and John Dickinson to justify colonial resistance to Great Britain. It also singularly declares American intentions "to die free men rather than live as slaves." The document is then dispatched for proclamation to the Continental army outside Boston. Together with the *Olive Branch Petition,* it further underscores the divided sentiments and loyalties of the delegates.

July 8
NORTH: American forces under Major Benjamin Tupper and Captain John Crane start probing the British defenses by overrunning a small detachment at Boston Neck (Roxbury) and burning a guardhouse.

July 9
NORTH: General George Washington convenes a war council at Cambridge, Massachusetts, to evaluate current affairs. He and his officers decide against fortifying Dorchester Heights so as not to provoke a strong British reaction; hence, this strategic feature remains unoccupied by either side. The army is also reorganized into three divisions under Major Generals William Heath, Artemas Ward, and Nathanael Greene.

July 10
NORTH: Brigadier General Horatio Gates outlines instructions for recruiting into the Continental army; African Americans, British deserters, and youths under 18 remain ineligible.
SOUTH: The Americans capture a British supply vessel with 14,000 pounds of gunpowder at Tybee Island, off the mouth of the Savannah River, Georgia.

July 12
SOUTH: American militia under James Mayson seize Fort Charlotte, South Carolina, 50 miles inland from Augusta on the Savannah River.

July 13
DIPLOMACY: Commissioners are appointed by the Continental Congress to hold councils with the Native Americans of the Six Nations to keep them from aligning with the British.
NORTH: British forces under General Henry Clinton probe American defenses at Roxbury, Boston, totally dispersing them. Clinton will later regret that he lacked sufficient force to launch an all-out assault against this ill-prepared assemblage.

July 14
POLITICS: King George III receives a petition from John Wilkes, lord mayor of London, beseeching him to cease military operations against the colonies and pursue reconciliation.

July 16
Naval: Jeremiah O'Brien entices the officers of two British schooners, HMS *Diligent* and *Tatamagouche,* ashore at Machias, Massachusetts (Maine), where they are seized along with accompanying vessels.

July 18
Politics: The Continental Congress recommends that the colonies pass uniform organization and equipage standards for the state militias, and also provide armed vessels for the protection of harbors and coasts.
North: General Philip J. Schuyler arrives at Fort Ticonderoga to find the garrison undermanned, poorly supplied, and inadequately prepared for protracted military operations.

July 20
Politics: The first national day of public humility, fasting, and prayer, adopted by Congress on June 12, 1775, is observed.
North: A swift raid conducted by Marinus Willett and Alexander McDougall captures Royal stores at Turtle Bay (East 42nd Street) on Manhattan Island. These are quickly forwarded to American forces besieging Boston.

July 21
Politics: Benjamin Franklin's proposed plan for Articles of Confederation and Perpetual Union is received by the Continental Congress. The item is tabled for future consideration, as are recommendations that American ports be opened to trade over nonexportation measures of the Continental Association.
North: Massachusetts militia under Major Joseph Vose raid Nantasket Point in Boston Harbor and also destroy the lighthouse on Great Brewster Island. The Americans suffer two wounded.

July 23
South: Patriot leader William H. Drayton arrives in the South Carolina backcountry to stir up revolutionary sentiment, but he is thwarted by a strong Loyalist presence. Drayton subsequently orders the Patriot militia to assemble and begin arresting Loyalist leaders.

July 24
North: General Philip J. Schuyler dispatches a small reconnaissance party under Major John Brown into Canada to gather intelligence about Montreal and ascertain attitudes of the inhabitants.

July 25
Politics: The Continental Congress formally assumes command and control functions over the Continental army.
North: Dr. Benjamin Church gains appointment as the first surgeon general of the Continental army over Paul Revere's objections that he is a British informant.

The first rifle company, commanded by Captain Michael Doudel of York, Pennsylvania, arrives at Cambridge, Massachusetts.

July 26
Politics: Having fulfilled the position for many years with the royal government, Benjamin Franklin becomes postmaster general of the new Post Office Department.

July 27
Politics: The Continental Congress establishes the Army Medical Department.
North: In Dorset, New Hampshire, the Green Mountain Boys nominate Seth Warner as their new lieutenant colonel. Ethan Allen is unceremoniously dropped as the unit's leader.

July 29
Politics: The Continental Congress promulgates a redemption plan for printed currency and mandates that individual colonies must each assume responsibility for their respective share of the payments. They also establish chaplain and judge advocate general departments within the Continental army.

July 31
Politics: The Continental Congress formally rejects Lord Frederick North's reconciliation plan as approved by Parliament in February. This called for an end to taxes on all colonies that raise revenue to support British officials and military personnel, but Congress has continued to insist that colonial legislatures alone can determine the use of monies raised.
North: Massachusetts militia under Major Benjamin Tupper attack Nantasket Point a second time, killing seven Royal Marines, wounding five, and capturing 33. American losses total two killed and one wounded.

August 1
Politics: The Continental Congress adjourns its fateful session and votes to reconvene on September 12, 1775.

August 3
North: General George Washington convenes a war council at his headquarters in Cambridge, Massachusetts, to discuss the critically low state of American gunpowder, which is poorly stored and susceptible to dampness and deterioration. They resolve to appeal to the colonies for fresh supplies.

August 6
South: The Virginia Convention appoints Patrick Henry a colonel of the 1st Regiment of state militia.

August 8
North: Captain Daniel Morgan arrives at Cambridge with his contingent of Virginia riflemen. The sharpshooters gain immediate notoriety for insubordination and disregard of military etiquette.

August 9–10
Naval: The British sloop HMS *Falcon* accosts two American schooners off the coast of Gloucester, Massachusetts, capturing one. However, when Captain John Linzee pursues the fugitive into Gloucester Harbor, he is repulsed by intense fire and

sustains three killed, one wounded. The British also lose two barges and 26 prisoners before heading back to sea once the American vessel is recaptured.

August 14
NORTH: Major John Brown completes his reconnaissance mission in Canada and reports back to General Philip J. Schuyler at Ticonderoga. He intimates that the French population and Indians are neutral while Saint Johns is lightly garrisoned by 300 men. Schuyler is encouraged to invade.

August 23
POLITICS: King George III of Great Britain issues his *Royal Proclamation of Rebellion,* declaring the colonies "misled by dangerous and ill designing men." By promising draconian measures against any public official deemed treasonous, this decree eliminates the possibility of reconciliation.

August 24
NORTH: Captain John Lamb and 60 men successfully capture the New York City battery and haul the cannon off despite the presence of the 64-gun HMS *Asia,* anchored nearby. When the British send a barge ashore to investigate, they are repelled with the loss of one man. The warship consequently unleashes a broadside against the battery, which triggers a mass exodus from the city.

August 26
POLITICS: The Rhode Island legislature directs that its delegates to the Continental Congress propose the creation of a Continental navy.
NORTH: General John Sullivan dispatches 1,200 men to build fortifications on Ploughed Hill, Boston, from which American artillery can range the harbor. But as Sullivan finishes his task he is bombarded by two floating British batteries. In the exchange that follows, one of the batteries is sunk by American artillery while Sullivan incurs three killed and two wounded.

August 28
NORTH: While General Philip J. Schuyler dithers about a prospective Canadian invasion in Albany, General Richard Montgomery assembles a force of 1,200 men at Fort Ticonderoga and embarks on Lake Champlain for Ile aux Noir without authorization.

August 30
NORTH: An ailing General Philip J. Schuyler approves Montgomery's decision to invade Canada and heads north with an additional 500 men to join him.
NAVAL: HMS *Rose* bombards Stonington, Connecticut, for repelling a foraging party, killing two citizens.

September 1
POLITICS: King George III refuses to receive the *Olive Branch Petition* issued by the Continental Congress.

September 2
NAVAL: General George Washington charters the 78-ton schooner *Hannah* of Beverly, Massachusetts, under Captain Nicholas Broughton to attack British transports and supply vessels off Boston Harbor. It is considered the first American warship.

September 6
NORTH: American forces under General Philip J. Schuyler assemble at Ile aux Noir, Quebec, before proceeding down the Richelieu River to Saint Johns. The defenders consist of 200 British soldiers and some Indians under Major Charles Preston. Having debarked near the fort, an American party is ambushed by Indians, with eight dead and nine wounded to a British loss of five killed and five wounded. Discouraged, Schuyler withdraws to Ile aux Noir for the evening.

A Canadian expedition of 1,054 men under Colonel Benedict Arnold sails from Newburyport, Massachusetts, and makes for the mouth of the Kennebec River. There they will disembark and wend their way through the Maine wilderness until reaching Quebec. The mission is undertaken without any prior knowledge or approval from Congress, and with a bare minimum of supplies and inadequate knowledge of the terrain to be encountered. Unknown at the time, Arnold's projected 20-day trek will last 45 days and cover 350 miles—twice the anticipated distance.

September 7
NAVAL: The armed schooner *Hannah* of Beverly, Massachusetts, seizes the transport HMS *Unity*, the first seagoing prize of the war; its valuable supply of gunpowder and arms is immediately forwarded to American forces outside Boston.

September 10
NORTH: General Philip J. Schuyler, having been reinforced at Ile aux Noir by an additional 700 men, leads a second advance against Saint Johns. His 1,700 soldiers attempt an ineffectual nighttime attack but their columns collide in the darkness and fire upon one another, so Schuyler withdraws to Ile aux Noir. Two days later General Richard Montgomery succeeds him as commander of American forces.

Disgruntled Pennsylvania riflemen, chafing under regular military order, mutiny briefly and are relocated from Cambridge to Prospect Hill. Surrounded by regular troops, the riflemen surrender their leaders, who are tried for insubordination and fined. All are then returned to the siege lines at Boston.
NAVAL: HMS *Nautilus*, grounded off Beverly, Massachusetts, while chasing an American schooner, is subsequently fired upon by militia units. The ship eventually frees itself and escapes with several wounded.

September 11
NORTH: A war council headed by General George Washington convenes to discuss the possibility of a direct attack upon Boston. After weighty deliberation all offensive action against the city is judged impracticable at *that* time.

September 13
POLITICS: The Second Continental Congress reconvenes with a delegation from Georgia, the first occasion on which all 13 colonies have provided representation.

September 15
SOUTH: American militia storm and capture Fort Johnson in Charleston, South Carolina, before it can be dismantled by British troops. The first Patriot flag of the colony is then unfurled over its ramparts. Royal governor William Campbell,

assessing his position as hopeless, immediately seeks refuge aboard the sloop HMS *Tamar* offshore.

September 16
NORTH: At Ile aux Noir, Quebec, General Richard Montgomery replaces an ailing Philip J. Schuyler as commander of forces in Canada. Reinforcements under Colonel Seth Warner bring American strength up to 2,000 effectives, although the British garrison at Saint Johns also rises to 500 men. Nevertheless, Montgomery resolves to commence a formal siege. Schuyler, meanwhile, returns to Fort Ticonderoga.

SOUTH: A truce is signed between William H. Drayton and the Loyalist, Colonel Thomas Fletchell, to circumvent the outbreak of hostilities and civil war in the South Carolina backcountry. The Loyalists are forced to agree not to join an invading British army, should one materialize, while the Patriots are sworn to respect the lives and property of Loyalists.

September 18
NORTH: Major John Brown and 135 Americans ambush a British supply train near Fort Chambly, Quebec. Brown is subsequently reinforced by an additional 500 men under Colonel Timothy Bedel, who helps thwart British efforts to recapture the train. Eight Indians are killed in exchange for two Americans wounded.

NAVAL: Admiral Samuel Graves orders all merchant vessels searched for flint, a quartz stone used as ballast, which if found, is to be thrown overboard. In this manner he hopes to cut off a possible supply of musket flints to the rebels. Graves also learns that he is to be replaced as North American naval commander by year's end.

September 19
POLITICS: The Continental Congress appoints the Secret Committee, successively under Thomas Willing and Robert Morris, to solicit clandestinely military arms and stores from abroad.

NORTH: General Richard Montgomery deploys 350 men on the Richelieu River to interdict HMS *Royal Savage* from entering Lake Champlain. He then begins a formal siege of Saint Johns, Quebec.

September 23
NORTH: The American expedition under Colonel Benedict Arnold departs Gardiner, Massachusetts (Maine), and advances through the wilderness in three divisions, each separated by a one-day interval.

September 24
POLITICS: The British cabinet under Lord North vows to pursue war with America "with the utmost vigor."

September 25
NORTH: General Richard Montgomery dispatches Colonel Ethan Allen to Chambly to recruit Canadian volunteers, but Allen encounters the returning force under Major John Brown en route. Together they decide to launch a two-pronged attacked on Montreal with 200 men. However, Governor-General Guy Carleton detects the weakness of Allen's advance (Brown fails to cross) and orders 35 soldiers and 200

On September 25, 1775, a small detachment of Americans under Colonel Ethan Allen launches a foolhardy attack near Montreal that results in Allen's capture. *(U.S. Army Center of Military History)*

Canadian volunteers under Captain Walter Butler to sortie. Allen is overwhelmed and captured, along with 40 soldiers, in a swift riposte. The Americans suffer a further seven killed to a British total of three slain and two wounded.

September 26
DIPLOMACY: Americans convene a peace conference with numerous Indian tribes at Pittsburgh, Pennsylvania. Representatives of various Ohio Valley tribes, the Continental Congress, and the British Indian Department are all present. After some deliberation, the Indians pledge their neutrality while Congress recognizes the Ohio River as the boundary between settlements and the frontier.
NORTH: General Thomas Gage is informed that he is being recalled to England for "consultations," a euphemism that effectively ends his military career. He is succeeded by General William "Billy" Howe, an immensely popular officer.

October 3
POLITICS: Rhode Island delegates at the Continental Congress urge the construction of a Continental navy. This is the first formal call for a naval arm.

October 4
POLITICS: Congress establishes a committee consisting of Benjamin Franklin, Thomas Lynch, and Benjamin Harrison to visit General George Washington's headquarters in Cambridge, Massachusetts. There they will inquire as to the status of military preparations and encourage him to capture Boston by December, if possible.
NORTH: Army surgeon general Benjamin Church is court-martialed for corresponding with the British. General George Washington, constrained by the Articles of War, refers the matter of punishment to the Continental Congress.

October 6
NORTH: The Canadian expedition of Colonel Benedict Arnold sails up the Kennebec River and reaches the Norridgewock Falls, where his men have to portage their numerous bateaux and other vessels by hand.

October 7
NAVAL: Admiral Samuel Graves authorizes British naval vessels to conduct punitive raids along the New England coast to dissuade privateering operations. A small force under Captain James Wallace arrives off Bristol, Rhode Island, and bombards the town until it agrees to surrender 40 sheep. The British vessel then departs without further incident; two civilians are killed.

October 10
NORTH: General Thomas Gage sails back to London, having been relieved of duties as commander in chief of British forces in North America.
NAVAL: The armed schooner *Hannah* under Captain Nicholson Broughton encounters Captain John Collins of the British sloop HMS *Nautilus* and flees to Beverly Harbor, Massachusetts, grounding there. The tide quickly ebbs, and while *Nautilus* tries to escape, it also runs ashore. Swarms of angry militiamen under Colonel Henry Herrick pelt the British vessel for four hours before it refloats and escapes with one killed and one wounded.

October 13
POLITICS: The Continental Congress authorizes Colonel John Glover to convert several transport vessels into warships and also approves construction of two armed warships as the nucleus of a new national navy. A marine committee consisting of Silas Deane, Christopher Gadsden, and John Langdon is then appointed to oversee such matters.

October 17
NORTH: A force of 625 men, including 350 newly recruited Canadians, under Colonels James Livingston and Timothy Bedel paddles down the St. Lawrence River, bypasses Saint Johns, and invests Fort Chambly, Quebec.
NAVAL: Royal Navy warships HMS *Canceaux*, eight guns, and *Halifax*, six guns, under Captain Henry Mowat drop anchor off Falmouth (Portland, Maine), Massachusetts, and send an ultimatum ashore, demanding the town's surrender. When refused,

Mowat bombards the waterfront for nine hours and landing parties go ashore to complete the destruction. Ultimately, fire engulfs 400 buildings and 15 vessels. The extent of destruction outrages New Englanders and fans the flames of resentment against Great Britain.

October 18
NORTH: American forces outside Fort Chambly, Quebec, float two nine-pound cannon down the Richelieu River and begin bombarding that post. Their fire finally convinces Major John Stopford to surrender 88 soldiers of the 7th Regiment along with many valuable supplies. More important, the water route from Saint Johns is now severed.

Governor William Tryon of New York escapes to the safety of HMS *Duchess of Gordon* in New York Harbor to avoid arrest. This vessel will serve as his headquarters for almost a year.

October 24
SOUTH: Governor John Murray, Lord Dunmore, lands six tenders at Hampton Creek, Virginia, in an attempt to destroy Norfolk. After bombarding and capturing nearby Hampton, they are met and driven off by riflemen under Colonel William Woodford with loss. Five vessels are sunk while two run aground and are captured by the Americans.

October 25
NORTH: The Canadian expedition under Colonel Benedict Arnold struggles to surmount a flooded countryside and freezing weather in the vicinity of Dead River. He loses the 300-man division of Colonel Roger Enos when they vote to return home.

October 26
NORTH: General David Wooster reinforces the siege of Saint Johns with 335 Connecticut troops and is soon joined by Major Barnabas Tuthill with an additional 225 New Yorkers.

October 27
POLITICS: A congressional committee recommends the construction or purchase of five frigates of 32 guns, five of 28 guns, and three with 24 guns.

October 28
NORTH: General William Howe issues a proclamation forbidding all Boston inhabitants from leaving the city under penalty of death. Henceforth all men of military age are also required to enroll in militia companies for the city's defense.

The American expedition under Colonel Benedict Arnold, having weathered incredible hardships and deprivations for a month, finally reaches the divide between the St. Lawrence and Atlantic watersheds. He resolves to press ahead while his soldiers are reduced to eating dogs and shoe leather.

October 30
POLITICS: Congress authorizes construction of a 36-gun and a 20-gun frigate. It also expands the Naval Committee by adding four new members: John Adams, Joseph Hewes, Stephen Hopkins, and Richard H. Lee.

North: Governor-General Guy Carleton, seeking to lift the siege of Saint Johns, advances with 800 soldiers and Indians and attempts to cross the St. Lawrence River at Longueuil, Quebec. They are engaged by Lieutenant Colonel Seth Warner's Green Mountain Boys and forced back. An attempt to flank the defenders also fails, so Carleton withdraws.

The American expedition under Colonel Benedict Arnold reaches Sertigan, Quebec, where supplies are purchased for the hungry, half-frozen soldiers.

November 2
Politics: The Naval Committee votes to purchase and rename eight merchant vessels as men-of-war; *Alfred*, 24 guns; *Columbus*, 18; *Andrew Doria*, 14; *Cabot*, 14; *Providence*, 12; *Hornet*, 10; *Wasp*, eight; and *Fly*, eight.
North: After staunchly defending Saint Johns, Quebec, for 55 days, Major Charles Preston concludes that he has no alternative but surrender. He then yields 500 prisoners and 41 artillery pieces to General Richard Montgomery. British losses include 25 killed during the siege, while Major John Andre, a future spy, is among those captured. The advance to Montreal is now open, but the delay incurred wastes two months of good weather and forces the Americans to wage a costly winter campaign for the rest of Canada.

November 4
Politics: The Continental Congress reorganizes the Continental army at Boston into a force of 20,372 officers and men, the majority of whom will remain under arms only through the end of 1776.

November 5
North: General Richard Montgomery leads a belated advance against Montreal under rainy and muddy conditions.
Naval: Esek Hopkins is appointed the first commodore of the Continental navy by the Continental Congress. He then assumes command of four armed commercial vessels outfitting at Philadelphia; the *Cabot*, the *Alfred*, the *Columbus*, and the *Andrew Doria*.

November 7
Politics: The House of Commons summarily rejects the *Olive Branch Petition*.

The Continental Congress amends the Articles of War to include treason as a capital crime.
North: The Rhode Island General Assembly removes Governor Joseph Wanton from office.
South: Governor John Murray, Lord Dunmore, declares Virginia under martial law and orders all law-abiding citizens to flock to his standard or be considered traitors. He also issues an emancipation proclamation offering freedom to any African-American slaves who join the British army. This provocative act ultimately backfires and ensures a considerable unity among disparate rebel forces.

November 8
Politics: The Continental Congress directs the Secret Committee to purchase arms and ammunition through the West Indies by trading American products.

November 9
NORTH: Colonel Benedict Arnold's command, reduced to 675 men by sickness and exposure, concludes a remarkable 450-mile trek through the Maine wilderness by reaching the St. Lawrence River opposite Quebec.

General William Howe is instructed by Secretary of the Colonies William Legge, Lord Dartmouth, to consider evacuating Boston and proceeding to New York to begin offensive operations. Howe, lacking sufficient shipping to convey both troops and numerous Loyalists wishing to leave, and not yet directly threatened by the Americans, declines to move at present.

Riflemen under Colonel William Thompson repulse a 500-man British foraging party at Phipp's Farm on Lechmere Point, Boston. The British lose two killed for two American wounded but manage to abscond with 10 cows. The Americans subsequently erect a water battery at this point.

November 10
POLITICS: Lord George Germain becomes secretary of state for the colonies, principally because of his hard-line support for crushing the nascent rebellion.

The Continental Congress authorizes two battalions of Continental marines to supplement its embryonic naval force. Captain Samuel Nicholas becomes the first commissioned officer of the Continental marine corps.

November 11
NORTH: Governor-General Guy Carleton hurriedly evacuates Montreal and withdraws his remaining 150 soldiers eastward along the St. Lawrence River to Quebec.
NAVAL: Captain Simon Tuft and the ship *Defiance,* while blockading Hog Point near Charleston, South Carolina, are attacked by British ships HMS *Tamer* and *Cherokee.* He nonetheless manages to scuttle four hulks without any casualties.

November 13
NORTH: American forces vigorously advance under General Richard Montgomery and receive Montreal's surrender. Meanwhile, Colonel Benedict Arnold, having rested his exhausted command for several days, crosses the St. Lawrence River at night and lands before the town of Quebec.

November 14
SOUTH: Governor John Murray, Lord Dunmore, leads 350 British soldiers from Norfolk against a smaller body of militia under Colonel William Woodford. They clash at Kemp's Landing on the Elizabeth River, Virginia, and the Americans withdraw after losing nine killed and 14 wounded.

November 15
NORTH: Colonel Benedict Arnold's command of 700 men occupies the Plains of Abraham, outside of Quebec City, and unsuccessfully attempts to bluff the 1,200-man garrison under Lieutenant Colonel Allan MacLean into surrendering. He subsequently concludes that 2,000 men and several cannon are necessary for its capture.

November 16
POLITICS: Outspoken Whig Edmund Burke introduces a bill in the House of Commons insisting that, because the colonies lack parliamentary representation, only

November 17
Politics: Parliament overwhelmingly defeats Edmund Burke's reconciliation bill, 210 to 105.
North: Colonel Henry Knox is appointed commander of the new Continental Regiment of Artillery, signaling the birth of that arm. He is also dispatched to Fort Ticonderoga to retrieve British ordnance captured there.
Naval: Charlottetown (on Prince Edward Island) is captured and sacked by American privateers.

November 18
South: A force of 1,800 Loyalists under Colonel Patrick Cunningham invests 600 Americans under Colonel Andrew Williamson at Fort Ninety Six, South Carolina. The contestants spend the next two days pot-shotting each other, with few losses to either side.

November 19
North: Colonel Benedict Arnold withdraws 20 miles from Quebec to avoid a possible attack by Lieutenant Colonel Allan MacLean. He sets up camp at Point aux Trembles for the next two weeks to await developments while MacLean prepares for the defense of the city. Meanwhile, the British flotilla on the St. Lawrence is detained at Sorel by adverse winds. An American force under Colonel John Brown brings up artillery and bombards the British into submission; General Richard Prescott, 145 rank and file, several armed ships, eight smaller craft, and stores pass into captivity. Governor-General Guy Carleton escapes by only the barest of margins.

November 21
South: Patriot militia under Colonel Andrew Williams, having nearly exhausted their gunpowder, conclude a truce with a larger Loyalist force at Fort Ninety Six, South Carolina. Henceforth the Americans will destroy their fortifications, release all their prisoners, and return to their homes unmolested. A 20-day cease-fire also ensues to permit the leaders of both factions to confer in Charleston. Of little consequence militarily, the "siege" of Fort Ninety Six marks the beginning of a protracted civil war throughout the South.

November 25
Politics: The Continental Congress authorizes privateering against English shipping and urges the creation of Admiralty courts to dispense the prize money.
South: Colonel William Woodford and 300 Virginia militia are dispatched to Suffolk to protect military supplies gathered there. His approach induces Governor John Murray, Lord Dunmore, to intercept him below the Elizabeth River at Great Bridge.

November 27
Naval: Captain John Manley, commanding the armed schooner *Lee,* captures the British ordnance brig HMS *Nancy* off Cape Ann, Massachusetts. This vessel is heav-

ily laden with military stores, including 2,000 muskets, 100,000 flints, 31 tons of musket balls, and a 2,700-pound mortar dubbed "Congress," all of which are immediately forwarded to the Continental army at Boston.

November 28
POLITICS: John Adams and the Naval Committee establish regulations for governing the nascent Continental navy, in effect, formally creating that force. These ordinances prescribe rates of pay, rations, discipline, and division of prize money.

November 29
DIPLOMACY: The Committee of Secret Correspondence to Conduct Foreign Relations is created by the Continental Congress to acquire loans and military supplies from sympathetic European governments—in effect, an embryonic Department of State. It is authorized to dispatch agents to friendly European powers to accomplish those ends. The members appointed are Benjamin Franklin, John Jay, John Dickinson, Benjamin Harrison, and Thomas Johnson.
SOUTH: A militia force of 1,000 men under Colonel William Woodford assumes strong defensive positions along the west bank of the Elizabeth River, Virginia, and awaits the approach of Governor John Murray, Lord Dunmore. The Americans hope to thwart British intentions of seizing Suffolk.

December 1
NORTH: A small column of 300 men under General Richard Montgomery sails down the St. Lawrence River to bolster Colonel Benedict Arnold at Point aux Trembles. Despite the onset of winter, supply shortages, and expiring enlistments, the siege of Quebec begins two days later with 800 men.

December 3
NAVAL: Lieutenant John Paul Jones unfurls the 13-stripe Grand Union Flag over the *Alfred* at Philadelphia. This represents the first American ensign ever hoisted aboard a warship.

December 6
POLITICS: The Continental Congress responds to King George III's rejection of the *Olive Branch Petition,* repeating vows of allegiance and protesting Parliament's unconstitutional actions. Independence is never mentioned.

December 7
NORTH: Richard Montgomery advances in rank to major general, although he will be killed before the promotion takes effect.

December 8
DIPLOMACY: In Paris, Charles Gravier, comte de Vergennes, declares that King Louis XVI has renewed his injunction against loading munitions aboard American vessels in port. However, the law is never seriously enforced.
NORTH: General Richard Montgomery demands Quebec's surrender; when Governor-General Guy Carleton refuses, American forces begin an ineffectual bombardment.

Colonel Henry Knox departs Fort Ticonderoga, New York, and begins transporting captured British ordnance 300 miles east to Boston. His train consists of 40 sleds drawn by 80 oxen and must negotiate rough terrain in mid-winter.

December 9
SOUTH: Governor John Murray, Lord Dunmore, appears before Great Bridge on the Elizabeth River, Virginia, with 600 Loyalists, 200 soldiers, and several former slaves. Though greatly outnumbered by American forces under Colonel William Woodford on the western side of the bridge, he orders Captain Samuel Leslie to force a passage across the causeway. Leslie is tricked into thinking that Woodford's defenses are unmanned and carelessly approaches without any precaution until the Americans suddenly rise and pour a heavy fire into the column. The British and Loyalists lose heavily yet form up for another charge, which results in further carnage. Dunmore finally withdraws after suffering 13 killed and 49 wounded to one American wounded. Woodford suddenly seizes the initiative and charges across the bridge, trapping the British behind their fortifications. Dunmore escapes under cover of darkness and his forces subsequently evacuate Norfolk.

December 10
NORTH: Expiring enlistments induce many Connecticut soldiers to leave Boston, underscoring a problem that vexes the Continental army throughout the war.
NAVAL: Captain James Wallace of HMS *Rose* leads 200 British marines and sailors on a raid against Conanicut Island, Rhode Island, in which 16 homes are burned and 100 livestock seized. The Americans lose two killed, seven wounded, and two captured.

December 13
SOUTH: Virginia militia under Colonel William Woodford, flush with their recent success at Great Bridge, occupy the port of Norfolk.

December 14
POLITICS: The Continental Congress mandates creation of a 13-seat marine committee, with one member from each colony, to augment the Naval Committee. It is tasked with purchasing and outfitting all warships authorized by that body.

December 21
POLITICS: Parliament authorizes the Confiscation Act for seizing rebel property. If shipping is involved, then crewmembers so taken are subject to impressment into the Royal Navy.

December 22
POLITICS: Parliament passes the Prohibitory Act to interdict and dissuade all possible foreign trade with the rebellious colonies. Violators are henceforth subject to impoundment.

The Continental Congress authorizes construction of five 32-gun, five 28-gun, and three 24-gun frigates to be named *Hancock, Randolph, Raleigh, Warren, Washington, Congress, Effingham, Providence, Trumbull, Virginia, Boston, Delaware,* and

Montgomery. This pits a force of 14 vessels and 332 guns against a Royal Navy establishment of 89 warships mounting 2,576 guns. Dudley Saltonstall, Abraham Whipple, John B. Hopkins, and Nicholas Biddle also receive captain's commissions. Esek Hopkins gains appointment as the nation's first naval commander in chief.

SOUTH: A force of 1,400 South Carolina militia under Colonels Richard Richardson, Thomas Polk, Alex Martin, and William Thompson gather to help quell a growing Loyalist movement. This force surprises and annihilates a smaller Loyalist detachment at Great Cane Brake on the Reedy River, killing six and taking 130 prisoners. Several of the most wanted Loyalist leaders are also apprehended.

December 23
POLITICS: King George III, by dint of royal proclamation, closes the colonies to all foreign commerce and trade as of the following March.

December 28
DIPLOMACY: The Committee of Secret Correspondence in Philadelphia receives French agent Archard de Bonvouloir, who assures the Americans of his government's sympathy and intention to ignore any clandestine effort to raise money and arms illegally in France.

December 30
NORTH: In a desperate gamble, General Richard Montgomery and Colonel Benedict Arnold lay out a plan for attacking Quebec, then garrisoned by 1,800 British regulars and militia under Governor-General Guy Carleton. It is a two-pronged affair, with Arnold taking 600 men along the banks of the St. Charles River while Montgomery leads 300 from Cape Diamond down a narrow path, south of the city. At a given signal, both columns will attack and try to capture the Lower Town, believed to be lightly defended.

December 31
NORTH: Outnumbered, short of supplies, and faced with expiring enlistments, General Richard Montgomery and Colonel Benedict Arnold launch a desperate attack on the 1,800-man garrison of Governor-General Guy Carleton during a howling blizzard. Montgomery personally leads the charge against a fortified position and is among the first killed by enemy fire. Arnold's 600-man column enjoys better success and overruns several enemy positions, but he is wounded in the leg and evacuated. His successor, Major Daniel Morgan, continues attacking the barricades and enjoys some minor success but is ultimately surrounded and forced to surrender. The Americans have 30 killed, 42 wounded, and 425 prisoners to a British tally of five killed and 13 wounded. Arnold gathers up his surviving soldiers and reestablishes a loose siege of the city.

1776

January 1
NORTH: General David Wooster assumes temporary command of American forces in Canada.

A new flag with 13 alternating white and red stripes and a blue field is unfurled for the first time at Cambridge, Massachusetts. In his general orders, General George Washington declares the beginning of a "new" army.

SOUTH: A British fleet commanded by Governor James Murray, Lord Dunmore, anchors off Norfolk, Virginia, and demands provisions. When the citizens refuse to comply the fleet commences a lengthy bombardment of the town and lands parties that torch the wharves and storehouses along the waterfront. Both sides suffer six killed or wounded.

January 2
SOUTH: The fires at Norfolk continue into the night, destroying 54 houses. The local committee of safety orders the remainder of the town burned to deny its use to the British. The property of local Loyalists is thus likewise consumed, resulting in 860 structures destroyed.

January 3
SOUTH: Royal governor Josiah Martin of North Carolina receives authorization from Secretary for the Colonies William Legge, Lord Dartmouth, to raise an army of 20,000 Loyalists from among that colony's large Scottish highlander population. This force is to rendezvous at Brunswick no later than February 15 and cooperate with a British military expedition expected off the coast that spring.

January 4
NORTH: A British burial detail uncovers the frozen remains of General Richard Montgomery outside Quebec City, and Governor-General Guy Carleton orders that it be interred with military honors. Montgomery's body reposed in Canada until 1818, when it was reburied at St. Paul's Church, New York.

General George Washington writes and assures the Continental Congress that he will attack Boston as soon as an opportunity arises.

January 5
NORTH: New Hampshire delegates meeting at Portsmouth vote to becomes the first independent state. They then replace the colonial charter with a new constitution mandating a president and a bicameral legislature.

NAVAL: The Continental Congress orders Commodore Esek Hopkins to sea with orders to clear the Virginia and Carolina coasts of marauding British vessels.

January 6
NORTH: General William Howe, eager to rid himself of his annoying subordinate General Henry Clinton, dispatches him from Boston on an expedition to Cape Fear, North Carolina. There he is to rendezvous with another squadron sailing from Cork, Ireland, under Commodore Peter Parker and General Charles Cornwallis. It is hoped that their combined forces will encourage a Loyalist resurgence throughout the southern colonies.

In New York, Alexander Hamilton founds the Provincial Company of Artillery of the Colony of New York with himself as colonel—this is the oldest, most continuous unit of the U.S. Army and survives today as Battery D, 5th Field Artillery.

January 8
North: A raid by Major Thomas Knowlton against Charlestown, Massachusetts, interrupts a performance of General John Burgoyne's farce *The Blockade of Boston*. The audience, assuming this is part of the play, laugh uproariously, but the Americans subsequently take five prisoners and burn several houses.

January 9
Politics: After a long delay, the Continental Congress finally promotes Colonel Benedict Arnold to brigadier general. Their neglect remains a source of resentment with the mercurial leader.

Thomas Paine publishes his seminal polemic *Common Sense* in Philadelphia, which electrifies the American polity and further enhances the stage for independence from Great Britain. "Everything that is right or reasonable pleads for separation," Paine emoted. "The blood of the slain, the weeping voice of nature cries, 'tis time to part." It is addressed squarely at common people and denounces King George III as the "Royal Brute." This tract proves to be one of the most influential pamphlets in history and enjoys a print run of half a million copies—unprecedented for its day.

January 10
South: Former royal governor Josiah Martin of North Carolina, onboard HMS *Scorpion*, urges Loyalists to gather at Brunswick, south of Wilmington, and cooperate with a forthcoming British expedition. He hopes to raise a force of 20,000 soldiers, including large contingents of Scottish highlanders.

January 11
Politics: The Maryland Convention, convening at Annapolis, sides with assemblies in New Jersey, Delaware, and Pennsylvania, by rejecting independence in favor of moderation. The colony's delegates at the Continental Congress are likewise instructed to pursue rapprochement with Great Britain and be receptive toward any conciliatory gestures from the king or Parliament.

January 12
North: British forces under Captain James Wallace and Rhode Island militia sustain a three-hour fight for possession of Patience, Hope, and Prudence Islands in Narragansett Bay. The British sustain three casualties, then withdraw.

January 15
North: Volunteers out of Newbury, Massachusetts, man three whaleboats and capture a British provisions ship.

January 17
North: General Philip J. Schuyler and 3,000 New York militia advance upon Johnson Hall, home of Loyalist Sir John Johnson. Johnson has amassed a force of 700 Loyalists and Indians but surrenders without a shot. Schuyler's victory thus eliminates any Loyalist threat emanating from the Albany region.
South: The Virginia Convention orders that all African Americans caught fighting for the British are to be resold to the West Indies.

NAVAL: Commodore Esek Hopkins sails from Philadelphia with his squadron of eight warships, although ice on the Delaware River prevents him from getting to sea. Samuel Tucker is also commissioned captain in the Continental navy and receives command of the frigate *Franklin*.

January 19
POLITICS: The Continental Congress approves of reinforcements for Canada from New Hampshire, Connecticut, Pennsylvania, and New Jersey. Furthermore, General George Washington is ordered to dispatch a battalion from Cambridge while Colonel Moses Hazen is authorized to raise a regiment in Canada.
NORTH: Colonel John Haslet is appointed head of the newly raised Delaware Continentals, one of the few American formations equipped with bayonets.

January 20
SOUTH: General Henry Clinton departs from Boston with 1,500 men on a naval expedition to Cape Fear, North Carolina, to assist royal governor Josiah Martin and await reinforcements. Once joined by Commodore Peter Parker and General Charles Cornwallis, his first task is to seize Wilmington as a base for future operations.

January 23
NORTH: The committee of safety in Elizabethtown, New Jersey, is informed that a British supply vessel, HMS *Blue Mountain Valley*, is anchored off the coast. Colonels William Alexander and Elias Dayton are directed to capture the intruder and lead four boatloads of volunteers 40 miles out from Sandy Hook, New York. The unsuspecting British, assuming the approaching craft are fishermen, are quickly subdued and brought into port.

January 24
POLITICS: The Continental Congress begins deliberations on independence and a committee is appointed under James Wilson of Pennsylvania. The recent failure of the Canadian expedition prompts them to investigate founding a war office to better coordinate military measures.
NORTH: Colonel Henry Knox arduously transports 44 cannon and 16 mortars from Fort Ticonderoga to American forces at Cambridge, Massachusetts. He accomplishes this remarkable trek of 300 miles in the dead of winter and without the benefit of wagons or roads. His arrival decisively tips the military equation at Boston in favor of the Americans.

January 25
POLITICS: The Continental Congress authorizes the Marine Committee, with one member from each state, to oversee affairs of the American fleet.

January 26
NAVAL: Admiral Samuel Graves is replaced as supreme naval commander in American waters by Admiral Molyneux Shuldham.

February 4
NORTH: A detachment of the Continental army under General Charles Lee occupies New York City just as the expedition under General Henry Clinton drops anchor in the harbor.

February 6
SOUTH: Colonel Robert Howe abandons Norfolk, Virginia, having completed the task of burning all remaining structures to the ground. The once thriving commercial center is now desolate and depopulated.

February 7
NORTH: Colonel William Alexander arrives in New York at the head of 1,000 New Jersey troops to reinforce the garrison.

February 13
POLITICS: In Philadelphia, James Wilson submits his 6,000-word draft concerning the prospects of independence from Great Britain. However, the recent publication and wild reception of Thomas Paine's *Common Sense* negates the document's relevance, and it is unceremoniously tabled.

February 15
SOUTH: Lieutenant Colonel Donald MacDonald musters 1,400 Loyalist Highlanders at Cross Creek, North Carolina, although only one-third possess arms. He nonetheless begins marching to the coast to join British forces expected there.

February 16
NORTH: General George Washington, anxious over weeks of inactivity in Boston, proposes a large-scale attack across the frozen waters of the bay with 16,000 men. However, he defers to his officers when they suggest that seizing strategic Dorchester Heights and planting newly arrived artillery there is more expedient. This move is calculated to force General William Howe either to leave his entrenchments and fight or to evacuate the city entirely.

February 17
POLITICS: The Continental Congress orders General Charles Lee to succeed General Philip J. Schuyler as head of the Northern Department.
NAVAL: Commodore Esek Hopkins, having sailed from Philadelphia a month earlier, finally reaches open water with a small squadron of eight armed and refitted merchantmen. Present for this first cruise of the nascent Continental navy are the 24-gun frigate *Alfred,* the 20-gun frigate *Columbus,* the 14-gun brigs *Cabot* and *Andrew Doria,* the sloops *Providence* and *Hornet,* and the schooners *Fly* and *Wasp*—mounting a total of 110 guns. Hopkins is ordered by Congress to drive Lord Dunmore's fleet out of the Chesapeake and scour the southern coastline for British privateers, but he uses a discretionary clause to attack Nassau in the Bahamas instead.

February 18
SOUTH: A Loyalist force of 1,500 men under Lieutenant Colonel Donald MacDonald, en route to Brunswick, North Carolina, confronts Patriot forces dug in behind Rockfish Creek. The Loyalists use boats to cross the river upstream and continue on their way.

February 23
SOUTH: Loyalists under Lieutenant Colonel Donald MacDonald advance toward Brunswick, North Carolina, but are blocked by Patriot militia under Colonel

Richard Caswell at Corbett's Ferry. MacDonald then builds a temporary bridge across the Black River and continues his march. At this juncture the 80-year-old MacDonald is taken ill and replaced by Captain Alexander Macleod.

February 27
POLITICS: The Continental Congress establishes the Northern, Middle and Southern Departments for the Continental army.
SOUTH: An American force of 1,900 men under Colonels James Moore, Alexander Lillington, John Ashe, and Richard Caswell confronts 1,500 Scottish Loyalists under Captain Alexander Macleod at Moore's Creek Bridge, North Carolina. Inexplicably, Macleod storms the bridge in full view of the defenders only to discover that the Americans have removed the planks and greased the poles. The attack flounders, Macleod is killed along with 30 soldiers, and 850 prisoners are secured. The Americans suffer one killed and one wounded in the three-minute affair. The defeat forces the British to abandon plans for converting nearby Wilmington into a base of operations, along with Governor Josiah Martin's plan to reestablish royal authority.

February 28
NORTH: General George Washington writes to African-American scribe Phillis Wheatley, thanking her for a poem written in his honor.

February 29
DIPLOMACY: The Continental Congress deliberates the possibility of entering formal trade agreements with France and Spain, which can only properly manifest when independence has been achieved. The debate sputters on for several hours without resolution.

March 1
NORTH: New York delegates pressure the Continental Congress to withdraw General Charles Lee as commander of the Northern Department and restore General Philip J. Schuyler. Henceforth, Lee is appointed commander of the Southern Department, headquartered at Charleston, South Carolina.
NAVAL: The American naval squadron of Commodore Esek Hopkins rendezvouses off the Bahaman island of Abaco, prior to launching a coordinated attack upon the capital of New Providence (Nassau). Of the eight vessels that departed Philadelphia in January, the schooners *Fly* and *Wasp* were previously damaged in a collision and returned home.

March 2
NORTH: American artillery in Boston provide a nighttime diversion by bombarding the city from Cobble Hill, Lechmere Point, and Roxbury while troops simultaneously occupy Dorchester Heights. British counterfire kills six and wounds five.

March 3
DIPLOMACY: The Continental Congress appoints Connecticut delegate Silas Deane as agent to France and dispatches him there to purchase military supplies. He is also authorized to sound out the foreign minister, Charles Gravier, comte de Vergennes, as to the possibility of an alliance.

South: Royal governor James Wright of Georgia attacks Savannah with naval reinforcements under Commodore Andrew Barkley; 11 merchant vessels are seized in the harbor. General Lachlan McIntosh, shorthanded and tasked with defending the city, does nothing to stop these depredations. However, the marauders are subsequently driven from their base camp on Hutchinson's Island by fire ships drifted in their direction. Both sides lose six killed and wounded.

Naval: The American naval squadron under Commodore Esek Hopkins attacks and captures New Providence on Nassau, the Bahamas, with sailors and 200 marines under Captain Samuel Nicholas. Governor Montfort Browne surrenders after a token defense at Fort Montagu. Hopkins lingers two weeks loading 88 cannon, 15 mortars, and quantities of gunpowder. This is the navy's first planned offensive and goes off smoothly. However, Hopkins's dilatory pace allows the governor to ship off 150 casks of gunpowder before he arrives.

March 4

North: General John Thomas and Colonel Richard Gridley lead 2,000 men on a nighttime foray to seize Dorchester Heights, concealed by an American artillery diversion to obscure the noise of digging. His men work arduously through the night and complete an impressive array of earthworks and fortifications by daybreak. These are promptly occupied by 10 companies of Continentals and riflemen. Cannon are soon brought up to Nook's Hill and Castle William, and their appearance completely astonishes the defenders. Admiral Molyneux Shuldham, the Royal Navy commander in Boston, insists that General William Howe either eliminate the threat to his fleet or evacuate the city altogether. Howe carefully considers the former option and prepares 2,200 men to attack Castle William that evening. Unfortunately, a storm prevents the troops from deploying, so Howe decides his position is no longer tenable. He prepares for the evacuation of Boston.

March 9

North: British and American artillery engage in a lengthy duel at Nook's Hill, Boston, which drives off unsheltered Continental infantry with five killed.

Naval: The Maryland warship *Defense,* assisted by two militia companies, attacks and drives off HMS *Otter* from Chariton Creek, Virginia.

March 12

South: A British naval expedition commanded by General Henry Clinton arrives off Cape Fear, North Carolina, and awaits reinforcements under Commodore Peter Parker. However, Clinton learns of the Loyalist defeat at Moore's Creek Bridge and recalculates his mission.

March 14

Politics: The Continental Congress strongly recommends disarming all Loyalist sympathizers.

March 17

North: General William Howe concludes an 11-month siege by finally evacuating Boston, taking 9,000 troops and 1,000 Loyalists onboard 125 ships. He has reached an understanding with General George Washington that, providing his retreat is uninterrupted, Boston will not be burned. However, the British troops plunder a number of residences against orders before exiting. The town is then reoccupied by American soldiers under General Artemas Ward. Washington, meanwhile, fears that Howe will sail for New York City and makes preparations to shift men and materiel to its defense.

March 19
Politics: The Continental Congress tables a motion by Samuel Chase that would have permitted attacks on British merchant vessels by the Continental navy. It instead encourages the practice of privateering.

March 20
Diplomacy: The Continental Congress instructs a deputation consisting of Benjamin Franklin, Samuel Chase, Charles Carroll, and the Reverend John Carroll to visit Canada and entreat the people to join the rebellion. They also wish to assure Canadians that their rights of worship, as Roman Catholics, will be preserved.
North: The victorious Continental army occupies Boston after a siege of nearly a year. But the Americans warily watch the British fleet, anchored five miles distant at Nantasket Roads, as it pauses to take on fresh water and other supplies.

March 23
Politics: The Continental Congress formally authorizes privateering against all British shipping and begins issuing letters of marque.

March 25
Politics: In light of the British evacuation of Boston, the Continental Congress authorizes a gold medal to be struck in honor of General George Washington.

March 26
South: The South Carolina General Assembly enacts a new government to replace its colonial charter, with John Rutledge as president.

March 27
Naval: The last Royal Navy vessels depart Nantasket Roads, five miles below Boston, and make sail for Halifax, Nova Scotia. A few remaining warships maintain a loose blockade of the city.

April 1
North: Some 1,124 Loyalist refugees from New England arrive in Halifax, Nova Scotia, the first of 40,000 who will settle there during the Revolution.

April 2
North: General David Wooster marches from Montreal to Quebec City with reinforcements and supersedes General Benedict Arnold. Arnold, meanwhile, falls off his horse and is forced to leave.

April 4
Naval: Captain Abraham Whipple and the 20-gun frigate *Columbus* induces the six-gun schooner HMS *Hawke* to surrender off Block Island, Rhode Island. This is the first enemy warship actually taken at sea.

April 5
NAVAL: The frigate *Alfred* under Commodore Esek Hopkins seizes the British bomb brig HMS *Bolton* under Lieutenant Edward Sneyd.

April 6
POLITICS: The Continental Congress reacts against Parliament's American Prohibitory Act and opens its ports to all nations except Great Britain. Henceforth, Spain, France, and the Netherlands are free to engage in commercial activities with the colonies. Meanwhile, Moderates caution compatriots that summarily rejecting the British Navigation Acts constitutes de facto independence.

NAVAL: The American naval squadron under Commodore Esek Hopkins engages Captain Tyringham Howe and the Royal Navy's 20-gun frigate HMS *Glasgow* off Block Island, Rhode Island, but fails to capture it after a three-hour running battle. The sloop *Cabot* is severely damaged in the chase and hauled off as the *Alfred* succeeds it in the van. Howe continues to maneuver brilliantly and severely damages *Alfred's* steering with a lucky shot. He then skillfully eludes his pursuers, which now include the *Andrew Doria* and *Columbus,* and successfully puts into Newport. Hopkins is subsequently censured for his performance; the Americans lose 10 killed and 14 wounded to British losses of one killed and three wounded.

April 7
NAVAL: While cruising off the Virginia Capes, Captain John Barry and the 16-gun brig *Lexington* capture the British sloop HMS *Edward* after a sharp, four-hour encounter. The Americans lose two killed and two wounded to one Briton dead and one injured. This is the first British vessel actually seized in a ship-to-ship engagement.

April 8
NAVAL: The eight-ship squadron under Commodore Esek Hopkins drops anchor in New London, Connecticut, concluding its only sortie in strength.

April 9
POLITICS: The Continental Congress adopts a resolution mandating an end to the slave trade.

NAVAL: The American schooner *Wasp* seizes the British brig *Betsey* in Christina Creek, Delaware Bay.

April 12
SOUTH: The Halifax Resolves are passed by the North Carolina Provisional Congress, which, for the first time, authorizes delegates to the Continental Congress to endorse independence.

April 13
NORTH: General George Washington arrives at New York from Boston and begins preparing its defenses. He fears that if the British capture the city they can seriously infringe on communications between the northern and southern colonies.

April 15
NAVAL: The warships *Warren* and *Providence* are launched and commissioned at Providence, Rhode Island.

April 18
South: The vanguard of Commodore Peter Parker's approaching fleet reaches Cape Fear, North Carolina.

April 20
North: Admiral Marriot Arbuthnot is commissioned lieutenant governor of Nova Scotia.

April 21
North: HMS *Scarborough* drops anchor at Halifax, Nova Scotia, and unloads numerous Loyalist refugees, including former royal governor James Wright of Georgia.

April 29
Diplomacy: A deputation under Benjamin Franklin, Samuel Chase, and Charles Carroll arrives at Montreal to encourage Canadians to desert the Crown. The Canadians, Catholic and French-speaking, fear assimilation by their southern neighbors and remain aloof to the deputation's overtures.

May 1
North: General John Thomas succeeds General David Wooster as commander of American forces in Canada, by now reduced to 1,900 poorly equipped men. He prepares to abandon the siege of Quebec while Governor-General Guy Carleton, awaiting reinforcements, bides his time within the city.

May 2
Diplomacy: After concluding negotiations with Arthur Lee, Charles Gravier, comte de Vergennes, convinces King Louis XVI to secretly approve 1 million livres in aid for the colonies. He also receives similar pledges from the Spanish government. The king subsequently directs Pierre-Augustin Caron de Beaumarchais to establish a dummy company, Roderigue, Hortalez et Cie, for the purpose of funneling clandestine aid to America.

North: A fleet of 15 British vessels begins ascending the St. Lawrence River, with reinforcements commanded by General John Burgoyne. Among these is the first large contingent of Hessian mercenaries under General Baron Friedrich von Riedesel.

May 3
Diplomacy: General William Howe and Admiral Richard Howe are authorized by King George III to serve on a forthcoming peace commission. Admiral Howe is also appointed commander in chief of all Royal Navy forces in American waters. Moreover, Lord George Germain insists that fighting will continue until each colony acknowledges the supremacy of Parliament.

South: A British expedition under Commodore Peter Parker and General Charles Cornwallis arrives off Cape Fear, North Carolina, and joins up with ships already there under General Henry Clinton.

May 4
Politics: The Rhode Island General Assembly expunges all written allegiances to King George III from its charter and declares itself independent under the title State of Rhode Island and Providence Plantations.

May 6
NORTH: Ships bearing British reinforcements drop anchor at Quebec under General John Burgoyne, which brings the garrison strength up to 13,000 men. Thus augmented, Governor-General Sir Guy Carleton dispatches a 900-man reconnaissance in force to examine the American encampment. General John Thomas is unable to prevent his remaining 250 men from panicking, and the camp is summarily abandoned. Many wounded soldiers and several artillery pieces are shamefully surrendered without a fight. Carleton, however, declines to pursue and continues landing the remainder of his troops ashore.
SOUTH: The Virginia Convention supersedes the House of Burgesses as the state's representative assembly.

May 8–9
NAVAL: British warships HMS *Roebuck* under Captain Andrew S. Hammond and *Liverpool* under Captain Henry Bellew wander too far up Christiana Creek, near Wilmington, Delaware, and are attacked by 13 armed galleys of the Pennsylvania navy. The vessels are driven downstream while the Americans suffer one killed and 12 wounded.

May 10
POLITICS: The Continental Congress authorizes a resolution encouraging all 13 colonies to form new, independent governments. John Adams, Richard H. Lee, and Edward Rutledge also chair a committee tasked with writing a preamble for the resolution prior to its public pronouncement.
NAVAL: Lieutenant John Paul Jones receives the 12-gun sloop *Providence,* his first command.

May 15
POLITICS: The Virginia Convention instructs Richard H. Lee and his fellow delegates in Congress to approve independence from England. Hot debate ensues over John Adams and his preamble to a resolution weighing independent governments in individual colonies, being so written as to actually endorse independence from Great Britain.

May 16
POLITICS: The Philadelphia committee of safety offers six pence for every pound of lead or lead products turned over for military purposes.
NORTH: Major Henry Sherburne leads a column of 150 American soldiers from Montreal to reinforce the small American post at the Cedars, 40 miles distant. It quickly dwindles to 100 men through desertion.

May 17
NORTH: An ailing General John Thomas assembles his shattered command at Sorel on the St. Lawrence River and decides to retreat toward Chambly, Quebec.
NAVAL: Captain John Mugford of the schooner *Franklin* attacks and seizes the supply ship HMS *Hope,* along with 1,500 barrels of gunpowder and scores of entrenching tools. That night a British cutting-out expedition of 200 men takes 12 boats and attacks the *Franklin* and privateer *Lady Washington* near Nantasket Roads, Mas-

sachusetts, but is bloodily repulsed with a loss of 70 men. The Americans sustain two killed, including Captain Mugford; the British admit to only seven dead.

May 18
NAVAL: Captain Nicholas Biddle departs the Delaware Capes aboard the 14-gun *Andrew Doria,* taking 10 prizes over the next four months.

May 19
NORTH: The 50 men of Britain's 8th Regiment under Captain George Forster, backed by 200 Indians, attack 400 American militia under Major Isaac Butterfield at the Cedars, halfway between Montreal and Quebec. The militia, abandoned by Colonel Timothy Bedel, initially defends its small wooden post until Foster assures Butterfield that the Indians will not massacre them. They then capitulate.

May 20
NORTH: An American relief force of 100 men under Major Henry Sherburne is ambushed near Vaudreuil, Quebec, by soldiers and Indians under Captain George Forster. The Americans lose 28 killed and several wounded before Sherburne surrenders.

May 24
POLITICS: General George Washington arrives in Philadelphia to confer with the Continental Congress over the course of events. Two new committees are subsequently appointed, one to oversee the ensuing campaign and another to explore the possibility of recruiting Native Americans to the war effort.

May 26
NORTH: Ever-energetic General Benedict Arnold marches from Montreal against Captain George Forster's British and Indians at Quinze Chiens, overtaking them. Rather than risk a massacre of nearly 487 prisoners, Arnold and Forster reach an agreement whereby the captives are freed in exchange for releasing a like number of British later on. The affair partially erases the disgrace of The Cedars seven days earlier.

May 31
SOUTH: Commodore Peter Parker's fleet finally assembles in full strength off Cape Fear and sails for Charleston, South Carolina, in concert with forces under General Henry Clinton.

June 1
NORTH: General John Sullivan supersedes General John Thomas at Saint Johns, Quebec, as commander of American forces in Canada. He brings 3,300 men with him and is further strengthened by a brigade of Pennsylvania troops under General William Thompson. Sullivan briefly entertains a second siege of Quebec City.

June 2
NORTH: General John Thomas succumbs to smallpox at Chambly, Quebec.

June 4
SOUTH: General Charles Lee arrives at Charleston and succeeds Colonel William Moultrie of the 2nd South Carolina Regiment as commander of the local garrison.

However, Moultrie remains in command of Fort Sullivan on Sullivan's Island, Charleston Harbor. This is constructed with two walls of palmetto logs separated by 16 feet of beach sand, mounts 31 cannon, and boasts a garrison of 420 men.

June 6
NORTH: General John Sullivan orders General William Thompson and 2,000 men on an expedition down the St. Lawrence River to Trois-Rivières (Three Rivers) to capture a fort strategically located midway between Montreal and Quebec, along with its garrison of 800 men. He is accompanied by Colonels Anthony Wayne, William Irvine, Arthur St. Clair, and William Maxwell. The men utilize small boats in order to sneak up on the enemy.

June 7
POLITICS: Virginian Richard H. Lee, outraged over Great Britain's importation of Hessian mercenaries, finally sounds the tocsin for American independence. He quickly urges creation of foreign alliances, along with adoption of articles of confederation. Lee's resolution is seconded by John Adams, delegate from Massachusetts, but Congress tables discussion for an additional day.
SOUTH: Denied a base at Wilmington, North Carolina, the British amphibious expedition under Commodore Peter Parker and General Henry Clinton appears off Charleston, South Carolina, and crosses the sandbar into the harbor. British troops disembark on Long Island to reconnoiter.
NAVAL: The 12-gun American privateer *Yankee Hero* succumbs to the frigate HMS *Melford* under Captain John Burr after a gallant two-hour struggle off Newburyport, Massachusetts.

June 8
NORTH: A force of 2,000 Americans under General William Thompson lands near Trois-Rivières, Canada, and advances overland to its objective in the dark. En route the Americans are betrayed by their Canadian guide and led into a chest-deep swamp, delaying their advance for several hours. They are also spotted by the British vessel HMS *Martin* and fired upon, which alerts the garrison. Unknown to Thompson, the town is occupied by several thousand newly arrived British regulars under General John Burgoyne. Colonel Anthony Wayne's column makes first contact with the enemy and initially forces them back, but British reinforcements drive the Americans off. Worse, a detachment of light infantry under General Simon Fraser arrives by boat and lands in the American rear, encircling them. Thompson's entire command stampedes into the swamp and retreats in confusion.

June 9
NORTH: Americans under General William Thompson are hotly pursued from Trois-Rivières back to their original debarkation point and are shocked to learn that their boats have deserted them. Thompson, his situation hopeless, surrenders while General Anthony Wayne cuts his way through and marches back to Sorel with 1,100 men. The entire operation has been a disaster for the Americans, who lose 40 killed and 236 prisoners. British casualties amount to eight killed and nine wounded.

Facing insurmountable odds, General Benedict Arnold abandons Montreal and marches 300 men for Saint Johns with alacrity. Beforehand he strips the navy yard of tools and timber, shipping them ahead to Fort Ticonderoga.

June 10
DIPLOMACY: King Charles III of Spain offers clandestinely to supply the United States with arms and supplies and hands over 1 million livres to the dummy company of Roderigue, Hortalez et Cie.
POLITICS: The Continental Congress, at the urging of more conservative members, postpones any consideration of independence until July.

June 11
POLITICS: The Continental Congress appoints a committee consisting of Thomas Jefferson, John Adams, Benjamin Franklin, Robert R. Livingston, and Roger Sherman to explore drafting a possible declaration of independence. Two more committees are then appointed to explore a confederation scheme of governance and a plan to negotiate treaties with foreign powers.

June 12
POLITICS: John Dickinson is appointed to chair a congressional committee tasked with drafting a plan for governance under articles of confederation, assisted by one delegate from each colony. The foreign treaty committee consists of Dickinson, John Adams, Benjamin Franklin, Benjamin Harrison, and Robert Morris. Congress also resolves to establish a five-member board of war and ordnance to function as a war office.
SOUTH: The Virginia Convention at Williamsburg adopts the Declaration of Rights, drafted by George Mason. He inculcates long-established English political precepts enunciated in the Magna Carta, the Petition of Rights, and the Bill of Rights.

June 13
POLITICS: The Continental Congress establishes the five-member Board of War and Ordnance to better oversee administration of the Continental army, along with the Department of Army Headquarters.
NORTH: General John Sullivan, in light of recent developments, cancels the invasion of Canada and prepares to withdraw almost 8,000 tattered soldiers back to American soil.
NAVAL: American artillery under General Benjamin Lincoln drive HMS *Renown* from Boston Harbor, finally breaking the British blockade there.

June 14
NORTH: Governor-General Guy Carleton advances to Trois-Rivières with 8,000 soldiers under Generals John Burgoyne and Friedrich von Riedesel. General John Sullivan begins embarking men and supplies at Sorel for an eventual return to Crown Point, New York. This move signals the end of the American invasion.

June 16
NORTH: General Benedict Arnold conducts a rearguard action at Chambly and continues retreating.

South: General Henry Clinton lands 2,000 men and 500 sailors on Long Island in Charleston Harbor and orders them to wade across and attack American defenses on Sullivan's Island. The maneuver proves untenable when their route proves inundated with deep shoals.

Naval: Captain Seth Harding, commanding a squadron consisting of the *Lee, Franklin, Lynch, Warren,* and *Defense,* captures the British transports HMS *George* and *Arabella* in Boston Harbor. The former, partly manned by soldiers of the 71st Highlanders, resists stiffly and surrenders only after losing 12 killed and 13 wounded. Among the 170 captives taken is Lieutenant Colonel Archibald Campbell; the Americans sustain nine wounded.

June 17
Politics: The Continental Congress is stunned by news of the defeat at Trois Rivieres and authorizes General Horatio Gates to replace General John Sullivan as commander of northern forces.

North: Montreal is reoccupied by British forces under Governor-General Guy Carleton, who commences preparations for invading northern New York.

June 20
North: American forces under Colonel Rufus Putnam begins construction of Fort Washington on Manhattan's northern end. Though spacious, it remains an open earthwork lacking a palisade, barracks, water supply, or bomb-proof magazines. Its sole defensive virtue is in sitting 230 feet above sea level and astride the Hudson River, from which the defenders hope its cannon can interdict the British passage upstream.

June 21
North: The New Jersey Provincial Congress deposes and arrests royal governor William Franklin—Benjamin Franklin's son—and begins drafting a state constitution. It also sends a new delegation to the Continental Congress with instructions to support any resolution declaring independence, installing a confederation, and ratifying treaties with foreign powers.

June 23
South: Thomas Jefferson composes a draft state constitution for consideration by the Virginia Convention.

June 24
North: Ragged American forces under Generals John Sullivan and Benedict Arnold cannot contain the British advance guard at Ile aux Noir, and Sorel, Quebec. Sullivan concedes the inevitable and orders an immediate withdrawal back to Crown Point, New York. His soldiers are hobbled by disease, hunger, and lack of equipment.

June 28
Politics: Thomas Jefferson submits his draft of the Declaration of Independence to the Continental Congress for consideration after slight alterations by John Adams and Benjamin Franklin.

The Maryland Convention unanimously authorizes its delegates at the Continental Congress to vote for independence.

NORTH: American soldier Thomas Hickey, former member of General George Washington's bodyguard, is publicly hanged in New York for conspiring to betray the general to the British. The execution is attended by 20,000 spectators.

SOUTH: After innumerable delays due to a sandbar and unfavorable tidal conditions, British naval forces under Commodore Peter Parker begin an attack on Charleston. They first engage a small American garrison under Colonel William Moultrie on Sullivan's Island, in the city's harbor. Parker draws up a double line of eight warships mounting 260 guns and bombards the fort for 10 hours. However, the unique properties of the palmetto logs enable them simply to absorb the British cannon shot with virtually no harm to the defenders. When a lucky shot brings down the fort's flagstaff, Sergeant William Jasper bravely mounts the parapet under fire and reraises the standard. Moultrie's batteries, meanwhile, riddle the commodore's flagship, HMS *Bristol*. This vessel is hit no less than 70 times, its captain is killed, and Parker wounded. Worse, when the British attempt slipping three frigates around the fort to enfilade it, they ground in shoal waters. The 20-gun HMS *Actaeon* cannot be refloated and is abandoned and burned by her own crew. By 9 P.M. Parker signals his fleet to withdraw. British losses are 64 killed and 161 wounded, to an American total of 17 dead and 20 wounded. The late royal governor of South Carolina, William Campbell, is also mortally wounded. Moultrie's victory makes him a national hero and secures Charleston from British control for another two and a half years.

June 29
NORTH: A large amphibious expedition of 127 ships under Admiral Molyneux Shuldham and General William Howe starts arriving off Sandy Hook, New York, with 10,000 troops aboard.

NAVAL: British naval vessels chase the American ship *Nancy* off Cape May, New Jersey, until it grounds. Captain Lambert Wickes then arrives to assist and orders gunpowder supplies opened and the ship set afire. The crew flees as the British board the burning ship, which suddenly explodes, killing several seamen. American militia then begin firing upon the survivors, who retreat back to their vessels.

SOUTH: The Virginia House of Burgesses in Williamsburg discards its colonial charter in favor of a new constitution. Patrick Henry is then elected governor by the legislature.

July 1
POLITICS: The issue of independence sparks a heated debate in the Continental Congress, at the conclusion of which only nine colonies are fully pledged in support. Supporters on both sides begin an intense lobbying effort over the next day and evening.

SOUTH: Lingering frontier resentment explodes into the Cherokee War when enraged Indians hit American settlements from Georgia to Virginia. Major Andrew Williams, seconded by Andrew Pickens, begins raising a force of 450 militia to counter their activity.

The British withdraw from Charleston on June 28, 1776, after 10 hours of battle. *(U.S. Army Center of Military History)*

July 2
POLITICS: The Continental Congress ratifies the Declaration of Independence from Great Britain 12-0, with New York abstaining. This seminal document, drafted by Thomas Jefferson, Benjamin Franklin, John Adams, and Roger Sherman, becomes the cornerstone of American political philosophy and tradition. Delaware delegate

Caesar Rodney rides furiously to Philadelphia from Delaware to attend the proceedings and dramatically arrives splattered with mud. He votes in favor.
NORTH: New Jersey adopts a new state constitution—along with the first statute granting women's suffrage.

July 3
NORTH: The British expeditionary force under General William Howe begins disembarking 10,000 troops on Staten Island in preparation for offensive operations.

July 4
POLITICS: The Declaration of Independence is signed by President John Hancock and Secretary Charles Thompson of the Second Continental Congress and forwarded to state assemblies for eventual ratification.

July 5
NORTH: General Horatio Gates arrives at Crown Point, New York, and succeeds General John Sullivan as head of the Northern Department.

July 6
NAVAL: The Continental sloop *Sachem* captures the British privateer *Three Brothers* off the Delaware River.

July 7
DIPLOMACY: Silas Deane arrives in Paris on a mission to ascertain French sympathies and solicit military and financial support.
NORTH: Sir John Johnson, a recent refugee from Albany, New York, is authorized by Governor-General Guy Carleton to recruit the king's Royal Regiment from among fellow Loyalists.

General John Sullivan rows the length of Lake Champlain and finally arrives at Crown Point, New York, with 8,000 exhausted, dispirited men. General Philip J. Schuyler subsequently orders them to fall back an additional 10 miles to the perceived safety of Fort Ticonderoga.

July 8
NORTH: The first public reading of the Declaration of Independence occurs outside the Pennsylvania State House (Independence Hall), Philadelphia. The crowd reacts with applause, church bells, and parades.
SOUTH: General Andrew Lewis masses a small force of 10 infantry companies, backed by a battery of 18-pounder cannon, in preparation for storming Gywnn Island at the mouth of the Rappahannock River. Since May this locale has served as de facto headquarters of royal governor John Murray, Lord Dunmore, from which he has launched numerous raids against the coastline. Dunmore enjoys the advantage of two small warships, the *Dunmore* and HMS *Otter*, in addition to artillery of his own, but his men are wracked by disease and in poor shape.

July 9

North: The Declaration of Independence is proclaimed to the assembled Continental army in New York. The provincial congress then initiates work on a new constitution while the statue of King George III at Bowling Green is ignominiously pulled down and melted into 40,000 musket balls.

South: Virginia militia under General Andrew Lewis bombards Gywnn Island, headquarters for former royal governor John Murray, Lord Dunmore. American artillery fire forces several British warships to ground themselves and also silences Dunmore's battery on the western end of the island. Murray himself is wounded by cannon fire and decides that Gywnn Island cannot be held, so he flees with his small fleet up the Potomac River that night. He also abandons 30 African-American soldiers, former slaves now fighting for the British but too ill to move. The island is occupied the following morning by 200 soldiers without incident. One American officer dies when his defective mortar explodes.

July 11

Naval: Captain Lambert Wickes and the brig *Reprisal* commence a cruise that seizes four British merchantmen by month's end.

July 12

Politics: John Dickinson outlines his plans for a confederation government to the Continental Congress with a draft consisting of 13 articles.

South: Colonel Elijah Clarke and a detachment of Georgia militia rout a band of Cherokee at the juncture of the Broad and Savannah Rivers, killing four and losing three killed and four wounded.

Naval: Admiral Richard Howe arrives off Staten Island with 150 ships conveying 11,000 additional soldiers for his brother, General William Howe. The frigates HMS *Phoenix* and *Rose* are then dispatched up the Hudson River and anchor off Tappan Zee to interdict American communications there. En route they engage numerous American shore batteries, killing six and wounding three. Meanwhile, General George Washington arrives back at New York City to confer with Admiral Howe's peace emissaries; these he briefly entertains and politely dismisses.

July 15

Politics: Having previously abstained, the New York delegation to the Continental Congress presents a resolution from the state convention granting approval of the Declaration of Independence.

South: American militia under Major John Downs successfully defend Lindley's Fort on Rayborn Creek, South Carolina, against marauding Cherokee and Loyalists, the latter being dressed as Indians. Having stymied their attack, the defenders sortie and scatter their opponents, taking nine prisoners. American losses are two killed and 13 wounded.

July 16

South: Governor John Murray, Lord Dunmore, temporarily lands at St. George's Island, Maryland, apparently intending to raid Mount Vernon and capture Martha Washington. However, they are intercepted by local militia and driven off.

July 18
DIPLOMACY: John Adams frames the "Model Treaty" for anticipated diplomatic relations with other countries.

July 19
POLITICS: The Continental Congress at Philadelphia votes to have the Declaration of Independence unanimously signed by all 55 delegates.

July 20
SOUTH: Cherokee under Chief Dragging Canoe attack Eaton's Station on the Holston River, North Carolina, losing 13 killed before withdrawing. The defenders had been tipped off in advance by Nancy Ward, the Cherokee War Woman. The Indians also unsuccessfully besiege Fort Caswell, Tennessee, but manage to inflict 40 casualties upon the defenders.

July 21
SOUTH: The British fleet under Commodore Peter Parker and General Henry Clinton abandons Charleston, South Carolina, and sails for New York.

July 23
SOUTH: Governor John Murray, Lord Dunmore, raids several plantations on the Potomac River before being driven off by Prince William County militia at Occoquan Creek, Virginia.

July 27
NAVAL: Captain Lambert Wickes and his 18-gun brig *Reprisal* are approached by the 16-gun sloop of war HMS *Shark* under Captain John Chapman, at St. Pierre Harbor, Martinique. When the British commander declares that he does not recognize *Reprisal's* new Grand Union flag, Wickes identifies himself with a broadside. Fighting commences and the guns of a nearby French fort eventually intervene. The *Shark* withdraws under fire and the British government subsequently protests France's breach of neutrality.

July 29
SOUTH: North Carolina general Griffith Rutherford leads 2,400 men on an invasion of Cherokee territory, assisted by South Carolina militia under Major Andrew Williamson and Virginia forces commanded by Colonel William Christiansen.

August 1
NORTH: Commodore Peter Parker, with Generals Henry Clinton and Charles Cornwallis, arrives at New York to reinforce General William Howe. The British expeditionary force of 32,000 men is the largest ever assembled in North America and includes 8,000 Hessians under General Leopold von Heister.
SOUTH: Major Andrew Williamson and 330 South Carolina militia are ambushed by 1,200 Cherokee under Loyalist Alexander Cameron at Seneca. They are defeated, as is a detachment coming to their aid under Colonel Andrew Pickens. However, the militiamen subsequently regroup and attack the deserted settlement at Essenecca Town (Seneca Ford), South Carolina, burning houses and stored corn. The Ameri-

cans suffer three killed and 14 wounded. Among the dead is Francis Salvador, the first Jew elected to a legislature in the New World and the first of his faith to fall in defense of his country.

August 2
POLITICS: The Declaration of Independence is formally signed by all 55 members of the Continental Congress.

August 3
NAVAL: Five American galleys under Lieutenant Colonel Benjamin Tupper unsuccessfully attack HMS *Phoenix* and *Rose* at their anchorage off Tappan Zee, New York. They lose two killed and 12 wounded.

August 4
SOUTH: American militia under Major Andrew Williamson attack and burn Cherokee settlements at Sugar Town, Soconee, and Keowee, South Carolina. Over the next eight days they reduce six more villages to ashes.

August 5
NORTH: General Nathanael Greene writes to General George Washington, advising him that New York City is probably indefensible and ought to be burned down to deprive the British of a useful port.

August 7
NAVAL: The American privateer *Hancock* under Captain Wingate Newman captures the British transport HMS *Reward* and brings it into Portsmouth, New Hampshire, as a prize. Among its cargo is a shipment of turtles intended for Prime Minister Lord Frederick North.

August 8
SOUTH: American militia under Major Andrew Williamson defeat the Cherokee at Oconore, South Carolina.

August 11
SOUTH: Major Andrew Williamson and his South Carolina militiamen attack and defeat a large party of Cherokee at Tamassee, South Carolina. The Americans lose six killed and 17 wounded while 16 dead warriors are left on the field.

August 12
POLITICS: The Continental Congress encourages desertions from the British army by granting free land as a bounty.
SOUTH: Colonel Andrew Pickens and 25 South Carolina militiamen are ambushed by an estimated 200 Cherokee near Lower Town. Pickens arrays his men in a defensive circle protected by high grass and orders them to fire in relays until relieved by troops under his brother.

August 16
DIPLOMACY: Admiral Richard Howe, writing from his flagship HMS *Eagle* off Staten Island, New York, contacts his friend Benjamin Franklin in Philadelphia, informing him of his authority to conduct peace negotiations.

NAVAL: The Americans use fire rafts to attack HMS *Phoenix* at Tappan Zee, New York; the tactic fails but convinces the British commanders to sail back down the Hudson River.

August 20
POLITICS: The Continental Congress prints copies of the Articles of Confederation for circulation.
NORTH: General Nathanael Greene, commanding American forces on Long Island, is struck down by fever and succeeded by General John Sullivan.

August 21–October 8
NAVAL: Captain John Paul Jones and the 12-gun sloop *Providence* depart Delaware, capturing 16 prizes over the next three months.

August 22
NORTH: General William Howe disembarks 8,000 troops at Gravesend Bay, Long Island, and advances inland. General George Washington counters by deploying six additional regiments on Brooklyn Heights while General William Heath, in northern Manhattan, makes preparations to march south with reinforcements if necessary.

August 23
NORTH: American forces under Colonel Edward Hand skirmish with Hessian troops commanded by Colonel Karl von Donop at Bedford Pass, Long Island, and are forced to withdraw.

August 24
NORTH: In another major change of command, General Israel Putnam supplants General John Sullivan as commander of troops on Long Island as the Americans brace for a British attack upon Brooklyn Heights. The newly arrived Putnam, unfortunately, knows little about the topography of the area.
NAVAL: General Benedict Arnold, having assembled a motley collection of schooners, sloops, and gondolas, sails from Crown Point to engage a British fleet bearing south on Lake Champlain.

August 25
NORTH: General William Howe lands two Hessian brigades under General Leopold von Heister on Long Island as reinforcements and marches toward Flatbush. The British general now has 22,000 soldiers at his disposal, including 8,000 Germans. General George Washington also rushes up additional troops, bringing the defenders of Long Island to 19,000 men—but only 9,000 are in the lines to face Howe.

August 26
NORTH: General George Washington assumes command of American forces on Long Island and reinforces Brooklyn Heights with new troops and fortifications. General William Howe, meanwhile, observes a gap in the American lines at Valley Grove (Jamaica Pass), and that evening he dispatches 10,000 men under General Henry Clinton and Colonel Hugh Percy to turn their left flank. Advancing stealthily in the night, they skirmish with a small cordon of troops posted there, killing two and wounding three, but their presence otherwise goes unnoticed.

August 27

NORTH: The Battle of Long Island commences as General James Grant launches a large diversionary attack upon the American right. Then the main British column under General Henry Clinton expertly turns the American left at Jamaica Pass and takes the division of General John Sullivan from behind. Sullivan himself is captured while leading a small party of soldiers forward to reconnoiter. His men scatter as the British begin expertly rolling up their line. A large diversionary attack is also launched against the American center by General Leopold von Heister to pin the remaining troops down. General William Alexander fights well and repels several determined attacks until he is also surprised from behind by a force under Clinton and captured. The surviving Americans scamper back to the defenses at Brooklyn Heights and brace for the inevitable final assault. Inexplicably, General William Howe is content to stop pursuing and commence siege operations, which grants the badly rattled Americans a welcome respite. The conquest of Long Island costs the British only 377 casualties, including 65 killed, while the Americans have approximately 300 dead and 1,100 taken prisoner.

NAVAL: Captain John Paul Jones on the 12-gun sloop *Providence* captures the British brig *Britannia*.

The Battle of Brooklyn, August 27, 1776, is a major tactical victory for the British. *(U.S. Army Center of Military History)*

August 28
North: General William Erskine takes 700 British troops and overwhelms a 100-man detachment of New York militia under General Nathaniel Woodhull at Jamaica, Long Island.
South: Andrew Williamson and General Griffith Rutherford march with 2,000 North and South Carolina militiamen to engage the Cherokee in the western mountains.

August 29–30
North: General George Washington, cornered by superior British numbers, skillfully evacuates Brooklyn Heights for Manhattan Island at night, assisted by the mariners of Colonel John Glover. In six hours a total of 9,500 men, replete with horses, cannon, and equipment, are ferried across without detection and conveniently covered by an early morning fog. It is a remarkable maneuver.
Naval: Captain Abraham Whipple and the 24-gun frigate *Columbus* seize four British merchantmen while cruising off the New England coast.

September 2
Diplomacy: General John Sullivan, recently paroled by the British, arrives at Philadelphia bearing a letter from Admiral Richard Howe requesting to meet with a delegation of private citizens. The Continental Congress agrees to debate an appropriate response.

September 3
Politics: The Continental Congress instructs General George Washington not to burn New York City if he decides to evacuate. However, the actual decision to retreat remains in his hands.
Naval: Captain John Paul Jones of the 12-gun brig *Providence* again departs Delaware Bay, this time for Bermuda, on a cruise that ultimately nets 16 prizes.

September 5
Diplomacy: The Continental Congress declines to send a delegation of private citizens to meet with Admiral Richard Howe, but it will allow an authorized committee to parley with him.

September 6
Diplomacy: Benjamin Franklin, John Adams, and Edward Rutledge are appointed to a committee tasked with meeting Admiral Richard Howe.
Naval: Inventor David Bushnell supervises deployment of his experimental submarine *Turtle* against Admiral Richard Howe's flagship, HMS *Eagle,* then anchored off Staten Island. The actual attack is conducted by Sergeant Ezra Lee, who is forced to fight strong currents in order to bring his vessel alongside. He then makes several unsuccessful attempts to attach an explosive device under *Eagle*'s hull, but cannot penetrate its copper sheathing. Lee then abandons his attempt and withdraws, releasing his explosive to detonate harmlessly on the surface. Thus, history's first submarine attack proves unsuccessful, but it greatly alarms enemy naval commanders, who accused the Americans of making "infernal machines."

September 7
NORTH: A war council convened by General George Washington ponders whether or not to evacuate New York and reaches a compromise solution: The city will remain garrisoned by General Israel Putnam's division while forces under General Nathanael Greene defend Kip's Bay. General William Heath's command is then ordered to guard Harlem Heights with 9,000 men.

September 9
POLITICS: The Continental Congress discards the designation "United Colonies" in favor of a new name, "United States."

September 10
NORTH: The army of Governor-General Guy Carleton departs Canada and begins marching down the Lake Champlain corridor into New York.

British forces seize Montresor's Island in New York's East River, from which they can simultaneously threaten Harlem and Knightsbridge.

September 11
POLITICS: The Continental Congress formally approves the name United States of America as its new title for the former British colonies.

DIPLOMACY: A three-hour peace conference convenes earnestly on Staten Island between Admiral Richard Howe, Benjamin Franklin, John Adams, and Edward Rutledge but avails nothing. The admiral possesses authority only for referring proposals back to London while the Americans refuse to rescind their Declaration of Independence.

September 12
NORTH: In the face of a rapidly deteriorating situation, General George Washington abandons Manhattan and commences ferrying his troops to the mainland.

Captain Nathan Hale volunteers to remain on Long Island as a spy for the United States.

September 15
NORTH: General William Howe interrupts American evacuation efforts by landing en masse at Kip's Bay, on the east side of Manhattan, covered by five Royal Navy warships. His goal is to split the island in two and possibly seal the Americans off in the lower half. A total of 86 British cannon sweep the beach for nearly an hour, at which point 4,000 crack British and Hessian troops embark on 84 flatboats under General Henry Clinton. The defending force of 450 Connecticut militia under Colonel William Douglas flees the scene almost immediately, as do two brigades under Colonels James Wadsworth and John Scott. The British thus land without meeting an organized resistance and quickly seize a beachhead before lunging inland. General George Washington gallops to the scene and is aghast at what transpires. He furiously attempts to rally the survivors but, despite threats and entreaties, a rout ensues. Additional efforts by General Israel Putnam forcefully stem the tide, and Washington orders a withdrawal up Manhattan's west side to Harlem Heights. Meanwhile,

General Charles Cornwallis leads a second wave of 9,000 men ashore, who march inland to sever the American retreat. Washington and his men escape by the narrowest of margins, thanks largely to the determined stand of brigades under Colonels John Glover and William Smallwood. Kip's Bay is a minor disaster for the Americans, who incur 367 casualties along with various supplies and 67 cannon captured. British losses are 14 dead and 150 wounded.

September 16
NORTH: Following the rout at Kip's Bay, General George Washington arrays his remaining troops on Manhattan into three distinct lines, consisting of divisions under Generals Nathanael Greene, Israel Putnam, and Joseph Spencer. On the morning of the 16th, Washington dispatches 120 Connecticut Rangers under Major Thomas Knowlton to reconnoiter the British lines. Approaching Morningside Heights they become embroiled in a fire fight with British and Hessian troops under General Alexander Leslie, who halts them. Britain's 42nd Regiment, the noted Black Watch, then successfully flanks the Americans and forces them back. Adding insult to injury, British horns derisively begin playing tunes reminiscent of a fox hunt. But Washington, observing the British advance, quickly draws up plans to entrap them in the Hollow Way by reinforcing Knowlton and instructing him to lure the enemy forward. Both sides then continue feeding additional troops into the fray, even though the distinguished Knowlton is killed in action. However, as the brigade under General John Nixon comes up, Leslie apparently loses heart and falls back to Morningside Heights. The Americans, heartened by the rare sight of British backsides, press them vigorously and at 2 P.M. Washington recalls his troops. The Battle of Harlem Heights clearly proves that the raw Americans can fight well if properly led. Worse, the action proves a setback for General William Howe, who postpones further action for over a month. American casualties total 16 killed and 40 wounded to a British loss of 14 killed and 154 wounded.

September 17
DIPLOMACY: The Continental Congress considers John Adams's Plan of Treaties to expedite a possible forging of links to France.

September 18
POLITICS: The Continental Congress authorizes creation of 88 battalions of infantry from among the 13 states according to their population and implores that soldiers enlist for the duration of the war to avoid the burden of expiring enlistments.

September 19
SOUTH: A detachment of South Carolina militia under Major Andrew Williamson is ambushed and surrounded by Cherokee warriors at Black Hole. Williamson holds his ground as long as possible before ordering an assault upon his antagonists, routing them. The Americans suffer 13 killed and 18 wounded.

September 20
POLITICS: The Continental Congress modifies the Articles of War governing the Continental army to better address long-standing problems of discipline, administration, and organization.
NORTH: Delaware adopts a new state constitution.

September 21
NORTH: New York City is swept by several fires, some apparently set by incendiaries, and 300 buildings are either destroyed or damaged. British authorities also arrest and detain Nathan Hale on Long Island for spying when he is recognized by a Loyalist cousin.

September 22
NORTH: Captain Nathan Hale, a former schoolteacher, is executed by the British for espionage in New York City and dies declaring "I regret that I have but one life to lose for my country." He becomes the new nation's first martyr.

September 23
NORTH: A force of 240 American militia under Lieutenant Colonel Michael Jackson attacks Montressor's (Randalls) Island, New York, with 240 men in three boats. The first craft lands, but when the other two fail to provide support, the Americans are forced back, losing two killed, four wounded, and 28 captured. Several officers and men in the other boats are court-martialed for dereliction of duty.

General Benedict Arnold's flotilla of 15 vessels reaches Bay St. Armand, 10 miles south of his final destination at Valcour Island, Lake Champlain.

September 24
DIPLOMACY: The Continental Congress approves the Model Treaty as the basis of negotiating with European governments. It stipulates that "free ships make free goods" and affirms the freedom of neutrals to trade in noncontraband items. France, in particular, is asked to grant most-favored-nation status to American exports.

September 26
DIPLOMACY: The Continental Congress authorizes Benjamin Franklin, Silas Deane, and Thomas Jefferson to serve as commissioners to France and secure arms, munitions, and military professionals—especially, trained engineers. Arthur Lee subsequently replaces Jefferson.

September 28
NORTH: Pennsylvania adopts a new state constitution, a unicameral legislature, and a bill of rights.

October 3
POLITICS: The Continental Congress approves a loan of $5 million at 4 percent interest to help finance the war effort; additional money is expected from France shortly. It also authorizes that a frigate and two cutters be purchased in Europe.

October 4
NORTH: Governor-General Guy Carleton, commanding 13,000 men, orders his fleet of five warships, 20 gunboats, and 28 lesser craft down Lake Champlain.

October 9
NAVAL: Royal Navy warships HMS *Phoenix* and *Roebuck* force their way up the Hudson River between Fort Washington on Manhattan Island and Fort Lee in New

Jersey. American gunners inflict 27 casualties yet fail to stop the British, who go on to destroy numerous vessels, including the transport carrying the submarine *Turtle*.

October 10
POLITICS: The Continental Congress institutes the rank of captain for the Continental navy and formally commissions 24 officers in that grade.

October 11
NORTH: Over the protests of subordinates, General William Howe orders 4,000 soldiers loaded onto transports where, escorted by 80 Royal Navy warships, they are to pass through the treacherous waters of Hell's Gate to the Bronx, New York, and land and march eight miles overland to Kingsbridge. By this expedient the British commander hopes finally to trap the American army entrenched at Harlem Heights and seal its fate. The convoy sails that night under cover of a thick fog, appearing intact off Throg's Neck.

NAVAL: A ramshackle American flotilla of 15 small vessels under General Benedict Arnold is attacked by a much larger armada of 25 warships under Lieutenant Thomas Pringle off Valcour Island, Lake Champlain, New York. Arnold has sequestered his little fleet in the shallow water between Valcour Island and the New York shore, where the prevailing wind blows south. The British initially sail past the Americans and have to beat back against the wind to engage them. Arnold

The Battle of Valcour Island, October 10, 1776, an American tactical defeat but a strategic triumph *(Paul Garnett Studios)*

deploys his ships in a defensive arc and they pummel the British squadron as it advances and anchors. The schooner HMS *Carleton* is heavily damaged and has to be towed away by several gunboats. However, firepower from the frigate HMS *Inflexible* proves overpowering and damages several smaller American vessels, sinking two. Nightfall ends the engagement and, under cover of a dense fog, Arnold slips his 13 surviving vessels past the British squadron through a hole in their lines. American losses are 107 killed or injured with 110 captured; British losses are negligible.

October 12
NORTH: General Charles Cornwallis lands 4,000 troops at Throg's Neck, New York, in an attempt to flank American forces ensconced on Harlem Heights. However, the position they disembark at is swampy and beset by rising tides. Consequently, once the nearby ford becomes inundated by water, the only avenue of advance is across a bridge and crossway. Fortunately for the Americans, Colonel Edward Hand and 30 soldiers of his 1st Pennsylvania Rifle Regiment are nearby to harass the enemy. They defeat British and Hessians attempting to cross at the ford as an additional 1,800 defenders rush up to defend the bridge and causeway. Stymied at every approach, British forces are trapped at Throg's Neck for six days, and the delay incurred allows American forces to escape envelopment.

October 13
NAVAL: The British Lake Champlain fleet under Lieutenant Thomas Pringle catches the remnants of General Benedict Arnold's flotilla at Split Rock, New York. Arnold fights a desperate rearguard action but runs an additional six vessels ashore at Buttonmold Bay, burns them, and marches overland to Crown Point. Five remaining vessels are also burned there and the crews continue on foot to Fort Ticonderoga. British command of Lake Champlain is complete but achieved too late in the season to facilitate military operations.

October 14
NORTH: General Benedict Arnold and Colonel Thomas Hartley abandon Crown Point, New York, and retrograde to Fort Ticonderoga. Governor-General Guy Carleton magnanimously paroles 110 American captives but—in a momentous decision—abandons his advance upon Fort Ticonderoga due to approaching winter. This becomes a major strategic victory for the otherwise struggling United States, which otherwise could not have contained such a large British force.

October 16
NORTH: General George Washington convenes a war council and is joined by General Charles Lee, recently arrived from South Carolina. They decide finally to evacuate Harlem Heights and cross over to White Plains. But 2,000 men will remain at Fort Washington to obstruct the Hudson River as long as possible.
NAVAL: The Continental Congress censures Commodore Esek Hopkins for disregarding its instructions and attacking New Providence instead of clearing the southern coastline of the Royal Navy.

October 17

NORTH: General Hugh Mercer leads a successful raid upon British positions on Staten Island, New York, capturing supplies and several prisoners.

October 18

POLITICS: Congress commissions Polish soldier of fortune Tadeusz Kościuszko as a colonel of engineers.

NORTH: General William Howe is determined to end the impasse on Manhattan Island, but he declines to engage directly General George Washington on Harlem Heights. Instead, having tasked General Hugh Percy with keeping the Americans preoccupied, he attempts another end run around Washington's flank to cut him off at King's Bridge. Washington, fortunately, catches drift of the move and orders a general withdrawal from Manhattan toward White Plains. Nevertheless, 4,000 men under Generals Henry Clinton and Charles Cornwallis are transported by ships to Pell's Point (New Rochelle), New York, and ordered to intercept the fleeing Americans. Once ashore they encounter a brigade of 750 Massachusetts Continentals under Colonel John Glover, who deploys his men in three distinct lines. As the British advance to contact, the first regiment under Colonel Joseph Reed emerges from behind a stone wall and pours point-blank musket fire into them. This tactic sows confusion in the British ranks, but they eventually regroup and resume advancing. Reed then falls back and the British march a short distance until Colonel William Shepard's regiment suddenly springs up from behind another stone wall, firing into their ranks. The British again bolt back for a short distance before resuming their march. At this juncture another regiment under Colonel Loammi Baldwin rises from behind a stone wall and fires, which again staggers the enemy advance.

The contending forces trade volleys for several minutes until it is perceived that Cornwallis has slipped behind the Americans and threatens to cut them off. Glover then sounds the retreat to Dobb's Ferry, which is performed in good order. The British decline to pursue. Colonel Glover is subsequently thanked by Washington and General Charles Lee for a splendid rearguard action that delays a superior foe and allows the main army to escape entrapment. American losses are six killed and 13 wounded; the British admit to only three killed and 20 wounded, although estimated losses are probably higher.

October 22

NORTH: General George Washington completes his relocation to White Plains and abandons the village of Mamaroneck. This will subsequently be occupied by the Queen's American Rangers under the celebrated Major Robert Rogers. American forces under Colonel John Haslet are subsequently ordered to attack the village and they manage to surprise the advance guard. The remaining rangers sharply counterattack and drive off the Americans. Haslet fails in his mission and sustains three killed and 12 wounded but inflicts 30 Loyalist casualties and takes 36 prisoners.

October 26

DIPLOMACY: Benjamin Franklin and Arthur Lee depart Philadelphia for France onboard the *Reprisal* under Captain Lambert Wickes. They carry new instructions requiring them to purchase eight ships-of-the-line and secure diplomatic recognition from the European community at large.

October 27
NORTH: At White Plains, British forces skirmish heavily with a brigade commanded by General Alexander McDougall, which is gradually reinforced by Delaware Continentals under Colonel John Haslet. The Americans lose 15 killed and 15 wounded.

A British probing attack against Fort Washington, New York, utilizing both land and naval forces, is driven back with loss.

October 28
NORTH: General William Howe leads 13,000 men against General George Washington's force of 14,500 at White Plains, New York. The Americans occupy a three-mile line behind the shallow Bronx River, with divisions under Generals Israel Putnam and William Heath on the right and left flanks respectively, while Washington holds the center. But the Americans have no sooner deployed than a resplendent British army under General William Howe arrives and parades itself in full view of the defenders to awe them. After brushing aside 1,500 skirmishers under General Joseph Spencer, Howe perceives that the eminence of Chatterton Hill is the key to Washington's right flank and makes preparations to storm it. General Alexander Leslie with two infantry regiments, and assisted by a force of Hessians, receives the task. Washington draws the same conclusion as to the heights and rushes 2,000 reinforcements there under his aide, Colonel Joseph Reed. Colonel Rufus Putnam, senior engineer present, is instructed to construct as many trenches as time will allow. The defenders under General Alexander McDougall resist gamely, pin Leslie's column at the ford, and repulse several determined efforts to cross the Bronx River. Suddenly, the Hessian regiment of Colonel Johann Rall turns the American right flank and, backed by British cavalry, begins rolling up the defenders. At this juncture Washington sounds a retreat, and the defenders withdraw intact. Howe again strangely declines to pursue and simply bivouacs his army upon Chatterton Hill. The Americans subsequently relocate to stronger positions at North Castle Heights, abandoning Fort Independence in the process. Washington's losses total 59 killed, 65 wounded, and 39 captured; the British and Hessians sustain 336 killed and wounded between them.

October 30
POLITICS: To improve the prospects of recruitment for the Continental navy, the Continental Congress authorizes crews to share in one-half the prize money of all vessels taken. Up until now, most seamen have preferred the more lucrative practice of privateering.

October 31
NORTH: The army under General George Washington continues entrenching in and around North Castle Heights.

November 1
NAVAL: Captain John Paul Jones commences a cruise aboard the 24-gun sloop *Alfred* that will culminate in the capture of nine vessels, including HMS *Active,* which has six guns, off Nova Scotia.

November 2
North: An American officer deserts to General Hugh Percy on Manhattan, carrying with him detailed plans of nearby Fort Washington.

November 4
North: In one of history's most momentous decisions, Governor-General Guy Carleton abandons Crown Point, New York, and begins withdrawing back to Canada for the winter. This act grants the struggling Americans a badly needed respite and a year to prepare their defenses.

November 5
North: General William Howe, mindful of losses incurred at Bunker Hill, concludes that any assault upon the American position at North Castle Heights will prove prohibitive. He then marches to Dobbs Ferry on the Hudson River to receive reinforcements under General Hugh Percy.

November 7
North: A force of 180 American militia under John Allen and Jonathan Eddy marches from Machias, Massachusetts (Maine), to Fort Cumberland, Nova Scotia.
Naval: British warships continue skirting Forts Washington and Lee, along with various hulks sunk on the Hudson River, with apparent impunity.

November 8
North: General George Washington writes to General Nathanael Greene bemoaning Fort Washington's inability to obstruct movement on the Hudson River and the mounting possibility of abandoning it, but he grants Greene discretionary authority to remain there.

November 9
North: General George Washington ferries most of his army across the Hudson River into New Jersey.
South: Maryland enacts a new state constitution.

November 10
North: American militia under Colonel Jonathan Eddy commence a siege of Fort Cumberland, Nova Scotia, but Colonel Joseph Goreham, commanding 200 men, refuses a surrender summons and awaits reinforcements.

November 12
North: Generals George Washington and Nathanael Greene confer again over the utility of Fort Washington and fail to reach a conclusion.
Naval: Captain John Paul Jones, commanding the 20-gun brig *Alfred,* captures the British armed transport *Mellish* by luring it away from an escorting frigate. Its valuable store of 10,000 winter uniforms and other military supplies is then hurriedly dispatched to the American army in Pennsylvania.

November 13
North: American forces are repulsed in an attack upon Fort Cumberland, Nova Scotia.

General George Washington, ordered by the Continental Congress to preserve a sizable force at Fort Washington, New York, arrives at Fort Lee, New Jersey, to discuss that matter with General Nathanael Greene. Greene prevails upon Washington to maintain the garrison there.

November 15
NORTH: The British begin constructing artillery batteries to cover a crossing of the Harlem River prior to attacking Fort Washington, New York.

November 16
NORTH: Early in the morning, Generals George Washington, Nathanael Greene, Hugh Mercer, and Israel Putnam arrive at Fort Washington, New York, on an inspection tour—when they suddenly realize that an imminent British assault is developing. The four generals quickly recross the Hudson River and take up positions at Fort Lee, New Jersey, on the opposite shore, to observe. The fort is garrisoned by 2,800 men under Colonel Robert Magaw, who spreads them out among various satellite fortifications. Meanwhile, General William Howe has devised a three-pronged attack to capture the looming post with 8,000 men. The first column of 3,000 Hessians under General Wilhelm von Knyphausen will attack Fort Washington from the north. A second force of 2,000 British under General Hugh Percy will simultaneously hit outlying fortifications to the south, while the third column under General Charles Cornwallis will advance from the base of Laurel Hill and move upland.

The British attack kicks off at 7 A.M. but is delayed several hours, and the contest does not become general until around noon. Percy and Cornwallis have little difficulty defeating the isolated segments of the garrison, who stream back into Fort Washington. However, the northern thrust under Knyphausen traverses rough, wooded terrain defended by Pennsylvania riflemen and is repulsed five times. In the course of battle Margaret Corbin replaces her slain husband at a battery and serves a gun until wounded. A final charge by the Hessians stampedes the defenders back into the fort, which is now dangerously overcrowded. Magaw, lacking a water supply and defenseless from an artillery bombardment, decides to capitulate at 3 P.M. It is a stinging reverse for the Americans, who have 53 killed, 96 wounded, and 2,818 captured, along with scores of valuable supplies and arms lost. British casualties are 20 killed and 102 wounded while the Hessians suffer 58 dead and 272 injured. The bastion is subsequently renamed Fort Knyphausen in honor of its captor. New York City is now firmly in British hands and will remain so for the rest of the war.
NAVAL: The *Andrew Doria* under Captain Isaiah Robinson arrives at the Dutch island of St. Eustatius, West Indies, and receives a first, if unofficial, salute to an American flag by a foreign government. British diplomatic protests result in Dutch disavowal of the action and dismissal of the island's governor.

November 18
NAVAL: The Continental Congress authorizes construction of the 74-gun ship-of-the-line *America* and five additional frigates mounting 36 guns apiece.

November 19–20
NORTH: Eager to maintain the initiative, General William Howe dispatches General Charles Cornwallis with 5,000 men on flatboats across the Hudson River at

Closter, New Jersey. General Nathanael Greene is fortuitously alerted to their approach and quickly abandons Fort Lee, closely pursued by Hessian jaegers under Major Johann Ewald. However, Cornwallis is after the fort, not Greene, so the American retreat is unimpeded. The British capture 300 tents, 1,000 barrels of flour, 50 cannon, and 150 prisoners. Fortunately for the Americans, Greene energetically removed a vast store of gunpowder days before the attack. General George Washington also continues withdrawing and eventually unites with Greene at Hackensack.

November 21
NORTH: General George Washington abandons the New York region altogether, advances across New Jersey and makes for the Delaware River and Pennsylvania. General Charles Lee and 5,000 men remain at North Castle, New York, while General Edward Heath commands an additional 3,200 men at Peekskill.

November 22
NORTH: American forces launch a second attack upon Fort Cumberland, Nova Scotia, and are rebuffed again.

November 25
NORTH: In New York, Colonel Guy Johnson, Indian superintendent, informs Lord Germain that the Seneca and other nearby tribes are now willing to side with the British.

November 28
NORTH: General Charles Cornwallis occupies Newark, New Jersey, as the Americans flee to Brunswick.

November 29
NORTH: American forces besieging Fort Cumberland, Nova Scotia, are repelled by reinforcements from Halifax. The British seize over 100 prisoners, who are promptly paroled and sent home.

General George Washington arrives at Brunswick, New Jersey, and is reinforced by 1,200 shoeless and shirtless men under General William Alexander.
NAVAL: The American warship *Reprisal* under Captain Lambert Wickes anchors at Quiberon Bay, France, with diplomatic commissioners Benjamin Franklin, Silas Deane, and Arthur Lee aboard. His is the first Continental navy vessel to ply European waters.

November 30
NORTH: In light of recent successes, General William Howe offers to pardon all Americans declaring their allegiance to the Crown within the next 60 days.

More than 2,000 Maryland and New Jersey militia abandon General George Washington's army once their terms of enlistment expire. Severely weakened, the Americans continue retiring before the British.

December 1
NORTH: General Charles Cornwallis nearly catches the Americans as they cross the Raritan River, but the bridge is destroyed, and the British halt at Brunswick.

December 2
North: General Charles Lee finally crosses the Hudson River and marches into New Jersey.

December 3
North: The army under General George Washington trudges into Trenton, New Jersey, and assembles boats necessary for crossing the Delaware River into Pennsylvania and safety.

December 4
Diplomacy: Benjamin Franklin and Richard Lee reach St. Nazaire and continue on to Paris by land.

Naval: Captain Lambert Wickes and the *Reprisal* depart France to begin a successful raid into the Bay of Biscay.

December 5
North: The American army at Trenton receives reinforcements in the form of the Pennsylvania Associators, a paramilitary organization, and a German-speaking regiment commanded by Colonel Nicholas Haussegger.

December 6
North: General William Howe catches up with General Charles Cornwallis at Brunswick and orders his pursuit to resume.

December 7
North: General George Washington makes an aborted advance upon Princeton with 1,200 men, but he encounters the fleeing forces of General William Alexander and together they fall back upon Assumpink Creek.

Newport, Rhode Island, is occupied by 6,000 men under General Henry Clinton and Commodore Peter Parker for use as a naval base.

December 8
North: General Richard Prescott lands a picked force of grenadiers and light infantry at Weaver's Cove, Rhode Island, scattering a nearby militia detachment and absconding with cannon and livestock.

Light infantry under General Charles Cornwallis advances through Trenton, New Jersey, and reaches the shore of the Delaware River at Assumpink Creek. There they are cannonaded and halted by batteries under General William Alexander on the opposite shore. The British sustain 13 wounded and withdraw.

December 11
North: General George Washington ferries his army over the Delaware River and marches back into Pennsylvania to await militia reinforcements. To prevent being pursued farther he also confiscates every boat within 75 miles of the crossing point. General Charles Cornwallis subsequently occupies Trenton a few hours later, which throws Philadelphia into a panic. General Israel Putnam consequently arrives there to restore order.

American militia conduct a successful raid behind British lines by seizing cattle and other livestock at Woodbridge, New Jersey.

December 12
Politics: The Continental Congress, alarmed by the British approach, abandons Philadelphia, Pennsylvania, and reconvenes in Baltimore, Maryland. Before departing it grants General George Washington near-dictatorial powers to prosecute the war until the crisis subsides. The Regiment of Light Dragoons under Colonel Elisha Sheldon is authorized by Congress, thereby establishing the American mounted arm.

December 13
North: General Charles Lee foolishly bivouacs in a tavern at Basking Ridge, New Jersey, three miles from the main American encampment at Morristown. When Loyalists apprise the British of his arrival they dispatch 25 men of the 16th Light Horse under Lieutenant Colonel William Harcourt (Lee's former subordinate) there, snaring Lee, killing two, wounding two, and capturing five.

December 14
North: General William Howe finally suspends his pursuit of General George Washington and orders the British army into winter quarters. He takes the largest detachment back to New York while Hessians under Colonel Karl von Donop are dispersed in an arc around Amboy, New Brunswick, Princeton, and Trenton.

December 15
Diplomacy: British agents in Paris approach Benjamin Franklin with offers of reconciliation but stop short of recognizing independence.
North: Generals William Heath and George Clinton raid Hackensack, New Jersey, snaring several British soldiers and arresting 509 Loyalists. A quantity of military supplies is also removed before British reinforcements arrive.

General George Washington is forced to issue an official proclamation denying any intention of burning Philadelphia to prevent its capture by the British.

December 18
South: North Carolina adopts a new state constitution.

December 19
Politics: Thomas Paine, volunteer aide de camp to General Nathanael Greene at Philadelphia, publishes the first of 13 installments to his *American Crisis,* with its memorable declaration, "These are times that try men's souls: The summer soldier and the sunshine patriot will, in this crisis, shrink from the service of his country: but he that stands it NOW deserves the love and thanks of man and woman. Tyranny, like Hell, is not easily conquered. Yet we have this consolation with us, that the harder the conflict, the more glorious the triumph." General George Washington, moved by such lofty prose, orders the tract proclaimed to every unit in the army. His shivering soldiers are likewise inspired and resolve to fight on.
Naval: The 16-gun brig *Lexington* under Captain William Hallock is captured by the frigate HMS *Pearl,* under Captain Thomas Wilkinson. However, the crew under Master's Mate Richard Dale subsequently recaptures the vessel and sails it to Baltimore.

December 20
Politics: The Continental Congress reconvenes in Baltimore, Maryland, while General George Washington assures them that he will use his new powers only to further the war effort. He also mobilizes more recruits and militiamen to offset declining manpower.
North: General John Sullivan, now commanding the division of General Charles Lee, crosses the Delaware River and reinforces the main American army at Newtown, Pennsylvania, with 2,000 men.

In light of recent successes, General William Howe writes to Lord Germain proposing a campaign to capture Philadelphia. This marks a dramatic shift in the British strategy pursued since the start of the war, which emphasized isolating New England from the rest of the colonies.

December 21
Diplomacy: Silas Deane, Benjamin Franklin, and Arthur Lee meet in Paris with congressional authority to negotiate treaties and secure loans.

December 22
North: Colonel Samuel Griffith leads 500 soldiers across the Delaware River; once reinforced by local militia, he attacks the Hessian outpost at Mount Holly, New Jersey. His forces are rebuffed by reinforcements under Colonel Karl von Donop and eventually withdraw.

December 24
North: In light of prevailing adversity, General George Washington realizes that the "game is nearly up" unless he stages a spectacular military coup. During a war council held at the Merrick House in Bucks County, Pennsylvania, he accordingly proposes a bold offensive against the exposed Hessian detachment garrisoning nearby Trenton. His officers agree unanimously. To underscore the gravity of their situation—and determination—"Victory or death" becomes the password.
South: Former general Richard Caswell become the first elected governor of North Carolina.

December 25
North: In a desperate gamble before his army disintegrates, General George Washington ferries his forces over the Delaware River and back into New Jersey on Christmas night. An attack by three columns is put in motion: Washington leads the main advance directly upon Trenton while two militia columns under General James Ewing and Colonel John Cadwalader will traverse farther down on either flank. Cadwalader's 1,900 men are to pin down the Hessian garrison at Bordentown as a diversion while Ewing and 700 men will seize the bridge at Assumpink Creek, trapping the Hessian garrison inside Trenton. Washington successfully crosses 2,400 shivering but high-spirited men and 18 cannon at McKonkey's Ferry, assisted by the mariners of Colonel John Glover's regiment. They then march a farther 19 miles to their objective in the cold and dark. Unknown at the time, neither Ewing nor Cadwalader were able to keep their rendezvous due to bad weather and icy conditions.

South: A party of American surveyors is attacked and massacred by Shawnee warriors under Chief Captain Pluggy at Limestone Creek, Kentucky.

December 26

North: The 2,400 Americans attack and surprise the 1,400-man Hessian garrison under Colonel Johann Rall at Trenton, New Jersey. Advancing under cover of a terrible ice storm, General George Washington divides his army into two columns under Generals Nathanael Greene and John Sullivan, and attacks the town from the north and northeast. Rall, who had been warned of an impending assault by General James Grant, is caught completely unprepared for the onslaught and struggles to form a defensive perimeter. However, the Hessians are blasted by the cannon of Colonel Henry Knox and outflanked by General Hugh Mercer's brigade. Rall manages to rally some of his men in an orchard outside of town but is fatally wounded by gunfire. His men then surrender en masse without further struggle. Hessian losses are 22 killed, 92 wounded, and 918 captured, along with six cannon taken. Only 400 manage to escape. American losses amount to two frozen to death and five wounded.

General Washington leads a victory over the Hessians in the Battle of Trenton, December 26, 1776. *(U.S. Army Center of Military History)*

Among the latter is Lieutenant James Monroe, a future president. Through this single stroke, brilliantly conceived and masterfully executed, Washington keeps the flagging revolution alive. The victors then withdraw back across the Delaware River, prisoners and booty in tow.

December 27
POLITICS: The Continental Congress votes to extend General George Washington's dictatorial powers for conducting the war and authorizes the raising of 22 additional infantry battalions. Colonel Henry Knox is promoted to brigadier general.
NORTH: General John Cadwalader finally manages to push his militia column across the frozen Delaware River, advances upon Burlington, New Jersey, and finds it deserted. He hastily informs General George Washington that the British and Hessians have contracted their lines since his victory at Trenton and urges him to return.

December 30
NORTH: Emboldened by success at Trenton, General George Washington recrosses the Delaware River into New Jersey with 2,000 men and reoccupies the town. There he learns that Generals Charles Cornwallis and James Grant have amassed 8,000 men at Princeton and are advancing upon him in force. Rather than retreat he orders up General Thomas Mifflin's 1,600 militiamen from Bordentown along with other detachments. The general then addresses the men, whose enlistments have expired, and urges them to remain under arms for another six weeks.

Colonel Joseph Reed, accompanied by seven mounted troopers, engages and defeats a small British detachment along the Delaware River near Trenton, taking 12 prisoners.

December 31
SOUTH: General George Rogers Clark petitions the Virginia Convention to annex the Kentucky settlement and provide directly for its defense. He does so to preempt settlers under Daniel Boone from organizing it as an independent state.
NAVAL: Between March 1776 and year's end, American naval forces of all types have captured 342 British ships.

1777

January 1
DIPLOMACY: The Continental Congress, convening at Baltimore, appoints Benjamin Franklin commissioner to the court of Spain. Meanwhile, Hessian prisoners are paraded through the streets of Philadelphia.
NORTH: General James Grant arrives at Princeton, New Jersey, with 1,000 men; he then departs, ordering 600 men to guard Brunswick. General Charles Cornwallis, previously intent upon returning to England, cancels his trip and rides to Princeton at the head of 6,000 men. General George Washington, meanwhile, collects 5,100 men and 40 cannon at Trenton, the bulk of whom are badly trained and equipped militia. For that reason he entrenches them along the south bank of Assumpink Creek and awaits developments. He also dispatches a brigade under a French volunteer, General Alexis Roche de Fermoy, with orders to delay any British

advance from Princeton. When Fermoy subsequently abandons his troops, command passes over to Colonel Edward Hand.

January 2
NORTH: British forces under General Charles Cornwallis, 5,500 strong, attempt to corner and engage the Americans at Trenton; Cornwallis has left 1,200 soldiers under Lieutenant Colonel Charles Mawhood at Princeton to guard supplies. As Cornwallis advances he encounters the American vanguard under Colonel Edward Hand and heavy skirmishing ensues. The Americans yield ground tenaciously at Shabbakonk Creek, delaying the British advance by three hours. It is 5 P.M. and growing dark before Cornwallis arrives with his main body before Washington's encampment. He immediately assumes that the Americans are trapped there, with the Delaware River to their back. Initial attempts to cross the bridge over Assumpink Creek under fire are rebuffed by accurate American artillery under General Henry Knox, so Cornwallis relents and prepares to "bag the fox" on the following day. However, in a major oversight, he fails to send a light force over the creek to pin the Americans within their works. General George Washington, however, has concluded that the British depots at Princeton and Brunswick have been badly weakened and boldly decides to make a nighttime march upon the former. He leaves 400 men behind to stoke campfires and continue digging to decoy the British. The Americans then slip 1,600 soldiers and 3,600 militia around the British right flank under cover of darkness. Cornwallis remains unaware of the ruse until the following morning. Losses for the day amount to six Americans killed and 10 wounded to 10 British dead, 20 wounded, and 25 captured.

NAVAL: Commodore Esek Hopkins learns that a British frigate, HMS *Diamond*, has grounded in Narragansett Bay. Taking command of the sloop *Providence* under Abraham Whipple, he tries attacking the British vessel in concert with a militia battery on land, but to no avail. Hopkins twice takes the unusual step of rowing ashore to confer with the militia commander and on the second trip his launch drifted away, leaving him stranded. Once the tide returns HMS *Diamond* frees itself and escapes intact.

January 3
NORTH: With General Charles Cornwallis idle before Trenton, General George Washington attacks a British outpost at Princeton, New Jersey. His advance guard of 350 men under General Hugh Mercer first encounters a similar force under Lieutenant Colonel Charles Mawhood of the 17th Regiment en route to Trenton on the same road. A stiff fight ensues and the Americans are routed after Mercer is fatally wounded. Mawhood, continuing to advance, also disperses a militia force under General John Cadwalader. Suddenly, Washington makes a battlefield appearance, rallies his men within musket shot of the enemy, and surges back across the field. Mawhood is unable to withstand this new onslaught and bayonets his way off the field. About 200 British then take cover in Nassau Hall at Princeton College, but they are flushed by Colonel Alexander Hamilton's cannon. The Americans subsequently capture large quantities of military stores and supplies, but the troops, though flush with victory, are exhausted. Washington therefore abandons plans to attack Brunswick and makes for the safety of Morristown and a winter encampment.

British losses are 28 killed, 58 wounded, and 323 captured; the Americans suffer 23 killed and 20 wounded. Ironically, Cornwallis arrives at Princeton after a hard slog and just in time to see the Americans depart. He immediately assumes they are en route to Brunswick and pushes his men there in the darkness.

January 4
NORTH: General Charles Cornwallis trudges into Brunswick following an all-night march while the main American force is miles away, reposing at Pluckemin, New Jersey.

January 5
NORTH: In order to maintain the initiative, General George Washington orders General William Heath, then in the Hudson Highlands, to stage a mock attack upon New York City.

January 6
NORTH: General George Washington marches his exhausted army north into the Watchung Mountains and encamps for the winter at Morristown, New Jersey. This places him menacingly astride British lines of communication while other American detachments under General William Maxwell recapture Hackensack and Elizabethtown, inflicting 10 casualties and netting 40 prisoners. British control of New Jersey is now restricted to the immediate vicinities of Brunswick and Amboy.

January 10
NORTH: Dr. John Morgan, director-general of army hospitals, is summarily dismissed from his post by the Continental Congress.

General William Howe orders all British forces withdrawn from central and western New Jersey for the winter. Advanced detachments remain at Amboy and Brunswick to guard the approaches to New York.
NAVAL: American artillery drives off HMS *Cerberus* from East Passage, Rhode Island, killing six.

January 15
NORTH: Colonel Oliver Spencer leads 300 New Jersey militia on a raid against Hessian forces at Connecticut Farms, New Jersey, taking 70 prisoners.
NAVAL: Captain Lambert Wickes of the 18-gun brig *Reprisal* commences a cruise that takes five prizes along the coast of France and Spain over the next month.

January 16
NORTH: The region of New England known as the New Hampshire Grants declares independence from New York and New Hampshire and establishes the "Republic of New Connecticut" (Vermont).

January 18
POLITICAL: The Continental Congress finally authorizes the names of all signers of the Declaration of Independence to be printed and made public.
NORTH: General William Heath, with the divisions of Benjamin Lincoln, Charles Scott, David Wooster, and Samuel H. Parsons, invests Fort Independence (King's

Bridge), New York. However, his 3,400 troops fail to cow the 2,000-strong Hessian garrison into submission and a siege commences.

January 20
NORTH: General Philemon Dickinson, commanding 400 militia and riflemen, drives off a British foraging party of comparable size at Somerset Courthouse, New Jersey, capturing prisoners, wagons, and horses. The Americans sustain four killed.

January 23
POLITICS: The Continental Congress passes the Naval Construction Act of 1777 mandating construction of a 36-gun and a 28-gun frigate.

January 25
NORTH: The Hessian garrison at Fort Independence, New York, sallies en masse and drives off larger American forces from Lancey's Mills.

January 29
NORTH: General William Heath withdraws from the vicinity of Fort Independence, New York, after a farcical two-week siege. He is harshly reprimanded by General George Washington in consequence.

February 2
SOUTH: Loyalists under Lieutenant Colonel Lewis Fuser invest the small fortified post of Fort McIntosh, Georgia, near the Florida border.

February 4
SOUTH: Georgia adopts a new state constitution.

Captain Richard Winn, commanding the 75-man garrison at Fort McIntosh, Georgia, surrenders to Loyalist forces before reinforcements under Lieutenant Colonel Francis Marion arrive. The Americans lose four killed, three wounded, and 68 captured.

February 7
POLITICS: Parliament authorizes privateering against United States shipping and issues letters of marque.

February 15
POLITICS: The Continental Congress, faced with spiraling inflation due to the onslaught of paper currency, adopts a New England recommendation to enforce rigid price controls. Other states are encouraged to follow suit.

February 19
POLITICS: The Continental Congress awards major general commissions to William Alexander, Thomas Mifflin, Adam Stephen, Arthur St. Clair, and Benjamin Lincoln. Benedict Arnold angrily tenders his resignation for being overlooked again, but General George Washington sympathetically encourages him to reconsider.

February 21
POLITICS: The Continental Congress elevates Colonel Anthony Wayne to brigadier general.

February 23
NORTH: General William Maxwell leads troops on a successful attack against a British foraging party near Rahway, New Jersey, inflicting many casualties. American losses are five killed and nine wounded.

February 25
POLITICS: In London, Lord Germain appoints General John Burgoyne to share a joint command of troops in Canada with Governor-General Guy Carleton.

February 27
POLITICS: The Continental Congress adjourns its session in Baltimore and returns to Philadelphia.

February 28
POLITICS: In London, General John Burgoyne outlines his elaborate strategy to detach New England from the rest of the colonies by attacking down the Lake Champlain corridor with 8,000 men. The main strike force is to be assisted by a smaller column that will land at Oswego, New York, and advance up the Mohawk River Valley. The two forces will then unite in preparation for a final drive upon Albany. With control of the Hudson River valley in British hands, New England will be effectively cut off and isolated from the rest of the colonies. It is assumed that British forces under Generals William Howe and Henry Clinton, at New York, will coordinate their efforts with Burgoyne and march northward.

March 3
POLITICS: Lord Germain approves the plan of General John Burgoyne but he also grants General William Howe permission to attack Philadelphia from the sea. However, Howe will receive only 5,000 men as reinforcements.
NAVAL: The American 14-gun brig *Cabot* under Captain Joseph Olney runs aground off Nova Scotia and is captured by British frigate HMS *Milford* under Captain John Burr. The crew manage to reach shore, steal a schooner, and sail for Boston.

March 8
NORTH: American troops under General William Maxwell defeat a small British force at Amboy, New Jersey, sustaining three wounded.

March 12
POLITICS: With New Jersey cleared of British forces, the Continental Congress reconvenes in Philadelphia. It has been deluged by foreign officers seeking employment with the Continental army and now advises American agents to discourage future applicants unless they speak good English and enjoy pristine recommendations.

March 14
NORTH: The Continental army at Morristown dwindles precipitously to 3,000 men as desertions and expiring enlistments thin its ranks. Faced with acute supply shortages, General George Washington has little recourse but to requisition food from civilians.

March 23–24
North: A British amphibious force of 500 men sails up the Hudson River and destroys the American supply depot at Peekskill, New York, driving off a small garrison under General Alexander McDougall. The Americans are reinforced the following day by 80 men under Lieutenant Colonel Marinus Willett, who attacks and boldly drives the marauders off. Peekskill is a small action, with British losses of 15 killed and wounded to an American tally of two killed and five wounded. But the raid alarms General George Washington sufficiently enough for him to dispatch an additional eight regiments there under General William Heath.

March 26
Politics: Lord Germain finalizes orders for the upcoming campaign, instructing Governor-General Guy Carleton to transfer the bulk of his forces to assist both General John Burgoyne and Lieutenant Colonel Barry St. Leger in their respective advances upon Albany.

Naval: The Continental Congress dismisses Commodore Esek Hopkins from the Continental navy for disrespect and failure to follow orders.

April 2
North: General William Howe advises Lord Germain that manpower deficiencies require him to cancel an overland thrust against Philadelphia and proposes transporting them by ship to Chesapeake Bay. Though tactically sound, this expedient removes any chance of cooperating with the forces of General John Burgoyne.

April 10
Politics: In Paris, France, Silas Deane recruits Marie-Joseph du Motier, marquis de Lafayette, and Baron Johann de Kalb for service.

April 11
Politics: The Continental Congress appoints Dr. William Shippen to serve as director-general of the Continental army's medical services. He has previously submitted a plan for reorganizing this department that met with congressional approval.

April 13
North: Throughout the spring, American detachments fight and harass the remaining British outposts in New Jersey. General Charles Cornwallis, while on a foraging expedition, suddenly leads 2,000 men against 500 Americans at Bound Brook. General Benjamin Lincoln, who should have been forewarned of any British approach by militia forces, is completely surprised in camp by the onslaught. However, he handles his men adroitly and escapes intact after losing three cannon, six killed, and 20 captured. The defeat persuades General George Washington to redeploy his advanced posts to place them at mutually supporting distances if attacked.

April 14
Politics: The Continental Congress establishes a large magazine at Springfield, Massachusetts, which will gradually evolve into the famous Springfield Arsenal.

April 17
POLITICS: The Continental Congress reorganizes the Committee of Secret Correspondence into the Committee for Foreign Affairs, with Thomas Paine as secretary.

April 19
NAVAL: Captain Dudley Saltonstall in the 28-gun frigate *Trumbull* captures two British transports off New York.

April 20
POLITICS: The marquis de Lafayette and Baron Johann de Kalb depart France for America, having been recruited by American agent Silas Deane.
NORTH: New York adopts a new state constitution.

April 21
NORTH: A British raiding force of 1,850 men is organized on the Hudson River under former governor, now general, William Tryon. They set sail that evening for a raid upon nearby Danbury, Connecticut.

April 25
NORTH: Governor William Tryon lands 1,850 men at Compo Beach on the Saugatuck River and advances against the American depot at Danbury, Connecticut, 23 miles distant. The town falls without a struggle the next day and is sacked and burned. Fortunately for the Americans, a large cache of cannon and ammunition stored there had been removed prior to the attack. Tryon, rather than retrace his steps, decides to return to the fleet by marching via Ridgefield.

April 27
NORTH: As Governor William Tryon's 1,850 raiders march along the road to Ridgefield, Connecticut, they suddenly encounter 500 American militia collected by General Benedict Arnold and Gold S. Silliman. Another force of 200 under General David Wooster begins nipping at the British rear, taking 40 prisoners. Once Wooster is killed, Tryon then outflanks the defenders and drives them off, nearly capturing Arnold in the process. The following day the British resume their march.

April 28
NORTH: General Benedict Arnold manages to collect an additional 700 militia and several cannon at Saugatuck Bridge and awaits Governor William Tryon's approach. But, aided by a Loyalist guide, the British successfully circumvent Arnold's position and arrive at Compo Hill above the embarking point. The Americans, heavily reinforced to 3,000 militia, harry and press the British withdrawal until a successful bayonet charge by General William Erskine drives them off. Tryon then departs, having suffered 25 dead, 177 wounded, and 29 missing to an American tally of 20 killed and 75 wounded. Tryon's raid proves costly without affecting much damage to the enemy.

May 1
Diplomacy: The Continental Congress appoints Arthur Lee to succeed Benjamin Franklin as commissioner to Spain.

May 2
Politics: The Continental Congress finally promotes Benedict Arnold to major general but, in another perceived slap, he remains junior in seniority to the five men preceding him.
West: Lieutenant William Linn delivers 98 barrels of gunpowder to Fort Henry, (West) Virginia, to defend that post and its residents against Loyalists and Indians.

May 3
Naval: Captain Gustavus Conyngham and the 10-gun lugger *Surprise* seize the British mail packet *Prince of Orange* in the English Channel; he removes his prize to Dunkirk, France. However, strong British diplomatic pressure results in Conyngham's arrest.

May 5
Politics: The Continental Congress appoints Joseph Reed brigadier general.
North: The Continental army under General George Washington at Morristown is built up to 9,000 men, well armed with muskets and other military supplies from France. The force now consists of five divisions commanded by Nathanael Greene, Adam Stephan, John Sullivan, Benjamin Lincoln, and William Alexander.

May 6
North: General John Burgoyne arrives and replaces Governor-General Guy Carleton as commander of British forces in Canada.

May 7
North: General George Washington issues a general order outlawing cards, dice, and other endemic forms of avarice among soldiers.

May 10
North: General Adam Stephan attempts to surprise the 42nd Highlanders at Piscataway, New Jersey, and is routed with 27 killed and about 40 prisoners. Stephan also egregiously misrepresents the action in his official report. British losses are eight killed and 19 wounded.

May 15
South: The camp of Georgia militiamen under Colonel John Baker is attacked by Indians at Sawpit, Florida, who abscond with several horses. The horses are recovered the following day and Baker remains in the vicinity awaiting Continental army reinforcements under Colonel Samuel Elbert.

May 17
South: British, Indians, and Loyalists under Lieutenant Colonel Thomas Brown and Major James Mark Prevost again attack and this time rout an American detachment of 109 men under Colonel John Baker at Thomas's Swamp, Florida. The advance under

Brown ambushes the Americans in camp and, while fleeing helter-skelter, they run directly into Prevost's British regulars positioned in their rear. The Americans lose eight dead and 31 prisoners. The Indians massacre several captives before order is restored.

May 20
SOUTH: Cherokee under Chief Oconostota sign the Treaty of Dewitt's Corner and forfeit all their remaining land in South Carolina to the United States. However, Chief Dragging Canoe refuses to accept the terms and heads south to join the Creek Confederacy and possibly continue the struggle.

May 23
NORTH: Lieutenant Colonel Return J. Meigs embarks 225 men at Guilford, Connecticut, and crosses Long Island Sound at night in 13 whaleboats. After landing he attacks Loyalists at Sag Harbor, New York; the Americans destroy 12 vessels, kill six soldiers, and take 90 captives without loss.

May 28
NORTH: General George Washington departs his camp at Morristown, New Jersey, and enters the field with 8,000 men. These redeploy at Middlebrook Valley in order to watch British movements on roads in and out of Philadelphia and Brunswick. General John Sullivan also commands an advance guard at Princeton.
NAVAL: Captain Lambert Wickes of the 18-gun brig *Reprisal* departs Nantes, France, in concert with the 16-gun brig *Lexington* and the 10-gun cutter *Dolphin*. This is the first American squadron to ply European waters and they capture 18 prizes by late June.

June 7
NAVAL: The 24-gun frigate *Boston* under Captain Hector McNeill and the 32-gun frigate *Hancock* under Captain John Manley engage the 28-gun British frigate HMS *Fox* under Captain Patrick Fotheringham. Both *Hancock* and *Fox* are badly damaged in a long running fight, which finally ends when the *Boston* overtakes them. When McNeill claims the vessel, Manley angrily demands that he remove his prize crew. American losses are four killed and six wounded.

June 12
NORTH: General Arthur St. Clair arrives to take command of Fort Ticonderoga, New York. He has 2,500 men under brigadiers Alexis Roche de Fermoy, John Paterson, and Enoch Poor. St. Clair finds the fort in poor condition and surrounded by nearby hills that are sufficiently high and close enough for enemy artillery. The Americans erroneously conclude that the largest of these, Mount Defiance, is too steep and overgrown to be accessible.

General William Howe concentrates 18,000 soldiers at Amboy, New Jersey, and advances to Brunswick. There forces under General Charles Cornwallis and Leopold von Heister entice the Americans to give battle, but the maneuver fails.

June 13
NORTH: General John Burgoyne assembles over 7,000 British and German soldiers at Saint Johns, Quebec, for his forthcoming invasion, assisted by Generals Simon

Fraser, William Phillips, and Friedrich von Riedesel. He is also accompanied by 400 Indians, 139 cannon, 28 gunboats, and sufficient bateaux to transport the army down Lake Champlain.

SOUTH: The marquis de Lafayette and Baron Johann de Kalb arrive at Georgetown, South Carolina, and proceed to make their way to Philadelphia.

June 14

POLITICS: The U.S. flag, traditionally attributed to Philadelphia seamstress Betsy Ross, is adopted as the national symbol by Congress. It consists of 13 alternating red and white stripes, and 13 white stars on a blue field, one for each state in the Union. In 1916 President Woodrow Wilson designates this date as Flag Day.

NORTH: General Charles Cornwallis leads a large force to the Millstone River in New Jersey and attempts to cross at Somerset Courthouse. He is engaged there by 200 militiamen and repulsed with two killed and 13 wounded. American losses are nine killed and 30 injured.

NAVAL: Captain John Paul Jones is appointed to lead the 18-gun sloop *Ranger* on a mission to harry the English coast.

June 17

NORTH: The army of General John Burgoyne, 7,000 strong, departs Saint Johns, Quebec, and begins marching south into American territory. General Simon Fraser pushes the British advance guard ahead of the main body and toward Crown Point, New York.

Colonel Daniel Morgan and his Virginia riflemen harass British troops building fortifications at Somerset Courthouse, New Jersey.

June 19

NORTH: General William Howe recalls his columns under General Leopold von Heister from Middlebrook, New Jersey, while General George Washington deploys an advance guard under General William Maxwell between New Brunswick and Amboy to detect any British movements against the American left flank.

June 20

NORTH: General John Burgoyne, after concentrating his army at Cumberland Head on Lake Champlain, unleashes a pompous proclamation against the Americans that elicits contempt and ridicule. Meanwhile, the main British column begins its slow descent upon Crown Point, New York.

General Philip J. Schuyler, though ill, arrives for a council of war at Fort Ticonderoga. It is agreed that the fort should hold out as long as possible before being abandoned and that the garrison under General Arthur St. Clair should then escape by boat to Mount Independence.

June 22

NORTH: American forces under Colonels Daniel Morgan and Anthony Wayne brush against the British rear guard at Brunswick, New Jersey, as they retire toward Staten Island. General George Washington shadows General William Howe as far as Quibbletown until the British rapidly deploy forces at Middlebrook to outflank him. The affair ends inconclusively with American losses of three killed and three wounded; British casualties are unknown.

June 23

NORTH: The Hessian leader General Leopold von Heister having been contentiously disposed, General William Howe is ordered home by the landgrave of Hessen-Kassel. He is replaced by General Wilhelm von Knyphausen.

A force of 1,800 British, Loyalists, and Indians under Colonel Barry St. Leger departs Montreal and heads down the St. Lawrence River and Lake Ontario for the port at Oswego, New York. In addition to his complement of regulars, he is assisted by Loyalist and Indian forces under Sir John Johnson, John Butler, and Chief Joseph Brant. It is anticipated that St. Leger's foray will distract American attention from the main British thrust down the Lake Champlain corridor under General John Burgoyne. However, once informed that the only real obstacle in his path, Fort Stanwix, is weak and poorly defended, St. Leger forgoes the inconvenience of lugging heavy siege artillery along.

June 26

NORTH: The advance guard under General Simon Fraser decamps from Crown Point and begins advancing upon Fort Ticonderoga while General John Burgoyne follows up with the main body.

General William Howe continues a series of maneuvers to outflank General George Washington. General Charles Cornwallis, moving through Woodbridge, marches two columns out of Amboy, New Jersey, in an attempt to catch and destroy General William Alexander at Short Hills (Metuchen). Both sides suffer 100 casualties apiece, but the Americans also lose three cannon. Washington uses the delay to reposition his army into prepared positions around Middlebrook. Having failed to provoke an engagement on favorable terms, Howe withdraws his entire force to Staten Island.

June 27

NAVAL: Captain Lambert Wickes concludes a successful foray into the very chops of the English Channel. His squadron, consisting of the *Lexington, Reprisal,* and *Dolphin,* returns to Nantes after seizing 18 prizes. While returning to the French coast he encounters the 74-gun HMS *Burford* under Captain George Bowyer off Ushant, and orders his two accompanying raiders to make for port. Wickes then entices his antagonist for a few hours and a lengthy pursuit unfolds. He is forced to jettison his armament and, by sailing close inland at night, convinces the British to finally abandon the chase.

June 30

NORTH: General William Howe departs New Jersey and concentrates his large army on Staten Island.

July 1

NORTH: General John Burgoyne, having traversed lake Champlain with 7,000 soldiers, lands and advances upon Fort Ticonderoga, encamping only three miles from his objective. The British will advance down the west bank of the Hudson River while the Hessians descend the east bank.

July 2

NORTH: Generals William Phillips and Simon Fraser eject American forces from their encampment at Mount Hope while a third force under General Friedrich von

Riedesel encircles Mount Independence from the rear. General John Burgoyne then dispatches a surrender demand to Fort Ticonderoga, which is refused.

July 4
POLITICS: The United States celebrates the first anniversary of its independence with fireworks and toasts.

NORTH: Having occupied Mount Hope, General John Burgoyne dispatches an engineer to reconnoiter nearby Mount Defiance. When it is ascertained that this position is suitable for bombarding Fort Ticonderoga, General William Phillips commences dragging his cannon up the slopes. He overcomes considerable difficulties, mounts his pieces, and makes possible a plunging fire upon the fort.

NAVAL: Captain John Paul Jones unfurls the new American flag for the first time on the Continental warship *Ranger* at Portsmouth, New Hampshire.

July 5
NORTH: General Arthur St. Clair, cognizant of the danger to Fort Ticonderoga, summons a war council and decides to abandon that post without further delay.

July 6
NORTH: General Arthur St. Clair loads all his ill soldiers and equipment onto bateaux and moves them by water. He also orders Colonel Pierce Long to march 500 men overland to Skeensboro, New York. Long complies but, finding the stockade there weakly defended, he burns it and continues on to Fort Anne. St. Clair, meanwhile, evacuates Fort Ticonderoga under the cover of darkness and makes for Castleton, Vermont. En route Colonel Seth Warner and 150 men are detached as a rear guard. In the course of the night he is reinforced by the 11th Massachusetts and 2nd New Hampshire regiments, bringing his numbers up to 1,100. Warner, however, disregards orders to withdraw to the main body and encamps for the night at Hubbardton, Vermont. He is unaware that his encampment has been observed by the British advance guard under General Simon Fraser. Encouraged by lax security, the British plan a surprise attack on Warner's camp.

July 7
NORTH: At dawn General Simon Fraser surprises the American camp under Colonel Seth Warner at Hubbardton, Vermont, capturing most of their supplies and baggage train. The defenders give way initially but then rally upon Zion Hill, which the British proceed to attack. A protracted firefight ensues as both sides maneuver for advantage and the Americans begin pressing Fraser back. Disaster looms for the British as their more numerous adversaries begin turning both flanks amidst heavy woodland skirmishing. Suddenly, a small Hessian contingent under General Friedrich von Riedesel appears on the field, singing psalms and making as much noise as possible to give the illusion of greater numbers. The Americans initially stand their ground before this new onslaught, but a bayonet charge ordered by Fraser sweeps them from the field. Though victorious, the British fail in their objective of capturing the American rear guard. Warner's losses are 30 killed, 96 wounded, and 228 captured. The British sustain 39 killed and 127 wounded, disproportionately suffered by elite light infantry and grenadier companies.

General John Burgoyne detaches Lieutenant Colonel John Hill and 190 men of the 9th Foot from Fort Ticonderoga to capture Fort Anne, New York, 10 miles distant. After traveling all day on bad roads and across burned bridges Hill reaches his destination that evening but pauses to assess events. His suspicions are confirmed when a "deserter" arrives in the British lines and informs Hill that the defenders number around 1,000 men. That evening the American slips back into his own lines and informs Colonel Pierce Long of Hill's apparent weakness.

NAVAL: British warships HMS *Rainbow,* 44 guns under Commodore George Collier, *Flora,* 32 guns, and *Victor,* 10 guns, capture the 32-gun frigate *Hancock* under Captain John Manley after a 30-hour chase off Halifax, Nova Scotia. Manley possesses a faster vessel and should have easily escaped but he mistakenly shifts his water casks forward to alter his ship's trim; this makes *Hancock* sit lower frontally and robs him of valuable speed. The British also recapture the frigate *Fox. Hancock* is subsequently impressed into British service as HMS *Iris.* American losses are one killed and 188 captured.

July 8

NORTH: The Vermont Convention convenes in Windsor and approves a state constitution that endorses universal manhood suffrage and abolishes slavery. However, statehood will not be achieved until 1791.

A small British force under Lieutenant Colonel John Hill is attacked outside Fort Anne, New York, by American forces under Colonel Pierce Long, recently reinforced by 400 militia under Colonel Henry Van Rensselaer. The contending forces skirmish heavily for two hours before the valiant Hill is forced into a last-ditch stand upon a wooded hillside. Suddenly, the attackers are disconcerted by approaching Indian war whoops—the advance guard of a relief force commanded by General William Phillips. Long hurriedly withdraws, burns Fort Anne, and immediately falls back upon Fort Edward on the Hudson River. The Americans lose 30 prisoners, Hill sustains three killed and 25 wounded.

General William Howe begins embarking his army on board the fleet at New York.

July 9

NORTH: General George Clinton becomes the first elected governor of New York.

General John Burgoyne arrives with the bulk of his army at Skeensboro and deploys Hessians under General Friedrich von Riedesel at Castleton to shield his advance. Thereafter, however, the British advance is increasing hampered by rough, wooded terrain infinitely better-suited to the American style of "brush fighting."

Major William Barton leads a raiding party of 40 men into Newport, Rhode Island, and captures British general Richard Prescott in bed.

July 16

NAVAL: Captain Gustavus Conyngham departs Dunkirk, France, on the 14-gun sloop *Revenge;* his ensuing sweep of British home waters nets 20 prizes.

July 17
NORTH: The General Court of New Hampshire commissions John Stark a brigadier general of militia. Stark swears to refuse any orders from either the Continental Congress or Continental army officers. Within a week he recruits 1,500 soldiers.

July 20
SOUTH: The Overhill Cherokee finally submit to the Treaty of Long Island, which cedes all remaining territory in western North Carolina to state authorities.

July 23
NORTH: Declining to assist the efforts of General John Burgoyne, General William Howe sails from New York with 267 vessels and 18,000 soldiers for Chesapeake Bay. Once apprised of this move, General George Washington redeploys the divisions of John Sullivan, Adam Stephan, Benjamin Lincoln, and William Alexander throughout the Philadelphia vicinity.

Count Kazimierz Pulaski arrives at Marblehead, Massachusetts, with a letter of introduction from Benjamin Franklin.

July 25
POLITICS: The Continental Congress votes Colonel William Barton an elegant sword for his recent capture of General Richard Prescott.
NORTH: General John Burgoyne marches southward upon Fort Anne while General Philip J. Schuyler musters 2,600 soldiers and 1,600 militia under Generals Arthur St. Clair and John Nixon to oppose him. Generals Benedict Arnold and Benjamin Lincoln are also en route, but a council of officers decides that Fort Edward cannot adequately be garrisoned.

July 26
NORTH: Lieutenant Colonel Barry St. Leger begins marching 1,800 British troops, Loyalists, and Indians from Oswego, New York, along the Mohawk River valley in support of General John Burgoyne's army. His first objective is capturing the American post at Fort Stanwix (Rome), New York.

July 27
POLITICS: The 19-year-old marquis de Lafayette and Baron Johann de Kalb arrive at Philadelphia seeking major-general commissions from the Continental Congress, although that body, besieged by foreigners, wavers on the decision.
NORTH: Loyalist settler Jane McCrea is murdered by British Indians at Fort Edward, New York, an atrocity that spurs American recruitment. General John Burgoyne declines to punish his Indians for fear of losing their support.

July 29
NORTH: General Philip J. Schuyler abandons Fort Edward, New York, and begins withdrawing down the Hudson River Valley toward Saratoga, 30 miles above Albany. He so successfully obstructs the progress of General John Burgoyne's juggernaut with felled trees and other obstacles that the British cover only 23 miles over the next 24 days.

July 30
NORTH: The main British column under General John Burgoyne occupies Fort Edward, New York.

General John Stark leads his New Hampshire militia from Portsmouth and marches toward Manchester.

Colonel Nicholas Herkimer is advised by friendly Oneida scouts that a British column is advancing up the Mohawk River toward Fort Stanwix; he quickly starts mobilizing the Tryon County militia to begin assembling at Fort Dayton, New York, for a relief expedition.

July 31
POLITICS: The marquis de Lafayette is commissioned a major general by the Continental Congress but he remains without pay or a command.
NORTH: General George Washington receives word that the British fleet has been spotted off the Delaware Capes so he orders his forces across the Delaware River and into Pennsylvania to defend Philadelphia.

August 1
NORTH: The British army under General John Burgoyne, having spent a month traversing difficult, wooded terrain, finally reaches the Hudson River, New York.

General George Washington, formally introduced to the marquis de Lafayette, takes an immediate liking to the young officer and grants him a staff position.

August 2
NORTH: Lieutenant Colonel Barry St. Leger, advancing up the Mohawk River, besieges a small garrison of 550 men of the 3rd New York Regiment under Colonel Peter Gansevoort at Fort Stanwix, New York. Assisted by Lieutenant Colonel Marinus Willett, Gansevoort has greatly strengthened his works while an additional 200 reinforcements slip in just prior to the British arrival. St. Leger, having paraded his force in front of the garrison, then demands its surrender under the pain of an Indian massacre. Noting that the British lack any heavy artillery, Gansevoort refuses. The British then establish three base camps around the fort and encircle it with a light skirmisher screen.

Word of General William Howe's lack of cooperation reaches General John Burgoyne at Fort Ticonderoga, but he is undeterred from striking south toward Albany.
NAVAL: Accurate gunfire from shore drives HMS *Renown* away from Dutch Harbor Island, Rhode Island.

August 3
NORTH: General Philip J. Schuyler arrives at Stillwater, New York, at the head of 4,500 soldiers. This places him 12 miles below Saratoga.

August 4
POLITICS: The Continental Congress appoints General Horatio Gates to replace General Philip J. Schuyler as commander of the northern army.
NORTH: Colonel Nicholas Herkimer departs Fort Dayton with a relief column of 800 men and begins marching to Fort Stanwix, New York. However, his efforts are keenly

observed by Molly Brant, who dispatches a runner to the British camp. Meanwhile, Indians accompanying Lieutenant Colonel Barry St. Leger's force surround Fort Stanwix and commence yelling for several hours in an attempt to unnerve the defenders. His demand that the garrison surrender is nonetheless summarily refused.

August 5

NORTH: Lieutenant Colonel Barry St. Leger learns from Molly Brant that an American relief expedition is headed toward Fort Stanwix, and he dispatches 200 Loyalists and a large number of Indians under Chief Joseph Brant to engage them. This leaves his campground woefully under-guarded, a situation that does not go unnoticed at Fort Stanwix.

Lieutenant Colonel John Campbell leads 200 British soldiers on a raid against American artillery positions at North Ferry, Rhode Island. The battery is stormed, eight casualties inflicted, and four prisoners taken.

August 6

NORTH: General Nicholas Herkimer and his 800 militiamen are ambushed by Loyalists and Indians under Cornplanter, Joseph Brant, Sir John Johnson, and Major Walter Butler at Oriskany Creek, New York, six miles from Fort Oriskany. The Americans are filing through a deep ravine that is densely wooded on either flank when the Indians attack, chasing off the rear guard and surrounding Herkimer and his wagon train. The troops come close to panicking but Herkimer, wounded in both legs, calmly lights his pipe and directs the battle. A sudden rainstorm affords the hard-pressed Americans a brief respite, and Herkimer effectively reorganizes his defensive ring on a wooded plateau west of the creek. He also instructs his men to fight in pairs, with one firing and one standing guard. The Indians charge repeatedly to close quarters and vicious hand-to-hand fighting ensues, but Herkimer's perimeter holds fast. At one juncture Butler tries a ruse by having a company of Loyalists turn their buff-lined green coats inside out to pass themselves off as reinforcements from Fort Stanwix, but the ploy fails when one officer recognizes a Loyalist neighbor. After fighting for six hours and sustaining heavy losses, the Indians sullenly withdraw, forcing the Loyalists back with them. The Americans also fall back to Fort Dayton, concluding the most savage encounter of the war. American losses are in the range of 200 killed outright, 50 wounded, and 200 captured while the Indians may have sustained as many as 150 casualties.

Simultaneously, a sortie of 250 men from Fort Stanwix under Lieutenant Colonel Marinus Willett ravages the British camp of Lieutenant Colonel Barry St. Leger. Willett does not lose a man and returns with five British flags, 21 wagon loads of supplies, and Sir John Johnson's personal papers. St. Leger's Indians, having already borne considerable losses, are now bereft of tents and blankets and completely discouraged. They begin deserting in large numbers.

August 7

NORTH: Summoned again to surrender by the British, Colonel Peter Gansevoort refuses. However, he accepts a three-day truce and makes plans to dispatch Lieutenant Colonel Marinus Willett to Fort Dayton for reinforcements.

August 8
NORTH: General John Stark marches into Bennington, Vermont; this American supply depot is soon the object of British attention.

August 9
NORTH: Lieutenant Colonel Marinus Willett slips through British siege lines at Fort Stanwix, New York, and arrives at Fort Dayton to request reinforcements. With Burgoyne's column only 29 miles away at Fort Edward and only 4,500 men to oppose them, General Philip J. Schuyler agrees to the risky scheme.

August 10
NORTH: General Philip J. Schuyler dispatches an 800-man relief force from Stillwater, New York, to Fort Stanwix under Generals Benedict Arnold and Ebenezer Learned.

August 11
NORTH: Faced with mounting supply shortages, General John Burgoyne dispatches 374 Brunswick dragoons, 30 Hesse-Hanau artillerists, and approximately 500 Loyalists and Indians from the British camp at Fort Miller. Their commander, Lieutenant Colonel Friedrich Baum, is ordered to procure supplies and horses at Bennington, Vermont. He is also tasked with recruiting as many sympathetic citizens to the British cause as possible; their numbers are rumored to be numerous. Curiously, Baum himself does not speak a word of English.

August 13
NORTH: General John Burgoyne departs Fort Edward, and makes preparations to ferry his army across the Hudson River prior to advancing upon Saratoga. Meanwhile, he dispatches a Hessian column under Lieutenant Colonel Friedrich Baum on a harassment raid in the vicinity of Cambridge, New York; a heavy skirmish develops.
NAVAL: Inventor David Bushnell unsuccessfully attacks HMS *Cerberus* with a spar torpedo.

August 14
NORTH: Hessians and Loyalists under Lieutenant Colonel Friedrich Baum scatter 200 militiamen at Sancoick (Van Schaick's Mill), New York. Somewhat surprised by this hostile reception, Baum contacts General John Burgoyne and declares his intention to attack any remaining Americans on the following day. He also requests reinforcements.

August 15
NORTH: General John Stark, collecting his forces outside Bennington, is informed of the approach of 400 men under Colonel Seth Warner, boasting his manpower to 2,000. He also dispatches several spies into the nearby German camp, posing as Loyalists, who relay accurate information as to enemy numbers and dispositions. Lieutenant Colonel Friedrich von Baum, disturbed by the great number of rebels before him, orders his troops to begin constructing breastworks. That day Lieutenant

Colonel Heinrich Breymann also departs Fort Edward with 800 grenadiers and Brunswick light infantrymen to reinforce Baum, 25 miles distant.

August 16
NORTH: General John Stark orders an elaborate double envelopment of enemy forces dug in and around Bennington, Vermont. Lieutenant Colonel Friedrich von Baum has erred in dispersing his men over too wide a defensive arc, where they are not in mutual supporting distance and are liable to be knocked off piecemeal. Stark is cognizant of this deficiency and orders a complicated double envelopment of Baum's entire position while he, leading the main column, assails them frontally. American columns under Colonels Nicholas Moses and Samuel Herrick march stealthily through the deep woods around both of Baum's flanks, routing the Loyalists and Indians positioned there. To Stark, this is the prearranged signal to launch the main assault over the bridge, which he leads in person. Baum's dragoons, trained to fight as dismounted infantry, are ensconced behind their muddy redoubt and resist fiercely. They keep up a hot fire upon the Americans for two hours before a lucky cannon shot ignites their supply wagon. Once their ammunition is gone, Baum orders the troopers to draw sabers and charge downhill on foot; he is mortally wounded. The victorious Americans then sweep over the redoubt, capturing his entire command. Stark allows his men to plunder the enemy camp systematically.

At 5 P.M. Breymann's column made its unexpected appearance on the battlefield and momentarily threw the victorious Americans into confusion. The Germans presented a solid front and were pressing Stark's men back when they were suddenly assailed on both flanks by Colonel Seth Warner's command. Breymann fought well until sunset when his ammunition expired and the Germans fled in confusion back to the British camp. Bennington was a remarkable victory for the largely untrained American militia; for a loss of 30 killed and 40 wounded they slew 200 of the enemy and seized 700 prisoners, along with their baggage and artillery. The first nail in General John Burgoyne's coffin had been driven home.

August 17
NORTH: General John Burgoyne learns of Colonel Friedrich von Baum's defeat at Fort Miller and prepares his army for combat operations.

August 19
NORTH: General Horatio Gates arrives at Stillwater and succeeds General Philip J. Schuyler as commander of northern forces, then numbering 4,500 men.

August 21
NORTH: A relief expedition of 950 men under General Benedict Arnold reaches Fort Dayton, New York, and halts to regroup. He then dispatches the half-witted Hon Yost Schuyler into the British camp with word that his army is "more numerous than the leaves on the trees," which frightens the Indians into retreating.

On his own initiative, General John Sullivan embarks 1,000 troops from Elizabethtown, New Jersey, on a large-scale raid upon Staten Island, New York. They land in two separate detachments and march inland against two different objectives but are ultimately thwarted by the British 52nd Foot under General John Campbell. Sullivan then badly bungles his withdrawal, and many soldiers are abandoned for want

General John Stark strategically surrounds an unsuspecting Hessian force and leads another Patriot victory at the Battle of Bennington, August 16, 1777. *(National Guard Bureau)*

of transport. The Americans sustain 28 killed and 172 captured while British losses are around 130. The general is subsequently court-martialed and acquitted.

General George Washington, flummoxed as to the destination of General William Howe's armada, summarizes that the British are sailing against Charleston, South Carolina.

August 22
NORTH: General Samuel H. Parsons and 500 men attack a Loyalist outpost at Setauket (Long Island), New York, and are repulsed by 150 defenders under Lieutenant Colonel Richard Hewlett.

The Americans receive positive intelligence that the British fleet has entered Chesapeake Bay and General George Washington orders detachments under Generals John Sullivan and Francis Nash to concentrate at Chester, Pennsylvania.

August 23
NORTH: General Benedict Arnold's relief column approaches Fort Stanwix, precipitating a panic in the camp of Colonel Barry St. Leger. The British flee and embark

just ahead of the vengeful Americans, abandoning valuable supplies. Arnold then garrisons the fort with an additional 700 men and hurriedly marches back to Saratoga with his remaining 1,200 soldiers. The left wing of General John Burgoyne's invasion, upon which so much hinges, has failed him completely.

August 24
NORTH: General George Washington parades 16,000 troops through Philadelphia en route to meet the British.

August 25
NORTH: General William Howe debarks 15,000 men at Head of Elk, Maryland, having spent 32 days at sea. His forces are quite emaciated by the voyage so he grants them three days' rest prior to marching on Philadelphia. He is particularly interested in plundering local farms to replace horses and draft animals that died in transit.

August 28
NORTH: The Continental army is augmented by creation of the Light Infantry Regiment, an elite formation consisting of 100 men and officers drawn from the cream of six brigades. It is constituted to replace the rifle battalion under Colonel Daniel Morgan, now detached to the Northern Department, and is assigned to the brigade of General William Maxwell.

Sharp skirmishing ensues as General Charles Cornwallis leads a division of British troops northward to Elkton, Maryland, while General Wilhelm von Knyphausen crosses the Elk River and seizes Cecil Courthouse. They hope to catch the American army in a pincer movement and crush it.

August 31–September 1
WEST: Colonel William Sheppard and a garrison of 42 men at Fort Henry (Wheeling, West Virginia) are besieged by 400 Indians under Simon Girty. After ambushing and massacring a detachment from the fort, the Indians attack the remaining 19 soldiers without success. Major Samuel McCulloch manages to escape and plunges his horse down a 150-foot cliff to bring reinforcements. The following day a relief column of 40 mounted riflemen arrives and drives off the attackers. American losses total 23; Indian casualties are unknown.

September 2
NAVAL: The 32-gun frigate *Raleigh* under Captain Thomas Thompson and the 24-gun sloop *Alfred* under Captain Elisha Hinman boldly attack an English merchant convoy at night before being driven off by the Royal Navy.

September 3
NORTH: The vanguard of General Charles Cornwallis's British column advances toward the Christiana River, encountering the American rear guard under General William Maxwell at Cooch's Bridge, Delaware. The Hessian jaegers and Anspach chasseurs under Lieutenant Colonel Ludwig von Wurmb quickly deploy to engage their adversary, who are fighting Indian-style from behind trees. After stout resistance, the American position is turned and carried by the jaegers while Maxwell falls back to White Clay Creek and rejoins the main army. His flight is

accelerated by a determined Hessian bayonet charge that flushes the Americans from two prepared positions. General William Howe arrives shortly after the battle and personally congratulates Colonel Wurmb for a fine action. Hessian losses total three killed and 20 wounded; the Americans lose around 40. For the United States, this is the first battle waged under the new stars and stripes flag.
NAVAL: The American frigate *Raleigh* under Captain Thomas Thompson badly damages the sloop HMS *Druid*, then escorting a convoy, but adverse winds prevent its capture. The British lose six killed and 26 wounded to one American slain and two injured.

September 4
NORTH: A body of 100 militiamen under General Ezekiel Cornell attacks a British foraging party from HMS *Juno* on Prudence Island, Rhode Island, but is driven off. The British lose three killed and complete their mission.

September 6
NORTH: Generals Nathanael Greene and Adam Stephen concentrate their two divisions at Newport, Pennsylvania, while General William Maxwell maintains defensive positions along White Clay Creek.

September 9
NORTH: General George Washington, wary of the British slipping around his right flank and attacking Philadelphia, deploys his army behind Chadd's Ford on Brandywine Creek, Pennsylvania.

September 10
NORTH: General William Howe, cognizant that attacking the American position behind Brandywine Creek would prove prohibitive, initiates a wide flanking movement calculated to turn the American right. He orders General Charles Cornwallis with 9,000 men northward from Kennett Square to cross the Brandywine higher up at Trimble's Ford and Jeffrie's Ford before sweeping in from behind. The Americans, fixated by events farther south, have totally neglected this avenue of approach and concentrated their forces in and around Chadd's Ford. Furthermore, to hold the army of General George Washington in place, Howe details General Wilhelm von Knyphausen and 7,000 Hessians to demonstrate before Brandywine Creek as a diversionary maneuver.

September 11
NORTH: British general John Campbell attacks and captures Elizabethtown, Newark, and Passaic, New Jersey.

Early in the morning the light troops of General Wilhelm von Knyphausen lead his columns in motion and advance upon American outposts commanded by General William Maxwell, driving them across Brandywine Creek. Knyphausen then brings up some cannon and bombards the Americans to distract them from events farther upstream as General Charles Cornwallis executes his flanking movement. This is accomplished promptly and by 2:30 P.M. sizable British forces begin positioning themselves behind the American right flank. General George Washington and his staff, confused by conflicting military intelligence, are almost ready to attack across the Brandywine and destroy Knyphausen until they recognize the threat posed by Cornwallis. Washington immediately orders the divisions of General Adam Stephen, William Alexander, and John Sullivan to pivot and meet them. These units have no sooner changed their front than Cornwallis attacks around 4:00 P.M. and, after much hard fighting, begins collapsing the American right. The marquis de Lafayette, in his first general action, sustains a leg wound in trying to rally the shaken defenders. Washington counters by weakening his center and left by ordering up the divisions of Generals Anthony Wayne and Nathanael Greene in support. The brigades of General George Weedon and John Peter Muhlenberg fight tenaciously and allow the shattered units of Sullivan to reform.

No sooner has Washington's situation temporarily stabilized than Knyphausen suddenly throws his whole weight across Brandywine Creek, now poorly defended, and drives the Americans back. The defenders fight well initially but yield to numbers and lose an entire artillery battery. The British then commence a determined advance across the battlefield, while Washington, judging the affair lost, withdraws in orderly fashion. Brandywine costs the British 90 killed and 480 wounded to an American tally of 1,200 killed and wounded, plus 11 cannon captured. Howe has triumphed again tactically, but Washington, though trounced, extricates himself to fight another day.

September 12
NORTH: General Horatio Gates, now commanding 6,000 men, begins occupying the strategic bluff of Bemis Heights near the Hudson River. This places him 24 miles north of Albany, New York, and 10 miles south of the main British encampment at Saratoga. He then directs Polish-born engineer Colonel Tadeusz Kościuszko to construct redoubts and fortified lines, further strengthened by an abatis.

General George Washington falls back to the falls of the Schuylkill River near Germantown and informs the Continental Congress that his men remain in good spirits.

September 13
NORTH: General John Burgoyne abandons his earlier plans for crossing the Hudson River opposite Albany, and instead erects a pontoon bridge at Fort Miller. He subsequently encamps two miles north of Saratoga, still believing that reinforcements from the west and south are forthcoming.

September 14
NORTH: General George Washington repositions his army at White Horse Tavern to avoid being outflanked.
NAVAL: Captain Lambert Wickes is released from prison in France and allowed to depart St. Malo aboard the *Reprisal*.

September 15
NORTH: General John Burgoyne shifts his army southward to Fishkill, New York, placing him within five miles of the American army under General Horatio Gates along Bemis Heights. British movements are reduced to a crawl due to rain, felled trees, and other obstacles created by his adversaries.

The Continental Congress commissions Baron Johann de Kalb a major general after he threatens to sue for breach of contract. He thus becomes a general without a command. Count Kasimierz Pulaski is also elevated to brigadier general while the position Commander of Horse is created for him.

September 16
NORTH: American and British forces under Generals Anthony Wayne, William Maxwell, and Wilhelm von Knyphausen skirmish briefly at White Horse Tavern (Warren), Pennsylvania, before a heavy downpour concludes the engagement. General George Washington then retires his army in the direction of Reading Furnace to replenish his ruined ammunition supply.

September 17
POLITICS: In light of the impending crisis, the Continental Congress prepares to flee Philadelphia a second time, for York, Pennsylvania, and grants General George Washington temporary dictatorial powers to conduct the war.

Generals Charles Cornwallis and Wilhelm von Knyphausen occupy Valley Forge, capturing valuable supplies.

September 18
NORTH: Colonel John Brown and 1,500 men stage a brief raid upon the British-held Fort Ticonderoga, then garrisoned by 900 men under General William Powell. Taking advantage of lax security, Brown attacks and captures all the posts surrounding the fort, seizing 300 prisoners and releasing 100 American captives. But lacking heavy artillery, Brown is unable to storm the fort itself and draws off. The affair underscores the vulnerability of British communications with Canada.

A British foraging party is attacked and captured only three miles from the main American position at Bemis Heights, New York. Such close proximity induces General John Burgoyne to organize a massive reconnaissance in force to ascertain the American position and seize a hill on their left for mounting artillery. He draws his army into three columns: the left flank of 1,800 soldiers under General Simon Fraser; the center composed of 1,100 soldiers under General James Hamilton; and the left wing consisting primarily of 1,100 German troops under General Friedrich von Riedesel.

September 19
POLITICS: The Continental Congress, fearing the British advance upon Philadelphia, flees for the second time and reconvenes in Lancaster, Pennsylvania.
NORTH: General John Burgoyne orders his three columns to advance against the army of General Horatio Gates at Freeman's Farm. Their advance traverses wooded, hilly terrain that obstructs a clear view of the battlefield and impedes their progress. However, Gates ignores General Benedict Arnold's advice to sally en masse and defeat the three columns piecemeal. The British left under General Simon Fraser is roughly handled by the riflemen and light infantry of Colonel Daniel Morgan and Lieutenant Colonel Henry Dearborn, but they fight their more numerous opponent to a draw. The center under General John Burgoyne butts up against the brigade of General Enoch Poor, which outnumbers the British two-to-one, and a

seesaw battle of attrition ensues. A violent conflict of several hours confers little advantage to either party, with American marksmanship largely negating British advantages in discipline and training. By now Gates is finally convinced by Arnold to reinforce his struggling line, and General Ebenezer Learned's brigade is committed to the fray. At one point, the reserves under General William Phillips charge and rescue the 62nd Regiment from being surrounded. But the Americans, by dint of sheer numbers, press forward and the British gradually yield ground. Arnold again pleads to Gates for reinforcements to clinch the deal, but Gates refuses and orders him back to camp. Arnold ignores this last directive completely and forges ahead—he will be removed as second in command.

Burgoyne, fearing that his center is collapsing, recalls the German column under General Friedrich von Riedesel, who force-marches and redeploys to assist the main body. Leaving only a token guard behind to watch the supplies and bateaux, Riedesel pulls his men out of line and leads them through an intervening swamp. The timely and sudden appearance of Hessian troops unnerves the American right wing, which falls back in good order, and the contest peters out. By 5 P.M. the British enjoy uncontested control of the battlefield but have achieved a pyrrhic victory. American losses are 80 killed, 200 wounded, and 36 missing, nearly half what Burgoyne has suffered: 556 men, including several regimental officers singled out by sharpshooters.

General George Washington, having replenished his munitions, marches to Perkiomen Creek on the Schuylkill River to thwart an impending British thrust against Philadelphia.

NAVAL: The 10-gun cutter HMS *Alert* under Captain John Bazeley captures Captain Henry Johnson and the 16-gun brig *Lexington* after the latter runs out of ammunition off Ushant, France. American losses in this embarrassing reverse are seven killed, 11 wounded, and 77 captured, to a British tally of three killed and two wounded.

September 20

NORTH: General John Burgoyne prepares to attack American troops manning the defensive positions of General Horatio Gates, which are short of ammunition and disorganized after the fighting at Freeman's Farm. However, he is dissuaded by General Simon Fraser, whose elite light troops are badly in need of rest. Gates then avails himself of British inactivity to occupy a strategic hill on his left flank, which renders him impervious to any attack from that sector.

General Anthony Wayne's brigade of 1,500 men takes up positions in the rear of General William Howe's army at Paoli, Pennsylvania, intending to attack Howe's baggage train should he cross the Schuylkill River. This places Wayne within only four miles of the main British camp.

September 21

NORTH: General John Burgoyne receives an urgent dispatch from General Henry Clinton outlining his plans to advance from New York with 4,000 men to provide a useful diversion for the American army of General Horatio Gates. However, Clinton never declares any intention to link up with Burgoyne's beleaguered main column. This information causes Burgoyne to cancel an impending attack against

Gates's weakened line—which might very well have succeeded—instead he orders his army to begin entrenching and await reinforcements. This is a dangerous prospect for Burgoyne as his food stocks are already running low.

General William Howe, seeking to secure his lines of communication prior to crossing the Schuylkill River, dispatches General Charles Grey to drive off General Anthony Wayne's brigade from its camp at nearby Paoli, Pennsylvania. Grey advances at night with three regiments in front and two in reserve under Lieutenant Colonel Thomas Musgrave, the whole being guided by local Tories. Furthermore, to eliminate any chance of premature discharge, he orders his men to remove the flints from their muskets and rely completely upon the bayonet. Marching order and noise discipline are excellent. Wayne has been tipped off by locals that attack is imminent, so he strengthens his pickets and orders his men to sleep on their arms. But so stealthily does Grey approach and eliminate the sentries that he subsequently charges directly into Wayne's encampment without opposition. A savage hand-to-hand melee erupts, but the Americans, the majority of whom lack bayonets, are gradually forced off the field. Wayne manages to extricate all his cannon but loses eight wagons to this avalanche of cold steel. American losses are 53 killed, 100 wounded, and 71 captured, while Grey incurs six dead and 22 injured. Having eliminated this threat to the British rear, he quickly reassembles his command and rejoins the main body under Howe. Hereafter, he is celebrated as "no-flint" Grey.

September 22
NORTH: General George Washington maneuvers his army to Pott's Grove, Pennsylvania, to forestall British flanking movements.

September 23
NORTH: General William Howe steals a lead on the Americans by countermarching at night and safely crossing the Schuylkill River at Flatland's Ford, Pennsylvania. This interposes the British army between General George Washington's forces and the city of Philadelphia.

September 24
NORTH: American troops under Colonel John Brown move up Lake George and raid Diamond Island, New York. Unfortunately, an alert Tory warns the British garrison of their approach and, after a brief bombardment, Brown withdraws to his boats. This action again underscores the vulnerability of British lines of communication to Canada.

September 26
NORTH: General Charles Cornwallis occupies Philadelphia to the cheers of Loyalist inhabitants and subsequently establishes his camp at Germantown, six miles north of the latter. General George Washington repositions himself again by moving his army to Pennypacker's Mill along the Perkiomen River.

September 27
POLITICS: The Continental Congress convenes for a single day in Lancaster, Pennsylvania, before moving to York.

WEST: Indians fighting for the British ambush an American detachment under Captain William Foreman at the Narrows, West Virginia, killing 22 out of 40 militiamen.
NAVAL: The 24-gun frigate *Delaware* under Captain Charles Alexander, intent upon bombarding British fortifications along Philadelphia's waterfront, runs aground in the Delaware River and is pounded by British artillery until it surrenders.

September 30
POLITICS: The Continental Congress reconvenes again in York, Pennsylvania, which functions as the capital of the United States for nine months, until June 1778.

October 1
NAVAL: Captain Lambert Wickes is lost when the brig *Reprisal* flounders in a storm off Newfoundland Banks; only the cook survives.

October 2
NORTH: General William Howe turns his attention to the Delaware River as a source of supply and begins scouring its banks of American defenders. He begins by attacking the outpost at Billingsport, New Jersey, then guarded by 100 Pennsylvania militiamen. The famous 42nd Highlanders (Black Watch) under Colonel Thomas Sterling easily flushes the defenders, who burn their redoubt and flee without firing a shot. Howe next turns his attention toward the enemy fortifications along the riverbank.

General George Washington, sensing an opportunity to attack, carefully relocates his men to within 15 miles of the British main camp at Germantown, Pennsylvania.

October 3
NORTH: Heavily reinforced, General Henry Clinton decamps from New York with 4,000 men and heads up the Hudson River toward Tarrytown. He hopes to provide a diversion in support of General John Burgoyne, still struggling at Saratoga.

General George Washington, informed by spies that General William Howe remains encamped at Germantown, Pennsylvania, determines to attack and surprise him. Various British detachments left at Philadelphia, Billingsport, and elsewhere have reduced Howe's army to 8,000 men while Washington, newly reinforced by Pennsylvania and New Jersey militia, possesses over 11,000. The Americans then devise a complicated plan to envelop and destroy Howe. Militia brigades under Generals John Armstrong and William Smallwood are to move out in a wide sweeping arc and place themselves behind Howe's right and left flanks. As it turns out, both columns prove ineffectual, either arriving late or getting lost. The main attack upon the center will be conducted by the divisions of Generals John Sullivan and Anthony Wayne, with 3,000 men, while General Nathanael Greene marches 5,000 men and overpowers the British right. Washington carefully leaves camp that evening and marches all night toward the British position.

October 4
NORTH: General John Burgoyne summons a war council to discuss his rapidly deteriorating situation near Saratoga, New York. Over the objections of his officers he decides to heavily probe the American defensive positions one more time prior to launching a final, successful attack.

General George Washington resumes offensive operations by mounting an attack upon General William Howe at Germantown, Pennsylvania. The division of General John Sullivan makes first contact with the enemy, pushing back British light infantry and the 40th Regiment under Lieutenant Colonel Thomas Musgrave. As the Americans press on, Musgrave and his men occupy the two-story stone house of Loyalist Benjamin Chew and barricade themselves. This obstacle trips up Sullivan's attack, for General Henry Knox convinces Washington not to leave a fortified position in his rear. The Americans lack heavy artillery, so for the next several hours the light brigade of General William Maxwell unsuccessfully attempts to storm the Chew house, taking heavy losses. Washington's movements are further complicated by the onset of a thick ground fog that reduces vision to a few yards.

The British, surprised by the ferocity of the American assault, are taken further aback when General Nathanael Greene's division suddenly bursts out of the fog and hits their right flank. Troops under General John Peter Gabriel Muhlenberg drive the British hard, but the division of General Adam Stephen becomes separated from the main body and accidentally attacks General Anthony Wayne's men from behind. Confusion breaks out in the American ranks and Howe, sensing an opportunity, orders an advance across the field. Sullivan and Wayne slowly give ground to forces commanded by General Charles Grey while on the right Greene loses the entire 9th Virginia Infantry under Colonel George Matthews when it is surrounded. Washington tries to rally his forces but they continue retreating and the engagement slowly winds down by 10 A.M. Howe pursues for about 10 miles before returning to camp. American losses at Germantown are 152 killed (including General Francis Nash), 521 wounded, and 400 captured, to a British tally of 70 dead, 450 injured, and 14 missing. Washington's overly ornate strategy proves beyond the capacity of his amateur troops to perform, but they retire in good spirits.

October 5
NORTH: General Henry Clinton advances through the New York Highlands with 4,000 men and captures Verplanck's Point at Tarrytown without a struggle.
NAVAL: Admiral Richard Howe arrives in Delaware Bay with his fleet.

October 6
NORTH: General Henry Clinton crosses 1,200 soldiers over the Hudson River to attack Fort Clinton, while a 900-man detachment under Lieutenant Colonel Archibald Campbell attacks nearby Fort Montgomery. General George Clinton fights stoutly and finally extricates 600 defenders under cover of darkness. The British sustain 200 casualties to 250 Americans injured and 67 cannon captured. Considering the difficulty of the terrain traversed, Clinton wins an impressive victory that greatly facilitates British navigation of the Hudson River.
NAVAL: The American frigates *Congress,* 28 guns, and *Montgomery,* 24 guns, are burned on the North and Hudson Rivers, respectively, to prevent their capture.

October 7
NORTH: General John Burgoyne, outnumbered and low on supplies, launches a reconnaissance in force against the American right flank at Bemis Heights. The British draw themselves up into three columns with the right commanded by

General Simon Fraser, the center under General Friedrich von Riedesel, and the left flank held by a single grenadier battalion lead by Major John Dyke-Acland. All told, only 1,500 soldiers are available to Burgoyne for this perilous operation. As the British deploy, they are observed by General Horatio Gates, who, in a rare display of initiative, orders a prompt counterattack. The brigade of General Enoch Poor closes with Dyke-Acland's grenadiers, completely dispersing them, while Colonel Daniel Morgan routes an assortment of Canadians and Indians protecting the British right. Riedesel's Hessians stoutly resist in the center until General Benedict Arnold arrives and invigorates the American drive.

Arnold, acting without orders, impetuously leads General Ebenezer Learned's brigade on a series of successful charges that dislodge the Hessians from several strong positions and sends them scampering into redoubts. General Fraser distinguishes himself while forming up the rear guard and successfully withstands several attacks until he is singled out by marksman Timothy Murphy and mortally wounded. Burgoyne then orders a full-scale withdrawal as Arnold gathers up additional men for an attack across the line. Several more entrenchments are carried at bayonet point, although Arnold sustains a serious leg injury. But the impetus of his attack carries the Americans into the Breymann redoubt, which falls after heavy fighting and the death of Lieutenant Colonel Heinrich Breymann. With disaster looming, Burgoyne vigorously cobbles together his remaining forces around the Great Redoubt and prepares for a last stand when nightfall terminates the contest. British losses are 176 killed, 200 wounded, and 200 captured along with 10 cannon. The American loss is significantly lower; 50 killed and 150 wounded. Burgoyne has little choice now but to withdraw toward Saratoga—pursued by a force nearly three times his size.

General George Washington relocates his army to Valley Forge, Pennsylvania, encamping there for the winter.

October 8

NORTH: As British forces advance up the Hudson River, Generals George Clinton and James Clinton fall back to New Windsor, New York, joining forces with General Israel Putnam.

General Henry Clinton occupies Constitution Island opposite West Point, New York. He also contacts General John Burgoyne, noting that only General William Howe, and not he, can issue orders to unite their respective commands. Loyalist Daniel Taylor then conveys the message in a hollow silver bullet.

October 9

NORTH: General John Burgoyne withdraws his army, reduced by losses to 5,800 men, up to the heights of Saratoga, impeded by rain and rough terrain. He occupies his old camp the following day.

A quick raid by Governor William Tryon destroys a small American outpost at Continental Village, New York.

October 10

NORTH: After inexplicable bouts of inactivity, General Horatio Gates begins pursuing the retreating army of General John Burgoyne by advancing upon Saratoga.

British artillery begins bombarding Fort Mifflin, Pennsylvania, on the Delaware River. Several batteries have been constructed on nearby Province and Carpenter's Islands and commence firing at close range. The fort's earthen walls afford defenders under Lieutenant Colonel Samuel Smith little protection.

October 12

NORTH: General Horatio Gates, having pursued the British army to Saratoga, withdraws a short distance after perceiving General John Burgoyne's forces drawn up in battle array and ready to receive him. Gates then dispatches Colonel Daniel Morgan's riflemen and other light troops to harass the British in camp. Moreover, once General John Stark's brigade of 1,100 New Hampshire militia makes its belated appearance north of Burgoyne's camp, it eliminates any chance of a British retreat.

General Thomas Conway begins surreptitiously writing letters critical of General George Washington to General Horatio Gates, suggesting that he should replace Washington as commander in chief. This is the start of the so-called Conway Cabal.

The fighting at Saratoga goes on for weeks between the Americans and the British. A turning point arrives with the death of Britain's General Fraser, causing Burgoyne to withdraw and the Americans to proclaim victory on October 17, 1777. *(U.S. Army Center of Military History)*

Lieutenant Colonel Samuel Smith, commanding Fort Mifflin, leads a desperate sortie against the nearby British batteries. His 400 men attempt to storm the guns but are outflanked by the defenders and withdraw to the fort. The Americans nonetheless take 54 prisoners.

October 13
NORTH: With the Americans blocking all access to the Hudson River, officers on General John Burgoyne's staff unanimously vote to commence negotiations for eventual surrender.

October 14
NORTH: General John Burgoyne requests terms under a flag of truce and negotiations begin in earnest. General Horatio Gates initially demands "unconditional surrender" but eventually agrees to an armistice. Meanwhile, the Americans capture Loyalist Daniel Taylor, discover General Henry Clinton's message in a hollowed-out silver bullet, and hang him as a spy.

October 15
NORTH: The siege of Fort Mifflin intensifies as four British batteries, assisted by the warships HMS *Roebuck* and *Vigilant,* pound the American position at close range. Lieutenant Colonel Samuel Smith and his outgunned defenders have little recourse but to hunker down behind their muddy walls and endure the iron onslaught.

October 16
NORTH: Generals Horatio Gates and John Burgoyne meet in person to conclude surrender terms, or more precisely, a "convention," at Saratoga. They agree that Burgoyne's army will be allowed to march to Boston and embark upon ships for England, never to return to America.

General Henry Clinton dispatches General John Vaughan and a flotilla under Captain James Wallace on a second foray up the Hudson River, and they burn Esopus (Kingston), New York, in an effort to support British forces at Saratoga. This places British reinforcements 45 miles from Albany, the closest assistance rendered to General John Burgoyne's doomed force.

October 17
POLITICS: The Continental Congress establishes a three-member Board of War and Ordnance to oversee military administration and army operations. Prospective members are not to be members of Congress, hopefully to minimize potential conflicts of interest.
NORTH: General John Burgoyne surrenders 5,728 men, 5,000 muskets, and 37 cannon to General Horatio Gates under terms of the "Convention of Saratoga." The two staffs then enjoy a spell of fraternization, with mutual toasts to General George Washington and King George III. For the first time in history an entire British army has been captured intact. Moreover, victory at Saratoga demonstrates the viability of the American Revolution, which induces France to pursue formal diplomatic relations and switch from covert to overt military aid.

October 19
NORTH: General William Howe concentrates his entire army at Philadelphia prior to offensive operations.

October 21
NORTH: Colonel Karl von Donop ferries 1,800 Hessians across the Delaware River and encamps at Haddonfield, New Jersey, prior to assaulting Fort Mercer. He volunteers his men for the dangerous task partially to erase their dishonor at Trenton 10 months earlier. In doing so, he prepares to attack a heavily fortified position without scaling ladders or axes to overcome the defenses. Meanwhile, the 1,000-man garrison under Colonel Christopher Greene, having strengthened its works, calmly awaits the enemy's approach.

October 22
NORTH: At Fort Mercer, New Jersey, Colonel Karl von Donop issues a surrender ultimatum to Colonel Christopher Greene, who refuses. Von Donop then decides to attack immediately rather than await support from British vessels in the Delaware River. He deploys his men into two columns and charges. The first column attacks the northern face of the fort; the Americans let them approach, withholding fire until the Germans are literally under their guns. Greene suddenly gives the command to fire and the Hessians are literally scythed down in droves. Their confusion is compounded by a fleet of American gunboats anchored in the river, whose fire also enfilades their columns. After three more charges the Hessians withdraw in disorder. Meanwhile, von Donop personally leads a attack against the southern face of Fort Mercer, with identical results. The Germans manage to clear the abattis when they are staggered by heavy musket and cannon fire. Von Donop falls, fatally wounded, and is abandoned on the ground. The attack then sputters out, with the Hessians losing 371 casualties and 120 prisoners. The Americans suffer 14 dead and 23 injured.

General William Howe, sensing a lack of political support from the government, requests to be relieved of command.

October 23
NAVAL: Admiral Richard Howe orders part of his fleet to engage the American garrison at Fort Mifflin, on an island in the Delaware River. Six warships then penetrate the chevaux de frise blocking the river, but good shooting by armed galleys under Commodore John Hazelwood drives the ship of the line HMS *Merlin,* 64 guns, and the 18-gun HMS *Augusta* aground at Hog Island. Both are grounded and burned; *Merlin* is the largest British vessel lost in the war.

October 28
NORTH: Captain James Wilkinson, aide to General Horatio Gates, arrives at York to announce the victory at Saratoga to Congress. He also broaches a confidential letter by General Thomas Conway to an aide of General William Alexander which thoroughly denigrates Washington's military abilities.

November 1
Politics: The Continental Congress elects Henry Laurens president to replace outgoing John Hancock.

November 2
North: General Adam Stephen is charged with drunkenness at the Battles of Brandywine and Germantown and for lying about an unsuccessful skirmish at Piscataway. General George Washington orders his court-martial and then marches the army to strong positions at Whitemarsh, Pennsylvania. From here he can survey British movements in and around Philadelphia while still within supporting distance of Forts Mercer and Mifflin on the Delaware River.
Naval: Captain John Paul Jones departs Portsmouth, New Hampshire, and sails for France in the 18-gun sloop *Ranger*.

November 3
North: General William Alexander alerts General George Washington of General Thomas Conway's possible subterfuge against him.

November 6
Politics: The Continental Congress appoints General Thomas Mifflin, Colonel Timothy Pickering, and Colonel Robert H. Harrison to the newly created Board of War.

November 8
North: Surviving British forces evacuate Fort Ticonderoga, New York, and withdraw to Crown Point.

November 10
North: The British, taking advantage of a new channel opened up by the Delaware River, bring up heavy cannon, warships, and floating batteries to pound Fort Mifflin, Pennsylvania, into submission. The 450-man garrison under Lieutenant Colonel Samuel Smith resists tenaciously and attempts repairing breaches and other damage during the night, but his muddy works are being ground down by heavy fire and inclement weather. When Smith is wounded, he is replaced by Major Simeon Thayer.

November 12
North: General Kazimierz Pulaski attacks and defeats the British in a small skirmish at Whitemarsh, Pennsylvania, losing two men to seven.

November 14
North: Colonel Thomas Conway tenders his resignation to the Continental Congress, ostensibly over its refusal to promote him.

Under the cover of darkness, General James M. Varnum ferries 450 men from his brigade into Fort Mifflin, Pennsylvania, to bolster the garrison. American artillery facing Province Island also manage to sink a British floating battery on the Delaware River.

November 15
POLITICS: After a year and a half of debate, the Continental Congress formally adopts the Articles of Confederation as a means of national governance and dispatches it to the state legislatures for ratification. However, the process proves tortuously slow and the actual government will not be in place until March 1, 1781.
NAVAL: Fort Mifflin, having sustained five days of intense shelling, is further pummeled by the warships HMS *Somerset, Iris, Roebuck, Pearl,* and *Liverpool.* At one point, frigates HMS *Vigilant* and *Fury* slip to within 20 yards of the fort and add to the conflagration. With 350 cannon throwing out 1,000 heavy balls every 20 minutes, Major Simeon Thayer finally abandons his muddy charge. The Americans sustain 300 casualties, and the survivors flee under the cover of darkness. British losses are seven killed and five wounded.

November 17
NORTH: American army detachments at Blue Bell Tavern, Pennsylvania, are attacked and heavily defeated by the 33rd Regiment under General Charles Cornwallis, losing five killed and 33 captured. The British sustain three killed.

November 18
NORTH: General Charles Cornwallis crosses the Delaware River at Billingsport and pushes on with 6,000 men against Fort Mercer. General Nathanael Greene is charged with holding onto that beleaguered post for as long as possible. However, before he can issue orders to that effect General James M. Varnum and Colonel Christopher Greene jointly decide to abandon the post against impossible odds.

November 20
NORTH: American forces under Colonel Christopher Greene are ordered to abandon Fort Mercer, New Jersey, effectively surrendering control of the Delaware River to the British. Commodore John Hazelwood also burns the American warships *Andrew Doria, Hornet,* and *Wasp,* while state vessels *Sachem, Washington, Independence,* and *Mosquito* in Delaware Bay are likewise torched to prevent capture. British control of the Delaware River is now secure, although Forts Mifflin and Mercer have delayed General William Howe for two months.

A general court-martial finds General Adam Stephen guilty of gross misconduct in the face of the enemy and he is dismissed from the service.

November 21
POLITICS: The Continental Congress, alarmed over allegations of embezzlement leveled by Arthur Lee, recalls Silas Deane from Paris to answer the charges.

November 23
NAVAL: Captain John Paul Jones, commanding the *Ranger,* seizes two large brigs and sends them to France as prizes.

November 25
NORTH: In his first action at Gloucester, New Jersey, the marquis de Lafayette leads 300 men in a heavy skirmish against a larger Hessian detachment and defeats them.

November 26
NAVAL: Admiral Richard Howe anchors at Philadelphia with 62 vessels to resupply British forces stationed there.

November 27
POLITICS: The Continental Congress recommends that states confiscate all Loyalist property, an act that triggers a mass exodus to Canada and Europe. It also names General Horatio Gates as president of the Board of War, along with Thomas Mifflin and Richard Peters. These men represent a clique unfavorably disposed toward General George Washington and are well situated to discredit him.

November 28
DIPLOMACY: The Continental Congress appoints John Adams to succeed Silas Deane as commissioner to France.

December 1
NORTH: Baron Friedrich von Steuben arrives at Portsmouth, New Hampshire, with a letter of introduction from Benjamin Franklin.

December 2
NAVAL: Captain John Paul Jones arrives at Nantes, France, with the sloop *Ranger*.

December 4
DIPLOMACY: News of the American victory at Saratoga reaches Paris, and Foreign Minister Charles Gravier, comte de Vergennes, now becomes receptive to a formal military alliance.

December 5
NORTH: General William Howe marches his army from Philadelphia in an attempt to surprise General George Washington at Whitemarsh, but his movements are detected by cavalry under Captain Allan McLane. The Americans are also forewarned by the heroic actions of spy Lydia Darragh. Meanwhile, British soldiers and American militia exchange fire in heavy skirmishes along Chestnut Hill, and General James Irvine, along with 17 men, is captured.

December 6
DIPLOMACY: Charles Gravier, comte de Vergennes, congratulates the American commissioners on the success at Saratoga and encourages them to resume pursuing a military alliance with France. The effort has been temporarily placed on hold in the wake of Philadelphia's fall.

December 7
NORTH: General Charles Grey probes American positions at Edge Hill, Pennsylvania, and pushes back several hundred defenders under Colonels Daniel Morgan and Mordecai Gist, but concludes the position is impervious to attack. Captain Allan McLane also repulses a Hessian bayonet charge with his dragoons, rescuing General Joseph Reed from capture. Fighting then sputters out along the line as General William Howe again declines to commit forces to a frontal assault. That night he

withdraws his army in stages and southward toward Bethlehem Pike. General George Washington, disappointed that the British do not attack his entrenchments, suffers around 100 casualties; the British admit to 12 casualties.

December 10
NORTH: Colonel Samuel Webb and 73 men from his regiment, while being transported across Long Island Sound, are attacked by HMS *Falcon* and captured.

General Charles Cornwallis leads a successful raid at Gulph's Mills (Matson's Ford), Pennsylvania, that rustles 2,000 sheep and cattle.

December 11
NORTH: General George Washington orders his army out of Whitemarsh and marches to Valley Forge via the Schuylkill River at Matson's Ford. Meanwhile, General Charles Cornwallis and 3,500 men depart Philadelphia on a foraging expedition. He makes a sudden appearance at Black Horse Tavern and skirmishes with militia forces under General Enoch Potter, posted there as a guard. The Americans are forced back in disorder just as the van of General John Sullivan's division advances down the same road. An impasse ensues and, with no further fighting in the offing, Cornwallis plunders nearby farms for supplies and slogs back to Philadelphia. Washington, unsure of British intentions, lingers at Whitemarsh another week before finally striking out for winter encampment at Valley Forge. Total casualties are probably 50 to 100 on each side.

December 12
DIPLOMACY: In Paris, Charles Gravier, comte de Vergennes, informs the American commissioners that French entry into the war is contingent upon Spain's approval. He requires an additional three weeks to receive a reply from the government in Madrid.

December 13
POLITICS: The Continental Congress authorizes two inspector generals for the Continental army, who are independent of the commander in chief and answer only to the Board of War.

December 14
POLITICS: The Board of War ignores General Thomas Conway's previous resignation and appoints him inspector general of the army—another slap at General George Washington.

December 15
DIPLOMACY: In Paris, British diplomats discuss the possibility of political reconciliation with Benjamin Franklin.

December 17
DIPLOMACY: Louis XVI, buoyed by the victory at Saratoga, orders his Council of State to extend full diplomatic recognition to the United States and authorizes negotiations for a formal treaty of alliance. Henceforth, American commissioner Benjamin Franklin ignores all British appeals for a cease-fire.

December 19
NORTH: An exhausted 9,000 men of the Continental army, driven from Philadelphia, straggle into Valley Forge, Pennsylvania, to spend an arduous winter. Located only 20 miles from the city, it allows General George Washington to protect his supply routes while affording him the ability to strike at the British. But a severe trial by cold and deprivation ensues, and 2,500 men—nearly a third of the army—eventually die of illness and exposure.

December 23
NORTH: General George Washington, wary of recent congressional inquiries about military affairs, invites several members to Valley Forge to discuss leadership issues. At the heart of the issue is General Thomas Conway's seeming attempt to have him replaced by General Horatio Gates. However, the so-called Conway Cabal fails to trigger any congressional motions to remove Washington, and the conspirators are ultimately disgraced.

December 27
NORTH: A vindictive Continental Congress votes not to allow the paroled army of General John Burgoyne to leave Boston until the convention he signed is ratified by King George III. General William Heath is also inundated with facetious instructions designed to keep the "Convention army" hostage for several months.

December 31
NAVAL: By year's end, American warships of all types have seized 464 vessels from the British.

1778

January 2
SOUTH: Colonel George Rogers Clark confers with Governor Patrick Henry in Williamsburg, Virginia, about seizing control of the Mississippi-Ohio River Valley. Such a move would curtail Shawnee threats to the frontier and also facilitate land speculation. He has previously won the support of such state luminaries as Thomas Jefferson, George Mason, and Richard H. Lee. Governor Henry acquiesces, and Clark, to disguise his real purpose, declares his intention to help defend Kentucky settlements.
NAVAL: Commodore Esek Hopkins is formally dismissed as naval commander in chief by the Continental Congress; no successor is ever appointed.

January 5
NAVAL: Explosive mines floated down the Delaware River by American inventor David Bushnell kill four British sailors on a barge. British naval forces subsequently expend much time and ammunition detonating the mines as they float into view. The incident inspires poet and Navy Board commissioner Francis Hopkinson to compose his satyrical poem, "Battle of the Kegs."

January 8
DIPLOMACY: In Paris, Charles Gravier, comte de Vergennes, announces France's intention to seek a formal military alliance with the United States.

NORTH: The Continental Congress accuses General John Burgoyne of failing to abide by the terms of his surrender convention, further delaying the departure of his captive army.

January 10
POLITICS: The Continental Congress appoints several members, along with Board of War members Horatio Gates, Thomas Mifflin, and Timothy Pickering, to confer with the commander in chief at Valley Forge.

January 13
NORTH: His army withering away from exposure and malnutrition at Valley Forge, General George Washington appeals to the Continental Congress for immediate supplies of food and clothing.

January 19
POLITICS: General Horatio Gates is warmly received at York as he is installed as president of the Board of War.

January 20
POLITICS: In light of the recent flare-up over the Conway letters, Horatio Gates, Thomas Mifflin, and Timothy Pickering are excused from visiting General George Washington at Valley Forge.
NORTH: Captain Henry Lee, then raiding British outposts near Valley Forge, Pennsylvania, is attacked in turn by 200 British dragoons. He and seven men seek refuge in Spread Eagle Tavern and noisily trick the British into thinking that American reinforcements are arriving. For this quick-witted action Lee is promoted by Congress to major.

January 22
POLITICS: Completely ignoring the ongoing ordeal at Valley Forge, the Continental Congress begins contemplating a new expedition into Canada.

January 23
POLITICS: The Board of War, in a nod to the Continental Congress, appoints the marquis de Lafayette to lead the Canadian expedition, seconded by General Thomas Conway. General John Stark is invited to serve with them, but he declines.

January 27
NAVAL: The sloop *Providence* under Captain John P. Rathbun again captures New Providence (Nassau) in the Bahamas, and raises the Stars and Stripes over a foreign stronghold for the first time. He also captures five vessels and releases 20 American prisoners after driving off the 16-gun British privateer *Gayton*.

January 28
NORTH: The marquis de Lafayette expresses his contempt for General Thomas Conway to congressional president Henry Laurens, refusing to serve with him. Laurens, a strong ally of General George Washington, now suspects the Board of War of complicity in the former "Conway Cabal."

February 4
NORTH: General William Heath announces the Continental Congress's resolutions respecting the Saratoga Convention of General John Burgoyne, which further delays the army's return to England.

Baron Friedrich von Steuben arrives at York, Pennsylvania, still bereft a command, and offers to serve as an unpaid volunteer.

February 6
DIPLOMACY: Four weeks of negotiations by Benjamin Franklin, Arthur Lee, Silas Deane, and French foreign minister Charles Gravier, comte de Vergennes, conclude with a two-part Franco-American entente. This consists of a treaty of amity and commerce with reciprocal favored-nation status for trade, and a treaty of alliance. All told the French alliance stipulates direct military intervention should war erupt between France and Great Britain. It further grants the United States the right to campaign against Canada and Bermuda while the French enjoy a free hand throughout the West Indies. This is a decisive development in the American Revolution, which now assumes the dimensions of a global conflict. From a diplomatic standpoint, the United States will not enter again into such a binding agreement until formation of the North Atlantic Treaty Organization (NATO) in 1949.

February 8
WEST: Captain Daniel Boone and 27 militiamen are taken captive by Shawnee under Chief Blackfish.

February 9
NORTH: General George Washington pens an angry missive to General Horatio Gates, rebuking him for ambiguous posturing throughout the "Conway Cabal." This note apparently ends any attempt by Gates and his alleged cohorts to have Washington removed; the matter then quietly subsides.

February 14
DIPLOMACY: John Adams departs Hough's Neck, Massachusetts, on board the warship *Boston* under Captain Samuel Tucker and sails for Bordeaux, France.

NAVAL: French cannon at Quiberon Bay salute the new American flag flying aboard the *Ranger* under Captain John Paul Jones. This is regarded as the first "official" salute from a sovereign nation.

February 16
POLITICS: Lord Germain accepts General William Howe's resignation, although Howe is ordered to remain on station until a successor is appointed.

February 17
POLITICS: Lord Frederick North, determined to preempt the Americans from ratifying a treaty with France, offers to suspend all the inflammatory acts passed by Parliament since 1763. Charles James Fox and Edmund Burke applaud the decision—then lampoon the prime minister in Parliament with news of the recent French alliance.

February 19
NORTH: The marquis de Lafayette expresses to General George Washington his displeasure over the forthcoming Canadian expedition and his disgust with the Board of War for even considering it.

February 23
NORTH: The American army at Valley Forge is bolstered by the arrival of a former Prussian officer, Baron Friedrich von Steuben, who institutes the first systematic training routine in American history. Steuben, who has misrepresented his credentials, is neither a baron nor a general, but his efforts prove nonetheless instrumental in rendering the Continental army a more effective force.

February 26
POLITICS: The Continental Congress, desperate to make up for manpower shortages in the military, authorizes the first draft in American history by allowing states to transfer men from militia to the regular regiments for nine months.
NAVAL: Captain John Barry and a boatload of 27 men surprise and capture the schooner HMS *Alert*, along with 110 prisoners and four transports.

February 28
NORTH: A proposed constitution for Massachusetts is overwhelmingly rejected by various town meetings. The legislature is then instructed to arrange a special convention to pen a new constitution.

March 2
NORTH: The congressional committee visiting Valley Forge makes numerous recommendations to the Continental Congress respecting the reorganization of basic procedures. That august body then appoints a reluctant General Nathanael Greene to be quartermaster general of the army.

March 7
POLITICS: Lord George Germain appoints General Henry Clinton to succeed General William Howe as commander in chief of British forces in North America.
NAVAL: Captain Nicholas Biddle, commanding the 32-gun frigate *Randolph*, encounters the much larger 64-gun HMS *Yarmouth* under Captain Nicholas Vincent off Barbados. The two vessels close in the darkness and fight fiercely for 20 minutes until Biddle and 311 of his men die when their vessel suddenly explodes—only four survive and are rescued by the British. This constitutes the greatest single loss of naval personnel until the sinking of the battleship USS *Arizona* in December 1941. British losses are five killed and 12 wounded.

March 8
POLITICS: In light of the French alliance, Lord Frederick North promulgates a new military strategy predicated upon the fleet of Admiral Richard Howe raiding coastal locations throughout New England. General Henry Clinton also receives permission for another attack on Charleston, South Carolina, to begin separating the southern states.

March 9

NAVAL: On a West Indian cruise, the 16-gun sloops HMS *Ariadne* and *Ceres* under Captains Thomas Pringle and James R. Dacres encounter the 20-gun frigate *Alfred* under Captain Elisha Hinman and the 32-gun frigate *Raleigh* under Captain Thomas Thompson. The British should have been easily overpowered but, during a lengthy chase and battle, Hinman receives little assistance from nearby *Raleigh* and the *Alfred* strikes its colors. The Americans lose 181 captives.

March 10

NAVAL: The frigate *Boston* under Captain Samuel Tucker, while conveying John Adams to France, captures the 14-gun privateer *Martha*.

March 12

NORTH: Though not officially part of the United States, Vermont adopts a government under Governor Thomas Chittenden.

March 13

DIPLOMACY: The French ambassador to London duly informs Secretary of State Thomas Thynne of the treaty of commerce between his country and the United States. War between the two nations is now widely anticipated, so Lord North recalls the English ambassador from Paris and cancels all prior instructions to General Henry Clinton.

POLITICS: The Continental Congress terminates the anticipated Canadian campaign and orders the marquis de Lafayette and General Johann de Kalb to resume their posts within the army.

SOUTH: Loyalist rangers under Lieutenant Colonel Thomas Brown attack Fort Barrington, Georgia. They cleverly surprise the garrison by swimming a quarter-mile across the Altamaha River and capture the fort with the loss of one killed and four wounded. American losses are two killed, four wounded, and 23 captured.

March 16

DIPLOMACY: Parliament authorizes Frederick Howard, earl of Carlisle, to head a peace commission with the Americans in Philadelphia. Unlike previous efforts, Carlisle is endowed with broad authority to conduct direct negotiations. Furthermore, they will acquiesce to all colonial demands—except independence.

March 17

NORTH: Colonel Charles Mawhood, having sailed from Philadelphia with 1,200 men, lands at Salem, New Jersey, on a mission to reconnoiter the adjoining region and gather forage and cattle.

March 18

NORTH: Colonel Charles Mawhood conducts a successful ambush against one of General Anthony Wayne's foraging parties at Quintin's Bridge, New Jersey. He dispatches 70 men from the 17th Regiment to distract the Americans while the remainder of his force assumes an ambuscade. Judging the moment right, Mawhood orders his men to fall back precipitously, which entices 300 militiamen under Colonel Asher Holmes into pursuing. About 200 Americans take the bait, rebuild the planks over the bridge, and advance carelessly until a party of rangers under Major John Graves Simcoe emerges from the two-story Wethersby's Tavern in their rear. Opening fire, they inflict 40 American casualties for the loss of one dead. The militia scampers off in confusion, chased by 30 British hussars until the remaining 100 Americans remove the drawbridge over the creek.

At Valley Forge, Pennsylvania, General Friedrich von Steuben makes history by taking 120 select men from the army and personally instructing them in his simplified, 10-motion version of the famous Prussian drill system. Within days they become completely proficient and are subsequently broken up and distributed among their own regiments to serve as drillmasters. The entire process is continuously replicated, and by the time the army reemerges from winter quarters, all ranks possess a discipline and fighting order heretofore lacking. Von Steuben's seemingly innocuous contribution proves a major factor in the ultimate American victory.

March 19
SOUTH: South Carolina ratifies a new state constitution.

March 20
DIPLOMACY: Benjamin Franklin, Arthur Lee, and Silas Deane are formally received at the court of King Louis XIV. Later, Franklin and the king privately reassure each other of their determination to fulfill all treaty obligations.

March 21
POLITICS: Lord George Germain directs General Henry Clinton to dispatch 5,000 men to the West Indies to seize the French island of St. Lucia, to send an additional 3,000 to Florida to reinforce Pensacola and St. Augustine, and to march the bulk of the army from Philadelphia to New York. This strategy marks a dramatic shift in priorities from preserving colonial rule to expanding Caribbean possessions.
NORTH: Colonel Charles Mawhood attacks a small American militia guard at Hancock's Bridge, New Jersey, in an attempt to gain supplies. The previous evening he dispatched Major John Graves Simcoe and the Queen's Rangers on flatboats down the Delaware River to land behind the Americans. Meanwhile, Lieutenant Colonel Edward Mitchell is to approach the enemy frontally with his 27th Regiment. However, the bulk of the militia are withdrawn before an attack materializes, and all that remains is a guard of 30 men. These are fast asleep in Judge Hancock's house when Simcoe eliminates their sentries, forces his way inside, and bayonets all to death. A nearby American patrol is also ambushed with a further loss of six men. However, during the attack two prominent Loyalists are also killed by mistake. Their mission complete, Simcoe and Mitchell return to Salem, New Jersey, to rejoin Colonel Mawhood. The extent of the killing makes the Americans level charges of atrocity against the victors.

March 26
POLITICS: Congressmen Francis Dana and Nathaniel Folsom introduce legislation to provide Continental army officers with half-pay for life or their widows with pensions. A furious debate ensues.

March 27
Naval: The American frigate *Providence* under Commodore Abraham Whipple perilously escapes from Narragansett Bay by running a gauntlet of 11 British vessels and gets to sea. However, the 20-gun frigate *Columbus* under Captain Hoystead Hacker is driven ashore by a British squadron and burned off Point Judith, Rhode Island, to prevent capture.

March 28
Politics: The Continental Congress authorizes General Kazimierz Pulaski to raise his own cavalry legion.

March 30
Politics: The Continental Congress stipulates that American captives Charles Lee and Ethan Allen are to be exchanged for British general Richard Prescott. Furthermore, all Loyalists presently in captivity who have served with the British army will be tried as traitors. This interference nearly derails a prior agreement between Generals George Washington and William Howe to exchange Lee for Prescott.

March 31
Diplomacy: John Adams, accompanied by his 10-year-old son and future president John Quincy Adams, arrives at Bordeaux, France.

Naval: The new 28-gun frigate *Virginia* under Captain James Nicholson runs aground in Chesapeake Bay and is attacked by British frigates HMS *Emerald* and *Conqueror*. Nicholson promptly rows himself to shore after authorizing Lieutenant Joshua Barney to surrender the vessel for him.

April 5
Politics: The Continental Congress allows General John Burgoyne and some staff officers to sail for England but the bulk of the Convention Army remains in captivity.

April 8
Diplomacy: John Adams arrives in Paris to serve as the new commissioner to France.

April 9
Politics: Jeremiah Wadsworth gains appointment as commissary general of purchases with authority from the Continental Congress to overhaul the inefficient Commissary Department.

April 10
Naval: Captain John Paul Jones and the 18-gun sloop *Ranger* depart Brest, France, for an extended raid into British home waters.

April 11
Naval: A French squadron of 12 ships of the line and several frigates departs Toulon under Admiral Charles-Hector-Théodat, comte d'Estaing. This movement causes great consternation in London for, if united with the main French fleet at Brest, d'Estaing could pose a direct threat to the British Isles. Admiral Augustus Keppel therefore opposes division of the British home fleet by sending additional ships to

America or the Straits of Gibraltar. He is seconded by John Montagu, earl of Sandwich and First Lord of the Admiralty. However, Lord Germain feels it imperative to oppose d'Estaing at the straits before he can reach America.

April 12
Diplomacy: The forthcoming Carlisle Commission is rounded out by the addition of William Eden and George Johnstone. In the past both Carlisle and Johnston evinced support for American positions in Parliament and, furthermore, Carlisle is a close associate of Charles James Fox, another outspoken Whig. Prime Minister Lord Frederick North nonetheless remains pessimistic about the commission's chance for success.

April 14
Politics: Henry Laurens, president of the Continental Congress, sends a reprimand to General George Washington for questioning congressional prerogatives respecting the exchange of prisoners or the treatment of Loyalists. Washington, taking the rebuke in stride, tactfully thanks the Congress for its sagacious advice.

April 16
Diplomacy: Members of the Carlisle Commission set sail from Portsmouth, England, accompanied by General Charles Cornwallis, the newly appointed second in command for North America.

April 21
North: Elias Boudinot, commissary of prisons, arranges to exchange Charles Lee for Richard Prescott. Lee's first action is to visit Congress to complain how other officers have been promoted over him. Lee also personally derogates General George Washington's leadership abilities to Boudinot.

April 22
Diplomacy: The Continental Congress passes a motion branding anyone who accedes to terms established by the forthcoming Carlisle Commission as an enemy of the United States.
Naval: Captain John Paul Jones, commanding the 18-gun brig *Ranger,* lands 31 men ashore and briefly seizes the English towns of Whitehaven and St. Mary's Island. The crewmembers then spike cannon in the local fort, burn several vessels, and return to their ship unmolested. This act constitutes the first hostile invasion of British soil since 1667.

April 23
North: General Charles Lee is formally exchanged for General Richard Prescott at King of Prussia Tavern, Pennsylvania.
Naval: Captain John Paul Jones accosts St. Mary's Island, intending to kidnap the earl of Serlkirk as a hostage, but he is absent from his estate. Lady Serlkirk's family silver is seized instead, but Jones eventually returns it with an apology.

April 24
Naval: Captain John Paul Jones and the *Ranger* encounter the 20-gun sloop HMS *Drake* anchored at Carrickfergus, Ireland. The British initially assume he is one of

their own privateers and dispatch an officer in a boat, who is taken prisoner. The *Drake* then puts to sea and hails the *Ranger,* at which point Jones underscores his identity by crossing *Drake's* bow and delivering a crushing broadside. A one-sided battle of 65 minutes ensues before the British surrender and Jones tows his prize back to Brest. The Americans lose two killed and six wounded to British losses of four killed, 19 wounded, and 150 prisoners.

Captain John Young loses the 10-gun sloop *Independence* when it runs aground off Ocracoke Inlet, North Carolina.

April 27
POLITICS: Acting upon intelligence received from Holland, Lord George Germain is convinced that the French fleet is headed for America. He desperately entreats the ministry of Lord Frederick North to dispatch part of the home fleet in pursuit.

NAVAL: The Continental Congress mandates the purchase of 12 additional warships.

April 29
POLITICS: After heated debate, the government of Lord Frederick North decides to reinforce Admiral Richard Howe's fleet with an additional 13 ships of the line under Admiral John Byron.

April 30
NORTH: The Americans stretch a great chain across the Hudson River to impede British movements upstream.

May 1
NORTH: A British force of 700 light infantry under Robert Abercrombie attacks a 60-man American outpost under General John Lacey at Crooked Billet Tavern, Pennsylvania. Hit simultaneously in the front and flank, Lacey's command is nearly surrounded by British rangers under Lieutenant Colonel John Graves Simcoe and defeated. The Americans withdraw with 26 killed, nine wounded, 30 prisoners, and the loss of their baggage. The British suffer nine wounded.

May 4
DIPLOMACY: The Continental Congress ratifies the treaties of alliance and of amity and commerce with France, but requests that two articles be rescinded. By war's end the French donate 10.5 million livres in subsidies and 35 million livres in loans to the American war effort.

May 5
POLITICS: The Continental Congress appoints General Friedrich von Steuben as inspector general upon the recommendation of General George Washington. In this capacity he composes the *Blue Book,* the first American drill manual, which is further refined by his aides Alexander Hamilton and John Laurens.

May 6
NORTH: News of the recent alliance with France is joyously received by the army at Valley Forge, and they march in review. Their newfound discipline and precise maneuvering, instilled over the winter by General Friedrich von Steuben, is immediately apparent.

May 8
NORTH: General Henry Clinton arrives in Philadelphia as commander in chief of British military forces in America.

The frigates *Effingham* and *Washington*, along with 42 other vessels, are destroyed at Bordentown, New Jersey, seven miles from Philadelphia, by a 700-man British raiding party.

NAVAL: Captain John Paul Jones and the *Ranger* dock at Brest, France, with the captured *Drake* and 200 British prisoners.

May 11
POLITICS: William Pitt, earl of Chatham and a vocal proponent of colonial rights, dies suddenly in Parliament.

May 12
WEST: Colonel George Rogers Clark departs the Redstone Settlement on a voyage down the Monongahela River to meet with reinforcements gathering at the falls of the Ohio.

May 14
POLITICS: Naval minister John Montagu, earl of Sandwich, delays the embarkation of Admiral John Byron's fleet over continuing concern as to the French fleet's probable destination.

May 15
POLITICS: The Continental Congress authorizes half-pay for Continental army officers, although the tenure is for seven years, not life—provided that they serve for the duration of the war.

May 16
NAVAL: The frigates HMS *Proserpine* and *Enterprise* confirm that Admiral Charles-Hector-Théodat, comte d'Estaing's fleet has cleared the Straits of Gibraltar and is steering for the open sea.

May 18
NORTH: An elaborate feast, christened *Meschianza* (Italian for medley), is organized in Philadelphia by Major John Andre for the departing British commander in chief, General William Howe.

General George Washington grants the marquis de Lafayette command of a 2,200-man corps of observation and orders him to watch British lines between the Delaware and Schuylkill Rivers. Lafayette accordingly deploys Generals Enoch Poor and James M. Varnum on Barren Hill and within sight of British forces. Captain Allan McLane is sent ahead to scout with 50 Oneida warriors.

May 19
NORTH: General William Howe, eager to capture the marquis de Lafayette and humiliate the Franco-American alliance, dispatches General James Grant and 5,000 men to outflank the Americans at Barren Hill while he leads the main body. Grant manages to cover 20 miles without detection and slips in behind Lafayette without his knowledge. Meanwhile, Howe takes his remaining 6,000 men out of

Germantown to confront the Americans and catch them between two fires. To that end he dispatches General Charles Grey to hit the American left flank. By daybreak the unwitting Americans are nearly cornered. Fortunately, the British are detected at the last minute by the ever-vigilant Captain Allan McLane, who warns Lafayette of their approach.

May 20
NORTH: The marquis de Lafayette cleverly conceals his small force on a steep slope behind Barren Hill. As General James Grant advances to within range the Americans suddenly reemerge into view and feign an all-out attack. Grant dithers and Lafayette, using a road apparently unknown to his adversaries, masterfully slips across the Schuylkill River to safety. A British pursuit avails nothing and there are about 40 casualties to either side. His clever ploy foiled, General William Howe orders his forces back to Philadelphia.

SOUTH: General Robert Howe arrives at the Altamaha River with 550 Continentals and militiamen, intending to attack General Augustin Prevost at St. Augustine, Florida. However, his plans go immediately awry when militia officers refuse to follow orders and the maneuver fails.

May 24
NORTH: The British 22nd Regiment under Lieutenant Colonel John Campbell advances from Newport, Rhode Island, and burns the nearby towns of Warren and Bristol. His withdrawal is harassed by militia under Colonel William Barton.

General William Howe concludes his American service by sailing from Philadelphia on board HMS *Cerberus*, the same vessel that brought him to America two years earlier.

May 27
POLITICS: The Continental Congress overhauls the organization of the Continental army while adding a provost corps and three engineering companies.

May 28
WEST: Colonel George Rogers Clark debarks at the falls of the Ohio River only to discover that promised reinforcements have failed to materialize. He is only joined by a few volunteers and stops to train them before continuing further.

NORTH: General Benedict Arnold is appointed the future governor and commander of the Philadelphia garrison by General George Washington.

May 30
NORTH: Mohawk Indians under Chief Joseph Brant burn the settlement of Cobbleskill, New York, killing many settlers and capturing others. A body of 22 militiamen is also dispersed and slaughtered. This raid initiates a long series of frontier actions, the only viable British tactic in New York after Saratoga.

May 31
NORTH: General Richard Prescott attacks and torches several mills in Tiverton, Rhode Island, before being repelled by local militia.

June 2
NAVAL: The frigate HMS *Proserpine* arrives at Falmouth bearing intelligence that the French fleet is headed for America.

June 6
DIPLOMACY: The Carlisle Commission arrives in Philadelphia to negotiate an end to hostilities. They offer autonomy under the British Crown but refuse to recognize American independence.

June 9
NAVAL: The fleet of Admiral John Byron finally debarks from Plymouth, England, and makes for the American station. He endures a storm-tossed transit, justifying his reputation as "Foul-Weather Jack."

June 10
NORTH: A special convention in New Hampshire begins deliberations on a new state constitution.

June 13
POLITICS: The Continental Congress deliberates on Lord Frederick North's conciliatory proposals and insists upon British recognition of American independence.
NAVAL: The Channel fleet of 21 ships of the line and three frigates sorties from Plymouth under Admiral Augustus Keppel to protect British shipping passing by Brest, France, and to keep a watchful eye on the French fleet anchored there.

June 16
NORTH: General Henry Clinton prepares to evacuate the Philadelphia region and dismantles all his redoubts and fortifications.

June 17
DIPLOMACY: The Continental Congress drafts a declaration to the Carlisle Commission reiterating its intention to make peace as soon as King George III recognizes American independence and withdraws his forces.
NAVAL: Admiral Augustus Keppel encounters two French frigates off the English coast at the Lizard, one of which fires a broadside at the approaching British. This announces France's declaration of war on Great Britain and its commitment to military intervention on behalf of the United States. When Keppel seizes the *Belle Poule,* one of the offending frigates, captured documents reveal that the main French fleet at Brest is making preparations to sail with 27 warships. The British then return promptly to Falmouth for reinforcements.

June 18
NORTH: General Henry Clinton, fearing a blockade by French vessels, evacuates the last of his 10,000 soldiers from Philadelphia, crosses the Delaware River, and heads for New York. A further 3,000 Loyalists, fearful of being abandoned, embark with the British fleet. Nine months of occupation ignominiously conclude and the Americans are greatly heartened. Meanwhile, Captain Allan McLane's cavalry company quickly nets 32 British stragglers outside of Philadelphia.

June 19

NORTH: General George Washington, alert to General Henry Clinton's intentions, rouses the Continental army and decamps from Valley Forge, Pennsylvania. He then marches 14,500 men to intercept the fleeing British.

General Benedict Arnold, escorted by a regiment of dragoons, enters Philadelphia and settles in as military governor. He still suffers from leg wounds incurred at Saratoga and is even further distracted after encountering Margaret Shippen, daughter of a noted Loyalist.

NAVAL: The frigate *Boston* under Captain Samuel Tucker captures two merchant brigs in the North Atlantic.

June 20

POLITICS: The Continental Congress is somewhat chagrined that only three states, New York, Virginia, and New Hampshire, have ratified the Articles of Confederation.

June 22

POLITICS: The Continental Congress summarily rejects 37 revisions, proposed by the states, to the Articles of Confederation.

June 23

NORTH: American and British forces skirmish at Crosswick, New Jersey, as the two armies begin drawing closer.

June 24

NORTH: General George Washington continues shadowing General Henry Clinton and encamps at Hopewell, New Jersey, only 15 miles from the main British camp at Allentown, Pennsylvania. During a war council he recommends attacking Clinton, a decision that the majority of officers oppose. Consequently, advanced troops under Generals William Maxwell and Philemon Dickinson will continue harassing Clinton's flank and rear guards.

June 25

NORTH: Fearful of being intercepted at Brunswick, General Henry Clinton divides his army into two columns with General Wilhelm von Knyphausen leading the advance and General Charles Cornwallis commanding the rear. Clinton remains in the center with the baggage train as the whole force marches toward Monmouth Courthouse, New Jersey. General George Washington dispatches his own advance guard of 4,000 men under the marquis de Lafayette to assail Clinton's flank if possible. The main army then encamps at Cranbury for the night.

June 26

WEST: Colonel George Rogers Clark shoots the rapids of the Ohio River with 175 men in flatboats and sails west toward the Illinois territory.

June 27

POLITICS: The Continental Congress adjourns its final session at York and votes to reconvene at Philadelphia.

North: General George Washington summons another war council and decides to engage General Henry Clinton's rear guard. The marquis de Lafayette has been entrusted with 4,000 advanced troops, but General Charles Lee, nominal second in command, insists upon leading the affair. Washington assents and grants him another 1,000 troops.

Naval: Admiral Augustus Keppel drops anchor off Spithead, England, and pleads for reinforcements. His recalcitrance greatly unsettles both king and cabinet members, who believe that British shipping from Gibraltar and the West Indies is now easy prey for privateers operating from Brest. Once Keppel receives four more ships of the line, bringing his total complement to 24 warships, he is immediately ordered back on station. He eventually acquires six more vessels, raising his total to 30.

June 28
North: General George Washington, seeking to strike the British hard with his invigorated army, attacks General Henry Clinton's rear guard at Monmouth, New Jersey. The Americans under General Charles Lee fight well initially, having been brought up to par with their European counterparts by the drill and discipline of General Friedrich von Steuben. However, Lee badly bungles the advance with contradictory orders and wholesale confusion erupts. He then compounds his mistake by ordering a retreat, which Clinton views as a ripe opportunity to counterattack. The Americans draw off in disarray as the British advance—until Washington suddenly appears in the van. He vocally excoriates Lee for allowing disorder to reign and forms a new defensive line.

As Clinton advances, confident of victory, he suddenly confronts the divisions of Generals Anthony Wayne, Nathanael Greene, and William Alexander, drawn up to receive him. The British charge several times and are repulsed by well-aimed volleys while the artillery of General Henry Knox posted on nearby Combs Hill enfilades their right flank. It is at this juncture that Mary Ludwig Hays (Molly Pitcher) distinguishes herself by replacing her husband in combat and manning a cannon. The ensuing battle peters out in the intense summer heat, and Clinton withdraws in good order. Monmouth is a tactical draw with the Americans sustaining 72 killed, 161 wounded, and 132 missing, while British losses are estimated at 350. More important, American forces have finally withstood their veteran British counterparts in the open field.

June 29
South: General James Screven and 900 Georgia militia attack and drive Loyalist rangers under Colonel Thomas Brown into Cabbage Swamp, St. Mary's River, Florida.

June 30
North: The British army under General Henry Clinton reaches Sandy Hook and boards transports bound for New York City. Several hundred Hessians have deserted since the clash at Monmouth.

July 2
Politics: The Continental Congress resumes its deliberations back at Philadelphia.
North: General Frederick Haldimand becomes Governor-General of Canada.

The Battle of Monmouth, June 28, 1778. The mass confusion on the part of the American soldiers leads to the court-martial and dismissal of General Charles Lee. *(U.S. Army Center of Military History)*

July 3–4
NORTH: A force of 1,200 Indians and Loyalists under Captain Walter Butler and Cornplanter attack Forty Fort in the Wyoming Valley of western Pennsylvania. Colonel Zebulon Butler, the garrison commander, refuses to surrender his 368 men and is subsequently tricked into a pursuit once the raiders depart. As the Americans rush headlong after the enemy, the British burn several blockhouses at Wintermoot's Fort to promote further the illusion of withdrawal. Suddenly Colonel Butler finds himself assailed on both flanks by Seneca warriors and the Royal Greens, and his line collapses in a carefully staged ambush. The vengeful raiders kill and scalp 227 of the fleeing soldiers; only 60 make it back to Forty Fort. Major Butler reports the loss of two rangers and one Indian killed, with eight more wounded.

July 4
NORTH: General Charles Lee, angered by the treatment accorded him after the Battle of Monmouth, demands a court-martial. The trial convenes at Brunswick, New Jersey, with General William Alexander presiding. Lee is accused of disobeying orders, misbehavior in the face of the enemy, and disrespect toward his commanding officer.

Captain Walter Butler accepts the surrender of Forty Fort, Pennsylvania, and his forces go on to devastate the Wyoming Valley, burning eight forts and 1,000 homes, and absconding with 1,000 head of cattle. It proves one of the most devastating raids in the entire war.

West: Colonel George Rogers Clark, with 175 men, surrounds the distant post of Kaskaskia (Illinois) at the confluence of the Mississippi and Kaskaskia Rivers. He then leads a party of men directly through the open gate, enters the commander's house, and receives his surrender. Though successful, Clark is careful to assuage the local French settlers with word of the recent treaty between France and the United States, and they quickly switch allegiances.

July 5

North: The British army under General Henry Clinton is gradually ferried from Sandy Hook to New York by the fleet of Admiral Richard Howe.

July 6

West: The frontier outpost at Cahokia (Illinois) surrenders to an American detachment commanded by Captain Joseph Bowman.

South: A force of 300 Georgia militia under Colonel Elijah Clarke advances to attack and capture a Loyalist-held bridge over Alligator Creek, Georgia. En route they skirmish heavily with rangers under Colonel Thomas Brown and the Americans pursue them. Both forces then stumble headlong into an oncoming group of British regulars, who cannot differentiate between the two, and a confused firefight erupts. At length the outnumbered Americans withdraw after losing three killed and nine wounded to a British tally of one killed and seven wounded. This defeat signals the end of American efforts to seize East Florida.

Naval: The Royal Navy successfully embarks remaining elements of General Henry Clinton's army from Sandy Hook to New York.

July 8

North: General George Washington selects West Point, New York, as the site of his new headquarters.

Naval: The 15-vessel fleet of Admiral Charles-Hector-Théodat, comte d'Estaing, arrives off the Delaware Capes, delayed by unfavorable winds and too late to trap Admiral Richard Howe's squadron. He still enjoys local naval superiority by mounting 834 guns to Howe's 534 and sails for New York seeking him out.

July 9

North: British naval units raid and burn Fairfield, Connecticut.

July 10

Naval: Admiral Louis, comte d'Orvilliers, departs Brest with a fleet of 32 vessels under orders to cruise open water for a month and avoid a general engagement.

July 11

Politics: The Continental Congress authorizes use of the term "United States of America" on all paper currency issued.

Naval: The French squadron of 12 ships of the line under Admiral Charles-Hector-Théodat, comte d'Estaing, arrives off Sandy Hook, New York, for combined operations with American forces. However, his ships cannot cross sandbars obstructing the harbor while British vessels under Admiral Richard Howe assume defensive positions to rake them should they approach.

British naval forces attack and burn Norwalk, Connecticut.

July 14
West: Colonel George Rogers Clark solicits help from Father Pierre Gibault to obtain the peaceful surrender of Vincennes. Gabriel then departs for the fort with letters addressed to the French community there.

July 18
North: Mohawk under Chief Joseph Brant attack and burn the settlement at Andrustown, New York, massacring several inhabitants.

July 20
West: Volunteer forces under Colonel George Rogers Clark occupy Vincennes (Indiana) without resistance, thanks to the support of the local priest, Father Pierre Gibault.

July 22
North: General George Washington confers with Admiral Charles-Hector-Théodat, comte d'Estaing, and agrees that the local waters are too constricted for combined operations. Washington then suggests he sail to Newport, Rhode Island, and the comte agrees. General John Sullivan is subsequently dispatched there with 1,000 men to begin joint operations.

July 23
Naval: The French and English fleets under Admirals Louis, comte d'Orvilliers, and Augustus Keppel sight each other off Ushant Island in the English Channel. A protracted contest of maneuvering begins, with d'Orvilliers striving to avoid a pitched battle.

July 24
Politics: Congressional delegates from Delaware, New Jersey, and Maryland withhold signing the Articles of Confederation unless all states with western land claims surrender them to the United States.

July 27
Naval: British and French fleets clash in an indecisive battle along the Brittany coast off Ushant, France. As Admiral Augustus Keppel (30 ships, 2,280 guns) closes upon the French rear, Admiral Louis, comte d'Orvilliers, with 27 ships and 1,950 guns, suddenly turns about, and the two fleets engage in a long and stately firing pass. Both sides suffer damage and losses, but the French withdraw at nightfall, and Keppel, with several vessels wallowing dangerously, declines pursuit. Casualties in this tepid action total 133 British killed and 375 wounded to 163 dead French and 573 wounded. Keppel is subsequently charged by his rearguard commander, Sir Hugh Palliser, with mishandling the battle and is court-martialed. Whig leader Charles James Fox also moves to have John Montagu, earl of Sandwich, removed as head of the Naval Ministry. An internecine political row ensues and Keppel is eventually declared innocent. Hereafter, British naval commanders will be less

beholden to the traditional and inflexible Permanent Fighting Instructions, first established in 1703.

July 28
Politics: Silas Deane reports to a congressional committee to justify his behavior in Paris. Specifically, he must refute charges of profligacy and misuse of public funds leveled against him by Richard Lee.

July 29
Naval: Admiral Charles-Hector-Théodat, comte d'Estaing, arrives off Newport, Rhode Island, to cooperate with American forces under General John Sullivan. However, the Americans will not arrive in force for another week, and Britain's General Robert Pigot, commanding 6,700 men, prepares for a siege behind newly raised fortifications. He hopes for timely reinforcement from the British fleet at New York under Admiral Richard Howe.

July 30
North: General George Washington positions his army at White Plains to enforce a land blockade of New York City.
Naval: Admiral Charles-Hector-Théodat, comte d'Estaing, sails several ships into Narragansett Bay and begins landing troops on Conanicut Island near Newport. General John Sullivan also arrives on the scene and confers with d'Estaing about strategy. They agree upon a French feint that will land troops on Aquidneck Island above Newport and force a British withdrawal into the city. The Americans will simultaneously occupy the vacated lines and advance artillery against Newport. Their combined forces will then storm the city under cover of d'Estaing's guns.

August 1
North: Colonel Ichabod Alden and 250 men of the 7th Massachusetts Continentals reach the settlement of Cherry Valley, New York, to bolster the garrison.

August 2
Politics: France formally declares war against Great Britain.

August 4
North: The marquis de Lafayette arrives in Rhode Island and convinces both General John Sullivan and Admiral Charles-Hector-Théodat, comte d'Estaing, to abandon their proposed feint against Aquidneck Island in favor of an immediate joint assault.

August 5
Naval: The approach of two French frigates under Admiral Pierre-André de Suffren up the Sakonnet Passage, Rhode Island, causes the British to beach the frigates HMS *Cerberus, Juno, Orpheus, Flora,* and *Lark,* burning them. Several other warships are scuttled in Newport harbor to obstruct the French approach.

August 6
Naval: General Henry Clinton, informed that Newport is under attack, orders Admiral Richard Howe to disperse the French fleet. The British have recently been

bolstered by the arrival of Admiral John Byron's squadron and now possess 20 ships and 914 guns to Admiral Charles-Hector-Théodat, comte d'Estaing's 15 vessels and 834 guns.

August 7
NORTH: General John Sullivan amasses a force of 10,000 men at Tiverton, Rhode Island, including veteran brigades of Generals James M. Varnum and John Glover.

August 9
NORTH: General John Sullivan awaits additional reinforcements before moving against the British garrison at Newport, Rhode Island. However, upon learning that the British have abandoned their northern defenses he marches troops across the Sakonnet River to occupy the area. This maneuver, taken without consulting the French, inexplicably angers the touchy Admiral d'Estaing and nearly scuttles combined operations.

NAVAL: The fleet of Admiral Richard Howe arrives off Newport, Rhode Island, and prepares for battle as soon as the winds are favorable. D'Estaing quickly orders all personnel ashore to embark at once and he sails.

August 10
SOUTH: The Georgia state government appeals to General Benjamin Lincoln for military assistance to prevent the British from further territorial gains.

NAVAL: The fleet of Admiral Charles-Hector-Théodat, comte d'Estaing, enjoys favorable winds as it exits Narragansett Bay, but it comes under fire from British land batteries at Newport. Admiral Richard Howe continues maneuvering cautiously, waiting to seize the weather gauge.

August 11
NORTH: A court-martial in Paramus, New Jersey, convicts General Charles Lee of insubordination and suspends him from command for a year.

August 12
NAVAL: The fleets of Admirals Richard Howe and Charles-Hector-Théodat, comte d'Estaing, are closing for a final confrontation off Newport, Rhode Island, when both are scattered and badly damaged by a sudden squall.

August 15
NORTH: General John Sullivan begins siege operations in earnest by establishing several batteries and driving the British from their outer perimeter.

August 19
NORTH: American artillery under General John Sullivan deploys and begins bombarding Newport, Rhode Island, but the following day the French fleet arrives in battered condition and Admiral Charles-Hector-Théodat, comte d'Estaing, declares his intention to abandon the siege and sail to Boston for repairs. Sullivan is aghast by his abrupt departure and pleads with the French to remain 48 hours, but they refuse. The French also remove their 3,000-man infantry contingent.

August 22
Naval: The French fleet under Admiral d'Estaing sails to Boston for repairs, forcing General John Sullivan to lift the siege of Newport, Rhode Island. The equally battered fleet of Admiral Richard Howe also departs for New York to refit.

August 23
Naval: The fleet of Admiral Augustus Keppel sails from Portsmouth to engage the French fleet in the English Channel, but Admiral Louis, comte d'Orvilliers, has since escaped to the Bay of Biscay.

August 24
Naval: Captains Abraham Whipple and Samuel Tucker, commanding the warships *Providence* and *Boston*, respectively, assisted by the sloop *Ranger*, capture three merchant vessels in the North Atlantic.

August 26
Diplomacy: George Johnstone, a member of the British Carlisle Commission, attempts to bribe Congressmen Joseph Reed, Robert Morris, and Francis Dana, and is ordered home.

August 28
North: General John Sullivan, beset by desertions and abandoned by French allies, begins withdrawing from Newport, Rhode Island. Wary of a British pursuit, the Americans assume strong defensive positions south of Quaker Hill and entrench, expecting the worst. The left flank is commanded by General Nathanael Greene, while the center and right are directed by General John Sullivan. The marquis de Lafayette is conspicuously absent, having ridden 70 miles to Boston to convince the French fleet to reconsider.

August 29
North: British forces under General Robert Pigot sortie from Newport and attack General John Sullivan's retiring army below Quaker Hill. General Francis Smith drives back the American light infantry of Colonel John Laurens until encountering the veteran brigade of General John Glover on Butt's Hill. After a stout clash Smith hastily falls back to Quaker Hill and fighting dies down along Sullivan's left. Concurrently, the American right is assailed by a large force of jaegers, which captures a number of outworks. Their success is abetted by heavy fire from several surviving British warships offshore. General Nathanael Greene responds by bringing up artillery, which drive vessels farther off. Pigot then orders his Hessians to assault the entire line, but they stall in front of a redoubt stoutly held by Colonel Christopher Greene's 1st Rhode Island Light Infantry Regiment, composed mainly of African Americans. The Hessians subsequently bypass the redoubt and crash into the American line, pushing it back. General Greene promptly counterattacks with General James M. Varnum's Continentals and General Solomon Lovell's Massachusetts militia, driving the Germans off in confusion. Pigot then suspends the action and Sullivan resumes his withdrawal. American losses are 30 killed, 137 wounded, and 44 missing; the British tally is 38 killed, 210 wounded, and 44 missing.

August 31
NORTH: A relief expedition of 5,000 men arrives at Newport, Rhode Island, under General Henry Clinton, but American forces under General John Sullivan have since withdrawn north into Bristol. Clinton then detaches General Charles Grey to raid along the Massachusetts coast.

British rangers under Lieutenant Colonel John Graves Simcoe ambush Chief Nimham and his warriors at Indian Field, New York, killing 40. The Indians have been cooperating with the Americans.

September 4
DIPLOMACY: The United States concludes a treaty of amity and commerce with the city of Amsterdam, Netherlands, an act infuriating the British government.

September 6
NORTH: A British raiding force under General Charles Grey lands at Clark's Neck, Massachusetts, and burns the towns of New Bedford and Fair Haven, along with 70 vessels, houses, and mills.
CARIBBEAN: French naval forces under Governor Francois-Claude Amour, marquis de Bouille, land 2,000 troops and overwhelm a 500-man British garrison on the island of Dominica, Lesser Antillies.

September 7–16
WEST: Shawnee under Blackfish attack and unsuccessfully besiege Boonesborough, Kentucky. Fortunately, the garrison has been forewarned by Daniel Boone, recently escaped from Indian captivity, and a stout defense is mounted. The garrison loses one killed and three wounded.

September 8
NORTH: General Charles Grey directs a raid upon Martha's Vineyard, Massachusetts, destroying property and seizing 10,000 sheep and 300 oxen for the British army.

September 11
NAVAL: Admiral James Gambier arrives at New York City to succeed temporarily Admiral Richard Howe as commander of British naval forces in America. His tenure proves brief and uneventful.

September 13
NORTH: A force of 450 Loyalists and Indians under Chief Joseph Brant and Captain William Caldwell attacks German Flats (Herkimer, New York) on the Mohawk River. The 700 settlers are forewarned of the enemy's approach by a scout and seek refuge in nearby Fort Herkimer and Fort Dayton. Consequently only four settlers are killed, but 100 houses, barns, and other buildings are torched. Unable to storm the forts, the raiders depart without further incident.

September 14
DIPLOMACY: The Continental Congress appoints Benjamin Franklin minister plenipotentiary to France, replacing the three-man commission.

September 16
NORTH: Colonel Mordecai Gist perceives an impending ambush orchestrated by Lieutenant Colonels John Graves Simcoe and Banastre Tarleton at Saw Mill River (Westchester), New York, and escapes intact.

September 22
NORTH: General Charles Cornwallis and 5,000 men are dispatched across the Hudson River into New Jersey on a large-scale foraging expedition and to harass nearby American outposts.

September 26
POLITICS: The Continental Congress appoints General Benjamin Lincoln to succeed General Robert Howe as commander of the Southern Department but without consulting General George Washington.

September 27
NORTH: General Charles Cornwallis, having overrun American outposts at Liberty Pole and New Bridge, New Jersey, is alerted by Loyalists that a detachment of 100 American dragoons is sequestered at nearby Old Tappan. Determined to eliminate them, he authorizes General Charles Grey to take four regiments and attack the following morning. Cornwallis himself leads a supporting column but gets lost in the night and plays no part in the action.

NAVAL: Captain John Barry, commanding the 32-gun frigate *Raleigh*, is attacked on the Maine coast by a British squadron consisting of the 50-gun HMS *Experiment* under Captain James Wallace and *Unicorn*, 28 guns, under Captain John Ford. Barry fights skillfully for several hours until his foretop mast suddenly topples. When the *Raleigh* subsequently grounds on Fox Island, he and 85 crewmen escape on foot. The Americans lose three dead, 22 wounded, and 135 captive, to a British tally of 10 killed.

September 28
NORTH: In the early morning hours General Charles Grey advances upon a detachment of 100 sleeping 3rd Continental Dragoons under Lieutenant Colonel George Baylor at Old Tappan, New Jersey. Having been guided through the dark by Loyalists, Grey orders his men to remove their flints and rely solely upon cold steel. At 3 A.M. six infantry companies surround the barn where Baylor and his men are sleeping and attack relentlessly. In the wild melee that follows, 16 Americans are killed, 16 wounded, and 38 captured; Baylor himself is fatally injured and captured. The British sustain no losses.

October 3
DIPLOMACY: Thwarted in their dealings with the Continental Congress, members of the Carlisle Commission print an offer of reconciliation to the American people at Philadelphia, with full pardons for any individuals accepting it over the next 40 days.

October 4
NORTH: A small Royal Navy flotilla under Captain Henry Collins lands 400 men of the 5th Regiment and New Jersey Volunteers under Captain Patrick Ferguson at

Chestnut Creek, New Jersey, and then proceeds against Little Egg Harbor, a noted privateering center. The entire village and 10 vessels are torched while a cavalry legion under Count Kazimierz Pulaski encamps at nearby Middle of the Shore. As a precaution, Pulaski deploys an advanced guard of 50 soldiers on Mincock Island to observe British movements.

October 5
NORTH: Using rowboats, a British raiding party of 250 men under Captain Patrick Ferguson surprises a detachment of cavalry commanded by Count Kazimierz Pulaski at Mincock Island, New Jersey. The British efforts are abetted by a near lack of sentries, and they charge into the camp of sleeping soldiers, bayoneting five, wounding 20, and taking five captive before reinforcements arrive from the mainland. British losses are three killed and three wounded.

October 6–8
NORTH: The 4th Pennsylvania Continentals under Lieutenant Colonel William Butler destroy the Indian settlement at Unadilla, New York. Chief Joseph Brant is not present, however, and the raiders burn several dwellings before retiring unmolested.

October 7
WEST: Lieutenant Colonel Henry Hamilton sets out from Detroit with 225 soldiers, French militia, and local Indians to recapture Vincennes. He is heartened to learn that Colonel George Rogers Clark has since withdrawn most of the garrison.

October 13
NORTH: General Charles Cornwallis, lately foraging in New Jersey with 5,000 men, is ordered back to New York and departs without interference.

October 22
NORTH: Captain Walter Butler amasses a force of 320 Seneca Indians, 150 Loyalist rangers, and 50 men of the 8th Regiment at Windsor, New York, prior to marching upon the American settlement at Cherry Valley, New York. They are eventually joined by an additional 100 Mohawk under Chief Joseph Brant.

October 28
DIPLOMACY: The Committee for Foreign Affairs dispatches new instructions to Benjamin Franklin in Paris and informs John Adams that his mission there is completed.
NAVAL: Major Silas Talbot, commanding the sloop *Hawke*, carefully approaches the eight-gun schooner HMS *Pigot* on the Sakonnet River, Rhode Island. He had previously mounted a kedging anchor on the bowsprit of his vessel, situated to rip away anti-boarding nets as it passes. Talbot then boards his adversary with such alacrity that the British are driven below deck and surrender. No casualties are reported but 45 captives are taken.

October 31
NAVAL: The fleet of Admiral Augustus Keppel, beset by mounting sickness, returns to Portsmouth to refit and rest for the winter.

November 2
CARIBBEAN: The British government, tired of local merchants on Bermuda selling supplies and goods to the Americans, installs a sizable garrison on the island to halt the practice.

November 4
NORTH: General Henry Clinton dispatches General James Grant and 5,800 men from New York to the West Indies.
NAVAL: The French fleet under Admiral Charles-Hector-Théodat, comte d'Estaing, departs Boston and commences a cruise of the West Indies without informing General George Washington. The fledgling Franco-American alliance has thus far achieved little beyond a ruffling of feathers.

November 8
NORTH: Colonel Ichabod Alden, commanding the 7th Massachusetts Regiment at Cherry Valley, New York, is alerted that Loyalists and Indians are en route to attack his garrison. He dismisses the threat, allowing officers to remain billeted away from the men and takes no special precautions. Worse, Alden refuses families of nearby settlers to enter the fort.

November 10
NORTH: A raiding party under Chief Joseph Brant and Captain Walter Butler captures and interrogates a patrol dispatched from Cherry Valley, New York, and ascertains useful intelligence about its defenses.

November 11
NORTH: A combined Loyalist/Indian force under Captain Walter Butler and Chief Joseph Brant ravages the American settlement at Cherry Valley, New York. They attack under the cover of a rainstorm and surprise the garrison under Colonel Ichabod Alden, who is killed along with 40 settlers. A further 30 prisoners are taken but released soon after. The extent of the devastation induces General George Washington to mount retaliatory action against the Indians that summer.

November 19
SOUTH: British forces under Lieutenant Colonel James Mark Prevost ambush and defeat a small American force under Colonel John Baker at Spencer's Hill, Georgia.

November 20
NORTH: New Jersey ratifies the Articles of Confederation.

November 24
SOUTH: British forces under Lieutenant Colonel James Mark Prevost skirmish heavily with mounted Georgia militia under Colonel John Baker and drive them off from Bulltown Swamp. Prevost continues advancing and brushes aside additional militia under Colonel John White at Medway Church, Georgia. The raiders burn the church and several other buildings. American losses are three wounded.

November 25
SOUTH: British forces under Lieutenant Colonel Lewis Fuser attack Sunbury, Georgia, and take the town but cannot dislodge Colonel John McIntosh from nearby Fort Morris.

November 26
POLITICS: Maryland remains the only state not to have ratified the Articles of Confederation.

November 27
DIPLOMACY: The British Carlisle Commission sails home from New York, having failed to achieve a negotiated peace settlement.
NORTH: Lieutenant Colonel Archibald Campbell departs New York with 3,500 men and makes for the Georgia coast. There he will join forces with General Augustin Prevost in an attack upon Savannah.
NAVAL: Admiral Richard Howe returns to England while Admiral John Byron replaces him as commander of British naval forces in America.

November 30
NORTH: General George Washington completes his land blockade of New York City. His troops occupy a semicircle with a radius of 40 miles while he coordinates movements from his headquarters at Middlebrook, New Jersey.

December 4
SOUTH: General Benjamin Lincoln arrives at Charleston, South Carolina, as commander of the Department of the South.

December 5
POLITICS: The Continental Congress stamps its approval on General Charles Lee's court-martial sentence, and he is relieved of command for a year. Meanwhile, Silas Deane publishes his defense and attacks Arthur Lee and others in the *Pennsylvania Packet*.

December 9
WEST: Virginia annexes the conquests of General George Rogers Clark as the county of Illinois. Captain John Todd is selected as governor.

December 10
POLITICS: John Jay is elected president of the Continental Congress.
NAVAL: The squadron of Commodore William Hotham drops anchor at Bridgetown, Barbados, to reinforce the fleet of Admiral Samuel Barrington. Offensive operations against St. Lucia commence shortly after under General James Grant.

December 11
NORTH: The army under General George Washington enters winter quarters at Middlebrook, New Jersey, positioning itself for a rapid advance into Delaware to counter any possible attacks upon Philadelphia.

NAVAL: The French fleet under Admiral Charles-Hector-Théodat, comte d'Estaing, arrives at Martinique, Lesser Antilles, from Boston.

December 12
CARIBBEAN: Admiral Samuel Barrington and General James Grant successfully capture the French naval base at St. Lucia, West Indies, with 5,800 men drawn from the New York garrison. The troops no sooner land at Grand Cul de Sac and secure control of the island than the fleet of Admiral d'Estaing arrives bearing 9,000 troops. The British entrench and await developments.

December 13
NAVAL: Admiral John Byron departs Newport, Rhode Island, and begins a sweep through the West Indies in search of the French fleet.

December 15
NAVAL: The French fleet under Admiral Charles-Hector-Théodat, comte d' Estaing, attacks British shore batteries at Carenage, St. Lucia, but is driven off. He then enters the bay of Grand Cul de Sac to engage a smaller British fleet under Admiral Samuel Barrington. D'Estaing launches two determined attacks upon the anchored British line yet fails to dislodge it. The French fleet then sails north and debarks 9,000 troops at Anse du Choc Bay.

December 17
WEST: A combined British/Indian force of 500 men under Lieutenant Colonel Henry Hamilton recaptures Vincennes (Indiana) from Captain Leonard Helm. Hamilton intends to attack Kaskaskia the following spring to drive off Colonel George Rogers Clark. He then dismisses most of his Indian and militia contingent to their homes for the winter. Helm and three other Virginians are taken captive.
NAVAL: A whaleboat commanded by Lieutenant Seth Chapin captures a British vessel off Newport, Rhode Island.

December 18
CARIBBEAN: A French fleet under Admiral Charles-Hector-Théodat, comte d'Estaing, attacks the La Vigie Peninsula, St. Lucia, with 9,000 men but is masterfully repelled by General James Grant. The attack miscarries badly against fortified British positions and the French withdraw after losing 400 killed and 1,200 wounded; Grant's losses are 13 killed and 158 wounded.

December 21
NORTH: General George Washington departs his headquarters at Middlebrook, New York, to confer with congressional leaders in Philadelphia. General William Alexander is left in command.

December 23
SOUTH: A British squadron under Commodore Hyde Parker lands 3,500 soldiers under Lieutenant Colonel Archibald Campbell on Tybee Island at the mouth of the

Savannah River. Meanwhile, General Robert Howe collects 700 soldiers and 150 militia at Sunbury and marches to defend the city.

December 25
NORTH: Loyalists under Major Mansfield Bearmore launch a botched attack against Young's House, New York, capturing the owner and several Americans but accidently killing a Tory prisoner.
SOUTH: Lieutenant Colonel Archibald Campbell, who is awaiting reinforcements from General Augustin Prevost, receives welcome intelligence that Savannah is weakly defended and that American troops under General Benjamin Lincoln are quite distant. Emboldened by this information, Campbell elects to attack now rather than wait for reinforcements under Prevost.

December 28
SOUTH: British forces under Lieutenant Colonel Archibald Campbell begin landing at Girardeau's Plantation, opposite Tybee Island, Georgia, and are briefly bombarded by two American galleys. Once onshore Lieutenant Colonel John Maitland's 71st Highlanders brush aside a picket of 50 Continentals and move inland undetected.
CARIBBEAN: The French garrison on St. Lucia formally surrenders to General James Grant once the fleet under Admiral d'Estaing returns to Martinique.

December 29
SOUTH: Lieutenant Colonel Archibald Campbell successfully leads 3,500 men against General Robert Howe, who strongly positions 1,200 troops astride the road to Girradeau with swamps on either flank and a stream to his front. Howe, however, ignores a suggestion by Colonel Samuel Elbert to flood nearby rice fields and make them impassable. But the American position is still strong and Campbell is preparing to assault it frontally until a slave named Quamino Dolly offers to lead him down an obscure route through the swamps. Campbell then marches a picked unit of 20 light infantry down the secret trail, which emerges on the American right, while other troops demonstrate noisily to their front. At a given signal, the British attack the Americans from behind just as British artillery opens up on their encampment. Howe's force, hit frontally and on the flank, crumbles quickly and is chased into Musgrove Swamp, where many Continentals are killed and captured. In a stunning reversal of fortunes, Savannah falls to Campbell after inflicting 83 dead, 11 injured, and 453 prisoners on the Americans for a loss of three killed and 10 wounded. The British also capture 48 cannon, 23 mortars, and numerous ships still at anchor. The city remains in British hands for the rest of the war.

1779

January 1
POLITICS: The Continental Congress, unswayed by General Henry Clinton's assurances that King George III has signed the Saratoga Convention, refuses to abide by its terms. The captured British army is then marched under armed guard from Boston to Virginia.

North: General George Washington advises the Continental Congress not to become ensnared with a new campaign against Canada, fearing that France will gain control of the region after the war.

January 6
South: General Augustin Prevost advances north from Florida with 2,000 British troops and besieges the 223-man garrison under Major Joseph Lane at Fort Morris, Sunbury, Georgia.

January 9
South: Major Joseph Lane surrenders Fort Morris to General Augustin Prevost after the latter brings up artillery to bombard his position. Losses are four Americans killed and seven wounded to one Briton dead and three injured. Eastern Georgia is now completely under British sway.

January 10
Diplomacy: Conrad-Alexandre-Rayvenal de Gerard, French minister to the United States, seeks positive affirmation of the recent alliance from the Continental Congress.
South: Colonel John Boyd, a Georgia Loyalist, departs Savannah with 600 men and begins marching for South Carolina to assist Loyalist efforts there.

January 11
Naval: The frigate *Alliance* departs Boston under Captain Pierre Landais, conveying the marquis de Lafayette back to France. It is the only warship jointly commanded by the allies.

January 14
Diplomacy: The Continental Congress assures the French minister in Philadelphia that the United States remains bound to observe all treaty commitments with France and will not seek a separate peace treaty without prior consultation.

January 20
Politics: A congressional committee is appointed to investigate allegations against Silas Deane.

January 23
Politics: Lord George Germain finalizes British strategy for General Henry Clinton, including plans to drive the Americans from the Hudson Highlands and to reestablish royal government in New York.

Beset by chronic manpower shortages, the Continental Congress accepts General George Washington's recommendation and authorizes a $200 bounty to both new recruits and soldiers who reenlist.
West: A large party of Indians under Simon Girty attacks and besieges Fort Laurens, Ohio, but fails to evict the garrison.

January 26
South: A force of 230 Loyalists under Colonel Thomas Brown attacks Patriot militia holed up in the Burke County Jail, Georgia. Despite repeated attacks Brown cannot dislodge the defenders and draws off, having inflicted five killed and seven wounded for a loss of three dead and seven captured.

January 29
South: Lieutenant Colonel Archibald Campbell advances up the Savannah River toward Augusta, Georgia, and is ambushed by militia under General Samuel Elbert and Colonel John Twiggs. The British suffer about 20 casualties but nonetheless seize Augusta, finding it abandoned by American forces. The British now control the entire state, and long-suppressed Loyalist sympathizers begin flocking to the king's colors. Remaining Patriots are either forced into an oath of allegiance or face property confiscation.

February 1
North: Delaware ratifies the Articles of Confederation.

February 2
North: General George Washington ends consultations with the Continental Congress and departs for his headquarters at Middlebrook, New Jersey.

February 3
Politics: Joseph Reed, president of the Pennsylvania Council, brings charges of abuse and mismanagement against General Benedict Arnold. Arnold angrily demands an investigation to clear his name.

South: General William Moultrie is sent by General Benjamin Lincoln to defend Port Royal Island, South Carolina, against possible attack. He places 300 militia, a handful of Continentals, and some cannon directly on the road to Beaufort then awaits the enemy's approach. Two companies of British appear under Major William Gardiner and are handily repulsed by the defenders with 50 casualties. Moultrie loses eight killed and 22 wounded.

February 4
Politics: The Continental Congress endows General George Washington with authority to take any appropriate measure deemed necessary to enhance and improve the Continental army. He is also authorized to resolve all disputes involving rank below that of brigadier general.

Naval: Captain John Paul Jones receives command of a dilapidated French merchant ship, the *Duc de Duras,* which he renames *BonHomme Richard* in honor of Benjamin Franklin. He spends the next six months scouring France for guns and other naval implements.

February 5
West: Colonel George Rogers Clark, informed of Vincennes's capture, gathers 127 men and commences a 180-mile march from Kaskaskia in midwinter. He also dispatches Lieutenant Colonel John Rogers and the armed galley *Willing* down the Mississippi River to intercept any British movements there.

South: Colonel John Boyd departs from Spartanburg, South Carolina, with a force of 600 newly recruited Loyalists and takes up a line of march for Augusta, Georgia. There he hopes to augment the British garrison under Lieutenant Archibald Campbell.

February 10
SOUTH: Colonels Andrew Pickens, John Dooly, and Elijah Clarke, commanding 350 Georgia and South Carolina militia, pursue 80 Loyalist cavalry under Lieutenant Colonel John Hamilton into Carr's Fort, Georgia. The Americans then cut the fort's water supply and make preparations to burn it down when they learn of Colonel John Boyd's column approaching. Rather than risk having them reinforce the British garrison at Augusta, Pickens immediately disengages and redeploys his men to meet them. Loyalist losses are nine killed and three wounded.

February 11
SOUTH: Colonel John Boyd, commanding 600 Loyalists, attempts to cross the Savannah River at Cherokee Ford, South Carolina, only to find his path obstructed by a small fort called McGowan's Blockhouse. It is held by 47 Georgia and South Carolina militiamen under Captain James Little, who also commands two small swivel guns. Boyd withdraws his force and marches five miles downstream, constructs rafts, and finally crosses the river at Vann's Creek.

February 12
SOUTH: Captain James Little's Patriot militia, reinforced by 60 South Carolina militiamen, abandons the security of McGowan's Blockhouse and tries to halt Colonel John Boyd's Loyalists from crossing the Savannah River at Vann's Creek (Cherokee Ford) but are defeated. The survivors return to the safety of their fort, having lost six killed, 10 wounded, and 16 captured.

February 13
SOUTH: Lieutenant Colonel Archibald Campbell, informed of General Benjamin Lincoln's approach with a large American force, hastily abandons Augusta and marches for Savannah. En route he is closely trailed by militia forces under General John Ashe.

February 14
SOUTH: Loyalists under Colonel John Boyd cross the Savannah River at Kettle Creek, Georgia, and encamp for the evening—unaware that the British garrison at Augusta has departed for Savannah. Colonels Andrew Pickens and Elijah Clarke, meanwhile, encircle Boyd's camp unobserved and deploy to his rear. They suddenly lead 350 men in a concerted attack upon the Loyalist position. Assaulted on three sides, Boyd's troops fight well initially but are eventually routed, losing 40 killed (including Boyd) and 70 captured. The Americans sustain nine dead and 23 injured, but Pickens declines to recapture Augusta and withdraws.

February 15
DIPLOMACY: To further induce Spain's participation in the war, French minister Gerard advises the Continental Congress to give due consideration to the status of Florida and navigation rights on the Mississippi River when drawing up peace terms.

February 18

POLITICS: The Continental Congress authorizes creation of an inspector general's department under a major general. Friedrich von Steuben serves as first department head.

WEST: Colonel George Rogers Clark and his exhausted little band arrive at the Wabash River to repose before the final push against Vincennes. Ten miles of flooded, icy plains remain to be crossed in bitterly cold weather.

February 23

DIPLOMACY: A congressional committee assigned to draw up definitive peace terms, consisting of Gouverneur Morris, Thomas Burke, John Witherspoon, and Samuel Adams, makes its final report. Among other things, it recommends establishment of minimum boundaries, evacuation of all British forces, acquisition of fishing rights off Newfoundland, free navigation of the Mississippi River and, above all, irrevocable British recognition of American independence.

WEST: Colonel George Rogers Clark's expedition traverses icy, flooded prairies and arrives at Horseshoe Plain. There he learns from a prisoner that Lieutenant Colonel Henry Hamilton is ignorant of his approach and holds Vincennes with only a small garrison. Clark then dispatches messengers to warn French residents

George Rogers Clark tricks Lieutenant Colonel Henry Hamilton into surrendering Fort Sackville at the Battle of Vincennes by having his soldiers wave many flags to give the appearance of a larger force. *(U.S. Army Center of Military History)*

to remain in their homes while British sympathizers are advised to shelter at Fort Sackville with Hamilton. The Americans then noisily encircle the fort to deceive the British of their actual strength. Clark, to underscore his determination, summarily orders four captured Indians executed and scalped in full view of the garrison. When Hamilton still refuses to surrender, the frontiersmen begin peppering the defenders with accurate rifle fire. The British lose six artillerists without getting off a shot.

British Indians ambush a detachment of the 13th Virginia Regiment outside Fort Laurens, Ohio, killing 16 men, but a subsequent attack upon the fort is repulsed.

February 25
POLITICS: The Continental Congress raises five companies of rangers for the protection of the Pennsylvania frontier.
WEST: After a daylong siege interrupted by occasional parleys, Lieutenant Colonel Henry Hamilton surrenders 79 men to Colonel George Rogers Clark at Vincennes. This is Clark's consummate victory and bequeaths to the United States control of the entire Illinois territory. An estimated 20,000 settlers will colonize the region by the time the Revolutionary War ends.

February 26
NORTH: Governor William Tryon of New York lands 600 troops at Horseneck Landing, Connecticut, and attacks 150 militiamen commanded by General Israel Putnam. The Americans are routed, and Putnam escapes only after dramatically plunging down a steep hill. Tryon then proceeds to plunder and burn the village. British losses are two dead and 20 captured.

February 27
SOUTH: General John Ashe stops pursing retreating British units and halts at Briar Creek, Georgia. While there he begins repairing the recently burned bridge and awaits reinforcements before resuming his march to Savannah.

March 3
SOUTH: American militia under General John Ashe and Colonel Samuel Elbert, en route to join the main force at Purysburg, Georgia, remain at Briar Creek to rebuild the bridge there. They are unaware that 900 British under Lieutenant Colonel James Mark Prevost have arrived from Florida. Prevost approaches undetected on a wide circuitous march and silently deploys two battalions of the 71st Highlanders astride the American rear. The ensuing attack routs 1,200 defenders, who suffer 150 dead and 162 captured, along with all their camp and baggage equipment. British losses are five killed and 11 wounded. For the time being, this ends American efforts to reconquer Georgia.

March 9
POLITICS: To counter lagging recruitment, the Continental Congress finally authorizes a $200 bounty to any soldier enlisting for the duration of the war. The states are also encouraged to raise 80 battalions of infantry, by either recruitment or draft, to meet their quotas.

March 11
Politics: The Continental Congress authorizes a corps of engineers within the Continental army.

March 13
Naval: A naval squadron consisting of the *Warren*, 32 guns, under Commodore John B. Hopkins; *Queen of France*, 28 guns, under Captain Joseph Olney; and *Ranger*, 18 guns, under Captain Thomas Simpson, departs Boston to cruise the eastern seaboard.

March 14
Politics: Colonel Alexander Hamilton composes a letter to President John Jay of the Continental Congress extolling the virtues of African Americans and encouraging Georgia and the Carolinas to recruit slaves into the army. He also argues that any military service should be rewarded with freedom.

March 28
West: A 500-man relief force under General Lachlan McIntosh arrives at Fort Laurens, Ohio, and disperses an Indian force lurking there under Simon Girty.

March 29
Politics: To combat persistent manpower shortages in South Carolina and Georgia, the Continental Congress formally suggests that they recruit 3,000 African Americans into the army and emancipate them after the war. Furthermore, Congress pledges to compensate owners with $1,000 per slave.

March 30
Naval: American warships *Warren, Queen of France,* and *Ranger* under Commodore John B. Hopkins capture a 14-gun British privateer off Cape Henry.

April 1–30
West: When Cherokee chief Dragging Canoe rejects treaties signed in 1777 and threatens war, Virginia and North Carolina raise 900 men under Colonel Evan Shelby to conduct punitive raids into Tennessee.

April 3
Diplomacy: Spanish foreign minister Conde de Floridablanca offers to mediate a peace between Great Britain and France, and guarantee Spain's neutrality, if the British surrender Gibraltar. The offer, as expected, is summarily rejected by the British.

April 6
Naval: Commodore John B. Hopkins's squadron consisting of *Warren, Queen of France,* and *Ranger* captures the armed schooner *Hibernia* and seven supply vessels off Cape Henry.

April 8
North: General Benedict Arnold marries Margaret Shippen, daughter of a leading Philadelphia Loyalist. She is a highly capable British intelligence operative and undoubtedly influences him to switch sides.

April 12
Diplomacy: France and Spain conclude the Convention of Aranjuez, formalizing an alliance against Great Britain. The Spanish regime is eager for a chance to recover its lost assets of Gibraltar, Florida, and Jamaica, pledging not to make a separate peace treaty with Great Britain. In return, France will receive Senegal, Dominica, and Newfoundland. Spain, however, declines to recognize American independence and views the United States as a potential threat to holdings in Louisiana and Mexico.

April 14
North: Major Gose Van Schaick departs Fort Stanwix, New York, with 500 men on a 180-mile raid through Onondaga territory.

April 20
North: A force of 550 Continental soldiers under Major Gose Van Schaick attacks the Indian settlement at Onondaga Creek, New York. The bulk of the inhabitants escape into the woods, but the raid manages to kill 17 warriors, capture 37, and burn 50 houses including the Onondaga Castle. The Americans then depart with their booty for Fort Schuyler.

April 23
South: Governor John Rutledge of South Carolina uses his emergency powers to raise 4,000 militia and assist the army of General Benjamin Lincoln. Thus augmented, Lincoln crosses the Savannah River and advances upon Augusta.

April 24
Naval: Admiral Marriot Arbuthnot sails from Torbay, England, with British and Hessian reinforcements bound for General Henry Clinton in New York. He also succeeds Admiral John Byron as commander of naval forces in American waters.

April 26
North: British naval forces raid Tinton Falls, New Jersey, although they fail to capture several American officers living there.

Major Patrick Ferguson attacks a militia detachment under Colonel Asher Holmes at Shrewsbury, New Jersey, wounding two and capturing 20.

Strong Indian forces unsuccessfully attack Fort Hand, Pennsylvania, while the militia loses two killed.

April 29
South: General Augustin Prevost launches an offensive by crossing 2,500 men over the Savannah River and advancing upon Charleston, South Carolina. Colonel Alexander McIntosh decides to abandon Purysburg and withdraws his 220 men to Black Swamp. There he unites with 1,000 soldiers under General William Moultrie, who in turn withdraws to Coosahatchie Bridge.

April 30
South: North Carolina and Virginia troops under Colonel Evan Shelby conduct additional punitive raids against Chickamauga villages in Tennessee.

May 1
WEST: The Americans repulse a British attempt to capture Cahokia, Illinois.

May 5
NORTH: A combined amphibious expedition under Commodore George Collier and General Edward Mathew sails from New York on a raid against Virginia. Their goal is to devastate the tobacco trade, which constitutes a large part of rebel finance.

May 7
NAVAL: The American 12-gun sloop *Providence* under Captain Hoysted Hacker takes the 12-gun brig HMS *Diligent* in the Atlantic. American losses are four killed and 10 wounded to a British tally of eight killed and 19 wounded.

May 9
SOUTH: Commodore George Collier and General Edward Matthews storm Fort Nelson at Portsmouth, Virginia, with 1,800 men and disperse 100 defenders under Major Thomas Matthews. The British then march unopposed to nearby Gosport and Norfolk, which are also plundered and torched. By the time the British withdraw they have burned 28 vessels and seized 1,000 hogsheads of tobacco.

May 10
NORTH: Philadelphia Loyalist merchant Joseph Stansbury, acting on behalf of General Benedict Arnold, engages Major John Andre in New York over the possibility of switching his allegiance to the British.

May 11
SOUTH: General William Moultrie force-marches to Charleston, South Carolina, a step ahead of pursuing British forces under General Augustin Prevost. Assisted by Governor John Rutledge, he musters 600 militia and rejects Prevost's demand to surrender. General Kazimierz Pulaski, meanwhile, impetuously mounts a sortie of his own and charges a detachment of British dragoons at Haddrel's Point. The Americans are handily defeated, sustaining 146 casualties, with an additional 155 missing to a British loss of 26 killed and 103 wounded. The outnumbered British nevertheless withdraw onto James Island.

May 12
SOUTH: General Augustin Prevost hastily retreats from Charleston in the face of advancing reinforcements under General Benjamin Lincoln. Having crossed over to Johns Island, he fortifies Stono Ferry on the mainland.

May 21
POLITICS: The Continental Congress requests that the states advance $45 million to help ameliorate a mounting financial crisis.

May 23
NORTH: To demonstrate his sincerity toward defecting, General Benedict Arnold secretly forwards General Henry Clinton detailed information on American defenses at West Point.

May 24
SOUTH: The amphibious expedition under Commodore George Collier and General Edward Mathew departs Portsmouth, Virginia, after concluding a successful, three-week raid that netted 17 prize ships, freed 90 Loyalist prisoners, and liberated 500 African-American slaves. The invaders have also sunk 130 vessels of various description.

May 26
POLITICS: The Continental Congress tasks John Dickinson with drafting an appeal to the states for new taxes to assist the war effort.

May 28
NORTH: General Henry Clinton amasses 6,000 soldiers at Kingsbridge, New York, in preparation for a lightning strike against the American stronghold at West Point. Two days later they ascend the Hudson River on 70 sailing vessels under Commodore George Collier and with 150 flat-bottomed scows.

June 1
NORTH: Generals Henry Clinton and John Vaughan lead 6,000 British troops against the American outpost at Stoney Point and subsequently bombard nearby Fort Lafayette on Verplanck's Point.

June 3
NORTH: The American garrison of 70 soldiers at Verplanck's Point surrenders to General Henry Clinton. This leaves the British in control of Kings Ferry, an important choke point on the Hudson River only 12 miles below the strategic West Point. The fortified post at Stony Point across the river is also abandoned by its defenders and occupied without a fight.
SOUTH: Thomas Jefferson succeeds Patrick Henry as governor of Virginia.

June 5
NORTH: New Hampshire town meetings reject a proposed state constitution.

June 6
NAVAL: American frigates *Boston*, under Captain Samuel Tucker, and *Confederacy*, under Captain Seth Harding, capture three British vessels, including the 24-gun privateer *Pole*.

June 12
POLITICS: The Continental Congress receives a strongly worded appeal from army officers endorsing General George Washington's position on lifetime half-pay after the war.
NORTH: General George Washington dispatches Major Henry Lee to ascertain intelligence as to British defenses and fortifications at Stony Point.

June 16
DIPLOMACY: The Spanish ambassador in London declares his country's intention to obtain "justice" by any means necessary after Britain's rejection of mediation. In light of the Convention of Aranjuez, Prime Minister Lord Frederick North considers this note tantamount to a declaration of war.

North: General Francis McLean sails from Halifax, Nova Scotia, with 700 men of Britain's 74th and 82nd Regiments to the Penobscot River, Massachusetts (Maine), to erect a fort on the Bagaduce Peninsula. He is tasked with securing supplies of lumber for Royal Navy masts and dispatching raiding parties into the neighboring countryside. McLean is capably assisted by Captain Henry Mowat and three Royal Navy sloops mounting 54 cannon.

South: General Augustin Prevost withdraws from Stono Ferry, leaving Lieutenant Colonel John Maitland behind with a rear guard of 900 men.

June 17

Politics: Lord John Cavendish makes an appeal in Parliament for a complete military mobilization for war against Spain and France, even at the price of abandoning the conflict in America. It is rejected by wide margins.

North: General James Clinton departs his base camp at Canajoharie, New York, and begins dragging his bateaux 20 miles overland to Lake Otsego, prior to uniting with the main American force under General John Sullivan.

Caribbean: French naval forces under Admiral Charles-Hector-Théodat, comte d'Estaing, capture the island of St. Vincent. This is undertaken in preparation for an assault against Barbados.

June 20

South: General Benjamin Lincoln leads 1,400 men across the Ashley River and attacks the British rear guard of 900 soldiers under Lieutenant Colonel John Maitland at Stono Ferry, South Carolina. Anticipating a coordinated effort with forces commanded by General William Moultrie, who never appears, Lincoln throws forward his left and right wings under Generals Jethro Sumner and Isaac Huger, and they drive back men of the 71st Highlanders. However, the Americans waver while clearing an abattis. Maitland's defenses, centered upon a strong redoubt manned by Hessians, resist fiercely and are augmented by reinforcements ordered up by General Augustin Prevost. His attack fails and Lincoln withdraws, briefly pursued by the victorious British. Considering the disparity of numbers engaged, it was a humiliating defeat for Lincoln, who loses 146 dead and 155 wounded. The victorious Maitland sustains 23 killed and 103 wounded but continues withdrawing toward Beaufort.

June 21

Politics: Spain under King Charles III declares war against Great Britain, acting upon French promises of assistance to regain Gibraltar and Florida. However, while denying overt political recognition to the United States, Spain continues to secretly supply subsidies and loans. The Spanish quickly surround Gibraltar to initiate a naval blockade and a protracted bombardment begins. British forces under General George Augustus Eliott, mustering 5,300 defenders, dig in and await the inevitable onslaught.

June 23

North: General John Sullivan begins massing troops at Wyoming Valley, Pennsylvania, for a large-scale incursion into Six Nations Indian territory. However, food and supply shortages will detain him there for another month.

June 24
South: Lieutenant Colonel John Maitland retreats from Stono Ferry, South Carolina, to Beaufort on Port Royal Island, and establishes another fortified strongpoint.

June 28
South: Militia under Colonel John Twiggs attack a company of British grenadiers at Hickory Hill, Georgia, killing eight, wounding nine, and taking 28 prisoners.

June 30
North: General James Clinton assembles his small army and supplies at Otsego Lake prior to rendezvousing with the main American army under General John Sullivan.
Naval: A French fleet of 25 ships of the line, 12 frigates, and 5,000 troops under Admiral Charles-Hector-Théodat, comte d'Estaing, hoists anchor at Fort Royal, Martinique, and sails for Barbados. Shortly after, adverse winds force him to change his destination to Grenada.

July 1
South: Virginia's governor Thomas Jefferson orders all Loyalist inhabitants to be processed for deportation.

July 2
North: Captain Allan McLane ably reconnoiters Stony Point, New York, under a flag of truce, and his report convinces General George Washington that it is vulnerable to a daring night assault. To facilitate the task, General Anthony Wayne receives command of the elite Light Infantry Regiment.

A column of 360 soldiers and 70 dragoons under Lieutenant Colonel Banastre Tarleton marches to Poundridge, New York, intent upon dislodging the American garrison. He attacks and drives off 90 troopers of the 2nd Continental Dragoons under Colonel Elisha Sheldon. However, once American militia begin firing from behind fences and buildings, Sheldon rallies his men and counterattacks. Tarleton then withdraws in good order, having sustained two casualties and inflicted 10.

July 3
North: Governor William Tryon amasses 2,500 picked Hessian, British, and Loyalist troops at Whitestone, New York, for a punitive expedition into Connecticut.
Caribbean: A French fleet under Admiral Charles-Hector-Théodat, comte d'Estaing, captures the West Indian island of Grenada, taking 159 British soldiers and 300 militia captive, along with 30 merchant ships.

July 5
North: A raiding party of 2,500 men under Governor William Tryon anchors in New Haven Harbor and lands in the face of resistance from General Andrew Ward and four militia regiments. The defenders are scattered with a loss of 23 killed, 15 wounded, and 12 captured, while Tryon loses 12 killed, 43 wounded, and 25 missing. Vengeful British troops plunder the town before withdrawing with 40 prisoners.

July 6
North: General George Washington personally reconnoiters the British fortifications at Stony Point, New York, and remains convinced they can be taken by assault.
Naval: French and British naval forces under Admirals Charles-Hector-Théodat, comte d'Estaing, and John Byron clash off the Caribbean island of Grenada. Byron, saddled with faulty intelligence, attacks his adversary with 21 ships of the line under the mistaken belief that the French possess only 16. In fact, d'Estaing possesses 25 vessels and they riddle the four vessels comprising the British van, disabling them. Byron is on the point of being overpowered when his rearmost vessels come up and save him. D'Estaing, however, declines to press his advantage and withdraws back to St. George's Bay. Byron's fleet, badly damaged, limps home to St. Kitts. The British sustain losses of 183 killed and 346 wounded to a French tally of 190 dead and 759 wounded; Grenada remains in French hands.

July 7
Naval: Lieutenant Colonel Silas Talbot, commanding the 12-gun sloop *Argo*, captures the British privateer *Lively* after a five-hour battle. Two British merchants vessels are subsequently taken shortly after.

July 8
North: Governor William Tryon lays waste to the coastal town of Fairfield, Connecticut, burning 83 houses and 100 barns, churches, and schools. The local militia stands briefly before retreating. Tryon reports nine killed, 30 wounded, and five missing. American losses are nine dead.

July 9
Politics: The Continental Congress, eager to end waste and profligacy in military procurement, urges the states to investigate all persons associated with supply departments and prosecute those guilty of misdeeds at government expense.
North: British raiders burn and loot Green Farms, Connecticut, before advancing upon Norwalk.
South: Don Bernardo de Gálvez, governor of Louisiana and Florida, is authorized by the Spanish government to capture British possessions up the Mississippi River and along the Gulf of Mexico.

July 11
North: British forces descend upon Norwalk, Connecticut, and proceed to burn 130 houses, 100 barns, and several vessels. An attempted stand by 50 militia is brushed aside and the Americans lose four killed and seven wounded. Governor William Tryon then embarks and returns to New York.

July 15
North: The British stronghold at Stony Point, New York, garrisoned by 600 men under Lieutenant Colonel Henry Johnson, 17th Regiment, succumbs to a brilliant night attack by General Anthony Wayne. The 1,350 Americans attack in two columns, with the left under Colonel Richard Butler, the right under Wayne, and a third column under Major Hardy Murfee mounting a diversion in the center. Taking a page

from his own bitter experience at Paoli, Wayne orders his men to remove all musket flints and to trust in cold steel. A moonless night and the lack of British patrols allow the Americans to approach undetected until the last few yards, when they began chopping through the abatis. Meanwhile, Murfee's diversion in the center induces Johnson to sortie six companies of infantry after him, emptying the fort of defenders. Wayne and Butler then scale the heights and storm the post after vicious hand-to-hand fighting. The first "American" in the fort proves to be Lieutenant Colonel François de Fleury, a French volunteer. Thus Stony Point, regarded by the British as "Little Gibraltar," falls in only 30 minutes at a cost of 63 killed, 70 wounded, and over 543 captured. Wayne's losses are 15 killed and 83 wounded.

July 17
NORTH: General George Washington inspects Stony Point, declares it impractical to defend, and orders it stripped and abandoned. General Henry Clinton, meanwhile, assembles an expedition to retake the fort.

July 18
NAVAL: While cruising in a fog off Newfoundland, Commodore Abraham Whipple's squadron, consisting of frigates *Providence* and *Queen of France,* and sloop *Ranger,* under Captain John P. Rathbun, finds itself in the midst of a 150-ship British convoy escorted by a 74-gun ship-of-the-line. Whipple, masquerading as a British warship, takes several unsuspecting vessels captive. Rathbun also successfully infiltrates the convoy and takes several prizes under the very noses of British cannon. The Americans seize a total of 11 vessels with cargos totaling $1 million and safely convey nine of their prizes back to Boston.

July 19
NORTH: Mohawks and Loyalists under Chief Joseph Brant attack the settlement of Minisink, New York, to gather food and booty. Their objective is to divert General James Clinton from joining an expedition into the Six Nations territory under General James Sullivan.
NAVAL: An amphibious expedition of 1,600 men, 19 armed vessels, and 24 transports leaves Boston for the Penobscot River under Commodore Dudley Saltonstall, assisted by Generals Solomon Lovell and Peleg Wadsworth of the Massachusetts militia. The celebrated rider, Colonel Paul Revere, commands the expedition's artillery. This sortie employs three Continental navy vessels and the entire Massachusetts state navy for a total of 344 guns. Furthermore, it is undertaken as a private venture, without notifying Congress.

July 22
NORTH: Militia forces under Colonel John Hawthorn and Lieutenant Colonel Benjamin Tusten pursue Chief Joseph Brant with 149 men. Despite signs that the raiding party is quite sizable, the vengeful soldiers insist upon pressing ahead. Brant spots his pursuers and doubles back to ambush them. While returning from the Delaware River at Port Jervis, New York, the Americans are successfully attacked by Brant and massacred. Only 30 survive.

July 24
NAVAL: The American expedition under Commodore Dudley Saltonstall arrives at Penobscot River, Massachusetts (Maine), and begins siege operations against British-held Fort George, a hastily constructed dirt fortification.

July 25
NAVAL: The squadron of Commodore Dudley Saltonstall timidly engages three British sloops under Captain Henry Mowat in Penobscot Bay and then retires. For the rest of the campaign, Saltonstall feels his square-rigged vessels cannot safely maneuver in the confined waters of the Bagaduce River, where they can easily be bombarded by British shore batteries.

July 26
POLITICS: The Continental Congress awards Lieutenant Colonel François de Fleury a silver medallion for conspicuous gallantry in the capture of Stony Point, New York. He is the first foreigner so honored.
NORTH: A party of 150 U.S. and Massachusetts marines under Captain John Welsh lands and charges British positions on Nautilus Island, Penobscot Bay, capturing four cannon. Colonel Paul Revere then plants several heavy guns and induces Captain Henry Mowat to relocate his three sloops farther up Penobscot Bay. The Americans lose three killed.

July 28
NORTH: General Solomon Lovell lands and prepares to attack the British at Penobscot. A stiff uphill fight ensues on the western face of the Bagaduce Peninsula, but the contingent of U.S. Marines drives the British up the slopes and back into Fort George. With the high ground secured, the attackers begin constructing siege batteries. The action costs the Americans 20 killed and 30 wounded, while the British lose 12 killed, eight wounded, and 10 captured. A small battery of three cannon is also seized.

July 30
WEST: A force of 240 Kentucky settlers under Colonel John Bowman attacks the Indian village of Chalahgawtha, Ohio, but is unable to dislodge 35 defenders in a fort. As the Americans withdraw they are pursed by the Indians, who persistently shoot down stragglers. An exasperated Bowman finally orders a charge upon the snipers, who return to their village after killing 30 militiamen and wounding 60.

July 31
NORTH: American leaders at Penobscot, Massachusetts (Maine), hold a war council to weigh objectives and options. General Solomon Lovell proposes that the fleet of Commodore Dudley Saltonstall attack and destroy three British sloops in the harbor. But, in a display of recalcitrance, Saltonstall withholds naval gunfire until after Fort George is taken. The impasse continues for several days as morale among American forces plummets.

General John Sullivan and 2,500 soldiers depart Wyoming, Pennsylvania, to commence punitive operations in central and western New York against Six Nation

Indian villages. His force includes the cream of the army, including the battle-hardened brigades under Generals Enoch Poor and William Maxwell.

August 2
NAVAL: An American squadron consisting of frigates *Deane* under Captain James Nicholson and *Boston* under Captain Samuel Tucker, in concert with the sloop *Thorn*, depart Chesapeake Bay on a cruise that seizes eight prizes.

August 3
DIPLOMACY: The French minister, Chevalier Anne-César de La Luzerne, arrives at Boston with John Adams and is lodged in the home of John Hancock.
NAVAL: Commodore George Collier sails from New York with a small fleet and 1,500 soldiers, intending to aid the defenders of Penobscot Bay.

August 5
NORTH: American cavalry under General John Glover attack and defeat Loyalists under Oliver De Lancey at Morrisania (Bronx), New York, taking 15 prisoners. While returning they are engaged by British cavalry under Lieutenant Colonel John Graves Simcoe, losing two killed and two wounded.

August 7
NORTH: American forces at Penobscot, Massachusetts (Maine), hold another war council but General Solomon Lovell and Commodore Dudley Saltonstall remain at loggerheads over the issue of cooperation. They agree simply to petition Boston for additional reinforcements.
NAVAL: Lieutenant Colonel Silas Talbot and the 12-gun sloop *Argo* engage the 14-gun Loyalist privateer *Dragon* under Captain Stanton Hazard off Rhode Island. A stiff four-hour battle ensues until Talbot's antagonist's mainmast topples and she strikes. Shortly afterward the British privateer brig *Hannah* hoves into view, which Talbot promptly attacks and captures with the help of the American vessel *Macaroni*.

August 9
NORTH: General James Clinton departs Lake Otsego, New York, and marches for Tioga to join the main American force under General John Sullivan.

August 11
NORTH: General Solomon Lovell directs 250 Massachusetts militiamen under his command to occupy an abandoned British battery to lure British defenders out from Fort George, Pensobscot, Maine, into an ambush. The British respond by dispatching 55 soldiers who charge upon the defenders, routing them.
WEST: Colonel Daniel Brodhead and 600 militiamen depart Pittsburgh and march up the Allegheny River to attack Indian villages in northern Pennsylvania. Meanwhile, General John Sullivan's main body marches into Tioga to join elements arriving there under General James Clinton.

August 12
NORTH: American forces at Penobscot, Massachusetts (Maine), receive positive instructions from the Massachusetts War Board in Boston directing Commodore

Dudley Saltonstall to attack and sink three British sloops anchored in the harbor. The Americans then prepare to make an all-out assault against Fort George.

August 13
NAVAL: Commodore George Collier enters the Penobscot River with 10 vessels and 1,600 soldiers, breaking the blockade there. Commodore Dudley Saltonstall unceremoniously flees upriver and burns all his ships. Within three days Collier has eliminated the entire squadron of 43 vessels and inflicted 474 casualties for a loss of 13 men. Damage to Massachusetts alone is estimated at $8 million. This proves the largest American naval defeat of the war.

Commodore John Paul Jones, commanding *Bonhomme Richard*, departs L'Orient, France, accompanied by the frigates *Alliance* and *Pallas*, the brig *Vengeance*, and the cutter *Le Cerf*. Jones intends to raid British home waters.

August 15
WEST: American frontiersmen under Captain Samuel Brady lead the advance of Colonel Daniel Brodhead's punitive expedition against the tribes of western Pennsylvania. They then manage to ambush a war party of 40 Indians under Chief Bald Eagle on the Upper Allegheny River, killing the chief and several warriors without loss.

August 16
NAVAL: An amphibious expedition of 4,000 men under Admiral Charles-Hector-Théodat, comte d'Estaing, sails from Le Cap-François, St-Domingue (Haiti), bound for Savannah, Georgia.

August 17
DIPLOMACY: The Continental Congress promulgates minimum terms for negotiating peace with Great Britain and demands independence, definite boundaries, British evacuation of American territory, and navigation rights on the Mississippi River.

SOUTH: Don Bernardo de Gálvez of Louisiana departs New Orleans with several hundred Acadian militiamen, African-American volunteers, and pro-Spanish Choctaw Indians on an expedition against Fort Bute (Manchac) and Baton Rouge, Louisiana.

August 19
NORTH: Major Henry Lee deploys 300 Virginia and Maryland troops to attack Paulus Hook, the last remaining British outpost in New Jersey. It is defended by 350 British, Hessians, and Loyalists under Major William Sutherland. Lee carefully reconnoiters his objective with the help of the noted scout, Captain Allan McLane, and detaches 200 men from his 2nd Partisan Corps for the task. His men are then divided into three groups but, en route, roughly half become lost in the dark and the attack is delayed four hours. The British sentries are alert that night and fire upon the approaching column, but Lee manages to get his men across the ditch, over the palisade, through an abatis, and into the fort. The ensuing bayonet attack succeeds in overrunning the garrison save for about 50 Hessians in a blockhouse, who refuse

to surrender. Lee then withdraws, prisoners in tow, and is closely pursued by Loyalists under Colonel Abraham Van Buskirk. His retreat is endangered when boats expected to ferry them across the Hackensack River do not materialize, which adds another 14 miles to the march. The Loyalists overtake Lee at Liberty Pole Tavern but are driven off by fresh troops directed there by General William Alexander. This sharp little action costs the British 58 killed and 150 captured in exchange for two killed, three wounded, and seven captured. The Continental Congress subsequently orders a special medal struck for Lee.

General James Clinton and his 1,500 men reinforce the main army of General John Sullivan at Tioga, Pennsylvania. Their combined expedition has been long-delayed by supply shortages.

August 25
NAVAL: Admiral Marriot Arbuthnot drops anchor in New York and succeeds Admiral John Byron as commander of naval forces. He also brings with him 3,000 soldiers as a reinforcement for General Henry Clinton.

August 26
NORTH: Generals John Sullivan and James Clinton depart Tioga and begin marching up the Chemung River into Six Nation territory.

August 29
NORTH: Generals John Sullivan and James Clinton, mustering 4,000 men, attack and defeat 1,200 Loyalists and Indians under Captain Walter Butler and Chief Joseph Brant at Newtown (Elmira), New York. The Americans proceed straight into an ambush until General Enoch Poor manages to circle behind the defenders and sends them scampering into the woods. Sullivan loses three killed and 33 wounded, while the British lose five killed and 36 wounded; Indian losses are unknown but probably heavy. No prisoners are taken by either side.

September 1
POLITICS: In a rare moment of fiscal sobriety, the Continental Congress resolves not to issue $200 million in bills of credit. This is done in face of the spiraling depreciation of paper currency.

September 3
POLITICS: The Continental Congress reverses itself and resolves not to issue further bills of credit under any circumstances.
NAVAL: John Paul Jones and his squadron sail along the western coast of Great Britain intent upon raiding the port cities of Leith, Edinburgh, and Newcastle-upon-Tyne.

September 4
NORTH: General John Sullivan directs the burning of Catherine's Town, New York, and resumes marching toward Kindaia.

September 5
NORTH: General John Sullivan attacks and burns the Seneca village of Kindaia, New York.

Major Benjamin Tallmadge and 150 dismounted dragoons debark from Shippan Point, Connecticut, cross Long Island Sound, and surprise 500 Loyalists at Lloyd Neck, New York. The bulk are captured and Tallmadge returns to Shippan Point without loss.

September 7
NORTH: General John Sullivan advances upon the Seneca village of Kanadaseagea, New York, burning it.
SOUTH: The British outpost of Fort Bute (Manchac), Louisiana, falls to Spanish forces under Don Bernardo de Gálvez. He now controls the water route down the Amite River and Lakes Maurepas, Ponchartrain, and Borgne directly to the Gulf of Mexico. The Don proceeds next against Baton Rouge.

September 10
NORTH: General John Sullivan's expedition reaches the major Iroquois settlement at Canandaigua, New York, and the ensuing destruction consumes two days.

September 11
NAVAL: A French force under Admiral Charles-Hector-Théodat, comte d'Estaing, approaches Savannah, Georgia, with 22 ships of the line, 10 frigates, and 3,900 men. He begins landing his men at Beaulieu's Plantation, eight miles south of the city, and initially works in concert with a small detachment of American forces under General Kazimierz Pulaski.

September 12
SOUTH: Don Bernardo de Gálvez, with 1,000 men and 13 cannon, surrounds and invests a 300-man British garrison under Colonel Alexander Dickson. The Spanish begin an immediate bombardment and commence digging siege trenches.

September 13
POLITICS: President of the Continental Congress John Jay asks states to levy taxes for funding the national treasury.
NORTH: Indians and Loyalists under Captain Walter Butler ambush a militia detachment under Lieutenant Thomas Boyd near the Indian village of Geneseo, New York, killing 22 men and torturing two prisoners to death. American forces burn the entire village shortly after.

September 14
NORTH: The punitive expedition under General John Sullivan lays waste to the Indian capital of Genesee, New York, burning 40 Seneca and Cayuga villages en route. However, he fails to press his attack against Fort Niagara, an important Loyalist entrepot and staging area for raiding activities. This allows British and Indian partisans to regroup.
WEST: Colonel Daniel Brodhead concludes his 400-mile raid against Indian villages and returns to Pittsburgh.
NAVAL: Captain John Paul Jones sorties from L'Orient, France, in the frigate *Bonhomme Richard,* accompanied by four French vessels.

September 16
SOUTH: General Benjamin Lincoln marches down from Charleston and arrives at Savannah with 1,500 troops to assist siege efforts there. Admiral Charles-Hector-Théodat, comte d'Estaing, demands General Augustin Prevost's surrender in the name of King Louis XVI but subsequently grants the British a 24-hour truce to consider terms. Prevost uses the time to bring up 800 reinforcements under Lieutenant Colonel John Maitland and otherwise strengthen his defenses.

September 17
NAVAL: Lieutenant Colonel Silas Talbot resigns from the Continental army and becomes a captain in the Continental navy. He remains the only military officer so commissioned.

September 21
DIPLOMACY: Chevalier de La Luzerne presents his credentials in Philadelphia as the new French minister to the United States.
SOUTH: Spanish forces under Don Bernardo de Gálvez attack and capture Baton Rouge, West Florida, along with 375 British prisoners under Lieutenant Colonel Alexander Dickson. Spanish control now extends to Natchez and other points along the Mississippi River.

September 22
NAVAL: Captain John Paul Jones captures two British ships off Flamborough Head and espies a large convoy anchored at the mouth of the Humber River.

September 23
SOUTH: French and American troops begin digging trenches outside Savannah, although allied officers begin quarreling among themselves. The fast approaching onset of the hurricane season also necessitates a removal of the French fleet to safer waters.
NAVAL: Captain John Paul Jones, commanding the 42-gun *Bonhomme Richard* and sailing off the British coast near Flamborough Head, encounters a 40-ship convoy escorted by two British warships: the new, copper-bottomed 44-gun frigate HMS *Serapis* under Captain Richard Pearson and the 20-gun sloop *Countess of Scarborough*. The Americans are assisted by the smaller French vessels, *Vengeance, Pallas,* and *Alliance.* Pearson orders the convoy into port and bravely places his ship between them and the enemy squadron. It is late in the evening before Jones can close with his quarry and a desperate engagement commences. Creaky *Bonhomme Richard* and the smartly handled *Serapis* trade broadsides for several hours in the moonlight, with the American getting the worst of it. Suddenly, Pearson loses the headwind while attempting to rake and Jones rams his stern. The two vessels then snare each other's rigging, and fighting continues at close quarters for two more hours. Finally, a grenade is dropped down a hatch on the *Serapis* by Lieutenant Nathaniel Fanning, which ignites an ammunition chest and convinces Pearson to strike. The British colors are lowered by Lieutenant Richard Dale. American casualties total 150 out of 237 present; the British sustain 170. The *Countess of Scarborough* surrenders to the French 10 minutes later, but *Bonhomme Richard* is so riddled that it sinks two days later.

September 24
SOUTH: British forces defending Savannah, Georgia, launch a determined sortie against French siege positions, losing four killed and 15 wounded but inflicting at least 70 casualties.

September 27
DIPLOMACY: The Continental Congress authorizes John Adams to negotiate peace with the British in Paris. John Jay also becomes minister to Spain with authority to negotiate treaties of alliance and commerce.

September 28
POLITICS: The Continental Congress elects Samuel Huntington to succeed John Jay as president.

September 30
NORTH: General John Sullivan marches 4,000 men back to Fort Sullivan, Pennsylvania, concluding his long raid against the Indian heartland. In four months he has torched over 40 villages and 160,000 bushels of corn, dislocating the Iroquois nation and forcing it to spend the ensuing months half-starved and exposed to the ravages of winter.
SOUTH: The British garrison at Natchez, Louisiana territory, falls to the Spanish forces of Don Bernardo de Gálvez.

October 2
POLITICS: The Continental Congress mandates that blue cloth will replace green and brown as the official color of the Continental army uniform.

October 3
NAVAL: The squadron of John Paul Jones reaches Texel, Holland, skillfully evading pursuit by eight British warships.

October 4
WEST: Indian forces under Simon Girty ambush Colonel David Rogers at the confluence of the Licking and Ohio Rivers, killing 57 men out of 70. They also capture a shipment of 600,000 Spanish dollars destined for New Orleans.
SOUTH: American and French leaders reject a truce by General Augustin Prevost so that he can allow women and children in Savannah to escape. That day the allied siege canons begin a steady but ineffectual bombardment of British defensive works.

October 8
SOUTH: The allied siege of Savannah, Georgia, progresses steadily, but Admiral Charles-Hector-Théodat, comte d'Estaing, grows impatient and wishes to settle matters by a *coup de main*. General Benjamin Lincoln initially demurs, but plans are drawn up to have militia forces under General Isaac Huger feint across the line while the main allied column of 4,000 men attacks the Spring Hill redoubt. Unfortunately, General Augustin Prevost has been informed of allied plans by a deserter and positions his best troops there to receive the impending attack.

October 9
SOUTH: At dawn Franco-American forces under Admiral d'Estaing and General Benjamin Lincoln storm the British fieldworks surrounding Savannah, Georgia. The expected diversion by militia under General Isaac Huger fails to materialize when they get lost in a swamp, as do three out of four allied assault columns. The only force to proceed, 1,200 French infantry and Continentals under General Lachlan McIntosh and Colonel John Laurens, charges repeatedly against the prepared works and is handily repulsed. A detachment under Colonel Francis Marion manages to scale the glacis and mount the parapet before being driven back. General Kazimierz Pulaski then leads an ill-advised cavalry charge against British artillery and is mortally wounded. D'Estaing himself is hit twice, rallying his men and leading them back into the fray before the effort finally collapses. Allied losses are 244 killed and 584 wounded, with a further 120 captured. The British under General Augustin Prevost lose only 155 killed and wounded. The French-American alliance sustains another tremendous blow.

October 11
NORTH: General Henry Clinton orders Newport, Rhode Island, abandoned and the 3,000-man garrison withdrawn to support operations down south.

October 17
NORTH: General George Washington directs the Continental army to begin taking up quarters at Morristown, New Jersey.

October 19
NAVAL: The French squadron under Admiral d'Estaing sails from the Georgia coast and makes for the West Indies to avoid the hurricane season.

October 21
DIPLOMACY: The Continental Congress elects Henry Laurens to serve as agent to the Netherlands and to negotiate a loan and treaties of amity and commerce.

October 22
NORTH: The New York Provincial Congress approves an ordnance authorizing confiscation of Loyalist property and also declaring former governors Lord Dunmore and William Tryon public enemies.

October 25
NORTH: The British withdraw their 3,000-man garrison from Newport, Rhode Island, to bolster the southern war effort.

A British raiding party storms Van Vechten's Bridge, New Jersey, burning several boats intended for the American army. While withdrawing they also seize the town of Hillsborough, freeing several Loyalist prisoners and burning Somerset Courthouse. They then escape, pursued by local militia.

October 26
NORTH: Lieutenant Colonel John Graves Simcoe is captured in an American ambush at South River Bridge, New Jersey. The Americans lose one killed and three wounded, while the Queen's Rangers sustain three killed and six captured.

October 28
Politics: The Continental Congress replaces the Marine Committee with the five-man Board of the Admiralty and empowers it to oversee naval matters.
South: General Benjamin Lincoln lifts the siege of Savannah and retrogrades to Charleston, South Carolina.

November 7
North: Colonel Charles-Armand, marquis de Rouerie, succeeds the fallen Kazimierz Pulaski as head of the Pulaski Legion. In this capacity he captures a small Loyalist detachment under Major Mansfield Bearmore at Jefferd's Neck, New York.

November 20
Naval: A squadron under Commodore Abraham Whipple, consisting of the frigates *Boston, Providence,* and *Queen of France,* and sloop *Ranger,* is dispatched to aid in the defense of Charleston, South Carolina.

November 25
Politics: Despite a torrent of criticism for failures in America and accusations by Charles James Fox that the king is abusing ministerial authority, the administration of Lord North survives a vote of no confidence in Parliament.

November 29
Politics: The year's final issue of $10 million in paper money is passed by the Continental Congress, bringing the total amount dispensed to $242 million.

December 1
North: General George Washington leads 12,000 troops into quarters at Morristown, New Jersey. It proves another harsh winter of deprivation, and the force will be plagued by desertion, mutiny, and low morale.

December 23
North: The court-martial of General Benedict Arnold convenes in Philadelphia, although he is charged with relatively minor offenses.
Naval: Admiral George Rodney sails from Portsmouth with 22 ships of the line and eight frigates. His mission is to convoy 300 transports to relieve the garrison at Gibraltar.

December 26
North: General Henry Clinton embarks from New York with the fleet of Admiral Marriot Arbuthnot—8,700 men on board 90 transports and 10 warships. He is destined for Charleston, South Carolina, which decisively shifts the focus of war southward. Clinton places a 10,000-man garrison under General Wilhelm von Knyphausen to secure New York in his absence, the first time a foreign officer has been entrusted with such an important command.

December 31
Naval: By year's end, the Americans have lost 269 vessels while capturing 516.

1780

January 1
NORTH: A mutiny occurs at the West Point garrison, and 100 members of a Massachusetts regiment are allowed to depart. They are subsequently brought back, pardoned, and allowed to rejoin the army.
SOUTH: American guerrillas begin an ongoing campaign against British outposts in the vicinity of Augusta, Georgia.

January 2
NORTH: The Continental army at Morristown endures extreme hardships at its winter encampment, owing to extremely low temperatures and a lack of blankets, shelter, and clothing.

January 8
NAVAL: Captain John Barry sails with the 32-gun frigate *Alliance* on an Atlantic cruise that nets three merchantmen.

Admiral George Rodney encounters a Spanish convoy of 20 ships under Commodore Don Juan di Yardi and south of Cape Finisterre. He attacks, capturing several transports and a 64-gun ship of the line.

January 9
NORTH: General George Washington appeals to states bordering New Jersey to help provide his shivering, hungry troops at Morristown with food and clothing.

January 10
NORTH: General Charles Lee writes an offensive letter to the Continental Congress and is summarily dismissed from the service; he retires to his estate and plays no further role in the war.

January 15
NORTH: Braving frigid weather, General William Alexander marches 2,500 men from Elizabeth Point, New Jersey, across the channel ice on sleighs against Staten Island. The British are alerted as to his movement, however, and retire behind prepared fortifications that the Americans were unaware of. After a day of plundering and fruitless maneuvering, Alexander returns to New Jersey after taking 17 prisoners and losing three killed.

January 16
NAVAL: A British fleet of 22 ships of the line and 14 frigates under Admiral George Rodney intercepts a Spanish squadron of 11 warships off Cape St. Vincent under Admiral Juan de Langara. Despite near-gale conditions, Rodney—ill with gout and confined to bed—eagerly closes with his outnumbered opponent and signals a general chase. The ensuing "Moonlight Battle" proves a rout and the British capture five new ships of the line. Another Spanish vessel sinks with a loss of 600 lives. Rodney's convoy then successfully reaches Gibraltar.

January 18
NORTH: An American raiding party under Captain Samuel Lockwood captures a Loyalist colonel, Isaac Hatfield, at Eastchester, New York, only to be dispersed by pursuing cavalry. The Americans end up losing 23 killed and 40 captured.

January 21
NORTH: American militia under General Samuel H. Parsons repel an attack by Loyalists under Lieutenant Colonel James de Lancey at West Greenwich, New York, killing 16, wounding 32, and capturing 17.

January 25
NORTH: British forces retaliate for the Staten Island raid by seizing and burning parts of Newark and Elizabethtown, New Jersey.

January 26
NORTH: General Benedict Arnold, court-martialed for financial speculation and malfeasance while commanding Philadelphia, is found guilty on two minor specifications. He is then mildly reprimanded by General George Washington—and indignantly fumes over the sentence.

January 27
NORTH: To alleviate the suffering of his troops, General George Washington drastically overhauls supply procedures in New Jersey, dividing that state into 11 districts and requisitioning specific food allotments from each. The scheme works well, and the influx of food improves the health and morale of the troops

January 28
WEST: Fort Nashborough (Nashville) is founded on the Cumberland River to secure the Tennessee and North Carolina region from Indian raids.

February 1
SOUTH: A British amphibious force of 14,000 men under Admiral Marriot Arbuthnot and General Henry Clinton arrives at Tybee Island, off Savannah, Georgia, for a brief rest and refit. Meanwhile, the American garrison at Charleston, South Carolina, musters only 3,200 men under General Benjamin Lincoln. He desires to retreat but is pressured by Governor John Rutledge and city officials to remain.

February 3
NORTH: A British/German force of 550 men under Lieutenant Colonel Chapple Norton departs Fort Knyphausen (Fort Washington), New York, and advances against an American outpost at nearby Mt. Pleasant. His target is 450 Continentals of the 10th Massachusetts under Lieutenant Colonel Joseph Thompson, billeted in and around Young's House. Norton gains their rear and defeats them with losses of 14 killed, 37 wounded, and 76 captured. The British sustain five killed and 18 wounded.

February 9
POLITICS: The Continental Congress suggests that the states draft an additional 35,000 men for the army, as well as monthly contributions of $1.2 million to the

national treasury. The states are bedeviled by ongoing financial crises of their own and are loath to scarf up more money for the war effort.

South: The Spanish expedition of Don Bernardo de Gálvez reaches Mobile Bay, where he disembarks 750 soldiers. Lieutenant Governor Elias Durnford elects to defend Fort Charlotte, an old brick fortification, and await reinforcements.

February 10
South: The combined expeditionary force under Admiral Marriot Arbuthnot and General Henry Clinton drops anchor off Charleston, South Carolina.

Spanish forces under Don Bernardo de Gálvez invest the British outpost at Mobile, West Florida.

February 11
South: The combined forces of Admiral Marriot Arbuthnot and General Henry Clinton enter North Edisto Inlet and land troops on John's Island. This places the enemy only 30 miles south of Charleston, but the Americans under General Benjamin Lincoln make no effort to interfere.

February 14
South: General Henry Clinton occupies Stono Ferry and James Island near Charleston in order to entrap the American garrison within their works. General Benjamin Lincoln, meanwhile, continues strengthening his fortifications.

February 23
South: The British Legion under Lieutenant Colonel Banastre Tarleton overruns a patrol of South Carolina militia near Charleston, killing 10 and capturing 14.

February 24
South: Colonel William Washington's cavalry engages and repels mounted troops under Lieutenant Colonel Banastre Tarleton along the Ashley River, North Carolina. The Americans subsequently withdraw to Monck's Corner.

February 28
Diplomacy: Czarina Catherine II of Russia founds the League of Armed Neutrality in concert with Sweden and Denmark. It aims to protect neutral commerce against all belligerents, a stance that further weakens British efforts to cut international trade to the colonies. The league is ultimately joined by the Netherlands, the Holy Roman Empire, Prussia, Portugal, and the Kingdom of the Two Sicilies.

March 1
North: In an attempt to eliminate slavery gradually, the Pennsylvania assembly emancipates all African-American children born after 1780. This is the first abolitionist ordinance in America.

March 3
South: General Benjamin Lincoln, commanding the American garrison at Charleston, is reinforced by the arrival of 700 Continental soldiers from North Carolina. However, militiamen continue streaming out of the city.

March 5
South: Governor John Rutledge enlists the labor of 600 slaves to construct earthen defenses at Charleston, including a stonework redoubt dubbed "The Citadel," the future site of a military academy.

March 8
South: General James Patterson captures an American detachment under Lieutenant James Ladon at Salkehatchie, South Carolina.

March 14
South: Don Bernardo de Gálvez and 1,400 men attack Fort Charlotte (Mobile), the capital of British West Florida. Two days later the 300-man garrison under Lieutenant Governor Elias Durnford surrenders after a relief column from Pensacola fails to materialize in time. The Spanish, while losing eight killed and 12 wounded, have been assisted by the American sloop *West Florida* under Captain William Pickles.

March 18
Politics: The Continental Congress authorizes the Forty to One Act, through which Continental paper money will be redeemed at one-fortieth of its face value. This move is calculated to bring a halt to spiraling inflation.

March 20
South: Commodore Abraham Whipple, commanding naval units at Charleston, withdraws his small fleet up the Cooper River and sinks several as hulks to obstruct British vessels. Admiral Marriot Arbuthnot, meanwhile, begins maneuvering his fleet into bombardment positions off the coast by slipping five frigates over the sandbar.
Naval: A British squadron of three ships of the line under Captain William Cornwallis engages a large French convoy under Commodore Jean, comte de La Motte-Picquet, off Monte Christi, San Domingo. An indecisive, running battle with four French ships of the line ensues until Cornwallis receives reinforcements. The French then withdraw intact.

March 22
North: General Wilhelm von Knyphausen, commanding the New York garrison, leads a small raid against Hackensack, New Jersey, to obtain supplies. He returns without incident.
Naval: Admiral Luc Urbain, comte de Guichen, arrives at Fort Royal, Martinique, with 16 French ships of the line and a large convoy of transports.

March 23
North: A British raiding party of 600 men under Lieutenant Colonels John Howard and Duncan McPherson rout a detachment of 250 men from the 5th Pennsylvania Regiment under Major Christopher Stuart, wounding two and seizing 65 captives at a cost of 10 killed, 18 wounded, and 30 missing.
South: Cavalry forces of Colonel William Washington and Lieutenant Colonel Banastre Tarleton clash indecisively at Pon Pon, South Carolina; the Americans incur 10 casualties.

March 25
SOUTH: General Henry Clinton's army is augmented by the arrival of Major Patrick Ferguson and his American Rangers.

March 26
SOUTH: Colonel William Washington bests Lieutenant Colonel Banastre Tarleton in fighting at Rantowles, South Carolina, taking seven prisoners.

March 29
SOUTH: General Henry Clinton marches 7,000 men across the Ashley River and commences the siege of Charleston, South Carolina. With British troops positioned across the neck of Charleston peninsula, the American garrison under General Benjamin Lincoln is effectively sealed off.

April 1
SOUTH: The British make good progress in their siege and break a parallel trench within 800 yards of Charleston's defenses.

April 2
NORTH: Indians and Loyalists under Chief Joseph Brant strike Harpersfield, New York, killing several and taking 19 prisoners.

April 3
NORTH: General George Washington orders General Johann de Kalb to Charleston, South Carolina, with a small brigade of Maryland and Delaware Continentals.

April 6
SOUTH: By dint of hard slogging, General William Woodford evades British forces and slips into Charleston, South Carolina, with 750 Virginia Continentals.

April 8
SOUTH: Admiral Marriot Arbuthnot runs seven frigates and several transports past the guns of Fort Moultrie, anchoring in the harbor and further tightening the noose around Charleston, South Carolina.

April 9
WEST: American and Spanish traders are attacked by British Indians at Little Maquoketa River, Iowa.

April 10
SOUTH: Regardless of the mounting danger, General Benjamin Lincoln declines escaping from Charleston by crossing Biggin Bridge over the Cooper River. Once the first series of parallel trenches is completed, General Henry Clinton calls upon the Americans to surrender. Lincoln refuses.

April 13
SOUTH: British artillery and warships commence a month-long bombardment of Charleston, South Carolina.
NAVAL: A French fleet of 23 ships of the line and five frigates escorts a large convoy from Fort Royal, Martinique, under Admiral Luc Urbain, comte de Guichen.

He has on board 3,000 troops and intends to capture the British-held island of Barbados.

April 14
SOUTH: Although Charleston is closely besieged, there remains an obscure, viable escape route across the Cooper River leading to Monck's Corner, 30 miles distant. It is garrisoned by a force of 500 militia and cavalry under General Isaac Huger, who also guards a large train of supplies intended for the city's defenders. However, a combined infantry/cavalry column of 1,400 men under Lieutenant Colonel Banastre Tarleton and Major Patrick Ferguson arrives outside the American camp around 3 A.M. Pressing forward, Tarleton surprises the American pickets and charges directly into Huger's camp. Ferguson then follows up with a savage bayonet attack and the defenders, who fail to make a coordinated stand, are completely routed. Huger and his second in command, Colonel William Washington, barely escape. The Americans suffer 14 dead, 13 wounded, and 67 captured to a British total of three wounded. Tarleton also seizes 200 horses as new mounts, along with 42 wagons of supplies. This victory closes the only remaining communications route out of Charleston.

April 15
NORTH: An American outpost under Lieutenant Samuel Bryson is overrun at New Bridge, New Jersey.

April 16
NORTH: A detachment of the 3rd Pennsylvania Regiment under Major Thomas L. Byles is captured by 300 Hessians under Colonel Johann Du Puy at Paramus, New Jersey. American losses are four killed, six wounded, and 40 captured.

April 17
NAVAL: A British fleet under Admiral George Rodney encounters French naval forces under Admiral Luc-Urbain, comte de Guichen, off Dominica. The two fleets are cruising north in parallel lines, and Rodney intends to fall upon Guichen's center and rear when the opportunity presents itself. However, the French admiral suddenly wears his fleet around and begins sailing south. Rodney does likewise and, sensing an advantage, orders his ships to close with the enemy's center and rear. Unfortunately, the English captains completely misinterpret this and, instead of concentrating their firepower against segments of the French fleet, simply engage in a traditional line action. A bloody, indecisive battle ensues before both fleets draw off. British losses are 120 killed and 354 wounded versus 222 killed and 537 wounded French. Barbados is spared an invasion, but Rodney angrily castigates subordinates for misunderstanding his instructions.

April 18
SOUTH: Lord Francis Rawdon delivers additional British reinforcements to Charleston, bringing besieging forces up to 10,000 combatants.

April 20
SOUTH: British trenches are scarcely 250 yards from Charleston, so General Benjamin Lincoln summons another war council. His officers ponder capitulation, but

Lieutenant Governor Christopher Gadsden urges them to fight on, threatening a civilian uprising if they surrender.

April 21
SOUTH: General Benjamin Lincoln parleys with General Henry Clinton and requests a surrender with honors of war, which is refused.

April 23–24
SOUTH: An American sortie by 200 Virginia troops storms the first line of British siege works at Charleston, South Carolina. They take 12 prisoners for the loss of three men but are too weak to inflict substantial damage.

April 25
SOUTH: British forces under General Henry Clinton commence a third series of parallel trenches only 30 yards from American lines at Charleston, South Carolina.

April 28
NORTH: The marquis de Lafayette returns to Boston after a year's absence, bearing commissions of lieutenant general and vice admiral for General George Washington.

A congressional committee comprised of Philip J. Schuyler, John Matthews, and Nathaniel Peabody calls upon General George Washington at his Morristown, New Jersey, headquarters.

May 5
SOUTH: American partisans capture 18 British soldiers after a brief skirmish at Wambaw, South Carolina.

May 6
SOUTH: Lieutenant Colonel Banastre Tarleton and 150 troopers from the British Legion pounce on 350 militiamen under Colonels Abraham Buford and William Washington at Lenud's Ferry, South Carolina. The Americans are in the act of uniting with a third force under Col. Anthony White when Tarleton suddenly appears, scattering all three. The British inflict 40 casualties and take 65 prisoners. The 18 British captives seized a day earlier are also freed.

May 7
SOUTH: Fort Moultrie, guarding the entrance to Charleston, South Carolina, surrenders to the British with a loss of 200 men. Sullivan's Island is occupied on the following morning.

May 11
SOUTH: British siege guns are so close to Charleston, South Carolina, that they begin firing hot shot directly into the town. The ferocity of the bombardment prompts the civilian authorities to ask General Benjamin Lincoln to capitulate rather then risk further destruction.

May 12
SOUTH: General Benjamin Lincoln surrenders 5,400 men, 6,000 muskets, and 400 cannon to General Henry Clinton at Charleston after a six-week siege. The militia are paroled and allowed to return home but the Continentals pass into

captivity. Commodore Abraham Whipple, the frigates *Providence, Boston,* and the sloop *Ranger* are also lost. In the course of the siege, Lincoln has sustained additional losses of 89 killed and 138 wounded. Clinton, who suffered only 76 killed and 189 wounded, prepares to return to New York. General Charles Cornwallis is appointed to theater commander in his absence. This is the biggest disaster to befall American arms in the war and the largest American capitulation until the fall of Bataan in 1942.

May 14
SOUTH: Colonel Abraham Buford retreats toward Hillsboro, being the last organized American force in all of South Carolina.

May 15
NAVAL: After several days of indecisive maneuvering, Admiral George Rodney and 21 ships of the line intercept Admiral Luc-Urbain, comte de Guichen, in the St. Lucia Channel. Variable winds prevent a full-scale engagement from developing and thus only the British van and French rear are able to close. The fleets then draw off and return to maneuvering. British losses are 21 killed and 100 wounded to a French total of 26 dead and 52 injured.

May 18
SOUTH: General Charles Cornwallis marches inland with 2,500 veteran troops to stamp out remaining resistance in South Carolina.

May 19
NAVAL: The fleets of Admirals George Rodney and Luc Urbain, comte de Guichen, spar for three hours off Martinique in another indecisive contest. The British lose ship of the line *Cornwallis,* along with 47 killed and 113 wounded, while French losses are recorded as 45 killed and 95 wounded.

May 21
NORTH: Sir John Johnson and Chief Joseph Brant lead a combined Loyalist/Indian force of 600 men that attacks settlements at Johnstown, New York, killing scores and taking 40 prisoners.

May 22
NORTH: Sir John Johnson sends half of his raiding force of 400 Loyalists and 200 Indians against the village of Caughnawaga, which is burned.

May 23
NORTH: Having pillaged their way through the Mohawk Valley, Loyalist and Indian raiders under Sir John Johnson attack and burn Johnstown, New York, and then retire unmolested.

May 25
NORTH: Two Connecticut regiments, subsisting on one-eighth of their assigned rations and being five months arrears in pay, mutiny at Morristown, New Jersey, and ignore appeals by Colonel Return J. Meigs. The rebellion is subsequently quelled by Pennsylvania troops without bloodshed, but the incident underscores the Continental Congress's inability to either fund or victual the army.

WEST: British captain Henry Bird departs Detroit at the head of 250 French militia and Lake Indians to attack the American garrison at the Falls of the Ohio River (Louisville). En route he will be joined by 700 additional warriors.

May 26
WEST: Captain Fernando de Leyba and the 310-man Spanish garrison at St. Louis (Missouri) repulse an attack by 300 British soldiers and 900 Indians under Captain Emmanuel Hesse.
NAVAL: Poet Philip Freneau is captured at sea when his vessel is accosted by the frigate HMS *Iris*.

May 27
SOUTH: General Charles Cornwallis, unable to overtake fleeing Americans with infantry, dispatches 170 cavalry and 100 mounted infantry under Lieutenant Colonel Banastre Tarleton ahead of the main column. His orders are to pursue and destroy Colonel Abraham Buford before he reaches the safety of North Carolina. Tarleton drives his men mercilessly over dusty roads and under a blazing sun, covering 105 miles in only two days and almost captures Governor John Rutledge.

May 29
SOUTH: British forces under Lieutenant Colonel Banastre Tarleton encounter an American force under Colonels Abraham Buford and William Washington at Waxhaws Creek, South Carolina. Buford, with 400 men of his 3rd Virginia Continentals, refuses an offer to surrender and draws his men up in a single line while his baggage train and artillery leave the field. Though outnumbered two-to-one, the British commander decides to attack the American left and center frontally while simultaneously turning their right. Buford erroneously instructs his men to withhold their fire until the British horsemen are at 10 paces; this enables Tarleton to reach the single row of infantry intact and crash through it. A wild melee ensues as the troopers begin sabering the fleeing survivors and Tarleton's horse is killed under him. The enraged British and Loyalists respond by bayoneting several prisoners before order is restored. Buford's unit ceases to exist, with losses of 113 killed, 150 wounded, and 203 captured. The heavy death toll will generate accusations of atrocity and the ominous charge of "Tarleton's Quarter" is now established. The British sustain three killed and 12 wounded, having crushed the last organized resistance in South Carolina.

Resurgent American militia disperse a Loyalist gathering at Winnsboro, South Carolina.

June 1
NAVAL: A bloody, drawn battle is waged north of Bermuda between the 28-gun frigate *Trumbull* under Captain James Nicholson and the 32-gun British privateer *Watt* under Captain John Coulthard. In one of the toughest fights of the war, Nicholson batters the British hull with several broadsides while Coulthard concentrates on the American masts and rigging. The combat ceases after several hours and both vessels limp home to safety. The Americans lose 17 killed and 31 wounded to a British total of 13 dead and 79 wounded.

June 3

SOUTH: A victorious General Henry Clinton proclaims to the residents of South Carolina that all men of military age must actively declare their allegiance to the Crown and enlist on its behalf or be considered rebels.

NAVAL: The American privateer *Pickering* under Captain Jonathan Haraden, cruising off the Spanish island of Bilbao, encounters an unidentified vessel in the darkness. This turns out to be the much larger 22-gun British privateer *Golden Eagle*, which is taken without a shot. Then while entering Bilbao Harbor, the *Pickering* is set upon by the even larger 42-gun privateer *Achilles.* Haraden, however, cleverly drops anchor near the shoals, forcing his antagonist to approach head-on under accurate cannon fire. At length *Achilles* is badly damaged and retreats while hundreds of milling Spaniards laud the victors.

June 6

NORTH: Encouraged by reports of extreme duress in the American camp at Morristown, General Wilhelm von Knyphausen sorties from New York with 6,000 men and advances into New Jersey.

June 7

POLITICS: Massachusetts installs the first state constitution ever ratified by a popular vote. It also contains a clearly prescribed Bill of Rights, which serves as a basis for outlawing slavery.

NORTH: Colonel Elias Dayton, with his 3rd New Jersey Regiment and some militia, engages 2,500 Hessians and British under General Wilhelm von Knyphausen at Connecticut Farms, New Jersey. The militia perform better than expected but are slowly driven back until reinforced by General William Maxwell's Continental brigade. Knyphausen, astounded by the sheer numbers of levies flocking onto the battlefield, assumes he cannot cross the Rahway River bridge and halts his advance. American casualties are recorded as 15 killed and 40 wounded; Hessian losses are unknown but British general Thomas Sterling is among the slain. Rather than retreat to New York, Knyphausen entrenches at De Hart's Point to maintain a presence in New Jersey.

June 8

SOUTH: Content with the progress of the war in the South, General Henry Clinton sails back to New York. The aggressive General Charles Cornwallis remains behind as theater commander.

June 9

WEST: British captain Henry Bird arrives at the Ohio River with 900 militia and Indians, but the natives refuse to proceed farther and attack Lousville. They persuade him to raid less-heavily defended settlements along the Licking River.

NAVAL: The 26-gun Massachusetts frigate *Proctector* under Captain John F. Williams engages and defeats the 32-gun privateer *Admiral Duff* under Captain Richard Stranger off Newfoundland. American losses are one killed and five wounded; only 55 British are saved after the prize suddenly explodes.

June 11
POLITICS: Massachusetts adopts a new constitution asserting that "all men are born free and equal," extending these principles by inference to African American slaves.

June 13
POLITICS: The Continental Congress appoints General Horatio Gates commander of the Southern Department—without informing or consulting General George Washington.
SOUTH: Colonel John Moore begins rallying 1,300 North Carolina Loyalists to support the royal cause at his home near Ramsour's Mill. He ultimately hopes to join and support the army of General Charles Cornwallis.

June 20
SOUTH: Colonel Francis Locke leads 1,200 American militia against a Loyalist force of comparable size under Colonel John Moore at Ramsour's Mill, North Carolina. The Loyalists deploy along the crest of a ridge with excellent fields of fire, but the Americans begin infiltrating through the nearby woods. A stiff fight ensues between poorly trained amateurs on either side, and a bloody impasse results until the Americans edge their way around Loyalist flanks. Moore's men are subsequently routed and he flees the field. Both sides suffer 150 casualties in this clumsily managed affair. However, the victory will further weaken British attempts to increase Loyalist support and discourage their participation.
NAVAL: British captain William Cornwallis and five ships of the line encounter a French force of seven warships under Commodore Charles-Louis, chevalier de Ternay, off Monte Christi, San Domingo. The French are escorting a convoy carrying troops destined for Rhode Island; Cornwallis attacks, damaging several vessels.

June 21
SOUTH: General Johann de Kalb arrives at Hillsboro, North Carolina, at the head of 1,400 Continentals under Colonels William Smallwood and Mordecai Gist. His appeals for food and supplies go ignored by the local populace.

June 22
WEST: A British/Indian expedition under Captain Henry Bird attacks Ruddle's Station, Kentucky, with 1,000 men, mostly Indians. A few shots from Bird's artillery convince the 300 settlers to surrender, but as soon as the gates are opened the warriors rush inside, massacring several.
NORTH: After enduring an exceptionally harsh winter, General George Washington moves the Continental army from Morristown, New Jersey.

June 23
NORTH: A combined British/Hessian expedition under General Wilhelm Knyphausen advances from Elizabethtown, New Jersey, and attacks American positions at Springfield. They immediately encounter stout resistance from New Jersey militia under General Philemon Dickinson at the bridge over Galloping Hill Road, which

further stiffens following the arrival of General William Maxwell's brigade. A determined frontal assault fails to dislodge the defenders, so Knyphausen resorts to an enveloping movement. When this maneuver also recoils, Knyphausen simply brings his superior numbers to bear against the regiments of Colonel Elias Dayton and Israel Angell, forcing them back from Springfield. Simultaneously, another British force hits Americans under Colonel Henry Lee defending the bridge over the Vauxhall Road. Again, British numbers prevail after hard fighting and General Nathanael Greene finally orders his men withdrawn to the safety of Short Hills. Though victorious, the extent of American resistence causes Knyphausen to question the sagacity of his offensive, and that evening he orders a retreat back to the coast. Vengeful New Jersey militia harass him every step of the way until the Hessians and British cross over to Staten Island. The defense of Springfield cost the Americans 13 killed, 49 wounded, and nine missing. British and Hessian losses are unrecorded but presumed in the vicinity of 300.

July 11
NORTH: A 5,500-man French army under General Jean-Baptiste, comte de Rochambeau, lands at Newport, Rhode Island, and finds the place nearly deserted by the Americans. General William Heath eventually arrives to welcome him.

July 12
SOUTH: An American militia force of 90 men under Colonels William Hill and Thomas Neal surprises and annihilates a 115-man detachment of the British Legion under Captain Christian Huck at Williamson's Plantation, South Carolina. The Loyalists, having pitched their camp between two rail fences, are unable to maneuver and are rapidly cut down; Huck is among the slain. The Americans inflict 90 men killed and wounded for the loss of one dead.

July 13
SOUTH: American militia under Colonels Elijah Clarke and John Thomas wipe out a Loyalist detachment at Cedar Springs, North Carolina, killing 35. American losses are four killed and 23 wounded.
NAVAL: A British fleet under Admiral Thomas Graves arrives off Sandy Hook, New York, to reinforce Admiral Marriot Arbuthnot.

July 16
NORTH: British and Indian raiders surprise Captain William Philips's ranger company at Fisher Summit, Bedford County, Pennsylvania, killing 10 and capturing their commander.

July 19
NAVAL: The British squadron under Admiral Marriot Arbuthnot anchors off Newport and blockades French vessels anchored there.

July 20
SOUTH: Partisans under Colonel William R. Davie defeat a larger Loyalist force under Major John Carden at Flat Rock, South Carolina.

July 21
NORTH: General Anthony Wayne is dispatched with 2,000 Pennsylvania Continentals to reduce a 70-man British stockade at Bull's Ferry, New Jersey. He bombards the enemy with four six-pounder cannon, which prove too light to inflict serious damage, and fails to evict the garrison. When word of approaching British reinforcements arrives, Wayne cancels the attack altogether and hastily falls back to Totowa. This unsuccessful affair costs the Americans 15 killed and 49 wounded while British losses total around 50.

July 25
SOUTH: General Horatio Gates assumes command of the Southern Department at Coxe's Mill, North Carolina, succeeding General Johann de Kalb, who reverts to commander of the Delaware and Maryland Continental brigade.

July 27
SOUTH: General Horatio Gates orders an advance against the important British supply depot at Camden, South Carolina. At this time he has only a brigade of Maryland and Delaware Continentals under General Mordecai Gist, and the mounted legion of Colonel Charles Armand. Moreover Gates, against the advice of his officers, deliberately chooses a barren, direct route to Camden rather than a circuitous one via Salisbury and Charlotte. The favored approach is 50 miles longer but would pass through a friendlier, well-stocked region. The path chosen is strongly Loyalist in tenor, barren, and poorly suited for victualing hungry troops.

July 30
SOUTH: An 600-man militia force under Colonels Isaac Shelby, Elijah Clarke, and Charles McDowell convinces Colonel Patrick Moore and the Loyalist garrison of Thickety Fort (Fort Anderson), South Carolina, to surrender without a fight. The militia seizes 93 captives.

August 1
NORTH: Chief Joseph Brant and his Indians raid the settlements at Canajoharie, New York, killing 15, capturing 50, and burning 53 buildings. But he declines to attack Fort Plank, then occupied by a regiment commanded by Colonel Peter Gansevoort, and withdraws with his booty and captives.
SOUTH: General Thomas Sumter and 600 militia unsuccessfully besiege a Loyalist outpost at Rocky Mount, South Carolina. Lacking artillery, Colonel Thomas Neal charges but fails to dislodge 150 defenders under Lieutenant Colonel George Turnbull. The Americans withdraw after a severe fight and losses of about 12 men apiece.

American militia under Colonel Elijah Clarke engage a Loyalist force of 210 men at Green Springs, South Carolina. The British have been dispatched by Major Patrick Ferguson to hunt down and capture Clarke, who routs them in a sharp engagement lasting 15 minutes. Both sides lose roughly 30 men apiece, although the British dead are abandoned on the ground.

American militia under Majors Tristam Thomas and James Gillespie attack a mixed British/Loyalist flotilla under Colonel Ambrose Mills floating down the Pee Dee River at Hunt's Bluff, South Carolina. The Americans then deploy several "Quaker cannon," which bluff the enemy into surrendering without a shot. A British supply vessel moving upstream is also taken.

August 2
NORTH: Chief Joseph Brant, commanding 500 Loyalists and Indians, attacks Fort Plank (Canajoharie), New York, along the Mohawk River and takes several prisoners but fails to winkle out the defenders and withdraws.

August 3
SOUTH: General Francis Marion and 20 guerrillas join General Horatio Gates as his army crosses the Pee Dee River en route to Camden, South Carolina. Gates, who has no use for irregulars, promptly sends them off on an extended scouting mission.

August 4
WEST: The British expedition of Captain Henry Bird concludes when he reaches Detroit with 150 American prisoners. An equal number have been massacred by the Indians en route, which leads to retaliatory expeditions into Shawnee lands.

August 5
NORTH: General Benedict Arnold campaigns hard to become commander of strategic West Point, New York, and is finally appointed by General George Washington. Unbeknownst to all, he has intended to betray that strategic post to the British since May 1779.
SOUTH: General Richard Caswell and 2,000 North Carolina militia join General Horatio Gates's army at Lynches Creek, South Carolina. The famished troops gorge themselves on green peaches and corn en route, which results in extreme gastronomic distress.

August 6
SOUTH: A militia band under General Thomas Sumter attacks the 500-man Loyalist outpost under Major John Carden at Hanging Rock, South Carolina, in concert with forces under Major William R. Davie. The 800 Americans are initially successful on the left and center but pause to loot the enemy camp. This delay allows Connecticut Loyalist infantry to form a square, supported by two small cannon, and beat back successive attacks. The approach of British Legion dragoons from nearby Rocky Mount induces Sumter to call off the battle and retire. The Americans nonetheless inflict 192 casualties for a loss of 12 killed and 41 wounded. Hanging Rock is subsequently abandoned as an outpost.

August 8
WEST: Colonel George Rogers Clark and 1,000 men pursue the Shawnee from their main settlement at Chillicothe to the fortified town of Piqua. There he attacks and heavily defeats the Indians, killing 73 in exchange for 20 dead and 40 injured.
SOUTH: Militia commanded by Colonels Elijah Clarke and Isaac Shelby are ambushed by Loyalist forces under Major Patrick Ferguson at Cedar Springs, South

Carolina. However, the Americans quickly turn the tables on their antagonists, driving them off. American losses are four killed and 23 wounded.

August 9
West: Colonel George Rogers Clark defeats Shawnee warriors on the Little Miami River, Ohio, and torches their village.
South: A British column under General Charles Cornwallis departs Charleston, South Carolina, and hurriedly marches to reinforce Lieutenant Colonel Francis Rawdon at Camden. He takes with him 2,200 battle-hardened veterans.

August 11
South: General Horatio Gates, while crossing Lynches Creek, skirmishes with the British advance guard under Lieutenant Colonel Francis Rawdon. The Americans flank Rawdon's position by fording the creek and he withdraws in good order. This places Gates only 15 miles northeast of Camden, South Carolina.

August 14
South: General Horatio Gates reaches Rugeley's Mills, South Carolina, where he is reinforced by 800 Virginia militia under General Edward Stevens, and continues advancing toward Camden. He also dispatches 400 men to join the partisans of General Thomas Sumter, who intends to raid a British supply train.

August 15
South: General Horatio Gates receives additional reinforcements in the form of 100 Maryland Continentals and 300 North Carolina militia. However, he errs in issuing a molasses ration, which plays havoc upon the digestive tracts of his men. Ironically, as the Americans continue marching toward Camden, they encounter General Charles Cornwallis advancing north along the same road in the pre-dawn darkness. A brief skirmish ensues after which both sides establish camps and await daybreak.

American militia and Continentals under Colonel Thomas Taylor are detached by General Thomas Sumter to attack Fort Carey (Wateree Ford), South Carolina. Taylor is successful, capturing Colonel Isaac Carey, 30 prisoners, and 36 wagon loads of provisions. They then retire to Sumter's camp, snaring an additional 70 British prisoners and eight wagons en route.

General Francis Marion handily defeats a larger Loyalist force at Port's Ferry, South Carolina.

August 16
South: General Horatio Gates prepares to engage British forces under General Charles Cornwallis at Camden, South Carolina. The battlefield is an open field surrounded on either flank by swamps and pine forests. Gates has slightly less than 4,000 soldiers, mostly militia but built around a solid nucleus of Maryland and Delaware Continentals under Generals Johann de Kalb and Mordecai Gist. Colonel William Smallwood commands the 1st Maryland Regiment in reserve, while cavalry under Colonel Charles Armand covers the left flank. However, Gates errs grievously by placing all his Virginia and North Carolina militia along his center and left flank, where they oppose some of the best regiments in the British army. Cornwallis, true to his European training, deploys his elite units, such as the Royal Welch Fusiliers,

on his right flank, the traditionally accepted "post of honor." His left consists of regulars and Loyalists under Lieutenant Colonel Francis Rawdon, with the British Legion under Lieutenant Colonel Banastre Tarleton in reserve.

After a brief artillery exchange the British advance and Colonel Otho H. Williams, sensing some disorder in their approach, suggests an immediate attack on their right. Gates complies, but his raw militiamen receive one volley from the enemy before fleeing en masse. The North Carolina militia occupying the center likewise depart and in short order only de Kalb's Marylanders hold their positions. These troops rebuff several British attacks, but Cornwallis quickly wheels his entire right flank upon the unsuspecting Americans, still covered in smoke and unaware they stand alone. By the time de Kalb realizes his danger it is too late and his Continentals are nearly surrounded. He goes down fighting, fatally injured with 11 wounds as the remaining soldiers break and flee the field. Gates himself has spurred his horse and ignominiously galloped off at the first sign of disaster, not stopping until he reaches Charlotte, 60 miles distant. Only 700 survivors join him there three days later. American losses are estimated at 250 killed and over 800 wounded; Cornwallis lost a trifling 68 killed and 256 wounded. This battle literally erases all organized American resistance in South Carolina; Cornwallis subsequently orders Tarleton to hunt down the partisan band of General Thomas Sumter, then operating in the area.

August 18

SOUTH: Lieutenant Colonel Banastre Tarleton catches the guerrillas under General Thomas Sumter off guard at Fishing Creek, South Carolina, and routs them. Sumter's force, exhausted from a forced march and laden with wagons and prisoners, is unable to outpace its pursuers. Worse, Sumter inadvertently allows them to encamp at Fishing Creek, South Carolina, with minimal safeguards, blissfully ignorant that Tarleton is nearby, observing his movements. The British then suddenly charge into the American camp, coming between the militia and their stacked arms, and rout them. For the loss of 16 men, the British kill 150 Americans and capture 300 more. Sumter barely survives this humiliating defeat but immediately begins rallying his survivors to fight again. In concert with Camden, his defeat signals the end of organized resistance in South Carolina and the invasion of North Carolina by General Charles Cornwallis.

American militia under Colonels Isaac Shelby, Elijah Clarke, and James Williams are sent to attack a British/Loyalist force under Colonel Alexander Innes encamped near Musgrove Mill, South Carolina. An advance guard of 25 men attacks the camp and entices the enemy to pursue, and they charge headlong into a devastating ambush. The Americans inflict 63 killed, 90 wounded, and 70 captured for the loss of four dead and eight injured. This is the first American triumph since the defeat at Camden and partially lifts morale.

August 20

SOUTH: General Francis Marion surprises a British detachment under Captain Jonathan Roberts at Great Savannah (Nelson's Ferry), South Carolina. The British have apparently bivouacked on the plantation of General Thomas Sumter, well-known to the Americans, who soundly defeat Roberts. Marion takes 24 captives and also repatriates 150 American prisoners.

September 1
NORTH: John Hancock becomes the first popularly elected governor of Massachusetts.

September 3
DIPLOMACY: Henry Laurens, on a diplomatic assignment to the Netherlands, is captured off the coast of Newfoundland by HMS *Vestal* and imprisoned at the Tower of London. The British also retrieve his official papers, which reveal the extent to which the Netherlands has clandestinely assisted the Americans.

September 4
SOUTH: General Francis Marion, with 50 militiamen, routs a detachment of 250 Loyalists under Major Micajah Ganey at Blue Savannah, South Carolina. He allows the enemy to walk into a carefully staged ambush that routs the advance guard, then charges full tilt into their ranks. Such aplomb unnerves Ganey's men, and the majority simply drop their weapons and flee into the swamps along Little Pee Dee River. Marion loses three men wounded.

September 9
SOUTH: Defying the orders of his superior, General Charles Cornwallis begins preparing for his invasion of North Carolina by advancing upon Charlotte.

September 12
SOUTH: Major Patrick Ferguson, pushing into western North Carolina, engages an American force at Cane Creek. This marks the farthest extent of the British advance.

September 14–18
SOUTH: A body of 430 American militia under Colonels Elijah Clarke and James McCall besiege Loyalists and Indians under Colonel Thomas Brown at Augusta, Georgia. The Americans charge and displace the enemy Indians from several outposts until encountering a fortification called the White House. The Loyalist garrison steadily repulses them, inflicting 60 casualties, and the Americans finally withdraw in the face of a relief column from Fort Ninety Six. Brown subsequently hangs 13 wounded patriots from a staircase.

September 20–22
NORTH: Generals George Washington and Jean-Baptiste, comte de Rochambeau, conduct a preliminary strategy conference at Hartford, Connecticut. Washington strongly suggests attacking New York, but the French decline until they have a larger fleet in the area. Rochambeau also favors a campaign in the Chesapeake region, but nearly a year transpires before this can manifest.

September 21
NORTH: General Benedict Arnold decides to betray West Point to the British and secretly meets with Major John Andre. However, when Andre's ship HMS *Vulture* sails off, he is stranded behind enemy lines and spends the night at the home of a local Loyalist.

South: A force of 150 American militia under Colonel William R. Davie surprises a 60-man detachment of the British Legion under Major George Hanger at Wahab's Plantation, North Carolina. Noting a lack of sentries, Davie sends several marksmen into a nearby building to distract the British. He then leads a mounted charge down a lane traversing the plantation, routing Hanger's command. The entire detachment is nearly annihilated, losing 12 killed and 47 wounded. Davie has one man wounded.

September 23
North: Major John Andre dons civilian garb and attempts to pass through American lines. He carries concealed in his boot information about West Point's defenses provided by General Benedict Arnold. While passing through an American checkpoint, he is apprehended by three militiamen, who discover secret documents acquired from Arnold. A letter is hastily dispatched to Arnold's headquarters, informing him of the capture—and his treacherous plot begins unraveling.

September 25
North: His perfidy uncovered, General Benedict Arnold flees to the British warship HMS *Vulture*, anchored in the Hudson River, and formally joins the British side. The captive major John Andre is then slated to be tried as a spy.

September 26
South: A large gathering of "over the mountain men" occurs at Sycamore Shoals (Johnson City), Tennessee, as Colonels Isaac Shelby and John Sevier prepare to confront the Loyalists of Major Patrick Ferguson in North Carolina. They are joined by Colonel William Campbell and 400 Virginians, Colonel Joseph McDowell with 160 North Carolinians, and additional soldiers under Colonel Benjamin Cleveland.

American militiamen under Colonel William R. Davie engage the advance guard of General Charles Cornwallis's army at Charlotte, North Carolina. The British Legion, temporarily led by Major George Hanger, trots into town and confronts 20 militiamen posted behind a stone wall. Davie and his small command, backed by 70 riflemen under Major Joseph Graham, withstand two determined charges. Cornwallis then arrives on the scene, berates his embarrassed troopers, and orders light infantry under Lieutenant Colonel James Webster to turn the American right flank. Davie then withdraws in good order, losing six killed and 13 wounded; British losses are around 22.

September 27
South: Major Patrick Ferguson, aware that the western militiamen are drawing together in strength against him, withdraws from the Catawba River, North Carolina, and marches south toward the perceived safety of King's Mountain, South Carolina.

September 29
South: General Francis Marion and 50 militiamen engage a Loyalist contingent of comparable size under Colonel John Ball at Black Mingo Creek, South Carolina. After an initial repulse, Marion rallies his men and routs the enemy, killing and capturing 20 of them. American losses are two killed and eight wounded, while the Loy-

alists incur three killed and 13 wounded. The victorious Marion then withdraws back to the swamps of eastern South Carolina.

October 1
SOUTH: Colonel William Campbell of Virginia accedes to the command of a large force of western militiamen gathering in Gilbert Town, North Carolina, to oppose the advance of Major Patrick Ferguson. Campbell is seconded by Colonels Isaac Shelby and John Sevier.

October 2
NORTH: Major John Andre is hung as a spy at Tappan, New York. His calmness and stoicism impress all the American officers present.
SOUTH: Colonel Daniel Morgan, hobbled by arthritis, returns to active duty and reports to the headquarters of General Horatio Gates at Hillsboro, North Carolina.

October 3
POLITICS: The Continental Congress reduces the standing establishment of the Continental army to 58 regiments of infantry, four of artillery, and four of cavalry.

October 4
SOUTH: General Charles Cornwallis, while advancing through North Carolina, directs Major Patrick Ferguson in the direction of King's Mountain, South Carolina, to guard his flank as the main column presses on toward Charlotte.

October 5
DIPLOMACY: The Continental Congress approves the principles behind the League of Armed Neutrality espoused by Catherine II of Russia. It also initiates an investigation of General Horatio Gates for his shameful performance at Camden.

October 7
POLITICS: The Continental Congress, acting upon the advice of General George Washington, appoints General Nathanael Greene commander of the Southern Department.
SOUTH: American militia forces under Colonels William Campbell, Isaac Shelby, Benjamin Cleveland, and John Sevier entrap a large body of Loyalists under Major Patrick Ferguson at King's Mountain, South Carolina. Ferguson arrays his King's American Rangers, 900 strong, along the top of a wooded eminence whose slopes are heavily forested and afford the Americans cover as they approach. The frontiersmen, numbering 1,100 men, quickly surround Ferguson's position and begin ascending the slopes Indian-style, firing as they go. The Loyalists responded with several downhill bayonet charges that rolled the attackers back but exposed them to highly accurate rifle fire from their front and flanks. Within the hour Shelby works his way up the southern crest and forces Ferguson back upon his main encampment. Surrounded and with soldiers falling fast around him, Ferguson rallies a few mounted men and tries escaping but is pierced by six bullets and killed. The Loyalists then try to surrender but are dealt a taste of "Tarleton's Quarter," and several are shot down before the colonels can restore order. Ferguson's entire force is annihilated, with 157 dead, 163 wounded, and 698 prisoners. The Americans,

by contrast, lose 28 killed and 64 wounded in a very lopsided engagement. This disaster strips General Charles Cornwallis of his best light infantry, and he consequently suspends his advance into North Carolina for three months. It also revives the American hopes while Loyalist support for the British throughout the region is suppressed.

October 9
NAVAL: The Continental sloop *Saratoga* under Captain John Young captures three British brigs before vanishing without a trace off the Delaware Capes.

October 10
NORTH: A quick raid by 770 Loyalists and Indians under Major Christopher Carleton nets the entire 75-man garrison of Fort Anne, New York, under Captain Seth Sherwood.

October 11
NORTH: Loyalists and Indians under Sir John Johnson and Joseph Brant capture Fort George, New York, and raid settlements in the vicinity of southern Lake George.

October 13
POLITICS: The Continental Congress promotes Colonel Daniel Morgan to brigadier general at Hillsboro, North Carolina, and he receives command of the light troops.

October 14
POLITICS: The Continental Congress appeals to the states to provide their quotas of flour, pork, and hay to sustain the war effort.
SOUTH: General Charles Cornwallis, deprived of badly needed light troops, withdraws to Winnsboro, South Carolina, to rest and refit over the winter.

October 15
NORTH: Alexander Leslie sails with 2,500 men from New York on an extended raid in Virginia to support the efforts of General Charles Cornwallis in North Carolina. His orders are to hit the coast line, wreck forts, and capture supplies. General Henry Clinton also weighs the possibility of establishing Portsmouth as a permanent base for operations against Richmond and the interior.
SOUTH: Don Bernardo de Gálvez sails from Havana, Cuba, with 3,800 men en route to Pensacola.

October 16
NORTH: A force of 800 Loyalists and Indians under Sir John Johnson and Chief Joseph Brant attack the Schoharie Valley settlements, New York, burning several buildings. However, they are unable to dislodge the 200-man garrison at Middle Fort. When Major Melancthon L. Woolsey attempts to surrender, he is forced by noted marksman Timothy Murphy and others to fight on.

October 18
NORTH: Loyalists and Indians under Sir John Johnson attack the settlement at Caughnawaga, New York, burning it to the ground.

October 19
North: Sir John Johnson and a mixed force of 1,000 Loyalists and Indians attack and defeat a body of 130 militiamen under Colonel John Brown at Fort Keyser, New York. They then lay waste the nearby village of Stone Arabia. However, the militiamen subsequently regroup around reinforcements brought up by General Robert Van Rensselaer, who pursues and counterattacks the raiding force at Klock's Field. The vengeful Americans brush aside a force of Mohawk and Hessians but cannot dislodge Johnson's main force, sequestered behind improvised breastworks. The presence of some small Loyalist cannon dissuades Van Rensselaer from attacking further and Johnson manages a hasty retreat after abandoning his guns and baggage.

October 21
Politics: The Continental Congress, after heated debate, accedes to General George Washington's petition and grants half-pay to Continental army officers for life.

October 22
North: Captain Walter Vrooman, leading a 60-man detachment, pursues the raiding force of Sir John Johnson until he is ambushed at Kanadesega, New York, losing four killed and 56 captured.

October 25
North: Massachusetts formally adopts a new state constitution.
South: General Francis Marion and 150 partisans surprise Loyalists under Colonel Samuel Tynes at Tearcourt Swamp, South Carolina. Attacking simultaneously in three columns, they rout their opponents, killing three, wounding 14, and capturing 23 without loss. Marion also captures 80 horses and many valuable supplies.

November 4
Politics: The Continental Congress implores states to comply with obligations to fulfill quotas of flour, pork, and hay to support the army. Many states are fiscally strapped, however, and find it impossible to provide more.

November 8
South: General Charles Cornwallis dispatches Major James Wemyss of the 63rd Foot from Winnsboro, South Carolina, to hunt down partisans commanded by General Thomas Sumter. Wemyss commands 210 mounted infantry of his own regiment and an additional 40 dragoons from the British Legion.

November 9
South: A British raiding column of 250 men of the 63rd Regiment under Major James Wemyss surprises 600 Americans under General Thomas Sumter at Fishdam Ford, South Carolina. The British charge directly into the American camp undetected but, highlighted by campfires, they sustain heavy losses. Sumter is roused from sleep only moments before a party of dragoons charges his tent looking for him, and he escapes. The British overrun the American camp and are on the point of driving a party of Georgia militia into the river, when South Carolina troops under Colonel Thomas Taylor hits them with a heavy enfilade fire. After a hard fight the British withdraw

with seven killed and 25 captured, including Wemyss. Sumter loses four killed and 14 wounded and likewise beats a hasty retreat to Hawkins Mill on the Tyger River.

November 15
SOUTH: After nearly a month of fruitless campaigning, General Alexander Leslie concludes his Virginia raid and departs Portsmouth for New York. The damage he has inflicted is less than hoped for and does little to assist British efforts farther south.

American militia under General Francis Marion attempt to seize the town of Georgetown, South Carolina, which is defended by an 80-man British garrison, recently reinforced by 200 Loyalist militia. The two sides skirmish briefly at White's Bridge, and Marion concludes he lacks sufficient strength to attack and withdraws. He loses two killed and three wounded to a British tally of three dead and 12 captured.

November 20
SOUTH: Hotly pursued, General Thomas Sumter and Colonel Elijah Clarke take 1,000 men and make a determined stand against 400 British dragoons and infantry under Lieutenant Colonel Banastre Tarleton at Blackstock's Plantation, South Carolina. The Americans are strongly posted with the Tyger River guarding their rear and right flank, while several plantation buildings on a hill form their left. Additional troops line the woods and await the British advance. Tarleton first commits the 63rd Regiment to a frontal assault that drives the militia up the hill, from which an ambush is sprung upon them from the buildings. While this drama unfolds, a body of mounted militia manages to slip around the rear of the British dragoons and deliver a point-blank volley that empties many saddles. Tarleton, his army crumbling around him, orders his dragoons to charge frontally and they are heavily repulsed. But at this critical juncture Sumter is severely wounded and disabled. The British then withdraw from the field and the Americans pursue them a short distance, returning with several captured horses. Tarleton well admits to a loss of 50 men, while the Americans sustained three killed and four wounded. Sumter is again victorious but out of action for several weeks.

November 23
NORTH: A party of 80 dismounted troopers from the 2nd Continental Dragoons under Major Benjamin Tallmadge debarks from Fairfield, Connecticut, and crosses Long Island Sound at night. At dawn they storm Fort St. George (Brookhaven), New York, guided by Tallmadge, a native of the town. The Americans kill seven and seize 54 prisoners for one man wounded. They also burn 300 tons of hay intended as forage before falling back unmolested.

November 30
NORTH: Major Henry Lee gains promotion to lieutenant colonel and receives a legion of 300 dragoons and three companies of picked infantry. He drills them into one of the most feared and efficient formations in the Continental army.

December 3
SOUTH: General Nathanael Greene arrives at Charlotte, North Carolina, assuming command of the Southern Department from the disgraced General Horatio Gates.

With only 2,500 Continentals and militia he boldly initiates offensive operations against larger British forces.

December 4
South: Colonel William Washington employs a pine log, or "Quaker gun," to dupe Colonel Henry Rugeley and 115 Loyalists to surrender at Rugeley's Mill, South Carolina.

December 8
South: Lieutenant Colonel John Sevier and 250 North Carolina militia heavily defeat the Cherokee at Boyd's Creek along the French Broad River, losing only one man.

December 12
Diplomacy: Great Britain recalls its ambassador from the Netherlands.
South: General Francis Marion, commanding 700 men, intercepts a party of 200 recruits from the British 64th Regiment under Major Robert McLeroth at Halfway Swamp as they march toward Winnsboro. Rather than fight, both leaders parley and agree to arrange a battle between respective "champions." McLeroth, however, tries to steal away from the encampment. The Americans pursue briefly and withdraw after indecisive skirmishing. Consequently, McLeroth is removed from command and replaced by Major John Campbell.

December 16
South: Colonel John Sevier leads 300 Tennessee militia against the Cherokee at Boyd's Creek, killing 28 for the loss of three wounded.

December 17
Diplomacy: The Continental Congress appoints Francis Dana as minister to Russia, despite his totally unfamiliarity with the language. He nonetheless strives to lay a foundation for good relations between the two countries.

December 19
South: Disregarding the risks, General Nathanael Greene daringly splits his forces by sending General Daniel Morgan and 600 men on a wide sweep through South Carolina. He is at liberty to attack the rear of General Charles Cornwallis's army but is also instructed to rejoin Greene at Cheraw if the British move against American forces gathered there.

December 20
Politics: Having examined the captured papers of Henry Laurens, Great Britain declares war on the Netherlands over its clandestine trade with America.
North General Benedict Arnold, now fighting for the British, sails from New York with 1,600 troops on an expedition against Virginia.

December 26
South: The army of General Nathanael Greene establishes a base camp at Cheraw, South Carolina, to gather local recruits and possibly strike at General Charles Cornwallis should he advance into North Carolina.

December 28
South: A force of 280 American cavalry and mounted infantry under Colonels William Washington and James McCall routs a body of Loyalists of comparable size under Colonel Thomas Waters at Hammond's Store (Abbeville), South Carolina, killing or wounding 150 and taking 40 prisoners. The Americans sustain one killed and inflict a crippling blow to Loyalist interests. General Charles Cornwallis, angered by the extent of casualties, dispatches Lieutenant Colonel Banastre Tarleton against the raiders.

December 30
South: General Benedict Arnold's expedition lands at Hampton Roads, Virginia, and commences a lengthy raid up the James River.

December 31
Naval: At year's end the British have lost 596 vessels to an American tally of 237.

1781

January 1
Politics: The Continental Congress makes a final issue of $191 million in paper money as the American economy verges on collapse.
North: A mutiny among the Pennsylvania line erupts at Mount Kemble, New Jersey, over expired enlistments. Roughly 2,000 men leave camp determined to march on Philadelphia and present their grievances to the Continental Congress. General Anthony Wayne, who sympathizes with the mutineers, harangues them to return to camp but is ignored.
South: A British expedition of 1,800 men under General Benedict Arnold brushes aside 200 American militia near Jamestown, Virginia, and prepares to march on Richmond.

January 2
South: A Spanish expedition consisting of 60 militia and 60 Indians under Captain Eugene Pourre departs St. Louis (Missouri) and marches for the British-held outpost of Fort St. Joseph, Michigan.

January 3
South: A British expedition of 100 regulars and 500 Indians under Colonel von Hanxleden sails from Pensacola to attack Spanish forces defending Fort Charlotte in Mobile Village.

January 4
North: The marquis de Lafayette, Arthur St.Clair, and John Laurens approach mutinous troops at Princeton, New Jersey, but fail to persuade them to ground arms. General Henry Clinton, apprised of difficulties in the American camp, also dispatches agent John Mason to solicit their defection.

January 5
South: General Benedict Arnold and Lieutenant Colonel John Graves Simcoe scatter 200 Virginia militia defending Richmond. They then offer to spare the city if their

troops are allowed to confiscate tobacco supplies, but Governor Thomas Jefferson refuses. For two days Arnold's forces plunder and burn several buildings before finally withdrawing unmolested to Portsmouth.

NAVAL: Captain Seth Harding and the 32-gun frigate *Confederacy* capture two British brigs in the North Atlantic.

January 6

POLITICS: The Continental Congress overhauls the Committee of Foreign Affairs and renames it the Executive Secretary of Foreign Affairs.

NORTH: Colonel James Reed, representing the Continental Congress, arrives at Maidenhead, New Jersey, and commences communicating with the mutineers at Princeton. British agent John Mason also begins secret negotiations with the disgruntled soldiers.

SOUTH: General Charles Cornwallis, apprised that General Nathanael Greene has split his forces in two, does likewise and dispatches Lieutenant Colonel Banastre Tarleton and 1,100 men after light troops commanded by General Daniel Morgan.

January 7

SOUTH: A 150-man Spanish garrison under Lieutenant Ramon del Castro repulses a determined attack upon Mobile by a British raiding force out of Pensacola commanded by Colonel Johann von Hanxleden. Spanish losses are 14 killed and 23 wounded. The attackers incur 38 casualties.

January 8

NORTH: Mutinous Pennsylvania soldiers accept Colonel James Reed's offer of amnesty and his pledge to have the Continental Congress honor all prior commitments to them. The mutiny ends and those soldiers eligible for discharge are allowed to leave.

SOUTH: Lieutenant Colonel John Graves Simcoe and 40 mounted rangers are dispatched from Westover to disperse 150 American militia gathered at Charles City Court House, Virginia. Simcoe surprises his quarry in a well-executed night attack, killing 20 and capturing eight. British losses are one killed and three wounded.

January 10

DIPLOMACY: To harmonize international relations better, an office for foreign affairs is established by the Continental Congress. However, months lapse before the positions are actually filled.

SOUTH: A large British raiding force under General Benedict Arnold departs Westover, Virginia, on a plundering expedition down the James River.

January 11

NORTH: British agent John Mason is hanged as a spy in Princeton, New Jersey.

January 14

SOUTH: An American militia detachment under Colonel Peter Horry fights a confused skirmish with Loyalists under Lieutenant Colonel William Campbell of the Queen's Rangers at Waccamaw Neck, South Carolina. The Americans lose one wounded to a Loyalist tally of three killed and two captured.

January 16
SOUTH: The British Legion of Lieutenant Colonel Banastre Tarleton steals a march upon the light troops of General Daniel Morgan by crossing the Pacolet River at night and advancing rapidly upon his camp. The Americans hastily scamper off, abandoning their breakfast to the enemy, and fall back until reaching a meadow locally known as Hannah's Cowpens. Morgan does not dare risk crossing the nearby Broad River with enemy troops so near, so that night he devises a plan to defeat the impetuous Tarleton. He ingeniously arrays his men into three distinct lines: the first, composed of Georgia riflemen, is instructed to fire two volleys at British officers, then retire. The second line, consisting of North and South Carolina militiamen under General Andrew Pickens, is likewise ordered to fire two volleys before retreating. Morgan's third line consists of redoubtable Maryland and Delaware Continentals under Colonel John E. Howard, who are to stand fast on the hilltop and swap volleys with the enemy while cavalry under Colonel William Washington simultaneously strike Tarleton's flank. It was a perilous undertaking, given that any American withdrawal was cut off by the river in their rear. But Morgan gambled upon the famed impetuousness of his adversary to assist him.

January 17
SOUTH: After a dogged chase, Colonel Banastre Tarleton and 1,100 troops catch up with General Daniel Morgan's fleeing forces at Cowpens, South Carolina. As anticipated, he immediately attacks without proper reconnaissance and plunges headlong into the trap awaiting him. The first and second lines of Morgan's force fire skillfully and retire, knocking down many officers. The British, though staggered, come on and engage the veteran Continentals under Colonel John E. Howard, who suddenly feign a retreat and give ground. At a given signal, Morgan has his regulars suddenly turn around and deliver a point-blank volley into the disorganized pursuers, which stuns them. The cavalry of Colonel William Washington then charges over the hill and flanks the British while General Andrew Pickens rallies his militia and does the same. It is a superbly executed double envelopment and Tarleton's army literally disintegrates. After trading cuts with Colonel Washington, he ignominiously flees the field once his surviving cavalry refuse to charge. Cowpens is an American tactical masterpiece and a crushing blow to General Charles Cornwallis, who has now lost his remaining light troops. British casualties total 110 killed, 229 wounded, and 600 prisoners out of 1,110 men. American losses are only 12 killed and 61 wounded.

January 19
SOUTH: The raiding expedition of General Benedict Arnold, having plundered Cobham and Smithfield, Virginia, defeats a militia force gathered at Hood's landing and takes up winter quarters at Portsmouth to await reinforcements.

General Charles Cornwallis, informed of the defeat at Cowpens, begins arduously pursuing American forces under General Nathanael Greene across the northernmost reaches of North Carolina. He hopes to destroy either Greene or General Daniel Morgan piecemeal before their detachments can unite.

January 20–27
NORTH: New Jersey troops at Pompton, New Jersey, mutiny and march out of camp, ignoring their officers' attempts to negotiate. The soldiers get as far as Chatham when they are finally persuaded to return to camp at Pompton.

The Battle of Cowpens is a major tactical victory for the Americans, January 17, 1781. *(U.S. Army Center of Military History)*

January 21
NORTH: General George Washington dispatches General Robert Howe with 500 soldiers to suppress the rebellious New Jersey soldiers.

January 22
NORTH: American forces under Lieutenant Colonel William Hull attack a Loyalist outpost at Morrissania (Bronx), New York, under Lieutenant Colonel James De Lancey. The Americans then withdraw, having inflicted 50 casualties and taken 52 prisoners for a loss of five killed and 13 wounded.

January 24
SOUTH: Cavalry and partisan forces and Colonel Henry Lee and General Francis Marion raid Georgetown, South Carolina, 60 miles north of Charleston. Their attack flounders, but the Americans capture Colonel William Campbell and several ranking officers sleeping in a tavern. But, being unable to storm a British-held fort without artillery, both leaders withdraw.

January 25
SOUTH: In a daring move General Charles Cornwallis lightens his force by burning his baggage and supplies at Ramsour's Mill, North Carolina, and resumes doggedly pursuing American forces under General Nathanael Greene.

January 26
NORTH: General Robert Howe suppresses the mutiny of New Jersey troops with 600 loyal troops; two of the ringleaders are subsequently executed, and the rebellion ends.

January 30
SOUTH: The forces of Generals Nathanael Greene and Daniel Morgan unite along the Catawba River, hotly pursued by the British under General Charles Cornwallis.

February 1
POLITICS: The Continental Congress determines to create additional executive offices to govern finance, war, and maritime matters.
SOUTH: General Charles Cornwallis, while crossing Cowan's Ford on the Catawba River, is obstructed by 300 militiamen under General William L. Davidson on the opposite bank. For a few tense moments Generals Charles O'Hara and Alexander Leslie are thrown from their horses and nearly drown in the strong current. Fortunately the British find another ford farther downstream and they cross to take the Americans from behind. Meanwhile, the Coldstream Guards claw their way onto the opposite bank, form up, and charge the Americans. Davidson is killed attempting to rally his men, who scatter. The total American loss is four killed and three wounded; the British sustain four killed and 36 wounded.

British cavalry under Lieutenant Colonel Banastre Tarleton cross the Catawba River, advance 10 miles, and encounter an American militia detachment milling around at Tarrant's Tavern, North Carolina. Tarleton's quick advance apparently surprises the militia, who are routed after a brief fight. Both sides sustain roughly 10 casualties apiece, but the defeat discourages further partisan attacks in the region.

Wilmington, North Carolina, is occupied by 450 British soldiers under Major James Craig, and Loyalists begin rallying to him there.

February 3
SOUTH: General Daniel Morgan, ailing from arthritis, quits the army and returns home. Command of the light troops then passes to Colonel Otho H. Williams, while the American army continues retreating to the Dan River and Virginia.
CARIBBEAN: An expedition of 3,000 men under Admiral George Rodney and General John Vaughan attacks and captures the Dutch island of St. Eustatius, West Indies, depriving the Americans of a major supply source. Moreover, 150 vessels are taken along with 2,000 American captives. Showing no favoritism, Rodney vigorously plunders British merchants suspected of trading with the enemy; the ensuing lawsuits keep the admiral tied up in court for years.

February 5
NAVAL: Combined Franco-Spanish forces wrest control of Minorca from the British while an additional 30,000 troops mass for an eventual attack upon Gibraltar under the duc de Crillon.

February 6
POLITICS: The Continental Congress, groping for better control of the economy, establishes a Department of Finance at the behest of financier Robert Morris, a leading economic authority.

February 7
Politics: The Continental Congress replaces the Board of War with the Department of War but proves unable to find a compromise candidate to serve as secretary of war. Concurrently, General Alexander McDougall is appointed secretary of marine to head up affairs previously controlled by the Board of Admiralty.

February 9
South: The army of General Nathanael Greene reaches Guilford Courthouse, North Carolina, closely pursued by British troops under General Charles Cornwallis. Greene subsequently holds a war council, and the majority of officers favor retreating until more militia swell his ranks.

February 12
West: The 120-man Spanish expedition under Captain Eugene Pourre surrounds the British outpost at Fort St. Joseph, Michigan, and obtains its surrender. They are assisted by the sudden appearance of 200 Pottawatomie warriors, eager to share in one-half the spoils of conquest. Pourre departs for St. Louis a day later.

February 13
South: Colonel Henry Lee and his legion suddenly turn upon pursuing British forces under Lieutenant Colonel Banastre Tarleton at Dix's Ferry, North Carolina, routing them in a swift action and killing 18. American losses are one dead.

General Nathanael Greene, closely pursued by General Charles Cornwallis for 200 miles, slips across the Dan River into Virginia to resupply and refit. The British, lacking boats and engineers, finally quit. Cornwallis now controls the Carolinas but his lines of communication are perilously stretched and susceptible to roving bands of guerrillas.

February 18
South: General Charles Cornwallis abandons his chase and trudges back toward Hillsboro, North Carolina. Colonels Otho H. Williams and Henry Lee are immediately dispatched across the Dan River and back into North Carolina to harass the withdrawing British and their outposts.

February 19
South: General Thomas Sumter marshals his men for an attack against Fort Granby on the Congaree River, South Carolina. Major Andrew Maxwell and his British garrison of 300 soldiers are prepared for the strike and repulse the Americans, who then begin siege operations. Once Sumter learns that Lieutenant Colonel Francis Rawdon has dispatched a battalion to reinforce the garrison, he immediately withdraws.

February 21
South: Partisans under General Thomas Sumter attack a British garrison at Belleville, South Carolina. The Americans, lacking artillery, are forced to engage in a sniping contest with the defenders. Sumter, meanwhile, moves off with part of his command to ambush a 20-wagon British supply convoy. However, when word arrives of a relief column from Camden, Sumter again abandons the siege and retreats.

February 22
SOUTH: General Charles Cornwallis raises the royal standard and summons regional Loyalists to rally under his standard at Hillsboro, North Carolina. One of the first units to respond is a 300-man infantry battalion under Colonel John Pyle of Chatham County, who is ordered to rendezvous with Lieutenant Colonel Banastre Tarleton.

February 23
SOUTH: General Nathanael Greene, rearmed and reinforced by 600 Virginia militia, crosses his army over the Dan River into North Carolina and advances upon Hillsboro.

February 25
NORTH: The marquis de Lafayette departs Peekskill, New York, with 1,200 picked infantry to try to halt British depredations in Virginia. He will be assisted there by an additional 1,200 French troops who are to arrive by sea.
SOUTH: American partisans under General Francis Pickens and Colonel Henry Lee unexpectedly encounter a 300-man Loyalist force under Colonel John Pyle at Haw River, North Carolina. Pyle mistakes Lee's force for Lieutenant Colonel Banastre Tarleton's British Legion and allows it to approach and intermingle with his men. At a given signal Pickens, hiding in the nearby woods, opens fire and the American troopers join in the fray. They quickly kill 93 men and take 200 prisoner. The defeat has an immediate dampening effect on Loyalist sympathies throughout the region.

February 28
SOUTH: General Thomas Sumter frontally assaults strongly held Fort Watson, South Carolina, and is bloodily repulsed, with losses of 18 killed and 38 captured. His third defeat in one month undermines morale and encourages desertions.

Delayed by a storm, Don Bernardo de Gálvez again sails from Havana with 1,500 men for Pensacola, East Florida.

March 1
POLITICS: The Articles of Confederation, submitted to the states four years earlier, is finally ratified by Maryland and enacted. This grants the new Confederation Congress authority to weigh matters of war, peace, and foreign relations but denies it any ability to raise taxes or regulate commerce. It also assumes a new moniker, "The United States in Congress Assembled," under President Samuel Huntington. This form of governance remains in place until the Constitution is ratified in 1789.

March 2
SOUTH: Cavalry and mounted infantry under Colonel Henry Lee skirmish with Lieutenant Colonel Banastre Tarleton at Clapp's Mill, North Carolina. The Americans sustain eight casualties, the British 21.

March 3
SOUTH: The marquis de Lafayette reaches Head of Elk, Maryland, and embarks on boats for Annapolis. There he expects to be reinforced by French forces arriving by sea.

March 6
NORTH: General George Washington arrives at Newport, Rhode Island, to confer with General Jean-Baptiste, comte de Rochambeau, over strategy.
SOUTH: The British advance guard under Lieutenant Colonels James Webster and Banastre Tarleton attacks an unguarded militia camp under Colonel William Campbell at Wetzell's Mill, North Carolina. As the Americans flee across a stream, they are reinforced by soldiers under Colonels Henry Lee and William Washington and rally. The Coldstream Guards stall while pursuing in midstream under heavy fire, until small parties ford farther downstream and strike at the American flanks. Campbell withdraws again until reinforced by Continentals under Colonel John E. Howard. At this point Webster disengages and the fighting stops. Both sides suffer approximately 30 casualties apiece but, more important, the light troops under Colonel Otho H. Williams, shadowing the main British body under General Charles Cornwallis, slip across the Haw River to safety.

General Thomas Sumter attacks a party of Loyalists under Major Thomas Fraser at Radcliffe's Bridge on the Lynches River, South Carolina. The Americans drive their enemy hard, forcing them into a swamp, and then withdraw. American losses are 10 killed and around 40 wounded.

Partisans under Colonel Francis Marion fight off a mixed British/Loyalist detachment under Lieutenant Colonel John Watson at Wiboo Swamp, South Carolina. The Americans lose six killed and 12 wounded.

March 8
NAVAL: A French squadron under Admiral Charles-René Sochet, chevalier Destouches, leaves Rhode Island conveying 1,200 reinforcements for the marquis de Lafayette in Virginia. They are subsequently pursued by the British fleet under Admiral Marriot Arbuthnot.

March 9
SOUTH: Don Bernardo de Gálvez arrives at Pensacola with 35 ships and 7,000 men. He confronts a small but determined garrison of 1,600 men under General John Campbell behind stout fortification.

March 12
POLITICS: James Madison, delegate from Virginia, recommends stronger governmental powers to force the states to fulfill all federal obligations.

March 14
SOUTH: General Nathanael Greene, augmented by militia drafts to 4,400 men, assumes a strong defensive position at Guilford Courthouse, North Carolina, and awaits the approaching British. Taking a leaf from General Daniel Morgan, he posts his army on sloping ground and into three distinct lines. The first consists of North Carolina militia behind a rail fence, who are under orders to fire two volleys then retire. These are further buttressed by the presence of two small cannon in the center. The second line is Virginia militia and riflemen positioned in a dense wood, supported on either flank by cavalry under Colonels Henry Lee and William Washington. Greene's final line consists of 1,400 veteran Maryland and Virginia Continentals under Colonel Otho H. Williams and Isaac Huger.

March 15

SOUTH: General Charles Cornwallis finally confronts a larger American force under General Nathanael Greene at Guilford Courthouse. The British, mustering only 1,900 veteran bayonets, march 12 miles to the battlefield and immediately deploy around 1:30 P.M. The right wing of two regiments is commanded by General Alexander Leslie, the left of two regiments by Lieutenant Colonel James Webster, and the guards and reserves under General Charles O'Hara. The British advance upon the first line, taking heavy losses but routing them. Sorting themselves out, they proceed upon the Virginians in the woods, who put up stout resistance before finally being overpowered. The American flanks hold, however, and Cornwallis is forced to wheel his men right and left to confront their enfilading fire, while bringing up Guard and grenadier regiments to fill his center. Fighting on the flanks forms separate actions as the remaining British march ahead.

Sensing victory in his grasp, Cornwallis enthusiastically advances upon Greene's veteran Continentals on the hilltop, who respond with crushing volleys and a bayonet charge. The British are staggered in their tracks and nearly routed when Colonel William Washington's cavalry assail their flank, but Cornwallis suddenly orders his own artillery to fire grapeshot into the struggling mass. The two sides separate, but the British rally first and resume advancing. Greene, rather than risk having his army destroyed, signals a withdrawal and the Americans draw off intact. Guilford Courthouse is a dearly bought British victory; Cornwallis loses 93 killed and 439 wounded

The Battle of Guilford Courthouse, March 15, 1781 *(U.S. Army Center of Military History)*

—one-fourth of his army. American losses are 78 dead, 185 injured, and 1,046 missing, mostly militiamen. Cornwallis is unable to sustain such attrition and abandons his conquest of North Carolina. He spends the next several days tending his wounded.

March 16
NAVAL: The Battle of Cape Henry is waged as France's Admiral Charles-René Sochet, chevalier Destouches, arrives off Chesapeake Bay with reinforcements for the marquis de Lafayette. There he encounters the British fleet under Admiral Marriot Arbuthnot, whose copper-bottomed ships have allowed him to arrive slightly earlier, and gives battle. Both sides possess eight warships apiece, although the British enjoy superiority in firepower. The contestants battle in heavy seas and run past each other, trading broadsides, but the British superiority in cannon is neutralized once rough water compels them to keep their lower gun ports closed. Arbuthnot also fails to signal for close action; consequently, his van drifts from the battle line and is roughly handled. After one hour of fighting, Destouches timidly withdraws to Newport, Rhode Island, having sustained 72 killed and 120 wounded. Arbuthnot has lost 30 killed and 73 wounded, but his rigging is badly cut up and he declines to pursue. Nonetheless, the French surrender control of Chesapeake Bay to Britain and fail to reinforce Lafayette. Arbuthnot thus remains able to supply and reinforce the army of General Benedict Arnold in Virginia.

March 19
SOUTH: General Charles Cornwallis, his conquest of North Carolina thwarted by heavy losses, marches all surviving soldiers to Wilmington, 200 miles distant.

March 20
SOUTH: General William Phillips arrives at Portsmouth, Virginia, with 2,000 men and orders to take command of forces presently under General Benedict Arnold. His strategy is to do as much damage to the tobacco-based Virginia economy as possible and deprive the Americans of much-needed food and money.

March 22
NAVAL: The main French fleet under Admiral François-Joseph-Paul, comte de Grasse, departs Brest with 20 ships of the line, three frigates, and 150 transports with 5,000 soldiers. He then makes for the West Indies.

March 24
SOUTH: Colonels Elijah Clarke and James McCall engage and destroy a band of Loyalists under Major James Dunlap at Beattie's Mill, South Carolina. The Loyalists lose 35 men killed and 40 taken prisoner; Dunlap, a particularly treacherous partisan, is murdered while in captivity.

March 26
SOUTH: The marquis de Lafayette marches from Annapolis to Head of Elk, Maryland, without promised reinforcements.

April 1
SOUTH: General Nathanael Greene, reduced to 1,500 soldiers, breaks camp at Ramsey's Mills, North Carolina, and resumes offensive operations against Lieutenant

Colonel Francis Rawdon, commanding British forces in South Carolina and Georgia. The British are scattered throughout these states in isolated outposts, and Greene intends to reduce them one by one.

April 2
NAVAL: Captain John Barry, commanding the 36-gun frigate *Alliance,* is accosted by British privateers *Mars* and *Minerva* off the French coast and captures both vessels.

April 7
SOUTH: General Charles Cornwallis and 1,435 soldiers wearily trudge into Wilmington, North Carolina, to rest, refit, and be resupplied by the Royal Navy.

April 11
SOUTH: Partisans under Colonel William Harden capture the garrison at Fort Balfour, South Carolina, taking 90 captives.

April 14
POLITICS: The Confederation Congress votes Captain John Paul Jones and his men its thanks, and he appears in person to accept the accolades.

April 15
SOUTH: American forces until General Francis Marion and Colonel Henry Lee attack the strong Loyalist garrison at Fort Watson, South Carolina, despite the plucky defenders and a lack of artillery.

NAVAL: The 32-gun American frigate *Confederacy* under Captain Seth Harding is cornered by British frigates HMS *Orpheus,* 32 guns, and *Roebuck,* 44 guns, off the Delaware Capes and surrenders without a fight. The vessel is then taken into British service as HMS *Confederate.*

April 16
SOUTH: Resurgent American militia under General Andrew Pickens and Colonel Elijah Clarke surround and besiege Augusta, Georgia, in the absence of British forces. The Loyalist garrison under Colonel Thomas Brown grimly determines to resist as long as possible.

NAVAL: A French squadron of five ships of the line under Admiral Pierre-André de Suffren de Saint-Tropez surprises a larger British force under Admiral George Johnstone at neutral Porto Praya, Cape Verde Islands. The French catch the British at anchor and heavily pummel Johnstone's squadron. However, de Suffren's captains tepidly fail to support him, and at length he is forced to draw off. French losses are 309 to a smaller British total of 166. However, de Suffren so heavily damages Johnstone's force that he postpones his planned invasion of the Dutch colony at the Cape of Good Hope. De Suffren capitalizes upon the delay to reinforce that post before proceeding into the Indian Ocean.

April 18
SOUTH: General Benedict Arnold sorties from Portsmouth, Virginia, with 2,500 men to continue raiding.

April 19
South: General Nathanael Greene and 1,550 men occupy the old battlefield of Camden, South Carolina, prior to marching upon Charleston.

April 23
South: General Charles Cornwallis departs Wilmington, North Carolina, and advances into Virginia with 1,500 men. Lieutenant Colonel Francis Rawdon succeeds him as field commander of British forces in Georgia and the Carolinas.

General Francis Marion and Colonel Henry Lee continue attacking Fort Watson, South Carolina, despite a lack of artillery. The problem is solved when Colonel Hezekiah Maham proposes building a platformed log crib so that riflemen can deliver a plunging fire into the British camp. The garrison then surrenders 114 men while American losses total two killed and six wounded. Thereafter, constructing "Maham towers" becomes a standard American tactic.

April 24
South: General Nathanael Greene encamps 1,500 veteran soldiers at Hobkirk's Hill, two miles from the main British position at Camden, South Carolina. He fully expects to rest his men and attack Lieutenant Colonel Francis Rawdon within a few days.

April 25
South: General Benedict Arnold, reinforced by 2,000 troops under General William Phillips, attacks 1,000 militia under General John Peter Gabriel Muhlenberg at Petersburg, Virginia. Muhlenberg puts on a good front and deploys his men on Blandford Hill as if to invite a frontal assault. Advancing in two columns under Lieutenant Colonels Robert Abercrombie and John Graves Simcoe, the British have little difficulty in driving the militia from their position but the Americans withdraw in good order. Muhlenberg loses about 10 killed to a British tally of one killed and 10 wounded.

Rather than be attacked, Lieutenant Colonel Francis Rawdon scrapes together 900 men at Camden and advances upon General Nathanael Greene at Hobkirk's Hill, South Carolina. Rawdon avoids the roads and takes a line of march through the woods, avoiding detection until it is nearly too late. The Americans are cooking at the time but assume strong defensive positions as the British/Loyalist force enters the field. Seeing that Rawdon is attacking along a very narrow front, Green orders parts of his Maryland and Virginia Continentals under Colonels Otho H. Williams and Isaac Huger to advance and envelop the British from both flanks.

The Americans are making good progress when Rawdon's second line steps up, extends its own flanks, and ends up outflanking the Americans. At this juncture the men of the usually solid 1st Maryland Regiment under Colonel John Gunby inexplicably bolt and panic ensues along the American line. As the Continentals fall back to redress their ranks, Rawdon sounds the charge and the Americans scatter. Worse, Greene's artillery is threatened and only direct intervention by the general saves it from capture. The sudden appearance of cavalry under Colonel William Washington prevents Greene's withdrawal from becoming a rout, and the Americans leave the field in good order. Greene's losses are 19 dead, 115 wounded, and 136 missing. However, Rawdon loses 38 killed and 220 wounded, nearly one-fourth of his army, and does not pursue.

Don Bernardo de Gálvez begins a formal siege of Pensacola, West Florida, defended by 1,600 English under General John Campbell.

April 27
SOUTH: General Benedict Arnold scatters American militia at Osborne's, on the James River, Virginia, and engages the 20-gun ship *Tempest*, the 26-gun *Renown*, and the 14-gun *Jefferson* offshore. A chance shot cripples the *Tempest*, and when her crew abandons ship, the others do likewise. Arnold ultimately burns 24 small ships gathered at Hampton Roads. A large store of tobacco is also confiscated.

British forces under General William Phillips destroy Chesterfield Court House, Virginia, burning various buildings and supplies.

April 29
SOUTH: The marquis de Lafayette arrives at Richmond with 1,200 men to reinforce the beleaguered defenders. He succeeds General Friedrich von Steuben and is ordered to keep the town from being recaptured.
NAVAL: A British blockading force off Fort Royal, Martinique, under Admiral Samuel Hood is suddenly accosted by a French fleet of 150 warships and transports commanded by Admiral François-Joseph-Paul, comte de Grasse. Hood maneuvers skillfully but is badly outgunned and cannot prevent the convoy from reaching Fort Royal. After each side sustains roughly 300 casualties, Hood retires to St. Kitts with several battered vessels.

April 30
SOUTH: Generals Benedict Arnold and William Phillips retire to their main camp at Portsmouth, Virginia.

May 4
SOUTH: General Thomas Sumter and 500 partisans lay siege to Fort Granby, South Carolina, defended by Major William Maxwell and 300 soldiers. Sumter does so in defiance of orders from General Nathanael Greene, who requested his troops as a reinforcement. He subsequently departs for a raid upon Orangeburg, leaving Colonel Thomas Taylor to conduct operations in his absence.

May 7
SOUTH: Lieutenant Colonel Francis Rawdon receives 50 reinforcements at Camden, South Carolina, and again marches against the army of General Nathanael Greene. Greene, anticipating the strike, withdraws nine miles to strong defensive positions that dissuade Rawdon from attacking. The British then retire back to Camden.

May 8
SOUTH: Partisan forces under General Francis Marion surround the fortified mansion of Rebecca Brewton Motte and demand the Loyalist garrison's surrender. When they refuse, the two sides exchange shots over the next four days.

May 9
SOUTH: Don Bernardo de Gálvez, commanding 7,000 Spanish troops, captures Pensacola from General John Campbell after blowing up his main powder magazine

with a lucky cannon shot. The Spanish are initially repulsed but subsequently occupy parts of the ruined fortification, prompting a British surrender. For a cost of 74 dead and 198 wounded, de Gálvez has inflicted 105 casualties, secured 1,100 prisoners, and acquired ample supplies of guns and ammunition. He now enjoys undisputed possession of West Florida, which will remain in Spanish hands until 1819.

May 10
SOUTH: Lieutenant Colonel Francis Rawdon abandons Camden, South Carolina, and withdraws toward Charleston. He also orders all British outposts in the interior evacuated, save for Fort Ninety Six.

May 11
SOUTH: The garrison at Orangeburg, South Carolina, surrenders 15 British and 70 Loyalist prisoners to General Thomas Sumter.

May 12
SOUTH: The British garrison under Lieutenant Charles McPherson at Fort Motte, South Carolina, surrenders its 150-man garrison to Colonel Henry Lee and General Francis Marion following a four-day siege. To accelerate their capitulation, the Americans assaulted the fort with fire-tipped arrows. The elderly widow who owned the mansion not only agreed to the tactic but also produced the bow and arrows for the attack! The Americans sustain two dead.

May 13
SOUTH: The talented British general William Phillips dies suddenly of typhoid fever at Petersburg, Virginia, and command of British forces reverts back to General Benedict Arnold.

May 14
POLITICS: The Confederation Congress caves in to Robert Morris's demands for complete control of national fiscal matters, along with the ability to handpick his subordinates. Among them is the Jewish financier Haym Salomon. With these conditions met Morris finally assumes his role as superintendent of finance.
NORTH: A Loyalist raiding party under Colonel James de Lancey surprises an American outpost at Croton River, New York, killing Colonel Christopher Greene and wounding 42 soldiers.

May 15
SOUTH: Colonel Henry Lee captures Fort Granby, South Carolina, and takes 352 British and Hessian prisoners under Major Andrew Maxwell. He first tries coaxing their surrender with generous terms, including full honors of war, but it is his firing of a single cannon shot that convinces the garrison to yield. Moreover, Maxwell, a notorious plunderer, is allowed to carry off two wagonloads of booty. American militia present under Colonel Thomas Taylor are greatly angered by Lee's generosity and at one point threaten to kill the prisoners.

May 18
NORTH: Loyalist prisoners stage a large breakout from Newgate Prison, Connecticut, on the site of an abandoned copper mine.

May 20
North: General George Washington confers with his French counterpart, General Jean-Baptiste, comte de Rochambeau, in Wethersfield, Connecticut. Both agree upon a joint operation against New York City, hopefully in concert with Admiral François-Joseph-Paul, comte de Grasse's powerful fleet, then cruising the West Indies. He also dispatches General Anthony Wayne with 1,000 men to reinforce the marquis de Lafayette in Virginia.
South: General Charles Cornwallis slogs into Petersburg, Virginia, strengthened to 7,200 men by detachments under General Benedict Arnold.

May 21
South: Colonel Henry Lee captures two companies of Loyalists and needed supplies at Fort Galphin, South Carolina, securing 126 prisoners for the loss of one man. Because this outpost serves as a depot for the superintendent of Indian Affairs, many valuable trading goods are also confiscated. Its capture signals that the noose around Augusta is tightening.

May 22
South: General Nathanael Greene besieges Fort Ninety Six, South Carolina, one of several British posts still dotting the interior. However, he possesses less than 1,000 men and lacks heavy artillery, while the 550 Loyalists under Colonel John Cruger are determined to resist. Colonel Tadeusz Kościuszko initially digs his trenches too close to the fort, and the defenders periodically sortie and disrupt them. New trenches are constructed farther back, along with a Maham tower allowing riflemen to shoot into the camp.

May 23
South: Colonel Henry Lee, assisted by militia under Colonel Elijah Clarke, captures Fort Grierson in Augusta, Georgia, killing or capturing the entire 80-man Loyalist garrison. The commander, Colonel James Grierson, a particularly brutal partisan, is murdered in captivity. Lee proceeds to besiege nearby Fort Cornwallis.

May 24
South: General Charles Cornwallis departs Petersburg, Virginia, and marches toward Richmond. General Benedict Arnold leaves for New York.

May 26
Politics: The Confederation Congress accepts a proposal by Robert Morris to establish a national bank. His efforts to stabilize the national economy are further enhanced by the receipt of 6 million French livres.
North: General Anthony Wayne, en route to Virginia from York, Pennsylvania, quells a minor mutiny among his troops by executing seven ring leaders, then proceeds without further delay.

May 28
South: The approach of General Charles Cornwallis forces the evacuation of Richmond, Virginia.
Naval: The 36-gun frigate *Alliance* under Captain John Barry, returning from a mission to France, is attacked by the 16-gun HMS *Atalanta* and 14-gun HMS *Trepassy* in calm waters. Using sweeps, the British ships row themselves out to raking posi-

tions near Barry's stern and he is wounded by grapeshot. He is carried below seriously injured, but, after crew members suggest surrendering, Barry orders them to return him topside. Shortly after, the wind springs up and *Alliance* outmaneuvers its opponents, capturing both. The Americans lose eight killed and 19 wounded to a British tally of 12 killed, 29 wounded, and 169 captured.

June 1
NORTH: General Henry Clinton, angered by General Charles Cornwallis's disregard for instructions, suggests that he either advance toward the Delaware Region or withdraw by sea back to New York. But Cornwallis, enjoying political support from Lord George Germain, disobeys again and intends campaigning in Virginia.

June 2
CARIBBEAN: The French fleet under Admiral François-Joseph-Paul, comte de Grasse, captures the British island of Tobago in the West Indies.

June 3
NORTH: General Henry Clinton receives intercepted dispatches by General George Washington to Congress, outlining his intention to gather strength and attack New York City.
SOUTH: Lieutenant Colonel Banastre Tarleton takes 180 troopers of his British Legion and 70 soldiers from the 23rd Royal Welsh Fusiliers on a raid against Charlottesville, Virginia, in an attempt to snare Governor Thomas Jefferson and his legislature.

June 4
SOUTH: Lieutenant Colonel Banastre Tarleton attacks Charlottesville, Virginia, after tearing across 70 miles in 29 hours. His sudden appearance causes Governor Thomas Jefferson and the legislature to flee, being warned only minutes in advance by militia captain John Jouett. Jefferson departs minutes ahead of Tarleton's cavalry, which captures military stores and tobacco. They also seize seven legislators, including Daniel Boone. Meanwhile, the assembly flees and sets up at Staunton, 40 miles to the west.

June 5
SOUTH: Lieutenant Colonel John Graves Simcoe directs a raid of 400 men against Point of Fork (at the confluence of the Fluvanna and Rivanna Rivers), Virginia, that tricks General Friedrich von Steuben into retreating. The British then double back and capture badly needed supplies along with 30 American prisoners.

American militia under General Andrew Pickens and Colonel Henry Lee capture Fort Cornwallis, Augusta, Georgia, after three failed assaults. Lee orders a Maham Tower to be constructed, which allows for plunging rifle fire into the enemy camp. He subsequently adds a small cannon, at which point the Loyalist defenders lose heart and finally surrender. The Americans have inflicted 52 killed and taken 334 prisoners for a loss of 40 men. They also capture Colonel Thomas Brown, a leading and heartily despised Loyalist.

June 6
SOUTH: An American militia detachment under Colonel Isaac Hayne, having captured Loyalist general Andrew Williamson, is charged and defeated by Loyalist cav-

alry under Major Thomas Fraser. The Americans lose 14 killed and one wounded, and Hayne is captured.

June 8
SOUTH: General Nathanael Greene, besieging Fort Ninety Six, is reinforced by soldiers under General Andrew Pickens and Colonel Henry Lee. Loyalists under Colonel John Cruger sortie the following morning, seizing a cannon and wounding several soldiers. Meanwhile, at Camden, Lieutenant Colonel Francis Rawdon collects three regiments and begins marching to relieve the fort.

June 9
NORTH: The French army of General Jean-Baptiste, comte de Rochambeau, begins marching from Newport, Rhode Island, toward New York.
SOUTH: A 400-man raiding force under Lieutenant Colonel John Graves Simcoe attacks Seven Islands, Virginia, sacking and burning several tobacco warehouses.

June 10
SOUTH: General Anthony Wayne arrives in Virginia with his brigade of 1,000 men to reinforce the marquis de Lafayette and Friedrich von Steuben, bringing their total strength up to 4,500 veteran soldiers.

June 11
DIPLOMACY: The Confederation Congress appoints the United States peace commission, consisting of John Adams, John Jay, Henry Laurens, and Benjamin Franklin. Thomas Jefferson is also appointed but declines to serve.

June 12
SOUTH: The marquis de Lafayette assumes strong defensive positions along Mechunck Creek to forestall a British offensive against Charlottesville. General Charles Cornwallis declines to attack and marches back to Richmond.

June 15
DIPLOMACY: The Confederation Congress modifies the 1779 peace instructions and authorizes conditions of independence and sovereignty only; peace commissioners are free to pursue other considerations at their discretion. Benjamin Franklin, however, adamantly refuses to bargain away navigation rights on the Mississippi River as the price for additional help from France and Spain.

June 18
SOUTH: Having completed a third parallel, American forces under General Nathanael Greene assault Fort Ninety Six, South Carolina. His objectives are Fort Holmes and its attendant star redoubt. The Americans are initially successful and clear the abattis, but are driven back by a determined Loyalist sortie. With British reinforcements rapidly approaching, Greene prepares to abandon the siege.

As Lieutenant Colonel Francis Rawdon marches to the relief of Ninety Six, he is shadowed by a large force of militia under Colonel Charles Myddleton. When the Americans began harassing the British rear guard, the aggressive Rawdon suddenly turns on his antagonists, routing them.

June 19
South: General Nathanael Greene abandons his siege of Fort Ninety Six, South Carolina, upon the approach of a British relief column under Lieutenant Colonel Francis Rawdon. The Americans sustain 55 killed, 70 wounded, and 20 captured, to a British tally of 27 killed and 58 wounded. This is one of the longest sieges of the war, having commenced May 22.

June 24
North: General George Washington marches his army to Peekskill, New York, awaiting the arrival of General Jean-Baptiste, comte de Rochambeau.

June 26
North: A party of 40 American soldiers under Captain Amos Morse is ambushed and captured by British forces at Rahway Meadow, New Jersey.
South: The marquis de Lafayette decides to attack and destroy a British raiding column commanded by noted light infantry leaders Lieutenant Colonel John Graves Simcoe and Major Johann Ewald. The British are surprised in camp at Spencer's Tavern by a cavalry charge under Major William McPherson, which stuns the defenders but fails to rout them. British cavalry then hit the American flank in return as Ewald deploys his jaegers to meet an oncoming rush by American riflemen. After an intense exchange of fire between the competing marksmen, Ewald's Hessians charge and force the Americans back through the woods. Pressing ahead he encounters a group of Continental infantry under Colonel Richard Butler and pauses to regroup. At this juncture Simcoe, sensing he is badly outnumbered, retreats and abandons his dead and wounded on the field. They speedily withdraw in good order toward Williamsburg, six miles distant, where the main force under General Charles Cornwallis reposes. An aroused Cornwallis hurriedly leads his army back to the battlefield only to find it deserted and returns to camp. Lafayette's gambit fails to destroy Simcoe's elite force but both sides conduct themselves well in a hard-fought action. American losses are given as nine killed, 14 wounded, and 14 missing; the British admit to 10 killed and 23 wounded.

June 29
South: British forces abandon Fort Ninety Six and withdraw toward the coast.

July 3
North: When General Benjamin Lincoln fails to receive French reinforcements at Fort Knyphausen (King's Bridge), New York, he refuses to attack such a strong post. The Hessians under Lieutenant Colonel Ernest von Prueschenck sortie briefly and some skirmishing ensues, but the attackers withdraw to their fortifications. Cavalry under Colonel Armand-Louis, duc de Lauzun, arrive too late to participate and Lincoln retreats. American losses are six killed and 52 wounded.

July 4
South: General Charles Cornwallis crosses the James River at Jamestown Ford and advances toward Williamsburg with 7,000 men. He anticipates that the youthful marquis de Lafayette will be tempted to interfere with his crossing and makes preparations to surprise him at Green Spring. Several "deserters" are dispatched to the

American camp, informing them that only the British rear guard remains on the north bank.

Naval: Admiral Thomas Graves relieves Admiral Marriot Arbuthnot as naval commander in North America, at New York.

July 5
South: The marquis de Lafayette, deceived by deserters sent by General Charles Cornwallis that the British rear guard is marooned on the north bank of the James River, dispatches 900 men under General Anthony Wayne from his camp at Tyree's Plantation. He also receives contradictory intelligence that the entire British army is lurking at Green Hill and urges caution.

July 6
North: The armies of Generals George Washington and Jean-Baptiste, comte de Rochambeau, unite at Dobbs Ferry, New York. The highly professional, spit-and-polish French veterans are astonished by the ragtag condition of their Continental allies.

South: General Charles Cornwallis unleashes an effective ambush at Green Spring, Virginia, nearly capturing General Anthony Wayne as the latter advances upon what appears to be the British rear guard. Cornwallis judiciously lures his quarry across the river while the bulk of his army deploys in the woods surrounding the causeway. The trap is successfully sprung but Cornwallis is thwarted by the aggressive delaying tactics of Wayne. For several tense moments Wayne's small command trades volleys with the entire British army before he suddenly orders his 900 men to charge bayonets. The marquis de Lafayette also arrives with some light infantry at the last moment and assists in the evacuation. The ploy forces Cornwallis to halt his advance, at which point Wayne skillfully extricates his command under heavy fire. The Americans suffer 28 killed, 99 wounded, and 12 missing, to a British total of around 75 casualties.

July 9
North: Loyalists and Indians under John Doxtader attack Currytown, New York, burning houses and taking several prisoners.

South: General Charles Cornwallis dispatches cavalry under Lieutenant Colonel Banastre Tarleton from Cobham, Virginia, on an extended raid into the state's heartland.

July 10
North: Militia under Colonel Marinus Willett attack John Doxtader's 300-man raiding party at Sharon Springs Swamp, New York. After some preliminary skirmishing, he lures Doxtader into a crescent-shaped ambush, routing him and inflicting 40 casualties. Willett loses five killed and nine wounded.

July 17
South: A British detachment of 600 men under Colonel John Coates, 19th Regiment, is attacked by partisans under Francis Marion, Henry Lee, and Thomas Sumter at Quimby's Bridge, on the Cooper River, South Carolina. Against the advice of Lee and Marion, Sumter orders Colonel Thomas Taylor to assault frontally a

strong position; he is repulsed with heavy losses. Other attacks elicit similar results and at length the Americans withdraw, suffering 60 casualties while inflicting six killed and 38 wounded. Sumter's mishandling of affairs engenders hard feelings, and Taylor swears that he will never serve under him again.

July 20
SOUTH: General Charles Cornwallis is ordered by General Henry Clinton to depart Richmond, Virginia, and march to Williamsburg on the coast. Once there he is to establish a strong base from which his army can be supplied and reinforced from the sea.

July 21
NORTH: Generals George Washington and Jean-Baptiste, comte de Rochambeau, reconnoiter the outskirts of New York, concluding that they lack the men and equipment necessary for a successful siege.

July 24
SOUTH: A cavalry column under Lieutenant Colonel Banastre Tarleton, having raided 400 miles across the Virginia interior, rejoins the main British army at Suffolk. This spectacular endeavor inflicts only minor damage upon the Americans while wearing out many valuable horses.

July 25
SOUTH: British forces burn the town of Georgetown, South Carolina, just ahead of advancing American forces.

July 26
NORTH: Engineering general Louis Duportail advises General George Washington that 20,000 troops are needed to attack New York with any prospect of success. This represents more manpower than the allies can muster, so the prospects of a southern campaign appear increasingly attractive. The only catalyst required is word from the French fleet.

August 1
SOUTH: General Charles Cornwallis arrives at Yorktown at the tip of the Virginia peninsula, astride the York River, and begins entrenching. He also fortifies Gloucester Point on the opposite shore, entrusting its defense to Lieutenant Colonel Banastre Tarleton.

A force of 280 British and 80 Loyalists under Major James Craig marches from Wilmington, North Carolina, on a 75-mile raid to New Bern.

August 4
SOUTH: South Carolina militia officer Isaac Hayne is executed by Lieutenant Colonel Francis Rawdon for violating his parole. His death sparks an outcry among the populace and further hardens attitudes toward the British.

August 5
NAVAL: Admiral Hyde Parker's British squadron of five ships of the line and two frigates is escorting a British convoy of 120 ships from the Baltic when it encounters

an unidentified force off Dogger Bank in the North Sea. This turns out to be a small Dutch squadron under Admiral Johann Arnold Zoutman, commanding six ships of the line and one frigate, which is also protecting a large convoy of vessels. The merchantmen bear away to their respective home ports as Parker and Zoutman close for action, and an intense slugging match ensues at close range. After several hours of fighting neither side can claim an advantage, so they mutually haul off. The Dutch suffer 545 casualties to 453 English in one of the costliest naval engagements of the entire war.

Admiral François-Joseph-Paul, comte de Grasse, departs Cap-François, Haiti, with 28 ships of the line and 3,300 infantry, and sails for Chesapeake Bay. In an audacious gamble, he leaves no major warships behind to protect French interests in the Caribbean. He also charts a course through the storm-tossed Old Bahama Channel off Cuba, the last route British naval strategists would have anticipated. De Grasse has until October 15 to conclude naval operations before the hurricane season arrives.

August 6
NORTH: A force of 60 Loyalists and Indians under Donald McDonald raids Shell's Bush, New York, but is unable to pry John Christian Shell, his wife, and six sons from a two-story blockhouse. The Shell family peppers their antagonists with musket fire while McDonald sustains a mortal leg wound while prying open a door with a crowbar. The raiders sullenly withdraw, having lost 11 killed and six wounded.

August 9
NAVAL: Captain James Nicholson surrenders the 28-gun frigate *Trumbull* to the 32-gun frigate HMS *Iris* and 18-gun brig *General Monck* after three-fourths of his crew, British deserters, refuse to fight. Nicholson, assisted only by Lieutenants Richard Dale, Alexander Murray, and a handful of men, stoutly resists for half an hour. Ironically, their captors are the former American warships *Hancock* and *General Washington*. Nicholson loses five killed, 11 wounded, and 175 prisoners.

August 10
POLITICS: Robert R. Livingston is appointed the first secretary of foreign affairs by the Confederation Congress.

August 13
SOUTH: A force of 200 partisans under General Francis Marion, having marched 100 miles to join forces with Colonel William Hardin at Parker's Ferry, South Carolina, sets up an ambush for 200 British dragoons under Major Thomas Fraser. After deploying his men along a causeway, Marion lures the enemy into attacking, and they are repelled by a severe discharge. Fraser rallies and charges two more times before finally retreating, having lost around 100 killed and wounded. Marion sustains no losses.

August 14
NORTH: Generals George Washington and Jean-Baptiste, comte de Rochambeau, receive electrifying news from Admiral François-Joseph-Paul, comte de Grasse, of his impending arrival at Chesapeake Bay. His missive occasions a joyous outburst from the nominally taciturn Washington, and he immediately proposes altering

allied strategy. Previously fixated on New York, he now favors rapidly marching to Virginia and entrapping the British at Yorktown. Rochambeau concurs completely and the allies make preparations to expedite their 400-mile trek in secrecy.

August 19
SOUTH: A British raiding force of 250 soldiers and 80 Loyalists under Major James Craig arrives from Wilmington, North Carolina, and burns the town of New Berne.

August 21
NORTH: Generals George Washington and Jean-Baptiste, comte de Rochambeau, secretly decamp and head south to Virginia with 6,000 men. They leave 2,500 men under General William Heath to deceive General Henry Clinton into thinking that New York is about to be attacked. Furthermore, false orders are written and allowed to fall into enemy hands, while the construction of bread-baking ovens in New Jersey gives the impression of a permanent French presence there. Clinton is completely duped by their subterfuge.

Mohawk raiders under Chief Joseph Brant and Simon Girty capture three American scouts on the Great Miami River, Ohio. From them they learn of the approach of 107 Pennsylvania militiamen under Colonel Archibald Lochry. Brant sends runners to Scioto Falls requesting reinforcements as he prepares to ambush the unsuspecting Americans.

August 22
NORTH: New York militia under Colonel Albert Pawling defeat a large party of Loyalists and Indians under Captain William Caldwell at Warwarsing, Ulster County, New York, inflicting three killed and four wounded.

August 23
SOUTH: General Nathanael Greene, having rested his men after the rigors of Fort Ninety Six, decamps from High Hills along the Santee River and advances upon British forces at Eutaw Springs, South Carolina.

August 24
WEST: Colonel Archibald Lochry's detachment of Pennsylvania militia lands on the banks of the Great Miami River, Indiana. Suddenly they are ambushed and destroyed by Indians under Chief Joseph Brant, who captures or kills the entire force. American losses are 36 killed and 55 prisoners. The latter's fate will remain unknown for two years until the survivors are finally paroled at Quebec.
NAVAL: A French squadron carrying 1,000 troops departs Newport, Rhode Island, under Admiral Jacques, comte de Barras, and makes for Chesapeake Bay.

August 27
NAVAL: Admiral Samuel Hood arrives in Chesapeake Bay with 14 ships of the line and spoiling for a fight but, finding the bay devoid of enemy ships, he sails for New York to join the main fleet under Admiral Thomas Graves.

August 30
NAVAL: A French fleet of 24 ships of the line under Admiral François-Joseph-Paul, comte de Grasse, arrives off the Virginia Capes, securing all water approaches to

Yorktown, and begins transferring 3,000 soldiers to the marquis de Lafayette at Jamestown, Virginia.

August 31
NAVAL: Admiral Thomas Graves, reinforced by the squadron under Admiral Samuel Hood, departs New York with 19 ships of the line and sails for Chesapeake Bay.

September 2
NORTH: General Henry Clinton, finally cognizant of American intentions, alerts General Charles Cornwallis of an impending attack. Wishing to provide a diversion for Cornwallis, he orders General Benedict Arnold on an amphibious expedition against New London, Connecticut, to capture military stores gathered there. Arnold embarks that day with 1,732 soldiers of the 38th, 40th, and 54th Regiments of Foot, and various Loyalist detachments.

The combined forces of Generals George Washington and Jean-Baptiste, comte de Rochambeau, file through Philadelphia. Washington allows several long-suffering Continental units, their pay several months in arrears, to petition Congress for redress. Robert Morris arranges a loan from Rochambeau to comply, and the army resumes its march to Head of Elk, Maryland.

September 5
NAVAL: The fleets under Admirals François-Joseph-Paul, comte de Grasse, and Thomas Graves commence sparring for control of Chesapeake Bay. The French muster 24 ships of the line (1,788 guns) while the British possess only 19 (1,402 guns). As the battle develops, the British hold the weather gauge, but Graves refuses to depart from traditional fighting instructions and maneuvers slowly. He further errs by allowing the French to depart the bay singly and form their battle line, instead of attacking them while they deploy, as Admiral Samuel Hood has suggested. Both fleets then approach each other in light winds that allow only eight British vessels and 15 French vessels of their respective vans to engage. These vessels are badly pummeled after a two-and-a-half-hour exchange that concludes at nightfall. The British warships, badly outgunned, suffer considerably, and HMS *Terrible* has to be scuttled. Graves's own flagship, HMS *London,* is also badly damaged. French losses amount to 220; the British sustain 79 killed and 230 wounded. This inconclusive battle nonetheless exerts a strategic significance for General Charles Cornwallis—still sequestered at Yorktown and not yet relieved.

September 6
SOUTH: General Benedict Arnold leads 1,732 soldiers on a punitive raid against New London, Connecticut. Dividing his force into two columns, the first easily storms the unfinished battery at Fort Trumbull on the west bank of the Thames River. Across the river Fort Griswold is defended by 158 men under Lieutenant Colonel William Ledyard of the militia. The British form up their assault columns and charge uphill under heavy fire, gaining the southern and northeastern walls. However, Lieutenant Colonel Edmund Eyre is slain at their head, along with several ranking officers, for a total of 48 killed and 145 wounded. At this point Ledyard attempts to surrender but is apparently murdered by the enraged English troops, who subsequently rampage and bayonet 85 defenders to death. An addi-

tional 35 are wounded and 37 captured. After burning 143 buildings in New London and Groton, the raiders embark. The extent of American losses further blackens Arnold's reputation.
NAVAL: The 24-gun privateer *Congress* under Captain George Geddes engages the 16-gun sloop HMS *Savage* under Captain Charles Stirling off Charleston, South Carolina. After a four-hour battle the British vessel is badly damaged and is boarded by marines under Captain Allan McLane as Stirling strikes his flag.

September 7
NORTH: Indians surprise and wipe out an American detachment under Lieutenant Solomon Woodworth at Fort Plain, New York. American losses are 26 killed and four wounded.

September 8
SOUTH: The Franco-American army reaches Head of Elk, Maryland, and prepares to embark on a sealift provided by the French navy.

General George Washington, en route to Williamsburg, Virginia, stops overnight to sleep at Mount Vernon—his first visit home in six years.

As General Nathanael Greene advances upon Eutaw Springs, South Carolina, with 2,450 men, he encounters a slightly smaller force of 1,800 under Lieutenant Colonel Alexander Stewart of the 3rd Regiment (Irish Buffs). The Americans approach his camp stealthily, surprising and capturing a party of 40 foragers. Minutes later a party of Loyalist cavalry is also bagged, although Major John Coffin escapes and alerts Stewart to the danger. The British are consequently drawn up in battle array when Greene attacks them in three lines. American militia in the first rank under Generals Francis Marion and Andrew Pickens fight exceptionally well and loose no less than 17 volleys before yielding to a counterattack. The British then charge directly into Greene's second line, consisting of veteran Continental infantry from Maryland and Virginia under Colonel Jethro Sumner, and fall back in confusion. The Americans quickly counterattack along the line and surge victoriously into Stewart's camp.

Greene seems poised to win a battle finally when his soldiers begin plundering. Meanwhile, a picked body of British light infantry and grenadiers under Major John Majoribanks take defensive positions in a thicket on Stewart's right flank and defies all American attempts to eject them. Colonel William Washington's cavalry tries and is heavily repulsed, with Washington captured. Majoribanks subsequently joins Stewart's remaining men in a large, fortified brick house in the rear, from which they pour in a heavy fire upon the milling Americans. Stewart then orders a charge across the field, and the disorganized Continentals begin giving ground. The heroic Majoribanks is killed, but Greene, wishing to avert disaster, orders his army disengaged and the British keep the field. Eutaw Springs is one of the hardest fought actions of the war and produces the highest proportional casualties of any battle. Greene loses 138 killed, 375 wounded, and 41 missing, while Stewart suffers 85 killed, 351 wounded, and 257 missing—a loss rate of 42 percent. Furthermore, British losses prove irreplaceable, so Stewart immediately withdraws back to Charleston. Greene has lost his final battle, but the Carolina interior is now largely free of British influence.

September 10
NAVAL: A squadron of eight ships of the line and numerous transports under Admiral Jacques, comte de Barras, slips by the British squadron of Admiral Thomas Graves and arrives in Chesapeake Bay, bringing badly needed French siege artillery. His arrival brings the strength of the French fleet up to 36 ships of the line. Admiral François-Joseph-Paul, comte de Grasse, now enjoys uncontested control of Chesapeake Bay; he also captures British frigates HMS *Iris* and *Richmond* as they try to depart.

September 12
SOUTH: A force of 1,000 Loyalists under Colonels David Fanning and Hector McNeill surprises an American detachment at Hillsboro, North Carolina, capturing Governor Thomas Burke and several ranking legislators. However, as the Loyalists withdraw they are attacked in turn by 400 Continental soldiers under General John Butler at Cane Creek. The Loyalists drive off their assailants but sustain 35 killed (including Colonel McNeill) and 92 wounded. The Americans have 40 killed, 110 wounded, and 210 prisoners.

NAVAL: Admiral Thomas Graves, after loitering in the vicinity of Chesapeake Bay for several days, concludes that he is badly outnumbered by the French and he makes for New York to gather reinforcements. This single act forfeits control of the sea to the allies; British forces under General Charles Cornwallis are now sealed within their works at Yorktown by Admiral François-Joseph-Paul, comte de Grasse.

September 14
SOUTH: Advance elements of the combined armies under Generals George Washington and Jean-Baptiste, comte de Rochambeau, reach Virginia and are transported to Williamsburg by French naval units.

Despite the gathering allied force before him, General Charles Cornwallis receives assurances from General Henry Clinton that an expedition is assembling in New York for his relief and should arrive no later than October 5. This letter has the effect of dissuading Cornwallis from cutting his way out of the peninsula and escaping toward the interior before siege lines are established.

September 15
SOUTH: The allies stage an impressive review of 17,000 men at Williamsburg, Virginia. Present are American divisions under the marquis de Lafayette, Benjamin Lincoln, and Friedrich von Steuben. The French army has assembled seven crack infantry regiments assisted by engineering, cavalry, and artillery elements. The British at nearby Yorktown under General Charles Cornwallis scarcely muster half that number.

September 17
SOUTH: General George Washington, accompanied by General Henry Knox and Louis Duportail, confers with Admiral François-Joseph-Paul, comte de Grasse, aboard his flagship *Ville de Paris* of 110 guns, then the largest warship in the world. A detailed strategy is finalized whereby the French contribute several heavy artillery pieces from their fleet. Ultimately, seven redoubts and six batteries will be established around the British position. Washington's return to the army is delayed by adverse winds until September 22.

September 23
SOUTH: Trapped at Yorktown, General Charles Cornwallis contacts General Henry Clinton in New York and cautions him to "hear the worse" if reinforcements are not quickly forthcoming.

September 28
SOUTH: The massed Franco-American force advances from Williamsburg, marches 12 miles, and formally invests British positions at Yorktown, Virginia. In response, General Charles Cornwallis abandons his outer works and retires to fortifications nearer the town. He wishes to spare as many of his soldiers' lives as possible until General Henry Clinton arrives to relieve him.

September 30
SOUTH: The allies readily occupy the outer ring of General Charles Cornwallis's defenses, which accelerates their timetable for planting siege artillery and digging trenches. Meanwhile, Lieutenant Colonel Banastre Tarleton defends the British toehold at Gloucester, across the bay, from French forces under the comte de Choisy and Colonel Armand-Louis, Duc de Lauzun. His men surprise and defeat an American reconnaissance party under Colonel Alexander Scammell, who is mortally wounded while in British custody.

October 1
SOUTH: American batteries planted in the captured outworks begin pounding British defenses at Yorktown, Virginia.

October 3
SOUTH: Cavalry under Lieutenant Colonel Banastre Tarleton and Colonel Armand-Louis, Duc de Lauzun, collide at Gloucester, Virginia, across the bay from Yorktown. During the melee, Tarleton seeks to engage Lauzun personally but is accidentally unhorsed. Lauzun then attempts to capture the fallen leader but is prevented by several troopers of the British Legion. Tarleton escapes unharmed but the French capture his horse and drive his remaining cavalry back to their lines. A standoff also develops between portions of the crack 23rd Royal Welsh Fusiliers and a select Virginia militia battalion under General George Weedon. Fighting eventually peters out and the British withdraw to safety. The allies apparently lose five killed and 27 wounded to a British total of 13 killed and wounded.

October 6
SOUTH: General George Washington symbolically breaks the ground for the first parallel trench at Yorktown, Virginia. Within days 1,500 sappers and engineers are hard at work digging the first parallel only 600 yards from the British outer defenses, and 2,000 yards long.

A quick raid by American partisans upon the British depot at Monck's Corner, South Carolina, nets 80 captives.

October 9
SOUTH: Massed firepower from 100 French and American cannon begins relentlessly pounding British defenses at Yorktown, burning the frigate HMS *Charon* and several transports anchored in the nearby York River.

October 10

NORTH: Major Lemuel Trescott and 100 of the 2nd Continental Dragoons capture Fort Slongo (Threadwells Neck), Long Island, along with 21 Loyalist prisoners.

October 12

SOUTH: The initial allied trench at Yorktown is completed and a second one commences only 300 yards from the British defensive works. However, because the fatigue parties are under fire from British-held Redoubts Nos. 9 and 10, plans are drawn up to reduce these strong points.

October 14

SOUTH: At 8 P.M., a combined assault under Colonels Alexander Hamilton and Guillaume de Deux-Ponts captures Redoubts Nos. 9 and 10 in Yorktown's defense perimeter. Hamilton's 400 Americans go forward without flints and using bayonets only. They quickly scramble over the abatis and parapet, seizing Redoubt No. 10 in only 10 minutes. Deux-Ponts has a much rougher go at Redoubt No. 9, taking 30

General Washington and the comte de Grasse surrounded British forces under General Cornwallis at Yorktown, leading to the eventual surrender of Cornwallis and a decisive victory for the Americans in their Revolution. *(U.S. Army Center of Military History)*

minutes and sustaining more casualties. Both redoubts are subsequently incorporated into allied siege lines, allowing additional cannon to be mounted at even closer range. American losses are nine killed and 31 wounded; the French lose 15 killed and 77 wounded. The British tally is 18 killed and 73 captured.

October 16
SOUTH: General Charles Cornwallis, in a desperate attempt to buy time, launches a heavy sortie of 350 men under Lieutenant Colonel Robert Abercrombie The British initially overrun a French battery and spike the cannon but are driven back with eight killed and 12 captured. That evening an attempt by Cornwallis to ferry his force across the York River to Gloucester is also foiled by bad weather.

October 17
SOUTH: With no succor in sight, a drummerboy mounts the British parapet and beats for a parley. A British officer is then blindfolded and brought into the headquarters of General George Washington with a request to negotiate terms.

October 18
SOUTH: A military commission under Colonel John Laurens and Viscount Louis-Marie Noailles meets with a British deputation about surrender terms. General George Washington insists upon unconditional surrender and adamantly refuses honors of war to the British—the exact terms imposed upon General Benjamin Lincoln at Charleston in May 1780. The British have no choice but to submit.

October 19
SOUTH: General Charles O'Hara formally surrenders 8,081 men of the Yorktown garrison. He initially approaches a group of French officers and attempts to tender his sword to General Jean-Baptiste, comte de Rochambeau, but is sternly redirected to the American side. General George Washington then allows his second in command, General Benjamin Lincoln, to accept it on his behalf. General Charles Cornwallis, feigning illness, declines to be present. The British bands then strike a tune appropriately called "The World Turned Upside Down" as the defenders dejectedly march out and stack arms. British combat losses total 156 killed, 326 wounded, and 70 missing. The French lose 60 killed and 197 wounded; the Americans 23 dead and 56 injured. All ranking British officers are subsequently paroled and sent to New York. This capitulation concludes major military operations on land and devastates British political will to continue the struggle.

October 20
DIPLOMACY: Robert R. Livingston finally assumes the post of secretary for foreign affairs. It has taken nearly 10 months for the Confederation Congress to confirm a compromise candidate for the office.

October 21
NAVAL: The American privateer *Indian* captures the ship *Venus,* the first of seven vessels taken on an Atlantic cruise.

October 22
NORTH: Philadelphia erupts into euphoric celebrations as Colonel Tench Tilghman hurriedly arrives with news of the British surrender at Yorktown.

October 24
NORTH: A 750-man Loyalist/Indian force under Major John Ross attacks and burns the settlement at Warrenbush, New York.

October 25
NORTH: A force of 750 Loyalists and Indians under Major John Ross, then ravaging the Mohawk Valley, is attacked by 400 New York militia under Colonel Marinus Willett at Johnstown Hall, New York. Wavering on Willett's flanks allows the raiders to escape under cover of darkness, but they incur 65 casualties to an American total of 35. Willett then vigorously pursues the marauders.

October 27
SOUTH: A combined amphibious force of 7,000 men under Admiral Thomas Graves and General Henry Clinton makes its belated appearance off Chesapeake Bay and promptly returns to New York when apprised of the British surrender. However, General George Washington fails to convince either General Jean-Baptiste, comte de Rochambeau, or Admiral François-Joseph-Paul, comte de Grasse, to accompany him back to New York for a proposed attack.

October 30
POLITICS: The Confederation Congress finally appoints General Benjamin Lincoln as the first secretary of war.
NORTH: Colonel Marinus Willett, commanding 400 New York militia and 60 Oneida warriors, overtakes a body of Loyalists and Indians at West Canada Creek (Jerseyfield), New York. The Americans engage and defeat the rear guard, killing Major Walter Butler and wounding seven. This proves the last incursion by Loyalist and Indian forces into the region.

November 5
DIPLOMACY: The United States obtains a large loan from the Netherlands.
NAVAL: The French fleet under Admiral François-Joseph-Paul, comte de Grasse, decamps Chesapeake Bay and sails for the West Indies.

November 6
SOUTH: Colonel Elijah Clarke and his militia ambush a party of pro-British Indians in Wilkes County, Georgia, killing 40 and capturing 40.

November 7
SOUTH: A body of 300 Loyalists under William Cunningham massacres a detachment of 30 American militiamen under Captain George Turner at Cloud's Creek, South Carolina. During surrender negotiations a young soldier shoots a Loyalist and slaughter ensues.

November 10
SOUTH: A division of men under General Arthur St. Clair marches from Yorktown to reinforce General Nathanael Greene in North Carolina.

November 18
SOUTH: British forces under Major James Craig evacuate Wilmington, North Carolina, removing all Loyalists who care to depart.

November 25
POLITICS: National dismay arises as Parliament learns of the defeat at Yorktown. Lord George Germain exclaims, "Oh, God, it is all over!"
CARIBBEAN: A French naval expedition under Admiral François-Claude-Amour, marquis de Bouille, recaptures St. Eustatius from the British, taking 700 prisoners.

November 26
NAVAL: The French fleet under Admiral François-Joseph-Paul, comte de Grasse, drops anchor at Martinique in preparation for a campaign against Barbados.

November 27
SOUTH: American militia under Colonels Isaac Shelby and Hezekiah Maham capture Fair Lawn, South Carolina, from the British.

December 1
SOUTH: Major John Doyle, commanding 850 men at Fort Dorchester, South Carolina, abandons his post to advancing forces under General Nathanael Greene. Unknown to Doyle, the Americans number only 400 men.

December 10
NAVAL: Admiral Luc Urbain, comte de Guichen, departs Brest with 19 ships of the line and a large convoy of transports, headed for the West Indies.

December 12
NAVAL: Admiral Richard Kempenfelt, with 12 ships of the line, attacks and defeats a combined Franco-Spanish convoy under Admiral Luc Urbain, comte de Guichen, at the Second Battle of Ushant, off the coast of France. After shadowing the enemy for several hours, a severe squall breaks up the enemy formation and juxtaposes the transports between French and British warships. Kempenfelt moves in quickly and captures 15 vessels.

December 13
POLITICS: News of the victory at Yorktown induces the Confederation Congress to declare a day of thanksgiving and prayer.

December 20
POLITICS: Disregarding appeals from Lords Frederick North and George Germain, King George III stubbornly refuses to end the war.

December 22
North: His mission to America completed, the marquis de Lafayette embarks at Boston and returns to France.

December 28–29
South: Colonel Henry Lee is rebuffed in his attempt to storm Johns Island, South Carolina, defended by British regulars under Major James H. Craig. Colonel John Laurens is supposed to attack with one column, but a second force under Major James Hamilton fails to cross the Wapoo Creek and the operation miscarries.

December 31
Politics: The Confederation Congress formally charters the Bank of North America in Philadelphia upon the urging of Robert Morris.

Naval: The year ends with only two American vessels, the frigates *Alliance* and *Deane,* remaining in commission. Wartime losses at sea amount to 625 British ships and 317 American.

1782

January 1
North: Loyalists commence evacuating America in large numbers and make for Nova Scotia and New Brunswick.

January 5
South: British forces evacuate Wilmington, North Carolina.

January 7
Politics: The National Bank opens for business in Philadelphia to bolster a flagging economy and mitigate a monetary crisis.

January 9
Caribbean: A French naval expedition of 24 ships of the line and several transports under Admiral François-Joseph-Paul, comte de Grasse, lands 6,000 troops at Basseterre, on the island of St. Kitts, West Indies. The British garrison of 700 men withdraws nine miles to Brimstone Hill and entrenches.

January 12
South: General Anthony Wayne crosses the Savannah River with 570 men and commences marching across Georgia.

January 14
Naval: News of the French attack upon St. Kitts prompts Admiral Samuel Hood, anchored at Barbados, to sail immediately and assist. En route he stops briefly at St. John's, Antigua, and takes 700 soldiers aboard as reinforcements.

January 22
Caribbean: A strong French squadron under Captain Armand-Guy-Simon de Coetnempren attacks and captures the former Dutch colony of Demerara from the English, seizing several small Royal Navy sloops in the process.

January 23
SOUTH: General Anthony Wayne routs Creek Indians under Chief Guristersigo who attack his camp at night near Savannah, Georgia, killing 18 warriors.

January 25–26
NAVAL: A British fleet under Admiral Samuel Hood approaches St. Kitts, West Indies, intending to surprise French forces under Admiral François-Joseph-Paul, comte de Grasse. The French are alerted to his arrival and sortie from Frigate Bay, intending to attack. After some maneuvering, Hood decides to sail directly into Basseterre harbor while de Grasse preoccupies himself with attacking the British rear. Hood's fleet then drops anchor in a solid line as planned and beats back another French attack. Unable to defeat his wily opponent, de Grasse draws off while Hood disembarks 700 badly needed reinforcements; a brilliant deception on Hood's part. French losses are 107 killed and 207 wounded to a British tally of 72 dead and 244 injured.

February 11
POLITICS: Lord George Germain resigns as secretary of state, although King George III still refuses to sue for peace.

February 12
CARIBBEAN: British forces on St. Kitts surrender to a French expeditionary force under Admiral François-Joseph-Paul, comte de Grasse, who then departs for Martinique to refit.

February 17
NAVAL: The American Revolution spills over into the distant Indian Ocean as the squadron of Admiral Pierre-Andre de Suffren begins cruising the Coromandel Coast off southeastern India. His opponent, Admiral Edward Hughes, who captured six transports the previous night, next confronts de Suffren de Saint-Tropez off Sadras. The French possess 11 ships of the line, the British nine, and an intense encounter ensues. Suffren enjoys the weather gauge and severely pounds the British van and Hughes's flagship HMS *Superb*. Hughes is nearly captured, but the wind shifts to the English, the rear comes up to rescue Hughes, and Suffren breaks contact.

February 22
NAVAL: A French squadron under Admiral Jacques, comte de Barras, bloodlessly captures the English island of Montserrat.

February 25
SOUTH: General Francis Marion attacks a large British force under Colonel Benjamin Thompson at Wambaw Creek Bridge, South Carolina, but is repulsed with a loss of 20 killed and 12 prisoners.

February 27
POLITICS: Stunned by the defeat at Yorktown, the House of Commons votes for King George III to accept peace with America, now referred to as the "former colonies."

March 4
Politics: The House of Commons passes a resolution denouncing any individual seeking to prolong hostilities with America as an enemy of king and country.
North: A raid conducted by Continentals under Lieutenant Colonel William Hull against Morrisania, New York, nets 52 prisoners and incurs 25 casualties.

March 5
Politics: The House of Lords dejectedly empowers King George III to enact peace negotiations with its "former colonies."

March 7–8
West: Vengeful Pennsylvania militia under Colonel David Williamson corral and massacre 96 peaceful, Christian Delaware Indians at Gnadenhutten, Ohio, with blunt instruments. On the following day additional Moravian Indians are forcibly moved to the settlement and similarly slaughtered. The Pennsylvania assembly subsequently condemns the act as "disgraceful to humanity."

March 19
West: Colonel Benjamin Logan dispatches 40 horsemen under Captain James Estill from Estill's Station (Kentucky) in pursuit of Wyandot raiders who have savaged a settlement at Strode's Station.

March 20
Politics: Rather than lose a vote of no confidence, Lord Frederick North resigns as prime minister.

March 22
Politics: Charles Watson-Wentworth, marquess of Rockingham, forms a new government and initiates direct peace negotiations in Paris.
West: A party of 25 Kentucky cavalrymen under Captain James Estill surprises a body of Wyandot warriors in camp at Little Mountain, Kentucky. The Americans open fire, killing several warriors; a bitterly contested firefight then ensues with heavy losses on both sides. At length the militiamen are outflanked and retreat. There are only seven survivors—Estill being among the dead. Monk, an African-American slave who fought with distinction and saved several of his white comrades, is rewarded with his freedom.

March 24
North: A British naval/Loyalist force of 120 men attacks the privateering center at Tom's River, New Jersey, driving off the local militia company and burning several homes. American losses are seven killed, four wounded, and 13 captive, to two British killed and six wounded.

April 1
North: General George Washington establishes his headquarters at Newburgh, New York, while his troops, their pay several months in arrears, start to grumble.

April 4
Politics: Charles Watson-Wentworth, marquess of Rockingham, appoints General Guy Carleton commander in chief of British forces in North America. He is then

instructed to avoid offensive operations, prepare to evacuate United States territory, and accommodate all Loyalists wishing to leave.

April 8
NAVAL: Captain Joshua Barney, commanding the 16-gun sloop *Hyder Ally,* is chased by the 20-gun brig HMS *General Monck* and the 16-gun privateer *Fair American.* He lures the former into the restricted waters of Delaware Bay, instructing his helmsman to do the opposite of whatever command he yells. The *General Monck,* taken in by this deception, mimicks its quarry until *Hyder Ally* suddenly crosses its bow, delivering a fatal broadside. The British surrender after sustaining 20 killed and 33 wounded. American losses are three killed and 12 wounded.

Admiral François-Joseph-Paul, comte de Grasse, sorties from Fort Royal, Martinique, with 33 ships of the line to protect a 123-ship French convoy headed from Dominica to join Spanish forces assembling off San Domingo for a combined attack upon Jamaica. Word of his movement induces the British fleet of 36 ships of the line under Admiral George Rodney at St. Lucia to raise anchor and pursue them.

April 9
NAVAL: Admiral Samuel Hood overhauls Admiral François-Joseph-Paul, comte de Grasse's fleet off Dominica, and a fight breaks out between the British van of eight vessels and 15 French warships constituting the rear division. The balance of Rodney's fleet is unable to come up owing to light winds and Hood is perilously outnumbered, but de Grasse proves reluctant to close. A protracted bombardment at long range ensues and ceases with nightfall. The French ships then gradually rejoin their convoy and sail off to Guadelupe. Hood impetuously pursues over the next two days before finally breaking contact.

April 12
DIPLOMACY: Peace negotiations informally commence between Benjamin Franklin and British representative Richard Oswald in Paris; John Adams is in the Netherlands, John Jay is in Spain, and Henry Laurens remains imprisoned in London. Franklin begins judiciously but doggedly pursuing formal recognition of independence, fishing rights off Newfoundland, and free navigation on the Mississippi River.
NORTH: Captain Joshua Huddy, a New Jersey militia officer captured in March, is hung by Loyalists for the death of Philip White. General George Washington retaliates by selecting a captive British officer, Captain Charles Asgill, to likewise hang in retaliation.
NAVAL: Admiral George Rodney engages the French fleet of Admiral François-Joseph-Paul, comte de Grasse, midway between Guadeloupe and Dominica, crushing it in a decisive engagement at the Saintes. The two fleets assume a traditional battle line and make a slow firing pass at each other. Suddenly, the wind veers and de Grasse's ships begin losing their compact order. As gaps begin appearing, Rodney orders several of his ships to steer directly toward the French and pierce their line. This is accomplished and a second force under Admiral Samuel Hood also breaks through de Grasse's struggling formation. After several hours of fighting at a disadvantage the remaining French vessels flee. Rodney's unorthodox tactics effectively destroy the French capacity to resist; moreover, he captures de Grasse and his huge 110-gun flagship, *Ville de Paris.* For the loss of 243 killed and 816 wounded,

the British capture five warships and inflict 3,000 casualties and prisoners. However, Rodney incurs a degree of controversy by declining to pursue vigorously; Hood will angrily insist that had he been in charge he might have snared the entire force. The Saintes is the most decisive British naval victory of the war, but it occurs too late to affect the outcome of events.

The squadrons of Admirals Pierre-Andre de Suffren and Edward Hughes clash again off the northwest coast of Ceylon (Sri Lanka). Both sides possess 11 ships of the line, but Suffren catches the British close to shore and unable to maneuver. Again, Hughes's flagship HMS *Superb* takes a tremendous pounding, while the *Monmouth*, reduced to tatters, refuses to surrender. Fighting concludes at nightfall and both antagonists remain within sight of each other for a week while conducting repairs. Suffren subsequently withdraws to his base at Cuddalore on April 22.

April 19
Diplomacy: John Adams secures diplomatic recognition of the United States from the Netherlands and immediately begins negotiations for a large loan.

April 20
Naval: A large expeditionary force of 59 warships, 1,600 sailors, and 2,000 troops under Governor Juan Miguel de Caxigal departs Havana, Cuba, and sails for New Providence (Nassau) in the Bahamas. Among them is the 40-gun American frigate *South Carolina* under Commodore Alexander Gillon.

April 24
South: American forces under Captain Ferdinand O'Neal wage a fierce and unsuccessful skirmish with British troops at Dorchester, South Carolina, losing nine captives.

May 7
Caribbean: A large Spanish naval expedition under Governor Juan Manuel de Caxigal seizes New Providence from 600 regulars, 338 militia, and 800 sailors under Governor John Maxwell of Great Britain. No fighting occurs and the ensuing occupation is characterized by mildness. However, after receiving news of Admiral François-Joseph-Paul, comte de Grasse's recent defeat at the Saintes, Caxigal cancels plans to invade Jamaica and returns to Havana. He leaves behind a small, 300-man garrison.

May 9
North: General Guy Carleton arrives in New York and relieves General Henry Clinton as supreme military commander in North America. He then begins orchestrating a complete British withdrawal.

May 22
North: At Newburgh, New York, General George Washington angrily dismisses a suggestion from Colonel Lewis Nicola that he install himself as king of the newly independent nation. "Banish these thoughts from your mind," the general insists, "and never communicate as from yourself or anyone else, a sentiment of the like nature." Taken aback by this rebuke, Nicola is profusely contrite and writes three letters of apology.

May 25
West: A party of 480 Pennsylvania militia under Colonel William Crawford departs Mingo Town, Pennsylvania, on a raid through the Sandusky region of Ohio.

June 4–6
West: A detachment of 480 Pennsylvania militiamen under Colonel William Crawford conducts an ill-fated expedition against Indians of the upper Ohio River Valley. En route they are ambushed at Sandusky by a mixed Indian/Loyalist force under Captain William Caldwell. The British manage to scrape together 100 men from Butler's Rangers, some artillery, and large numbers of Lake Indians and Shawnee under noted scout Simon Girty, whose arrival tips the balance. The fighting lasts two days before the Americans are finally surrounded and defeated. A detachment under Major David Hamilton manages to cut through the encirclement and escape. The Americans nonetheless lose eight killed and 27 wounded outright and several prisoners—including Colonel Crawford—are slowly tortured to death. British and Indian losses are five killed and 11 wounded.

June 7
Diplomacy: The Netherlands formalizes a $1 million loan to the United States.

June 13
West: Survivors of the recent expedition to Sandusky arrive back at Mingo Town, Pennsylvania, under Colonel David Williamson.

June 23
Diplomacy: John Jay arrives in Paris from Madrid to assist in peace negotiations. In time he perceives that French minister Charles Gravier, comte de Vergennes, is maneuvering to place French and Spanish priorities ahead of their treaty obligations with America.

June 24
North: Lieutenant Colonel Henry Hamilton is appointed lieutenant governor of Canada.

July 1
Politics: William Petty, earl of Shelburne, succeeds Charles Watson-Wentworth, marquess of Rockingham, as prime minister following the latter's sudden death.
Naval: American privateers raid Lunenberg, Nova Scotia.

July 6
Naval: The 11-warship French squadron of Admiral Pierre-Andre de Suffren, having embarked from Cuddalore with various troops, sails south to attack and capture the British base at Negapatam. En route he is intercepted by Admiral Edward Hughes, also with 11 ships, who gives battle off Negapatam. The two lines clash for several hours and at one point the French *Servere* surrenders, but the crew refuses to obey their captain's command and successfully avoids capture. Thwarted in his goal to capture Negapatam, Suffren retires back to Cuddalore and refits.

July 11
SOUTH: British forces under former governor James Wright evacuate 4,000 Loyalists and 5,000 African-American slaves from Savannah, Georgia, concluding two and a half years of occupation.

July 13
NORTH: Chief Joseph Brant directs a raid against the village of Hannastown, Pennsylvania but fails to carry the stockade.

July 20
POLITICS: The Confederation Congress adopts the Great Seal of the United States, which has been under development since July 1776.

July 29
DIPLOMACY: The mother of captured British officer Captain Charles Asgill, who is scheduled to be executed for the death of an American prisoner in April, visits Paris and pleads with Charles Gravier, comte de Vergennes, for help in sparing his life. Vergennes, visibly moved, informs King Louis XVI and the queen, who then authorize him to appeal to General George Washington. The Confederation Congress subsequently votes for Asgill's unconditional release.

August 7
NORTH: General George Washington institutes the Purple Heart, or Badge of Military Merit, for distinguished military service to the country. Three soldiers are initially honored.

August 8
NORTH: A small British garrison at Fort Prince of Wales, Hudson Bay (Canada), surrenders to three French warships.

August 14–17
WEST: A mixed Loyalist/Indian raiding party of 340 men under Simon Girty and Captain William Caldwell besieges Bryan's Station, Kentucky, but is repulsed. A relief force is roughly handled by the Indians, but 17 troopers manage to join the defenders inside the fort. The Americans suffer four killed and three wounded. Girty and Caldwell call off the attack after losing five Indians killed and several more wounded, and they fall back to the ruins of Ruddell's Station, ransacked the previous year. En route they also deliberately mark their trail as if inviting the Americans to follow.

August 18
WEST: An American relief column of 182 men under Colonel Hugh McGary departs Bran's Station and pursues Simon Girty's raiding party across the Licking River, Kentucky, despite signs of an impending ambush. Daniel Boone, the noted scout, is familiar with the area and advises McGary against crossing directly. Instead he proposes dividing the force and sending half to ford the river several miles downstream and catch the raiders from behind. He also implores his commander to await reinforcements under Colonel Benjamin Logan. But McGary, having been accused of cowardice by some soldiers for delaying, resolves to attack.

August 19
West: Colonel Hugh McGary divides his force of 182 mounted Kentuckians into three columns and surges across the lower Blue Licks. Assembling on the opposite bank, they begin ascending the high ground when Simon Girty's Indians suddenly rise from cover, fire a devastating volley, and charge. McGary's right and center quickly collapse while his left-most column, under Daniel Boone, struggles to hold its ground. The surviving Kentuckians then flee across the river in panic, leaving the Indians to scalp and mutilate the wounded. The Americans lose 77 men in 15 minutes and a further seven are captured and slowly tortured to death. Among the slain is Boone's youngest son, Israel Boone. Girty reports seven killed and 10 wounded.

August 24
West: Colonel Benjamin Logan and 470 mounted Kentuckians arrive at the Blue Licks battlefield and spend several hours interring the dead. Colonel Daniel Boone recovers his son's remains and conveys them back to Boone's Station for burial.

August 27
South: American forces under General Mordecai Gist unsuccessfully skirmish with a British foraging party at Combahee Ferry, South Carolina, losing two killed and 19 wounded. Colonel John Laurens, the son of Henry Laurens, is among the slain. The foragers return to Charleston unimpeded.

August 28
Naval: The French squadron of Admiral Pierre-Andre de Suffren attacks and captures the important British base at Trincomalee, Ceylon (Sri Lanka).

September 2
Naval: France receives the 74-gun ship of the line *America*, the first such vessel constructed in the United States, to compensate it for the loss of the *Magnifique*, which grounded and sank in Boston Harbor.

September 3
Naval: The British squadron of 12 ships of the line under Admiral Edward Hughes arrives off Trincomalee, Ceylon (Sri Lanka), to wrest it back from the French. Admiral Pierre-André de Suffren de Saint-Tropez then sorties out of the harbor to engage him with 14 ships of the line. For three hours the antagonists flail away at each other and Suffren's flagship *Heros* loses a mainmast. But a draw ensues and fighting ceases by nightfall. While withdrawing back into Trincomalee the warship *L'Orient* grounds on a reef and sinks; Hughes, unable to recapture the base, sails back to Madras.

September 9
Diplomacy: In Paris, John Jay discerns that Charles Gravier, comte de Vergennes, has dispatched his secretary to London to begin secret negotiations with England behind America's back. Benjamin Franklin, alerted to the deception, now insists that the British deal with the United States as a single entity, not 13 separate colonies.

September 10
SOUTH: General Andrew Pickens leads 316 South Carolina militiamen on a second campaign against the Cherokee. He then enters Georgia and is joined by additional militia under Colonel Elijah Clarke.

September 13–14
NAVAL: The British garrison at Gibraltar under General George Augustus Eliott decisively repels a large French-Spanish assault upon that peninsula. The French cleverly employ 10 floating batteries designed by Michaud D'Argon, which are stoutly constructed and considered impervious to cannon fire. Eliott counters this innovation with one of his own: red-hot shot heated in ovens prior to being fired. By day's end all 10 batteries have been sunk, with a loss of 2,000 lives.

WEST: Fort Henry, Virginia, is unsuccessfully besieged for three days by 300 Indians and Loyalists. The attackers try making an improvised cannon out of a hollow tree, but it explodes harmlessly. The defenders then repulse several attempts to scale the walls at night, at which point the siege ends.

September 19
POLITICS: Secretary of State for the Colonies William Petty, Lord Shelburne, acknowledging a *fait accompli,* authorizes his agents in Paris to negotiate with the United States as a sovereign entity and not simply 13 colonies.

September 20
WEST: Colonel John Sevier defeats the Cherokee under Dragging Canoe at Lookout Mountain, Tennessee, which finally suppresses the last of the hostile bands.

September 24–28
NAVAL: Captain John Barry and the 32-gun frigate *Alliance* capture four heavily-laden British merchant ships bound for Jamaica.

September 27
DIPLOMACY: Representatives from Britain and the United States commence formal peace negotiations in Paris.

September 30
NAVAL: At Tangier Sound, Chesapeake Bay, six British barges attack the Maryland barge *Protector* under Commodore Hezekiah Whaley and capture it, sustaining 25 casualties. The Americans lose 25 killed, 29 wounded, and 40 captured.

October 1
DIPLOMACY: Benjamin Franklin and John Jay indicate to their British counterparts a willingness to negotiate and ignore prior pledges to France—in exchange for a better deal from England.

October 5
DIPLOMACY: British and American negotiators in Paris conclude a preliminary draft of peace terms that defines national boundaries, evacuates British forces, affords American fishing rights off Newfoundland, and ensures free navigation of the Mississippi River.

October 8
DIPLOMACY: John Adams finalizes a treaty of friendship and commerce with the Netherlands.

October 11
NAVAL: Admiral Richard Howe skillfully conducts a 186-ship relief convoy into Gibraltar, running the blockade.

October 20
NAVAL: A British fleet under Admiral Richard Howe is scattered by a severe storm off Gibraltar and blown into the Mediterranean. A combined Franco-Spanish fleet blockading the peninsula is likewise dispersed, and the two antagonists spend several hours sorting themselves out. At length Howe takes up defensive positions off Cape Spartel, Morocco, with 35 ships of the line. The allied fleet of 46 ships of the line under Admiral Córdoba catches up with him before timidly probing his line with a long-range artillery duel. The British easily repel an attempt to close and the battle gradually tapers off. Both sides suffer around 600 casualties apiece, but Howe manages to keep Gibraltar's lines of communication open.

October 26
DIPLOMACY: John Adams arrives in Paris to help finalize peace negotiations.

November 1
DIPLOMACY: American peace commissioners in Paris, ignoring instructions from Congress, engage their British counterparts—without consulting the French as per the French alliance.

November 4
SOUTH: Americans and British fight a final skirmish near St. Johns Island, South Carolina, which occasions the death of Captain William Wilmot, 2nd Maryland Continentals, and four soldiers. Four others are wounded. Wilmot is the last American officer to fall in the war.

November 5
DIPLOMACY: Henry Laurens, newly freed from prison, joins the American diplomatic circle in Paris.

November 10
WEST: General George Rogers Clark leads 1,050 mounted riflemen on a punitive raid against Shawnee villages around present-day Piqua, Ohio, concluding the last battle of the Revolutionary War. The Indians lose 10 killed and 10 wounded.

November 30
DIPLOMACY: Benjamin Franklin, John Jay, Henry Laurens, and John Adams conclude the Treaty of Paris with the British government. The document ignores Spanish protests over lands east of the Mississippi River and also fails to inform the French of the proceedings—a violation of the 1778 French alliance. However, the treaty is not technically in effect until ongoing conflicts with France and Spain are also resolved, and the Confederation Congress will not actually ratify the document until January 14, 1784.

December 14
SOUTH: British forces under General Alexander Leslie evacuate Charleston, South Carolina, taking along 3,800 Loyalists and 5,000 newly liberated African Americans. The city is then occupied by troops under General Nathanael Greene.

December 15
DIPLOMACY: French minister Charles Gravier, comte de Vergennes, remonstrates against being left out of peace negotiations with Great Britain, but a crisis is thwarted after deft consultations with Benjamin Franklin. To underscore his mastery of diplomacy, Franklin also manages to secure a new loan of 6 million livres from the French government.

December 20
NAVAL: The 40-gun American frigate *South Carolina* under Captain John Joyner surrenders to the 54-gun HMS *Diomede* under Captain Thomas L. Frederick and the 40-gun frigate *Quebec* off the Delaware Capes. American losses are three killed, three wounded, and 450 prisoners.

December 24
NORTH: General Jean-Baptiste, comte de Rochambeau, embarks from Boston with his army and makes for the West Indies.

1783

January 6
NORTH: General Alexander McDougall, Colonel John Brooks, and Colonel Matthias Ogden petition the Confederation Congress for back pay and other amenities. There is a growing sense among military officers that Congress cannot successfully discharge its obligations toward the army—or the nation.

January 20
DIPLOMACY: Peace terms between Great Britain, France, and Spain are concluded in Paris.

February 3
DIPLOMACY: The government of Spain extends belated diplomatic recognition to the United States.

February 4
POLITICS: King George III officially declares an end to hostilities with America.

February 6
NAVAL: Franco-Spanish forces formally conclude their unsuccessful siege of Gibraltar. The British victory is made possible through splendid, close coordination between military forces and the Royal Navy. British losses are 350 killed and 1,000 wounded; the allies suffer approximately twice that.

February 14
POLITICS: Through a unique shift in British ministerial politics, Prime Minister William Petty, earl of Shelburne, resigns and is replaced by Charles James Fox. Fox

accedes to power only by entering into a coalition arrangement with his former archnemesis, Lord Frederick North.

February 15
DIPLOMACY: The United States gains diplomatic recognition from Portugal.

March 8
POLITICS: Secretary of Finance Robert Morris, faced with a huge national debt and uncooperative state governments, threatens to raise taxes and impose duties, using the powers implied under the Articles of Confederation.

March 10
NORTH: The Newburgh Conspiracy unfolds as Major John Armstrong anonymously circulates letters complaining about the Confederation Congress's failure to honor its promises to the army. The letters demand direct action and stipulate that all officers meet to discuss the matter on the following day.

NAVAL: To Captain John Barry and his 36-gun frigate *Alliance* goes the honor of waging the last American naval action of the war. En route from France and accompanied by the French frigate *Duc de Lauzun* under Captain John Green, they are set upon by the British frigates HMS *Alarm,* 32 guns, *Sybil,* 28 guns, and the 18-gun sloop *Tobago* off Florida. Barry cooly closes with the *Sybil,* under Captain James Vashon, and withholds firing until within pistol shot. He then unlooses a devastating broadside that cripples the British ship. *Sybil* is dismasted and helpless but Barry moves off to cover the *Duc de Lauzun,* then transporting a half-million dollars in specie, and sails home. The Americans lose one killed and nine wounded; British losses are unknown but presumed heavier.

March 11
NORTH: General George Washington, alarmed by threats of violence against the Confederation Congress implied in the Newburgh Conspiracy, forbids a gathering on the subject and summons his officers for a general meeting to be held on the 15th.

March 15
NORTH: At Newburgh, New York, General George Washington harangues his officers about duty and honor and strongly denounces military force against lawful authority. He personally promises that all grievances will be addressed by the Confederation Congress. Swayed by his example, the officers subsequently vote to disavow the Newburgh Conspiracy and reaffirm their loyalty to the American government.

March 24
POLITICS: The Confederation Congress recalls all armed vessels under the American flag.

April 1
NAVAL: A Loyalist expeditionary force under Colonel Andrew Deveaux sails from St. Augustine, Florida, to Nassau in the Bahamas. He commands a motley collection of boats and approximately 270 volunteers.

April 11
Politics: The Confederation Congress officially declares an end to hostilities with Great Britain.

April 15
Diplomacy: A provisional draft of the Treaty of Paris is ratified by the Confederation Congress. Eight years have lapsed since the first shots were fired. Congress also orders all naval prisoners of war released.

April 17
West: A party of 100 Loyalists and 50 Indians under Captain James Colbert attacks Fort Carlos, Arkansas, seizing 11 captives, but is unable to evict the remaining 40-man garrison under Captain Rayondo DuBreuil.

April 18
Politics: The Confederation Congress suggests paying off the national debt through a revenue system, but the recommendation is defeated by delegates from New York.
Caribbean: Spanish forces surrender the Bahamas to a Loyalist expedition under Colonel Andrew Deveaux, who then paroles his captives and allows them to return to Havana.

April 24
West: Captain James Colbert abandons the siege of Fort Carlos, Arkansas, and releases his prisoners upon hearing of the peace treaty.

April 26
North: The last remaining Loyalists, 7,000 strong, evacuate New York. More than 100,000 have departed for Europe or Canada since 1775 after their property was confiscated. The British government subsequently institutes a commission to pay claim damages, and £3.3 million will ultimately be dispensed.

May 13
North: The Society of the Cincinnati, an influential veteran's organization, is established at Newburgh, New York. Over 2,000 officers join and George Washington is elected president-general.

May 26
North: The bulk of the Continental army demobilizes save for a small formation retained to observe the British evacuation of New York. They return home without pay but are granted promissory notes worth three months' pay to be redeemed at a subsequent date.

June 4
Politics: Robert R. Livingston resigns as secretary for foreign affairs.

June 13
North: Disgruntled members of a Pennsylvania regiment protest lack of pay and threaten to march on the capital. Secretary of War Benjamin Lincoln tries to calm the soldiers but is ignored.

Sergeants Elijah Churchill and William Brown receive the newly created Badge of Merit from General Washington in May 1783. *(U.S. Army Center of Military History)*

June 14
NORTH: Faced with the prospect of confronting angry Pennsylvania troops in Philadelphia, the Confederation Congress votes to adjourn and flees to Princeton, New Jersey. General George Washington dispatches troops in their support.

June 15
POLITICS: The Confederation Congress, beset by angry soldiers, adjourns its session and is allowed to depart through their ranks.

June 17
POLITICS: The Confederation Congress votes to reconvene at Princeton, New Jersey, while the mutinous soldiers disband in Philadelphia without further protest.

Naval: The French squadron of Admiral Pierre-André de Suffren de Saint-Tropez eludes a British squadron searching for him off the east coast of India and puts into the port of Cuddalore, then closely besieged by land forces. Suffren nonetheless gleans off 1,200 artillerists and soldiers to supplement his crew and returns to sea.

June 20

Naval: Admirals Pierre-Andre de Suffren and Edward Hughes conclude three days of maneuvering and commence battle off the closely besieged base at Cuddalore. The French squadron of 15 ships of the line and its British counterpart, which possesses 16, fight furiously over three hours, but the result is another tactical draw. Unable to secure an advantage, Hughes withdraws to Madras while Suffren returns to help break the siege of Cuddalore. Word of the Treaty of Paris arrives shortly after, and hostilities cease around the world.

July 2

Politics: The British government closes West Indian ports to American trade unless the cargo is carried in British bottoms.

July 8

North: Massachusetts becomes the first New England state formally to abolish slavery.

July 28

Diplomacy: Francis Dana is recalled from St. Petersburg as the American agent to Russia; he has spent two fruitless years attempting to secure diplomatic recognition from Czarina Catherine II but was perpetually handicapped by his inability to speak either French or Russian.

September 3

Diplomacy: The Treaty of Paris is formally concluded between the United States and Great Britain, officially ending the Revolutionary War. America now has its independence and controls a huge swath of land east of the Mississippi River and up to the Great Lakes region. The British also sign separate treaties with Spain and France.

October 7

South: The government of Virginia emancipates all African-American slaves who fought in the Continental army.

October 15

Politics: The Confederation Congress approves an Indian policy for dealing with the Northwest Territory, shifts the national boundary westward, and instructs agents to deal with the tribes separately in order to divide them.

October 18

North: General George Washington issues orders to departing soldiers of the Continental army at Rocky Hill, New Jersey, bidding them an affectionate farewell. He is especially keen to solicit their support for a strong federal government, whatever form that may take.

October 31
NORTH: New Hampshire finally ratifies a new state constitution.

November 2
NORTH: General George Washington issues final orders to the Continental army and bids it farewell. Though disbanding, he exhorts them that "they should carry with them into civil society the most conciliating dispositions; and that they should prove themselves not less virtuous and useful as citizens, than they have been persevering and victorious as soldiers."

November 3
NORTH: The Continental army is formally disbanded by congressional fiat.

November 11
SOUTH: Annapolis, Maryland, becomes the temporary national capital until August 1784.

November 25
NORTH: The last British forces embark on ships in New York Harbor and are replaced by soldiers under General George Washington and Governor George Clinton.

November 26
SOUTH: The Confederation Congress convenes its new session at Annapolis, Maryland, and thereafter alternates residences with Trenton, New Jersey, until a new capital is established.

December 3
NORTH: The Continental army, constricted in size to 500 rank and file, is ordered to guard public stores gathered at West Point, New York.

December 4
NORTH: The remaining British forces finally evacuate Staten Island, New York. General George Washington subsequently takes leave of his officers in a tearful ceremony at the Fraunces Tavern.

December 23
SOUTH: Having led his nation to victory and independence, General George Washington, pursuant to the wishes of Congress, resigns as commander in chief at Annapolis, Maryland, and tenders his resignation to President Thomas Mifflin. An incredulous King George III subsequently declares that Washington will become "the greatest man in the world."

A new age begins.

Adams, Abigail (1744–1818)
advocate for women's rights, first lady

Abigail Smith was born in Weymouth, Massachusetts, on November 11, 1744, the daughter of a well-to-do Congregationalist minister. She was raised in a culture affording few educational or social opportunities for women, yet was encouraged by her father to study and inculcate literature, philosophy, religion, and the classics. She evinced intellectual properties at a young age and became quite adept as a witty, poignant correspondent. Abigail met John ADAMS in 1759 when he was an aspiring attorney and married him four years later. The union proved a happy one for both parties and produced five children, including John Quincy Adams, a future president.

In 1774 John Adams departed his farm in Weymouth to attend the First Continental CONGRESS, and Abigail assumed her role as head of the household. She proved capable as a business woman and a farmer, coping with John's 10-year absence by intensely corresponding with fellow intellectuals such as Mercy Otis WARREN and Thomas JEFFERSON. The twilight of colonial rule in America also occasioned intense political discussion and she totally immersed herself in the arena of ideas. In fact, while Adams completely embraced the newly emerging ideology of republicanism, she sought to extend its benefits to women. She was especially concerned with abolishing the practice of coverture, whereby married women could not possess property or pursue business activities on their own. "Remember the Ladies," she penned her husband in March 1776, "and be more favorable and generous to them than your ancestors. Do not put such unlimited power in the hands of the Husbands. Remember all men would be tyrants if they could." Adams also eloquently inveighed against slavery and racial discrimination and appealed to lawmakers to grant young girls equal opportunities for education. She viewed the ongoing revolution as a perfect opportunity to redress these grievances while still upholding the existing social order.

In 1783 Adams accompanied her husband to Europe after he gained appointment as minister to The Hague. She actively partook of the social, cultural, and intellectual life of the upper classes there, particularly in Paris and London, and the excesses she observed convinced her that the United States was the most virtuous nation in the world. In 1789 John was selected the first vice president under George WASHINGTON, and Abigail accompanied him back to Philadelphia. Eight years later she became first lady when her husband became the second president of the United States. This placed her at the epicenter of national politics and, in an age when compliancy was expected from women of all classes, she gained notoriety through a partisan and outspoken defense of her husband against critics like Jefferson and James MADISON. Abigail exuded such strong opinions that critics accused her of manipulating the president's political decisions, and newspaper columns derided the first lady as "Her Majesty." She was profoundly hurt by John's loss of the presidency to Jefferson in 1800 but gradually abandoned her support for the Federalists when they refused to condemn Great Britain for attacks upon American shipping and commerce.

Abigail Adams died of typhus on October 28, 1818, the personification of republican womanhood and a role model for her generation. Her copious correspondence reveals a perceptive mind, a strong will, and a determination to better define women's place in society through piety, education, and equality. From the standpoint of intellect and vision, she was in many respects the first lady of the Revolution.

Further Reading
Akers, Charles W. *Abigail Adams, An American Woman.* New York: Longman, 2000.
Berkin, Carol. *America's Revolutionary Mothers: Women in the Struggle for Independence.* New York: Knopf, 2005.
Bohrer, Melissa L. *Glory, Passion, Principle: The Story of Eight Remarkable Women at the Core of the American Revolution.* New York: Atria Books, 2004.
Levin, Phyllis L. *Abigail Adams: A Biography.* New York: St. Martin's Griffin, 2001.
Roberts, Cokie. *Founding Mothers: The Women Who Raised Our Nation.* New York: William Morrow, 2004.
Withey, Lynne. *Dearest Friend: A Life of Abigail Adams.* New York: Simon & Schuster, 2001.

Adams, John (1735–1826)
American politician, second president of the United States

John Adams was born in Braintree, Massachusetts, on October 30, 1735, the son of a prosperous farmer and town official. He was well educated locally and gained admittance to Harvard University in 1751, intending to join the clergy. But the experience of higher education broadened his outlook and, after serving briefly as a teacher, he studied law under noted Worcester attorney James Putnam. Adams was admitted to the bar in 1755 and spent much of his time alternating between Braintree and Boston practicing law. In 1764 he married Abigail Smith in a celebrated and happy union that lasted 54 years. The turning point in his career occurred in 1765 with the passage of the STAMP ACT, and Adams became a noted dissenter over British imperial policy. In time he was joined by vocal agitators like James OTIS and his cousin Samuel ADAMS, gaining local notoriety by publishing various protests in the *Boston Gazette.* In 1768 he enhanced his legal and political reputation by defending merchant John HANCOCK against charges of smuggling. But while increasingly concerned for the future of liberty, Adams remained firmly committed to the rule of law. In 1770 he joined fellow attorney Josiah QUINCY in defending British officers and soldiers implicated in the notorious BOSTON MASSACRE. In the process he ended up portraying local sailor Crispus ATTUCKS as an instigator behind the violence. His was an unpopular decision, but Adams remained unswervingly committed to doing what was right rather than what was popular. As tensions between Parliament and the colonies escalated, especially in the wake of the COERCIVE ACTS, he became convinced that reconciliation was impossible. Consequently, in 1774 he was elected to the First Continental CONGRESS in Philadelphia as one of its most outspoken radicals.

Over the next three years Adams made indelible contributions to the eventual split with Great Britain and the gradual move toward independence. In the spring of 1776 he used his influence to have George WASHINGTON confirmed as commanding general of the Continental ARMY, a ploy undertaken to placate southern suspicions of New England. He subsequently served on the Board of War and Ordnance and proved instrumental in helping create a colonial navy to challenge the British at sea. A revolutionary with limits, he also criticized the radicalism of Thomas PAINE's incendiary polemic *COMMON SENSE* as dangerously naive. On May 10, 1776, Adams performed his most influential service by authoring resolutions culminating in the DECLARATION OF INDEPENDENCE the following July. In the debate that followed, he also demonstrated his legislative mastery by capably steering the document through Congress and soliciting support from the more moderate factions. Throughout this period he also wrote and published extensively and persuasively in defense of American independence. By the time he departed Philadelphia in 1777, an exhausted Adams had served on 90 committees, chairing no less than 25 of them.

In 1778 Adams commenced an equally important phase of his career when he was dispatched to France to replace Silas DEANE as a diplomatic agent. Blunt, impatient, and irritable, he accomplished little beyond angering and insulting French minister Charles Gravier, comte de VERGENNES, Arthur LEE, and Benjamin FRANKLIN. Adams subsequently removed himself from Paris and relocated to the Netherlands to negotiate successfully diplomatic recognition, a loan, and a treaty of amity with the Dutch. In 1779 he briefly returned to Massachusetts to work on the new state constitution, but two years later Congress ordered him back to France for peace negotiations. Adams, to the irritation of Franklin and John JAY, stridently insisted upon fishing rights off the Canadian coast and succeeded. He was subsequently one of the signatories to the Treaty of PARIS on September 3, 1783. In 1785 he gained appointment as minister to Great Britain, but postwar hostilities largely negated his attempts at promoting better relations.

In 1789 Adams returned home and was selected to serve as the first vice president of the United States under the newly adopted Constitution. Impatient and garrulous as ever, he quickly pronounced it "the most insignificant office that ever the invention of man contrived." Adams nonetheless served capably as a national figure, and in 1796 he narrowly defeated Thomas Jefferson to become the second president.

Adams served a single term in high office, and his tenure was wracked by acrimony. The national polity was split between conservative Federalists headed by Alexander HAMILTON and liberal Democratic-Republicans under Jefferson over the exact nature the new American government should assume. Tensions were further exacerbated following the French Revolution of 1789 and strident calls for war by the Federalists. Adams, however, preferred diplomacy to hostilities and, despite a flurry of warfare at sea known as the Quasi-War, 1798–1800, he managed to secure an honorable treaty and an end to harassment of American commerce. Hamilton and his allies were outraged and failed to support Adams in the 1800 presidential elections. He finished an ignominious third behind Jefferson and Aaron Burr, and departed the capital a bitter, disillusioned man. He spent the balance of his life secluded back in Massachusetts, where personal and political reconciliation with Jefferson took several years to achieve. Adams died on his farm in Quincy, Massachusetts, on July 4, 1826, part of the brilliant political coterie that steered the colonies toward independence and provided a steady hand at the helm once nationhood was achieved. He was foremost among the founding fathers.

Further Reading

Diggins, John P., ed. *The Letters of John and Abigail Adams.* New York: Penguin Books, 2004.

Ferling, John. *Setting the World Ablaze: Washington, Adams, Jefferson, and the American Revolution.* New York: Oxford University Press, 2000.

Grant, James L. *John Adams: Party of One.* New York: Farrar, Straus, and Giroux, 2005.

McCullough, David. *John Adams.* New York: Simon & Schuster, 2001.

Staloff, Darren. *Hamilton, Adams, Jefferson: The Politics of Enlightenment of the American Founding.* New York: Hill & Wang, 2005.

Taylor, Robert J., ed. *Papers of John Adams,* 11 vols. Cambridge, Mass.: Belknap Press of Harvard University Press, 1977–2003.

Vidal, Gore. *Inventing a Nation: Washington, Adams, and Jefferson.* New Haven, Conn.: Yale University Press, 2003.

Adams, Samuel (1722–1803)
American politician

Samuel Adams was born in Boston, Massachusetts, on September 27, 1722, the son of a prosperous brewer. After graduating from Harvard College in 1740, Adams tried his hand at a number of legal and commercial professions, failing miserably. His father's death in 1748 left him a sizable inheritance but he typically squandered it through neglect and after 1756 was forced to accept the position of tax collector. Adams served in this capacity until 1764, until his accounts revealed him to be several thousand pounds in arrears. But by this time he had become steeped in local politics and displayed considerable aptitude as an organizer and propagandist. Adams then found his calling as a political gadfly.

Adams's talent for political invective and agitation first manifested in 1764 when he helped orchestrate minor protests against the SUGAR ACT. However, the following year, with the adoption of the notorious STAMP ACT, Adams refined his niche as a political incendiary. He wrote and published forceful essays condemning taxation without representation and warned fellow colonists of a conspiracy to infringe upon their rights as Englishmen. In concert with John HANCOCK, he also helped recruit and organize the notorious SONS OF LIBERTY to enforce boycotts of British goods and intimidate dissenters. He proved particularly effective at instigating popular resentment against royal governors Francis BERNARD and Thomas HUTCHINSON. The unrest he stirred was sufficient enough to convince Parliament to repeal the Stamp Act in 1766. The following year they instituted the TOWNSHEND DUTIES on imports, and once again Adams sounded the clarion call for protest. In the wake of the infamous BOSTON MASSACRE, Adams headed a delegation that visited Governor Hutchinson and successfully demanded that British troops leave the city. In 1772 Adams was instrumental in organizing a committee of correspondence to better disseminate resistance to British policies throughout the state and colonies. Through a succession of escalating events like the TEA ACT, the BOSTON TEA PARTY, and the COERCIVE ACTS, he remained at the forefront of political resistance and was marked for arrest by the new royal governor, General Thomas GAGE. In June of that year he helped prod the provincial capital to relocate to Salem, Massachusetts, where it met behind locked doors to chose delegates to the First Continental CONGRESS in 1774. Not surprisingly, Adams was selected as a delegate, and once at Philadelphia he continued his inflammatory rhetoric and posturing.

By April 1775, on the cusp of revolution, one objective of British forces dispatched to Lexington and Concord was the arrest of Adams and Hancock, whose names were conspicuously absent from a proposed British amnesty. Between 1775 and 1783 Adams served as a Massachusetts delegate to the Second Continental Congress, but his activities there were largely eclipsed by his cousin, John ADAMS. In fact, Adams's role during the Revolution proved relatively minor, and he failed to distinguish himself legislatively. Nonetheless, he was a signatory to the DECLARATION OF INDEPENDENCE and the ARTICLES OF CONFEDERATION, both of which steered the nascent United States on a collision course with Great Britain. In 1780 he returned home briefly to champion a new state constitution drawn by his more famous cousin. The war ended in 1783, and Adams served in the Massachusetts state senate. In 1788 he failed in a bid to return to Congress and subsequently joined a state convention called to ratify the new federal constitution. This he did with some reluctance, for Adams feared the adoption of strong, centralized authority and, with it, arbitrary governance. In 1789 he was also elected lieutenant governor under Hancock, and from 1793 to 1797 he served as governor. Again, he acquitted himself capably but without distinction. Adams remained alarmed by the growing authority of the Federalist Party, and in 1800 he favored Thomas JEFFERSON for president over his cousin John Adams. He died in Boston on October 2, 1803, one of the master polemicists of the American Revolution.

Further Reading

Alexander, John K. *Samuel Adams: America's Revolutionary Politician.* Lanham, Md.: Rowman & Littlefield, 2002.

Beagle, Jonathan M. " 'The Cradle of Liberty': Faneuil Hall and the Political Culture of Eighteenth-century Boston." Unpublished Ph.D. diss., University of New Hampshire, 2003.

Cushing, Harry A., ed. *The Writings of Samuel Adams.* New York: G. P. Putnam's Sons, 2001.

Irvin, Benjamin H. *Samuel Adams, Son of Liberty, Father of Revolution.* New York: Oxford University Press, 2002.

McMahon, John E. "Dividing the Kingdom: John Cleaveland, Samuel Adams, and the Rationale for Revolution in Eighteenth-Century New England." Unpublished Ph.D. diss., Clark University, 2004.

Wright, Conrad E. *Revolutionary Generation: Harvard Men and the Consequences of Independence.* Amherst: University of Massachusetts Press, 2005.

African Americans

By 1775 African Americans numbered 500,000 or roughly 25 percent of the North American population. Of these, only 10 percent were free, the rest subject to slavery or indenture. Nonetheless, many blacks had been at the forefront of political unrest in Massachusetts, and on March 5, 1770, Crispus ATTUCKS was killed at the so-called BOSTON MASSACRE, becoming the first African American to die for his country. As events unfolded, African Americans constituted a potential source of willing manpower for the Continental ARMY, but CONGRESS and many state political establishments loathed tapping into them, for political and economic reasons. The southern colonies, where the bulk of the African-American population was concentrated, were indelibly intertwined in issues relating to slavery and proved reluctant to sacrifice these economic benefits. Plantation owners were also unwilling to see slaves armed and trained for fear of fomenting an insurrection. For this reason Congress initially outlawed the recruitment of slaves into the armed forces and depended solely upon white volunteers. General George WASHINGTON, upon assuming command of Continental forces at Cambridge in July 1775, took this exclusion a step further and forbade the recruitment of blacks in general, slave and free alike. However, as manpower shortages became chronic due to a lack of white volunteers, the prospect of African-American recruitment became much more palatable, at least in the northern colonies. Several blacks were also successfully employed as spies, with James LAFAYETTE being the most conspicuous example.

Ironically, the first African-American military unit was recruited by Governor John MURRAY, Lord Dunmore, of Virginia, who issued a proclamation emancipating any slave who joined the British side. Consequently, around 300 former slaves were enrolled in the "Ethiopian Regiment," which campaigned in Virginia until the British were finally expelled in the spring of 1776. Thereafter, it became standard British policy to recruit blacks for military service in exchange for freedom, especially in the south. By war's end, the bulk of these were evacuated and resettled either in Canada or the West Indies. The United States promulgated no consistent policy toward African Americans, and hence many blacks were allowed to serve in the ranks, frequently as paid substitutes for unwilling whites. After September 1776, when Congress authorized creation of 88 battalions of troops, state officials simply glossed over the fact that blacks were enlisted whenever the white population failed to provide its quota of troops. Once manpower levels became critical, Washington reversed himself, and on January 2, 1777, he authorized the enlistment of free blacks wherever possible. The practice was most prevalent in New England, where slavery was weakest, and African Americans joined in comparatively large numbers. The famous unit to emerge from such practices was the 1st Rhode Island Light Infantry Regiment under Colonel Christopher GREENE, which was racially mixed, if heavily black, and led by white company-grade officers. They distinguished themselves during the Battle of Rhode Island on August 29, 1778, and repelled several determined Hessian attacks. All told, by war's end most American units had armed blacks marching directly in the ranks and, when permitted to serve, they did so with distinction. Many of these soldiers were consequently manumitted from slavery in exchange for their military service.

The armies of Spain and France had no such prohibitions against black enlistment, and both Governor Bernardo de GÁLVEZ and Admiral Charles-Hector-Théodat, comte d'ESTAING, employed considerable numbers of French- and Spanish-speaking blacks in Louisiana, at the siege of Savannah, and elsewhere. In 1779 South Carolina representative and army officer John LAURENS extolled the virtues of black soldiery and urged the governments of his native state and Georgia to recruit large numbers of slaves into the army in exchange for freedom. It was a viable plan to address chronic manpower shortages, but deep-seated enmity toward African Americans precluded its adoption.

African Americans enlisted in the military faced varying degrees of racial discrimination that militated against promotions and occupations held. Conditions proved far more accommodating in the Continental NAVY, state navies, and in PRIVATEERING, where far less emphasis was placed on race than ability. For many years prior to the Revolution, many free blacks and former slaves were attracted to service in either the merchant marine or the Royal Navy because the harsh living conditions aboard were still better than those encountered on land. Consequently, ship crews frequently contained a much higher percentage of African Americans than found ashore, and they received a fairer share of the prize monies allotted to all hands. The Royal Navy was also quick to enlist the services of African Americans as pilots, cooks, and gun crewmen, and they served throughout the war.

By 1783 around 5,000 African Americans had served in either the Continental army or navy, acquitting themselves well. They filled a critical niche in manpower needs, anticipating the role they would perform 80 years later during the Civil War, when liberty, denied them during the Revolution, was finally realized.

Further Reading

Bilal, Kolby. "Black Pilots, Patriots, and Pirates: African-American Participation in the Virginia State and British Navies during the American Revolution in Virginia." Unpublished master's thesis, College of William and Mary, 2000.

Buckley, Gail. *American Patriots: The Story of Blacks in the Military from the Revolution to Desert Storm.* New York: Random House, 2001.

Knoblock, Glenn A. *"Strong, Brave Fellows": New Hampshire's Black Soldiers and Sailors of the American Revolution, 1775–1784.* Jefferson, N.C.: McFarland, 2003.

Lanning, Michael L. *Defenders of Liberty: African-Americans in the Revolutionary War.* New York: Citadel Press, 2000.

Philyaw, L. Scott. " 'A Slave for Every Soldier': The Strange History of Virginia's Forgotten Recruitment Act of 1 January, 1781," *Virginia Magazine of History and Biography* 109, no. 4 (2001): 367–386.

Quintal, George. *Patriots of Color: "A Peculiar Boasting and Merit": African Americans and Native Americans at Battle Road and Bunker Hill.* Washington, D.C.: National Park Service, 2002.

Shirley, Paul. "Tek Force wid Force," *History Today* 54, no. 4 (2004): 30–35.

Swan, Jon. "America's Forgotten Patriots," *MHQ* 13, no. 1 (2000): 34–41.

Alamance, Battle of (May 16, 1771)

For many years prior to the American Revolution, the western provinces of North Carolina exuded deep-seated animosities toward the colonial political establishment located along the coast. Their main grievance was a lack of political representation, excessively high taxation, and the open graft of sheriffs, tax collectors, and other appointed officials. By 1768 this discontent manifested itself in the creation of the so-called Regulators, an English term denoting citizens intent upon governmental reform. Initially, the inhabitants of the Piedmont region were peaceful and repeatedly petitioned the government for redress, but none proved forthcoming. Governor William TRYON, a hard-line conservative administrator, acknowledged abuses in the system, and he warned officials not to abuse the privileges of office. But he also sternly admonished the westerners about civil disobedience and the rising tide of violence against authority. When the Regulators continued disrupting local court systems, Tryon induced the legislature to pass the Johnson Riot Act in January 1771, which equated unruly behavior with treason. Civil disobedience and unrest in the western counties continued unabated, however, and when the Superior Court of Hillsboro ceased functioning due to regulator interference and intimidation, Tryon persuaded the legislature to authorize an expedition to crush dissenters and restore order.

By April 1771, Tryon and Colonel Richard CASWELL had assembled a force of roughly 1,100 Royal militia at New Bern, the colonial capital. An additional 300 men were gathered under General Hugh WADDELL at Cape Fear, with orders to join Caswell at Hillsboro. Meanwhile, the regulators gathered a force of 3,000 frontiersmen and, while lacking a single leader, waxed united in their opposition to the establishment. Waddell departed Cape Fear as ordered and proceeded as far as the Yadkin River, when he was confronted by large numbers of Regulators on May 9, 1771. Outnumbered and fearing that his men were in sympathy with the rebels and would not fight, he withdrew his column back to Salisbury. Tryon, meanwhile, advanced with the main force from Hillsboro and encamped near Alamance Creek. Despite a brave front, the seriousness of the situation convinced many in the Regulator camp to petition the governor for redress one last time, but Tryon rejected the appeal and demanded their surrender. When the rebels refused, both sides prepared to give battle.

On May 16, 1771, Tryon's 1,100 militia confronted 2,000–3,000 ill-disciplined, ill-armed regulators across a field near Alamance Creek. As the two lines drew to within 300 yards, Tryon began shelling his opponents with several small cannon, weapons to which the Regulators could not respond. After a short interval the governor ordered his well-trained Royal militia forward and a general exchange broke out. The frontiersmen, many of whom were crack shots, dropped many of their opposites but could not withstand Tryon's advance. Regulators began falling back in groups while knots of men continued resistance, but within two hours all had been swept from the field. Tryon lost nine killed and 61 wounded while the Regulators are thought to have sustained 20 dead and several more wounded and evacuated, along with 12 captured. One Regulator leader was summarily hung on the spot and six more went to the gallows in June. Tryon also forced 6,000 inhabitants of the Piedmont region to sign oaths of allegiance to the Crown before returning to New Berne. Many historians consider Alamance to be the opening round of the American Revolution and, as such, an expression of resistance against colonial oppression and misrule. Contemporaries, however, simply regarded it as a move to restore law and order to an unruly portion of the colony—no British troops were involved. Furthermore, many hundreds of former Regulators apparently dismissed their grievances and fought as LOYALISTS when revolutionary hostilities commenced four years later.

Further Reading

Gammons, P. Keith. "Revivalist Rhetoric and the North Carolina Regulator Rebellion." Unpublished Ph.D. diss., University of North Carolina at Greensboro, 2001.

Kars, Marjoleine. *Breaking Loose Together: The Regulator Rebellion in Pre-Revolutionary North Carolina.* Chapel Hill: University of North Carolina Press, 2002.

Lee, Wayne E. *Crowds and Soldiers in Revolutionary North Carolina: The Culture of Violence in Riot and War.* Gainesville: University Press of Florida, 2001.

Powell, William S., James K. Huhta, and Thomas J. Franham, eds. *The Regulators in North Carolina: A Documentary History, 1759–1776.* Raleigh, N.C.: State Department of Archives and History, 1971.

Powell, William S. *The War of the Regulation and the Battle of Alamance, May 16, 1771.* Raleigh, N.C.: Department of Cultural Resources, 1976.

White, Howard. *The Battle of Alamance, May 16, 1771.* Burlington, N.C.: Burlington Chamber of Commerce, 1955.

Alexander, William (1726–1781)
American military officer

William Alexander was born in New York City on December 26, 1726, the son of a Scottish Jacobite refugee and a mother who was also a successful merchant. He enjoyed an affluent upbringing and a fine education, becoming particularly adept at mathematics. Given his abilities and social connections, Alexander served in the Seven Years' War against France as secretary to General William Shirley. In 1756 he accompanied Shirley to England when the latter was summoned there to account for his failed expedition against Fort Niagara. Alexander remained in England several years thereafter, acquiring a taste for aristocratic circles and aspiring to become part of the landed gentry. For this reason he claimed to be descended from the fifth earl of Stirling, Scotland, a title that had elapsed in 1739. The Scottish courts ruled in his favor, but the House of Lords rejected his petition.

Brigadier General William Alexander, head of the Northern Department *(Independence National Historical Park)*

Alexander nevertheless adopted the title of Lord Stirling and signed all his official correspondence under that moniker.

Alexander returned to America in 1761, where he cultivated a life of luxury in New York and New Jersey and served on the councils of both colonies. In 1775 he was expected to declare his allegiance for the British Crown but surprised contemporaries by opting for the Patriot side. He was stripped of his official offices but then won appointment as colonel of the 1st New Jersey Militia Regiment. In this capacity he outfitted a small expedition in concert with Colonel Elias DAYTON on January 23, 1776, by rowing 70 men several miles out to sea and capturing the British transport *Blue Mountain Valley*. CONGRESS responded by promoting him to brigadier general in March 1776 and directing him to take command of New York City's defenses. Alexander spent several months erecting Forts Lee and Washington until he was superseded by General George WASHINGTON. The two men struck up a close acquaintance and Washington appointed him to command a brigade under General Israel PUTNAM. During the Battle of LONG ISLAND on August 27, 1776, Alexander tenaciously covered the American right flank with 1,600 men and repelled several determined attacks by General James GRANT. However, when British forces suddenly appeared in his rear, he led a series of desperate charges that enabled the bulk of his command to escape. Alexander then surrendered to General Leopold von HEISTER but was exchanged shortly after. He subsequently fought well during the Battles of WHITE PLAINS and especially TRENTON, where he blocked the retreat of Hessian forces gathered there.

In February 1777 Alexander was promoted to major general and took charge of a division. The following month Washington carelessly deployed his division at Short Hills, New Jersey, beyond immediate support, and it was strongly attacked by British forces under General Charles CORNWALLIS on June 26, 1777. The Americans fought tenaciously but were forced to withdraw after losing three cannon. Alexander nonetheless served with distinction at the Battles of BRANDYWINE and GERMANTOWN that fall. He conducted his troops exceedingly well at MONMOUTH on June 28, 1778, against General Henry CLINTON and later headed the court-martial that convicted General Charles LEE of insubordination. That fall he became the first senior officer apprised of Colonel Thomas CONWAY's machinations against Washington and alerted his superior to that fact. Washington responded to his loyalty by appointing him commander of the army at Valley Forge while he conferred with Congress in Philadelphia over the winter. Alexander also directed forces that covered the retreat of Colonel Henry LEE following the successful storming of Paulus Hook, New Jersey, on August 19, 1779.

Washington placed great trust in Alexander's leadership and in December 1779 he offered him command of the Southern Department, but the general declined on grounds of poor health. He consequently became head of the Northern Department, headquartered at Albany, New York, from which he established and ran an excellent intelligence system. In January 1780 Alexander conducted an ill-advised raid upon Staten Island that was badly drubbed, but the following June he rendered valuable services to General Nathanael GREENE at the Battle of Springfield, New Jersey. That September he also convened the board that sentenced Major John ANDRE to death for spying. Chronic gout ended Alexander's military activities in December 1782, although he remained near his headquarters. He died in Albany on January 15, 1783, one of Washington's most dependable commanders and trusted subordinates. In the republican-minded American officer corps, he was also the only senior leader to be addressed by his honorific title of Lord Stirling.

Further Reading

Carey, Arthur T. "The Military Career of Major General William, 'Earl' of Stirling." Unpublished master's thesis, University of Scranton, 1969.

Fehlings, Gregory E. " 'Act of Piracy': The Continental Army and the Blue Mountain Valley," *New Jersey History* 115, nos. 3–4 (1997): 60–70.

Helmke, George E. *Lord Stirling, William Alexander: Country Gentleman and New Jersey's Military Leader in the War for Independence.* Basking Ridge, N.J.: Historical Society of the Somerset Hills, 2000.

Morrissey, Brendan. *New York, 1776: The Continental Army's First Battles.* Oxford: Osprey, 2004.

Nelson, Paul D. *William Alexander, Lord Stirling.* Tuscaloosa: University of Alabama Press, 2004.

Taafe, Stephen R. *The Philadelphia Campaign, 1777–1778.* Lawrence: University Press of Kansas, 2003.

Valentine, Alan C. *Lord Stirling.* New York: Oxford University Press, 1969.

Allen, Ethan (1738–1789)
American militia officer

Ethan Allen was born in Litchfield, Connecticut, on January 21, 1738, the son of a successful farmer. During the French and Indian War, 1755–63, he served with the militia and subsequently acquired a large tract of land, the so-called New Hampshire Grants, in present-day Vermont. When the New York legislature also laid claim to this region, Allen, a large and imposing individual, raised his own vigilante militia, the Green Mountain Boys. These were bands of frontier ruffians that burned settler houses if they possessed New York leases, and intimidated sheriffs sent to restore order. Allen's notoriety peaked in 1770 when New York governor William TRYON offered a large reward for his capture. Not surprisingly, when fighting erupted at Lexington and CONCORD in April 1775, Allen and his four brothers threw in their lot with the Patriots and redirected their energies toward independence.

In April 1774 Allen was petitioned by the Connecticut assembly to capture the British post at Fort Ticonderoga, New York, then lightly garrisoned. He eagerly complied and mustered 200 of his Green Mountain Boys but en route encountered Colonel Benedict ARNOLD on an identical mission. The two haughty leaders then forged an uneasy alliance and successfully surprised the sleeping British garrison on May 10, 1775. When the fort's commander asked by whose authority he would dare attack the king's garrison, Allen reputedly thundered "in the name of great God Jehovah and the Continental Congress!" News of this seemingly easy conquest electrified the colonies and made Allen one of the war's earliest heroes. Moreover, the 78 cannon he captured proved instrumental in forcing the British from Boston in March 1776. However, Allen's headstrong style of command and apparent disdain for military discipline alienated many soldiers, and when the Green Mountain Boys were inducted into the Continental ARMY, they unceremoniously dumped him in favor of Lieutenant Colonel Seth WARNER.

Undeterred, Allen subsequently joined the army of General Philip J. SCHUYLER as a scout in September 1775, during the ill-fated invasion of Canada. The restless leader plunged ahead of the army to confer with the Canadians and possibly sow dissension in their ranks. Allen performed capably in that role and was authorized to recruit and command a regiment of Canadians for the army of General Richard MONTGOMERY, then besieging Saint Johns, Quebec. While on a scouting mission, Allen conspired with Colonel John Brown to attack and seize the city of Montreal with only 300 men. When Brown's force failed to materialize, the impetuous Allen proceeded to attack anyway and was captured by a swift riposte under Governor-General Guy CARLETON. He was sent to England in chains and endured three years of hunger and deprivation before being exchanged on May 6, 1778. When his narrative of captivity was published, the hardships it detailed further stoked public sentiment against Great Britain.

Once back Allen was commissioned a colonel in the Continental army and assigned to the forces at Valley Forge, but his penchant for recklessness preceded him and he failed to receive a command. Angered by the snub, Allen resigned his commission to become a major general of militia in the New Hampshire Grants, in which he had a vested interest. He pushed local authorities hard to adopt a "state" constitution for the region—over vocal opposition from New York. When that failed, along with numerous petitions to CONGRESS to recognize Vermont's statehood, Allen began clandestinely corresponding with Governor-General Frederick HALDIMAND of Canada over the possibility of annexing the region as an independent British province. This cabal was diffused by the British surrender at YORKTOWN in 1781, and Allen was never implicated in this erstwhile treasonable plot.

After the war, Allen continued his ceaseless efforts to have Vermont admitted into the United States. He died in Burlington on February 11, 1789, two years before that eventuality; he remains one of the most colorful frontier figures of the Revolutionary War and a driving force behind Vermont statehood.

Further Reading
Allen, Ethan. *A Narrative of Colonel Ethan Allen's Captivity.* Acton, Mass.: Copley Publishing Group, 2000.
Bellesiles, Michael A. *Revolutionary Outlaws: Ethan Allen and the Struggle for Independence on the Early American Frontier.* Charlottesville: University Press of Virginia, 1993.
Duffy, John J., and Eugene A. Coyle. "Green Brush vs. Ethan Allen: A Winner's Tale," *Vermont History* 70 (summer–fall 2002): 103–110.
———, eds. *Ethan Allen and His Kin: Correspondence, 1772–1819, A Selected Edition in Two Volumes.* Hanover, N.H.: University Press of New England, 1998.
Madden, Edward H., and Marian C. Madden. "Ethan Allen, His Philosophical Side," *Transactions of the Charles S. Peirce Society* 35, no. 2 (1999): 270–283.
Ranzan, David. " 'Thus a War Has Begun': The Capture of Fort Ticonderoga and Its Influence on the American Revolution." Unpublished master's thesis, East Stroudsburg University, 2002.

Andre, John (1750–1780)
English military officer, spy
John Andre was born in London on May 2, 1750, the son of a Swiss businessman. Coming from a long line of French Huguenots who sought refuge in Geneva, he was exceptionally well educated, becoming fluent in French, German, and English. However, Andre chaffed working at his father's countinghouse, and in 1770, following a failed love affair, he joined the famous Royal Welch Fusiliers

as a lieutenant. He subsequently relocated to the electorate of Hanover to continue his education and demonstrated genuine talent for poetry and art. In 1774 he was recalled to his regiment and dispatched to Canada as part of the garrison. The following year he fought at the defense of Saint Johns, Quebec, and was taken prisoner by American forces under General Richard MONTGOMERY. He endured several months of harsh imprisonment in Carlisle, Pennsylvania, before being exchanged and reassigned as a captain with the 26th Regiment of Foot in New York. In this capacity Andre came to the attention of General William HOWE, who recommended him as an aide-de-camp for newly arrived general Charles GREY. Grey took an immediate liking to his youthful charge, and the two fought closely throughout the Philadelphia campaign of 1777. During the occupation of that city, Andre became closely involved with one of its leading belles, Margaret SHIPPEN, daughter of a leading LOYALIST merchant. In May 1778 Andre demonstrated his flair for theatrics by arranging the *Meschianza*, an elaborate farewell party, for the outgoing general Howe. Andre then accompanied Grey back to New York when the British abandoned Philadelphia. Before leaving he gave Shippen, by now a love interest, a lock of hair as a memento.

Grey left for England in July 1778 and Howe's successor, General Henry CLINTON, suitably impressed by this bright young blade, appointed him a staff officer. Andre performed well during the siege of CHARLESTON, South Carolina, in May 1780, and Clinton subsequently appointed him his chief of military intelligence. In this capacity Andre was responsible for coordinating the network of English and Loyalist spies throughout the New York region. However, his role grew exceedingly complicated after April 1779, when he was contacted by emissaries representing American general Benedict ARNOLD, now governor of Philadelphia and husband of the former Margaret Shippen. Arnold indicated his intention to provide the British with valuable intelligence in exchange for money, but neither Andre nor Clinton felt Arnold was trustworthy, as he was being court-martialed for fiscal improprieties. A year lapsed before Andre pursued the matter again, this time with fatal consequences.

Arnold resumed his traitorous correspondence in June 1780 and finally convinced General Clinton of his sincere desire to change sides. In September 1780 Andre was ordered to confer with the rogue leader and exchange money for the defenses of West Point, New York, a strategic defensive position. However, Clinton explicitly ordered him to remain in uniform at all times so as not to be charged with espionage if caught. Andre complied, boarded the ship HMS *Vulture*, and ascended the Hudson River to rendezvous with Arnold on September 12, 1780. The meeting concluded successfully, and Andre was returning to his ship when he learned that it had been driven downstream by American cannon fire. Undeterred, he spent the evening with a local Loyalist and then resumed his journey on foot through American lines—dressed in civilian clothes. En route he was apprehended by three militiamen who found incriminating evidence in his shoe. Andre was about to be sent back to General Arnold's headquarters when the Patriot spymaster, Major Benjamin TALLMADGE, suspected treachery and prevented Andre's transfer.

On September 29, 1780, Andre was tried at Tarrytown, New York, by a military board and convicted of espionage. At no time did the young officer deny the charges and he coolly accepted his fate—death by hanging. At this juncture General Clinton pleaded with General George WASHINGTON to spare the life of his young aide in exchange for several American prisoners, but Washington wanted only one man—Arnold. When Clinton refused, Andre was sent to the gallows on October 2, 1780. The American officers present were struck by the solemnity of the scene and the heroic serenity of the accused. Washington himself confessed that Andre had met his fate "with that fortitude which was to be expected from an accomplished man and gallant officer." In 1821 Andre's remains were removed to England and reinterred at Westminster Abbey, where a small monument arose in his honor.

Further Reading

Baber, Jean. *The World of Major Andre: An Accomplished Man and a Gallant Officer.* Fort Washington, Pa.: Copy Factory, 1994.

Cray, Robert E. "Major John Andre and the Three Captors: Class Dynamics and Revolutionary Memory Wars in the Early Republic, 1780–1831," *Journal of the Early Republic* 17, no. 3 (1997): 371–397.

Hagman, Harlan. *Nathan Hale and John Andre: Reluctant Heroes of the American Revolution.* Interlaken, N.Y.: Empire State Books, 1992.

Kaplan, Roger. "The Hidden War: British Intelligence Operations during the American Revolution," *William and Mary Quarterly* 47, no. 1 (1990): 115–138.

Lodge, Henry C., ed. *Major Andre's Journal.* New York: Arno Press, 1968.

Walsh, John E. *The Execution of John Andre.* New York: Palgrave, 2001.

Angell, Israel (1740–1832)
American military officer

Israel Angell was born in Providence, Rhode Island, on August 24, 1740, the son of a cooper. He pursued his father's business until 1775, when he received a major's commission in Colonel Daniel Hitchcock's Rhode Island Regiment. After serving at the siege of Boston, Angell was promoted to colonel of the newly raised 2nd Rhode Island Regiment on January 13, 1777, and accompanied it throughout the Philadelphia campaign. He fought well at the Battle of BRANDYWINE and was subsequently brigaded with the 1st Rhode Island Regiment under Colonel Christopher GREENE during the heroic defense of Fort Mercer, New Jersey, October 22 to November 21, 1777. There he conspicuously exposed himself while bloodily repulsing a determined Hessian attack on the first day of the siege. In 1778 his troops were also closely engaged in the victory at MONMOUTH, winning additional plaudits.

Angell made his military mark at Springfield, New Jersey, on June 23, 1780, while commanded by fellow Rhode Islander General Nathanael GREENE. The 2nd Rhode Island Regiment then formed part of a brigade under General William MAXWELL and was ordered to hold the Galloping Hill Road bridge spanning the Rahway River. Another force under Colonel Henry LEE likewise guarded the nearby Vauxhall Bridge. Hessian general Wilhelm von KNYPHAUSEN attacked in force with 5,000 veteran British and German troops, but Angell and his men resisted for 40 minutes, inflicting many casualties. Thwarted in his frontal assault, Knyphausen threw a column around the American left to turn Angell's position, and he withdrew until reinforced by New Jersey militia. Knyphausen then called off his attack, burned the village of Springfield, and retreated back to New York. Several American units had distinguished themselves in combat, but Angell's performance was singled out for praise by General George WASHINGTON.

In January 1781 both Rhode Island regiments were consolidated into a single command, and Angell resigned rather than be demoted to lieutenant colonel. He resumed work as a cooper, remarried three times, and sired 17 children before dying in the town of Smithfield on May 4, 1832.

Further Reading

Angell, Israel. *Diary of Colonel Israel Angell.* New York: Arno Press, 1971.

Boyle, Lee, ed. "The Israel Angell Diary, 10 October 1777–28 February 1778," *Rhode Island History* 58, no. 4 (2000): 107–138.

Fleming, Thomas. *The Forgotten Victory: The Battle for New Jersey, 1780.* New York: Reader's Digest Press, 1973.

Lovell, Louise L. *Israel Angell, Colonel of the 2nd Rhode Island Regiment.* New York: Knickerbocker Press, 1921.

Walker, Anthony. *So Few the Brave: Rhode Island Continentals, 1775–1787.* Newport, R.I.: Seafield Press, 1981.

Arbuthnot, Marriot (ca. 1711–1794)
English naval officer

Marriot Arbuthnot was born in Weymouth, England, around 1711, and little is known of his parentage or upbringing. He joined the Royal

Navy in 1729, rose to lieutenant in 1732, and made captain by 1747. Arbuthnot was actively engaged in the Seven Years' War against France and was present at the victory of Quiberon Bay on November 2, 1759. After a tour of duty commanding the naval base at Portsmouth, he transferred as naval commissioner at Halifax, Nova Scotia, in 1771, where he also served as lieutenant governor. After the Revolutionary War broke out in April 1775 Arbuthnot was active in reinforcing Fort Cumberland against Patriot forces and also took measures against American privateers in that area. His career thus far had been competent, if undistinguished, and in January 1778 he was recalled to England for consultations. There, much to his surprise, he was made commander in chief of naval forces in North America by Naval Minister John MONTAGU, earl of Sandwich. In light of the fact that the British war effort required leaders of foresight and determination—qualities stodgy Arbuthnot clearly lacked—his appointment would prove a fateful one.

Arbuthnot returned to New York in May 1779 and replaced the highly aggressive and capable commodore George COLLIER at New York. He then entered into a contentious relationship with General Henry CLINTON, the army's top commander, for these two irascible leaders regarded each other with thinly disguised contempt. That spring, when the fleet of France's Admiral Charles-Hector-Théodat, comte d'ESTAING was heading for America, Arbuthnot ignored Clinton's pleas to reinforce the garrison at Newport, Rhode Island, and remained in port. Fortunately for the British, d'Estaing was consumed by an ineffectual siege of Savannah, Georgia, but again the Royal Navy could not be prodded into assisting. In December 1779, Arbuthnot roused himself long enough to transport Clinton's army south during the siege of CHARLESTON, South Carolina. Over the next five months he sullenly cooperated with the army and secured the city's surrender the following May. Arbuthnot then returned north and, when informed of the approach of another French fleet under Admiral Louis, comte de Ternay, headed for Newport, he stood fast at anchor. Harsh prodding

Royal Navy Admiral Marriot Arbuthnot *(National Maritime Museum, Greenwich, London)*

from Clinton finally induced him to blockade the army of General Jean-Baptiste-Donatien de Vimeur, comte de ROCHAMBEAU, in Rhode Island once he had been reinforced by a squadron under Admiral Thomas GRAVES. But when Arbuthnot again refused to initiate action against the invaders, Clinton began pressing the ministry for his replacement.

In September 1780 Arbuthnot received a letter from Admiral George B. RODNEY indicating that he was assuming command of naval forces in North America. The old admiral, furious over subordination to an officer many years his junior, protested loudly to the government and threatened to resign. However, once Rodney sailed to the Leeward Islands, Arbuthnot returned to command at New York and the matter was dropped. In the spring of 1780 the traitorous general Benedict ARNOLD alerted superiors that a French fleet under Admiral Charles-René, comte Destouches, was approaching Chesapeake Bay with reinforcements, intending to cut Arnold off in Virginia. Clinton then gingerly persuaded the old admiral to sortie his squadron and engage the enemy in open battle. Arbuthnot reluctantly complied, and on March 16, 1781, he found Destouches waiting for him off Cape Henry. The battle was joined, but Arbuthnot discarded any tactical advantages he might have enjoyed by invoking uninspired, textbook tactics. Destouches noted that the British, with a strong wind to their backs, dared not open their lower gun ports for fear of flooding. He then doubled back for another firing pass, battering them considerably. The French ultimately withdrew, but Arbuthnot, with several ships heavily damaged, could not follow. His poor performance provided the Admiralty with a pretext for his removal, and on July 4, 1781, he was replaced by Graves.

Arbuthnot was never censored for his dismal behavior in North America and, in fact, he was promoted to full admiral in 1793. However, he failed to secure another active command and died in London on January 31, 1794, one of the more inept naval leaders of the Revolutionary War. Overall, his presence proved detrimental to the conduct of the British naval effort.

Further Reading

Andreopoulos, George J., and Harold E. Selesky, eds. *The Aftermath of Defeat: States, Armed Forces, and the Challenge of Recovery.* New Haven, Conn.: Yale University Press, 1994.

Clark, Ernest A. "The Error of Marriot Arbuthnot," *Nova Scotia Historical Review* 8, no. 2 (1988): 94–107.

Gardiner, Robert, ed. *Navies and the American Revolution.* Annapolis, Md.: Naval Institute Press, 1996.

Greene, William. *The Memoranda of William Greene, Secretary to Vice Admiral Marriot Arbuthnot in the American Revolution.* Providence: Rhode Island Historical Society, 1924.

Syrett, David. *The Royal Navy in American Waters, 1775–1783.* Brookfield, Vt.: Gower Publishing Co., 1989.

Tilley, John A. *The British Navy and the American Revolution.* Columbia: University of South Carolina, 1987.

Armand, Charles (Armand-Charles Tuffin, marquis de la Rouerie) (1750–1793)
French military officer

Charles-Armand Tuffin, Marquis de la Rouerie was born in Brittany, France, on January 1, 1750, the scion of an old aristocratic family. He entered the Royal House Guards at the age of 10 and gradually acquired the reputation of a dashing, headstrong officer. His military career nearly ended when he dueled with, and severely wounded, a nephew of King Louis XVI over a woman and was dismissed. The young marquis sought solace among a community of Trappist monks for several years but news of the American Revolution fired his imagination. In 1776 he secured a letter of introduction from American agent Silas DEANE and sailed for the America. He boat was nearly seized by British warships in Chesapeake Bay; rather than be captured, he jumped overboard,

French military officer Charles-Armand Tuffin. General Washington, impressed with the marquis's ability, put him in command of the Continental cavalry after the death of General Pulaski. *(Atwater-Kent Museum)*

swam to shore, and proceeded nearly 100 miles on foot to Philadelphia. There he delivered dispatches to the Continental CONGRESS and tendered his services to the American cause. General George WASHINGTON was very impressed by this youthful aristocrat and authorized him to raise and outfit a body of rangers at his own expense.

Armand, who had stopped using his aristocratic surname, first led a German-speaking contingent in the sharp engagement at Short Hills, New Jersey, on June 26, 1777, losing 30 soldiers out of 80 but personally rescuing a cannon from capture. He was subsequently commissioned a colonel and assigned to serve under General Kazimierz PULASKI, chief of all Continental cavalry. Armand fought with distinction at BRANDYWINE and White Marsh, and on November 24, 1777, during a swift raid against Gloucester under the marquis de LAFAYETTE, he seized 60 Hessian prisoners for the loss of one man. Congress then authorized him to raise his own mixed infantry/cavalry legion, the "Free and Independent Chasseurs," to conduct partisan warfare in and around New York City. In one spectacular 1779 raid he captured a high-ranking LOYALIST officer who was still in bed. After General Pulaski was killed in October 1779, Armand transferred south to assume command of his unit. There the two commands were combined to form a new unit, Armand's Legion. He fought well but futilely under General Horatio GATES at the Battle of CAMDEN in August 1780. His cavalry was posted in reserve on the left flank but could not stave off the ensuing rout. Several weeks of recruiting followed, but Armand was soon able and eager to resume field operations against the British. However, he expressed disillusionment for Congress's failure to recognize his merits through promotion.

In 1781 Armand returned to France, partly to brood and partly to raise supplies, money, and support for the American cause. The king also forgave his youthful indiscretions and inducted him into the prestigious Order of St. Louis. Armand returned to America in August 1781 and partook in the siege of YORKTOWN, Virginia. Because his unit had dwindled through combat and sickness to insignificance, he tendered his services to General Washington as a foot soldier. In this capacity he accompanied Colonel Alexander HAMILTON on the assault against Redoubt No. 10, becoming the first officer over the parapet, and helped secure its surrender. Again, Washington officially lauded the young aristocrat for his bravery and in 1782 Congress finally promoted Armand to brigadier general and chief of all Continental cavalry. He spent the final months of the war in Georgia and South Carolina under General Nathanael GREENE, mopping up isolated British outposts.

Armand returned home in 1784 as a celebrated war hero, but by then France was on the brink of a social cataclysm. When the French Revolution erupted in 1789 he tried to remain aloof, like many of his class, but was repelled by the mounting excesses of the Jacobins. Armand led royalist forces in the rebellious area known as the Vendée with considerable success until the Prussian defeat at Valmy in 1792. Armand died of a heart attack on January 30, 1793, after hearing of the king's execution. He was a capable partisan leader and one of the few foreign officers that Washington held in high esteem.

Further Reading

Armand, Charles T[sic]. "Letters of Col. Armand," *Collections of the New York Historical Society for the Year 1878* 11 (1879): 287–396.

Haarman, Albert W. "General Armand and His Partisan Corps, 1777–1783," *Military Collector and Historian* 12 (winter 1960): 97–102.

Kite, Elizabeth. "Charles-Armand Tuffin, Marquis de la Rouerie," *Legion d'honneur Magazine* 10 (1940): 451–462.

Stutesman, John H. "Colonel Armand and Washington's Cavalry," *New York Historical Society Quarterly* 45 (January 1961): 5–42.

Ward, Townsend. "Charles Armand Tuffin, Marquis de la Rouerie," *Pennsylvania Magazine of History and Biography* 92 (1878): 1–34.

Whitridge, Arnold. "The Marquis de la Rouerie, Brigadier General in the Continental Army," *Massachusetts Historical Society Proceedings* 79 (1967): 47–63.

Armstrong, John (1717–1795)
American militia officer

John Armstrong was born in County Fermanagh, Ireland, on October 13, 1717, and trained as a surveyor. He relocated to Pennsylvania in the mid-1740s and settled in the Kittanning area of the Susquehanna River Valley. Politically ambitious, he gained election to the Pennsylvania assembly in 1749, and he advanced the interests of land developers in his region. He subsequently helped found the town of Carlisle and in 1773 was a founding trustee of the future Dickinson College. When the French and Indian War broke out, Armstrong surveyed and cut wilderness roads for General Edward Braddock. The following year he led a force of 350 frontiersmen against the Delaware Indian settlement at Kittanning, killing the war leader Captain Jacobs, burning French supplies, and releasing several prisoners. Thereafter he was applauded as the "Hero of Kittanning." Though a small action, it helped secure the western region of Pennsylvania from Indian attack for several years. In 1758 he accompanied the advance of General John Forbes during the campaign against Fort Duquesne and personally raised the flag over that captured post. In 1763 he was also active in military matters during the so-called Conspiracy of Pontiac. As war clouds with Great Britain gathered, Armstrong opposed Imperial policies and joined the local COMMITTEE OF CORRESPONDENCE to support the citizens of Boston. He also recommended the candidacy of a close associate, James WILSON, to represent Pennsylvania in CONGRESS.

In March 1776 Armstrong became the first brigadier general commissioned by Congress and four months later rendered valuable assistance during the attack on CHARLESTON, South Carolina, that summer. However, he resented being overlooked for promotion and resigned from the Continental ARMY in April 1777 to serve with state forces. As a brigadier general of militia Armstrong was present at BRANDYWINE in September 1777 but occupied the far left of General George WASHINGTON's line and saw little fighting. The following month his brigade was entrusted with an important feint against General William HOWE's left flank at GERMANTOWN, but he encountered HESSIAN troops en route and withdrew from the field. During the winter of 1777–78 Armstrong advanced to major general of Pennsylvania militia. The following February he resigned his commission to represent his state in Congress. While present he opposed the recall of Arthur LEE from Paris and called for severe punishment of extreme LOYALISTS. Armstrong left Congress in August 1780 and returned to private life back at Carlisle. In this capacity he lent his reputation, which was considerable in western Pennsylvania, to such causes as revising the state constitution and adopting the federal constitution. Armstrong served briefly again in Congress, 1787–88, before dying at Carlisle on March 9, 1795, a mediocre military leader but a popular frontier figure in his state.

Further Reading

Armstrong, John. "Letters of John Armstrong of Kittanning to Gen. William Irvine," *Historical Magazine* 8 (January 1864): 16–21.

Crist, Robert G. "John Armstrong: Proprietor's Man." Unpublished Ph.D. Diss., Pennsylvania State University, 1981.

Flower, Milton E. *John Armstrong, First Citizen of Carlisle.* Carlisle, Pa.: Cumberland County Historical Society, 1971.

Heathcote, Charles W. "General John Armstrong—A Capable Pennsylvania Officer and Colleague of Washington," *Picket Post* 66 (November 1959): 4–12.

King, J. W. "Colonel John Armstrong," *Western Pennsylvania Historical Magazine* 10 (July 1927): 129–145.

Stradley, Wilson. "General John Armstrong," *Valley Forge Journal* 5, no. 2 (1990): 117–128.

army, Continental

The biggest obstacle facing American independence after 1775 was the British army, consisting of several thousand highly trained, well-led professional soldiers. The vaunted redcoats were subject to harsh discipline, rigorous drilling, and enjoyed capable, professional leadership that rendered them formidable adversaries. Quite often, the mere sight of an advancing line of scarlet-clad infantry, bayonets leveled menacingly, was enough to send lesser troops tearing from the field of battle. The qualitative superiority of the opposition ensured that American militia, despite sometimes capable performances, were unequal to the task of expelling the British by themselves. The nascent United States required a new military force that approximated its European-style adversaries in performance, yet would be consistent with the emerging republican ideology underscoring the revolution itself. Because standing military establishments had long been viewed as instruments of tyranny, the solutions adopted would prove uniquely American and a reflection of prevailing political realities.

The Continental army had its origins in New England military forces hastily raised in the wake of the Battles of Lexington and CONCORD. These numbered upward of 15,000 men, but the leaders of Massachusetts, wishing to expand popular support for the war against Great Britain, tendered control of their men to the Continental CONGRESS in Philadelphia. Congress willingly complied, and on June 14, 1775, it also authorized the raising of 10 companies of riflemen from Pennsylvania, Maryland, and Virginia, to join the soldiers already gathered outside Cambridge, Massachusetts. On the following day Congress made the fateful appointment of General George WASHINGTON of Virginia as commander in chief—a position he held over the next eight years. Thus was born the Continental army, intended as the principal instrument of victory over Britain. Washington, once he assumed command at Cambridge in July, began systemizing plans for an even larger military establishment, with 26 regiments of infantry, one of riflemen, and one of artillery, totaling 20,372 men. The most notable feature of this plan was the call for one-year enlistments for all ranks, made on the assumption of a relatively short war. But Washington and Congress proved overly optimistic, and within six months the army was dwindling due to expiring enlistments, desertions, and combat losses. By September 1776 Congress was forced to expand the Continental army into 88 battalions, distributed among various states, with a combined manpower ceiling of 80,000. The exigencies of war also required it to extend enlistment terms to three years or the duration of the war, in exchange for cash bounties, and parcels of land following discharge. The United States, with its population of 2.5 million, could have easily raised and sustained a force of 35,000 men, but at no time during the entire war could Washington muster more than 15,000 soldiers—with 10,000 closer to the norm. This sheer lack of trained volunteers proved a daunting proposition for the Continental army throughout its existence, resulting in heavy reliance upon episodic state militias while campaigning in the field. To help offset these deficiencies, many states allowed recruitment of AFRICAN AMERICANS into the ranks, where they served with distinction.

Compounding Washington's difficulties were intractable problems of supply. Due to breakdowns in state funding, the inability of Congress to provide funds, and the general unreliability of private contractors, his soldiers routinely lacked such basic necessities as food, clothing, weapons, gunpowder, and camp equipage. Remedial efforts were further hampered by the lack of a professionally trained quartermaster department. Talented officers like Nathanael GREENE, Thomas MIFFLIN, Stephen MOYLAN, and Timothy PICKERING all tried to improve supply functions within the army, but they remained beset by lack of funding and properly trained subordinates. Toward the end of the war, many hungry, unpaid soldiers mutinied and returned home rather then endure such deprivation further, but the bulk of the Continental army fulfilled its obligations manfully. Washington was further beset by a lack of uniform disciplinary standards among recruits, a daunting proposition when tangling with professionally trained British and HESSIAN adversaries. Many soldiers acquired their first exposure to discipline in the militia, each of which possessed its own peculiar system of drill, and hence could not be readily exercised with other units differently trained. It was not until the arrival of the Prussian drillmaster, General Friedrich Wilhelm von STEUBEN, at Valley Forge in the winter of 1777 that systematic military discipline was instilled into the troops. In fact, his famous *Blue Book* remained the standard army drill manual until 1813, and it persisted in militia usage up through the 1830s. Results were striking: Commencing with the Battle of MONMOUTH in 1778, the Continental army demonstrated a military proficiency closely approximating its British adversaries. The revolution's survival was now basically assured.

The Continental army won its share of victories throughout the Revolutionary War and gradually improved as it garnered experience, but the United States remained militarily weak and required direct assistance from France before the war was won. Nonetheless, the force made indelible contributions to the ultimate victory, perhaps in spite of itself. Congress certainly failed to heed Washington's pleas to maintain a small standing force during peacetime, for in 1784 it summarily disbanded the Continental army, reducing it to a force of 80 privates and a few captains to guard military stores. Consequently, the hard lessons of war were forgotten and perilously reacquired during a rematch with Great Britain in the War of 1812.

Further Reading

Benninghoff, Herman O. *Valley Forge, a Genesis for Command and Control, Continental Army Style.* Gettysburg, Pa.: Thomas Publications, 2001.

Bodle, Wayne K. *The Valley Forge Winter: Civilians and Soldiers in War.* University Park: Pennsylvania State University Press, 2002.

Buchanan, John. *The Road to Valley Forge: How Washington Built the Army That Won the Revolution.* Hoboken, N.J.: John Wiley and Sons, 2004.

Chadwick, Bruce. *The First American Army: The Remarkable Story of George Washington and the Men behind America's Fight for Freedom.* Naperville, Ill.: Sourcebooks, 2005.

Cox, Caroline. *A Proper Sense of Honor: Service and Sacrifice in George Washington's Army.* Chapel Hill: University of North Carolina Press, 2004.

Kestnbaum, Meyer. "Citizen-Soldiers, National Service, and the Mass Army: The Birth of Conscription in Revolutionary Europe and North America," *Comparative Social Research* 20 (2001): 117–144.

———. "Citizenship and Compulsory Military Service: The Revolutionary Origins of Conscription in the United States," *Armed Forces and Security* 27, no. 1 (2000): 7–36.

Knouff, Gregory T. *The Soldiers' Revolution: Pennsylvanians in Arms and the Forging of Early American Identity.* University Park: Pennsylvania State University Press, 2004.

Martin, James K., and Mark E. Louden. *A Respectable Army: The Military Origins of the Republic, 1763–1789.* Wheeling, Ill.: Harlan Davidson, 2006.

Arnold, Benedict (1741–1801)
American military officer, spy

Benedict Arnold was born in Norwich, Connecticut, on January 14, 1741, the son of an alcoholic father. He weathered a troubled childhood and deserted his militia unit twice during the French and Indian War before finally settling down as a successful merchant in New London. Initially patriotic, he raised a militia company and marched it to Cambridge, Massachusetts, after the Battles of Lexington and CONCORD in April 1775. He also convinced the Committee of Public Safety to commission him colonel of an expedition intending to capture British-held Fort Ticonderoga, New York, where valuable arms and ammunition were stored. En route, Arnold encountered a similar force under Colonel Ethan ALLEN, and the two men struck up an uneasy alliance pursuing this objective. After the fort surrendered on May 10, 1775, Arnold commandeered a ship and made a sudden raid up Lake Champlain that captured Saint Johns, Quebec. The feeble nature of Canadian defenses induced him to approach General George WASHINGTON to mount an expedition through the Maine wilderness to seize the strategic city of Quebec. Permission was granted and Arnold, displaying his trademark energy and strong leadership, led 1,100 men through the wilderness on an epic march that September. On November 8, 1775, he shepherded 700 half-starved, exhausted survivors onto the Plains of Abraham and commenced a loose siege. The following month he was reinforced by another 300 soldiers under General Richard MONTGOMERY, and the two leaders decided to attack the city before expiring enlistments forced their withdrawal. On the night of December 31, 1775, both charged under the cover of a howling blizzard and were disastrously repulsed; Montgomery was slain while Arnold sustained a leg wound and was evacuated. The siege of Quebec resumed and CONGRESS, in light of Arnold's energetic exploits, commissioned him a brigadier general in the Continental ARMY.

In the spring of 1776 Governor-General Guy CARLETON was heavily reinforced from England and began pushing the outnumbered Americans out of Canada. Arnold countered the threat by constructing a small flotilla of gunboats on Lake Champlain, down which the British were obliged to pass. Carleton was thus forced to expend valuable time, money, and effort acquiring a fleet of his own; the two forces clashed off Valcour Island on October 11–13, 1776. Arnold's scratch-built squadron was decisively beaten, but the delays incurred forced Carleton to postpone his invasion of New York for another year. Arnold's sacrifice had bought the struggling United States a precious interval to strengthen its northernmost defenses. However, Congress failed to extend him any laurels for such Herculean feats and, in fact, callously promoted five men with less seniority to major general. Arnold was appreciably livid by the slight but was persuaded by Washington to remain in the service. He then returned home to mull things over in Connecticut where, on April 25, 1777, he helped organize defenses that repelled a large-scale raid by Governor William TRYON of New York. Congress then finally promoted him to major general but without granting him the requisite seniority. Again, Arnold angrily threatened to resign, but Washington prevailed on his friend to persevere.

In the summer of 1777, General John BURGOYNE led a major British offensive down the Lake Champlain corridor into New York, which shook Arnold out of his lethargy. He eagerly joined the army of General Philip J. SCHUYLER near Albany and forcefully marched a relief expedition toward the beleaguered post of Fort Stanwix, New York, that August. His approach forced General Barry ST. LEGER to abandon the siege, denying Burgoyne valuable reinforcements. Arnold then hurriedly rejoined the main army, which by now had reverted to General Horatio GATES, a somewhat vacillating, long-winded Englishman. The impetuous Arnold made no attempt to disguise his contempt for Gates. However, when Burgoyne attempted to probe the American position at FREEMAN'S FARM on September 19, 1777, Arnold collected troops, dashed into battle without orders, and stopped the British cold. He was convinced that Gates deliberately withheld troops to deny him a victory, and relations between the two men plummeted to the point where Arnold was relieved of

American general and British spy Benedict Arnold *(Anne S. K. Brown Military Collection, Brown University Library)*

command. He returned to sulking in his tent, Achilles-like, until Burgoyne launched another probe at BEMIS HEIGHTS on October 7, 1777. Arnold, a veritable whirlwind in battle, collected his forces—again without orders—attacked the HESSIANS, and drove them from their fortifications. He sustained a second, serious leg wound in close-quarter fighting but sealed Burgoyne's fate. Gates, as commander, could claim victory, but Congress finally rewarded Arnold's aplomb under fire by restoring his backdated seniority. Washington also appointed him commander of the Philadelphia garrison in June 1778.

Arnold took up his post at Philadelphia, still brimming with resentment, and was further alienated when charges of fiscal impropriety were leveled against him. He also apparently became infatuated with Margaret "Peggy" SHIPPEN, the lovely 18-year-old daughter of a prominent local LOYALIST, whom he ultimately married. For reasons not entirely clear, in April 1779 Arnold commenced a traitorous correspondence with General Henry CLINTON at New York, offering to trade intelligence for money. Over a year lapsed before Clinton came to trust Arnold's sincerity, especially when he offered to turn over defense plans for strategic West Point, New York, to the British. Feigning disability, Arnold had previously convinced Washington to appoint him to the command of West Point, and he was well-positioned to betray it. Clinton then dispatched his head of intelligence, Major John ANDRE, to meet Arnold, but the plot was exposed when Andre was caught and hanged. Arnold made his escape to the British side, where he was commissioned a brigadier general. He subsequently conducted several destructive raids against his former compatriots in Virginia and Connecticut throughout 1781. The following year he sailed to England to meet with King GEORGE III but found his erstwhile hosts decidedly chilly. Arnold spent the rest of his life in Canada and the West Indies as a merchant but failed to pay off his gambling debts. He died in London on June 14, 1801, friendless, countryless, and unmourned. Benedict Arnold made indelible contributions to victory in the American Revolution and his piques over lack of recognition were not unjustified, but in the context of American history he remains the embodiment of treason and betrayal.

Further Reading

Desjardin, Thomas A. *Through A Howling Wilderness: Benedict Arnold's March to Quebec, 1775.* New York: St. Martin's Press, 2006.

Hallahan, William H. *The Day the Revolution Ended.* New York: Wiley, 2004.

Niderost, Eric. "Tarnished Hero's Victory at Lake Champlain," *Military Heritage* 7, no. 2 (2205): 44–53, 78.

Powell, Walter L. *Murder or Mayhem? Benedict Arnold's New London, Connecticut, Raid, 1781.* Gettysburg, Pa.: Thomas Publications, 2000.

Roberts, William C. *Victory in Defeat: Valcour Island and the American Revolution.* Henderson, Tenn.: Freed-Hardeman University Press, 2003.

Sale, Richard T. *Traitors: The Worst Acts of Treason in American History from Benedict Arnold to Robert Hanssen.* New York: Berkley Books, 2003.

Wallace, Audrey. *Benedict Arnold: Misunderstood Hero?* Shippensburg, Pa.: Burd Street Press, 2003.

Wilson, Barry. *Benedict Arnold: A Traitor in Our Midst.* Ithaca, N.Y.: McGill-Queen's University Press, 2001.

Articles of Confederation

With the onset of open hostilities against Great Britain in the spring of 1775, members of the Second Continental CONGRESS began advocating a formal governmental structure to better coordinate colonial affairs. That year Benjamin FRANKLIN proposed his "Articles of Confederation and Perpetual Union," but, in so much as the issue of independence had yet to be resolved, no further action was taken. But within a year, as the notion of independence gathered currency in the face of British intransigence, new emphasis was placed on acquiring the machinery of central governance to administer national needs. In June 1776 Representative John DICKINSON headed a committee tasked with drawing up a proposal and he responded with the Articles of Confederation, which, in effect, was America's first constitution. This called for rule by a unicameral legislature, or congress, without the interference of an executive or judicial branch. Moreover, the powers of government were closely prescribed and enumerated while the bulk of political power remained with the states. The government could manage foreign affairs, raise armies and navies, and conclude treaties with foreign countries and Native Americans. However, it lacked powers of taxation and could not uniformly regulate trade and commerce between states. Moreover, even if Congress passed laws, they were nonbinding unless individual states chose to enforce them. The inherent weakness of the central government bore marked testimony to America's recent experience with British imperial power, especially the issue of taxation. Many politicians feared replacing one form of tyranny with another, so the Articles of Confederation appeared to be a viable compromise between political philosophy and wartime expedience.

Debate on the Articles of Confederation was warm, lucid, and erudite, with the greatest disagreement arising along three main points. The first, representation, was solved when all states were given equal status and one vote. The second, appropriation, was settled on the basis of contributing money to Congress based upon the value of privately owned land. The third and most contentious issue proved to be control of western lands. Certain states like Virginia claimed large swaths of territory in the interior, while others, like Maryland, had no claims and insisted that such territories must be ceded to Congress in advance. The issues took several years to resolve successfully. Months of debate and delay ensued before Congress approved the articles and passed them on to state legislatures for ratification. Part of the problem was the British occupation of Philadelphia in the summer of 1777, so passage of the new government occurred in York, Pennsylvania, on November 17 of that year. Then commenced a long and tortuous path to ratification. Many states ratified the articles speedily, but Maryland proved a consistent obstacle until the issue of western lands was resolved. Not until Virginia governor Thomas JEFFERSON willingly surrendered all western land claims to Congress did the Maryland legislature finally give its assent. Hence on March 1, 1781, when the war was nearly over, the Articles of Confederation were unanimously passed by all the states and enacted. The United States, heretofore an ad hoc assemblage of 13 disjointed colonies, formally transformed itself into a confederation government.

In practice the Articles of Confederation proved unwieldy, even in times of peace. Bereft of the ability to raise money, the government remained financially hamstrung and at the whim of states for revenue. Moreover, states continually annulled laws intended to rationalize interstate commerce with uniform standards and practices. The inability to regulate foreign commerce also induced nations like Great Britain to raise trade barriers without the risk of retaliation. Nor could the government require states to provide military manpower along the frontier at a time of mounting Indian unrest. By 1787 the shortcomings of the Articles were so manifold that a constitutional convention met in Philadelphia to draw up a new form of truly centralized government, although with appropriate checks and balances befitting republican governance. The Articles of Confederation were thus replaced by the new federal Constitution as of March 4, 1789, although many of its provisions and political sentiments were incorporated by the new document.

Further Reading
Bailyn, Bernard. *To Begin the World Anew: The Genius and Ambiguities of the American Foundation*. New York: Alfred A. Knopf, 2003.
Dougherty, Keith L. *Collective Action under the Articles of Confederation*. New York: Cambridge University Press, 2001.
Ferling, John E. *A Leap in the Dark: The Struggle to Create the American Republic*. New York: Oxford University Press, 2003.
Jennings, Francis. *The Creation of America: Through Revolution to Empire*. New York: Cambridge University Press, 2000.
Kersh, Rogan. "The Rhetorical Genesis of American Political Union," *Polity* 33, no. 2 (2000): 229–257.

Kromkowski, Charles A. *Recreating the American Republic: Rules of Apportionment, Constitutional Change, and American Political Development, 1700–1870.* New York: Cambridge University Press, 2002.

Robinson, Ward, and Christopher Eaton, eds. *Founding Character: Words and Documents That Forged a Nation.* Santa Clarita, Calif.: Roan Adler Publishers, 2003.

Ashe, John (ca. 1720–1781)
American militia officer

John Ashe was born near Albemarle Sound, North Carolina, around 1720, the son of a successful politician. Being well educated, he briefly attended Harvard College in 1746 but dropped out due to lack of interest. He subsequently held minor civil posts back home and served as a militia captain during the 1747 Spanish attack upon Brunswick. His political fortunes advanced in 1752, when Ashe replaced his uncle as speaker of the colonial legislature and finally found his niche. Over the next two decades he emerged as one of the colony's leading politicians and an outspoken champion of resistance to British imperial policies. In 1765 he privately warned hard-line royal governor John TRYON that the STAMP ACT would in all likelihood be resisted violently if enforced. Ashe underscored that fact by leading the local SONS OF LIBERTY in riots against the homes of tax officials. However, in 1771 he sided with Tryon during the regulator disturbances and led a company of militia during the Battle of ALAMANCE in which the rebels were crushed. In January 1775 Ashe once again reverted to his role as political agitator, and he joined the New Hanover Committee of Safety to coordinate enforcement of the boycott against British goods following the COERCIVE ACTS. When Ashe was informed that royal governor Josiah MARTIN intended to reinforce Fort Johnson, Wilmington, with British troops, he led an armed expedition that burned it to the ground on July 17, 1775.

Despite his reputation as a leading patriot, Ashe failed to win appointment as colonel of the 1st North Carolina Continental Infantry, which went to his brother-in-law, James MOORE. Undeterred, he raised a company of rangers and took to the field against Scottish LOYALISTS of the Cape Fear region. On February 9, 1776, he bore a conspicuous role in the American victory at Moore's Creek Bridge and received promotion to brigadier general of militia for the Wilmington district. He served capably, rising to major general in 1778. The following spring he received orders to reinforce General Benjamin LINCOLN in South Carolina, and in February 1779 he led a force of 1,600 North Carolina militia and Georgia Continentals across the Savannah River. He joined up with Lincoln at Charleston and was ordered back toward the interior with a view toward retaking Augusta, Georgia, from the British. When British general Archibald CAMPBELL evacuated Augusta, Lincoln ordered Ashe to pursue. The Americans advanced as far as Briar Creek, Georgia, where they were stopped by the flooded Savannah River.

Ashe lingered in camp two weeks waiting for an opportunity to cross and renew his chase. But security proved lax and he was unaware that Campbell had detached Colonel Mark James Prevost with 900 British regulars to attack him. On March 3, 1779, Prevost successfully completed a circuitous, 50-mile march through the wilderness that placed him in the rear of the American camp. The British battle line formed within 500 feet of Ashe's position before he realized the danger. Prevost's regulars completely scattered the poorly armed, badly trained militia, although they had a harder time subduing the Georgia Continentals under Colonel Samuel ELBERT on the right flank. Nonetheless, surprise was complete and Ashe lost 150 men killed and 173 men captured. Prevost's losses were five killed and 11 wounded. Ashe managed to escape the rout and demanded a court of inquiry, which exonerated him, but the debacle at Briar Creek effectively terminated his military career. It also ended American attempts to recapture Georgia for several years.

Ashe returned home and resettled in Wilmington. In the spring of 1781 that town fell to advancing British troops, and he was wounded and captured. Ashe endured several months of close confinement and deprivation, through which he contracted smallpox. He was paroled due to illness and died at Wilmington on October 23, 1781. A mediocre military leader, Ashe is best remembered as one of the leading pre-Revolutionary leaders of North Carolina.

Further Reading
Cox, William E. "Brigadier General John Ashe's Defeat in the Battle of Briar Creek," *Georgia Historical Quarterly* 57, no. 2 (1973): 295–302.
Heidler, David S. "The American Defeat at Briar Creek, 3 March, 1779," *Georgia Historical Quarterly* 66, no. 3 (1982): 317–331.
Hooper, Archibald M. *A Memoir of Gen. John Ashe of the Revolution*. Wilmington, N.C.: Printed at the Office of the *Daily Herald*, 1854.
Howard, Joshua B. " 'Things Here Wear a Melancholy Appearance': The American Defeat at Briar Creek," *Georgia Historical Quarterly* 88, no. 4 (2004): 477–498.
Johnston, Peter R. *Poorest of the Thirteen: North Carolina and the Southern Department in the American Revolution*. Haverford, Pa.: Infinity Pub., 2001.
Wheeler, Milton. "The Role of the North Carolina Militia in the Beginning of the American Revolution." Unpublished Ph.D. diss., Tulane University, 1969.

Attucks, Crispus (ca. 1723–1770)
African-American sailor

Crispus Attucks was born around 1723 in the vicinity of Framingham, Massachusetts, and has been traditionally regarded as of mixed African-American and Natick Indian ancestry. He was probably a slave and sold to Deacon William Brown sometime before 1750, the year that he escaped. Attucks, like many African Americans and Native Americans, found gainful employment as a sailor or whaler. He matured into a large individual over six feet tall and heavily built, exuding the intimidating mien typical of his profession. On March 5, 1770, he was in Boston when a street disturbance broke out between some local rowdies and a lone British sentry on King Street. Tensions had been high in Boston over British imperial policy, and the populace was increasingly resentful of British forces, whom they derided as "Lobsterbacks." On this day Private Hugh White of the 29th Regiment apparently struck a belligerent child for taunting him and a crowd, principally sailors and dockworkers, milled around his guardhouse. Attucks, who was armed with piece of cordwood, advanced in the direction of King Street with the mob, remonstrating against White in a threatening manner. The commotion brought out Captain Thomas Preston and eight other soldiers, who confronted the angry citizens and warned them off. Angry words were exchanged and the Bostonians began pelting the soldiers with snowballs. Tensions suddenly escalated when Attucks apparently strode up to White and knocked him down. The soldiers suddenly lost all composure and fired into the crowd, killing Attucks and fatally injuring three others. Word spread quickly of the affair, which soon became propagated as the BOSTON MASSACRE to further inflame passions against British rule.

On March 8, the bodies of Attucks and the other victims were placed in state at Faneuil Hall, where an estimated 12,000 people paid their respects and escorted the remains to the Granary burial ground. Legal action was also brought against Captain Preston and his men, who were charged with murder. Between November 27 and December 5, 1770, the soldiers were effectively defended by attorneys John ADAMS and Josiah QUINCY, with six being acquitted and two found guilty of the lesser charge of manslaughter. In his arguments Adams painted Attucks as a provocateur, "a stout fellow whose very looks were enough to frighten any person." Nonetheless, he enjoyed national notoriety as America's first martyr of the Revolution and a local hero. In 1888 the state of Massachusetts erected a memorial to Attucks on Boston Commons that was designed by the celebrated sculptor Augustus Saint-Gaudens.

Further Reading
Fiske, John. "Crispus Attucks," *Negro History Bulletin* 33, no. 3 (1970): 58–67.

James, Stephen E. "The Other Fourth of July: The Meanings of Black Identity at American Celebrations of Independence, 1770–1863." Unpublished Ph.D. diss., Harvard University, 1997.

Kaplan, Sidney, and Emma N. Kaplan. *The Black Presence in the Era of the American Revolution.* Amherst: University of Massachusetts Press, 1989.

Neyland, James. *Crispus Attucks.* Los Angeles: Melrose Square Pub., 1995.

Payne, Samuel B. "Was Crispus Attucks the First to Die?" *New England Journal of History* 57, no. 2 (2001): 1–10.

Rediker, Marcus. "The Revenge of Crispus Attucks; or, the Atlantic Challenge to Americans Under History," *Labor* 1, no. 4 (2004): 35–45.

Bailey, Anne (1742–1825)
American messenger and scout

Anne Hennis was born in Liverpool, England, the daughter of a soldier. Orphaned at an early age, she came to America and settled in Staunton, Virginia, to live with relatives. Four years later she married Richard Trotter, a frontiersman and Indian fighter, and relocated with him to the wilderness. When Governor James MURRAY, Lord Dunmore, solicited soldiers for a war against the Shawnee in 1771, Trotter responded and was killed at the Battle of Point Pleasant on October 10 of that year. This loss induced Anne to embrace fully the life of a frontier scout and avenge her husband's death. Throughout the Revolution, she scouted and carried messages for Patriot forces in present-day West Virginia. She also became well known to the Native Americans indigenous to the region, and they purportedly called her "The White Squaw of the Kanawha." Reputedly, Bailey was a crack shot, good with a knife, and could down whiskey with the most grizzled frontiersmen. Bestride her horse named Liverpool, she became a popular figure in western Virginia and served capably throughout the Revolutionary War. Her apparently fearlessness and indifference to danger also gave rise to the nickname Mad Ann.

In 1785 Anne married John Bailey, who belonged to a group of frontier rangers and was nominally stationed at Fort Lee (now Charleston, West Virginia). Indian resentment against continuous white encroachment on their land erupted into violence in 1791, and the Shawnee began raiding the Kanawha region. It was here that Anne performed her most celebrated deed. When a large force of Indians besieged Fort Lee, she was selected to ride to Fort Savannah (now Lewisburg, West Virginia) and secure badly needed gunpowder for the garrison. Anne readily complied, bravely traversed 50 miles of hostile territory, and returned with the requisite ammunition in only three days. Her endeavors certainly spared Fort Lee from destruction and enhanced an already legendary reputation for daring and endurance. In 1817 Anne relocated with her son to Gallipolis, Ohio, where she died on November 22, 1825, still celebrated in story and verse as the "Great Heroine of the Kanawha."

Further Reading

Cole, Adelaide M. "Anne Bailey, Woman of Courage," *Daughters of the American Revolution Magazine* 114, no. 3 (1980): 322–325.

Cook, Roy B. " 'Mad Anne' Bailey at Fort Lee," *West Virginia Review* (July 1934): 282–286.

Hall, Grace M. "Anna Bailey in West Virginia Tradition," *West Virginia History* 17 (October 1955): 22–85.

Hammond, Neal O., and Richard Taylor. *Virginia's Western War, 1775–1786.* Mechanicsburg, Pa.: Stackpole Books, 2002.

Hintzen, William. *A Sketchbook of the Border Wars of the Upper Ohio Valley, 1769–1794: Conflicts and*

Resolutions. Manchester, Conn.: Precision Shooting, 2001.

Lewis, Virgil A. *Life and Times of Anna Bailey, the Pioneer Heroine of the Great Kanawha Valley.* Charleston, W.Va.: Butler Print Co., 1891.

Bancroft, Edward (1744–1821)
Loyalist spy

Edward Bancroft was born in Westfield, Massachusetts, on January 9, 1744, the son of a farmer. He ran away to join the merchant marine in 1763 and spent several years in Surinam on a plantation. There Bancroft became intrigued by poisonous plants and dyes used by indigenous peoples and decided to pursue medicine. He subsequently studied for two years at St. Bartholomew's Hospital, London, and in 1767 earned his license to practice. Besides a lucrative medical profession, Bancroft also dabbled in literature and fitted comfortably within London's intellectual circles. In this capacity he met and befriended noted American scientist Benjamin FRANKLIN, who recommended him for membership in the prestigious Royal Society in 1773. When the Revolutionary War broke out in 1775, Bancroft professed his sympathy for the rebels and Franklin suggested that he be employed by the United States as a spy. The following year he was formally recruited by Silas DEANE, then an American agent in France. Unbeknownst to the Americans, Bancroft was already a double agent on the payroll of Paul Wentworth, head of the British secret service. As Deane's secretary he had immediate access to all confidential correspondence regarding American diplomacy, most of which was immediately duplicated and relayed to British intelligence within days.

For the next seven years Bancroft lived in Paris with Deane, sending a steady stream of useful information back to his handlers in London. Foremost was news of the newly signed FRENCH ALLIANCE with the United States, the complete contents of which were in British hands within 48 hours. Bancroft and Deane also used military intelligence, particularly the defeat of General John BURGOYNE, to manipulate the stock market, and both profited hugely by selling stocks short while prices were high. After Deane was recalled from Paris in 1778, Bancroft continued spying adroitly for both sides. His usefulness to the British declined after the war ended in 1783, the same year in which Deane, now labeled a traitor, relocated to London and was supported by Bancroft. Deane mysteriously died on a ship in 1789, and Bancroft, given his expertise with poisons, was suspected of complicity in the murder. He continued experimenting with various plant dyes used in calico printing, received several patents, and accumulated considerable wealth. Bancroft died in London on September 8, 1821, a respected member of the Royal College of Physicians. The exact nature of his espionage was not fully understood until his memoir was uncovered nearly a century later.

Further Reading

Anderson, Godfrey T., and Dennis K. Anderson. "Edward Bancroft, M. D., F. R. S., Aberrant Practitioner of Physick," *Medical History* 17, no. 4 (1973): 356–367.

Bakeless, John. *Turncoats, Traitors, and Heroes.* New York: Da Capo Press, 1998.

Boies, Bessie. "Edward Bancroft: A British Spy." Unpublished master's thesis, University of Chicago, 1908.

Einstein, Lewis. *Divided Loyalties: Americans in England during the War of Independence.* London: Gobden-Sanderson, 1933.

Mahoney, Harry T. *Gallantry in Action: A Biographical Dictionary of Espionage in the American Revolutionary War.* Lanham, Md.: University Press of America, 1999.

Pearl, William D. "New Perspectives on Dr. Edward Bancroft." Unpublished master's thesis, George Washington University, 1969.

Barney, Joshua (1759–1818)
American naval officer

Joshua Barney was born in Baltimore, Maryland, on July 6, 1759, the son of a farmer. He joined the merchant marine at the age of 11, and within three years had risen to first mate. In January 1775, when the captain of his vessel died at sea, young Barney took control, safely conducted it to a French port, and successfully concluded all business transactions. Upon returning home later that year he joined the Continental NAVY as a ship's mate onboard the sloop *Hornet*. Barney initially sailed as part of Commodore Esek HOPKINS's flotilla, but returned home when his ship suffered damage in a collision. Transferring to the schooner *Wasp*, Barney sailed again, distinguished himself in several engagements, and received his lieutenant's commission. He next joined the sloop *Sachem* as executive officer and helped subdue a British privateer. Barney transferred once more to the *Andrea Doria*, facilitated seizure of the privateer *Racehorse*, and was put aboard the captured ship as prize master. However, he himself was then captured by HMS *Perseus*, exchanged, and rejoined the *Andrea Doria* at Philadelphia.

Barney partook of the unsuccessful defense of Philadelphia against General William HOWE in the spring of 1777, when the *Andrea Doria* was burned to prevent capture. He subsequently relocated to Baltimore to serve as second in command of the brand new frigate *Virginia* under Captain James NICHOLSON. Unfortunately, this vessel ran aground off Hampton, Virginia, on March 31, 1778, and was captured by HMS *Emerald*. Captain Nicholson had rowed himself ashore to prevent capture, so Barney fell captive a second time. After four months on a prison hulk in New York, he was exchanged and served on board several privateers. In October 1780 he joined the Continental navy sloop *Saratoga* out of Philadelphia, and helped take the British privateer *Charming Molly*. Barney served as prize master and was captured again by HMS *Intrepid* before making homeport. He ended up in the notorious Mill Prison, Plymouth, England, and staged several unsuccessful escape attempts. Barney finally succeeded in March 1782 with the help of American sympathizers and made his way back to Philadelphia. When there were no slots available for him on Continental navy ships, Barney took command of the Pennsylvania state navy vessel *Hyder Ally*, a converted

American naval officer Joshua Barney cleverly snared two British warships in Delaware Bay in 1782. *(Independence National Historical Park)*

merchant vessel. On April 8, 1782, while cruising Delaware Bay, he fell in with three British warships and, in a brilliant display of seamanship, captured two of them, including the 30-gun frigate *General Monk*. This was taken into Pennsylvania service as the *General Washington*, and Barney commanded it until the end of the war. In 1784 he became the last of the Continental navy captains to be discharged.

After the Revolution, Barney pursued business interests for a decade and in 1794, when the U.S. Navy was founded, he became one of its first six captains. However, friction with Silas TALBOT over seniority resulted in his resignation, and in 1796 Barney accepted a commission in the French navy. He retired in 1802 with the rank of commodore and returned to Baltimore. When the War of 1812 commenced in June 1812, Barney outfitted the privateer *Rossie* and took 18 prizes. The following year he was made master commandant with a local rank of captain and led a gunboat flotilla guarding Chesapeake Bay. In this capacity he harassed British warships for nearly a year until 1814, when Admiral George Cockburn landed 4,000 troops and attacked Washington, D.C. Barney, commanding only 500 sailors and marines, bravely held his ground at Bladensburg, Maryland, while the militia ran. He was wounded and captured but Admiral Cockburn, impressed with his bravery, paroled him. After the war the city of Washington honored him with an elaborate sword and promotion to captain. Barney died in Pittsburgh, Pennsylvania, on December 1, 1818, an outstanding naval leader of the young republic.

Further Reading

Footner, Hulbert. *Sailor of Fortune: The Life and Adventures of Commodore Joshua Barney, U.S.N.* New York: Harper & Bros., 1940.

Levin, Alexandra L. "How Joshua Barney Outwitted the British at Norfolk," *Maryland Historical Magazine* 73, no. 2 (1978): 163–167.

Miller, Nathan. *Sea of Glory: The Continental Navy Fights for Independence, 1775–1783.* Mount Pleasant, S.C.: Nautical and Aviation Pub. Co., 2000.

Norton, Louis A. *Joshua Barney: Hero of the Revolution and War of 1812.* Annapolis, Md.: Naval Institute Press, 2000.

Wilkinson, Dave. "Legend of Joshua Barney: Forgotten Hero of the American Revolution," *Oceans* 9 (November 1976): 4–13.

Barry, John (1745–1803)

American naval officer

John Barry was born in County Wexford, Ireland, on January 1, 1745, and he became a cabin boy in the merchant marine at the age of 10. He settled in Philadelphia in 1761 and rose to prominence as a ship's captain. When the Revolution erupted in April 1775, he donated his ship, *Black Prince,* to the fledgling Continental NAVY, and it was converted into the armed vessel *Alfred.* On March 14, 1776, Barry was himself commissioned captain and assigned to the brig *Lexington.* He was tasked with protecting American commerce around Delaware Bay, and on April 6, 1776, he engaged and captured the tender HMS *Edward.* This was the first combat victory for the navy and, the following June, Barry ran his ship alongside the stranded Pennsylvania brig *Nancy,* off-loaded valuable supplies of gunpowder, and set charges that exploded just as the British boarded the stricken vessel. In recognition of his prowess, CONGRESS ranked Barry seventh on its list of navy captains in October 1776. It further distinguished him with command of the new, 32-gun frigate *Effingham,* then under construction at Philadelphia. Rather than be idle, Barry raised a company of artillerists from among his crew, joined the army of General George WASHINGTON, and fought with distinction at the victories of TRENTON and PRINCETON that winter. Subsequent British advances forced him to burn the *Effingham* on its stocks, so in February 1778 Barry led a four-boat expedition into Delaware Bay that netted three British vessels laden with valuable mili-

American naval officer John Barry won the first American naval combat victory, on April 6, 1776. *(Naval Historical Center)*

tary supplies. General Washington personally commended Barry for his gallantry and he received a new command, the frigate *Raleigh,* in September 1778.

Barry took to sea immediately but the sheer weight of the Royal Navy began bearing down upon the tiny American navy. On September 25, 1778, while cruising from Boston to Penobscot, Maine, the *Raleigh* was attacked by HMS *Experiment* and HMS *Unicorn* and driven close to shore. There Barry lost his topsail and had little recourse but to beach his ship, burn it, and escape overland. In February 1779 he assumed control of the Pennsylvania state navy brig *Delaware* and served as commodore of an ad hoc squadron that cruised the West Indies. He subsequently took a turn at privateering, again with some success. By this time Barry had also befriended Secretary of War Henry KNOX, who used his influence to secure him command of the frigate *Alliance.* This was one of the last remaining American ships of war still in serviceable condition, and Barry was entrusted with important diplomatic missions.

In February 1780 Barry sailed from Philadelphia with John LAURENS and Thomas PAINE as diplomatic envoys to France. En route he engaged and captured the British brig *Alert* and safely delivered his charges at L'Orient on March 30, 1780. On his return voyage Barry captured the privateers *Mars* and *Minerva* on April 2, 1780, but two months later faced his greatest naval challenge. On May 23, 1780, the *Alliance* was caught in becalmed waters and attacked by the British warships *Atalanta* and *Trepassy.* Using sweeps to row themselves off Barry's stern, they opened a heavy fire that wounded him and he was carried below deck. Barry, as tenacious as ever, refused to yield, and the moment the winds sprang up he ordered himself carried to the main deck, where he outfought and captured his antagonists. In the fall of 1781 Barry was chosen to convey the marquis de LAFAYETTE back to France and, on his return jaunt, he put into Havana, Cuba, to convoy a gold shipment. On March 10, 1783, the *Alliance* sighted and engaged HMS *Sybil* off Cape Canaveral, Florida.

Barry severely pummeled his opponent before being driven off by additional warships in this, the final naval encounter of the Revolutionary War.

After the Revolution, Barry resumed his maritime activities until March 1794, when he became senior captain of the newly founded U.S. Navy. He oversaw construction of the huge 44-gun frigate *United States,* and when the so-called Quasi-War with France broke out in 1798, he sailed into the Caribbean in search of privateers. For the second time in his career he headed a squadron of warships as commodore, and on February 3, 1799, his vessels fought and captured the *L'Amour de La Patrie* off Martinique. Barry resigned from the navy in 1801 on the grounds of poor health and died in Philadelphia on September 13, 1803. Like his famous contemporary John Paul JONES, he was considered a "father of the U.S. Navy" and a purveyor of its fighting traditions.

Further Reading
Bradford, James C., ed. *Command under Sail: Makers of the American Naval Tradition, 1775–1780.* Annapolis, Md.: Naval Institute Press, 1985.
Clark, William B. *Gallant John Barry, 1745–1803: The Story of a Naval Hero of Two Wars.* New York: Macmillan, 1938.
Everett, Barbara. "John Barry, Fighting Irishman," *American History Illustrated* 12, no. 8 (1977): 18–25.
McManemin, John A. *Captains of the Continental Navy.* Ho-Ho-Kus, N.J.: Ho-Ho-Kus Pub. Co., 1981.
Miller, Nathan. *Sea of Glory: The Continental Navy Fights for Independence.* Mount Pleasant, S.C.: Nautical and Aviation Press, 2000.
Melville, Phillips. "Lexington-Brigantine of War, 1776–1777," *U.S. Naval Institute Proceedings* 86, no. 4 (1960): 51–59.

Barton, William (1748–1831)
American militia officer
William Barton was born in Tiverton, Rhode Island, on May 26, 1748, and he trained as a hatter. When fighting broke out in April 1775, he joined a militia company, was elected captain, and spent several months at the siege of Boston. Barton was apparently an effective leader because on August

19, 1776, he gained promotion to major. From December 1776 Rhode Island had been partially occupied by British forces stationed at Newport, at the southern end of the state. Their commander, General Richard Prescott, who had previously been captured and exchanged for General John SULLIVAN, proved himself a haughty and abusive occupier. When word was received that American general Charles LEE had fallen prisoner at Basking Ridge, New Jersey, on December 12, 1776, Barton began drawing up a daring scheme to seize Prescott in order to exchange him.

On the evening of July 4, 1777, Barton set out from Tiverton with four whaleboats and 35 volunteers. They dropped down as far as Warwick Neck before resting, and subsequently crossed Narragansett Bay on the night of July 9. It was well known that Prescott made his headquarters at the Overing House outside of Newport, about a mile from the bay, with a guard consisting of only eight soldiers. Barton and his men rowed silently with muffled oars past three British frigates in the harbor, landed, and advanced inland. The Americans moved stealthily and with dispatch, came upon the Overing House and quickly silenced the sentries. They then battered down the door and seized Prescott, still in his night shirt. Barton then quickly departed with his captive, rowed across the bay, and delivered his prisoner to authorities in Warwick, before the British could respond. The nominally arrogant Prescott reputedly commended his captor for his boldness.

Barton's success facilitated an exchange between the captured Lee and Prescott in April 1778. For his efforts he was lauded by CONGRESS, which gave him a vote of thanks and an elaborate sword. The Rhode Island general assembly also showered him with praise, promoting him to lieutenant colonel of militia. Throughout the siege of Newport in 1778 Barton served as aide-de-camp to fellow Rhode Islander Nathanael GREENE, but his subsequent military career proved anticlimactic. He commanded militia forces in and around Tiverton, skirmishing occasionally with British raiding parties, and in one such action near Warren in 1778 was severely wounded. Barton ended the war commanding a special corps of light infantry with the rank of colonel.

After the war, Barton partook of politics and became a leading figure in the unsuccessful campaign to have Rhode Island ratify the new federal constitution in 1788. He also became involved in a long-standing legal contretemps with the state of Vermont over a land grant he somehow acquired after the war. When a local court issued a judgment against him in 1811, Barton stubbornly refused to pay the fine, citing grounds of principle. He was then placed under house arrest for 14 years in Danbury until the judgment was paid. In 1825

American militia officer William Barton was promoted to lieutenant colonel of militia after he successfully kidnapped British general Richard Prescott on July 9, 1777. *(Brown University Archives)*

the marquis de LAFAYETTE, who had apparently befriended Barton during the Newport campaign, was passing through Vermont on his nationwide tour and heard of his old friend's incarceration. Lafayette promptly paid the fine and Barton was released to return home. He died in Providence on October 22, 1831, one of Rhode Island's most celebrated revolutionary heroes.

Further Reading

Carter, Peyton. *The Bartons' Quest for Liberty: One Family's Sojourns through Rhode Island and Virginia during the Nation's Formative Years.* Salem, Mass.: Higginson Book Co., 2003.

Falkner, Leonard. "Capture of the Barefoot General," *American Heritage* 11, no. 5 (1960): 28–31, 48–100.

Hagler, Don N., comp. *General Orders, Rhode Island: December 1776–January 1778.* Bowie, Md.: Heritage Books, 2001.

Luke, Myron H. "William Barton, Patriot," *Daughters of the American Revolution Magazine* 111, no. 3 (1977): 228–231.

Mazet, Horace S. "From Revolutionary War Hero to Vermont Prisoner," *American History Illustrated* 16, no. 10 (1982): 10–11, 46–47.

Swan, Frank H. *General William Barton.* Providence, R.I.: Roger Williams Press, 1947.

Baum, Friedrich (d. 1777)

German army officer

Nothing is known of Friedrich Baum's birth or background, other than he was apparently a tough, professional officer with the Brunswick Dragoon Regiment (mounted infantry). He departed the German duchy in February 1776 as part of a large Brunswick contingent hired by Great Britain to fight against the United States. Baum's command was attached to troops under General Friedrich von RIEDESEL, and consisted of 336 cavalrymen sporting bicorne hats, bright blue jackets, and armed with both carbines and sabers. It was assumed that the unit would acquire its mounts while in Canada. After arriving at Quebec in the summer of 1777, Baum was assigned to the army of General John BURGOYNE, then deep in preparing for a major offensive down New York's Lake Champlain corridor. The invasion kicked off in late June and on July 7, 1777, won a victory over the rebels at Hubbardton, in present-day Vermont. But by August Burgoyne's juggernaut bogged down in heavily wooded, inhospitable terrain and was experiencing supply shortages. Intelligence had been received that livestock and foodstuff were available a few miles away at BENNINGTON in the neighboring New Hampshire Grants (Vermont). Accordingly, on August 8, 1777, Burgoyne ordered Baum to take 800 men through central Vermont, seizing cattle and horses along the way, and also to recruit numerous LOYALIST sympathizers known to be in the region. The choice of Baum for this mission was curious for he spoke no English and was unfamiliar with the territory.

Baum's column departed Burgoyne's camp on August 11, 1777, with 374 Brunswick dragoons, 50 jaegers (riflemen), 30 artillerists, and 300 Loyalists, Canadians, and Indians. He moved slowly through the woods in good German fashion, periodically stopping his column to dress and realign the ranks. The following day his men exchanged fire with American militia at Cambridge, which prompted Baum to write Burgoyne and request reinforcements as a precaution. He was also rather perturbed that the expected throng of Loyalists had yet to flock to his colors. He then dug several redoubts in the vicinity of Bennington to await developments. Unknown to Baum, General John STARK was rapidly approaching at the head of 1,400 militia. He arrived undetected and sent several spies into the German camp, who feigned friendliness while making accurate notations of its size and strength. On the morning of August 16, 1777, once the Americans had nearly surrounded Baum's encampment, Stark gave the order to attack.

Baum was somewhat taken aback by the ferocity of the American assault, which had nearly enveloped his position. The Germans fought back fiercely from behind their redoubts, although Stark deliberately marched his men around them in order to get the Germans to waste ammunition. As their fire slackened, the Americans charged and picked the emplacements off piecemeal. Baum, commanding the last redoubt, saw the hopelessness of his position and resorted to a desperate maneuver. His surviving men drew sabers and charged downhill upon the Americans, attempting to break through and flee. Seven dragoons actually cut their way to freedom and eventually trudged into Burgoyne's camp, but Baum was mortally wounded and captured. He died in the American camp on August 18, 1777, his defeat ensuring that Burgoyne lacked sufficient food and draft animals for the ongoing struggle at Saratoga.

Further Reading
Arndt, Karl J. R. "New Hampshire at the Battle of Bennington: Colonel Baum's Mission and Bennington Defeat as Reported by a German Officer under General Burgoyne's Command," *Historical New Hampshire* 32, no. 4 (1977): 198–227.
Ketchum, Richard M. "Bennington," *MHQ* 10, no. 1 (1997): 98–111.
Lansing, Amy E. "Baum's Raid," *Quarterly Journal of the New York State Historical Association* 9 (January 1928): 45–56.
Parks, Joseph W. R. *The Battle of Bennington*. Old Bennington, Vt.: Bennington Museum, 1976.
Stephens, Thomas. "In Deepest Submission: The Hessian Mercenary Troops of the American Revolution." Unpublished Ph.D. diss., Texas A & M University, 1998.
Wohl, Michael S. "The German Auxiliary Troops of Great Britain in the Saratoga Campaign." Unpublished master's thesis, Tulane University, 1976.

Bemis Heights, Battle of (October 7, 1777)

Following his defeat at FREEMAN'S FARM on September 19, 1777, General John BURGOYNE found himself in difficult straits, being both short of supplies and increasingly outnumbered. The recent withdrawal of General Barry ST. LEGER from Fort Stanwix had also deprived him of valuable reinforcements. He flirted with the idea of withdrawing across the Hudson River and retreating toward Canada, but a letter from General Henry CLINTON arrived suggesting that reinforcements were en route from the south. Buoyed by this intelligence, Burgoyne sought to try conclusions with the American army under General Horatio GATES one more time, despite the lack of proper reconnaissance. Gates, in fact, had recently been strengthened by the arrival of thousands of militia, which brought his total strength up to 11,000 combatants—twice Burgoyne's strength. But rather than strike the enemy decisively he seemed disposed to dig in and let events unfold from behind his numerous fortifications. Burgoyne, however, was eager to try conclusions and on October 7, 1777, he initiated a major reconnaissance in force prior to launching a formal attack. He did so against the advice of his officers, but "Gentleman Johnny" was too adept a gambler not to incur the risk one last time.

Having only 5,000 men at his disposal, Burgoyne parceled them out carefully, with only a few light troops under the redoubtable earl of Balcarres available to guard his right flank. The center was held by General Friedrich von RIEDESEL and his HESSIANS, backed by an additional British regiment. Burgoyne's left consisted of collected grenadier companies under Major John Acland, strongly posted on a hillside. All were drawn up into a single line before advancing upon the American line. Gates, observing these events from the confines of his fieldworks, ordered riflemen under Colonel Daniel MORGAN to harass Burgoyne's right while other troops under General Enoch POOR closed with his left. Poor's assault was adroitly and aggressively handled, and it completely overwhelmed Major Acland's grenadier battalion, capturing him. On the left, Morgan's sharpshooters kept up a heavy and accurate fire against the British, repeatedly driving them back. However, these rallied under the inspired bravery of General Simon FRASER and sharply counterattacked. Fraser exposed himself so conspicuously that he was singled out by marksman Timothy MURPHY and mortally wounded. His incapacitation deprived Burgoyne of one of his best combat officers, and the tide of battle swung irrevocably against him.

While his flanks collapsed, Burgoyne's center initially held against repeated attacks by General Ebenezer LEARNED's brigade. Combat swayed to and fro with loss to both sides but the impasse appeared intractable. At this critical juncture, General Benedict ARNOLD, acting against orders and without a formal command, appeared in the swirl of battle and began directing affairs on the flanks. He energetically assaulted Balcarres's light troops in their redoubt and was repulsed, but enjoyed better success against the Hessians under Lieutenant Colonel Heinrich Breymann. As the Americans knifed through this last barrier, Arnold received a severe leg wound, but the impetus of his attack nearly carried them into the British camp. Balcarres's redoubt was subsequently stormed from behind and taken. Burgoyne, fast losing control of events, finally signaled a withdrawal to his starting position at Freeman's Farm where his beleaguered command rallied and stood fast. By sunset fighting had petered across the line, and the bested British were fortunate to hold their part of field. Gates, however, remained ensconced behind his fortifications, a passive spectator to this dramatic turn of events.

Bemis Heights proved the death knell of the British invasion. Burgoyne had lost 600 of his best troops while Gates incurred only 150 casualties. Once it became apparent that Clinton was, in fact, not going to render material assistance, the game was nearly up. Burgoyne had little recourse but to gather up his remaining soldiers, withdraw to nearby Saratoga, and await the inevitable onslaught.

Further Reading

Harding, H. DeForest. "Saratoga: Turning Point of the Revolution," *Manuscripts* 53, no. 4 (2001): 299–308.

Ketchum, Richard M. *Saratoga: Turning Point in America's Revolution.* New York: Holt, 1997.

Phifer, Mike. "Campaign to Saratoga," *Military Heritage* 2, no. 1 (2000): 40–51, 94.

Morrissey, Brendan. *Saratoga, 1777: Turning Point of a Revolution.* Oxford: Osprey, 2000.

Nester, Joseph B. "The Battle of Saratoga." Unpublished master's thesis, East Stroudsburg University, 2001.

Seymour, William. "Turning Point at Saratoga," *Military History* 15, no. 5 (1999): 46–52.

Bennington, Battle of (August 16, 1777)

As the Americans withdrew down the Champlain Valley before the approaching army of General John BURGOYNE, they methodically employed scorched earth tactics to deny anything of use to the enemy. Burgoyne, needing to secure livestock for his baggage train and horses to mount his cavalry, was eager to have the situation ameliorated as quickly as possible. Lieutenant Colonel Friedrich BAUM, commanding 374 Brunswick Dragoons within Burgoyne's army, suggested that he be allowed to forage for supplies and animals throughout the region called the New Hampshire Grants (present-day Vermont). Burgoyne, sensing that the mission was easily accomplished, concurred and encouraged Baum to solicit cooperation from LOYALIST sympathizers known to reside in that vicinity. On August 11, 1777, Baum conducted 800 rank and file—dismounted cavalry, Germans, Loyalists, Canadians, and Indians—eastward from Fort Miller, New York. No serious resistance was anticipated, so Baum proceeded slowly, halting his column periodically to dress ranks, and on the 12th he reached the village of Cambridge. There he seized a handful of prisoners and 150 oxen. Proceeding to Van Schaick's Mill on the Walloomac River, the Germans again skirmished periodically with American militia, and Baum was perplexed that the Loyalists did not turn out in force to greet him. As a precaution he dispatched a messenger back to Burgoyne, requesting immediate reinforcements. He then marched six miles farther past the mill and began entrenching on top of the hills overlooking the vicinity of Bennington.

Unknown to Baum, General John STARK had been alerted to his approach and was marching hard to engage him with 1,400 men. He conducted his 20-mile march south from Manchester under tight marching security and the Germans remained unaware of his arrival on the 14th. Stark then sent a stream of "deserters" into the enemy camp who feigned friendship while carefully noting numbers of troops and their dispositions. This information was rapidly conveyed to Stark, who was bivouacked four miles north of Bennington and began formulating a plan of attack. The Americans concluded that Baum's fortifications were dispersed and not within mutual supporting distance, so Stark gambled on the dangerous expedient of dividing his force first to surround and then to envelop the Germans. Rainy weather on August 15 kept both armies confined to camp, but on the following day Stark dispatched 300 rangers under Colonel Samuel Herrick to attack the German right flank from the south and west while another force, under Colonel Moses Nicholas, hit them from the north. This attack, when launched, would be the signal to deliver the main blow in a frontal assault with 1,200 soldiers. It was a complicated scheme for raw troops in exceedingly rough terrain, but Stark knew the mettle of his men and determined to strike a blow.

On August 16, the flank attacks of Herrick and Nicholas went off as planned. In fact, when Baum first perceived the approaching Americans, he calmly passed them off as Loyalists finally flocking under his banner. A stiff firefight dissipated this delusion and the Americans quickly dispersed numerous Loyalists and Indian contingents on the flanks. Only Baum's Hessians, secure behind their redoubt, stood firm. Stark then led the main thrust at the German center, having them advance and feign retreat repeatedly to have the enemy waste ammunition at long range. The ploy worked perfectly, and when Baum's fire slackened due to lack of bullets, the Americans charged and clambered over the redoubt. Rather than surrender, Baum ordered his dragoons to put down their muskets, draw their sabers, and charge downhill on foot. It was an act of desperation, and only seven Germans managed to cut their way through to Burgoyne's camp. Baum was not among them; he had been mortally wounded and captured.

As the victorious Americans were systematically plundering the German camp, they were startled by the sudden appearance of a new German column of 600 men under Lieutenant Colonel Heinrich Breymann. Breymann had been dispatched by Burgoyne on the 15th and made the 25-mile journey at a leisurely pace. The Hessians went forward with leveled bayonets and began driving the disorganized mob back when Stark was suddenly reinforced by 300 fresh troops under Colonel Seth WARNER. This new infusion of strength stiffened the Americans and they counterattacked along the line. Breymann began an orderly withdrawal that degenerated into a rout once his ammunition ran out. The fighting died down at evening; Burgoyne had lost a total of 200 veteran soldiers killed and 700 captured. Stark, flush with victory, sustained around 70 killed and wounded. Considering the rawness of the militia involved, Bennington was a startling victory for the Americans and the first indication of the capable resistance Burgoyne would encounter.

Further Reading
Jepson, George H. *Herrick's Rangers.* Bennington, Vt.: Hawden, 1977.
Ketchum, Richard M. "Bennington," *MHQ* 10, no. 1 (1997): 98–111.
Mann, David L. "Bennington: A Clash between Patriot and Loyalist," *Historical New Hampshire* 32, no. 4 (1977): 171–188.
Parks, Joseph W. R. *The Battle of Bennington.* Old Bennington, Vt.: Bennington Museum, 1976.
Resch, Tyler. *Bennington's Battle Monument: Massive And Lofty.* Bennington, Vt.: Beech Seal, 1993.

Bernard, Francis (1712–1779)
English governor

Francis Bernard was born in Berkshire, England, in July 1712, the son of a prominent Anglican minister. He was well educated at St. Peter's College, Westminster, and Christ Church, Oxford, being admitted to the bar in 1737. Bernard maintained a successful law practice and subsequently served as commissioner of bails for Lincoln, York, and Nottingham. In 1741 he further advanced his political fortunes by marrying Amelia Offley, a cousin of viscount Barrington. As Bernard and Barrington became good friends, the latter helped arrange his appointment as royal governor of New Jersey in 1758. In this capacity Bernard distinguished himself as an energetic leader, well versed in the nuances of colonial law. He concluded a peace treaty with the Delaware Indians, raised troops for the French and Indian War, and granted Quakers representation on the council. Bernard even managed to have English authorities modify their stance on prohibiting paper money to ease New Jersey's economic problems. His short tenure was uniformly successful and resulted in an appointment as royal governor of Massachusetts in 1760. This seemingly plumb promotion proved to be a turning point in his career—and the colony's.

Bernard assumed his office on August 2, 1760, and made an initial mistake by appointing Thomas HUTCHINSON, a nonlawyer, as his chief justice. The position had been promised to long-established attorney James OTIS, and the favoritism alienated many within the ruling elite. For four years Bernard ran the colony efficiently amid general praise, but attitudes toward him cooled considerably following the SUGAR ACT of 1764 and the STAMP ACT of 1765. Bernard sought to accommodate colonial concerns and suggested that they be enabled to raise their own Imperial taxes based on quotas established by Parliament. He even considered the Stamp Act misguided but felt, nonetheless, that the rule of law should prevail in such matters. This became increasingly problematic in the wake of mob actions orchestrated by the SONS OF LIBERTY against tax officials and their homes. When Bernard tried maintaining order, he became popularly identified with the "English conspiracy" to rob colonials of their rights. And, once the TOWNSHEND DUTIES were approved by Parliament in 1767, the Massachusetts General Court sought to ratchet up colonial resistance through its famous circular letter. Bernard, at the instigation of Secretary for the Colonies Lord Hillsborough, subsequently demanded that the assembly retract its letter, and they refused. He responded in July 1768 by suspending the General Court.

In light of deteriorating public order, Bernard strongly suggested to the government that additional troops be sent to Boston. These arrived in October 1768 and led to a crescendo of condemnation by agitators such as Samuel ADAMS. Far from intimidating the colonials, the presence of British troops only heightened the friction between colony and homeland. Bernard's regime was effectively ended in April 1769 when he composed several letters to Lord Hillsborough urging that the colony's charter be revoked and a royal one be substituted so that the governing council could be appointed by the king. Unfortunately, when his correspondence was surreptitiously obtained by the editors of the *Boston Gazette* and published, public uproar ensued. The governor lost his remaining political support and the General Court demanded his removal from office. The government apparently agreed and Bernard was recalled to England in August 1769 amid an outpouring of relief. Hutchinson was then appointed governor in his place, which in time also added to colonial frustrations.

Bernard's mishandling of affairs in Massachusetts did not weigh heavily against him back in England, for he received a baronetcy, an honorary doctorate from Oxford, and appointment as customs commissioner for Ireland. He died in Aylesbury, Buckinghamshire, on June 16, 1779, an earnest and able administrator but unable to fathom the depth of colonial resentment against British Imperial policy.

Further Reading

Channing, Edward, and Archibald C. Coolidge, eds. *The Barrington-Bernard Correspondence and Illustrative Matter, 1760–1770.* New York: Da Capo Press, 1970.

Jones, Ruth. "Governor Bernard Francis and His Land Acquisitions," *Historical Journal of Massachusetts* 16, no. 2 (1988): 121–134.

Nicolson, Colin. *The 'Infamas Govener' Francis Bernard and the Origins of the American Revolution.* Boston: Northeastern University Press, 2001.

Nobles, Gregory H. *Divisions throughout the Whole: Politics and Society in Hampshire County, Massachusetts, 1750–1775*. Cambridge: Cambridge University Press, 2002.

Raphael, Ray. *The First American Revolution: Before Lexington and Concord*. New York: New Press, 2002.

Sents, Aeilt E. "Francis Bernard and English Imperial Reconstruction." Unpublished Ph.D. diss., University of Missouri, 1973.

Biddle, Nicholas (1750–1778)
American naval officer

Nicholas Biddle was born in Philadelphia, Pennsylvania, on September 10, 1750, the son of a successful merchant. He entered the merchant marine at the age of 13 and once survived two months on a deserted island following a shipwreck. In 1770 Biddle joined the Royal Navy as a midshipman and three years later accompanied Captain Constantine J. Phipps on an exciting expedition to the Arctic region for the Royal Geographic Society. Among Biddle's messmates was a young Horatio Nelson, the future admiral. In 1775 Biddle returned to Philadelphia and volunteered his services to the nascent Continental NAVY and became one of its first six captains. Consequently he received command of the armed galley *Franklin* and patrolled the Delaware coastline. But, thirsting for action, Biddle requested a transfer and gained appointment as captain of the 18-gun brig *Andrea Doria*. He then accompanied Commodore Esek HOPKINS on a successful foray against the Bahamas in 1776 and, on the return leg of the voyage, captured two British transports carrying 400 Highland troops en route to Boston. In recognition of Biddle's abilities, he next obtained command of the 32-gun frigate *Randolph*, the first of 13 vessels constructed for the Continental navy.

Biddle sailed with the *Randolph* in February 1777, despite his criticism that the masts, which had been in storage for 18 years, were probably rotted. True to his observations, Biddle's mainmast tore away in the middle of a heavy storm, necessitating his putting into Charleston, South Carolina, for repairs. He then took to sea again and made for the West Indies. His cruise was particularly successful and included capturing 20-gun privateer

American naval officer Nicholas Biddle, known for his boldness, was one of the first captains of the Continental navy. *(Independence National Historical Park)*

True Briton. No sooner had the *Randolph* returned to Charleston in December 1777 than the Royal Navy blockaded the port for three months, but Biddle used the delay to outfit additional vessels for a new expedition. The British had departed by the time the *Randolph* sailed again in February 1778, accompanied by a company of the 1st South Carolina Regiment acting as marines, and four smaller warships of the South Carolina state navy. Biddle then shepherded his flotilla back to the West Indies.

On March 7, 1778, Biddle was cruising 60 miles east of Barbados when he was approached by a huge warship in the darkness. This turned out to be the 64-gun HMS *Yarmouth* under Captain Nicholas Vincent, who drew up within hailing distance and demanded to know Biddle's identity. With gun ports ready, he reputedly fired back "This is the Continental frigate *Randolph*!" and unloosed a broadside. A fiery exchange commenced in the night with Biddle's well-drilled crews firing three times to every British salvo. He exposed himself recklessly in combat, was hit by a bullet in the leg, yet refused to relinquish command. Biddle ordered a chair brought to the quarterdeck and he continued to direct the action personally. *Yarmouth* took a pounding and sustained considerable damage in the exchange until a lucky shot struck and ignited *Randolph's* gunpowder magazine. The frigate exploded and sank suddenly, killing 311 crew members, including Biddle; four survivors were subsequently rescued by the *Yarmouth*. The loss of so capable a sailor was a severe blow to the fledgling American navy, but Biddle's brief career conveyed important traditions of bravery and seamanship.

Further Reading
Biddle, Edward. "Captain Nicholas Biddle (Continental Navy) 1750–1778," *U.S. Naval Institute Proceedings* 43, no. 125 (1917): 1993–2003.
Clark, William B. *Captain Dauntless: The Story of Nicholas Biddle of the Continental Navy.* Baton Rouge: Louisiana State University Press, 1949.
———, ed. "The Letters of Nicholas Biddle (1771–1777)," *Pennsylvania Magazine of History and Biography* 74 (July 1950): 348–405.
Miller, Nathan. *Sea of Glory: The Continental Navy Fights for Independence, 1775–1783.* Mount Pleasant, S.C.: Nautical and Aviation Press, 2000.

Biron, Armand-Louis de Contaut, duc de.
See LAUZUN, ARMAND-LOUIS DE CONTAUT, DUC DE

Boone, Daniel (1734–1820)
American militia officer
Daniel Boone was born in Reading, Pennsylvania, on November 2, 1734, into a Quaker family. He matured in the Yadkin district of North Carolina, took readily to outdoor life, and became an accomplished hunter and marksman. When the French and Indian War broke out in 1755, Boone accompanied General Edward Braddock on his ill-fated expedition against Fort Duquesne as a teamster and barely escaped the slaughter that followed. He then fought with General John Forbes in the capture of that outpost in 1758 and became a leading exponent of Indian woodland tactics. Restless by nature, in 1767 Boone led a small expedition into Kentucky and helped establish a migratory route through the famous Cumberland Gap. Native Americans, the Shawnee in particular, both resented and resisted this white encroachment, and Boone endured harrowing escapes in countless skirmishes. When Virginia governor John MURRAY, Lord Dunmore, instigated a war with the Shawnee in 1775, Boone secured appointment as his personal messenger. In this capacity he rescued a party of surveyors working behind Indian lines who were unaware that hostilities had commenced. But, like many Americans living on the

American militiaman Daniel Boone hoped to establish the state of Kentucky with his settlement, Boonesborough. *(James Audubon Museum)*

frontier, he resented the PROCLAMATION OF 1763 and its impositions against settling beyond the Trans-Appalachian region. Boone nevertheless fulfilled a lifelong ambition by establishing Boonesborough in 1775, from which he hoped to organize the state of Kentucky.

When the Revolutionary War erupted in April 1775, Boone was inducted into the militia as a captain. In February 1778 his hunting party of 21 men was surrounded and captured by a large contingent of Shawnee warriors and taken to Detroit for ransoming. There Boone was interviewed by Governor Henry HAMILTON and subsequently adopted into the family of Chief Black Fish. He lived like an Indian for several months, becoming affectionately attached to his new family but also biding his time. When informed that the Shawnee were mustering 400 warriors for an attack upon Boonesborough, he escaped and rode 160 miles in five days to alert the garrison. When the Indians besieged and attacked the settlement on September 7, 1777, Boone was on hand to help defeat them. Around this time he also ran afoul of Colonel George Rogers CLARK, who was determined to prevent Boone and other settlers from establishing a new state and was working to organize Kentucky as a Virginia county. In February 1781 Governor Thomas JEFFERSON promoted Boone to lieutenant colonel and he subsequently won election to the state legislature. That June he was briefly taken prisoner at Charlottesville during a lightning raid by Lieutenant Colonel Banastre TARLETON. He returned to Kentucky shortly afterward, losing his brother Edward to an Indian ambush en route.

The American victory at YORKTOWN in late 1781 did little to mitigate the ferocity of Indian warfare against scattered and thinly populated frontier enclaves. On August 19, 1782, a roving band of Indians and LOYALISTS under Captain Simon GIRTY besieged Bryan's Station until a relief column approached. The Indians then fled to the vicinity of Blue Licks, deliberately leaving signs of their withdrawal. Boone, an experienced frontiersman, suspected a ruse and advised against pursuing. However, his commander, Colonel John Todd, proved reluctant to have his bravery questioned by delaying. He ordered his Kentucky militia forward and they crossed the Blue Licks on August 19, 1782. True to Boone's dire predictions, Girty and his Indians were laying in ambush and sprang it with deadly effectiveness. The Americans lost 70 men killed and scalped, including Boone's youngest son, Israel. Boone hid his body in the undergrowth and returned several days later to render a proper burial.

After the war, Boone became embroiled in protracted legal disputes over land in Kentucky and by 1799 had lost all his titles. That year he relocated to Missouri, then under Spanish control, where he served as a magistrate. When the United States acquired that area through the Louisiana Purchase of 1803, he was again deprived of his land titles. It was not until 1814 that CONGRESS finally restored his holdings. Boone died in St. Charles County, Missouri, on September 26, 1820, a skilled Indian fighter and an iconic symbol of the American frontier.

Further Reading

Adam, Michael C. C. "An Appraisal of the Blue Licks Battle," *Filson Club History Quarterly* 75, no. 2 (2001): 181–203.

Hammond, Neal O. *Daniel Boone and the Defeat at Blue Licks*. Sumter, S.C.: Boone Society, 2005.

Hammond, Neal O., and Richard Taylor. *Virginia's Western War, 1775–1786*. Mechanicsburg, Pa.: Stackpole Books, 2002.

Hindraker, Eric, and Peter C. Mancall. *At the Edge of Empire: The Backcountry of British North America*. Baltimore: Johns Hopkins University Press, 2003.

Graves, James. "Fatal Decision at Blue Licks," *Military History* 19, no. 3 (2002): 34–40.

Nester, William R. *The Frontier War for American Independence*. Mechanicsburg, Pa.: Stackpole Books, 2004.

Boston Massacre (March 5, 1770)

Parliamentary imposition of such unpopular bills as the QUARTERING ACT of 1765, the STAMP ACT of 1765, and the TOWNSHEND DUTIES of 1767, created an atmosphere of confrontation and overt hostilities throughout the colonies. Nowhere was this more prevalent than in Boston, Massachusetts, long a hotbed of resistance to imperial tax schemes. The ensuing unrest often gave way to violence against customs and revenue officials, so in November 1768 no less than four British infantry regiments were deployed there to maintain order. By 1770 only two regiments, the 14th and 29th, remained, but brawls between them and dockworkers and the SONS OF LIBERTY were a frequent occurrence. Resentment crested on March 5, 1770, a cold snowy day when Private Hugh White of the 29th Regiment, while guarding his sentry box, was rudely harassed by a youth. White unwisely struck at his tormentor with his musket butt in exasperation, and the youth ran off seeking assistance. Shortly afterward, an unruly mob of 400 dockworkers and ship hands assembled on King Street under Crispus ATTUCKS and began approaching the guard box. Confronted by a hostile throng, White called for assistance and at length Captain Thomas Preston, a corporal, and seven privates came to his succor. The presence of armed soldiers did little to intimidate the crowd, which began throwing snowballs and ice chunks. Preston warned his men to stand their ground and not fire, but apparently Attucks or one of the rioters struck White with a snowball, knocking him down. The soldier responded by rising and firing into the crowd, at which point the remainder of the patrol also discharged their weapons. When the smoke cleared Attucks and another man lay dead, three more civilians were mortally injured, and two more were wounded.

The so-called Boston Massacre proved itself a publicity bonanza for radicals such as Samuel ADAMS and Paul REVERE, who propagandized the incident simply as the latest example of British injustice. Word of it spread like wildfire throughout the other colonies, increasing public anger against England. When Adams formed a deputation demanding that Governor Thomas HUTCHINSON remove all British troops from the city immediately, Hutchinson initially refused but, upon further reflection, authorized their transfer to Castle William in Boston Harbor. To diffuse public tensions further, the offending soldiers were arrested and charged with the murder of five citizens.

The trial of Captain Preston and his men occurred in the following October and November and generated great public interest. Ironically, the soldiers were defended by two strident critics of British policy, John ADAMS and Josiah QUINCY, who felt that the rule of law must prevail. In court both men labored to prove that the mob had instigated the affair and, not surprisingly, a sympathetic jury acquitted all ranks of murder. However, two soldiers were found guilty of manslaughter and branded on the thumb as punishment. Curiously, Bostonians evinced little dissent following Preston's acquittal; apparently, most citizens concurred that the mob was, in fact, at fault. But the "Boston Massacre" continued the long series of British missteps that exacerbated colonial tensions and ultimately fueled greater resistance.

Further Reading
Butts, Robert H. "The Boston Massacre Trials: The Adamses and Whig Divides." Unpublished master's thesis, Texas A & M University, 2001.
Hansen, Harry. *The Boston Massacre: An Episode of Dissent and Violence.* New York: Hastings House, 1984.
Newman, Michael. "Interpreting the British Position on the Boston Massacre: An Analysis of the Key Players and Main Events Surrounding the 1770 Affair." Unpublished honors thesis, State University of New York, Binghamton, 2000.
Ruchir, Gupta. "The Effect of Massacres on Regional and National Independence Movements." Unpublished master's thesis, State University of New York, Binghamton, 2001.
Zobel, Hiller B. *The Boston Massacre.* New York: W. W. Norton, 1996.

Boston Tea Party (December 16, 1773)
Since the repeal of the TOWNSHEND DUTIES in April 1770, a relative calm had settled over the nominally restless port of Boston. However, news of Lord Frederick NORTH's decision to impose the TEA ACT rekindled long-simmering resentment

against imperial revenue policies. This fear of renewed taxation, coupled with the expansion of monopolies such as had been granted the East India Tea Company, spurred quiescent Massachusetts radicals into action. Samuel ADAMS, backed by the SONS OF LIBERTY, publicly swore not to allow British tea ships to discharge their cargo in Boston. This time the extremists were backed by leading figures like John HANCOCK and Josiah QUINCY, who formed a COMMITTEE OF CORRESPONDENCE to coordinate better resistance throughout the colony. However, Governor Thomas HUTCHINSON proved equally adamant that the supremacy of government be upheld, regardless of public sentiment. He instructed that the tea ships, once docked, not leave Boston Harbor until all duties on their seemingly superfluous cargo had been paid. The groundwork had thus been laid for a major confrontation—of some kind. When the tea vessel *Dartmouth* anchored at Boston on November 18, 1773, Adams quickly assembled a mob that crowded the wharfs and blocked any attempt to offload its cargo. However, the radicals were operating under a timetable, for if the tea was not unloaded within 20 days, customs required it to be confiscated and sold anyway. This had the effect of undercutting the boycott against British goods. The captain of the *Dartmouth*, Francis Rotch, met with customs officials and requested clearance to leave for England but was refused. As the deadline approached, Adams felt some dramatic gesture was necessary to end the impasse while sending an unmistakable protest back to Parliament.

Toward the end of November, Adams orchestrated a mass gathering of 5,000 individuals at the Old South Meeting House to draft resolutions demanding the tea's return. When this failed, the Sons of Liberty were inducted into a deliberate act of political protest. On the night of December 16, 1773, Adams harangued another mass crowd at the Old South Meeting House, whipped them into a fury, and the "Boston Tea Party" unfolded. Sixty men, loosely disguised as Indians, marched down to the wharves and boarded the vessels *Dartmouth*, *Eleanor*, and *Beaver*. Accompanied by the cheers of several hundred spectators, they systematically seized 342 casks of tea and unceremoniously hurled them into Boston Harbor. The rioters, however, proved circumspect: No one was injured in the fracas and no other property was damaged by the time they withdrew into the night. When word of the action spread to other colonies, similar anti-tea vandalism occurred at New York and Annapolis. But it was Boston, long a maelstrom of antigovernment agitation, that would be singled out for its temerity.

The British government was appreciably livid over what it construed as a direct challenge to its authority over colonial affairs. King GEORGE III was especially taken aback by his American subjects, declaring, "We must master them or totally leave them to themselves." It then fell upon Lord NORTH to concoct an appropriate imperial response to the affront, which culminated in passage of the COERCIVE ACTS that closed Boston Harbor until Massachusetts compensated for the tea destroyed. Both sides were now set upon a seemingly irrevocable collision course: What had begun as benign defiance against imported beverages began spiraling toward a confrontation just short of armed struggle.

Further Reading

Breen, T. H. *The Marketplace of Revolution: How Consumer Politics Shaped American Independence*. New York: Oxford University Press, 2004.

Carter, Mary J., and Michael Kaplan. *The Ruling Passion: Reflections on a Society under Siege*. Weston, Mass.: Font & Center Press, 1998.

Dunsworth, Emily M. " 'Headquarters of the Revolution': Colonial Boston's Green Dragon Coffeehouse." Unpublished master's thesis, University of St. Thomas, 2005.

Larabee, Benjamin W. *The Boston Tea Party*. Unpublished Master's thesis, University of St. Thomas, 2005.

Thomas, Peter D. G. *Tea Party to Independence: The Third Phase of the American Revolution, 1773–1776*. New York: Oxford University Press, 1991.

Young, Alfred F. *The Shoemaker and the Tea Party*. Boston: Beacon Press, 1999.

Boudinot, Elias (1740–1821)
American politician

Elias Boudinot was born in Philadelphia on May 2, 1740, the son of a prosperous silversmith. His family subsequently relocated to New Jersey, where he passed though Princeton College and founded a successful legal practice in 1760. Boudinot eventually settled at Elizabethtown, gaining there a fortune from speculation and mercantile activities. Despite his close ties with land and monied interests, Boudinot was a Whig by inclination and a critic of British imperial policy. He was a particularly ardent opponent of royal governor William Franklin, son of Benjamin FRANKLIN, who had been Boudinot's neighbor in Philadelphia. As the crisis with Great Britain approached in 1774, Boudinot volunteered his services for the colony's COMMITTEE OF CORRESPONDENCE, served as chairman of the Committee of Safety, and was voted a delegate to the extralegal Provincial Congress. Here Boudinot proved instrumental in securing a large cache of gunpowder and dispatching it to General George WASHINGTON at Boston. However, he opposed an attempt by New Jersey to declare its independence in April 1776 and ultimately hoped for reconciliation with the motherland.

When hostilities commenced Boudinot tendered his services as aide-de-camp to General William Livingston of the New Jersey militia. General Washington then prevailed upon Boudinot to serve as commissary general of prisoners. This proved an arduous task requiring him to ensure the well-being of British captives while carefully monitoring the treatment of American prisoners. Ultimately he dispensed $30,000 out of his own pocket to obtain food and clothing for his charges. Boudinot served efficiently and in 1778 he was elected to the Continental CONGRESS from New Jersey. His principal role was as advocate for western land claims by the middle states, a stance that brought him into conflict with Virginia's James MADISON. In July 1781 he was reelected and the following year Boudinot became president of Congress, a largely ceremonial post that technically made him chief executive of the nation. He helped conduct day-to-day affairs of the national legislature and, following the resignation of Robert R. LIVINGSTON, he also functioned as the de facto secretary of foreign affairs. In this capacity Boudinot was a signatory to the preliminary peace treaty with England on April 15, 1783. His presidential term was generally constructive until the mutiny of the Pennsylvania Line in June 1783, after which he orchestrated the removal of Congress from Philadelphia to Princeton, New Jersey.

After the war Boudinot resumed his legal and financial activities back in New Jersey until 1790, when he returned to Congress under the new federal Constitution. He was staunchly Federalist in outlook and a close ally of Alexander HAMILTON and his fiscal policies. In 1795 Boudinot was appointed superintendent of the national mint, which he capably administered until 1805. Once back in civilian life he delved into political literature and strongly attacked the writings of Thomas PAINE for their supposedly anti-religious bent. Profoundly religious himself, Boudinot also founded the American Bible Society in 1816, of which he was also first president. He spent the remainder of his life giving freely to charities and philanthropic causes before dying in Burlington, New Jersey, on October 24, 1821.

Further Reading
Boudinot, Elias. *Journal of Events in the Revolution.* New York: Arno Press, 1968.

Boyle, Joseph L., ed. *'Their Distress Is Almost Intolerable': The Elias Boudinot Letterbook, 1777–1778.* Bowie, Md.: Heritage Books, 2002.

Carlson, Jonas. "Elias Boudinot: A Study of Religion, Politics, and Economics during the American Revolutionary Era." Unpublished master's thesis, University of Nebraska, Kearney, 2001.

Clark, Barbara L. *E. B.: The Story of Elias Boudinot IV, His Family, Friends, and His Country.* Philadelphia: Dorrance, 1977.

Robertson, Cheryl. "Elias Boudinot: A Case Study of Ethnic Identity and Assimilation." Unpublished master's thesis, University of Delaware, 1980.

Tunis, Edwin. *The Tavern at the Ferry.* Baltimore: Johns Hopkins University Press, 2002.

Brady, Samuel (1756–1795?)
American militia officer

Samuel Brady was born at Shippensburg, Pennsylvania, in 1756, the son of a militia officer. He relocated with his family to the wilderness region along the Susquehanna River, becoming steeped in the ways of Indian culture and warfare. When the Revolutionary War broke out in 1775, Brady joined a Pennsylvania rifle company commanded by Captain John Lowden and accompanied it to Boston. He was subsequently promoted to lieutenant and fought in most of the large engagements of the northeast, including PRINCETON in January 1777, where he rescued Colonel Edward HAND from capture. Brady also fought well at the Battle of BRANDYWINE on September 11, 1777, where he was severely wounded. He then distinguished himself at MONMOUTH on June 28, 1778, winning promotion to captain. Brady eventually joined the frontier forces of Colonel Daniel BRODHEAD at Pittsburgh in 1779. While home he learned that his father and brother had been massacred by Indians and, according to folklore, he swore eternal vengeance against them.

Brady became a legendary frontier figure of whom many tales are told. Most are impossible to verify but in August 1779 he ambushed a large party of Shawnee warriors in canoes, killing Chief Bald Eagle. He thereafter committed several daring reconnaissance missions against hostile tribes in the Sandusky region of the Ohio territory. Brady was hotly pursued on several occasions and invariably managed to outwit his antagonists. The warriors, singularly impressed by his marksmanship and fighting ability with a knife, christened him "Big Snake." His most celebrated escape occurred sometime in 1780, when, being confronted by a deep gorge across a stream, he dropped his rifle and leapt an estimated 22 feet to the other side. The incident has since been passed down in frontier lore as "Brady's leap." After the war Brady settled down in Wellsburg, (West) Virginia, and married a Miss Drucilla Swearingen in 1786. He died in West Liberty, (West) Virginia, around 1795, a renowned scout, frontiersman, and Indian fighter.

Further Reading
Barr, Daniel P. "The Indian Hunter: Captain Samuel Brady and the American Revolutionary War on the Western Pennsylvania Frontier," *Journal of America's Military Past* 27, no. 2 (2000): 4–18.
Brady, William Y. *Captain Sam Brady, Indian Fighter.* Washington, Pa.: Brady Pub. Co., 1950.
DeMay, John A. *The Settler's Forts of Western Pennsylvania: Thank You Ann Hupp, and You, Too, Sam Brady.* Apollo, Pa.: Clossier Press, 1997.
Fall, Ralph E. "Captain Samuel Brady (1756–1795), Chief of Rangers, and His Kin," *West Virginia History* 29, no. 3 (1988): 203–233.
Hintzen, William. *A Sketchbook of the Border Wars of the Upper Ohio Valley, 1769–1794: Conflicts and Resolutions.* Manchester, Conn.: Precision Shooting, 2001.
Nester, William R. *The Frontier War for American Independence.* Mechanicsburg, Pa.: Stackpole Books, 2004.

Brandywine, Battle of (September 11, 1777)

Having debarked 13,000 men at Head of Elk, Maryland, on August 25, 1777, General William HOWE began a concerted advance upon the American capital at Philadelphia. Continental forces under General George WASHINGTON then positioned themselves along Brandywine Creek, Pennsylvania, roughly mid-point between Head of Elk and Howe's objective. It appeared a deceptively strong position, but Washington, mustering only 8,000 regulars and 3,000 militia, had to disperse his men at various points along the creek to cover all possible fords and crossing points. The left flank at Pyle's Crossing was held by militia under General John ARMSTRONG, the center at Chadd's Ford was commanded by General Nathanel GREENE, while General John SULLIVAN, who also directed the divisions of Generals Adam STEPHEN and William ALEXANDER, guarded Brinton's and Painter's Fords on the extreme right. The British had reconnoitered the American position on September 10, and Howe concocted a strategy reminiscent of the Battle of LONG ISLAND a year earlier. One division of 5,000 men under General Wilhelm von KNYPHAUSEN would demonstrate to Washington's front, fixing his attention there. Concurrently, the remaining 8,000 would accompany Howe and General Charles CORNWALLIS on a circuitous march several miles around the American right flank before crossing Trimble's and Jeffrey's Fords, taking them in the rear. It was a relatively simple strategy but, conducted under intense summer heat, an arduous one.

In the morning of September 11, Knyphausen's men advanced and drove back the outer picket under General William MAXWELL across Brandywine Creek. Knyphausen then held back from assaulting the main American line and simply brought up a few batteries to bombard it. Washington assumed this was a feint and anticipated that the British intended turning his right flank. He then ordered Sullivan to turn his line 90 degrees across Howe's expected line of march to oppose him. He also made preparations to cross Brandywine Creek in overwhelming force and destroy Knyphausen's division to his front. At this critical juncture Washington received contradictory intelligence suggesting that the British were not trying to turn his flank, so he ordered Sullivan's movement halted and also called off his main attack. The Americans were still in the act of redeploying when Howe's main column suddenly materialized at Osborne Hill to their rear around 2 P.M. The British had just come off a grueling 17-mile march and Howe ordered the men to repose before committing them to battle. During the impasse Sullivan hurriedly assumed new positions before Howe ordered a general advance at around 4 P.M. Fighting was particularly intense around Battle Hill and Sullivan slowly gave ground before superior numbers and discipline. Washington, desperate to stave off disaster, then ordered Greene to detach the brigade of Generals George WEEDON and John Peter MUHLENBERG to reinforce Sullivan. This force completed a four-mile march in only 45 minutes and shored up the American right before it gave way. Greene eventually followed with more troops, but the British surging line proved irresistible. Back at the center, Knyphausen, biding his time as Greene gradually weakened his position, suddenly attacked across Brandywine Creek in force. The Americans under General Anthony WAYNE were hard-pressed to stop them and withdrew after losing a battery of 11 guns. Washington then ordered a general withdrawal under fire, which was completed in good order. The Americans extricated themselves bloodied but intact.

The reverse at Brandywine sealed the fate of Philadelphia and it fell to the British on September 26, 1777. Washington suffered more than 1,200 casualties to Howe's 577 killed and wounded, but on the balance the Continental ARMY performed well. However, defeat reflected badly on his leadership abilities as, for the second time in a year, the American right flank had been turned with near-disastrous consequences. Howe himself had conceived an excellent battle plan that placed the bulk of his forces in the enemy's rear, but his dilatory execution allowed the Americans to avoid a complete disaster. Furthermore, the capture of Philadelphia, while a propaganda windfall, proved of little consequence strategically and employed troops that might better have been sent to reinforce General John BURGOYNE.

Further Reading
Cullen, Joseph P. "Brandywine Creek," *American History Illustrated* 15, no. 5 (1980): 8–13, 40–43.
Eastby, Allen G. "Setback for the Continental Army," *Military History* 15, no. 5 (1998): 58–64.
Martin, David G. *The Philadelphia Campaign, June 1777–July 1778.* Cambridge, Mass.: Da Capo Press, 2003.
McQuire, Thomas J. "British Images of War at Brandywine and the Tredyffrin Encampment," *Pennsylvania Heritage* 28, no. 4 (2002): 24–31.
Mowaday, Bruce E. *September 11, 1777: Washington's Defeat at Brandywine Dooms Philadelphia.* Shippensburg, Pa.: White Mane Press, 2002.
Taaffe, Stephen R. *The Philadelphia Campaign, 1777–1778.* Lawrence: University Press of Kansas, 2003.

Brant, Joseph (ca. 1743–1807)
Loyalist Mohawk chief

Joseph Brant (Thayendaneagea) was born around 1743, a member of the Wolf Clan of the Mohawk, which constituted a part of the six-nation assembly known as the Iroquois Confederation. He spent much of his youth in the household of Sir William Johnson, superintendent of Indian affairs and common-law husband of his sister, Molly BRANT. As such he received a British-style education at Eleazar Wheelock's Indian Charity School in Lebanon, Connecticut, becoming fluent in English and a devout Anglican. An aspiring warrior, he fought alongside British troops throughout the French and Indian War, 1755–63, and again in Pontiac's Rebellion. After 1765 Brant proved instrumental in translating the bible and other religious tracts into the Mohawk tongue. When the elder Johnson died in 1774 and was succeeded by his nephew, Guy JOHNSON, Brant functioned as his personal secretary and interpreter. After the American Revolution broke out in April 1775, both Brant and Johnson relocated their families from New York to Quebec for safety reasons. There he was interviewed by Governor-General Guy CARLETON and sent on a diplomatic mission to London. Brant was widely feted in the English capital, had his portrait done by Sir Joshua Reynolds, and was introduced to King GEORGE III. He was also commissioned a captain of Indians and returned to America firmly committed to the British cause.

Once home, Brant tried coaxing unity among the Six Nations but failed, as the Oneida and Tuscarora elected to side with the Americans. He then returned to Quebec to recruit a body of Mohawk warriors to fight for the Crown. In the summer of 1777 Brant accompanied Lieutenant Colonel Barry ST. LEGER on his expedition up the Mohawk River in support of General John BURGOYNE. During the siege of Fort Stanwix, New York, his sister informed him that the Americans were mounting a relief expedition of their own. Brant and 300 Indians, assisted by LOYALISTS under Captain Walter BUTLER, ambushed Colonel Nicholas HERKIMER at ORISKANY Creek on August 6, inflicting and sustaining heavy losses. Thereafter the British retreated back to Canada while Indians and Loyalists resorted to a bloody hit-and-run insurgency against the frontier settlements of New York and Pennsylvania. These culminated in the bloody, November 11, 1778, destruction of Cherry Valley, New York, in which he tried and failed to spare civilian lives. On July 22, 1779, Brant cleverly ambushed and destroyed a pursing militia detachment at Minisink, New York. The Americans countered the following summer by dispatching General John SULLIVAN on a retaliatory expedition into the Iroquois heartland. On August 29, 1779, the American defeated Brant

Mohawk warrior and ardent Loyalist, Joseph Brant continually sought unity among the Six Nations of the Iroquois. *(Fenimore Art Museum, Cooperstown, New York)*

and Butler at Newtown (Elmira) New York, after which nearby Indian villages were razed to the ground. This destruction spurred the Iroquois into greater efforts, and that fall Brant accompanied Sir John JOHNSON on destructive raids in the Mohawk and Schoharie valleys. In recognition of his contributions and military skills, he was also promoted to colonel of Indians. In April 1781 Brant took his warriors west to defend Detroit against an anticipated attack by Colonel George Rogers CLARK. On August 26, 1781, he ambushed an American detachment under Colonel Archibald Lochry on the Ohio River, annihilating it.

Brant always sought unity amongst the Six Nations, but his position was continually undercut by Chief RED JACKET of the Seneca, who argued for making a separate peace treaty with the Americans. In any event, by war's end most Indian territory in New York was in American hands, a fact that Great Britain acknowledged in the TREATY OF PARIS. Feeling betrayed by his erstwhile allies, Brant conferred with Governor-General Frederick HALDIMAND in Quebec about a possible land grant in Upper Canada. When discussions failed, he made a second pilgrimage to England in 1785 and received land grants along the Grand River, Ontario. Brant spent the rest of his life working on behalf of dispossessed Mohawk, and he also founded the first Anglican church for Indians in Upper Canada. He died on his family estate on November 24, 1807.

Further Reading
Allen, Robert S. *His Majesty's Indian Allies: British Indian Policy in the Defense of Canada, 1774–1815.* Toronto: Dundurn Press, 1992.
Calloway, Colin G. *The American Revolution in Indian Country: Crisis and Diversity in Native American Communities.* New York: Cambridge University Press, 1995.
Kelsay, Isabelle T. *Joseph Brant, 1743–1807: Man of Two Worlds.* Syracuse, N.Y.: Syracuse University Press, 1984.
Mann, Barbara A. *George Washington's War on Native America.* Westport, Conn.: Praeger, 2005.

Taylor, Alan. *The Divided Ground: The Northern Borderland of the American Revolution.* New York: Alfred A. Knopf, 2006.
Tiro, Karim M. "A 'Civil War'?: Rethinking Iroquois Participation in the American Revolution," *Early American Culture* 4 (2000): 148–165.
Watt, Gavin K. *The Burning of the Valleys: Daring Raids from Canada against the New York Frontier in the Fall of 1780.* Buffalo, N.Y.: Dundurn Press, 1997.

Brant, Molly (ca. 1735–1783)
Mohawk interpreter and facilitator

Molly Brant (Konwatsi tsiaienni) was probably born in the Mohawk village of Canajoharie, New York, around 1735. She was the elder sister of future war chief Joseph BRANT and, like him, received a rudimentary English education and early exposure to Christianity. She came to prominence within the tribe after 1759 by marrying the noted superintendent of Indian affairs, Sir William Johnson, in a Mohawk ceremony. The union produced eight children, and Brant became renowned as a gifted hostess at the family estate at Johnson Hall, New York. She also used her husband's position to increase her own influence among the Mohawk, and she eventually became regarded as a clan matron. Consistent with Mohawk traditions and culture, she was constantly employed as an interpreter and facilitator for her husband's tribal dealings. Sir William died in 1774 and Brant relocated from Johnson Hall to her traditional home in Canajoharie, living in comparative splendor and running several trading ventures. When the Revolutionary War commenced the following year, she remained firmly in the British camp and, in concert with her brother, convinced the majority of Mohawk to follow suit. Despite pressures to migrate to Canada from nearby Patriot communities she steadfastly refused to do so and expended much energy assisting LOYALIST refugees and gathering military intelligence.

Brant's greatest service to England came in August 1777 during the siege of Fort Stanwix, New York, by forces under Lieutenant Colonel Barry ST. LEGER. From her home she observed an American relief expedition commanded by Colonel Nicholas HERKIMER, and she dispatched an Indian runner to warn the British in advance. St. Leger responded by ordering his Indians to ambush the intruders at ORISKANY on August 15, 1777, which was attended with much slaughter. Frontier attitudes consequently hardened on both sides, and Brant was finally driven from her home by vengeful whites. She eventually relocated her family to a reservation near Montreal but in 1779 moved back to the Niagara frontier to keep in contact with her people. She continued to act as a useful adviser until the end of the war.

After 1783 Brant eventually settled at Cataraqui (Kingston), Ontario, at the invitation of Governor-General Frederick HALDIMAND, and she received a government pension of 100 pounds a year—the largest accorded any Native American to that time. She remained active in community and Anglican church affairs until her death in Kingston on April 16, 1796. Molly Brant remains one of the most influential women leaders in Iroquois history.

Further Reading
Blakeley, Phyllis R., and John N. Grant. *Eleven Exiles: Accounts of Loyalists of the American Revolution.* Toronto: Dundurn Press, 1982.
Huey, Lois M. *Molly Brant: A Legacy of Her Own.* Youngstown, N.Y.: Old Fort Niagara Association, 1997.
Kenney, Maurice. *Tekonwatoni, Molly Brant, 1735–1795.* Fredonia, N.Y.: White Pine Press, 1992.
Rhoden, Nancy L., and Ian K. Steele. *The Human Tradition in the American Revolution.* Wilmington, Del.: Scholarly Resources, 2000.
Swineheart, Kiel D. "The Wild Place: Sir William Johnson among the Mohawks, 1715–1783." Unpublished Ph.D. diss., Yale University, 2002.
Thomas, Earle. *The Three Faces of Molly Brant: A Biography.* Kingston, Ont.: Quarry, 1996.

Brodhead, Daniel (1736–1809)
American military officer

Daniel Brodhead was born in Albany, New York, on September 17, 1736, the son of a merchant. He matured on the frontier in Bucks County, Pennsylvania, where he familiarized himself with nearby Indian tribes and their customs. An attack upon his home, "Brodhead Manor," in December 1755 greatly hardened his attitude toward Native Americans, and he was always disposed to fight them whenever necessary. By 1773 Brodhead had relocated to Reading, where he established political connections to Benjamin FRANKLIN and was appointed surveyor general of the colony. Once the Revolutionary War commenced in April 1775, Brodhead threw his lot in with the Patriots and organized a COMMITTEE OF CORRESPONDENCE for Bucks County.

Brodhead's military career began in March 1776 when he gained appointment as lieutenant colonel of the Pennsylvania State Rifle Regiment, which he accompanied to New York City. He fought well in the debacle at LONG ISLAND that August, when he narrowly escaped capture, and served as acting battalion commander until March 1777. He then gained promotion to colonel of the 8th Pennsylvania Regiment. In this capacity Brodhead served under General Benjamin LINCOLN at Brunswick, New Jersey, on April 12, 1777, and subsequently fought as part of General Anthony WAYNE's brigade at BRANDYWINE, Paoli, GERMANTOWN, and Whitemarsh. Following a harsh winter at Valley Forge, General George WASHINGTON transferred Brodhead to Fort Pitt in western Pennsylvania as part of General Lachlan McINTOSH's command. Brodhead, a garrulously disposed individual, disliked McIntosh intensely and openly regarded him as incompetent. He nonetheless accompanied his extended raid up the Ohio River against Fort Detroit in September 1778, where he helped construct Fort McIntosh. McIntosh then canceled the proposed expedition and a furious Brodhead complained to Washington about his ineptitude. Consequently, McIntosh was relieved and Brodhead succeeded Brodhead as commander of the Western Department. McIntosh always suspected Brodhead was acting behind his back and their dispute nearly ended in a duel.

In August 1779 Brodhead undertook his largest wartime endeavor by launching a punitive expedition against the Seneca Indians of New York, in concert with a major offensive under General John SULLIVAN. Accordingly, he led 605 men, including celebrated scout Samuel BRADY, up the Allegheny River against slight resistance and burned several Indian villages before finally returning to Fort Pitt that September. The following month a deputation of Delaware Indians arrived at Fort Pitt to conclude a treaty with him. When, in the spring of 1781, the renegade Simon GIRTY convinced the Delaware to switch sides, Brodhead mounted another expedition against them. That fall he transferred as colonel of the 2nd Pennsylvania Regiment but quarreled with his officers and was relieved in September 1781. Brodhead was subsequently exonerated by a court-martial and, at Washington's behest, he advanced to brigadier general on September 30, 1783.

After the war Brodhead resumed his surveying activities and became an influential political figure along the Pennsylvania frontier. An ardent Federalist, he urged adoption of the Constitution in 1788 and also supported the policies of Alexander HAMILTON throughout the 1790s. Brodhead died in Milford, Pennsylvania, on November 15, 1809, a capable frontier leader.

Further Reading

Appel, John C. *General Daniel Brodhead: Patriot in War, Civil Servant in Peace.* Stroudsburg, Pa.: Monroe County Historical Society, 1970.

———. "Colonel Daniel Brodhead and the Lure of Detroit," *Pennsylvania History* 38, no. 3 (1971): 265–282.

Brady, William Y. "Brodhead's Trail up the Allegheny," *Western Pennsylvania Historical Magazine* 37 (March 1954): 19–31.

Gabarino, William. *Indian Wars along the Upper Ohio: A History of the Indian Wars and Related Events along the Upper Ohio and Its Tributaries.* Midway, Pa.: Midway Pub., 2001.

Nestor, William R. *The Frontier War for American Independence.* Mechanicsburg, Pa.: Stackpole Books, 2004.

Trussell, John B. B. *The Sullivan and Brodhead Expeditions.* Harrisburg: Pennsylvania Historical and Museum Commission, 1976.

Brown, Thomas (1750–1825)
Loyalist

Thomas Brown was born in Whitby, England, in 1750, the son of a prosperous shipowner. In 1774 he arrived in Georgia and acquired a large land grant near Augusta, which he developed into a plantation. When fighting erupted in April 1775 radical elements began agitating for Georgia to join the Continental Association to support a ban on British goods. Brown, an ardent LOYALIST, opposed such a move and was marked by the local SONS OF LIBERTY for harassment. On August 2, 1775, they seized him, scalped him, burned his feet, broke his skull, and paraded him around in an ox cart. Brown eventually recovered from his injuries and made his way to the backcountry of South Carolina. There, in concert with royal governor William Campbell, he drew up plans to use local Cherokee Indians against the insurgents. When the provincial congress issued a warrant for his arrest, Brown and many of his Loyalist expatriates fled to East Florida. Shortly after arriving he began recruiting the East Florida Rangers with himself as lieutenant colonel.

In time Brown emerged as one of the most vicious Loyalist partisans operating on the southern frontier. Commencing in 1776 authorities in Georgia mounted no less than three expeditions into Florida to evict him, but his rangers and Indians defeated them all. After Savannah fell to Lieutenant Colonel Archibald CAMPBELL in December 1778, Brown linked up with British forces and helped spearhead the advance upon Augusta. Campbell then fell back when anticipated Indian support did not materialize and was pursued by American forces under General John ASHE. On March 3, 1779, the British, aided by Brown, suddenly turned on Ashe and routed him at Briar Creek, Georgia. His rangers then formed part of the Savannah garrison, where, on October 9, 1779, they proved instrumental in repulsing an attack mounted by General Benjamin LINCOLN and Admiral Charles-Hector-Théodat, comte d'ESTAING. That same year Brown was promoted to superintendent of the Indian Department for the southwest and actively sought assistance from neighboring Creek and Cherokee nations. He then returned to Augusta, fortified it, and made it a center of Loyalist activity for the rest of the state.

In September 1780 Brown was suddenly attacked by Georgia militia under Colonel Elijah CLARKE, which besieged Brown in the Mackay House for four days. The approach of a British relief column induced the Americans to withdraw hastily, and Brown vindictively hanged 13 prisoners from the stairwells for violating their parole. Brown next constructed Fort Cornwallis on the Savannah River to deter future attacks. However, on May 22, 1781, the combined forces of Colonel Henry LEE and General Andrew PICKENS invested the fort and fierce fighting ensued. After two weeks the Americans constructed a fortified Mahan Tower to shoot into Brown's camp, and he was forced to surrender on June 6, 1781. He remained under close confinement until being exchanged shortly after. His last wartime role was in defending Savannah before finally surrendering to General Anthony WAYNE. Brown subsequently conducted a large party of Loyalists to Florida and helped them resettle along the St. Johns River in 1782.

After the war Brown relocated to the Bahamas, where he became active in local politics. In 1805 he received a large estate on St. Vincent island and lived the rest of his life as a wealthy planter. He died there on August 3, 1825, one of the most hated figures of Revolutionary Georgia.

Further Reading

Cashin, Edward J. *The King's Ranger: Thomas Brown and the American Revolution on the Southern Frontier.* Athens: University of Georgia Press, 1989.

Hall, Leslie. *Land and Allegiance in Revolutionary Georgia.* Athens: University of Georgia Press, 2001.

Olson, Gary D. "Dr. David Ramsay and Lt. Col. Thomas Brown: Patriot Historian and Loyalist Critic," *South Carolina Historical Magazine* 77, no. 4 (1976): 257–267.

Risher, Charles A. "Propaganda, Dissension, and Defeat: Loyalist Sentiment in Georgia, 1763–1783." Unpublished Ph.D. diss., Mississippi State University, 1976.

Searcy, Martha C. *The Georgia-Florida Contest in the American Revolution, 1776–1778.* Tuscaloosa: University of Alabama Press, 1985.

Spach, John. "The Struggle for Augusta in 1781 Witnessed Military Brilliance and the Ugly Settling of Scores," *Military History* 20, no. 2 (2003): 12–14.

Buford, Abraham (1749–1833)
American military officer

Abraham Buford was born in Culpepper County, Virginia, on July 31, 1749, the son of a landowner. In 1775 he helped raise a company of militiamen at the behest of the Virginia Convention and helped fight in various battles against John MURRAY, Lord Dunmore, the royal governor. On November 13, 1776, Buford left the militia to serve in the Continental Line as a major with the 14th Virginia Regiment. He served competently, rising to colonel of the 5th Virginia Regiment by May 1778. Little is known of his actual military career, but he was apparently present in the north throughout General George WASHINGTON's endeavors. However, following the capture of Savannah in December 1778, the locus of fighting shifted southward and Buford, now colonel of the 11th Virginia Infantry, was ordered to Charleston, South Carolina. He accordingly marched 400 recruits south as far as the Santee River when he learned that the city had been captured by General Henry CLINTON on May 12. American resistance had collapsed in South Carolina, and General Isaac HUGER ordered Buford to retrace his steps back to Hillsboro, North Carolina. En route he was to gather numerous supplies to prevent them from falling into enemy hands. When intelligence of Buford's column became known to General Charles CORNWALLIS, he immediately began pursuing with 2,500 soldiers but could not overtake the fleeing Americans. He then dispatched a fast-moving column of 270 mounted LOYALISTS and cavalry under Lieutenant Colonel Banastre TAR-

LETON, who chased and rapidly closed with Buford's command. On the morning of May 29, 1780, the British confronted him at Waxhaws, South Carolina, about 10 miles east of Lancaster.

The ensuing battle was the defining moment in Buford's military career—and that of the Revolution in the South. Knowing he outnumbered Tarleton 400 to 270, he refused the latter's invitation to surrender and the British drew themselves up to attack. Buford then egregiously erred by placing his men in a single rank while sending his artillery pieces off the field with the baggage train. Finally, he ordered his men to withhold their fire until the cavalry were 10 paces away. Tarleton charged head on and received Buford's fire, but his momentum carried the cavalry through his ranks before the Americans could reload. The troopers then started slashing away at the defenders and were promptly joined by some British regulars who plied their bayonets mercilessly. Tarleton's horse was hit, and he went down at the height of the battle, which convinced many British that he was killed. They consequently went on a rampage, killing many Americans as they tried to surrender. Before Tarleton could remount and restore order, 113 of Buford's men had been killed and 203 captured. British losses totaled 19 dead and wounded. Buford himself escaped on horseback. It has never been established if Waxhaws was actually a massacre or not, but it occasioned the notion of "Tarleton's Quarter," a synonym for butchery. This immediately hardened the attitudes of Patriots and Loyalists fighting throughout the South. Thereafter vengeful atrocities were committed by both sides.

Buford was not held responsible for the disaster at Waxhaws and he subsequently served as colonel of the 3rd Virginia Regiment. He retired from the army at the end of the war and spent several years as surveyor of Lincoln County, Virginia. Buford eventually relocated to Scott County, Kentucky, where he died on June 30, 1833, having presided over one of the most singular disasters to befall American arms.

Further Reading
Edgar, Walter B. *Partisans and Redcoats: The Southern Conflict That Turned the Tide of the American Revolution.* New York: Morrow, 2001.
Gordon, John W. *South Carolina and the American Revolution: A Battlefield History.* Columbia: University of South Carolina Press, 2003.
Hayes, John T. *Massacre: Tarleton and Lee, 1780, 1781.* Fort Lauderdale, Fla.: Saddlebag Press, 1997.
Power, J. Tracy. " 'The Virtue of Humanity Was Totally Forgotten': Buford's Massacre, May 29, 1780," *South Carolina Historical Magazine* 93, no. 1 (1992): 5–14.
Rider, Thomas A. "Massacre or Myth? No Quarter at the Waxhaws, 29 May 1780." Unpublished master's thesis, University of North Carolina, Chapel Hill, 2002.
Russell, David L. *The American Revolution in the Southern Colonies.* Jefferson, N.C.: McFarland, 2000.

Bunker Hill, Battle of (June 17, 1775)

After the Battles of Lexington and CONCORD in April 1775, Boston was besieged by a Patriot force of 15,000 militia under General Artemas WARD. The 6,000-man British garrison under General Thomas GAGE, badly outnumbered, took no offensive action against this ill-clad, partially trained mob and remained secure behind its fortifications. However, rumors circulated in the American camp that Gage was about to advance from the city and attack. To circumvent this, Ward chose to fortify the hills on the Charlestown Peninsula, bring up guns, and command the adjacent harbor. On the evening of June 16, 1775, General Israel PUTNAM, Colonel William PRESCOTT, and chief engineer Colonel Richard GRIDLEY led 1,200 soldiers from Cambridge onto Charlestown Heights and commenced digging strong breastworks on top of Breed's Hill. Actually, Putnam had been ordered to occupy nearby Bunker Hill, which was higher and farther back than the site chosen, but Putnam preferred to place his cannon as close to the enemy as possible. On the morning of the 17th, Gage was astounded to see such an elaborate system of defenses spring up literally overnight and he held a council of war. Ships of the Royal Navy and a nearby British battery on Copp's Hill commenced a heavy fire upon the rebels, but they ignored it

Despite the British victory at the Battle of Bunker Hill, American militia performed well against the most powerful military force in the world. *(U.S. Army Center of Military History)*

and continued digging in. The American position, while strong, was exposed and easily cut off by landing troops at the neck of the peninsula. General Henry CLINTON implored his superior to outflank the American position to minimize the risk of casualties, but Gage decided that the rebels had overplayed their hand and a show of strength was now essential. He then ordered the main assault entrusted to Generals William HOWE and Robert PIGOT while Clinton commanded the reserves and John BURGOYNE the artillery. All these seasoned, professional regulars reasonably expected the rebels to flee at the first sight of British bayonets.

By noon some 2,500 soldiers and marines had been ferried across the harbor and landed at the tip of the Charlestown Peninsula. Howe had devised a simple but effective plan for dealing with the Americans. He would send Pigot and the 38th and 43rd Regiments directly up the slope to overrun the main earthworks. On his right, a combined grenadier battalion and the 5th and 53rd Regiments would charge the rail fence along the beach and dispatch the defenders before rolling up American positions on top of the hill. It was a sultry summer day when the scarlet line of infantry, each man carrying 80-pound knapsacks, formed in precise ranks and began ascending the slope. Colonel Prescott, a cool veteran of the French and Indian War, stood on the ramparts to inspire his men and admonished them not to fire until they perceived "the whites of their eyes." Accordingly, Colonel John STARK allowed the British line to approach to within 100 paces before unleashing a crackling fusillade that sent redcoats reeling back down the hill. Farther left, Pigot's assault on the main fortification was also bloodily repulsed. Howe quickly reformed his men and led them up the hill again. Once more the Americans calmly allowed the enemy to approach to within a few yards, then cut them down with concentrated musketry. It was an amazing scene to behold the backsides of the world's greatest infantry, and the defenders stared in disbelief at the corpse-strewn hillside. However, calls for replenishing ammunition went unheeded and, in the distance, the British were forming up again for yet another assault.

Howe, miraculously unhurt, vigorously rallied his shaken men and ordered them to drop their backpacks. He also ordered up the reserves under Clinton and a battalion of royal marines under Major John PITCAIRN to assist. The fateful signal to advance was given, and Howe led his men back up the slopes, now slippery with blood. For a third time the Americans held their fire until close range, when redcoats dropped in swaths. The British line staggered momentarily but disregarded its losses and continued advancing. At this critical juncture the defenders' ammunition gave out and the British pitched into them with cold steel. A vicious melee erupted along the line as the Americans—lacking bayonets—were forced out of their works. Resistance crumbled and the defenders fled pell mell for the rear while Colonel Thomas KNOWLTON provided covering fire from behind a rail fence. The victorious British were simply too exhausted to pursue, and the fighting petered out.

Bunker Hill was a shocking Pyrrhic victory for the British, who lost 1,154 men out of 2,500 committed. Casualties among officers were also heavy and a tribute to rebel marksmanship. American losses, appreciably less severe, were also heavy and came to 140 killed and 271 wounded, including General Joseph WARREN, who fought as a volunteer. Bunker Hill, while a loss, was a major propaganda victory for the colonials, as their untrained, untested militia had bloodied Europe's best trained army. The battle also failed to lift the siege of Boston, which remained in place until the British evacuation of March 1776.

Further Reading
Brooks, Victor. *The Boston Campaign, April 1775–March 1776.* Conshohocken, Pa.: Combined Pub., 1999.
Carr, Jaqueline B. *After the Siege: A Social History of Boston in the Wake of Revolution.* Boston: Northeastern University Press, 2004.
Cray, Robert E. "Bunker Hill Refought: Memory Wars and Partisan Conflicts, 1775–1825," *Historical Journal of Massachusetts* 29, no. 1 (2001): 22–52.
Edgar, Gregory T. *Reluctant Break with Britain.* Bowie, Md.: Heritage Books, 1997.
Morrissey, Brendan. *Boston, 1775: The Shot Heard Around the World.* Westport, Conn.: Praeger, 2004.
Schwartz, F. D. "The Battle of Bunker Hill," *American Heritage* 51, no. 3 (2000): 109–111.

Burgoyne, John (1723–1792)
English army officer
John Burgoyne was born in London on February 24, 1723, the scion of an old aristocratic family. He joined the army at the age of 15 and, by dint of his impeccable family credentials, was allowed into the 3rd Horse Guards. In 1742 he transferred to the 13th Dragoons as a coronet (ensign), but Burgoyne's promising military career was interrupted two years later when he eloped with Lady Charlotte Stanley, daughter of the earl of Derby. Her father angrily cut them off from the family inheritance, while he and his spouse lived happily in London. Eventually, Burgoyne's gambling debts forced him to sell his commission and the couple moved to France. There he became fluent in French and began a lifelong interest in theater and writing plays. In 1755 Burgoyne and his wife were finally reconciled with earl Derby, who now used political influence to regain Burgoyne's commission. Burgoyne subsequently served as lieutenant colonel of the elite Coldstream Guards during early phases of the Seven Years' War with France. He also raised and equipped the 16th Regiment of Light Dragoons, the first such light cavalry outfit

in the English army. While on leave in 1762 he successfully stood for a seat in Parliament, and the following year gained distinction by heading a series of charges that routed several Spanish camps and captured a general. Throughout his military career Burgoyne was unique among contemporaries by insisting that soldiers be treated with respect and humanity. Despite a reputation for pomposity and an addiction to gambling, he gained promotion to major general in 1773. In the spring of 1775 he arrived in Boston along with Generals William HOWE and Henry CLINTON. Barely engaged at the June 17, 1775, Battle of BUNKER HILL, he composed several letters highly critical of his superior, General Thomas GAGE, and lobbied his friends back in London for more active employment.

In the spring of 1776 Burgoyne, recently promoted to lieutenant general, arrived at Quebec to serve under Governor-General Guy CARLETON. In this capacity he commanded forces that gradually drove off General Benedict ARNOLD from the Trois-Rivières district. However, he disliked serving under the stodgy Carleton and returned to England that fall to concoct what, to his mind, was a potentially war-winning strategy. Burgoyne, a smooth talker who went by the sobriquet "Gentleman Johnny," won the trust and confidence of Lord George GERMAIN and advocated detaching New England from the rest of the colonies by a large offensive down the Lake Champlain corridor. Here his 8,000 men would be assisted by an ancillary movement by 1,500 LOYALISTS and Indians under Lieutenant Colonel Barry ST. LEGER, who would march east along the Mohawk River and rendezvous with him near Albany. He also counted on a significant thrust up the Hudson River from New York City by General Howe. Germain agreed in principle to the plan, and the ebullient Burgoyne posited himself as the right man to lead it. The war office concurred, but for some reason Germain failed to issue unequivocal orders to Howe for his support. As it turned out, when Burgoyne advanced down from Canada, he marched alone.

General John Burgoyne was a leader of considerable merit; however, defeat at the Battle of Bennington caused his strategic planning and position to deteriorate rapidly. Painting by Sir Joshua Reynolds *(Frick Collection)*

Burgoyne arrived back at Quebec in May 1777 and began assembling one of the finest armies ever deployed overseas by Great Britain. This totaled 7,500 British and HESSIAN regulars, 400 Indians, and 100 Loyalists. His commanders, Generals Friedrich von RIEDESEL, Simon FRASER, and William PHILLIPS, regarded as among the best officers in their grade. In late June Burgoyne's juggernaut rolled down from Canada, driving the army of General Arthur ST. CLAIR from Fort Ticonderoga. On July 7, 1777, Fraser and Riedesel surprised and defeated Colonel Seth WARNER at Hubbardton, Vermont, capturing his baggage train. However, the British commander underestimated the heavily wooded terrain opposing him and progress continued at a snail's pace. Moreover, a new commander, General Horatio GATES, fell back repeatedly before the British, luring them deeper into the wilderness around Saratoga. By late summer Burgoyne was experiencing supply shortages, so he dispatched a column of 800 Hessians under Colonel Friedrich BAUM to comb the Vermont countryside for horses and other livestock. On August 16, 1777, this force was suddenly annihilated by militia under General John STARK at BENNINGTON. Burgoyne at this juncture would have been justified in calling a retreat, but he refused to lose face. Instead, he took his army across the Hudson River and began inching his way toward Gates's position entrenchments.

Despite his offensive posture, Burgoyne's strategic position was rapidly deteriorating. St. Leger had been rebuffed at Fort Stanwix by Colonel Peter GANSEVOORT and, worse, General Howe had moved large numbers of troops away from New York City for his campaign against Philadelphia. General Henry Clinton, meanwhile, undertook a modest diversion on Burgoyne's behalf by capturing forts in the New York highlands, but little else. Burgoyne nonetheless decided to end the impasse by mounting a reconnaissance in force against the American lines at FREEMAN'S FARM on September 19, 1777. After a stiff fight his veteran troops were unexpectedly defeated by General Benedict ARNOLD, with a loss of 600 men. Burgoyne waited in vain for his promised assistance and, once it failed to arrive, a council of war suggested that he withdraw back to Canada. Ever the gambler and obsessed with enhancing his reputation, he ordered one more sortie against the American lines. On October 7, 1777, he attacked at BEMIS HEIGHTS, but suffered another repulse, the loss of an additional 600 men, and the death of General Fraser. Outnumbered nearly three to one by the Americans, who fast closed in around him, Burgoyne finally ordered a withdrawal back to Saratoga. As feared, he was completely surrounded by Gates's army and forced to surrender on October 17, 1777. This was the first time in history that a British army had capitulated intact; worse, victory here ensured that France, with the urging of Charles Gravier, comte de VERGENNES, would enter the conflict on America's behalf.

Burgoyne and his senior officers were paroled, but the bulk of his army remained in captivity under the rules of a convention signed with Gates, which CONGRESS refused to ratify. He arrived back in London requesting a court-martial to clear his name, but a vindictive and angry King GEORGE III refused and stripped him of all military titles. Burgoyne remained in disgrace until 1781 when the new Whig administration of Charles WATSON-WENTWORTH, Lord Rockingham, appointed him commander in chief of Ireland. The Tories returned to power the following year and he was sacked once more. Burgoyne then formally withdrew from public life and worked dutifully as an aspiring playwright. He died in London on August 4, 1792, sharing with Lord Germain a reputation as "the man who lost America."

Further Reading
Ketchum, Richard M. "The Man Who Lost it All," *MHQ* 11, no. 2 (1999): 88–97.
Mintz, Max. *The Generals of Saratoga.* New Haven, Conn.: Yale University Press, 1990.
Morrissey, Brendan. *Saratoga, 1777: Turning Point of a Revolution.* Oxford: Osprey, 2000.
Murray, Stuart. *The Honor of Command: General Burgoyne's Saratoga, June–October, 1777.* Bennington, Vt.: Images from the Past, 1998.
Nestor, Joseph B. "The Battle of Saratoga." Unpublished master's thesis, East Stroudsburg University, 2001.
Phifer, Mike. "The Campaign to Saratoga," *MHQ* 2, no. 1 (2000): 40–51, 94.
Seymour, William. *The Price of Folly: British Blunders in the War for American Independence.* Washington, D.C.: Brassey's, 1995.

Burke, Edmund (1729–1797)
English politician
Edmund Burke was born in Dublin, Ireland, on January 12, 1729, the son of a prosperous attorney. Having weathered an unhappy childhood, he attended Trinity College and subsequently obtained a law degree at Middle Temple, London. However, Burke declined a law practice in favor of

pursuing belle lettres, so he spent many years writing and publishing. In 1765 he became personal secretary to Charles WATSON-WENTWORTH, marquis of Rockingham, a leading, reform-minded Whig politician. The marquis recognized Burke's political potential and arranged for him to win a seat in Parliament. A gifted orator with a penchant for detail, he quickly emerged as a Whig leader and theorist in his own right. In fact the role of the opposition leader dovetailed perfectly with Burke's strident, combative disposition, and he carved out a niche as the leading foil to the polices of King GEORGE III. He was strongly supportive of America in 1765 and argued eloquently for repealing the STAMP ACT and the TOWNSHEND DUTIES. Unlike his American counterparts, Burke never doubted the legitimacy of Parliament's ability to levy taxes—he simply questioned the wisdom of such tactics. In light of the hostility they generated toward the mother country, he argued it was better for the colonies to tax themselves than lose them through unrest. In 1770 Burke further expressed his interest in New World affairs by becoming agent for the New York assembly.

The BOSTON TEA PARTY of December 1773 stimulated a vengeful Parliament to draft punitive legislation, most notably the COERCIVE ACTS, which demanded financial redress for properties lost. The Rockingham Whigs unilaterally opposed the move for fear of precipitating a major upheaval, and Burke forcefully remonstrated against continuance of the TEA ACT. As relations with the colonies worsened in March 1775, Burke delivered a three-hour diatribe against the policies of Prime Minister Lord Frederick NORTH and introduced resolutions calling for outright reconciliation. He did so less out of respect for American rights than for pragmatic reasons of empire. "Magnanimity in politics is not seldom the truest wisdom," he declared. "A great empire and little minds go ill together." His plans were rejected and, after the Revolutionary War commenced in April 1775, he promulgated another reconciliation plan. Burke insisted that Parliament abandon its notion of taxing the colonies and, furthermore, called on it to recognize the Continental CONGRESS as an official colonial entity to reckon with. His sagacious proposal again went down to defeat by a wide margin, 210 votes to 105.

Burke remained a leading opposition figure throughout his entire political career, and spent the war years doing his best to embarrass the administration of Lord North. When the North cabinet fell in the spring of 1782, Rockingham briefly assumed power as prime minister and set Great Britain irrevocably on the path to peace talks. Burke served briefly in the government as paymaster general, and then resumed his seat when the government fell a few months later. He returned to office for a few months, lost it within weeks, and never again held a ministerial post. Burke subsequently gained greater renown as a strident critic of the French Revolution—and he drew clear distinctions between that upheaval and recent events in America. Burke maintained that the United States was forced to defend itself against bad governmental policies, much as happened during the Glorious Revolution of 1688. The French, he maintained, were simply tearing down tried and tested institutions of governance in the vain hope that something better would emerge from the ashes. He then penned perhaps his most renowned tract, *Reflections upon the Revolution in France,* which drew in turn a sharp riposte from Thomas PAINE in the form of his *Rights of Man.* Burke died at his estate in Beaconsfield, Buckinghamshire, on July 9, 1797, a leading political orator and theorist of the second half of the 18th century.

Further Reading
Bromwich, David, ed. *On Empire, Liberty, and Reform.* New Haven, Conn.: Yale University Press, 2000.
Bullard, Paddy. "Contexts for Edmund Burke's Rhetoric, 1756–1780." Unpublished Ph.D. diss., University of Oxford, 2001.
Conway, Stephen. *The British Isles and the War of American Independence.* New York: Oxford University Press, 2000.
Elofson, W, M., and John A. Woods, ed. *The Writing and Speeches of Edmund Burke,* vol. 3: *Party, Parliament,*

and the American Revolution. New York: Oxford University Press, 1996.

Mellon, Stanley, and Philip Dynia. "Jefferson and Burke," *Consortium on Revolutionary Europe, 1750–1850. Selected Papers* (1995): 58–64.

Ward, Lee. *The Politics of Liberty in England and Revolutionary America.* New York: Cambridge University Press, 2004.

Bushnell, David (1740–1824)

American inventor

David Bushnell was born in Saybrook, Connecticut, on August 30, 1742, the son of farmers. He attended Yale College in 1771 and there grew fascinated by the possibility of underwater explosions. An inventive tinkerer by nature, Bushnell successfully combined a blackpowder charge with a clockwork timing device, thereby creating the first naval mine. As he set about conceiving a practical delivery system for this unique weapon, the onset of the Revolutionary War in 1775 lent greater urgency to his work. By the fall of that year he had designed and engineered the *American Turtle* (or simply *Turtle*), a primitive, if ingenious, submarine. It was so christened on account of its appearance, like two turtle shells lashed together, but proved perfectly functional. Manned by a single occupant, it was powered by hand-cranked screw propellers and a system of water pumps to admit or expel water, thereby controlling a rise or descent. The pilot was provided with a small conning tower possessing several windows, which also contained a depth gauge and a compass naturally lit by phosphorus. Its offensive power lay with Bushnell's earlier clock-mine, which was attached to a metal screwing device designed to penetrate the copper sheathing of warship hulls. Once the mine was attached and released, the timing mechanism engaged and the *Turtle* had one hour to leave the vicinity before the 150-pound powder charge was detonated by a flintlock device. Bushnell arranged a successful demonstration for General Israel PUTNAM in the Thames River, and he urged the government to continue funding the development of this weapon system.

Bushnell's *Turtle* made naval history in the summer of 1776, with an attack on a huge British fleet anchored off New York City under Admiral Richard HOWE. Bushnell being ill, the attack was to be conducted by Sergeant Erza Lee. On the night of September 6, 1776, the *Turtle* was towed offshore by two whaleboats and released, after which Lee approached the fleet under his own power. The transit proved arduous owing to contrary tides, but after great exertions Lee pulled alongside the 64-gun ship of the line HMS *Eagle*, Howe's flagship. Lee then tried repeatedly boring through the ship's copper sheathing but he kept hitting an iron bar. With his air nearly exhausted, the attempt was abandoned, and the mine was allowed to float free. It subsequently exploded with a tremendous roar and alerted the slumbering sailors that they were under attack. With a little more luck Lee may very well have succeeded in sinking the *Eagle* and thus spelled the end of wooden warships. Bushnell subsequently launched a handful of attacks on solitary vessels; all were defeated by currents or inexperienced operators. The *Turtle* itself was lost the following October when a transport carrying it was sunk by British cannon fire in the Hudson River.

Bushnell remained undeterred by failure and he continued tinkering with naval mines and other explosives. On August 13, 1777, he released a large mine that floated toward HMS *Cerberus,* then anchored in Black Point Bay. The tides carried it right up to that vessel but the device was snared by a small schooner and exploded, killing three sailors. In December 1777 Bushnell tried again by releasing 20 large keg-mines off Bordentown, New Jersey. One detonated near a British row boat, killing several sailors, and the attack so unnerved the British fleet that it spent the rest of the day shooting up kegs—and anything else that floated by. The event was satirized by poet Francis Hopkinson in his composition "Battle of the Kegs" (1778).

Bushnell returned to Saybrook, much ridiculed, in the spring of 1778, and he was briefly detained by LOYALISTS. After his release he joined the Continental ARMY as a captain of sappers and miners and served competently for the rest of the war. After his discharge he briefly visited France before resurfacing in Georgia around 1795. He practiced medicine in Warrenton, Georgia, until his death there in 1824. Despite his failures, Bushnell is regarded as the father of modern undersea warfare.

Further Reading
DeLuca, Richard. " 'An Effort of Genius': A New Look at David Bushnell and the Connecticut Turtle," *Connecticut History* 42, no. 1 (2003): 1–18.
Diamant, Lincoln. *Dive! The Story of David Bushnell and His Remarkable 1776 Submarine (and Torpedo).* Fleischmanns, N.Y.: Purple Mountain Press, 2003.
Leary, Joseph. "The Turtle Dives Again," *American Heritage of Invention & Technology* 11, no. 4 (1996): 18–26.
Grant, Marion H. *The Infamous Machines of Saybrook's David Bushnell: Patriot Inventor of the American Revolution.* Old Saybrook, Conn.: Bicentennial Committee, 1976.
Lefkowitz, Arthur S. *Bushnell's Submarine: The Best Kept Secret of the American Revolution.* New York: Scholastic Non-fiction, 2006.
Speck, Robert M. "The Connecticut Water Machine versus the Royal Navy," *American Heritage* 32, no. 1 (1980): 32–38.

Butler, John (1728–1796)
Loyalist officer and interpreter

John Butler was born in New London, Connecticut, on April 28, 1728, the son of an army officer. He relocated with his family to the Mohawk Valley, New York, in 1742, becoming immersed in the language and culture of the neighboring Iroquois tribesmen. By the time the French and Indian War commenced in 1755, Butler was working as an interpreter for the Indian Department superintendent, Sir William Johnson. In this capacity he accompanied Johnson in his successful campaign against Fort Sainte Frederic (Crown Point, New York), being promoted to captain of Indians. Butler next fought under General James Abercromby at Fort Carillon (Ticonderoga) and at the capture of Fort Frontenac under General John Bradstreet. After rejoining Johnson in a successful bid to acquire Fort Niagara, he accompanied General Jeffrey Amherst's advance against Montreal. The war ended in 1763 and Butler resumed his work for the Indian Department while also acquiring a large estate near Johnstown, New York. There he commanded a local militia regiment as lieutenant colonel under Guy JOHNSON.

When tensions between Great Britain and its colonies exploded in the spring of 1775, Patriot activity forced the Johnsons and the Butlers to flee New York for Upper Canada. However, Butler's wife and children were captured and spent nearly five years in captivity near Albany. When Johnson departed Canada for a trip to England that fall, Butler was appointed Indian Department deputy superintendent by Governor-General Guy CARLETON. He was under strict instructions to keep the Six Nations neutral in the fighting and succeeded admirably. However, the following year General John BURGOYNE reversed British policy and actively solicited Indian support for military operations. Butler was selected to lead a force of 350 Seneca under Chiefs Joseph BRANT and CORNPLANTER as part of Lieutenant Colonel Barry ST. LEGER's offensive up the Mohawk River in the summer of 1777. When St. Leger's campaign stalled before Fort Stanwix that August, Butler helped arranged a clever ambush that nearly destroyed an American relief column under Colonel Nicholas HERKIMER at ORISKANY. The siege lifted two weeks later and Butler fled back to Canada, where he was commissioned a major in the British army and authorized to raise a corps of LOYALIST partisans. Thus was born Butler's Rangers, one of the most feared irregular units of the Revolutionary War.

In July 1778, Butler led 500 Iroquois warriors under Old King, Johnson's Royal Greens, and his own regiment, on a raid through the Susquehanna region of northern Pennsylvania. He swept through the Wyoming Valley on July 3–4, 1778, upending a force of Continentals under Major Zebulon BUTLER, killing and scalping upward of 300 men. The marauders then devastated several villages and took many hostages in what came to be known as the "Wyoming Valley Massacre." Historians continue disputing this allegation, as Butler labored diligently to restrain those Native Americans under his command from committing atrocities. But the sheer extent of his success induced the Americans to mount a punitive expedition into the Iroquois heartland the following summer, and on August 29, 1779, Butler was soundly defeated by General John SULLIVAN at Newtown, New York. The surviving rangers and warriors made their way to Fort Niagara, which Butler converted into a base of operations, and within a year he was back raiding frontier settlements. Foremost among these was a protracted attack upon the Schoharie Valley, October 15–19, 1780. None of these actions, however, could turn the tide of war in favor of Great Britain.

After the Revolution, Butler and his family departed New York and resettled in the region of Newark, Upper Canada (Ontario). There he received an ample pension from the British government and also continued as deputy superintendent of the Six Nations. Butler strove hard for many years to mitigate the suffering of displaced Indians who had lost everything after mistakenly siding with England. He died at Newark on May 13, 1796, and Chief Joseph BRANT of the Mohawk eulogized "there are none remaining who understand our manners and customs as well as he did." In light of his settlement activities, Butler is still regarded as a founding father of modern Canada.

Further Reading
Allen, Robert S. *The Loyal Americans: The Military Role of the Loyalist Provincial Corps and Their Settlement in British North America, 1775– 1784*. Ottawa: National Museum of Man, 1983.
The Butler Bicentenary: Commemorating the 200th Anniversary of the Death of Colonel John Butler. Niagara-on-the-Lake, Ont.: Colonel John Butler Branch, The United Empire Loyalists Association of Canada, 1997.
Francavilla, Lisa A. "The Wyoming Valley Battle and 'Massacre': Images of a Constructed American History." Unpublished master's thesis, College of William and Mary, 2002.

Watt, Gavin. *The Burning of the Valleys: Daring Raids from Canada against the New York Frontier in the Fall of 1780*. Toronto: Dundurn Press, 1997.
Williamson, James R., and Linda A. Fossier. *The Susquehanna Frontier: Northeastern Pennsylvania during the Revolutionary Years*. Wilkes-Barre, Pa.: Wilkes University Press, 1997.

Butler, Richard (1743–1791)
American military officer

Richard Butler was born in Dublin, Ireland, on April 1, 1743, the son of petty aristocracy. His family migrated to Pennsylvania in 1748, where he eventually farmed and became closely acculturated with Native American tribes on the frontier. In 1763 Butler fought in Pontiac's Rebellion as a militia ensign, and he subsequently established a thriving Indian trade factory near Fort Pitt. When the Revolution erupted in 1775 he was dispatched by state authorities to various Shawnee and Delaware settlements in the Ohio territory to secure their neutrality and was partially successful. A year later he was commissioned into the 8th Pennsylvania Regiment, the so-called Kittanning Regiment, as a major. He fought well throughout the northern frontier, being closely associated with Colonel Daniel MORGAN's command at Saratoga in 1777. The following year Butler gained promotion to colonel of the 9th Pennsylvania Regiment and played a prominent role in the victory at MONMOUTH in August 1778. Butler then transferred over to General Anthony WAYNE's command where, on July 16, 1779, he led an important charge against the right flank of British defenses at Stony Point. When soldiers of the Pennsylvania Line mutinied in January 1781, Butler was among the few officers whom the rebels trusted enough to negotiate with, and he helped diffuse the crisis. That spring he shifted his men south to serve in Virginia under the marquis de LAFAYETTE. On June 26, 1781, Butler participated in the successful skirmish against Lieutenant Colonel John Graves SIMCOE at Spencer's Tavern, and he also fought well in Wayne's desperate rearguard action at Green Spring the following July 6. After additional fighting at

YORKTOWN, Butler accompanied Wayne south into Georgia to assist General Nathanael GREENE in a major mop-up operation. Butler elected to remain in the tiny military establishment after the war and was promoted to brigadier general as of September 1783.

In March 1784 the Confederation CONGRESS appointed Butler an Indian commissioner and authorized him to enforce U.S. land claims over the northwestern tribes. He visited the Shawnee repeatedly, in concert with George Rogers CLARK, Samuel H. PARSONS, and other military figures, and finally extracted a favorable treaty by 1786. However, the government was weak militarily and could not enforce its aggressive claims upon Indian land. When the Miami and other tribes revolted in 1791, defeating a small expedition under Colonel Josiah Harmar, Butler became second in command of a larger force under General Arthur ST. CLAIR. On November 4, 1791, St. Clair's army was overrun by warriors under Chief Little Turtle and disastrously routed. Butler, who fought bravely as usual, was critically wounded twice and insisted that his wounded younger brother Edmund be evacuated in his place while he remained behind. Butler died at the hands of Indians that day and his body was never recovered. He was one of four brothers engaged during the Revolution, and Lafayette reputedly declared, "When I want a thing well done I send a Butler to do it!"

Further Reading
Butler, Richard. "General Richard Butler's Journal of the Siege of Yorktown," *Historical Magazine* 8 (March 1864): 102–112.
Edel, Wilbur. *Kekionga!: The Worst Defeat in the History of the U.S. Army.* Westport, Conn.: Praeger, 1997.
Frederic, Harold. *Path of Blood: The Untold Story of the Kittanning PA. Regiment in the American Revolution.* Kittanning, Pa.: W. C. Frederick III with W. J. McMaster, Sr., 1998.
Pozar, Stephen M. *Richard Butler, Patriot.* Butler, Pa.: Butler County Historical Society, 2001.
Williams, Edward G. "Fort Pitt in the Revolution on the Western Frontier," *Western Pennsylvania Historical Magazine* 52, no. 2 (1976): 129–152.

Butler, Walter (1752–1781)
Loyalist military officer

Walter Butler was born at Butlersburg (Fonda), New York, in 1752, the son of John BUTLER, a British Indian Department interpreter. He displayed an interest in military life and in 1768 was commissioned in the militia. Two years later he relocated to Albany to study law but his endeavors were interrupted by the Revolutionary War in April 1775. An outspoken LOYALIST, Butler and his father fled for Canada after his mother and sister became captives of the Americans. Once in Canada he assumed command of a mixed Loyalist-Indian force, and on September 25, 1775, he helped orchestrate the capture of Colonel Ethan ALLEN at Longue-Pointe, Quebec. Butler then ventured to England, received an ensign's commission in the 8th Regiment, and returned to Canada the following spring. Butler fought well at the victory of the Cedars in May 1776, winning promotion to lieutenant. He spent the winter at Fort Niagara with orders from Governor-General Guy CARLETON to keep the Seneca nation neutral in the fighting. The following summer he accompanied a large Indian contingent under Chiefs Joseph BRANT and CORNPLANTER as part of Lieutenant Colonel Barry ST. LEGER's expedition up the Mohawk River. He fought well in the ambush of Colonel Nicholas HERKIMER at ORISKANY on August 6, 1777, but did not accompany the army back to Canada. Instead, he rather foolishly marched into the Mohawk Valley under a flag of truce to recruit other Loyalists and was arrested. General Benedict ARNOLD sentenced him to hang for espionage, but former acquaintances of Butler's interceded and had him placed under house arrest. He then spent several months under close confinement at Albany before escaping in April 1778 and rejoining the army in Canada.

In 1778 Butler joined his father's regiment of partisan fighters, the feared Butler's Rangers, and commenced a long series of raids against frontier settlements in New York and Pennsylvania. That fall he received his first independent command of 200 rangers and 600 Seneca and attacked the village of Cherry Valley, New York, on November 11, 1778. He proved unable to storm the fort, so he burned the village and crops. However, Butler completely lost control of his Indians, who massacred 31 women and children—one of the war's worst atrocities. Neither Butler nor Brant could stop the rampaging warriors, still smarting over losses incurred at Oriskany the year before. He did manage to spare several citizens who were then held as hostages until his family members were released at Albany. In the summer of 1779 Butler fought against the punitive expedition of General John SULLIVAN at Newtown, fell ill, and spent several months recuperating in Montreal. He did not take to the field again until the summer of 1780, when he accompanied a large-scale raid against the Mohawk Valley under Major John Ross. However, the raiders were defeated and vigorously pursued by Colonel Marinus WILLETT in a series of skirmishes. The Americans closely hounded Ross's rear guard at West Canada Creek on October 30, 1781, and in the fighting Butler was killed and scalped by an Oneida warrior. Completely and perhaps unfairly vilified by the Americans, Walter Butler was among the most feared raiders of the beleaguered Mohawk Valley; locally, news of his death is said to have occasioned greater celebration than the victory at YORKTOWN.

Further Reading
Browne, Douglas G. "Butlers of Butlersburg," *Cornhill Magazine* 124, no. 51 (1921): 601–616.
Callahan, North. *Royal Raiders, the Tories of the American Revolution.* Indianapolis: Bobbs-Merrill, 1963.
Cruikshank, Ernest A. "Memoir of Captain Walter Butler," *Royal Canadian Institute Transactions* 4 (1892–93): 284–298.
Kenney, James F., ed. "Walter Butler's Journal of an Expedition along the North Shore of Lake Ontario, 1779," *Canadian Historical Review* 1 (December 1920): 381–391.
Miller, Hanson O. *Raiders of the Mohawk: The Story of Butler's Rangers.* Toronto: Macmillan, 1960.
Watt, Gavin. *The Burning of the Valleys: Daring Raids from Canada against the New York Frontier in the Fall of 1780.* Toronto: Dundurn Press, 1997.

Butler, Zebulon (1731–1795)
American military officer

Zebulon Butler was born in Ipswich, Massachusetts, on January 23, 1731, and was raised in Lyme, Connecticut. He joined the militia during the French and Indian War and partook of the capture of Havana, Cuba, in 1762. Afterward he led Connecticut settlers into the Wyoming Valley of Pennsylvania, which was jointly claimed by both colonies and, after settling in Westmoreland Township, he served as a local military authority. During the so-called Yankee-Pennamite Wars, waged concurrently with the Revolution, the Pennsylvania militia repeatedly tried evicting the settlers by force. On December 20, 1775, Butler helped repel an attack by Pennsylvanians at the Nanticoke Gap. He then became governor of the Susquehanna Company and was elected to the Connecticut assembly. Once the Revolution commenced in 1775 Butler rejoined the militia, was commissioned a lieutenant colonel, and fought under General George WASHINGTON throughout the New Jersey campaign. In March 1778 he rose to colonel of the 2nd Connecticut Regiment and that summer took leave of the army to return to his home in the Wyoming Valley. About this time forces of LOYALISTS and Native Americans began raiding American frontier settlements in New York and Pennsylvania for the purpose of denying much-needed food supplies for the Continental ARMY. In June 1778 Major John BUTLER led a force of some 900 Loyalists and Indians across New York and down into the Wyoming Valley. Butler, once apprised of this looming menace, hastily evacuated all citizens into the relative safety of nearby Forty Fort while he retained command of 368 poorly trained militia and a handful of veteran Continentals. A council of war held on July 3, 1778, decided against defending the fort and persuaded Butler to attack the marauders instead.

Butler's small command departed Forty Fort that morning and marched upriver about two miles when scouts discovered the Loyalist encampment at Fort Wintermoot. The Americans approached stealthily, intending to surprise their opponents, when they were suddenly fired upon by two Indian sentries. Butler then made the fateful decision to charge ahead with his regulars in the center, his militia on the right flank, and other militia under Colonel Nathan Denison on the left. The Loyalist Butler allowed the outnumbered Americans to advance to within point-blank range before springing an effective ambush that routed both flanks. The Continentals stood bravely in the center until hit from all directions by vengeful rangers and Indians. A rout ensued and Butler hastily rode off on horseback while 300 of his men were slaughtered. He and a handful of survivors eventually made it back to Fort Wilkes-Barre. The Loyalists and Indians then received Forty Fort's surrender and plundered the inhabitants. The Wyoming "Massacre" was one of the war's biggest defeats for the Americans.

Butler was never held accountable for his defeat at Wyoming, and the following year he accompanied General John SULLIVAN on his punitive expedition into the Six Nations heartland. In 1780 he fulfilled a tour of garrison duty at West Point, New York, before Washington ordered him back to Fort Pitt to help soothe testy relations between Connecticut and Pennsylvanian troops then mustering out at war's end. Butler left the army and returned to the Wyoming Valley as one of its leading citizens. He died at Wilkes-Barre, Pennsylvania, on July 28, 1795.

Further Reading
Butler, Zebulon. "Orderly Book of Col. Zebulon Butler, at Wyoming, From Aug. 1, 1778 to Oct. 28, 1778," *Proceedings and Collections of the Wyoming Historical and Geological Society* 7 (1902): 106–130.
Francavilla, Lisa A. "The Wyoming Valley Battle and 'Massacre': Images of a Constructed American History." Unpublished master's thesis, College of William and Mary, 2002.
Kashatus, William C. "The Wyoming Valley Massacre: The Surpassing Horror of the American Revolution, July 3, 1778," *Valley Forge Journal* 4, no. 2 (1988): 107–122.
Ousterhout, Anne M. "Frontier Vengeance: Connecticut Yankees vs Pennamites. In the Wyoming Valley," *Pennsylvania History* 62, no. 3 (1995): 330–363.
Williamson, James R. *Zebulon Butler: Hero of the Revolutionary Frontier*. Westport, Conn.: Greenwood Press, 1995.
Williamson, James R., and Linda A. Fossier. *The Susquehanna Frontier: Northeastern Pennsylvania during the Revolutionary Years*. Wilkes-Barre, Pa.: Wilkes University Press, 1997.

Byron, John (1723–1786)
English naval officer

John Byron was born near Newstead Abbey, Nottingham, England, on November 8, 1723, a son of Baron William Byron. He went to sea as a cabin boy in 1731 and nine years later rose to midshipman. In this capacity Byron accompanied the Pacific voyage of Commodore George Anson around the tip of South America aboard the transport *Wager*. When he was shipwrecked off the coast of Chile in May 1741, he and his crewmates endured incredible hardship for four years until rescued by a passing French vessel. Upon returning to England Byron rose to lieutenant and fought well in the War of the Austrian Succession. He again distinguished himself for bravery during the Seven Years' War, 1755–63, and on July 8, 1760, fought and won the last naval engagement on the Restigouche River, Canada. Byron became a captain in 1764 and was appointed to command the frigate HMS *Dolphin*, the Royal Navy's first copper-bottomed warship. He then took a small flotilla of vessels on a secret circumnavigation of the world that lasted 22 months. Byron, lacking the patience and imagination of a seasoned explorer, sailed virtually in a straight line across the Pacific and missed every island not directly in his path. Also, his penchant for encountering stormy weather garnered him the less than flattering sobriquet of "Foul-Weather Jack." In January 1769 he became governor of the naval colony at Newfoundland, Canada, which he ran capably until replaced by Admiral Molyneux SHULDHAM in 1772. The following year

Byron was elevated to rear admiral and rose again to vice admiral on June 29, 1778, while stationed in England.

Byron's activities during the Revolutionary War were brief but controversial. When the British learned that a French fleet under Admiral Charles-Hector-Théodat, comte d'ESTAING, had departed Toulon and was headed for America, he received command of a squadron to intercept him. Byron, dogged by ships and crews in poor condition, finally weighed anchor from Plymouth on June 9, 1778, three weeks behind the French. While crossing the Atlantic he encountered—true to form—a tremendous gale that scattered his fleet of 14 vessels. Byron was forced to put into Halifax for repairs, and it was not until September 25, 1778, that he reported to Admiral Richard HOWE at Newport, Rhode Island. There he weathered another surprise when Howe announced his intention to resign and, distrusting his aged subordinate Admiral James GAMBIER, summarily turned command of the North American station over to Byron.

Byron, having refitted his squadron, departed New York harbor on October 18, 1778, and had no sooner cleared Long Island Sound than *another* huge storm battered his fleet, wrecking two ships and scattering the rest. A further eight weeks lapsed before his command was thoroughly repaired, and Byron finally resumed his hunt for d'Estaing on December 13, 1778—six months after leaving Plymouth! He cruised the West Indies for several more months before encountering the French off the newly captured island of Grenada on July 6, 1779. Believing that he outnumbered his quarry when, in fact, d'Estaing possessed 25 ships to his 21, Byron signaled for a general engagement before his entire fleet could came up. The British thus committed themselves piecemeal against a formed French battle line and the lead four warships were dismasted. A potential disaster loomed for Byron before his own line was completely formed, but d'Estaing timidly broke off the engagement and returned to Grenada. The British then withdrew to make repairs and, in their absence, d'Estaing sailed off to initiate the siege of SAVANNAH. Byron's seemingly endless string of misadventures played havoc with his health and spirits, so on October 10, 1779, he returned to England to recuperate. In September 1780 he made senior vice admiral but never again held an active command. Byron died in London on April 10, 1786, possibly the unluckiest sailor in the Royal Navy. However, he gained a measure of immortality when noted poet Lord Byron—his grandson—used his shipwreck narrative as the basis for the poem *Don Juan*.

Further Reading

Bonner-Smith, David. "Byron in the Leeward Islands in 1779," *Mariner's Mirror* 30 (January 1944): 38–48, 81–92.

Cock, Randolph. "Precursors of Cook: The Voyages of the Dolphin, 1764–8," *Mariner's Mirror* 85, no. 1 (1999): 30–52.

Gureny, Alan, ed. *The Loss of the Wager: The Narratives of John Bulkeley and John Byron.* Woodbridge, U.K.: Boydell, 2004.

Shankland, Peter. *Byron of the Wager.* New York: Coward, McCann, & Geoghegan, 1975.

Syrett, David. *The Royal Navy in American Waters, 1775–1783.* Brookfield, Vt.: Gower Publishing, 1989.

Tilley, John. *The British Navy and the American Revolution.* Columbia: University of South Carolina Press, 1987.

C

Cambray-Digny, Louis, chevalier de (1751–1822)

French military officer

Louis-Antoine-Jean-Baptiste, chevalier de Cambray-Digny was born in Italy to French parents in 1751. Returning home, he became an officer candidate in the artillery ca. 1770 but was discharged when no vacancies were available. In June 1778, he arrived in America and tendered his services to the Continental CONGRESS as an engineering officer and was posted in Col. Louis DUPORTAIL's engineering corps with a rank of lieutenant colonel. Cambray-Digny first saw action during the MONMOUTH campaign, and he then transferred to western Pennsylvania to serve as engineering officer under General Lachlan MCINTOSH. In this capacity, he accompanied the American advance into Ohio that fall and directed construction of Fort McIntosh, 30 miles northwest of present-day Pittsburgh, which became an important frontier entrepot. In February 1779, Congress ordered Cambray-Digny south to join the army of General Benjamin LINCOLN. He was present at both the unsuccessful ATTACK ON SAVANNAH in October 1779 and the equally unfortunate siege of CHARLESTON in spring 1780. Cambray-Digny fell captive when the city fell on May 12, 1780, but was quickly paroled. He then requested a leave of absence to return to France, which was granted in October 1782. He apparently elected to remain in France and was discharged from the Continental ARMY as a brevet colonel on November 15, 1783. Cambray-Digny died at his home in the Department of the Somme in 1822, a minor player in a very large conflict.

Further Reading

Agnew, Daniel. *Fort McIntosh: Its Times and Men.* Beaver, Pa.: Beaver Area Heritage Foundation, 1971.

Carlisle, Ronald C. "Louis-Antoine-Jean-Baptiste, le chevalier de Cambray-Digny: French Volunteer in the American Revolution." Unpublished master's thesis, University of Pittsburgh, 1977.

Carver, Frank F. *Fort McIntosh: The Story of Its History and Restoration of the Site.* Beaver, Pa.: Beaver Area Heritage Foundation, 1993.

Nicolai, Martin L. "Subjects and Citizens: French Officers and the North American Experience, 1755–1783." Unpublished Ph.D. diss., Queen's University, 1992.

Walker, Paul K. *Engineers of Independence: A Documentary History of the Army Engineers in the American Revolution, 1775–1783.* Washington, D.C.: Office of the Chief of Engineers, 1981.

Camden, Battle of (August 16, 1780)

The loss of Charleston, South Carolina, in May 1780 induced CONGRESS to dispatch General Horatio GATES, the "Hero of Saratoga," to replace the captured General Benjamin LINCOLN as commander of the Southern Department. On July 25, 1780, Gates rode into the camp of General Johann de KALB at Deep River, North Carolina, presented his credentials, and took command. He had at that time a veteran brigade of Maryland and Delaware Continentals under General Mordecai GIST, plus remnants of the Pulaski Legion commanded by Colonel Charles ARMAND. With this small force Gates decided to resume offensive operations against the British and it departed on July 25, 1780. Gates marched with celerity but the path he chose, the shortest possible route, had been picked clean of supplies and foodstuffs by months of warfare and offered few prospects of resupply. The men were thus forced to subsist in large measure off unripened corn and apples, which induced chronic gastronomic distress. As the Americans pressed southward they were gradually reinforced by North Carolina militia under General Richard CASWELL, which swelled their ranks to 4,200 men—mostly raw and untrained. Gates's first objective was to attack an outnumbered British outpost at Camden, South Carolina, then held by Lieutenant Colonel Francis RAWDON. However, word of his approach had reached General Charles CORNWALLIS at Charleston and, always eager for a fight, Cornwallis hurriedly pressed north with 1,000 veteran troops to engage Gates.

Ironically, the opposing forces marched headlong down the same road and collided at about five miles north of Camden. After some confused skirmishing they separated and encamped at a respectful distance for the night. Dawn arose on August 16 to find Gates deploying his men in a traditional European manner, with his best troops on the right flank, the accepted post of "honor." This rendered his left flank dependent upon the skittish behavior of North Carolina and Virginia militia, whose martial qualities were dubious at best. Gates nonetheless enjoyed a two-to-one numerical superiority and the additional advantage of secure flanks as both contestants were hemmed in between swamps. Unfortunately for the Americans, Cornwallis had likewise adopted a European deployment with his very best troops, including the crack Welsh Fusiliers, on his right—arrayed against Gates's militia. Gates further compounded his errors by stationing himself too far to the rear and was thus unable to influence battlefield events.

Skirmishing between the two armies commenced at daybreak and Colonel Otho Holland WILLIAMS, Gates's adjutant, perceived what he thought was confusion on the British right. Galloping back to Gates he strongly suggested that the Virginia militia attack immediately and exploit it. Gates agreed and ordered General Edward Stevens forward. However, the raw Virginians had no sooner advanced a few yards toward the British when they halted and began firing sporadically. Cornwallis seized upon this hesitation by ordering his right flank under Lieutenant Colonel James Webster to charge en masse. The sight of British bayonets proved too much for the levies and, after a few scattered volleys, they unceremoniously fled the field. Their panic also unnerved the nearby North Carolina militia under Caswell, which also took it its heels. Having stampeded Gates's left and center from the battlefield, Cornwallis had his soldiers wheel left and take de Kalb's continental in their flank. The Americans, hotly pressed from the front and enshrouded by smoke, failed to see the danger and were almost completely surrounded. De Kalb's men fought with heroic bravery but in the end he was mortally wounded and his command nearly destroyed. The entire American army then fled the field in panic, closely hounded by cavalry under Lieutenant Colonel Banastre TARLETON. The debacle was complete.

Having lost the battle at Camden, Gates disgraced himself by fleeing from the battlefield on horseback and not stopping until he reached Charlotte, 120 miles distant. His army had been virtually annihilated, losing 250 killed and 800 wounded, to a British loss of only 324 men. Cornwallis was now at leisure to commence his invasion of North Carolina and knock the southern colonies out of the war. The victory also produced a surge of LOYALIST activity in South Carolina, with hundreds of volunteers flocking to the king's banners. So devastating was Camden to the American cause that for many months only the partisans of General Thomas SUMTER could mount organized resistance.

Further Reading

Buchanan, John. *The Road to Guilford Courthouse: The American Revolution in the Carolinas.* New York: Wiley, 1997.

Gordon, John W. *South Carolina and the American Revolution: A Battlefield History.* Columbia: University of South Carolina Press, 2003.

Morrill, Dan L. *Southern Campaigns of the American Revolution.* Mount Pleasant, S.C.: Nautical and Aviation Press, 1993.

Pancake, John S. *This Destructive War: The British Campaign in the Carolinas, 1780–1782.* Tuscaloosa: University of Alabama Press, 2003.

Russell, David L. *The American Revolution in the Southern Colonies.* Jefferson, N.C.: McFarland, 2000.

Whitfield, R. Bryan. "The Preservation of Camden Battlefield." Unpublished master's thesis, Wake Forest University, 1980.

Campbell, Archibald (1739–1791)
English military officer

Archibald Campbell was born in Inveraray, Argyllshire, Scotland, on August 24, 1739, the son of a judge. He joined the Corps of Engineers as a young man and saw wide-ranging service in Guadelupe, Dominica, and Bengal. In 1768 the British East India Company elevated him to chief engineer, which position he held for the next four years. Campbell returned to Scotland in 1773 to inherit an estate and run for Parliament, and two years later he became lieutenant colonel of the newly raised 71st (or Fraser's) Highland Regiment. He then sailed for Boston Harbor, unaware that the city had been evacuated by General William HOWE three months earlier, and both he and his regiment were taken prisoner by Captain Seth HARDING on June 16, 1777. Captivity was initially quite cordial, with Campbell provided a house at Reading, servants, and relative freedom of movement. Conditions radically worsened, unfortunately, with word that American prisoners like Charles LEE and Ethan ALLEN suffered mistreatment while in captivity. Consequently, the Continental CONGRESS ordered all British prisoners kept in "safe and close custody." For Campbell this meant transferring to an unheated jail cell in Concord, New Hampshire, where he successfully petitioned General George WASHINGTON for better treatment. On May 6, 1778, he was formally exchanged for Allen and released from confinement.

Campbell reported to General Henry CLINTON in New York City and, despite his relative lack of combat experience, was selected for a difficult mission. On November 27, 1778 he boarded a naval squadron with 3,500 men and sailed south against Savannah, Georgia, to initiate offensive operations in the south. Surprisingly, Campbell, having survived a storm-tossed transit, conducted his affairs with consummate skill. On December 29, 1778, his armada brushed aside several American gunboats and splashed ashore at Girardeau's Plantation, only two miles below Savannah. His first concern was a small defending force of 700 Continentals and militia under General Robert HOWE, positioned across the road on Fairlawn Plantation. Howe's camp, flanked by seemingly impassible swamps, was strong but Campbell personally reconnoitered it by climbing a nearby tree. Then, aided by a slave named Quamino Dolly, he sent part of his force down a secret trail around the American right flank while other troops made noisy demonstrations to Howe's front. At a given signal, the 71st Highlanders suddenly charged from the flank, routing the Americans, killing 83, and capturing 453. Campbell's loss was only three killed and 10 wounded. Savannah then fell under British control for the rest of the war.

Campbell installed himself as acting governor of Georgia, the only part of the United states to be reclaimed as a colony, and boasted of being "the first British officer to rent a stripe and a star from the rebel flag." He nonetheless proved an enlightened leader, treating former rebels civilly while encouraging LOYALISTS to join the militia. In January 1779 he was replaced by General Augustin PREVOST, who arrived from Florida with reinforcements. Campbell subsequently commanded an

Archibald Campbell, the conqueror of Georgia *(National Gallery of Art)*

expedition into the heart of Georgia to capture Augusta, then a center of rebel activity. He did so with alacrity and the town fell without a struggle on January 31, 1779, but partisan forces began harassing his lines of communication. Worse, Cherokee and Loyalist sympathizers failed to materialize, and when intelligence was received that a large American army under General Benjamin LINCOLN was approaching from South Carolina, Campbell hastily withdrew back to Savannah on February 14. After a brief visit to England that summer he was assigned to the island of Jamaica as brigadier general. Campbell saw no further action in the war, and in 1784 he was elevated to major general. He returned home the following year to receive the prestigious Order of Bath, and in 1786 boarded a ship bound for India. There he served as governor of Madras state under Governor-General Charles CORNWALLIS. He again distinguished himself by leniency toward the natives and efficient administration of public affairs. Campbell came home for the last time in 1789, briefly reoccupied his seat in Parliament, and died in London on March 31, 1791. Though little regarded today, Campbell was one of the most efficient British officers of the Revolutionary War.

Further Reading

Campbell, Colin, ed. *The Journal of Lieutenant Colonel Archibald Campbell During the Invasion of Georgia, 1777–1779*. Darien, Ga.: Ashantilly Press, 1981.

Davis, Robert S., ed. *Encounters on a March through Georgia, in 1779: The Maps and Memorandums of John Wilson, Engineer, 71st Highland Regiment*. Sylvania, Ga.: Partridge Pond Press, 1986.

Howe, Archibald. "Letters and Memoirs of Sir Archibald Campbell, Prisoner of War, Captured in Boston Bay, June 17, 1776," *Bostonian Society Publications* 12 (1915): 275–286.

Nunis, Doyce B., ed. "Colonel Archibald Campbell's March from Savannah to Augusta, 1779," *Georgia Historical Quarterly* 45 (September 1961): 275–286.

Walcott, Charles H. *Sir Archibald Campbell of Inverneill: Sometime Prisoner of War in the Jail at Concord, Massachusetts*. Boston: Printed for the Author by T. Tood, 1898.

Wilson, David K. *The Southern Strategy: Britain's Conquest of South Carolina and Georgia, 1775–1780*. Columbia: University of South Carolina Press, 2005.

Campbell, Arthur (1743–1811)
American militia officer, politician

Arthur Campbell was born in Augusta County, Virginia, on November 3, 1743, the son of Scotch-Irish immigrants. He served as a ranger during the French and Indian War, 1755–63, and was captured by the Wyandot Indians. Campbell returned home after two years of captivity at Detroit and trained at the Augusta Academy as a surveyor and lawyer. He thereafter married and relocated to the Holston River region, serving as a major of militia during the Indian war of Governor John MURRAY, Lord Dunmore, in 1774. The following year, after the First Continental CONGRESS requested all colonies to create various committees, Campbell was elected to the county Committee of Safety. He subsequently attended the Fifth Virginia Convention as a delegate, and voted in favor of a state constitution and a bill of rights. In 1776 Campbell was elected to the new Virginia House of Delegates, in which he served six terms. He also became indelibly associated with land speculation in the western part of the state. Such activities convinced Campbell that the eastern political establishment was too remote and too indifferent to understand the needs or aspirations of western settlers—especially speculators like himself—so he opposed efforts by leaders like George Rogers CLARK to annex new Kentucky settlements as state counties. As such he made more than his share of political enemies but also acquired a fortune in land, amassing 15,000 acres at various locations.

In addition to his political activities, Campbell was active and highly visible in the defense of southwestern Virginia. As colonel of the 17th Virginia Militia, he helped organize companies, built forts, and protected the region from attacks by LOYALISTS and Indians. Like his cousin, General William CAMPBELL, Arthur was ruthlessly disposed toward Loyalists, terrorized many, and executed a few. In the fall of 1780 he proved instrumental in cooperating with Colonels Isaac SHELBY and John SEVIER during the KING'S MOUNTAIN campaign, which resulted in the death of Major Patrick FERGUSON. That December he accompanied Sevier on numerous forays against Chief DRAGGING CANOE and burned numerous villages and settlements as far south as present-day Tennessee. Campbell apparently developed the innovative tactic of riflemen fighting while on horseback, which added greater mobility to frontier militia. The Indians were roughly handled in several battles and finally submitted to the Treaty of Long Island on July 20, 1781.

After the war Campbell resumed his political and land speculation activities. Strongly opposing the government's handling of western lands, he became closely allied to secessionist movements in the newly settled areas of Tennessee and Kentucky. In 1785 Governor Patrick HENRY had Campbell stripped of all appointed offices and threatened to charge him with treason if he persisted in secessionist activities. Campbell relented and in 1786 was elected back to the House of Delegates. Two years later he emerged as a leading Federalist in favor of adopting the new Constitution. President George WASHINGTON subsequently appointed him an Indian agent in 1793, and he also helped establish a mail route between Staunton and Abingdon. Campbell died at the future site of Middleboro, Kentucky, on August 8, 1811. A competent frontier soldier and an ambitious speculator, his political agitation provided an impetus in forming the new states of Kentucky and Tennessee in the 1790s.

Further Reading
Campbell, Arthur. "Two Letters to Arthur Lee," *New York Public Library Bulletin* 7 (May 1907): 162–163.
Hagy, James W. "Arthur Campbell and the Origins of Kentucky: A Reassessment," *Filson Library History Quarterly* 55, no. 4 (1981): 344–374.
———. "Arthur Campbell and the West," *Virginia Magazine of History and Biography* 90, no. 4 (1982): 456–471.
Kastor, Peter J. " 'Equitable Rights and Privileges': The Divided Loyalties in Washington County, Virginia, during the Franklin Separatist Crisis," *Virginia Magazine of History and Biography* 105, no. 2 (1997): 193–226.
Kincaid, Robert L. "Colonel Arthur Campbell: Frontier Leader and Patriot," *Historical Society of Washington County Publications* 2nd Ser., 1 (1965): 2–18.
Quinn, Hartwell L. *Arthur Campbell: Pioneer and Patriot of the Old Southwest.* Jefferson, Va.: McFarland, 1990.

Campbell, William (1745–1781)
American militia officer
William Campbell was born in Augusta County, Virginia, in 1745, the son of a prosperous landowner and farmer. He was well educated at the Augusta Academy (later Washington and Lee Uni-

versity) before relocating to the Middle Fork of the Holston River, where he became justice of the peace in April 1773. The following year Campbell, a 300-pound giant whom friends nicknamed "Old Round About," raised a militia company to fight in the Indian war of Governor John MURRAY, Lord Dunmore. When the Revolutionary War broke out in April 1775, he commanded a rifle company as part of Virginia forces operating under Colonel William WOODFORD. In February 1776 Campbell was commissioned a captain in the 1st Virginia Regiment under Colonel Patrick HENRY; he subsequently married Henry's sister two months later. However, Campbell disliked campaigning far from the frontier, and in October 1776 he resigned from the army and went home. He then rejoined the militia in anticipation of renewed violence with the neighboring Cherokee but, when war failed to materialize, he served as a boundary commissioner to draw up a line dividing Virginia from Indian land. Campbell proved himself a popular figure among fellow frontiersmen, and in 1780 they elected him colonel of a rifle regiment from Washington County. In this capacity he terrorized local LOYALISTS, burning their property and apparently executing several without trial. He also proved effective in quashing a Loyalist effort to seize the lead mines of Montgomery County. In 1780 Governor Thomas JEFFERSON ordered him to lead militia forces back into Cherokee territory to renew negotiations for peace, which were successfully concluded. That year he also won a seat in the Virginia House of Delegates but rarely sat in sessions due to military activities.

In the fall of 1780 Campbell fulfilled his greatest military service by campaigning against the Loyalist forces assembled by Lieutenant Colonel Patrick FERGUSON in North Carolina. Gathering 400 volunteers, Campbell conducted them to Sycamore Shoals, where he parleyed with the likes of Isaac SHELBY, John SEVIER, Joseph McDOWELL, and Joseph WINSTON, being elected "leader." He then marched in hot pursuit of Ferguson, who had assumed a strong defensive position atop KING'S MOUNTAIN. On October 7, 1780, Campbell's command surrounded the Loyalists and attacked. He conspicuously exposed himself recklessly, yelling "shout like Hell and fight like devils!" and gradually worked his troops up the slopes. When Ferguson was killed and his force annihilated, Campbell was slow in restoring order and several prisoners were apparently murdered. However, his victory deprived General Charles CORNWALLIS of valuable light troops and forced him to postpone his invasion of North Carolina by several months.

Campbell subsequently joined the army of General Nathanael GREENE in North Carolina. On March 6, 1781, he fought alongside Colonel Otho Holland WILLIAMS in a desperate rearguard action at Wetzell's Mills against cavalry commanded by hard-charging Lieutenant Colonel Banastre TARLETON. He next fought at Guilford Courthouse on March 15, 1781, as part of Colonel Henry LEE's command on Greene's right flank. A hard tussle ensued and the Americans were driven off with loss and Campbell bitterly remonstrated against what he considered Lee's lack of support. But in light of sterling service, he was promoted to brigadier general of militia in June 1781 and assigned to the army of the marquis de LAFAYETTE. Declining health forced Campbell to take a leave of absence the following month, and he reposed at his wife's half-brother's home at Rocky Hills, Huntington County. He died there on August 22, 1781, one of the war's most imposing and successful militia commanders.

Further Reading
Crowson, E. T. "Colonel William Campbell and the Battle of King's Mountain," *Virginia Cavalcade* 30, no. 1 (1980): 22–29.
Dameron, J. David. *King's Mountain: The Defeat of the Loyalists, October 7, 1780.* Cambridge, Mass.: Da Capo Press, 2003.
Hairr, John. *Guilford Courthouse: Nathanael Greene's Victory in Defeat, March 15, 1781.* Cambridge, Mass.: Da Capo Press, 2002.
Hammond, Neal O., and Richard Taylor. *Virginia's Western War, 1775–1786.* Mechanicsburg, Pa.: Stackpole Books, 2002.

Malgee, David G. "A Frontier Biography: William Campbell of King's Mountain." Unpublished master's thesis, University of Richmond, 1983.

Riley, Agnes G. S. *Brigadier General William Campbell, 1745–1781*. Abingdon, Va.: Historical Society of Washington County, 1985.

Carleton, Guy (1724–1808)
English military officer

Guy Carleton was born on September 3, 1724, in Strabane, Ireland, the son of a Protestant landowner. Exposure to a majority Roman Catholic population at an early age inoculated him against prevailing religious biases and prepared him for his subsequent career. Carleton joined the army in 1742, and nine years later he had risen to lieutenant colonel of the elite 1st Foot Guards. In this capacity he fought at the capture of Louisbourg in 1758 and accompanied General James Wolfe during the conquest of Quebec the following year. Carleton was severely wounded but recovered and performed capably at Belle Isle, France, in 1761. He was wounded again at Port Andro and during the capture of Havana in 1762 as a colonel. In light of his demonstrated competence, Carleton next received appointment as lieutenant governor of Quebec in 1766, and full governor the following year.

Carleton inherited a delicate situation in predominantly Roman Catholic, French-speaking Canada, but he discharged his duties with tact and finesse, making subjugation much more palatable. To overcome sullen cooperation from the locals, he took active measures to protect their religious and judicial beliefs. And, by carefully catering to and befriending the ruling provincial elite, he won their overt support and loyalty to England. Carleton's good work resulted in promotion to major general in 1772 and two years he later proved instrumental in having Parliament pass the controversial QUEBEC ACT. This measure not only guaranteed the religious freedoms of Canadians, it also extended the boundaries of Quebec down the Mississippi Valley, thereby restricting westward expansion by the English colonies. Ironically, the majority Protestant population of America viewed this legislation as a part of a conspiracy and it helped hasten the onset of revolution. By the time Carleton returned from England late in 1774 as governor-general of Quebec, North America was on the cusp of a major political and military upheaval.

British military officer and governor-general of Quebec, Guy Carleton *(National Archives of Canada)*

In the spring of 1775 the British commander in chief, General Thomas GAGE, felt sufficiently threatened by events in Boston to strip Canada of all but 800 British soldiers and reinforce his own garrison. The province's military weakness was further highlighted when the bulk of Canadians declined his appeal to join the local militia. Many officials with the Indian Department such as John BUTLER and Guy JOHNSON also strongly argued that Native Americans be used militarily against the rebels. However, Carleton, schooled in the art of "civilized" warfare, rejected these appeals and expressly instructed that the Indians be kept under tight control. The relative weakness of Canada was further underscored in the fall of 1775 when Generals Philip J. SCHUYLER and Richard MONTGOMERY led a small invading army up the Champlain corridor. Carleton gave ground slowly and was almost captured when Montreal surrendered on November 13, 1775, but he determined to defend Quebec City to the last extremity. That final outpost was gradually besieged by small forces under General Benedict ARNOLD, who was eventually reinforced by Montgomery's column. The two Americans then launched a desperate, all-out assault in a blinding snowstorm on December 31, 1775, and were bloodily repulsed by Carleton's active defenses. Montgomery was killed and Arnold had little recourse but to reestablish a loose blockade of the city. In March 1776 British reinforcements under General John BURGOYNE arrived at Quebec and Carleton began rolling the invaders back. After crushing the Americans at Trois Rivieres that April, Carleton's forces chased General John SULLIVAN out of Canada and began building a fleet for pursuing the Americans into northern New York. This endeavor took several months and it was not until October that the British sailed down Lake Champlain. There they encountered Arnold's small flotilla at Valcour Island on October 10, 1776, and totally defeated it. Carleton was now free to advance upon strategic Fort Ticonderoga but the lateness of the season, combined with recurrent supply problems, induced him to retire to Canada until the following spring. This fateful decision gave the hard-pressed Americans a badly needed respite and possibly cost Britain the war. Carleton nonetheless received a knighthood and promotion to lieutenant general for his services.

Canada was saved but the colonies were still in revolt. Secretary of state for the colonies George GERMAIN waxed indignant over what he perceived as Carleton's timidity and replaced him with Burgoyne in the following spring. When that general was chosen as commander for the massive invasion of New York to be launched in the summer of 1777, Carleton, highly offended, resigned as governor-general of Canada. He nevertheless pledged complete support for Burgoyne's campaign, which culminated in his surrender at Saratoga that October. Carleton was then recalled to England and replaced by General Frederick HALDIMAND. He served as governor of Armagh, Ireland, until 1782 when the new Whig government appointed him to succeed General Henry CLINTON as commander in chief at New York. Carleton spent the next year evacuating British military personnel and LOYALISTS while enforcing provisions of the TREATY OF PARIS that had ended the war. He then sailed back to England and received the title Lord Dorchester.

In 1786 Carleton was again tapped to serve as governor-general of Canada for a third time. Under his supervision that colony was subdivided into Upper (Ontario) and Lower Canada (Quebec), each with its respective assemblies. He also authored far-reaching plans for uniting all of British North America under a single federation, which proved vastly ahead of its time. Carleton finally departed Canada in 1796, having largely laid the foundation for a future nation to arise. He died in Stubbings, England, on November 10, 1808, one of the most effective military administrators of his age. That Canada emerged as a viable nation under the British North America Act of 1867 bears mute testimony to his sagacious foresight.

Further Reading
Doerr, Lambert. "Lord Dorchester's Views on the Problems of Canada during the Last Period of His Governorship, 1791–1796." Unpublished Ph.D. diss., University of Ottawa, 1964.
Gorn, Michael H. "To Preserve Good Humor and Perfect Harmony: Guy Carleton and the Governing of Quebec, 1776–1784." Unpublished Ph.D. diss., University of Southern California, 1978.
Jones, Eldon L. "Sir Guy Carleton and the Close of the American War of Independence, 1782–83." Unpublished Ph.D. diss., Duke University, 1968.
LeRoy, Perry E. "Sir Guy Carleton as a Military Leader during the American Invasion and Repulse in

Canada, 1775–1776," 2 vols. Unpublished Ph.D. diss., Ohio State University, 1960.

Milsop, John P. "A Strife of Pygmies: The Battle of Valcour Island," *MHQ* 14, no. 2 (2002): 86–94.

Nelson, David P. *General Sir Guy Carleton, Lord Dorchester: Soldier-Statesman of Early British Canada.* Madison, N.J.: Fairleigh Dickinson University Press, 2000.

Stevens, Paul L. "His Majesty's 'Savage' Allies: British Policy and the Northern Indians during the Revolutionary War: The Carleton Years, 1774–1778." Unpublished Ph.D. diss., State University of New York at Buffalo, 1984.

Caswell, Richard (1729–1789)
American politician, militia officer

Richard Caswell was born on August 3, 1729, in Baltimore, Maryland, the son of a merchant, and he relocated to North Carolina in 1746. He then commenced a four-decade career in public service as deputy clerk of the Johnson County Court. By 1771 he was functioning as speaker of the General Assembly, and that year he also commanded militia forces under Governor William TRYON at the Battle of ALAMANCE on May 16. He was consequently appointed a judge by Tryon's successor, Governor Josiah MARTIN. However, as tensions with Great Britain increased, Caswell became increasingly identified with revolutionary activity. He served periodically on several COMMITTEES OF CORRESPONDENCE and in 1774 was elected a delegate to the First and Second Continental CONGRESS. By 1776 he was functioning as colonel of militia again and rendered valuable service to the Patriot cause on February 27, 1776, by defeating LOYALIST forces under General Donald MacDonald at Moore's Creek Bridge. This victory was decisive in keeping North Carolina in the Patriot column. He then presided over the Fifth Provincial Congress, tasked with framing a new state constitution, and in December 1776 they elected Caswell the first governor of North Carolina.

Caswell proved himself a capable, energetic leader and was instrumental in placing his state on a wartime footing. He oversaw the recruitment and training of troops, the acquisition of supplies to feed them, and the raising of funds to sustain them. In 1780 a grateful state legislature rewarded him with a major generalship of militia, the only individual to hold that rank during the war. In this capacity he joined the army of General Horatio GATES during his advance into South Carolina. Disaster then struck at the battle of CAMDEN on August 17, 1780, in which Caswell and his North Carolina militia abandoned the center of the American line and precipitately fled. However, his political career did not suffer in consequence, and he continued supervising militia matters until the end of the war. During this period Caswell was also elected governor no less than six times, more than any state politician until the 20th century. In 1782 he became comptroller general and subsequently represented North Carolina at the constitutional convention in Philadelphia, in which he opposed ratification. Caswell became governor for the seventh time in 1785, served two more years, and died in office at Fayetteville on November 10, 1789. Given the longevity and effectiveness of his tenure in office, he is considered the father of modern North Carolina.

Further Reading

Alexander, Clayton B. "The Training of Richard Caswell," *North Carolina Historical Review* 23, no. 1 (1946): 13–31.

———. "Richard Caswell: Versatile Leader of the Revolution," *North Carolina Historical Review* 23, no. 2 (1946): 199–141.

———. "Richard Caswell's Military and Later Public Services," *North Carolina Historical Review* 23, no. 3 (1946): 287–312.

Butler, Lindley. "The Coming of the Revolution in North Carolina, 1763–1776." Unpublished Ph.D. diss., University of North Carolina at Chapel Hill, 1971.

Morgan, David T., and William J. Schmidt. *North Carolinians in the Continental Congress.* Winston-Salem, N.C.: J. F. Blair, 1976.

———. "From Economic Sanctions to Political Separation: The North Carolina Delegation to the Continental Congress, 1774–1776," *North Carolina Historical Review* 52, no. 3 (1975): 215–234.

Charleston, attack on (June 28, 1776)

By the spring of 1776 British attempts to crush the American Revolution had stalemated at Boston, and the government sought new approaches to end the impasse. At the behest of William Legge, Lord Dartmouth and secretary of state for the colonies, General Henry CLINTON was dispatched from Boston with a fleet under Commodore Peter PARKER and to rendezvous off Cape Fear, North Carolina, with another squadron bearing additional troops under General Charles CORNWALLIS. It was hoped that a show of strength would induce LOYALISTS throughout the south to rally behind the king's banner. The plan quickly went astray on February 27, 1776, when militia under Colonel Richard CASWELL crushed a large detachment of Scottish Loyalists at Moore's Creek Bridge. Thus, when Clinton arrived off Cape Fear the following month he could not expect local reinforcements. Worse, Cornwallis endured a storm-tossed Atlantic transit that delayed his appearance until May. Clinton, now bereft of a mission, was preparing to head back north until Admiral Parker, who had reconnoitered harbor facilities at Charleston, South Carolina, perceived their unfinished state. He strongly suggested an attack against Fort Sullivan and Clinton concurred. The combined expedition finally anchored off the city on June 7, 1776, after nearly three months of inactivity.

The inhabitants of Charleston had anticipated an attack from the sea for several months and worked furiously at preparing local defenses. Foremost of these was Fort Sullivan on Sullivan's Island, a three-sided fortification boasting 16-foot-wide sand walls fenced off with soft palmetto logs, which had a tendency to absorb cannon balls. The fort itself mounted 25 cannon of various calibers and housed a garrison of 420 men under Colonel William MOULTRIE of the state militia. Charleston itself was defended by 6,500 Continentals and militia under recently arrived General Charles LEE. Lee, who fancied himself a military expert, thought Fort Sullivan was too exposed, likely to be overwhelmed, and wanted it abandoned. However, he was overruled by Governor John RUTLEDGE, who felt the fort was the city's best line of defense against the Royal Navy. The ensuing British attack developed painfully slow, due to a lack of charts, treacherous tides, and the confusing series of waterways leading to the city. Clinton initially sought to land 2,500 men on Long Island, for he believed that the narrow channel between it and Sullivan's Island was shallow and could be crossed at low tide. A landing occurred on June 16, but the inlet proved rife with shoals and strong currents, making passage impracticable. The men encamped there for two more weeks as Parker struggled over the best approach into the harbor.

It was not until June 28, 1776, nearly a month after arriving, that the British prepared to advance upon Charleston. Parker drew up his fleet into two lines and assumed bombardment positions in the harbor. Moultrie, chronically short of gunpowder, ordered his gunners to fire and aim slowly, making every shot count. A general exchange commenced between the fleet and the fort over several hours. Fort Sullivan proved exceptionally resilient, with its sand and palmetto walls absorbing or deflecting the storm of shot poured upon it. At the height of the exchange a British ball cut down the South Carolina flag, and Sergeant William JASPER bravely mounted the parapet in full view of the fleet and restored it. American gunnery also proved far more effective and struck Parker's vessels repeatedly. The crisis of the day occurred when three frigates tried moving around Fort Sullivan for an enfilade fire and then grounded. Two vessels subsequently freed themselves but HMS *Actaeon* remained firmly caught on a shoal and was burned to prevent capture. The British fleet also sustained a terrific pounding, with many casualties. Parker's flagship HMS *Bristol* suffered severely and one lucky shot cut its anchor cable. The crew was unable to prevent the ship from swinging around and presenting its stern to the defenders, who poured in a hot raking fire. Heavy casualties ensued, and the commodore suffered the additional indignity of a shot passing between his legs, tearing his pants off. At nightfall Parker signaled to disengage, and his fleet sullenly withdrew from the harbor.

The British bombardment of Charleston ended in a near-disastrous repulse. The Royal Navy suffered over 225 casualties, with *Bristol* alone accounting for 40 dead and 71 wounded. Moultrie's loss was recorded as 17 killed and 20 wounded. Clinton's men, who took no part in the affair, remained exposed on Long Island for another three weeks before re-embarking, and the expedition finally dropped anchor off New York on July 31, 1776. Parker's defeat at Charleston was significant because it secured South Carolina's independence for four more years. Significantly, the Palmetto insignia of the Fort Sullivan garrison was subsequently incorporated into the South Carolina state flag.

Further Reading
Farley, M. Foster. "Battering Charleston's Palmetto Walls," *Military History* 18, no. 2 (2001): 38–44.
Gordon, John W. *South Carolina and the American Revolution: A Battlefield History.* Columbia: University of South Carolina Press, 2003.
Lipscomb, Terry W. *The Carolina Lowcountry, April 1775–June 1776 and the Battle of Fort Moultrie.* Columbia: South Carolina Department of Archives and History, 1994.
Reid, Ronald M. "The Battle of Sullivan's Island," *American History* 33, no. 5 (1999): 34–39, 70–72.
Russell, David L. *Victory on Sullivan's Island: The British Cape Fear/Charleston Expedition.* Haverford, Pa.: Infinity, 2002.
Wilson, David K. *The Southern Strategy: Britain's Conquest of South Carolina and Georgia, 1775–1780.* Columbia: University of South Carolina Press, 2005.

Charleston, siege of (February 11–May 12, 1780)

In the winter of 1779 General Henry CLINTON, commander in chief of British forces, desired to break the stalemate on the northern frontier by a rapid conquest of the southern colonies. He would begin his campaign by attacking and seizing the port of Charleston, South Carolina, the south's richest city and the site of his earlier repulse in June 1776. Accordingly, on December 26, 1779, he departed New York with 8,700 men and a fleet of 90 transports and 10 warships commanded by Admiral Marriot ARBUTHNOT, which carried 650 cannon and an additional 5,000 sailors and marines. The whole sustained a storm-tossed voyage that left several ships damaged, and on January 30, 1780, the fleet dropped anchor off Savannah, Georgia, to refit. It was not until February 11 that Clinton entered the North Edisto Inlet and landed troops on various islands off the city's coast.

Charleston at this time was defended by General Benjamin LINCOLN, commanding a force of 1,600 veteran Continentals and 2,000 militia. He was assisted by Commodore Abraham WHIPPLE and his fleet of six small warships. Perceiving himself as badly outnumbered, Lincoln broached the topic of retreating with state officials, but Governor John RUTLEDGE insisted that he remain and fight. Lincoln therefore foresook any action that might have saved his army, although Rutledge requisitioned 600 slaves to construct earthworks and other defenses. He also requested Whipple to sink several of his ships in the harbor as an obstruction to the British fleet, which was accomplished. Before the British jaws clamped entirely around Charleston, Lincoln received additional troops in the form of 700 Virginia Continentals under General William WOODFORD. Clinton, meanwhile, continued systematically ringing the city with outposts at Stono Ferry and on James Island. In March he was reinforced by LOYALIST units commanded by Lieutenant Colonel Banastre TARLETON and Major Patrick FERGUSON. Events offshore proved equally disconcerting as Arbuthnot began working his frigates across the bar and into the harbor. Once Clinton had slipped men across the Ashley River and onto the peninsula leading to Charleston, the city was nearly shut off from outside help. The British then began digging an intricate system of siege lines and trenches, pushing their siege guns even closer to the city.

On April 1, 1780, Clinton's sappers broke ground within 800 yards of Charleston's outer ring of defenses. Arbuthnot also ran six of his frigates past crumbling Fort Moultrie and anchored off James Island, completely closing off all water approaches. British siege batteries then progressed steadily and on April 14 they commenced firing into the city, inflicting a steady stream of damage. At this late juncture Lincoln could still have withdrawn across a little-used route on the Cooper River leading to Monk's Corner, but on April 15 a cavalry column under Tarleton smashed into the defenders under Colonel Isaac HUGER, routing them. Lincoln was trapped and on April 19 Clinton summoned him to surrender. The general refused but only after Lieutenant Governor Christopher GADSDEN threatened him with a civilian uprising. On April 24 the Americans launched a desperate sortie against the British emplacements, which did some damage but was repulsed. Given the hopelessness of his predicament Lincoln then offered to surrender if the British agreed to honors of war—in effect, allowing his army to escape—but Clinton, smelling blood, declined. The British were further buoyed by the arrival of Lieutenant Colonel Francis RAWDON on April 18, who brought an additional 2,500 men into camp. Clinton then began constructing his second series of parallel trenches only 250 yards from the city, while Arbuthnot's marines stormed ashore on Sullivan's Island, capturing Fort Moultrie and its 200-man garrison. Clinton again demanded Lincoln's surrender and again was refused. On May 9, the British batteries began a concerted, destructive bombardment of Charleston with heated shot, and inhabitants petitioned Lincoln to avoid the destruction of the city. Surrounded, outnumbered, and unable to defend his charge, Lincoln finally capitulated on May 12, 1780.

The siege and capture of Charleston was the biggest American defeat of the war on land. Clinton captured nearly 5,000 prisoners, 400 artillery pieces, and 6,000 muskets. The militia were subsequently paroled and allowed to go home, but the Continentals passed into harsh captivity. Organized resistance in South Carolina had begun to crumble. Worse, Charleston was hastily converted into a base of operations from which General Charles CORNWALLIS launched his destructive invasions of North Carolina and Virginia. Clinton's vaunted southern strategy had commenced on a highly promising and, for the Americans, perilous note.

Further Reading

Borick, Carl P. *A Gallant Defense: The Siege of Charleston, 1780.* Columbia: University of South Carolina Press, 2003.

Buchanan, John. *The Road to Guilford Courthouse: The American Revolution in the Carolinas.* New York: Wiley, 1997.

Deaton, Stanley K. "Revolutionary Charleston, 1765–1800." Unpublished Ph.D. diss., University of Florida, 1997.

Gordon, John W. *South Carolina and the American Revolution: A Battlefield History.* Columbia: University of South Carolina Press, 2003.

Russell, David L. *The American Revolution in the Southern Colonies.* Jefferson, N.C.: McFarland, 2000.

Wilson, David K. *The Southern Strategy: Britain's Conquest of South Carolina and Georgia, 1775–1780.* Columbia: University of South Carolina Press, 2005.

Chastellux, François-Jean de Beauvoir, marquis de (1734–1788)

French military officer, writer

François-Jean de Beauvoir was born in Paris on May 5, 1734, scion of an old aristocratic family with strong traditions of service to France. Consistent with his illustrious forebears, he joined the Auvergne Regiment as a lieutenant at the age of 13 and pursued a military career. But Chastellux was also well educated and steeped in Enlightenment precepts. He was particularly interested in the latest scientific theories and in 1755 became the first Frenchman inoculated for smallpox. That same year the Seven Years' War commenced and he saw extensive campaigning in Germany. In 1759, at the age of 21, he was colonel of the Marches Regiment and, two years later, the Guyenne Regiment. In 1761, after the victory at Wolfenbüttel, Chastellux had the honor of presenting captured enemy standards to King Louis XVI. Intellectually gifted, he acquired national renown by writing philosophical tracts and also acquired fluency in English. At one point he translated and adapted Shakespeare's *Romeo and Juliet* for the French stage. His pamphlet entitled *An Essay on Public Happiness* (1772), in which he evinced great concern for the poor, won him plaudits as a philosopher and he was inducted into the prestigious French Academy in 1775. He enhanced his reputation as a cultured individual by partaking of the intellectual life at the famous Paris salons, but Chastellux had also became a brigadier general in January 1769. When the American expedition of General Jean-Baptiste Donatieu de Vireur, comte de ROCHAMBEAU, was outfitting in France, he gained promotion to major general and was appointed nominal third in command.

Chastellux sailed with the fleet from Brest on May 1, 1780, and arrived at Newport, Rhode Island, the following July 11. He found the New World fascinating and penned several captivating passages in his revealing memoir, *Travels in North America in the Years 1780, 1781, and 1782* (1786). He also accompanied the French army from Newport on its march to YORKTOWN, rendering invaluable services as a liaison between Rochambeau and General George WASHINGTON during numerous staff conferences. Given his fluency in English and ability to function smoothly in social circles, he became popularly regarded as the "diplomat of Rochambeau's army." After the war Chastellux remained behind in Philadelphia where he reveled in the social and scientific circles of polite society. Given his credentials, he gained easy admittance into the Order of the Cincinnati, the American Philosophical Society, and the American Academy of Arts and Sciences. He also received honorary degrees from William and Mary College and the University of Pennsylvania. Chastellux finally returned to France in 1783, where he was installed as military governor of Longwy. Two years later he inherited the hereditary title of marquis before dying of a sudden illness in Paris on October 24, 1788. His memoir of military service remains an important narrative of Revolutionary America.

Further Reading

Adams, Randolph G. *The Burned Letter of Chastellux.* New York: American Society of the French Legion of Honor, 1935.

Carson, George B. "The Chevalier de Chastellux, Soldier and Philosophe." Unpublished master's thesis, University of Chicago, 1942.

Chastellux, Francois Jean. *Travels in North America in the Years, 1780, 1781, and 1782*, 2 vols. Chapel Hill: Published for the Institute of Early American History and Culture at Williamsburg, Va., by the University of North Carolina, 1963.

Gury, Jacques. "A Letter to David Garrick," *Notes and Queries* 23, no. 76 (1911): 504–506.

Washington, George. *General Washington's Letters to the Marquis de Chastellux.* Charleston, S.C.: C. C. Sebring, 1977.

Clark, George Rogers (1752–1818)
American militia officer

George Rogers Clark was born in Charlottesville, Virginia, on November 19, 1752, the son of a farmer. Largely self-educated, he worked as a surveyor and also gained a reputation by leading numerous expeditions into unsettled regions of Kentucky. Clark first attracted military attention by serving as a scout during the war of Governor John MURRAY, Lord Dunmore, against the Shawnee in 1774. He was a captain of militia when the Revolution erupted the following year and proved instrumental in helping organize frontier defenses against marauding Indians. Clark realized that this unrest was instigated by the British in Detroit, and in 1777 he approached Governor Patrick HENRY for a campaign against them. He was also determined to keep settlers like Daniel BOONE from seceding from Virginia and prevailed upon the legislature to annex Kentucky as a state county. When Clark finally obtained permission for his campaign, along with promotion to lieutenant colonel, he immediately took to the field with 175 rough-hewed frontiersmen.

Clark departed Kentucky in May 1778 and rode flatboats for 120 miles down various rivers, then marched another 120 miles through pristine wilderness, before arriving at his first goal—

Kaskaskia. This French settlement fell without a shot being fired on July 4, 1778, as did the nearby settlement of Cahokia. They then rapidly pushed onto their final objective, the village of Vincennes, which also fell without a fight on July 20. At a single stroke Clark had acquired the Northwest Territory for the United States. However, Virginia authorities failed to supply him with sufficient manpower or supplies to attack Detroit and he withdrew to Kaskaskia for the winter. Meanwhile, Lieutenant Governor Henry HAMILTON, commanding British and Indian forces at Detroit, was organizing an expedition of his own. Informed that Vincennes had been abandoned by the Americans, he pushed forward with a mixed force of 500 soldiers, LOYALISTS, and Indians, easily recapturing the settlement in December 1778. Hamilton lacked the necessary supplies to attack Kaskaskia that winter, so he discharged his Indians and waited for spring. Clark entertained no such respite. When word of Hamilton's activities reached him he rounded up 150 volunteers and led them on a grueling midwinter trek back to Vincennes on February 6, 1779. Braving freezing cold and icy water, they slogged silently toward their quest and completely surrounded a very surprised Governor Hamilton on the 25th. The garrison put on a determined front initially and resisted for two days before Hamilton surrendered. By dint of remarkable powers of endurance, Clark once again restored American supremacy to the Old Northwest.

In January 1781 Clark was back in Virginia pushing Governor Thomas JEFFERSON for a new expedition against Detroit, but interest in the frontier had waned. He then fought briefly against the invasion commanded by General Benedict ARNOLD before being promoted to brigadier general of militia. In this capacity Clark returned to Kentucky and led several punitive expeditions against the Shawnee for participating at the Battle of Blue Licks. He subsequently assisted the Spanish garrison at St. Louis to repel a combined English-Indian assault in 1782. By the end of the war Clark's endeavors came to fruition when Great Britain recognized American claims to the Illinois Territory through terms of the TREATY OF PARIS.

After the war Clark fell deeply into debt, and Virginia authorities refused to reimburse him for wartime expenses. He then served as an Indian commissioner on the frontier and led an expedition against the Wabash tribes in 1786 before running afoul of General James Wilkinson's intrigues and losing his commission. He had little recourse but to indulge in several military and colonizing schemes at the behest of Spain and in 1793 received a major general's commission from France in anticipation of its reconquest of Louisiana. None of these projects materialized, and by 1799 Clark had returned to Kentucky disgraced and in debt. He died in Louisville on February 13, 1818, a forgotten architect of American frontier expansion. In 1918 the U.S. government erected a $1 million memorial to him at Vincennes.

American militia officer George Rogers Clark led a successful surprise attack on British lieutenant governor Henry Hamilton at Vincennes in 1779. *(Filson Historical Society, Louisville, Kentucky)*

Further Reading

Allen, Janis M. "Kinship, Class, and Land: The Influence of George Rogers Clark on the Post-Revolutionary Settlement of Clarkesville, Indiana." Unpublished master's thesis, University of Louisville, 2002.

Carstens, Kenneth C., and Nancy S. Carstens, eds. *The Life of George Rogers Clark, 1752–1818: Triumphs and Tragedies*. Westport, Conn.: Praeger, 2004.

Clark, George R. *The Conquest of the Illinois*. Carbondale: Southern Illinois University Press, 2001.

Risjord, Norman K. *The Revolutionary Generation*. Lanham, Md.: Rowman & Littlefield, 2001.

Schmidt, Ethan A. "Wilderness Warrior: The Life of George Rogers Clark." Unpublished master's thesis, Emporia State University, 2001.

Stalker, Michael D. "George Rogers Clark and the Revolutionary War in the Northwest." Unpublished master's thesis, East Stroudsburg University, 2002.

Clarke, Elijah (ca. 1742–1799)

American militia officer

Elijah Clarke was probably born in Edgecombe County, South Carolina, around 1742. He relocated to Georgia in 1773, taking up residence in the future Wilkes County region. When the Revolution broke out in April 1775 Clarke became one of the most vocal supporters of war against England. He initially served as a captain of militia under Colonel John Dooley and was wounded in a battle against LOYALIST troops at Alligator Creek, East Florida, on June 30, 1778. Bravery and talent for partisan warfare resulted in his promotion to lieutenant colonel, and on February 14, 1779, he commanded the left flank of Patriot forces under General Andrew PICKENS in their smashing victory over Loyalists at Kettle Creek, Georgia. However, by 1780 Lieutenant Colonel Archibald CAMPBELL had subdued most of the state for the Crown. Colonel Dooley and most of his men were paroled and sent home, but Clarke remained in the field. He proved himself an enterprising guerrilla and extracted a heavy toll from British and Loyalist garrisons at Musgrove Mills, Cedar Springs, Augusta, Fishdam Ford, Long Cane, and Blackstocks, sometimes operating in conjunction with General Thomas SUMTER but usually alone. In time his reputation and backwoods popularity rivaled that of Pickens, Sumter, and Francis MARION. He frequently crossed over into South Carolina to raid and forage, and was briskly pursued by the Loyalist column under Major Patrick FERGUSON before the latter was confronted and destroyed at KING'S MOUNTAIN in October 1780. When Clarke was seriously wounded again at Long Cane, his men volunteered for service under General Daniel MORGAN and bore a prominent role in the January 17, 1781, victory of COWPENS. Reputedly, Morgan had specifically requested their participation in this encounter.

Clarke bore a special grudge against the noted Loyalist Thomas BROWN and his rangers. On September 14–18, 1780, he besieged Brown at Augusta, Georgia, and endured four days of vicious fighting before falling back upon the approach of a British relief column. The vindictive Brown subsequently hung several wounded prisoners and also devastated Wilkes County in retaliation. Clarke led his 500 followers safely through Cherokee land to escape pursuit before finally encamping in Tennessee. With the revival of Patriot fortunes in the south, Clarke returned to fighting and captured several Loyalist outposts. He again invested Colonel Brown at Augusta from May 22 to June 5, 1781, although the assistance of Colonel Henry LEE and General Pickens was required to finally subdue his adversary. At war's end his status as Georgia's leading partisan was confirmed by receipt of the confiscated estate of Loyalist Thomas Waters.

Clarke subsequently served in the state General Assembly from 1781 to 1790, and he also became a major general of Wilkes County militia. However, his restless nature led him astray when he became involved in French schemes to conquer Spanish East Florida for France. In February 1794 he led an armed force into Florida and established the "Trans-Oconee Republic" with himself as provisional leader. When the United States refused to recognize his efforts, the venture withered and Governor George Matthews issued a writ for his arrest. Clarke was tried and acquitted; his final years were spent in relative poverty. He died in Richmond County, Georgia, on January 15, 1799, the most popular Georgia folk hero of the Revolutionary War.

Further Reading
Bridges, Edwin. "To Establish a Separate and Independent Government," *Furman Review* 5 (1974): 11–17.
Davis, Robert S. *Georgians in the Revolution: At Kettle Creek (Wilkes Co.) and Burke County.* Easley, S.C.: Southern Historical Press, 1986.
Hays, Louise F. *Hero of the Hornet's Nest: A Biography of Elijah Clarke, 1733 to 1799.* New York: Stratford House, 1946.
Murdock, Richard K. "Elijah Clarke and Anglo-American Designs on East Florida," *Georgia Historical Quarterly* 35 (July 1951): 174–190.
Singleton, Lucy A. "Ingenuity in Hornet's Nest," *Daughters of the American Revolution Magazine* 109, no. 2 (1975): 108–111.
Spach, John. "The Struggle for Augusta in 1781 Witnessed Military Brilliance and the Ugly Settling of Scores," *Military History* 20, no. 2 (2003): 12–14.

Cleveland, Benjamin (1738–1806)
American militia officer

Benjamin Cleveland was born in Prince William County, Virginia, on May 26, 1738, son of a house-joiner. He received only a rudimentary education and spent his early manhood addicted to such vices as drinking, womanizing, and fighting. In 1769 he relocated to the Yadkin River valley, North Carolina, and started a plantation named Round About. During this time Cleveland befriended noted scout Daniel BOONE and was tutored in the arts of scouting and bush fighting. In 1772 Cleveland and four companions recklessly explored the Cherokee hunting grounds of Kentucky, when they were seized by Indians, robbed of their possessions, and released unharmed. Yet, displaying the audacious streak for which he was renown, Cleveland subsequently returned to various Indian lodgements to recover his property. When the Revolutionary War erupted in 1775, Cleveland briefly served as a lieutenant in the 2nd North Carolina Continental Infantry but found the inherent discipline too constraining. Thereafter he preferred serving as a captain of rough and tumble militiamen and gained notoriety for extracting unbridled frontier justice against LOYALISTS. His reputation for ruthlessness soon rivaled that of David FANNING. Cleveland initially served under Colonel James MOORE at the crushing victory of Moore's Creek Bridge, February 26, 1776, and subsequently accompanied General Griffith RUTHERFORD in campaigns against the Over Hill Cherokee villages. He then rose to the rank of colonel of the Wilkes County militia in 1778, while also holding numerous political offices, including justice of the peace and commissioner of confiscated estates. He next managed to parley his burgeoning popularity into a viable political career by winning seats in both the House of Commons and the Senate, 1778–80.

As a frontier military figure of some repute, Cleveland performed his greatest service during the British invasion of North Carolina in 1780. That fall, British forces under General Charles CORNWALLIS advanced from South Carolina and sent a flanking column of Loyalists under noted partisan leader Major Patrick FERGUSON toward the backwoods country. Ferguson then warned its rough-hewed inhabitants either to submit to the king's authority or be punished with "fire and sword." This insolence only served as a rallying cry for such "Over the Mountain Men," and Cleveland rendezvoused with the likes of Colonels William CAMPBELL, John SEVIER, and Isaac SHELBY at Quaker Meadows on the Catawba River. There, Campbell was elected leader of the 1,000 frontiersmen, and they finally cornered Ferguson at KING'S MOUNTAIN on October 7, 1780. He then led one of four columns in a relentless uphill attack that saw Ferguson slain and his command nearly annihilated. After the victory, he was conspicuous in executing several Loyalist prisoners whom he accused of robbery and other crimes. Cleveland proved so merciless toward the king's supporters that the superior court at Salisbury handed down an indictment on two murder counts, but the governor and the assembly quickly arranged for a wartime pardon.

After the war, Cleveland lost his plantation to a faulty claim and moved onto the Tugaloo River in Oconee County, South Carolina. There he served as associate justice alongside Andrew PICKENS, becoming notorious for sleeping—and snoring loudly—through trials. By the time of his death at Tugaloo in October 1806, the gluttonous Cleveland weighed 450 pounds and was popularly known as "Old Round About." But in his prime he formed part of a boisterous and vindictive backwood gentry that scorned authority, settled old scores violently, and decisively thwarted British control of the frontier.

Further Reading
Addison, Stephen O., Polly Fowler, and Cheryl Hunt. *Colonel Benjamin Cleveland, Hero of King's Mountain.* Cleveland, Tenn.: S. O. Addison, 1993.
Dameron, J. David. *King's Mountain: The Defeat of the Loyalists, October 7, 1780.* Cambridge, Mass.: Da Capo Press, 2003.
Dildy, David S. "North Carolina's Revolutionaries in Arms: The Battle of King's Mountain." Unpublished master's thesis, College of William and Mary, 1997.
Hindraker, Eric, and Peter C. Mancall. *At the Edge of Empire: The Backcountry of British North America.* Baltimore: Johns Hopkins University Press, 2002.
Waugh, Betty L. "The Upper Yadkin Valley in the American Revolution: Benjamin Cleveland, Symbol of Continuity." Unpublished Ph.D. diss., University of New Mexico, 1971.
Wise, Larry A. "Frontier Leadership and Transition: Benjamin Cleveland and the North and South Carolina Backcountry, 1777–1806." Unpublished master's thesis, Wake Forest University, 1993.

Clinton, George (1739–1812)
American military officer, politician

George Clinton was born in New Britain, New York, on July 26, 1739, the son of a farmer. Educated at home, he served on a privateer during the French and Indian War, 1755–63, and also joined the militia on a campaign against Fort Frontenac. Afterward Clinton studied law, was admitted to the bar in 1764, and gained election to the colonial assembly in 1768. At a time of increasing unrest over imperial strictures, he became clearly identified as a leader of the radical, anti-British faction. In 1770 he was one of a handful of politicians that voted against jailing Alexander MCDOUGALL, and that year he enhanced his social and political standing by marrying into the prominent Tappan family. Once the crisis emerged in 1774, Clinton positioned himself at the forefront of unrest by chairing a colonial COMMITTEE OF CORRESPONDENCE and being elected to the Second Continental CONGRESS as a delegate. In this capacity he voted for the DECLARATION OF INDEPENDENCE but never signed that document after becoming preoccupied with military affairs back home. In 1776 Clinton was made a brigadier general of militia and he energetically organized the troops and defenses of Ulster County. His talent for leading and motivating men came to the attention of General George WASHINGTON, who commissioned him a brigadier general in the Continental ARMY.

Clinton's military career proved less than salubrious. Entrusted with the defense of the Hudson River and Highlands in the summer of 1777, he lacked the troops and wherewithal to stop a determined offensive by General Henry CLINTON from New York City. His biggest failure was to prevent the capture of Forts Clinton and Montgomery with his brother, General James CLINTON, on October 6, suffering the loss of 250 casualties and 67 cannon. However, the tenacity with which he conducted his defense persuaded the British not to reinforce the beleaguered army of General John BURGOYNE at Saratoga. Clinton enjoyed much greater success in the political arena, where, in June 1777, he was elected the first governor under the new state constitution. His victory over General Philip J. SCHUYLER was achieved by appealing to common farmers and average citizens and presaged the eventual decline of the aristocracy in New York politics. As a war governor, Clinton was in his element and performed useful work raising and equipping troops and bolstering frontier defenses against Indian attacks while mercilessly hounding LOYALISTS and confiscating their property. He also worked hard to prevent parts of Vermont, claimed by New York, from seceding under Colonel Ethan ALLEN. Clinton's popularity as New York's chief executive can be gauged by his five consecutive reelection victories while in office. In 1788 he came out against ratification of the new federal constitution, fearing that a strong central government would curtail state powers. However, once the document was ratified, he unflinchingly supported the administration of President Washington.

Clinton voluntarily resigned from power in 1795 although he remained active in political circles by criticizing the Federalist policies of John JAY and Alexander HAMILTON. In 1800 he was persuaded by Aaron Burr to come out of retirement and seek the governorship again, which he did, and remained in office until 1804. That year he successfully ran as President Thomas JEFFERSON's vice president, and in 1808 he served President James MADISON in the same capacity. But Clinton despised Madison, and in 1811 he cast the deciding vote against rechartering the expired Bank of the United States. He died in Washington, D.C., on April 20, 1812, the first vice president to die in office. Clinton also proved instrumental in helping New York make the difficult wartime transition from colony to statehood.

Further Reading

Clinton, George. *Public Papers of George Clinton, First Governor of New York, 1777–1795, 1801–1805*, 10 vols. New York: AMS Press, 1973.

Fingerhut, Eugene R., and Joseph S. Tiedemann. *The Other New York: The American Revolution Beyond New York City, 1763–1787*. Albany: State University of New York Press, 2005.

Kaminski, John P. *George Clinton: Yeoman Politician of the New Republic*. Madison, Wis.: Madison House, 1993.

Musket, Jerome. *George Clinton, New York Governor During Revolutionary Times*. Charlotteville, N.Y.: Sam-Har Press, 1974.

Pagano, Francis B. "An Historical Account of the Military and Political Career of George Clinton, 1739–1812." Unpublished Ph.D. diss., St. John's University, 1956.

Smith, Gregory, and James M. Johnson. "Interpreting the Battle for the Hudson River Valley: The Battle of Fort Montgomery," *Hudson River Valley Review* 20, no. 1 (2003): 14–26.

Clinton, Henry (1730–1795)
English military officer

Henry Clinton was born in Newfoundland, Canada, on April 16, 1730, the son of Admiral George Clinton, governor of that province. His father subsequently gained appointment as royal governor of New York, where Clinton first developed an interest in military affairs by joining the militia. He returned to England in 1751 and used family connections to secure a lieutenant's commission with the elite Coldstream Guards. In this capacity he served with distinction during later phases of the Seven Years' War against France and ultimately served as aide-de-camp to Prince Ferdinand of Brunswick. By 1772 Clinton had risen to major general and, like many budding aristocrats, he also successfully stood for a seat in Parliament. His career hit an unexpected rough spot following the death of his young wife, which traumatized him severely, and three years lapsed before he could resume military duty. In the winter of 1774 his cousin, the duke of Newcastle, arranged for his transfer to North America. Clinton arrived at Boston in May 1775 along with Generals William HOWE and John BURGOYNE, where they reported to General Thomas GAGE, the British commander in chief.

Clinton, a shy, somewhat querulous individual, did not harmonize well with contemporaries, and they routinely ignored his oftentimes sound military advice. He nonetheless fought bravely at the costly British victory at BUNKER HILL on June 17, 1775. When Gage was recalled to England the following October, Howe was made supreme commander with Clinton as his second in command. The two men clashed repeatedly over strategy and objectives, and in the winter of 1776 Howe dispatched him on an expedition against South Carolina, to rid himself of interference. On June 28, 1776, Clinton watched as Commodore Peter

PARKER's fleet conducted an unsuccessful attack on CHARLESTON, which was repelled with loss. Both men returned to New York and rejoined Howe. Clinton seriously considered tending his resignation but the government persuaded him to remain. He bore a conspicuous role in the victory over General George WASHINGTON at LONG ISLAND on August 27, 1776, expertly outflanking and rolling up defenders under General Israel PUTNAM. But the two British commanders again clashed over military priorities, with Howe wishing to capture as much territory as possible, while Clinton insisted that Washington's army be destroyed in detail. In December 1776 Howe again wished to free himself of his testy subordinate and dispatched Clinton on another amphibious expedition against Newport, Rhode Island.

Henry Clinton, the longest-serving British commander in chief in North America *(R. W. Norton Art Gallery, Shreveport, Louisiana)*

In the spring of 1777 Clinton returned to England, generally disgusted by Howe's conduct of affairs, and again tendered his resignation. However, Lord George GERMAIN, suffering from a shortage of senior officers, persuaded him to stay on and, as an additional sop, arranged for him to be knighted and promoted to lieutenant general. Clinton returned to New York and was entrusted with its defense while Howe campaigned overland against Philadelphia. The general railed against what he viewed as a waste of time and resources, and in October 1777 he scraped together sufficient manpower to advance into the New York highlands to support General John BURGOYNE at Saratoga. He expertly dislodged the troops of General George CLINTON from Forts Clinton and Montgomery but lacked the resources to assist further. After Burgoyne's embarrassing surrender at Saratoga that month, the British administration decided to shake up its high command in North America. Howe was allowed to resign and come home in May 1778 while Clinton assumed his role as British commander in chief.

When Clinton took control of the army at Philadelphia, he felt exposed to an attack by the French fleet and decided to march overland back to New York. He was intercepted by Washington's army at MONMOUTH, New Jersey, on June 28, 1778, and a drawn battle ensued. The British drew off in good order and assumed a defensive posture in the city for the next three years. Clinton's attempts to regain the strategic initiative were greatly hindered by the appointment of Admiral Marriot ARBUTHNOT, a stubborn, quarrelsome individual who did everything in his power—or so it seemed to Clinton—to obstruct combined operations. He also felt obliged to keep an eye on his talented and ambitious subordinate, General Charles CORNWALLIS, who was clearly eager to succeed him. With a strategic draw in the north, Clinton devised a clever strategy intended to bolster LOYALIST participation in the war effort and detach the southern states from the rebellion. In December 1778 he ordered Lieutenant Colonel Archibald CAMPBELL to attack Savannah, Georgia, which was successfully accomplished. A year later Clinton himself led a large expedition of several thousand men against South Carolina. The ensuing siege of CHARLESTON proved disastrous to American arms, and in May 1780 General Benjamin LINCOLN surrendered 5,500 men. It was the greatest British victory of the war and a perilous strategic loss for the United States. Clinton then departed for New York, leaving Cornwallis with 8,000 veterans to continue their conquest of the south.

Back in New York, there was little Clinton could accomplish militarily beyond an occasional foray into Connecticut under General William TRYON. He scored something of a coup in September 1780 by arranging for the defection of General Benedict ARNOLD, but this was accomplished at the cost of his most trusted aide, Major John ANDRE, who was arrested and executed for spying. Worse, the aggressive Cornwallis, backed politically by Lord Germain, unilaterally abandoned Clinton's methodical strategy and plunged headlong into costly invasions of North Carolina and Virginia. Clinton's predictions of dire consequences manifested in the October 1781 campaign at YORKTOWN, when Generals Washington and Jean-Baptiste, comte de ROCHAMBEAU, stole a march on the British and invested Cornwallis before Clinton could react. The general arranged a relief expedition for his unruly subordinate with 8,000 fresh troops, but he arrived at Chesapeake Bay eight days after the British capitulation on October 24, 1781. In the spring of 1782 the new Whig administration of Charles WATSON-WENTWORTH, marquis of Rockingham, replaced Clinton with General Guy CARLETON at New York.

Clinton returned to England an angry and dejected man, blamed by many for the loss of America. Unwilling to be scapegoated, Clinton fired back with several political pamphlets and castigated Gage, Howe, and Cornwallis for their lack of leadership. He subsequently lost his parliamentary seat in 1784 but regained it six years later. Clinton's reputation was gradually rehabilitated, and in 1793 he became a full general commanding the strategic garrison at Gibraltar. He died there in that capacity on December 23, 1795, a capable strategist but too abrasive and impolitic to function successfully as commander in chief.

Further Reading
Borick, Carl P. *A Gallant Defense: The Siege of Charleston, 1780*. Columbia: University of South Carolina Press, 2003.
Gruber, Ira D. "The Education of Sir Henry Clinton," *Bulletin of the John Rylands University Library of Manchester* 72 (1990): 131–153.
Schecter, Barnet. *The Battle for New York: The City at the Heart of the American Revolution*. New York: Walker & Co., 2002.
Wilcox, William B., ed. *The American Rebellion: Sir Henry Clinton's Narrative of His Campaigns, 1775–1782*. New Haven, Conn.: Yale University Press, 1954.
———. *Portrait of a General: Sir Henry Clinton in the War of Independence*. New York: A. A. Knopf, 1964.
Wilson, David K. *The Southern Strategy: Britain's Conquest of South Carolina and Georgia, 1775–1780*. Columbia: University of South Carolina Press, 2005.

Clinton, James (1736–1812)
American military officer

James Clinton was born in New Britain, New York, on August 9, 1736, the son of a farmer and elder brother of George CLINTON. After receiving his education at home, Clinton joined the Ulster County militia as an ensign in 1756 and, as a captain, accompanied the expedition of General James Bradstreet against Fort Frontenac in 1758. After the French and Indian War, Clinton returned home and settled in New Britain, where he maintained ties to the militia. These contacts held him in good stead after June 1775, when he was appointed colonel of the 3rd New York Infantry. With it he accompanied the expedition of General Richard MONTGOMERY against Canada and fought at the disastrous repulse at QUEBEC on December 29, 1775. He subsequently secured the colonelcy of the 2nd New York Regiment the following March, and on August 9, 1776, Clinton advanced to brigadier general in the Continental ARMY. Along with his brother, he was entrusted with the defense of the Hudson Highland region, centered upon Forts Clinton and Montgomery. In the fall of 1777 General Henry CLINTON launched a major offensive up the Hudson River in order to assist General John BURGOYNE at Saratoga. The brothers were badly outnumbered but fought bravely until being forced to abandon their posts. Clinton himself was among the last Americans to leave and sustained a bayonet wound to the leg in the act of retreating. The following year he assumed command of the Northern Department, based at Albany, and shored up frontier defenses against attacks by Indians and LOYALISTS. In April 1779 he also led a major sweep of Tryon County but failed to encounter any opposition.

Clinton's largest contribution to the war occurred in the summer of 1779 as part of the punitive expedition commanded by General John SULLIVAN. He was ordered to concentrate 1,500 troops at the south end of Lake Otsego, New York, before marching along the Mohawk River and linking up with the main column in Pennsylvania. To facilitate his journey Clinton constructed a dam, allowed the water to rise, then broke it—which gave his heavily laden boats sufficient depth to float downstream. After rendezvousing with Sullivan at Tioga on August 22, 1779, they advanced into the Iroquois heartland, burning villages and crops at they went. Clinton then met and defeated the forces of Chief Joseph BRANT and John BUTLER at Newton (Elmira), New York, on August 29, driving them off after a stiff battle. After advancing as far as the Genessee country, and having destroyed 40 Indian villages and thousands of bushels of crops, the expedition returned safely. Clinton then resumed command of the Northern Department until August 1781, when his brigade was ordered south by General George WASHINGTON. He was there attached to the division of General Benjamin LINCOLN and participated in the siege and surrender of YORKTOWN in October 1781. Clinton remained in the army for two more years and saw no more fighting, but CONGRESS promoted him to brevet major general as of September 1783.

After the war Clinton returned to New Britain to farm and speculate in land. In 1784 he was selected to head a boundary commission for determining the border between New York and Pennsylvania, and in 1788 he became a delegate to the state constitutional convention. There he opposed adoption of the new federal constitution for its lack of a viable bill of rights. Clinton died at Little Britain on December 22, 1812; his son, DeWitt Clinton, was a future governor of New York.

Further Reading
Bush, Clesson S. "The Other Clinton," *Hudson Valley Regional Review* 13, no. 1 (1996): 20–39.
Campbell, William W. *Lecture on the Life and Services of General James Clinton.* New York: W. Osborn, 1839.
Clinton, James. "James Clinton's Expedition," *New York History* 13 (1932): 433–438.
Diamant, Lincoln. *Chaining the Hudson: The Fight for the River in the American Revolution.* New York: Fordham University Press, 2004.
Fischer, Joseph R. *A Well-Executed Failure: The Sullivan Campaign against the Iroquois, July–September, 1779.* Columbia: University of South Carolina Press, 1997.
Smith, Gregory, and James M. Johnson. "Interpreting the Battle for the Hudson River Valley: The Battle of Fort Montgomery," *Hudson River Valley Review* 20, no. 1 (2003): 14–26.

Closen, Ludwig von (1752–1830)
French military officer
Hans Christoph Frederick Ignatz Ludwig von Closen-Haydenburg was born in Monsheim, Bavaria, on August 14, 1752, the son of a distinguished army officer. His aristocratic family had fielded soldiers since medieval times, most recently in the employ of France, so at the age of 14 he joined the German-speaking Royal Deux-Ponts Regiment in 1769 as a sublieutenant. In this capacity he befriended the lieutenant colonel of his regiment, Guillaume de DEUX-PONTS. Closen proved himself a diligent officer, rose steadily through the ranks, and reached second captain in April 1780. The young German was then selected to accompany the expedition of General Jean-Baptiste, comte de ROCHAMBEAU, to America that summer

and, after arriving in Newport, Rhode Island, in July he was appointed the general's aide-de-camp. As a staff officer Closen was required to perform courier duties, and he traveled throughout the northern United States, usually delivering important dispatches to General George WASHINGTON. His fluency in English and smooth manners made him a popular figure at both headquarters. Closen then accompanied the French forces on their march from New England to Virginia in the summer of 1781, and he rode ahead of the main column carrying dispatches for Admiral François-Joseph, comte de GRASSE, in Chesapeake Bay. Closen was present throughout the siege of YORKTOWN and particularly distinguished himself in the October 14 night assault against British-held Redoubt No. 9. He spent the rest of the year touring Virginia with Rochambeau and finally departed America in December 1782.

After brief stops in Venezuela and the West Indies, Closen arrived in France in 1783, where he was admitted to the Order of Military Merit, gained promotion to colonel, and again served as an aide to Rochambeau in 1791. By this time the French Revolution had unfolded in all its fury, making the life of any aristocratic officer extremely perilous. Closen nevertheless remained in the king's employ, finally rising to major general in July 1792. However, he resigned his commission weeks later and relocated to Bavaria to prevent his family estates from being confiscated. Closen never again held a military rank and contentedly served as a state bureaucrat. After Napoléon's victory against Prussia in 1806 he was appointed sub-prefect in the department of Rhine and Moselle. Closen continued serving capably until his death in Mannheim, Baden, on August 9, 1830. The detailed journal he kept of his military experiences in America is among the best detailed and most enlightening to emerge from the Revolutionary War.

Further Reading

Acomb, Evelyn M., ed. *The Revolutionary Journal of Baron Ludwig von Closen, 1780–1783.* Chapel Hill: University of North Carolina Press, 1958.

Bowen, Clarence W. "A French Officer with Washington and Rochambeau," *Century Magazine* 73 (February 1907): 531–538.

Kennett, Lee. *The French Forces in America, 1777–1783.* Westport, Conn.: Greenwood Press, 1977.

Scott, Samuel F. *From Yorktown to Valmy: The Transformation of the French Army in an Age of Revolution.* Niwot: University Press of Colorado, 1998.

Selig, Robert A. "Storming the Redoubts," *MHQ* 8, no. 1 (1995): 18–27.

Coercive Acts (1774)

The BOSTON TEA PARTY may have been an indelible colonial protest against what was popularly perceived as arbitrary rule, but it drew an unexpectedly sharp response from the British government. Word of the deed infuriated both King GEORGE III and Parliament and, in a speech delivered on March 17, 1774, the usually placid monarch demanded coercive action to bring the colony of Massachusetts into line. Having capitulated to the colonies on the STAMP ACT and the TOWNSHEND DUTIES, Prime Minister Lord Frederick NORTH felt it essential that the unquestioned supremacy of Crown and Parliament now be underscored in bold relief. This gave rise to four successive pieces of legislation known collectively as the Coercive Acts. Their impact on the conduct of colonial rule was unprecedented, and the Americans, who were at the receiving end, came to regard these punitive measures as "Intolerable Acts."

On March 18, 1774, Lord North shepherded the Boston Port Bill through Parliament with little dissent. It effectively closed the port of Boston to all trade and commerce until its inhabitants compensated the East India Company for tea lost at the infamous Tea Party. Though aimed directly at Boston, it manifested unintended consequences across the sea. Politicians in other colonies viewed it as a direct threat to their own well-being, for if the government could arbitrarily seal off Boston, then any dissenting region was liable for the same treatment. Thus many inhabitants who in the past waxed indifferently or cautiously in their support for anti-British measures began to get involved.

The next nefarious legislation to pass was the Massachusetts Government Act, which Parliament approved on May 20, 1774. This mandated drastic changes by replacing the existing colonial charter with a royal one, thus promoting greater governmental control at the expense of popular sovereignty. Under its provisions the Massachusetts General Court summarily forfeited its ability to appoint members to the ruling council and, henceforth, the king would alone appoint them, along with judges and civil officials. A prohibition on town meetings was also enacted and no gathering of citizens would be tolerated without permission from a royal authority. Trial juries were also to be selected by sheriffs, who were themselves representatives of royal authority. By extending royal authority and influence into every community in Massachusetts the British government hoped to curb what it deemed as an excessive democratic impulse. This willful diminution of local control and participation in decision-making processes alarmed the assemblies of other colonials, for now no charter was immune to parliamentary dictates.

To crack down on the apparent inability to try and prosecute smugglers and other criminals who violated imperial regulations, Parliament also passed the Impartial Administration of Justice Act on May 20, 1774. It allowed Crown officials to relocate the trial of any individual from local juries to those in another colony or back in England. This measure violated the closely held American precept of trial by one's peers, especially since defendants would also be required to pay all expenses associated with moving. This legislation met with a chorus of condemnation from moderates such as Edmund BURKE, Charles James FOX, William PITT, and Charles WATSON-WENTWORTH, marquis of Rockingham, but their remonstrances went unheeded. Another action involved renewal of the QUARTERING ACT on June 2, 1774, which authorized direct billeting of troops in private housing. A fifth, unrelated bill, the QUEBEC ACT, also passed on June 22, 1774. This did not directly affect the American colonies, per se, but did grant linguistic and religious freedom to French-speaking Roman Catholic inhabitants of Canada. It also extended the borders of Quebec down the Mississippi River Valley, thereby erecting a barrier to further westward movement. Many Americans on the frontier considered such prohibitions an infringement upon their rights and further proof of a conspiracy to deny them the rights of Englishmen.

If by adoption of such measures the British government intended to intimidate the colonial polity it was sadly mistaken. In fact, the Coercive Acts served as a catalyst for mounting defiance against imperial prerogatives and a greater urgency to resist. Colonial legislatures subsequently authorized various COMMITTEES OF CORRESPONDENCE to coordinate better their resistance to British rule. The acts also engendered an outpouring of sympathy, heretofore lacking, for the inhabitants of Boston from across the colonies. This, in turn, stimulated widespread nonimportation of British goods until the Coercive Acts were retracted. Resistance to parliamentary rule ultimately congealed by the fall of 1774, when the First Continental CONGRESS convened in Philadelphia. The delegates gathered there in deadly earnest to air grievances, petition, and seek redress before the outbreak of hostilities rendered such diplomatic niceties moot.

Further Reading

Ammerman, David. *In the Common Cause: American Response to the Coercive Acts of 1774.* Charlottesville: University Press of Virginia, 1974.

Cook, Don. *The Long Fuse: How England Lost the American Colonies, 1760–1785.* New York: Atlantic Monthly Press, 1995.

Schwarz, Michael. "The Boston Port Act: Politics, Humanitarianism, and the Growth of Intercolonial Unity on the Eve of the American Revolution, 1774–1775." Unpublished master's thesis, Ohio University, 2001.

Thomas, Peter D. G. *Tea Party to Independence: The Third Phase of the American Revolution, 1773–1776.* New York: Oxford University Press, 1991.

Webb, Paul L. "A Comparative Study of the Common Cause: Responses of New York and Virginia to the Coercive Acts." Unpublished Ph.D. diss., Ohio State University, 1977.

Collier, George (1738–1795)
English naval officer

George Collier was born in London on May 11, 1738, into a common household. He joined the Royal Navy in 1751 and, by dint of good service, received his lieutenant's commission three years later. Collier made captain in 1762 and in 1775 he was dispatched on a secret mission to North American prior to the outbreak of hostilities. The exact nature of his errand has never been revealed, but he was knighted by King GEORGE III in consequence. In May 1776 he received command of the frigate HMS *Rainbow* and joined the fleet under Admiral Richard HOWE for service against the Americans. That August he was anchored off New York during General William HOWE's defeat of General George WASHINGTON on LONG ISLAND and described his "inexpressible" astonishment when the fleet did not move to intercept the American retreat. He was subsequently dispatched with a squadron to Nova Scotia in November 1776, where he landed troops that broke up the American siege of Fort Cumberland. Collier subsequently orchestrated naval activities against American privateers, ultimately snaring 76 enemy vessels. On July 7, 1777, he capped these efforts by capturing the 32-gun frigate *Hancock* under Captain John MANLEY. Collier's reputation held him in good stead when, in April 1779, he replaced the outgoing and highly unpopular admiral James GAMBIER as acting commander in chief with a local rank of commodore.

In addition to his nautical talents, Collier was one of the few naval officers able to work smoothly with his army counterpart at New York, General Henry CLINTON. In May 1779 he prevailed upon Clinton to lend him 2,000 troops under General Edward Mathews for a protracted raid against the Virginia coast. On May 10 his men landed at Fort Nelson and advanced inland, torching the towns of Norfolk and Suffolk with little resistance. For the next two weeks his fleet scoured the lightly defended coastline, seizing vessels, burning supplies, and removing anything of use to the enemy. By the time Collier returned

British naval officer George Collier led the most successful naval attack on the part of the Royal Navy against the Americans, in Penobscot Bay, Massachusetts (Maine), August 1779. *(National Maritime Museum of Greenwich, London)*

with his squadron to New York, he had absconded with 28 ships and more than 1,000 hogsheads of tobacco, a vital cash commodity for the rebels. Collier next accompanied Clinton up the Hudson River, where, on June 1, 1779, he assisted in the capture of Fort Verplanck and Stony Point. He subsequently rendered valuable assistance to Governor William TRYON during a protracted raid along the Connecticut coast. Compared to his predecessors, the naval establishment now possessed a commander who was skilled, compliant, and highly aggressive—precisely what the British war effort needed.

Collier's moment of triumph occurred in August 1779, when he received word that an American expedition under Commodore Dudley SALTONSTALL of Massachusetts had invested a British fort in Penobscot Bay, Massachusetts (Maine).

Mustering every available warship, he sailed with alacrity for Penobscot, intending to trap the Americans in the bay. On August 13 he accomplished exactly that and drove the Americans upriver, where they beached and burned their vessels. In all, Collier accounted for 38 rebel warships, the largest tally ever taken by a single action. He then returned in New York fully expecting a promotion—only to find that he had been replaced by the tottering admiral Marriot ARBUTHNOT. Angered by a lack of recognition, Collier demanded and received a transfer back to home waters.

Collier joined the Channel Fleet in 1780, partook of the relief efforts at Gibraltar, and captured the Spanish frigate *Leocadia* on the return leg of the voyage. Yet because he lacked both aristocratic pedigree and family patronage, his career languished, and he never again held an independent command. Collier then retired from active service to stand for a seat in Parliament in 1784. He lingered there in obscurity for nearly a decade until 1793, when he finally made rear admiral. Collier rose to vice admiral in retirement the following year before dying in London on April 6, 1795. He was among the Revolutionary War's most talented naval commanders—and among the least utilized.

Further Reading
Buel, Richard. *In Irons: Britain's Naval Supremacy and the American Revolutionary Economy.* New Haven, Conn.: Yale University Press, 1998.
Corbin, Gary. "Disaster at Penobscot Bay." Unpublished master's thesis, State University of New York at Brockport, 1992.
Sharp, Arthur G. "The Penobscot Expedition: An Exercise in Futility," *Military History* 20, no. 5 (2003): 50–57.
Syrett, David. *The Royal Navy in American Waters during the Revolutionary War.* Brookfield, Vt.: Gower Publishing Co., 1989.
Tilley, John A. *The British Navy in the American Revolution.* Columbia: University of South Carolina Press, 1987.
Tucker, Louis L., ed. "To My Inexpressible Astonishment: Admiral Sir George Collier's Observations on the Battle of Long Island," *New York Historical Society Quarterly* 48, no. 4 (1964): 292–305.

committees of correspondence

As friction escalated with Great Britain over imperial policy, many colonies responded with committees of correspondence to coordinate and share information between each other. Such bodies were intra-colonial at first, but as resistance expanded they reached out to counterparts elsewhere. The first committee of correspondence was formed by the New York assembly in the wake of the SUGAR ACT and STAMP ACT of 1764. The British crackdown following the GASPÉE AFFAIR of 1772 also induced the Virginia House of Burgesses to invoke similar measures and begin corresponding with other assemblies. However, the practice achieved its biggest impetus and greatest results in Massachusetts. Boston being on the cutting edge of colonial unrest, it fell upon agitators like Samuel ADAMS, James OTIS, and Joseph WARREN to establish the city's first committee in 1772. By the following spring nearly half the towns and districts in Massachusetts had responded favorably and established committees of correspondence. After the TOWNSHEND DUTIES were repealed, a general lessening of tensions ensued, but Adams warned compatriots that crisis had been averted but only temporarily and that the polity had better prepare for continuing onslaughts against their liberties. He and other radicals kept the Boston committee of correspondence particularly active, and the ill-conceived TEA ACT of 1773 gave them a convenient pretext for inciting greater resistance. In December 1773, the Boston committee orchestrated public events culminating in the BOSTON TEA PARTY of that month. Committees expanded further in Massachusetts and elsewhere in the wake of the punitive COERCIVE ACTS of 1774, and within a year virtually every colony save Pennsylvania possessed at least one.

Two types of committee of correspondence evolved in the period between 1772 and 1775, when they were most effective. The first were intercolonial committees established by colonial assemblies and tasked with communicating with legislative bodies elsewhere. The second, the local committees, wielded even greater influence as the political matrix of revolution unfolded. In practice they were initially propaganda wings for anti-British sentiment, but they gradually assumed authoritative roles once fighting commenced at Lexington and CONCORD in April 1775. As British authority disintegrated, committees began functioning more and more like governmental agencies in its place. The committees assumed local and colony-wide administrative duties, which, in turn, helped mobilize popular support for revolution. They were a uniquely American response to the evolving political crisis and helped prepare local political institutions for eventual self-rule.

Further Reading
Brown, Richard D. *Revolutionary Politics in Massachusetts: The Boston Committee of Correspondence and the Towns, 1772–1774.* Cambridge, Mass.: Harvard University Press, 1970.
Hagan, Brian S. "A Rhetorical Analysis of Letters of the Boston Committee of Correspondence." Unpublished master's thesis, University of New Mexico, 1995.
Hertz, Carolyn D. "The Committees of Correspondence, Inspection, and Safety in Old Hampshire County, Massachusetts, during the American Revolution." Unpublished master's thesis, University of Massachusetts, Amherst, 1993.
Reed, Robert. "Loyalists, Patriots, and Trimmers: The Committee System in the American Revolution, 1774–1776." Unpublished Ph.D. diss., Cornell University, 1988.
Watson, Alan D. "The Committees of Safety and the Coming of the American Revolution in North Carolina, 1774–1776." *North Carolina Historical Review* 73, no. 2 (1996): 131–155.

Common Sense

Although the struggle against British political tyranny had commenced nine months earlier, by January 1776 the colonies had edged no closer to declaring independence. A major obstacle was that the majority of Americans retained a close, even cherished, kinship with their monarch and the notion of English citizenship. But that same month the radical pamphleteer Thomas PAINE stepped into the void with *Common Sense,* an electrifying discourse that altered the political landscape of the revolution and, with it, the world. In succinct, precise language easily fathomed by commoners, Paine railed against continuation of monarchical governance for the intrinsic weakness, corruption, and tyranny it ultimately conveyed. He willfully asserted that, far from benevolent, the British Crown negated virtue by dint of its great wealth while impoverishing the nation through ill-advised policies. The only method of ensuring America's survival was by rejecting King GEORGE III, whom he denounced as the "Royal brute of England," and establishing a republican form of government, one answerable to the people alone. In sum, *Common Sense* helped crystallize opposition not only to the British monarchy but the very notion of kingship itself.

Paine cleverly buttressed his railings with biblical passages and allegories, employing a vernacular verse that Americans of the time easily inculcated. He also presented legalistic Enlightenment principles of the great English political philosopher John Locke in simplistic terms, highlighting for average people their stake in the ongoing struggle. Paine forcefully articulated that the will of the people, not the divine right of kings, was the surest and most reliable guarantor of happiness. These complex issues, distilled through the prism of Paine's fiery prose, heightened the tenor of political dialogue throughout the colonies.

While writing *Common Sense,* Paine turned frequently for advice to Dr. Benjamin RUSH and Benjamin FRANKLIN, who read the manuscript and helped critique it. The polemic had an electrifying effect on the population and added popular currency and renewed impetus toward independence. *Common Sense* enjoyed an initial print run of 100,000 copies, making it the most widely read political tract until that time. General George WASHINGTON was so impressed that he ordered it read to soldiers at every military camp in America. The issues raised by *Common Sense,* and the principles it invoked, intellectually paved the ground for the DECLARATION OF INDEPENDENCE, only six months hence. For this reason it remains the most influential political tract of human history and a major catalyst behind the final break with Great Britain.

Further Reading
Ferguson, Robert A. "The Commonalities of Common sense," *William and Mary Quarterly* 57, no. 3 (2000): 465–504.
Ferling, John E. *A Shot in the Dark: The Struggle to Create the American Republic.* New York: Oxford University Press, 2003.
Kashatus, William C. "Revolution with Ink and Pen," *American History* 34, no. 6 (2000): 52–54, 56–59.
Liell, Scott. *46 Pages: Thomas Paine, Common Sense, and the Turning Point to American Independence.* Philadelphia: Running Press, 2003.
Paine, Thomas, and Tony Benn, ed. *Common Sense and the Rights of Man.* London: Phoenix, 2000.
Paine, Thomas, and Thomas P. Slaughter. *Common Sense and Related Writings.* New York: St. Martin's Press, 2001.

Concord, Battle of (April 19, 1775)

Having been alerted by General Thomas GAGE that Massachusetts was in a state of rebellion, Lord William Dartmouth, secretary of state for the colonies, opined that "force should be repelled by force." On April 14, 1775, Gage received precise orders from the government instructing him to take whatever actions deemed necessary to enforce royal authority. The general immediately ordered the Boston garrison to cobble together an 800-man expeditionary force containing all the elite flank companies (light infantry and grenadiers) to be commanded by Lieutenant Colonel Francis SMITH and Major John PITCAIRN of the royal marines. This force was to march secretly at night for the village of Concord, where arms and gunpowder were known to be stored and, if possible, arrest radical leaders Samuel ADAMS and John HANCOCK. This was not the first time that Gage had dispatched armed men into the interior for the purpose of seizing colonial arms; on September 2, 1774, a British column raided nearby Cambridge and returned with little more then threats from local militia. When Smith departed on the night of April 18, 1775, he did so under complete secrecy to avert possible detection. Given the British army's opinion of colonial militia, and a somewhat sneering assumption that the mere sight of redcoats with fixed bayonets would deter outbreaks of violence, serious resistance was not anticipated.

Unfortunately for Gage, the colonial intelligence network was alert and immediately cognizant of his scheme. Joseph WARREN, a local radical leader, immediately dispatched several riders, including Paul REVERE, to alert the countryside by crying "The regulars are coming out!" and warn Adams and Hancock to flee. Early on the morning on April 19, 1775, Captain John Parker mustered his company of 70 MINUTEMEN in Lexington, a few miles east of Concord, through which the British column would most likely pass. By daybreak Smith's force, which had endured a tiring night march through a downpour, trudged into Lexington and confronted Parker's force. Parker rather wisely deployed his men on Lexington Green, astride their route of march but safely out of their way. The British commanders felt it unwise to leave potentially hostile troops on their lines of communication back to Boston, so Major Pitcairn rode up to the Americans and ordered them to disband and disperse. Parker concurred and was in the act of leaving the field when a shot rang out of nowhere. It has never been ascertained precisely who fired; it was most likely a minuteman's weapon that accidentally discharged as he departed the scene. But the fatigued, rain-soaked British regulars reacted by firing several volleys at the milling militia, killing eight and wounding 10. It took several minutes for Pitcairn to restore order and resume his march to Concord. Once Smith brought up the rear of the column, they arrived at their destination to find that the military stores in question had been removed. The British then reassembled on the road and tramped off the way they had come.

News of the fighting at Lexington, however, had an electrifying effect on the local populace. Many had resigned themselves to the eventuality of war and minutemen companies began assembling for combat. A preliminary skirmish was fought at North Bridge, which claimed several lives and emboldened the rebels to act further. Pushing ahead of Smith's columns in uncoordinated groups, they took up ambush positions on either side of the road and peppered the densely packed column with rolling musketry as it passed. Redcoats toppled and Smith was obliged to send his light infantry off the road to scour the woods for rebels. An intensive firefight ensued over the next 20 miles, with the highly trained regulars keeping order under very heavy musketry. Smith was wounded, Pitcairn unhorsed, and their command seemed on the verge of being overwhelmed by myriads of militiamen, when suddenly help arrived in the form of 1,000 soldiers under Colonel Hugh PERCY just east of Lexington. This new infusion of strength checked the rebel onslaught long enough for Percy to reform the troops and continue marching. The Americans kept up their relentless running battle until Percy, anticipating a large colonial ambush, suddenly turned and veered into Charlestown. This concluded the battle of Concord, in which the British lost 273 men to a casualty count of 146 Americans. It reflected the greatest credit upon the British army, men and officers alike, who maintained excellent marching and fire discipline under dire circumstances. However, blood had been prodigiously shed, and the war between Briton and American, long anticipated, now began in earnest.

Further Reading
Andrews, Joseph L. *Revolutionary Boston, Lexington, and Concord: The Shots Heard 'Round the World!* Beverly, Mass.: Commonwealth Editions, 2002.
Bracken, Jeanne M. "The First to Die," *American History* 31, no. 1 (1996): 24–27, 62–63.
Gross, Robert. *The Minutemen and Their World.* New York: Wiley and Wang, 2001.
Hallahan, William H. *The Day the Revolution Began.* New York: Avon Books, 1999.
Kehoe, Vincent J-R. *The British Story of the Battles of Lexington and Concord on the Nineteenth of April, 1775.* Los Angeles: Hale & Co., 2002.

Morrissey, Brendan. *Boston, 1775: The Shot Heard Round the World.* Westport, Conn.: Praeger, 2004.

Congress, Continental

The First and Second Continental Congresses were collective bodies of elected delegates struggling from 1775 to 1783 to address the seemingly endless litany of problems associated with emergent nationhood. Unprecedented in colonial politics to that date, they represented the first time that 13 disparate entities attempted speaking with one voice. The First Continental Congress had its origins in colonial reaction to the COERCIVE ACTS of 1774, adopted by Parliament to punish Massachusetts for its complicity in the BOSTON TEA PARTY. Such arbitrary and punitive action triggered alarm in other colonies, which felt that they might be next, and calls for an assembled congress echoed through assemblies in Rhode Island, New York, Pennsylvania, and Virginia. On June 17, 1774, the Massachusetts General Court appealed to all colonies for delegates to attend a general meeting in Philadelphia. When Congress finally convened at Carpenter's Hall, Philadelphia, on September 5, 1774, every colony but Georgia was in attendance. During preliminary maneuvers, the delegates adopted the practice of one vote per colony while the conduct of affairs was entrusted to a senior officer, the president. Peyton Randolph of Virginia was the first individual elected to that post, after which Congress began weighing the contentious issues before it.

The First Continental Congress assembled principally to seek redress from Great Britain, specifically Parliament, which delegates believed had violated their rights as Englishmen. On September 17, members adopted the so-called Suffolk Resolves, first passed in Massachusetts, which declared the Coercive and other acts unconstitutional. It also encouraged colonies to begin funding and equipping militia forces to defend themselves, as necessary. There was little or no discussion of independence from England at this juncture. In fact, when LOYALIST delegate Joseph

GALLOWAY of Pennsylvania promulgated a scheme for establishing a colonial council and dominion status within the British Empire, it lost by only a single vote. Congress next passed a series of resolutions affirming rights to life, liberty, and property, based on long-accepted principles of the English constitution. It also issued calls for repealing all illegal measures passed by Parliament since 1763. Congress then adopted punitive measures of its own by endorsing a widespread boycott of British goods (nonimportation) through the Continental Association. But, as a final sop to moderation, it also dispatched the Olive Branch Petition directly to King GEORGE III, pledging its allegiance to the Crown and seeking his intercession against Parliament on its behalf. The body then adjourned on October 26, 1775, having voted first to reconvene the following May if no action were taken.

When the Second Continental Congress met again at Philadelphia on May 10, 1775, the tempo and tenor of political events throughout North America had changed significantly. The recent outbreak of fighting at Lexington and CONCORD now underscored the solemnity and urgency of their endeavors. With John HANCOCK elected the new president, delegates began addressing their rapidly deteriorating relationship with England and several possible solutions. They also began assuming the traditional duties of a provisional government to better coordinate the nascent war effort. In this regard their most important decision was confirmation of Virginian George WASHINGTON as commander in chief of the new Continental ARMY. To promote unity with southerners, he was nominated by John ADAMS of Massachusetts on June 15, 1775, thus forestalling any lingering suspicions about New England. That October provisions were also made for the founding and outfitting of a new Continental NAVY under Commodore Esek HOPKINS. As before, public sentiment for national independence scarcely evinced itself, but the onset of hostilities, Britain's flat refusal to consider concessions, and the use of hired HESSIANS against the populace irrevocably nudged the polity that way. The call for a complete fissure was then strikingly abetted through publication of Thomas PAINE's sensational monograph *COMMON SENSE* in January 1776. By July 2, 1776, with reconciliation all but dead and Britain massing its forces for a war of conquest, a motion finally advanced resolving that "these United Colonies are, and of right ought to be free and independent states." Two days later the DECLARATION OF INDEPENDENCE, a seminal event in human history, was finally approved by Congress. Events had come full circle.

Congress spent the balance of the war years consolidating its ability to rule and formalizing a structure to facilitate governance. On November 17, 1777, it adopted the ARTICLES OF CONFEDERATION, America's first constitution, which formalized a weak, unicameral legislature with clearly delineated powers. The most important power of all—taxation—was left entirely to individual states and essentially hobbled the country's ability to wage war, but this was an acceptable concession to promote ratification. The articles were finally ratified on March 1, 1781, and Congress finally acquired a constitutional basis and, with it, long-sought legitimacy to govern. Another significant improvement was the shifting of governmental responsibility from committees to executive departments tasked with specific military, naval, and monetary considerations. In sum the Continental Congresses were far from perfect instruments of governance, especially in a period of war, but probably represented the only practical expedient acceptable to the mind set of the day. After the war Congress hobbled along ineffectively until March 4, 1789, when a more centralized scheme under the new federal constitution.

Further Reading

Baack, Ben. "Forging a Nation State: The Continental Congress and the Financing of the War of American Independence," *Economic History Review* 54, no. 4 (2001): 639–656.

Davis, Derek. *Religion and the Continental Congress, 1774–1789.* New York: Oxford University Press, 2000.

Ferling, John E. *A Leap in the Dark: The Struggle to Create the American Republic.* New York: Oxford University Press, 2003.

Hardinge, H. DeForest. "Nine Months in York," *Manuscripts* 56, no. 4 (2004): 309–319.

Horgan, Lucille. *Forged in War: The Continental Congress and the Origins of Military Supply and Acquisition Policy.* Westport, Conn.: Greenwood Press, 2002.

Mires, Charlene. *Independence Hall in American Memory.* Philadelphia: University of Pennsylvania Press, 2002.

Myers, Joseph P. "Inventing the Republic: The Continental Congress, Institutional Formation, and the Revolution of American National Identity." Unpublished Ph.D. diss., Temple University, 1999.

Conway, Thomas (1735–1800?)
French military officer

Thomas Conway was born in Kerry, Ireland, on February 27, 1735, and he immigrated to France with his parents while a child. At 14 he enrolled in the expatriate Irish Brigade of the French army and rose rapidly through ability. A colonel by 1772, he sought out American agent Silas DEANE at Paris in 1776 and was promised a brigadier general's commission should he sail to America. Conway reached Morristown, New Jersey, on May 8, 1777, received his commission, and fought well under General William ALEXANDER, Lord Stirling, at BRANDYWINE and GERMANTOWN. Feeling unappreciated, Conway approached General George WASHINGTON for a promotion to major general but was refused. Washington feared that elevating a foreigner with less seniority over the heads of native generals would severely impact army morale. Apparently, Conway greatly resented what he considered a slight and penned a scathing appraisal of Washington's command abilities to General Horatio GATES, the recent victor of Saratoga. In it he suggested that Gates ought to supplant Washington as commander of American forces. This was not an unusual sentiment, especially in light of Washington's inability to defend New York or, more recently, Philadelphia. When a drunken major James Wilkinson, Gates's aide-de-camp, mentioned Conway's letter to General Alexander, he immediately notified his superior that a cabal was afoot intent upon replacing him.

Washington did, in fact, have his share of enemies in the army and CONGRESS, such as Thomas MIFFLIN, who took deliberate steps to embarrass him and provoke his resignation. In December 1777 they arranged for Conway's promotion to major general and assignment as inspector general of the army, an office accountable not to Washington but rather to a newly created board of war—staffed by Gates. Washington, angered by what can only be construed as a conspiracy, angrily denounced Gates and Conway in letters and made his displeasure known to allies in Congress. The plot then quickly unraveled once both men made halting attempts to rationalize such seemingly inexplicable behavior. Conway was also unhappy with his subordination to the youthful marquis de LAFAYETTE on a proposed expedition against Canada and haughtily threatened to resign. He was dumbfounded when Congress summarily accepted it. Conway was also subsequently wounded in a duel with General John Cadwalader for disparaging remarks he made about Washington. He then sullenly returned to France, where he rose to major general and died in exile around 1800. His position as inspector general was subsequently filled by the infinitely more tractable baron Friedrich von STEUBEN.

Further Reading

Brenneman, Gloria E. "The Conway Cabal: Myth or Reality," *Pennsylvania History* 40 (April 1973): 169–177.

Kohn, Richard H. "The Coup D'etat That Failed," *New York Historical Society Bulletin* 12 (1975): 30–36.

O'Keefe, Steven. "An Investigation into the Existence of the Conway Cabal." Unpublished master's thesis, St. Bonaventure University, 1999.

Rossman, Kenneth. "Conway and the Conway Cabal," *South Atlantic Quarterly* 41 (1948): 32–38.

Russell, Preston. "The Conway Cabal," *American Heritage* 46, no. 1 (1995): 84–91.

Conyngham, Gustavus (1747–1819)
American naval officer

Gustavus Conyngham was born in County Donegal, Ireland, in 1747, and in 1763 he migrated to Philadelphia to work in the merchant marine. Adept as a sailor, by 1775 he commanded the brig *Charming Peggy* and was tasked with obtaining illicit military supplies from the Netherlands. Word of his activities slipped out to the English consulate, which vigorously protested to the Dutch government. Conyngham quickly fled and ventured to Paris, France, where he approached American agent Benjamin FRANKLIN about joining the Continental NAVY. Franklin then commissioned him a captain on March 1, 1777, and arranged for him to purchase a small vessel for the American cause. Conyngham then sailed from Dunkirk with his 10-gun lugger *Surprise* and quickly subdued two English prizes. Again, his activities triggered a diplomatic contretemps when the British ambassador protested and threatened retaliatory action against the French fishing fleet. The French government, officially neutral, promptly confiscated Conyngham's ships, placed him in irons, and returned the captured ships to England. His commission was also seized and sent to the court at Versailles, where it vanished for over a century. The intrepid raider was soon released, however, and he quickly acquired a new and bigger vessel, the *Revenge*. Commencing in May 1777 Conyngham cruised the English Channel for 22 months, capturing or sinking 60 British ships—an unprecedented feat. His success was not lost on the British and, because they refused to recognize his commission, they dubbed him the "Dunkirk Pirate," promising severe retribution if he were ever caught.

After operating out of France for several months, Conyngham next shifted his activities to La Coruña, Spain, and raided British shipping in the Bay of Biscay. Britain brought pressure to bear on the Spanish government, and he was eventually ejected. He then sailed to the West Indies, securing several more prizes before dropping anchor at

American captain Gustavus Conyngham cruised the English Channel for 22 months beginning in 1777, capturing or sinking a record 60 British ships. *(Naval Historical Center)*

Philadelphia in February 1779. After refitting the *Revenge* as a privateer, he cruised the coast off New York until captured by HMS *Galatea* that May. As promised, the British treated him as a pirate and subjected him to horrific conditions at Old Mill Prison in Plymouth. Conyngham managed to escape on his third attempt, made his way to Holland, and briefly joined the crew of Captain John Paul JONES on the *Alliance*. He next arrived in Spain, acquired a new privateer named *Tartar* and was again snared by the Royal Navy on May 17, 1780. Another round of incarceration at Mill Prison ensued, although Conyngham was eventually released and exchanged in January 1781. He returned home looking to fill a slot in the Continental NAVY and spent the rest of the war waiting for a warship.

Afterward Conyngham rejoined the merchant marine and proved reasonably successful. However, the Continental CONGRESS would not recognize his claims for compensation as his original commission had been lost and, worse, he was accused of collaborating with the disgraced Silas DEANE while in Paris. Conyngham spent the rest of his life futilely pursuing official recognition for his deed and died in Philadelphia a disillusioned man on November 27, 1819. He was nonetheless one of the Revolutionary War's most daring and successful sea raiders.

Further Reading
Barnes, James. *With the Flag in the Channel.* New York: Appleton, 1902.
Bowen-Hassell, E. Gordon, Dennis M. Conrad, and Mark L. Hayes. *Sea Raiders of the American Revolution: The Continental Navy in English Waters.* Washington, D.C.: Naval Historical Center, 2003.
Coleman, Eleanor S. *Captain Gustavus Conyngham, U.S.N., Pirate or Privateer, 1747–1819.* Washington, D.C.: University Press of America, 1982.
Conyngham, Gustavus. "Narrative of Captain Gustavus Conyngham, U.S.N., While in Command of the 'Surprise' and the 'Revenge,'" *Pennsylvania Magazine of History and Biography* 22 (1899): 479–488.
Jones, Charles H. *Captain Gustavus Conyngham; A Sketch of the Services He Rendered in the Cause of Independence.* Philadelphia: Pennsylvania Society of the Revolution, 1903.
Nesser, Robert W., ed. *Letters and Papers Relating to the Cruises of Gustavus Conyngham; A Captain of the Continental Navy, 1777–1779.* New York: Printed for the Naval History Society by the DeVinne Press, 1915.

Corbin, Margaret (1751–1800)
American camp follower, artillery woman

Margaret Cochrane was born in Franklin County, Pennsylvania, on November 12, 1751, the daughter of Scotch-Irish settlers. She was orphaned at the age of five when an Indian attack killed her father and carried off her mother, and she was raised by an uncle. In 1772 she married William Corbin of Virginia, who subsequently served as a matross in Captain Thomas Procter's company of the 1st Continental Artillery. Like many women of her day, Corbin followed her husband around as a camp follower. She was present in this capacity during the battle of Fort Washington on November 16, 1776, in which William died in combat. Undeterred, she began serving an artillery piece in his place and fired it several times before being struck by grapeshot from HMS *Pearl* in the river below. She was severely wounded and lost the use of one arm. After Fort Washington's surrender Corbin was allowed to leave, and she relocated to Philadelphia as an invalid.

In time Corbin's condition was made known to the Pennsylvania Executive Council, which granted her a small sum of money and referred her case to the Continental CONGRESS. The Board of War, impressed by her reputation as "Captain Molly," then voted her a soldier's half-pay for life on July 29, 1779. She was also allotted one free suit of clothing per year or the equivalent in money. Corbin was thus the first woman of the Revolutionary War to receive a disability pension for military service. She was also formally discharged from the military in April 1783.

Afterward Corbin was allowed to join the Corps of Invalids at West Point, New York, where she apparently married again. Her new husband was also a cripple, and the couple lived several years in grinding poverty. In 1782 Congress allowed her to receive a daily ration of rum due veteran soldiers. She died at Highland Falls, New York, on January 16, 1780, in an unmarked grave. Corbin's remains were subsequently rediscovered and, through the intervention of the Daughters of the American Revolution (DAR), she was interred at the U.S. Military Academy in 1926 with full military honors. Her grave remains marked by a bronze memorial. Given Corbin's association with artillery, she is often confused with Mary Ludwig HAYS, or "Molly Pitcher," a common nickname for camp followers of the time.

Further Reading

Downey, Fairfax. "Girls behind the Guns," *American Heritage* 8, no. 1 (1955): 46–48.

Hall, Edward. *Margaret Corbin, Heroine of the Battle of Fort Washington, 16 November, 1776.* New York: American Scenic and Historic Preservation Society, 1932.

Liberman, Joe. "Amid the Demoralizing Loss of Fort Washington, Margaret Corbin Emerged as America's First Wartime Hero," *Military History* 15, no. 6 (1999): 12–15.

Ross, Emily. "Captain Molly: Forgotten Heroine of the Revolution," *Daughters of the American Revolution Magazine* 106, no. 2 (1972): 108–111, 186.

Teipe, Emily J. "Will the Real 'Molly Pitcher' Please Stand Up?" *Prologue* 31, no. 2 (1999): 118–126.

Thompson, D.W., and Merri Lou Schaumann. "Goodbye, Molly Pitcher," *Cumberland County History* 6 (summer 1989): 3–26.

Cornplanter (ca. 1740–1836)

Seneca chief

Cornplanter (Gyantwakia) was born around 1740 at Conawaugus (Avon), New York, the son of John Abeel, a Dutch Indian trader, and a Seneca squaw. He was raised by his mother as part of an influential tribal family and amply demonstrated his merits as a warrior while still young. When the Revolutionary War broke out in April 1775 and the Six Nations of the Iroquois Confederacy were pressured by both sides to join, Cornplanter, by now a respected war chief, cautioned neutrality. This put him in opposition to the pro-British Mohawk under Chief Joseph BRANT, who urged war. It was not until August 1777 that the Seneca lifted up hatchets against the Americans, and Cornplanter led a tribal delegation accompanying the expedition of Lieutenant Colonel Barry ST. LEGER. In this capacity he participated in the siege of Fort Stanwix, New York, and subsequently led his warriors to victory over Colonel Nicholas HERKIMER at ORISKANY on August 6, 1777. The British then withdrew their regular forces from New York and resorted to hit and run guerrilla raids against frontier settlements.

Cornplanter was actively engaged in many raids against American communities, particularly at Wyoming Valley, Pennsylvania, on July 3, 1778, when he helped destroy a force of 400 pursuing soldiers under Colonel Zebulon BUTLER. The following November he assisted Captain Walter BUTLER during a devastating attack upon Cherry Valley, New York. The success of Indian and LOYALIST raiders prompted General George WASHINGTON to authorize a large-scale punitive campaign against the Six Nations the following summer. On August 28, 1779, an army under General John SULLIVAN attacked and defeated the Indians and Loyalists at Newtown (Elmira), New York, initiating a scorched earth policy throughout the region. The Seneca were forced to lay low for the winter, but by the summer of 1780 Cornplanter was back in the field conducting raids against Canajoharie and the Schoharie Valley, New York. In the former attack he actually captured his father and offered to take him into his tribal household as an honored guest, but when he declined the chief released him.

After the war Cornplanter became a frequent sight at numerous treaty signings, whereby the United States slowly confiscated Indian land. The Indians were powerless to stop such encroachment, but Cornplanter defended his people with dignity and resolve. In this capacity he was denounced by RED JACKET, who stridently opposed land sales in a bid to boost his reputation among fellow tribesmen. Nevertheless, the American government tapped him to visit warring tribes of the Ohio River region in 1792, where he argued unsuccessfully for a cessation of hostilities. Afterward the government of Pennsylvania awarded him a large land grant on the Allegheny River. At this time the Seneca were experiencing a religious revival led by Cornplanter's brother Handsome Lake, and when his position as chief was threatened he expelled the controversial mystic to another reservation. After the War of 1812 broke out the aged chief tendered his services to the United States and was politely declined, although

Seneca chief and warrior Cornplanter joined Loyalists to fight against American forces. After the war he negotiated many treaties with the new country and offered his services in the War of 1812. *(New York Historical Society)*

his son Henry O'Bail fought with distinction. Cornplanter, one of the fiercest Seneca warriors, died on his land grant on February 18, 1836, widely mourned. In 1871 the state of Pennsylvania erected a marble shrine atop his grave as a token of continuing respect.

Further Reading

Beck, Harold T. *Cornplanter Chronicles: A Tale of the Legendary Seneca Chief*. Custer City, Pa.: Mountain Laurel Pub., 2001.

Fitzpatrick, Michael G. "The Canandaigua Treaty: A Saga of War and Peace on the Old Frontier, 1775–1795." Unpublished master's thesis, St. Bonaventure University, 2000.

Francello, Joseph A. *Chief Cornplanter (Gy-ant-wa-kia) of the Senecas*. Allentown, Pa.: Glasco Pub., 1998.

Taylor, Alan. *The Divided Ground: The Northern Borderland of the American Revolution*. New York: Alfred A. Knopf, 2006.

Tiro, Karim M. "A 'Civil' War? Rethinking Iroquois Participation in the American Revolution," *Explorations in Early American Culture* 4 (2000): 148–165.

Williams, Glenn F. *Year of the Hangman: George Washington's Campaign against the Iroquois*. Yardley, Pa.: Westholme, 2005.

Cornstalk (ca. 1720–1777)
Shawnee chief

Cornstalk (Hokoleskwa) was probably born in western Pennsylvania around 1720, a member of the Mekoche division of the Shawnee Indian nation. Little is known of his youth, but it is surmised that he sided with France throughout the French and Indian War against England, and subsequently supported Pontiac's Rebellion in 1763. He was briefly taken hostage and brought to Fort Pitt but escaped back to his home village. Afterward he served as a voice of moderation and conciliation with whites and sought peaceful accommodation. That same year, to forestall the outbreak of future hostilities, Parliament passed the PROCLAMATION OF 1763, which forbade white settlements beyond the Appalachian Mountains. Never seriously enforced and outright ignored by settlers, it failed to placate Native Americans in their dire quest to preserve traditional hunting grounds. In 1768 the Iroquois of New York apparently ceded their claim to Kentucky, and Virginia's royal governor, John MURRAY, Lord Dunmore, was determined to seize as much land as possible. Using the recent massacre of illegal squatters on Indian land as a pretext, he ordered a full mobilization of the militia in what has come to be known as "Lord Dunmore's War." Cornstalk repeatedly parleyed with the governor to forestall violence, but the whites proved inflexible and unrelenting. When Cornstalk's own brother, Silver Heels, was shot and wounded outside Fort Pitt on a peace mission, the Shawnee had no choice but to raise the war hatchet. They did so unsupported, as the Cherokee under OCONOSTOTA and other tribes had been bribed by officials into staying neutral.

At length the English launched two large columns of militia into the heart of Shawnee territory, one commanded by the governor and the other by Colonel Andrew LEWIS. Badly outnumbered, Cornstalk decided to pounce on the nearest force before both could unite. On October 10, 1774, his warriors ambushed Lewis at Point Pleasant at the mouth of the Kanawha River (modern West Virginia) and a tremendous battle ensued. Both sides sustained around 150 casualties before Cornstalk decided that the contest was lost and withdrew. When Lord Murray caught up with him, he readily acceded to the Treaty of Camp Charlotte, which renounced all Shawnee claims to Kentucky.

Once the Revolutionary War broke out in 1775, Cornstalk advised his people to reject overtures from both Americans and Britains and remain neutral. He managed to pursue a peaceful course despite two years of armed provocation, and in November 1777 he visited Fort Randolph at Point Pleasant to assess white intentions. These became perfectly clear when he and his son were seized, detained, and finally murdered in their jail cell. The Shawnee were enraged by his death, which precipitated a frontier conflict that lasted until 1795, more than a decade following American independence.

Further Reading
Barr, Daniel P. "Contested Land: Competition and Conflict along the Upper Ohio River, 1774–1784." Unpublished Ph.D. diss., Kent State University, 2001.
Calloway, Colin G. " 'We Have Always Been the Frontier': The American Revolution in Shawnee Country," *American Indian Quarterly* 16, no. 1 (1992): 39–52.
Hinderacker, Eric. *Elusive Empires: Constructing Colonialism in the Ohio Valley, 1763–1800.* New York: Cambridge University Press, 1997.
Hurt, R. Douglas. *The Ohio Frontier: Crucible of the Old Northwest, 1720–1830.* Bloomington: Indiana University Press, 1996.
McConnell, Michael M. *A Country Between: The Upper Ohio Valley and Its Peoples, 1724–1774.* Lincoln: University of Nebraska Press, 1992.

Morgan, John G. *A Point in History: The Battle of Point Pleasant.* Huntington, W.Va.: Discovery Press, 2001.

Cornwallis, Charles (first marquis and second earl Cornwallis) (1738–1805)
English military officer

Charles Cornwallis was born in London, England, on December 31, 1738, the scion of an established aristocratic family. Educated at Eton, he was trained in military art by a Prussian officer, distinguished himself throughout the Seven Years' War, and by 1762 was colonel of the 33rd Regiment. That year his family connections held him in good stead when he became aide-de-camp to King GEORGE III. Despite his association with wealth and privilege, Cornwallis proved himself a Whig by inclination and outwardly sympathetic to the colonies. A member of both the House of Commons and Lords as of 1760, he opposed the STAMP ACT and worked for its repeal. Cornwallis rose to major general in 1775 and, while he opposed war with America, dutifully volunteered his services to the king. In the spring of 1776 he accompanied General Henry CLINTON in the ill-fated attack on CHARLESTON on June 28 and subsequently landed at New York to served under General William HOWE. As the Continental ARMY under General George WASHINGTON was soundly driven into New Jersey that fall, Cornwallis commanded the advance guard and pursued the fleeing Americans up to the Pennsylvania border. Like many British officers, he believed that the war was nearly over and applied to visit England and attend his sick wife when Washington suddenly struck back at TRENTON on December 26, 1776. Cornwallis canceled his trip, rode 50 miles back to camp, and aggressively attacked Washington's camp. However, the "Old Fox," as he came to be known, brilliantly side-stepped Cornwallis and successfully stormed PRINCETON on January 3, 1777. Cornwallis then returned to England, loudly criticized by Clinton and others for allowing the Americans to escape.

Cornwallis returned to America in the spring of 1777 and accompanied General Howe's campaign against Philadelphia. On September 11, 1777, he led a brilliant flanking action that nearly routed the Americans at BRANDYWINE and figured prominently in blunting Washington's determined counterthrust at GERMANTOWN on October 4, 1777. He then returned to England to confer with Lord George GERMAIN, where the two men struck common ground in their dislike for the sullen, uncommunicative General Clinton. Cornwallis consequently received promotion to lieutenant general and returned to America, still subordinated to Clinton but making no secret of his desire to succeed him as commander in chief. Cornwallis again fought capably at the drawn battle of MONMOUTH on June 28, 1778, after which he visited England a third time to bury his wife. Cornwallis acutely felt her loss and sought to compensate through further military distinction. He received his chance in the spring of 1780 when General Clinton decisively shifted the locus of war southward.

Cornwallis was present at the successful siege of CHARLESTON in May 1780, and once Clinton returned to New York he finally received his long-coveted independent command of 8,000 men. In a display of tactical wizardry he aggressively smashed the Americans under General Horatio GATES at CAMDEN on August 16, 1780, and unleashed the cavalry of Lieutenant Colonel Banastre TARLETON to beat down various bands of partisans. It appeared that Cornwallis was on the verge of conquering North Carolina when a sudden resurgence by frontiersmen destroyed his light infantry under Major Patrick FERGUSON at KING'S MOUNTAIN on October 7, 1781. Defeat here forced the British back into South Carolina for several months, and during this interval the American position was demonstrably improved with the arrival of Cornwallis's foil, General Nathanael GREENE. Preliminary maneuvering by Tarleton against General Daniel MORGAN resulted in complete destruction of British forces at COWPENS on January 17, 1781, prompting Cornwallis to give a vigorous chase of the fleeing Americans, but to no avail. Two months later Greene posted his entire army of 4,500 men on a strong position at GUIL-FORD COURTHOUSE and bid the British to attack. Cornwallis, aggressive as ever, took the bait on March 15, 1781, and attacked with 1,900 men, winning a costly victory. He then fell back on his communications to Wilmington before committing one of the war's fateful decisions. Tired of Clinton's slow and methodical strategy and politically backed by Lord Germain in London, Cornwallis violated orders and plunged directly into Virginia to join British forces already stationed there.

For several weeks during the summer of 1781 Cornwallis enjoyed a measure of success against episodic militia forces. However, after failing to trap the army of the marquis de LAFAYETTE at Green Spring on July 6, 1781, he fell back to YORKTOWN, where he entrenched and awaited reinforcements. The moment of decision was at hand.

British general Charles Cornwallis, an honorable and proud officer, led a brilliant attack against American soldiers at Brandywine and countered General Washington's move toward Germantown in October 1777. *(National Portrait Gallery, London)*

Generals Washington and Jean-Baptiste, comte de ROCHAMBEAU, quickly executed a speedy march from New York to Virginia with 15,000 troops and trapped Cornwallis within his works. When the Royal Navy under Admiral Thomas GRAVES failed to dislodge a French fleet under Admiral François-Joseph-Paul, comte de GRASSE, on September 5–10, 1781, the British had little recourse but surrender. On October 19, 1781, the proud Cornwallis was forced to capitulate 8,081 men, thereby concluding the major military operations on land. The Revolutionary War, for all intended purposes, had ended.

Cornwallis was exchanged and returned home but, shielded by his political connections, no blame was attached to him for the disaster. He then engaged in a lengthy pamphlet war against Clinton until 1786, when he gained appointment as field marshal and governor-general of India. He served capably there and in Ireland before dying at Ghazipur, India, on October 5, 1805. A brave leader of real merit, Cornwallis failed to adjust his strategy and tactics to the realities of war in the New World. By perpetually underestimating his adversaries and failing to see events beyond the next battlefield, he laid the seeds for Britain's ultimate defeat.

Further Reading

Hairr, John. *Guilford Courthouse: Nathanael Greene's Victory in Defeat, March 15, 1781.* Cambridge, Mass.: Da Capo Press, 2002.

Hallahan, William H. *The Day the Revolution Ended.* New York: Wiley, 2004.

Ketchum, Richard M. *Victory at Yorktown: The Campaign That Won the Revolution.* New York: Henry Holt, 2004.

Konstam, Angus. *Guilford Courthouse, 1781: Lord Cornwallis's Ruinous Victory.* Westport, Conn.: Praeger, 2004.

Patterson, Benton R. *Washington and Cornwallis: The Battle for America, 1775–1783.* Lanham, Md.: Taylor Trade Pub., 2004.

Wilson, David K. *The Southern Strategy: Britain's Conquest of South Carolina and Georgia, 1775–1780.* Columbia: University of South Carolina Press, 2005.

Cowpens, Battle of (January 17, 1781)

In early January 1781 American forces under General Nathanael GREENE departed North Carolina and slipped across the border into South Carolina. He had previously divided his little army by sending a 600-man detachment under General Daniel MORGAN westward in an attempt to lure British forces while he advanced upon a major supply depot at Cheraw. British general Charles CORNWALLIS, once apprised of this seemingly fatal maneuver, immediately sought to destroy the Americans piecemeal before they could unite. On January 6, 1781, Lieutenant Colonel Banastre TARLETON, commanding the feared British Legion, rode off with 1,000 picked men to hunt down and destroy Morgan. Tarleton, as usual, drove his troops mercilessly and quickly gained on the Americans, who began withdrawing toward the Broad River. When it became apparent to Morgan that he could not outrun the hard-charging Tarleton, and that his retreat was cut off by the river to his rear, his chose to stand and fight at an obscure pasture known locally as the Cowpens. This was a small, open field with few natural obstacles and a slight rise at the northern end, where Morgan posted his forces, now reinforced to 1,000 men by the arrival of partisans under General Andrew PICKENS.

Although Cowpens offered few tactical advantages to defenders and, in fact, appeared to facilitate Tarleton's famous cavalry tactics, Morgan deployed his men with skill and guile. His first rank consisted of sharpshooters who were instructed to fire three volleys at the oncoming British—hitting as many officers as possible—and then fall back behind the rise. The second line consisted of Pickens's partisans, good fighters and crack shots, but still unequal to meeting the redcoats head on. These men were also ordered to unleash three volleys before retiring in good order behind the third and final line. This consisted of a small brigade of Maryland Continentals under Colonel Otho Holland WILLIAMS, who deployed them across the high ground in full view of the enemy. Lurking behind the whole was a squadron of Continental dragoons under Colonel William WASHINGTON, with orders to remain hidden until the last moments of battle. All told, Morgan's tactics represented a clever use of his limited manpower and played brilliantly to the strength of each group. He also counted on Tarleton's renowned impetuosity to work in his favor and ultimately carry the day. Morgan was confident his stratagem would succeed, and on the night before battle he visited all ranks, carefully reviewing what was expected of them and exhorting them to fight bravely.

Early on the morning of January 17, 1781, Tarleton's cavalry trotted within range of Morgan's pickets, who emptied several saddles before falling back. The main British body then appeared after a forced march and speedily deployed with light infantry in the center and dragoons on either flank. True to form Tarleton, without bothering to reconnoiter Morgan's position, galloped up and ordered an immediate advance. The battle unfolded precisely as planned: The British marched up in excellent discipline under a withering fire and the militiamen continually fell back as ordered. As Tarleton's main line finally closed with Williams's Continentals, he ordered the 17th Light Dragoons to pursue and destroy the fleeing militia. Before this maneuver transpired, the last line of Americans held firm and punished the oncoming British with accurate volleys. An unexpected crisis erupted when Williams ordered his men to meet a body of Highlanders moving around his flank and several commanders interpreted the move as a retreat. Confusion in the American line emboldened the British, who charged the top of the rise, only to have Williams's command suddenly halt, face out, and deliver a devastating point-blank volley in their faces. At this precise moment Colonel Washington's dragoons charged out from behind the hill and fell upon Tarleton's right. The now rallied militia also suddenly reappeared and attacked his left. The British line collapsed under this double envelopment while Tarleton frantically ordered his British Legion troopers to charge. They fled in turn and the British commander, after trading sword cuts with Washington, galloped off in headlong flight.

Cowpens was a tactical masterpiece that greatly lifted morale throughout the south. "Bloody Ban" had been severely chastised and his army destroyed with a loss of 100 killed, 229 wounded, and 600 captured. Morgan reported only 12 killed and 61 wounded. In concert with the prior defeat at KING'S MOUNTAIN, the victory deprived Cornwallis of his best light troops and further hobbled his attempts to conquer North Carolina.

Further Reading

Babits, Lawrence E. *A Devil of a Whipping: The Battle of Cowpens.* Chapel Hill: University of North Carolina Press, 2001.

Bearss, Edwin H. *The Battle of Camden: A Documented Narrative and Troop Movement Maps.* Johnson City, Tenn.: Overmountain Press, 1996.

Buchanan, John. *The Road to Guilford Courthouse: The American Revolution in the Carolinas.* New York: Wiley, 1997.

Keithly, David. "Poor, Nasty, and Brutish, Guerilla Operations in America's First Civil War," *Civil Wars* 4, no. 3 (2001): 35–69.

Larsen, Eric H. "Catch Him and Smash Him," *U.S. Naval Institute Proceedings* 129, no. 7 (2003): 74–77.

Russell, David L. *The American Revolution in the Southern Colonies.* Jefferson, N.C.: McFarland, 2000.

Swisher, James K. "Duel in the Backwoods," *Military Heritage* 4, no. 3 (2002): 50–57.

Crawford, William (1732–1782)
American militia officer

William Crawford was born in Frederick County, Virginia, in September 1732, a son of Scotch-Irish farmers. Raised in a wilderness environment he took readily to military life and distinguished himself as a militia captain during the ill-fated expedition of General Edward Braddock in 1755. In this capacity he struck up cordial relations with Colonel George WASHINGTON, and they remained lifelong friends. After the war Crawford relocated to various localities in western Pennsylvania, which were jointly claimed by Pennsylvania and

Virginia. He amassed a personal fortune through land speculation, surveying, and the Indian trade, in all of which he proved adept. In 1770 Crawford became Washington's personal land agent for the Monongahela River Valley. He was also active in Governor John MURRAY, Lord Dunmore's war against the Ohio Valley tribes in 1774 and burned two Mingo villages. Once the Revolutionary War broke out he was commissioned colonel of the 7th Virginia Regiment, commanding it at LONG ISLAND, TRENTON, PRINCETON, and GERMANTOWN. In the fall of 1777 Crawford was reassigned to Fort Pitt, Pennsylvania, where he quarreled with General Lachlan MCINTOSH over military matters and gradually aligned himself with opposing factions under Colonel Daniel BRODHEAD. He subsequently served both men in various campaigns against the nearby Delaware and Seneca Indians. In 1781 Crawford resigned his commission and returned to his home on the frontier.

In the spring of 1782 Crawford left retirement to lead an expedition against the tribes of the Ohio River Valley. While conventional military actions against England had ceased in 1781, the Indians kept up an internecine struggle of frontier raids that claimed many settlers. Crawford, a veteran frontier fighter, conceived a punitive foray aimed at punishing hostile Delaware in their main camp. In May 1782 he led a force of 482 raw militia into the Ohio wilderness and was almost immediately detected by the Indians. On June 6 they ambushed his force, wiping out his baggage train and inflicting heavy loss. Crawford led his men out of the encirclement that night, but became separated from the main force and fell captive. The Indians, smarting from the recent massacre of Christian Delaware at Gnadenhutten in March, promptly set about torturing their captives for several days. Crawford endured their torment until June 11, 1782, when he was burned at the stake. Reportedly, the notorious LOYALIST scout Simon GIRTY, a former acquaintance of Crawford, did nothing to save him, a misdeed that increased American hatred for Girty.

Further Reading

Brown, Parker B. "The Search for the Colonel William Crawford Burn Site: An Investigative Report," *Western Pennsylvania Historical Magazine* 68, no. 1 (1985): 43–66.

Fitzpatrick, Alan. *Wilderness War on the Ohio: The Untold Story of the Savage Battle for British and Indian Control of the Ohio Country During the American Revolution.* Benwood, W.Va.: Fort Henry Publications, 2003.

Garabino, William. *Indian Wars along the Upper Ohio: A History of the Indian Wars and Related Events along the Upper Ohio and Its Tributaries.* Midway, Pa.: Midway Pub., 2001.

Hintzen, William. *A Sketchbook of the Border Wars of the Upper Ohio Valley, 1769–1794: Conflicts and Resolutions.* Manchester, Conn.: Precision Shooting, 2001.

Nestor, William R. *The Frontier War for American Independence.* Mechanicsburg, Pa.: Stackpole Books, 2004.

Scholl, Allen W. *The Brothers Crawford: Colonel William, 1722–1782, and Valentine, Jr., 1724–1777.* Bowie, Md.: Heritage Books, 1995.

Currency Act (1764)

Colonial financial affairs had been in a state of flux for over a century. To alleviate endemic shortages of hard currency, a consequence of the mercantile system, colonies began issuing paper money to facilitate the conduct of day-to-day economic life. However, uniform standards were nonexistent and the actual value of scrip varied from colony to colony. Furthermore, because paper notes were highly susceptible to depreciation, merchants in England complained to Parliament about their inability to collect colonial debts at face value. Anxious to placate such a valuable constituency, Prime Minister George GRENVILLE prevailed upon Parliament to pass the Currency Act of 1764. This mandated that no colony could print future stocks of paper money, and those bills already in circulation had to be withdrawn by a specified deadline. More important, the act outlawed the use of paper currency as legal tender throughout North America. Hereafter all bills and transactions were to be conducted in pounds sterling. From a political standpoint, the Currency Act represented a victory for the hard-money, conservative interests of England, whose success was achieved largely at colonial expense.

In sum, the Currency Act made no attempt to reform or standardize the use of paper money but rather abolished it altogether. It singularly failed to appreciate or even consider the resultant economic chaos imposed on a colonial economy almost completely dependant upon scrip. Within months working class elements of society were also deprived of an inexpensive and functional means of conducting business matters and repaying debts. The act further exacerbated a trade deficit with the homeland, and colonial assemblies protested loudly, but to no avail. Parliament, through this haughty imposition, managed to alienate the merchant classes within its colonies and set a precedent for continuing government interference in economic matters.

Further Reading

Cook, Don. *The Long Fuse: How England Lost the American Colonies, 1760–1785.* New York: Atlantic Monthly Press, 1995.

Edgar, Gregory T. *The Reluctant Break with Britain: From Stamp Act to Bunker Hill.* Bowie, Md.: Heritage Books, 1997.

Ernest, Joseph A. *Money and Politics in America, 1755–1775: A Study in the Currency Act of 1764 and the Political Economy of Revolution.* Chapel Hill: University of North Carolina, 1973.

Sosin, Jack M. "Imperial Regulation of Colonial Paper Money, 1764–1773," *Pennsylvania Magazine of History and Biography* 88, no. 2 (1964): 174–198.

Dale, Richard (1756–1826)
American naval officer

Richard Dale was born in Norfolk County, Virginia, on November 6, 1756, the son of a shipwright. He joined the merchant marine at the age of 12 and had risen to first mate by 1775. When the Revolutionary War broke out, he tendered his services to the Virginia state navy as a lieutenant until his capture the following year. LOYALIST friends prevailed upon him to switch sides, and he subsequently served on a British tender. On July 27, 1776, his vessel was captured by Captain John BARRY of the Continental brig *Lexington,* who was so impressed by the young sailor's bearing that he convinced him to rejoin the Americans. Dale consequently received a midshipman's commission in the Continental NAVY and accompanied several cruises through the West Indies and English Channel until September 1777, when he was captured again by HMS *Alert.* He was then confined to the notorious Mill Prison at Plymouth, engineered several escape attempts, and finally reached France in early 1779. There he signed on with Captain John Paul JONES as a gunnery officer onboard the *Bonhomme Richard.* Dale fought bravely during the capture of HMS *Serapis* on September 23, 1779, receiving a severe wound. He nonetheless led the first armed party to board the British vessel and helped strike its flag. Dale next transferred with Jones to the frigate *Alliance* and then *Ariel,* again rendering useful service. In June

American naval officer Richard Dale was captured by the British three times during the course of the war. Painting by John Ford *(U.S. Naval Academy Museum)*

1781 he joined the frigate *Trumbull* under Captain Samuel Nicholson and was captured a third time by the British ships *Monk* and *Iris* the following August. Following a brief captivity Dale was exchanged and ended the war as captain of the privateer *Queen of France.*

After the war Dale resumed his maritime activities and made several trips to China. However, in 1794, after the Barbary pirates began seizing American vessels for ransom, he was commissioned one of six captains in the new United States Navy. He subsequently served throughout the Quasi-War with France, 1798–1800, and later resigned in a dispute over rank with Captain Thomas Truxtun. The issue of Dale's seniority was resolved by President Thomas JEFFERSON, who then dispatched him on an expedition against the Barbary pirates in 1801. He reached the Mediterranean that July and spent several months blockading the port of Tripoli before returning home in March 1802. Dale resigned his commission later that year and moved to Philadelphia where, in the War of 1812, he served on the city's defense committee. Dale died in Philadelphia on May 23, 1826, a leading naval figure of his day.

Further Reading

Brown, John H. *American Naval Heroes.* Boston: Brown, 1899.
Hannon, Bryan. *Three American Commodores.* New York: J. Tartell, 1935.
Ireland, Bernard. *Naval Warfare in the Age of Sail: 1650–1850.* London: Cassell, 2000.
Miller, Nathan. *Sea of Glory: The Continental Navy Fights for Independence.* Mountain Pleasant, S.C.: Nautical and Aviation Press, 2000.
———. *The Age of Fighting Sail, 1775–1815.* New York: Wiley, 2000.
Morris, Charles. *Heroes of the Navy in America.* Philadelphia: J. B. Lippincott, 1907.

Darragh, Lydia (ca. 1729–1789)
Quaker midwife and spy

Lydia Barrington was born in Dublin, Ireland, around 1729; in 1753 she married William Darragh, a clergyman's son, through which union she had nine children. She soon after migrated with her family to Philadelphia, becoming a respected member of the Quaker community there. Darragh, a small, fragile-looking woman, found employment in the arduous business of midwifery and also sewed burial clothing for the deceased. She was present in the city in October 1777 when it was captured by British forces under General William HOWE. Thereafter, her house on 2nd Street was directly across from the general's headquarters. As a nurse, Darragh apparently enjoyed some freedom of movement between the lines and attended to sick refugees. She also became quite alarmed when her son rejected his Quaker leanings and joined the Continental army as a lieutenant.

Darragh's greatest contribution to the Revolution occurred on the evening of December 2, 1777. Apparently the British determined to use her house for a strategy session and, being Quakers, no subterfuge was suspected. Darragh and her family were summarily told by officers to go to bed while the meeting convened, but she placed her ear to the keyhole and overheard their intentions. Apparently Howe had decided upon a secret nighttime march from Philadelphia to Whitemarsh, Pennsylvania, where he hoped to surprise the army of General George WASHINGTON in camp. Darragh opened up her needle book and furiously jotted down details of the operation, intending to convey them to American headquarters personally. On the morning of December 4 she told her husband that she was going to Pearson's Mill, several miles from town, to purchase flour. With an empty sack over her shoulder, she then received permission to pass through the British lines and began walking 13 miles toward the American camp. After hiking several hours she fortuitously encountered an American cavalry patrol commanded by Colonel Thomas Craig, an old acquaintance. Once informed of her intent, Craig safely deposited Darragh at a nearby house and hurriedly galloped off to Washington's headquarters with the information. Consequently, when Howe appeared before Whitemarsh on December 6, the Americans were ready and rebuffed all attempts to attack them.

Darragh continued living in Philadelphia after the war, dying there on December 28, 1789. Many versions of her famous deed exist, which may in fact be apocryphal, but a character very much like Lydia Darragh surfaced in the memoirs of Elias BOUDINOT, who at that time was in charge of army intelligence for the Philadelphia region.

Further Reading
Bohrer, Melissa L. *Glory, Passion, Principle: The Story of Eight Remarkable Women at the Core of the American Revolution.* New York: Atria Books, 2004.
Darragh, Henry. "Lydia Darragh, One of the Heroines of the Revolution," *Publications of the City Historical Society of Philadelphia* no. 13 (1916): 277–303.
Jackson, John W. *Whitemarsh, 1777, Impregnable Stronghold.* Fort Washington, Pa.: Historical Society of Fort Washington, 1984.
Taafe, Stephen R. *The Philadelphia Campaign, 1777–1778.* Lawrence: University Press of Kansas, 2003.

Davidson, William Lee (1746–1781)
American militia leader

William Lee Davidson was born in Lancaster County, Pennsylvania, in 1746, and he accompanied his family to North Carolina four years later. He joined the militia in 1767 and assisted Governor William TRYON in resolving a boundary dispute with the Cherokee Indians. When war erupted in 1775 Davidson served with the Rowan County Committee of Safety and was subsequently commissioned a major in the 4th North Carolina Infantry in April 1776. He then fought under Colonel Francis NASH at the battle of GERMANTOWN on October 4, 1777, winning promotion to lieutenant colonel. After tours in other regiments and a harsh winter at Valley Forge, he led the new 3rd North Carolina Infantry down south in 1779. He missed the siege of CHARLESTON in May 1780, owing to an extended family visit, and was not present when his regiment was captured. Davidson then transferred to the militia and commanded a battalion at the Battle of Ramseur's Mills, on June 20, 1780. He fell severely wounded at Coulson's Mills a few weeks later and spent the next two months recuperating. Davidson was then promoted to brigadier general and replaced General Griffith RUTHERFORD, who had been captured. For several months he operated guerrilla bands in concert with Colonel William DAVIE against numerous LOYALIST outposts. In December 1780 Davidson reported for duty under General Daniel MORGAN at the Pacolet River and was off on recruiting service when the Battle of COWPENS was won, January 17, 1781.

At this time the British under General Charles CORNWALLIS were strongly pursuing the forces of General Nathanael GREENE, and Davidson was instructed to guard the Catawba River crossings with his 300 militiamen. On February 1, 1781, British advanced forces under Generals Alexander LESLIE and Charles O'HARA began fording under fire from Davidson's militia on the other bank. Both British generals lost their horses in midstream and nearly drowned, but elements of the Guards brigade managed to cross farther upstream and threatened to take the Americans from behind. Davidson then rallied his soldiers and attacked the British before they could consolidate their bridgehead, when he was shot and killed. The action ended with cavalry under Lieutenant Colonel Banastre TARLETON harrying the fleeing militia and defeating them again at Tarrant's Tavern later that day. Davidson's remains were eventually recovered and buried. Davidson College, North Carolina, was so christened in his honor.

Further Reading
Bartholomees, J. Boone. "Fight or Flee: The Combat Performance of the North Carolina Militia in the Cowpens-Guilford Courthouse Campaign, January–March, 1781." Unpublished Ph.D. diss., Duke University, 1977.
Buchanan, John. *The Road to Guilford Courthouse: The American Revolution in the Carolinas.* New York: Wiley, 1997.
Davidson, Chalmers G. *Piedmont Partisan: The Life and Times of Brigadier General William Lee Davidson.* Davidson, N.C.: Davidson College, 1951.
Graham, William A. "General William Lee Davidson," *North Carolina Booklet* 13 (July 1913): 11–39.
Rankin, Hugh F. *The North Carolina Continentals.* Chapel Hill: University of North Carolina Press, 1971.

Williams, Samuel C. "Generals Francis Nash and William Lee Davidson," *Tennessee Historical Quarterly* 1, no. 3 (1942): 250–268.

Davie, William Richardson (1756–1820)
American militia leader

William Richardson Davie was born in Egremont, England, on June 20, 1756, the son of a manufacturer. He migrated with his family to the Waxhaws district of South Carolina in 1763. He was well-educated at a local academy and subsequently passed through the College of New Jersey (Princeton) with honors in 1776. He then returned home to study law and serve in the local militia, but in April 1779 Davie was commissioned a lieutenant in the Continental ARMY and commanded a cavalry troop under Colonel Kazimierz PULASKI. In this capacity he fought under General Benjamin LINCOLN at Stono Ferry, Georgia, on June 20, 1779, receiving severe injuries. Davie needed several months to recuperate before retaking the field in the spring of 1780. At that time he raised a cavalry troop at his own expense and operated as part of guerrilla forces under General Thomas SUMTER. Davie fought well at Hanging Rock, South Carolina, on August 6, 1780, winning promotion to colonel. Sumter's ensuing defeat at Fishing Creek on August 18, 1780, left Davie with the only band capable of organized resistance. On September 21, 1780, he planned and fought his finest action at Wahab's Plantation, North Carolina. Taking 80 cavalry and 70 riflemen, Davie surprised a detachment of the feared British Legion under Major George HANGER, routing them in a charge that inflicted 60 casualties and captured 96 horses. North Carolina was then being occupied by General Charles CORNWALLIS, who advanced rapidly upon the capital at Charlotte. On September 21 Davie, accompanied by only 20 riflemen, ambushed the British advanced guard on the outskirts of town and drove them off. This stout fight was promptly concluded once the British brought up more men, but it halted Cornwallis's entire army for several minutes.

The turning point of the war in the south occurred in December 1780 when General Nathanael GREENE arrived in North Carolina with a small force of Continentals. Upon hearing of Davie's prowess and administrative abilities, Greene ordered him to become his commissary general—an arduous and largely thankless task. Davie protested his transfer but finally accepted it and performed well. His efforts kept Greene's army supplied and functioning long enough to finally best the British in North Carolina. After the war Davie resumed legal activities and also ran for the state legislature in 1786. Two years later he was a leading figure at the Constitutional Convention and strongly endorsed ratification. In 1789 Davie proved a moving force behind chartering the University of North Carolina at Chapel Hill. He was elected governor in 1799 and also received an appointment as brigadier general in the U.S. Army during the difficulties with France. After venturing to France as a peace commissioner and then negotiating a treaty with the Tuscarora Indians in 1802, he retired to his plantation in Lancaster County, South Carolina. In 1812 President James MADISON thought highly enough of Davie to offer him a major general's commission, but he declined. Davie died at home on November 29, 1820, one of the most adept partisan leaders of the Revolutionary War.

Further Reading

Buchanan, John. *The Road to Guilford Courthouse: The American Revolution in North Carolina.* New York: Wiley, 1997.

Edgar, Walter B. *Partisans and Redcoats: The Southern Conflict That Turned the Tide of the American Revolution.* New York: Morrow, 2001.

Hamilton, Joseph G. R., and Kemp P. Battle. *William Richardson Davie, A Memoir.* Chapel Hill: The University, 1907.

Robinson, Blackwell P. *The Revolutionary War Sketches of William R. Davie.* Raleigh, N.C.: Department of Cultural Resources, 1976.

Tomberlin, Bruce M. "William Richardson Davie." Unpublished master's thesis, University of North Carolina, 1942.

Dayton, Elias (1737–1807)
American military officer

Elias Dayton was born in Elizabethtown, New Jersey, on May 1, 1737, the son of a militia officer. He inherited an interest in military life from his father, joined the colonial militia in 1756, and fought with General James Wolfe at Quebec in 1759. Dayton subsequently campaigned at Detroit during Pontiac's uprising in 1763, prior to resettling back at Elizabethtown as a merchant. He then served on the local committee of safety in December 1774 and, after hostilities with Great Britain broke out, was commissioned colonel of the 3rd New Jersey Continentals in January 1776. He then assisted General William ALEXANDER by capturing the British transport vessel *Blue Mountain Valley* off Sandy Hook on January 23, 1776. Dayton then marched his men to New York, where they helped construct Fort Stanwix and Fort Dayton. His regiment subsequently rejoined the main army under General George WASHINGTON outside Philadelphia, fighting well at BRANDYWINE and GERMANTOWN in 1777. The following year Dayton performed exceptionally well at MONMOUTH on June 28, 1778, and severely harassed the retreating British. In 1779 he transferred to the division under General John SULLIVAN and accompanied him during his extended raid into the Iroquois heartland. After orchestrating the destruction of Runonvea, New York, he transferred back to his native state of New Jersey as part of General William MAXWELL's brigade.

In June 1780 General Wilhelm von KNYPHAUSEN left New York and invaded New Jersey with a large force. Dayton, still with Maxwell, fought well during the Battle of Springfield on June 23, 1780, greatly assisting the enemy's repulse there. The following winter he proved instrumental in helping to suppress the mutiny of the New Jersey Line at Pompton in January 1781. The following March he assumed command of the 2nd New Jersey Continentals and accompanied General Washington into Virginia that fall. Dayton was present at YORKTOWN, where he commanded a brigade of 1,300 troops. And, at a time when other officers sought out high political office, Dayton remained in the army until the very end of hostilities. Just prior to his discharge he was promoted to brigadier general at Washington's behest.

After the war Dayton resumed his merchant activities back in Elizabethtown and also gained election to the state assembly. He then served as major general of militia and as a member of CONGRESS, 1787–88, before dying at Elizabeth on October 22, 1807.

Further Reading

Coriell, Mrs. Abner S. "Major General Elias Dayton, 1737–1807," *Union County Historical Society Proceedings* 2 (1923/1934): 204–211.

Dayton, Elias. " 'The Drum Beats to Arms . . . ': Two Letters from Yorktown and a Missing Map," *Princeton University Library Chronicle* 31, no. 3 (1970): 209–213.

———. "Papers of General Elias Dayton," *New Jersey Historical Society Proceedings* 9 (1864): 175–194.

Dayton, Hughes. "Elias Dayton, Brigadier General, Continental Line of New Jersey," *Society of the Cincinnati in the State of New Jersey. Historical Papers* (1901): 17–31.

Fehlings, Gregory E. "Act of Piracy: The Continental Army and the Blue Mountain Valley," *New Jersey History* 115, nos. 3–4 (1997): 60–70.

Fleming, Thomas. *The Battle of Springfield*. Trenton: New Jersey Historical Society, 1975.

Lender, Mark F. *The New Jersey Soldier*. Trenton: New Jersey Historical Commission, 1975.

Deane, Silas (1737–1789)
American diplomat

Silas Deane was born in Groton, Connecticut, on December 24, 1737, the son of a blacksmith. He passed through Yale College in 1761 and was admitted to the bar but evinced a great talent for business and social climbing. Buoyed by two wealthy marriages, he eagerly pursued land speculation in western Pennsylvania and amassed a considerable fortune. Deane was also aware of his growing political profile in Connecticut, so in 1767 he actively opposed the TOWNSHEND DUTIES and subsequently served on the local COMMITTEE

OF CORRESPONDENCE. In 1772 he gained election to the colonial assembly, which he deftly used as a springboard for further advancement. In the fall of 1774 he was chosen by the assembly to accompany Roger SHERMAN and Eliphalet Dyer to the Continental CONGRESS as delegates. Deane distinguished himself by securing the funds for the Fort Ticonderoga expedition of Colonels Benedict ARNOLD and Ethan ALLEN. However, he did not get along with Sherman personally, and by the end of 1775 the Connecticut assembly failed to reelect him to CONGRESS. Unperturbed, Deane continued circulating among his fellow merchant delegates in Philadelphia, and in March 1776 he was appointed American agent to France. That fact that he spoke no French and was completely unversed in the nuances of diplomacy was further proof of his influence with fellow delegates.

Deane arrived at Paris in the spring of 1776, where he was to purchase clandestinely arms and equipment for the Continental ARMY. To that end he maneuvered with noted playwright Pierre A. C. de Beaumarchais and helped orchestrate efforts by the dummy company Roderigue, Hortalez et Cie to funnel arms and money to America. The venture proved successful, and the weapons he procured greatly assisted the victory at Saratoga in October 1777. However, Deane erred gravely by befriending and enlisting Dr. Edward BANCROFT as a spy, for he was actually an English double agent. In this manner Bancroft inadvertently compromised American diplomatic secrecy at the highest levels. Meanwhile, Deane had also been tasked with recruiting professional European army officers to assist the fledgling war effort. He proved singularly unqualified for so sensitive a mission and commissioned a number of incompetent adventurers, although two conspicuous successes were the marquis de LAFAYETTE and Johann de KALB. Nonetheless, Congress began evincing suspicions over Deane's handling of finances, and in December 1776 it dispatched Benjamin FRANKLIN and Arthur LEE to "assist" him in his duties.

Together with his new mentors, Deane helped persuade Charles Gravier, comte de VERGENNES, to tender diplomatic recognition to the United States and cement a formal alliance. He was on hand to sign the FRENCH ALLIANCE in February 1778, whereby military and economic assistance was transformed from covert to overt. However, Lee remained highly suspicious of Deane's motives and openly charged him with profiteering and misuse of public funding. Lee's influential friends in Congress heeded his remonstrances, and by August 1778 Deane had been summoned back to Philadelphia to answer these charges. A political row ensued as Deane forcefully defended himself, and neither side could prove conclusively or refute the accusations. Proceedings for and against Deane proved so vitriolic that Henry LAURENS, president of Congress, resigned his position and was replaced by John JAY, a Deane ally. After a two-year struggle Deane, nearly bankrupt, returned to England to secure evidence that would clear his name. Instead he ended up penning a series of letters to political friends suggesting that America should seek reconciliation with Great Britain. When these letters subsequently appeared in a LOYALIST newspaper, Deane was publicly condemned as a traitor. He remained abroad for the rest of his life, usually in the house of his friend Dr. Bancoft. Both men, having previously manipulated the stock market with insider diplomatic intelligence, could have been prosecuted for this and other schemes. On September 23, 1789, Deane boarded a ship in London, then suddenly fell ill and died. Historians have since speculated that he may have been poisoned by Bancroft to preclude any chance of revealing their prior activities.

Further Reading
Bill, Shirley A., and Louis Gottschalk. "Silas Deane's 'Worthless' Agreement with Lafayette," *Prologue* 26 (1994): 18–22.

Bloom, Richard. "Silas Deane: Patriot or Renegade?" *American History Illustrated* 13 (November 1978): 32–42.

Coy, James H. *Silas Deane, Patriot or Traitor?* East Lansing: Michigan State University Press, 1975.

Goldstein, Kalman. "Silas Deane: Preparation for Rascality," *Historian* 43, no. 1 (1980): 75–97.

Halsted, Janet G. "Silas Deane: Intelligence Agent and Ambassador for the Continental Congress." Unpublished master's thesis, Southern Connecticut State University, 1999.

Obringer, David. "Silas Deane: The Disillusionment of a Patriot." Unpublished master's thesis, St. Bonaventure University, 1985.

Declaration of Independence (July 4, 1776)

By the spring of 1776, American resentment against 12 years of parliamentary missteps crested in moves toward independence from Great Britain. Prior to this point most colonial leaders were undecided, or even openly opposed, to the notion of severing ties with the motherland. Not surprisingly, many inhabitants evinced a strong attachment to Britain and waxed proudly in their rights as Englishmen. Thus, when the First Continental CONGRESS convened in Philadelphia in 1774, they met largely for the purpose of denouncing Parliament, endorsing economic retribution in the form of boycotts, and petitioning King GEORGE III for redress. Reconciliation, not independence, was the common denominator behind such actions. The outbreak of hostilities at Lexington and CONCORD in April 1775 neatly coincided with the gathering of the Second Continental CONGRESS in May but, again, the issue of independence remained a secondary concern. In fact, moderate factions represented by John DICKINSON remonstrated continually against it and, furthermore, submitted the so-called Olive Branch Petition to the monarch, pledging continuing allegiance to the English Crown. However conciliatory American intentions may have been at this juncture, they went unnoticed by the English government. In August 1775 the king not only refused to receive Dickinson's petition, he also unilaterally declared the colony of Massachusetts in a state of open rebellion. This stance, coupled with the Prohibitory Act of December 1775, which authorized naval blockades of the colonies, prohibitions against their trade, and the impressment of their sailors, served to harden attitudes on both sides of the Atlantic. The final nail in reconciliation's coffin was the decision to hire thousands of HESSIANS, or German mercenaries, for military service in America, which made the colonial polity recoil.

In January 1776 the impetus for independence quickened dramatically when the radical English expatriate Thomas PAINE issued his famous polemic, COMMON SENSE. It called for colonials to completely reevaluate their relationship to, not simply the British Empire, but also the very concept of monarchy itself. Paine's use of clear, forceful writing, which enunciated complex Enlightenment precepts in language suitable for a mass audience, began mobilizing public sentiment in favor of independence from England. Colonial legislatures, taking cues from this upsurge in popular support, started instructing delegates in Philadelphia to approve independence when and if the issue came up for a vote. Congress began testing the waters that February when delegate James WILSON of Pennsylvania composed a rambling, 6,000-word document calculated to prepare the public for independence—but which was immediately tabled for further discussion. On June 7, 1776, Virginia delegate Richard Henry LEE initiated the turning point by formally introducing a motion for a break with Britain. To facilitate the outcome, a committee comprised of Thomas JEFFERSON, John ADAMS, Robert R. LIVINGSTON, and Roger SHERMAN was tasked with drafting a statement about independence. Even at this late date many delegates from the Middle Colonies proved hesitant to embrace such radicalism, and it was not until July 2, 1776, after nearly a month of heated debate, that Lee's motion finally carried. Jefferson had labored to draft a formal declaration of independence and, once vetted by Adams and Franklin, it was introduced to the delegates and passed on July 4, with New York abstaining. It contained only three proposals, but the first, and by far the most important, unequivocally declared that ". . . these United Colonies are, and of Right ought to be, Free and Independent States." President of Congress John HANCOCK then directed that the document be disseminated to all the colonies for public scrutiny and consumption. The declaration was finally signed by 56 delegates on August 2, 1776. It remains a seminal document in American history.

As an expression of political thought, the Declaration of Independence was steeped in Enlightenment principles, chiefly those of English political theorist John Locke, and was presented in Jefferson's lofty and artfully crafted prose. It also drew upon the philosophy of natural law to underscore the consent of the governed as the sole legitimate basis for governance and enunciated no less than 18 specific grievances against the king. The Declaration of Independence was first read to a crowd at Philadelphia on July 8 and greeted with wild enthusiasm. The delegates at the Second Continental Congress had finally achieved the political legitimacy they coveted. Moreover, after a year of armed struggle, the revolutionaries now possessed a concrete objective for which to fight: a nation of their own.

Further Reading
Armitage, David. "The Declaration of Independence and International Law," *William and Mary Quarterly* 59, no. 1 (2002): 39–64.
Bailyn, Bernard. *To Begin the World Anew: The Genius and Ambiguity of the American Founders.* New York: Alfred A. Knopf, 2003.
Barthelmas, Della G. *The Signers of the Declaration of Independence: A Biographical and Genealogical Reference.* Jefferson, N.C.: McFarland, 2003.
Dershowitz, Alan M. *America Declares Independence.* Hoboken, N.J.: John Wiley & Sons, 2003.
Gerber, Scott D. *The Declaration of Independence: Origins and Impact.* Washington, D.C.: Congressional Quarterly, 2002.
Gragg, Rod. *The Declaration of Independence: The Story Behind America's Founding Document and the Men Who Created It.* Nashville, Tenn.: Rutledge Hill Press, 2005.
McIlwane, Charles H. *The American Revolution: A Constitutional Interpretation.* Clark, N.J.: Lawbook Exchange, 2005.

Deux-Ponts, Guillaume de (1754–1807)
French military officer

Wilhelm von Forbach (Guillaume de Deux-Ponts) was born in Zweibrücken, in Germany's Rhineland, in 1754, son of Christian IV, duke of Zweibrücken —one of the 300 or so principalities of what later became Germany. Because his mother was a French woman of common origin, he was cut from the line of succession to the Crown but allowed to enroll in Zweibrücken's tiny, one-regiment army. Since 1757, when the duke reached an agreement with King Louis XV of France, this regiment had found regular employment as part of the French army, where it was known as the Royal Deux-Ponts. Deux-Ponts himself joined the regiment as a lieutenant in 1772 and within five years had risen to lieutenant colonel. In the fall of 1779 the French government began mobilizing an expeditionary force to assist the Americans, and General Jean-Baptiste, comte de ROCHAMBEAU, its commander, specifically requested the Royal Deux-Ponts to accompany him —a singular honor. It embarked at Brest on April 6, 1780, and, after a voyage of 70 days, disembarked at Newport Rhode Island. Deux-Ponts remained in garrison with his troops for nearly a year before marching first to New York and then to Virginia in concert with American forces under General George WASHINGTON. The allies then penned in a British army under General Charles CORNWALLIS at YORKTOWN, systematically ringing his position with an intricate system of siege lines.

On the night of October 14, 1781, Deux-Ponts, assisted by Major Ludwig von CLOSEN, was tasked with storming Redoubt No. 9, a significant point of the British defenses. This was undertaken in concert with a simultaneous American attack under Colonel Alexander HAMILTON upon Redoubt No. 10. Taking 400 veteran grenadiers and chasseurs of the Royal Deux-Ponts and Gatinais regiments, Deux-Ponts charged the works under the cover of darkness, meeting stiff resistance. The French lost 20 percent of their manpower in a brief, savage fight of only seven minutes, but the redoubt was taken. As Deux-Ponts hastily reorganized his line against a possible counterattack, he was wounded by fragments tossed by a cannonball and evacuated. The French army nevertheless hailed him as the hero of Yorktown and he received the honor of transporting captured British flags back to King

Louis XVI in Paris. There the king also awarded him with the prestigious Order of St. Louis and command of the 3rd Chasseur Regiment.

Deux-Ponts continued in the employ of France until July 25, 1791, when he resigned after being implicated in the attempted flight of the king from revolutionary France. He then sought and received employment in Bavaria and commanded the palace guard of Maximilian I. He died there in 1807, a lieutenant general.

Further Reading
Deux-Ponts, William de. *My Campaigns in America: A Journal Kept by Count William de Deux-Ponts, 1780–81.* Boston: J. K. Wiggin and W. P. Lunt, 1868.
Selig, Robert A. "George Washington's German Allies," *Journal of the Johannes Schwalm Historical Association* 6, no. 4 (2000): 52–59; 7, no. 1 (2001): 43–53; 7, no. 2 (2002): 29–43.
———. "Storming the Redoubts," *MHQ* 8, no. 1 (1995): 18–27.
———. "A German Soldier in New England during the Revolutionary War: The Account of George Daniel Flohr," *Newport History* 65, no. 2 (1993): 48–65.
Tross, Rudolph K. *The Zweybrucken or Royal Deux-Ponts Regiment and Yorktown.* Translated and edited by Wolf Prow. Yorktown, Va.: York County Bicentennial Committee, 1981.

Dickinson, John (1732–1808)
American politician

John Dickinson was born in Talbot County, Maryland, on November 13, 1732, the son of a judge. He initially studied law in Philadelphia before venturing to England and receiving his law degree from London's Middle Temple in 1757. Dickinson returned home and opened a law practice in Philadelphia while also serving in the Delaware assembly. In 1762 he relocated to Philadelphia and was elected to the Pennsylvania legislature, where he clashed with Benjamin FRANKLIN and Joseph GALLOWAY over proprietary government. However, with the passage of the STAMP ACT in 1764, Dickinson emerged as a leading and articulate spokesman for the colonial opposition. He subsequently served with the Stamp Act Congress and drafted a declaration demanding its repeal. However, unlike many radicals, Dickinson was firmly in the moderate camp; while he opposed tax measures as unconstitutional, he never advocated violence or breaking with Great Britain. In 1767 Parliament passed the TOWNSHEND DUTIES, and Dickinson responded with his famous pamphlet, *Letters from a Farmer in Pennsylvania,* which supported nonimportation of British goods but—again—stood squarely in the corner of reconciliation.

The rapidly escalating confrontation between Britain and its colonies culminated in the COERCIVE ACTS of 1774, whereupon Dickinson was elected a delegate to the First Continental CONGRESS. There he again condemned parliamentary arbitrariness over the issue of taxation and urged the colonies to make preparations for defending themselves. After fighting began in April 1775, Dickinson was elected a delegate to the Second Continental Congress. But he clung stubbornly to hopes for better relations with England and crafted the so-called Olive Branch Declaration for King GEORGE III. In it the signers pledged their continuing allegiance to the English Crown and called upon the monarch to repeal the Coercive Acts and other illegal measures. When the king summarily refused to receive the petition, the political stock of moderates like Dickinson declined measurably. He nevertheless voted against the DECLARATION OF INDEPENDENCE in July 1776; once independence was ratified, he removed himself from Congress and accepted a colonelcy in the Pennsylvania militia. Before leaving, Dickinson also helped write the ARTICLES OF CONFEDERATION to establish a legitimate government.

Dickinson participated in the New Jersey campaign of 1776, lost his seat in Congress, and was reelected from Delaware. After withdrawing from politics and the military for further reflection, he rejoined the militia as a private and fought at the battle of BRANDYWINE as a private. He subsequently served as a brigadier general of the Pennsylvania militia but saw no further action. In 1779 he resumed his seat in Congress but resigned two years later to serve as president of the Executive Council of Delaware. In 1787 Dickinson attended the Constitutional Convention back in Philadelphia, where he advocated adoption of stronger, centralized government. In 1800 he aligned himself with the Democratic-Republicans and campaigned on behalf of Thomas JEFFERSON for the presidency. Dickinson died in Wilmington, Delaware, on February 14, 1808. Never popular among his more radical contemporaries, they nonetheless respected his expository talents and regarded him as the "penman of the Revolution."

Further Reading
Ahern, Gregory S. " 'Experience Must Be Our Only Guide': John Dickinson and the Spirit of American Republicanism." Unpublished Ph.D. diss., Catholic University of America, 1997.
DeValinger, Leon. "John Dickinson and the Federal Constitution," *Delaware History* 22, no. 4 (1987): 299–308.
Flower, Milton E. *John Dickinson, Conservative Revolutionary.* Charlottesville: Published for the Friends of the John Dickinson Mansion by the University Press of Virginia, 1983.
McDonald, Forrest, and Ellen McDonald. "John Dickinson, Founding Father," *Delaware History* 23, no. 1 (1988): 24–38.
Munroe, John A. *Colonial Delaware: A History.* Wilmington: Delaware Heritage Press, Delaware Heritage Commission, 2003.

Dickinson, Philemon (1739–1809)
American militia officer

Philemon Dickinson was born in Talbot County, Maryland, on April 5, 1739, the son of a judge. He was a younger brother of John DICKINSON. In 1759 he graduated from the College of Philadelphia (University of Pennsylvania) and briefly clerked in a law office with his brother. Dickinson abandoned law shortly after and withdrew to run his father's estates. In 1767 he married and relocated to a farm outside of Trenton, New Jersey. He was still residing there in 1775, when a colonelcy in the New Jersey militia was proffered. He accepted and the following October rose to brigadier general while also holding a seat in the state's provincial congress.

Unlike many militia officers, Dickinson fought well during General George WASHINGTON's retreat across New Jersey and particularly distinguished himself at the Battle of TRENTON, December 24, 1776. In the heat of battle he unflinchingly shelled and damaged his own house, then being used as an enemy command post. Dickinson continued leading his untrained men aggressively, and on January 20, 1777, he attacked and routed a British foraging party at Somerset Courthouse, capturing three dozen wagons and over 100 horses. The following June he rose to major general and commander in chief of New Jersey militia. In this capacity he repelled an attack upon Trenton by Major John Maitland on May 9, 1778, and performed useful service during the pursuit of General Henry CLINTON out of Philadelphia. Dickinson and his 800 men felled trees and destroyed bridges in his path, slowing Clinton down long enough for Washington to advance with the main body and fight the Battle of MONMOUTH, June 28, 1778. The following August he stood as a second while his cousin, General John Cadwalader, dueled with General Thomas CONWAY over his disparaging remarks about General Washington. Dickinson and his militia also fought surprisingly well during the repulse of General Wilhelm von KNYPHAUSEN at Springfield on June 23, 1780.

Throughout the war years, Dickinson was also active politically. Despite his popularity with the troops, he failed in three bids to become governor of New Jersey in 1778–80, although in 1782 he gained appointment as a delegate to the Second Continental CONGRESS. Two years later he functioned as vice president of the New Jersey state council, and in 1784 he joined Robert MORRIS and Philip J. SCHUYLER on a commission tasked with locating a new federal capital. In 1790 Dickinson was tapped to serve out the remainder of William Paterson's term in the U.S. Senate, where he remained until 1793. The energetic Dickinson died at Trenton on February 4, 1803, one of the war's most accomplished militia leaders.

Further Reading

Dickinson, Wharton. "Philemon Dickinson, Major General, New Jersey Militia—Revolutionary Service," *Magazine of American History* 7 (December 1881): 420–427.

Fleming, Thomas. *The Battle of Springfield.* Trenton: New Jersey Historical Society, 1975.

Kwasny, Mark V. *Washington's Partisan War, 1775–1783.* Kent, Ohio: Kent State University Press, 1996.

Lefkowitz, Arthur S. *The Long Retreat: The Calamitous American Defense of New Jersey, 1776.* New Brunswick, N.J.: Rutgers University Press, 1999.

Lender, Mark F. *The New Jersey Soldier.* Trenton: New Jersey Historical Commission, 1975.

Yesenko, Michael. *Connicut Farms, June 7, 1780.* Union, N.J.: The Author, 1993.

Dragging Canoe (ca. 1750–1792)
Cherokee chief

Dragging Canoe (Tsiyu-Gunsini) was born around 1750 near the Little Tennessee River, a son of Chief Attakullakulla of the Overland Cherokee tribes. Nothing is known of his youth, but by 1775 he was a significant war chief among the Overland peoples of Tennessee and positioned to challenge the authority of existing senior chiefs like OCONOSTOTA. In this capacity he vehemently opposed the Treaty of Sycamore Shoals, which ceded the region of Kentucky and a large swath of Tennessee to colonials. The treaty was nonetheless concluded, and Dragging Canoe angrily stormed out of the session, promising Indian agent Richard Henderson to turn this region into "a dark and bloody ground." The chief then began plotting attacks on American frontier settlements in the vicinity of Watauga, Tennessee. In July 1776, just as hostilities were about to commence, Dragging Canoe's plan was revealed to the Americans by his cousin, Nancy WARD, herself an important tribal figure. Her action spared many lives and Dragging Canoe's attack was eventually defeated at Island Flats by reinforcements commanded by John SEVIER. The hostile Cherokee bands then retreated to their villages but made repeated forays against the North Carolina, Virginia, and Georgia frontiers. The following year vengeful Patriot forces destroyed the offending villages, and Dragging Canoe relocated his followers to new settlements on Chickamauga Creek, deep inside Tennessee. Aided by British supplies from Florida, he continued his campaign of frontier harassment. The Americans countered by raiding his Chickamauga villages in 1779 and 1782, which again forced him to resettle farther west. After these villages were finally destroyed in 1784 Dragging Canoe agreed to suspend hostilities.

The onset of peace did little to mitigate Dragging Canoe's intractable hostility to white encroachment. In 1791 Tennessee territorial governor Willie Blount entered into negotiations with the tribe and many Cherokee leaders, exhausted by their struggle, readily acquiesced to American demands for land. Dragging Canoe, as usual, strongly dissented. He spent the last months of his life attempting to build a southern Indian confederation to repel the invaders and met repeatedly with noted Creek chief Alexander MCGILLIVRAY and others. He died on his return trip at Running Water Village, Tennessee, on March 1, 1792, before his dreams could be realized. Dragging Canoe ultimately failed in his attempt to curb land sales, but he mounted the only serious opposition to white encroachment for two decades.

Further Reading

Alderman, Pat. *Nancy Ward, Cherokee Chieftainess, Dragging Canoe, Chickamauga War Chief.* Jefferson City, Tenn.: Overmountain Press, 1978.

Cox, Brent A. "Heart of the Eagle: Dragging Canoe and the Emergence of the Chickamauga Confederacy." Unpublished master's thesis, University of Memphis, 1996.

Dennis, Jeffrey W. "American Revolution and Native Americans: The South Carolina Experience." Unpublished Ph.D. diss., University of Notre Dame, 2002.

Evans, E. Raymond. "Notable Persons in Cherokee History: Dragging Canoe," *Journal of Cherokee Studies* 2, no. 1 (1977): 176–189.

Hatley, M. Thomas. *The Dividing Paths: Cherokees and South Carolinians through the Era of Revolution.* New York: Oxford University Press, 1993.

Rhoden, Nancy L., and Ian K. Steele, eds. *The Human Tradition in the American Revolution.* Wilmington, Del.: Scholarly Resources, 2000.

Drayton, William Henry (1742–1779)
American politician

William Henry Drayton was born at Drayton Hall, South Carolina, in September 1742, the son of a wealthy planter. Like many aristocratic sons he was educated in England and attended Westminster School and Oxford. Drayton came home in 1763 and enhanced his wealth and social standing by marrying into the colony's richest family. In 1765 he also gained a seat in the General Assembly, where he evinced conservative attitudes toward imperial relations with England. Drayton vigorously defended the STAMP ACT of that year and, consequently, lost his seat in the following election. He then went on to write and publish *The Letters of a Freeman*, which condemned the growing practice of nonimportation. In the face of mounting unpopularity, Drayton decided to visit England in 1771 for a sinecure to recognize his loyalty to the Crown. He was widely feted at court and consequently received appointment to the provincial council back in Charleston. Drayton came home and was seated, but his ambitions for advancement were continually thwarted by the practice of appointing Englishmen to all positions of high office. He applied for numerous colonial offices and judgeships only to have them filled by what he deemed as "strangers." By August 1774 an angry Drayton was ready to change sides, and he inveighed against the British government for imposition of the COERCIVE ACTS against Boston. His outspoken defiance led to suspension from the provincial council in March 1775.

When hostilities finally commenced in April 1775, Drayton became one of South Carolina's most outspoken proponents of rebellion. He was elected to the provincial congress, led raids against British armories, and helped secure money and weapons for the militia. In July the revolutionary council on safety dispatched him on a six-week tour of the Carolina backcountry to drum up support for the rebellion. His efforts were largely negated by a sizable LOYALIST presence but he did manage to conclude a neutrality agreement with their leaders at Fort Ninety Six in September. Drayton subsequently served as president of the provincial congress and helped establish a state navy while authorizing attacks upon Royal Navy vessels at Charleston to precipitate a war with England. Failing that, on February 6, 1776, he openly endorsed independence from Great Britain and sponsored a state constitution to replace the old royal charter. He then served as chief justice of South Carolina until his election to the Second Continental CONGRESS in February 1778.

Drayton proceeded to Philadelphia and energetically chaired or participated in almost 90 committees. Here he sought to protect southern interests and stridently opposed all attempts at reconciliation with England. Strong-willed and outspoken, he made several enemies in his brief stay at Philadelphia, most notably fellow South Carolinian Henry LAURENS. He also openly questioned the commitment of General Charles LEE to the revolution and nearly fought a duel. Over it, Drayton's promising career as a national figure of note suddenly ended on September 4, 1779, when he died of typhus.

Further Reading

Bledsoe, Julia G. "The Failure of Colonial Government and the American Revolution in South Carolina." Unpublished master's thesis, College of William and Mary, 1996.

Dabney, William M. *William Henry Drayton and the American Revolution.* Albuquerque: University of New Mexico Press, 1962.

Drayton, William H. *The Letters of a Freeman, etc.; Essays on the Non-Importation Movement in South Carolina Collected by William Henry Drayton.* Columbia: University of South Carolina Press, 1976.

Horne, Paul A. "William Henry Drayton and the Articles of Confederation," *Proceedings of the South Carolina Historical Association* (1990): 23–29.
Krawczynski, Keith. *William Henry Drayton: South Carolina Revolutionary Patriot*. Baton Rouge: Louisiana State University Press, 2001.
Snapp, J. Russell. "William Henry Drayton: The Making of a Conservative Revolutionary," *Southern History* 57, no. 4 (1991): 637–658.

Dumas, Mathieu (1753–1837)
French military officer

Mathieu Dumas was born in Montpelier, France, on November 23, 1753, part of an aristocratic family. He became a cadet in 1769 and four years later was commissioned a second lieutenant with the Medoc Regiment in May 1773. By spring 1780, when General Jean-Baptiste Donatien de Vimeur, comte de ROCHAMBEAU, was assembling a general staff for his forthcoming American expedition, Dumas, an excellent and enterprising young officer, advanced to captain and became one of his six aides-de-camp. He arrived with the French fleet at Newport in late summer 1780 and the following September attended the conference with General George WASHINGTON at Hartford, Connecticut. The following month Rochambeau tasked him with finding winter quarters for the cavalry legion of Comte Armand Louis de LAUZUN in nearby Lebanon, and he competently fulfilled his charge. In August 1780 Dumas accompanied the main French army from New York on its epic march to YORKTOWN, Virginia, to partake of the siege of General Charles CORNWALLIS. On October 17, 1781, he attended the surrender ceremonies and turned back General Charles O'HARA's attempt to yield his superior's sword to Rochambeau. In a final play of chivalry, Dumas curtly directed O'Hara over to the American side and General George Washington. He remained in Virginia with the main force and subsequently rose to chief of staff on a proposed expedition to the Caribbean but ultimately returned to France as a major in July 1783. His published memoirs capture many important details of French military operations in America.

Back home Dumas served with the general staff of the army, and he served on military missions to Turkey, 1784–85, and the Netherlands in 1787. That year he participated in the unsuccessful defense of Amsterdam against the Prussians, returned to Paris, and gained promotion to colonel. After the French Revolution commenced in 1789 Dumas quickly allied himself with progressive forces under the marquis de LAFAYETTE and he sat with the legislative assembly. However, the bloody excesses of the Jacobins forced him to flee the country, and he remained exiled until summoned home by Napoéon in 1799. Dumas then resumed his military career under the First Empire, seeing distinguished service against Austria, Prussia, Spain, and Russia. He was captured at Dresden in 1813 and, after the restoration of King Louis XVII the following year, he fulfilled military administrative functions. Dumas supported Napoéon during the 100 Days' Campaign, was stripped of his offices after the restoration, yet fell back into favor and ended up on the council of state and as a peer of France by 1830. He died in Paris on October 16, 1837, a valuable witness to two revolutions.

Further Reading
Chartrand, Rene. *The French Army in the American War of Independence*. London: Osprey, 1991.
Dumas, Mathieu. *Memoirs of His Own Time: Including the Revolution, the Empire, and the Restoration*, 2 vols. Philadelphia: Lea & Blanchard, 1839.
Duncan, Kenneth A. "Mathieu Dumas: A Biography." Unpublished Ph.D. diss., University of St. Andrews, 1974.
Howard, C. Rice, and Anne S. K. Brown. *The American Campaigns of Rochambeau's Army, 1780, 1781, 1782, 1783*, 2 vols. Princeton, N.J.: Princeton University Press, 1972.
Nicolai, Martin L. "Subjects and Citizens: French Officers and the North American Experience, 1755–1783." Unpublished Ph.D. diss., Queen's University, 1992.
Scott, Samuel F. *From Yorktown to Valmy: The Transformation of the French Army in an Age of*

Revolution. Niwot.: University Press of Colorado, 1998.

Duportail, Louis (1743–1802)
French military officer

Louis Le Beque de Presle Duportail was born in Pithiviers, France, on May 14, 1743, the son of a king's councillor. Like many aristocrats, he prepared for a military career by attending the engineering school at Mezières, from which he graduated in 1765. Duportail served capably for a decade, rose to captain, and gained the reputation of an efficient engineer before presenting his credentials to Benjamin FRANKLIN in 1776. He was then hired as an engineer and dispatched by boat to America, arriving there in the spring of 1777. Duportail became a colonel in the Continental ARMY and joined the staff of General George WASHINGTON on July 29, 1777. The American military was then in dire need of professional expertise and the youthful aristocrat acquitted himself well in various capacities. After fighting at BRANDYWINE and GERMANTOWN he rose to brigadier general and commandant of the Corps of Engineers as of November 17, 1777. He subsequently endured a grueling winter at Valley Forge and spent the time imposing a unified command structure on his troops, as well as expertly fortifying the American encampment. He next fought at MONMOUTH on June 28, 1778, before being dispatched to supervise construction of defenses in the Hudson Highlands. There he reputedly quarreled with Colonel Tadeusz Kościuszko over building techniques before transferring to South Carolina as part of the army of General Benjamin LINCOLN. Duportail partook in the siege of CHARLESTON but arrived too late to greatly contribute to affairs and fell captive in May 1780. He was exchanged a few weeks later before returning to Washington's staff in New York.

In spring 1781 Duportail functioned as an important military adviser when Washington conferred with his French counterpart, General Jean-Baptiste-Donatieu de Vireur, comte de ROCHAMBEAU, over a proposed attack upon New York.

French officer Louis Duportail was a key military adviser to General Washington in 1781. *(Independence National Historical Park)*

In view of allied weakness, he urged caution and the attack was canceled. Duportail subsequently accompanied Washington on his decisive march to YORKTOWN and planned the intricate siege lines that forced General Charles CORNWALLIS to capitulate that October. As a reward for his contributions to victory, he was promoted to major general the following November. Duportail returned to France in 1783, where he served as a brigadier general and helped reorganize the Neapolitan army, 1783–88. Following the outbreak of the French Revolution he gained appointment as minister of war in November 1790 but served only a year before gaining promotion to major general and command of the Moulins region in January 1792. But Duportail, owing to his friendship with the firmly royalist marquis de LAFAYETTE, fell under increasing political suspicion as the revolutionary violence escalated. Anticipating the worst, he resigned from office in December 1792 and fled France for America. He lived on a small farm outside Philadelphia, warmly welcomed by his former friends, until his name was struck from the proscription list. Duportail sailed back to France to join the army of Napoléon Bonaparte in 1802 but died en route and was buried at sea. Despite his youth, he was one of the most capable and popular French officers employed by the United States.

Further Reading

Buzziard, Raleigh B. "Washington's Most Brilliant Engineer," *Military Engineer* 41 (September–October 1949): 358–365.

Heathcothe, Charles W. "General Chevalier Louis Lebeque Duportail—Devoted to the United States and Washington," *Picket Post* no. 63 (February 1959): 14–21.

Kite, Elizabeth. *Brigadier General Louis Lebeque Duportail, Commandant of Engineers in the Continental Army, 1777–1783*. Baltimore: Johns Hopkins University Press, 1933.

Nicolai, Martin L. "Subjects and Citizens: French Officers and the North American Experience, 1755–1783." Unpublished Ph.D. diss., Queen's University at Kingston, 1992.

Walker, Paul K. *Engineers of Independence: A Documentary History of the Army Engineers in the American Revolution, 1775–1783*. Washington, D.C.: Historical Division, Office of the Chief of Engineers, 1981.

Watts, Arthur P. "A Newly Discovered Letter of Brigadier General Duportail," *Pennsylvania History* 1 (April 1934): 103–106.

Elbert, Samuel (ca. 1740–1788)
American military officer

Samuel Elbert was probably born around 1740 in Prince William Parish, South Carolina, the son of a Baptist minister. Orphaned as a child, he eventually settled in Savannah, Georgia, and flourished as a merchant. Marriage into one of the colony's wealthiest families ensured his social and political status, and by 1769 he was closely identified with conservative elements of the Patriot faction. Elbert fully embraced resistance toward Great Britain and joined both the local SONS OF LIBERTY and the extralegal Georgia Provincial Congress. His military experience was restricted to a stint in the Georgia Grenadiers as a captain, but in early 1776 he became lieutenant colonel of the 1st Georgia Continental Infantry under Lachlan MCINTOSH. In this capacity he confronted and rebuffed a Royal Navy attempt to take on supplies at Savannah in March 1776 during the so-called Battle of the Riceboats. This act further enhanced his reputation, and the following September he succeeded McIntosh as colonel of the regiment when the latter rose to brigadier general. However, owing to a political struggle between that officer and the president of Georgia, Elbert became the compromise candidate to lead an ill-fated invasion of British-held East Florida. In 1777 and again in 1778 Elbert led two malnourished, undermanned, and undersupplied columns against LOYALISTS under Colonel Thomas BROWN. He managed to capture several outposts and vessels before manpower and supply shortages forced him back. That fall he formed part of Savannah's defenses under General Robert HOWE and was present at the defeat of Fairlawn Plantation on December 29, 1778, when Lieutenant Colonel Archibald CAMPBELL secretly turned the American position. Elbert managed to escape the disaster and fled to South Carolina with the remnants of his command.

Elbert gradually reconstituted the 1st Georgia Continentals, and the following spring he formed part of the army under General John ASHE. On March 3, 1779, the Americans were encamped at Briar Creek when a British force under Colonel Mark Prevost managed to gain their rear and charged. Ashe's force, composed mostly of raw militia, wilted under the assault but Elbert's regulars stood firmly on the right flank, allowing them to escape. A staunch fight ensued before the Continentals were overwhelmed and captured. Elbert remained a prisoner until his exchange in June 1781. He then joined the army of General George WASHINGTON at YORKTOWN, where he commanded the "general deposit of stores and military arms." In recognition of his military service Elbert was promoted to brevet-brigadier general in 1783 along with major general of the Georgia militia.

After the war Elbert worked diligently to rebuild his commercial activities, and in 1785 the legislature appointed him governor by a unanimous vote. His single term in office proved uneventful save for legislation chartering the state university. Afterward poor health restricted Elbert to a succession of minor offices, and he died in Chatham County at the age of 48 on November 1, 1788. Despite an uneven and unlucky career in the field, he is regarded as Georgia's most capable military leader of the war.

Further Reading
Elbert, Samuel. "Order Book of Samuel Elbert, Colonel and Brigadier General in the Continental Army," *Georgia Historical Society Collections* 5 (1902): 5–191.
Heidler, David S. "The American Defeat at Briar Creek, 3 March 1779," *Georgia Historical Quarterly* 66, no. 3 (1982): 317–331.
"Letters, Colonial and Revolutionary," *Pennsylvania Magazine of History and Biography* 42 (January 1918): 75–85.
Purcell, Clarice E. "The Public Career of Samuel Elbert." Unpublished master's thesis, University of Georgia, 1951.
Searcy, Martha C. *The Georgia-Florida Contest in the American Revolution, 1776–1778.* Tuscaloosa: University of Alabama Press, 1985.
Smith, Gordon B. "The Georgia Grenadiers," *Georgia Historical Quarterly* 64, no. 4 (1980): 405–415.

Estaing, Charles-Hector-Théodat, comte d' (1729–1794)

French naval officer

Charles-Hector-Théodat, comte d'Estaing, was born in Château de Ruvel, Auvergne, France, on November 24, 1729, part of an ancient aristocratic family. His father was a lieutenant general and, as such, he was preened for a military career early in life. D'Estaing served as an officer during the War of the Austrian Succession and rose to colonel at the age of 19. He then served with distinction throughout the Seven Years' War, 1756–63, gaining promotion to brigadier general at age 27. While campaigning in India he was captured by the English, released, and captured again while serving on a French privateer. D'Estaing endured a spell of harsh confinement for violating his parole and came to hate the English. By war's end he had risen to lieutenant general and was installed as governor-general of Saint-Domingue (Haiti) in 1763. Being interested in naval affairs he used his social standing to acquire the rank of vice admiral in 1777.

After the FRENCH ALLIANCE with the United States was concluded in the spring of 1778, D'Estaing assumed command of the first French forces to intervene in the Revolutionary War. He departed Toulon on April 13, 1778, and caused quite a stir among British naval officials, but he sailed leisurely and crossed the Atlantic in three months. This dilatory pace enabled General Henry CLINTON to evacuate Philadelphia without interference from the French fleet. D'Estaing subsequently dropped anchor off New York in July, where he found a smaller English squadron under Admiral Richard HOWE deployed and waiting to receive him. However, d'Estaing felt the harbor insufficiently deep to work his vessels inland so he canceled an attack in favor of joint operations against Newport, Rhode Island. There he was to cooperate closely with American forces under General John SULLIVAN, but d'Estaing, a haughty aristocrat, could scarcely disguise his contempt for such rag-tag allies. Worse, once Howe's fleet was reinforced and also arrived off Newport to assist the garrison of General Richard PIGOT, d'Estaing promptly abandoned the siege, recalled his forces to the fleet, and sallied to give battle. On August 10, 1778, both combatants were badly damaged by a sudden storm and d'Estaing declared his intention to sail to Boston for repairs. His departure abandoned Sullivan to carry on the siege alone. Resentment against French behavior culminated in violence against d'Estaing's officers on September 8, 1778. When he subsequently sailed for the West Indies—without informing General George WASHINGTON— he left the Franco-American alliance in near tatters.

D'Estaing enjoyed better success advancing French interests in the Carribean. In June and July 1779 he captured the British-held islands of St.

French naval officer the comte d'Estaing commanded the first French military force to aid the Americans against the British, in 1778. *(Bridgeman Art Library)*

Vincent and Grenada and, on July 6, he roughly handled a British fleet commanded by Admiral John BYRON. However, many subordinates privately complained that he broke off the action too early and should have easily captured Byron's fleet intact. Nonetheless, on August 16, 1779, d'Estaing boarded 4,000 troops and sailed from Haiti for the Georgia coast, there to cooperate with forces under General Benjamin LINCOLN. He arrived ahead of the Americans and began a siege of SAVANNAH that proved so leisurely that British forces under General Augustin PREVOST were reinforced and strongly entrenched. Once American troops under Lincoln arrived matters proceeded apace, but d'Estaing waxed anxiously about the onset of stormy weather. He therefore goaded his ally into a premature assault against the British works. The ensuing battle of Savannah on October 9, 1779, proved disastrous for the allies, who lost 800 men in one of the costliest engagements of the war. D'Estaing bravely led his troops sword in hand and was badly wounded twice. He then embarked his troops and set sail for France on October 21 to the dismay of his American allies. Ironically, his effort at Savannah induced General Clinton to remove finally the British garrison at Newport, winning by default what he had failed to secure by force of arms.

Back at the French court there were few recriminations over d'Estaing's failures in America, and he forcefully lobbied to dispatch another fleet under Admiral François-Joseph-Paul, comte de GRASSE, in 1781. The following year he was slated to command a large Franco-Spanish expeditionary force but the war ended before he sailed. After the war d'Estaing continued as a high-ranking military officer, even after the breakout of the French Revolution in 1789. He was promoted to admiral and appointed commander of the Versailles National Guard by January 1792, but his close association with the French monarchy rendered him a marked man. On April 28, 1794, he was arrested and executed by radicals in Paris. Coalition warfare is difficult under the best of circumstances, and d'Estaing, overbearing, overly sensitive, and brave to the point of foolishness, was scarcely an ideal player. His record in America was less than successful but amply demonstrated France's commitment to the Patriot cause and, more important, helped pave the way for future cooperation.

Further Reading

Cogar, William B., ed. *New Interpretations in Naval History: Selected Papers from the Ninth Naval History Symposium.* Annapolis, Md.: Naval Institute Press, 1991.

Dull, Jonathan R. *The French Navy and American Independence: A Study in Arms and Diplomacy, 1774–1787.* Princeton, N.J.: Princeton University Press, 1975.

Freeman, H. Ronald. *Savannah under Siege: The Bloodiest Hour of the Revolution.* Savannah, Ga.: Freeport Pub., 2002.

Gardiner, Robert., ed. *Navies and the American Revolution, 1775–1783.* Annapolis, Md.: Naval Institute Press, 1996.

Hattendorf, John. *Newport, the French Navy, and American Independence.* Newport, R.I.: Redwood Press, 2004.

Syrett, David. "D'Estaing's Decision to Steer for Antigua, 20 November, 1779," *Mariner's Mirror* 61, no. 2 (1975): 155–162.

Ewald, Johann (1744–1813)

German army officer

Johann Ewald was born in the German state of Hesse-Kassel on March 30, 1774, the son of a shopkeeper. Despite lowborn status he was attracted to military service and joined the Regiment Gila as a private in 1760 at the age of 16. He saw active duty in the Seven Years' War, 1756–63, being severely wounded and promoted to ensign. Excellent service saw him transferred to the Guard Regiment as a second lieutenant in 1766 but, because he lacked a noble pedigree, he was subsequently transferred to a line unit. In February 1770 his promising career almost ended when he was wounded in a frivolous duel and lost an eye. Fortunately, Ewald recovered and was allowed to study military science at the Collegium Carolinum. He then began publishing numerous and well-received texts on light infantry tactics. Ewald's renown in Germany was such that he received promotion to captain in the elite *Liebjager* Corps, a unit of rifle-equipped sharpshooters usually reserved for aristocrats. Two years later the landgrave of Hesse-Kassel decided to lease his army to Britain for service in America, and Ewald became one of several thousand HESSIANS earmarked for duty in the New World.

Ewald disembarked at New York on October 14, 1776, and was committed to battle within days of arriving. His elite troops proved themselves to be the bane of enemy outposts, for they could shoot and maneuver in wooded terrain as easily as the vaunted American riflemen opposing them. In time, Ewald's jaegers became one of the most feared units in the British army, and he struck up a close relationship with General Charles CORNWALLIS. Cornwallis tapped him to lead the decisive turning action at BRANDYWINE on September 11, 1777, where he was conspicuously engaged in fighting around Battle Hill. Ewald performed similar useful work at MONMOUTH on June 28, 1778, and helped save the British baggage train from capture. His unit was then actively employed by General Henry CLINTON throughout the siege of CHARLESTON in May 1780 and bore a conspicuous role in its surrender. Ewald subsequently accompanied Clinton back to New York and so missed the initial phases of Cornwallis's southern campaign. Throughout the summer of 1781 his jaegers were attached to forces in Virginia commanded by renegade General Benedict ARNOLD, and usually acted in concert with the Queen's Rangers under Lieutenant Colonel John Graves SIMCOE. On June 26, 1781, Ewald and Simcoe fought off a very determined attack by riflemen under Colonel Richard BUTLER at Spencer's Tavern, Virginia, until ordered to retreat. He was then present throughout the siege of YORKTOWN in the fall of 1781 and taken prisoner there. Transferred to Long Island as a prisoner, Ewald contracted a fever and nearly died. Fortunately he recovered and, as a token of respect for a gallant enemy, General Henry KNOX allowed him to inspect the defenses of West Point, New York.

Ewald and his surviving jaegers returned to Germany in May 1784, and he resumed his military service for the landgrave of Hesse-Kassel. The following year he published his most celebrated text, *Essay on Partisan Warfare,* which was hailed by King Frederick the Great of Prussia as the best treatise on the subject. However, Ewald's military advancement remained thwarted by his common birth, so in 1788 he transferred his allegiance to the royal Danish army. He performed competently there for 25 years and helped uphold Danish neutrality during the Napoléonic Wars. In 1809, forces under his command killed the renegade Prussian hussar officer, Major Ferdinand von Schill, gaining him promotion to lieutenant general. Ewald continued serving loyally until his death in Kiel, Germany, on June 25, 1813. In theory and in practice, he is considered one of the fathers of light infantry service. His memoir of service in America is also regarded as among the most lucid penned during the Revolutionary War.

Further Reading

Atwood, Rodney. *The Hessians: Mercenaries from Hessen-Kassel in the American Revolution.* New York: Cambridge University Press, 1980.

Ewald, Johann von. *Diary of the American War: A Hessian Journal.* New Haven, Conn.: Yale University Press, 1979.

———. *Treatise on Partisan Warfare.* New York: Greenwood Press, 1991.

Lobdell, Jared C. "Six Generals Gather Forage: The Engagement at Quibbletown, 1777," *New Jersey History* 102, nos. 3–4 (1984): 34–49.

Selig, Robert A. "Light Infantry Lessons from America? Johann von Ewald's Experiences in the War for Independence," *Studies in Eighteenth Century Culture* 23 (1993): 111–129.

Taylor, Peter K. "The Household's Most Expendable People: The Draft and Peasant Society in 18th Century Hessen-Kassel." Unpublished Ph.D. diss., University of Iowa, 1987.

Fanning, David (ca. 1755–1825)
Loyalist

David Fanning was born in Amelia County, Virginia, around 1755 and orphaned at an early age. He was raised in Johnson County, North Carolina, by a county justice and subsequently resettled on Raeburn's Creek in western South Carolina in 1773. He farmed and traded with nearby Cherokee Indians until the Revolution commenced in 1775. Accosted and robbed by Patriot militias, Fanning then cast his lot with the LOYALISTS and partook of military activity that captured a large Patriot force at Fort Ninety Six in November of that year. However, he was himself captured by victorious Patriots at Big Cane Brake on December 22, 1775, and imprisoned for the first of 14 times. Between confinements, Fanning proved himself an active and enterprising partisan officer who skirmished continually with American forces in what evolved into a bloody, backwoods civil war. However, by August 1779 most Loyalists were discouraged by heavy losses and Fanning, like many others, accepted a conditional pardon proffered by Governor John RUTLEDGE. He remained inactive for many months until British success at the siege of CHARLESTON and the Battle of CAMDEN rekindled the flames of Loyalist resentment. Civil strife began anew, with Fanning as one of its most artful and successful exponents.

Once the forces of General Charles CORNWALLIS invaded South Carolina in the fall of 1780, Fanning secured steady supplies of ammunition and vigorously recruited Loyalists to his band. Success proved fleeting, however, and after the American victory at KING'S MOUNTAIN, Fanning relocated operations to Deep River in North Carolina. He proved so successful that, in July 1781, Fanning transferred operations to newly captured Wilmington. There he became a colonel of Loyalist militia, and he actively raided and skirmished throughout the Carolinas, becoming one of the South's most feared partisan leaders. On September 12, 1781, Fanning scored his biggest success by taking 950 men on a surprise attack against Hillsboro, the de facto Patriot capital. His attack completely overthrew the defenders and netted Governor Thomas Burke, along with 200 prisoners. On his return to Wilmington that same afternoon he was in turn attacked at Lindley's Mill by 400 Patriots under General John Butler, who drove the Loyalists hard and might have won save for Fanning's leadership. Desperately wounded, he finally defeated the Americans and his prisoners were safely delivered. Fanning's military fortunes declined rapidly after the British withdrawal from Wilmington in November 1781, although he waged a bitter guerrilla struggle against Patriot settlements well into 1782. The following year Fanning accepted another conditional truce from the government and suspended his military activities. He then arrived in Charleston for eventual deportation to Florida in

1783. As a measure of his success as a guerrilla, Fanning was one of three men expressly forbidden by the North Carolina legislature from ever returning to the state.

After drifting several months, Fanning ultimately ended up in New Brunswick, Canada, accompanied by thousands of Loyalist refugees. There he served as part of the legislative assembly until convicted of a rape charge in 1800. Fanning successfully appealed a death sentence and was banished from New Brunswick for life, so he resettled at Digby, Nova Scotia. There he acquired considerable wealth as a shipbuilder and merchant before his death on March 14, 1825. Though reviled as a bloody partisan, Fanning was, in truth, no more violent or savage than many of his Patriot neighbors, and his experience exemplified the harsh nature of Revolutionary warfare in the backwoods regions. Fanning also bequeathed to posterity a revealing set of memoirs, one of the few written from a Loyalist perspective.

Further Reading
Butler, Lindley S., ed. *The Narrative of Col. David Fanning.* Davidson, N.C.: Briar Patch Press, 1981.
Culpepper, Kinda P. "Blood, the Tie That Binds: The Role of Scottish Clans in North Carolina Loyalism during the Revolutionary Era." Unpublished master's thesis, Western Carolina University, 1998.
Hairr, John. *Colonel David Fanning: The Adventures of a Carolina Loyalist.* Erwin, N.C.: Averasboro Press, 2000.
Massey, Gregory De Van. "The British Expedition to Wilmington, January–November, 1781," *North Carolina Historical Review* 66, no. 4 (1989): 387–411.
Newlin, Algie I. *The Battle of Lindley's Mill.* Burlington, N.C.: Alamance Historical Association, 1975.
Troxler, Carole W. *The Loyalist Experience in North Carolina.* Raleigh: North Carolina Dept. of Cultural Resources, Division of Archives and History, 1976.

Fanning, Nathaniel (1755–1805)
American naval officer

Nathaniel Fanning was born in Stonington, Connecticut, on May 31, 1755, and he entered the merchant marine at an early age. When the Revolutionary War commenced in 1775 he apparently joined a privateer and three years later, while serving onboard the *Angelica,* fell captive. A year at Forton Prison, Plymouth, lapsed before he was exchanged in 1779 and made his way to L'Orient, France. There he met and signed on as a midshipman under Captain John Paul JONES of the *Bonhomme Richard.* On September 23, 1779, Fanning served as captain of the maintop during the famous encounter against Captain Richard PEARSON of HMS *Serapis.* During intense fighting he lost most of his crewmates but took on additional sailors and helped clear the British topmasts. Once the two ships locked their rigging he crawled over a British yardarm and lobbed several grenades down an open hatch. The ensuing explosion killed 20 Britons and helped clear the main deck. Pearson subsequently struck his colors, and Jones lauded Fanning as "one cause among the prominent in obtaining the victory." He continued serving with Jones on the *Alliance* and the *Ariel* before resuming his privateering activities in 1781. He then served aboard several French vessels, being captured twice and quickly exchanged. Fanning also accepted a lieutenant's commission in the French navy but resigned following the onset of peace.

After the war Fanning returned to the United States, married, and rejoined the merchant marine. He enjoyed a successful career and later joined the U.S. Navy as a lieutenant in 1803. While performing gunboat duty at Charleston, South Carolina, Fanning died of yellow fever on September 30, 1805. He is best remembered for a highly detailed memoir outlining his tour of duty under Jones. In it he harshly criticized his superior for boorish and oftentimes cruel behavior toward crew members and fellow officers. It is considered one of the more lucid naval recollections to emerge from the Revolutionary War.

Further Reading
Barnes, John S., ed. *Fanning's Narrative: The Memoirs of Nathaniel Fanning, an Officer of the American Navy, 1778–1783.* Bowie, Md.: Heritage Books, 2003.

———. *The Log of the Serapis-Alliance-Ariel, under the Command of John Paul Jones, 1779–1780*. New York: Printed for the Naval History Society by the De Vinne Press, 1911.

Brooks, Walter E. *History of the Fanning Family*, 2 vols. Worcester, Mass.: Private Printing, 1905.

Miller, Nathan. *Sea of Glory: A Naval History of the American Revolution*. Mount Pleasant, S.C.: Nautical and Aviation Pub., 2000.

Schaeper, Thomas J. *John Paul Jones and the Battle off Flamborough Head: A Reconsideration*. New York: P. Lang, 1989.

Walsh, John E. *Night on Fire: The First Complete Account of John Paul Jones's Greatest Battle*. New York: McGraw-Hill, 1978.

Ferguson, Patrick (ca. 1744–1780)
English military officer

Patrick Ferguson was born in Scotland around 1744, the son of a jurist. He studied military science at an academy in London and in 1759 became a coronet in the Royal North British Dragoons. Recurring sickness rendered his military career intermittent for several years but, while recuperating in 1770, Ferguson conceived the idea of a viable breech-loading rifle for infantry use. He successfully developed a prototype "Ferguson Rifle" in 1775, which could fire six shots per minute as opposed to only two for a musket. More important, it could be loaded and fired while in a prone position. Ferguson prevailed upon the Woolwich arsenal to manufacture 100 rifles while he recruited a company of sharpshooters for service in America. The riflemen arrived in New York in May 1777 as part of British forces under General William HOWE and accompanied him during his campaign against Philadelphia. Ferguson fought well at the battle of BRANDYWINE on September 11, 1777, while assigned to the right wing under General Wilhelm von KNYPHAUSEN. At one point he apparently had General George WASHINGTON lined up in his sights but could not bring himself to shoot the tall, imposing officer. Ferguson's men performed exceptionally well, but he was wounded in the arm and Howe, in a fit of military conservatism, ordered their weapons re-

British military officer Patrick Ferguson developed the breech-loading rifle (six shots per minute) in 1775 and subsequently assembled a team of sharpshooters to serve in America. *(National Park Service, King's Mountain National Military Park, South Carolina)*

moved and stored. His successor, General Henry CLINTON, viewed Ferguson as an enterprising partisan officer and employed him on several raids into New Jersey. On October 4–5, 1778, he surprised a detachment under Colonel Kazimierz PULASKI, inflicting heavy losses. The following year he recruited a LOYALIST unit entitled the "American Volunteers," which accompanied Clinton throughout the siege of CHARLESTON, South Carolina. There Ferguson performed useful light infantry service in concert with two other noted leaders, Lieutenant Colonels John Graves SIMCOE and Banastre TARLETON.

With the fall of Charleston in May 1780, General Charles CORNWALLIS assumed control as theater commander and planned several aggressive forays into the interior. Ferguson, who accepted duties as inspector general of Georgia and Carolina Loyalist militia, began recruiting and training soldiers for a grueling campaign in the Carolina backcountry. In September 1780 Cornwallis began a concerted invasion of North Carolina in which Ferguson's column of 1,000 picked light infantry constituted his left wing. He had been specifically instructed to rally Loyalists to the king's banner from the hinter-most regions of the state, as well as cow Patriot militia into submission with threats and punitive measures. The American Volunteers subsequently acquired a vile reputation by burning and plundering households thought to be sympathetic to the Patriots. However, when Ferguson ordered the "over the mountain men" residing in Tennessee to submit to British rule or face fire and sword, they rallied in large numbers to meet his challenge. By October 1780 roughly 1,100 rough-hewed frontiersmen led by William CAMPBELL, Benjamin CLEVELAND, Isaac SHELBY, and John SEVIER gathered for battle and marched against the Loyalists. Ferguson, undaunted, retreated a short distance into South Carolina before occupying a strong defensive position at KING'S MOUNTAIN. On October 17, 1780, the rifle-armed Americans surrounded Ferguson and began fighting their way up the bloody slopes. Ironically, the Loyalists were still armed with muskets and gradually were whittled down. Rather than be captured, Ferguson spurred his horse down a slope and tried to escape when several well-aimed rifle bullets found him. He was the only non-American casualty of the 157 killed, 163 wounded, and 698 captured Loyalists taken that day. Consequently, Ferguson's disaster stripped the British army of some of its best light forces, stopped Cornwallis in his tracks, and postponed the invasion of North Carolina by several months.

Further Reading

Dameron, J. David. *King's Mountain: The Defeat of the Loyalists, October 7, 1780.* Cambridge, Mass.: Da Capo Press, 2003.

Gilchrist, Marianne M. *Patrick Ferguson: "A Man of Some Genius."* Edinburgh, U.K.: NMS Enterprises, 2003.

Gordon, John W. *South Carolina and the American Revolution: A Battlefield History.* Columbia: University of South Carolina Press, 2003.

Hoskins, William J. "Patrick Ferguson and the American Revolution." Unpublished master's thesis, University of South Dakota, 1984.

Swisher, James K. "Fatal Miscalculation," *Military Heritage* 2, no. 5 (2001): 68–77.

Wicker, Tom. "Turning Point in the Wilderness," *MHQ* 11, no. 1 (1998): 62–71.

Fiske, John (1744–1797)
American naval officer

John Fiske was born in Salem, Massachusetts, on April 11, 1744, the son of a clergyman. He went to sea as a cabin boy and by 21 was master of his own brigantine. When difficulties with England manifested in 1775 he also served on the Salem Committee of Safety and Correspondence. The following year, after Massachusetts had founded a state navy, he became the second captain commissioned after Jeremiah O'BRIEN. On April 20, 1776, Fiske assumed command of the brigantine *Tyrannicide* and quickly subdued four prizes by the following July. In February 1777 he shifted his flag to the brigantine *Massachusetts* and sailed in concert with other state vessels commanded by Captains Jonathan HARADEN and John Coulston during a concerted raid upon English shipping. The miniature squadron secured 25 prizes before returning to Salem the following July. Subsequent voyages in the *Massachusetts* netted more captures until October 1777, when Fiske was charged with fiscal impropriety by another naval officer. A public hearing subsequently cleared his name, but he declined to serve further in the state navy. The following year Fiske was proffered command of the vessel *Hazard*, but he refused, citing its weak armament.

The experience of war rendered Fiske a wealthy man, and after 1783 he resumed his maritime activities by purchasing ships and outfitting them for work in the Mediterranean and East Indies. In 1791 he became master of the Salem Marine Society and used his influence to install navigational aids along the Massachusetts coast. Despite his naval background, Fiske also gained appointment as major general of militia in 1792 and labored hard to improve the conditions of common soldiers. He died in Salem on September 28, 1797, a skilled sailor in a city renowned for maritime prowess.

Further Reading
Allen, Gardner W. *Massachusetts Privateers of the Revolution.* Boston: Massachusetts Historical Society, 1927.
Bentley, William. *A Funeral Discourse, Delivered in the East Meeting-House, Salem, on the Sunday after the Death of Major General John Fiske.* Salem, Mass.: Thomas C. Cushing, 1797.
Gardner, Frank A. "The Tyrannicide," *Massachusetts Magazine* 1 (April 1908): 103–107.
———. "The Massachusetts," *Massachusetts Magazine* 1 (July 1908): 195–199.
McManemin, John A. *Captains of the State Navies during the Revolutionary War.* Ho-Ho-Kus, N.J.: Ho-Ho-Kus, 1984.
Morse, Sidney G. "New England Privateering in the American Revolution." 2 vols. Unpublished Ph.D. diss., Harvard University, 1941.

Fox, Charles James (1749–1806)
English politician

Charles James Fox was born in London on January 24, 1749, a son of Henry Fox, Third Baron Holland of Foxley. As an aristocrat he was superbly educated at Eton and Oxford, displaying an impressive command of the classics, recitation, and elocution. Fox matured into a highly intelligent individual, with strong personal and political convictions, considerable charm, and a dynamic, attractive personality. He also exhibited a profound reckless streak in his private behavior, becoming addicted to gambling, drinking, and womanizing at an early age. In 1768 his father purchased a seat for him in the House of Commons, and he discovered his niche as a parliamentary debater with few equals.

Fox initially sided with the royal party, aligned himself with Lord Frederick NORTH, and generally supported British tax and trade policies up to the period of the BOSTON TEA PARTY. However, he also displayed cavalier attitudes toward party loyalty by taking up the cause of radical politician John WILKES. North nonetheless appointed him to minor posts on the Admiralty board, where he distinguished himself only for dissolute behavior. He resigned from office after disagreeing with North over the Royal Marriages Act, briefly accepted another minor post with the Treasury Board, and was finally dismissed in 1774 for opposing North's leadership. From this point on, with little interruption, Fox became the personification of Whig opposition to royal policy. As such, the straitlaced King GEORGE III, who disapproved of his flamboyance, worked assiduously behind the scenes to deny him public office.

Beginning in 1775, Fox reversed his stance on the American colonies and became one of the government's most strident critics. He accused Lord North of orchestrating dangerous, disruptive policies that threatened the very stability of the empire. Furthermore he argued for a repeal of all legislation adversely affecting colonial relations since 1763. Fox waxed critical of the conduct of military affairs and proved scathing in his denunciation of Lord George GERMAIN. He thus became the leading spokesman for opposition Whigs associated with Lord Charles WATSON-WENTWORTH, Lord Rockingham. Fox made repeated calls for reconciliation with the colonies until 1778, when, after the American victory at Saratoga and the commencement of the FRENCH ALLIANCE, he demanded recognition of American independence. Fox sincerely believed that an honorable peace would preserve favorable trade relations that had flourished prior to the Revolutionary War and also permit England to concentrate on fighting France.

With the Revolution winding down in 1782, the opposition Whigs finally returned to power under Lord Rockingham, who installed Fox as foreign secretary. In this capacity he advanced the cause of peace by opening negotiations with Benjamin FRANKLIN in Paris and preparing to recognize unconditionally American independence. However, after Rockingham's death in July 1782, control of the government passed to Prime Minister William PETTY, earl of Shelburne, a close ally of George III, who wanted the issue of independence negotiated. Fox could not be reconciled with this shift in priorities, and he resigned before the TREATY OF PARIS was concluded. The following year he and his former adversary Lord North united to undermine Shelburne's administration, and he resumed his post as foreign secretary. It proved an unworkable alliance, and that same year George III and William Pitt the Younger managed to dissolve North's coalition. Fox spent the remaining two decades as an opposition leader.

Fox, despite his reputation as a wastrel, proved himself an unswerving champion of political liberty and limitations upon government power. He unabashedly admired the French Revolution even as its violence expanded and his own influence waned because of it. In 1806 he was again appointed foreign secretary and sought to strengthen British ties to the United States. Fox died in London on September 13, 1806, a genuine friend of America and one of the most influential parliamentarians of the 18th century.

Further Reading
Conway, Stephen. *The British Isles and the War of American Independence.* New York: Oxford University Press, 2000.
Davis, Michael T. *Radicalism and Revolution in Britain, 1775–1848: Essays in Honor of Malcolm I. Thomas.* New York: St. Martin's Press, 2000.
Derry, John W. *Politics in the Age of Fox, Pitt, and Liverpool.* New York: Palgrave, 2001.
Mitchell, L. G. *Charles James Fox.* New York: Oxford University Press, 1992.
Phillips, Kevin P. *The Cousins' Wars: Religion, Politics, and the Triumph of Anglo-America.* New York: Basic Books, 2000.
Ward, Lee. *The Politics of Liberty in England and Revolutionary America.* New York: Cambridge University Press, 2004.

Francisco, Peter (ca. 1760–1836)
American soldier

Peter Francisco was around four years old when he was put ashore at Hopewell, Virginia, by an unknown merchant vessel and abandoned. He was subsequently adopted and raised by Judge Anthony Winston, Patrick HENRY's nephew, and was exposed to burgeoning republican ideology as he matured. Francisco grew into a giant of a man, literally, and was reputedly six feet, six inches in height and weighed 260 pounds. He joined the 10th Virginia Continental Infantry at the age of 15 and first saw combat at BRANDYWINE, September 11, 1777. Badly wounded, Francisco met and befriended the equally youthful marquis de LAFAYETTE, then being treated for injuries in battle. Francisco subsequently fought at GERMANTOWN and Fort Mifflin that year and was wounded again at MONMOUTH on June 28, 1778. The following year he formed part of the forlorn hope that stormed Stony Point on July 16, 1779, and was reputedly the second man to scale the British defenses. In this action he wielded a five-foot broadsword given to him by General George WASHINGTON, slaying two grenadiers.

Francisco enlisted in a militia regiment after his army enlistment expired, and he was present at the debacle of CAMDEN, South Carolina, on August 16, 1780. Despite the rout, he apparently hauled off a 1,000-pound cannon on his back to prevent its capture and then single-handedly rescued his commander, Colonel William Mayo, from being captured. Francisco then attached himself to Colonel William WASHINGTON's legion and fought at GUILFORD COURTHOUSE on March 15, 1781. In the thick of the fight as always, he allegedly killed 11 British soldiers and was found desperately wounded under a pile of enemy corpses. Francisco recovered and next tangled with nine troopers of Lieutenant Colonel Banastre TARLETON's British Legion at Ward's Tavern, Virginia. He slew two soldiers, scattered the rest, and made his escape. His last recorded activity was during the siege of YORKTOWN in 1781. After the war Francisco married and served as a combination blacksmith/tavern owner.

In 1823 he relocated to Richmond to serve as master of arms in the House of Delegates. The following year he was on hand to greet his old friend Lafayette during the latter's triumphal tour of America. He died in Richmond in 1836 around the age of 70. Being of Portuguese descent, he acquired a folkloric status among that ethnic community and is commemorated every March 15 by "Peter Francisco Day" in Virginia, Massachusetts, and Rhode Island.

Further Reading
Cook, Fred J. *What Manner of Men: Forgotten Heroes of the American Revolution.* New York: Morrow, 1959.
Eanes, Greg. *Tarleton's Southside Raid: Prelude to Yorktown.* Burkeville, Va.: E & H Pub. Co., 2002.
Edgar, Walter B. *Partisans and Redcoats: The Southern Conflict That Turned the Tide of the American Revolution.* New York: Morrow, 2001.
Gustaitis, Joseph. "One Man Army," *American History* 29, no. 4 (1994): 56–60.
Hamilton, Charles H. *Peter Francisco, Soldier Extraordinary.* Richmond, Va.: Whittet & Shepperson, 1976.
Moon, William A. *Peter Francisco: The Portuguese Patriot.* Pfafftown, N.C.: Colonial Publishers, 1980.

Franklin, Benjamin (1706–1790)
American politician, diplomat

Benjamin Franklin was born in Boston, Massachusetts, on January 17, 1706, the son of a candle maker. Scarcely educated, he worked with his brother as a printer's apprentice before immigrating to Philadelphia in 1723 with only a Dutch dollar and a copper shilling in his pocket. Fortunately, Franklin soon proved himself to be one of the most industrious, multitalented individuals of that or any other age, a man whose outward simplicity and friendly demeanor masked a cunning, percipient mind. By 1746 Franklin was highly successful as printer of the *Pennsylvania Gazette* and *Poor Richard's Almanac*, two colonial best sellers that allowed him to retire at the age of 42. He then parlayed his wealth and talent into numerous civic projects such as founding the Library Company of Philadelphia, the American Philosophical Society, and the College of Philadelphia. To this litany of accomplishments must be added his considerable skill as a scientist and inventor, whose efforts at developing the Franklin stove, bifocal glasses, and the lightning rod culminated with membership in England's Royal Philosophical Society. Franklin also proved quite adept at politics, and he served several years with the Pennsylvania assembly.

Between 1757 and 1762, and 1764 and 1775, Franklin also served as Pennsylvania's agent in London, where he became embroiled in the ongoing dispute over British imperial policies. He appeared before Parliament on several occasions, to protest the STAMP ACT of 1765, the TOWNSHEND DUTIES of 1767, the TEA ACT of 1773, and the COERCIVE ACTS of 1774. As colonial postmaster Franklin also surreptitiously obtained letters of Massachusetts governor Thomas HUTCHINSON, which were published and increased the political turmoil. When called to task for this misdeed and dismissed, he confidently predicted that if the king's ministers dispatched troops to America, "they will not find a rebellion; they may indeed make one." His final act in England was arranging for radical pamphleteer Thomas PAINE to immigrate to Pennsylvania. Franklin returned to Philadelphia in the spring of 1775, fully committed to the American cause. As a member of the Second Continental CONGRESS, he proffered sagacious advice to Thomas JEFFERSON during the drafting of the DECLARATION OF INDEPENDENCE and subsequently served on a peace commission that conferred with Admiral Richard HOWE on Staten Island in 1776. The following year he received his most daunting assignment, representing the fledgling United States at the court of Louis XVI in Versailles. The first real American diplomat, Franklin moved easily within diplomatic circles, appearing in homespun clothes and a beaver hat and posting himself as a man of the "New World." He became hailed as a celebrity at the French court and also worked with Foreign Minister Charles Gravier, comte de VERGENNES, in delicate negotiations over clandestine aid. In concert with Silas DEANE and Henry LEE, he crafted and signed two treaties comprising the essential

FRENCH ALLIANCE in February 1778, which allowed for direct military intervention on behalf of the Patriots. In 1782 he discarded congressional instructions not to negotiate a peace treaty unacceptable to France and secretly bargained with British agents. The resulting TREATY OF PARIS in 1783, which he signed with John ADAMS and Henry LAURENS, established the Mississippi River as the western boundary of the new nation at the expense of SPAIN, France's ally. Franklin's smooth personal diplomacy subsequently convinced Vergennes to accept the fait accompli graciously.

Franklin came home to an independent nation in the spring of 1785 to resume his distinguished career in politics. He served as president of the Supreme Executive Council of Pennsylvania and the Pennsylvania Society for the Abolition of Slavery. In 1788 he represented his state at the Constitutional Convention in Philadelphia and urged all delegates to adopt the newly framed federal constitution unanimously. In recognition of his litany of achievements in various fields, Franklin received honorary degrees from Harvard, Yale, Oxford, St. Andrews, and William and Mary College. He died in Philadelphia on April 17, 1790, after indelible and long-lasting contributions to science, his state, and the nation.

Further Reading
Gaustad, Edwin S. *Benjamin Franklin.* New York: Oxford University Press, 2004.
Houston, Alan, ed. *Franklin: The Autobiography and Other Writings on Politics, Economics, and Virtue.* New York: Cambridge University Press, 2004.
Isaacson, Walter. *Benjamin Franklin: An American Life.* Waterville, Maine: Thorndike, 2004.
Lemay, J. A. Leo. *The Life of Benjamin Franklin.* Philadelphia: University of Pennsylvania Press, 2005.
Morgan, Edmund S. *Benjamin Franklin.* New Haven, Conn.: Yale University Press, 2002.
Schiff, Stacy. *A Great Improvisation: Franklin, France, & the Birth of America.* New York: Henry Holt, 2005.
Strodes, James. *Benjamin Franklin: The Essential Founding Father.* Washington, D.C.: Regnery Press, 2003.
Wood, Gordon S. *The Americanization of Benjamin Franklin.* New York: Penguin Press, 2004.

Fraser, Simon (ca. 1729–1777)
English military officer

Simon Fraser was born in Balnain, Scotland around 1729. He commenced his military career in 1747 by joining the Dutch army and subsequently transferred to the English service in 1755. Fraser proved himself a competent officer and fought at Quebec under General James Wolfe in 1759. His experience in the North American wilderness also convinced him of a need for the continuing development of light infantry. By 1760 he functioned as aide-de-camp to the duke of Brunswick and fought exceptionally well throughout the Seven Years' War. His finest accomplishment occurred at Wezen on November 9, 1761, where he attacked and drove off 400 French troops with only 50

British colonel Simon Fraser commanded the 24th Regiment, one of the few British formations capable of performing as light infantry. He was renowned as a brave and daring officer. *(Clan Fraser Society of Canada)*

handpicked men. A decade later he was colonel of the 24th Regiment and, through dint of specialized training, it became one of the few British formations capable of light infantry tactics. In April 1776 Fraser was entrusted with command of five regiments that were shipped to Canada as reinforcements for Governor-General Guy CARLETON, then besieged in Quebec. On June 8, 1776, he led a force of 6,000 crack troops that routed a force of comparable size under General William THOMPSON at Trois-Rivières. Consequently, Carleton granted him a local rank of brigadier general and command of the Advanced Corps. Fraser then spearheaded the British drive into the Champlain Valley with excellent results until Carleton, wary of campaigning in winter so far from his lines of communication, returned to Canada. Fraser put the next several months to good use by drilling his troops in the essentials of light infantry warfare. Under his tutelage they became quite as adept at forest fighting as their American counterparts.

In the spring of 1777 a new commander, General John BURGOYNE, arrived at Quebec to launch a new invasion of northern New York with 8,000 seasoned troops. As expected Fraser commanded a brigade of 1,200 light troops and was joined by Generals William PHILLIPS of the artillery and Friedrich von RIEDESEL, who led the HESSIANS. The campaign commenced in June 1777, when Fraser's men spearheaded the British juggernaut south toward Fort Ticonderoga. His troops effectively screened Burgoyne's advance, seized nearby Mount Defiance from the Americans, and convinced General Arthur ST. CLAIR to abandon the fort without a fight. Fraser, who personally ran up the English flag over Ticonderoga, then took off in pursuit of the enemy, chasing him as far as Hubbardton, Vermont. There, on July 7, 1777, he managed to surprise the American rear guard under Colonel Seth WARNER and drove them out of their camp. A confused, swirling fight unfolded in the woods as the Americans began pressing the outnumbered British back, but Fraser was saved by the sudden appearance of General Riedesel's troops. The Americans lost 200 prisoners, and Fraser immediately assumed the point once Burgoyne's main body arrived. By August the British were firmly positioned at Saratoga in anticipation of a final drive upon the state capital of Albany.

Burgoyne, having badly underestimated the terrain and extent of opposition arrayed against him, experienced supply shortages by late summer, and on September 19, 1777, he conducted a reconnaissance in force against defensive lines under General Horatio GATES. Fraser was only lightly engaged on the right flank at FREEMAN'S FARM, where he drove off the vaunted riflemen of Colonel Daniel MORGAN. He then strongly urged Burgoyne to pursue the defeated enemy, but the general withdrew to camp. Mounting supply shortages prompted Burgoyne to test American resolve again, and he launched a probe of BEMIS HEIGHTS. As usual, Fraser was in the thick of the fray, and he continually rallied his outnumbered men in the face of determined attacks by General Benedict ARNOLD. His bravery and indifference to danger proved so conspicuous that Arnold reputedly informed rifleman Timothy MURPHY, "That is a gallant officer, but he must die." Murphy then climbed a tree and fired three shots at long range, mortally wounding Fraser on the last attempt. After the British were repulsed he was tended at the tent of Baroness Fredericke RIEDESEL and died the next morning. Fraser's death stunned Burgoyne's army and, when American cannon mistakenly bombarded his funeral procession, General Gates ordered them to cease and fire a salute to a fallen enemy instead. The heroic Fraser died as he lived—recklessly, at the head of his troops. He was among the best light infantry officers of the Revolutionary War.

Further Reading

Carman, W. Y. "The Burial of General Simon Fraser, Saratoga, 1777," *Journal of the Society for Army Historical Research* 48 (summer 1970): 62–65.

Fraser, Simon. "General Fraser's Account of Burgoyne's Campaign on Lake Champlain and the Battle of Hubbardton," *Proceedings of the Vermont Historical Society* (1899): 139–147.

Luzader, John F. *Documentary Study of the Death and Burial of General Simon Fraser*. Stillwater, N.Y.: Saratoga National Historic Park, 1958.

Nestor, Joseph B. "The Battle of Saratoga." Unpublished master's thesis, East Stroudsburg University, 2001.

Phifer, Mike. "Campaign to Saratoga," *Military Heritage* 2, no. 1 (2000): 40–51, 94.

Williams, John A. *The Battle of Hubbardton: The American Rebels Stem the Tide*. Montpelier: Vermont Division for Historic Preservation, 1988.

Freeman's Farm, Battle of (September 19, 1777)

In June 1777, General John BURGOYNE led a British force of nearly 9,000 men down the Champlain Valley from Canada and into northern New York. He achieved good progress initially, dislodged the American garrison at Ticonderoga without firing a shot, and also defeated their rear guard at Hubbardton, Vermont. But as Patriot forces under General Philip J. SCHUYLER fell back into densely wooded terrain, they burned bridges, felled trees, and created other obstacles that severely impeded Burgoyne's progress. On September 13, 1777, the British crossed the Hudson River on a bridge constructed of bateaux and encamped near Saratoga, a few miles from the American position at BEMIS HEIGHTS. There further progress was blocked by additional forces under General Horatio GATES, now numbering upward of 7,000 men, ensconced behind entrenchments constructed by Colonel Tadeusz KOŚCIUSZKO. By this time Burgoyne's supply situation was approaching critical, especially after the defeat of Lieutenant Colonel Friedrich BAUM at BENNINGTON on August 16, 1777. His force had now dwindled to roughly 5,000 effectives, and the general resolved to conduct a large reconnaissance in force of Gates's line near Freeman's Farm. If successful, he hoped to follow through with a decisive attack that would clear his path to Albany, 24 miles distant.

On September 19, 1777, Burgoyne deployed his men in a wooded area in the vicinity of Freeman's Farm. His right consisted of 1,500 picked troops and Indians under General Simon FRASER, who advanced toward a clearing. The British left consisted of 1,100 HESSIANS under the resourceful General Friedrich von RIEDESEL, who marched down a river road. Burgoyne then accompanied the remaining 1,100 men under General James Hamilton, who comprised the center column. This was a risky maneuver: Each British force moved over difficult terrain, and they were shielded from each other by intervening woods, so Burgoyne potentially risked defeat in detail. Nevertheless Gates declined any offensive moves for the time being and passively observed their movements from behind his fortifications. However, his forceful and unruly subordinate, General Benedict ARNOLD, urged the general to launch an attack of his own. At length Gates consented to sending a force of riflemen under Colonel Daniel MORGAN and some light infantry to contest the British right. A hot fight ensued whereby the marksmen picked off numerous officers but gradually yielded the field to British bayonets. Moreover, as Burgoyne advanced in the center he met and engaged a stream of American reinforcements intending to assist Morgan's hard-pressed command. A protracted struggle ensued with both sides alternately taking and giving ground. Arnold pleaded with Gates for additional troops to clinch the victory but the general refused and directed Arnold back into his own lines—an order he ignored. After several hours of stalemate, Burgoyne's casualties mounted to the point where his command of the field seemed threatened and he ordered Riedesel to reinforce the center. The Hessians then conducted a protracted march through a swamp and suddenly appeared on the American flank with 500 men and several cannon. Riedesel then pressed forward at bayonet point and drove his assailants off. The Americans, low on ammunition, simply fell back in good order to their fortified lines.

The fighting tapered off by nightfall, and the British were firmly in possession of the field. However, Burgoyne had suffered heavy losses, particularly in officers, totaling upward of 600 men. The 63rd Regiment alone, which at one point was nearly surrounded in the day's fighting, lost 80 percent of its strength. Gates suffered far less in proportion to the forces committed, sustaining only 300 casualties. Faced with such heavy attrition and unable to make up for his losses, Burgoyne felt obliged to fall back to camp. A heavy day of fighting and sacrifice availed the British little and in fact demonstrably weakened them for the upcoming struggle.

Further Reading
Hardinge, H. DeForest. "Saratoga: Turning Point of the Revolution," *Manuscripts* 53, no. 4 (2001): 299–308.
Ketchum, Richard M. *Saratoga: Turning Point of America's Revolutionary War.* New York: H. Holt, 1997.
Morrissey, Brendan. *Saratoga, 1777: Turning Point of a Revolution.* Oxford: Osprey, 2000.
Nestor, Joseph B. "The Battle of Saratoga." Unpublished master's thesis, East Stroudsburg University, 2001.
Phifer, Mike. "Campaign to Saratoga," *Military Heritage* 2, no. 1 (2000): 40–50, 94.
Seymour, William. "Turning Point at Saratoga," *Military History* 16, no. 5 (1999): 46–52.

French alliance (1778)

The onset of the Revolutionary Bourbon War in 1775 represented a unique opportunity for France, as American aspirations for independence dovetailed nicely with its own desire for avenging the loss of Canada in the French and Indian War. The French also surmised that, in an age of mercantilism, the corresponding loss of American colonies would severely weaken England's economic and naval dominance of Europe. As early as November 1775, when the Continental CONGRESS founded the Committee of Secret Correspondence to solicit foreign aid from abroad, French foreign minister Charles Gravier, comte de VERGENNES, began orchestrating a carefully crafted scheme of clandestine assistance. Vergennes was also keen to keep the animosity between the combatants boiling long enough to preclude any attempt at reconciliation. The bogus company of Roderigue, Hortalez et Cie was established in 1776 by noted French dramatist Pierre-Augustin Caron de Beaumarchais to funnel arms and supplies to the rebels; by 1783 French aid would amount to 35 million livres in loans and 10 million livres in grants to the Americans. Congress countered by dispatching Silas DEANE as the American agent in Paris, followed by Benjamin FRANKLIN and Henry LEE. But France professed neutrality during initial and somewhat sputtering phases of the war until the prospect of American victory justified the risk of confronting Great Britain. The victory of Saratoga in October 1777—won in large measure with weapons provided by France—proffered a convenient pretext for intervention. That December Vergennes informed the Americans of King Louis XVI's intention to enter into a formal alliance with the United States. It proved a major point in the conduct of military affairs and, by altering the strategic balance, ultimately decisive.

After several weeks of negotiations, France and the United States signed two treaties on February 6, 1778, which formalized their mutual endeavors to defeat Britain in the New World. The Treaty of Amity and Commerce conferred diplomatic recognition to the United States along with the mutual granting of most favored nation status for trade purposes. The second document, the Treaty of Alliance, stipulated direct French intervention in the American conflict should Great Britain resort to war against France. Furthermore, neither party was to seek a separate peace with England without each other's consent. The United States also vowed to help protect French possessions throughout the West Indies, while France pledged not to seek any territory in Canada held prior to 1763. Congress, spurning a new spate of English reconciliation proposals, formalized the two treaties on May 4, 1778. The French then dispatched two powerful squadrons under Admirals Charles-Hector-Théodat, comte d'ESTAING, and François-Joseph-Paul, comte de GRASSE, along with a sizable military contingent under General Jean-Baptiste, comte de ROCHAMBEAU. This infusion of roughly 12,000 soldiers, 63 warships, and 22,000 sailors allowed the United States to persevere and ultimately win a stunning triumph over the British at YORKTOWN in October 1781. The French incurred 2,112 casualties and battle deaths by war's end. Concurrently, France successfully pursued a military alliance with SPAIN, which, while Spain refused to recognize the Americans, allowed the armies of Governor Bernard de GÁLVEZ to clear Florida of the British.

The period of Franco-American amity was not long-lived and began unraveling in the wake of France's own revolution of 1789. Throughout the 1790s Presidents George WASHINGTON and John ADAMS viewed continuation of the alliance as potentially dragging the United States into ongoing European conflicts. Relations between France and the United States deteriorated into open conflict during the so-called Quasi War of 1798, which lasted at sea for two years. It was not until Napoléon Bonaparte agreed to the Convention of 1800 that the French alliance was formally revoked. The United States would not enter into such a binding military alliance again until the North Atlantic Treaty Organization (NATO) arose in 1949.

Further Reading

Hoffman, Ronald, and Peter J. Alberts, eds. *Diplomacy and Revolution: The Franco-American Alliance.* Charlottesville: Published for the United States Capitol Historical Society by the University Press of Virginia, 1981.

Hudson, Ruth S. *The Minister from France: Conrad-Alexandre Gerard, 1729–1790.* Euclid, Ohio: Lutz, 1994.

Morton, Brian N., and Donald C. Spinelli. *Beaumarchais and the American Revolution.* Lanham, Md.: Lexington Books, 2003.

Ross, Maurice. *Louis XVI: America's Founding Father, with a Survey of the Franco-American Alliance in the Revolutionary Period.* New York: Vantage Press, 1976.

Schaeper, Thomas J. *France and America in the Revolutionary Era: The Life of Jacques-Donatien Leray de Chaumont, 1725–1803.* Providence, R.I.: Berghahn Books, 1995.

Gadsden, Christopher (1724–1805)
American politician

Christopher Gadsden was born in Charleston, South Carolina, on February 16, 1724, the son of a British merchant marine officer. He was educated in England and worked in a Philadelphia mercantile house before serving as a purser aboard the warship HMS *Aldborough*. In 1741 he inherited a small fortune and established himself as a successful planter. Gadsden won a seat in the colonial assembly in 1757, where he served for the next 27 years and clashed repeatedly with royal governors. The STAMP ACT of 1765 pushed Gadsden into the ranks of the radical Whig opposition, where he emerged as a leading spokesman for anti-British sentiment and helped organize the local SONS OF LIBERTY. Fiery and articulate, Gadsden represented his colony at the Stamp Act Congress that year, and in 1767 he performed similar services against the TOWNSHEND DUTIES. He was also outspoken in his support for the British radical John WILKES. By 1770 Gadsden was the de facto leader of South Carolina's resistance movement, although, despite his reputation as the Samuel ADAMS of the south, he never preached violence against British authority. In 1774 Gadsden was elected a delegate to the First Continental CONGRESS, where he singularly impressed and befriended John ADAMS, and subsequently attended the Second Congress. As part of the Naval Committee, he designed the rattlesnake-adorned "Don't Tread on Me" flag, which became the personal pennant of Commodore Esek HOPKINS.

Gadsden returned to Charleston in January 1776 to stand in the extralegal provincial congress, where he took the unprecedented stand of advocating independence from Great Britain. He also served as colonel of the 1st South Carolina Regiment. In this capacity he was present throughout the British attack on CHARLESTON in June 1776 and bore a minor role in helping Colonel William MOULTRIE repel the British fleet. On September 17, 1776, Congress promoted him to brigadier general in the Continental ARMY, although his military service had basically ended. Back at the provincial congress, Gadsden proved a major force behind adoption of a new state constitution, although he managed to alienate the influential John RUTLEDGE. Thereafter, his political activities were restricted to secondary offices such as lieutenant governor. Gadsden was present through the British siege of CHARLESTON, where he foolishly prevailed upon General Benjamin LINCOLN to defend the city at all costs rather than retire. In May 1780 he was taken prisoner by General Henry CLINTON, paroled, then arrested by General Charles CORNWALLIS and interned at St. Augustine, Florida, for 10 months.

In 1781 Gadsden was released from close confinement and tendered the post of governor, but he declined. He then resumed his activity in the assembly for several years and also conducted the family business. In the 1780s Gadsden's most important work was in the state convention that ratified the federal constitution, and he also helped draft a new state constitution. Throughout the 1790s he was a staunch Federalist ally of Presidents George WASHINGTON and John Adams. Gadsden died in Charleston on August 28, 1805, one of the earliest advocates of national independence.

Further Reading
Bledsoe, Julia G. "The Failure of Colonial Government and the American Revolution in South Carolina: A Long View." Unpublished master's thesis, College of William and Mary, 1996.
Godbold, E. Stanley, and Robert H. Woody. *Christopher Gadsden and the American Revolution.* Knoxville: University of Tennessee Press, 1982.
Horne, Paul A. "Forgotten Leaders: South Carolina's Delegation to the Continental Congress, 1774–1789." Unpublished Ph.D. diss., University of South Carolina, 1988.
Matchett, S. R. " 'Unanimity, Order, and Regularity': The Political Culture of South Carolina in the Era of Revolution." Unpublished Ph.D. diss., University of Sydney, 1980.
McDonough, Daniel J. *Christopher Gadsden and Henry Laurens: The Parallel Lives of Two American Patriots.* Selinsgrove, Pa.: Susquehanna University Press, 2000.
Weir, Robert M., ed. *The Writings of Christopher Gadsden, 1746–1808.* Columbia: University of South Carolina Press, 1966.

Gage, Thomas (1719–1787)
English military officer

Thomas Gage was born in Firle, England, in 1719, son of Thomas, First Viscount Gage. As an aristocrat he was educated at Westminister School alongside George GERMAIN and William HOWE and entered the army in 1741 as a lieutenant in the 48th Regiment. Gage, a competent officer, rose steadily through the ranks, and by 1755 he functioned as lieutenant colonel of the 44th Regiment. In this capacity he accompanied General Edward Braddock on his ill-fated expedition against Fort Duquesne in western Pennsylvania and fought bravely at the disastrous ambush at Monongahela on July 9, 1755. He also met and befriended an obscure colonel of Virginia militia, George WASHINGTON, and the two men corresponded over the next two decades. Gage fought well throughout the ensuing French and Indian War, and in 1760 General Jeffrey Amherst appointed him governor of Montreal. Three years later he became commander in chief of British North America, headquartered at New York. Gage experienced firsthand the rising tide of resentment against colonial rule when he asked the New York assembly for funding to comply with the QUARTERING ACT of 1765, and it refused. Nonetheless, Gage served capably, if cautiously, over the intervening years—without precise instructions from London on how to cope with mounting unrest. He sailed home in February 1773 for consultations and the following year returned as royal governor of Massachusetts to replace the unpopular Thomas HUTCHINSON and enforce parliamentary will.

Gage's presence reflected Britain's political determination to clamp down on unruly Massachusetts, and it fell upon him to preside over seminal events such as the wildly unpopular COERCIVE ACTS, which included shutting down the port of Boston. Such actions did little to endear either the military or Parliament to the colonials, and Gage worked in constant fear of provoking some kind of armed confrontation. The pot further simmered at the hands of professional agitators such as Samuel ADAMS, John HANCOCK, and their cohorts in the violent SONS OF LIBERTY. When accommodation proved beyond his grasp, Gage ordered preemptive strikes against caches of colonial arms to forestall an open breach. On September 1, 1774, he dispatched a column of 260 soldiers to Charlestown for the purpose of seizing cannon and gunpowder; the mission proceeded peacefully, but thousands of angry residents massed in the town on the following day to protest. In the absence of direct orders from London, Gage proved unwilling to do more than harass supplies. In February 1775 he

Parliament appointed Thomas Gage as royal governor of Massachusetts in 1774 in an attempt to defuse mounting unrest in the colony. Painting by John Singleton Copley *(Yale Center for British Art)*

Colonel Francis SMITH and Major John PITCAIRN to seize colonial supplies sequestered at Concord, Massachusetts. This act precipitated the first battles of the Revolutionary War at Lexington and CONCORD, and the surviving British soldiers were lucky to be rescued by Colonel Hugh PERCY and return to Boston intact. Thereafter Gage was besieged in the city by 20,000 hostile militia until reinforcements arrived under Generals Howe, Henry CLINTON, and John BURGOYNE the following spring. Stung by charges of inactivity, he overreacted to colonial seizure of high ground in Charlestown harbor by authorizing the Battle at BUNKER HILL on June 17, 1775, whereby the British lost half their force. This disaster served only to embolden the rebels elsewhere, and Lord George Germain finally recalled Gage to England for "consultations" in October 1775. His mishandling of political and military affairs helped precipitate the very Revolutionary War he sought so hard to avoid, and for several years he remained without a military command. But in 1782 Gage was elevated to lieutenant general and appointed to prepare the defenses of Kent against a possible French invasion. He died in London on April 2, 1787, an honest, earnest military bureaucrat but incapable of comprehending—let alone containing—the forces of revolution.

ordered Colonel Alexander LESLIE to seize military contraband stored at Salem; this time the British aborted their mission in the face of a hostile public reception. Gage, who had pleaded for upward of 20,000 troops to help restore order and was refused, finally received the authorization he coveted on April 14, 1775, in a tersely written letter from Secretary of State for the Colonies William Legge, earl of Dartmouth. Legge upbraided the general for his seeming timidity and ordered him to arrest the leaders of the Massachusetts Provincial Congress, especially Adams and Hancock. He was also at liberty to seize any arms caches that he was aware of.

On April 18, 1775, Gage issued fateful orders for a column of 800 picked men under Lieutenant

Further Reading

Alden, John R. *General Gage in America: Being Principally a History of His Role in the American Revolution.* Baton Rouge: Louisiana State University Press, 1948.

Brooks, Victor. *The Boston Campaign, April 1777–March 1776.* Conshohocken, Pa.: Combined Pub., 1999.

Carter, Clarence E., ed. *The Correspondence of General Thomas Gage with the Secretary of State, 1763–1775,* 2 vols. Hamden, Conn.: Archon Books, 1969.

Clarfield, Gerald H. "The Short, Unhappy Civil Administration of Thomas Gage," *Essex Institute Historical Collections* 109, no. 2 (1973): 138–151.

Edgar, Gregory T. *Reluctant Break with Britain: From Stamp Act to Bunker Hill.* Bowie, Md.: Heritage Books, 1997.

Hallahan, William H. *The Day the Revolution Began: 19 April, 1775.* New York: Avon Books, 1999.

Galloway, Joseph (ca. 1731–1803)
American politician, Loyalist

Joseph Galloway was born in West River, Maryland, around 1731, the son of a successful farmer. He studied law in Philadelphia and established himself as one of that city's most prominent attorneys. In 1753 Galloway further enhanced his social standing by marrying a daughter of the wealthy Growden family, whose father was speaker of the colonial assembly. Galloway himself was elected to the assembly in 1756, where he formed a deep and abiding friendship with Benjamin FRANKLIN. Together they wielded an alliance aimed at removing the proprietary rule of the Penn family and converting Pennsylvania into a Crown Colony. In this capacity both gained an adversary in fellow delegate John DICKINSON who felt that new British authority would invariably trample upon constitutional rights. The turning point in Galloway's distinguished political career came in 1765 with the passage of the STAMP ACT. As newly elected speaker of the assembly, he was stunned by riots against British authority and began articulating views sympathetic toward Parliament's right to tax the colonies. In 1767, after passage of the controversial TOWNSHEND DUTIES, Galloway strongly refuted Dickinson's pamphlet *Letters from a Farmer in Pennsylvania* by reiterating Parliament's right to tax the colonies—but argued that legislators could somehow dissuade them from doing so. Such views placed him at odds with fellow assembly members, including Franklin, who came to resent his evolving LOYALIST sympathies. But Galloway remained popular among more conservative elements, and in 1774 they elected him a delegate to the First Continental CONGRESS.

Like many conservatives, Galloway attended Congress convinced that the growing rift with England could be mitigated without the threat of violence. Furthermore, he felt that Britain's oftentimes slapdash colonial practices ought to be systematized into a formal arrangement based on constitutional law and precedents. On September 28, 1774, he introduced his "Plan of Union" to Congress, whereby colonials would receive both representation in Parliament and a say in the revenue matters affecting them. It mandated creation of an intercolonial American legislature headed by a president-general who was appointed by the king. New laws could not be enacted without the consent of both the new legislature and Parliament. It was a pragmatic and effective solution to long-standing colonial grievances and was defeated by only a single vote. So threatening did more radical elements construe Galloway's plan that they voted to expunge all mention of it from Congressional records. Furthermore, in October 1774 Dickinson became speaker of the Pennsylvania assembly, and he used his influence to remove Galloway from Congress.

Galloway remained on the fringes of political debate until July 1776, when the Second Continental Congress authorized the DECLARATION OF INDEPENDENCE from Great Britain. Rather than partake of what he considered treason, Galloway left Philadelphia and repaired immediately to New York. There he was a frequent visitor to the headquarters of General William HOWE and urged him to attack the rebel capital at Philadelphia. This was accomplished in October 1777, and once the city fell to the British, Galloway was installed as superintendent. His principal accomplishment was to effectively suppress Patriot sentiments within the city and intercept the flow of supplies intended for General George WASHINGTON's army at Valley Forge. However, the British subsequently abandoned Philadelphia in the summer of 1778, and Galloway returned to New York with them, a thoroughly detested figure. He next ventured to London and appeared before the House of Commons to criticize the war effort and assure the government of widespread Loyalist support throughout the colonies. After the war ended in 1783 Galloway petitioned the Pennsylvania assembly for permission to return home, but it refused and confiscated his vast estates. Galloway thereafter lived on a pension in England for many years before dying in Watford, Hertfordshire, on August 29, 1803. Ironically, his "Plan of Union" anticipated by nearly a century what ultimately became the British Commonwealth.

Further Reading

Ferling, John E. *The Loyalist Mind: Joseph Galloway and the American Revolution.* University Park: University of Pennsylvania Press, 1977.

Galloway, Joseph. *Selected Tracts,* 3 vols. New York: Da Capo Press, 1974.

Hinshaw, George. *Joseph Galloway: Loyalist Spokesman.* Maryville: Northwest Missouri State University, 1981.

Jacobson, David L. "John Dickinson of Joseph Galloway, 1764–1776: A Study in Contrasts." Unpublished Ph.D. diss., Princeton University, 1959.

Lively, Bruce R. "The Speaker and His House: The Impact of Joseph Galloway upon the Pennsylvania Assembly, 1755–1776." Unpublished Ph.D. diss., University of Southern California, 1975.

Newcomb, Benjamin H. *Franklin and Galloway: A Political Partnership.* New Haven, Conn.: Yale University Press, 1972.

Gálvez, Bernardo de (1746–1786)

Spanish military officer

Bernardo de Gálvez was born near Málaga, SPAIN, on July 23, 1746, into a prominent military family. He attended the military academy at Ávila before receiving his lieutenant's commission and distinguishing himself in fighting against Portugal in 1762. Promoted captain, he next ventured to Mexico to serve under his uncle, Jose de Gálvez, then visitor-general to New Spain. Gálvez again distinguished himself in combat against the Apaches along the Rio Grande and subsequently received command of Nueva Vizcaya and Sonora. In 1775 he returned to Spain to fight in the war against Algiers, was promoted to lieutenant colonel, and was allowed to teach at the Ávila academy. The following year he arrived at New Orleans, Louisiana, as acting governor-general and formally assumed that role on January 1, 1777. In this capacity, Gálvez proved an energetic and able ruler who reduced taxes, expanded agriculture, increased trade with neighboring British colonies, and facilitated French, German, and American immigration into the province. Fluent in French, Gálvez also enhanced his social status at New Orleans by marrying into one of the leading Creole families. In time he became an extremely popular administrator.

When the Revolutionary War commenced in 1775, Gálvez proved sympathetic to the rebels less for altruistic reasons than that they weakened Spain's traditional enemy, England. He thereby acted in concert with American agent Oliver Pollock and secretly funneled money and supplies to George Rogers CLARK, while harassing British traders in his waters. He had been warned months in advance that war with England was pending, and Gálvez, rather than allow his relatively weak colony to be attacked, sought a preemptive strike. Accordingly, once Spain declared war in May 1779,

Spanish officer and governor-general of Louisiana Bernardo de Gálvez declared war against the British in 1779 and successfully countered British forces along the Mississippi Valley. *(Museum of Mobile, Alabama)*

he attacked isolated British posts along the Mississippi Valley. In August 1777 Forts Bute, New Richmond, and Pamure fell quickly to Gálvez and his polyglot force of Spanish troops, AFRICAN-AMERICAN volunteers, French and German militia, and Choctaw Indians. With the Mississippi Valley secure, he next assembled a fleet of warships to attack neighboring Mobile, Alabama, which fell on March 14, 1780. Success here resulted in promotion to major general, and Gálvez spent several months preparing for what would prove his greatest challenge: Pensacola. He relocated his headquarters from New Orleans to Havana, Cuba, and began amassing the requisite men and ships for this formidable task. Incessant bad weather delayed his expedition for several months, and it was not until February 1781 that Gálvez was able to sail. He did so without assistance from the Spanish fleet, whose commander, Don José Calbo de Irazabel, feared that the waters off Pensacola ran too shallow for his vessels.

Pensacola proved a tough nut to crack. It was defended by 900 British and German troops commanded by General John Campbell and well fortified. Gálvez landed several thousand troops on March 9, 1781, and began a formal siege that proceeded slowly. Fighting proved tenacious and he was wounded twice as the trenches advanced. However, on May 8, 1781, the Spanish fired a lucky cannon shot that ignited a British powder magazine and demolished part of Pensacola's defenses. Campbell felt compelled to surrender on May 10, and West Florida passed once again into Spanish hands. In recognition of his conquests, King Carlos III promoted Gálvez to lieutenant general, captain-general of Cuba, and governor of Louisiana. He was also created a conde and granted a coat of arms with the inscription "Yo Solo" (I alone), in reference to his singular determination to attack Pensacola without naval cooperation. Because of his efforts, provisions of the TREATY OF PARIS in 1783 returned all of Florida to Spain.

After the war Gálvez returned to Mexico as viceroy of New Spain. He ruled effectively and efficiently before dying of a fever in Mexico City on November 30, 1786. By cutting off supplies to British forces and tying down troops throughout the Gulf, he made valuable contributions to the American cause.

Further Reading

Coker, William S., and Robert E. Rea, eds. *Anglo-Spanish Confrontation on the Gulf Coast during the American Revolution.* Pensacola, Fla.: Gulf Coast History and Humanities Conference, 1982.

Fleming, Thomas. "Bernardo de Galvez," *American Heritage* 33, no. 3 (1982): 30–39.

Galvez, Bernardo de. *Yo Solo: The Battle Journal of Bernardo de Galvez during the American Revolution.* New Orleans: Polyanthos, 1978.

Grissett, Mary L. "The Foundations of Spanish Louisiana." Unpublished master's thesis, Valdosta State College, 1990.

LaFarelle, Lorenzo G. *Bernardo de Galvez: Hero of the American Revolution.* Austin, Tex.: Eakin Press, 1992.

Williams, Harold D. "Bernardo de Galvez and the Anglo-American Struggle for the Trans-Appalachian West, 1777–1779." Unpublished master's thesis, Creighton University, 1969.

Gambier, James (1723–1789)
English naval officer

James Gambier was born in 1723, the descendant of Huguenot refugees. He joined the Royal Navy at an early age and had risen to lieutenant by 1743. He subsequently rendered useful service at Louisbourg in 1758, and at Guadelupe, Martinique, and Quiberon Bay the following year. Gambier, however, proved something of a dullard, and in 1766 he received command of the guardship HMS *Yarmouth* at Portsmouth. Four years later he transferred his flag to Halifax, Nova Scotia, as commander of the North American station. Following an additional stint as comptroller of victualling, he was replaced there by Admiral Samuel GRAVES and transferred back to Portsmouth as resident commissioner. On January 23, 1778, Gambier's seniority prompted the naval ministry under Lord John

Montagu, earl of Sandwich, to promote the tottering leader to rear admiral. He arrived in New York on May 23, 1778, as second in command under Admiral Richard Howe.

Gambier's reputation as a cranky, uninspiring subordinate did little to improve relations with Admiral Howe, who simply ordered him confined to New York harbor. While Howe was away with the fleet, Gambier also clashed with the British commander of land forces, General Henry Clinton, which further eroded his reputation. When Howe left for England in the fall of 1778, Gambier briefly succeeded him as naval commander in chief, until the arrival of Admiral John Byron. Like his predecessor, Byron had little use for Gambier's whining, although, when Byron sailed for the West Indies, Gambier was again senior naval officer by default. In April 1779 the government finally recalled him to England. His brief tenure was undistinguished save for complaints by him—and about him—and the British naval and military establishments breathed a collective sigh of relief following his departure. In accordance to the seniority system, he advanced to vice admiral on September 26, 1780, and two years later gained appointment as commander in chief of the Jamaica station. He was also forced to publish a pamphlet defending his behavior against numerous political and naval critics. Poor health necessitated Gambier's return home in 1783, and he finally died in London on January 8, 1789. His service in North America was marked by incompetence, whiny diatribes to Sandwich about lack of manpower, ships, and respect from his peers, and constituted a nadir for Royal Navy leadership in this conflict. Fortunately his successor, Captain George Collier, was an aggressive officer who greatly revived Britain's naval fortunes.

Further Reading

Billias, George A., ed. *George Washington's Opponents.* New York: William Morrow, 1969.

Gardiner, Robert, ed. *Navies and the American Revolution, 1775–1783.* Annapolis, Md.: Naval Institute Press, 1996.

Syrett, David. " 'This Penurious Old Reptile': Rear Admiral James Gambier and the American Revolution," *Historical Research* 74, no. 183 (2001): 63–76.

———. *The Royal Navy in American Waters, 1775–1783.* Brookfield, Vt.: Gower Publishing Co., 1989.

Tilley, John. *The British Navy and the American Revolution.* Columbia: University of South Carolina Press, 1987.

Gansevoort, Peter (1749–1812)
American military officer

Peter Gansevoort was born in Albany, New York, on July 17, 1749, a descendant of wealthy Dutch settlers. While lacking in military experience, he used family connections to secure a major's commission in the 2nd New York Infantry on July 2, 1775, and he accompanied the ill-fated expedition of General Richard Montgomery into Canada. He emerged from defeat with a fine military reputation, and in July 1776 Gansevoort advanced to lieutenant colonel. The following November he assumed command of Fort George on Lake Champlain as colonel of the 3rd New York Infantry. In April 1777 he was appointed commander of Fort Stanwix, New York, over Colonel Elias Dayton and began rebuilding the walls of his tottering charge. Gansevoort's foresight proved essential, for that summer a 1,700-man British/Indian expedition under Lieutenant Colonel Barry St. Leger landed at Oswego, New York, and threaded its way up the Mohawk River Valley. This column intended to approach the rebel capital of Albany from the west and eventually link up with the main British force under General John Burgoyne, coming from the north. Gansevoort stood squarely in this path.

The ensuing defense of Fort Stanwix proved a critical turning point in the northern campaign. Gansevoort, ably seconded by Lieutenant Colonel Marinus Willett, received a small reinforcement of 200 men just as the British approached and so commanded 750 soldiers. He flatly refused a surrender summons from St. Leger because the British lacked heavy artillery to batter down Fort Stanwix's walls. Furthermore, because the majority of St.

Leger's force was comprised of Native Americans, Gansevoort and his men preferred to die in combat rather than risk being massacred in captivity. The garrison remained safely hunkered behind its fortifications until August 6, 1777, when St. Leger dispatched the bulk of his army to ambush Colonel Nicholas HERKIMER at ORISKANY. Once fighting began, Gansevoort ordered his troops to sortie under Colonel Willett, and they severely damaged the British camp without loss. On August 22, 1777, St. Leger abandoned the siege following the approach of another relief column commanded by General Benedict ARNOLD, and Burgoyne never received his badly needed reinforcements.

For his valiant stand at Fort Stanwix, Gansevoort received the thanks of CONGRESS and a new command in Albany. In the summer of 1779 he formed part of General John SULLIVAN's punitive expedition into the Iroquois heartland, and he personally burned the lower Mohawk castle. In March 1781 the New York provincial congress appointed him a brigadier general of militia, although he saw no further fighting. Gansevoort remained active in military affairs after the war and he rose to major general of militia in 1793. He also served as an Indian agent and military agent within the northern department of the army. Gansevoort received a brigadier general's commission in February 1809 and held that rank until his death in Albany on July 2, 1812. His stand at Fort Stanwix in 1777 proved an essential component of America's victory in the north.

Further Reading
Edgar, Gregory T. *"Liberty or Death!" The Northern Campaigns in the American Revolutionary War.* Bowie, Md.: Heritage Books, 1999.
Kenney, Alice P. *The Gansevoorts of Albany: Dutch Patricians in the Upper Hudson Valley.* Syracuse, N.Y.: Syracuse University Press, 1969.
Lewis, Jane A. "Blood Red Dawn: The New York Campaigns of the War of Independence." Unpublished Ph.D. diss., Union Institute, 2001.
Lowenthal, Larry, ed. *Days of Siege: A Journal of the Siege of Fort Stanwix in 1777.* New York: Eastern Acorn Press, 1983.
Luzader, John F. *The Construction and Military History of Fort Stanwix.* Washington, D.C.: U.S. Office of Archaeological and Historic Preservation, 1969.
Watt, Gavin K. *Rebellion in the Mohawk Valley: The St. Leger Expedition of 1777.* Toronto: Dundurn, 2002.

Gaspée affair (June 9, 1772)
Rhode Island, by dint of its numerous waterways and secluded estuaries astride Narragansett Bay, had been a smuggler's haven throughout the 18th century. In fact, illicit trade of one sort or another had become an important staple of the colonial economy, and several leading citizens actively embraced it. To curtail such activity, Admiral John Montagu assigned the schooner HMS *Gaspée* under Lieutenant William Dudingston to patrol the waters of Narragansett Bay, then examine and seize all suspicious vessels. Dudingston proved particularly adept in his duties, and complaints from

American general Peter Gansevoort refused to surrender Fort Stanwix to British officer St. Leger in 1777. *(Munson-Williams-Proctor Institute)*

the local merchant community prompted the sheriff of Providence County to issue a warrant for his arrest on the basis of illegal seizures. The turning point in this ongoing matter came on June 9, 1772, when the *Gaspée,* hot on the trail of the *Hannah,* a known smuggling craft, suddenly ran aground off Warwick Point and could not be refloated. Word of Dudingston's plight quickly reached the Providence wharves, and a group of citizens, headed by leading merchant John Brown, determined to increase his discomfiture even further.

On the evening of June 9, 64 citizens and several boats under Abraham WHIPPLE left Providence under muffled oars and made for Warwick Neck, seven miles distant. Around 10 o'clock that evening they approached the *Gaspée* and were challenged by a sentry. Whipple thundered back that he carried an arrest warrant for Lieutenant Dudingston, who was subsequently wounded in an exchange of gunfire. The citizens quickly overpowered the *Gaspée's* crew, driving them into the hold, and they made preparations to burn their vessel. They then burned it to the waterline. Poor Dudingston endured the further humiliation of being arrested and detained until Admiral Montagu paid a heavy fine for his release. British authorities were enraged by this assault upon one of his majesty's warships, and they initiated a full-scale investigation. Despite that fact that the perpetrators were well known and a large reward was posted for incriminating information, no individuals came forward. Worse still from an American standpoint, the British government authorized the commission to arrest and deport any guilty parties back to England for trial. This provision clearly violated long-accepted colonial practices of trial by one's peers and added to growing perceptions of British arbitrariness. Another important outcome of the *Gaspée* affair was to convince the Virginia House of Burgesses to establish its first COMMITTEE OF CORRESPONDENCE.

Further Reading
DeVaro, Lawrence J. "The Impact of the Gaspée Affair on the Coming of the Revolution, 1772–1773." Unpublished Ph.D. diss., Case Western University, 1973.
Dukes, Richard S. "The Gaspée Incident as a Clash of Cultures." Unpublished master's thesis, University of Alabama, 1989.
Lovejoy, David S. *Rhode Island Politics and the American Revolution, 1760–1776.* Providence, R.I.: Brown University Press, 1958.
May, W. E. "The Gaspée Affair," *Mariner's Mirror* 63, no. 2 (1977): 129–135.
Simister, Florence P. *The Fire's Center: Rhode Island in the Revolutionary Era.* Providence: Rhode Island Bicentennial Foundation, 1979.
York, Neil L. "The Uses of Law and the Gaspée Affair," *Rhode Island History* 50, no. 1 (1992): 2–21.

Gates, Horatio (1728–1806)
American military officer

Horatio Gates was born in Maldon, England, in 1728, the son of a tradesman. Because his mother was a housekeeper for the duke of Leeds, he received help in purchasing a lieutenant's commission in 1749. Gates proved himself competent as an officer, fought well throughout the French and Indian War in America (1755–63), and struck up friendly relations with Colonel George WASHINGTON of the Virginia militia. He subsequently campaigned at Martinique in 1761, rising to major. However, Gates's lack of social connections or a family pedigree militated against further advancement, and in 1765 he angrily resigned his commission. In 1772 Gates relocated to Virginia at the behest of Washington, who helped him acquire a plantation and join the petty gentry. When the Revolutionary War erupted in April 1775, Gates threw in his lot with the Americans, being one of the few officers in the Continental ARMY with professional military training. That June he joined Washington's staff outside Boston as his adjutant general, displaying a genuine aptitude for drilling troops and military administration. However, Gates was driven by ambition to secure a field command of his own and used all his political influence to obtain one. His demonstrated talent, coupled with pressing needs for experienced leadership, finally induced CONGRESS to promote him to major general as of May 16, 1777. He initially assigned to take command of American forces in Canada, but after those troops had retreated back to New York he was assigned to serve under General Philip J. SCHUYLER, commander of the Northern Department. Gates was unhappy at being subordinated to an officer he felt was inferior in merit and talent to himself, and his complaints to friends in Congress resulted in other assignments in New Jersey and Pennsylvania. Finally, on August 4, 1777, he was authorized to relieve the ailing Schuyler and assume control of the Northern Department.

Gates fortuitously arrived and took command just as a major British offensive from the north under General John BURGOYNE was bogging down in the forested terrain east of Albany. He deployed his 7,000 troops directly in Burgoyne's path, entrenched, and allowed the British to dissipate themselves in frontal assaults. However, Gates was fortunate in having such capable subordinates as Colonel Daniel MORGAN and the ever active General Benedict ARNOLD on hand to transform encounters such as FREEMAN'S FARM (September 19, 1777) and BEMIS HEIGHTS (October 7, 1777) into clear American victories. When Burgoyne, cut off from Canada, short on supplies, and surrounded by superior numbers, finally capitulated on October 19, 1777, Gates became hailed as the "Hero of Saratoga." His conduct, while minimal, proved competent, and his newfound status as a national icon only stoked his ambitions further.

Discontent over lackluster generalship by General Washington led to dissent from Colonel Thomas CONWAY, who suggested that Gates be appointed supreme commander in his place. Gates was gradually drawn in and partially implicated in a plot over the winter of 1777–78. The so-called Conway Cabal quickly unraveled, and Gates disavowed all knowledge of the affair, but relations between the two former friends cooled considerably. Over the next two years he assumed various commands in New York and Massachusetts but eventually manipulated his political influence to

A former British officer, General Horatio Gates became known as the "Hero of Saratoga" due to his victories at Freeman's Farm and Bemis Heights. *(Independence National Historical Park)*

secure another field command. In the spring of 1780 Gates's machinations succeeded with an appointment as commander of the Southern Department, recently reeling from the loss of General Benjamin LINCOLN and his army. He assumed command without the knowledge or consent of General Washington, who preferred General Nathanael GREENE for the post. Nonetheless, Gates arrived in North Carolina in July 1780, collected his ragtag forces, and began an ill-fated offensive into South Carolina. His poorly fed and half-trained troops finally confronted a smaller but highly professional force under General Charles CORNWALLIS at CAMDEN on August 16, 1780, and, owing to Gates's faulty deployment of troops, were disastrously routed. The general also ruined his erstwhile military reputation by shamefully fleeing the battlefield and riding over 120 miles nonstop to Hillsboro, North Carolina. He managed to cling to command until December 1780, when Greene cordially if unceremoniously relieved him.

Gates never again held a significant command in the war. He demanded and received a court of inquiry to clear his name, but it never materialized. He briefly served on Washington's staff at Newburgh, New York, in 1783 and retired from the army in semi-disgrace. Gates lived several years on his Virginia plantation until 1790, when he manumitted his slaves and relocated to New York City. He died there on April 10, 1806, one of the war's most controversial senior officers.

Further Reading
Ketchum, Richard M. *Saratoga: Turning Point of America's Revolutionary War.* New York: H. Holt, 1997.
Maass, John R. *Horatio Gates and the Battle of Camden—"That Unhappy Affair," August 16, 1780.* Camden, S.C.: Kershaw County Historical Society, 2001.
Mintz, Max. *The Generals of Saratoga: John Burgoyne and Horatio Gates.* New Haven, Conn.: Yale University Press, 1990.
Morrissey, Brendan. *Saratoga, 1777: Turning Point of a Revolution.* Westport, Conn.: Praeger, 2004.
Nelson, Paul D. *General Horatio Gates: A Biography.* Baton Rouge: Louisiana State University Press, 1976.
Nestor, Joseph B. "The Battle of Saratoga." Unpublished master's thesis, East Stroudsburg University, 2001.

George III (1738–1820)
king of Great Britain

George William Frederick Hanover was born in London on June 4, 1738, the son of Frederick, Prince of Wales, and Princess Augusta of Saxe-Gotha. A mediocre student, he was the first king of the Hanoverian dynasty for whom English was a native tongue. During his youth George was tutored by John Stuart, earl of Bute, with whom he enjoyed deep emotional bonds. He rose to the throne in 1760 after the death of George II, his grandfather, and set about trying to reclaim powers for the throne lost to Parliament in the previous century. As a man, George III was scrupulously moral, thrifty, and devoted to Princess Charlotte of Mecklenburg-Strelitz, his wife of 50 years. He was also a strict constitutionalist who never challenged his ministers and invariably accepted their decisions. When not engaging in political struggles, he totally immersed himself in farming—a lifelong passion. But the young king was also willful and stubborn, especially while asserting what he regarded as kingly prerogatives. He initially made Lord Bute prime minister in 1760; his tenure in office proved a public relations disaster owing to incompetence, and over the next decade George appointed a variety of indifferent successors. Of these, George GRENVILLE exuded immediate impact on the colonies by promulgating the STAMP ACT of 1765, a defining moment in the first British Empire. Colonial resentment resulted in its repeal, which was then followed by imposition of the equally unpopular TOWNSHEND DUTIES, whose measures, in due course, were also lifted. However, by 1770 British affairs were under the sway of Lord Frederick NORTH, who saw parliamentary authority challenged by colonial assemblies, so he instituted the TEA ACT to reassert the government's right to tax its colonies. The king fully supported North over what he perceived as a relatively insignificant measure, and no problems were anticipated.

The English government was genuinely surprised when colonial resentment culminated in the BOSTON TEA PARTY of December 1773, a direct strike against Parliament and the rule of law. Again, the king concurred with Lord North's imposition of the COERCIVE ACTS to obtain financial restitution for property destroyed, which further strained Britain's relationship to the colonies. After fighting broke out in April 1775, George III was aghast at the extent of resentment against his rule, and the following August he refused to receive the "Olive Branch Petition" submitted by the Second Continental CONGRESS. He also declared the colonies in a state of rebellion against the Crown and authorized military preparations to force them back into the fold. Not surprisingly, he viewed his actions, and those of his ministers, as

King George III was a modest and orderly monarch who bore the brunt of American resentment of the British in the colonies. *(National Portrait Gallery, London)*

perfectly consistent with his responsibility as sovereign and head of state. Worse, he feared that tolerating disobedience here might induce Ireland to rebel against British authority as well. Further compounding this intractability was his reluctance to question the conduct of the war as waged by ministers Lord George GERMAIN and John MONTAGU, earl of Sandwich, neither of which proved overtly competent.

Prior to the war, George III was viewed as a benign father figure by the majority of Americans, who felt that their struggle was against Parliament. But, through an unforeseen turn of events, the king was transformed by American radicals from a modest, orderly monarch into a poster child for political oppression. In January 1776, English expatriate Thomas PAINE excoriated the role of monarchy in human affairs through his brilliant polemic COMMON SENSE. Six months later, Thomas JEFFERSON proffered a litany of 18 grievances against the king in the DECLARATION OF INDEPENDENCE. George III was hardly the tyrant portrayed in that seminal document, but the notion gained currency with significant parts of the American polity. The king's stubborn refusal to consider any option other than abject surrender also boded ill for any attempt at reconciliation with his former subjects. His willingness to hire mercenary HESSIAN soldiers to fight against his subjects was also held by many as proof of his tyrannical intentions. By 1779 the fluctuating fortunes of the British war effort had convinced many in Parliament that the war could not be won, and leading Whigs like Edmund BURKE and Charles James FOX demanded an end to hostilities. George III, true to his nature, stubbornly refused to yield even after Lord North threatened to resign in the wake of the YORKTOWN disaster of 1781. North's government collapsed shortly after, and it fell upon the administration of Charles WATSON-WENTWORTH, marquis of Rockingham, to begin peace negotiations in earnest. The TREATY OF PARIS, whereby Great Britain recognized American independence, was finally realized in 1783 and marked a low point in the Hanoverian dynasty's fortunes.

Despite the loss of America, George III went on to compile a reign of impressive longevity and achievements. A second British Empire arose upon the ashes of the first, and by the end of his reign Great Britain was experiencing the first twinges of the Industrial Revolution. During his reign Britain also emerged as the world's leading military power, with direct roles in containment of the French Revolution and the defeat of Napoléon by 1815. However, the king suffered severely from a hereditary mental disorder that occasioned bouts of insanity, and in 1810 his son, the future George IV, assumed the role of prince regent. George III died in London on January 29, 1820, a figure thoroughly vilified in American history to that point but more popularly regarded and beloved at home as "Farmer George."

Further Reading

Cannon, John. "George III and America," *Historian* no. 85 (2005): 20–26.

Conway, Stephen. *The British Isles and the War of American Independence*. New York: Oxford University Press, 2000.

Ditchfield, G. M. *George III: An Essay in Monarchy*. New York: Palgrave Macmillan, 2002.

Gould, Eliga H. *The Persistence of Empire: British Political Culture in the Age of the American Revolution*. Chapel Hill: University of North Carolina Press, 2000.

O'Shaughnessy, Andrew J. "'If Others Will Not Be Active, I Must Drive': George III and the American Revolution," *Early American Studies* 2, no. 1 (2004): 1–46.

Walpole, Horace. *Memoirs of the Reign of King George III*. Edited by Derek Jarrett, 4 vols. New Haven, Conn.: Yale University Press, 2000.

Germain, George (1716–1785)
English politician

George Sackville was born in London on January 26, 1716, a son of the first duke of Dorset. He was well-schooled at the Westminster School and Trinity College, Dublin, before entering the army as a cavalry captain in 1737. He served well in the War of the Austrian Succession and became a major general by the time of the Seven Years' War, 1756–63. However, owing to a misinterpretation of orders during the Battle of Minden in 1759, Sackville failed to charge home as ordered and was court-martialed. He was found guilty of disobedience, cashiered, and a vindictive King George II ordered the verdict written into every orderly book in the English army. Unrepentant, Sackville worked vigorously over the next 15 years to remove this stigma from his name. In 1770 he improved his social status by marrying the wealthy Lady Betty Germain on the condition that he adopt her surname. He willingly obliged and was thereafter known as Lord Germain. Germain also gained a measure of political respectability by befriending the youthful King GEORGE III and becoming a hard-line proponent for his monarch's policies—especially the taxing of the colonies. By aligning himself with Prime Minister Lord Frederick NORTH, Germain finally achieved personal vindication when he gained appointment as secretary of state for the colonies in November 1775. In this capacity he became instrumental in conducting warfare against the rebellious American colonies over the next six years.

In office, Germain proved himself highly skilled at military administration and bore direct responsibilities for recruiting, training, and transporting thousands of soldiers across the Atlantic Ocean to America. Such a feat would tax the abilities of any minister operating at the end of a 3,000-mile-long supply line, but British armies were basically well-supplied and adequately supported throughout the war. And, whatever his shortcomings as a strategist, he certainly displayed more courage and conviction than the vacillating Lord North. But Germain, like most of his contemporaries, completely misjudged the nature of the conflict he was embroiled in. He refused to believe that the majority of Americans were unfaithful to the Crown and, in fact, counted on the support of nonexistent LOYALISTS throughout the struggle. Nor was he above partisan politics with respect to senior military leadership. Germain openly disliked Guy CARLETON, William HOWE, and Henry CLINTON because of disagreements over strategy. Whenever possible, he also found convenient pretexts for interfering with his commanders in the field, a habit that invariably held fatal results for the British. Worse, he openly played to favorite subordinates such as the flamboyant John BURGOYNE and the overly aggressive Charles CORNWALLIS, even when their actions clashed with the orders of superiors. Thus disasters like Saratoga and YORKTOWN were by and large a direct result of Germain's backhanded machinations and inclination to meddle. His inability to formulate a coherent strategy to win the war and unwillingness to let his generals actually conduct it without interference largely negated Britain's sizable war effort.

The loss of the war by 1782 and the public uproar that followed induced both Germain and North to resign from office. As in the aftermath of Minden, he again found himself a despised figure and the butt of political humor. George III helped soften the blow by appointing him viscount Sackville and allowing him to sit in the House of Lords, but he never again held the public's confidence. Germain died at Withyham, England, on August 26, 1785, reviled by many as the man who lost America.

Further Reading

Brown, Gerald S. *The American Secretary, the Colonial Policy of Lord George Germain, 1775–1778.* Ann Arbor: University of Michigan Press, 1963.

Gould, Eliga H. *The Persistence of Empire: British Political Culture in the Age of the American Revolution.* Chapel Hill: University of North Carolina Press, 2000.

Hibbert, Christopher. *Redcoats and Rebels: The American Revolution through British Eyes.* New York: Norton, 2002.

Lenman, Bruce. *Britain's Colonial Wars, 1688–1783.* New York: Longman, 2001.

Seymour, William. *The Price of Folly: British Blunders in the War of American Independence.* Washington, D.C.: Brassey's, 1995.

Valentine, Alan C. *Lord George Germain.* Oxford: Oxford University Press, 1962.

Germantown, Battle of (October 4, 1777)

After the fall of Philadelphia on September 26, 1777, British forces under General William HOWE began dispersing for other assignments. Howe had advanced and encamped at Germantown, Pennsylvania, a few miles north of the city, yet left behind sizable detachments under General Charles CORNWALLIS to guard his lines of communication. Meanwhile several infantry regiments were also detached to evict the American garrison at Billingsport, Delaware, leaving him with roughly 8,000 soldiers at his immediate disposal. General George WASHINGTON monitored these developments carefully, for he had built up his own force to 11,000 soldiers and militia and clearly outnumbered Howe in the field. Such a disparity prompted him to launch a bold counterstroke to defeat the British and force them to evacuate Philadelphia. Washington and his staff devised a rather complicated, four-pronged attack to be delivered at dawn on the morning of October 4. Two militia columns under Generals John ARMSTRONG and William SMALLWOOD would cover the right and left flanks, respectively, to pin down enemy forces there and provide a diversion. The main thrust would then arrive in the center as the divisions of Generals John SULLIVAN and Nathanael GREENE arrived on the field. Sullivan, with 3,000 men, would hit the British center-left along the Germantown Road while Greene, commanding 5,000 of Washington's best soldiers, would simultaneously crash into the center-right, overwhelming it. This was an aggressive riposte, especially after the recent defeat at BRANDYWINE, but Washington waxed confident that his maneuver would catch Howe unawares and pummel him.

In practice, Washington's plan proved overly complex and beyond the ability of his amateur ARMY to execute successfully. The Americans kicked off their attack early in the morning of October 4, 1777, and covered 15 miles in the darkness, but their movements quickly went astray. On the right, Armstrong arrived too late to afford much assistance while Smallwood, on the left, apparently got lost and failed to reach the battlefield at all. Movement was also rendered increasingly difficult when a thick fog settled over the contested area. The initial attack by Sullivan's column commenced at dawn but remained unsupported and exposed on its flanks. As anticipated, the British were surprised and driven back by the advance guard under Colonel Thomas CONWAY and cavalry under Captain Allen McLANE. However, men of the 40th Regiment under Lieutenant Colonel Thomas Musgrave hastily occupied Clivedon, a fortified, twin-story stone house owned by Judge Benjamin Chew, and barricaded themselves inside. Musgrave, in light of the recent "massacre" at Paoli, warned his men that the Americans were probably in no mood to take prisoners and urged all ranks to fight to the death. Sullivan continued pressing forward his attack past Musgrave's detachment, but when Washington came up with his staff, General Henry KNOX remonstrated about leaving a sizable British force in the army's rear. Colonels Alexander HAMILTON and Timothy PICKERING, however, urged their commander to maintain the initiative and simply bypass Clivedon. After quick reflection, Washington concurred with Knox and ordered General William MAXWELL's brigade to winkle the defenders out. The Americans charged the stone house repeatedly and took heavy losses, but they lacked the heavy artillery necessary to batter its stout walls down. After hard fighting, the Americans simply cordoned off Clivedon and proceeded with the main attack under General Anthony WAYNE. However, the delay had cost Washington a precious hour, which Howe put to use consolidating his defenses.

Greene's division also pushed off late, but the brigade of General Peter MUHLENBERG charged entirely through the British line and penetrated as far as their camp. Thus far the American plan had succeeded surprisingly well, but disaster struck when General Adam STEPHEN inexplicably pulled his troops out of line in the fog and meandered across the field. Perceiving enemy forces to their front, they mistakenly began firing into the backs of Wayne's command. Confusion ensued as the two forces engaged each other and struggled to sort themselves out, at which point Howe orchestrated a vigorous counterstroke. British forces under General Charles GREY drove back the milling Americans at bayonet point and rescued the garrison at Clivedon. General Francis NASH was then mortally wounded by a cannon shot while the 9th Virginia Continentals under Colonel George Mathews were suddenly cut off by General James GRANT and surrendered 400 soldiers. With Cornwallis fast approaching with reinforcements from Philadelphia, Washington correctly judged the battle lost and ordered a withdrawal at 10 A.M. The Americans had 673 casualties and lost 400 prisoners to a British tally of 551—a two-to-one margin. Howe's highly disciplined regulars clearly prevailed in this stiff encounter, and Philadelphia remained in British hands; the Americans had little recourse beyond occupying their freezing accommodations at Valley Forge. But Germantown demonstrated Washington's capacity for aggressive leadership along with the resiliency and willingness of his tattered soldiers to fight. Though thwarted in victory by an overly ambitious strategy, bad luck, and tactical mismanagement, the Americans had given a good account of themselves, and their morale improved commensurately.

Further Reading
Brownlow, Donald G. *A Documentary History of the Battle of Germantown.* Gettysburg, Pa.: Gettysburg Historical Society, 1955.
Edgar, Gregory T. *The Philadelphia Campaign, 1777–1778.* Bowie, Md.: Heritage Books, 1998.
Jackson, John W. *With the British Army in Philadelphia, 1777–1778.* San Rafael, Calif.: Presidio Press, 1979.
Martin, David C. *The Philadelphia Campaign, June 1777–July 1778.* Cambridge, Mass.: Da Capo Press, 2003.
McGuire, Thomas J. *The Surprise of Germantown, or, the Battle of Clivedon.* Gettysburg, Pa.: Thomas Publications, 1994.
Niderost, Eric. "Victory Denied by the Fog of War." Military Heritage 6. no 4 (2005): 46–55.
Taafe, Stephen R. *The Philadelphia Campaign, 1777–1778.* Lawrence: University Press of Kansas, 2003.

Gerry, Elbridge (1744–1814)
American politician

Elbridge Gerry was born in Marblehead, Massachusetts, on July 17, 1744, the son of a merchant. He passed through Harvard College in 1762 and returned to his hometown to manage the family business. However, like many colonials, he was shocked by the BOSTON MASSACRE and entered politics as an anti-British agitator. He gained election to the Massachusetts General Court in 1772, becoming a protege of radical leader Samuel ADAMS. As relations with Great Britain deteriorated, Gerry served on the Marblehead COMMITTEE OF CORRESPONDENCE and subsequently composed the noted circular letter dispatched to other colonies in 1773. The following year, when the British COERCIVE ACTS closed down the port of Boston, Marblehead served as the new entrepot for the city, and Gerry skillfully collected and distributed supplies intended for the inhabitants. In 1774 he served with the extralegal Massachusetts provincial congress, being tasked with procuring supplies and weapons for various MINUTEMEN companies throughout the colony. On the night of April 18, 1775, just prior to the battles of Lexington and CONCORD, he barely escaped capture from a tavern at Menotomy, which was on the British marching route.

In 1776 Gerry was elected to the Second Continental CONGRESS, where he functioned as an early and forceful proponent of breaking ties with England. He subsequently signed the DECLARATION OF INDEPENDENCE, embraced the ARTICLES OF CONFEDERATION, and served on numerous committees dealing with finance. His business expertise held him in good stead when he undertook raising supplies and arms for the Continental ARMY, which he personally distrusted. Moreover, his political viewpoints began exhibiting a maddening inconsistency. Throughout the period of the so-called Conway Cabal, he appeared to support both Colonel Thomas CONWAY and George WASHINGTON and, while fearing standing armies, Gerry argued strenuously in favor of long-term enlistments and officers' half-pay for life. Curiously, he denounced the FRENCH ALLIANCE and believed that Benjamin FRANKLIN had been duped by his hosts into an entangling arrangement. Gerry also functioned as a purveyor of supplies to the army and, in a period of shameless profiteering, he acquitted himself honestly and efficiently. In 1780 he disagreed with fellow delegates over pricing formulas for military supplies and stormed out of Congress. Gerry remained at Marblehead for the remainder of the war to conduct business affairs and manage several privateers. Gerry also found time to secure a seat in the lower house of the state legislature before resuming his seat in Congress, 1783–85.

The post-Revolution period found the United States grappling with the inadequacies of the Articles of Confederation, and political movements arose to replace that arrangement with one promoting stronger, centralized government. In 1787 Gerry attended the Constitutional Convention in Philadelphia as a chairman where, again, his inconsistencies antagonized fellow delegates. Gerry advocated centralized governance—yet denounced it as a threat to republicanism. After orchestrating the great compromise between small and large states—in effect, saving the Constitution—Gerry then railed against its adoption because a bill of rights to guarantee personal liberties was lacking. He returned to Massachusetts and agitated against ratification, citing inadequate representation, the perils of a potentially oppressive judiciary, and ambiguous legislative powers. But Gerry's advice was generally heeded and a bill of rights was finally appended to the Constitution. He was then elected to Congress in 1789 as an anti-Federalist but, once again, he changed his tack and firmly supported the new government. Gerry finally left Congress in 1793 and returned home to rail against the pro-British tendencies of the Federalists.

In 1797 Gerry added to his quixotic reputation when President John ADAMS appointed him to a three-man committee tasked with reducing tensions with Revolutionary France. When the French minister Talleyrand and his secret agents X, Y, and Z demanded bribes, two members left Paris in disgust, but Gerry remained behind seemingly smug in the knowledge that his presence would prevent war. Adams then ordered him home in semi-disgrace, and he launched several failed attempts for the Massachusetts governorship. Gerry finally won the governor's mansion in 1810, where he pioneered the practice of "Gerrymandering," namely, manipulating congressional districts to give his Democratic-Republican party greater power. In 1813 he was tapped by President James MADISON to serve as vice president to replace the deceased George CLINTON. He performed capably in that role during most of the second war with England before dying in office on November 23, 1814. His wife, who died in 1849, was the last surviving spouse of a Declaration of Independence signer.

Further Reading

Billias, George A. *Elbridge Gerry: Founding Father and Republican Statesman.* New York: McGraw-Hill, 1976.

Flynn, Patrick B. "The Papers of Elbridge Gerry." Unpublished master's thesis, Clark University, 1994.

Jefferies, Lynn A. "Elbridge Gerry and the American Revolution, 1772–1787." Unpublished master's thesis, Miami University, 1973.

Gardiner, Clinton H., ed. *A Study in Dissent: The Warren-Gerry Correspondence, 1776–1792.* Carbondale: Southern Illinois University Press, 1968.

Knight, Russell W. "Fire, Smoak, and Elbridge Gerry," *Essex Institute Historical Collections* 106, no. 1 (1970): 32–45.

Kramer, Eugene. "The Public Career of Elbridge Gerry." Unpublished Ph.D. diss., Ohio State University, 1955.

Gillon, Alexander (1741–1794)

American naval figure

Alexander Gillon was born in Rotterdam, Holland, the son of a wealthy merchant. Well educated and multilingual, he entered the shipping business by 1764 and eventually settled at Charleston, South Carolina. Throughout the period of difficulties with Great Britain he waxed indifferently as to politics, until the practice of nonimportation infringed upon his ability to conduct business. He was then brought before the local Liberty Tree Committee and charged with violating the trade ban; then, only reluctantly, he joined the Patriot side. Thereafter, Gillon's principal motivation for loyalty appears to have been financial. In 1775 he commenced his political career by sitting in the second provincial congress and secured a lucrative contract for munitions through the Continental CONGRESS. He also served as a captain in the German Fusiliers throughout 1777 before prevailing upon the local government to appoint him commodore of the South Carolina state navy in February 1778. After briefly sailing on two Connecticut privateers he left for Europe in November 1778, now tasked with obtaining three frigates in exchange for South Carolina goods.

From the onset Gillon's mission was surrounded by controversy and shady dealings. Having conferred with American agent Benjamin FRANKLIN in Paris, he arrived in the Netherlands to purchase his warships with credit provided by the French government. Previously, he had conspired with Arthur LEE against John Paul JONES to ensure that command of the new frigate *Alliance* remained in French hands. On May 30, 1780, having promised the Chevalier Luxembourg one-fourth of the share of all prizes, Gillon managed to lease the powerful 41-gun frigate *L'Indien,* the largest warship to be employed by the United States, which he promptly rechristened *South Carolina.* However, bad weather prevented his departure, and Gillon was nearly bankrupted by expenditures until he received a new infusion of cash through American agent and fellow South Carolinian John LAURENS. He finally departed in August 1781 and spent several months intriguing in Spain before arriving at Havana, Cuba, in January 1782. There he became involved in the Spanish expedition against the Bahamas commanded by Governor Cagigal of Cuba, enticed by the prospect of plundering British warehouses. Gillon accompanied 61 Spanish transports against the island, which surrendered without a fight on May 6, 1782, but the conditions of surrender established by Cagigal forbade plundering. Disgusted, Gillon abandoned his allies and arrived penniless at Philadelphia on May 28, 1782.

Gillion was not long in port before he was detained by legal matters advanced by Luxembourg's agents for monies past due. Worse, the *South Carolina* sailed on to Charleston without him that December and was captured by the British. Gillon escaped paying financial restitution for his role in this farce, but his native state proved liable and was unable to settle the matter satisfactorily until 1814. All told, Gillon's escapade represented a huge monetary loss for South Carolina. Curiously, this sordid affair little diminished Gillon's personal popularity, and he reentered politics by holding a succession of state offices commencing in 1783. Once back in the legislature he espoused anti-British stances and strongly urged confiscation of all LOYALIST property. In 1793 Gillon was elected to the new federal Congress and died while serving in this capacity, at his home, on October 6, 1794. He was a controversial—if somewhat inept—figure of the time, and his motives remain difficult to accurately assess.

Further Reading

Grimball, Berkeley. "Commodore Alexander Gillon of South Carolina, 1771–1794." Unpublished master's thesis, Duke University, 1951.

Groth, Gwin L. "Alexander Gillon, an Asset or a Liability to South Carolina." Unpublished master's thesis, Wake Forest University, 1971.

Lewis, James A. *Neptune's Militia: The Frigate South Carolina during the American Revolution.* Kent, Ohio: Kent State University Press, 1999.

Middlebrook, Louis F. *The Frigate South Carolina: A Famous Revolutionary Warship.* Salem, Mass.: Essex Institute, 1929.

Stone, Richard G. " 'The South Carolina We've Lost': The Bizarre Saga of Alexander Gillon and His Frigate," *American Neptune* 39, no. 3 (1979): 159–172.

Topping, Aileen M. "Alexander Gillon in Havana, 'This Very Friendly Port,' " *South Carolina Historical Magazine* 83, no. 1 (1982): 34–49.

Girty, Simon (1741–1818)

Loyalist interpreter and scout

Simon Girty was born near Harrisburg, Pennsylvania, in 1741, the son of a farmer. He never acquired an education and was illiterate through life. At the age of 10, Girty lost his father in a drunken duel and, during the French and Indian War, his entire family was captured by Delaware Indians. After watching his grandfather burned at the stake, Girty and his three brothers were then divided up among the tribes as hostages. He was taken among the Seneca and adjusted well to captivity; after living among them for eight years he became fluent in Iroquois and well versed in the nuances of tribal life and warfare. Girty was finally released at Fort Pitt in 1759, and thereafter he sought work as an interpreter. He functioned in this capacity during Lord Dunmore's War with the Shawnee in 1774, where he befriended the noted scout Simon Kenton. When the Revolutionary War erupted the following year, Girty initially sided with the Patriots and was dispatched into the Ohio territory to secure the neutrality of tribes living there. But, given much to drink and raucous behavior, he was continually in and out of trouble with American authorities and decided to switch sides. In March 1778, Girty, accompanied by his brothers James and George, escaped to Detroit and tendered his services to Lieutenant Governor Henry HAMILTON. He was immediately attached to the Indian Department as a scout and interpreter and soon gained an infamous reputation along the western frontier.

Commencing in 1779, Girty led several combined LOYALIST/Indian raids from Detroit and scored several striking successes. His warriors massacred several detachments outside of Fort Laurens, Ohio, and, on October 4, 1779, he ambushed an American detachment under Colonel David Rogers, killing 57 men and capturing 600,000 Spanish dollars. The following year he accompanied an even larger expedition into Kentucky under British captain Henry Bird, which seized two forts and secured over 300 hostages —including his former friend Kenton, whose release he arranged. Girty performed well in his scouting and combat activities but, when he confronted Mohawk chief Joseph BRANT for bragging, Brant slashed him across the face with a sword. Such disfigurement only enhanced his standing among the warriors, and in August 1782 Girty took them on another long raid through Ohio. On June 4–5, he successfully ambushed and defeated a column under Colonel William CRAWFORD, gaining lasting infamy for allowing that officer to be tortured for several days before being burned at the stake. Girty then continued into Kentucky to attack numerous, isolated settlements. Having unsuccessfully besieged Bryant's Station on August 15, he feigned a retreat in the face of an oncoming relief column and posted his Indians and rangers along the heights of the Blue Licks River. Girty made no attempt to disguise his location, which prompted the Kentuckians under Major Hugh McGary to charge across the stream and directly into a deadly ambush. Seventy Americans died on August 19, 1782, including the youngest son of noted scout Daniel BOONE, before Girty withdrew to Detroit.

The end of the Revolutionary War did little to mitigate Indian hostilities against American encroachment along the northwestern frontier. For a decade Girty consistently attended tribal councils and urged war against the United States. In 1791 he accompanied the warriors of Chief Little Turtle of the Miami in their smashing victory over Generals Arthur ST. CLAIR and Richard BUTLER. Three years later he unsuccessfully fought against General Anthony WAYNE at the decisive victory of Fallen Timbers, whereby the Indians finally sued for peace. When Detroit finally passed over to American hands in 1795, Girty relocated to Amherstburg, Ontario, and continued working for the British Indian Department. Melancholy and increasingly alcoholic, he fled his home in 1813 when American forces stormed western Ontario in the War of 1812. The aged scout finally died at Amherstburg on February 18, 1818, a brutal man and the product of a brutal frontier. Though reviled for ruthlessness, Girty was no better or worse than many contemporaries on either side of the frontier struggle.

Further Reading
Colwell, David G. "The Causes and Accuracy of the Reputation of Simon Girty in American History," *Pittsburgh History* 77, no. 1 (1994): 30–42.
Fitzpatrick, Alan. *Wilderness War on the Ohio: The Untold Story of the Savage Battle for British and Indian Control of the Ohio Country during the American Revolution.* Benwood, W.Va.: Fort Henry Publications, 2003.
Frederick, Harold. *The Damnation of Simon Girty.* Havelock, N.C.: The Print Shop, 1991.
Rhoden, Nancy L., and Ian K. Steele, eds. *The Human Tradition in the American Revolution.* Wilmington, Del.: Scholarly Resources, 2000.
Richards, James K. "A Clash of Cultures: Simon Girty and the Struggle for the Frontier," *Timeline* 2, no. 3 (1985): 2–17.
Truman, Timothy. *Wilderness: The True Story of Simon Girty, the Renegade.* Lancaster, Pa.: 4 Winds Publishing Group, 1989.

Gist, Mordecai (1742–1792)
American military officer

Mordecai Gist was born in Reisterstown, Maryland, on February 22, 1782, the son of a merchant. He came from a family steeped in military service, and his uncle, Nathaniel Gist, had fought alongside Colonel George WASHINGTON during the French and Indian War. Gist, who found success as a merchant, proved himself an ardent Patriot; following the onset of difficulties with Great Britain, he served as a captain with the Baltimore Independent Company. On January 14, 1776, Gist was commissioned major in the 1st Maryland Continental Infantry under Colonel William SMALLWOOD and accompanied that officer to New York. His regiment served as part of the division commanded by General William ALEXANDER, Lord Stirling, and fought exceptionally well during the defeat at LONG ISLAND, August 27, 1776. Gist defended his position tenaciously against superior forces directed by General James GRANT and facilitated the escape of Alexander's force. After Williams fell wounded at WHITE PLAINS on October 28, 1776, Gist was promoted lieutenant colonel to succeed him and guided the regiment throughout the New Jersey campaign. Shortly after, he transferred to the 3rd Maryland Continentals and led them competently at GERMANTOWN on October 4, 1777.

Gist eventually transferred back to Maryland to recruit and on January 9, 1779, he gained promotion to brigadier general and was assigned to the Southern Department under General Johann de KALB. In this capacity Gist's 2nd Maryland Brigade fought superbly at the disaster of CAMDEN on August 16, 1780, and tenaciously defended the American left until nearly surrounded. After Kalb fell mortally wounded, Gist cut his way free with a handful of troops and subsequently received the thanks of Congress. Gist spent the balance of the year recruiting and procuring supplies for newly arrived forces under General Nathanael GREENE. In the summer of 1781 he marched to Virginia and commanded a brigade at YORKTOWN. He then returned to the Carolinas with a light brigade as Greene conducted mop-up operations against isolated British posts. On August 27, 1782, Gist was at Combahee Ferry outside Charleston, South Carolina, when he learned of a large British/LOYALIST force rowing down the nearby river and decided to intercept them. When his advanced guard was ambushed in tall grass, resulting in the death of Colonel John LAURENS, Gist hurried up with his cavalry elements and fought the enemy to a standstill. Pressing on, he subsequently attacked and captured an armed galley at Port Royal Ferry. This was one of the last conventional engagements of the war.

Gist resigned his commission on November 3, 1783, and retired to a plantation in Charleston. He died there on August 2, 1792, a competent regimental commander from a state highly regarded for its Continental infantry. His son, aptly christened States Rights Gist, fought and died as a Confederate brigadier during the Civil War.

Further Reading

Batt, Richard J. "The Maryland Continentals, 1780–1781." Unpublished master's thesis, Tulane University, 1974.
Blakeslee, Katherine W. *Mordecai Gist and His American Progenitors.* Baltimore: Daughters of the American Revolution, Mordecai Gist Chapter, 1923.
Gist, Mordecai. "Letter of Mordecai Gist to Col. Munford," *Maryland Historical Magazine* 4 (December 1909): 369–372.
Kilbourn, John D. *A Short History of the Maryland Line in the Continental Army.* Baltimore: Society of the Cincinnati of Maryland, 1992.
Lynch, Branford G. "Brigadier General Mordecai Gist," *Daughters of the American Revolution Magazine* 15 (December 1931): 720–724.
Tacyn, Mark A. " 'To the End': The First Maryland Regiment and the American Revolution." Unpublished Ph.D. diss., University of Maryland, College Park, 1999.

Glover, John (1732–1797)
American military officer

John Glover was born in Salem, Massachusetts, on November 5, 1732, the son of a carpenter. His father died while he was young, and he subsequently relocated to nearby Marblehead with his mother. There Glover became involved in fishing and shipping activities and by 1770 had acquired a small fleet of vessels. He was also attracted by military affairs and in 1759 received an ensign's commission in the local militia. Because English economic measures like the SUGAR ACT of 1764 had adversely affected his business affairs, Glover became active in politics by joining the local COMMITTEE OF CORRESPONDENCE. He rose to colonel of the Marblehead militia just prior to the outbreak of violence in April 1775 and marched his regiment to Cambridge to partake of the siege of Boston. His unit was renamed the 14th Massachusetts Continental Infantry, which was unique in the Continental ARMY for being composed of professional sailors. They wore blue coats and white caps denoting their special status and could handle boats and other small craft regardless of weather conditions. In August 1775, General George WASHINGTON asked him to outfit a number of private armed vessels to interdict enemy shipping along the coast, and his schooner *Hannah* became one of America's earliest warships. After British forces evacuated Boston in March 1776, Glover accompanied Washington to New York City as the theater of war shifted westward.

The Americans were badly defeated by General William HOWE at the Battle of LONG ISLAND on August 27, 1776, and trapped with their siege works along Brooklyn Heights. Glover's mariners then performed a minor miracle by evacuating

American sailor and officer John Glover is considered to be one of the most accomplished soldiers of the Revolutionary War. *(New York Public Library)*

Washington's 9,000 soldiers and their artillery across the East River to Manhattan under cover of darkness—and British noses—on August 29–30. Howe subsequently pursued the Americans with a successful landing at Kip's Bay on September 15, 1776, where Glover contained the beachhead long enough for General John SULLIVAN's brigade and General Henry KNOX's cannon to escape intact. The Americans continued retreating and on October 13, 1776, Glover's 750 men fought nearly 4,000 British troops to a standstill at Pelham Bay in another celebrated delaying action. He then accompanied Washington throughout the arduous retreat across New Jersey until they reached the safety of Pennsylvania. On the night of December 25, 1776, Glover's mariners again proved instrumental to the American cause when they ferried 2,400 troops and 18 cannon across the Delaware River in a howling snowstorm, then marched several miles overland to block the HESSIAN garrison at TRENTON from retreating. Shortly after, Glover fought well at PRINCETON, then rowed the army back, prisoners in tow, across the Delaware. These harrowing exploits, conducted over 36 hours in sub-zero weather, established the "Marblehead mariners" as among the toughest outfits of the American army. Glover's unit then disbanded owing to expiring enlistments, and he shortly after returned home to attend to his ailing wife.

In February 1777 Glover was tendered the appointment of brigadier general, but he declined to accept until personally asked by Washington. He then took to the field that summer as part of forces fighting under General Horatio GATES at Saratoga, and he subsequently escorted the so-called Convention Army of General John BURGOYNE into captivity at Cambridge. The following year he commanded a brigade under the marquis de LAFAYETTE during the ill-fated siege of Newport, Rhode Island, and spent several months commanding the Providence garrison. In 1780 Glover assumed command of the Hudson River Highlands and served on the board that convicted English major John ANDRE of espionage. Poor health finally necessitated Glover's retirement from the army on July 22, 1782, and he returned to Marblehead to recuperate. After the war Glover resumed his business activities with some success and also served as a delegate to the Massachusetts Constitutional Convention of 1787. Two years later he gained election to the General Court, serving there until his death in Marblehead on January 30, 1797. Glover was one of the most accomplished American officers of his grade.

Further Reading

Billias, George A. *General John Glover and His Marblehead Mariners.* New York: Holt, 1960.

Hearn, Chester G. *George Washington's Schooners: The First American Navy.* Annapolis, Md.: Naval Institute Press, 1995.

Knight, Russell W., ed. *General John Glover's Letterbook, 1776–1777.* Salem, Mass.: Essex Institute, 1976.

McKenzie, Matthew G. *Barefooted, Bare Leg'd, Bare Breeched: The Revolutionary War Service of the Mass-*

achusetts Continental Line. Boston: Massachusetts Society of the Cincinnati, 1995.

Myers, J. Jay. "George Washington's Dire Straits," *American History* 36, no. 2 (2001): 22–30.

Swanson, Susan C. "Colonel Glover's Stand at Pelham," *American History Illustrated* 15, no. 2 (1980): 14–22.

Golden Hill, Battle of (January 19, 1770)

Commencing in 1765, when Parliament passed the revised QUARTERING ACT, inhabitants of New York displayed increasing resentment toward imperial policy. The following year, to celebrate repeal of the earlier STAMP ACT, the local SONS OF LIBERTY orchestrated raucous celebrations on the New York City commons, centered upon a newly erected flagstaff. In the context of the times, this pole became popularly regarded as the "Tree of Liberty." Soon after, the colonial assembly refused General Thomas GAGE's request for funding to comply with provisions of the Quartering Act and was suspended. Such contention gnawed away at relations between civilians and the military, and on August 10, 1766, British soldiers deliberately cut down the flagstaff. The Sons of Liberty then defiantly erected a new one, which occasioned heated confrontations between the two groups. On March 18, 1767, New Yorkers again marked celebration of the Stamp Act's repeal, and again British soldiers removed the Liberty Pole. Tensions were further exacerbated that year following passage of the TOWNSHEND DUTIES on imports, which crystalized political opposition to British policies.

Events in New York City crested in the late fall of 1769 when new elections added several moderate delegates to the colonial assembly. These members promptly authorized requisite funding for the Quartering Act, which greatly angered anti-British factions. Alexander MCDOUGALL, head of the local Sons of Liberty, then composed a scathing pamphlet entitled *To the Betrayed Inhabitants of the City and Colony of New York*, aimed at inflaming popular passions. Relations were also strained by a sluggish economy in which unemployed dockworkers competed with soldiers for scarce jobs. On January 17, 1777, several soldiers, angered by anti-British broadsides, again removed a Liberty Pole in the city square. The next day angry colonials seized two soldiers caught distributing broadsides of their own and intended turning them over to the local sheriff. More soldiers then arrived to rescue their friends, at which point workers began picking up weapons, withdrew to a wheatfield known as Golden Hill, and taunted the soldiers to follow. Thoroughly provoked, the British waded into the mob with bayonets, and a violent riot erupted and lasted for several hours. One man was killed and scores injured by the time order was finally restored. Thereafter all soldiers were restricted to their barracks and could not venture out in public unless accompanied by an officer. The "battle" of Golden Hill was the first outbreak of large-scale violence against British soldiers in America and anticipated what followed at the BOSTON MASSACRE six weeks later.

Further Reading

Boyer, Lee R. "Lobster Boys, Liberty Boys, and Laborers in the Streets of New York's Golden Hill and Nassau Street Riots," *New York Historical Quarterly* 57, no. 4 (1973): 280–308.

Gilje, Paul A. *The Road to Mobocracy: Popular Disorder in New York City, 1763–1834.* Chapel Hill: Published for the Institute of Early American History and Culture by the University of North Carolina Press, 1987.

Humphrey, Thomas J. *Land and Liberty: Hudson Valley Riots in the Age of Revolution.* DeKalb: Northern Illinois University Press, 2004.

Lee, Wayne E. "Careful Riot, Virtuous War: The Legitimization of Public Violence in Eighteenth Century New York." Unpublished Ph.D. diss., Duke University, 1999.

Pencak, William, Matthew Denis, and Simon P. Newman, eds. *Riot and Revelry in Early America.* University Park: University of Pennsylvania Press, 2002.

Grant, James (1720–1806)

English military officer

James Grant was born in Ballindalloch, Scotland, in 1720, and he joined the British army in 1744 as a captain in the famous 1st Regiment of Foot, the

Royal Scots. In this capacity he fought well at Fontenoy and Culloden in 1745. He arrived in America as a major of the 77th Highlanders in 1757, and the following year both he and Andrew LEWIS were taken prisoner during a botched reconnaissance outside French-held Fort Dusquesne, Pennsylvania. Grant remained a prisoner at Montreal until 1760, when he was exchanged and promoted to lieutenant colonel of the 40th Regiment. He next deployed to South Carolina, where, in 1761, he led a successful raid against Cherokee commanded by Chief OCONOSTOTA. Two years later Spain ceded Florida to Great Britain, and Grant replaced Colonel Frederick HALDIMAND as governor. He proved himself an amiable and competent administrator but found himself constantly quarreling with colonial officials throughout this wild and backward territory. Grant took ill and returned to England in 1771 to recuperate, being replaced by William MOULTRIE. Once home he found time to secure a seat in Parliament and partook of early debates concerning the Revolutionary War. At one point he declared that he could march from one end of the colonies to the other with only 5,000 men—a boast he subsequently retracted. Because of his previous experience in America, Grant gained promotion to colonel of the 55th Regiment in December 1775, and the following spring he arrived at Boston as part of General William HOWE's entourage. Shortly after, he was promoted to brigadier general.

Grant fought at the Battle of LONG ISLAND on August 27, 1776, where he performed useful service by pinning down the division of General William ALEXANDER. He then served under General Charles CORNWALLIS during the advance across New Jersey and succeeded that officer after he departed for England. Grant proved somewhat contemptuous of the Americans and assured the HESSIAN commander, Colonel Johann RALL, at TRENTON that they posed no threat. Disaster ensued and this misjudgment did little to enhance his reputation among contemporaries. Grant subsequently commanded a division in operations directed against Philadelphia during the fall of 1777 and fought reasonably well at BRANDYWINE and GERMANTOWN, winning promotion to major general. In the late spring of 1778, when General Howe was preparing to return to England, he orchestrated one final campaign to ensnare advanced forces under the marquis de LAFAYETTE at Barren Hill. On May 28 Grant was ordered to conduct a circling movement to catch his opponent from behind, and he positioned his troops without difficulty. However, when Lafayette suddenly feigned an attack against the British, Grant apparently panicked and assumed defensive positions, allowing his quarry to escape. Howe was appreciably furious at the successful deception and, like many officers, refused to talk to Grant during the march back to Philadelphia.

British general James Grant frequently misjudged American soldiers, leading many contemporaries to believe he was militarily inept. *(Private Scottish Collection)*

In June 1778 General Henry CLINTON assumed command of British forces and directed an overland march back to New York. Grant was ordered to act as the rear guard in the event that General George WASHINGTON made a sudden lunge at the column. Washington did exactly that on June 28, but Grant, slow as ever, failed to deflect the blow, and the British took heavy losses at the Battle of MONMOUTH. Shortly after, Clinton received instructions from Lord George GERMAIN to detach 5,800 men from his army for service in the Caribbean; eager to rid himself of such a plodding performer he assigned Grant to the task. Grant captured the French island of St. Lucia on December 12, 1778, and spent several days fortifying his charge against a possible counterattack. Six days later a fleet under Admiral Charles-Hector-Théodat, comte d'ESTAING, arrived and landed several thousand troops on St. Lucia, whom Grant expertly repulsed at Vigie with 1,600 casualties on December 18, 1778. He returned to England on August 1, 1779, advanced to lieutenant general in 1782, and died at Ballindalloch on April 13, 1806. Grant fought well on occasion but his performance was generally uneven.

Further Reading

Grant, Alastair M. *General James Grant of Ballindalloch, 1720–1806.* London: A. M. Grant, 1930.

McCue, Margaret C. "Lieutenant Colonel James Grant's Expedition against the Cherokee Indians, 1761." Unpublished master's thesis, University of South Carolina, 1967.

Nelson, Paul D. *General James Grant: Scottish Soldier and Royal Governor of Florida.* Gainesville: University Press of Florida, 1993.

Opal, C. Cannon. "Lieutenant Colonel James Grant's Governorship of East Florida, 1764–1771." Unpublished master's thesis, University of South Carolina, 1973.

Rogers, George C. "The Papers of James Grant of Ballindalloch Castle, Scotland," *South Carolina Historical Magazine* 77, no. 3 (1976): 145–160.

Schafer, Daniel L. *St. Augustine's British Years, 1763–1784.* St. Augustine, Fla.: St. Augustine Historical Society, 2002.

Grasse, François-Joseph-Paul, marquis de Grasetilly, comte de (1722–1788)
French naval officer

François-Joseph-Paul, comte de Grasse, was born in Bar-sur-Loup, France, on September 12, 1722, part of an old aristocratic family. After attending the Gardes de la Marine at Toulon in 1735, he served as a page to the grand master of the Knights of Malta. De Grasse then entered the French navy in 1740 and fought in the War of the Austrian Succession. He matured into a lofty figure well over six feet in height and exceedingly cool under fire. De Grasse was captured at the Battle of Cape Finisterre on May 2, 1747, and spent his detention studying the English and their naval institutions. He functioned as a lieutenant commander when the Seven Years' War erupted in 1755 and fought in the unsuccessful defense of Louisbourg. He made captain in 1762 and spent several years commanding both vessels and stations in the West Indies and Mediterranean. On June 1, 1778, de Grasse rose to commodore and commanded several ships at the indecisive Battle of Ushant on the following July 27. This encounter formally signified France's entry into the Revolutionary War, and the following summer he accompanied the expedition of Admiral Charles-Hector-Théodat, comte d'ESTAING, to the West Indies. He fought well at the Battle of Grenada on July 6, 1779, wherein a British squadron under Admiral John BYRON was worsted, and subsequently served throughout the ill-fated siege of SAVANNAH. When d'Estaing returned to France later that year, de Grasse temporarily assumed command of French naval forces in the Caribbean. After fighting at Martinique under Admiral Luc Urbain, comte Guichen, on April 17, 1780, he sickened and went home to recuperate. There, on March 22, 1781, de Grasse advanced to admiral and commander of a 150-ship expeditionary force bound for the West Indies. He then hoisted his pennant on the 110-gun ship of the line *Ville de Paris,* then the world's largest warship. The choice of de Grasse was fortuitous for he proved both an accomplished sailor and a willing coalition partner.

De Grasse anchored at Saint-Domingue (Haiti) on August 12, 1781, when he received a letter from General Jean-Baptiste, comte de ROCHAMBEAU, requesting assistance. The admiral wrote back informing him that his squadron would be in the vicinity of Chesapeake Bay from September to October, and then sailed with 3,000 reinforcements. De Grasse's reply proved decisive, for it prompted Rochambeau and his American counterpart, General George WASHINGTON, to speedily march from New York to YORKTOWN, Virginia, and entrap the army of General Charles CORNWALLIS there. True to his word, de Grasse stationed himself at Chesapeake Bay on August 26 and began offloading troops and supplies until the appearance of a British force of 19 warships under Admiral Thomas GRAVES on September 5. De Grasse promptly sallied with 24 warships of his own and gave battle for several hours. Both sides maneuvered and made firing passes at each other, but the conflict off the Virginia Capes otherwise proved indecisive. For several more days the two fleets made repairs and stood off from each other. However, once de Grasse was reinforced by additional ships under Admiral Jacques, comte de Barras, on September 10, 1781, the British promptly retreated to New York. This left the army of General Cornwallis stranded without support, and he ultimately surrendered on October 19, 1781.

After the victory at Yorktown, both Washington and Rochambeau pleaded for de Grasse to remain behind for possible combined operations against New York, but he feared the approaching hurricane season and returned to the West Indies on November 4, 1781. On February 12, 1782, he captured the British-held island of St. Kitts despite valiant efforts by Admiral Samuel HOOD to reinforce the garrison. De Grasse then conducted a series of running battles with a new adversary, Admiral George Brydges RODNEY, who finally brought the French to bay at Iles de Saintes on April 12, 1782. De Grasse, with slightly fewer ships, drew up his traditional line of battle only to have it pierced in three places by the more aggressive Rodney and Hood. The French decisively lost 3,000 men and seven warships, while de Grasse was taken prisoner aboard the *Ville de Paris*. Conducted back to England, Prime Minister William PETTY, Lord Shelburne, approached him to serve as an intermediary between the two governments during peace talks. After the war ended in 1783 de Grasse fell under criticism for his defeat at the Saintes, which he blamed on certain subordinates. In May 1784 he requested and received an official court of inquiry that cleared his name, but King Louis XVI nonetheless exiled him from the court. De Grasse spent the remainder of his life in semi-disgrace on his estate at Tilly, where he died on January 14, 1788. He was easily the most effective French naval commander to assist the United States and, in terms of deportment and cooperativeness, a vast improvement over his haughty predecessor. After the French Revolution commenced in 1789, all five of his children fled to America, where they became

French naval officer the comte de Grasse commanded allied revolutionary forces in the Caribbean and the decisive Yorktown campaign. *(U.S. Naval Institute)*

citizens and received pensions from the United States government in recognition of their father's contributions to independence. In 1984 the U.S. Navy further honored him by commissioning the destroyer USS *Comte de Grasse*.

Further Reading

Dull, Jonathan R. *The French Navy and American Independence: A Study of Arms and Diplomacy, 1774–1787*. Princeton, N.J.: Princeton University Press, 1975.

Gardiner, Robert, ed. *Navies in the American Revolution, 1775–1783*. Annapolis, Md.: Naval Institute Press, 1996.

Institut françois de Washington (D.C.). *Compilation of General Washington and Comte de Grasse, 1781, August 17–November 4*. Washington, D.C.: Government Printing Office, 1931.

Lewis, Charles L. *Admiral De Grasse and American Independence*. Annapolis, Md.: United States Naval Institute, 1945.

Selig, Robert A. "Francois Joseph Paul, Comte de Grasse, The Battle off the Virginia Capes, and the Victory at Yorktown," *Colonial Williamsburg* 21, no. 5 (1999): 26–32.

Valliant, Joseph N. "Revolution's Fate Sealed at Sea," *Military History* 12, no. 4 (1995): 46–53.

Graves, Samuel (1713–1787)

English naval officer

Samuel Graves was born in England on April 17, 1713, and joined the Royal Navy at an early age. He rose to lieutenant in 1739, campaigned at Cartagena two years later under his uncle, Admiral Thomas Graves, and rose to captain by 1743. Graves then commanded the frigate HMS *Duke* throughout the Seven Years' War, 1755–63, and distinguished himself in combat at Basque Roads in 1757 and Quiberon Bay in 1759. Graves rose to rear admiral in 1772 and vice admiral in 1774, a reflection of his overall military ability. He also enjoyed close ties with the naval minister, Lord John MONTAGU, earl of Sandwich, who in July 1774 appointed him commander in chief of Royal Navy forces in American waters. Graves had never previously held an independent command, and he arrived at Boston on June 30, 1774, amid the tumult of revolutionary unrest. He discovered at that time that his command consisted of seven sloops and 14 smaller vessels, all of which were inadequate for patrolling the thousand-mile coastline of North America. At that time the Boston Port Act, part of the COERCIVE ACTS, had closed that port to commercial activity. Given his scanty naval resources, Graves proved unsuccessful at suppressing smugglers who plied the waters to and from Boston with near impunity. He also proved unable to establish close ties with his army counterpart, General Thomas GAGE. Worse of all, both remained flummoxed as to how to contain and extinguish the fires of rebellion.

Like any naval commander in such a predicament, Graves pleaded with superiors at the naval ministry for reinforcements, especially small, shallow-draft warships that could maneuver in the tight harbor channels. Instead he received the large ships of the line, HMS *Asia, Boyne,* and *Somerset,* which looked impressive at anchor but were impractical for cornering such elusive adversaries. The Revolutionary War commenced in April 1775, and Graves strongly suggested that Gage completely fortify Boston and burn the outlying regions of Roxbury and Cambridge to deny them to the rebels. He also urged the army to construct fortifications upon Charlestown and Dorchester Heights to preclude their possession by the enemy. Gage took no action until the Americans had seized the high ground overlooking Boston Harbor, which culminated in the disastrous Battle at BUNKER HILL. With the failure of Gage to win a decisive victory, Graves and the Royal Navy fell under increasing pressure to take offensive action, despite his lack of ships, armament, and manpower. He did so reluctantly and finally authorized outfitting of several converted merchantmen with army howitzers. This slapdash force, commanded by Lieutenant Henry Mowat, was then authorized to raid hostile enclaves along the Massachusetts coast.

On October 18, 1775, Mowat attacked and burned the village of Falmouth, Massachusetts (now Maine), an act that further inflamed regional passions against the British. Graves was then criticized by army officers and naval ministers for not attempting to do more. On September 17, 1775, Lord Sandwich resigned to the inevitable and relieved Graves of command. He was replaced by Admiral Molyneaux SHULDHAM on December 30, 1775, an officer of less seniority. Graves returned home an angry, dejected man and demanded a court-martial to clear his name, but the Admiralty, which had not charged him with misconduct—or, for that matter, anything—politely hedged. He thus remained bereft of an active command for several years and refused to accept the Portsmouth naval facilities as a sinecure to silence him. Graves was gradually promoted through seniority to admiral of the blue in 1778 and of the white in 1782, but his naval career had effectively ended at Boston. He retired to his estate and died at Hembury Fort, England, on March 8, 1787. Whatever naval ability Graves possessed, his 18-month tenure in North America proved both frustrating, embarrassing, and counterproductive. Like General Gage, he was unprepared to cope with the difficulties before him and essentially hamstrung by scanty resources.

Further Reading

French, Allen. "The Hallowell-Graves Fisticuffs, 1775," *Massachusetts Historical Society Proceedings* 63 (1931): 23–48.

Tilley, John A. "The Development of American Revolutionary Naval Policy, April 1775–July 1776," *Nautical Research Journal* 25, nos. 1, 3, 4 (1979): 69–78, 119–126, 195–199.

Tracy, Nicholas. *Navies, Deterrence, and American Independence: Britain and Seapower in the 1760s and 1770s.* Vancouver: University of British Columbia Press, 1988.

Wahll, Andrew J., ed. *Henry Mowat: Voyage of the Canceaux, 1764–1776.* Bowie, Md.: Heritage Books, 2003.

Yerxa, Donald A. "Admiral Samuel Graves and the Falmouth Affair: A Case Study in British Imperial Pacification, 1775." Unpublished master's thesis, University of Maine, Orono, 1974.

———. "Vice Admiral Graves and the North American Naval Squadron, 1774–1776," *Mariner's Mirror* 62, no. 3 (1976): 371–385.

Graves, Thomas (1725–1802)
English naval officer

Thomas Graves was born in Thanckes, Cornwall, on October 23, 1725, the son of an admiral. He went to sea with his father and in 1743 received a lieutenant's commission in the Royal Navy. Graves proved himself a capable seaman, rose to captain by 1755, and commanded the 20-gun frigate HMS *Sheerness* during the Seven Years' War. His career hit a rough patch on December 26, 1755, when, during a night chase, he refused to engage a French vessel perceived as much larger than his own. When it turned out that the enemy in question was actually a large Indiaman (transport), Graves was court-martialed for failing to engage the enemy and publicly reprimanded. In 1761 he assisted in repelling a French squadron off Newfoundland and spent the next three years as governor of that province. Graves then fulfilled a long and uneventful stint in home waters and the West Indies before being promoted to admiral in 1779.

On July 13, 1780, Graves convoyed a squadron of six large warships from England to New York. En route he just missed intercepting a French squadron under Admiral Charles-Louis d'Arac de Ternay off Narragansett Bay, which was convoying men and equipment for the army under the marquis de LAFAYETTE near Chesapeake Bay. This was typical of the bad luck that dogged him throughout his tenure in American waters. Graves subsequently served as second in command under Admiral Marriot ARBUTHNOT and helped enforce a blockade of Rhode Island waters for several months. Graves then accompanied his superior to Chesapeake Bay, Virginia, to engage a French fleet under Admiral Charles-René, chevalier Destouches, on March 16, 1781. The British won the skirmish but were roughly handled, and Arbuthnot requested to be relieved. Permission was granted on July 4, 1781, but Graves found

British admiral Thomas Graves arrived too late to aid General Cornwallis at the Battle of Yorktown. *(National Maritime Museum, Greenwich, London)*

himself suddenly superseded by Admiral Robert Digby, a man with less seniority than himself. This awkward arrangement was apparently the result of the machinations of the naval minister, Lord John MONTAGU, earl of Sandwich, who was also Digby's brother-in-law. Graves, who was himself married to the sister of Prime Minister Lord Frederick NORTH, could have contested the appointment but accepted it for the good of the service. Digby, in any case, courteously allowed Graves to maintain command of the fleet at New York.

At this juncture, naval power in the Revolutionary War was about to assert itself upon strategic and military events as it never had previously. In the fall of 1781 the army of General Charles CORNWALLIS ensconced itself on the tip of the YORKTOWN peninsula, Virginia, where it was quickly surrounded by larger forces commanded by Generals George WASHINGTON and Jean-Baptiste, comte de ROCHAMBEAU. The allies were further strengthened by the arrival of a powerful French squadron of 24 ships under Admiral François-Joseph-Paul, comte de GRASSE. The British army commander, General Henry CLINTON, was eager to reinforce Cornwallis with men and supplies before he was overpowered and pleaded with Graves to break the French blockade of Chesapeake Bay. Graves agreed in principle to the move but dithered at New York until reinforced by the squadron of Admiral Samuel HOOD. During the impasse another French squadron under Admiral Jacques-Melchior, comte de Baras, prepared to sail from Newport, Rhode Island, with men and supplies for the allies at Yorktown. Graves finally departed New York with 19 vessels and engaged de Grasse on September 5, 1781, at the Second Battle of the Virginia Capes. The two fleets drew up their traditional battle lines and made a long running pass at each other, although Graves allowed his van to distance itself from the main body, where it was mauled. The British also enjoyed the weather gauge for most of the battle, but Graves performed rigidly and failed to exploit it. After several hours of indecisive fighting, the British drew off. He remained in the vicinity for several more days until de Grasse was reinforced by Baras and then returned to New York on September 13, 1781, to refit. Abandoned by the navy, Cornwallis was thus unable to stave off the allied siege lines and finally surrendered on October 19. One week later Graves reappeared off Yorktown with 7,000 reinforcements for Cornwallis, but it was too late. Allied sea power had proved decisive.

No official blame was attached to Graves for his failure to relieve Cornwallis, but Admirals Hood and George RODNEY treated him shabbily thereafter. He returned to England in 1782 after losing his flagship in a squall and finally arrived in a transport vessel. Graves continued in the service with little fanfare and rose to vice admiral in 1787 and full admiral in 1794. He subsequently distinguished himself by fighting under Admiral Richard HOWE at the "Glorious First of June," being severely wounded. Graves then retired from the service, received a title within the Irish peerage, and died at Cadhay, Devon, on February 9, 1802. He was a capable sailor, but his strict adherence to the Royal Navy's "Fighting Instructions" cost him a chance to beat the French at Yorktown and possibly alter the outcome of the war.

Further Reading
Andreopoulos, George J., and Harold E. Selesky, eds. *The Aftermath of Defeat: States, Armed Forces, and the Challenge of Recovery.* New Haven, Conn.: Yale University Press, 1994.
Breen, Kenneth. "Graves and Hood at the Chesapeake," *Mariner's Mirror* 66, no. 1 (1980): 53–64.
Chadwick, French E., ed. *The Graves Papers and Other Documents Relating to Naval Operations of the Yorktown Campaign, July–October, 1781.* New York: Arno Press, 1968.
Sullivan, J. A. "Graves and Hood," *Mariner's Mirror* 69, no. 2 (1983): 175–194.
Syrett, David. *The Royal Navy in American Waters during the Revolutionary War.* Columbia: University of South Carolina Press, 1998.
Valliant, Joseph N. "Revolution's Fate Sealed at Sea," *Military History* 12, no. 4 (1995): 46–53.

Greene, Christopher (1737–1781)
American military officer

Christopher Greene was born in Warwick, Rhode Island, on May 12, 1737, the son of a prominent judge. Trained as a merchant, he joined the Kentish Guards militia as a lieutenant in 1774, and the following year he became a major in Colonel James M. VARNUM's Rhode Island Regiment. Greene next marched under his cousin, General Nathanael GREENE, to partake of the siege of Boston and there volunteered his services to General Benedict ARNOLD during the arduous march into Canada. Greene, promoted to lieutenant colonel, fought during the ill-fated attack upon QUEBEC, December 31, 1775, and was captured.

Lieutenant Colonel Christopher Greene commanded the Rhode Island Light Infantry, primarily composed of African Americans and one of the best combat units of the Continental army. *(Brown University Archives)*

Exchanged 18 months later—having sworn he would never surrender again—Greene was appointed colonel of the 1st Rhode Island Infantry. In this capacity he joined the main army in New Jersey and was tasked with defending Fort Mercer on the Delaware River with 400 men. On October 22, 1777, General William HOWE dispatched 1,800 HESSIANS under Colonel Karl von Donop to storm Fort Mercer, and Greene summarily rejected his surrender demand. When the Hessians attempted storming the works, Greene ordered his men to withhold their fire until the very last minute and cut the attackers down in droves. Von Donop was one of 400 casualties inflicted by this heroic defense; Greene was subsequently voted a sword from CONGRESS.

Shortly after Greene assumed command of the Rhode Island Light Infantry, a force composed primarily of freed AFRICAN-AMERICAN slaves. Under his strict regimen it soon emerged as one of the best combat units in the Continental ARMY. It formed part of a force under General John SULLIVAN that unsuccessfully besieged British-held Newport, Rhode Island, in August 1778. When the British garrison under General Robert PIGOT suddenly sortied on August 28 and attacked the retreating Americans at Quaker Hill, Greene's regiment repulsed three determined Hessian charges and saved Sullivan's flank. In recognition of his abilities, he next received command of American defenses along the Croton River, New York. This was a no-man's-land characterized by LOYALIST raids under Colonel James de Lancey. On May 14, 1781, de Lancey launched a surprise attack that successfully stormed Greene's headquarters at the home of Richard Davenport. He fought back sword in hand but was eventually killed along with several other officers. Greene's congressional sword was eventually delivered to his son, with a highly complimentary letter by Secretary of War Benjamin LINCOLN.

Further Reading
Boyle, Joseph L. *"Death Seemed to Stare": The New Hampshire and Rhode Island Regiments at Valley Forge.* Baltimore: Clearfield, 2005.
Browne, Gregory M. "Fort Mercer and Fort Mifflin: The Battle for the Delaware River and the Importance of the American Riverine Defenses during Washington's Siege of Philadelphia." Unpublished master's thesis, Western Illinois University, 1996.
Greene, M. A. "Christopher Greene, the Hero of Red Bank," *American Monthly Magazine* 2, no. 5 (1893): 521–526.
Puckerin, Gary A. *The Black Regiment in the American Revolution.* Providence, R.I.: Afro-American Studies Program, Brown University, 1978.
Raymond, Marcius D. *Colonel Christopher Greene: A Paper Read before the Sons of the Revolution of New York, April 26, 1902.* Tarrytown, N.Y.: Argus Print, 1902.
Walker, Anthony. *So Few the Brave: Rhode Island Continentals, 1775–1783.* Newport, R.I.: Seafield Press, 1981.

Greene, Nathanael (1742–1786)
American military officer

Nathanael Greene was born in Warwick, Rhode Island, on August 7, 1742, into a Quaker household. He trained as a merchant and operated his father's iron foundry but also displayed a great interest in military affairs. Consequently, he was expelled from the Society of Friends for attending a military parade, and in 1770 he helped establish a noted militia formation, the Kentish Guards. Greene sought to become an officer but, owing to an ungainly limp, he was restricted to serving as a private. He joined the colonial general assembly in 1772, where his knowledge of military affairs gained him an appointment as brigadier general of colonial forces in May 1775. In this capacity Greene led the Rhode Island Corps of Observation to Boston, where he was introduced to General George WASHINGTON. Washington immediately recognized his talent for command and organization and persuaded the Continental CONGRESS to make him a brigadier general in the Continental ARMY in June 1775. At that time Greene was the military's youngest senior officer. Greene performed capably throughout the siege of Boston and subsequently accompanied Washington back to New York as a major general. Sickness precluded his participation in the disastrous Battle of LONG ISLAND on August 27, 1776, and he later mistakenly advised Washington to defend Fort Washington, which fell to the British on November 15, 1776. But Greene then capably supervised the evacuation of nearby Fort Lee and helped lead the hurried retreat across New Jersey. On December 25, 1776, he redeemed himself by fighting well at the surprising victory at TRENTON, where he blocked the HESSIAN retreat, and performed equally useful service at PRINCETON on January 3, 1777. In light of Greene's good service and military sagacity, which improved markedly with experience, Washington came to trust his judgment implicitly.

Greene next fought at the defeat of BRANDYWINE, where his tenacious defense of the American center staved off disaster. He then turned in a mixed performance at GERMANTOWN, where fog and command confusion resulted in a late appearance on the battlefield. However, Greene's next important contribution to the war effort came in March 1778, when Washington asked him to serve as quartermaster general. Supply functions in the army were seemingly on the brink of collapse, and Greene only reluctantly agreed to shoulder responsibility for such a logistical nightmare, but he evinced a solid talent for administration and literally saved the army from starvation. His tenure as quartermaster general was briefly interrupted by fighting at MONMOUTH on June 28, 1778, and by accompanying the army of General John SULLIVAN during the unsuccessful campaign to liberate his native state of Rhode Island that August. After resuming quartermaster functions and efficiently rendering essential work there, Greene regained a field command by succeeding General Benedict ARNOLD as commander of the strategic New York Highlands. In this capacity he was president of the tribunal that sentenced Major John ANDRE to death for spying.

Greene's greatest contribution to American independence arrived in the fall of 1780, when Washington tapped him to succeed the disgraced General Horatio GATES as commander of the Southern Department. This region had been disastrously overrun by British forces after the siege of CHARLESTON and the Battle of CAMDEN, but Greene arrived in North Carolina undeterred by the odds. He immediately set about recruiting and reforming his shattered army, paying particular attention to its logistical arrangements. In the spring of 1781 Greene undertook the perilous expedient of dividing his small army by sending General Daniel MORGAN on a sweep of North Carolina, which forced General Charles CORNWALLIS to do the same. The much feared cavalry leader, Lieutenant Colonel Banastre TARLETON, trotted off in pursuit of Morgan, but British endeavors came to grief with the spectacular American victory at COWPENS on January 17, 1781. Cornwallis himself commenced a dogged pursuit of Morgan that ended weeks later when Greene successfully withdrew his army across the Dan River into Virginia. The Americans then cobbled together 4,400 men and Greene immediately switched back to offensive operations. His reconstituted army assumed defensive positions at GUILFORD COURTHOUSE and bid the British to come on. On March 19, 1781, Cornwallis achieved his long-sought confrontation with the Americans and carried the day, but in victory he lost one-quarter of his army. Greene then unleashed the partisan forces of Generals Thomas SUMTER, Francis MARION, and Thomas PICKENS to harass British lines of communication as Cornwallis sullenly abandoned North Carolina for Virginia. Greene was now at leisure to advance into the Carolinas to attack numerous and isolated British outposts. By default he had lost a battle with Cornwallis yet won a major strategic victory.

For the next several months Greene successfully campaigned against British forces in his

Brigadier General Nathanael Greene assumed command of the Southern Department in 1780 and successfully campaigned against British forces, although he lost every battle. *(Independence National Historical Park)*

accustomed style. On April 25, 1781, he encamped at Hobkirk's Hill, South Carolina, intending to attack the outnumbered forces of Lieutenant Colonel Francis RAWDON, but the British struck first and drove the Americans from the field. Rawdon's losses were prohibitive, however, and he was forced to withdraw toward Charleston. Greene quickly rebounded from this loss and attacked again at Eutaw Spring, South Carolina, on September 8, 1781, only to be heavily repelled by the tactically adroit lieutenant colonel Alexander STEWART. But, again, British losses greatly exceeded Greene's, and Stewart was compelled to abandon his hard-won position. By December 1781 Greene had completely expelled British forces from the interior of South Carolina, reducing them to a handful of enclaves along the coast. Miraculously, he accomplished this by losing every engagement! Consequently, the governments of South Carolina and Georgia were reconstituted and rewarded him with both land and money. Congress also voted him a sword for his seemingly impossible triumph. In fact, Greene's success established him as the premier American strategist of the war, second only to Washington in overall importance. But the "Fighting Quaker" shrugged off his well-earned accolades and modestly declared, "We fight, get beat, rise, and fight again." It is the stuff of legend.

After the war, Greene spent several years sorting out his personal finances and skirted bankruptcy until he purchased an estate in Savannah, Georgia. He died there suddenly on June 19, 1786, at the age of 44, apparently of a stroke. His death was widely mourned, especially by Washington, who saw his brilliant southern campaign as a major cause behind the ultimate American victory.

Further Reading

Anderson, Lee P., and Lisa Skrowronski. *Forgotten Patriot: The Life and Times of Major General Nathanael Greene.* Parkland, Fla.: Universal Publishers, 2002.

Conrad, Dennis M., and Roger N. Parks, eds. *The Papers of General Nathanael Greene,* 12 vols. Chapel Hill: University of North Carolina Press, 1994–2004.

Golway, Terry. *Washington's General: Nathanael Greene and the Triumph of the American Revolution.* New York: Henry Holt, 2005.

Hairr, John. *Guilford Courthouse: Nathanael Greene's Victory in Defeat.* Cambridge, Mass.: Da Capo Press, 2002.

Kennedy, Michael D. "Major General Nathanael Greene's Role in the Southern Campaign of the American Revolution, December 1780–December 1781." Unpublished master's thesis, Jackson State University, 1997.

Leeman, William P. "Rhode Island's Controversial General Nathanael Greene and the Continental Congress, 1776–1780," *Rhode Island History* 59, no. 3 (2001): 84–100.

Grenville, George (1712–1770)
English politician

George Grenville was born in Buckinghamshire, England, on October 14, 1712, a son of Richard Grenville, earl of Temple. He received an aristocratic education at Eton and Oxford, was admitted to the bar, and successfully stood for a seat in Parliament in 1741. Grenville, a talented politician, rose steadily through the ranks of government through ability and the patronage of his brother-in-law, William PITT the Elder. He successively held positions as lord of the Admiralty in 1744, lord of the treasury in 1747, treasurer of the navy and privy councillor as of 1754, and secretary of state in 1762. His career reached its pinnacle in 1763, when Grenville became both prime minister and chancellor of the Exchequer. At that time Great Britain had triumphed over France in the Seven Years' War (French and Indian War in America), but he inherited a nation awash in debt. To help Britain meet its pecuniary responsibilities he began casting around for new and heretofore untapped sources of revenue.

Not surprisingly, Grenville turned to the North American colonies to help subsidize the burdens of empire. Specifically, he wanted them to partly shoulder the expenditures of maintaining army garrisons for their protection. This was the impetus behind the so-called Grenville Acts, which included the CURRENCY ACT of 1764, the SUGAR ACT of 1764, and, above all, the STAMP ACT of 1765.

Collectively these had the effect of raising revenues and imposing parliamentary controls upon a previously neglected colonial economy. But neither Grenville nor King GEORGE III could have foreseen the hostile reaction toward such seemingly innocuous matters. In fact, the colonial intelligentsia immediately railed against the practice of "taxation without representation" in Parliament, which gradually spawned deep-seated mistrust of, and mounting resistance to, imperial rule. Colonials found provisions of the Stamp Act, which mandated stamps on everyday commodities such as paper and even dice, particularly odious and summoned the Stamp Act Congress to meet in New York. This was the first instance of organized resistance in colonial history and a harbinger of events to follow. More intractable still was the growing suspicion that a parliamentarian "conspiracy" to rob them of their rights as Englishmen was afoot. More practically, dissent was further underscored by rioting and violent acts directed at revenue officials.

Grenville's tenure as prime minister proved raucous and unhappy. In addition to unpalatable tax programs, he further alienated popular sentiments by prosecuting the noted radical John WILKES. Grenville's ministry proved appreciably short-lived, and he was replaced by Charles WATSON-WENTWORTH, Lord Rockingham, in 1765. The new prime minister was clearly sympathetic toward the colonies and he induced Parliament to rescind the Stamp Act in 1766. Grenville, however, staunchly defended his measures, voted against their repeal, and warned the king "that if any man ventured to defeat the regulations laid down for the colonies he should look upon him as a criminal and a betrayer of his country." Thereafter he remained a leading opposition figure in Parliament, not so much liked as respected, until his death in London on November 13, 1770. Thus Grenville, whose actions did so much to precipitate the Revolutionary War, died without witnessing the consequence of his labors.

Further Reading
Bullion, John L. *A Great Necessary Measure: George Grenville and the Genesis of the Stamp Act, 1763–1765.* Columbia: University of Missouri Press, 1982.
Cook, Don. *The Long Fuse: How England Lost the American Colonies, 1760–1785.* New York: Atlantic Monthly Press, 1995.
Cornish, Rory T. *George Grenville, 1712–1770: A Bibliography.* Westport, Conn.: Greenwood Press, 1992.
Edgar, Gregory T. *Reluctant Break with Britain: From Stamp Act to Bunker Hill.* Bowie, Md.: Heritage Books, 1997.
Johnson, Allen S. *A Prologue to Revolution: The Political Career of George Grenville (1712–1770).* Lanham: University Press of Maryland, 1997.
Lawson, Philip. *George Grenville: A Political Life.* New York: Oxford University Press, 1984.

Grey, Charles (1729–1807)
English military officer

Charles Grey was born in Howick, England, in 1729, a son of Sir Henry Grey, baronet of Northumberland. He joined the army as an ensign in 1748 and rose steadily through the ranks due to ability. Grey was tapped to serve as aide-de-camp to Ferdinand, duke of Brunswick, during the Seven Years' War and greatly distinguished himself at Minden in 1757. By 1761 he was a lieutenant colonel of the 98th Regiment and active throughout the reduction of Belle Isle off the coast of Brittany. The following year he fought well at the capture of Havana, Cuba, before being placed on half-pay. Even in civilian life Grey sustained his reputation for military excellence, and in 1772 he was allowed back into the service as aide to King GEORGE III with a rank of colonel. He served in this capacity for five years, and it was not until the spring of 1777 that Grey reported for service in America as part of the forces under General William HOWE. Grey received command of the Third Brigade with a local rank of major general, and enjoyed the services of a talented young aide, Major John ANDRE. Grey subsequently accompanied Howe's amphibious descent upon Philadelphia in August 1777 and commanded the reserves at BRANDYWINE. This victory cleared the way for a British march upon Philadelphia, but Howe was closely trailed by an American brigade commanded by General Anthony WAYNE. Rather than attempt crossing the Schuylkill River with hostile forces to his rear, Howe detailed Grey to eliminate this threat.

On September 20, 1777, LOYALISTS informed Grey as to the precise location and composition of Wayne's brigade at Paoli, Pennsylvania. He then formulated a stealthy strike against the American camp that night. Gathering up the 42nd and 44th Regiments, along with a detachment of the 16th Light Dragoons, he marched through the darkness with complete tactical silence. And, as a further precaution, Grey ordered the flints removed from all muskets to preclude any chance of an accidental discharge. The British passed on through the darkness, eliminated Wayne's sentries, and successfully approached his encampment. Grey's men then fell like a thunderbolt on the unsuspecting Americans, bayoneting many in their tents and driving them from their camp. Wayne was lucky to escape with his artillery train, having suffered over 200 casualties—principally to cold steel. Grey's losses were far fewer and the Americans, from the sheer savagery of his success, subsequently labeled Paoli a "massacre." It also garnered Grey his infamous nickname of "No Flint."

Grey's next major action was at GERMANTOWN on October 4, 1777, when General George WASHINGTON sought to surprise Howe's army in its camp. The Americans came close to succeeding but foundered upon unexpectedly staunch resistance from the fortified Clivedon mansion. In the confusion that followed, Grey personally led a bayonet charge down Germantown Avenue that drove off the Americans and rescued the British garrison. Washington then drew his forces off for a miserable winter at Valley Forge while the British enjoyed the relative comforts of Philadelphia. Grey himself reposed in the house of Benjamin FRANKLIN, where he criticized Howe for his leniency toward the Americans. As a professional soldier, he believed that only direct and brutal applications of military force would crush the rebellion. Howe was subsequently replaced by General Henry CLINTON, and Grey followed him back to New York. There his brigade was utilized for numerous raids along the

Major General Charles Grey won a striking victory at Paoli, clearing the way for a British march upon Philadelphia. *(Anne S. K. Brown Military Collection, Brown University Library)*

New England coast and, on September 6–8, 1778, he ravaged the island of Martha's Vineyard, seizing an estimated $300,000 worth of property. Grey was next posted under General Charles CORNWALLIS and ordered into the New York highlands. On September 28, 1778, Cornwallis ordered him to eliminate an American cavalry force that had carelessly encamped at nearby Old Tappan, New Jersey. As at Paoli, Grey took a small but veteran infantry force, removed their flints, and took the enemy campsite at bayonet point. The 3rd Continental Dragoons under Colonel George Baylor was eliminated as a fighting force, further proof of Grey's proclivity for night attacks. Again, given the disparity of losses, the Americans accused the British of perpetrating a massacre.

In the fall of 1778 Grey was finally recalled to England, where he rose to major general and conducted numerous campaigns against Revolutionary France in Holland and the West Indies. Created First Earl Grey in 1806, he died at Howick on November 14, 1807, possibly the most efficient British general of the Revolutionary War. Had a leader of such single-minded ferocity been in charge of military affairs at the onset of the struggle, the Revolutionary War might have taken an entirely different turn.

Further Reading
Lynn, Robert A. "Paoli Massacre," *Military Heritage* 1, no. 3 (1999): 60–67.
McGuire, Thomas J. *Battle of Paoli*. Mechanicsburg, Pa.: Stackpole Books, 2000.
Nelson, Paul D. *Sir Charles Grey, First Earl Grey: Royal Soldier, Family Patriarch*. Madison, N.J.: Fairleigh Dickinson University Press, 1996.
Railton, Arthur R. "Grey's Raid: The Island's Biggest Historical Event," *Dukes County Intelligencer* 38, no. 3 (1997): 107–143.
Taafe, Stephen R. *The Philadelphia Campaign, 1777–1778*. Lawrence: University Press of Kansas, 2003.
Yetwin, Neil B. "Who Was General Charles Grey, the Man the Vineyard Hated?" *Dukes County Intelligencer* 35, no. 3 (1994): 146–152.

Gridley, Richard (1711–1796)
American military officer

Richard Gridley was born in Boston, Massachusetts, on January 3, 1711, the son of a currier and militia officer. He apprenticed as a merchant, but his abilities at mathematics induced him to study military engineering at Castle William in Boston Harbor. Here he was ably instructed by Britain's Captain John H. Bastide, and in 1744 Gridley received a lieutenant colonel's commission in the colonial artillery for an expedition against Louisbourg. He handled his affairs admirably and was rewarded with a regular army commission. For many years thereafter Gridley worked on fortifications at Boston and along the Maine frontier. When the French and Indian War commenced in 1755, he became colonel and chief engineer in the expedition against the French fort at Crown Point, New York. Three years later Gridley participated in the second capture of Louisbourg and was also on hand during the capture of Quebec in 1759. In recognition for his distinguished services, the Crown rewarded 3,000 acres in New Hampshire and a half-pay pension for life. However, he was rebuffed in his attempt to establish a seal fishery on the Magdalen Islands at the mouth of the St. Lawrence River. This rejection apparently induced him to join the anti-British movement. In 1770 Gridley purchased a foundry in Stoughtonham, where he contemplated casting artillery pieces in the event of war with England. When fighting commenced in April 1775, he tendered his services to the colonial government and became chief engineer and commander of artillery. Gridley also received an appointment as major general of militia, but this was eventually rescinded.

Despite his years, Gridley actively participated in early phases of the Revolutionary War in Massachusetts. As chief engineer, it fell upon him to erect fortifications overlooking Charlestown Harbor on the night of June 16, 1775. Gridley intended to fortify BUNKER HILL as ordered, but General Israel PUTNAM insisted that the work be raised upon Breed's Hill, closer to the water. He then fought bravely during the British capture of the heights and sustained a leg wound. That month Gridley was also absorbed into the Continental ARMY as its first chief engineer. On the night of March 4, 1776, he again performed impressively by raising—overnight—an intricate series of breastworks and batteries upon Dorchester Heights. General William HOWE was so startled by this singular act that he ordered Boston evacuated altogether. In light of his age Gridley surrendered his title as senior artillerist to General Henry KNOX in November 1775, but he remained chief engineer of the Eastern Department until his retirement from the army in December 1780.

In addition to his engineering duties, Gridley's foundry also manufactured the first cannon and howitzers ever cast in America. After the war he successfully pursued farming and milling at his home in Canton. He was not invited to attend victory celebrations in Boston after the war ended for, as a Universalist, he was not considered Christian. Gridley died in Canton on June 21, 1796, highly regarded as the father of American military engineering.

Further Reading
Huntoon, Daniel V. T. "Major General Richard Gridley," *Magazine of History* 7, nos. 5–6 (1908): 278–283, 336–342; 8, no. 1 (1908): 29–38.
McAfee, Michael J. *Artillery of the American Revolution, 1775–1783*. Washington, D.C.: American Defense Preparedness Association, 1974.
Morrissey, Brendan. *Boston, 1775: The Shot Heard Round the World*. Westport, Conn.: Praeger, 2004.
Parkman, Aubrey. *Army Engineers in New England: The Military and Civil Work of the Corps of Engineers in New England, 1775–1975*. Waltham, Mass.: U.S. Army Corps of Engineers, New England Division, 1978.
Walker, Paul K. *Engineers of Independence: A Documentary History of the Army Engineers in the American Revolution, 1775–1783*. Washington, D.C.: Office of the Chief of Engineers, 1981.

Guilford Courthouse, Battle of (March 15, 1781)

The American victory at COWPENS, South Carolina, on January 17, 1781, so angered General Charles CORNWALLIS that he immediately pursued General Daniel MORGAN's small command to crush him. Morgan swiftly retreated northward until he reunited with the main American army under General Nathanael GREENE in the vicinity of Guilford Courthouse, North Carolina, on February 8, 1781. Surveying what he considered a fine defensive position, Greene sought to battle the pursuing British but was dissuaded from doing so by his officers. The Americans then continued retiring across the Dan River into Virginia, at which point Cornwallis finally relented and withdrew. Greene remained quiescent until early March, when he received 1,000 militia and 550 veteran Continental infantry as reinforcements. This brought his total complement up to 4,400 men, and he slipped back into North Carolina, looking for a fight. The Americans then occupied the locality of Guilford Courthouse and, knowing Cornwallis's aggressive demeanor, awaited the inevitable British onslaught.

Greene had taken Morgan's spectacular success in stride and sought to emulate his militia-oriented tactics. He thus deployed his army in three distinct lines, each with its own role to play. The first rank consisted of 1,000 North Carolina militiamen under Generals John Butler and Pinketham Eaton, who placed themselves behind a rail fence fronting an open field. Because the British were obliged to cross this field to close with Greene's main body, he instructed the militiamen to fire only two rounds at the enemy before retiring in good order. Bolstering these inexperienced troops were the veteran cavalry of Colonels William WASHINGTON and Henry LEE, deployed on their left and right flanks. The second American line arose a quarter-mile farther back, where Greene posted 1,000 Virginia riflemen and militia under Generals Edward Stevens and Robert Lawson. These sharpshooters occupied a thick belt of woods ideal for their style of combat and were specifically instructed to drop as many British officers as possible. Their position was strengthened by the presence of two small cannon in the center of the line. Greene's final formation consisted of four veteran Continental regiments under Colonels Isaac HUGER and Otho Holland WILLIAMS. They occupied a small rise overlooking another field that the British had to traverse once they cleared the woods. This deployment reflected Greene's belief that his raw and inexperienced militia, comprising the bulk of his army, were unable to withstand battle-hardened British regulars in a stand-up fight. He hoped that they could hold their ground long enough to inflict incremental losses upon their opponent, in effect "softening up" Cornwallis's army before it encountered his best troops. The ploy was typical of Greene's generalship, a calculated risk yet a seemingly functional one.

Cornwallis no sooner learned of Greene's preparations at Guilford Courthouse than he made immediate preparations to engage him. On the morning of March 19, 1781, he accordingly roused 1,900 soldiers from their tents and marched them 12 miles without breakfast. After cavalry under Lieutenant Colonel Banastre TARLETON skirmished with Greene's pickets, Cornwallis began forming the men for battle. His right consisted of two regiments under General Alexander LESLIE, while the left contained two regiments commanded by Lieutenant Colonel James Webster. The British reserves, consisting of the Guards brigade and HESSIAN jaegers, remained under Colonel Charles O'HARA. The battle commenced around noon, when the redcoats advanced in perfect formation across the field and took fire from the North Carolina militia. Ignoring losses, they marched to within 40 paces of the Americans, fired off a volley of their own, and then charged bayonets. The levies predictably wilted before the onslaught, and Cornwallis's men cleared the fence and advanced until encountering Virginia militia and riflemen in the woods. However, the general was forced to pivot his outmost units to engage Lee and Washington's cavalry, which stood firm on either flank, and then brought up O'Hara's reserve before plunging into the woods. The Americans proved adept at fighting in such broken terrain, but British and German professionals slowly evicted them, and the riflemen yielded after inflicting considerable loss. The victorious British again sorted themselves out, pressed out of the woods, and confronted Greene's third and final line. The moment of decision seemed at hand.

The Maryland and Virginia Continentals of Huger and Williams allowed the British to approach to within a few yards of their position before cutting loose with a heavy volley and charging bayonets downhill. Colonel Webster was killed, and the British line faltered until O'Hara came up with the Guards to renew the action. At this critical juncture one of the Maryland regiments gave way, but Colonel Washington rescued the American center by hitting the Guards from behind with his troopers. A writhing melee erupted across the battlefield, and Cornwallis, fearful of losing control of events, decisively ordered his own cannon fired directly into the struggling mass. Americans and Britons fell in swaths, but this new onslaught completely halted Greene's counterattack. The well-trained British promptly reformed their ranks ahead of their adversaries and renewed their attack, at which point Greene gave the order to retreat. The Americans fell back in good order, but Cornwallis held the field—and little else.

The British, by dint of superb discipline and bravery, prevailed at Guilford Courthouse, but it was a Pyrrhic victory. Cornwallis lost one-quarter of his army—over 500 casualties—to an American tally of 78 dead, 185 wounded, and 1,046 missing, principally militia who deserted. Under such conditions pursuit was impossible, so the British fell back toward their base at Wilmington in preparation for abandoning North Carolina altogether. Greene thereby lost the battle but achieved a strategic victory: With Cornwallis destined for Virginia, his own army was now free to press southward to liberate the Carolinas.

Further Reading

Bartholomees, James B. "Fight or Flee: The Combat Performance of the North Carolina Militia in the Cowpens-Guilford Courthouse Campaign, January–March, 1781." Unpublished Ph.D. diss., Duke University, 1978.

Buchanan, John. *The Road to Guilford Courthouse: The American Revolution in the Carolinas.* New York: Wiley, 1997.

Hairr, John. *Guilford Courthouse: Nathanael Greene's Victory in Defeat, March 15, 1781.* Cambridge, Mass.: Da Capo Press, 2002.

Konstam, Angus. *Guilford Courthouse, 1781: Lord Cornwallis's Ruinous Victory.* Westport, Conn.: Praeger, 2004.

Russell, David L. *The American Revolution in the Southern Colonies.* Jefferson, N.C.: McFarland, 2000.

Haldimand, Frederick (1718–1791)
English military officer

Frederick Haldimand was born in Yverdon, Canton Vaud, Switzerland, on August 11, 1718, the son of a town official. He evinced an interest in military affairs early on and joined the renowned Prussian army as an officer in 1741. Haldimand fought well in several battles and in 1748 he transferred and became a lieutenant colonel of Swiss Guards within the Dutch army. Six years later the English army was experiencing a shortage of trained senior officers, so he switched allegiances once again to become lieutenant colonel of the 60th Regiment, the famed Royal Americans. In this capacity Haldimand distinguished himself in fighting throughout the French and Indian War, 1754–63, where he helped pioneer light infantry tactics. In 1760 General Jeffrey Amherst granted him the honor of receiving the surrender of Montreal where, as a French-speaking officer, he also served as a liaison between British and French camps. Haldimand advanced to colonel in 1762, but higher rank and command proved impossible owing to the prevailing prejudice against foreigners in the British army. He therefore served as second in command under General Thomas GAGE within the Montreal district. Haldimand functioned capably and without complaint, so in 1765 he became commander of the Southern District, headquartered at Pensacola, with the rank of brigadier general. In 1773 he was replaced by Colonel James GRANT, promoted to major general, and again served as assistant commander in chief of British forces under General Gage. When Gage returned to England in 1774, Haldimand became acting commander in chief at Boston in his absence. Once the Revolutionary War erupted in April 1775, Haldimand was one of the most experienced senior officers available to the British, yet he remained shunted aside due to his foreign birth. He was forced to accept a token position as inspector general of the West Indies throughout 1776, and it was not until the following year that Lord George GERMAIN, who had provoked the resignation of General Guy CARLETON, appointed him governor-general of Quebec. Bad weather and the frozen St. Lawrence prevented Haldimand's return to Quebec until June 26, 1778.

Canada at this time was not directly threatened by an American invasion, but Haldimand juggled a vastly complicated situation. He inherited a vast, sparsely populated region whose inhabitants were dubiously loyal at best. But, despite the marginal British troops accorded him, Haldimand built forts and strengthened local defenses against any future attacks. To facilitate the transportation of men and supplies, he authorized construction of Canada's first canals in 1779. He also determined to cement the French-speaking majority's allegiance by adhering closely to the provisions of the QUEBEC

Colonel Frederick Haldimand was appointed governor-general of Quebec in 1778 and authorized construction of Canada's first canals in 1779. *(National Portrait Gallery, London)*

ACT, which safeguarded French law, language, and religion. He accomplished this by alienating the tiny English-speaking minority, who more or less dominated the economy of the province and sought the imposition of English law and customs. Haldimand's smooth diplomacy precluded any chance that French Canadians might support a French attempt at reconquest once France entered the war. In a total departure from Carleton's policy, Haldimand also actively recruited Native American tribesmen into the war effort and dispatched them on repeated raids along the New York and Pennsylvania frontiers. Thus, chiefs like Joseph BRANT and CORNPLANTER, assisted by LOYALIST rangers under Colonels John BUTLER and John JOHNSON, effectively raised havoc behind enemy lines and forced the Americans to expend men and supplies defending themselves. Their stark success provoked a large retaliatory effort in the summer of 1779 under General John SULLIVAN, which resulted in a flood of Indian refugees at Fort Niagara in western New York. Haldimand, fortunately, mitigated their hardships by efficiently feeding and housing his allies over the winter. Due to irregularities within the Indian Department, Haldimand also demanded and received the resignation of Superintendent Guy JOHNSON over sloppy administration. Consequently, the Indians and Loyalists were back raiding the New York frontier by 1780, with frequently devastating results.

In addition to his usual preoccupations, Haldimand found time to promote political subterfuge by corresponding with American militia commander Ethan ALLEN over allowing Vermont to be annexed by Canada as an independent region. These negotiations amounted to nothing but did have the effect of neutralizing the Champlain Valley as a potential avenue of invasion. By war's end Haldimand had conducted his affairs effectively, and he faced an even greater challenge in settling thousands of Indian and Loyalist refugees fleeing the United States. Once again he met his responsibilities skillfully and successfully, considering the sheer magnitude of the task. He was especially insistent that English-speaking Loyalists settle west of the Ottawa River (present-day Ontario) to preserve the special nature of French Canada. Yet in 1782 the government of Lord William PETTY, Lord Shelburne, suddenly replaced him with Carleton. Apparently the government feared a potential French invasion of Canada and could not tolerate Canada's military affairs being dictated by a foreigner. Rather than submit to this latest indignity, Haldimand resigned as governor-general and finally returned to England in 1785. There he was inducted into the prestigious Order of the Bath, all the while remonstrating over Britain's willingness to abandon its Native American allies during peace negotiations. Haldimand spent his last few years shuttling between London and his native birthplace. He died at Champetit, Switzerland, on June 5, 1791, one of the most competent—and underutilized—British officers of the Revolutionary War.

Further Reading

Dendy, John O. "Frederick Haldimand and the Defense of Canada, 1778–1784." Unpublished Ph.D. diss., Duke University, 1972.

Haldimand, Frederick. "The Haldimand Papers," *Michigan Pioneer Collections,* vols. 9, 10, 11 (1886–87).

Hatvany, Matthew G. "Overcoming Ethnic and Social Barriers in Colonial British America: The 'Meritorious' Career of Frederick Haldimand," *Historian* 58, no. 3 (1996): 589–604.

Leuthy, Ivor C. E. "General Sir Frederick Haldimand," *Canadian Ethnic Studies* 3 (June 1971): 63–75.

Rea, Robert R. "Brigadier Frederick Haldimand—the Florida Years," *Florida Historical Quarterly* 54, no. 4 (1976): 512–531.

Whitfield, Faye V. "The Geography of the British Northern Interior Frontier Defense during the Haldimand Revolutionary War Administration of Quebec, 1778–1782." Unpublished Ph.D. diss., McMaster University, 1994.

Hale, Nathan (1755–1776)
American military officer, spy

Nathan Hale was born in Coventry, Connecticut, on June 6, 1755, the son of successful farmers. An exceptional student, he entered Yale College at the age of 14 and graduated with honors four years later. Among his classmates at the time were William Hull and Benjamin TALLMADGE, future military officers. Hale intended to serve as a schoolmaster and held teaching positions at East Haddam and New London before revolutionary violence broke out. However, in the wake of battles at Lexington and CONCORD, Massachusetts, he delivered a forceful speech on behalf of American independence before joining the 7th Connecticut Militia Regiment as a lieutenant. In this capacity Hale served throughout the siege of Boston, rising there to captain. When his enlistment expired that December, he joined the newly constituted 19th Connecticut Regiment in January 1776. The siege of Boston ended the following March, and Hale subsequently accompanied his regiment back to New York. There he spent several months constructing fortifications and is attributed with helping to seize a British tender under the guns of HMS *Asia* in May 1776. Hale's regiment was not actively engaged in the disastrous defeat at LONG ISLAND on August 27, 1776, and he fell back to New York City with the main army under General George WASHINGTON. There he apparently joined the elite Connecticut Rangers under Lieutenant Colonel Thomas KNOWLTON and was assigned to patrol the shorelines of the city. That September General Washington was desperate for military intelligence about British forces under General William HOWE and made repeated solicitations for volunteers to spy on Long Island.

Despite his lack of training in espionage, Hale bravely stepped forward and volunteered for this dangerous and difficult mission. Apparently Captain William Hull tried dissuading him from accepting such a perilous assignment but without success. Hale was transported to Long Island disguised as a Dutch schoolmaster and carried his Yale diploma as proof of employment. Hale's activities are not completely known but, in any event, Howe's successful landing at Kip's Bay on September 15, 1776, rendered his mission redundant. With New York City now in British hands he apparently felt compelled to obtain intelligence there and bravely crossed over. Unfortunately, on September 21, 1776, Hale was apprehended, probably by Lieutenant Colonel Robert ROGERS, and found to be carrying incriminating evidence. A story also exists that he was recognized by a LOYALIST cousin, who alerted British Authorities. Brought before General Howe, he readily admitted the nature of his activities and was sentenced to hang without a trial on the morrow. Early on September 22, 1776, Hale was marched five miles outside the city and placed upon a gallows. He then uttered his famous declaration, "I regret I have but one life to lose for my country," and died at the age of 21. His body was then left to hang for several days as a public warning and was subsequently interred in an unmarked grave. But Hale's adroitness in the face of death favorably impressed several British officers present, and it fell upon Captain John Montressor, under a flag of truce, to relay his heroic passing to the Americans. He has since become enshrined as the first martyr of the Revolutionary War and a model of heroic sacrifice. Hale is commemorated by a granite memorial in his hometown of Coventry and a bronze statue in the capitol at Hartford.

Further Reading
Bryne, Leonard. "Nathan Hale: A Testament to Courage," *New England Galaxy* 16 (1975): 13–22.
Cray, Robert E. "The Revolutionary Spy as Hero: Nathan Hale in the Public Memory, 1776–1846," *Connecticut History* 38, no. 2 (1999): 85–104.
Hagman, Harlan L. *Nathan Hale and John Andre: Reluctant Heroes of the American Revolution.* Interlaken, N.Y.: Empire State Books, 1992.
Mahoney, Harry T., and Marjorie L. Mahoney. *Gallantry in Action: A Biographic Dictionary of Espionage in the American Revolutionary War.* Lanham, Md.: University Press of America, 1999.
Thompson, Edmund R. *Secret New England: Spies of the American Revolution.* Portland, Maine: The Provincial Press, 2001.

Hamilton, Alexander (1757–1804)
American military officer

Alexander Hamilton was born at Nevis, British West Indies, on January 11, 1757, the illegitimate son of a Scottish merchant and his Huguenot mistress. Orphaned at an early age, he was raised by his aunts and apprenticed as a merchant. Hamilton, despite his youth, displayed a near-genius for financial matters and was allowed to run his family company as a teenager. In 1772 he ventured to New York to attend King's College (Columbia University), where he distinguished himself academically and also tested the waters of revolutionary politics. Hamilton became an active figure in anti-British agitation by giving speeches, writing pamphlets, and joining a militia company. In the summer of 1776 he received a captain's commission in a New York Artillery unit and fought at the battles of LONG ISLAND and WHITE PLAINS, winning praise from General Nathanael GREENE. Hamilton then handled his guns adroitly during the victory of PRINCETON on January 3, 1777, where he first came to the attention of General George WASHINGTON. Washington was so impressed by Hamilton's deportment and grasp of military matters that he promoted him to lieutenant colonel and his aide-de-camp. Hamilton was only 20 years old at the time. He nonetheless performed valuable services as a staff officer, and Washington depended on his usually sound advice.

Hamilton was also reckless and brave and, during the Battle of MONMOUTH in June 1778, he led a desperate charge that rescued General Charles LEE's division from being trapped. He subsequently testified against Lee during his court-martial. In 1780 he also advanced his political fortunes in New York by marrying into the family of General Philip J. SCHUYLER. Hamilton continued as part of Washington's entourage until February 1781, when friction over the latter's refusal to grant him a combat command ended in his dismissal. He then transferred to the staff of the marquis de LAFAYETTE during the YORKTOWN campaign. In one celebrated incident, Hamilton bravely—if foolishly—ordered his elite light infantry battalion to the ramparts in full view of the British, where they flawlessly performed the manual of arms and astonished the defenders. On the night of October 14, 1781, Hamilton led one of two allied columns that stormed Redoubts No. 9 and 10, the success of which spelled the doom of General Charles CORNWALLIS and his army. Hamilton remained in uniform until December 1783, when he retired with a rank of brevet colonel. His military experience convinced him that the new nation required stronger, more centralized governance than that afforded by the ARTICLES OF CONFEDERATION. To this end he played a major role in fomenting army discontent during the NEWBURGH CONSPIRACY but subsequently backed down and alerted Washington to the existence of a cabal.

In the postwar period, Hamilton gained a measure of immortality as one of the nation's political avatars. Here his quest to graft a stronger, centralized administration upon the tottering new nation proved decisive. Hamilton served in the Continental CONGRESS from 1782 to 1783, before returning to New York to practice law. But at the Annapolis Convention in 1786, and at the Constitutional Convention at Philadelphia in 1787, he was a driving force behind adoption of the proposed federal constitution. Then, in concert with James MADISON and John JAY, he penned the majority of lucid arguments favoring it in the celebrated *Federalist Papers,* long regarded as a masterpiece of American political thought. When the Constitution was finally ratified in 1789, Hamilton again served Washington, now president as his secretary of the treasury. Again, Hamilton's exceptional grasp of economics and his brilliant presentations before Congress proved vital in establishing a national economy. His stance also stoked mounting opposition to Federalist policies from less inclined Democratic-Republicans such as Madison and Thomas JEFFERSON. When the Quasi War with France erupted in 1798, President John ADAMS appointed Hamilton inspector general of the army with a rank of brigadier general. However, Hamilton's profound disagreement with Adams over the issue of war and his willing embrace of standing professional armies assisted the election of Jefferson in 1800. This was achieved behind the scenes when Hamilton preferred Jefferson, his ideological adversary, to the grasping and ambitious Aaron Burr as president. In 1804 he also managed to undercut Burr as governor of New York, which resulted in a celebrated duel. Hamilton died of his wounds on July 12, 1804, an accomplished soldier, a master politician, and one of America's most influential founding fathers.

Further Reading

Chernow, Ron. *Alexander Hamilton.* New York: Penguin Press, 2004.

Harper, John L. *American Machiavelli: Alexander Hamilton and the Origins of U.S. Foreign Policy.* New York: Cambridge University Press, 2004.

Knott, Stephen F. *Alexander Hamilton and the Persistence of Myth.* Lawrence: University Press of Kansas, 2002.

Randall, Willard S. *Alexander Hamilton: A Life.* New York: HarperCollins, 2003.

———. "Fighting Federalist," *MHQ* 15, no. 1 (2002): 64–75.

Selig, Robert A. "Storming the Redoubts," *MHQ* 8, no. 1 (1995): 18–27.

Staloff, Darren. *Hamilton, Adams, Jefferson: The Politics of Enlightenment and the American Founding.* New York: Hill and Wang, 2005.

Hamilton, Henry (ca. 1734–1796)
English military officer

Henry Hamilton was probably born in Dublin, Ireland, around 1734, the son of an Irish parliamentarian. He received a classical education and joined the army in 1755 as an ensign in the 15th Regiment. Hamilton arrived in America in 1758 and proved himself a capable combat officer. He fought with distinction at Louisbourg in 1758, Quebec in 1759, and Montreal in 1760. In 1767 he rose to captain and took control of the Trois-Rivières and Crown Point garrisons. Hamilton also struck up cordial relations with his superior, Governor-General Guy CARLETON, who recommended him for the civil service. After the QUEBEC ACT was passed in 1774, the British government began organizing a formal government for Canada and Hamilton was tapped to serve as lieutenant governor. He arrived at Detroit on November 9, 1775, and began the difficult and lengthy task of imposing law and order upon a raucous frontier society. And, because the Revolutionary War had broken out the previous spring, Hamilton wasted no time organizing local French inhabitants and English settlers into a viable militia. He remained cognizant of the inherent military weakness of his charge and went to great lengths to secure friendly relations with the Native American tribesmen of the region. For two years he successfully defended British interests against American and Spanish intrusions yet, upon Governor-General Carleton's insistence, kept the Indians out of the fighting.

In the spring of 1777 Hamilton received positive instructions from Lord George GERMAIN to solicit military assistance from the tribes. He was also instructed to organize raids into the neighboring Ohio Valley to tie down American military resources there while General John BURGOYNE invaded New York. Hamilton complied and, in concert with noted renegade Simon GIRTY, he authorized numerous and bloody forays against colonial frontier settlements. Yet despite explicit instruction to keep the Indians on a short leash, Girty and other scouts allowed them to massacre captives. Hamilton consequently and mistakenly gained an unsavory reputation as the "Hair-buyer" for allegedly encouraging such misdeeds. Still he possessed just enough resources to launch a major raid upon Wheeling, Virginia (now West Virginia) in September 1777 before losing most of his warriors to Burgoyne. Hamilton nevertheless performed useful work for the Crown by efficiently administering his charge and securing his main base at Detroit from possible attack.

On July 4, 1778, the tempo of confrontation between the British and American settlers increased exponentially when Colonel George Rogers CLARK led a small expedition that captured the French settlement of Vincennes in the Illinois territory. This placed an American lodgement perilously close to Detroit and Hamilton acted with characteristic energy. He quickly organized and outfitted an expedition of his own that departed Detroit on October 7, 1778, with 500 militia and Indians. Braving snowdrifts and flooded rivers, he recaptured Vincennes without a struggle on December 17, 1778. Believing it too cold for protracted operations, Hamilton then dismissed the bulk of his warriors and settled in for the winter with a garrison of 80 men. However, he had completely underestimated the resolve of Colonel Clark, who quickly rounded up 150 frontiersmen and headed north. After an epic march under horrific conditions they surprised and surrounded Hamilton at Vincennes, initiating a loose siege. Badly outnumbered and realizing that the game was up, Hamilton surrendered to Clark on March 8, 1779, and was led back to Virginia a celebrated prisoner.

Once Hamilton arrived at Williamsburg, Governor Thomas JEFFERSON ordered him placed in irons and solitary confinement. The British strongly protested his treatment, and it took the intercession of General George WASHINGTON before the irons were removed. He remained incarcerated until paroled and exchanged in 1781 when he returned to England. However, upon the recommendation of Governor-General Frederick HALDIMAND, Hamilton returned to Canada as the new lieutenant governor in June 1782. This time he proved unable to smooth the fractious enmity between English and French inhabitants and was recalled by 1785. Three years later Hamilton received a far more palatable assignment as governor of Bermuda, which he handled with his usual dispatch, and the island's capital—Hamilton—was subsequently named in his honor. He then accepted the governorship of Dominica in 1794, dying there in office on September 26, 1796. Hamilton was an effective military leader and conscientious bureaucrat throughout his long tenure in North America; his reputation as the notorious "Hair-buyer" is more the product of frontier myth than reality.

British officer Henry Hamilton was surprised by George Rogers Clark at Vincennes. *(Houghton Library, Harvard University)*

Further Reading

Allen, Robert S. *His Majesty's Allies: British Indian Policy in the Defense of Canada, 1774–1815.* Toronto: Dundurn Press, 1992.

Havinghurst, Walter. *Proud Prisoner.* Williamsburg, Va.: Colonial Williamsburg, 1964.

Jaebker, Orville J. "Henry Hamilton: British Soldier and Colonial Governor." Unpublished Ph.D. diss., University of Indiana, 1955.

Sheehan, Bernard W. " 'The Famous Hair Buyer General': Henry Hamilton, George Rogers Clark, and the American Indian," *Indiana Magazine of History* 79, no. 1 (1983): 1–28.

Stevens, Paul L. " 'Placing Proper Persons at Their Head': Henry Hamilton and the Establishment of the British Revolutionary Era Indian Department," *Old Northwest* 12, no. 3 (1986): 279–317.

Walsh, Martin W. "The Native American Sketches of Henry Hamilton," *Michigan History Magazine* 81, no. 3 (1997): 20–27.

Hancock, John (1737–1793)

American politician

John Hancock was born in Braintree, Massachusetts, on January 23, 1737, the son of an impoverished clergyman. Orphaned at an early age he was subsequently adopted by his uncle Thomas Hancock, then one of the richest merchants in the colonies. Hancock was well educated and graduated from Harvard College in 1754, at which point he was groomed to take over the family business. To expand his personal horizons he visited England in 1760 and witnessed the coronation of King GEORGE III. He also cultivated a taste for the nouveau riche living characteristic of his later life. Hancock then returned to Boston, where, in 1764, he inherited his uncle's business and family fortune. Propelled to the front ranks of the colonial elite, he next developed an interest in politics, especially after the STAMP ACT of 1765. Hancock quickly emerged as a leading spokesman for anti-British agitation. He developed a close relationship with radicals under Samuel ADAMS, emerging as one of the resistance movement's most visible leaders. Hancock's popularity soared further in June 1768 after customs officials seized his vessel *Liberty* and accused him of violating the SUGAR ACT of 1764. Hancock waxed defiant and received public sympathy through one of Boston's biggest riots on June 10, 1768—after which British troops were garrisoned in the city. Hancock further capitalized upon his newfound celebrity by winning a seat in the General Court in 1769 and then heading the Boston committee investigating the BOSTON MASSACRE of March 5, 1770. In 1773 he vociferously denounced the TEA ACT and the following year served as president of the extralegal Massachusetts provincial congress. General Thomas GAGE, the royal governor, then specifically excluded him and Adams from a general amnesty program. In 1775 both men were alerted by Paul REVERE that British troops were en route to arrest them prior to the Battle of CONCORD and they fled to Philadelphia.

In May 1775 Hancock served as a delegate to the Second Continental CONGRESS and quickly rose to become president of that body. In this capacity he was the first individual to sign the DECLARATION OF INDEPENDENCE in August 1776, using bold script twice the size of other delegates so that the king could recognize his name without glasses. Hancock coveted and fully expected to be made commander in chief of the Continental ARMY—despite his lack of military experience—and did not mask his disappointment when George WASHINGTON was chosen. Hancock stepped down in October 1777 in favor of Henry LAURENS, and his remaining career in Philadelphia proved undistinguished. Feeling he could wield greater impact at home he returned to Massachusetts in 1778 and became a major general of militia. Hancock then commanded 5,000 state troops throughout the Rhode Island campaign of General John SULLIVAN, but his performance there proved only marginal.

Hancock wielded much greater impact upon local politics by dint of his wealth and conspicuous patronage, so in 1780 the citizens elected him their first governor. He served nine terms, from 1780 to 1785 and 1789 to 1793, while also attending the Massachusetts constitutional convention of 1788. Hancock initially expressed reservations about the new government, but his qualified support proved essential for ratification. Throughout his public career, Hancock never displayed any great capacity for politics or original thought, but he was nevertheless a committed Patriot who spent lavishly out of his own pocket both to foment and to sustain the revolutionary movement. He died at home in Quincy on October 8, 1793.

Further Reading
Angelis, Angelo T. "Pregnant with Future Consequences: Political Culture in Revolutionary Massachusetts, 1775–1787." Unpublished Ph.D. diss., City University of New York, 2002.
Brandes, Paul D. *John Hancock's Life and Speeches: A Personalized Vision of the American Revolution, 1763–1793*. Lanham, Md.: Scarecrow Press, 1996.
Finklestein, Robert Z. "Merchant, Revolutionary, and Statesman: A Reappraisal of the Life and Public Services of John Hancock, 1737–1793." Unpublished Ph.D. diss., University of Massachusetts, 1981.
Fowler, William M. *The Baron of Beacon Hill: A Biography of John Hancock*. Boston: Houghton Mifflin, 1980.
Unger, Harlow G. *John Hancock: Merchant King and American Patriot*. New York: Wiley, 2000.
Wright, Conrad E. *Revolutionary Generation: Harvard Men and the Consequences of Independence*. Amherst: University of Massachusetts Press, 2005.

Hand, Edward (1744–1802)
American military officer

Edward Hand was born in King's County, Ireland, on December 31, 1744, and he studied medicine at Trinity College, Dublin. After graduating in 1766 he joined the British army as a surgeon's mate in the 18th Royal Irish Regiment, and the following year his unit shipped to Pennsylvania. Hand served many years with the garrison at Fort Pitt, where he also dabbled in land speculation and befriended George WASHINGTON. He purchased his ensign's commission in 1772, but then resigned two years later to establish a private practice in Lancaster. During the period leading up to the break with Great Britain, Hand became closely identified with the Patriot faction, and in 1775 he became lieutenant colonel of a rifle regiment commanded by Colonel William THOMPSON. In this capacity he marched to Massachusetts and participated in the siege of Boston, where his riflemen garnered a reputation as crack shots but wildly undisciplined. Hand nevertheless performed capably, and in March 1776 he rose to colonel of the redesignated 1st Continental Infantry. He subsequently accompanied the army to New York and fought well at the defeat of LONG ISLAND on August 27, 1776. Moreover, Hand performed exceptionally well at Trog's Neck on October 12, 1776, where his riflemen completely stymied a landing by General Charles CORNWALLIS and allowed Washington's main force to escape. After similar good service at WHITE PLAINS, Hand retreated across New Jersey that winter. On January 2, 1777, he again dogged Cornwallis's advance at Assumpink Creek long enough for Washington to sidestep the British and win the Battle at PRINCETON. In light of his good conduct and close ties to Washington, Hand gained promotion to brigadier general on April 1, 1777.

Hand reported for duty at Fort Pitt in the late spring of 1777, where he was tasked with protecting western Pennsylvania settlements from Indians and LOYALISTS. He tried consistently to organize a punitive expedition against tribes of the Ohio River Valley but was thwarted by persistent shortages of men and supplies. It was not until February 1778 that Hand collected 500 soldiers for his much-ridiculed "Squaw Campaign," which failed to reach Sandusky due to bad weather and led to accusations of his being a Tory sympathizer. Hand, however, provided every possible assistance to Colonel George Rogers CLARK and his campaign to conquer the Illinois territory. Unable to accomplish much more, he petitioned Washington for a transfer and was replaced by General Lachlan MCINTOSH in November 1778.

Hand subsequently replaced General John STARK as commander of the Albany region and throughout the summer of 1778 he rendered valuable services as part of General John SULLIVAN's campaign into the Iroquois heartland. After a stint at Morristown, New Jersey, he repaired to the New

York Highlands and sat on the board that convicted Major John ANDRE of spying in October 1780. The following month he received command of a special light infantry brigade under the marquis de LAFAYETTE before succeeding Colonel Alexander SCAMMELL as adjutant general on Washington's staff. He was at the victory at YORKTOWN in this capacity a year later and proved instrumental in helping squelch the army's unrest at NEWBURGH, New York, in 1782. Hand was elevated to major general on September 1, 1783, shortly before resigning from active duty.

Back in civilian life, Hand served in the Continental CONGRESS, 1784–85, and the Pennsylvania assembly, 1785–86. A staunch Federalist, he was appointed customs collector of Pennsylvania's Third District by President Washington in 1791 and again served as adjutant general during the so-called Whiskey Rebellion of 1794. When war loomed with France four years later Hand was commissioned major general and adjutant general of the Provisional Army by President John ADAMS. However, having opposed the election of Thomas JEFFERSON in 1800, he lost his position as customs collector. Hand died at his home in Rockford, Pennsylvania, on September 3, 1802, reputedly while his accounts with the government were being audited for irregularities.

Further Reading
Bowden, J. A., ed. *The Unpublished Revolutionary Papers of Major General Edward Hand of Pennsylvania, 1777–1784.* New York: Privately Printed, 1907.
Craig, Michel W. *General Edward Hand, Winter Doctor.* Lancaster, Pa.: Rock Ford Foundation, 1984.
Fitzpatrick, Paul J. "General Edward Hand and Rock Ford," *Social Science* 44 (January 1969): 3–11.
Forry, Richard R. "Edward Hand: His Role in the American Revolution." Unpublished Ph.D. diss., Duke University, 1976.
Heathcote, Charles W. "General Edward Hand—A Capable Pennsylvania Military Officer and Colleague of Washington," *Picket Post* no. 69 (July 1960): 14–22.
Orrill, Lawrence A. "General Edward Hand," *Western Pennsylvania Historical Magazine* 25 (September–December 1942): 99–112.

Hanger, George (ca. 1751–1824)
English military officer

George Hanger was born near Berkshire, England, around 1751, a son of Gabriel, baron Coleraine. He was educated at Eton before spending a year at the University of Göttingen in Hanover, Germany. Though a bright student, Hanger exuded rakish qualities and was exceptionally fond of women, drinking, and gambling. He also claimed to have fought three duels before the age of 20 and fancied himself a crack shot with a rifle. While in Hanover, Hanger had an opportunity to view the Prussian army of Frederick the Great on maneuvers and decided upon a military career. He was consequently gazetted ensign in the elite 1st Foot Guards on January 31, 1771, and served capably but resigned his commission after being passed over for promotion four years later. Hanger then used his German contacts to secure a captain's commission in the Feld Jaeger Corps of Hesen-Kassel in January 1776, an elite formation reserved for aristocrats. When the landgrave decided to rent his HESSIAN soldiers out to King GEORGE III as mercenaries, Hanger sailed to America from Portsmouth on March 15, 1776. He fought in various campaigns throughout 1776–77, and by 1778 he had assumed command of a Hessian jaeger company drawn from all such regiments in the army. This formation was subsequently disbanded in November of that year, but Hanger next led a number of composite infantry/rifle formations under the noted light infantry leader Major Patrick FERGUSON. In this capacity he accompanied General Henry CLINTON on his amphibious expedition against South Carolina in the spring of 1780 and served as aide-de-camp throughout the ensuing siege of CHARLESTON. He then received an appointment under Ferguson as deputy inspector of militia but managed to effect a transfer to the British Legion after meeting Lieutenant Colonel Banastre TARLETON. The raucous, hard-drinking aristocrats shared much in common, and Hanger was installed as Tarleton's second in command.

During this phase of the war in the south the British Legion, a green-coated cavalry unit recruited from American LOYALISTS, acquired one of the most fearsome reputations of any unit in an already formidable British army. Hanger proved himself to be a cheerful and capable subordinate under Tarleton, but clearly lacked his ability to lead cavalry. When General Charles CORNWALLIS invaded North Carolina in the fall of 1780, the British Legion spearheaded the move until Tarleton contracted yellow fever. Hanger then assumed command and recklessly encamped at Wahab's Plantation on the evening of September 21, 1780. That evening he was surprised by partisan forces under Colonel William R. DAVIE and routed with the loss of 12 killed, 47 wounded, and 96 horses captured. The British Legion was subsequently reconstituted and tasked with leading the British advance into Charlotte on September 26, 1780. Rather than act in concert with his light infantry, Hanger carelessly rode into the village unsupported—and directly into another ambush orchestrated by Davie. American riflemen, lined up behind a wall, shot down the British troopers as they repeatedly charged, and it took the direct intervention of General Cornwallis to steady their ranks. Hanger, badly wounded in the skirmish, later contracted yellow fever and was evacuated to the West Indies to recuperate. He returned to New York in July 1781, and two years later he accompanied Governor-General Guy CARLETON on one of the last troop ships to evacuate America.

Back in London, Hanger displayed his talents as a flamboyant wastrel and ended up in debtor's prison, 1798–1800. He then found employment as a coal merchant, gambler, and all-around rake. Hanger also pushed a variety of pamphlets on military affairs, gambling, hunting, and marksmanship, at all of which he was quite adept. When the barony of Coleraine was tendered to him in 1814 he refused it, preferring instead to socialize with the equally profligate Prince of Wales, the future King George IV. Hanger died in London on March 31, 1824, a self-styled military expert and regarded as one of the leading eccentrics of his day.

Further Reading
Buchanan, John. *The Road to Guilford Courthouse: The American Revolution in the Carolinas.* New York: Wiley, 1997.
Edgar, Walter B. *Partisans and Redcoats: The Southern Conflict That Turned the Tide of the American Revolution.* New York: Morrow, 2001.
Gordon, John W. *South Carolina and the American Revolution: A Battlefield History.* Columbia: University of South Carolina Press, 2003.
Hanger, George. *The Life, Adventures, and Opinions of Colonel George Hanger.* New York: Johnson & Stryker, 1801.
Melville, Lewis. "Eighteenth-Century Men about Town," *Fortnightly Review* 89 (April 1908): 658–661.
Nifong, Michael R. "In Provincial Service: The British Legion in the American Revolution, 1778–1783." Unpublished master's thesis, University of North Carolina at Chapel Hill, 1976.

Hanson, John (1721–1783)
American politician
John Hanson was born at Mulberry Grove, Charles County, Maryland, on April 3, 1721, the son of a planter. Of his youth and education little is known, but in 1744 he married a wealthy landowner and within a decade possessed 1,300 acres in Charles County. Hanson entered the public arena in 1750 when he was elected sheriff and seven years later won a seat in the lower house of the Maryland general assembly. There he gained a reputation as an honest and efficient bureaucrat with particular expertise in finance. As friction between Great Britain and its colonies grew in the 1760s, Hanson was more and more identified with opposition interests. He publicly denounced the STAMP ACT of 1765 and drew up the instructions for Maryland delegates attending the Stamp Act Congress in New York. In 1769 he also signed the Nonimportation Resolution adopted by Maryland to protest the TOWNSHEND ACTS. That same year Hanson relocated to Frederick County to function as a merchant and partake of extralegal political activities protesting British policy. In 1774 he chaired a town meeting to protest imposition of the COERCIVE ACTS, and the following year he declared that

armed force might be necessary to resist British tyranny. After the Revolutionary War commenced in April 1775 Hanson lent his fiscal and organizational expertise to arming and equipping soldiers for the Continental ARMY. Consequently, soldiers from Frederick County became the first southerners to join the forces gathering under General George WASHINGTON. Commencing in 1777 the citizens of his county returned him to the general assembly five successive times and two years later he was appointed a delegate to the Continental CONGRESS.

Once seated at Philadelphia, Hanson expressed alarm over the slapdash and profligate monetary policies of Congress. He therefore favored stronger governance under the ARTICLES OF CONFEDERATION but nonetheless withheld Maryland's ratification until Virginia and other states surrendered their western territorial claims to Congress. When Virginia finally complied, Hanson and fellow delegate Daniel Carroll formally ratified the articles, which authorized the nation's first government structures. Despite his previous obstructionist stances, fellow delegates thought highly enough of Hanson to elect him the first "President of the United States in Congress Assembled" on November 5, 1781. This was not, by any means, an executive position, for the articles contained no such provision. Rather, this was strictly a ceremonial role to facilitate the day-to-day proceedings of Congress while in session. Hanson thus corresponded with state governors, dispatched various resolutions to state assemblies, and helped orchestrate daily legislative functions. It was during his tenure that peace talks with England commenced and the actual framework of government, the departments, first manifested. His most memorable activity in Congress was receiving the sword of General Charles CORNWALLIS from a victorious General Washington in November 1781. Hanson, whose health had been failing, left Congress after one year as president and retired from office. He died in Oxon County, Maryland, on November 15, 1783, much less a founding father than a highly trusted and conscientious public servant. Technically speaking, he remains the nation's first "president."

Further Reading

Carlsson, Sten. "John Hanson's Swedish Background," *Swedish Pioneer Quarterly* 29 (January, 1978): 9–20.

Klos, Stanley L. *President Who? Forgotten Founders.* Carnegie, Pa.: Estoric.com, 2004.

Kremer, J. Bruce. *John Hanson of Mulberry Grove.* New York: A. & C. Boni, 1938.

Levering, Ralph B. "John Hanson, Public Servant," *Maryland Historical Magazine* 71, no. 2 (1976): 13–33.

Nelson, Jacob A. *John Hanson and the Inseparable Union.* Boston: Meader Pub. Co., 1939.

Stoeckel, Herbert J. *The Strange Story of John Hanson, First President of the United States.* Hartford, Conn.: Hanson House, 1956.

Haraden, Jonathan (1745–1803)
American naval officer

Jonathan Haraden was born in Gloucester, Massachusetts, on November 11, 1744, and he went to sea as a cabin boy. He proved himself a competent sailor, so in July 1776, after the Revolutionary War had commenced, Haraden received his commission as a lieutenant in the Massachusetts state navy. He then accompanied Captain John FISKE onboard the sloop *Tyrannicide* and completed two successful cruises that year. In 1777 Haraden succeeded Fiske as captain of *Tyrannicide,* which was converted into a faster-sailing brigantine. He then accompanied Fiske's vessel *Massachusetts* on an extended raid in European waters and took, among 25 prizes, a transport full of HESSIAN troops. He subsequently eluded a hotly pursuing British squadron before effecting a narrow escape. Haraden returned to Boston in August 1777 and enjoyed another successful cruise of the West Indies that year.

In the summer of 1778 Haraden left the state service to become a privateer commanding the 16-gun vessel *General Pickering.* He spent a year conveying cargoes to Spain and captured several armed prizes on the return leg of his voyages. By now Haraden had emerged as one of the most tactically astute naval commanders of the war. While cruising off Sandy Hook in October 1779, he encountered three British vessels totaling 32 guns, yet managed to isolate and defeat them all in only 90 minutes. In June 1780 Haraden was cruising the Bay of Biscay, when he encountered the larger 22-gun schooner *Golden Eagle* at night. Boldly running his vessel alongside he bluffed his larger opponent into surrendering without a shot. Haraden then took his prize into the port of Bilbao on June 3, 1780, and was accosted there by the privateer *Achilles* of 42 guns. Haraden quickly abandoned his prize to the intruder and positioned himself in shoal waters, allowing him to rake his opponent head on. For three hours the *Achilles* tried closing with its smaller opponent under a hail of cannon fire and drew off a badly damaged Haraden, who, running low on ammunition, loaded his guns with a supply of crowbars that severely injured his antagonist's rigging and contributed to his victory. He then sortied and quickly recaptured the *Golden Eagle* to the cheers of thousands of Spaniards who lined the shore to watch the one-sided engagement. Haraden was subsequently hailed as a hero and carried aloft on their shoulders throughout the city.

Haraden's luck finally ran out in February 1781 after Admiral George RODNEY captured the Dutch island of St. Eustatius, and all American vessels unknowingly entering its harbor were snared. He was quickly exchanged and subsequently took charge of the 14-gun *Julius Caesar* out of Salem. In June 1782 he skillfully fought off a British ship and brig for three hours before escaping. At the end of the war Haraden returned to Salem to engage in maritime activities before dying there on November 23, 1804, an intrepid American sea dog. During his career he reputedly captured a total of 1,000 British cannon from his various prizes.

Further Reading

Allen, Gardner W. *Massachusetts Privateers of the Revolution.* Boston: Massachusetts Historical Society, 1927.

Cook, Fred J. *What Manner of Men: Forgotten Heroes of the American Revolution.* New York: William Morrow, 1959.

Gardner, Frank A. "Captain Jonathan Haraden," *Massachusetts Magazine* 2 (October, 1909): 191–199.

McManemin, John A. *Captains of the State Navies during the Revolutionary War.* Ho-Ho-Kus, N.J.: Ho-Ho-Kus Pub. Co., 1984.

Morse, Sidney G. "New England Privateering in the American Revolution," 2 vols. Unpublished Ph.D. diss., Harvard University, 1941.

Paine, Ralph D. "Jonathan Haraden—Privateersman," *Outing* 52 (April 1900): 37–45.

Harding, Seth (1734–1814)
American naval officer

Seth Harding was born in Eastham, Massachusetts, on April 17, 1734, and relocated to Norwich, Connecticut, around 1760. Having joined the merchant marine at a young age he eventually owned his own ship and settled in Liverpool, Nova Scotia, by 1771. However, once the Revolutionary War began in 1775, Harding returned to Connecticut, joined the state navy, and received command of the brig *Defiance*. He was first deployed in and around Boston Harbor where, on June 12, 1775, he captured the British armed transport *George* and with it, several hundred Scottish troops of the 71st Highland Regiment under Lieutenant Colonel Archibald CAMPBELL. Subsequent commands included a new brig, also called *Defiance*, and the *Oliver Cromwell*. Harding enjoyed considerable success in both vessels, so in September 1778 he was commissioned a captain in the Continental NAVY.

In June 1779 Harding departed New London commanding the new 32-gun frigate *Confederacy*. However, he was hard-pressed to attract sufficient crew members and at one point impressed several French prisoners being exchanged by the British. He then accompanied Captains Samuel TUCKER and Samuel NICHOLSON of the frigates *Boston* and *Deane*, respectively, on a lengthy cruise of the Atlantic, seizing the privateer *Pole,* 24 guns, the schooner *Patsey* of six, and several merchantmen.

The following October Harding was detailed to transport John JAY, minister to SPAIN, across the Atlantic, along with French minister Conrad Alexandre Gerard. En route *Confederacy* weathered a tremendous storm and was completely dismasted, but Harding's skilled seamanship kept her afloat, and he managed to reach Martinique for repairs. On April 15, 1781, Harding was convoying several French and American vessels near the Delaware Capes when he was suddenly accosted by HMS *Roebuck,* 44 guns, and *Orpheus,* 32 guns, and forced to strike. He was paroled in early 1782, assumed command of the privateer *Diana,* but was again captured near Jamaica. Harding was once more released and taken aboard the frigate *Alliance* under Captain John BARRY. On March 10, 1783, he participated in the fight again HMS *Sybil* and fired the last naval shot of the Revolutionary War.

Afterward Harding resumed his activities in the merchant marine and actively traded among the Virgin Islands. To facilitate this, at one point he applied for and received Danish citizenship. By 1786 Harding was weakened from old wounds and settled at New York City in poverty. There he petitioned CONGRESS for a pension and in 1807 was awarded half-pay for life. Harding died in Schoharie, New York, on November 20, 1814, a talented commander of the young American navy.

Further Reading

Cohen, Sheldon S. "We Dare Oppose Them": The Connecticut State Navy in the American Revolution," *Connecticut Historical Society Bulletin* 47 (July 1982): 74–96.
Hearn, Chester G. *George Washington's Schooners: The First American Navy.* Annapolis, Md.: Naval Institute Press, 1995.
Howard, James L. *Seth Harding, Mariner: A Naval Picture of the Revolution.* New Haven, Conn.: Yale University Press, 1930.
McManemin, John A. *Sea Raiders from Connecticut during the American Revolution.* Ho-Ho-Kus, N.J.: Ho-Ho-Kus Pub. Co., 1995.
Miller, Nathan. *Broadsides: The Age of Fighting Sail, 1775–1815.* New York: Wiley, 2000.

Morgan, William J. *Captains to the Northward: The New England Captains in the Continental Navy.* Barre, Mass.: Barre Gazette, 1959.

Hayne, Isaac (1745–1781)
American militia officer

Isaac Hayne was born in Colleton County, South Carolina, on September 23, 1745, the son of a planter. He enjoyed a life of relative luxury and won a seat in the royal assembly by 1770. Once the Revolutionary War commenced in 1775 he enrolled in a local militia unit, rising to the rank of colonel. Among his other preoccupations at the time was managing the Aera Ironworks, which manufactured ammunition for American forces. Hayne was apparently present during the siege of CHARLESTON under General Henry CLINTON and taken prisoner when the city fell in May 1780. Being a militiaman, he was paroled and allowed to return home without interference. However, on June 3, 1780, Clinton proclaimed that all inhabitants of South Carolina were obliged to sign an oath of allegiance to the Crown or be considered enemy combatants. Hayne, whose wife and children were seriously ill, ventured to Charleston and signed the oath—with the understanding that he was not obliged to take up arms against his former compatriots.

Hayne basically complied with the terms of his parole and refused to join and fight for either Patriot or LOYALIST units operating in his area. However, in the summer of 1781, the declining fortunes of British arms in South Carolina, plus the pressure of former friends, convinced him that the terms of his parole were now irrelevant, and he rejoined the militia as a colonel. That July Hayne and a number of other scouts captured Loyalist general Andrew Williamson near Charleston. However, the city's commander, Lieutenant Colonel Nisbet Balfour, dispatched 90 dragoons under Major Thomas Fraser to rescue him. Galloping hard, they overtook Hayne's group on July 8, 1781, killed 14 Americans, and took him prisoner. Hayne was then imprisoned in Charleston for three weeks before being informed that he would face a military tribunal for violating his parole. He vigorously protested his predicament, but the British were determined to set an example for others. On July 31, 1781, the theater commander, Lieutenant Colonel Francis RAWDON, declared that Hayne was to be executed for spying and parole violations, a decision reached after an informal hearing. The citizens of Charleston then petitioned the British for his release, but on August 4, 1781, Hayne was led to the gallows and hanged. The Americans were appreciably incensed, and General Nathanael GREENE threatened to execute any British officer of equal rank that fell into his hands. If through this harshness the British sought to intimidate South Carolinians from joining the rebels, they miscalculated badly, for Hayne was immediately enshrined as a martyr. Moreover, the nature of his death served as a rallying point for increased enlistments and further hardened the already callous attitudes of a bloody civil war.

Further Reading
Bowden, David K. *The Execution of Isaac Hayne.* Lexington, S.C.: Sandlapper Store, 1977.
Dawson, Henry B. "Lord Rawdon and the Duke of Richmond on the Execution of Colonel Isaac Hayne," *Historical Magazine* 12 (September 1866): 269–272.
Richardson, Marcus, Mrs. "Asgill for Hayne: A Life for a Life," *American Historical Register* (January 1895): 455–460.
Webber, Mabel L. "Records Kept by Colonel Isaac Hayne," *South Carolina Historical of Geological Magazine* 10 (July, October 1909): 145–170, 220–235, 11 (January, April, July 1910): 27–38, 92–106, 161–172.

Hays, Mary (1754–1832)
American camp follower, soldier
Mary Ludwig was born in Trenton, New Jersey, on October 13, 1752, the daughter of German immigrants. In 1769 her family relocated to Carlisle, Pennsylvania, where she subsequently found domestic work in the household of Dr. William IRVINE. That year she apparently met and married John Hays, a barber who enlisted with the 1st Pennsylvania Artillery Regiment in December 1775 as a gunner. Two years later he transferred to Colonel Irvine's 7th Pennsylvania Infantry as a private. Hays, like thousands of camp followers in the war, accompanied her husband into the field, performing mundane but useful services such as cooking, washing, and nursing the injured. On June 28, 1778, both John and Mary Hays were present at the Battle of MONMOUTH, where the former, having previously served as an artillerist, was detached from his regiment to help man the cannon. The day was extremely hot, with Mary and scores of other women carrying buckets of water to cool the guns and their crews. At some point during the battle, John Hays collapsed either from heat exhaustion or wounds. Tradition holds that Mary threw down her pitcher, picked up her husband's rammer, and ably served his piece for the rest of the engagement. In the course of battle a cannon ball apparently tore through her skirt, but she ignored the danger and continued working. Her bravery came to the attention of General Nathanael GREENE, who arranged an introduction with General George WASHINGTON. Washington personally thanked Hays for courage under fire and promoted her to sergeant. In this manner she became universally applauded as "Molly Pitcher," although this was a commonly used appellation for camp followers at that time.

Hays remained in the army as a washerwoman for eight years without further notoriety, and following her discharge she returned to Carlisle as a servant. When husband John died in 1787 she married another veteran, John McCauley, who was apparently semi-disabled, and spent the rest of her days supporting him. After he died in 1809 Hays endured a period of obscurity until 1822, when she petitioned the Pennsylvania general assembly for assistance: It voted her a $40 per year annuity in recognition of her services. She died in Carlisle on January 22, 1832, and received a military funeral. During the Revolutionary Centennial in 1876, Hays was further honored with a special marker placed over her grave. Her story is sometimes confused with that of another female artillerist, Margaret CORBIN, but the two remain enshrined in the national mythology, if not in fact.

Further Reading

Berkin, Carol. *America's Revolutionary Mothers: Women in the Struggle for Independence*. New York: Knopf, 2005.

Bohrer, Melissa L. *Glory, Passion, and Principle: The Story of Eight Remarkable Women at the Core of the American Revolution*. New York: Atria Books, 2003.

Martin, David G. *A Molly Pitcher Source Book*. Hightstown, N.J.: Longstreet House, 2003.

———. *The Story of Molly Pitcher*. Hightstown, N.J.: Longstreet House, 2000.

Roberts, Cokie. *Founding Mothers: The Women Who Raised Our Nation*. New York: William Morrow, 2004.

Teipe, Emily J. "Will the Real Molly Pitcher Please Stand Up?" *Prologue* 31, no. 2 (1999): 118–126.

Hazelwood, John (ca. 1726–1800)
American naval officer

John Hazelwood was born in England around 1726; he joined the merchant marine as a young man, and by 1753 was an accomplished mariner based in Philadelphia. In July 1775 he advised the Pennsylvania committee of safety about naval defenses for the city, and that December he received command of a flotilla of fire rafts and a rank of captain. For most of 1776 Hazelwood worked on riverine defenses throughout Pennsylvania and New York to the satisfaction of employers, for in 1777 he received promotion to commodore. In September of that year he became commander of the Pennsylvania state navy, a wretched little force tasked with defending Philadelphia's water approaches along the Delaware River. Hazelwood had at his disposal the Continental sloop *Montgomery*, two floating batteries, a handful of armed sloops and schooners, 13 armed galleys, and some smaller craft. The Delaware River defenses were further augmented by hastily constructed Fort Mercer in New Jersey under Colonel Christopher GREENE and Fort Mifflin on the river itself, under Lieutenant Colonel Samuel SMITH. Once Philadelphia fell to British forces under General William HOWE on September 2, 1777, he sought to clear the river of its defenders to avoid dependance upon overland supply routes. Several warships were detached from the British fleet of Admiral Richard HOWE, which made their way up the river to engage the forts.

On October 23, 1777, Hazelwood's flotilla, in concert with Forts Mifflin and Mercer, bombarded a squadron of six British warships as they maneuvered upstream. The attacks from his galleys proved particularly effective and, after a struggle of several hours, the ship of the line HMS *Augusta*, 64 guns, and the sloop *Merlin*, 18 guns, were run aground and burned to prevent capture. *Augusta* became the largest British warship lost in either the Revolutionary War or the War of 1812. Hazelwood's victory delayed the British advance for a month, and Congress voted him an elegant sword. It was not until November 10 that the Royal Navy returned—in overwhelming force. This time the flotilla of the Pennsylvania state navy rendered little support, and Hazelwood eventually scuttled them all upstream. In 1778 the state navy was disbanded altogether, although he retained his rank. Hazelwood spent the balance of the war as commissioner of purchases for the Continental ARMY and afterward returned to the merchant marine. He died in Philadelphia on March 1, 1800, having gallantly contributed to his city's defense.

Further Reading

Browne, Gregory M. "Fort Mercer and Fort Mifflin: The Battle for the Delaware River and the Importance of the American Riverine Defenses during Washington's Siege of Philadelphia." Unpublished master's thesis, Western Illinois University, 1996.

Gifford, Edward S. *The American Revolution in the Delaware Valley*. Philadelphia: Pennsylvania Society of Sons of the Revolution, 1976.

Jackson, John W. *Fort Mifflin: Valiant Defender of the Delaware*. Philadelphia: Old Fort Mifflin Historical Society Preservation Committee, 1986.

———. *The Pennsylvania Navy, 1775–1781: The Defense of the Delaware*. New Brunswick, N.J.: Rutgers University Press, 1974.

Leach, Josiah G. "Commodore John Hazelwood, Commander of the Pennsylvania Navy in the Revolution," *Pennsylvania Magazine of History and Biography* 26 (April 1902): 106.

Heath, William (1737–1814)
American military officer

William Heath was born in Roxbury, Massachusetts, on March 13, 1737, the son of successful farmers. He followed into his father's profession although displaying an avid interest in military affairs. He then served with the local militia for several years before transferring to the Ancient and Honorable Artillery Company of Boston and gradually rose to commander. During the period leading up to hostilities with Great Britain, Heath became identified with anti-British agitation, and he published numerous newspaper articles advocating colonial military preparedness. In 1774 he became a colonel of the Suffolk militia while simultaneously holding seats in the Massachusetts provincial congress and on its COMMITTEE OF CORRESPONDENCE. In recognition of his military expertise, Heath gained appointment as brigadier general of militia on February 9, 1775. Two months later he hastily arrived at the Battle of CONCORD and helped harass the withdrawing forces of Colonel Hugh PERCY. He then assumed command of milling American forces outside Cambridge until relieved by General Artemas WARD. Heath then controlled reserve forces during the Battle of BUNKER HILL on June 17, 1775, and subsequently organized American defenses at Roxbury. Heath rose to major general of militia on June 20, 1775, and two days later he was commissioned a brigadier general in the Continental ARMY. He functioned capably throughout the siege of Boston and then accompanied General George WASHINGTON with his men to New York City.

Heath saw relatively little fighting in and around New York, being deployed mostly on the northern end of Manhattan. On August 9, 1776, he gained promotion to major general and assumed command of both the Third Division and the defenses of the Hudson Highlands. During Washington's retreat from New York, Heath refused an order by General Charles LEE to transfer the bulk of his forces to his command in New Jersey. Within days Washington had won the Battles of TRENTON and PRINCETON, and he ordered Heath to keep the enemy off balance by attacking Fort Independence, New York. On January 17, 1776, Heath complied as ordered and demanded the garrison's immediate surrender, but it refused. The Americans then spent several days attempting to maneuver around the fort in a snow storm while their artillery bombardment proved ineffectual. Heath's ineffectiveness emboldened the defenders, and on January 25 they sortied and routed the besiegers at Delancey Mills. Heath then called off the attack, resulting in a private reprimand from Washington. He never again held a combat command.

Heath assumed command of the Boston garrison, where he performed useful work training troops and forwarding supplies. In the fall of 1777 he was allowed to command troops that escorted the captured "convention" army of General John BURGOYNE from Saratoga, New York, to Cambridge, where they remained in limbo for several months. Heath then resumed command of the Hudson Highlands district rather than accept an offer from the Second Continental CONGRESS to serve on the newly constituted Board of War. Heath's tenure at West Point, New York, remained uneventful, save for several months in 1780 when he ventured to Rhode Island to assist the newly arrived army of General Jean-Baptiste, comte de ROCHAMBEAU. Back at West Point he proved instrumental in helping to quell a mutiny of the Massachusetts Line on January 1, 1780, and in August 1781 he assumed an offensive posture outside New York to cover the march of Washington and Rochambeau to YORKTOWN.

Heath mustered out on July 1, 1783, and returned to Roxbury. There he resumed his political activities by serving at the constitutional convention in 1788, where he supported ratification. He next served in the state senate, 1791–92, and also as a probate judge for Norfolk County. During the 1790s, Heath became an ardent proponent of Thomas JEFFERSON and railed against the government's potential powers of taxation. In 1798 he failed to secure a seat in Congress but was elected lieutenant governor in 1806. Heath's final political activity was opposing the War of 1812 under President James MADISON. He died in Roxbury on January 24, 1814, the oldest-surviving major general of the Revolution.

Further Reading
Dolan, Graham P. "Major General William Heath and the First Years of the American Revolution." Unpublished Ph.D. diss., Boston University, 1966.
Heath, William. *Memoirs of Major General William Heath.* Freeport, N.Y.: Books for Libraries Press, 1970.
———. "The Heath Papers," *Massachusetts Historical Society Collections,* 5th ser., vol. 4 (1878); 7th ser., vol. 4 (1904), vol. 5 (1905).
Heathcote, Charles W. "General William Heath—An Earnest Patriot and Friend of Washington," *Picket Post* no. 78 (October 1962): 4–9.
Nichols, Fessenden A. "The Life and Public Services of General William Heath," *Roxbury Historical Society Year-Book for 1920,* 12–24.
O'Connell, Lenaham. *William Heath: Late Major General, Army of the Revolution, and First Judge of Probate, Norfolk County, Massachusetts.* Boston: Elizabeth-James Press, 2001.

Heister, Leopold von (1707–1777)
Hessian military officer

Leopold von Heister was born in the German principality of Hessen-Kassel in 1707. Details of his military career are little known, but he apparently served his sovereign, Landgrave Frederick II, long and well for many years. In December 1775 the landgrave concluded an extensive agreement with King GEORGE III of England to provide 12,000 veteran soldiers to fight in the Revolutionary War. Heister, a lieutenant general and Frederick's most senior officer, was appointed commander of all HESSIAN forces. While instructed to fight for the British, he was also under strict orders to protect the lives of his monarch's subjects where possible. Accordingly, Heister mustered his men at Portsmouth, England, and steadfastly refused to sail until everything was in proper German order. This delay infuriated George III, whose forces were hard-pressed for manpower, and he ordered the Hessians to depart in May 1776. Heister arrived at Halifax, Nova Scotia, with 7,800 men only to learn that the main British army under General William HOWE had already sailed for New York. The Hessians made their tardy appearance just as Howe was preparing major offensive operations against the army of General George WASHINGTON. Relations between the two strong-willed commanders were cordial initially, but Heister resented what he considered Howe's tactical interference by ordering his units deployed in two ranks instead of the traditional three. Howe, meanwhile, respected Heister's ability as a commander but gradually came to resent what he construed as an obstructionist attitude toward orders. Furthermore, Heister was, from the standpoint of rank, the secondmost-senior figure of all British forces in America. The war minister, Lord George GERMAIN, to preclude any chance that a foreigner would accede to command, granted the third-ranking officer, General Henry CLINTON, a "dormant commission" to succeed Howe should Howe be killed or incapacitated. Such arrangements, when they became known, did little to foster unity between the two allies.

Heister fought well at the victory of LONG ISLAND on August 27, 1776, and demonstrated how effective his veteran troops were, once arrayed against a rabble. Indeed, the Americans very much feared the reputation of their German opponents. Heister held the British center as ordered, advanced stolidly, and ultimately forced the surrender of General William ALEXANDER. Two months later he again performed competently, if cautiously, at WHITE PLAINS on October 28, 1776. But his refusal to risk or endanger the lives of his charge unnecessarily created increasing friction between himself and Howe. When Howe began complaining to Germain about Heister's perceived recalcitrance, the minister began looking for a pretext to replace him with a more pliable subordinate. The break came during final phases of the American withdrawal across New Jersey that December. In light of cold weather Howe called off the chase and left the state dotted with British and Hessian garrisons for the winter. Unfortunately, the Hessian garrison at TRENTON under Colonel Johann RALL, while closest to the enemy, was among the weakest. Before this situation was brought to the attention of Heister, Washington suddenly struck back at Trenton on December 26, 1777, annihilating Rall's command. Howe quickly blamed Heister for the disaster and Germain then formally requested his recall. Frederick II obliged him, and the elderly general was ordered back home on June 23, 1777. He was replaced by his nominal second in command, General Wilhelm von KNYPHAUSEN. Howe briefly paid Heister a friendly visit before he departed America on July 19, 1777, but the two leaders remained scarcely on speaking terms. The elderly general arrived back at Hessen-Kassel on October 13, 1777, completely angered and bewildered by his recall. His lengthy professional career apparently ending in disgrace, he died suddenly on November 19, 1777. As a token of appreciation for services rendered, Heister's widow received a settlement from the landgrave and a pension from the English king.

Further Reading

Atwood, Rodney. *The Hessians: Mercenaries from Hesse-Kassel in the American Revolution.* New York: Cambridge University Press, 1980.

Burgoyne, Bruce E., ed. *Enemy Views: The American Revolutionary War as Recorded by the Hessian Participants.* Bowie, Md.: Heritage Books, 1996.

Heinemeier, Dan C. *A Social History of Hesse: Roman Times to 1800.* Arlington, Va.: Heinemeier Publishing, 2002.

Hoffman, Elliott W. "The German Soldiers in the American Revolution," 2 vols. Unpublished Ph.D. diss., University of New Hampshire, 1982.

Stephens, Thomas R. "In Deepest Submission: The Hessian Mercenary Troops in the American Revolution." Unpublished Ph.D. diss., Texas A & M University, 1999.

Henry, Patrick (1736–1799)
American politician

Patrick Henry was born in Hanover County, Virginia, on May 29, 1736, a part of the lesser frontier gentry. He was educated at home and tried his hand at managing a business, but failed. He then read law by himself and passed the bar exam in 1760. Henry proved adept as a backcountry attorney and made a name for himself by winning the so-called Parson's Cause with his trademark stirring oratory. This case initiated Henry's reputation as a leading critic of British imperial policy, and in May 1765 he won a seat in the Virginia House of Burgesses. Here he unleashed torrents of invective against the STAMP ACT of 1765 and, when the cry of "treason" went up among some legislators, he thundered back "If this be treason, then make the most of it!" Henry went on to propose a series of seven resolves against Parliament, none of which passed, but these were subsequently published as the *Virginia Resolves* and circulated among the colonies. Over the next decade Henry established himself as one of the most strident and forceful critics of Great Britain and harangued his compatriots with an eloquence and passion that held many spellbound. In 1774 he was elected to the First Continental CONGRESS, where he allied himself with Massachusetts radical John ADAMS and sought to make common cause with all colonies then struggling with the motherland. Convinced that armed conflict was inevitable, Henry was actively involved in recruiting and mobilizing the Virginia militia. On March 23, 1775, at a gathering of local forces, he delivered his most famous speech by declaring "Is life so dear, or peace so sweet, as to be purchased at the price of chains and slavery? Forbid it, Almighty God! I know not what course others may take, but as for me, give me liberty or give me death!" Henry's firebrand rhetoric was never more emphatic and resonates to this day.

Once fighting commenced at Lexington and CONCORD in April 1775, Henry emerged as a foil to Virginia's governor John MURRAY, Lord Dunmore, who had summarily dismissed the House of Burgesses. When the governor ordered royal marines to seize a cache of colonial gunpowder at Williamsburg, Henry confronted the governor with a party of militia and demanded that he compensate the colony. In the spring of 1775 Henry attended the Second Continental Congress and, curiously, proved reluctant to advocate completely breaking ties with Britain. This reticence put him somewhat at odds with other radicals present, and at length he abandoned his seat to effect a greater influence at home. Henry was initially appointed colonel of the 1st Virginia Militia Regiment but subsequently lost that post due to political enemies. He next worked hard on a new state constitution, which was approved on June 29, 1776, and became the state's first elected governor. In this capacity, he oversaw Virginia's political and military contributions to the war in a smooth and efficient manner. In 1778 Henry proved instrumental in supplying and supporting the expedition of George Rogers CLARK against the Illinois territory, which reduced British influence in the Old Northwest. He proved a popular executive, winning two more consecutive terms in office before being succeeded by Thomas JEFFERSON in 1779. Henry rejoined the House of Delegates in 1780, remaining there another four years.

Henry gained reelection to the governorship from 1784 to 1786, and the legislature from 1786 to 1790. However, during the struggle to replace the flawed ARTICLES OF CONFEDERATION with a new federal constitution, he was staunchly opposed to the scheme. Specifically, Henry feared that centralized governance would erode states' rights and he insisted upon the addition of a bill of rights to preserve personal liberties. The constitution was then modified and ratified by 1789, and Henry resumed his legal activities at home. Throughout the 1790s President George WASHINGTON tendered Henry the posts of secretary of state and chief justice, but he declined. By this time he had also become estranged from his former ally Jefferson and joined the Federalist Party in opposition. In January 1799 he successfully ran for a new seat in the House of Delegates but died at his home in Red Hill, Virginia, on June 6, 1799.

Further Reading
Edwards, Gregory J. " 'Righteousness Alone Exults a Nation': Protestantism and the Spirit of the American Revolution." Unpublished Ph.D. diss., State University of New York at Buffalo, 2002.
Hack, Timothy. "Shaping a Revolution: The County Committees of Safety in Virginia, 1774–1776." Unpublished master's thesis, James Madison University, 2002.
Mayer, Henry. *A Son of Thunder: Patrick Henry and the American Republic.* Charlottesville: University Press of Virginia, 1991.
McCants, David A., ed. *Patrick Henry, the Orator.* New York: Greenwood Press, 1990.
McDonnell, Michael A. "The Politics of Mobilization in Revolutionary Virginia: Military Culture and Political and Social Relations, 1774–1783." Unpublished Ph.D. diss., University of Oxford, 1995.
Vaughn, David J. *Give Me Liberty: The Uncompromising Statesmanship of Patrick Henry.* Nashville, Tenn.: Cumberland House, 2003.

Herkimer, Nicholas (1728–1777)
American militia officer

Nicholas Herkimer was born in Herkimer, New York, in 1728, the son of German emigrants from the Rhineland Palatinate. He pursued farming and during the French and Indian War functioned as a lieutenant within the local militia. His principle task was defending the local blockhouse, Fort Herkimer (later Fort Dayton), from attack, which he accomplished successfully. Afterward Herkimer accumulated considerable wealth and became one of the county's most respected citizens. During the period leading up to the break with Great Britain, he became involved in Patriot affairs and chaired the Tryon County committee of safety. In January 1776 he accompanied General Philip SCHUYLER on an expedition against Johnson Hall, home of LOYALIST Sir John JOHNSON, and disarmed his personal force of Highlanders. Herkimer performed well in his various assignments, and when Schuyler departed he was appointed commander of the Tryon County militia with a rank of brigadier general. In this capacity Herkimer marshaled scanty resources to protect scattered frontier settlements against possible attack. In June 1777 Herkimer led 300 militiamen to a conference at Unadilla, home of Mohawk chief Joseph BRANT, where he tried unsuccessfully to secure Mohawk neutrality. When the meeting almost broke into a pitched battle, Herkimer managed to calm the participants and extricate his force without loss.

In August 1777, Herkimer was alerted by Colonel Peter GANSEVOORT, commander of Fort Stanwix on the Mohawk River, that a large British expedition had landed at Oswego and was marching en route. Herkimer therefore assembled the Tyron County militia, totaling 800 rank and file, and proceeded to his relief. While passing through Canajoharie, his column was observed by Molly BRANT, sister of the chief, who dispatched a runner to warn him. Meanwhile, Herkimer made steady progress toward his objective, although younger subordinates railed against the slow pace. Disregarding his well-founded caution, he force-marched his command through a thickly wooded region called ORISKANY and was ambushed by Indians and Loyalists under Major John BUTLER on August 6. A savage, hand-to-hand struggle ensued, with the Americans losing up to half their number. Herkimer, badly hit in the leg, had to be propped up against a tree to direct the engagement, all the while smoking his pipe. At length the enemy failed to dislodge his troops and fell back after the Fort Stanwix garrison sortied against the British camp. Herkimer then evacuated his survivors and endured a painful 35-mile trek back to Fort Dayton. His relief effort had failed.

Herkimer lingered in bed for 10 days until a relief column under Colonel Benedict ARNOLD arrived and tendered him the services of Arnold's French surgeon. Overruling the objections of Herkimer's own doctor, he proceeded to amputate the general's leg but failed to effectively close the wound. Herkimer died calmly in his bed on August 16, 1777. Unknown to him, the losses he inflicted upon the Indians at Oriskany demoralized them, and they deserted Lieutenant Colonel Barry ST. LEGER, forcing him to abandon the siege of Fort Stanwix. In this manner General John BURGOYNE, rapidly approaching Saratoga, was denied badly needed reinforcements.

Further Reading
Foote, Allan D. *Liberty March: The Battle of Oriskany.* Utica, N.Y.: North Country Books, 1998.
Patterson, Gerard A. "The Battle of Oriskany," *American History Illustrated* 11, no. 4 (1976): 8–17.
Piatt, Kevin P. "Opportunity Lost: The Battle of Oriskany and the Siege of Fort Stanwix." Unpublished master's thesis, California State University, Dominguez Hills, 1998.
Watt, Gavin K. *Rebellion in the Mohawk Valley: The St. Leger Expedition of 1777.* Toronto: Dundurn Press, 2002.
———. *The Flockey, 13 August 1777: The Defeat of the Tory Uprising in the Schoharie Valley.* King City, Ont.: G. K. Watt, 2002.

Hessians

By 1775 the English government of King GEORGE III had realized that its standing army of 15,000 troops, however well trained and led, was insufficient to the task of putting down a rebellion in North America. Conscription was politically impossible, and the recruitment and drilling of new forces would take time, so the British turned to the time-honored expedient of hiring foreign auxiliaries to flesh out their meager manpower. In a strictly legal parlance, these soldiers were distinct from mercenaries inasmuch as they were hired directly from the monarch of a sovereign state and not recruited individually. England found a ready and willing source of superb soldiery from among the 300 German principalities, many of whom were willing to rent out entire armies at a stipulated rate. Moreover, contracts with England required that sovereigns receive additional money for each of their subjects either killed or maimed in battle. The British, taking a long view of the struggle, hoped that this sudden influx of professional soldiers would help crush the rebellion quickly, thereby saving the government lives, money, and time. This was a realistic appraisal, considering that German soldiers were rigorously disciplined, led by older, professional officers, and enjoyed fearsome reputations. But in practice the recruitment of auxiliary soldiers backfired politically, for American propagandists highlighted the fact that the king now recruited hired killers to deprive citizens of their rights. Resentment toward foreign troops proved so ingrained that it was specifically listed in the DECLARATION OF INDEPENDENCE as a cause for severing ties with England.

Ultimately, between 1775 and 1783, Great Britain acquired roughly 29,000 German soldiers, collectively known as "Hessians." In fact, these originated from no less than six different principalities: Hessen-Kassel, Hessen-Hanau, Brunswick, Ansbach-Bayreuth, Anhalt-Zerbst, and Waldeck. All were savagely drilled in the Prussian-style discipline of the day and consequently fought coolly under fire. Owing to the wilderness conditions of North America, the British also insisted that the Germans abandon their traditional three-rank-deep formations in favor of a more flexible two-rank attangement. Such tactical interference generated some resentment among senior commanders like General Leopold von HEISTER but did not overtly diminish their fighting prowess. Many Germans also resented the fact that the British viewed them as second-class citizens, sent them on dangerous missions unsupported, and only infrequently called senior officers into staff meetings. The Americans, on the other hand, were openly terrified of them and sometimes the mere sight of their precisely advancing formations instilled panic.

In combat the Germans usually performed well. General Heister led them competently at the victories of LONG ISLAND and WHITE PLAINS in 1776, where they experienced little problem in defeating the American rabble. German valor proved so conspicuous during the capture of Fort Washington, New York, that General Wilhelm von KNYPHAUSEN was singled out for commendation by General William HOWE, and the post was subsequently renamed Fort Knyphausen in his honor. One light infantry officer, Major Johann EWALD, proved to be so worthy an opponent that he was honored by the Patriot general, Henry KNOX after the war. At Hubbardton, Vermont, on July 7, 1777, another German detachment under General Friedrich von RIEDESEL rescued British forces led by General Simon FRASER. However, smaller commands performing independent missions—for which they were not essentially trained—could and did meet with disaster. Hessians under Colonel Friedrich BAUM and Johann RALL at TRENTON in 1776 and BENNINGTON in 1777, were annihilated because they either underestimated the numbers opposing them or were contemptuous of their foes and refused to entrench. As the war unfolded and the Americans gradually lost their terror of the Hessians, the Americans employed various methods to induce their desertion, with some effect. By war's end the Hessian component had performed capably in every campaign from Canada to Florida. Of the 29,000 mustered, only 17,000 returned to Europe, the remainder either died of wounds and disease or simply chose to begin a new life in their adopted land.

Further Reading

Burgoyne, Bruce E., ed. *Most Illustrious Hereditary Prince—Letters to Their Prince from Members of the Hesse-Hanau Military Contingent in the Service of England during the American Revolutionary War.* Bowie, Md.: Heritage Books, 2003.

———. *The 3rd English-Waldeck Regiment in the American Revolutionary War.* Bowie, Md.: Heritage Books, 1999.

———. *Enemy Views: The American Revolutionary War as Recorded by the Hessian Participants.* Bowie, Md.: Heritage Books, 1996.

Hall, Cosby W. "French and Hessian Impressions: Foreign Soldier's Views of America during the Revolution." Unpublished master's thesis, College of William and Mary, 2003.

Katrizky, Linda. "Johann Gottfried Seume's Expedition with the Hessians to America, 1781–83," *Yearbook of German-American Studies* 32 (2002): 41–61.

Hinman, Elisha (1734–1805)
American naval officer

Elisha Hinman was born in Stonington, Connecticut, on March 9, 1734, the son of a merchant marine captain. He followed into his father's service at an early age and at the age of 19 commanded his own brig in the West Indies trade. In 1776 Hinman was commissioned a lieutenant in the Continental NAVY and was assigned to the brig *Cabot* under Captain John B. HOPKINS. In this capacity he accompanied the New Providence expedition of Commodore Esek HOPKINS and was present during the embarrassing encounter with HMS *Glasgow* on April 6, 1776. He nonetheless acquitted himself well and assumed command of the *Cabot* the following August.

On October 10, 1776, Hinman received promotion to captain, being 20th on the seniority list, and succeeded John Paul JONES as commander of the *Alfred*, a converted merchantman and one of the nation's earliest warships. Hinman conducted an uneventful cruise that fall, and in the spring of 1777 he was teamed up with Captain Thomas Thompson of the new frigate *Raleigh* and ordered to France. They took several vessels en route and on September 3, 1777, the small squadron attacked a lucrative British West Indian convoy. However, Hinman proved unable to engage owing to *Alfred*'s sluggish sailing qualities, and several highly valuable prizes escaped. After docking at L'Orient, France, on October 7, 1777, both ships made a return voyage in December. On March 9, 1778, they were observed by the British warships HMS *Ariadne* of 20 guns and *Ceres* of 16, a clearly inferior force. But as the British ships acted in tandem against the slower *Alfred*, Hinman was forced to surrender once Thompson abandoned him. In truth, the British ships should easily have been overpowered, and Thompson was subsequently discharged for incompetence. No blame was attached to Hinman, although he never held another Continental navy command.

After escaping from Forton Prison, England, Hinman returned to Connecticut, where he commanded the privateers *Deane* and *Marquis de Lafayette*. In 1779 he lent his nautical expertise to assisting the new frigate *Trumbull* out of the Connecticut River and into open water. After the war ended Hinman resumed his activities in the merchant marine for several years, and he declined President John ADAMS's invitation to command the new frigate USS *Constitution* in 1794. Four years later he joined the nascent Revenue Service (Coast Guard) as a captain and led the cutter *Argus* until his retirement in 1802. Hinman died at New London on August 29, 1805.

Further Reading
Clark, William B. "The Battle of Words: A Naval Episode of the Revolutionary War," *Minute Man* 41 (February 1951): 5–8.

Kern, Florence. *Jonathan Maltbies, U.S. Revenue Cutter Argus, 1791–1804.* Washington, D.C.: Alised Enterprises, 1976.

McKusker, John J. *Alfred: The First Continental Flagship, 1775–1778.* Washington, D.C.: Smithsonian Institute Press, 1973.

McManemin, John A. *Sea Raiders from Connecticut during the American Revolution.* Spring Lake, N.J.: Ho-Ho-Kus Pub. Co., 1995.

Middlebrook, Louis F. *History of Maritime Connecticut during the American Revolution, 1775–1783,* 2 vols. Salem, Mass.: Essex Institute, 1925.

Rogers, Ernest E. *Connecticut's Naval Office at New London during the War of the American Revolution.* New London: New London County Historical Society, 1933.

Hogun, James (d. 1781)
American military officer

James Hogun was born in Ireland, and he migrated to Halifax County, North Carolina, around 1751. As the ongoing crisis with Great Britain unfolded, he was increasingly drawn into revolutionary politics by serving on the local committee of safety and also won three successive seats in the extralegal provincial congress. After completing useful service on various military committees, Hogun was appointed a major in the Halifax County militia in April 1776 and then colonel of the 7th North Carolina Continental Infantry that

November. He spent several months energetically recruiting, equipping, and training his charge, which he then marched north to join the main American army under General George WASHINGTON. Hogun performed well under fire at BRANDYWINE and GERMANTOWN and later transferred to command the 3rd North Carolina Continental Infantry. After several months in this capacity Hogun was dispatched south to raise recruits for his old regiment, which he brought back to New York by September 1778. He spent several months in the vicinity of New York building fortifications near West Point until March 1779, when General Benedict ARNOLD requested to be relieved of duty as governor of Philadelphia. Washington selected Hogun for the task, and he remained there several months until the Continental CONGRESS appointed him and Jethro SUMNER brigadier generals from North Carolina. This was achieved by promoting him over the head of Colonel Thomas Clark, the acting brigadier. He then spent several months training and equipping the four regiments constituting the North Carolina brigade.

In the winter of 1779 Washington ordered Hogun south again with his brigade. There he was to augment the army of General Benjamin LINCOLN at Charleston, South Carolina. Hogun performed as asked, led his men on an arduous winter march, and arrived in March 1780, just as the city was being surrounded by British forces under General Henry CLINTON. Over the next two months his men bore a prominent role in defending the doomed city, which capitulated to the British on May 12, 1780. Clinton then promptly paroled the bulk of the defenders, being militia, but the Continentals were incarcerated as prisoners of war at nearby Haddrel's Point on Sullivan's Island. The men, restricted to confined, filthy conditions and poorly fed, gradually sickened. At one point the British offered to parole Hogun, but he elected to remain with his men and urge them to resist volunteering to serve as royal militia. After several months of deprivation and illness, Hogun died at Haddrel's Point on January 4, 1781, and was interred in an unmarked grave.

Further Reading

Borick, Carl P. *A Gallant Defense: The Siege of Charleston, 1780.* Columbia: University of South Carolina Press, 2003.

Clark, Walter. *Career of General James Hogun: One of North Carolina's Revolutionary Officers.* Raleigh: North Carolina Society, Daughters of the American Revolution, 1911.

———, ed. *The State Records of North Carolina,* 26 vols. Raleigh, N.C.: P. M. Hale, 1886–87; vols. 11–22.

Hogun, Neil. "General James Hogun: A Forgotten American hero," *Irish Sword* 17 (Summer 1990): 255–260.

Rankin, Hugh F. *The North Carolina Continentals.* Chapel Hill: University of North Carolina Press, 1977.

Saunders, William L., ed. *The Colonial Records of North Carolina,* 10 vols. Raleigh, N.C.: P. M. Hale, 1886–1890; vols. 9, 10.

Wheeler, Earl M. "The Role of North Carolina Militia in the Beginning of the American Revolution." Unpublished master's thesis, Tulane University, 1969.

Hood, Samuel (1724–1816)
English naval officer

Samuel Hood was born in Butleigh, Somerset, England, on December 12, 1724, and he entered the navy as a midshipman at the age of 16. Curiously, he served under Captain George RODNEY, an officer with whom his later career would be closely entwined. Hood proved himself an efficient leader, and he received his first command, the sloop HMS *Jamaica,* in 1754 at the relatively young age of 30. He fought well during the French and Indian War, capturing two French privateers while commanding HMS *Antelope,* 50 guns, in 1757, and the large frigate *Bellone* off Cape Finisterre in 1759. After another tour with Rodney in the Mediterranean, he was posted with the North American station at Halifax, although in 1769 he spent a year at Boston. Hood was then replaced by Admiral James GAMBIER in 1770 and returned to England to serve as commissioner of the Portsmouth dockyard and governor of the naval academy, 1778–80, where he became a baron. By now Hood had acquired the reputation of a capable but acerbic officer, one quick to find—and complain about—the shortcomings of others. But his efficiency impressed King GEORGE III during an inspection of the Portsmouth facilities, and in September 1780 Hood finally gained promotion to rear admiral. In January 1781 he was sent to the West Indies to serve under Rodney for a third time. Both men, brilliant leaders in their own right, maintained a tense but cordial relationship over what to do.

The principal British naval objective in the West Indies was a sizable French fleet under Admiral François-Joseph-Paul, comte de GRASSE. On April 29, 1781, Hood tried to prevent de Grasse from raising the blockade of Martinique, although outnumbered by 14 ships of the line to 19 for the French. After a heavy exchange of fire the British withdrew and rejoined the main force under Rodney. On August 1, 1781, Rodney returned to England on sick leave, and Hood rose to temporary commander of Caribbean forces. In this capacity he sailed on August 10 and tried to intercept de Grasse at Haiti, but the French had departed earlier than anticipated and plied an indirect route through the Bahama Channel to confuse their pursuers. Hood's faster-sailing copper-bottom warships nevertheless reached Chesapeake Bay ahead of his quarry; but, finding the area devoid of enemy ships, he sailed to New York and anchored there on August 28. Hood then became subordinated to Admiral Thomas GRAVES, a capable but rather cautious officer. Hood nevertheless prevailed upon his superior to sail at once for the Chesapeake, having divined that the French intended to entrap the army of General Charles CORNWALLIS there. Graves only grudgingly complied, and on September 5, 1781, the decisive Battle of the Virginia Capes was fought. Hood, placed in the rear, was scarcely engaged and watched Graves fritter away his opportunity for victory. He then accompanied the fleet back to New York on September 23 and helped outfit a relief expedition to rescue Cornwallis, but by the time he returned to the Chesapeake three weeks later the British had surrendered at Yorktown. Hood remained on station in New York until November 11, 1781, when he sailed off to Barbados to rejoin Rodney.

Admiral Samuel Hood of the Royal Navy served brilliantly in the West Indies. *(National Portrait Gallery, London)*

Meanwhile, de Grasse had invested the Caribbean island of St. Kitts in an attempt to abscond with as much British territory as possible. But on January 24, Hood appeared with military reinforcements and a slightly smaller fleet, which induced the French to attack. De Grasse accordingly left Frigate Bay at Basse-Terre in force, but adroit maneuvering by Hood allowed the British to avoid the blow and suddenly steal their way into de Grasse's former anchorage. It was a brilliant ploy and British reinforcements were delivered, but the island nevertheless finally surrendered on February 12, and Hood sailed off. Fortunately, Rodney arrived at Antigua with additional ships and intelligence that de Grasse was planning an attack upon the strategic island of

Jamaica. The British finally intercepted him off Dominica on April 9, where Hood's aggressive sailing placed the van ahead of the main body, and he received a drubbing. Three days later at the Saintes, both Rodney and Hood brought the French fleet to battle and decisively defeated them by breaking de Grasse's line in two places. However, Hood angrily remonstrated that Rodney had failed to vigorously pursue his defeated enemy, being content to capture de Grasse and his huge flagship *Ville de Paris*. It was nevertheless the decisive naval victory of the Revolutionary War and assured British domination of the seas for years to come. For his part, Hood received a title in the Irish peerage.

After the war Hood returned to the Mediterranean, where he served as commander in chief during the early phases of the French Revolution. His most important activity was the defense of Toulon Harbor in August–December 1793, in which he was driven out by the batteries of a little-known artillery captain named Napoléon Bonaparte. After several more years of commanding at Corsica, Hood finally retired from sea duty and became governor of the Greenwich Hospital. He died there on January 27, 1816, a tough, resolute leader but perpetually subordinated to men who lacked his aggressive fighting disposition. The combative Hood was one of the few British admirals whose career shone during the Revolutionary War and helped secure his reputation as one of the Royal Navy's outstanding leaders.

Further Reading
Billias, George A., ed. *George Washington's Opponent: British Generals and Admirals in the American Revolution.* New York: Morrow, 1969.
Breen, Kenneth. "Graves and Hood at the Chesapeake," *Mariner's Mirror* 66, no. 1 (1980): 53–64.
Hannay, David, ed. *Letters Written by Samuel Hood.* London: Navy Records Society, 1895.
Larabee, Harold A. *Decision at the Chesapeake.* New York: Clarkson R. Potter, 1964.
Sulivan, J. A. "Graves and Hood," *Mariner's Mirror* 62, no. 2 (1983): 175–194.

Syrett, David. *The Royal Navy in American Waters, 1775–1783.* Brookfield, Vt.: Gower Publishing Co., 1989.

Hopkins, Esek (1718–1802)
American naval officer

Esek Hopkins was born in North Scituate, Rhode Island, on April 26, 1718, the son of farmers. He joined the merchant marine as a youth and within a few years commanded his own fleet of vessels. Hopkins commanded a privateer throughout the French and Indian War, 1754–63, and accumulated enough wealth to purchase a 200-acre farm, along with considerable political influence. In October 1775 the Rhode Island legislature appointed him a brigadier general of militia and entrusted him with the state's defenses. However, his brother, Stephen Hopkins, former governor and now a member of the Continental CONGRESS's Marine Committee, arranged for his promotion to commodore and first commander in chief of the nascent Continental NAVY on December 22, 1775. This was a force in name only and consisted of eight merchant ships being outfitted with armament at Philadelphia. In January 1776 Hopkins arrived to take care of his charge, and he received instructions from Congress to drive British warships away from Chesapeake Bay and the southern coastline. In the event this proved impractical, he could invoke a discretionary clause enabling him to attack Nassau in the Bahamas. Given the fragile state of his fleet and the Royal Navy's formidable reputation, Hopkins understandably chose the latter course.

Hopkins sailed south on February 17, 1776, and anchored off Nassau on March 3, 1776. He then landed a party of sailors and marines under Captain Samuel NICHOLAS, which took the island's citadel without a struggle, seizing much needed stores of cannon and ammunition. The effort proceeded smoothly and, on the return voyage home, Hopkins encountered several British warships. Two smaller vessels were taken, but on April 6, 1776, the 20-gun frigate HMS *Glasgow* managed to elude the American squadron after inflicting considerable damage. In truth, Hopkins and his fleet of converted merchantmen were totally outclassed by a true warship manned by highly trained sailors. Such discrepancies mattered little to Congress, and it censured Hopkins for allowing his quarry to escape and for disregarding its instructions. Worse, his tiny squadron put into New London on April 8, 1776, and never sailed again.

Hopkins, a salty tongued, expressive individual with little regard for authority, soon proved to be his own worst enemy. For nearly two years he was unable to recruit enough sailors to man his ships for the simple reason that PRIVATEERING vessels paid crewmen twice as much. Moreover, he was perpetually short of money, equipment, and supplies, lack of which rendered the Continental navy nearly dysfunctional. Strong British naval forces also had him bottled up in Narragansett Bay for most of the year. For all these reasons he was unable to get to sea, while other leaders like John Paul JONES, Nicholas BIDDLE, and Abraham WHIPPLE scored marked successes on their own. Hopkins compounded his own unpopularity by doling out prize money gingerly, thereby alienating his own captains. When their complaints reached the ears of Congress, Hopkins was suspended from duty in May 1777. They subsequently learned that the gruff commodore had publicly ridiculed them, so on in January 1778 he was formally removed from command. This was accomplished over the objections of John ADAMS, who sympathized with the unenviable plight of his fellow New Englander. Hopkins never held another command, and a new commodore was never appointed to replace him.

Hopkins survived the controversy surrounding his dismissal and gained a seat in the Rhode Island general assembly from 1779 to 1786. During this period he also served as a trustee of Rhode Island College (today's Brown University). Hopkins died on his farm on February 28, 1802, a coarse, indiscreet leader placed in an impossible position. Few questioned his abilities as a seaman, but he proved unequal to the task of running the nation's new navy; a daunting task that, in any event, would have taxed the abilities—and patience—of men far more capable than himself.

Further Reading

Beck, Alverda S., ed. *The Letterbook of Esek Hopkins, Commander in Chief of the United States Navy, 1775–1777.* Providence: Printed for the Rhode Island Historical Society, 1932.

———. *The Correspondence of Esek Hopkins, Commander-in-Chief of the United States Navy.* Providence: Printed for the Rhode Island Historical Society, 1933.

Bradford, James C., ed. *Command under Sail: Makers of the American Naval Tradition, 1775–1850.* Annapolis, Md.: Naval Institute Press, 1985.

McCusker, John J. "The American Invasion of Nassau in the Bahamas," *American Neptune* 25, no. 3 (1965): 189–215.

Miller, Charles H. *Admiral Number One: Some Incidents in the Life of Esek Hopkins, 1718–1802.* New York: William-Frederick Press, 1962.

Miller, Nathan. *Sea of Glory: A Naval History of the American Revolution.* Mount Pleasant, S.C.: Nautical & Aviation Pub. Co., 2000.

Hopkins, John B. (1742–1796)
American naval officer

John Burroughs Hopkins was born in Providence, Rhode Island, on August 25, 1742, a son of merchant captain Esek HOPKINS. He followed into his father's profession and gradually sided with the colonists in their ongoing dispute with Great Britain. On June 9, 1772, Hopkins accompanied Abraham WHIPPLE during the capture and burning of a British revenue vessel during the GASPÉE AFFAIR. Once the Revolutionary War commenced he used his father's influence to secure a captain's commission in the new Continental NAVY as of December 22, 1775. In this capacity he took charge of the 16-gun brig *Cabot* and accompanied his father's expedition against New Providence. During the return voyage the American squadron encountered the 20-gun frigate HMS *Glasgow* off Block Island on April 5, 1776, and gave chase. Hopkins, badly outgunned by his opponent, suffered four dead and seven wounded, including himself. He recovered and, when Congress published its captain's list by seniority in October 1776, he was number 13. In the spring of 1777 Hopkins acceded to command of the newly launched, 32-gun frigate *Warren,* which remained blockaded in the Providence River by British naval forces for several months. In March 1778, Hopkins slipped out of Narragansett Bay under the cover of darkness and briefly cruised Bermuda, where two prizes were taken. He then put back into Boston on March 23, 1778, but was detained in port for nearly a year while recruiting a crew.

Hopkins emerged from Boston in March 1779 at the head of a small squadron consisting of his own *Warren,* the *Queen of France,* 28 guns, and the *Ranger,* 18 guns. He then cruised off Cape Henry, Virginia, for six weeks, snaring the New York LOYALIST privateer *Hibernia,* and seven ships of a nine-vessel convoy. Hopkins also apparently seized a number of British army officers on board along with considerable quantities of supplies and equipment. These successes validated his reputation as a competent naval leader, but after returning to Boston he was charged by the Congressional Marine Committee with exceeding orders. Hopkins was then stripped of command and the *Warren* reverted to Captain Dudley SALTONSTALL. Hopkins engaged in PRIVATEERING for the remainder of the conflict and led the Massachusetts ship *Tracy* until it was captured in 1781. He next commanded the Rhode Island sloop *Success* until war's end. At this juncture Hopkins returned to civilian life and lived in relative obscurity. He is known to have died in Providence on December 5, 1796.

Further Reading
McManemin, John A. *Captains of the Continental Navy.* Ho-Ho-Kus, N.J.: Ho-Ho-Kus Pub. Co., 1981.
Millar, John F., ed. *Building Early American Warships: The Journal of the Rhode Island Committee for Constructing the Continental Frigates Providence & Warren, 1775–1777.* Providence: Rhode Island Publications Society, 1988.
Miller, Nathan. *Sea of Glory: A Naval History of the American Revolution.* Mount Pleasant, S.C.: Nautical & Aviation Pub. Co., 2000.
Morgan, William J. *Captains to the Northward: The New England Captains in the Continental Navy.* Barre, Mass.: Barre Gazette, 1959.
Paullin, Charles O. *Out-Letters of the Continental Marine Committee and Board of Admiralty,* 2 vols. New York: Printed for the Naval History Society by the De Vinne Press, 1914.

Howard, John E. (1752–1827)
American military officer
John Eager Howard was born in Baltimore County, Maryland, the son of affluent landowners. He was well educated by tutors and joined the Maryland militia as a captain in July 1776. Howard formed part of the so-called Flying Camp under General Hugh MERCER and fought capably at WHITE PLAINS on October 28, 1776. On February 22, 1777, he transferred to the 4th Maryland Continental Infantry as a captain, garnering additional laurels at GERMANTOWN that fall. Howard transferred again to the 5th Maryland Continentals as a lieutenant colonel in March 1778 and distinguished himself at MONMOUTH the following summer. In October 1779 Howard became lieutenant colonel of the 2nd Maryland Continentals and followed his unit south as part of the army under General Horatio GATES. He served directly under General Johann de KALB at the disaster of CAMDEN on August 16, 1780, and was one of the few regular officers able to cut his way through and escape. He then spent several months reconstituting his shattered regiment before joining a new southern army commanded by General Nathanael GREENE. Greene appointed him to stiffen the militia forces of General Daniel MORGAN's brigade as it marched through North Carolina in early 1781.

Howard performed heroically at the January 17, 1781, Battle of COWPENS, when Morgan's cleverly deployed troops were attacked by veteran forces under Lieutenant Colonel Banastre TARLETON. Having peeled away the first two lines of Morgan's militia, the British marched forcefully upon Howard's Continentals, situated on the rise of a gentle slope. At this juncture, he apparently mistook Morgan's orders and began retreating in good order. The British, sensing victory, then broke out into a wild charge. Howard suddenly countermanded the withdrawal, faced about, and delivered a crushing volley into his opponent's ranks. The American line next surged downhill at bayonet point, assisted on either flank by militia under General Andrew PICKENS and the dragoons of Colonel William WASHINGTON. Tarelton's little army disintegrated under the onslaught and fled ignominiously from the field. In light of such superb behavior under fire, the Continental CONGRESS voted Howard a silver medal and its thanks.

Howard and his veteran Marylanders continued campaigning under Greene and throughout the south for the rest of the year. On March 15, 1781, he was closely engaged at GUILFORD COURTHOUSE and successfully covered the American retreat. The following month he was again at close quarters at Hobkirk's Hill, another fierce contest. On September 8, 1781, he fought at close range in the costly encounter at Eutaw Springs, in which he drove off the Irish "Buffs" after a lengthy bayonet fight. Howard was seriously wounded in the action and his command reduced to 30 survivors. The battered veteran saw no further fighting for the remainder of the war and returned to Maryland a hero.

Howard quickly parlayed his military reputation into a political career by becoming governor of Maryland in 1788–91, winning reelection twice. From 1796 to 1803 he also held a seat in the U.S. Senate and functioned as a political ally of President George WASHINGTON. In 1794 the government tendered him the office of secretary of war but Howard declined, as he did a brigadier general's commission in 1798. A staunch Federalist, he grew increasingly out of touch with the rising tide of Jeffersonian republicanism and failed three times to win back his Senate seat. In 1814 the elderly Howard raised troops for the defense of Baltimore but saw no action in the War of 1812. In 1816 he was tapped to serve as the Federalist vice presidential candidate under Rufus KING and was handily defeated. Howard died at Baltimore on October 12, 1827, one of the Revolutionary War's outstanding regimental officers.

Further Reading

Batt, Richard J. "The Maryland Continentals, 1780–1781." Unpublished Ph.D. diss., Tulane University, 1974.

Howard, Benjamin C. *A Memoir of the Late Col. John Eager Howard.* Baltimore: Keely, Hedian & Pict, 1863.

Howard, Cary. "John Eager Howard, Patriot and Public Servant," *Maryland Historical Magazine* 62, no. 3 (1967): 300–317.

Kilbourne, John D. *A Short History of the Maryland Line in the Continental Army.* Baltimore: Society of the Cincinnati of Maryland, 1992.

MacDonald, James M. "A Tale of Two Soldiers: John Eager Howard, Samuel Smith, and the New American Nation." Unpublished master's thesis, Appalachian State University, 1997.

Lieutenant Colonel John Eager Howard fought exceptionally at the Battles of White Plains, Cowpens, and Guilford Courthouse. *(Independence National Historical Park)*

Winsor, Justin, ed. "Col. John Eager Howard's Account of the Battle of Germantown," *Maryland Historical Magazine* 4 (December 1909): 314–320.

Howe, Richard (earl Howe, fourth viscount Howe (1726–1799)
English naval officer

Richard Howe was born in London, England, on March 19, 1726, the scion of an aristocratic family and elder brother to General William HOWE. He joined the Royal Navy at the age of 14 and partially circumnavigated the globe with the fleet of Admiral George Anson. Adept as a sailor, he rose to lieutenant in 1745, and two years later, after defeating two French privateers, Howe became a captain. He then held a succession of berths in the West Indies and Mediterranean before commanding the ship of the line HMS *Dunkirk*, which aided in the capture of the French warship *Alcide* on June 8, 1755 —the first naval shots of the French and Indian War. Significantly, when Howe's elder brother, George Augustus, was killed at the siege of Fort Ticonderoga in 1758, Massachusetts colony paid for an elaborate monument to his memory at Westminster Abbey in London. Howe never forgot this generous act and thereafter remained favorably disposed toward Americans. In 1762 he gained election to Parliament as a Whig and generally opposed the tax policies of various ministries. After serving effectively on the Admiralty board, Howe was promoted to rear admiral in 1770 and vice admiral in 1775. He also befriended American agent Benjamin FRANKLIN in London and conferred with him repeatedly about colonial matters. Howe, who exuded a stern, taciturn demeanor, was known as "Black Dick" by his sailors on account of his swarthy complexion, but his sense of fairness and concern for all hands rendered him a popular figure in the fleet.

When the Revolutionary War broke out in 1775, neither Howe nor his brother evinced great enthusiasm for fighting their fellow Englishmen in the colonies. Nonetheless, when asked to do so by King GEORGE III in February 1776, they felt duty-bound to oblige their monarch, and Richard Howe became commander in chief of naval forces in

British Admiral Richard Howe was favorably disposed toward Americans but performed his duty to the king and served admirably against his fellow Britishers. *(National Maritime Museum, Greenwich, London)*

American waters. As an added inducement, the king authorized both men to serve as peace commissioners should the opportunity avail itself. In the summer of 1776 Howe conducted a huge fleet of warships and transports from England to New York, where they assisted in driving the Americans under General George WASHINGTON from Long Island. However, Admiral Howe made no attempt to intercept the fleeing Americans by ship and they escaped to Manhattan. He then dispatched the captured general, John SULLIVAN, to the Continental CONGRESS to request peace negotiations. Accordingly, Howe shared a table with Franklin, John ADAMS, and Edward Rutledge at Staten Island on September 11, 1776, but negotiations faltered because he refused to acknowledge American independence. Admiral Howe next rendered valuable assistance during the capture of Fort Washington on November 16, 1776, another hard knock that the brothers hoped would bring the rebels to their senses. When this failed he secured Newport, Rhode Island, as a useful entrepot the following December. It now became apparent that the Americans were not interested in peace, so Howe and his brother began extensive preparations for a campaign against Philadelphia. He expertly landed British forces at Elk's Head, Maryland, in August 1777 and subsequently reduced American strongpoints along the Delaware River that fall. However, after the surrender of General John BURGOYNE, for which the Howes were roundly criticized, both men tendered their resignations. Meanwhile, the entry of France into the war in 1778 strained British resources to the limit, while Howe was also forced to contend with his incompetent subordinate, Admiral James GAMBIER. He then waited several months for his replacement to arrive and, during the interim, performed useful service by engaging the French fleet of Admiral Charles-Hector-Théodat, comte d'ESTAING, off Newport in August 1778. A battle was precluded by a sudden storm that damaged both fleets, but d'Estaing subsequently abandoned his commitments to Rhode Island and made for Boston to refit. Shortly after, Howe was replaced by Admiral John BYRON, and he returned to England rather disillusioned.

Howe was disgusted by what he perceived as underhanded policies of the prime minister, Lord Frederick NORTH, and naval minister John MONTAGU, earl of Sandwich, and he refused to serve them longer. It was not until 1782, when Charles WATSON-WENTWORTH, Lord Rockingham, became prime minister, that Howe accepted a post as head of the Channel Fleet. In this capacity he brilliantly relieved the besieged island of Gibraltar and fought off a combined French and Spanish fleet in the process. Howe became First Lord of the Admiralty in consequence, where he remained until 1788. He again commanded the Channel Fleet following the onset of the French Revolution and at the request of the king and won an important victory over Admiral Louis Villaret de Joyeuse during the so-called Glorious First of June in 1794. He was rewarded by becoming a Knight of the Garter, the first naval officer so honored. Howe retired from active service until 1797, when he arrived at Spithead to help quell a serious mutiny within the Channel Fleet. "Black Dick" was apparently the only naval leader whom sailors trusted and he helped peacefully settle the disturbance. Howe died in London on August 5, 1799, one of the leading naval figures of 18th-century England.

Further Reading

Calderhead, William J. "British Naval Failure at Long Island: A Lost Opportunity in the American Revolution," *New York History* 7, no. 3 (1976): 321–338.

Comtois, George. "The British Navy in the Delaware River, 1775 to 1777," *American Neptune* 40, no. 1 (1980): 7–22.

Duffy, Michael, and Roger Morriss, eds. *The Glorious First of June: A Naval Battle and Its Aftermath.* Exeter, U.K.: University of Exeter Press, 2001.

Gruber, Ira D. *The Howe Brothers and the American Revolution.* New York: Atheneum, 1972.

Le Fevre, Peter. *Precursors of Nelson: British Admirals of the Eighteenth Century.* Mechanicsburg, Pa.: Stackpole Books, 2000.

Syrett, David. *Admiral Lord Howe: A Biography.* Annapolis, Md.: Naval Institute Press, 2005.

Howe, Robert (1732–1786)
American military officer

Robert Howe was born in Bladen County, North Carolina, in 1732, the son of a wealthy planter. Educated in England, he inherited his father's fortune and, after 1764, was repeatedly elected to the colonial assembly. Howe also developed an interest in military affairs, for in 1766 he became a captain in the county militia and two years later rose to be colonel of an artillery unit. In this capacity he served under Governor William TRYON throughout the so-called Regulator Disturbance of 1774. However, he abandoned the royal government that year to attend the extralegal provincial congress at New Berne in 1774 and also served on the local COMMITTEE OF CORRESPONDENCE. On July 15, 1775, Howe led an expedition that removed the royal governor, Josiah MARTIN, from power, and that September he became colonel of the 2nd North Carolina Continental Infantry. Marching north to Virginia, he joined forces with Colonel William WOODFORD and helped defeat Governor John MURRAY, Lord Dunmore, at the Battle of Great Bridge on December 9, 1775. The following spring he was elevated to brigadier general in the Continental ARMY and ordered south.

Howe was present during the attack on CHARLESTON in July 1776 and served briefly under General Charles LEE. Previously, General Charles CORNWALLIS had led a quick raid against his plantation at Brunswick, on May 12, 1776, completely gutting it. Howe then received command of the Southern Department, with promotion to major general in October 1777. In the spring of 1778 he led an expedition against General Augustin PREVOST at St. Augustine, Florida, but was hobbled by pervasive sickness and supply shortages. His failure led to some rash comments by Lieutenant Governor Christopher GADSDEN, which culminated in a bloodless duel. Howe, seemingly unable to overcome operational deficiencies, lost command of the department to General Benjamin LINCOLN the following September. He was then ordered to defend Savannah, Georgia, against an impending British attack. On December 29, 1778, Howe deployed his forces capably along Fairlawn Plantation outside the town to confront the approaching expedition of Lieutenant Colonel Archibald CAMPBELL. But Campbell, assisted by local slaves, happened upon a secret path that enabled him to attack the American encampment from behind. Despite a valiant stand by Georgia and South Carolina Continentals under Colonels Samuel ELBERT and Isaac HUGER, the Americans were routed with a loss of 83 killed and 453 captured. Howe then demanded and received a court of inquiry that acquitted him of any blame for the disaster. However, his tenure as an independent commander ended and he transferred back to the northern theater.

Howe arrived at Philadelphia in time to head the court-martial of General Benedict ARNOLD at Philadelphia. He then formed part of General Anthony WAYNE's division that successfully stormed Stony Point on July 16, 1779, although both he and Major Rufus PUTNAM had failed to take nearby Verplanck's Point. In February 1780 Howe succeeded General William HEATH as commander of the Hudson Highlands region, and the following September he sat on the board of officers that condemned Major John ANDRE to hang for espionage. In January 1781 it fell upon Howe to quell a violent mutiny by the New Jersey Line, which he did after summarily executing three ringleaders. In June 1783 he performed similar work when Pennsylvania troops also rebelled and threatened the Continental CONGRESS in Philadelphia. Mindful of his ruthlessness, the soldiers allegedly disbanded upon hearing of his approach.

After the war Howe returned to his life as a planter, although two years later Congress appointed him a boundary commissioner to work with the western Indians. He then successfully stood for a seat in the state legislature but died in Bladen County on December 14, 1786, before filling it.

Further Reading

Bennett, Charles E., and Donald R. Lennon. *A Quest for Glory: Major General Robert Howe and the American Revolution.* Chapel Hill: University of North Carolina Press, 1991.

Lennon, Donald R. "The Graveyard of American Commanders: The Continental Army's Southern Department, 1776–1778," *North Carolina Historical Review* 67, no. 2 (1990): 133–158.

Naisawald, Louis V. "The Career of Major General Robert Howe, Continental Army." Unpublished master's thesis, University of North Carolina, 1965.

Ranlet, Philip. "Yorktown, Loyalism, and a British Spy at West Point," *Journal of America's Military Past* 29, no. 1 (2002): 42–57.

———. "Loyalty in the Revolutionary War: General Robert Howe of North Carolina," *Historian* 53, no. 4 (1991): 721–742.

Watson, Alan D., Dennis R. Lawson, and Donald R. Lennon. *Harnett, Hooper, and Howe: Revolutionary Leaders of the Lower Cape Fear.* Wilmington, N.C.: Lieut. Moore Memorial Commission, Lower Cape Fear Historical Society, 1979.

Howe, William (fifth viscount Howe) (1729–1814)

English military officer

William Howe was born in England on August 10, 1729, a son of the Second Viscount Howe. He was well educated at Eton and subsequently joined the duke of Cumberland's Light Dragoons as a coronet in 1746. Howe demonstrated a flair for military leadership; he rose repeatedly over the next 30 years due to bravery and skill. He fought at the siege of Louisbourg in 1758 and was deeply touched when the inhabitants of Massachusetts financed a memorial to his fallen brother George Augustus at Westminster Abbey. On the night of September 12, 1759, Howe personally led the forlorn hope up the heights to the Plains of Abraham, thereby enabling General James Wolfe's victory over General Montcalm. After garnering additional laurels at Montreal, Belle Isle, and Havana, Howe became something of a light infantry specialist, and in 1772 he authored a drill manual to train such troops. King GEORGE III was so impressed that he authorized every regiment in the British army to raise a company of light infantry. Politically speaking, however, Howe and his elder brother, Admiral Richard HOWE, were Whigs by inclination. As members of Parliament, both opposed governmental tax measures and openly expressed sympathy for the colonials. Both the Howes nonetheless responded to the king's wish for their service in America once the Revolutionary War erupted in 1775. Cognizant of their feelings on the subject, he also authorized them to serve as peace commissioners should the opportunity present itself.

In May 1775, Howe arrived in Boston on a ship carrying Generals Henry CLINTON and John BURGOYNE. The city at that time was effectively besieged by 15,000 American militia, and the commander, General Thomas GAGE, seemed in a quandary over what to do next. However, when rebels seized and fortified the heights overlooking Charleston Harbor on June 17, 1775, Howe was ordered to attack them at BUNKER HILL and drive them back. Victory was achieved at a terrible cost, which indelibly imprinted upon the general a need for caution. Once the dithering Gage was relieved that October, Howe superseded him, and the British remained ensconced behind their fortifications. He felt that he lacked the manpower to break out; then, on the evening of March 5, 1776, American engineers under Colonel Richard GRIDLEY seized nearby Dorchester Heights and deployed cannon captured from Fort Ticonderoga. Howe was initially inclined to attack the new entrenchments but was dissuaded by bad weather. Then, upon the advice and near insistence of Admiral Molyneux SHULDHAM, he ordered Boston evacuated.

Howe remained at Halifax, Nova Scotia, for the next three months, carefully gathering a new army. In August 1776 he accompanied the fleet of Admiral Howe to Staten Island, New York, where he disembarked 30,000 troops—the largest amphibious force ever assembled by Britain to that point—and began planning offensive operations. On August 27, 1776, Howe attacked the American army under General George WASHINGTON at LONG ISLAND, drubbing him badly. However, Howe and his brother forfeited a chance to annihilate the enemy as the Patriots withdrew from Brooklyn Heights, for neither interfered. Further deft maneuvering evicted the Americans from Manhattan Island and, between October 28 and November 15, Howe again beat them on the fields of WHITE PLAINS and Fort Washington. Washington now had no alternative but to evacuate New York altogether. But despite this litany of victories, Howe proved strangely dilatory in pursuing, and the Americans invariably escaped to fight another day. This mistake was painfully underscored after the British conducted a leisurely pursuit across New Jersey that December before establishing winter encampments across the state. Washington then suddenly turned on his antagonists at TRENTON and PRINCETON, inflicting small but embarrassing setbacks upon the British and their HESSIAN allies. Despite this dramatic reversal of fortune, Howe was knighted by the king for his otherwise competent services.

General William Howe served capably in the British military for over 30 years and is arguably one of the most controversial figures of the American Revolution. *(Anne S. K. Rowe Military Collection, Brown University Library)*

Over the winter Howe and his brother conceived ambitious plans to attack the American capital of Philadelphia that fall. They received permission from the war minister, Lord George GERMAIN, with the caveat that they should act in concert with a larger, northern thrust down the Champlain corridor under flamboyant general Burgoyne. At no time was Howe directly ordered to assist Burgoyne, although it would have made strategic sense. But the Howes seemed content to wage their own little war—and at their own pace. Instead of marching overland through New Jersey, Howe enacted an elaborate amphibious descent upon Elk River, Maryland, on August 25, 1777, followed by a push inland. On September 11, 1777, Washington made a valiant stand at BRANDYWINE in an attempt to stop him, but Howe executed a brilliant flanking action that drove his opponents from the field. He then dispatched General Charles GREY to eliminate a shadowing force under General Anthony WAYNE at Paoli, which was brutally accomplished with cold steel on September 21. Philadelphia fell on September 26; Washington next tried a surprise attack upon the British camp at nearby GERMANTOWN on October 4, 1777. After a stiff fight, the Americans were again driven off to spend a miserable winter at Valley Forge. However, Howe's successes proved illusory and were achieved at the cost of Burgoyne's army, which was surrounded at Saratoga and surrendered on October 17, 1777. When Howe and his brother were publicly criticized for failing to support the general, especially by Lord Germain, they both felt slighted by the government and tendered their resignations. On May 25, 1778, he turned command of the army over to the capable but querulous General Clinton and returned home. Prior to leaving, Howe and his officers engaged in an opulent going-away party, *Meschianza,* orchestrated by a popular staff officer, Major John ANDRE.

Back home, Howe demanded a parliamentary investigation to clear his name, and several top subordinates like General Grey and Charles CORNWALLIS stepped forward in his defense. He also engaged in an extensive war of pamphlets with Burgoyne and Germain over their respective culpability for the disaster at Saratoga. Howe's military career remained in limbo until the administration of Lord Frederick NORTH fell and was replaced by Charles WATSON-WENTWORTH, Lord Rockingham. Howe was raised to lieutenant general in 1792, then full general the following year, and he held several important posts during the initial phases of the French Revolution. After the death of Richard in 1799, Howe inherited the title of earl. Declining health promoted his resignation from the military in 1803, and he received the governorship of Plymouth as a sinecure. Howe died in that capacity on July 12, 1814, possibly the most controversial British general of the American Revolution. He was certainly a capable tactician, but his lack of a "killer instinct" deprived the British of several clear-cut chances to end the war victoriously. Historians have also speculated that Howe remained beholden to his Whiggish sympathies for the Americans and refused to hand the Tory government of North and Germain the victory they coveted.

Further Reading
Buchanan, John. *The Road to Valley Forge: How Washington Built the Army That Won the Revolution.* Hoboken, N.J.: John Wiley, 2004.
Gallagher, John J. *The Battle of Brooklyn, 1776.* New York: Sarpedon, 1995.
Gruber, Ira D. *The Howe Brothers and the American Revolution.* New York: Norton, 1972.
Lefkowitz, Arthur. *The Long Retreat: The Calamitous Defense of New Jersey, 1776.* New Brunswick, N.J.: Rutgers University Press, 1999.
Spear, Moncrieff, J. *To End the War at White Plains.* Baltimore: American Literary Press, 2002.
Taafe, Stephen R. *The Philadelphia Campaign, 1777–1778.* Lawrence: University Press of Kansas, 2003.

Huger, Isaac (1743–1797)
American military leader

Isaac Huger was born at Limerick Plantation, South Carolina, on March 19, 1742, and partially educated in Europe. He was a militia officer during the Cherokee conflict of 1760 and, once the Revolutionary War commenced in April 1775, he won a seat in the South Carolina provincial congress. In light of Huger's prior military service, he successively became lieutenant colonel of the 1st South Carolina Continental Infantry in June 1775 and colonel of the 5th Regiment in September 1776. Huger was initially posted with forces under General Robert HOWE and assigned to the defense of Savannah. However, on December 29, 1778, Howe's encampment at Fairlawn Plantation was successfully stormed by British forces under Lieutenant Colonel Archibald CAMPBELL. Huger, assisted by Colonel Samuel ELBERT, resisted staunchly Campbell's onslaught, but they were outflanked and defeated. For his otherwise good performance, Huger gained promotion to brigadier general on January 9, 1779, and was assigned to a new army assembling under General Benjamin LINCOLN. In this capacity he helped pursue the retreating forces of General Augustin PREVOST out of Georgia and fought bravely during the ill-fated attack upon Stono Ferry on June 20, 1779. Huger led the left wing in an unsuccessful maneuver, receiving severe injuries. After recovering, he accompanied Lincoln throughout the siege of SAVANNAH and commanded the Georgia and South Carolina militia during the disastrous assault of October 9, 1779.

The British siege of CHARLESTON unfolded in the spring of 1780, and Huger was posted outside the city at Monck's Corner. As General Henry CLINTON slowly extended his siege lines, this post became the only route for men and supplies into the city. For this reason, Lieutenant Colonel Banastre TARLETON was ordered to attack and disperse the Americans and completely cut Charleston off. Riding swiftly, on April 14, 1780, he managed to surprise Huger and Colonel William WASHINGTON in their camp. Tarleton was assisted by the fact that Huger had failed to post adequate sentries and inadvertently placed his cavalry ahead of his infantry. Tarleton scattered them both in a single charge, and Huger ended up losing 14 killed, 13 wounded, 67 captured along with 42 wagons, and nearly 200 horses to the victorious British. This spectacular defeat initiated the notorious career of Tarleton and also sealed Charleston's fate. Huger then ordered forces under Colonel Abraham BUFORD to quit South Carolina altogether, gather all available supplies en route, and retreat toward Hillsborough, North Carolina. But Tarleton promptly pursued and defeated Huger's subordinate at the notorious skirmish at Waxhaws on May 29, 1780. Organized resistance in South Carolina had collapsed.

Huger escaped any recrimination for the disaster at Monck's Corner, and he subsequently formed part of General Nathanael GREENE's reconstituted army. In this capacity he capably led the 4th and 5th Virginia Continentals at the bloody battle of GUILFORD COURTHOUSE on March 15, 1781, acquitting himself well. He again suffered severe wounds but recovered in time to command Greene's right wing at Hobkirk's Hill on April 15, 1781. Here his desperate stand with the 5th Virginia Continentals thwarted a determined attack by Lieutenant Colonel Francis RAWDON and saved the army from annihilation. Shortly afterward Huger was elected to the state general assembly, and the following year he was installed as vice president of the South Carolina Society of the Cincinnati. He died at Charleston on October 17, 1797, a competent but luckless regimental officer.

Further Reading
Borick, Carl P. *A Gallant Defense: The Siege of Charleston, 1780.* Columbia: University of South Carolina Press, 2003.
Buchanan, John. *The Road to Guilford Courthouse: The American Revolution in the Carolinas.* New York: Wiley, 1997.
Edgar, Walter B. *Partisans and Redcoats: The Southern Conflict That Turned the Tide of the American Revolution.* New York: Morrow, 2001.
Freeman, H. Ronald. *Savannah under Siege: The Bloodiest Hour of the Revolution.* Savannah, Ga.: Freeport Pub., 2002.
Wilson, David K. *The Southern Strategy: Britain's Conquest of South Carolina and Georgia, 1775–1780.* Columbia: University of South Carolina, 2005.

Huntington, Jedediah (1743–1818)
American military officer

Jedediah Huntington was born in Norwich, Connecticut, on August 4, 1743, the son of a highly prosperous merchant. Well educated at home, he graduated from Harvard College in 1763 before pursuing a master's degree at Yale. As the crisis with Great Britain developed, Huntington espoused the Patriot cause and joined the colonial militia in 1769 as an ensign. He was also active in the local chapter of the SONS OF LIBERTY. Adept as a soldier and well-connected politically, Huntington rose to colonel of the 20th Militia Regiment in 1774, and the following year, once hostilities commenced, he marched his charge to Boston. In the spring of 1776 he became colonel of the newly reorganized 17th Connecticut Continental Infantry, then part of General Joseph SPENCER's brigade, and subsequently accompanied General George WASHINGTON back to New York City after the siege of Boston ended. Huntington's regiment was actively engaged in the Battle of LONG ISLAND in August 1776, although it is unclear if Huntington commanded. Apparently, the following year he returned home to head the 1st Connecticut Continental Infantry and there assisted Generals Benedict ARNOLD and David WOOSTER in repelling Governor William TRYON's raid upon Danbury in April 1777. A month later Huntington advanced to brigadier general in the division of General Israel PUTNAM and was assigned to defend the strategic Hudson Highlands. He subsequently transferred to Washington's main force outside of Philadelphia in the fall of 1777 and sat on the court-martial exonerating General Anthony WAYNE for the defeat at Paoli. After a winter of hardship at Valley Forge, in which he labored successfully to keep his Connecticut troops fed and clothed, Huntington transferred to the division of General Charles LEE.

Huntington was present at the June 1778 Battle at MONMOUTH, and he was called to testify against General Lee at his court-martial. He then returned to the Hudson Highlands under General William HEATH and sat on the board that sentenced Major John ANDRE to death for spying in September 1780. Although he saw relatively little combat, Huntington exhibited exemplary organizational skills, and Washington frequently called upon him to round up and ship food and other necessities to the main army. Toward the end of the war he became a founding member of the Society of the Cincinnati and, in light of his useful contributions and faithful service, mustered out on October 3, 1783, with a rank of brevet major general.

Huntington returned to Connecticut to resume his family business, although he also dabbled in local politics. In 1789 President Washington appointed him collector of customs at New

London, which position he held over the next 26 years. Huntington died in New London on September 25, 1818, hardly a combat officer of the first rank but an accomplished administrator and a dependable soldier.

Further Reading
Callahan, North. *Connecticut's Revolutionary War Leaders*. Chester, Conn.: Pequot Press, 1973.
Damon, Douglas G. *The Bridge Not Taken: Benedict Arnold Outwitted*. Westport, Conn.: Westport Historical Society, 2002.
Diamont, Lincoln. *Chaining the Hudson: The Fight for the River in the American Revolution*. New York: Fordham University Press, 2004.
Heathcote, Charles W. "General Jedediah Huntington Rendered Patriotic Service for His Country," *Picket Post* no. 52 (May 1956): 12–18.
Huntington, Jedediah. "Letters of Jedediah Huntington," *Massachusetts Historical Society Collections* 5th ser., 9 (1885): 491–518.
———, and Joshua Huntington. *Huntington Papers: Correspondence of the Huntington Brothers Jedediah and Joshua Huntington during the Period of the American Revolution*. Hartford: Connecticut Historical Society, 1923.

Hutchinson, Thomas (1711–1780)
American politician

Thomas Hutchinson was born in Boston on September 9, 1711, son of a successful merchant and great-grandson of noted religious rebel Anne Hutchinson. He attended Harvard College at the age of 12 and entered his father's countinghouse three years later. A successful and affluent businessman in his own right, Hutchinson won a seat in the Massachusetts General Court in 1737, where he remained until 1749. His aptitude for debate and administration was widely recognized, and in 1740 he represented Massachusetts at the royal court during boundary disputes with New Hampshire. In 1754 he attended the noted Albany Congress in New York, where he and former fellow Bostonian Benjamin FRANKLIN advocated viable plans for a colonial union. An accomplished historian, Hutchinson also published a noted tract, *History of Massachusetts Bay*, in 1764. In light of his numerous talents, Governor Francis BERNARD appointed him lieutenant governor in 1758, and two years later he also assumed functions as chief justice. This aggregation of power alarmed individuals in the colonial body politic, notably Samuel ADAMS and James OTIS, who felt that men like Hutchinson represented a threat to personal and economic liberty. Ironically, Hutchinson sided with radical elements over the issuing of writs of assistance, nor did he accept the rationale of such provocative legislation as the SUGAR ACT of 1764 and the STAMP ACT of 1765. Where Hutchinson differed with many colonials was his unshakable belief that Parliament did, in fact, possess an inalienable right to tax the colonies. This stance made him a convenient target for the growing radical movement, whose violence and vehemence toward imperial authority proved beyond Hutchinson's comprehension. In fact, he simply maintained that his critics were motivated far more by economic self-interest than political principle.

The Stamp Act proved a turning point in the destiny of both Hutchinson and his colony. His failure to denounce it strongly, and the fact that his brother-in-law, Andrew Oliver, was appointed a stamp distributor, stirred the SONS OF LIBERTY to action, and on August 13, 1765, they torched his elaborate mansion. The Stamp Act's repeal in 1766 calmed the troubled political waters, but the following year Parliament imposed the TOWNSHEND DUTIES, which elicited similar outpourings of resentment. Hutchinson, with deep roots in the business community, went on record questioning the wisdom of this act, but he reiterated his support for British rule in general. These duties were also repealed and tempers once again slackened, to a state more akin to the calm before the storm.

By 1771 the government in London had tired of Governor Bernard's inability to stabilize Massachusetts, so he was recalled and replaced by Hutchinson. The radicals, now backed by the influential John HANCOCK, wasted no time and considerable quantities of ink branding the mild-mannered, soft-spoken leader as a tyrant. His political misfortunes crested in 1773 with the passage of the TEA ACT, which levied a small fee on the popular beverage. The colony again quaked in anger, but Hutchinson, who had a vested business interest in tea—and whose two sons were licensed to sell it—insisted upon the rule of law. In December of that year he summarily refused to allow several tea ships to depart Boston Harbor until their cargos were sold and the duties collected. This intransigence drew a sharp response from the radicals, who organized the BOSTON TEA PARTY in protest. Worse yet, Benjamin Franklin, then in London, absconded with several of Hutchinson's private letters that inferred that tougher measures ought to be taken by the government to enforce imperial rule. These missives, once published, generated an uproar against the governor, and the legislature voted for his immediate removal. With events again spinning out of control in Massachusetts, Parliament agreed, and it relieved Hutchinson in 1774. Ominously, his replacement was General Thomas GAGE, commander in chief of British forces in America.

In June 1774 Hutchinson relocated to London for his own safety, where he continued to plead for moderation and reconciliation with his former subjects. He met with no success and died there a broken, disillusioned man on June 3, 1780. In sum, Hutchinson was a decent, fair-minded individual and a scrupulously efficient administrator who always balanced the interests of his charge with greater obligations to the empire. But to the end he failed to fathom the depths of resentment toward parliamentary rule—a radicalism precluding any attempts at accommodation.

Further Reading

Beagle, Jonathan M. " 'In the Cradle of Liberty': Faneuil Hall and the Political Culture of Eighteenth-Century Boston." Unpublished, Ph.D. diss., University of New Hampshire, 2003.

Doherty, Brian A. "Thomas Hutchinson, Milton, and the Revolutionary Period, 1740–1780: A Thesis." Unpublished master's thesis, University of Massachusetts, Boston, 2000.

McFarland, Philip J. *The Brave Bostonians: Hutchinson, Quincy, Franklin, and the Coming of the American Revolution.* Boulder, Colo.: Westview Press, 1998.

Nobles, Gregory H. *Divisions throughout the Whole: Politics and Society in Hampshire County, Massachusetts, 1750–1775.* Cambridge: Cambridge University Press, 2002.

Raphael, Ray. *The First American Revolution: Before Lexington and Concord.* New York: Free Press, 2002.

Walmsley, Andrew S. *Thomas Hutchinson and the Origins of the American Revolution.* New York: New York University Press, 1999.

Irvine, William (1741–1804)
American military officer

William Irvine was born in Enniskillen, Ireland, on November 3, 1741, and he studied medicine at Dublin University. After serving as a surgeon in the Royal Navy during the Seven Years' War, he immigrated to Pennsylvania and settled at Carlisle. Irvine maintained a successful practice for many years, and throughout the growing crisis with Great Britain he voiced support for the colonies. In July 1774 he attended the provincial convention that opposed the COERCIVE ACTS and called for a general congress. In January 1776 Irvine joined the nascent Continental ARMY as colonel of the 6th Pennsylvania Continental Infantry. In this capacity he marched north to join the army in Canada under General John SULLIVAN, where he was captured at the disastrous encounter of Trois Rivieres on June 8, 1776. Irvine was exchanged and paroled in May 1778, and he rejoined the main army of General George WASHINGTON in time to fight at MONMOUTH that August. Here the wife of one of his soldiers, Mary Ludwig HAYS, gained a measure of notoriety as "Molly Pitcher." Afterward he served on the court-martial that tried and convicted General Charles LEE. Irvine rose to brigadier general as of May 1779 and assumed command of a Pennsylvania brigade. With it he fought under General William ALEXANDER during the ill-fated attack upon Staten Island in January 1780, and next supported General Anthony WAYNE's attempt to storm the Bull's Ferry blockhouse the following July. In November 1781 Irvine was ordered to take command of the western military department frontier with headquarters at Fort Pitt (Pittsburgh). He spent the rest of the war there, struggling with an endless litany of supply shortages, unruly troops, and hostile Indians. His principle military activity was organizing volunteers for the expedition of Colonel William CRAWFORD against the Ohio Valley tribes in June 1782, which was disastrously defeated. He finally resigned his commission on November 3, 1782.

In 1785 Irvine gained appointment as the agent responsible for parceling out western land to veteran soldiers. In this capacity he convinced government officials to purchase an area known as the Triangle from the Seneca. This region, located at the extreme northwestern edge of Pennsylvania, was then acquired to give the state access to Lake Erie. Irvine next held a seat in the Continental CONGRESS, 1786–88, and also served in the state constitutional convention of 1790. In 1793 he gained a seat in the federal Congress and a year later became a government emissary tasked with defusing the so-called Whiskey Rebellion in western Pennsylvania. When his mission failed, Governor Thomas MIFFLIN commissioned him major general of state militia, and he helped suppress this quixotic disturbance. In 1801 Irvine relocated to Philadelphia, where President Thomas JEFFERSON made him an intendant of military stores. He was also voted state president of the Society of the Cincinnati, which title he retained until his death in Philadelphia on July 29, 1804.

Further Reading

Butterfield, Consul W., ed. *Washington-Irvine Correspondence; The Officila Letters Which Passed between Washington and Brigadier General William Irvine, and between Irvine and Others Concerning Military Affairs in the West from 1781 to 1783.* Madison, Wis.: David Atwood, 1882.

Heathcote, Charles W. "General William Irvine—A Trusted Pennsylvania Officer and Friend of Washington," *Picket Post* no. 67 (February 1960): 6–14.

Irvine, William. "Selections from the Military Papers of Brig. Gen. William Irvine," *Pennsylvania Magazine of History and Biography* 40 (July 1916): 108–112.

Ridner, Judith. "William Irvine and the Complexities of Manhood and Fatherhood in the Pennsylvania Backcountry," *Pennsylvania Magazine of History and Biography* 124, nos. 1–2 (2001): 5–34.

Wainwright, Nicholas B. *The Irvine Story.* Philadelphia: Historical Society of Pennsylvania, 1964.

Williams, Edward G. *Fort Pitt and the Revolution on the Western Frontier.* Pittsburgh: Historical Society of Western Pennsylvania, 1978.

Jasper, William (ca. 1750–1779)
American soldier

William Jasper was probably born around 1750 near Georgetown, South Carolina. On July 7, 1775, he enlisted in a company of the 2nd South Carolina Continental Infantry commanded by Captain Francis MARION and, by dint of ability, rose rapidly to the rank of sergeant. The following September he reported for duty at Fort Johnson on James Island, Charleston Harbor, under Colonel William MOULTRIE. After performing several months of garrison duty Jasper's regiment redeployed to Fort Sullivan on Sullivan's Island and occupied this uncompleted structure constructed from sand dunes and palmetto logs. He was present on June 28, 1776, when the British fleet of Commodore Peter PARKER took up position 400 yards distant and unleashed a torrent of shot from 271 cannon. Owning to the absorbent qualities of palmetto logs, little damage was incurred despite a furious bombardment. However, one lucky shot cut down the distinct blue field/white crescent flag of the 2nd Regiment, and it tumbled down onto the sand. Without giving a thought to safety, Jasper jumped over the parapet, braved intense British fire, and recovered the standard. He then waved it aloft in full view of the enemy until it was tied to a sponge staff and remounted. For this conspicuous display of bravery, Governor John RUTLEDGE subsequently awarded Jasper his personal sword and a lieutenant's commission. Jasper, who was illiterate, declined the latter but requested retention in the service as a roving scout.

For many months into the war Jasper disguised himself and went behind enemy lines in Georgia to gather information for General Marion and General Benjamin LINCOLN. Many enterprising deeds are attributed to him, the majority too steeped in folklore to be accepted as factual. Sometime in 1779 Jasper rejoined the 2nd South Carolina in time for the ill-fated siege of SAVANNAH. He participated in the disastrous assault upon General Augustin PREVOST's redoubt at Spring Hill and was killed planting the regimental colors on October 9, 1779. Jasper emerged from the Revolutionary War as one of the south's leading heroes; no less than eight counties and several towns have been named in his honor. Lofty memorials have also been erected in his memory at Savannah and Charleston.

Further Reading

Farley, M. Foster. "Battering Charleston's Palmetto Walls," *Military History* 18, no. 2 (2001): 38–44.

Freeman, H. Ronald. *Savannah under Siege: The Bloodiest Hour of the Revolution.* Savannah, Ga.: Freeport Pub., 2002.

Jones, Charles C. *Sergeant William Jasper.* Albany, N.Y.: Munsell, Printer, 1876.

Jones, George F. "Sergeant Johann Wilhelm Jasper," *Georgia Historical Quarterly* 65, no. 1 (1981): 7–15.

Reid, Ronald M. "The Battle of Sullivan's Island," *American History* 33, no. 5 (1999): 34–39, 70–72.

Russell, David L. *Victory on Sullivan's Island: The British Cape Fear/Charleston Expedition.* Haverford, Pa.: Infinity, 2002.

Jay, John (1745–1829)
American politician, diplomat

John Jay was born in New York City on December 12, 1745, into one of the city's most influential families. Well educated at King's College (now Columbia University), he was admitted to the bar in 1768 and established a successful law practice. Jay was politically conservative by nature, although he generally sided with the mounting anti-British sentiment. In 1774 he married the wealthy Sarah Bruge Livingston, which further cemented his status within the colonial elite. That same year Jay served on the local COMMITTEE OF CORRESPONDENCE and was also elected to the First Continental CONGRESS. Not surprisingly, Jay initially opposed independence from Britain and argued for reconciliation—with war to be undertaken only as a last resort. He was not present when the DECLARATION OF INDEPENDENCE was signed on July 4, 1776, but did wholeheartedly embrace it once adopted. Jay was reelected to the Second Continental Congress, where he succeeded Henry LAURENS as president in December 1778. He also became deeply immersed in debates over foreign policy. Shortly after, Jay retired back to New York and helped draft the new state constitution with Gouverneur MORRIS; he was consequently installed as chief justice of the New York supreme court. In 1779 Congress tapped him to serve as minister plenipotentiary to SPAIN, being tasked with securing diplomatic recognition and financial aid. But the Spanish court, although a nominal ally of France, had no intention of recognizing American independence out of fear of triggering similar revolutions within its own colonies. Jay spent a frustrating two years in Madrid, where he managed to acquire a loan for $170,000, but little else.

In the spring of 1782, Jay arrived in Paris to join John ADAMS, Benjamin FRANKLIN, and Henry Laurens as a peace commissioner. He caused somewhat of a stir by insisting that the English address them as agents of the "United States of America," rather than merely "Colonial representatives." Getting this stance accepted incurred some delays but also underscored Jay's determination to have American independence recognized before negotiations commenced. He also harbored deep suspicions that French foreign minister Charles Gravier, comte de VERGENNES, was secretly negotiating with England behind the Americans' backs and sought to preempt them at their own game. Jay convinced Adams, Franklin, and Laurens to disregard instructions from Congress and seek the best possible terms for peace through secret negotiations of their own. Accordingly, he privately contacted Prime Minister William PETTY, Lord Shelburne, and proposed quickly terminating the war without French approval or knowledge. The British agreed and on November 30, 1782, preliminary peace accords were signed. The TREATY OF PARIS was formally concluded on September 3, 1783; it bequeathed to the United States, among other things, a boundary reaching westward to the Mississippi River.

Jay returned home in 1784, where he succeeded Robert R. LIVINGSTON as foreign affairs minister. At this time the shortcomings of national governance and the conduct of foreign affairs under the ARTICLES OF CONFEDERATION were painfully apparent, and Jay worked vigorously on behalf of ratifying a federal constitution in 1788. The following year President George WASHINGTON appointed him chief justice of the new, national Supreme Court. However, the United States was still weak militarily and increasingly buffeted by events arising from the barely began French Revolution. When Great Britain began seizing American shipping and sailors, Jay was dispatched to England to negotiate a peace treaty and avert war. The ensuing "Jay Treaty" caused a firestorm at home, for it closely reflected the pro-British political philosophy of Alexander

HAMILTON. Here the Americans agreed in principle to pay off staggering prewar debts in exchange for British-held fortifications in the Old Northwest and new, if restricted, access to the West Indian trade. More important, renewed conflict with England was averted and normalized relations became possible. But Democratic-Republicans like Thomas JEFFERSON railed against it, especially because issues of impressment and neutral trade were completely ignored. Jay then quit the government in 1795 to serve two terms as governor of New York. In 1801 he retired to private life in Bedford, New York, dying there on May 17, 1829. While overshadowed by many of his more luminous contemporaries, Jay made positive and indelible contributions to the new nation through astute diplomacy.

Further Reading
Brecher, Frank W. *Securing American Independence: John Jay and the French Alliance.* Westport, Conn.: Praeger, 2003.
Freeman, Landa M., Louise V. North, and Janet M. Wedge., eds. *Selected Letters of John Jay and Sarah Livingston.* Jefferson, N.C.: McFarland, 2004.
Glahn, Walter F. "John Jay: The Forgotten Founding Father." Unpublished master's thesis, East Stroudsburg University, 2001.
Kaminski, John P. "Shall We Have a King? John Jay and the Politics of Union," *New York History* 81, no. 1 (2000): 31–58.
Klein, Milton M. "John Jay and the Revolution," *New York History* 81, no. 1 (2000): 14–30.
Stahr, Walter. *John Jay: Founding Father.* New York: Hambledon & London, 2005.

Jefferson, Thomas (1743–1826)
American politician, third president of the United States

Thomas Jefferson was born in Albemarle County, Virginia, the son of a successful surveyor. He received an excellent primary education and subsequently attended William and Mary College. After graduating in 1762, Jefferson passed the bar five years later and established a lucrative practice. He then inherited his father's vast estate and, as part of the landed elite, successfully stood for a seat in the Virginia House of Burgesses in 1769. There he quickly allied himself to anti-British factions headed by Patrick HENRY. Jefferson, an outstanding intellectual steeped in the classics and well versed in English law, took the process a step further in 1774 when he composed and published *A Summary View of the Rights of British America,* asserting that Parliament possessed no right to tax the colonies and, more important, that their allegiance to the Crown was strictly voluntary. This document firmly catapulted him to the front ranks of the radical movement and as such he was elected to the First Continental CONGRESS in 1774. Jefferson, tall, gangly, and somewhat shy, quickly befriended the short, outspoken John ADAMS, who steered him toward a committee tasked with drafting the DECLARATION OF INDEPENDENCE in 1776. This proved Jefferson's moment: He went on to compose one of the seminal documents of United States history, a justification for the break with Britain and a legitimization of the revolution at hand. Couched in lofty prose, he declared that all men are created equal and that government was intended to serve, and not rule, the people; by this he meant all white males, not AFRICAN AMERICANS. Jefferson had previously wrestled with slavery and failed to promulgate a solution by himself. Nonetheless his declaration remains a masterpiece of political philosophy and a stirring example of Enlightenment thought in action. The document was approved by his fellow delegates on July 4, 1776, a day that has been enshrined as a national holiday.

Jefferson was reelected to Congress in 1777, but he relinquished his seat in favor of returning to Virginia. There he contributed heavily to the formulation of a new state constitution to replace the royal charter and distinguished himself by advocating separation of church and state. This last notion was initially viewed as far too radical and not adopted for nearly a decade. In 1779 Jefferson succeeded Henry as governor, but his tenure in office proved undistinguished. Within two years the state was invaded by British forces under General Benedict ARNOLD and Charles CORNWALLIS, and Jefferson responded ineffectually to the crisis.

Worse, on June 4, 1781, Lieutenant Colonel Banastre TARLETON launched a mounted raid on the capital at Charlottesville, and Jefferson, warned through the exertions of John JOUETT, only narrowly escaped capture. This experience underscored his mounting distaste for public office, and he withdrew to his opulent home at Monticello while the remainder of his term was finished by Thomas Nelson, Jr. This episode induced the legislature to conduct a formal inquiry, although Jefferson was subsequently cleared of any wrongdoing.

Jefferson returned to Congress in 1783, where he helped draft the "Ordinance of 1784," another important document intending to admit new western states into the union on equal footing with the thirteen original colonies; while not adopted, it served as the basis for the Northwest Ordinance of 1787, which also forbade slavery in the new territories. In 1784 Jefferson was selected to join Adams and Benjamin FRANKLIN in Paris to negotiate commerce treaties with France and Prussia. After replacing the aged Franklin as minister in 1785, he remained in Paris until the onset of the French Revolution four years later. The United States had since replaced the ARTICLES OF CONFEDERATION with the new federal Constitution, and President George WASHINGTON appointed his fellow Virginian the first secretary of state. In this capacity Jefferson entered the mounting ideological dispute with Alexander HAMILTON over the nature of American governance and the latter's seemingly pro-British views. He resigned from office in 1793 and three years later became vice president under President Adams. In 1800, he was elected president when Hamilton, his nominal ideological adversary, arranged for the House of Representatives to select him over Aaron Burr. He was also the first chief executive sworn into office at Washington, D.C., the new national capital. Overall, Jefferson enjoyed a highly successful tenure as chief executive and doubled the size of the nation through the Louisiana Purchase of 1803. The following year he authorized the Lewis and Clark Expedition to chart this vast wilderness region. Jefferson easily gained reelection in 1804, although he was increasingly caught up in the struggle between Great Britain and Napoléonic France. He was succeeded in office by James MADISON in 1808 and retired to private life as the "Sage of Monticello." Ever the scholar, in 1809 he donated 6,000 volumes of his personal library to the nascent Library of Congress, and in 1819 he served as the primary force behind the founding of the University of Virginia. Jefferson, who sustained an angry rupture with Adams in 1800, also sought and achieved reconciliation with his former friend, and they resumed their lifelong correspondence. He died at Monticello on July 4, 1826, on the exact day as Adams and precisely 50 years after the signing of the Declaration. Jefferson remains enshrined in the panoply of American heroes, for his impact on the American political landscape cannot be exaggerated. More than any other individual, he placed the budding American nation irrevocably down the path of republicanism.

Further Reading

Bailyn, Bernard. *To Begin the World Anew: The Genius and Ambiguities of the Founding Fathers.* New York: Vintage Books, 2004.

Eicholz, Hans L. *Harmonizing Sentiments: The Declaration of Independence and the Jeffersonian Idea of Self Government.* New York: P. Lang, 2001.

Ferling, John. *Setting the World Ablaze: Washington, Adams, Jefferson, and the American Revolution.* New York: Oxford University Press, 2000.

Golden, James L., and Eugene R. Sheridan, eds. *The Papers of Thomas Jefferson,* 28 vols. Princeton, N.J.: Princeton University Press, 2000.

Ollivant, Douglas A. "Jefferson's Pursuit of Happiness." Unpublished Ph.D. diss., Indiana University, 2003.

Staloff, Darren. *Hamilton, Adams, Jefferson: The Politics of Enlightenment and the American Founding.* New York: Hill and Wang, 2005.

Vidal, Gore. *Inventing a Nation: Washington, Adams, Jefferson.* New Haven, Conn.: Yale University Press, 2002.

Johnson, Guy (ca. 1740–1788)
Loyalist officer

Guy Johnson was born in County Meath, Ireland, around 1740, a son of John Johnson and a nephew

Loyalist officer and judge Guy Johnson issued a grand jury declaration against the Continental Congress in 1775. *(National Gallery of Art, Washington)*

to Sir William Johnson, the famous Indian agent. He immigrated to New York in 1756 and was taken into his uncle's household as a personal secretary. When the French and Indian War commenced in 1755, Johnson used family connections to obtain a lieutenant's commission in the local militia and he fought at the capture of Fort Niagara in 1759. However, in 1762 Sir William prevailed upon him to resign and work full time as an officer within the Indian Department as his personal representative to the Six Nations of the Iroquois Confederation. Johnson complied, married his uncle's daughter, and received a large estate, which he immodestly named Guy Hall. He also continued in military affairs, rising to colonel of the Tryon County militia, and functioned as a judge of the common pleas in 1772. Governor William TRYON then appointed him to the provincial assembly, and in 1774 General Thomas GAGE, commander in chief of British forces in America, elevated Johnson to acting superintendent of Indian Affairs following the death of Sir William. Johnson, who owed everything he had to patronage, was demonstrably loyal to the British government during the difficulties leading up to the Revolutionary War. His high social standing and outspoken LOYALIST leanings naturally rendered him a conspicuous target for inhabitants espousing the Patriot cause.

When the Revolution commenced in April 1775, the Tryon County committee of safety voted resolutions in favor of the Continental CONGRESS. Johnson, as a judge, issued a grand jury declaration against that body, which turned the county inhabitants against him. Relations were further estranged when both Johnson and his brother-in-law, John JOHNSON, broke up several committee meetings by force. But in May 1775, upon hearing that American militia under Colonel Ethan ALLEN were marching to arrest him, Johnson fled with his family for Oswego, New York. There he addressed 1,200 Indians and persuaded them to remain loyal to Great Britain before he passed onward to Quebec. There Johnson engaged in a simmering dispute with Governor-General Guy CARLETON, who disliked his entire clan personally and strove to undercut his standing within the Indian Department. He also refused Johnson's request that the Indians be utilized militarily against the rebels. Greatly angered, Johnson then sailed off to England with Joseph BRANT and Walter BUTLER to confer with high government officials. American secretary George GERMAIN seemed suitably impressed by his remonstrances, and in the spring of 1776 Johnson sailed home with a commission as Deputy of the Six Nations. Johnson failed to acquire control over the Canadian tribes, which went to Major John Campbell, but he was the sole authorized agent for the Iroquois Confederation. Unfortunately, Johnson dithered at New York for nearly three years, during which time Indian affairs were capably administered by John BUTLER. After finally arriving at Quebec in 1779, Governor-General Frederick HALDIMAND authorized him to work with the Butlers to coordinate Indian raids against New York's frontier settlements. The three men performed poorly together and, following General John SULLIVAN's successful raid into the Indian heartland, Johnson found himself both marooned at Fort Niagara and increasingly isolated from the decision-making process.

By 1782 Guy Johnson was totally preoccupied in providing food and shelter to thousands of displaced Native Americans. This entailed great expense, and as he was an apparently sloppy bookkeeper, Governor-General Haldimand accused him of corruption and installed John JOHNSON as his successor. Because Guy Johnson's extensive estates had been confiscated by the Americans, he ventured back to England to press his claims for compensation. He died in London on March 5, 1788, a talented but self-absorbed bureaucrat who did little to advance the interests of England or the Indians.

Further Reading
Allen, Robert S. *His Majesty's Allies: British-Indian Policy in Defense of Canada, 1774–1815.* Toronto: Dundurn Press, 1992.
Gibb, Harley L. "Colonel Guy Johnson, Superintendent of Indian Affairs, 1774–1782," *Papers of the Michigan Academy of Science, Arts, and Letters* no. 37 (1943): 596–613.
Hamilton, Milton V. "Guy Johnson's Opinions on the American Indian," *Pennsylvania Magazine of History and Biography* 77, no. 3 (1953): 311–327.
Mintz, Max M. *Seed of Empire: The Revolutionary Conquest of the Iroquois.* New York: New York University Press, 1999.
Reinhardt, Leslie. "British and Indian Identities in a Picture by Benjamin West," *Eighteenth Century Studies* 31, no.3 (1998): 283– 305.
Stevens, Paul L. "His Majesty's Savage Allies." Unpublished Ph.D. diss., State University of New York at Buffalo, 1984.

Johnson, John (1741–1830)
Loyalist officer
John Johnson was born near Amsterdam, New York, the illegitimate son of Sir William Johnson and a Dutch servant. At the age of 13 he accompanied his father as a volunteer throughout the French and Indian War and attended important Indian conferences. After briefly attending Benjamin FRANKLIN's College and Academy in Philadelphia in 1757, Johnson returned home to partake of militia affairs. He acquitted himself well during Pontiac's Rebellion in 1763, and two years later his father broadened his social horizons by sending him to England. There Johnson was knighted by King GEORGE III in preparation for inheriting his father's impressive estates. Part of this entailed ridding himself of a common law wife and two children in favor of marrying into the New York aristocracy. Following Sir William's death in 1774, Johnson acquired his vast domain of 200,000 acres along with numerous tenants. He also succeeded him as superintendent of Indian Affairs despite his preference for living as a county gentleman at a palatial home christened Johnson Hall. In recognition of his high social standing, Johnson was also created a major general of militia shortly before the onset of the Revolutionary War.

Prior to the outbreak of war with England, Johnson espoused LOYALIST sympathies for the Crown and also recruited numerous Scottish and English army veterans living on his land as a personal militia. He had approached Governor William TRYON and offered to organize the Mohawk Valley to support the British cause, but such moves deeply alarmed the resident Patriots. In January 1776 the Continental CONGRESS authorized General Philip J. SCHUYLER to gather an army and eliminate Johnson as a threat to the Albany region. This was accomplished, Johnson's supporters were disarmed, and he thereafter pledged neutrality but continued to be viewed with suspicion. In May 1776 Johnson fled with his family and many supporters to Quebec to escape possible arrest and tendered his services to Governor-General Guy CARLETON. He received a lieutenant colonel's commission in a new formation, the King's Royal Regiment (or Royal Greens), and was ordered to keep the Indians neutral for the time being. In August 1777 Johnson accompanied the expedition of Lieutenant Colonel Barry ST. LEGER up the Mohawk River and helped invest the American garrison at Fort Stanwix. On August 6, 1777, his Indians and rangers ambushed and dispersed the relief column of Colonel Nicholas HERKIMER at ORISKANY, but his papers and luggage were seized during a sortie from the fort. A disgruntled Johnson then fled back to Canada with St. Leger, where he became increasingly preoccupied with feeding and housing hundreds of Native American refugees.

Over the next three years Johnson gained a measure of infamy throughout the Mohawk Valley by leading combined Loyalist and Indian raids, usually in concert with Colonel John BUTLER and Chief Joseph BRANT. He enjoyed his greatest success in 1780, when the settlements at Schoharie, Caughnawaga, and Fort Hunter were laid to waste. At one point, his stealthy raiders briefly recaptured his former home at Johnson Hall. Such punitive measures proved destructive to the Americans and also forced them to divert badly needed men and resources to the Mohawk Valley—but failed to alter the outcome of events. In 1782 Governor-General Frederick HALDIMAND appointed him to succeed Guy JOHNSON as superintendent of Indian Affairs owing to the latter's fiscal irregularities. By war's end it became Johnson's painful duty to explain to his Indian consorts that their land was being confiscated by the victorious Americans. He also ventured back to England and pressed his own claims for compensation. Back in Canada he proved essential in helping to transport and resettle thousands of fleeing Loyalists and Indians at Cataraqui (Kingston). Johnson's work proved exemplary, and he fully expected to gain appointment as the first governor-general of newly created Upper Canada (Ontario) but became embittered when the post went to Colonel John Graves SIMCOE. After several more years in England Johnson finally settled in Quebec, where he gained an appointment with the Legislative Council of Lower Canada. In this capacity he became a common fixture among the United Empire Loyalists and a champion of Indian rights. Johnson died at Montreal on January 4, 1830, and was eulogized by Chief Brant as a "friend and fellow warrior." He is regarded as one of the founding fathers of Canada.

Further Reading

Blakeley, Phyllis R., and John N. Grant. *Eleven Exiles: Accounts of Loyalists of the American Revolution.* Toronto: Dundurn Press, 1982.

Bryce, Peter H. "Sir John Johnson, Superintendent General of Indian Affairs," *New York State Historical Association Proceedings* 7 (July 1928): 233–271.

Hamilton, Milton W. "An American Knight in Britain: Sir John Johnson's Tour," *New York History* 42 (April 1961): 119–144.

MacLachlan, Alan J. *John Johnson (1742–1820).* Toronto: Dundurn Press, 1977.

Thomas, Earle. *Sir John Johnson: Loyalist Baronet.* Toronto: Dundurn Press, 1986.

Watt, Gavin K. *The Burning of the Valleys: Daring Raids from Canada against the New York Frontier in the Fall of 1780.* Toronto: Dundurn Press, 1997.

Jones, John Paul (1747–1792)
American naval officer

John Paul was born in Kirkcudbrightshire, Scotland, on July 6, 1747, and at the age of 12 he sailed with merchant marine vessels from nearby Whitehaven. In the rough-hewed world of naval command he proved adept as a leader and rose rapidly through the ranks. On one occasion, when his ship's master died at sea, the youthful Paul skillfully brought his vessel into port, and he consequently received command of a ship at the age of 21. Paul, however, proved tyrannically disposed and something of a martinet; in 1770 he allegedly flogged a carpenter to death and was brought up on murder charges. Jones was cleared by an Admiralty court, but in 1773 he killed another sailor during a mutiny and fled to Virginia under the assumed name of John Paul Jones. When the Revolutionary War commenced two years later he was in Philadelphia and managed to receive a lieutenant's commission in the Continental NAVY from the Continental CONGRESS. In this capacity he served on the reconditioned merchantman *Alfred* under Commodore Esek HOPKINS and rendered valuable service during the successful capture of New Providence, the Bahamas, in March 1776. The following May, Jones received command of the sloop *Providence* as acting captain, and during his first Atlantic cruise he captured several prizes. That fall he transferred back at the helm of *Alfred* and, still in concert with *Providence,* scored several more successes off Nova Scotia before returning to Boston in December.

Jones, impetuous and ambitious, kept agitating for new and larger commands and received assistance from congressional friends like John HANCOCK and Robert MORRIS. In June 1777 he hoisted his flag aboard the new 18-gun sloop *Ranger* and sailed off to France to take charge of a frigate being constructed in the Netherlands for the United States. Upon arriving he learned that his vessel had been sold to France, so he sailed the *Ranger* from Brest on an extended raid into English home waters. There, on February 14, 1778, he met and defeated the 20-gun sloop HMS *Drake* off the Irish coast—this was the first Royal Navy vessel captured in British waters. The following April Jones returned to his old haunt at Whitehaven and landed a party intending to seize the earl of Selkirk as a hostage. Meanwhile, American minister Benjamin FRANKLIN finally managed to purchase the dilapidated 42-gun East Indiaman *Duc du Duras* in February 1779. Jones promptly renamed it *Bonhomme Richard* in honor of his benefactor and spent several months outfitting it at L'Orient with weapons and a new crew. That summer he took *Bonhomme Richard,* in concert with several French vessels, and cruised the Bay of Biscay. His flotilla snared 16 merchantmen, but Jones, eager for greater game, boldly returned to English waters in September 1779.

Jones skillfully circumnavigated the British Isles until September 23, 1779, when he encountered a convoy escorted by the 44-gun frigate HMS *Serapis* and the 22-gun sloop *Countess of Scarborough*. He moved quickly to attack while Captain Richard PEARSON of *Serapis* skillfully placed his vessel between Jones and the convoy. An intense night engagement erupted between Pearson's crack Royal Navy vessel and the creaking, water-logged *Bonhomme Richard*. As the two warships closed, Jones took a severe pounding from heavier British armament and, worse, lost several men when two of his own 18-pound cannon exploded. The two captains flailed away at point-blank range as Jones unsuccessfully attempted to grapple with his larger antagonist. At length, when Pearson inquired through his megaphone if the American wished to surrender, Jones shot back "I have not yet begun to fight!" Eventually both vessels were lashed together and Nathaniel FANNING managed to drop a grenade

American naval officer John Paul Jones is considered one of the founders of the United States Navy and was the only officer of the Continental navy to receive a congressional gold medal. *(Independence National Historical Park)*

down the *Serapis's* open hatch. The ensuing explosion temporarily cleared Pearson's top deck, and he struck his colors after three and a half hours of intense combat. Jones, who lost half his crew, spent several days trying to salvage the *Bonhomme Richard* but, badly riddled, it sank two days later. He then arrived back at Texel, the Netherlands, with his captives and was hailed for winning the most contested ship encounter of the Revolutionary War.

Jones returned to America in February 1781 commanding the borrowed warship *Ariel*. He had been previously promised the new French-built frigate *Alliance* but lost it due to the machinations of Arthur LEE and Alexander GILLON. Once home Jones received a gold medal and the Thanks of Congress, along with command of the new ship of the line, *America*. When this vessel was subsequently given to France as a gift, he revisited Paris to press claims for his prize vessels, and King Louis XVI made him a chevalier. After the war ended in 1782 and Congress began selling off its warships, Jones tendered his services to Czarina Catherine the Great of Russia, who made him an admiral of the Black Sea Fleet. Jones won several battles against the Turks before quarreling with superiors and returning to Paris. Jones died there in obscurity on July 18, 1792, and was interred in an unmarked grave. It was not until 1905 that his remains were identified and reburied in an elaborate ceremony at the U.S. Naval Academy in Annapolis, Maryland. Along with John BARRY, Jones is considered a founding father of the United States Navy, who bequeathed to the service valuable traditions of aggressive leadership and victory. He was the only officer of the Continental navy honored by a congressional gold medal.

Further Reading

Bowen-Hassell, E. Gordon, Dennis M. Conrad, and Mark L. Hayes. *Sea Raiders of the American Revolution: The Continental Navy in English Waters*. Washington, D.C.: Naval Historical Center, 2003.

Conrad, Dennis M. "John Paul Jones, the *Ranger*, and the Value of the Continental Navy," *Sea History* no. 1,000 (2002): 9–13.

Poirier, Noel B. "Raids Target Western England," *Naval History* 17, no. 4 (2003): 32–38.

Thomas, Evan. *John Paul Jones: Sailor, Hero, Father of the American Navy*. New York: Simon & Schuster, 2003.

Vansittart, Peter. *John Paul Jones: A Rebellious Spirit*. London: Robson, 2003.

Webbe, Stephen. "Revenge Raid on Whitehaven," *MHQ* 12, no. 3 (2000): 20–27.

Jouett, Jack (1754–1822)
American militiaman

John Jouett was born in Albemarle County, Virginia, on December 7, 1754, the son of a tavern owner, although little is known of his early years. By the advent of the Revolutionary War he was renowned throughout the county as a towering individual, over six feet, four inches in height, a crack shot with a rifle, and an expert horseman. He was also a captain in the local militia. Around midnight on the evening of June 3, 1781, Jouett was at the Cuckoo Tavern, 40 miles from the capital of Charlottesville, when he espied a hard-riding column of British cavalry under Lieutenant Colonel Banastre TARLETON passing by. These troops had been dispatched by General Charles CORNWALLIS to both "disturb the assembly" at Charlottesville and capture whatever stores found there. Jouett quickly comprehended Tarleton's objective, and the British had no sooner trotted from view than he mounted his own horse and galloped off. Taking barely used backcountry paths Jouett managed to cover 40 miles in a few hours and arrived at the estate of Monticello around 4:30 in the morning. He then roused Governor Thomas JEFFERSON from his slumbers, alerted him to the danger, and rode off to warn the assembly. Once this was accomplished, the legislators decided to convene at Staunton, roughly 40 miles distant, to elude their pursuers.

Jouett's exertions proved fortuitous, for by the time Tarleton's legion pounded into Charlottesville, it was deserted by all save a few military figures. The British quickly scattered a handful of defenders, rounded up Colonel Daniel BOONE and General Charles SCOTT, and burned numerous stores. But their preemptive strike against the Virginia government otherwise had failed. This was no fault of Tarleton's, who drove his men 70 miles from Hanover County to Charlottesville in only 24 hours—an impressive effort that otherwise would have undoubtedly seized Jefferson and the assembly. But the marauders drew off empty-handed, and grateful members of the legislature voted Jouett an elaborate sword and a brace of pistols in recognition of his services. In 1784 Jouette relocated with his family to Mercer County, Kentucky, where he eventually served in the assembly. He also owned and operated a dozen gristmills before dying there on March 1, 1822. Over time Jouett's ride became as famous in the south as Paul REVERE's similar effort was up north and is commemorated every June 3 with a horse race retracing his route to Monticello.

Further Reading

Ardery, William B. "The 'Other Ride' of the Revolution," *American History Illustrated* 6, no. 5 (2000): 41–42.

Dabney, Virginius. "Jack Jouett's Ride," *American Heritage* 13, no. 1 (1961): 56–59.

Jouett, Edward S. "Jack Jouett's Ride," *Filson Club Quarterly* 24 (April 1950): 141–156.

Maass, John. "'To Disturb the Assembly': Tarleton's Charlottesville Raid and the British Invasion of Virginia," *Virginia Cavalcade* 49, no. 4 (2000): 148–157.

Morse, Genevieve F. "Captain Jack Jouett," *Daughters of the American Revolution Magazine* 115, no. 7 (1981): 700–703.

Taylor, J. Y. "Jack Jouett, Forgotten Hero," *Daughters of the American Revolution Magazine* 110, no. 9 (1976): 1,380–1,382.

K

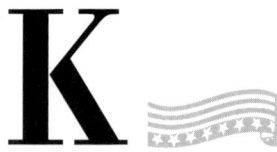

Kalb, Johann de (1721–1780)
French military officer

Johann de Kalb was born in Huttendorf, Bavaria, on June 19, 1721, into a peasant family. Restless and thirsting for adventure, he joined the French army at a young age and by 1743 was serving as a lieutenant in the Loewendal Regiment. Despite a lack of prior education Kalb possessed a flair for linguistics, becoming fluent in both French and English. He rose to major during the Seven Years' War and retired from the army in 1764 as a lieutenant colonel. That year he also married a clothing manufacturing heiress and settled down to the life of a country gentleman. It was not long before Kalb grew adventurous again, and in 1767 the French foreign minister Etienne-François, duc de Choiseul, dispatched him to America to gauge political sentiments there. He toured the colonies for four months and composed several detailed letters that declared that the colonials, while angry at England, were not ready for an alliance with France. Kalb then returned home and remained inactive for several years until November 1776, when King Louis XVI elevated him to brigadier general in anticipation of war with England. But Kalb, as usual, was unwilling to wait for war to happen, so he tendered his services to Silas DEANE, the American agent in Paris. At that time he represented himself as a baron using the aristocratic appellation de Kalb. Deane was suitably impressed and proffered him a major general's commission in the Continental ARMY. Kalb then sailed with the youthful marquis de LAFAYETTE to South Carolina in June 1777. After venturing a farther 800 miles to Philadelphia, he grew dismayed when the Continental CONGRESS commissioned Lafayette and seemed ready to

French general Johann de Kalb joined the Continental army and fought bravely at the Battle of Camden, where he was fatally wounded. *(Independence National Historical Park)*

renege on his offer. He angrily threatened to sue and was on the point of returning home when Congress relented, and he was commissioned on September 7, 1777. Reporting to General George WASHINGTON at Valley Forge, Pennsylvania, he favorably impressed all in his circle.

Washington rated Kalb's professionalism highly yet he remained without a suitable command throughout most of 1778. That year he was chosen to serve as a subordinate to Lafayette during a proposed invasion of Canada, which was ultimately canceled. He then fulfilled a series of small commands in New Jersey and the Hudson Highlands but yearned for an opportunity to distinguish himself in combat. It was not until April 1780 that Kalb was ordered to the relief of Charleston, South Carolina, and marched a small force of Maryland and Delaware Continental infantry, among Washington's best soldiers, to the south. En route he learned of General Benjamin LINCOLN's surrender on May 12, 1780, and paused in North Carolina to rest and regroup. Kalb was genuinely disturbed when the local militias did not turn out as reinforcements as promised, nor did nearby civilian centers offer him assistance in the way of food. He received an even bigger jolt that July when General Horatio GATES arrived to replace him as commander of the Southern Department. Kalb took the slight in stride and served as a highly competent subordinate.

Kalb felt the Americans were too poorly supplied to undertake offensive operations and counseled caution, but Gates ignored him. The little army then resumed marching south to attack the British at their important supply depot at CAMDEN, South Carolina, just as British forces under General Charles CORNWALLIS trudged north along the same road. The contestants collided at Camden on August 16, 1780, where Gates recklessly deployed militia forces along his left wing and center. A determined British attack swept the rabble away and then pivoted leftward to outflank Kalb's Continentals comprising the American right. Heavy screens of dust and smoke prevented Kalb from perceiving the danger until he was nearly overwhelmed. Rather then retreat, he manfully stood with his soldiers and, supported by redoubtable Colonels William SMALLWOOD, Otho Holland WILLIAMS, Mordecai GIST, and John E. HOWARD, charged several times to cut his way out. Kalb's outnumbered host was nearly decimated in the fighting, while he was unhorsed and captured after receiving 11 wounds. He died in British captivity on August 19, 1781, a former mercenary who had become personally and completely committed to the American cause. He is commemorated by six counties and several towns with the name De Kalb.

Further Reading

Farley, M. Foster. "Foreigners in the Continental Army," *Daughters of the American Revolution Magazine* 118, no. 9 (1984): 622–626, 699.

Kalb, Johann de. "Letter of Johann de Kalb, 1777," *American Historical Review* 15 (April 1900): 562–567.

Maass, John R. *Horatio Gates and the Battle of Camden—"That Unhappy Affair"—August 16, 1780.* Camden, S.C.: Kershaw County Historical Society, 2001.

Sifton, Paul G., ed. "La Caroline Meridional: . . . Two Unpublished Letters of Baron de Kalb," *South Carolina Historical Magazine* 66, no. 2 (1965): 102–108.

Whitridge, Arnold. "Washington's French Volunteers," *History Today* 24, no. 9 (1974): 593–603.

Zucker, A. E. *General de Kalb: Lafayette's Mentor.* Chapel Hill: University of North Carolina Press, 1966.

King's Mountain, Battle of (October 7, 1780)

The conquest of South Carolina by forces under General Charles CORNWALLIS allowed him to prepare an invasion of neighboring North Carolina, with a view toward eventually subjugating the entire American south. However, he underestimated the resilience of partisan bands under men like Isaac SHELBY, Elijah CLARKE, and Joseph MCDOWELL, who maintained constant pressure on British and LOYALIST outposts throughout the Carolina backcountry. Such resistance induced Cornwallis to throw out a column of Loyalist light infantry, 1,000 strong, to cover his left flank as he advanced on Charlotte. He specifically chose Major Patrick FERGUSON to head this flank guard, seeing that he was an enterprising light infantry officer who enjoyed a working rapport with his loyal American troops. The British commenced invading North Carolina on September 9, 1780, and Cornwallis methodically trudged toward his objective. Ferguson also advanced into the wilderness of Tryon County, routinely plundering the homes of suspected Patriots before halting at Gilbert Town. There he issued an ultimatum to inhabitants of the region, especially the "over the mountain men" residing in present-day Tennessee, that they swear allegiance to the Crown or face retribution with fire and sword. But Ferguson, like Cornwallis himself, completely underestimated the resolve of hardy frontier fighters in the face of such a challenge. Stung by his harsh rhetoric, they began amassing in large numbers at Sycamore Shoals under Shelby and John SEVIER on September 26 while awaiting the arrival of other groups from Virginia and North Carolina. A turning point in the war for the south was at hand.

At length, the Patriots cobbled together roughly 1,000 men from the Carolinas and Virginia, including bands under Colonels William CAMPBELL, Benjamin CLEVELAND, and Joseph WINSTON. After some debate Campbell was chosen the unofficial "leader," and the whole then set off in pursuit of Ferguson. The British subsequently learned of their approach through a deserter, and Ferguson withdrew in an orderly fashion until he reached King's Mountain, a low-lying hill just below the South Carolina border. Rather than marching 35 miles farther to rejoin the main column under Cornwallis, the proud Scot assumed defensive positions and decided to confront his antagonists. He deployed his musket-armed troops across the crest of this 60-foot-high plateau, whose slopes were heavily forested and provided ample cover to an attacker. Furthermore, Ferguson, although he possessed the time, made no attempt to cut down trees and form barricades against the coming onslaught. Having personally trained his men, he apparently enjoyed the highest possible confidence in their ability to dispense with what he openly disdained as rabble.

By October 7, 1780, Campbell had approached and surrounded King's Mountain, completely cutting off Ferguson's escape. Early in the morning the sharpshooting mountain men, armed with long-range rifles, began ascending the slopes and picking off Loyalists like squirrels. Far from attacking as a mob, the Americans formed four distinct columns at different points along Ferguson's defensive perimeter and launched a highly coordinated assault. Ferguson calmly allowed his antagonists to approach before launching a series of desperate bayonet charges downhill and driving the riflemen off. The Americans melted before this steely onslaught, but marksmen posted on the flanks continued picking off men and officers from afar. Three times the Loyalists ran the Americans back, only to leave the slopes littered with their dead and wounded. Unable to sustain such attrition, Ferguson withdrew his survivors into a compact circle at the northern end of the ridge as Campbell ordered his Americans to close. An intense firefight erupted in the underbrush as Loyalists continued falling before the unerring aim of frontier marksmen. Ferguson then realized that the battle was lost, and he endeavored to escape on horseback. But, unmistakably clad in a checkered hunting shirt, he was quickly identified and half a dozen bullets found their mark. At this juncture the remaining Loyalists attempted to surrender, but the Americans, fired by memory of "Tarleton's quarter," continued a killing spree. Campbell eventually established control over his men, and the fighting gradually ceased—as did Ferguson's entire command. Loyalist losses amounted to 157 killed, 163 wounded, and 698 captured, while the Americans suffered a trifling 28 killed and 64 wounded. This startling discrepancy is mute testimony to the effectiveness of frontiersmen in the art of bush fighting.

King's Mountain was a decisive American victory in so much as it eliminated some of General Cornwallis's best light infantry at a time when he needed their specialized skills the most. The defeat prompted him to call off suddenly the invasion of North Carolina, and he fell back toward Winnsboro, South Carolina, to regroup. For the Americans, King's Mountain signified the resurgence of organized resistance to the Crown and raised morale throughout the entire region. It also severely dampened future attempts to recruit Loyalists under the king's banner. Three months lapsed before the redcoats returned to North Carolina, where they would meet a similar fate at the Battle of COWPENS.

Further Reading
Buchanan, John. *The Road to Guilford Courthouse: The American Revolution in the Carolinas.* New York: Wiley, 1997.
Dameron, J. David. *King's Mountain: The Defeat of the Loyalists, October 7, 1780.* Cambridge, Mass.: Da Capo Press, 2003.
Gordon, John W. *South Carolina in the American Revolution: A Battlefield History.* Columbia, S.C.: University of South Carolina Press, 2005.
Messick, Hank. *King's Mountain: The Epic of the Blue Ridge 'Mountain Men' in the American Revolution.* Boston: Little, Brown, 1976.
Russell, David L. *The American Revolution in the Southern Colonies.* Jefferson, N.C.: McFarland, 2000.
Wicker, Tom. "Turning Point in the Wilderness," *MHQ* 11, no. 1 (1998): 62–71.

Knowlton, Thomas (1740–1776)
American military officer

Thomas Knowlton was born in West Boxford, Massachusetts, and raised in Ashford, Connecticut. He joined the militia during the French and Indian War, rising to lieutenant, and also accompanied the expedition that captured Havana, Cuba, in August 1762. Afterward he returned to Ashford to farm but maintained ties to the local militia as a captain. In April 1775, after word of the Battles of Lexington and CONCORD, Knowlton marched with his company to Cambridge, Massachusetts, and served throughout the siege of Boston. He fought at BUNKER HILL on June 17, 1775, as part of a force commanded by Colonel John STARK, then stationed behind a split-rail breastwork on the American left. Knowlton's force held its ground the entire day and threw back several British attempts to outflank them from the beach. Toward the end of the engagement he ably covered the American withdrawal back to the mainland. Praised for his coolness under fire, he became a major in the newly constituted 20th Connecticut Continental Infantry as of January 1776. On the 8th of that month Knowlton led a clever night raid into Charlestown that burned eight buildings and absconded with several prisoners. In a unique twist, General William HOWE and his staff were watching a theatrical satire in Charlestown entitled *The Siege of Boston,* when a uniformed soldier suddenly burst in with news of the raid. The startled audience, assuming it was part of the performance, howled in laughter until Howe ordered all officers to their stations.

Knowlton's unit subsequently accompanied the army of General George WASHINGTON back to New York the following summer, where, in August 1776, he advanced to lieutenant colonel. In this capacity he was present during the Battle of LONG ISLAND on August 17, 1776, and fought well with 100 soldiers while guarding Flatbush Pass. He then retreated back to New York City with the main force. There Washington authorized creation of a new corps of light infantry "rangers" to scout British positions ahead of the fighting. Knowlton ultimately recruited 120 volunteers, including Nathan HALE. It was Knowlton who allowed Hale to land behind British lines on Long Island after which he was caught and hanged as a spy. The British, meanwhile, staged a brilliant landing at Kip's Bay on September 15, 1776, and Washington pulled back along Morningside Heights to await developments. The following day, September 16, he ordered Knowlton to reconnoiter British positions at nearby Harlem Heights and possibly envelop a forward detachment of the 42nd Highlanders. Knowlton advanced bravely as ordered but, unfortunately, he attacked prematurely and hit the British flank by mistake. The Americans then pursued the fleeing enemy vigorously until they rallied behind a stone wall; Knowlton was killed in the act of urging his men on. Given his talent for commanding light infantry and the high esteem in which he was held, Knowlton's death was a genuine loss to the army. His elite unit, informally called "Congress's Own," was subsequently captured at the fall of Fort Washington the following November.

Further Reading
Callahan, North. *Connecticut's Revolutionary War Leaders.* Chester, Conn.: Pequot Press, 1973.
Coffin, Charles. *The Lives and Services of Major General John Thomas, Colonel Thomas Knowlton, Colonel Alexander Scammell, and Major General Henry Dearborn.* New York: Egbert, Hovey & King, 1845.
Cohen, Sheldon S. "The Death of Colonel Thomas Knowlton," *Connecticut Historical Society Bulletin* 30, no. 2 (1965): 50–57.
De Martino, Francis. "Colonel Francis Knowlton." Unpublished bachelor's thesis, St. Francis College, 1971.
Perley, Sidney. "Colonel Thomas Knowlton," *Essex Institute Historical Collections* 58 (April 1922): 89–100.
Woodward, Ashbel. *Memoir of Col. Thomas Knowlton of Ashford, Connecticut.* Boston: H. W. Dutton, 1861.

Knox, Henry (1750–1806)
American military officer

Henry Knox was born in Boston, Massachusetts, on July 25, 1750, the son of a shipwright. His father died when he was 12, forcing him to work in a bookstore and support his family. Knox, a huge, jovial man, over six feet tall and weighing over 300 pounds, opened his own bookstore in 1771 and catered exclusively to British army officers. He also developed an appetite for military literature, with a special interest in artillery. Knox remained indifferent to politics until the BOSTON MASSACRE of December 1770, after which he joined a local militia unit, the Boston Grenadier Corps. He did so despite the loss of two fingers in a hunting accident. When the Revolutionary War broke out in April 1775, Knox volunteered his services to General Artemas WARD and saw fighting at BUNKER HILL. He then struck up a deep and abiding friendship with General George WASHINGTON during the siege of Boston, and Washington influenced the Continental CONGRESS to secure him an appointment as colonel of the Continental Artillery Regiment. In this capacity, Knox was ordered to visit Fort Ticonderoga in December 1775 and retrieve the 59 British cannon seized there by Colonel Ethan ALLEN. Knox not only secured the cannon and transported them 300 miles in the dead of winter with a train of oxen, he also subsequently sighted them on Dorchester Heights the following March. This development convinced General William HOWE to evacuate Boston completely on March 17, 1776. For helping orchestrate this impressive American victory, Knox thereafter served as one of Washington's closest military and personal confidants.

Knox was soon regarded as the Continental ARMY's foremost authority on artillery. His cannon served with distinction at the Battles of LONG ISLAND, TRENTON, and PRINCETON, winning him applause from Washington and promotion to brigadier general. His performance at Trenton was particularly brilliant in so much as he organized the passage of Washington's army across the ice-choked Delaware River in concert with Colonel John GLOVER. In 1777 Knox's cannon further distinguished itself at BRANDYWINE and GERMANTOWN, and again the following year at MONMOUTH, all to the acclaim of his commander in chief. He was also responsible for establishing the famous Springfield Arsenal in Massachusetts, and the Artillery Academy at Morristown, Pennsylvania, a precursor to the U.S. Military Academy at West Point. The high point of Knox's military career transpired during the siege of YORKTOWN, where his well-handled artillery pounded the army of General Charles CORNWALLIS into submission by October 17, 1781. At this juncture Washington freely admitted that "the resources of his genius supplied the deficit of his means" and recommended his promotion to major general. Congress willingly complied, and on November 15, 1781, Knox—at age 31—became the youngest ranking officer in his grade. As the war wound down, Knox received command of strategic West

Point in the New York Highlands, where he cordially entertained a distinguished prisoner, Major Johann EWALD of the Hessian jaegers. Knox then led American forces that occupied New York City after the British finally withdrew. When Washington retired and bid his officers a tearful good-bye at Fraunces Tavern on December 4, 1783, Knox was the first to shake his hand in farewell. He then became acting commander in chief until Congress finally disbanded the army the following spring.

Unlike many contemporaries, Knox remained extremely active in military matters long after the Revolutionary War ended. In 1785 he succeeded General Benjamin LINCOLN as secretary of war under the ARTICLES OF CONFEDERATION, and he helped to found the Order of the Cincinnati, a political organization consisting of former army officers. He also took steps to contain militarily the outbreak of Shays's Rebellion in western Massachusetts in 1787, which stimulated calls for more centralized government. Knox openly endorsed ratification of the new federal constitution in 1789 and continued on as secretary of war under President Washington. In this capacity he dispatched Generals Arthur ST. CLAIR and Anthony WAYNE in various wars against the Northwest Indians, 1791–94, and also laid foundations for the new United States Navy. Knox remained cognizant of the nation's weakness and proposed a scheme for universal military training, but Congress was willing to adopt only a watered-down version, the Militia Act of 1792. This was a pale and generally inept imitation of his original plan and did little to enhance national preparedness. Knox finally resigned from office in December 1794 after Secretary of the Treasury Alexander HAMILTON tried usurping the functions of his office. He died at Thomaston, Maine (then part of Massachusetts), on October 25, 1806, one of the Revolution's outstanding senior leaders. Knox is also revered as father of the American artillery service.

Further Reading

Brooks, Victor. *The Boston Campaign: April 1775–March 1776.* Conshohocken, Pa.: Combined Pub., 1999.

Carter, Michael D. "Nation Building and the Military: The Life and Career of Secretary of War Henry Knox." Unpublished Ph.D. diss., West Virginia University, 1997.

Griffiths, Thomas M. *Major General Henry Knox and the Last Heirs to Montpelier.* Monmouth, Maine: Monmouth Press, 1991.

Lonergan, Thomas J. *Henry Knox: George Washington's Confidant, General of Artillery, and America's First Secretary of War.* Rockport, Maine: Picton Press, 2003.

Ranzan, David. " 'Thus a War Has Begun': The Capture of Fort Ticonderoga and Its Influence on the American Revolution." Unpublished Ph.D. diss., East Stroudsburg University, 2002.

Thompson, John M. "Citizens and Soldiers: Henry Knox and the Development of American Military Thought and Practice." Unpublished Ph.D. diss., University of North Carolina at Chapel Hill, 2000.

American Henry Knox transported the cannon that forced the British evacuation of Boston. *(Independence National Historical Park)*

Knyphausen, Wilhelm von (1716–1800)
Hessian military officer

Wilhelm von Knyphausen was born in Lutzburg, Hanover, on November 4, 1716, the son of an army officer. After studying at the Berlin Gymnasium, he entered the Prussian service in 1734 and rose steadily through the ranks due to ability. Knyphausen was a lieutenant colonel by the time he transferred his services to Friedrich II, landgrave of Hesse-Kassel, in 1763. He had acquired a reputation as a capable combat officer but also as a grim, humorless individual who projected a somewhat grave demeanor. Knyphausen was also something of an eccentric, much given to buttering bread with his thumb. After the Revolutionary War commenced in April 1775, King GEORGE III negotiated with Friedrich II and other German princes to hire thousands of German auxiliaries, known collectively as HESSIANS.

In the spring of 1776 Knyphausen assumed command of the Second Division from Hesse-Kassel and arrived at New York on October 18 with 4,000 troops as part of a larger British force commanded by General William HOWE. There he also joined the First Division under Lieutenant General Leopold von HEISTER, his nominal superior. At this time, the Americans under General George WASHINGTON had been all but driven from New York City save for a large dirt fortification called Fort Washington on the northern tip of the island. On November 16, 1776, it fell upon Knyphausen to storm this strongly fortified position. With one assault column under Colonel Johann RALL and the other directed by himself, he led his Hessians up the slopes in the face of heavy rifle and cannon fire. Many Germans were shot down, and Knyphausen exposed himself recklessly before a second British force under Colonel Hugh PERCY came up to assist. At this juncture the Americans under Colonel Robert Magraw surrendered to Knyphausen, who then calmly lit his pipe and watched quietly as the captives filed out. The Hessians sustained 58 killed and 202 wounded, but they captured 2,800 prisoners; Howe was so impressed by his performance that he renamed the captured post Fort Knyphausen in his honor.

Knyphausen remained in New York during the wintertime pursuit of Washington's force through New Jersey, which culminated in the surprise American victory at TRENTON on December 26, 1776, and the annihilation of Rall's detachment. General Howe used the disaster as a convenient pretext for General Heister's removal, and in July 1777 Knyphausen became the senior Hessian commander in America. In this capacity he bore a conspicuous role in the British victory at BRANDYWINE on October 10, 1777, by pinning Washington's force frontally while General Charles CORNWALLIS outflanked it. He also stridently enforced discipline and prevented his troops from committing atrocities or plundering the citizenry. He spent the winter at Philadelphia in the former house of General John Cadwalader and, when the British abandoned the city the following August, he compensated his host by paying rent for the time involved. As the British under General Henry CLINTON withdrew back to New York, Knyphausen commanded the baggage train and was not seriously engaged at MONMOUTH. Clinton apparently liked and trusted his Hessian consort, and he became one of the few foreign officers invited to attend high-level strategy sessions. When Clinton departed New York for his expedition against Charleston, South Carolina, in December 1779, Knyphausen succeeded him as commander of the entire New York region. He remained the only Hessian officer so honored during the war.

During Clinton's absence, Knyphausen was informed that Washington's army in neighboring New Jersey was beset by mutinies, and he decided to attack while they were still demoralized. In June 1780 he advanced with 6,000 men as far as Connecticut Farms, where he encountered swarms of angry militiamen and withdrew. A few weeks later Knyphausen attacked again at Springfield and met with another bloody repulse at the hands of General Nathanael GREENE. Thereafter, the elderly general was increasingly beset by health problems, and in May 1782 he sailed back to Germany; his replacement was the next senior German, Friedrich von Lossberg. Knyphausen was honored by Friedrich II for his services with an appointment as military governor of Kassel. He died while serving in this capacity on December 7, 1800, a consummate professional soldier and one of the few foreigners trusted by the British high command.

Further Reading

Andrews, Melodie. "Myrmidons from Abroad: The Role of the German Mercenary in the Coming of Independence." Unpublished Ph.D. diss., University of Houston, 1986.

Atwood, Rodney. *The Hessians: Mercenaries from Hesse-Kassel in the American Revolution.* New York: Cambridge University Press, 1980.

Deary, William P. "Toward a Disaster at Fort Washington, November, 1776." Unpublished Ph.D. diss., George Washington University, 1996.

Fleming, Thomas. *The Battle of Springfield.* Trenton: New Jersey Historical Society, 1975.

Stephens, Thomas R. "In Deepest Submission: The Hessian Mercenary Troops of the American Revolution." Unpublished Ph.D. diss., Texas A & M University, 1998.

"Wilhelm, Baron Innhausen and Knyphausen," *Pennsylvania Magazine of History and Biography* 16 (1892): 239–245.

Kościuszko, Tadeusz (1746–1817)
Polish military officer

Tadeusz Kościuszko was born in Mereczowsczyna, Poland (now Lithuania), on February 4, 1746, son of an army officer and part of the minor gentry. Orphaned at a young age, he attended the Royal Military School in Warsaw and eventually taught there with a rank of captain. In 1769 he was dispatched to study engineering and artillery at the Ecole Militaire in Paris, France, and returned home in 1774. Poland at that time had suffered the first of what would be three partitions by Prussia, Austria, and Russia, and its army was almost disbanded. Kościuszko concluded he had no future there and returned to Paris to study painting. He eventually learned of the ongoing revolution in America, which stoked his sense of adventure.

Kościuszko borrowed money from his brother and arrived by ship in Philadelphia on August 30, 1776, and introduced himself to members of the Continental CONGRESS. Having applied for an officer's commission, he then tendered his services to the state of Pennsylvania and found employment building fortifications along the nearby Delaware River. Congress then appointed him a colonel of engineers on October 18, 1776, and ordered him to join the Northern Department under General Philip J. SCHUYLER. Kościuszko subsequently made recommendations for strengthening the hills around Fort Ticonderoga, which were ignored. Consequently, when the army of General John BURGOYNE arrived at the fort in July 1777, it was hastily abandoned by the Americans. Kościuszko then joined the staff of newly arrived general Horatio GATES and helped select the battlefield at nearby Saratoga. He was specifically entrusted

Polish officer Tadeusz Kościuszko was appointed colonel of engineers by the Continental Congress. *(Independence National Historical Park)*

with constructing earthworks and fortifications in the vicinity of BEMIS HEIGHTS, where Burgoyne was ultimately defeated and surrendered that October.

In 1778 Kościuszko was next employed in strengthening the defenses in and around strategic West Point, New York. Two years later Gates transferred as commander of the Southern Department and invited him to join his staff. The young engineer readily complied, although he arrived after the disaster at CAMDEN, which resulted in Gates's dismissal. He then served under General Nathanael GREENE and proved instrumental in designing and constructing special flat-bottomed wagons that doubled as small boats. In this manner the hurriedly retreating Americans managed to cross the Dan River into Virginia ahead of pursuing British forces under General Charles CORNWALLIS. Kościuszko's next major task was besieging Fort Ninety Six in the South Carolina backwoods in May–June of 1781. Here he was criticized by others for failing to cut off the defender's water supply and for placing his initial earthworks so close to the fort that they were damaged by sorties. Throughout the rest of 1782 Kościuszko conducted intelligence-gathering missions near Charleston and also served as a cavalry officer. In October 1783 Congress rewarded him with promotion to brigadier general and American citizenship. He also became a founding member of the Society of the Cincinnati.

Kościuszko returned to Poland in 1784, after the second partitioning, and emerged as a leading figure in the drive for independence. As a lieutenant general he repulsed several Russian armies before being defeated in 1792. He returned two years later and fought in an abortive uprising against Russia and composed the "Act of Insurrection," based upon principles first espoused in the DECLARATION OF INDEPENDENCE. Kościuszko then fought furiously against the combined might of Prussia and Russia but was wounded in battle and imprisoned. He was allowed to leave Russia in 1797 and visit the United States to a hero's welcome. Congress then voted him $20,000 in back pay and a land grant of 500 acres in Ohio. Kościuszko also befriended Thomas JEFFERSON, and the two remained correspondents for life. He resettled at Paris in 1798 to write several treatises on horse artillery and engineering. Kościuszko was approached several times by Emperor Napoléon for military service, but he refused to serve unless the object was a free and independent Poland. One of his last acts was to authorize Congress to sell off his Ohio lands and invest the proceeds in a school for AFRICAN AMERICANS at Newark, New Jersey. He died in Solothurn, Switzerland, on October 15, 1817, a hero on two continents.

Further Reading
Froneck, Thomas. "Kosciusko," *American Heritage* 26, no. 4 (1975): 4–11, 78–81.
Kajencki, Francis C. "Kościuszko's Role in the Siege of Ninety-Six," *Polish American Studies* 54, no. 2 (1997): 9–22.
Kyte, George W. "Thaddeus Kosciuszko at the Liberation of Charleston," *South Carolina Historical Magazine* 84 (January 1983): 11–21.
Pula, James S. *Engineering American Independence: Tadeusz Kosciuszko's Role in the Northern Campaign.* New Britain: Polish Studies Program, Central Connecticut State University, 2000.
———. *Thaddeus Kosciuszko: The Purest Son of Liberty.* New York: Hippocrene Books, 1999.
Walker, Paul K. *Engineers of Independence: A Documentary History of the Army Engineers in the American Revolution, 1775–1783.* Washington, D.C.: Office of the Chief of Engineers, 1981.

Lacey, John (1755–1814)
American militia officer

John Lacey was born in Bucks County, Pennsylvania, on February 4, 1755, the son of Quaker parents. Despite his religious upbringing he displayed an interest in military affairs and was eventually expelled from the movement. In January 1776 he was commissioned a captain of the Bucks County militia, which subsequently became the 4th Pennsylvania Continental Infantry under Colonel Anthony WAYNE. Lacey accompanied Wayne throughout the rigors of the Canadian campaign before returning home that December. The following spring he reemerged as a sub-lieutenant tasked with organizing men and supplies throughout Bucks County. Lacey performed well in these limited tasks and on May 6, 1777, he became a lieutenant colonel of militia. In January 1778 Lacey was promoted to brigadier general at the age of 23, making him one of the youngest leaders on the American side. He also received a battalion of 450 men and was tasked with harassing the flow of supplies in and out of British-held Philadelphia.

On May 1, 1778, Lacey occupied an advanced post at Crooked Billet, about 15 miles northeast of the city. Sickness, desertion, and expiring enlistments had reduced his command to a mere 60 men, a fact that the British did not fail to notice. The night before, Lieutenant Colonel Robert Abercromby was dispatched with 400 soldiers to pin Lacey frontally at Crooked Billet while an additional 300 rangers under Lieutenant Colonel John Graves SIMCOE slipped up behind him. Lacey was almost completely surrounded before the first shot was fired, but he managed to retreat with the bulk of his men into a nearby woods and escaped annihilation. The Americans lost 26 killed and nine wounded, along with all their baggage, to a British tally of nine injured. This was the largest military action in Lacey's career, and on May 11 he resigned his commission and returned to Bucks County. In 1780 and 1781 he briefly resumed his militia activities at the behest of local authorities and commanded a brigade, but saw no further action. Concurrent with his militia activities, Lacey turned to politics and was elected to the state assembly in 1778 and the supreme executive council the following year. In 1782 he relocated his family to New Mills, New Jersey, to engage in manufacturing. While there he also served as justice of the peace and won a new seat in the state assembly. He died at New Mills on February 17, 1814, an earnest if ineffectual militia leader.

Further Reading
Copeland, Peter F. "Clothing of the 4th Pennsylvania Battalion, 1776–1777," *Military Collector and Historian* 18, no. 3 (1966): 69–74.

Davis, William W. H. *Sketch of the Life and Character of John Lacey, a Brigadier General in the Revolutionary Army.* Doylestown, Pa.: Privately Printed, 1868.

Heathcote, Charles W. "The Battle of Crooked Billet," *Daughters of the American Revolution Magazine* 86 (October 1952): 1,023–1,027.

Lacey, John. "Memoirs of Brigadier General John Lacey of Pennsylvania," *Pennsylvania Magazine of History and Biography* 25 (1901): 1–13, 191–207, 341–354, 498–515; 26 (1902): 101–111, 265–270.

Radbill, Kenneth A. "Quaker Patriots: The Leadership of Owen Biddle and John Lacey, Jr.," *Pennsylvania History* 45, no. 1 (1978): 47–60.

Zanine, Louis J. "Brigadier General John Lacey and the Pennsylvania Militia in 1778," *Pennsylvania History* 48, no. 2 (1981): 129–142.

Lafayette, James (ca. 1748–1830)

African-American slave, spy

James Armistead was born a slave around 1748, probably in New Kent County, Virginia. His surname originated with his owner William Armistead, who worked in Richmond during the Revolutionary War as a commissary of supplies. In the summer of 1781 an American army under the marquis de LAFAYETTE had partially garrisoned the state to thwart its conquest by British forces under General Charles CORNWALLIS. The Americans at that time sought better military intelligence to keep abreast of British intentions, so Lafayette issued a call for spies. Armistead then volunteered his services, with his master's permission, and apparently in the mistaken belief that, if successful, he would obtain his freedom. By July 1781 he had crossed over to the British camp at Portsmouth to work as a forager and his presence, constantly passing through the lines, raised little suspicion. Over the ensuing weeks Armistead was able to apprise Lafayette that the British were intending to depart Portsmouth by ship. The following August he brought back valuable information that Cornwallis was fortifying himself on the YORKTOWN Peninsula. Armistead was also willing to serve as a double agent and allowed himself to be "recruited" by the British to spy on their adversaries. In concert with Lafayette, he fed them steady streams of disinformation that made the American army appear heavily reinforced, when in fact it was quite weak. The strategic value of Armistead's efforts was seen that fall when the armies of General George WASHINGTON and Jean-Baptiste, comte de ROCHAMBEAU suddenly descended upon Yorktown, ensnaring Cornwallis there and forcing him to surrender on October 17, 1781. Afterward, when Cornwallis paid a courtesy call upon Lafayette's headquarters, he was somewhat surprised to see Armistead there.

For all his useful service to the nation, Armistead was not released from bondage but returned to his owner's household as a slave. In 1786, however, William Armistead supported his slave's petition to the legislature for manumission. Central to his plea was a letter written by Lafayette himself, in which he attributed Armistead with "essential services" during the war. Consequently, the legislature voted James Armistead his freedom while compensating William Armistead for the loss. Armistead, finally a free man, took the surname Lafayette in honor of his benefactor. In 1816, being older and in poor health, Lafayette petitioned the legislature for an annuity, and he received a small pension of $40 per year. Moreover, when the marquis de Lafayette returned to America in 1824 on his triumphal visit, James Lafayette was on hand to greet him at Yorktown and was joyously received. He died on his farm in New Kent County on August 9, 1830, one of the hundreds of AFRICAN-AMERICAN Patriots who obtained freedom in exchange for conspicuous service to the nation.

Further Reading

Fehrenbacher, Don E. *The Slaveholding Republic: An Account of the United States Government's Relations to Slavery.* New York: Oxford University Press, 2001.

Kaplan, Sydney, and Emma N. Kaplan. *The Black Presence in the Era of the American Revolution.* Amherst: University of Massachusetts Press, 1989.

Mahoney, Harry T. *Gallantry in Action: A Biographic Dictionary of Espionage in the American Revolutionary War.* Lanham, Md.: University Press of America, 1999.

Nell, William C. *The Colored Patriots of the American Revolution.* Salem, N.H.: Ayer Co., 1986.

Salmon, John. "A Mission of the Most Secret and Important Kind: James Lafayette and American Espionage in 1781," *Virginia Cavalcade* 31, no. 2 (1981): 78–85.

Lafayette, marquis de (La Fayette) (1757–1834)

French military officer

Marie-Joseph-Paul-Yves-Roch-Gilbert du Motier, marquis de La Fayette (or Lafayette) was born at Chavaniac, France, on September 6, 1757, into one of France's most distinguished aristocratic families. Orphaned at an early age, he inherited his family's fortune and joined the French army at the age of 13. Six years later he married into the influential Noailles family, which cemented his future to the inner circles of royal power and ensured him the leisurely life of a wealthy nobleman. He was commissioned a captain of dragoons in 1776, the same year in which he became aware of the Revolutionary War. Young and idealistic, Lafayette thrilled to the principles underscoring the DECLARATION OF INDEPENDENCE, and he sought to strike a personal blow for liberty in the New World—and possibly the Old. He approached Silas DEANE, the American agent in Paris, about the possibility of fighting for America and received a general's commission in the Continental ARMY. When his family refused to condone this decision, Lafayette chartered a boat in SPAIN at his own expense and was subsequently declared an outlaw by King Louis XVI. He nonetheless arrived at Charleston, South Carolina, in 1777, accompanied by his friend and mentor, Baron Johann de KALB. The 19-year-old Lafayette, while lacking military experience, approached the Continental CONGRESS for his promised commission and—after some dithering—it appointed him a major general, although without a specific command. In this capacity the youthful aristocrat joined the army of General George WASHINGTON, who was favorably impressed by his enthusiasm and martial bearing.

Lafayette first fought at BRANDYWINE in September 1777, receiving a leg wound and compliments for his bravery. On November 27, 1777, he led a detachment of 300 infantry at Gloucester, New Jersey, and defeated a larger body of HESSIANS

Marquis de Lafayette was declared an outlaw by King Louis XVI for his decision to join the Continental army as a general. *(Independence National Historical Park)*

in a heavy skirmish. Lafayette then accompanied the army into harsh winter quarters at Valley Forge, 1777–78, where he stoically endured the deprivation and won more of Washington's trust. The following spring he was dispatched with a larger command to the vicinity of Barren Hills, Pennsylvania, to watch British movements in and out of Philadelphia. British general William HOWE, wishing to snare the "boy general" as a going-away gift before departing for England, arranged a clever ambush. However, Lafayette saw through the ruse on May 28, 1778, and quickly bluffed General James GRANT into assuming defensive positions while he escaped intact. Washington responded to such incisive leadership with a division of light troops that Lafayette jointly commanded with General Charles LEE at Monmouth on June 28, 1778. He then led two brigades and accompanied General John SULLIVAN during the ill-fated expedition to Rhode Island that summer and unsuccessfully pleaded with France's Admiral Charles-Hector-Théodat, comte d'ESTAING, for greater cooperation. In January 1779 he requested and received a furlough to return to France and push for wider French involvement in the war.

Lafayette was initially arrested after landing on French soil, but the king pardoned him and promoted him to colonel. He also successfully convinced his monarch to commit greater resources to the American war effort and rejoined Washington in April 1780 with news of General Jean-Baptiste, comte de ROCHAMBEAU's impending arrival. The following summer he was dispatched to Virginia to reinforce and command American forces there under General Friedrich von STEUBEN. Lafayette spent several weeks sparring with British forces under General Charles CORNWALLIS, who made several unsuccessful attempts to overwhelm his youthful opponent. His finest moment as a general came at Green Spring on July 6, 1781, where quick intervention saved the advance guard of General Anthony WAYNE. Tipped off by AFRICAN-AMERICAN spy James LAFAYETTE, the young marquis carefully shadowed Cornwallis to YORKTOWN and helped seal him in his works. Once Washington and Rochambeau suddenly came down from New York to invest the peninsula, the British were forced to surrender on October 17, 1781. Lafayette commanded a light division throughout the siege and then made a final, goodwill tour of the nation before returning home in December 1781.

Lafayette was thoroughly imbued with a new sense of republicanism, and he championed social and political reform. The French Revolution of 1789 seemed to embrace these changes initially but quickly descended into an orgy of violence. Lafayette, commanding the National Guard, was forced to flee, and he was imprisoned by Austria until 1797. Freed by forces of Napoléon, he returned to France in 1800 a private citizen and distanced himself from the emperor. Once Napoléon was deposed in 1815, he resumed his crusade for democracy and liberty while serving in the Chamber of Deputies. In 1824 Lafayette conducted a final tour of the United States and was greeted with thunderous applause from a grateful nation. Back home he continued functioning as an outspoken champion of freedom until his death in Paris on May 20, 1834. Lafayette remains an enduring symbol of friendship between the two nations and is, quite appropriately, a hero on two continents.

Further Reading
Barra, Allen. "French Hero of the American Revolution," *American Heritage* 51, no. 3 (2000): 62–65.
Idzerda, Stanley J., ed. *Lafayette in the Age of the American Revolution: Selected Letters and Papers, 1776–1790,* 5 vols. Ithaca, N.Y.: Cornell University Press, 1977–83.
Kramer, Lloyd S. *Lafayette in Two Worlds: Public Culture and Personal Identities in an Age of Revolutions.* Chapel Hill: University of North Carolina Press, 1996.
Lane, Jason. *General and Madam de Lafayette: Partners in Liberty's Cause in the American and French Revolutions.* Lanham, Md.: Taylor Trade, 2003.
Poirier, Noel B. "Young General Lafayette," *MHQ* 12, no. 2 (2000): 32–41.
Unger, Harlow G. *Lafayette.* New York: Wiley, 2002.

Lamb, John (1735–1800)
American military officer

John Lamb was born in New York City on January 1, 1735, the son of a prosperous optician. He established himself as a merchant and liquor dealer by the time of the STAMP ACT of 1765, after which he became closely identified with anti-British organizations. Lamb also joined Alexander MCDOUGALL as one of the most active leaders of the New York SONS OF LIBERTY, in which he headed the COMMITTEE OF CORRESPONDENCE. Besides being a gifted orator and pamphleteer, Lamb was raucously disposed by nature and led numerous riots against stamp officials. He and his minions also intimidated local merchants into complying with the colonial practice of nonimportation. In 1767 Lamb orchestrated oftentimes violent protests against New York assembly members for compliance with provisions of the QUARTERING ACT of 1765. Arrested and charged with libel, he was eventually released and actively participated in protests arising from the TEA ACT and the COERCIVE ACTS in Boston. After fighting erupted at Lexington and CONCORD, Lamb organized raids of British depots at Turtle Bay in concert with Marinus WILLETT and prevented arms from leaving the city. On June 30, 1775, the provincial assembly appointed him captain of an artillery company, and he marched his guns north to join the army of General Richard MONTGOMERY in Canada.

Despite a well-deserved reputation for belligerence, Lamb proved himself to be an active and enterprising officer. He was present at the siege and capture of Saint Johns, Quebec, in November 1775 and subsequently assisted in the capture of Montreal a few days later. He then accompanied Montgomery on the march to Quebec City and joined forces there with Colonel Benedict ARNOLD. Lamb established a small siege battery to awe the defenders into submission, but his 12-pound cannon were completely overpowered by larger British ordnance defending the city. On December 31, 1775, Lamb participated in the ill-fated Attack on QUEBEC in which he was severely injured by grapeshot and captured. He lost his left eye but returned to active duty after being exchanged in August 1776. Lamb, now a colonel, was residing with his family at Stratford, Connecticut, when Governor William TRYON attacked nearby Danbury. Lamb energetically directed several pieces at Compo Hill on April 28, 1777, where he again sustained secere injuries. After recovering, Lamb reported for duty under General George CLINTON and was posted at Fort Clinton on the Hudson River. This post was attacked by General Henry CLINTON on October 5, 1777, and Lamb again distinguished himself by being virtually the last officer to spike his guns before the post was overrun.

Commencing in 1779 Lamb was appointed commander of artillery at West Point, New York, under General Arnold. In this capacity he openly questioned the latter's tendency to methodically reduce the garrison there, unaware of Arnold's impending treason. By 1781 he was the second-most senior artillerist next to General Henry KNOX and was allowed to command the bulk of American artillery during the siege of YORKTOWN. Lamb commanded over 100 field guns and orchestrated a devastating bombardment of British siege works there, prompting the surrender of General Charles CORNWALLIS on October 17, 1781. He mustered out of the Continental ARMY on September 30, 1783, with a rank of brigadier general.

Lamb resumed his interest in politics when he gained a seat in the New York assembly in December 1783. There he stridently opposed repatriating LOYALISTS or returning their property. The following year Governor Clinton appointed him collector of the port of New York, a significant sinecure. Up through 1788 Lamb also served as a vocal anti-Federalist by opposing ratification of the new federal constitution—and his house was nearly stormed by protesters. In August 1789 President George WASHINGTON reappointed Lamb collector, and he also served as vice president of the state's Society of the Cincinnati under Friedrich von STEUBEN. However, when a dishonest clerk embezzled money from the collector's office, Lamb was forced to sell off his property to cover missing funds. After 1797 he spent the rest of his life in relative poverty. Lamb died in New York on May 31, 1800, an irritable individual but an outstanding artillery officer.

Further Reading

Champagne, Roger J. "New York's Radicals and the Coming of Independence," *Journal of American History* 51, no. 1 (1964): 21–40.

Leake, John Q. *Memoir of the Life and Times of General John Lamb.* New York: Da Capo Press, 1971.

Ranlet, Philip. "The Two John Lambs of the Revolutionary Generation," *American Neptune* 42, no. 4 (1982): 301–305.

Shannon, Dennis M. " 'Restless Genius': John Lamb and Revolutionary New York." Unpublished Ph.D. Diss., University of California, Berkeley, 1994.

Sims, Lynn Lee. "The Military Career of John Lamb." Unpublished Ph.D. diss., New York University, 1975.

Laurens, Henry (1724–1792)
American politician

Henry Laurens was born in South Carolina on February 24, 1724, the son of a prosperous merchant. After being relatively well educated at home he sailed for England in 1744 and served three years in a countinghouse. By dint of hard work, Laurens went on to become one of South Carolina's wealthiest merchants and expanded his holdings into plantations and the rice trade. He was politically conservative by nature, but deteriorating relations between Great Britain and the colonies forced him gradually into the Patriot camp. During the STAMP ACT of 1765 his home was ransacked by radicals looking for stamped paper products; after the TOWNSHEND DUTIES of 1767 were enacted, three of Laurens's trading vessels were seized by customs officials. He retaliated by publishing extensively on the illegality of British trade practices but distanced himself from calls for violence or independence. Laurens again visited England in 1771 to supervise the education of his sons but railed against what he perceived as the corruption of English society. He returned home three years later completely committed to the cause of independence, although still on comparatively conservative terms. In 1775 Laurens commenced his political career by winning a seat in the extralegal first provincial congress, in which he later served as president. He also functioned as head of the committee of safety and helped to draft the new state constitution. Ever mindful of property rights, Laurens insisted on protecting the holdings of LOYALISTS and sparked the ire of more-radical elements under William Henry DRAYTON and Christopher GADSDEN.

In June 1777 Lauren was elected to the Second Continental Congress in Philadelphia and, the following November, he succeeded John HANCOCK as president. Over the following year he managed to usher important legislation through that fractious body, including the ARTICLES OF CONFEDERATION and the FRENCH ALLIANCE. However respected, Laurens revealed himself a stubborn individual with a prickly sense of honor who constantly inveighed against what he considered corrupt practices by other delegates. At one point he demanded a congressional investigation of financier Robert MORRIS, whose influence further eroded Laurens's popularity. He also became enmeshed in the contretemps surrounding Silas DEANE and finally resigned as president on December 9, 1778, in favor of John JAY. Laurens remained in Congress another year when he was nominated a commissioner to the Netherlands. He sailed from Philadelphia in August 1780, but his ship was captured off Newfoundland by the Royal Navy a month later. Laurens threw all his official dispatches overboard, but these were subsequently recovered and revealed the extent of Dutch assistance to America; the papers served as a convenient pretext for a declaration of war against Holland. British officials then charged Laurens with treason, rendered him a state prisoner, and harshly imprisoned him in the infamous Tower of London. Moreover, the government refused his claims of diplomatic immunity, denied him adequate food and medical attention, and his health suffered commensurately. In April 1782 Laurens was finally exchanged for General Charles CORNWALLIS and ordered to Paris as a peace commissioner. There he joined Benjamin FRANKLIN, John ADAMS, and John Jay during preliminary talks leading to the TREATY OF PARIS. Laurens himself did not sign the treaty, having returned to England to discuss business matters. He remained there two years as unofficial ambassador before returning to South Carolina in January 1785.

Once home Laurens labored to restore his business fortunes, which had suffered heavily during the war and British occupation. His health ailing, he refused all overtures to return to public life, despite being elected a delegate to the Constitutional Convention in 1788. He also remained severely depressed over the death of his son John LAURENS in 1782. Laurens died in Charleston on December 8, 1792, one of South Carolina's most important figures during its transition from colony to statehood.

Further Reading

Chestnutt, David R., Philip M. Hamer, and C. James Taylor, eds. *The Papers of Henry Laurens,* 16 vols. Columbia: University of South Carolina Press, 1968–2003.

Gudzune, Jeffrey R. "Crisis Manager of the American Revolution: Henry Laurens." Unpublished master's thesis, West Virginia University, 2005.

Hoffman, Ronald, and Peter J. Albert. *Peace and Peacemakers: The Treaty of 1783.* Charlottesville: Published for the United States Capitol Historical Society by the University Press of Virginia, 1986.

Hurt, John P. A. "The Epitome of Revolutionary Nationalism: The Politics of Henry Laurens, 1757–1779." Unpublished master's thesis, University of Missouri, St. Louis, 1993.

Kirschke, James J., and Victor J. Sensenig. "Steps Toward Nationhood: Henry Laurens (1724–92) and the American Revolution in the South," *Historical Research* 78, no. 200 (2005): 180–192.

McDonough, Daniel J. *Christopher Gadsden and Henry Laurens: The Parallel Lives of Two American Patriots.* Selinsgrove, Pa.: Susquehanna University Press, 2000.

Laurens, John (1754–1782)
American military officer

John Laurens was born in Charleston, South Carolina, on October 28, 1754, a son of noted planter Henry LAURENS. His father's wealth enabled him to be educated in England and Geneva, Switzerland, where he acquired fluency in French. Laurens returned home in 1777, when the Revolutionary War was in full swing and, with his father's influence, he secured a position as volunteer aide-de-camp to General George WASHINGTON. In this capacity Laurens fought bravely at BRANDYWINE and GERMANTOWN in 1777 and at MONMOUTH in 1778, being wounded in the latter two engagements. Understandably, he was quite loyal to his commander and dueled with General Charles LEE over disparaging remarks he made about Washington. Laurens was also unique in proposing that southern states recruit up to 3,000 AFRICAN AMERICANS and offer them freedom in exchange for military service. His radical proposal was summarily rejected by various state legislatures but proved far ahead of its time. In August 1778 he accompanied General John SULLIVAN on the ill-fated expedition against Rhode Island, where he served an as a liaison to the French fleet under Admiral Charles-Hector-Théodat, comte d'ESTAING. In 1779 the Continental CONGRESS tendered Laurens a lieutenant colonel's commission, and he again served on Washington's staff. That fall Laurens ventured south to Georgia to partake of the unsuccessful attack upon SAVANNAH. In the spring of 1780 he subsequently formed part of the garrison during the siege of CHARLESTON and was captured there along with General Benjamin LINCOLN on May 12, 1780.

After being exchanged, Laurens was dispatched to Paris in the spring of 1781, where he became secretary to Benjamin FRANKLIN. In this capacity he rather brazenly bypassed France's foreign minister, Charles Gravier, comte de VERGENNES, and appealed directly to King Louis XVI for help in securing a $10 million loan from the Netherlands. He succeeded and subsequently transported over $2 million of this grand total back home, receiving the thanks of Congress in consequence. He rejoined Washington's army at YORKTOWN, where, on October 14, 1781, he accompanied Colonel Alexander HAMILTON during the successful assault on Redoubt No. 10. Laurens then joined the viscount de NOAILLES in negotiating the surrender of General Charles CORNWALLIS. He insisted that the British endure the same harsh terms imposed on the Americans at Charleston in May 1780. Ironically, Cornwallis was also constable of the Tower of London, where Laurens's father was imprisoned. Shortly after, Laurens was elected to the South Carolina state assembly, but he declined to take his seat. Instead, he joined the army of General Nathanael GREENE, then combing the state for isolated British outposts. He was then posted with a light infantry force under Colonel Mordecai GIST and stationed near Charleston to observe British movements. On August 27, 1782, Laurens commanded men at an insignificant skirmish near Combahee Ferry, where he was killed. Given his ability as an officer and his popularity with the troops, Laurens's death was a significant loss.

Further Reading

Higgins, W. Robert, ed. *The Revolutionary War in the South—Power, Conflict, and Leadership.* Durham, N.C.: Duke University Press, 1979.

Laurens, John. *The Correspondence of Colonel John Laurens in the Years 1777–8.* New York: Arno Press, 1969.

Lefkowitz, Arthur S. *George Washington's Indispensable Men: The 32 Aides-de-camp Who Helped American Independence.* Mechanicsburg, Pa.: Stackpole Books, 2003.

Maslowski, Peter. "National Policy and the Use of Black Troops in the Revolution," *South Carolina Historical Magazine* 73, no. 1 (1972): 1–17.

Massey, Gregory D. *John Laurens and the American Revolution.* Columbia: University of South Carolina Press, 2000.

Weir, Robert M. "Portrait of a Hero: John Laurens Loved America, Not Wisely, but Too Well," *American Heritage* 27, no. 3 (1976): 16–19, 86–88.

Lauzun, Armand-Louis de Gontaut, duc de (comte de Biron; duc de Biron)
(1747–1793)

French military officer

Armand-Louis de Gontaut was born in Paris, France, on April 13, 1747, into an ancient aristocratic family with a long tradition of producing distinguished military officers. As a young nobleman, he was commissioned into the French Guards at the age of 13 and had achieved his captaincy by 1767. Lauzun subsequently acquitted himself well during the pacification of Corsica, and on September 1, 1778, he was authorized to raise a legion, or regiment, of foreign volunteers (Volontaires Étranger) for the army with a rank of colonel. This unit became known popularly as Lauzun's Legion, which combined elements of elite hussars (light cavalry) and light infantry. France declared war on England in 1779, and Lauzun (who later became duc de Biron) initially used his troops to subdue the English colony of Senegal. The following year he became part of the larger expedition dispatched to the United States under General Jean-Baptiste Donatien de Vimeur, comte de ROCHAMBEAU, and sailed with two squadrons of cavalry and two companies of infantry. Lauzun disembarked at Newport, Rhode Island, with the bulk of French forces, but his men were bivouacked at nearby Lebanon, Connecticut, for ease of forage. They spent a year in garrison there before accompanying Rochambeau on a march to join General George WASHINGTON at New York. Given the strength of British defenses and the relative weakness of the allies, Lauzun accomplished little beyond a handful of skirmishes.

In August 1781 allied forces under Washington and Rochambeau made a forced march from New York to YORKTOWN, Virginia, to entrap British forces under General Charles CORNWALLIS. Lauzun (then known as the comte de Biron) was detached as a flank guard throughout this transit and subsequently took post outside of Gloucester, Virginia, on the other bank of the York River. There he was tasked with confining the movements of Lieutenant Colonel Banastre TARLETON, who made clear his intention of personally "shaking hands with the duke." On October 3, 1781, Lauzun's cavalry managed to surprise a British foraging expedition, and Tarleton's British Legion galloped up in support. The two officers, immediately recognizing each other, drew sabers and charged, but Tarleton's horse collided with another, and he was thrown off. More British troopers arrived and prevented Lauzun from capturing his adversary, but the French held the field while sustaining three killed and 16 wounded. After Cornwallis's surrender in October, Lauzun was singled out to convey news of the victory back to King Louis XVI. He returned to America in 1782 to assume command of French forces following the departure of General Rochambeau and the following year sailed back with the last of his troops. In consequence of his excellent service, Lauzun gained promotion to major general.

In 1788 Lauzun inherited his uncle's hereditary title of Biron, and the following year he was elected to the Estates General from Quercy. The French Revolution commenced that same year, and he generally voted with the liberal aristocracy. In 1792 Lauzun was promoted to lieutenant general and dispatched to suppress a counterrevolution in the Vendée region of France. On July 11, 1793, however, Lauzun was suddenly arrested and charged with treason. He was executed by guillotine in Paris on December 30, 1793, a dashing and colorful military figure representative of his class.

Further Reading
Biron, Armand-Louis de Gontaut, duc de. *Memoirs of the Duc de Lauzun.* New York: New York Times, 1969.
Maugras, Gaston. *The Duc de Lauzun and the Court of Marie Antoinette.* London: McIlvaine, 1896.
Selig, Robert A. "The Duc de Lauzun and His Legion, Rochambeau's Most Troublesome, Colorful Soldiers," *Colonial Williamsburg* 21, no. 6 (1999–2000): 56–63.
———. *Rochambeau's Cavalry: Lauzun's Legion in Connecticut, 1780–1781.* Hartford: Connecticut Historical Commission, 2000.
Stevens, John A. "The Duke de Lauzun in France and America," *American Historical Magazine* 2 (July, September 1907): 292–298; 343–375.
Whitridge, Arnold. "Two Aristocrats in Rochambeau's Army," *Virginia Quarterly Review* 40, no. 1 (1964): 114–128.

Learned, Ebenezer (1728–1801)
American military officer

Ebenezer Learned was born in Oxford, Massachusetts, on April 28, 1728, the son of a landowner. During the French and Indian War he commanded a ranger company and subsequently rose to become a leading citizen in his town. Throughout the difficulties with England Learned espoused an increasingly radical line, and by 1774 he served in the extralegal provincial congress at Cambridge. When word of fighting at Lexington and CONCORD arrived at Oxford, Learned hastily mustered his company of MINUTEMEN and marched them to Cambridge. There, as part of the greater New England army under General Artemas WARD, he partook of the ensuing siege of Boston. Learned saw no further fighting, but his men did come under fire at Roxbury during the Battle of BUNKER HILL on June 17, 1775. The following June he was elevated to colonel of militia forces and, on January 1, 1776, he became colonel of the 3rd Massachusetts Continental Infantry. It was in this capacity that Learned played a vital role during the British evacuation of Boston. He served as a go-between for Generals George WASHINGTON and William HOWE, whereby the British departed without American interference and left the town intact. On March 17, 1776, Learned personally unbolted the town gates and led the first American detachment into the liberated city. His men then manned whaleboats and patrolled Boston Harbor while ships of the Royal Navy were still in local waters. Two months later declining health necessitated Learned's resignation, and he returned home to recuperate.

On April 2, 1777, Learned was appointed brigadier general by the Continental CONGRESS and assigned to the Northern Department under General Philip J. SCHUYLER. Here he performed useful service by removing supplies from Fort Ticonderoga before it fell to the army of General John BURGOYNE in July. As the defenders fell back around Forts Anne and Edward he also energetically organized American defenses before crossing over the Hudson River to join the main force gathering under General Horatio GATES. In August, Learned volunteered to accompany General Benedict ARNOLD on a forced march to relieve Fort Stanwix; their inexorable approach convinced British forces under Lieutenant Colonel Barry ST. LEGER to abandon their siege. He then hurried back to rejoin Gates at Saratoga just as Burgoyne's army crossed the Hudson River. On September 19, 1777, the British probed American positions at FREEMAN'S FARM and were roundly repulsed. Learned's brigade remained in reserve until the end of the battle and was released in time to rebuff a hand-picked force under General Simon FRASER. On

October 7, 1777, Burgoyne attacked again at BEMIS HEIGHTS with similar results and was almost swept away by Arnold's counterattack. Learned, positioned in the center of the American line, attacked and drove off HESSIAN troops holding the Breyman redoubt, thereby breaking the British right flank. After Burgoyne's surrender on October 7, 1777, Learned accompanied his men on a march to Valley Forge, Pennsylvania, where they endured a difficult winter. However, health problems again mandated his removal and on March 24, 1778, Learned resigned his commission a second time.

For the remainder of his life, Learned was a leading citizen at Oxford and also commenced a career in politics. In 1779 he served with the state constitutional convention, and in 1783 he successfully stood for a seat in the legislature. Learned also opposed the outbreak of Shays's Rebellion in 1786, despite the fact that most of his family were in sympathy with the rebels. He died at Oxford on April 1, 1801, a capable soldier when not sidelined by disabilities.

Further Readings
Daniels, George F. *History of the Town of Oxford, Massachusetts.* Oxford, Mass.: Pub. by the Author, 1892.
Heathcote, Charles W. "General Ebenezer Learned—A Courageous Patriot and Friend of Washington," *Picket Post* no. 59 (February 1958): 4–7, 34–36.
Ketchum, Richard M. *Saratoga: Turning Point of America's Revolutionary War.* New York: Henry Holt, 1997.
Learned, William L. *The Learned Family (Learned, Larned, Learnard and Lerned), Being Descendants of William Learned Who Was of Charlestown, Massachusetts, in 1632.* Albany, N.Y.: J. Munsell's Sons, 1882.
Nelson, Peter. "Learned's Expedition to the Relief of Fort Stanwix," *Quarterly Journal of the New York State Historical Association* 9 (October 1928): 380–385.
Nestor, Joseph B. "The Battle of Saratoga." Unpublished master's thesis, East Stroudsburg University, 2001.

Ledyard, William (1738–1781)
American militia officer

William Ledyard was born in Groton, Connecticut, on December 6, 1738. Little is known of his early life, but by 1775 he had cast his lot with the Patriots and served on the local COMMITTEE OF CORRESPONDENCE. The following year he was commissioned an artillery captain in the Connecticut militia and stationed at Fort Griswold in Groton, on the east bank of the Thames River. This fortification had been authorized by Governor Jonathan Trumbull in November 1775, although by 1781 it was still uncompleted. Still, this imposing work was nestled upon a hilltop rising 120 feet above the nearby river and mounted 22 cannon. Ledyard was by now lieutenant colonel of artillery and tasked with the defense of New London, a notorious haven for American privateers and a logical target for British retaliation. Not surprisingly, on September 6, 1781, an expedition commanded by the now-British general Benedict ARNOLD dropped anchor off New London, intending to storm the town and burn supplies. Arnold's force mustered three regular British regiments, replete with elite flank companies, and numerous HESSIAN and LOYALIST detachments, totaling 1,732. Ledyard commanded only 140 poorly trained militia, and he was chronically short of ammunition and other vital supplies.

As forces under Arnold stormed and burned New London, a force of 800 British landed on the Groton side of the river under Lieutenant Colonel Edmund Eyre, 54th Regiment. As his troops struggled to get ashore and work their way up the steep hill, he sent a message ahead demanding the fort's immediate surrender. Ledyard refused to comply without a fight and also spurned a second ultimatum. Eyre then personally led the flank companies of the 54th and 40th Regiments against the northeast corner of the bastion while a second force under Major Montgomery assailed the south and southwest faces. Ledyard's men kept up a hot fire upon the approaching British, especially when they stormed and seized the outer works of Fort Griswold. The struggle lasted 40 minutes, and in the confused fighting both Eyre and Montgomery were killed before their troops penetrated the fort. At this juncture Ledyard decided to surrender and tendered his sword to a nearby British officer. He was then run through and killed as the British commenced a general massacre of the survivors. Several minutes elapsed before order was restored, after which 85 Americans lay dead, 35 wounded, and 37 taken unhurt. British losses amounted to 48 killed and 145 wounded.

The capture of Fort Griswold proved a costly British success that failed to inflict major harm upon the Americans. Indeed, the biggest casualty was Arnold's reputation, even though he had not directed the action, and the incident only enhanced his aura of villainy. This battle was also the last major action of the Revolutionary War in the north. Ledyard and his men were subsequently entombed as martyrs, and in 1830 an impressive monument arose at Fort Griswold in their honor.

Further Reading
Burnham, Norman H. *The Battle of Groton Heights: A Story of the Storming of Fort Griswold, and the Burning of New London, on the Sixth of September, 1781.* New London: E. E. Darrow, 1917.
Overtirf, Bradley J. "The Groton Monument: The Construction of a Commemoration." Unpublished master's thesis, Trinity College, 2000.
Powell, Walter L. *Murder or Mayhem? Benedict Arnold's New London, Connecticut Raid, 1781.* Gettysburg, Pa.: Thomas Publications, 2000.
Rathbun, Jonathan. *Narrative of Jonathan Rathbun.* New York: New York Times, 1971.
Snow, Richard F. "Battle of the Revolution: Fort Griswold," *American Heritage* 24, no. 6 (1973): 69–72.
Wilson, David G. "Benedict Arnold's Last Raid, New London, Connecticut, September 6, 1781." Unpublished master's thesis, Southern Connecticut State University, 1994.

Lee, Arthur (1740–1792)
American politician

Arthur Lee was born in Westmoreland County, Virginia, on December 21, 1740, the son of a successful planter and member of one of that colony's most prestigious families. Richard Henry LEE was his elder brother. He was well educated at Eton in England and subsequently studied medicine at the University of Edinburgh. Lee then returned home and opened a practice at Williamsburg, but he forsook medicine in favor of politics and returned to England in 1768 to study law at Middle Temple. During this interval he also established himself as a major voice for colonial interests in Great Britain. He published many radically tinged polemics against British imperial policy, which brought him to the attention of Samuel ADAMS in Massachusetts, and he also befriended noted agitator John WILKES. Through Adams's patronage, Lee became an agent for Massachusetts in London, a title he shared with Benjamin FRANKLIN. By 1774 he also represented the First Continental CONGRESS by presenting several petitions to Parliament. After the Revolutionary War erupted in April 1775, Lee became an informant for Congress's Committee of Secret Correspondence. In this capacity he also met French dramatist Pierre-Augustin Caron de Beaumarchais and helped establish the dummy company Roderigue, Hortalez et Cie to funnel clandestine aid to the Americans. In 1776 Congress appointed Lee a commissioner in Paris to serve alongside Franklin and Silas DEANE. This proved his downfall; Lee, a paranoid, irritable individual, suspected Deane of treachery and profiteering and forwarded incriminating letters about him to Congress. He was only slightly less hostile to Franklin and openly questioned his patriotism and commitment to the war.

In February 1777, Lee was dispatched to SPAIN to secure money, supplies, and possible diplomatic recognition. After several months of wrangling he returned to Paris with a small loan and little else. Eager to rid themselves of this gadfly, Deane and Franklin next sent Lee on a diplomatic mission to the kingdom of Prussia, where Frederick the Great refused to see him. He then returned to Paris an angry, sullen man and continued his one-man diatribe against Deane. After helping sign the FRENCH ALLIANCE in February 1778, Lee finally succeeded in having Congress recall Deane for a formal investigation. The ensuing political fracas in Congress badly split that body into pro- and anti-Deane factions, which served to hobble the legislative process for nearly two years. When Deane was subsequently cleared of all improprieties, he then agitated to have Lee recalled from Paris, which was accomplished in September 1779. He was eventually replaced by John JAY.

Back home, Lee resumed his political activities by winning a seat in the Virginia House of Delegates in 1780. He was elected to Congress in 1782 and two years later joined a four-man commission tasked with securing 30 million acres of land from the Iroquois. He also furiously assailed the monied interests of financiers like New York's Robert MORRIS for overt profiteering. Lee quit Congress in disgust by 1785, although he continued with the Board of Treasury until it was eliminated under the new federal Constitution in 1789. Prior to this, Lee functioned as an anti-federalist, which did little to enhance his already quixotic reputation. He resumed his legal practice in Middlesex County, Virginia, and died there on December 12, 1792, one of the most cantankerous diplomats and politicians of his generation.

Further Reading
Abernathy, Thomas P. "The Origin of the Franklin-Lee Imbroglio," *North Carolina Historical Review* 15 (1983): 41–52.
Higgins, W. Robert, eds. *The Revolutionary War in the South—Power, Conflict, and Leadership.* Durham, N.C.: Duke University Press, 1979.
Moore, Stanley J. "The Character of Arthur Lee." Unpublished master's thesis, University of South Florida, 1977.
Potts, Louis W. *Arthur Lee: A Virtuous Revolutionary.* Baton Rouge: Louisiana State University Press, 1981.
Rhoden, Nancy L., and Ian K. Steele, eds. *The Human Tradition in the American Revolution.* Wilmington, Del.: Scholarly Resources, 2000.
Riggs, A. R., and Edward M. Riley. *The Nine Lives of Arthur Lee, Virginia Patriot.* Williamsburg: Virginia Independence Bicentennial Committee, 1976.

Lee, Charles (1731–1782)
American military officer

Charles Lee was born in Chester, England, on January 26, 1731, the son of a military officer. He joined the 44th Regiment as a lieutenant in 1751 and four years later ventured to America to fight in the French and Indian War. Lee accompanied General Edward Braddock on his disastrous expedition against Fort Duquesne, Pennsylvania, in 1755, where he met and befriended an obscure Virginia colonel named George WASHINGTON. Lee fought well at Fort Ticonderoga the following year, where he was severely wounded, and subsequently married the daughter of a Seneca Indian chief. In this capacity Lee acquired the tribal name Boiling Water from his decidedly testy disposition. After good performances at Fort Niagara in 1759 and Montreal in 1760, Lee returned to England, where he gained promotion to major of the 103rd Regiment. He then transferred to British forces fighting in Portugal under Brigadier General John BURGOYNE, garnering additional laurels while fighting the Spanish. However, when he was discharged and placed on half-pay, Lee's restless spirit compelled him to become a soldier of fortune. He ventured to Poland in 1762, where King Stanislaus Poniatowski made him a major general, and he fought against the Turks until 1770. Lee at that time received a written endorsement from the Polish monarch imploring King GEORGE III to readmit him into the British service, but the king declined. Greatly incensed, Lee migrated to Virginia in 1773, where he bought an estate in present-day West Virginia. There his simmering dissatisfaction with England manifested in sympathy for the Patriot movement.

Lee continued fuming until the outbreak of the Revolutionary War in April 1775 induced him to petition the Continental Congress for a general's commission. Because few senior American officers possessed extensive military service, he became the Continental ARMY's third-senior major general after Washington and Artemas WARD as of June 1775. When Ward was retired in 1776, Lee became next in line to succeed Washington, a position that may have clouded his military judgment. He initially served well during the siege of Boston and performed well as an administrator and drillmaster. Washington then sent him to New York to assess that city's defenses in the summer of 1776, but Congress suddenly transferred him to head the newly created Southern Department. Lee was present and technically in charge during the attack on CHARLESTON, South Carolina, in June 1776, although he was forced to share the victory with Colonel William MOULTRIE. Lee, now hailed as the "Palladiun of Liberty," transferred back to Washington's command that August for more fighting in New York. At this time he promulgated his belief that the American cause would best be served through creation of large-scale guerrilla forces with himself at their head. In light of Washington's drubbing at LONG ISLAND and Fort Washington, he was also increasingly contemptuous of his superior and made no attempt to hide his ambition to succeed him. Throughout the late fall of 1776, Lee repeatedly ignored Washington's orders to join him in New Jersey, ostensibly waiting for him to fail and be replaced. However, on December 13, 1776, Lee was captured in a tavern at Basking Ridge, New Jersey, and interred for 18 months. While a captive he apparently submitted a detailed plan for conquering the southern colonies to General William HOWE, but it is not known if this was actually a deception. Some historians have, in fact, ascribed treachery to Lee's motive, but the assertion remains unproven.

Lee was finally exchanged for captured general Richard Prescott in June 1778, and he rejoined the main army in New Jersey. Washington was then contemplating an attack upon the retreating forces of General Henry CLINTON and tendered him command of the light division, but Lee opposed the maneuver and declined. However, once the troops were given to the youthful marquis de LAFAYETTE, Lee changed his mind and demanded control. On June 27, 1778, he led this force against the British rear guard at MONMOUTH, but his tactical dispositions proved faulty. Lee ordered his men to retreat three times—an act nearly precipitating a rout—before Washington suddenly galloped up to reverse the tide. Lee was abruptly relieved of command, and he also resented his superior's verbal rebuke on the battlefield. He then demanded a court-martial to clear his name but was found guilty of insubordination and lack of respect toward his superior, being sentenced to one year's suspension. Lee then withdrew in a huff to his estate and harangued Congress with a series of insulting letters, demanding immediate reinstatement. His crass and carelessly uttered comments about Washington also resulted in duel with aide-de-camp John LAURENS, and Lee was severely wounded. A second duel with General Anthony WAYNE was in the offing for identical reasons. By January 1780 Congress angrily remonstrated about Lee's lack of respect, and it discharged him from the army entirely. He remained without a command for the rest of the war and died at Philadelphia on October 2, 1782. To his final days, Lee felt that he could conduct the war better than anybody else, but his arrogance and vitriolic disposition precluded any chance of securing a higher command.

Further Reading

Caterall, Ralph T. "Traitor or Patriot? The Ambiguous Career of Charles Lee," *Virginia Cavalcade* 24 (1975): 164–177.

Ethier, Eric. "Clash at Monmouth," *American History* 34, no. 4 (1999): 48–57.

Fleming, Thomas J. "The 'Military Crime' of Charles Lee," *American Heritage* 19, no. 3 (1968): 12–15, 83–89.

Morrissey, Brendan. *Monmouth Courthouse 1778: The Last Great Battle in the North.* Oxford: Osprey, 2004.

Murrin, Mary R., and Richard Waldron. *Conflict at Monmouth Court House: Proceedings of a Symposium Commemorating the Two-hundredth Anniversary of the Battle of Monmouth, April 8, 1978.* Trenton: New Jersey Historical Commission, 1983.

Thayer, Theodore. *The Making of a Scapegoat: Washington and Lee at Monmouth.* Port Washington, N.Y.: Kennikat Press, 1976.

Lee, Henry (1756–1818)
American military officer

Henry Lee was born in Prince William County, Virginia, on January 29, 1756, a scion of the important Lee family and, as such, part of the landed gentry. After attending the College of New Jersey (Princeton) in 1773 he began reading law, but the onset of the Revolutionary War in April 1775 interrupted his studies. Lee joined the militia as a cavalry captain and eventually served under General George WASHINGTON, a man whom he came to admire greatly. He also distinguished himself as an excellent partisan commander and his minor victory at Spread Eagle Tavern, New Jersey, on January 20, 1778, resulted in his promotion to major and a new command. This formation of three troops of cavalry and three companies of light infantry was subsequently renowned as "Lee's Legion" and became regarded as one of the best units in the Continental ARMY. Lee subsequently became a terror of British outposts in New Jersey and, on August 19, 1779, he staged a successful nighttime raid that seized Paulus Hook along with 158 prisoners. Lee was again promoted, to lieutenant colonel, and received one of only eight medals struck by the Continental CONGRESS. With the war in the north stalemated, his services were desperately needed in the Southern Department, so in the spring of 1781 he transferred to General Nathanael GREENE's army in North Carolina.

It was here that Lee firmly established his reputation as a dashing leader during partisan forays throughout the south. He covered the withdrawal of Greene's army to the Dan River and frequently acted in concert with guerrilla bands under Francis MARION and Andrew PICKENS. On February 25, 1781, he gained a measure of infamy by destroying a LOYALIST cavalry detachment at Haw River, apparently taking few prisoners. On March 15, 1781, he rendered valuable services at GUILFORD COURTHOUSE and, following the evacuation of British forces from the Carolinas under General Charles CORNWALLIS, his command was unleashed against isolated British garrisons dotting the interior. In quick succession he captured Forts Watson, Motte, Granby, and Augusta, and was also present during the unsuccessful siege of Fort Ninety Six, South Carolina, where he berated engineer Tadeusz KOŚCIUSZKO for failing to cut off the garrison's water supply. Reunited with Greene, he bore a conspicuous role at the Battle of Eutaw Springs on September 8, 1781, where hard fighting staved off a determined counterattack by Lieutenant Colonel Alexander STEWART. Shortly after, Lee galloped back north to Virginia, where he helped man the trenches at YORKTOWN. Back with Greene that fall, Lee next fought at Dorchester, South Carolina, on December 1, 1781, and in the aborted attack upon John's Island on the 29th. At length this hard-charging trooper was furloughed out of sheer exhaustion, and he retired from the military in February 1782, a national hero. But Lee remained depressed and embittered by his relatively low rank and a sense that he had been denied sufficient credit for numerous victories.

Major Henry Lee took command of a unit consisting of three troops of cavalry and three companies of light infantry that became known as "Lee's Legion," one of the best units of the Continental army. *(Independence National Historical Park)*

After the war Lee turned to politics and served in the Confederation Congress from 1785 to 1788 and as governor of Virginia from 1792 to 1795. A leading Federalist, he pushed hard for ratification of the new federal constitution in 1788, and in 1794 President Washington appointed him major general to quell disturbances, known as the "Whiskey Rebellion," in western Pennsylvania. When Washington died in 1799, it was Lee who eulogized him as "first in war, first in peace, first in the hearts of his countrymen." However, he proved incapable of managing money, and in 1809–10 Lee ended up in debtor's prison; he used the time to write his memoirs of the war, still highly regarded. In July 1812 Lee was badly injured during a riot in Baltimore while protecting his Federalist friend George Hanson and spent the next five years in the West Indies recuperating. There he corresponded with British governor George Beckwith on ways to end the ongoing War of 1812. Lee then returned to Georgia and was so enfeebled that General Greene's daughter tended to him on her plantation. "Light Horse Harry" Lee died at Cumberland Island, Georgia, on March 25, 1818, one of the partisan leaders of the Revolutionary War. He was also the father of the celebrated Confederate general, Robert E. Lee.

Further Reading

Hartmann, John W. *The American Partisan: Henry Lee and the Struggle for Independence, 1776–1780.* Shippensburg, Pa.: Burd Street Press, 2000.

Lee, Henry. *Memoirs of the War in the Southern Department of the United States.* New York: Da Capo Press, 1998.

Mitchell, Craig. "Assault on Paulus Hook: Everything that Could Go Wrong Did . . . ," *American History Illustrated* 16 (1982): 30–37.

Petrocci, Charles A. " 'Light Horse Harry' Lee Entered History with a Daring Night Attack on the Fort at Paulus Hook," *Military History* 17, no. 3 (2000): 16–18.

Royster, Charles. *Light Horse Harry Lee and the Legacy of the American Revolution.* New York: Knopf, 1981.

Troxler, Carole W. *Pyle's Defeat: Deception at the Race Path.* Graham, N.C.: Alamance County Historical Association, 2003.

Lee, Richard Henry (1732–1794)
American politician

Richard Henry Lee was born at Stratford Hall, Virginia, on January 20, 1732, the son of a successful planter and part of an influential Virginia family; he was the elder brother of Arthur LEE. Well educated at home by tutors, he next attended the Wakefield Academy in England before touring northern Europe for several years. Lee finally came home in 1751 to marry and establish his own estate at Chantilly. In 1757 he entered politics by serving as justice of the peace for Westmoreland County, and the following year he gained a seat in the House of Burgesses. Over the next decade Lee struck up close personal relationships with Patrick HENRY and Thomas JEFFERSON, becoming closely identified with radical, anti-British sentiments. In fact, Lee, an accomplished orator, was utterly explicit in his denunciation of imperial policy. After the STAMP ACT of 1765 he organized the Westmoreland Association to enforce nonimportation of British goods and, with the TOWNSHEND DUTIES of 1767, Lee proposed that individual colonies establish COMMITTEES OF CORRESPONDENCE to better coordinate resistance to England. In March 1773 Lee established the Virginia committee, and the following year, when Governor John MURRAY, Lord Dunmore, dissolved the legislature for overt sympathy toward the inhabitants of Boston, Lee and others convened at Raleigh's Tavern to draw up a new nonimportation agreement. He also called for an intercolonial assembly to debate the ongoing crisis; when Massachusetts forwarded this identical call a few weeks earlier, Virginia dispatched seven delegates, including Lee and Henry, to attend the First Continental CONGRESS. Along with Henry, he was among the most strident revolutionaries in attendance and a political force to reckon with.

In Philadelphia, Lee quickly established a working relationship with New England radicals like John ADAMS, and the two frequently acted in concert. He then sat on several committees that promulgated the Declaration of Rights, the Memorial to the People of British America, and other polemical appeals. But Lee's single most important act in Congress was introducing a resolution on June 7, 1776, mandating complete independence from Great Britain. After 18 months of warfare, this was the first time such a notion had been formally enunciated by American politicians. The resolution was then seconded by Adams and approved on July 4, 1776. Lee was not present to sign the document initially and placed his signature on it sometime in August. He then worked hard at drafting and passing the ARTICLES OF CONFEDERATION to establish a national government, along with an alliance with France. Because passage of the articles was threatened by the Maryland delegation, which demanded that Virginia renounce all claims on western lands, Lee influenced the House of Delegates to have such territory ceded to the new government. He also became caught up in the heated dispute between his brother Arthur and Silas DEANE of Connecticut, then a commissioner in Paris, and plied his vitriolic pen and oratory accordingly. He thus helped divide Congress into warring factions, which did nothing to assist the passage of badly needed legislation. When Lee's health began declining, he resigned his seat and returned home in 1779.

Lee returned to politics in 1780 by winning a seat in the House of Delegates, where he voted with other conservative planters. Curiously, he was also a lifelong opponent of slavery and the slave trade, and made several impassioned appeals to end both. Lee returned to Congress in 1784 and the following year briefly functioned as its president. Like many national leaders, Lee was cognizant that the Articles of Confederation afforded less than perfect governance, but he railed against adoption of more centralized rule. In 1787 he was elected to the Virginia Constitutional Convention but boycotted it to protest the lack of a bill of rights. He then composed his powerful polemic *Letters of the Federal Farmer to the Republican*, clearly delineating his anti-Federalist objections. The new government was ratified and functioning by 1789, and Lee was elected to the U.S. Senate, where he vociferously championed the addition of a bill of rights. Ill health again necessitated his departure from public life in 1792, and he died at Chantilly, Virginia, on June 19, 1794. For the brief time he served, Lee was among the most influential leaders in Congress.

Further Reading

Engal, Marc. "The Origins of the Revolution in Virginia: A Reinterpretation," *William and Mary Quarterly* 37, no. 3 (1980): 401–428.

Matthews, John C. *Richard Henry Lee*. Williamsburg: Virginia Independence Bicentennial Commission, 1978.

McDonald, Forrest, ed. *Empire and Nation*. Indianapolis: Liberty Fund, 1999.

McGaughy, J. Kent. *Richard Henry Lee of Virginia: A Portrait of an American Revolutionary*. Lanham, Md.: Rowman & Littlefield, 2004.

Virginia, Mary E. "Richard Henry Lee of Virginia: A Biography." Unpublished Ph.D. diss., State University of New York at Buffalo, 1992.

White, William E. "Charlatans, Embezzlers, and Murderers: Revolution Comes to Virginia." Unpublished Ph.D. diss., College of William and Mary, 1998.

Leslie, Alexander (ca. 1731–1794)
English military officer

Alexander Leslie was born in Scotland around 1731, a son of the noted fifth Earl of Leven and Melville. He joined the Foot Guards as a captain in March 1753 and two years later transferred to the 11th Regiment. By 1766 Leslie had risen to colonel of the 64th Regiment and was performing garrison duty at Halifax, Nova Scotia. In 1772 he accompanied his regiment to Boston as part of the attempt to restore authority to that increasingly unruly city. Three years later the possibility of violence between His Majesty's troops and subjects drew ever nearer, and the royal governor, Thomas GAGE, possibly to circumvent disaster, enacted a preemptive strike. Spies alerted him to the presence of several cannon at nearby Salem, home of the extralegal Massachusetts provincial congress, so on February 26, 1775, he ordered Leslie and the 64th Regiment to seize them. Owing to the sensitive nature of the mission, Leslie, then stationed at

Castle William in Boston Harbor, would be transported by boat under the cover of darkness. His departure went unobserved by the usually alert American intelligence apparatus but, having landed at Marblehead, the alarm went out as he tramped toward his objective. The British column was greeted by hostile citizens and militia, who raised the drawbridge over the North River and refused to let them cross. Anxious moments passed as Leslie threatened to open fire, but a last-minute agreement was reached whereby the British would cross over, march a few yards into town, then about-face and return. Thus Leslie's secret mission was reduced to a comic opera farce, but armed confrontation had been avoided.

Leslie next saw action as part of British forces commanded by General William HOWE in the summer and fall of 1776. A brigadier general, he fought at the Battle of Harlem Heights on September 16, 1776, and his stand incurred the death of Major Thomas KNOWLTON. Leslie was also present at WHITE PLAINS on October 28, 1776, in which his men attacked bravely and sustained heavy losses. That December he accompanied General Charles CORNWALLIS during the pursuit of American forces under General George WASHINGTON and commanded several advanced posts. However, on the night of January 2, 1777, Washington stole to within three miles of Leslie's camp at Maidenhead, New Jersey, without arousing the defenders and went on to win a victory at PRINCETON. Leslie nevertheless rendered capable, if undistinguished, service and on February 19, 1779, gained promotion to major general.

In the fall of 1780 Leslie was picked by General Henry CLINTON to lead an amphibious expedition from New York into Virginia, with a view toward seizing Richmond. His 2,500 men then landed at Portsmouth and proceeded up the James River until the mission was countermanded. Leslie then received orders to sail his detachment to Charleston, South Carolina, as reinforcements for General Cornwallis. He disembarked there on December 14, 1780, and hurriedly marched inland to assist Lieutenant Colonel Banastre TARLETON but failed to arrive before the British disaster at COWPENS on January 17, 1781. At length he countermarched and eventually joined the main column under Cornwallis in North Carolina. On February 1, 1781, Leslie and General Charles O'HARA were unhorsed while fording the Catawba River and nearly drowned. The following month he commanded the British right wing at GUILFORD COURTHOUSE, performing well in a tough, stand-up engagement. Declining health forced him back to New York for several months, and in November 1781 he returned to Charleston as overall theater commander. Leslie rose to temporary lieutenant general in January 1782 but, after the defeat at YORKTOWN, there was little the British could do but mark time. That summer he ordered the evacuation of Savannah, Georgia, and orchestrated the final British withdrawal from Charleston in December 1782. After the war Leslie returned to

British general Alexander Leslie orchestrated the British withdrawals from Savannah and Charleston in 1782. *(Private Scottish Collection)*

England where he became commander of military forces in Scotland. He died there on December 27, 1794, in consequence of injuries received during a riot.

Further Reading

Barnes, Eric. "All the King's Horses . . . and all the King's Men," *American Heritage* 11, no. 6 (1960): 56–59, 86–87.

Barnwell, Joseph W. "The Evacuation of Charleston by the British in 1782," *South Carolina Historical Magazine* 11 (January 1911): 1–26.

Hairr, John. *Guilford Courthouse: Nathanael Greene's Victory in Defeat, March 15, 1781.* Barnsley, U.K.: Leo Cooper, 2003.

McCowen, George S. *The British Occupation of Charleston, 1780–1782.* Columbia: University of South Carolina Press, 1972.

Newsome, Albert R., ed. "A British Orderly Book, 1780–1781," *North Carolina Historical Review* 9 (January–October 1932): 57–58, 163–186, 273–298, 366–392.

Philips, James D. "Why Colonel Leslie came to Salem," *Essex Institute Historical Collections* 90 (October 1954): 313–316.

Lewis, Andrew (1720–1781)

American army officer

Andrew Lewis was born in County Donegal, Ireland, on October 9, 1720, the son of an Irish tenant. His father fled to Virginia after allegedly killing his landlord in self-defense and established a new home in August County around 1732. Lewis subsequently worked as a surveyor and land speculator, amassing a minor fortune while also taking an interest in militia affairs. He was apparently a strapping figure, over six feet tall and exuding a somewhat grim countenance. In 1754 Lewis accompanied a young George WASHINGTON in the expedition that culminated in the surrender of Fort Necessity. Two years later he commanded the unsuccessful Sandy Creek expedition to reach the Ohio River, but food shortages canceled his endeavor. In 1758 he accompanied Major James GRANT on a reconnaissance of French forts on the Upper Ohio and was captured. After a brief internment at Montreal, Lewis was released and attended treaty negotiations with the Iroquois at Fort Stanwix in 1768. After the French and Indian War ended in 1763, he resumed his business endeavors throughout southwestern Virginia. His reputation was such that in 1774 Governor John MURRAY, Lord Dunmore, appointed him a brigadier general commanding one of two militia columns during the frontier disturbance known as Lord Dunmore's War. Lewis marched 800 men to the confluence of the Ohio and Kanawha Rivers, where, on October 10, 1774, he was vigorously attacked at Point Pleasant by Shawnee under Chief CORNSTALK. The Virginians were roughly handled initially but stood their ground after losing 81 killed and 140 wounded. Cornstalk's losses were also prohibitive, so he sued for peace and ultimately ceded all tribal territory south of the Ohio River. Victory here made Lewis a celebrity throughout Virginia.

As the Revolutionary War approached, Lewis supported the Patriot side and functioned on the local committee of safety. His military reputation also remained high, and in March 1776 the Continental CONGRESS appointed him brigadier general in the Continental ARMY. In this capacity Lewis performed his most useful work by confronting British and LOYALIST forces still operating in the state under the now-renegade Governor Dunmore. Since the beginning of the year Dunmore had established his base on Gwynn Island at the mouth of the Rappahannock River, from which he launched destructive raids inland. On July 8, 1776, Lewis approached the island with a brigade of Virginia troops and several cannon. A heavy bombardment drove off the small squadron covering the island, and the Virginians made preparations to cross. On July 10, after Gwynn Island was secured without further fighting, it was discovered that the defenders had suffered badly from smallpox and buried many of their soldiers.

Lewis's success removed the threat of British forces to Virginia until 1780. Meanwhile, he was angered about not being promoted to major general and threatened to quit. Washington, who knew Lewis and valued him as a military leader, urged him to stay on, but he resigned his commission on April 15, 1777, citing poor health. Thereafter he attended several peace conferences with the Indians and in 1780 served on Governor Thomas JEFFERSON's executive council. Lewis died in Bedford en route to his home on September 26, 1781, an early hero of the Revolutionary War.

Further Reading
Burton, Patricia. *Virginia Begins to Remember: Her Men Who Went to the Point in 1774: Opening of the American Revolution.* Birmingham, Mich.: Burton, 1980.
Campbell, Fay T. "Andrew Lewis and His Times." Unpublished master's thesis, West Virginia University, 1934.
Johnson, Patricia G. *General Andrew Lewis of Roanoke and Greenbrier.* Christiansburg, Va.: Johnson, 1980.
Morgan, John G. *A Point in History: The Battle of Point Pleasant.* Huntington, W.Va.: Discovery Press, 2001.
Raper, Margaret. "Andrew Lewis, Valley Patriot." Unpublished master's thesis, Mississippi State University, 1952.
Wrike, Peter J. *The Governor's Island: Gwynn's Island during the Revolution.* Gwynn, Va.: Gwynn's Island Museum, 1993.

Lincoln, Benjamin (1733–1810)
American military officer

Benjamin Lincoln was born in Hingham, Massachusetts, on January 24, 1733, the son of a successful farmer. He became active in local politics and also served in the Suffolk County militia, rising to lieutenant colonel as of 1774. After fighting broke out in April 1775, Lincoln marched his regiment to Cambridge, where the provincial congress appointed him state mustermaster. A bluff, popular figure, he was also elected to the Massachusetts council, through whose authority he became brigadier general of militia in February 1776. Lincoln performed capably throughout the siege of Boston, and he gained promotion to major general of militia as of May 1776. In this capacity he accompanied the army of General George WASHINGTON to New York, where, on October 28, 1776, he performed credibly at the Battle of WHITE PLAINS. As the Americans fell back across New Jersey that winter, Lincoln was dispatched to Rhode Island for additional reinforcements, and he returned in time for the siege of Fort Independence under General William HEATH in January 1777. He then rejoined Washington's main army at Morristown, New Jersey, where he became a major general in the Continental army as of February 1777. This appointment carried political overtones, as Lincoln lacked the seniority of other brigadiers, and General Benedict ARNOLD nearly resigned over the slight. By the summer of 1777 Lincoln was dispatched to join the Northern Department under General Philip J. SCHUYLER, and that August he helped organize the Vermont militia responsible for defeating Colonel Friedrich BAUM at the Battle of BENNINGTON. He subsequently served under General Horatio GATES and rendered valuable service at the Battle of BEMIS HEIGHTS on October 7, 1777, being severely wounded. Lincoln recuperated for nearly a year before resuming active duty.

In September 1778 the Continental CONGRESS appointed Lincoln commander of the hard-pressed Southern Department, which was accomplished with Washington's approval. Lincoln, who had never previously held an independent command, proved himself earnest but somewhat inept as both a tactician and a strategist. Apparently, many in Congress felt that his popularity with militia forces would bolster the use of that arm throughout the South. Lincoln advanced into Georgia in early 1779 but proved unable to prevent the capture of Savannah by Lieutenant Colonel Archibald CAMPBELL that December. He then thwarted an attack upon Charleston, South Carolina, by General Augustin PREVOST on May 12, 1779, and promptly pursued the retreating British. Unfortunately, he mounted a clumsy attack against their rear guard at Stono Ferry on June 29, 1779, and was handily repulsed. Five months later Lincoln again advanced into Georgia to join forces with a French expedition commanded by Admiral Charles-Hector-Théodat, comte d'ESTAING. Good progress was made during

General Benjamin Lincoln served admirably throughout the Revolution, and was the first secretary of war under the Articles of Confederation. *(Independence National Historical Park)*

the siege, but d'Estaing, anxious to depart before the onset of hurricane season, insisted on a premature assault, and Lincoln concurred. On October 9, 1779, the allies were badly repulsed during the attack on SAVANNAH and Lincoln, abandoned by the French, withdrew back to Charleston. He was still in garrison in January 1780 when a British expedition under General Henry CLINTON commenced the siege of CHARLESTON. Clinton's leisurely pace gave the Americans ample time to evacuate the city with their forces intact, but Lincoln fell under enormous political pressure from Governor John RUTLEDGE to remain behind and defend it. He felt obliged to comply and performed capably with limited resources but finally capitulated with 5,500 men on May 12, 1780—the biggest American defeat of the war. Lincoln was subsequently paroled and exchanged a few months later in time to join Washington's army again at YORKTOWN. Lincoln, the nominal second in command, commanded one of three divisions present and was appointed to receive the sword of General Charles CORNWALLIS from his subordinate, General Charles O'HARA. Shortly afterward Lincoln was tapped to serve as the first secretary of war under the ARTICLES OF CONFEDERATION; he served in this capacity until being replaced by General Henry KNOX on March 8, 1785.

Back in civilian life, Lincoln returned to farming and land speculation until 1787, when Governor James Bowdoin appointed him commander of militia forces that suppressed the rebellion of Daniel Shays. This he accomplished quickly and bloodlessly, averting what may have become a civil war in western Massachusetts. The following year he became lieutenant governor, a largely ceremonial post but one in which he clashed with Governor John HANCOCK. Lincoln also attended the Constitutional Convention in 1788, lending his vital support to its adoption. In 1789 President Washington appointed him to the lucrative post of Collector of the Port of Boston, where he remained until 1809. In 1789 and 1793 Lincoln also performed as a peace commissioner to the western Indians. The corpulent, gregarious general died in his home at Hingham on May 8, 1810, hardly an astute military leader of the Revolutionary War but still a capable, dependable subordinate, well liked by soldiers and superiors alike.

Further Reading
Borick, Carl P. *A Gallant Defense: The Siege of Charleston, 1780.* Columbia: University of South Carolina Press, 2003.
Damon, Allan L. "A Second in Command: Benjamin Lincoln and the American Revolution." Unpublished Ph.D. diss., Columbia University, 1994.
Freeman, H. Ronald. *Savannah under Siege: The Bloodiest Hour of the Revolution.* Savannah, Ga.: Freeport Pub., 2002.
Mattern, David B. *Benjamin Lincoln and the American Revolution.* Columbia: University of South Carolina Press, 1995.

Ward, Harry M. "George Washington's Solid General," *Virginia Quarterly Review* 72, no. 4 (1996): 764–768.

Wilson, David K. *The Southern Strategy: Britain's Conquest of South Carolina and Georgia, 1775–1780.* Columbia: University of South Carolina Press, 2005.

Little, George (1754–1809)
American naval officer

George Little was born in Marshfield, Massachusetts, on April 15, 1754, and he was drawn to life in the merchant marine at an early age. Upon the onset of the Revolutionary War in 1775 he joined the Massachusetts state navy as a second lieutenant and received command of the armed vessel *Boston*. He was subsequently captured by British forces and confined to the prisoner ship *Lord Sandwich* at Newport, Rhode Island, but effected his escape on March 7, 1778. Little then resumed his career in the state navy as an officer onboard the brigantines *Active* and *Hazard*. On May 3, 1779, he advanced to first lieutenant and accompanied Commodore Dudley SALTONSTALL on the ill-fated Penobscot expedition of that year. Little subsequently served with the ship *Protector* under Captain John F. WILLIAMS and acquitted himself well during the desperate victory over the large British privateer *Admiral Duff* on June 9, 1780. He himself was then taken prisoner when his vessel was captured by HMS *Roebuck* and *Medea* and thereafter confined to Mill Prison, Plymouth. At length Little and several other sailors managed to bribe a guard and escaped to France. He then returned to the United States in 1782 with a letter of recommendation from Benjamin FRANKLIN, gained promotion to captain, and received the state ship *Winthrop* as a command. Little cruised the New England coast with some success and captured several British ships in Penobscot Bay, scene of the earlier disaster. Having completed the final cruise of the state navy over the winter of 1782–83, Little resigned from the service on June 23, 1783, and returned to his farm in Marshfield.

Little resumed his naval career on March 4, 1799, when President John ADAMS commissioned him a captain in the new United States Navy. He then obtained command of the 28-gun frigate USS *Boston* and was ordered to cruise the Caribbean and defeat French privateers preying on American commerce during the so-called Quasi-War. Little enjoyed considerable success and took seven prizes, including a Danish vessel whose seizure had been approved by the American consul in Haiti. On October 12, 1799, Little scored his biggest triumph by engaging and defeating the 24-gun corvette *Le Berceau* off the American coast after a three-hour fight. However, back in Boston his career was sidelined by legal action pertaining to some of the vessels captured; in at least one instance he was ordered to pay damages by the U.S. Supreme Court. Little thus became the first American naval commander in history held accountable by international law. He died in Weymouth, Massachusetts, on July 22, 1809.

Further Reading

Allen, Gardner W. *Massachusetts Privateers of the Revolution.* Boston: Massachusetts Historical Society, 1927.

Gardner, Frank A. "State Sloop Winthrop," *Massachusetts Magazine* 4 (January–October 1911): 110–116.

Leiner, Frederick C. "Anatomy of a Prize Case: Dollars, Back-Deals, and Les Deux Agnes," *American Journal of Legal History* 39 (April 1995): 1–19.

McManeim, John A. *Revolution on the High Seas: A History of Maritime Massachusetts during the Revolutionary War.* Spring Lake, N.J.: Ho-Ho-Kus Pub. Co., 1988.

Morse, Sidney G. "New England Privateering in the American Revolution," 2 vols. Unpublished Ph.D. diss., Harvard University, 1941.

Palmer, Michael A. *Stoddert's War: Naval Operations during the Quasi-War with France, 1798–1801.* Annapolis, Md.: Naval Institute Press, 2000.

Livingston, Robert R. (1746–1813)
American politician

Robert Robert Livingston was born in New York City on November 27, 1746, into one of that colony's leading patrician families. Wealth afforded him a fine education at King's College (now Columbia University) in 1765, and he passed the bar exam in 1768. For many years up until the Revolutionary War erupted, Livingston was a law partner with John JAY, and both were increasingly drawn into political activities. In 1773 Governor William TRYON appointed him recorder of the city but, because of overt sympathy for the First Continental CONGRESS, he was removed in 1775. That same year the extralegal New York provincial congress elected him a delegate to the Second Continental Congress, where he served until 1776 and from 1779 to 1781. By dint of education, oratory, and perspicacity, Livingston emerged as a leader of the New York delegation, although he proved reluctant to break with England. For this reason he opposed Virginia delegate Richard Henry LEE's resolution for independence. In any event, lacking instructions from the provincial congress, he was not authorized to either vote for or sign the DECLARATION OF INDEPENDENCE on July 4, 1776. Shortly afterward he returned to New York and participated in the state constitutional convention. He worked closely with Jay and Gouverneur MORRIS in drafting the final document, which he rendered very conservative to retain power in the hands of the landed gentry. When the new constitution was ratified, Livingston became the state's first chancellor and temporarily governed New York until the election of Governor George CLINTON in June 1777. That same year British forces ravaged the Hudson Valley, and Livingston lost his home and other valuable properties.

In 1779 Livingston assumed Jay's seat in Congress when the latter became envoy to SPAIN. He served with little distinction until after the ARTICLES OF CONFEDERATION were adopted in 1781, and he became the nation's first secretary of foreign affairs. In this capacity Livingston engaged in orchestrating final peace negotiations with Great Britain, although he played only a relatively minor role in the TREATY OF PARIS. Worse, because Jay deliberately violated Livingston's instructions not to conclude negotiations without consulting France, the two former friends were never reconciled. But Livingston, a strident nationalist, was among the first national leaders to espouse American control of the Mississippi River. This proved an issue he would revisit in 1803.

After the war ended in 1783 Livingston resigned as secretary and was returned to the state legislature. He performed useful work there by helping mitigate long-standing boundary disputes with Massachusetts and in 1788 also participated in the federal Constitutional Convention. The following year he administered the oath of office to President George WASHINGTON in New York City, which again affirmed his position as a leading national figure. But over the ensuing decade Livingston gradually opposed the fiscal and political policies of Alexander HAMILTON, and he gradually shifted his political allegiance from the Federalists to the emerging Democratic-Republican Party of Thomas JEFFERSON. Livingston also openly admired the ongoing French Revolution, and in 1795 he excoriated the Jay Treaty for being overtly pro-British. Three years later he ran for and was resoundingly defeated by Jay for the governorship. Fortunately, the election of Jefferson to the presidency in 1800 proved a new lease for his political ambitions, and the following year Livingston replaced Gouverneur MORRIS as minister to France. It was here that he performed his most useful service to the country. Livingston, though dealing from a position of weakness, artfully prevailed upon First Consul Napoléon Bonaparte to sell remaining French holdings in North America before they were seized by Great Britain. Then, assisted by James MONROE, he signed the Louisiana Purchase of 1803—an act that literally doubled the size of the young republic. He returned home the following year and performed more useful work by financially backing noted inventor Robert Fulton and his steamboats. Livingston died on his estate on February 26, 1813, an entrenched aristocrat, yet a representative member of the revolutionary generation.

Further Reading
Brandt, Clare. "Robert R. Livingston, Jr.: The Reluctant Revolutionary," *Hudson Valley Regional Review* 4, no. 1 (1987): 8–20.

Champagne, Roger L. "New York's Radicals and the Coming of Independence," *Journal of American History* 51, no. 1 (1964): 21–40.
Dangerfield, George. *Chancellor Robert R. Livingston of New York, 1746–1833.* New York: Harcourt, Brace, Jovanovich, 1980.
Hughes, John. "The Issue of Sovereignty in the American Revolution and Its Impact on American Federalism." Unpublished master's thesis, Trinity College, 1998.
Launitz-Schurer, Leopold S. *Loyal Whigs and Revolutionaries: The Making of the Revolution in New York, 1765–1776.* New York: New York University Press, 1980.
Tully, Allan. *Forming American Politics: Ideals, Interests, and Institutions in Colonial New York and Pennsylvania.* Baltimore: Johns Hopkins University Press, 1994.

Long Island, Battle of (August 27, 1776)

General William HOWE, having been dislodged from Boston the previous spring, reappeared off New York in June 1776 on board a huge fleet commanded by his brother, Admiral Richard HOWE. The British were then further augmented by the arrival of Commodore Peter PARKER's squadron and additional soldiers under Generals Henry CLINTON and Charles CORNWALLIS. Howe now commanded upward of 32,000 veteran troops, including 8,000 HESSIANS, and intended to commence offensive operations against the much smaller army of General George WASHINGTON on Long Island. Accordingly, the British ferried some 15,000 troops from Staten Island to Gravesend on August 22, 1776, and marched inland. Washington at that time had deployed 9,000 men—roughly half his force—upon Brooklyn Heights, with additional forces strung eastward in the direction of Jamaica. Unfortunately the nominal commander, General Nathanael GREENE, had taken ill and was successively replaced by John SULLIVAN and Israel PUTNAM, neither of whom was acutely familiar with the terrain they occupied. Furthermore, American forces, bravely disposed but ill-trained for close-order combat, tried to cover the approaches through Gowanus, Flatbush, and Bedford but inadvertently neglected the strategic gap at Jamaica Pass farther east. This approach remained lightly defended, and once British reconnaissance relayed this intelligence to Howe, he began formulating a bold stroke against the American left. On the evening of August 26, 1776, General Clinton, Colonel Hugh PERCY, and 10,000 men marched off to seize Jamaica Pass and then turn leftward, in effect placing themselves behind Washington's army. Meanwhile, other British forces under General James GRANT and Hessians under General Leopold von HEISTER were deployed to demonstrate along the American front, pinning them down until they were surrounded.

Howe's offensive kicked off on the morning of August 27, 1776, when troops under Grant advanced through Gowanus Pass toward General William ALEXANDER's position. Meanwhile, the combined forces of Clinton and Percy captured Jamaica Pass without difficulty and marched in the pre-dawn darkness toward the American flank. As Heister's Hessians engaged Sullivan at Flatbush Pass, Sullivan failed to notice the danger looming in his rear and was quickly captured along with most of his men. The British juggernaut continued rolling up the American flank and center, despite a valiant stand by hard-pressed Maryland and Delaware Continentals under Colonel Mordecai GIST. At length Alexander likewise was forced to surrender while the surviving Americans scrambled to reach the fortifications at Brooklyn Heights. To that point the Battle of Long Island had been a splendid tactical triumph for the redcoats, who, by dint of careful planning and forceful execution, suffered only 377 casualties. The roughly handled Americans lost nearly 2,000 men killed, wounded, and captured.

A moment of decision seemed at hand but Howe, cognizant of heavy losses sustained at BUNKER HILL the year before, chose to formally invest Washington's defenses rather than storm them—an act that may have destroyed the American army outright. Fighting died down at sunset, and the British paused to commence siege operations over the next two days, which granted the rebels a badly needed respite. Washington had previously rushed troops and cannon from Manhattan up to Brooklyn Heights before realizing that his position was essentially hopeless. On the evening of August 29 he ordered a complete evacuation under the very noses of the British. Covered by darkness and facilitated by mariners under Colonel John GLOVER and General Alexander McDOUGALL, the Americans achieved a minor miracle. In only six hours roughly 9,500 soldiers and all their equipment were quickly and quietly transported to Manhattan without incident. Fortuitously, nature itself was working on behalf of the Americans. Throughout the evening and well into the day a thick fog settled into the area, reducing vison to a few hundred yards. A strong, contrary wind also kept Admiral Howe's ships from entering the East River and cutting their retreat. But the Battle of Long Island underscored Washington's ineptitude as a strategist, for he not only had divided his army on both sides of the East River but also had grossly underestimated Howe's numerical superiority. Close combat had also demonstrated the inability of raw American troops to withstand their veteran adversaries with cold steel. Defeat here signified an unbroken string of setbacks that only ended six months later with Washington's brilliant riposte at TRENTON.

Further Reading

Edgar, Gregory T. *Campaign of 1776: The Road to Trenton.* Bowie, Md.: Heritage Books, 1995.

Flanagan, James W. "Decisive Victory Let Go," *Military History* 7, no. 4 (1991): 30–37.

Gallagher, John J. *The Battle of Brooklyn, 1776.* Edison, N.J.: Castle Books, 2002.

Held, James E. "The Brooklyn Campaign," *Military Heritage* 3, no. 4 (2002): 54–63, 88.

Myer, J. Jay. "George Washington's Dire Straits," *American History* 36, no. 2 (2001): 22–30.

Schecter, Barnet. *The Battle for New York: The City at the Heart of the American Revolution.* New York: Walker & Co., 2002.

Lovell, Solomon (1732–1801)

American militia officer

Solomon Lovell was born at Abington, Massachusetts, on June 1, 1732, the son of a farmer. Orphaned at an early age he was raised by his grandfather and partially educated by the Reverend William Smith, better known as the father of Abigail ADAMS. Lovell eventually prospered as a farmer, and in 1756 he served in the Seven Years' War in a regiment commanded by Colonel Richard GRIDLEY. Afterward he resumed his career in husbandry and rose to social prominence at Weymouth. In 1771 he was elected to a seat on the General Court and also became a major in the 2nd Suffolk Militia Regiment. By 1775, following the onset of hostilities with Britain, Lovell was part of the Weymouth COMMITTEE OF CORRESPONDENCE and, on February 7, 1776, he was appointed colonel of his regiment. In this capacity he accompanied General John THOMAS during the occupation of Boston's Dorchester Heights, which prompted the British evacuation of that city. On June 24, 1777, Lovell gained promotion to brigadier general of the Suffolk County militia. The following month he led 1,200 militiamen into Rhode Island as part of the expedition commanded by General John SULLIVAN. He fought at the inconclusive Battle of Rhode Island on August 29, 1778, and was commended by Sullivan for his bravery.

Lovell performed his most important work in the summer of 1779. That June a small British force under General Francis Maclean occupied the Bagaduce Peninsula astride Penobscot Bay, Massachusetts (Maine), and constructed Fort George. The Massachusetts General Court then authorized a large amphibious expedition to evict them. Accordingly, Lovell, seconded by General Peleg WADSWORTH, commanded a force of 1,000 militiamen (including Colonel Paul REVERE) and joined up with a fleet of 39 vessels under Commodore Dudley SALTONSTALL. The Americans reached their objective on July 24, 1779, and, given the size of their force, little difficulty was anticipated. Unfortunately, operations broke down over a simmering dispute between Lovell and Saltonstall: The former wished the fleet to seize three British vessels in the harbor, while the commodore insisted that Fort George be reduced before he committed his vessels to such cramped waters. An embarrassing impasse ensued, and they bickered for two weeks while a British relief expedition under Commodore George COLLIER approached from New York to rescue the garrison. Its appearance off Penobscot on August 12, 1779, signaled the end of the operation, for Saltonstall quickly withdrew upriver and burned his ships. Lovell and his men then endured an arduous march through the Maine wilderness before reaching Boston.

Lovell was subsequently cleared of all charges for the Penobscot disaster by a committee, and he retained his command until 1782. That year he resigned from the militia to resume farming. He died in Weymouth on September 9, 1801, remembered mainly for his role in the Penobscot disaster.

Further Reading
Corbin, Gary. "Disaster at Penobscot Bay." Unpublished master's thesis, State University of New York, Brockport, 1992.
Elliott, Peter J. "The Penobscot Expedition of 1779: A Study in Naval Frustration." Unpublished master's thesis, University of Maine, Orono, 1974.
Kevitt, Chester B. *General Solomon Lovell and the Penobscot Expedition, 1779.* Weymouth, Mass.: Kevitt, 1976.
Nash, Gilbert. "Sketch of General Solomon Lovell," *Weymouth Historical Society Collections* 1 (1881): 19–92.
Nielson, Jon M. "Penobscot: From the Jaws of Victory—Our Navy's Worst Defeat," *American Neptune* 37, no. 4 (1977): 288–305.
Sharp, Arthur G. "The Penobscot Expedition: An Exercise in Futility," *Military History* 20, no. 5 (2003): 50–57.

Loyalists

The Loyalists represented those segments of American society that upheld the British Crown throughout the Revolutionary War. Their exact numbers are disputed historically but may have ranged upward of 500,000—nearly one-fifth of the total population. Occupationally they represented a wide cross section of society, including yeoman farmers, clergymen, highland tenants, wealthy land owners, and businessmen—in sum, virtually a mirror image of the Patriot community. Americans also lumped Native Americans and AFRICAN AMERICANS into their ranks through the simple expedient that these opposed Patriot goals during the war. As a group, Loyalists were distributed in all thirteen colonies but were disproportionately represented in New York, Pennsylvania, South Carolina, and Georgia. Patriots also frequently derided them through the label "Tory," which implied slavish political devotion to unrestrained monarchy when, in fact, most Loyalists embraced the notion of parliamentary supremacy. They did, however, make the logical extension of this supremacy to colonial affairs as well. Moreover, thoughtful Loyalist leaders like Joseph GALLOWAY of Pennsylvania bridled at the notion of unfair taxation and, like more radical factions, they waxed critical over imperial policy throughout the period from 1765 to 1775. But Loyalists and Patriots broke ranks over the issue of independence, with the former fearing the chaos and anarchy that war inevitably produced. Many Loyalists, especially recent immigrants, simply proved unwilling to part with their cherished relationship with King GEORGE III or with their English political identity. Such empathy wrent counties, communities, and even families asunder; Benjamin FRANKLIN was among the most pristine of Patriots, yet his eldest son William Franklin, governor of New Jersey, remained staunchly loyal to the Crown. Governor Thomas HUTCHINSON of Massachusetts, a mild-mannered, strict constitutionalist, was openly branded as a tyrant because of his devotion to imperial prerogatives. Such deeply ingrained allegiances, and the animosity they engendered, produced an atmosphere of profound hatred and oftentimes engendered blind retribution.

Militarily speaking, Loyalists wielded an impact upon British strategy far out of proportion to their actual numbers. Secretary of State for the Colonies George GERMAIN remained convinced that the majority of Americans were loyal, and he promulgated elaborate strategies contingent upon nonexistent support. As early as 1776 General

William HOWE warned the government that it could expect little help from the Loyalist community, but this cogent advice was ignored. In August 1777, General John BURGOYNE dispatched the column of Colonel Friedrich BAUM into Vermont, where he believed it would be welcomed with open arms—but instead went down to defeat at the Battle of BENNINGTON. But it was on the actual battlefields and frontiers of North America that Loyalists made their greatest impression. Many showed their sympathy for the Crown by taking up arms, either through enlisting in the British army or, more commonly, as part of Loyalist military units. New York alone provided an estimated 19,000 fighting men for the Crown. Several distinguished units arose, including Banastre TARLETON's American Legion, Francis RAWDON's Volunteers of Ireland, Patrick FERGUSON's American Rangers, John JOHNSON's Loyal Greens, Walter BUTLER's Tory Rangers, and John Grave SIMCOE's Queen's Rangers. These were among the most tactically adept—and feared—units in the British service and frequently played havoc among American militia units and frontier communities. Thousands of other Loyalists simply functioned as guerrillas fighting alongside roving bands of hostile Indians. In the south, where Loyalist and Patriot numbers were almost evenly matched, warfare frequently degenerated into a bloody civil war, with torture and murder of prisoners shamefully commonplace. Men like Thomas BROWN, David FANNING, and Simon GIRTY blazed a trail of infamy across the frontier, and their excesses elicited identical responses from the Patriot side. Off the battlefield, Loyalists also provided useful service to the Crown while employed in mundane but essential roles as spies, propagandists, guides, and ship pilots. In sum, they were a useful addition to the British war effort but were never available in sufficient numbers to alter the outcome of events.

Loyalists, the bulk of whom remained in the United States throughout the war, paid deeply for their beliefs by way of punitive laws. They were openly regarded as traitors and state legislatures frequently stripped them of political rights and confiscated their properties. Mobs also harassed, tarred and feathered, and sometimes even murdered them in overt acts of intimidation. British authorities were acutely aware of their indignities and insisted that the 1783 TREATY OF PARIS contain provisions to facilitate their eventual return home without fear of reprisal and compensation for losses. The Continental CONGRESS, while powerless to enforce such stipulations, magnanimously advised the states to show leniency toward all returnees. But many Patriots, particularly throughout the South, remained vindictively disposed toward their former neighbors, and large numbers of Loyalists concluded that it was simply too risky to go home. Consequently, over 100,000 refugees left the United States for new lives in Florida, the West Indies, and England. Loyalists made their biggest impact upon Canada, where 37,000 immigrants were settled in Ontario and New Brunswick, thereby creating new provinces virtually from scratch. The British government freely accepted responsibility for the well-being of the new inhabitants and paid millions of pounds in compensation (usually pensions or land grants) for prior losses. By the 1790s public hostility toward Loyalists had abated, and they were gradually reabsorbed into the mainstream of American society. Widespread prosecution ceased, but laws against Loyalists were not formally proscribed until after the War of 1812. Furthermore, those Loyalists fleeing to Canada possessed much longer memories. Once settled they founded the United Loyalists Association to bolster their political authority throughout the province. In this manner they rendered Ontario a bastion of festering anti-Americanism and mounted the strongest opposition to United States forces during the War of 1812.

Further Reading
Devoss, David. "Divided Loyalties," *Smithsonian* 34, no. 10 (2004): 62–68.
Harper, David B. "Ambitious Marylander: Caleb Jones and the American Revolution." Unpublished master's thesis, Utah State University, 2001.

Ketchum, Richard M. *Divided Loyalties: How the American Revolution Came to New York.* New York: Henry Holt, 2002.

Papas, Philip. "That Ever Loyal Island: Loyalism and the Coming of the American Revolution on Staten Island, New York." Unpublished Ph.D. diss., City University of New York, 2003.

Ranlet, Philip. *The New York Loyalists.* Lanham, Md.: University Press of America, 2002.

Thomas, William H. B. *Remarkable High Tories: Supporters of King and Parliament in Revolutionary Massachusetts.* Bowie, Md.: Heritage Books, 2001.

Van Buskirk, Judith L. *Generous Enemies: Patriots and Loyalists in Revolutionary New York.* Philadelphia: University of Pennsylvania Press, 2002.

Ludington, Sybil (1761–1839)
American messenger

Sybil Ludington was born in Fredericksburg, New York, on April 5, 1761, the daughter of Henry Ludington, a noted local militia officer. She was the oldest of 12 siblings when the Revolutionary War broke out and was tending to her home chores on the evening of April 26, 1777, when an exhausted messenger arrived for her father. He then relayed intelligence that British and LOYALIST forces under Governor William TRYON had burned the nearby town of Danbury, Connecticut, only 15 miles distant. Colonel Ludington, preoccupied by organizing his men, lacked a fresh messenger to spread the alarm to other parts of the county. He therefore dispatched 16-year-old Sybil, an accomplished rider, to alert the others. Galloping off into the darkness, she rode the entire 40-mile circuit around Putnam County, from Carmel to Stormville, knocking on doors and warning the owners. Consequently, the Americans mustered a force sufficiently large under Colonel Benedict ARNOLD to harass the raiders at Ridgefield, Connecticut, on the following day. In 1784 Ludington married a lawyer and settled down in Unadilla, New York, and remained there until her death on February 26, 1839. However, thanks to her exertions that night she became locally known as the "female Paul REVERE" and gradually acquired national fame as well. In 1961 an impressive statue was erected to her memory at Carmel, New York, while her home town of Fredericksburg renamed itself Ludington.

Further Reading

Berkin, Carol. *America's Revolutionary Mothers: Women in the Struggle for Independence.* New York: Alfred Knopf, 2005.

Berson, Robin K. *Young Heroes in World History.* Westport, Conn.: Greenwood Press, 1999.

Bohrer, Melissa L. *Glory, Passion, Principle: The Story of Eight Remarkable Women at the Core of the American Revolution.* New York: Atria Books, 2004.

Daquino, V. T. *Sybil Ludington: The Call to Arms.* Fleischmanns, N.Y.: Purple Mountain Press, 2000.

Jones, Keith. *Farmers against the Crown: A Comprehensive Account of the Revolutionary War Battle in Ridgefield, Connecticut, April 27, 1777.* Ridgefield: Connecticut Colonel Pub., 2002.

Roberts, Cokie. *Founding Mothers: The Women Who Raised Our Nation.* New York: William Morrow, 2004.

Madison, James (1751–1836)
American politician, fourth president of the United States

James Madison was born in Port Conway, Virginia, on March 16, 1751, the son of an affluent planter. Well educated by tutors at home and possessing a lucid, engaging intellect, he attended the College of New Jersey (Princeton) and obtained his bachelor's degree in 1771, after only two years of study. Short at five feet six inches tall, pale, and physically nondescript, Madison's appearance belied a brilliant, incisive mind. He proved extremely adept in the classics and became intrigued by the rise and fall of ancient republics. Madison also studied and inculcated the tenets of the Scottish Enlightenment. He returned home to ponder various careers in law and theology, yet was gradually drawn into the revolutionary activities of his day. Madison acquitted his first public service by winning election to the Orange County Committee of Safety in 1774, a minor experience that whetted his intellect—and appetite—for even greater political challenges. By May 1776 Madison had found his niche in politics. He sat in the Virginia convention tasked with drawing up a new state constitution and immediately impressed contemporaries with his profound intellect and political grasp. For this reason he won a seat in the new House of Burgesses, where he met and befriended another towering intellect, Thomas JEFFERSON; the two men remained confidants for life. Madison's most significant work here was in helping Jefferson craft and ultimately pass legislation disestablishing the Church of England as an official religion. This, in effect, initiated the greater move toward complete religious freedom under the First Amendment. Madison then failed to gain reelection because he refused to shower his constituents with liquor, as was the popular tradition. He nevertheless won a seat on the governor's council and advised Patrick HENRY on essential matters of state. By dint of erudition, reasoning, and political savvy, Madison's political reputation grew exponentially, and in December 1779 he gained a seat in the Second Continental CONGRESS.

In Philadelphia, Madison began exhibiting the political brilliance that characterized his subsequent career. He proved instrumental in coaxing the Virginia House of Delegates to renounce all claims to western lands, an issue that Maryland and other states had used to obstruct ratification of the ARTICLES OF CONFEDERATION. Yet, mindful of weakness inherent under the articles, he strove to strengthen the government by crafting amendments granting it the power to levy duties. The effort ultimately failed in state legislatures, but his endeavors portended events to come. He also supported Robert MORRIS's goal of establishing greater fiscal responsibility through new executive departments like the Department of Finance. Moreover, he favored strengthening the FRENCH ALLIANCE and the final TREATY OF PARIS. After the war ended in 1783 the diminutive leader returned to the House of Delegates, grimly fixed upon measures that would strengthen the national government.

Over the intervening years Madison functioned as a principal spokesman for greater centralized authority, a political notion that seemed to contradict the goals of the Revolution. When the Constitutional Convention met in Philadelphia in 1787–88, he authored and put forward the so-called Virginia Plan, which ultimately served as the basis for a new federal constitution. Unlike many politicians of his day, Madison did not fear centralized authority, but rather he embraced it as the best means of preventing chaos and thereby preserving liberties. To further this objective, he joined ranks with other nationalists like Alexander HAMILTON and John JAY and penned several essays delineating the advantages of a new constitution in a series of famous pamphlets entitled *The Federalist Papers*. He then proved essential in convincing the Virginia Convention to ratify the document in 1788 by overcoming entrenched resistance from Patrick Henry and George MASON. The final document so closely reflected Madison's political precepts that he is regarded as the "father of the U.S. Constitution" and the architect behind its unique system of republican governance.

Madison remained in the forefront of national politics over the next three decades, replacing Gouverneur MORRIS as minister to France in 1794, serving as secretary of state under President Jefferson, 1801–09, and ultimately president himself from 1809 to 1816. His tenure as chief executive proved tumultuous, for the young republic was increasingly ensnared by the ongoing Napoléonic conflagration. In June 1812 Madison convinced Congress to declare war on Great Britain, despite the military unpreparedness of the United States. He did so out of the conviction that war was the only way to preserve republicanism and prevent its subversion by British aggression on the high seas. A harrowing two years of war ensued, and he was succeeded by James MONROE, the third member of the "Virginia Dynasty," in 1816. Madison then retired to private life on his estate at Montpelier, Virginia. He died there on June 28, 1836, a little man whose public career wielded big implications for the United States. Madison's role in the Revolutionary War was relatively minor, but it set in motion his dogged determination to ensure that newfound liberties acquired therein would be preserved in perpetuity. For this reason Madison remains among the most significant of the Founding Fathers.

Further Reading

Banning, Lance. *The Sacred Fire of Liberty: James Madison and the Founding of the Federal Republic*. Ithaca, N.Y.: Cornell University Press, 1998.

Leibiger, Stuart E. *Founding Friendship: George Washington, James Madison, and the Creation of the American Republic*. Charlottesville: University Press of Virginia, 1999.

Mattern, David B., ed. *James Madison's Advice to My Country*. Charlottesville: University Press of Virginia, 1997.

Rakove, Jack N., and Oscar Handlin. *James Madison and the Creation of the American Republic*. New York: Longman, 2002.

Read, James H. *Power versus Liberty: Madison, Hamilton, Wilson, and Jefferson*. Charlottesville: University Press of Virginia, 2000.

Sheldon, Garrett W. *The Political Philosophy of James Madison*. Baltimore: Johns Hopkins University Press, 2001.

Manley, John (1746–1829)
American naval officer

John Manley was probably born at Torquay, England, around 1732, and he entered the merchant marine while young. He then immigrated to Marblehead, Massachusetts, where he successfully plied the waters between New England and the West Indies. When the Revolutionary War erupted in April 1775 Manley threw in his lot with the Patriots, and the following August General George WASHINGTON appointed him to command the schooner *Lee*, one of the nation's first warships. He was tasked with intercepting British shipping in and out of Boston Harbor while American forces besieged General Thomas GAGE in the city. On October 28, 1775, he seized the British brig *Nancy,* the first American prize of the war. Moreover, this vessel was heavily laden with valuable stores of gunpowder and cannon, which were immediately relayed back to the army. In January 1776 Washington appointed Manley commander of a small squadron of schooners to continue interdicting British supplies. He again enjoyed considerable success, so in April 1776 the Continental CONGRESS appointed him captain in the newly forming Continental NAVY. He was placed second in seniority on the published captain's list.

The following August Manley was appointed to take command of the new 32-gun frigate *Hancock,* then being constructed at Newburyport, Massachusetts. In this capacity he was forced to compete with another captain, Hector MCNEILL of the frigate *Boston,* for scarce seamen and supplies; in time the two developed a thinly veiled contempt for each other. Manley and McNeill then sailed in May 1777 to cruise for British prizes off the Grand Banks. On June 7, 1777, they encountered and subdued the 24-gun frigate HMS *Fox,* which was added to their small squadron. Proceeding ahead, Manley next encountered Captain George COLLIER and the 44-gun frigate HMS *Rainbow* and its escort *Flora* on July 7. Outgunned, he tried fleeing and should have easily outpaced the slower British ships but for his placement of heavy cargo in the *Hancock's* forward holds. This had the effect of dipping his vessel's bow lower than usual and sufficiently slowed it for Collier to keep apace. After a harrowing chase of 39 hours Manley—long deserted by McNeill—struck his colors on July 9 and was interned at New York.

In March 1778 Manley was exchanged, although the navy had suffered severe losses by that point and no warships were available. He then assumed command of a succession of privateers, including *Marlborough* and *Cumberland,* taking several prizes. In 1779 Manley was taken by HMS *Pomona* and imprisoned on Barbados. He engineered an escape, took the helm of the privateer *Jason,* and was captured again. Manley then remained nearly two years at Mill Prison in Plymouth before being exchanged, and in September 1782 he received the frigate *Hague* as a final command. That month, while cruising near Martinique, he was set upon by several larger British vessels and ran aground in the harbor. Manley fought a stiff action against steep odds but managed to work the *Hague* free and escape. This was apparently the last confrontation between commissioned warships during the Revolutionary War. Furthermore, while returning to Boston in January 1783, Manley attacked and seized the *Baille,* the final prize taken by the Continental navy. Thus he had taken both the first and last prizes of the conflict.

After reaching Boston, Manley was charged with misconduct by several of his subordinates, and he resigned his commission. He then resumed his work with the merchant marine until dying in Boston on February 12, 1793. A mediocre commander despite his seniority, Manley failed to exhibit the superior qualities of many contemporaries.

Further Reading
Dow, H. E. "Captain John Manley of the Continental Navy," *United States Naval Institute Proceedings* 52 (August 1926): 1,554–1,561.
Greenwood, Isaac T. *Captain John Manley, Second in Rank in the United States Navy, 1776–1783.* Boston: C. E. Goodspeed, 1915.
Hearn, Chester G. *George Washington's Schooners: The First American Navy.* Annapolis, Md.: Naval Institute Press, 1995.
Peabody, Robert E. *The Naval Career of Captain John Manley of Marblehead.* Salem, Mass.: Essex Institute, 1909.
Powers, Stephen T. "Robert Morris and the Courts-martial of Captains Samuel Nicholson and John Manley of the Continental Navy," *Military Affairs* 44, no. 1 (1980): 13–17.
Smith, Philip C. F. *Fired by Manley Zeal: A Naval Fiasco of the American Revolution.* Salem, Mass.: Peabody Museum of Salem, 1977.

Marion, Francis (ca. 1732–1795)
American militia officer

Francis Marion was born in Berkeley County, South Carolina, around 1732, the son of farmers. Frail and sickly as a child, he tried serving in the merchant marine but returned home to resume farming. His first brush with military service occurred in 1759, when he served as a lieutenant in a war against the Cherokee. At one point his company was ambushed and surrounded, but he conducted a dogged last stand that thwarted his antagonists. That Marion acquired a fine military reputation is surprising since he was poorly educated and remained semi-literate his entire life. But once hostilities commenced in April 1775, he sat in the provincial congress as a delegate and subsequently received a captain's commission in the 2nd South Carolina Continental Infantry. In this capacity he helped capture British arsenals throughout the state while rising to major. Marion further distinguished himself during the attack on CHARLESTON on June 28, 1776, by manning the guns of Fort Sullivan. By 1778 he had advanced to lieutenant colonel of his regiment and led it during the unsuccessful attack on SAVANNAH, Georgia, in October 1779. Marion should have accompanied his regiment during General Benjamin LINCOLN's ill-fated defense during the siege of CHARLESTON, but he was sidelined at home with a broken ankle. Charleston's surrender to General Henry CLINTON in May 1780 and the crushing American defeat of CAMDEN at the hands of General Charles CORNWALLIS that August effectively ended organized resistance to British arms. It thus fell upon men like Marion, Andrew PICKENS, and Thomas SUMTER to stoke the dying embers of revolution through concerted guerrilla warfare.

Operating from the interior, and usually based in a swamp or a bog for protection, Marion quickly gained notoriety as a talented partisan warrior. In his first action of August 20, 1780, he wiped out a LOYALIST force and freed 147 Patriot prisoners captured at Camden. Thereafter he struck hard and repeatedly at enemy lines of communication and supply, never hesitating to cut off and capture small British and Loyalist detachments where possible. Moreover, his men constantly shifted and changed locations to avoid being attacked themselves. Cornwallis, exasperated by the seeming ease of Marion's operations, dispatched the feared Lieutenant Colonel Banastre TARLETON to run down these ragtag guerrillas. At one point troopers of the British Legion had chased the fleeing Americans through 26 miles of swamp when Tarleton suddenly halted and declared, "As for this old fox, the Devil himself could not catch him." The sobriquet stuck, and from this point on Marion became celebrated as the "Swamp Fox" and a genuine hero of the revolutionary south. Unlike his more flamboyant contemporary Sumter, the priggish Marion was a strict disciplinarian who dressed modestly, never drank, and forbade his troops from plundering Loyalist property.

Marion's success crested in 1781, when Governor John RUTLEDGE promoted him to brigadier general of militia. That year he also formed a close relationship with General Nathanael GREENE in an intense war against British outposts dotting the Carolinas. Marion, usually in concert with the cavalry legions of Henry LEE and William WASHINGTON, repeatedly isolated, attacked, and usually captured British and Loyalist strong points. Another high point of his career arrived when he commanded a brigade of South Carolina troops at the hard-fought battle of Eutaw Springs in September 1781. His effective performance helped check a determined counterattack by Lieutenant Colonel Alexander STEWART and saved the Americans from being defeated piecemeal. By year's end the British abandoned their interior posts and withdrew to the vicinity of Charleston. Marion dogged their retreat closely, cutting off stragglers, and on August 29, 1782, he ambushed a column of British dragoons sent to attack him at Fair Lawn. After the war Marion turned to politics, serving in the state senate and pressing for the peaceful assimilation of Loyalists back into society. Marion died at Pond Bluff on February 27, 1795, one of the great guerrilla leaders of all time.

Further Reading

Edgar, Walter. *Partisans and Redcoats: The Southern Conflict That Turned the Tide of the American Revolution.* New York: William Morrow, 2001.

Fitz-Simmons, Daniel E. "Francis Marion, the 'Swamp Fox': An Anatomy of a Low-Intensity Conflict," *Small Wars and Insurgencies* 6, no. 1 (1995): 1–16.

Helsley, Alexia J. *South Carolinians in the War for Independence.* Columbia: South Carolina Department of History and Archives, 2000.

Risjord, Norman K. *The Revolutionary Generation.* Lanham, Md.: Rowman & Littlefield, 2001.

Thomsen, Paul A. "The Devil Himself Could Not Catch Him," *American History* 35, no. 3 (2000): 46–52.

———. "Guerilla Patriot: The Intelligence Gathering Efforts and Battle Tactics of Francis Marion," *American Intelligence Journal* 21, nos. 1, 2 (2002): 61–65.

Martin, Josiah (1737–1786)

English politician

Josiah Martin was born in Dublin, Ireland, on April 23, 1737, the son of a prominent Antigua sugar planter. He was initially groomed for law and briefly studied at the Inner Temple, London, before joining the island militia in 1754. Within three years Martin had risen to ensign in the 4th Regiment, and he saw action against Martinique and Guadelupe. He proved himself a competent officer, and by the end of the French and Indian War in 1763 he functioned as lieutenant colonel of the 22nd Regiment. However, poor health forced him to sell his commission in 1769, and he unknowingly requested friends in Parliament to help secure him a civil post in North America. Accordingly, on December 14, 1770, he gained appointment as royal governor of North Carolina—unknowingly destined to be the last such official.

Martin arrived at New Bern on August 12, 1771, and was cordially received. To better acquaint himself with his subjects, he spent the next three months touring the colony and getting acquainted with local officials. Unfortunately, North Carolina was being buffeted by the winds of revolution, and he proved unable to deal with a recalcitrant legislature. The main sticking point was the issue of "foreign attachment," whereby creditors could place liens on a merchant's property in England for failing to pay local debts. When Martin rejected such legislation he became scorned as an object of derision and political hatred. Thereafter the legislature blocked any law lacking the attachment clause, which led to the collapse of the colonial court system by 1773. Martin countered by trying to establish special criminal courts, but the legislature declined funding them. A major constitutional crisis then erupted in August 1774, when revolutionary leaders convened an extralegal provincial congress to choose delegates for the upcoming Continental CONGRESS. Martin, feeling that he lacked local support, fled to Fort Johnson on the Cape Fear River to await developments. When bands of Patriot militia began converging on his headquarters, Martin boarded the nearby vessel HMS *Cruizer* on June 1, 1775, which functioned as his headquarters for several months. There he concocted grandiose schemes for a LOYALIST-supported counterrevolution, based upon the large number of Scottish immigrants still subservient to the Crown. Officials in London read his correspondence closely, for they, like Martin, strongly believed that the majority of North Carolinians supported England. They began sending the governor and his supporters weapons and supplies and also promised him assistance in the form of a major amphibious expedition. Martin waited patiently aboard HMS *Cruizer* for several months, anticipating the day when he could retake the colony and reestablish royal authority. However, on February 27, 1776, the Loyalists were crushed by Patriot forces at Moore's Creek Bridge, and his long-anticipated resurgence withered.

Martin met with the British expedition under Commodore Peter PARKER and General Henry CLINTON when it arrived off Cape Fear on March 12, 1776. He then accompanied them during the ill-fated attack on CHARLESTON in June 1776 and withdrew to New York with the fleet. Martin spent the next three years trying to convince British authorities of his ability to rally Loyalists if given the resources. In December 1779, Clinton mounted a new expedition against South Carolina, and Martin fought at the ensuing siege of CHARLESTON as a volunteer. He then accompanied General Charles CORNWALLIS during the invasion of North Carolina, winning high praise for his ability as a soldier but still unable to explain the tepid Loyalist response. After fighting bravely at GUILFORD COURTHOUSE in March 1781, Martin took ill and returned to England. There he served on the American Loyalist Claims Commission, tasked with doling out compensation to refugees, before dying in London on April 13, 1786. For the time that he held office Martin governed well, but his tumultuous tenure as governor underscored his misjudgement of the mounting resentment against colonial rule.

Further Reading
Butler, Lindley S. "The Coming of the Revolution in North Carolina, 1763–1776." Unpublished Ph.D. diss., University of North Carolina, Chapel Hill, 1971.
Glass, David M. "Josiah Martin: An Examination of His Life Prior to His Becoming North Carolina's Last Royal Governor." Unpublished master's thesis, Wake Forest University, 1986.
Hartsoe, Kenneth D. "Governor Josiah Martin and His 1772 Journey to the North Carolina Backcountry." Unpublished master's thesis, San Jose State University, 2001.
Sheridan, Richard B. "The West Indian Antecedents of Josiah Martin, Last Royal Governor of North Carolina," *North Carolina Historical Review* 54, no. 3 (1977): 253–270.
Smith, Penelope. "Creation of an American State: Politics of North Carolina, 1765–1789." Unpublished Ph.D. diss., Rice University, 1980.
Stumpf, Vernon O. *Josiah Martin: The Last Royal Governor of North Carolina.* Durham, N.C.: Carolina Academic Press for the Kellenberger Historical Foundation, 1986.

Mason, George (1725–1792)
American politician

George Mason was born in Stafford County, Virginia, in 1725, the son of a wealthy planter. When his father died he was raised by his uncle, a noted lawyer, and became thoroughly steeped in jurisprudence. Mason inherited the family fortune and lived the life of a country squire. He also dabbled in land speculation, serving as treasurer of the Ohio Company and befriending George WASHINGTON in the process. Mason also held minor political offices, but he generally disdained public life and preferred working privately. Possessed of an incisive intellect and firmly grounded in legal, political, and moral issues, he nevertheless found himself in great demand following the STAMP ACT of 1765. After passage of the TOWNSHEND DUTIES in 1767, Mason crafted the Virginia Resolves, which more or less advanced the argument that Parliament lacked the right to tax the colonies without their consent. This document, once introduced into the House of Burgesses by Washington, so angered royal governor James MURRAY, Lord Dunmore, that he dissolved the legislature. As the imperial crisis deepened, so too did Mason's intellectual assault upon British practices. On July 18, 1774, he penned the famous Fairfax Resolves to protest the COERCIVE ACTS and reiterated colonial positions in even bolder terms. In a significant escalation of rhetoric, he formally accused the English government of attempting to enslave its colonies. Taken together his two documents intellectually framed the then emerging revolutionary ideology. His discourse proved so persuasive that it was accepted by the Continental CONGRESS as the rationale behind its existence. In 1775 Mason also sat with the Virginia Committee of Safety, which assumed control of the colony and ousted Governor Dunmore from power. He was then tasked with replacing the royal charter with a new constitution.

Mason's greatest intellectual contribution to American political philosophy occurred in May 1776 when he originated the Virginia Declaration of Rights. The concepts and wording so moved Thomas JEFFERSON that he freely inculcated its precepts and phrasing in his own DECLARATION OF INDEPENDENCE. Eventually, Mason's principles manifested in the U.S. Constitution as the first 10 amendments, or Bill of Rights. But celebrity notwithstanding, Mason himself declined the political limelight and never ventured to Philadelphia. He remained in the Virginia House of Delegates and helped sponsor the western campaigns of Colonel George Rogers CLARK to secure the state's western flank. By the time the war ended in 1783, he had already withdrawn from public life and returned to his estate to continue philosophical ruminations.

Mason reentered the public arena in 1787 as movement toward replacing the ARTICLES OF CONFEDERATION gathered steam, and he represented Virginia at the Constitutional Convention in Philadelphia. He initially supported the concept of more centralized governance but ended up opposing the constitution rendered by fellow Virginian James MADISON for failing to safeguard individual liberties with a bill of rights. He also railed against its compromise on slavery—which Mason regarded as an anathema to civilized rule. He then attended the Virginia Constitutional Convention as a delegate and, in concert with Patrick HENRY, nearly derailed the process. Once the new government was adopted and the Bill of Rights appended, he dropped his opposition and embraced the new government. Mason then resumed his life of seclusion until dying at Gunston Hall on October 7, 1792. From a political and philosophical standpoint—especially his steadfast and unapologetic defense of individual rights—he is regarded as the finest example of the "American Enlightenment." His contributions during the revolutionary period are not as well known as Jefferson or Madison's, but Mason's ideas and principles have permeated the very fabric of the American political system.

Further Reading

Bradford, Melvin E. *George Mason: Planter, Political Philosopher, and Statesman*. Lawrence: University Press of Kansas, 1994.

Engal, Marc. "The Origins of the Revolution in Virginia: A Reinterpretation," *William and Mary Quarterly* 37, no. 3 (1980): 401–428.

Rutland, Robert A. *George Mason and the War of Independence*. Williamsburg: Virginia Independence Bicentennial Commission, 1976.

———, ed. *The Papers of George Mason, 1752–1790*, 3 vols. Chapel Hill: University of North Carolina Press, 1970.

Schwartz, Stephan A. "George Mason," *Smithsonian* 31, no. 2 (2000): 142–154.

Wilkins, Roger W. *Jefferson's Pillow: The Founding Fathers and the Dilemma of Black Patriotism*. Boston: Beacon Press, 2002.

Maxwell, William (ca. 1733–1796)
American military officer

William Maxwell was born in County Tyrone, Ireland, around 1733 and he migrated with his parents to Sussex (now Warren) County, New Jersey, by 1747. He joined the provincial army at the onset of the French and Indian War in 1754 and fought at General Edward Braddock's defeat in western Pennsylvania. Maxwell subsequently served in various American regiments and was apparently present at Fort Ticonderoga in 1758 and most likely at the fall of Quebec in 1759. Maxwell remained in the service after the war and had risen to commissary officer at Fort Mackinac when the first rumblings of the Revolutionary War arose. He then resigned his commission and returned to New Jersey, where he served with the provincial congress and as chairman of the committee of safety. On November 8, 1775, he became colonel of the 2nd New Jersey Continental Infantry and in the spring of 1776 he accompanied General John SULLIVAN on a march to reinforce American forces in Canada. In this capacity he fought with General William THOMPSON at the defeat of Trois Rivieres on June 6, 1776. He then bitterly complained to CONGRESS when Colonel Arthur ST. CLAIR was promoted brigadier general ahead of him. Maxwell also vociferously opposed General Philip J. SCHULYER's intention to abandon Crown Point, New York, to the advancing forces of General Guy CARLETON. On October 23, 1776, Maxwell finally rose to brigadier general, and he served under General George WASHINGTON during the New Jersey campaign. He ended the year posted at Elizabethtown guarding the Jersey coast. He had since acquired the reputation of a brave combat officer but was uneven under fire and heavily dependent upon liquor.

In the spring of 1777 Maxwell assumed control of the Light Infantry Brigade, whose handpicked men were drawn from every regiment in the army. This unit arose to replace the riflemen of Colonel Daniel MORGAN, then operating in northern New York. Maxwell commanded his men adroitly at the Battle of Cooch's Bridge, Delaware, on September 3, 1777, the initial skirmish of General William HOWE's Philadelphia campaign. The Americans fought well until outflanked by HESSIAN adversaries and forced to fall back. This was reputedly the first conflict waged under the new "Stars and Stripes" flag recently adopted by Congress. Maxwell subsequently performed well at BRANDYWINE and GERMANTOWN that fall, although he was brought up on charges of excessive drinking. A court of inquiry proved inconclusive, so he returned to Valley Forge for the winter, leading a newly recruited New Jersey brigade. The following summer Maxwell's troops were closely engaged at MONMOUTH in August 1778, and he subsequently testified against General Charles LEE at his court-martial.

In the summer of 1779 Maxwell again joined General Sullivan, this time on his punitive expedition into the heart of Iroquois territory. Sullivan was well acquainted with his subordinate and had specifically requested his services. Maxwell performed well, and in August, when Sullivan sickened, he temporarily assumed control of the entire army. That fall he returned home with his brigade to New Jersey. In June 1780 he proved instrumental in organizing troops and militia to blunt the advance of General Wilhelm von KNYPHAUSEN at Connecticut Farms and Springfield. However, Maxwell grew discontented with the lack of recognition and tendered his resignation to Congress in the mistaken belief he could gain a promotion. But the ploy backfired when it was accepted, and command of Jersey troops consequently devolved upon Colonel William DAYTON. Maxwell tried and failed to achieve reinstatement, then resumed his interest in politics. In 1783 he served a term in the state legislature but otherwise failed to distinguish himself. The hard-drinking Maxwell died at Lansdowne, New Jersey, on November 4, 1796, brave and resolute but a decidedly mediocre commander.

Further Reading
Griffith, J. H. "William Maxwell of New Jersey in the Revolution," *New Jersey Historical Society Proceedings* 13, no. 2 (1894): 111–123.
Heathcote, Charles W. "General William Maxwell—an Earnest Patriot," *Picket Post* no. 467 (February 1955): 13–18.
Honeyman, A. Van Doren, ed. "General William Maxwell Correspondence," *New Jersey Historical Society Proceedings* 10 (April 1925): 176–180.
Minnock, Barbara J. *New Jersey in the American Revolution.* New Brunswick, N.J.: Rutgers University Press, 2005.
Ward, Harry M. *General William Maxwell and the New Jersey Continentals.* Westport, Conn.: Greenwood Press, 1997.
Yesenko, Michael R. *General William Maxwell and the New Jersey Brigade during the American Revolutionary War.* Union, N.J.: MRY Pub. Co., 1996.

McCrea, Jane (ca. 1752–1777)
Loyalist

Jane McCrea was born in Somerset County, New Jersey, around 1752, the daughter of a Presbyterian minister. Nothing is known of her childhood, but she had several brothers, some of whom joined the Continental ARMY during the Revolutionary War, while others became LOYALISTS. As McCrea grew up she also befriended David Jones, a local boy with whom a love interest arose. When the Revolution commenced, Jones relocated to the region of Fort Edward, New York, but the two lovers maintained their correspondence. In the summer of 1777 McCrea was invited by her brother, Colonel John McCrea of the New York militia, to move in with his family near Albany. She made the move but was contacted by Jones, then serving as a scout under General John BURGOYNE. He entreated her to meet him at Fort Edward to be married. She willingly obliged him and awaited her beau at the home of another Loyalist friend, Mrs. Sarah McNeil, a relative of General Simon FRASER. According to legend, McCrea and Mrs. McNeil were accosted by Native American scouts working for Burgoyne. Details are vague and varying but, en route to the British camp, McCrea was killed and scalped. Jones was waiting patiently for her when he sadly recognized her scalp, unmistakably distinguished by its long, flowing locks. Her body was subsequently discovered near Fort Edward and properly interred. In 1852 she was again laid to rest in the Union Cemetery north of Fort Edward.

McCrea's grisly demise had unforeseen and somewhat far-reaching consequences. The American commander at Saratoga, General Horatio GATES, wrote Burgoyne a scathing letter denouncing the latter's use of Indians against helpless civilians. Burgoyne, for his part, apologized for the matter, which he portrayed as an unfortunate incident. However, when he failed to punish the alleged offender for fear of alienating his tawny auxiliaries, Gates excoriated McCrea's murder as simply the latest example of British injustice toward colonials. In fact, the matter served as a propaganda windfall for the Patriots. Word spread quickly about the colonies and even to England, where no less a figure than Edmund BURKE chastised the government for employing Indians against its former subjects. Closer to home, McCrea also served as an unexpected rallying point for the local militia, who began flocking under the American banner. But, because the actual events surrounding McCrea remain obscure, wrapped in folklore, and shrouded by the mists of time, her exact contribution to the American cause—Burgoyne's downfall in particular—will never be known. Artist John Vanderlyn subsequently commemorated her passing in a celebrated painting, *The Murder of Jane McCrea,* which embodied Indian savagery toward non-combatants.

Further Reading
Cortesi, Lawrence. "The Tragic Romance of Jane McCrea," *American History Illustrated* 20, no. 2 (1985): 10–15.
Edgerton, Samuel Y. "The Murder of Jane McCrea: The Tragedy of an American Tableau d'Histoire," *Art Bulletin* 58 (December 1965): 481–492.
———. "The Murder of Jane McCrea and Vattemare's System of International Exchange," *Bulletin of the Fort Ticonderoga Museum* 11, no. 6 (1965): 336–342.
Koster, John. "Jane McCrea, Remembered as a Victim of American Indian Brutality, May Have Died under Different Circumstances," *Military History* 17, no. 2 (2000): 12–14.
Namias, June. *White Captives: Gender and Ethnicity on the American Frontier.* Chapel Hill: University of North Carolina Press, 1993.
Tomkinson, Grace. "Jane McCrea: A Martyr of the Revolutionary War," *Dalhousie Review* 49, no. 3 (1969): 399–403.

McDougall, Alexander (1732–1786)
American military officer

Alexander McDougall was born on the Isle of Islay, Scotland, sometime in 1732, the son of a dairyman. He immigrated to New York with his family as a child and eventually worked in the merchant marine. McDougall commanded several privateers during the Seven Years' War, making a small fortune that enabled him to settle in New York City. He subsequently flourished as a merchant but did not become involved in radical politics until 1769, when he published a fiery polemic entitled *A Son of Liberty to the Betrayed Inhabitants of the City and Colony of New York,* which criticized the colonial assembly for subsidizing the QUARTERING ACT. He was afterward arrested for libel and imprisoned when he refused to post bail. This defiance catapulted McDougall into the forefront of New York dissidents, and he was hailed as the "American John WILKES." In fact, so many distinguished supporters visited him in his jail cell that appointments became necessary. He was never brought to trial and eventually released until the assembly summoned him for questioning. When McDougall refused to answer questions, every member of that body voted to condemn him except Philip J. SCHUYLER, and he suffered incarceration again until March 1771. Thereafter McDougall became indelibly associated with anti-

British agitation. He attended a number of provincial congresses and also served on the local COMMITTEE OF CORRESPONDENCE. After helping arrange a provisional government in May 1775, McDougall was appointed colonel of the 1st New York Continental Infantry. He spent several months fortifying New York City but remained behind for recruiting purposes when his charge marched off to Canada. McDougall still favorably impressed General George WASHINGTON, and he influenced the Continental CONGRESS to have him appointed brigadier general in August 1776.

McDougall garrisoned New York City and missed the Battle of LONG ISLAND on August 27, 1776, but three days later he supervised Colonel John GLOVER's evacuation of American forces from Brooklyn Heights. He acquitted himself well at WHITE PLAINS on October 28, 1776, by his gallant stand at Chatterton's Hill against steep odds, and then accompanied the American withdrawal across New Jersey. McDougall endured a harsh winter at Valley Forge, which severely compromised his health, but went on to fight well at GERMANTOWN on October 4, 1777. Assisted by troops under General John P. MUHLENBERG, McDougall's brigade charged into the very center of town before being nearly surrounded. Three weeks later McDougall gained promotion to major general and received a health-related furlough at his own request. Over the next two years he succeeded General Israel PUTNAM as commander of the Hudson Highlands and served intermittently due to illness. In 1780 he replaced General Benedict ARNOLD as commander of strategic West Point, and performed capably until he won a seat in Congress that October. He served at Philadelphia for three months as secretary of the Marine Department but then donned his uniform and returned to West Point in March 1781. The following year McDougall had a dispute with his superior, General William HEATH, over the chain of command and was court-martialed. He was found guilty on one court of insubordination and returned to duty. As the war gradually wound down, many army officers began grumbling over back pay and other benefits that Congress had promised yet reneged upon, and McDougall served as an intermediary during sensitive negotiations. He was not officially connected with the so-called NEWBURGH CONSPIRACY but undoubtedly held sympathy for the rebels. McDougall later helped to found the Society of the Cincinnati, serving as first secretary-treasurer.

Afterward McDougall resumed his interest in politics by returning to Congress, 1784–85, and also fulfilled a term in the New York state senate, 1783–86. Thereafter he became closely associated with the faction of Alexander HAMILTON, who arranged for him to serve as first president of the newly chartered Bank of New York. McDougall died in New York on June 10, 1786, a capable military leader when not sidelined by poor health.

Further Reading
Champagne, Roger J. *Alexander McDougall and the American Revolution in New York.* Schenectady, N.Y.: Union College Press, 1975.
Diamant, Lincoln. *Chaining the Hudson: The Fight for the River in the American Revolution.* Bronx, N.Y.: Fordham University Press, 2004.
Egly, T. W. *History of the First New York Regiment, 1775–1783.* Hampton, N.H.: P. E. Randall, 1981.
Launitz-Schurer, Leopold S. *Loyal Whigs and Revolutionaries: The Making of the Revolution in New York, 1765–1776.* New York: New York University Press, 1980.
MacDougall, William L. *American Revolutionary: A Biography of General Alexander McDougall.* Westport, Conn.: Greenwood Press, 1977.
Shannon, Anna M. "General Alexander McDougall: Citizen and Soldier, 1732–1786." Unpublished Ph.D. diss., Fordham University, 1957.

McDowell, Joseph (1756–1801)
American militia officer

Joseph McDowell was born in Winchester, Virginia, on February 15, 1756, and he was raised in Burke County, North Carolina. In 1776 he rose to major in the militia regiment commanded by his elder brother Charles and fought against DRAGGING CANOE in the Cherokee War of that year.

Over the next four years McDowell engaged in minor skirmishes against roving bands of Indians and LOYALISTS in the Carolina backcountry, and in 1780 he joined forces with Colonel Isaac SHELBY to oppose the invasion of General Charles CORNWALLIS. The British advance occasioned a Loyalist resurgence and on June 10, 1780, McDowell thwarted an ambush near Ramseur's Mills. However, the American defeat at CAMDEN that August severely dampened all organized resistance, and the guerrillas disbanded for several weeks. It was not until the appearance of Major Patrick FERGUSON in the western counties that McDowell reassembled enough men to sustain field operations. He then joined a large gathering of "Over the Mountain Men" under Colonel William CAMPBELL and marched to engage Ferguson, who was annihilated at KING'S MOUNTAIN on October 7, 1780. Most of the Americans then dispersed, but McDowell's command of 190 mounted riflemen subsequently joined the army of General Daniel MORGAN in North Carolina. On January 17, 1781, he fought at the victory of COWPENS as part of Colonel William WASHINGTON's command. The following year McDowell served under his brother in another campaign against the Cherokee.

After the war McDowell stood for a seat in the state legislature, 1785–89 and 1791–95. He also attended the state constitutional convention and opposed ratification of that document for want of a bill of rights. Once the new government was organized in 1789, McDowell sat in the new federal CONGRESS from 1797 to 1799. He died in Burke County on August 11, 1801, and is commemorated by counties in both North Carolina and Virginia.

Further Reading

Babits, Lawrence E. *A Devil of a Whipping: The Battle of Cowpens.* Chapel Hill: University of North Carolina Press, 2001.

Dameron, J. David. *King's Mountain: The Defeat of the Loyalists, October 7, 1780.* Cambridge, Mass.: Da Capo Press, 2003.

Dildy, David S. "North Carolina Revolutionaries in Arms: The Battle of King's Mountain." Unpublished master's thesis, College of William and Mary, 1997.

Edgar, Walter B. *Partisans and Redcoats: The Southern Conflict That Turned the Tide of the American Revolution.* New York: Morrow, 2001.

Hinderaker, Eric, and Peter C. Mancall. *At the Edge of Empire: The Backcountry of British North America.* Baltimore: Johns Hopkins University Press, 2003.

Wheeler, Earl M. "The Role of the North Carolina Militia in the Beginning of the American Revolution." Unpublished Ph.D. diss., Tulane University, 1969.

McGillivray, Alexander (ca. 1759–1793)
Creek chief

Alexander McGillivray (Hippo-ilk-micco) was born in Little Tassie Village, present-day Alabama, around 1759, the son of a Scottish trader and a Creek woman of the Wind Clan. He was raised among his mother's people until the age of 14, when his father sent him to Savannah and Charleston to be educated. Fluent in Creek and English, McGillivray moved easily between both worlds and worked at his father's countinghouse, where he acquired an excellent grasp of business and economics. However, when the Revolutionary War broke out in 1775 his father, a LOYALIST, returned to Scotland while he was returned to his village among the Upper Creek. Because his tribe was matrilineal, authority passed down through the mother's side, and young McGillivray rose rapidly to positions of authority. At that time the British were also bolstering their slender resources in the South by turning the Creek and other tribesmen against the United States. To that end McGillivray was commissioned a colonel and appointed commissary officer of Indian affairs. He then led a series of raids against Augusta, Georgia, in 1779 to keep the Americans off balance. The following year he mustered 600 warriors to assist in the defense of Pensacola, which helped deter a Spanish conquest for many months. By the time the war ended in 1783 McGillivray was the most powerful leadership figure among the Upper Creek, and he also wielded considerable influence among the lower tribes.

By the terms of the TREATY OF PARIS, Great Britain forsook its Native American allies, and Indian land became the object of white encroachment and settlement. McGillivray, while determined to protect Creek lands, proved astute enough to realize that he could not singlehandedly challenge the United States, so in June 1784 he signed a treaty with SPAIN. This agreement granted the Indians a monopoly of trade conditions and a steady flow of weapons and gunpowder. Closer to home, McGillivray also established a force of "constables" to enforce his will among tribesmen and harass chiefs opposing him. He also determined to play one side off against the other, and that same year McGillivray made friendly overtures to the American government. State authorities in Georgia, eager for his favor, then granted him compensation for properties confiscated during the Revolutionary War. The chief hoped that personal diplomacy, backed by English money and Spanish weapons, could deter the waves of white settlers illegally occupying Indian lands. He also sough to erect a pan-tribal confederacy to oppose the United States by force of arms, if necessary.

Up through 1785 the Americans made no real effort to constrain white expansion, and McGillivray felt he had no option but war. He then unleashed his warriors against settlements across the southern frontier. State governments, dependent solely upon episodic militias, were powerless to stop the onslaught, as was the national government under the ARTICLES OF CONFEDERATION. McGillivray may very well have succeeded in restoring the Creek frontier to its 1773 boundaries, but he was sidelined by Spanish agents, who feared they might be drawn into a war with the Americans. Having cut off the flow of supplies in 1787, they insisted that McGillivray make peace. The chief did so sullenly and only after the governors renounced all claims to Creek land. After 1789, when the United States adopted more centralized governance—and a national army—under the Constitution, McGillivray's position was steadily undermined. The following year Indian agent Marinus WILLETT arrived to invite the chief to New York for a conference with President George WASHINGTON. In August 1790 McGillivray signed a treaty with the Americans that sacrificed Creek lands in Georgia in return for inviolable boundaries around remaining tribal homelands in Alabama. To sweeten the pot, he also received a brigadier general's commission with a yearly stipend of $1,200. But no sooner did McGillivray return home than he recommenced secret negotiations with Spain, obtained an annuity of $2,000, and denounced the American treaty in July 1792. McGillivray's dealings nonetheless angered many of his fellow Creek, and he fled to Pensacola in Spanish-held Florida. He died there on February 17, 1793, an astute power broker of the Old Southwestern frontier.

Creek chief Alexander McGillivray was commissioned as a colonel and commissary of Indian affairs by the British. *(Fordham University Library)*

Further Reading
Barnes, Celia. *Native American Power in the United States, 1783–1795.* Madison, N.J.: Fairleigh Dickinson University Press, 2003.

Edmunds, R. David, ed. *American Indian Leaders: Studies in Diversity.* Lincoln: University of Nebraska Press, 1980.

Langley, Linda. "The Tribal Identity of Alexander McGillivray: A Review of the Historical and Ethnographic Data," *Louisiana History* 46, no. 2 (2005): 231–239.

Martin, James K. *The American Revolution in Indian Country: Crisis and Diversity in Native American Communities.* New York: Cambridge University Press, 1995.

Saunt, Claudio. *A New Order of Things: Property, Power, and the Transformation of the Creek Indians, 1733–1816.* Cambridge: Cambridge University Press, 1999.

Wright, Amos J. *The McGillivray and McIntosh Traders on the Old Southwest Frontier.* Montgomery, Ala.: New South Books, 2000.

McIntosh, Lachlan (1727–1806)
American military officer

Lachlan McIntosh was born at Invernessshire, Scotland, on March 5, 1727, the son of a clan chieftain. He accompanied his family to Darien, Georgia, then a military colony. Dissatisfied with life as a planter, McIntosh relocated to Charleston, South Carolina, where he befriended and worked for Henry LAURENS in his countinghouse. He then moved back to Georgia and established a highly profitable rice plantation. McIntosh, who never expressed much interest in politics, was gradually drawn over to the radical side during the period of difficulties with Great Britain—at a time when most Scottish residents were firmly in the LOYALIST camp. He then served with the colony's provincial congress and in January 1776 ended up as the compromise candidate to win an appointment as colonel of militia. In this capacity McIntosh energetically threw himself into the task of defending Savannah from British attack but was perpetually hobbled by shortages of men, money, and materiel. Nonetheless, his allies in the Continental CONGRESS arranged a promotion to brigadier general within the Continental ARMY as of September 16, 1776. This appointment brought him into a collision course with Button Gwinnett, former governor and signer of the DECLARATION OF INDEPENDENCE, who also coveted the post. Their heated disagreement resulted in a bloody duel on May 16, 1777 whereby McIntosh was wounded and his opponent killed. Gwinnett's allies were making moves to have him charged with murder when McIntosh's friends arranged his transfer north to the army under General George WASHINGTON.

McIntosh arrived at Valley Forge in the winter of 1777, where he assumed command of a Carolina brigade. The following spring Washington appointed him to replace General Edward HAND as commander of the Western Department, with headquarters at Fort Pitt, Pennsylvania. Once again, McIntosh found himself with a large command hobbled by perpetual shortages of manpower and supplies. However, having surveyed the damage inflicted by Indians and Loyalists at the

Scottish settler Lachlan McIntosh was promoted to brigadier general in the Continental army in 1776. *(Independence National Historical Park)*

Wyoming Valley Massacre of July 1778, he resolved to drive the British out of Fort Detroit. Throughout the summer and fall he labored incessantly to amass the requisite troops and supplies, and also managed to recruit Delaware Indians to serve as scouts. But delays proved intractable, and the Americans could not commence operations before October, too late in the season to accomplish anything significant. McIntosh's chief engineer, Louis CAMBRAY-DIGNAY, did manage to erect Forts McIntosh and Laurens in the heart of Indian country to deter future attacks. But, running short of supplies and plagued by heavy rains, he canceled the campaign until the spring of 1779. Failure here caused enemies in Congress to lobby Washington for his removal, and in February 1779 he was replaced by Colonel Daniel BRODHEAD. Again, the two men disagreed strongly over Brodhead's suspected role in his dismissal, and they nearly dueled.

McIntosh subsequently transferred home as part of General Benjamin LINCOLN's army. In October 1779 he bore a conspicuous role in the ill-fated attack on SAVANNAH, where his Georgia and South Carolina Continentals lost heavily. He then accompanied Lincoln back to South Carolina to fight at the siege of CHARLESTON and was taken prisoner in May 1780. McIntosh remained in British hands until February 1782, when he was exchanged for General Charles O'HARA. He then learned that congressional adversaries had suspended his rank during captivity, and he campaigned to retrieve it. Through the intercession of Laurens and James MONROE, McIntosh gained reinstatement and promotion to major general as of September 1783. After the war he attempted to regain his former wealth, but his property had suffered severely during the war. McIntosh subsequently held a succession of state offices, served on numerous boundary commissions, and formed part of the deputation that greeted President Washington in Savannah in 1791. He died there on February 20, 1806, among Georgia's most controversial Revolutionary War leaders.

Further Reading

Cook, Betty. "The Strange Saga of General Lachlan McIntosh," *Daughters of the American Revolution Magazine* 12, no. 9 (1978): 888–891, 893.

Hawes, Lilla M., ed. *Lachlan McIntosh Papers in the University of Georgia Libraries.* Athens: University of Georgia Press, 1968.

Heathcote, Charles W. "General Lachlan McIntosh, Loyal American and Friend of Washington," *Picket Post* no. 55 (February 1957): 9–16.

Jackson, Harvey H. *Lachlan McIntosh and the Politics of Revolutionary Georgia.* Athens: University of Georgia Press, 2003.

Lamplugh, George R. " 'To Check and Discourage the Wicked and Designing': John Wereat and the Revolution in Georgia," *Georgia Historical Quarterly* 61, no. 4 (1977): 295–307.

Williams, Edward G. *Fort Pitt and the Revolution on the Western Frontier.* Pittsburgh, Pa.: Historical Society of Western Pennsylvania, 1978.

McLane, Allan (1746–1829)
American military officer

Allan McLane was born in Philadelphia on August 8, 1746, the son of a Scottish merchant. Well educated at home and in Europe, he married and settled in Kent County, Delaware, where he joined the local militia company. In September 1775 McLane was commissioned a lieutenant, marched to Virginia, and fought against Governor John MURRAY, Lord Dunmore, at the battle of Great Bridge in December 1775, and again at Norfolk in June 1776. He then transferred to the regiment of Colonel Caesar Rodney and joined the main army under General George WASHINGTON in New York. McLane acquitted himself well in the Battle of LONG ISLAND, where, on August 27, 1776, he and his company of mounted scouts captured an entire HESSIAN patrol. He then accompanied the American withdrawal across New Jersey, again fighting with distinction at TRENTON and PRINCETON, and gaining both promotion to captain and an independent command called McLane's Troop. Throughout the ensuing Philadelphia campaign, McLane and his cavalry, assisted by Oneida warriors, performed useful work scouting enemy lines and gathering intelligence. In December 1777 he obtained information from Lydia DARRAGH that British forces were planning a surprise attack on Washington's encampment at Whitemarsh, which was consequently thwarted in timely fashion. On May 20, 1778, McLane received word of another British advance, this time against the marquis de LAFAYETTE at Barren Hill, which was also deflected. After General Henry CLINTON evacuated Philadelphia in August 1778, McLane was among the first American soldiers to enter the city, and his prompt pursuit netted 30 British stragglers. His activities and striking success render him among the most accomplished partisan fighters of the Revolutionary War.

While at Philadelphia in 1779, McLane became suspicious of General Benedict ARNOLD's activities, and he alerted General Washington but was angrily rebuked. He then lost his independent command and was assigned to the legion of Colonel Henry LEE, distinguishing himself at the storming of Stoney Point, New York, and Paulus Hook, New Jersey, that summer. Unfortunately, McLane and Lee functioned poorly together and in 1780 he transferred south to join the army of General Benjamin LINCOLN in South Carolina. McLane arrived too late to participate in the siege of CHARLESTON, and subsequently served in Virginia under General Friedrich von STEUBEN. In the summer of 1781 he performed possibly his most important work by conveying Washington's appeal for help to Admiral François-Joseph-Paul, comte de GRASSE, whose fleet was then anchored at Haiti. The admiral readily complied and immediately sailed to Chesapeake Bay, trapping the army of General Charles CORNWALLIS at YORKTOWN. McLane spent the waning months of the war keeping an eye on Clinton's army in New York and was discharged in 1781 with the rank of major.

For several months McLane lived in Philadelphia, where he pursued business deals with financier Robert MORRIS. But, once back in Delaware, he developed a taste for politics and repeatedly won seats in the House of Assembly and the state privy council. In 1787 he attended the state constitutional convention and pushed for ratification; Delaware was the first state to endorse unanimously the Constitution. In 1797 President Washington appointed McLane to the lucrative post of customs collector at Wilmington, Delaware, where he served almost 30 years. He also operated a cutter at New Castle, which proved instrumental in seizing vessels for customs violations. Politically, McLane was an ardent Federalist, but after 1800 the new Democratic-Republican president, Thomas JEFFERSON, retained him as collector in light of his sterling service to the country. Throughout the War of 1812 he actively criticized Jefferson's successor, James MADISON, and commanded troops and fortifications of Wilmington. McLane died there on May 22, 1829, embittered by what he perceived as a lack of recognition for his many daring exploits.

Further Reading

Cook, Fred J. *What Manner of Men: Forgotten Heroes of the American Revolution.* New York: Morrow, 1959.

Crary, Catherine S. "The Tory and the Spy: The Double Life of James Rivington," *William and Mary Quarterly* 16, no. 1 (1959): 61–92.

Edson, Edith M. "A James Peale Puzzle: Captain Allan McLane's Encounter with British Dragoons," *Pennsylvania Magazine of History and Biography* 125, no. 4 (2001): 375–392.

———. "Allan McLane, James Peale, and Henry Bryan Hall: An Artistic Mystery Solved," *Delaware History* 28, no. 8 (1999–2000): 311–321.

Mahoney, Harry T. *Gallantry in Action: A Biographic Dictionary of Espionage in the American Revolutionary War.* Lanham, Md.: University Press of America, 1999.

Taafe, Stephen R. *The Philadelphia Campaign, 1777–1778.* Lawrence: University Press of Kansas, 2003.

McNeill, Hector (1728–1785)
American naval officer

Hector McNeill was born in County Antrim, Ireland, on October 10, 1728, and he immigrated to Boston while a child. He gravitated toward work in the merchant marine and during the Seven Years' War he leased his schooner *Lawrence* to the British government as a troop ship. While operating off the Canadian coast McNeill was captured by Indians and interned at Quebec. He was eventually exchanged, acquired another vessel, and plied the New England coastal trade. Curiously, McNeill was residing back at Quebec when the Revolutionary War broke and he was told by Governor-General Guy CARLETON either to join the militia or depart. McNeill chose the latter, and for several months thereafter he transported supplies for the besieging army under General Benedict ARNOLD. Following the American retreat from Canada in June 1776, McNeill appeared in Philadelphia, where he lobbied the Continental CONGRESS for a captain's commission in the Continental NAVY. Congress complied on June 15, and he was installed as that service's third-ranking captain. In this capacity McNeill received command of the new frigate *Boston*, then outfitting at Newburyport, Massachusetts. It took him nearly a year to properly man and outfit his ship when it became part of a two-ship squadron under Captain John MANLEY, the navy's second-rated officer and captain of the brand-new frigate *Hancock*. Both men proved stiff-necked, garrulous individuals who entertained a thinly veiled contempt for each other. On May 21, 1777, McNeill accompanied Manly on a sortie to the Grand Banks. On June 8, 1776, they managed to capture the 24-gun British frigate HMS *Fox* after a 90-minute action in which Manley did most of the fighting before McNeill swooped in to claim the prize. Manley then angrily ordered him to relinquish the *Fox* to his crew, which served only to embitter both commanders.

The three vessels continued cruising off the Grand Banks, where, on July 7, 1776, they ran afoul of the 44-gun British frigate HMS *Rainbow* under Captain George COLLIER and a smaller vessel, HMS *Flora*. Though outgunned, the well-trained Royal Navy had little problem dispensing with its opponents, and *Hancock* and *Fox* were both captured after a 39-hour chase. McNeill declined to support Manley throughout the fight and eventually fled for the safety of the Sheepscot River, Maine. He remained there a month amid rising criticism of his leadership. Once Manley was exchanged in the summer of 1778, both men were court-martialed, and McNeill was dismissed from the navy without ceremony. For the remainder of the war he commanded the Massachusetts privateers *Pallas* and *Adventure*. McNeill resumed his career in the merchant marine after the war; he was lost at sea on December 25, 1785.

Further Reading
Allen, Gardner W. *Captain Hector McNeill of the Continental Navy*. Boston: Massachusetts Historical Society, 1922.
Canney, Donald L. *Sailing Warships of the U.S. Navy*. Annapolis, Md.: Naval Institute Press, 2001.
McManemin, John A. *Captains of the Continental Navy*. Spring Lake, N.J.: Ho-Ho-Kus Pub. Co., 1981.
Miller, Nathan. *Sea of Glory: A Naval History of the American Revolution*. Charleston, S.C.: Nautical & Aviation Pub. Co., 2000.
Morgan, William J. "The Stormy Career of Captain McNeill, Continental Navy," *Military Affairs* 16 (fall 1952): 119–122.
Smith, Philip C. *Fired by Manley Zeal: A Naval Fiasco of the Revolution*. Salem, Mass.: Peabody Museum of Salem, 1977.

Meigs, Return J. (1740–1823)
American military officer
Return Jonathan Meigs was born in Middletown, Connecticut, on December 17, 1734, the son of a hatter. He was gradually drawn into militia affairs and, after the Revolutionary War commenced in April 1775, he led a company of light infantry to Cambridge, Massachusetts. In this capacity Meigs accompanied the Canadian expedition of Colonel Benedict ARNOLD as a major and was captured during the ill-fated attack on QUEBEC, December 31, 1775. Meigs was finally exchanged by June 1776 and returned home to become lieutenant colonel in Henry Sherburne's Additional Connecticut Regiment. He remained there until Governor William TRYON's raid against Danbury in April 1777, when General Samuel H. PARSONS selected him to mount a raid on Sag Harbor, Long Island. This action established Meigs as an

attentive and aggressive regimental officer. Taking 120 men in three sloops and 13 whaleboats, he traversed Long Island Sound on the evening of May 23, 1777, and silently stole ashore in the darkness. Pushing inland, Meigs completely surprised a large British/LOYALIST garrison, killing six, taking 83 captives, and burning 12 vessels and over 100 tons of hay. The Americans then safely returned to Guilford, Connecticut, the following day, having covered 100 miles without the loss of a man. The Continental CONGRESS consequently voted Meigs an elaborate ceremonial sword in his honor and he also became colonel of the 6th Connecticut Continental Line.

Meigs subsequently served in the Hudson Highlands as part of General Anthony WAYNE's division. Here he commanded one of four light infantry regiments that conspicuously fought at the storming of Stony Point in July 1779. He then resumed command of his regiment and, with it, helped subdue a mutiny of the Connecticut Line in May 1780. Meigs's services were especially appreciated by General George WASHINGTON, and he received a personal letter of thanks. However, when the Connecticut regiments were reorganized on January 1, 1781, Meigs tendered his resignation and took no further part in the fighting.

In 1787 Meigs served as a surveyor with the Ohio Company and helped found the settlement at Marietta, Ohio. In 1795 he again assisted General Wayne's army as commissary of clothing during the Old Northwest Indian War. In 1801 President Thomas JEFFERSON appointed him to his most important position, that of government agent to the Cherokee in Tennessee, which he held for two decades. At a time when most agents were either indifferent or corrupt in their dealings with Native Americans, Meigs was singularly distinguished by his devotion to the Cherokee, who gave him the name "White Path." He used every resource at his disposal to prevent white encroachment or violence against his charge and always dealt with their concerns honestly and effectively. He also favored the growth of agriculture and the gradual assimilation of Indians into white society. In 1808 he negotiated an important treaty between the tribe and the state of Tennessee. So effective was Meigs in his tribal relationships that the Cherokee unanimously supported the United States throughout the War of 1812. He died on the Hiwassee Reservation, Georgia, on January 28, 1823, an accomplished military officer and benefactor of the Cherokee. His son, Return Jonathan Meigs, Jr., was a governor of Ohio.

Further Reading

Callahan, North. *Connecticut's Revolutionary War Leaders*. Chester, Conn.: Pequot Press, 1973.

Dillard, James E. "Into the Sanctuary: Return Jonathan Meigs and U.S.-Cherokee Relations, 1801–1823." Unpublished master's thesis, Southern Illinois University, 1978.

Johnston, Henry P. "Return Jonathan Meigs, Colonel of the Connecticut Line of the Continental Army," *Magazine of American History* 4 (April 1880): 282–292.

McKeown, James S. "Return J. Meigs, United States Agent in the Cherokee Nation, 1801–1823." Unpublished Ph.D. diss., Pennsylvania State University, 1984.

Meigs, Return J. "Lt. Col. R. J. Meigs's Journal of Arnold's Expedition against Quebec," *Massachusetts Historical Society Collections* 2 (1886): 266–305.

Whaples, Meigs H. *A Historical Sketch of Return Jonathan Meigs: A Revolutionary Hero of Connecticut*. Colonel Jeremiah Wadsworth Branch, Connecticut Society, Sons of the American Revolution, 1990.

Mercer, Hugh (ca. 1725–1777)

American military officer

Hugh Mercer was born in Aberdeenshire, Scotland, around 1725, and he passed through the University of Aberdeen with a medical degree in 1744. That year he joined the Jacobite army of Prince Charles Edward, the Pretender, and fought at the disastrous engagement of Culloden on April 16, 1746. He then fled for America, settling in present-day Mercerville, Pennsylvania, to ply his profession. When the French and Indian War broke out in 1754 Mercer tendered his services to the provincial forces and fought in several notable actions. In September 1756 he accompanied Colonel John ARMSTRONG on his expedition against Indian villages at Kittanning and was severely wounded. Two years later he fought as a lieutenant colonel at the capture of Fort Duquesne, Pennsylvania, and subsequently commanded there. It was during this interval that he met and befriended Colonel George WASHINGTON of the Virginia Regiment. The war ended in 1763, and Mercer resettled at Fredericksburg, Virginia, to resume his medical practice. By 1775 he had embraced the Patriot cause, and that September he became colonel of all MINUTEMAN companies in the four adjoining counties. In January 1776 the provincial congress appointed him colonel of the 3rd Virginia Continental Infantry, which he drilled into a finely honed unit. But Washington, now commander in chief and lacking experienced senior officers, prevailed upon the Continental CONGRESS to make Mercer a brigadier general the following June.

A big, red-headed, fiery Scot, Mercer enjoyed a fine military reputation so Washington entrusted him to command the so-called Flying Camp, a mobile militia reserve. With it he tried assisting the main army throughout the New York campaign, but his force was perpetually plagued by desertions, lack of manpower, and supply shortages, so it disbanded that winter. Mercer still enjoyed Washington's complete confidence, and he bore a prominent role during the masterful counterattack at TRENTON on December 26, 1776, driving the HESSIAN garrison through the streets before cornering them in a nearby field. The Americans then fell back to Assumpink Creek to await an assault by General Charles CORNWALLIS; Mercer may have suggested the famous ruse of leaving their campfires burning. The British were duped as Washington adroitly sidestepped and marched upon PRINCETON, site of another small enemy garrison. Mercer, leading the advanced corps, scouted ahead of the main body, and on January 3 he ran headlong into a brigade of 1,200 British troops under Lieutenant Colonel Charles Mawhood of the 17th Regiment, a severe engagement erupted in the vicinity of Stony Brook Bridge. Rather than retreat, the imposing Scot plunged into battle against the better-trained redcoats, and his troops were forced back in stiff fighting. While attempting a rally, Mercer was shot off his horse, bayoneted several times by British soldiers, and fatally wounded. He was then borne to a nearby farmhouse, where Cornwallis graciously allowed Washington's leading physician, Dr. Benjamin RUSH, to attend to him. The popular Mercer died on January 12, 1776, a genuine loss to the American cause.

Further Reading

English, Frederick. *General Hugh Mercer, Forgotten Hero of the American Revolution.* New York: Vantage, 1975.

Heathcote, Charles W. "General Hugh Mercer—a Courageous Revolutionary Officer and Friend of Washington," *Picket Post* no. 72 (May 1961): 4–10.

Novak, Beatrice. "The Life of General Hugh Mercer." Unpublished master's thesis, University of Pittsburgh, 1936.

Philson, William C., and Rachel E. Darby. *Hugh Mercer: The Doctor General.* Mercer, Pa.: Mercer County Historical Society, 2001.

Sabine, David B. "Hugh Mercer: Patriot, Physician, Soldier," *Daughters of the American Revolution Magazine* 108, no. 9 (1974): 844–848.

Waterman, Joseph M. *With Sword and Lancet: The Life of General Hugh Mercer.* Richmond, Va.: Garrett, Massie, 1941.

Mifflin, Thomas (1744–1800)
American military officer

Thomas Mifflin was born in Philadelphia on January 10, 1744, the scion of prosperous Quaker merchants. Bright and ambitious, he passed through the College of Philadelphia (now the University of Pennsylvania) in 1760 at the age of 16 and formed a thriving business partnership with his brother. As a successful merchant, he roundly opposed British measures like the STAMP ACT of 1765 and the TOWNSHEND DUTIES of 1767, and Mifflin gradually became identified with the radical Whig resistance. As such he sat in the colonial assembly as of 1772 and espoused the Patriot viewpoint. Mifflin strongly championed the notion of an intercolonial body to resist British oppression, and in 1775 he won seats in the First and Second Continental CONGRESS. After war erupted in April 1775 Mifflin turned his attention to military matters, and he served as a major in the local militia. In this capacity he caught the eye of General George WASHINGTON, who appointed him aide-de-camp and lieutenant colonel on June 23, 1775. However, Mifflin remained a staff officer only briefly because, on August 14, 1775, he assumed critically important responsibilities as quartermaster general of the Continental ARMY. It became Mifflin's responsibility for the clothing and victualing of thousands of soldiers and, by dint of his business background and excellent administrative abilities, he appeared a logical choice for the slot. In reality, American military administration—at all levels off command—proved slapdash at best, and Mifflin failed to distinguish himself in office. He nonetheless rose to brigadier general in May 1776 and major general as of February 1777.

In truth, Mifflin's tenure as quartermaster general proved an unhappy one, for the young and frequently crass officer sought out a combat command. He accompanied the main army to New York in 1776 and acquitted himself well at LONG ISLAND, WHITE PLAINS, TRENTON, and PRINCETON. But with time Mifflin grew dissatisfied with Washington's performance as commander in chief, and he flirted briefly with Colonel Thomas CONWAY's aborted cabal to replace him. In October 1777 he resigned as quartermaster general and was replaced by Colonel Stephen MOYLAN. However, he retained his rank as part of the newly constituted Board of War under General Horatio GATES, also eager and willing to replace Washington if asked. Once the so-called Conway Cabal was exposed and fell through, Mifflin denied any complicity, but thereafter his relationship with Washington was appreciably strained.

Back in active duty, Mifflin failed to secure a significant command, and members of Congress accused him of embezzlement while quartermaster. He consequently resigned his commission in August 1778, but Washington declined to prosecute and the matter dropped. Despite this controversy Mifflin retained a degree of popularity in his home state, and in 1782 he won a seat in Congress. The following year he served as president of that body and performed memorable service by receiving the sword of Washington when he retired from the army on December 23, 1783. The two men were never completely reconciled.

After the war Mifflin remained a force in Pennsylvania politics, serving at the Constitutional Convention in 1787, as speaker of the state general assembly in 1785–88, and chairman of

American merchant and Continental Congress member Thomas Mifflin was appointed quartermaster general of the Continental army in 1775. *(Pennsylvania State Archives)*

the state constitutional convention in 1788–90. That year he handily defeated Arthur ST. CLAIR for the governorship, and he served three successful terms. In 1794 Mifflin raised and headed militia forces that put down the "Whiskey Rebellion" in the western part of the state at the behest of President Washington. Mifflin, however, grew increasingly profligate as he aged in office, and in 1799 he fled Philadelphia to escape creditors. He died penniless in Lancaster on January 20, 1800, and his funeral expenses were absorbed by the state.

Further Reading

Carp, E. Wayne. *To Starve the Army at Pleasure: Continental Army Administration and American Political Culture, 1775–1783.* Chapel Hill: University of North Carolina Press, 1983

Cometti, Elizabeth. "The Department of the Quartermaster and Clothier-General, 1775–1780." Unpublished Ph.D. diss., University of Virginia, 1939.

Heathcote, Charles W. "General Thomas Mifflin—Colleague of Washington and Pennsylvania Leader," *Picket Post* no. 62 (November 1958): 7–12.

Kortenhof, Kurt D. "Republican Ideology and Wartime Reality: Thomas Mifflin's Struggle as the First Quartermaster of the Continental Army, 1775–1778," *Pennsylvania Magazine of History and Biography* 122, no. 3 (1998): 179–210.

Lefkowitz, Arthur S. *George Washington's Indispensable Men: The 32 Aides-de-camp Who Helped American Independence.* Mechanicsburg, Pa.: Stackpole Books, 2003.

Risch, Erna. *Supplying Washington's Army.* Washington, D.C.: Government Printing Office, 1981.

minutemen

The concept of "citizen-soldiery" in Massachusetts dates back to the inception of that colony in the early 17th century, and such forces were deployed in various wars against the Indians and French up through 1763. Afterward a period of increasing tensions over imperial tax and trade policy raised the specter of widespread rebellion against royal authority, which, in turn, affected militia policy. The decisive turn occurred following the passage of the COERCIVE ACTS, punitive measures closing down the port of Boston, which prompted radical Whig leaders to begin organizing defenses for that colony. In September 1774 Worcester County leadership decided to completely reorganize its militia forces, then consisting of three regiments. All officers were discharged to purge the muster rolls of LOYALISTS, and all eligible males aged 16 to 60 were drafted into companies. New officers were then elected and the militia reorganized into seven new regiments. Moreover, it was decided that one-fourth of each regiment would be designated "minuteman" companies, a term first coined in 1756. These units were composed of 50 men, a captain, and two lieutenants and were construed as elite formations within the regular militia. In effect they functioned as a colonial rapid response force. Each minuteman was required to be fully armed and prepared for action within one minute of an alarm being sounded. Only the fittest and most capable young citizens were allowed to volunteer for minutemen service and, as such, they were expected to be available for military drill at least three times a week. Furthermore, each town and district was responsible for the arming and equipping of resident minutemen, in addition to their usual militia responsibilities. As relations with Great Britain unraveled, the minuteman movement gathered impetus in other counties. On October 26, 1774, the extralegal Massachusetts provincial congress required all towns and districts to reconstitute their militia along similar lines to Worcester. Mobilizing for war devolved upon Dr. Joseph WARREN, head of the Committee of Safety, who could call them out as necessary.

Over the intervening six months the clouds of war gathered, and the Massachusetts militia were assiduously drilling in wintertime. Such activity did not escape the attention of Governor Thomas GAGE's network of spies, and he authorized preemptive strikes at colonial arms caches to forestall the outbreak of violence. The well-drilled minutemen responded surprisingly well to a series of British provocations at Charlestown, Cambridge, and especially Salem in February 1775, where armed citizens peacefully confronted an armed expedition commanded by Colonel Alexander LESLIE. However, on the evening of April 18, 1775, a larger force under Lieutenant Colonel Francis SMITH marched at night toward colonial arms stored at Concord. The American intelligence network quickly detected this maneuver, and Dr. Warren dispatched Paul REVERE and other riders to alarm the countryside. On the morning of April 19, 1775, an advance British detachment under Major John PITCAIRN confronted the first minuteman company of Captain John Parker on Lexington Green. Shots were exchanged, blood shed, and the militia scattered, but the "shot heard round the world" became a rallying cry for nearby minutemen companies to act. Within hours they attacked and drove British troops of the 43rd Regiment from the North Bridge at CONCORD and effectively harried Smith's 20-mile retreat back to Boston. Only the timely intercession of reinforcements under Colonel Hugh PERCY spared the British column from annihilation by thousands of militia and minutemen swarming out of the woods. Considering the fearsome and well-deserved reputation of British arms, the day proved stunningly successful for the colonials.

Glory for the Massachusetts minutemen proved transient as, once additional troops commenced the siege of Boston, they were gradually absorbed into the new Continental ARMY. Still, on July 18, 1775, the Continental CONGRESS encouraged other colonies to form minuteman organizations, and they arose in Maryland, North Carolina, New Hampshire, and Connecticut. These units performed a useful service by covering those territories unoccupied by regular army units, protecting them from raids while also squelching Loyalist activities. In sum, the minutemen served briefly but left an indelible imprint upon the nation. As celebrated figures in national military mythology, they are commemorated by an imposing statue erected on Lexington battlefield. They fired the first shots for liberty.

Further Reading
Castle, Norman. *The Minute Men, 1775–1975.* Southborough, Mass.: Yankee Colour Corp., 1977.
Galvin, John R. *The Minutemen, the First Fight: Myths and Realities of the American Revolution.* Washington, D.C.: Brassey's, 1996.
Gross, Robert A. *The Minutemen and Their World.* New York: Hill and Wang, 2001.
Merk, Edward. "The Minutemen: A Significant Force Behind America's Revolutionary War." Unpublished master's thesis, California State University, Dominguez Hills, 1994.
Nichipor, Mark A. *The Battles of Lexington and Concord.* Petersborough, N.H.: Cobblestone Pub. Co., 2002.

Monmouth, Battle of (June 28, 1778)
No sooner had General Henry CLINTON acceded to the command of British forces in Philadelphia than he concluded that the recent FRENCH ALLIANCE made his position untenable and exposed him to attack from the sea. He accordingly ordered a withdrawal to New York City; lacking ships to make the transit entirely by water, he dispatched only his heavy artillery and LOYALIST refugees on all available craft. The main British force of 12,000 men would proceed north on foot. Clinton's departure on June 18, 1778, rapidly came to the attention of General George WASHINGTON at Valley Forge, who wished to resume an offensive posture. Washington had on hand 12,000 men, somewhat raggedly attired but well drilled by General Friedrich von STEUBEN over the previous winter. He gauged the tenor of his men and found them full of fight, so he ordered an immediate pursuit. Over the next few days his decision was challenged by the recently repatriated General Charles LEE, who felt that the troops were still unequal to British forces in the field. Washington initially complied with Lee's caution and dispatched only 1,400 troops under General William MAXWELL and Philemon DICKINSON to harass the British. By June 25, 1778, the Americans had advanced to within striking distance of Clinton's column, and Washington ordered advance troops under the marquis de LAFAYETTE to attack Clin-

ton's rear guard. Lee, who had been tendered command of these forces, initially declined yet, upon further reflection, suddenly reversed himself and pressed Washington to lead them, citing his seniority. When Lafayette graciously consented to subordination, Lee marched off with 5,000 men toward Monmouth Court House.

June 28, 1778, dawned swelteringly hot, and Lee boldly advanced upon the 2,000 men commanded by General Charles CORNWALLIS. But as the action unfolded Lee, who attacked without a battle plan, issued a stream of conflicting instructions and gradually lost control of the situation. His mishandling of units squandered what for Cornwallis might have been a perilous situation, and after several hours of inconclusive fighting he ordered a retreat. Over the next few minutes the Americans were ordered to fall back no less than three times, with vengeful British bayonets in full pursuit. A disaster seemed imminent, but at this critical juncture Washington came galloping up at the head of his main body. He viewed the ensuing confusing in disbelief, confronted Lee, and dressed him down in blistering fashion. Washington then rallied his shaken troops and deployed them in defensive positions as the rest of the troops arrived. His alacrity proved fortuitous as General Clinton also arrived with the balance of his army and attacked. The two forces were evenly matched in numbers as the British confidently advanced upon their ragtag opponents with cold steel. But, unlike previous engagements, the Americans stood their ground with surprising steadiness and unleashed devastating volleys against their antagonists. Both sides continued feeding additional troops into the fray, but Washington's men blasted back every advance. Intense heat forced Clinton to postpone further attacks and for several hours his artillery dueled with that of General Henry KNOX. During this interlude Mary Ludwig HAYS ("Molly Pitcher") performed her celebrated deed by manning an American artillery piece after her husband collapsed. All told, officers and soldiers of the Continental ARMY never performed better. For the disgraced Lee, it meant the end of his military career.

The battle eventually subsided with the growing darkness and both sides withdrew to lick their wounds. Monmouth, the last conventional battle in the north, proved a draw but was also significant in being the first instance when American troops withstood their British opposites on an open field. Battlefield laurels were equally shared and both sides lost about 360 casualties apiece, although Clinton also suffered an additional 600 desertions—mostly HESSIANS—over the next few days. Washington, sensing an opportunity to inflict serious harm on the British, sought to renew the conflict on the following day, but Clinton stole a march on him and escaped in the predawn hours. An entrenched stalemate then settled in along the northern theater, for Monmouth underscored that the days of easy victories over American forces had passed. This reality probably weighed heavily over the next few months when the bulk of British strategic operations shifted dramatically southward. The Americans were at liberty to celebrate their newfound martial prowess and the liberation of Philadelphia, which, while only symbolic, was encouraging.

Further Reading
Edgar, Gregory T. *The Philadelphia Campaign, 1777–1778.* Bowie, Md.: Heritage Books, 1998.
Ethier, Eric. "Clash at Monmouth," *American History* 34, no. 4 (1999): 48–57.
Martin, David G. *The Philadelphia Campaign, June 1777–July 1778.* Cambridge, Mass.: Da Capo Press, 2003.
Morrissey, Brendan. *Monmouth Courthouse, 1778: The Last Great Battle in the North.* Oxford: Osprey, 2004.
Taafe, Stephen R. *The Philadelphia Campaign, 1777–1778.* Lawrence: University Press of Kansas, 2003.
Wade, David R. "Washington Saves the Day at Monmouth," *Military History* 15, no. 2 (1998): 46–52.

Monroe, James (1758–1831)
American military officer, fifth president of the United States

James Monroe was born in Westmoreland County, Virginia, on April 28, 1758, the son of prosperous planters. He was attending William and Mary College when the Revolutionary War broke out in April 1775 and quit school to join the Continental ARMY. On September 28, 1775, Monroe became a second lieutenant in the 3rd Virginia Continental Infantry under Colonel Hugh MERCER and accompanied the regiment to New York. There he first saw combat at Harlem Heights on September 16, 1776, and volunteered to accompany the rangers of Major Thomas KNOWLTON. After additional fighting at WHITE PLAINS in October, Monroe was closely engaged at TRENTON on December 26, 1776, where he charged a HESSIAN battery with Colonel William WASHINGTON and fell dangerously wounded. Monroe recuperated and subsequently acquitted himself well at the Battles of BRANDYWINE and GERMANTOWN the following fall. His good conduct caught the attention of superiors, and on November 20, 1777, he became aide-de-camp to General William ALEXANDER, Lord Stirling, with the rank of major. In the summer of 1778 he again saw active duty at MONMOUTH but proved unable to secure further promotions and so resigned on November 20 of that year.

Back in civilian life Monroe decided to study law under Governor Thomas JEFFERSON, and the two men struck up a cordial, lifelong relationship. In 1781 Jefferson appointed him military commissioner with the rank of lieutenant colonel and dispatched him to study conditions in the southern army. The following year Monroe commenced his lengthy career in politics by winning a seat in the Virginia House of Delegates, from which he succeeded to the Confederation CONGRESS in 1783. Four years later he served in the state constitutional convention, where he opposed the new federal constitution for its centralized authority. But once the new government was ratified, Monroe successfully stood for a seat in the new U.S. Senate in 1790, and four years later President George WASHINGTON dispatched him to France as an envoy. He was recalled three years later and joined the anti-Federalist opposition then forming under the aegis of Jefferson and James MADISON. In 1799 Monroe was elected governor of Virginia and twice reelected. In 1802 President Jefferson appointed him envoy to France for a second time, and he marginally assisted Robert R. LIVINGSTON in signing the famous Louisiana Purchase the following year. Afterward Monroe served as minister to Great Britain, where he negotiated a commercial treaty in 1806, which was rejected for failure to address the emotional issue of impressment.

After holding additional offices in Virginia, Monroe became President Madison's secretary of state as of 1811. Here he conducted national affairs against the backdrop of increasing hostility with Great Britain, which culminated in the War of 1812. After August 1814 he also assumed the temporary portfolio as secretary of war and finally capped his ambitions by being elected the nation's fifth president in 1816. Monroe's administration coincided with a burgeoning sense of nationalism known as the Era of Good Feelings, and he continued to advance America's position on the global stage. In 1819 he became the first American president to traverse the nation on a goodwill tour, and he also waged a brief but successful war against the Seminole Indians of Florida. After an easy reelection bid in 1820, he arranged for the purchase of Florida from SPAIN and also signed the Missouri Compromise to forestall any outbreak of civil war over slavery. Monroe's biggest contribution came in 1823, when he promulgated the so-called Monroe Doctrine, which placed the Western Hemisphere off limits to further European colonization. Monroe was succeeded by John Quincy Adams, son of President John ADAMS, in 1822, and he retired to private life. He died in New York City on July 4, 1831, the last American executive to have fought in the Revolutionary War.

Further Reading

Cunningham, Noble E. *Jefferson and Monroe: Constant Friendship and Respect.* Charlottesville, Va.: Thomas Jefferson Foundation, 2003.

Hanser, Richard. *The Glorious Hour of Lt. Monroe.* New York: Athenaeum, 1976.

Moats, Sandra A. "The Last Republican: James Monroe's Tours and the Politics of Succession." Unpublished

Ph.D. diss., University of California, Los Angeles, 2002.
Preston, Daniel, and Marlena C. DeLong, eds. *The Papers of James Monroe.* Westport, Conn.: Greenwood Press, 2003.
Scherr, Arthur E. "The Changing Republicanism of James Monroe, 1787–1831: An Essay in the History of Political Ideas." Unpublished Ph.D. diss., City University of New York, 1979.
Sellers, John R. *The Virginia Continental Line.* Williamsburg: Virginia Independence Bicentennial Commission, 1978.

Montagu, John (1718–1792)
English politician

John Montagu was born in England on November 3, 1718, and he inherited the family title of fourth earl of Sandwich at the age of 11. He received a typical aristocratic education at Eton and Trinity College, Cambridge, before assuming a seat in the House of Lords in 1739. Adept at internecine Georgian politics, he served on several international conferences before becoming First Lord of the Admiralty in 1748. Thereafter Montagu became intrigued with naval matters and demonstrated a flair for administration. He also met and befriended the political rabble-rouser John WILKES and shared his revelries at the notorious Hellfire Club in Medmenham. Montagu reveled in his reputation as an excessive-living, gambling addicted rake who abandoned his wife for a favorite mistress. He also reputedly invented his namesake, the sandwich, as a means of eating beef without having to leave the gambling table. In 1763 Prime Minister George GRENVILLE appointed him secretary of state, although their feuding over a proposed alliance with Austria brought his ministry down by 1765. Montagu then turned against his erstwhile friend Wilkes and managed to expel him from the House of Commons, a move that did little to enhance his own popularity. Montagu now became popularly denigrated as "Jemmy Twitcher" after an unsavory line from *The Beggar's Opera*. Nonetheless, both King GEORGE III and Prime Minister Lord Frederick NORTH thought highly of his organizational abilities, so in 1771 he regained the appointment as Lord of the Admiralty.

Montagu was tasked with the modernization, maintenance, and deployment of the formidable Royal Navy. Unfortunately, he took charge of the navy at a time of fiscal entrenchment and military cutbacks. His budget was slashed, and he inherited a dispirited, undermanned force declining in morale and efficiency since the Seven Years' War. Worse, corruption was rife as offices were bought, naval stores stolen, and ships routinely dispatched abroad while still unseaworthy. But for all his flaws, Montagu remained a talented bureaucrat by the standards of the day, and he energetically set his charge down the path of modernity. His most important act was in adopting copper sheathing for all ship hulls to retard the growth of barnacles to grant them speed advantages over wooden-hulled French and Spanish adversaries. Montagu also introduced improvements in the field of ship-to-ship signaling to enhance communication. Finally, he pioneered the use of carronades on British warships—short-range, crew-killing artillery pieces of great effectiveness in line of battle. All told, in his third and longest tenure at the Admiralty, Montagu laid the foundations for a modernized naval force that finally came to fruition in 1805 under Admiral Horatio Nelson.

Where Montagu utterly failed as a naval administrator was in the field of naval strategy. When the Revolutionary War commenced in April 1775 he promised Admiral Samuel GRAVES in Boston an armada of new ships—which never arrived. He was then scarcely on speaking terms with Graves's successor, Admiral Richard HOWE, and was content to let direction of the war drift. After 1778, when the FRENCH ALLIANCE was signed, Montagu lacked the resources, money, and manpower to conduct what was essentially a world war. Fearful of a French invasion, he kept the bulk of his ships home while the Royal Navy stagnated in American waters. He efforts were further undermined by divisive political factors in the naval high command when Admirals Augustus

Keppel and Hugh Pallister accused each other of incompetence during the indecisive Battle of Ushant in July 1778, and both were court-martialed. Parliamentarian Charles James FOX used this discord to attack the Admiralty's performance in the war and demanded Montagu's ouster. Only Lord North's threat to resign kept him in office. But one of his last—and worst—decisions was to appoint Admiral Marriot ARBUTHNOT as commander of the North American station in February 1779. Arbuthnot's principal activity was to feud with General Henry CLINTON, which further hobbled the British war effort. Montagu left the Admiralty in March 1782 when North's government finally collapsed, his public reputation severely tarnished. He then settled into a comfortable retirement and lived in obscurity until his death on April 3, 1792. Along with Secretary of State George GERMAIN, he bears considerable responsibility for the loss of Britain's North American colonies.

Further Reading
Martelli, George. *Jemmey Twitcher: A Life of the Fourth Earl of Sandwich, 1718–1792.* London: Cape, 1962.
Padfield, Peter. *Maritime Supremacy and the Opening of the Western Mind: Naval Campaigns That Shaped the Western World.* London: Murray, 1999.
Rodger, N. A. M. *The Insatiable Earl: A Life of John Montagu, Fourth Earl of Sandwich, 1718–1792.* New York: Norton, 1994.
Syrett, David. *The Royal Navy in European Waters during the American Revolution.* Columbia: University of South Carolina Press, 1998.
Wickwire, Mary B. "Lord Sandwich and the King's Ships: British Naval Administration, 1771–1782." Unpublished Ph.D. diss., Yale University, 1962.
Williams, Michael J. "The Naval Administration of the Fourth Earl of Sandwich, 1771–82." Unpublished Ph.D. diss., University of Oxford, 1962.

Montgomery, Richard (1738–1775)
American military officer

Richard Montgomery was born in Dublin, Ireland, on December 2, 1738, the son of an Irish parliamentarian. He passed through St. Andrews and Trinity College before joining the British army in 1756 as an ensign in the 17th Regiment. In this capacity he fought actively throughout the French and Indian War, rendering exceptional service at the siege of Louisbourg, Crown Point, and Fort Ticonderoga. He climaxed his American activities in 1759 by campaigning under the celebrated general James Wolfe during the capture of Quebec. Montgomery subsequently saw action at Havana and Martinique, winning promotion to captain before returning home in 1765. He then became disillusioned by the lack of economic advancement and disenchanted with the political establishment. Montgomery also befriended noted Whigs Edmund BURKE and Charles James FOX, fully inculcating their perspectives on personal liberty. Facing few prospects in England, he then sold his commission in April 1772 and immigrated to New York. There he purchased a farm and expanded his social horizons by marrying the daughter of Robert R. LIVINGSTON. By the advent of revolution in April 1775, Montgomery was firmly committed to the Patriot cause, and he served in the first New York provincial congress. He had little use for politics, however, drawing upon his exemplary military record, Montgomery sought out a high command.

In June 1775 the Continental CONGRESS appointed Montgomery one of the first eight brigadier generals in the Continental ARMY. He was then posted back to the Northern Department under General Philip J. SCHUYLER, with instructions to prepare for an invasion of Canada. Montgomery, impatient as ever, fumed when Schuyler fell ill and decided to launch the attack without him. That September he departed Fort Ticonderoga with 2,000 ill-clad, poorly trained but enthusiastic troops and advanced into British-held Quebec. Schuyler eventually caught up with him in time to help commence the siege of Saint Johns, then defended by 750 men of the 7th Regiment. The Americans gradually overcame logistical shortfalls and plucky defenders, capturing that town and the nearby garrison of Fort Chambly by November 2, 1775. Having seized the first British

Richard Montgomery was the first American general to die for his country. *(Independence National Historical Park)*

regimental colors taken in the war, Montgomery then pushed 300 half-starved cohorts toward the next objective, Montreal. This city fell without a shot on November 13, having been readily evacuated by Governor-General Guy CARLETON. With the conquest of Canada in his grasp, Montgomery next ordered his men into boats, and they paddled down to the St. Lawrence River toward his final goal, the fortified citadel of Quebec.

Montgomery arrived at Quebec on December 3, 1775, where he linked up with 700 soldiers under Colonel Benedict ARNOLD. Together their combined force of 1,000 ragged, poorly clothed and malnourished men confronted twice their number of professionally trained British regulars behind stout fortifications. A stalemate ensued as the American army slowly withered and perished in the winter snow. Montgomery and Arnold were further daunted by the specter of expiring enlistments, which would eliminate their army altogether, so on December 31, 1775, they boldly launched an attack on QUEBEC under a blinding snowstorm. Montgomery bravely pushed his column against the barricades at Point Diamond, where he was cut down in a flurry of artillery and musket fire. His body, left behind in the snow, was recognized by the British and given a military funeral. In 1818 the United States petitioned the British government for his remains, and he was exchanged for those of Major John ANDRE. The impetuous Montgomery now reposes at St. Paul's Episcopal Church in New York City, commemorated there by a lavish monument. He was the first American general to die for his country.

Further Reading
Aimone, Alan. "The Siege and Capture of Fort Chambly and St. Johns in 1775," *Journal of America's Military Past* 28, no. 2 (2001): 4–18.
Cathcart, Rex. "The Death of Major General Richard Montgomery, 31 December, 1775," *Irish Sword* 18 (Summer 1991): 85–90.
Gabriel, Michael P. *Major General Richard Montgomery: The Making of an American Hero.* Madison, N.J.: Fairleigh Dickinson University Press, 2002.
Hatch, Robert. *Thrust for Canada: The American Attempt on Quebec in 1775–1776.* Boston: Houghton, Mifflin, 1979.
Shelton, Hal T. *General Richard Montgomery and the American Revolution: From Redcoat to Rebel.* New York: New York University Press, 1994.
Stanley, George F. G. *Canada Invaded, 1775–1776.* Toronto: Hakkert, 1973.

Moore, James (1737–1777)
American military officer
James Moore was born in New Hanover County, North Carolina, in 1737, the son of planters. He joined the militia as a captain during the French and Indian War in 1758 and commanded Fort Johnson on the Cape Fear River. Moore then sought out a career in politics and in 1765 he successfully stood for a seat in the lower house of the General Assembly. His politics were radicalized by the STAMP ACT of 1765, and thereafter he became closely associated with anti-British sentiments.

Nonetheless, Governor William TRYON appointed him an artillery colonel in 1768, and in 1771 he accompanied General Hugh WADDELL in campaigns against the regulators. But as the revolutionary movement gathered force, Moore joined the local SONS OF LIBERTY and also served on the county Committee of Safety. In 1775 he sat with the Third Provincial Congress, where, on September 1, he was appointed colonel of the 1st North Carolina Continental Infantry, with Francis NASH, his lieutenant colonel. It was in this capacity that Moore made his greatest contribution to the American cause. Previously, royal governor Josiah MARTIN had instigated a LOYALIST rebellion among numerous Highland residents of the Cape Fear region and ordered them to gather at Wilmington to join the anticipated British expedition commanded by General Henry CLINTON. But Moore carefully concentrated his 1,100 men behind Moore's Creek Bridge on February 27, 1776, and enticed the Highlanders to attack. When the impetuous Scots, numbering 1,600, willingly obliged they were resoundingly defeated in only three minutes of combat. This decisive victory freed North Carolina from a Loyalist threat for the next four years and allowed the Patriots to consolidate their hold. Curiously, Moore was absent from the battle and events were actually conducted by Colonel Richard CASWELL, but he received credit for masterfully marching and deploying his troops beforehand.

On March 1, 1776, the Continental CONGRESS appointed Moore a brigadier general in the Continental ARMY and tasked him with fortifying the port of Wilmington to secure it from British naval attack. The following September he succeeded General Charles LEE as commander of the Southern Department and divided his time between Wilmington and Charleston, South Carolina. Having recruited and trained a solid brigade of North Carolina regulars, Moore was next ordered north to join the main army under General George WASHINGTON. Unfortunately, he suddenly sickened and died at Wilmington on April 15, 1777.

The loss of such a talented officer severely hindered the Patriot cause in the south.

Further Reading

Butler, Lindley. "The Coming of the American Revolution in North Carolina, 1763–1776." Unpublished Ph.D. diss., University of North Carolina, Chapel Hill, 1971.

Cullen, Joseph P. "Moore's Creek Bridge," *American History Illustrated* 5 (January 1970): 10–15.

Lee, Wayne E. *Crowds and Soldiers in Revolutionary North Carolina.* Gainesville: University Press of Florida, 2001.

Rankin, Hugh F. *The Moore's Creek Bridge Campaign, 1776.* Burgaw, N.C.: Moores Creek Bridge Association, 1986.

———. *The North Carolina Continentals.* Chapel Hill: University of North Carolina Press, 1971.

Smith, Penelope S. "Creation of an American State: Politics of North Carolina, 1765–1789." Unpublished Ph.D. diss., Rice University, 1980.

Morgan, Daniel (ca. 1736–1802)
American military officer

Daniel Morgan was born in Hunterdon County, New Jersey, around 1736. He relocated to the Shenandoah Valley, Virginia, as a teenager and acquired the reputation of a hard-drinking frontier brawler. In 1755 he accompanied the ill-fated expedition of General Edward Braddock as a teamster and garnered the nickname "Old Wagoner." This brash and insubordinate frontiersman did not take kindly to spit-and-polish British discipline, and in 1756 he gained notoriety by striking an officer. He received 500 lashes in consequence, yet frequently joked the British had miscounted and still owed him one. In 1758 an Indian bullet passed through his cheek, disfiguring his face and contributing to an already fearsome demeanor. But military life nonetheless appealed to Morgan, and he fought as a ranger throughout Pontiac's Rebellion of 1763 and Lord Dunmore's War of 1774. The Revolutionary War commenced in April 1775, and the Continental CONGRESS authorized creation of a 10-company regiment of riflemen.

This act in effect founded the Continental ARMY, and Morgan was selected as captain of a Virginia company. He led it to Boston and joined the main army gathered there under General George WASHINGTON. In September 1775 Morgan volunteered to accompany Colonel Benedict ARNOLD on his grueling trek into Canada. He survived the hardships of several weeks in the Maine wilderness and linked up with forces under General Richard MONTGOMERY at Quebec on December 3, 1775. During the attack on QUEBEC on December 31, 1775, Morgan succeeded to the command once Arnold was wounded and Montgomery killed, but he was unable to penetrate the city's defenses and surrendered. After eight months in captivity Morgan was exchanged and created colonel of the 11th Virginia Continental Infantry. Washington, sensing the need for talented light infantry marksmen, also authorized him to raise a battalion of riflemen.

Morgan subsequently joined the Northern Army under General Horatio GATES and played pivotal roles in the Saratoga campaign against General John BURGOYNE. His marksmen shot down droves of British officers at the Battles of FREEMAN'S FARM and BEMIS HEIGHTS, further demonstrating the utility of riflemen in a wooded environment. One sharpshooter, Timothy MURPHY, is credited with mortally wounding the outstanding British battle leader General Simon FRASER on October 7, 1777. Gates openly gushed about Morgan's qualities in his official report and partly attributed Burgoyne's demise to his efforts. Morgan then transferred back to Washington's army in New Jersey, rendering valuable service at the Battle of MONMOUTH in August 1778. Anxious for a promotion, he was severely disappointed when General Anthony WAYNE became brigadier general in his place and requested an extended furlough in July 1779. Morgan then went home to sulk and await the outcome of events.

By September 1780, General Gates, recently savaged at the defeat of CAMDEN, appealed to Morgan to resume active service. He accepted a belated promotion to brigadier general that October and assumed command of light infantry forces under Gates's successor, General Nathanael GREENE. In January 1781 Greene advanced into North Carolina by throwing Morgan's light troops forward in a wide arc. The British leader, General Charles CORNWALLIS, divined an opportunity to crush the Americans piecemeal and dispatched the fearsome British Legion under Lieutenant Colonel Banastre TARLETON to crush him. Morgan had other plans for Tarleton. Realizing his opponent's penchant for impetuousness, he stationed his little army at COWPENS in three mutually self-supporting ranks and waited for the British to approach. When Tarleton appeared on January 17, 1781, he attacked blindly as Morgan had envisioned, crashed through the first two lines of militia, then stalled

Rogue frontierman Daniel Morgan was selected by the Continental Congress to captain a Virginia rifle regiment in 1775 and subsequently won the Battle of Cowpens. *(Independence National Historical Park)*

before a solid line of Continentals under Colonel John E. HOWARD. At a given signal, the militia and cavalry under Colonel William WASHINGTON suddenly materialized on either flank, enveloping their opponents and driving them from the field. Considering Tarleton's reputation, it was a stunning and seemingly inexplicable reversal of fortune at the hands of the "Old Wagoner." For a loss of only 12 dead and 61 wounded, Morgan killed over 200, captured over 600, and deprived Cornwallis of his finest light troops. Cowpens has since been regarded as the tactical masterpiece of the Revolutionary War and a factor in the ultimate British defeat.

Shortly following his stunning victory, Morgan, beset by rheumatism, withdrew from active service for the rest of the war in February 1781. He then became one of only eight recipients of a congressional gold medal and was hailed as a national war hero. Afterward Morgan prospered as a landowner in the Shenandoah; he donned his military uniform for the last time in 1794 while commanding troops during the so-called Whiskey Rebellion in western Pennsylvania. He also served one term in the U.S. House of Representatives as a Federalist as of 1797. Illnesses necessitated his withdrawal from public life soon after, and he died at Winchester, Virginia, on July 6, 1802. The sharpshooting, rough-hewed Morgan was probably the most accomplished light infantry leader of the Revolutionary War on either side.

Further Reading

Babits, Lawrence E. *A Devil of a Whipping: The Battle of Cowpens.* Chapel Hill: University of North Carolina Press, 2001.
LaCrosse, Richard B. *Revolutionary Rangers: Daniel Morgan's Riflemen and Their Role on the Northern Frontier, 1778–1783.* Bowie, Md.: Heritage Books, 2002.
Morgan, Anne P. *The Morgan Legacy: The Man Who Paved the Way to American Independence.* Ireland: A. Morgan, 1999.
Morgan, Richard L. *General Daniel Morgan: Reconsidered Hero.* Morgantown, N.C.: Burke County Historical Society, 2001.
Schaefer, Nancy S. "Abigail Morgan: Wife of the 'Old Waggoner.'" Unpublished master's thesis, University of Oklahoma, 2004.
Smith, Byron C. "White Savages in Hunting Shirts: The Rifleman's Costume of National Identity and Rebellion in the American Revolution." Unpublished master's thesis, University of Richmond, 2000.

Morris, Gouverneur (1752–1816)
American politician

Gouverneur Morris was born on his family estate at Morrisania (now Bronx), New York, on January 31, 1752, into one of that colony's most distinguished families. Well educated by tutors, he passed through King's College (now Columbia University) in 1768 with a law degree and gained admittance to the bar at the age of 19. Indelibly aristocratic, Morris originally opposed breaking from Great Britain on account of the chaos and instability it posed to landowners; in fact, several members of his family remained committed LOYALISTS. However, after the Battles at Lexington and CONCORD in April 1775 he evinced sympathy for the Patriot cause and won a seat in the extralegal provincial congress. Here he proved a vocal proponent of the Continental CONGRESS and also assisted John JAY and Robert R. LIVINGSTON in drawing up a new state constitution. Morris also wielded one of the most facile, politically expressive pens in America, and his writing skills were soon in great demand.

In 1777 Morris gained a seat in Congress itself, where he further distinguished himself with fine oratory. He signed the ARTICLES OF CONFEDERATION although, as part of the landed gentry, he feared mob rule and gravitated toward aristocratic control of the process. The following year Morris chaired the committee that met to discuss—and ultimately reject—the reconciliation proposal of Prime Minister Lord Frederick NORTH. He also drafted instructions for Benjamin FRANKLIN, then minister to France, and helped lay the negotiating principles by which the TREATY OF PARIS was negotiated and signed in 1783. But when Morris failed to support Governor George

CLINTON's faction at home, he was defeated in 1779 and lost his seat. He then relocated to Philadelphia in 1780 to pursue law and penned several significant essays on national finance that were published in the *Pennsylvania Packet*. This act brought him to the attention of Robert MORRIS (no relation), then superintendent of finance, who appointed him an assistant. In this capacity he originated the scheme for a decimal-based coinage that remains the basis of U.S. currency. Morris served in this capacity until 1787, when he represented Pennsylvania at the Constitutional Convention in Philadelphia. It was here, as an effective and articulate advocate for centralized government, that he made indelible contributions to the country. Morris delivered more speeches on behalf of the Constitution than any other delegate present and was subsequently appointed chair of the drafting committee that wrote it. Ever concerned with political stability, he initially proposed a strong executive elected for life, who in turn appointed a senior body, or senate, also with life terms. These proposals were rejected, but his notion of an electoral college and checks upon the executive by a two-thirds vote in the Senate were accepted. The famous constitutional preamble, "We the People of the United States, in order to form a more Perfect Union," also flowed from his expressive hand.

Once the new government was in place after 1789, Morris traveled to France on a business venture for Robert Morris and witnessed the outbreak of the French Revolution. The following year President George WASHINGTON dispatched him to London as a special agent to negotiate a commercial treaty, but he failed. In 1792 Morris was tapped to replace Thomas JEFFERSON as minister to France, and he secretly involved himself in attempts to spirit King Louis XVI out of the country. The Jacobins demanded his removal in 1794, and he was replaced by James MADISON. After touring Europe for several years he returned to New York and served as a Federalist in the U.S. Senate until 1803. In 1809 he married the controversial Anne Carey Randolph of Virginia, a controversial woman previously tainted by scandal and possibly murder, but the union proved a happy one. Throughout the last decade of his life Morris stridently criticized Jefferson, Madison, and the Democratic-Republicans who inherited the mantle of national leadership. He died in Morrisania on November 6, 1816, a distinguished patriot but insufferably aristocratic to the end.

Further Reading

Adams, William H. *Gouverneur Morris: An Independent Life*. New Haven, Conn.: Yale University Press, 2003.

Brookhiser, Richard. *Gentleman Revolutionary: Gouverneur Morris, the Rake Who Wrote the Constitution*. New York: Free Press, 2003.

Crawford, Alan P. *Unwise Passions: A True Story of a Remarkable Woman—and the First Great Scandal of Eighteenth-Century America*. New York: Simon & Schuster, 2000.

Kirschke, James J. *Gouverneur Morris: Author, Statesman, and Man of the World*. New York: Thomas Dunne Books, 2005.

Miller, Melanie R. "Gouverneur Morris and the French Revolution, 1789–1794." Unpublished Ph.D. diss., George Washington University, 2000.

Tiedeman, Joseph S. *Reluctant Revolutionaries: New York City and the Road to Independence*. Ithaca, N.Y.: Cornell University Press, 1997.

Morris, Robert (1734–1806)
American politician

Robert Morris was born in Liverpool, England, on January 31, 1734, the son of a tobacco exporter. He immigrated to Philadelphia in 1747 and eventually joined a shipping and mercantile house as a partner. Morris proved highly successful in business and quickly accumulated a fortune. Like many of his class, he strongly opposed the STAMP ACT of 1765, along with other imperial tax measures, but was relatively tepid toward revolutionary sentiment. When the Revolutionary War started in April 1775 Morris gradually shifted his allegiance over to the Patriots, thereby gaining a seat in the Pennsylvania assembly. He served as a member of the Council of Safety and on the local COMMITTEE OF CORRESPONDENCE before becoming a delegate to the Continental CONGRESS in November 1775. There Morris distinguished himself by his command of fiscal and monetary matters and served on several important bodies, including the Secret Committee of Trade and the Marine Committee, both of which were tasked with acquiring weapons and materiel for the Continental ARMY and NAVY. Morris performed well but raised conflict of interest charges by continuing his profitable activities, ostensibly at taxpayers' expense. On July 2, 1776, Morris absented himself from a vote on the DECLARATION OF INDEPENDENCE, which he felt was premature, but subsequently signed it the following August. He also became embroiled in the dispute between Silas DEANE and Arthur LEE, with the latter flatly accusing him of wartime profiteering. Morris then demanded and received a congressional inquiry, which cleared him of any malfeasance, but his reputation suffered and he resigned his seat in 1779.

American military fortunes reached their nadir in 1780–81 while the nation, thanks to the profligacy and economic mishandling of Congress, teetered toward fiscal insolvency. For that reason Morris was invited back to the government and appointed superintendent of finance as of February 20, 1781. He willingly obliged but only on the condition that he receive near-dictatorial powers to regulate governmental finance. Here he made indelible contributions to the war effort by reviving America's moribund national credit and, with it, the economy. He then wielded an iron hand to enforce public credit, oversee economic expansion, and even issue notes on his own signature, backed by his personal fortune. In this manner the United States received a $100,000 loan from Admiral Jean-Baptiste, comte de ROCHAMBEAU, with which Morris founded the Bank of North America—the nation's first credit institution. He then worked closely with General George WASHINGTON to pay for the movement of troops and supplies from New York to YORKTOWN, Virginia, in the summer of 1781, which ultimately won the war. The effectiveness of Morris's regimen can be gauged by the fact that the army was amply supplied for the first time in the war, all the debts he contracted for were paid off in full, and America's treasury even ended up with a small surplus. All told, his deft handling of public finance was a bravura performance that—in all likelihood—prevented the revolution from collapsing under the weight of wartime debt. His only serious misstep was in partly backing a proposed military mutiny to intimidate Congress through the NEWBURGH CONSPIRACY.

After the war, Morris also continued his efforts to strengthen national governance under the ARTICLES OF CONFEDERATION. Failing that, he attended the Annapolis Convention of 1786 and the Constitutional Convention of 1787 to push for a more centralized regime. When the new government materialized in 1789, President Washington tendered Morris the post of secretary of the treasury, but he declined in favor of serving as U.S. senator from Pennsylvania. Here the Federalist-inclined Morris championed the national economic programs of Alexander HAMILTON, and he also helped broker the deal whereby Virginia surrendered territory for a new national capital in exchange for assumption of state debts. However, Morris also widely engaged in land speculation in the Old Northwest and lost heavily. By 1798 he had accumulated debts of $3 million—unheard of for that period—and he spent the next three years in debtor's prison. Morris gained his release in 1801 and died quietly in Philadelphia a broken man on May 8, 1806. But during the Revolutionary War his financial wizardry was absolutely essential for the survival of the American republic; to charges of profiteering it may be stated that Morris helped his nation—and himself—with equal abandon.

Further Reading

Eicholz, Hans L. "The Bank of North America and the Transformation of Political Ideology in the Early National Pennsylvania." Unpublished Ph.D. diss., University of California, Los Angeles, 1992.

Gallagher, Mary A. Y. "Private Interest and the Public Good: Settling the Score for the Morris-Holker Business Relationship," *Pennsylvania History* 62, no. 2 (2002): 179–209.

Nuxoll, Elizabeth M., et al., eds. *The Papers of Robert Morris,* 9 vols. Pittsburgh: University of Pittsburgh Press, 1999.

Rappaport, George D. *Stability and Change in Revolutionary Pennsylvania: Banking, Politics, and Social Structure.* University Park: Pennsylvania State University Press, 1996.

Schoderbok, Michael P. "Robert Morris and Reporting for the Treasury under the U.S. Continental Congress," *Accounting Historians Journal* 26, no. 2 (1999): 1–34.

Simner, William G. *The Financier and the Finances of the American Revolution.* Washington, D.C.: Beard Books, 2000.

Moultrie, William (1730–1805)
American military officer

William Moultrie was born in Charleston, South Carolina, on November 30, 1730, the son of a physician. Little is known of his early life, but by the 1750s he was serving in the House of Assembly. In 1761 he gained appointment as a militia captain and joined Colonel James GRANT in his expedition against OCONOSTOTA and the Cherokee Indians. In 1772 Moultrie became a commissioner chosen to fix the boundary between the Carolinas, and in 1774 he advanced in rank to colonel of militia. That year Moultrie was also elected to the First Continental CONGRESS, but he declined to be seated. Instead, he remained at home to partake of the various provincial congresses and on June 17, 1775, he became colonel of the 2nd South Carolina Regiment. His first military action occurred in December of that year, when he stormed Sullivan's Island and captured a number of escaped AFRICAN-AMERICAN slaves. Over the next six months Charleston began preparing itself for a possible British onslaught, and Moultrie's regiment was entrusted with the defense of Fort Sullivan on Sullivan's Island. He disagreed with General Charles LEE, head of the Southern Department, that the post should be abandoned and solicited the help of President of the Assembly John RUTLEDGE to keep troops garrisoned there. On June 28, 1776, a large amphibious expedition under Commodore Peter PARKER and General Henry CLINTON sailed into the harbor to launch an attack on CHARLESTON. They approached with a view toward bombarding Fort Sullivan into submission and then landing troops to storm the city. Moultrie, who commanded only 435 men, 31 cannon, and sparse ammunition, nonetheless husbanded every round and made HMS *Bristol,* Parker's flagship, his main target. That vessel, along with other warships, suffered extensively from Fort Sullivan's accurate fire and gradually withdrew by evening. Moultrie's success denied the British a lodgement in the south for at least two years, and Congress voted him both its thanks

American colonel William Moultrie successfully repulsed the British amphibious fleet at Charleston and disrupted British operations in the south for two years. *(Gibbes Art Museum)*

and a promotion to brigadier general on September 16, 1776. Fort Sullivan was then christened Fort Moultrie in his honor while his regiment mustered into the Continental ARMY as regulars.

Moultrie spent the next two years raising and equipping troops, although greatly hindered by a lack of funding. In the fall of 1779 he functioned as a part of General Benjamin LINCOLN's army in the defense of South Carolina, and on February 3, 1779, he repulsed a British attack against Port Royal (Beaufort). Over the intervening months he maneuvered against British forces under General Augustin PREVOST in Georgia and partook of the attack upon Johns Island during the Stono Ferry operation of June 20, 1779. In the spring of 1780 Moultrie fought at the siege of CHARLESTON with Lincoln and was taken prisoner on May 12. He then declined several invitations to command a regiment at Jamaica and was finally exchanged for General John BURGOYNE on February 9, 1782. The war nearly being over he saw no further action and finally mustered out on October 15, 1782, the last officer promoted major general during the Revolutionary War.

Moultrie's wartime service rendered him a hero, and he parlayed his popularity into politics. After a term as lieutenant governor in 1783 he succeeded to the governor's mansion from 1785 to 1787 and again in 1792–94. His most significant work was in forbidding South Carolinians from participating in a Florida expedition proposed by Charles Genet, the French representative to the United States. In between terms as governor he also held a seat in the state senate and worked on ratifying a new state constitution. Moultrie retired from office in 1794 and turned to cultivating rice and cotton. He died at Northampton, South Carolina, on September 27, 1805, one of the Revolution's earliest war heroes.

Further Reading
Farley, M. Foster. "Battering Charleston's Palmetto Walls," *Military History* 18, no. 2 (2001): 38–44.
Griffiths, John W. " 'To Receive Them Properly': Charleston Prepares for War, 1775–1776." Unpublished master's thesis, University of South Carolina, 1992.
Hilborn, Nat, and Sam Hilborn. "A Show of Strength at Sullivan's Island," *South Carolina History Illustrated* 1, no. 3 (1970): 11–19, 51–60.
Levine, Ida L. "A Letter from William Moultrie at Charleston to George Washington at Mount Vernon, April 7, 1786," *South Carolina Historical Magazine* 83, no. 2 (1982): 116–120.
Moultrie, William. *Memoirs of the American Revolution.* New York: Arno Press, 1968.
Russell, David L. *Victory on Sullivan's Island: The British Cape Fear/Charles Town Expedition of 1776.* Haverford, Pa.: Infinity, 2002.

Moylan, Stephen (1734–1811)
American military officer

Stephen Moylan was born in Cork, Ireland, in 1734, the son of a prosperous merchant. Because he was Catholic his parents chose to educate him in Paris and he eventually entered the shipping business. Moylan immigrated to Philadelphia in 1768, where he became part of that city's social elite and also first president of the Friendly Sons of Ireland, an expatriate organization. As war with England approached in 1775 Moylan cast his lot with the Patriots, and his friend John DICKINSON introduced him to General George WASHINGTON. He then became muster-master of the Continental ARMY outside of Boston and was also entrusted with outfitting several privateers to raid British shipping in Boston Harbor. Moylan acquitted himself well, and in March 1776 he was made Washington's secretary. He served in this capacity until the summer, when Congress appointed him quartermaster general to replace the outgoing Thomas MIFFLIN with a rank of colonel. Unfortunately, the deficiencies inherent in this department proved beyond his capacity to remedy, and his performance proved marginal throughout the ensuing New York campaign. Moylan also proved ineffectual while attempting to block Admiral Richard HOWE's efforts to send warships up the Hudson River. By September he was replaced by Mifflin and returned to Washington's staff as a volunteer officer. Moylan, a boisterous, rashly brave individual, then distinguished himself in the fighting at PRINCETON in January 1777 and thereafter sought additional combat commands.

In January 1777 Moylan was authorized to raise a cavalry regiment from Pennsylvania with himself as its colonel. This was eventually mustered into service as the 4th Continental Light Dragoons and ordered to join forces with Polish officer Kazimierz PULASKI. However, the two high-spirited men disliked each other intensely and Moylan was eventually brought up on charges of insubordination and disrespect. He also rendered valuable services in scouting and reconnaissance missions for the main army, and his performance prior to the Battle of MONMOUTH in August 1778 proved particularly useful. Moylan also accompanied General Anthony WAYNE at the unsuccessful action at Bull's Ferry in June 1780, before taking his regiment south. There it was broken up into detachments and never saw combat as a complete unit. Moylan's whereabouts and activities for this period are little known, but he resurfaced with some of his troopers to reinforce the marquis de LAFAYETTE in Virginia in 1781. He was thus present for the finale at YORKTOWN, where he met and befriended the marquis de CHASTELLUX, who mentioned him extensively in his memoirs. Moylan was finally mustered out of the army in November 1783 with a final brevet promotion to brigadier general.

After the war Moylan returned to Philadelphia to resume his mercantile activities. In 1793 President Washington appointed him commissioner of loans in Philadelphia, and he also served as president of the Friendly Sons of St. Patrick. Moylan died in Philadelphia on April 13, 1811.

Further Reading
Collins, James L. "Irish Participation at Yorktown," *Irish Sword* 15, no. 58 (1982): 3–10.
Griffin, Martin I. J. *Stephen Moylan, Muster-master General, Secretary and Aide-de-Camp to Washington*. Philadelphia: Privately Printed, 1909.
Hearn, Chester. *George Washington's Schooners: The First American Navy*. Annapolis, Md.: Naval Institute Press, 1995.
Heathcote, Charles W. "General Stephan Moylan—A Trusted Officer of the Revolution," *Picket Post* no. 51 (February 1956): 23–28.
Monaghan, Frank. "Stephen Moylan in the American Revolution," *Studies: An Irish Quarterly Review* 19 (September 1930): 481–486.
Moylan, Stephen. "Selections from the Correspondence of Col. Stephen Moylan," *Pennsylvania Magazine of History and Biography* 37 (July 1913): 341–360.

Muhlenberg, John P. G. (1746–1807)
American military officer

John Peter Gabriel Muhlenberg was born in Trappe, Pennsylvania, on October 1, 1746, the son of a Lutheran minister. After attending the Academy of Philadelphia he was sent to the University of Halle, Germany, in 1763 but ended up at a countinghouse in Lübeck. Muhlenberg also took an interest in military matters, and he subsequently joined the Royal American Regiment within the British army. Muhlenberg was honorably discharged in 1767 and returned to Philadelphia to study theology. Three years later he opened up a congregation in Dunmore, Virginia, where he befriended and allied himself with radical leader Patrick HENRY. In 1772 he ventured to England to be ordained in the Episcopal Church, all the while retaining his Lutheran congregation. As the colonies ground toward war with Great Britain, Muhlenberg became increasingly radicalized and served on the local COMMITTEE OF CORRESPONDENCE. In 1774 he held a seat in the House of Burgesses while fulfilling his religious commitments, and in January 1776 he accepted a position as colonel within the Continental ARMY. At the end of a final sermon to his flock, Muhlenberg reputedly tossed off his gown and revealed his uniform underneath to parishioners, entreating them to uphold the Patriot cause. He then recruited the 8th Virginia Continental Infantry, which was overwhelmingly German in composition, and led it south.

Muhlenberg's first assignment was during the attack on CHARLESTON, South Carolina, in June 1776, where he assisted the forces of Colonel William MOULTRIE. By February 1777 he was summoned north to the main army under General George WASHINGTON and promoted to brigadier general. After a harsh winter at Morristown, Muhlenberg joined the brigade of General Nathanael GREENE and fought exceptionally well at the Battles of BRANDYWINE and GERMANTOWN. In the last engagement his deep penetration of the British right wing nearly won the battle for the Americans. After another harsh winter at Valley Forge, Muhlenberg rendered valuable service in the MONMOUTH campaign of August 1778, after which he joined forces with General Anthony WAYNE in New Jersey. He then commanded the reserves during Wayne's successful reduction of Stoney Point in July 1779. The following year he returned to Virginia to help fend off a powerful British invasion and functioned as second in command under General Friedrich von STEUBEN. In this capacity he fought an unsuccessful delaying action against General William PHILLIPS at Petersburg on April 25, 1781, and subsequently joined the division of the marquis de LAFAYETTE. Part of his command distinguished itself under Colonel Alexander HAMILTON in the October 14, 1781, capture of Redoubt No. 10 during the YORKTOWN campaign. On September 30, 1783, Muhlenberg retired from active service with the final rank of brevet major general.

Muhlenberg ended the war as a national hero, especially among his German constituents in Philadelphia, and he commenced a long and distinguished career in politics. He served with the state supreme executive council, rising to vice president under President Benjamin FRANKLIN, and was reelected three time to the national CONGRESS as a representative. In 1801 he successfully stood for a seat in the U.S. Senate but resigned shortly after when President Thomas JEFFERSON made him customs collector at Philadelphia. Muhlenberg died at Grey's Ferry near Philadelphia on October 1, 1807, the most distinguished German-American of the Revolutionary War.

Further Reading

"Gen. John Peter G. Muhlenberg," *Pennsylvania German* 3 (January 1902): 3–18.

Germann, Wilhelm. "The Crisis in the Early Life of General Peter Muhlenberg," *Pennsylvania Magazine of History and Biography* 37 (July–October 1913): 298–329, 450–470.

Heatchcote, Charles W. "General John Peter Gabriel Muhlenberg," *Picket Post* no. 42 (October 1953): 4–10.

Hocker, Edward W. *The Fighting Parson of the American Revolution.* Philadelphia: The Author, 1936.

Rightmyer, Thomas N. "The Holy Orders of Peter Muhlenberg," *Historical Magazine of the Protestant Episcopal Church* 30 (September 1961): 183–197.

Wallace, Paul. *The Muhlenbergs of Pennsylvania.* Philadelphia: University of Pennsylvania Press, 1950.

Murphy, Timothy (1751–1818)
American soldier

Timothy Murphy was born in Minisink, New Jersey, in 1751, a son of Irish immigrants. He was raised in the wilderness region of the Wyoming Valley, Pennsylvania, becoming quite adept as a woodsman and a marksman. Sometime after the Revolutionary War commenced, Murphy, a short, dark-haired, but steely individual, joined the Pennsylvania Battalion of Riflemen and marched to join the main American army at Boston. He then fought under General George WASHINGTON at LONG ISLAND, TRENTON, and PRINCETON, gaining considerable renown for his shooting and stalking skills. In July 1777 Murphy transferred to the Rifle Corps under Colonel Daniel MORGAN and was sent to reinforce the Northern Army under General Horatio GATES. In this capacity he rendered valuable assistance at the Battles of FREEMAN'S FARM and BEMIS HEIGHTS against British forces commanded by General John BURGOYNE. On October 7, 1777, General Benedict ARNOLD summoned Murphy to the front line and ordered him to draw a bead upon the heroic general Simon

FRASER at extreme range. Placing his Dickert rifle in the fork of a tree, he mortally wounded Fraser on his third shot and is also credited with killing Burgoyne's aide, Sir Francis Carr Clerke. In August 1778 Murphy's regiment was marginally engaged at MONMOUTH, but afterward he gained notoriety by capturing the coach of a British officer.

After Burgoyne's defeat, the British resorted to raiding the New York and Pennsylvania frontiers with bands of LOYALISTS and Mohawk Indians. Murphy then accompanied several companies of riflemen dispatched to the region for its defense. He partook in many bloody skirmishes—many of which remain shrouded in myth and thus difficult to verify—but Murphy excelled as a ruthless Indian fighter. In August 1779 he accompanied General John SULLIVAN's punitive expedition into the heart of Iroquois territory as a part of a company of scouts commanded by Lieutenant Thomas Boyd. On September 13, 1779, Murphy narrowly escaped death in an ambush that wiped out Boyd and 22 of his men. Sometime in the spring of 1780 Murphy and another rifleman were captured by the Iroquois and were being transported back to their village to be tortured and killed. That evening he and his companion apparently slipped their bonds and silently killed 11 of their captors while they slept before escaping. The following September Murphy was assigned to help defend Middle Fort in the Schoharie Valley. On October 16, that post was besieged by a large force of Loyalists and Indians under Major John JOHNSON, assisted by Chiefs Joseph BRANT and CORNPLANTER. The fort's cowardly commander, Major Melancthon Woolsey, wanted to surrender, but Murphy—knowing the fate that awaited him in the hands of vengeful Indians—stridently refused to capitulate. He then fired on several flags of truce and threatened to gun down Woolsey personally if he raised the white flag. At length Johnson was forced to draw off and left the garrison intact. In April 1781 Murphy joined the 3rd Pennsylvania Continental Infantry and fought under General Anthony WAYNE. He was present at the hard-fought engagement at Green Spring on July 6, 1781, and was later present at YORKTOWN. Murphy then mustered out of the Continental ARMY, returned to the Schoharie Valley, and spent the rest of the war skirmishing with hostile tribesmen. In recognition of his legendary feats of prowess, he was formally introduced to General Washington on August 3, 1783.

After the war Murphy returned to a life of relative obscurity while farming in upstate New York, and he died in Fultonham on June 27, 1818. Like his noted contemporaries Sam BRADY and Daniel BOONE, he was among the most influential frontiersmen of the Revolutionary War.

Further Reading
Alotta, Renard M. *The True Story of the Frontier Riflemen.* East Greenbush, N.Y.: R. M. Alotta, 2000.
Cook, Fred J. *What Manner of Men: Forgotten Heros of the American Revolution.* New York: William Morrow, 1959.
La Crosse, Richard B. *Revolutionary Rangers: Daniel Morgan's Riflemen and Their Role on the Northern Frontier, 1778–1783.* Bowie, Md.: Heritage Books, 2002.
O'Brien, Michael J. *Timothy Murphy, Hero of the American Revolution.* New York: Eire Publishing Co., 1941.
Smith, Byron C. "White Savages in Hunting Shirts: The Rifleman's Costume of National Identity and Rebellion in the American Revolution." Unpublished master's thesis, University of Richmond, 2000.
Van Dyke, Mark A. "Timothy Murphy: The Man and the Legend," *New York Folklore* 2, nos. 1–2 (1976): 87–110.

Murray, Alexander (1754–1821)
American naval officer

Alexander Murray was born at Chestertown, Maryland, on July 12, 1754, the son of a physician, and went to sea while still young. At the age of 18 he commanded his own vessel and regularly plied the Atlantic trade routes to Europe. When the Revolutionary War erupted in 1775 he enlisted in Colonel William SMALLWOOD's 1st Maryland Continental Infantry as a lieutenant and saw action in the Battles of WHITE PLAINS and Flatbush in 1776. However, while commanding a battery erected to interdict traffic along the Hudson River, he was injured by an exploding cannon and rendered nearly deaf. Murray largely surmounted his handicap and continued campaigning until sickness forced his retirement in 1777. While recuperating he applied to the Continental CONGRESS for an officer's commission in the Continental NAVY. Rather than wait for a response he commanded a succession of privateers, gaining a reputation as a dauntless but unlucky commander. Murray commanded the 18-gun schooner *General Mercer* for several months and succeeded to the larger *Saratoga,* which was captured in 1778. Exchanged shortly thereafter, he took control of the *Columbus* and *Revenge* but was taken a second time. Following his release Murray was finally commissioned a regular lieutenant on July 20, 1781, and assigned to the frigate *Trumbull* under Captain James NICHOLSON. He served on that vessel until it was captured by the British warships HMS *Iris* and *General Monk* on August 9, 1781. During the engagement nearly one-third of the crew, who were British deserters, refused to fight, and Murray, assisted by Richard DALE, fought on as long as possible. After his third release Murray acceded to command of the *Prosperity,* with which he secured several prizes in the West Indies. He subsequently accompanied the joint American-Spanish expedition against the Bahamas and nearly dueled with the Spanish commander over the insulting terms of surrender offered the British. Murray then transferred to the frigate *Alliance* under Captain John BARRY, remaining on that vessel until it was decommissioned in 1785. He was the last naval officer to hold a commission after the war.

Murray eventually settled in Philadelphia, where he worked as a merchant. In 1798 President John ADAMS expanded the nascent U.S. Navy for the limited Quasi War against France in the West Indies, and he became one of six newly commissioned captains. He then headed the 20-gun

American naval officer Alexander Murray served admirably on many vessels during the course of his career. *(Metropolitan Museum of Art, Rogers Fund)*

corvette *Montezuma* on several Caribbean sweeps until a bout of yellow fever forced him to convalesce ashore. A few months later he took charge of the captured 41-gun frigate *Insurgente* and convoyed several hundred American vessels throughout the region without loss. In 1800 Murray took charge of the new 38-gun frigate *Constellation,* and he replaced Captain Silas TALBOT as commander of the San Domingo station. In light of capable service he was retained after the "war" as sixth in seniority on the list of 12 captains.

In 1802 President Thomas JEFFERSON acted decisively against the depredations of the Barbary pirates and dispatched a powerful naval squadron to the North African shore. Murray resumed command of the *Constellation* again and blockaded the port of Tripoli for several months. He enjoyed a successful engagement with several enemy gunboats before transferring his flag to the frigate *John Adams* for an extended cruise of home waters. In 1807 he headed the court-martial that convicted Commodore James Barron for negligence in the notorious *Chesapeake Leopard* affair of that year and he subsequently served as the first commander of the Philadelphia Navy Yard. Murray was by then the navy's senior officer, but he missed action in the War of 1812 on account of his deafness. He died in Philadelphia on October 6, 1821, a venerable witness to several stirring events in American naval history.

Further Reading
Brown, John H. *American Naval Heroes*. Boston: Brown and Co., 1899.
"Life of Commodore Murray," *Port Folio* 3 (May 1814): 399–409, 619.
Miller, Nathan. *Sea of Glory: A Naval History of the American Revolution*. Mount Pleasant, S.C.: Nautical and Aviation Pub. Co., 2000.
Palmer, Michael A. *Stoddert's War: Naval Operations during the Quasi-War with France, 1790–1801*. Annapolis, Md.: Naval Institute Press, 2000.

Murray, John (1732–1809)
English politician

John Murray was born in Perthshire, Scotland, in 1737, a son of the Third Earl of Dunmore. After serving several years as a captain in the 3rd Foot Guards, he inherited his father's title as earl of Dunmore in 1756 and served as one of 16 peers representing Scotland in the English Parliament. There he displayed somewhat moderate sensibilities in his dealings with American issues and in 1770 he gained appointment as governor of New York through the offices of his brother in law, earl Gower. However, he served less than a year in this capacity before being replaced by William TRYON and was reassigned as governor of Virginia in 1771. Murray enjoyed considerable popularity initially, and he went to great lengths to befriend leading members of the landed gentry like George WASHINGTON. However, as the rising tide of resentment against British policies buffeted the colony he faced an increasingly intractable assembly, the House of Burgesses. By 1773 Murray was at loggerheads with the assembly over COMMITTEES OF CORRESPONDENCE and nonimportation, so he dissolved it. He summarily dismissed the assembly again in 1774 for its overt display of sympathy toward Boston during imposition of the COERCIVE ACTS. Perhaps as a method of deflecting attention away from imperial frictions and possibly to boost his own sagging popularity,

Virginia governor John Murray issued his controversial Emancipation Proclamation in 1775, offering freedom to any African American who fought on behalf of the British. *(Scottish National Portrait Gallery)*

Murray then fomented hostilities with the Shawnee Indians over western lands jointly claimed by Virginia and Pennsylvania. The Indians responded with a wave of attacks across the frontier that sent streams of refugees back across the Appalachian Mountains. In August 1774 Murray mustered a large contingent of militia and led it to the western frontier while a second column under Colonel Andrew LEWIS was to rendezvous with him. On October 10, 1774, Lewis met and engaged the principle Indian force under Chief CORNSTALK and defeated it after a bloody battle at Point Pleasant. Murray subsequently arrived and forced the Shawnee into favorable land concessions. This was the last colonial war in American history and it did much to revitalize Murray's political standing, if temporarily.

Once tensions exploded into war in April 1775 Murray resorted to increasingly arbitrary methods of enforcing royal rule in Virginia. On April 21, 1775, he ordered royal marines to seize a cache of colonial gunpowder at Williamsburg, which drew the wrath of Patrick HENRY and other legislators. The governor then backed down and compensated the colony for the property seized. With events spinning out of control and lacking sufficient British troops to protect him, Murray fled for the protection of the frigate HMS *Fowley* on June 8, 1775, where he maintained a floating government in exile over the next 14 months. Murray's most controversial act came on November 15, 1775, when he issued his Emancipation Proclamation to AFRICAN-AMERICAN slaves. This declaration promised freedom and a chance to fight for any individual who escaped and joined the British. Many slaves did, in fact, bolster the British ranks by enlisting in Lord Dunmore's Ethiopian Regiment, the first all-black military unit in American history. However militarily expedient, his tactics completely alienated the planting classes dependent upon slaves, and they vigorously threw their lot in with the Patriots. Both sides continued massing men and materiel until December 9, 1775, when the main rebel force appeared outside the port of Norfolk. Murray ordered an all-out attack in the battle of Great Bridge and was completely defeated by forces under General William WOODFORD. He then fled the mainland and established his headquarters on Gwynn Island offshore. On January 1, 1776, his fleet bombarded Norfolk and partially burned it to the ground, which did little to enhance his already sullied reputation. Murray then conducted a number of raids inland and solicited LOYALIST support until July 10, 1776, when Gwynn Island was successfully stormed by General Lewis. At this juncture Murray abandoned his struggle to restore royal authority and departed on August 7, 1776, for England.

Murray resumed his seat in Parliament until 1781 when he was ordered to accompany the army of General Charles CORNWALLIS back to Virginia. He was initially stationed at Charleston, South Carolina, to recruit when news of the surrender at YORKTOWN arrived. A disgruntled Murray then returned to England, where he labored several years on behalf of displaced Loyalists. In consequence of his useful services he was appointed governor of the Bahamas in 1786, where he established a lucrative trade relationship with Chief Alexander MCGILLIVRAY of the Creek. However, he fell from favor when his daughter married a younger son of King GEORGE III, a violation of the Royal Marriage Act, and he was dismissed in 1796. Murray then retired to his personal estate at Ramsgate, Kent, where he died on February 25, 1809. His tenure as the last royal governor of Virginia, well intended, proved unworkable and certainly precipitated the fall of British power there.

Further Reading

Barr, Daniel P. "Contested Land: Competition and Conflict along the Upper Ohio Frontier, 1744–1784." Unpublished Ph.D. diss., Kent State University, 2001.

Carey, Charles W. "Lord Dunmore's Ethiopian Regiment." Unpublished master's thesis, Virginia Polytechnic Institute and State University, 1995.

Crawford, David B. "Counter-revolution in Virginia: Patriot Response to Dunmore's Emancipation Proclamation of November 7, 1775." Unpublished master's thesis, Ball State University, 1993.

Fought, Leigh K. "Lord Dunmore's War, 1768–1774." Unpublished master's thesis, University of Houston, 1994.

Gara, Donald A. "Loyal Subjects of the Crown: The Queen's Own Loyal Virginia Regiment and Dunmore's Ethiopian Regiment," *Journal of the Society for Army Historical Research* 83, no. 333 (2005): 30–42.

Skidmore, Warren, and Donna Kaminsky. *Lord Dunmore's Little Wars of 1774: His Captains and Their Men Who Opened up Kentucky and the West to American Settlement*. Bowie, Md.: Heritage Books, 2002.

Nash, Francis (ca. 1742–1777)
American military officer

Francis Nash was born in Prince Edward County, Virginia, around 1742 and raised in the wilderness region of Hillsboro, North Carolina. An enterprising individual, he had succeeded in a number of occupations including merchant, attorney, and justice of the peace by 1763. The following year he represented Orange County in the colonial assembly and supported the state government during the period of Regulator difficulties. As such he served as a militia captain in the army of Governor William TRYON and fought at the Battle of ALAMANCE on May 16, 1771. In light of his service to the government he became judge of the court of oyer and terminer for Hillsboro district in 1774. However, the onset of fighting in April 1775 induced Nash to change allegiance to the Patriot side, and he sat in several of the extralegal provincial congresses. Nash eventually made colonel of militia based solely on his prior military experience and a reputation for bravery. On September 1, 1775, he became lieutenant of the 1st North Carolina Continental Infantry and succeeded James MOORE as colonel the following April. In this capacity he marched to South Carolina and was present during the attack on CHARLESTON, acquitting himself well. On February 5, 1777, the Continental CONGRESS made Nash a brigadier general in the Continental ARMY and ordered him on recruiting service prior to marching north to join the main force under General George WASHINGTON.

Nash accompanied the Carolina brigade as ordered and replaced Moore as commander following the latter's death at Wilmington in April 1777. Once in Pennsylvania he joined the division of General William ALEXANDER, Lord Stirling, and was present at the Battle of BRANDYWINE that September but not closely engaged. On October 4, 1777, Nash accompanied Alexander during the Battle of GERMANTOWN as part of the reserves. However, while crossing a fog-shrouded field his troops became engaged in confused fighting, and Nash was struck on the leg by a cannonball. He died three days later on October 7, 1777, lamented as a brave soldier. Nash County, North Carolina, and Nashville, Tennessee, were named in his honor.

Further Reading

Ashe, Samuel A., ed. *Biographical History of North Carolina,* 8 vols. Greensboro, N.C.: C. L. Van Noppen, 1908.

Rankin, Hugh F. *The North Carolina Continentals.* Chapel Hill: University of North Carolina, 1971.

Reed, John. "Tragic Sword: A Biography of Brigadier General Francis Nash, 1742–1777," *Bulletin of the Historical Society of Montgomery Country* 18 (fall 1972): 227–297.

Rogers, Linell C. "Francis Nash, Soldier and Patriot," *Tennessee Historical Magazine* 3, no. 4 (1937): 268–279.

Waddell, A. M.. Gen. *Francis Nash; An Address by Hon. A. M. Waddell.* Greensboro, N.C.: Guilford Battle Ground Co., 1906.

Williams, Samuel C. "General Francis Nash and William Lee Davidson," *Tennessee Historical Quarterly* 1, no. 3 (1942): 250–268.

navy, Continental

Given the extent of the American coastline, and the sheer oceanic distance between Great Britain and its colonies, sea power was destined to play a significant role in the Revolutionary War, if not a decisive one. Technically speaking, the first American naval victory occurred on June 11–12, 1775, when a handful of sailors under Jeremiah O'BRIEN attacked and seized the British vessels HMS *Margaretta* and *Unity* off Machias, Maine. But this was strictly a state affair and done in the absence of a national navy. During the siege of Boston, General George WASHINGTON contracted a score of private vessels to harass British shipping in and out of the harbor; in this regard the *Hannah* of Beverly is sometimes regarded as the first American "warship." On November 27, 1775, Captain John MANLEY of the schooner *Lee* scored the first significant capture by seizing the British transport *Nancy*, which contained many valuable military supplies. These antecedents, while minor, proved encouraging enough to members of the Second Continental CONGRESS, especially John ADAMS of Massachusetts, to consider establishment of a national naval arm. Not surprisingly, it fell upon the delegation from neighboring Rhode Island to first broach the idea of a Continental navy, and Adams pushed hard for its creation. On December 13, 1775, the Congressional Naval Committee authorized construction of 13 frigates—one for each colony—to serve as the nucleus of a new navy. That month a list of potential captains was also approved and Esek HOPKINS, whose brother Stephen sat on the Naval Committee, was appointed commodore of the still nonexistent force. It was not until the spring of 1776 that the Continental navy sortied in force from Philadelphia; Hopkins, ignoring congressional instructions, sailed against the Bahamas, which he successfully captured on March 3–4. This seemingly auspicious beginning belied the improvised, ad hoc, and frequently slap-dash administration of the Continental navy for the rest of the war, which rendered it unable to make much of an impact on the course of events.

Navies, then as now, were expensive to construct, maintain, and operate. For this reason Congress elected to forego construction of mighty ships of the line, each mounting 60 cannon or more, and concentrate instead on smaller, faster frigates. Such vessels, from the standpoint of speed and armament, were ideal, long-range commerce raiders, being both reasonably priced and manned. The Americans ultimately constructed 13 such vessels, which proved largely superior in sailing qualities to their British counterparts. Unfortunately, the Continental navy remained dogged by endemic manpower shortages from the outset. Discipline was harsh and pay irregular, and the navy found itself competing with privateers for scarce, trained manpower. Privateers not only enjoyed better living and working conditions, but the financial reward—prize money—was far more lucrative. The navy also suffered from a lack of trained combat personnel. Those individuals eventually commissioned as officers possessed extensive maritime experience handling commercial vessels, an arduous enough task, but frequently proved deficient in the art of commanding warships in battle. Consequently, by war's end only two American frigates, *Alliance* and *Deane*, remained in commission, while the others had either been taken or burned to prevent capture. After the FRENCH ALLIANCE was concluded in 1778, France's navy became the principle obstacle and concern for British naval planners, as the bulk of American vessels were simply nonexistent. This strategic dilemma anticipated by 30 years what would befall the equally tiny U.S. Navy during the War of 1812.

Perhaps the most compelling reason for the Continental navy's lack of success at sea was its adversary, the formidable Royal Navy. This battle-hardened force had suffered declines in combat effectiveness and seaworthiness since the Seven Years' War, largely due to the economy measures of Lord Frederick NORTH and his scheming lord of the Admiralty, John MONTAGU, but it enjoyed a century's experience in naval and personnel administration, permanent dockyards for upkeep, and superb fighting traditions. The Revolutionary War, in fact, represented a low point in the long history of this service, yet no Continental vessel could take any confrontation or engagement with British warships lightly, for veteran British captains were well versed in the nuances of naval combat. The best illustration of this longtime experience occurred on April 6, 1776, when the 20-gun frigate HMS *Glasgow* under Captain Tryingham Howe fended off Commodore Hopkins's entire squadron, damaging several vessels. Commodore George COLLIER, moreover, completely destroyed the Penobscot expedition of Captain Dudley SALTONSTALL on August 12, 1779, nearly gutting the Massachusetts state navy in the process. Other individuals such as Captain Richard PEARSON of HMS *Serapis* mounted formidable resistance before capitulating to superior force. Despite being stretched very thin, at no time during the war did the Royal Navy's 460 warships ever lose control of waters they occupied to the Americans, notwithstanding PRIVATEERING and occasional raids in home waters. By dint of training, tradition, and leadership, they restricted American naval activities to raiding and also bested French and Spanish fleets in a number of celebrated actions. Senior leaders like Admiral Richard HOWE, Samuel HOOD, and George Brydges RODNEY remain among the most famous names in naval history. Hopkins, the only senior American naval leader, was dismissed in January 1778, and no replacement was ever named.

Where the Continental navy did succeed was in establishing precedents for success in individual battle. In contrast to the timid French naval establishment, with its many beautiful and highly efficient vessels, Americans inherited the distinctly British mentality of placing one's vessel alongside that of an opponent—and fighting. Daring sailors like John Paul JONES, John BARRY, Gustavus CONYNGHAM, and Lambert WICKES fought well in a number of engagements—sometimes against steep odds—and usually prevailed. Their successes, small when set against the backdrop of the entire war, bequeathed to the nascent naval arm traditions of victory that would be expanded upon during the Quasi-War with France, the war against the Barbary pirates, and the War of 1812. The too small, too ineptly administered, and too undermanned Continental navy may have captured 196 vessels worth $6 million in prize money, but during this same period privateers seized 2,200 ships worth several times more. Yet for all its faults, the Continental navy provided solid foundations upon which a new force, the United States Navy, ultimately arose.

Further Reading
Blanchard, Christopher E. "Unconventional Maritime Warfare in the American Revolution: The Case against Creation of the Continental Navy." Unpublished master's thesis, University of San Diego, 1997.
Canney, Donald L. *Sailing Warships of the U.S. Navy.* Annapolis, Md.: Naval Institute Press, 2001.
Cogliano, Francis D. *American Maritime Prisoners in the Revolutionary War: The Captivity of William Russell.* Annapolis, Md.: Naval Institute Press, 2001.
Gardiner, Robert, ed. *Navies of the American Revolution, 1775–1783.* Annapolis, Md.: Naval Institute Press, 1996.
Gilje, Paul A. "Loyalty and Liberty: The Ambiguous Patriotism of Jack Tar in the American Revolution," *Pennsylvania History* 67, no. 2 (2000): 165–193.
Miller, Nathan. *Sea of Glory: A Naval History of the American Revolution.* Mount Pleasant, S.C.: Nautical and Aviation Pub. Co., 2000.
Silverstone, Paul H. *The Sailing Navy, 1775–1854.* Annapolis, Md.: Naval Institute Press, 2001.
Zeiler, Harris R. "The Maddest Idea in the World: The Origins of the United States Navy during the Revolution." Unpublished master's thesis, East Stroudsburg University, 1996.

Newburgh Conspiracy (March 1783)
A major weakness of the ARTICLES OF CONFEDERATION was the inability of the Continental and Con-

federation Congresses to raise money through direct taxation. Consequently, the Continental ARMY's pay usually remained many months in arrears, which caused serious mutinies among the Pennsylvania and Connecticut Line. As the Revolutionary War ground to its conclusion, many officers were likewise disenchanted that the legislature would prove able or willing to fulfill prior pledges to award them half-pay for life as a pension. When Congress refused to address the issue seriously, a conspiracy arose between nationalist factions, who preferred centralized authority with the ability to levy taxes, and disgruntled elements within the military. The nationalists, unofficially headed by Alexander HAMILTON, Robert MORRIS, and Gouverneur MORRIS, encouraged discontent in the army to frighten Congress into adopting national imposts as a prelude to stronger governance. To that end they solicited and received the cooperation of General Alexander MCDOUGALL in December 1782, who penned thinly veiled threats of mutiny and a possible march on Philadelphia if the army's concerns were not speedily addressed. When this effort failed to prompt congressional action, the conspirators approached the ever ambitious General Horatio GATES, stationed with the main army at Newburgh, New York, to orchestrate an actual mutiny.

At length it devolved upon Gates's aide-de-camp, John Armstrong, Jr., son of General John ARMSTRONG, to draft two anonymous letters on March 12, 1783. The first called for an unauthorized meeting of officers to "discuss" long-standing disputes with Congress, while a second strongly reiterated their grievances and urged them to take action. By this juncture, Hamilton and other nationalists realized that no military action of any kind—let alone a mutiny—would succeeded without the approval of General George WASHINGTON, who remained studiously circumspect in his dealings with an otherwise troublesome Congress. Hamilton then informed Washington that a conspiracy was afoot (without admitting his own culpability) and urged him to take action. The general, stung by a conspiracy at his own headquarters, canceled the intended meeting of officers, then summoned them to a personal audience on March 15. The room grew quiet as the imposing commander thanked the men for their patience and sacrifice—then excoriated the cabal against civilian authority as illegal and immoral. His stance instantly quashed any notion of mutiny, and the affair evaporated as quickly as it came. The net effect of the so-called Newburgh Addresses was to reaffirm the military's deference to civilian control and to further enhance Washington's reputation as a national figure. Meanwhile, Congress, having carped on its fiscal obligations toward the military, finally agreed to a pension of full salaries for the next five years, and the matter subsided.

Further Reading
Kohn, Richard H. "The Inside Story of the Newburgh Conspiracy: America and the Coup d'etat," *William and Mary Quarterly* 27, no. 2 (1970): 187–220.
Nelson, Paul D. "Horatio Gates at Newburgh, 1783: A Misunderstood Role," *William and Mary Quarterly* 29 (January 1972): 143–158.
Skeen, C. Edward. "The Newburgh Conspiracy Reconsidered," *William and Mary Quarterly* 31 (April 1974): 273–298.
Wensyel, James W. "The Newburgh Conspiracy," *American Heritage* 32, no. 3 (1981): 40–47.

Nicholas, Samuel (ca. 1744–1790)
American Marine Corps officer

Samuel Nicholas was born in Philadelphia around 1744, the son of a blacksmith. Active as a sportsman during his youth, he settled into the position of innkeeper and apparently performed some work for the merchant marine by the time the Revolutionary War commenced. On November 10, 1775, the Continental CONGRESS authorized creation of two battalions of marines to serve onboard ships of the nascent Continental NAVY. Shortly afterward, on November 28, 1775, Nicholas became both a captain and the first commissioned officer of marines in American history. In this capacity he recruited a company of 80 men and reported for duty onboard the converted merchantman *Alfred* under Commodore Esek

HOPKINS. By February 1776 no less than five companies of marines had been assembled, and they accompanied Hopkins's expedition against the Bahamas. On March 3, 1776, Nicholas commanded the first American landing force by leading 234 marines and 50 sailors ashore at New Providence Island (Nassau), which convinced Governor Montfort Browne to surrender after token resistance. Forts Montagu and Nassau were then promptly stripped of guns and ammunition and the stores removed to the fleet. On April 6, 1776, the returning American squadron encountered the 20-gun frigate HMS *Glasgow* off Block Island, and Nicholas was actively engaged in the battle. After anchoring at New London, Connecticut, Hopkins ordered Nicholas to Philadelphia with important dispatches.

Back home, Nicholas received new orders instructing him to recruit additional companies for new frigates still on the stocks, and he also gained promotion to major as of June 1776. The following December he took a detachment of 80 marines into the field as part of Colonel John Cadwalader's brigade and fought well in the Battles of Assumpink Creek and PRINCETON in January 1777. Thereafter he was increasingly drawn into training and administrative work for the marines, in effect functioning as their first commandant. Nicholas also performed unrelated work for financier Robert MORRIS by conveying large sums of money and military supplies between Philadelphia and Boston. In August 1779 he was instructed to raise an additional company of marines; two years later Nicholas requested sea duty on board the new ship of the line *America*. When this was denied he apparently resigned his commission. Nicholas then resumed his work as an innkeeper and died at Philadelphia on August 27, 1790, at the age of 46. In 1919 the U.S. Navy honored his memory by commissioning the destroyer *Nicholas*.

Further Reading

Fagan, Louis E. "Samuel Nicholas, First Officer of American Marines," *Marine Corps Gazette* 18, no. 3 (1933): 5–15.

Keenan, Jerry. "Ashore at New Providence," *By Valor and Arms* 2, no. 3 (1976): 22–29.

Lewis, Charles L. *Famous American Marines*. Boston: Page, 1950.

McClellan, Edwin N. "American Marines in the Revolution," *U.S. Naval Institute Proceedings* 49 (June 1923): 957–963.

Smith, Charles R. *Marines in the American Revolution: A History of the Continental Marines in the American Revolution*. Washington, D.C.: History and Museums Division, Headquarters, U.S. Marine Corps, 1975.

Stevens, Harold R. "Samuel Nicholas, Innkeeper–Marine," *Marine Corps Gazette* 37 (November 1953): 12–15.

Nicholson, James (ca. 1736–1804)
American naval officer

James Nicholson was born in Chestertown, Maryland, around 1736, although little is known of his family life. Apparently he joined the Royal Navy during the French and Indian War and fought at the siege of Havana in 1762. When the Revolutionary War commenced in April 1775, Nicholson tendered his services to the Maryland state navy and became captain of the *Defiance*. In this capacity he handily repelled the British vessel HMS *Otter* in Chesapeake Bay on March 9, 1776, and recaptured several prizes. Consequently he was commissioned a captain in the Continental NAVY on June 6, 1776, and, following the resignation of Esek HOPKINS in 1778, he became the senior naval officer. Apparently he owed his high rank to the Continental CONGRESS's need to balance the captain's list—heavily dominated by New Englanders—regionally. Nicholson then received command of the new frigate *Virginia*, still under construction in Baltimore, and he waited nearly two years ashore before it was completed. Nicholson also gained some notoriety by remedying crew shortages through impressment, for which he was suspended from duty for several months. Once the *Virginia* was fully rigged and manned, Nicholson had to negotiate a tight and efficient British blockade off Chesapeake Bay. On the evening of March 30, 1778, he managed to steal past the blockaders only to ground his vessel on a sandy shoal. On April 1, 1778, the *Virginia* was accosted by three British warships, and Nicholson, rather than be captured, hastily abandoned ship and rowed to shore. He left Lieutenant Joshua BARNEY to surrender the vessel in his place. Only the intervention of his political friends in Congress prevented him from facing a court-martial.

Nicholson remained without a command for the next 15 months until he finally received the 30-gun frigate *Trumbull* at New London. In May 1780 he sailed for the West Indies, where, on June 2, he encountered the larger, 32-gun privateer *Watt* north of Bermuda. An intense battle erupted at close range in which both ships were severely pummeled; *Trumbull* lost a mast, while *Watt* limped away. This was one of the most contested actions of the war and occasioned extremely heavy losses to the British vessel. Nicholson himself returned to Boston for a refit, and in the summer of 1781 he sailed for Havana. On August 8 he was intercepted by the 32-gun frigate HMS *Iris* and gave battle. Unfortunately, because three-fourths of *Trumbull's* crew consisted mainly of British deserters, they refused to fight. Nicholson, assisted by Lieutenants Richard DALE and Alexander MURRAY, resisted for an hour before the 18-gun sloop *General Monk* added its firepower to the fight and he surrendered. On November 29, 1781, he was cleared by a court of inquiry for the loss of his ship but received no further commands for the rest of the war.

Nicholson remained on active duty until April 1785, when he requested and received a leave of absence. He then served in the merchant marine out of New York City and eventually settled there as a respected figure. In April 1789 he commanded the barge that towed president-elect George WASHINGTON from New Jersey to the city for his inauguration. Nicholson then became a strong supporter of Thomas JEFFERSON and active in Democratic-Republican party matters. When Jefferson became president he granted Nicholson the sinecure of commissioner of loans for New York City as a reward. He died in New York on September 2, 1804, a high-ranking but generally inept naval leader of the Revolutionary War. In eight years of service Nicholson failed to capture a single enemy vessel, while losing two brand-new frigates of his own.

Further Reading

Fowler, William M. "The Non-Volunteer Navy," *U.S. Naval Institute Proceedings* 100, no. 858 (1974): 74–78.

———. "James Nicholson and the Continental Frigate Virginia," *American Neptune* 34, no. 2 (1974): 135–141.

McManemin, John A. *Captains of the Continental Navy.* Spring Lake, N.J.: Ho-Ho-Kus Press, 1982.

Miller, Nathan. *Sea of Glory: A Naval History of the American Revolution.* Mount Pleasant, S.C.: Nautical and Aviation Press, 2000.

Paullin, Charles O., ed. *Out-letters of the Continental Marine Committee and the Board of the Admiralty, August, 1776–September, 1780.* New York: Printed for the Naval History Society by the De Vinne Press, 1914.

Nicholson, Samuel (1743–1811)
American naval officer

Samuel Nicholson was born in Maryland in 1743, the younger brother of James NICHOLSON. He entered the merchant marine while young and was residing in England on business when the Revolutionary War began in April 1775. Nicholson subsequently made his way to Paris and worked with American agent Benjamin FRANKLIN to secure a captain's commission in the Continental NAVY. This was accomplished by December 10, 1776, at which point Nicholson returned to England and purchased the cutter *Dolphin*. Sailing across the channel to Calais, he outfitted his charge with cannon and as of May 1777 became part of a small squadron under Captain Lambert WICKES. Their raid proved extremely successful and so upsetting to English authorities that when Nicholson dropped anchor at Nantes, his vessel was confiscated. He remained technically in limbo until the FRENCH ALLIANCE was concluded in the spring of 1778, after which he received command of the

French-built 32-gun frigate *Deane*. Nicholson returned to the United States, where he assumed command of a small squadron consisting of *Deane*, the *Confederacy* under Captain Seth HARDING, and the *Boston* under Captain Samuel TUCKER. A quick sweep of the West Indies in July and August 1778 netted several captures, and Nicholson returned to Boston with 250 prisoners in his hold. He returned repeatedly to the West Indies over the next three years and in May 1782 seized the privateer *Jackal*, one of the last prizes taken by the Continental navy. However, when Nicholson arrived in Boston he was brought up on charges of "tyranny and oppression" and subjected to a court-martial. The ensuing trial vindicated his career, but by then he had acquired the reputation of a martinet.

Nicholson resumed his maritime activities after the war, but in June 1794 he was recommissioned a captain in the slowly evolving U.S. Navy; he ranked second in seniority after Captain John BARRY. Nicholson reported to Boston Harbor to supervise construction of a new and powerful 44-gun frigate, USS *Constitution*. He launched this famous vessel on October 21, 1797, and the following year he sailed into the Caribbean to partake in the Quasi-War against France. Finding his vessel too slow and bulky to catch agile French privateers, Nicholson mistakenly caught and released two unarmed English vessels, which landed him in trouble with Secretary of the Navy Benjamin Stoddert. He returned to Boston in April 1799, his active service days ended. In 1801, President Thomas JEFFERSON appointed him first superintendent of the Charlestown Navy Yard, where he also functioned as the navy's senior officer after Barry's death in 1803. Nicholson served capably and without further controversy until his own passing in Boston on December 29, 1811. His long naval career was somewhat nondescript, save only for serving as first commander of the famous "Old Ironsides."

Further Reading
Fitz-Enz, David G. *Old Ironsides: Eagle of the Sea.* Lanham, Md.: Taylor Trade Pub., 2004.

Martin, Tyrone G. *A Most Fortunate Ship: A Narrative History of Old Ironsides.* Annapolis, Md.: Naval Institute Press, 2003.
Miller, Nathan. *Sea of Glory: A Naval History of the American Revolution.* Mount Pleasant, S.C.: Nautical and Aviation Pub. Co., 2000.
Palmer, Michael A. *Stoddert's War: Naval Operations during the Quasi-War with France, 1798–1801.* Annapolis, Md.: Naval Institute Press, 2000.
Paullin, Charles O., ed. *Out-letters of the Continental Marine Committee and Board of Admiralty, August, 1776–September, 1780.* New York: Printed for the Naval History Society by the De Vinne Press, 1914.
Powers, Stephen T. "Robert Morris and the Courts-Martial of Captains Samuel Nicholson and John Manley of the Continental Navy," *Military Affairs* 44, no. 1 (1980): 13–17.

Nicola, Lewis (1717–1807)
American military officer

Lewis Nicola was probably born in France in 1717 and raised in Ireland. He joined the British army and served three decades before relocating to Philadelphia in 1766. Despite his preoccupation with military affairs, Nicolas was interested in publishing and promoting public enlightenment. In 1767 he established a circulating library of some 1,000 volumes, and he subsequently published *The American Magazine, or General Repository,* which contained useful scientific information. In 1769 Nicola helped negotiate creation of the famed American Philosophical Society and also published its yearly *Transactions*. A devoted public servant, in 1774 he rose to justice of the peace in Northampton County until difficulties with Great Britain persuaded him to return to military themes. He then published *A Treatise of Military Exercise, Calculated for the Use of the Americans* (1776) and also translated several military texts from the French. Nicola was made barracks-master of Philadelphia in 1776 and also appointed to command the town guards. During the British occupation of the city, 1777–78, he drew and published a useful map. The Continental CONGRESS then established a Corps of Invalids, namely, a force of crippled soldiers unfit for field service but still capable of guard work around encampments, and Nicola was appointed its colonel. Under his guidance, his veterans also imparted professional European-style training upon recruits for the Continental ARMY, the first time Americans were subjected to such discipline. General George WASHINGTON was so impressed by Nicola's efforts that in 1781 he transferred the Corps of Invalids to West Point, New York, site of the future military academy.

By May 1782 the Revolutionary War had been for all intents and purposes won, but the economy was in a shambles and Congress unable to meet its fiscal obligations to the nation and army. In light of this misrule, Nicola, then encamped with the main army at Newburgh, New York, apparently broached the idea to Washington that some kind of monarchy could effectively sort out the mess Congress had created. Antipathy toward Congress in the military was, in fact, widespread and eventually culminated in the NEWBURGH CONSPIRACY of March 1783. Washington recoiled at the thought and sternly rebuked Nicola with a tersely worded missive. That officer was taken aback by his commander's anger and, genuinely contrite, composed several effusive apologies. Washington then let the matter drop, although it was never made public. In November 1783 Nicola was discharged from the army with a rank of brevet brigadier general.

Nicola returned to Philadelphia, where he joined the Society of the Cincinnati and assumed useful work as manager of the city's workhouse. Still interested in military affairs, he also served as inspector of the city's militia brigades up through the 1790s. After retiring, Nicola relocated to Alexandria, Virginia, where he died on August 9, 1807. A competent regimental-grade officer and a devoted civil servant, he is best remembered for proffering his "monarchical" advice to Washington.

Further Reading
Bell, Whitfield. *Colonel Lewis Nicola, Advocate of Monarchy, 1782*. Philadelphia: Pennsylvania Society of the Cincinnati, 1983.

Haggard, Robert F. "The Nicola Affair: Lewis Nicola, George Washington, and American Military Discontent during the Revolutionary War," *Proceedings of the American Philosophical Society* 146, no. 2 (2002): 139–169.

Nixon, John (1727–1815)
American military officer

John Nixon was born in Framingham, Massachusetts, on March 1, 1727. He joined the colonial militia in 1745 and fought under Sir William Pepperell at Louisbourg. During the French and Indian War, Nixon served with Sir William Johnson at Crown Point, rising to captain. Afterward he settled in Sudbury as a farmer until the onset of difficulties with Great Britain prompted him to assume command of a local MINUTEMAN company. Once the Revolutionary War erupted in April 1775 he mustered his men in time to fight at CONCORD and subsequently participated in the siege of Boston. Nixon distinguished himself at BUNKER HILL on June 17, 1775, where he was wounded. After recovering he gained promotion to colonel of the 4th Massachusetts Continental Infantry and marched with General George WASHINGTON to New York as part of General Nathanael GREENE's division. There the Continental CONGRESS elevated him to brigadier general in August 1776 upon Washington's recommendation, and he garrisoned Governor's Island throughout the disastrous New York campaign. Nixon then shifted his troops back onto Manhattan Island, where they fought ably at the Battle of Harlem Heights on September 16, 1776. His command initially served with General Charles LEE's division, then fell back through New Jersey with the main army to form part of Colonel John Cadwalader's brigade. He proved unable to cross the Delaware River on the night of December 25, 1776, thus missing the Battle of TRENTON.

In the summer of 1777 Nixon's brigade was ordered north to reinforce the army of General Horatio GATES at Saratoga, New York. He reached Fort Edward on July 13, being criticized for taking four days to cover only 46 miles and ended up in the reserves. Nixon's force was therefore only marginally engaged in the Battles of FREEMAN'S FARM and BEMIS HEIGHTS that fall. In the latter engagement he was seriously injured by a cannonball. His brigade then pursued General John BURGOYNE as far as Fishkill, New York, on October 11, 1777, then paused when it encountered the entire British army drawn up in battle array. After Burgoyne surrendered, Nixon was chosen to escort his "Convention army" back to Cambridge and then withdrew from active service on a medical furlough. He briefly returned to service in October 1778 and sat on the court-martial of General Philip J. SCHUYLER. Declining health necessitated Nixon's retirement from the army on September 12, 1780, and he returned to Sudbury to resume farming. He died at Middlebury, Vermont, on March 24, 1815, a technically competent but otherwise mediocre commander.

Further Reading

Ketchum, Richard M. *Saratoga: Turning Point of America's Revolutionary War.* New York: Henry Holt, 1997.

Merriam, John M. "The Military Record of Brigadier General John Nixon of Massachusetts," *American Antiquarian Society Proceedings* 36 (April 1926): 38–70.

Morrissey, Brendan. *Boston 1775: The Shot Heard Around the World.* Westport, Conn.: Praeger, 2004.

Temple, Josiah H. *History of Framingham, Massachusetts: 1640–1885.* Somerset, N.H.: New England History Press in Collaboration with the Framingham Historical and Natural History Society, 1988.

Noailles, Louis-Marie, comte de (1756–1804)

French military officer

Louis-Marie de Noailles was born in Paris, France, on April 17, 1756, a son of Philippe, duc de Mouchy, and part of an ancient aristocratic family renowned for providing soldiers to the king. At the age of 17 he became an officer in the Company of Scottish Guards, the king's bodyguard, which had been commanded by members of the Noailles family since 1651. Noailles proved himself a competent young soldier, and by 1773 he was major of the Noailles Cavalry Regiment and colonel-general of hussars as of April 1779. Previously he had married the sister-in-law of the marquis de LAFAYETTE and became highly interested in the ideals of America's Revolutionary War. However, unlike Lafayette, his family prevailed upon him not to depart without permission, and he remained as quartermaster of the army in Normandy. Once the FRENCH ALLIANCE was concluded in the spring of 1778, Noailles readily volunteered himself for service in America, and the following year he joined Admiral Charles-Hector-Théodat, comte d'ESTAING, and his fleet in Haiti. In this capacity he commanded a company of light infantry during the capture of Grenada and subsequently served well during the ill-fated siege of SAVANNAH. After commanding the rear guard during d'Estaing's embarkation, Noailles accompanied the admiral back to France in early 1780, where he became second colonel of the Royal Soissonnais Regiment. Now part of General Jean-Baptiste-Donatien de Viveur, comte de ROCHAMBEAU's new expedition, he arrived with the fleet at Newport, Rhode Island, and remained in garrison for nearly a year. In the summer of 1781 Noailles gained a measure of fame by becoming the only officer to walk the entire distance between Newport and YORKTOWN, Virginia, alongside his men. He fought well in repelling a British sortie against French siege works and was selected, along with Colonel John LAURENS, to draw up terms for the surrender of General Charles CORNWALLIS. Noailles then returned to France, where he gained promotion to colonel of the Royal Dragoons in January 1782.

Once the French Revolution erupted in 1789 Noailles became deeply immersed in its politics. He served successively in the Assembly of Notables and the Estates General, where, on August 4, 1790, he dramatically proposed abolishing all traditional privileges of the nobility. The following November he was appointed commander of the Army of the North but resigned in May 1792 owing to its lack of discipline. Noailles, like all aristocrats, fell into disfavor when the radicals assumed power and he fled France; his wife remained behind and was eventually executed. After initially visiting England he settled in Philadelphia, Pennsylvania, as a banker. Working closely with financier Robert MORRIS, Noailles helped establish an asylum for French émigrés near Pittsburgh. In 1800 Napoléon removed Noailles from the proscription list, restored his property, and invited him home. He then relocated to Haiti and served as a brigadier general under Rochambeau's son. After defending the port of Mole for several months, Noailles slipped through a British blockade and made for Cuba, where he outfitted the privateer *Courrier*. On December 31, 1803, his vessel attacked and captured the larger British privateer *Hazard*, although he was fatally wounded in the encounter. Noailles died in Havana on January 7, 1804; his name was subsequently engraved on the Arc de Triomphe, or Arch of Triumph, in Paris.

Further Reading
Chartrand, Rene. *The French Army in the American War of Independence.* London: Osprey, 1991.
Forbes-Robinson, Diana. "Asylum in Azilum," *American Heritage* 27 (April 1976): 54–59.
Nicolai, Martin L. "Subjects and Citizens: French Officers and the North American Experience, 1755–1783." Unpublished Ph.D. diss., Queen's University of Kingston, 1992.
Scott, Samuel F. *From Yorktown to Valmy: The Transformation of the French Army in an Age of Revolution.* Niwot: University Press of Colorado, 1998.
Whitridge, Arnold. "French Émigrés in Philadelphia," *Virginia Quarterly Review* 44, no. 2 (1968): 205–301.
Wood, Anna, ed. "The Robinson Family and Their Correspondence with the Vicomte and Vicomtess De Noailles," *Newport History* 72, no. 249 (2003–04): 30–65.

North, Frederick (1732–1792)
English politician

Frederick North was born in London, England, on April 13, 1732, a son of Francis, First Earl of Guilford. As an aristocrat he was well educated at Eton and Oxford, and in 1754 he commenced his political career by winning a seat in the House of Commons. North proved himself intelligent and affable but also thick-skinned and capable of stinging retorts. In light of his obvious talents he held a succession of high political posts commencing in 1759, when he served as junior lord of the treasury. By September 1767 North succeeded Charles Townshend as chancellor of the Exchequer as part of the ministry under George GRENVILLE. In this capacity he generally supported British attempts to raise revenue in the colonies through taxation, and he generally favored the TOWNSHEND DUTIES. King GEORGE III greatly appreciated his staunchly Tory credentials and ability to effectively deal with Whig opposition in Parliament, so in 1770 he elevated North to prime minister—a position he held over the next 12 years.

For all his ability and good intentions, North's regime is indelibly associated with the loss of the American colonies. He was willing to stand by royal prerogatives and supported policies like the TEA ACT of 1773 to bail out the East India Company, and the COERCIVE ACTS to punish Massachusetts for the BOSTON TEA PARTY, even if these worked against his better judgment. Like many contemporaries, North simply misjudged the depth of American resentment toward perceived arbitrary policies and the reality that colonials, intellectually speaking, had long since parted company with the motherland. Once fighting broke out in April 1775, North tepidly supported British attempts to repossess their colonies, although he grew increasingly morose as to the conduct and course of events. As a war leader, he also chose to allow the day-to-day conduct of military and naval affairs to be run by his ministers George GERMAIN and John MONTAGU. Yet North remained flexibly disposed toward the Americans politically and willingly embraced virtually any demand short of independence. To that extent he authorized General William HOWE and Admiral Richard HOWE possibly to negotiate reconciliation in 1776. But, after the surrender of General John BURGOYNE in October 1777, North concluded that the war was unwinnable and repeatedly solicited the king for permission to resign. His monarch remained steadfast that the colonies must be reconquered and insisted that North remain in office. In 1778 he again sought political rapprochement with America through the ill-fated Carlisle Commission, which accomplished nothing. But the steady stream of British reverses led to stinging invective from notable Whigs such as Edmund BURKE and Charles James FOX, along with continually diminishing majorities in PARLIAMENT. The king stubbornly refused to relent, yet North felt he had no recourse but to support his monarch. It was not until the surrender of General Charles CORNWALLIS at YORKTOWN in October 1781 that he finally gathered the intestinal fortitude to confront his king. George III typically and stubbornly refused to recognize American independence, so North again tendered his resignation—this time backed by a threatened vote of confidence in Parliament. His cabinet finally relinquished power on March 20, 1782, and was replaced by William PETTY, earl of Shelburne.

North remained out of power for only a few months until he entered an unholy alliance with his former enemy Fox, who became de facto prime minister in April 1783. He then resumed duties as chancellor of the Exchequer, but the arrangement lasted only a few months and North left office the following December. At that point he broke with King George completely by refusing to serve as chancellor of the Exchequer under Charles WATSON-WENTWORTH, Lord Rockingham. By this time North was also beset by fading eyesight, and he withdrew from public life after 1786. Beyond occasionally addressing the House of Commons he took no part in national politics, and in 1790 he inherited his father's title as Second Earl of Guilford. North died in London on August 5, 1792, a capable politician and a loyal subject to his king, but indecisive and unwilling to strongly enforce policies that he personally did not embrace. He remains indelibly—and perhaps unfairly— associated with the dismemberment of the first British Empire.

Further Reading

Conway, Stephen. "From Fellow-Nationals to Foreigners: British Perceptions of the Americans, circa 1739–1783," *William and Mary Quarterly* 59, no. 1 (2002): 65–100.

Gould, Eliga H. *The Persistence of Empire: British Political Culture in the Age of the American Revolution.* Chapel Hill: University of North Carolina Press, 2000.

Smith, Charles D. *The Early Career of Lord North: The Prime Minister.* Rutherford, N.J.: Fairleigh Dickinson University Press, 1979.

Weintraub, Stanley. *Iron Tears: America's Battle for Freedom, Britain's Quagmire, 1775–1783.* New York: Free Press, 2005.

Whiteley, Peter. *Lord North: The Prime Minister Who Lost America.* Rio Grande, Ohio: Hambledon Press, 1996.

York, Neil L. *Turning the World Upside Down: The War of American Independence and the Problem of Empire.* Westport, Conn.: Praeger, 2003.

O'Brien, Jeremiah (1744–1818)
American naval officer

Jeremiah O'Brien was born at Kittery, Massachusetts (Maine), in 1744, the son of an Irish tailor. He relocated with his family to the frontier settlement of Machias in 1763 to engage in lumbering and also joined the first militia company organized there. By May 1775 word had been received of the Battles of Lexington and CONCORD, which induced residents to erect a liberty pole in the town square. A month later the armed schooner HMS *Margaretta* under Midshipman James Moore, and the sloops *Unity* and *Polly*, anchored off Machias and demanded to purchase lumber for British troops besieged in Boston. When Moore saw the liberty pole he summarily threatened to bombard the town if it were not removed, but he eventually backed down. On June 11, 1775, Moore was briefly captured ashore in church, but he escaped and made for sea. O'Brien then took a party of 40 volunteers, armed principally with axes, captured the *Unity*, and sailed off in pursuit. Moore was making for the open sea when he lost a mast to high winds, and the two vessels clashed on June 12, 1775. After a stiff hand-to-hand fight the Americans prevailed and captured the *Margaretta*, returning in triumph to Machias. This little affair is generally accepted as the first naval encounter of the Revolutionary War. In recognition of O'Brien's daring, the Massachusetts Provincial Congress passed a resolution praising him while the local Committee of Safety ordered O'Brien to arm *Unity* with cannon taken from his prize. The new vessel was subsequently rechristened *Machias Liberty*, and O'Brien then cruised the Bay of Fundy for several weeks. On July 16, 1775, he captured the eight-gun HMS *Diligent* and its tender *Tatamagouche* without a struggle. Both vessels were added to O'Brien's flotilla and incorporated as the first warships of the Massachusetts state navy.

O'Brien continued cruising the Maine coast for several months and made additional captures, but he felt that the provincial congress failed to adequately support him. He consequently quit the state service to engage in PRIVATEERING and commanded a succession of armed vessels. His largest ship, the 24-gun *Hannibal*, was captured by the British off New York, and O'Brien endured several months of harsh captivity onboard the prison hulk *Jersey* and at Mill Prison in Plymouth before engineering his escape. He finally returned to Machias in October 1782 and never went to sea again. A successful businessman and leading citizen, he was appointed collector of customs for the district of Machias in 1811 by President James MADISON. He died still serving in that capacity on September 5, 1818, the first American naval hero of the Revolutionary War.

Further Reading

Cahill, Thomas P. *A Short Sketch of the Life and Achievements of Captain Jeremiah O'Brien of Machias, Maine.* Worcester, Maine: Harrigan Press, 1936.

Giambattista, M. D. "Captain Jeremiah O'Brien and the Machias Liberty," *U.S. Naval Institute Proceedings* 96 (February 1970): 85–87.

Leamon, James S. *Revolution Downeast: The War for American Independence in Maine.* Amherst: University of Massachusetts Press, 1993.

McManemin, John A. *Revolution on the High Seas: A History of Maritime Massachusetts during the Revolutionary War.* Spring Lake, N.J.: Ho-Ho-Kus Press, 1988.

O'Connell, Joseph F. *Tribute to Capt. Jeremiah O'Brien: Address.* Washington, D.C.: Government Printing Office, 1937.

Sherman, Andrew M. *Life of Captain Jeremiah O'Brien, Machias, Maine, Commander of the First American Naval Flying Squadron of the War of the Revolution.* Morristown, N.J.: G. W. Sherman, 1902.

Oconostota (ca. 1710–1783)
Cherokee chief

Oconostota (Groundhog Sausage) was probably born in Chota (Monroe County, Tennessee) around 1710, a member of the powerful Cherokee nation. This tribe was strategically located in central Tennessee and northern Georgia, from which they influenced the Creek confederation to the south, white colonials to the east, and even the mighty Six Nations to the north. Oconostota gradually matured into a physically imposing individual and first entered the historical record in 1736 as part of the pro-French faction within the tribe. By dint of military prowess he assumed the mantle of Great Warrior (war chief) in 1738 and consolidated his control within the Overhill Cherokee towns dotting the Little Tennessee and Hiawassee Rivers. With time Oconostota gradually became more amicably disposed toward the English and conducted forays against Choctaw aligned with France. In 1755 he also led 500 warriors in the decisive victory of Taliwa, which expelled the Creek from northern Georgia. Despite his demonstrated loyalty to England, the colonial government of South Carolina regarded him with suspicion. When a bloody fight erupted between Cherokee and settlers in 1759, Oconostota made a good-faith gesture by visiting the capital of Charleston with 24 chiefs to preempt further violence. Instead, Governor William Lyttelton arrested the entire group and held them hostage until Oconostota turned over those Indians responsible for the recent murders. He refused and remained imprisoned until the Cherokee peace chief, Attakullakulla, arranged for his release. Oconostota was no sooner freed than he retaliated for the rest of the hostages by attacking Fort Prince George, killing Lieutenant Richard Coytmore. The garrison then retaliated by murdering its prisoners, and a brutal frontier war erupted.

Oconostota confirmed his reputation as a skilled warrior throughout the First Cherokee War. On June 27, 1760, he bloodily ambushed a column commanded by Colonel Archibald Montgomerie and also captured Fort Loudoun, luring the garrison out before slaughtering them. The following year England responded with an even larger expedition under Colonel James GRANT, who successfully dodged Oconostota's stratagems and despoiled the Cherokee homeland. The war finally concluded in 1761 with frightful losses and consequences for the Cherokee, but the conflict greatly enhanced the Great Warrior's standing. In 1763 he again sided with England by fighting the rebellion of Ottawa chief Pontiac, and in 1768 he ventured to New York to confer with noted Indian agent Sir William Johnson and conclude a peace treaty with the Iroquois. The British then vowed to protect Cherokee lands from white settlement, consistent with the PROCLAMATION OF 1763, but this did little to deter frontiersmen from illegal encroachment. Oconostota nonetheless remained on good terms with the English, and in 1774 he refused to join a coalition of tribesmen under the Shawnee CORNSTALK in their struggle against Governor John MURRAY, Lord Dunmore, of Virginia. The following year he concluded a treaty that ceded an additional 20 million acres of land to North Carolina rather than risk hostilities from which, he surmised, the Cherokee would suffer.

When the Revolutionary War erupted in 1775, the Cherokee enjoyed few options. Oconostota, embracing the inevitable, sided with Great Britain

Cherokee chief Oconostota became known among his people as Great Warrior for his actions against the British in 1736; he later confirmed this title during the First Cherokee War. *(Gilcrease Museum)*

and loosed his warriors against American settlements. In 1776 General Griffith RUTHERFORD led 2,400 men on a destructive raid against the Overhill Cherokee towns, and the aging chief sued for peace in July 1777. However, he proved unable to restrain restless young warriors under DRAGGING CANOE, who continued raiding Virginia and North Carolina. In 1780 American forces under Colonels Arthur CAMPBELL and John SEVIER launched another series of devastating raids against Cherokee villages, and again Oconostota sued for peace. He then resigned as chief in July 1782 and was succeeded by his son Tuckesee. The Great Warrior finally died at Chota in the spring of 1783, unable to stem a tide of white immigration overpowering a continent and its peoples.

Further Reading

Bryant, James A. "Between the River and the Flood: The Cherokee Nation and the Battle for European Supremacy in North America." Unpublished master's thesis, College of William and Mary, 1999.

Dennis, Jeffrey W. "American Revolutionary and Native Americans: The South Carolina Experience." Unpublished Ph.D. diss., University of Notre Dame, 2002.

Kelly, James C. "Oconostota," *Journal of Cherokee Studies* 3 (fall 1978): 221–238.

Kirby, James M. *The American Revolution in Indian Country: Crisis and Diversity in Native American Communities.* New York: Cambridge University Press, 1995.

Lee, Wayne E. "Fortify, Fight, or Flee: Tuscarora and Cherokee Defensive Warfare and Military Culture Adaptation," *Journal of Military History* 68, no. 3 (2004): 713–770.

Oliphant, John. *Peace and War on the Anglo-Cherokee Frontier, 1756–1763.* Baton Rouge: Louisiana State University Press, 2001.

O'Hara, Charles (ca. 1740–1802)
English military officer

Charles O'Hara was born around 1740, the illegitimate son of James O'Hara, then colonel of Britain's elite Coldstream Guards. His father groomed him for a life in the military, and in 1752 he arranged his appointment as coronet in the 3rd Dragoon Regiment. O'Hara proved himself a competent soldier and received a lieutenant's commission in the Coldstream Guards on January 14, 1756. He then served as aide-de-camp to the marquis of Grandy during the Seven Years' War in Europe, acquitting himself well. By 1762 O'Hara had risen to quartermaster of the army in Portugal with a brevet rank of lieutenant colonel. After commanding a penal regiment in Senegal in 1766, he rose to lieutenant colonel in the Coldstreams. O'Hara by this time had acquired the reputation of a stern disciplinarian, though he remained popular with the troops owing to his fondness for drinking, gambling, and womanizing. In 1778 he ventured to America and joined General William HOWE's army at Philadelphia and performed useful work with a commission tasked with prisoner exchanges. That summer Howe was succeeded by General Henry CLINTON, who ordered O'Hara to organize the defenses of Sandy Hook against possible attack by the French fleet. He served capably over the next two years and rose to brigadier general as of October 1780. In this capacity he was dispatched to reinforce General Charles CORNWALLIS in South Carolina, and the two men became immediate best friends. O'Hara at that time was also elected to command the elite Guards Brigade, a handpicked force with battalions from the three senior regiments of the British army: the Grenadier Guards, the Coldstream Guards, and the Scots Guards.

At this time the invigorated American army under General Nathanael GREENE was beginning to probe British-held regions of North Carolina. O'Hara received the honor of spearheading the British pursuit of Greene, and he fought a heavy skirmish while crossing Cowan's Ford across the Catawba River on February 1, 1781. The British pushed aside determined resistance by partisans under General William L. DAVIDSON, but O'Hara and General Alexander LESLIE nearly drowned when their horses were swept under by strong currents. Despite a hard chase, Greene outpaced his pursuers and slipped across the Dan River to Virginia and safety. A month later the Americans were heavily reinforced to 4,500 men, reentered North Carolina, and occupied good defensive positions at GUILFORD COURTHOUSE. On March 15 Cornwallis lunged at the mostly untrained Americans with 1,900 steely veterans and a severe engagement unfolded. O'Hara, commanding the British left, pitted his Guards against a solid line of Continentals and was twice severely wounded. As the British veterans began to give ground Cornwallis ordered his artillery fired directly into the struggling mass—over O'Hara's objections—and the Americans finally yielded the field. Cornwallis obtained victory at the exorbitant cost of a third of his army and subsequently retreated into Virginia. O'Hara was so badly injured that he was borne by litter for the entire trip. He recovered in time to resume his duties at the siege of YORKTOWN, where the British capitulated on October 19, 1781. Cornwallis, unable to face the indignity of surrender, asked O'Hara, his second in command, to appear in his place. However, when he tried to hand his sword to General Jean-Baptiste, comte de ROCHAMBEAU, he was curtly interrupted by Colonel Mathieu DUMAS, who then redirected him to the waiting Americans. The drama continued when General George WASHINGTON refused to accept the sword from anybody but Cornwallis, so O'Hara finally gave it to General Benjamin LINCOLN, Washington's own second in command.

O'Hara was exchanged in February 1782 and promoted to major general. After transporting reinforcements from New York to the West Indies he returned to England in 1784, where gambling debts necessitated his departure for Italy. In 1787 he became a staff officer on the strategic peninsula of Gibraltar and by 1792 functioned there as lieutenant governor. O'Hara rose to lieutenant general in 1793 and was engaged in defending Fort Mulgrave at Toulon when he was wounded and captured by a young Napoleon Bonaparte. Exchanged for Rochambeau's son two years later, he was reassigned as governor-general of Gibraltar and gained renown as the venerable "Cock of the Rock." The affable, licentious O'Hara, who sired a bevy of illegitimate children, died there on February 21, 1802. His will bequeathed a large endowment (70,000 pounds sterling) for the benefit of at least two mistresses and his many offspring.

Further Reading

Buchanan, John. *The Road to Guilford Courthouse: The American Revolution in the Carolinas.* New York: Wiley, 1997.

Griffin, William D. "General Charles O'Hara," *Irish Sword* 10 (summer 1972): 179–187.

Ketchum, Richard M. *Victory at Yorktown: The Campaign That Won the Revolution.* New York: Henry Holt, 2004.

Konstam, Angus. *Guilford Courthouse, 1781: Lord Cornwallis's Ruinous Victory.* Oxford: Osprey, 2002.

May, Robin. *The British Army in North America, 1775–1783*. New York: Hippocrene Books, 1997.

Rogers, George C., ed. "Letters of Charles O'Hara to the Duke of Grafton," *South Carolina Historical Magazine* 65, no. 3 (1964): 158–180.

Oriskany, Battle of (August 6, 1777)

On August 4, 1777, word of the siege of Fort Stanwix, New York, by 1,600 British, LOYALISTS, and Native Americans under Lieutenant Colonel Barry ST. LEGER caused a relief column to be organized at Fort Dayton, some 30 miles distant. This force, commanded by Colonel Nicholas HERKIMER of the Tryon County militia, consisted of some 800 men and 400 ox carts. Herkimer gathered and marched his charge immediately, preceded by 60 Oneida warriors acting as scouts. He had sent runners ahead of the column to alert Colonel Peter GANSEVOORT, the garrison commander, of his approach and the possibility of mounting a sortie should a general action develop. The Americans progressed slowly, owing to Herkimer's caution, and on the morning of August 6, 1777, a council of war disputed his approach. After a stormy session, Herkimer agreed to dispense with the usual safeguards and relieve the fort at all hazards. The commander complied against his better judgment, unaware that his preparations had been observed by Molly BRANT, sister of Chief Joseph BRANT, who sent runners of her own ahead to alert St. Leger. The British responded by sending Brant, CORNPLANTER, and a select Loyalist force under Major John BUTLER to intercept the unwary Americans along a narrow defile at Oriskany, roughly six miles from St. Leger's encampment. This proved to be a near-ideal location for an ambush, being a deep ravine with steep, heavily wooded sides. The Loyalists and Indians then carefully deployed their forces and awaited Herkimer's approach.

Around mid-morning on August 6, 1777, Herkimer led 400 men into the defile while a further 200 were detached to guard the ox carts. His Oneida scouts apparently missed the ambush, for the Americans were almost completely in the ravine when Brant and Cornplanter sprang their trap. The initial attack proved devastating but premature, as the bulk of Herkimer's rear guard recoiled and escaped. A confused firefight then erupted down the length of the ravine as the Loyalists hit the head of the column while the Indians fired into its flanks. Herkimer was quickly shot off his horse and seriously wounded while scores of militiamen fell killed and wounded. Rather than succumb to panic, the old Dutchman had himself propped up against a tree, took out his pipe, and began organizing a hasty defense. His calmness and steadfast behavior in the face of danger saved the day. The Indians repeatedly charged into the American perimeter seeking to penetrate; vicious hand-to-hand fighting erupted, and both sides sustained heavy losses before a heavy downpour temporarily halted the fighting.

Herkimer, notwithstanding a painful leg wound, availed himself of the impasse to rearrange and consolidate his lines in a small circle. Thereafter he instructed the militia to fight in pairs, with one shooting and the other covering as the Indians rushed them. Once the fighting resumed Brant's warriors attacked the defensive perimeter but were continually rebuffed. Loyalists under Butler also tried a subterfuge by reversing their green coats and buff facings and infiltrating the line while posing as reinforcements. The trick almost worked until a militiaman recognized one of his Tory neighbors in the ranks and fired on them. After six hours of internecine combat the Indians, depressed by the loss of several chiefs, broke ranks and began returning to camp. At this juncture Butler had no recourse but to break off the action and the Battle of Oriskany ended in a bloody draw.

Herkimer was unable to continue advancing, so his column turned around and limped back to Fort Dayton with hundreds of casualties; he would died of his wounds 10 days later. Meanwhile, Gansevoort took advantage of Butler's absence to launch a violent sortie against the main British encampment under Lieutenant Colonel Marinus WILLETT. The American easily brushed aside a small camp guard, looted and burned the Indian tepees, and made off with Major John JOHNSON's official papers. This development, coupled with heavy losses, totally dispirited St. Leger's Indians, who comprised nearly one-third of his force. As they began drifting away, he was apprised of a new and even larger relief column headed his way under the formidable General Benedict ARNOLD; he finally abandoned Fort Stanwix. The upshot of the Battle at Oriskany was a bloody tactical defeat for the Americans, who lost upward of 200 killed and wounded. However, it was a complete strategic reversal for the British; St. Leger's withdrawal meant that the main British column under General John BURGOYNE at Saratoga would be denied reinforcements at a critical juncture in the campaign.

Further Reading
Edgar, Gregory T. *"Liberty or Death!" The Northern Campaigns in the American Revolutionary War.* Bowie, Md.: Heritage Books, 1994.
Foote, Allan D. *Liberty March: The Battle of Oriskany.* Utica, N.Y.: North Country Books, 1998.
Piatt, Kevin P. "Opportunity Lost: The Battle of Oriskany and the Siege of Fort Stanwix." Unpublished master's thesis, California State University, Dominguez Hills, 1998.
Roberts, Donald. "Into the Trap," *Military Heritage* 5, no. 6 (2004): 44–51.
Watt, Gavin K. *The Flockey, 13 August 1777: The Defeat of the Tory Uprising in the Schoharie Valley.* King City, Ont.: G. K. Watt, 2002.
———. *Rebellion in the Mohawk Valley: The St. Leger Expedition of 1777.* Tonawanda, N.Y.: Dundurn Press, 2002.

Otis, James (1725–1783)
American politician

James Otis was born in Barnstable, Massachusetts, on February 5, 1725, the son of a merchant and brother of Mercy Otis WARREN. He graduated from Harvard in 1743, read law, and gained admittance to the Plymouth bar in 1758. Two years later Otis relocated to Boston, where he functioned as king's advocate general of the Vice-Admiralty Court, a position increasingly involved with customs affairs. In 1760 he also entered into a long, personal contretemps with Thomas HUTCHINSON, a former political ally who was appointed chief justice of the colony by Governor Francis BERNARD. Otis felt that the position was owed his father, James Otis, Sr., for his support in passing paper money legislation. Thus, from the onset of his professional career, Otis was personally placed on a collision course with royal authority. The pace and intensity of his defiance was heightened by the Admiralty Court's reliance upon writs of assistance. Past colonial defiance of the Molasses Act of 1733, invariably in the form of smuggling, had induced the court to issue such writs, which were general warrants enabling customs officials to search homes and warehouses without specifying exact locations or goods in question. Otis philosophically disagreed with the writs and resigned from the court rather than enforce them. Thereafter he functioned as the peerless defender of merchants and, in February 1761, Otis delivered a riveting, five-hour diatribe in court against the issuance of writs. John ADAMS, who was present and impressed by the power of his logic and his eloquent delivery, later declared that "American independence was then and there born."

Overnight Otis became a political celebrity in Boston, and in 1761 he was elected to the General Court (legislature). In this capacity he articulated finely tuned arguments against British tax and trade policies and also embarked on a successful career in polemics. His treatises, *A Vindication of the Conduct of the House of Representatives* (1762) and *The Rights of the British Colonies Asserted and Proved* (1764), openly and artfully challenged Parliament's right to tax the colonies without representation. In 1765 he bore a prominent role in the STAMP ACT Congress convening in New York, and he subsequently chaired the local COMMITTEE OF CORRESPONDENCE. However, upon further reflection, Otis gradually moderated his stance against Parliament and at no time embraced or advocated violence against royal authority. This placed him at odds with more radical elements under Samuel ADAMS, many of whom began questioning Otis's sanity. In fact, the former doyen of the radicals had become increasingly erratic in his personal behavior and oscillated his support between the Crown and the colonies.

Despite his waning reputation and faculties of thought, Otis passionately defended his loyalty as a British subject. When he learned that customs officials in Boston were denouncing him for treason, he published an acerbic riposte in the *Boston Gazette*. On September 5, 1769, he confronted Crown officer John Robinson in a coffeehouse and was struck on the head during a brawl. From then on Otis began a slow descent into insanity, and by 1771 he was declared the ward of his younger brother Samuel. He still managed to fight in the Battle of BUNKER HILL as a volunteer but eventually surrendered his seat in the legislature and took no further part in public discourse. Otis was dramatically killed by lightning on May 23, 1783, while viewing a thunderstorm. But his efficacy remains in providing Americans the intellectual foundation upon which the Revolutionary War would be waged.

Further Reading

Bell, Hugh F. "James Otis of Massachusetts—The First Forty Years, 1725–1765." Unpublished Ph.D. diss., Cornell University, 1970.

Breen, T. H. "Subjecthood and Citizenship: The Context of James Otis's Radical Critique of John Locke," *New England Quarterly* 71, no. 3 (1998): 378–403.

Galvin, John R. *Three Men of Boston*. Washington, D.C.: Brassey's, 1997.

Ray, Raphael. *The First American Revolution: Before Lexington and Concord*. New York: New Press, 2002.

Samuelson, Richard A. "The Constitutional Sanity of James Otis; Resistance Leader and Loyal Subject," *Review of Politics* 61, no. 3 (1999): 493–523.

Shaw, Peter. *American Patriots and the Rituals of Revolution*. Cambridge, Mass.: Harvard University Press, 1981.

Paine, Thomas (1737–1809)
English politician

Thomas Paine was born in Thetford, England, on January 19, 1737, the son of a corsetmaker. Poorly educated, he tried working at a succession of minor professions, failing each time. Paine also developed an interest in science and with it a passion for political rationalism. In 1762 he gained appointment as an excise collector but lost it in 1774 after petitioning Parliament to increase the wages of all excisemen. That year he also encountered Benjamin FRANKLIN, who encouraged him to immigrate to America and also provided him with letters of introduction. Paine, eager to escape creditors at home, arrived in Philadelphia in November 1774 to start life anew and found work as an editor with the *Pennsylvania Magazine*. Wielding a muscular prose that was as forceful as it was convincing, Paine wrote several essays condemning slavery and a host of political issues that brought him considerable notoriety. Given his dislike for England's political system and his own profound belief in freedom and equality, he easily slipped into radical circles of revolutionary America. But no one could have anticipated the reaction to his small pamphlet entitled COMMON SENSE, which he anonymously published in January 1776. This seminal pamphlet combined a fiery and unprecedented condemnation of kings and aristocracy that caught the American polity by storm and accelerated public sentiment toward the DECLARATION OF INDEPENDENCE that summer. *Common Sense* sold over 120,000 copies in only three months, rendering Paine an immediate political celebrity.

Paine eagerly demonstrated his devotion to the cause of American independence by joining the Continental ARMY as an aide-de-camp to General Nathanael GREENE. In this capacity he participated in the retreat across New Jersey, when the Revolution's fortunes were at their lowest ebb, and composed an equally stirring series of tracts entitled *The Crisis*. With the forceful eloquence that was his forte, Paine urged his fellow Americans to fight on, insisting that "These are the times that try men's souls." General George WASHINGTON was so impressed by its appeal that he ordered it read to soldiers in the field. Thereafter Paine was admitted to the Continental CONGRESS as secretary to the Committee of Foreign Affairs, where he became embroiled in the dispute between Silas DEANE and Arthur LEE in 1779 and was forced to resign. He thereafter functioned as clerk to the Pennsylvania state assembly and occasionally raised funds to buy supplies for Washington's army.

After the war Paine resumed his interest in technology, and in 1787 he ventured back to England to raise funds for a pierless iron bridge he had patented. There he befriended the noted liberal thinker Edmund BURKE but broke with him following the onset of the French Revolution in 1789.

Not surprisingly Paine supported the French revolutionaries, and when Burke attacked them with a publication, Paine countered with *The Rights of Man* (1791), which defended republicanism and called for an insurrection against the English monarchy. Again, his polemic met with startling success, selling over 200,000 copies in a few months, and was also translated into German and French. English authorities were naturally furious, declared the tract seditious, and ordered Paine's arrest. He fled to France, being warmly embraced by the Girondists, and was elected to the National Assembly. However, having expressed dismay over the violent excesses of the Jacobins, he was arrested and imprisoned. From his cell Paine composed his most controversial tract, the *Age of Reason* (1794), which attacked organized religion. As before, this polemic circulated widely in several languages and was roundly condemned by established churches and political establishments. Paine eventually gained his freedom through the intercession of James MONROE in November 1794, and he returned to the United States in 1802 somewhat discredited. He further stoked his unpopularity with published attacks upon President Washington and died in New York, all but forgotten, on June 10, 1809. But for the time in which he lived Paine was the most effective pamphleteer of two revolutions.

Further Reading

Fitzsimmons, David M. "Toward a New World Order: Thomas Paine and the ideology of Early American Foreign Relations." Unpublished Ph.D. diss., University of Michigan, 2002.

Foner, Eric. *Tom Paine and Revolutionary America*. New York: Oxford University Press, 2004.

Kaminski, John P. *Citizen Paine: Thomas Paine's Thoughts on Man, Government, Society, and Religion*. Lanham, Md.: Rowman & Littlefield, 2002.

Kaye, Harvey J. *Thomas Paine: Firebrand of the Revolution*. New York: Oxford University Press, 2000.

Larkin, Edward. *Thomas Paine and the Literature of Revolution*. New York: Cambridge University Press, 2005.

Vickers, Vikki J. " 'My Pen and My Soul Have Ever Gone Together': Thomas Paine and the American Revolution." Unpublished Ph.D. diss., University of Missouri, Columbia, 2002.

Paris, Treaty of (1783)

The surrender of General Charles CORNWALLIS at YORKTOWN in October 1781 constituted the end of major land operations in the Revolutionary War. In March 1782 it also brought about the end of Lord Frederick NORTH's ministry, for he resigned and was replaced by Charles WATSON-WENTWORTH, Lord Rockville, whose Whiggish inclinations prodded the British government toward an immediate peace settlement with the United States. Shortly after, Richard Oswald arrived in Paris to commence preliminary direct negotiations with American agent Benjamin FRANKLIN. Franklin welcomed the initiative, but he rejected the British stance of dealing with the colonies individually and also declined to violate the precepts of the FRENCH ALLIANCE by negotiating without French approval. The waters were further muddied following the death of Lord Rockville in July 1782 when his successor, William PETTY, Lord Shelburne, declined to recognize American independence outright. Around this time Franklin was buttressed by the arrival in Paris of John JAY, who immediately suspected that the French minister of foreign affairs, Charles Gravier, comte de VERGENNES, was secretly undermining the American position by supporting SPAIN's claims to lands between the Appalachian Mountains and the Mississippi River. Spain for its part harbored a genuine concern that a powerful United States could threaten its nearby territories in the New World. All told, competing diplomatic interests made peace negotiations to end the war a volatile mix. Fortunately for the United States, its neophyte commissioners more than matched their European counterparts in guile and audacity.

By August 1782 Jay felt impelled to disregard his orders from the CONGRESS to respect the Treaty of Alliance with France and not negotiate without its approval. He also discarded instructions not to press for the Mississippi River as a western boundary and seek only independence instead. Jay then approached the Shelburne administration with a willingness to deal directly with the British agents if they would allow Oswald to negotiate openly with the Americans, in effect, granting de facto diplomatic recognition. Shelburne, eager to break the Franco-American alliance in exchange for easier relations in the future, readily assented. The Americans, Franklin in particular, were disappointed that the British retained Canada, but Shelburne generously acknowledged American ambitions to mark the Mississippi River as their western boundary. Moreover, the British also granted the United States fishing rights off the Grand Banks, another generous concession. In return, the Americans pledged good faith efforts to pay off existing prerevolutionary debts at face value and take steps to return all confiscated property to LOYALISTS who remained behind. Considering the relative military weakness of the United States, such terms completely consummated its aspirations for nationhood. The preliminaries were signed in Paris on November 30, 1782; considering what both nations had endured for the past eight years, the arrangement was an intelligent compromise that laid the foundation for improved diplomatic relations and enhanced national growth.

No sooner had Vergennes been apprised of these developments than he angrily remonstrated to Franklin that terms of the Franco-American alliance had been breeched. Franklin soothed his sensibilities by pointing out that the preliminary articles did not violate their alliance through the simple expedient that they were not effective until hostilities between all the belligerents had ended—another stipulation of the alliance. This reality convinced Vergennes of the impracticality of waging war upon Spain's insistence that Gibraltar be recaptured and also weakened French motives to support their aspirations for land already claimed by the Americans. The French ultimately persuaded King Charles III to accept the island of Minorca and Florida as a sop instead. Thus France, beyond avenging its earlier loss of Canada to England, received little for its sacrifice beyond Senegal, Tobago, and horrific national debts that eventually toppled the monarchy. The Treaty of Paris was then signed by Franklin, Jay, John ADAMS, and Henry LAURENS on September 3, 1783, thereby formally concluding the Revolutionary War with England. Its actual implementation proved less than uniform, for some state legislatures refused to return Loyalist property and also hedged on settling prewar debts. The British, noting this hesitancy, deliberately ignored pledges to evacuate military posts in the Old Northwest until such conditions were met. It was not until the divisive Jay Treaty of 1795 that both sides felt compelled to honor all treaty obligations. But American independence had finally and irrevocably been recognized. More important, the Treaty of Paris represented a diplomatic coup by providing fixed boundaries far beyond those that the United States might have reasonably expected otherwise. This aggregation of new land proved a major factor in the rise of a new world power.

Further Reading
Challinor, Joan, and Robert L. Beisner. *Arms at Rest: Peacemaking and Peacekeeping in American History.* New York: Greenwood Press, 1987.
Dull, Jonathan R. *The Treaty of Paris, 1783: Its Origin and Significance.* Washington, D.C.: National Committee for the Bicentennial of the Treaty of Paris, 1983.
Gifford, Prosser, ed. *The Treaty of Paris (1783) in a Changing States System: Papers from a Conference, January 26–27, 1984.* Lanham, Md.: University Press of America, 1985.
Hoffman, Ronald, and Peter J. Albert, eds. *Peace and the Peacemakers: The Treaty of 1783.* Charlottesville: University of Virginia Pres, 1986.
Murray, Craig C. "Benjamin Vaughan (1751–1835): The Life of an Anglo-American Intellectual." Unpublished Ph.D. diss., Columbia University, 1989.
Stockley, Andrew. *Britain and France at the Birth of America: The European Powers at the Peace Negotiations, 1782–1783.* Exeter, U.K.: University of Exeter Press, 2001.

Parker, John (1729–1775)
American militia officer
John Parker was born in Lexington, Massachusetts, on July 13, 1729, where he settled and

worked as a farmer and a mechanic. He acquired military experience by fighting with provincial troops in the French and Indian War and saw combat at Louisbourg and Quebec. Some accounts also suggest he may have served as a ranger under the noted Major Robert ROGERS. As tensions escalated between Britain and its colonies, Parker volunteered his services again for the militia as a captain and received command of the local MINUTEMAN company. On the evening of April 18, 1775, an alert colonial intelligence system detected the approach of a British column under Lieutenant Colonel Francis SMITH, who was apparently en route to seize a cache of colonial stores and weapons at CONCORD. Parker then dispatched the alert and mustered about 130 minutemen on Lexington Common. With these he formed a cordon around the house of Reverend Jonas Clarke, where radical leaders John HANCOCK and Samuel ADAMS reposed. When it was clear that Smith's column would not reach Lexington that night, Parker then dismissed his men and went home.

Early on the morning of April 19, 1775, Parker was again alerted by runners that several companies of British light troops under Major John PITCAIRN were approaching the town. The alarm was again sounded, but Parker could cobble together only around 70 men on Lexington Common when the British arrived in force and began deploying. Pitcairn's men, who had been up all night marching through a rainstorm, were wet, tired, and in no mood for resistance. But Parker nonetheless deployed his men off to the side and awaited developments. Tradition has him declaring to his men, "Stand your ground. Don't fire unless fired upon. But if they mean to have a war, let it begin here," but his handful of militia could have hardly made much of an impression upon the British. Once his regulars assembled on the green, Pitcairn apparently rode up to the Americans and ordered them to disperse peacefully. Parker fully understood the implications for failing to do so and told his men to leave, and they did so. The confrontation seemed to subside when suddenly a musket fired—most likely the accidental discharge of a careless minuteman. But the redcoats, anxious and perceiving themselves under attack, loosed two volleys at the Americans and followed up with cold steel. Eight militiamen died and 10 were wounded before Pitcairn finally restored order—but a war had begun. Parker subsequently rallied his survivors and marched them to Concord, where they fought in the general action against Smith's rear guard later that day.

Parker, apparently terminally ill at the time, next participated in the siege of Boston. He was also in the vicinity of BUNKER HILL on June 17, 1775, but sickness precluded his participation. Parker died of disease on September 17, 1775, but remained long celebrated for commanding American forces in the first battle of the Revolutionary War. His stand at Lexington, inscribed with words that he may or may not have uttered, is commemorated by an impressive stone monument.

Further Reading
Gross, Robert A. *The Minutemen and Their World.* New York: Hill and Wang, 2001.
Hallahan, William H. *The Day the Revolution Began, 19 April 1775.* New York: Avon Books, 1999.
Kehoe, Vincent J-R. *The British Story of the Battle of Lexington and Concord on the Nineteenth of April 1775.* Los Angeles, Calif.: Hale & Co., 2000.
Morrissey, Brendan. *Boston 1775: The Shot Heard around the World.* Oxford: Osprey, 2003.
Nichipor, Mark A. *The Battles of Lexington and Concord.* Peterborough, N.H.: Cobblestone Pub. Co., 2002.
Parker, Theodore. *Genealogical and Biographical Notes of John Parker of Lexington.* Worcester, Mass.: Press of Charles Hamilton, 1893.

Parker, Peter (1721–1811)
English naval officer
Peter Parker was probably born in Ireland in 1721, the son of Admiral Christopher Parker. He served as a cabin boy upon several vessels before receiving his lieutenant's commission in the Royal Navy by 1741. After commanding a succession of warships in the Mediterranean and elsewhere, Parker rose to captain in charge of the frigate HMS *Margate*. He

then remained ashore on half-pay for several years while supervising construction of HMS *Woolwich*, which he commanded throughout the Seven Years' War. Parker functioned without a command for nearly a decade until 1773, when he finally obtained the 50-gun warship HMS *Bristol*. In February 1776 he was promoted to commodore of a small squadron of warships at Plymouth and entrusted with conveying several Irish regiments under General Charles CORNWALLIS to the Cape Fear region of North Carolina. This was part of an overarching strategy whereby he would cooperate with Governor Josiah MARTIN and General Henry CLINTON in a campaign to raise LOYALIST support. A rough Atlantic voyage ensued, and Parker's armada reached its destination to rendezvous with Clinton as planned, but the Loyalist resurgence upon which so much hinged had been crushed at Moore's Creek Bridge on February 21, 1776. After discussing their options, Parker and Clinton next decided for an attack on CHARLESTON, South Carolina, which was then viewed as weakly defended. They hoped its capture could then serve as a rallying point for Loyalists throughout the region.

Parker's fleet anchored off Charleston on June 1, 1776, but the lack of charts required him to sound the waters and wait for favorable tides before attacking. This provided a badly needed respite for the American defenders under Colonel William MOULTRIE, who worked steadily at improving the defenses of Fort Sullivan on Sullivan's Island. It was not until June 28, 1776, nearly a month after arriving, that Parker landed Clinton's troops on Long Island and worked his vessels into bombardment positions. A terrific cannonade ensued but, in so much as the Americans were well protected by Fort Sullivan's palmetto walls, whose spongy bark absorbed cannon fire, little damage resulted. But the few pieces Moultrie possessed were exceptionally well served, and he concentrated their fire upon HMS *Bristol*. Parker's vessel consequently had its cable shot away during the exchange, and it swung around, prompting a raking fire from the fort. The commodore bravely stood his post on the quarterdeck but was nearly killed by red-hot cannonballs that tore off his pants and burned him badly. The frigate HMS *Actaeon* also grounded and had to be burned to prevent capture. After 10 hours of combat and 250 casualties, Parker finally withdrew the fleet; his defeat at Charleston not only deprived the British of a southern lodgement for nearly three years, but its lopsided nature also boosted American morale.

Parker's squadron limped back to New York, where it joined the main fleet under Admiral Richard HOWE. He then participated in the landing of British troops on LONG ISLAND, which

Commodore Peter Parker launched the British attack on Charleston with fellow officer Henry Clinton. *(National Maritime Museum, Greenwich, London)*

resulted in an American withdrawal from New York City. In December 1776 Parker conveyed a small force under Clinton that seized Newport, Rhode Island, as a valuable naval base. There he gained promotion to rear admiral on April 28, 1777, and two months later became commander of the Jamaica station. Parker subsequently advanced to rear admiral in March 1779, and in August 1782 he returned to England carrying the captured French admiral, François-Joseph-Paul, comte de GRASSE, as his prisoner. This concluded his service in American waters, and Parker, now elevated to a baronetcy, spent several years commanding Portsmouth Harbor. In this capacity he met and befriended a youthful Lieutenant Horatio Nelson, the future victor of Trafalgar, and facilitated his early career. By his passing in London on December 21, 1811, Parker had succeeded Richard Howe as admiral of the fleet for his lengthy and capable services.

Further Reading
Farley, M. Foster. "Battering Charleston's Walls," *Military History* 18, no. 6 (2000): 38–45.
Miller, Nathan. *The Age of Fighting Sail, 1775–1815*. New York: Wiley, 2000.
Reid, Ronald D. "The Battle of Sullivan's Island," *American History* 33, no. 5 (1998): 34–39, 70–72.
Russell, David L. *Victory on Sullivan's Island: The British Cape Fear/Charleston Expedition*. Haverford, Pa.: Infinity, 2002.
Syrett, David. *The Royal Navy in American Waters during the Revolutionary War*. Columbia: University of South Carolina Press, 1998.
Tilley, John A. *The British Navy in the American Revolution*. Columbia: University of South Carolina Press, 1987.

Parsons, Samuel H. (1737–1789)
American military officer

Samuel Holden Parsons was born in Lyme, Connecticut, on May 14, 1737, the son of a preacher. He passed through Harvard College in 1756, read law, and opened a successful law practice near home. Parsons then won a seat in the colonial assembly in 1762, remaining there 14 years. In this capacity he outspokenly championed colonial rights and was also an early advocate of an intercolonial CONGRESS to coordinate political resistance. In 1770 he joined the militia as a major, and by 1775 he was serving with the local COMMITTEE OF CORRESPONDENCE. After hostilities commenced, Parsons became colonel of the 6th Connecticut Militia, and he supported efforts of Colonels Ethan ALLEN and Benedict ARNOLD to capture Fort Ticonderoga. He then marched his regiment to Cambridge, Massachusetts, to partake of the siege of Boston. There he mustered into the Continental ARMY with the same rank and subsequently accompanied General George WASHINGTON back to New York. In August 1776 he gained promotion to brigadier general and fought competently at LONG ISLAND, Harlem Heights, and WHITE PLAINS. Parsons particularly distinguished himself for bravery in the rout at Kip's Bay, September 15, 1776, assisting Washington in rallying his shaken soldiers. Afterward, Washington continually assigned him to the strategic Hudson Highlands region, where, on January 20, 1778, Parson's brigade constructed the first fortifications at West Point.

Parsons was a capable battle leader, but his latter career was restricted to small actions and raids. In July 1779 his men helped repel a determined British raid upon Norwalk, Connecticut, and the following December he succeeded General Israel PUTNAM as commander of the state division. Parsons advanced to major general in October 1780 and also sat on the court-martial of Major John ANDRE. In January 1781 his brigade conducted a successful raid upon British and LOYALIST positions at Morrisania, New York, and he received a Thanks of Congress. However, Parsons grew acutely concerned that depreciation of Continental currency threatened his fiscal holdings and he petitioned repeatedly for an early discharge to attend to personal affairs. When this was refused, General Henry CLINTON attempted to lure him over to the British side through his double agent, William Heron, but Parsons remained loyal. He was finally mustered out of the service in July

1782, greatly embittered that military service had left him nearly bankrupt.

After the war, Parsons remained eager to recoup his losses, so he resumed his law career and also speculated in western lands. In 1785 Congress appointed him a commissioner to obtain Indian lands throughout the Ohio Territory, and he also served as director of the Ohio Company, an organization specializing in parceling out land grants to army veterans. By October 1787 Parsons became the first judge of the Northwest Territory and the following year put down roots in the new settlement at Marietta, Ohio. A year later he began speculating among lands assigned to Connecticut's Western Reserve and, in his obsessive quest for profits, apparently conducted some shady transactions. Parsons was returning from a visit to the Salt Springs Tract when his canoe overturned on the Big Beaver River, drowning him on November 17, 1789.

Further Reading
Callahan, North. *Connecticut's Revolutionary War Leaders.* Chester, Conn.: Pequot Press, 1973.
Hall, Charles S. *Life and Letters of Samuel Holden Parsons, Major General in the Continental Army and Chief Judge of the Northwestern Territory, 1737–1789.* Binghamton, N.Y.: Otseningo, 1905.
Loring, George B. *A Vindication of General Samuel Holden Parsons against the Charge of Treasonable Correspondence during the Revolutionary War.* Salem, Mass.: Salem Press, 1888.
McGurdy, Charles J., and Charles S. Hall. "General Samuel Holden Parsons," *Magazine of American History* 21 (January 1889): 66–71.
Palmer, Dave R. *The River and the Rock: The History of Fortress West Point, 1775–1783.* New York: Greenwood Press, 1969.
Trumbull, Jonathan, and Joseph G. Woodward. *Vindications of Patriots of the American Revolution.* Connecticut Sons of the American Revolution, 1896.

Paterson, John (1744–1808)
American military officer

John Paterson was born in Farmington, Connecticut, in 1744, the son of a militia colonel. He graduated from Yale in 1762 and practiced law before relocating to Lennox, Massachusetts, in 1774. Paterson gradually became one of the foremost civil servants of the Berkshire region and also represented that town in the provincial congress. In 1775 he was appointed colonel of militia and, upon receipt of news about Lexington and CONCORD, he marched his regiment to Boston. There he built and occupied a fort on Prospect Hill, from which his men functioned as a reserve during the Battle of BUNKER HILL. In the ensuing siege of Boston his troops were particularly active in repulsing a British detachment at Lechmere Point on November 9, 1775. Paterson's command subsequently mustered into the Continental ARMY as the 15th Massachusetts Continental Infantry as of January 1, 1776. The following spring he accompanied General George WASHINGTON to New York and thence to Canada with Colonel William THOMPSON as reinforcements. It is not known if Paterson fought at the defeat of Trois-Rivières on June 8, 1776, but his regiment sustained 67 casualties there. He subsequently served at Fort Ticonderoga and Mount Independence and rejoined Washington's main army in New Jersey that winter. Paterson then fought in the victories at TRENTON and PRINCETON before rising to brigadier general on February 21, 1777.

In the summer of 1777 Paterson found himself attached to the army under General Arthur ST. CLAIR at Ticonderoga, and he fell back as British forces under General John BURGOYNE advanced. He subsequently served under General Horatio GATES at Saratoga and remained in reserve during the September 19, 1777, fight at FREEMAN'S FARM. Paterson then fought conspicuously under General Benedict ARNOLD at BEMIS HEIGHTS on October 7, 1777, where he helped storm the British redoubt held by Lord Balcarres. He fought bravely from the front until his horse was killed by a cannonball. Paterson wintered at Valley Forge with the main army and was in the vicinity of MONMOUTH, although not engaged. Paterson then joined troops garrisoning the strategic Hudson Highlands, principally near West Point, under General William HEATH. In September 1780 he sat on the board condemning Major John ANDRE to death and later formed part of the Philadelphia defenses. While present he inadvertently appointed Deborah SAMPSON, a woman soldier masquerading as a man, to be his aide-de-camp. Paterson was finally discharged from the service on September 30, 1783, with a rank of brevet major general.

Back in civilian life Paterson resumed his law practices at Lennox and also served as president of the state branch of the Society of the Cincinnati. He also continued his military services as commander of the Ninth Massachusetts Militia Division, and in 1786–87 he led them against antigovernment rebels during Shays's Rebellion. While at Pittsfield he urged and acquired the surrender of 90 armed insurgents, releasing them after they took an oath of allegiance. In 1791 Paterson relocated to Tioga County, New York, where he acquired a tract of land and represented that region in the state legislature. He then sat in the U.S. House of Representatives as a Democratic-Republican, from 1803 to 1805, while also serving as chief justice of Tioga and Broome counties. Paterson died in Lisle, New York, on May 13, 1806.

Further Reading
Booth, Bulkeley. "General John Paterson," *New England Magazine* 11 (September 1894): 42–51.
Egleston, Thomas. *The Life of John Paterson, Major General in the Revolutionary Army.* New York: G. P. Putnam's Sons, 1898.
Gardner, Frank A. "Colonel John Paterson's Regiment," *Massachusetts Magazine* 8 (January–April 1915): 27–42, 75–84.
Heathcote, Charles W. "General John Paterson—Ardent Patriot Who Loyally Supported Washington," *Picket Post* no. 58 (November 1957): 20–26.
Lee, William H. "An Address on the Life and Character of Major General John Paterson of the Revolutionary Army," *New York Genealogical and Biographical Record* 21 (July 1890): 99–112.

Pearson, Richard (1731–1806)
English naval officer
Richard Pearson was born in Westmoreland, England, in March 1731, and he joined the Royal Navy as a cabin boy at the age of 12. After completing several cruises on a variety of warships, he left the service for better-paying work in the merchant marine but rejoined as a fourth lieutenant just prior to the Seven Years' War. In this capacity he accompanied Admiral John Pocock to India and fought in several engagements throughout the Indian Ocean. On one occasion, when his captain was injured in a storm, Pearson took charge of HMS *Norfolk* and sailed it to safety. In light of competent service he advanced to captain in 1773 and spent the first three years of the Revolutionary War convoying vessels to Canada and guarding the St. Lawrence River. In 1779 Pearson received command of the new, copper-bottomed, 44-gun frigate HMS *Serapis,* unusual for its class by possessing two gun decks instead of one. That fall he was entrusted with escorting a small convoy home from the Baltic Sea in concert with the 16-gun schooner *Countess of Scarborough.* The Continental NAVY had been all but swept from the sea by the Royal Navy, so no serious interference was anticipated. However, as Pearson rounded Flamborough Head on September 23, 1779, he espied a red flag hoisted on nearby Scarborough Castle, indicating that hostile vessels were nearby. Around two o'clock in the afternoon strange sails were spotted on the horizon bearing down on the convoy. Pearson then signaled the merchant ships to disperse and tacked to place *Serapis* between them and the enemy.

The vessels in question were a small squadron of American and French warships commanded by Captain John Paul JONES. Jones commanded his own leaky East Indiaman *Bonhomme Richard,* the 20-gun frigate *Alliance* under Captain Pierre Landais, the 32-gun French frigate *Pallas,* and the 12-gun corvette *Vengeance.* Pearson appeared badly outnumbered on paper but, seeing that Jones wielded little or no control over his erstwhile allies, his odds steadily improved. It was nearly nightfall before adverse winds permitted the contestants to drift within firing range, and they commenced trading broadsides. The Americans got the worst of the exchange when two of their 18-

Captain Richard Pearson commanded the uniquely designed British vessel *Serapis*, which he lost to John Paul Jones in 1779. *(National Maritime Museum, Greenwich, London)*

pounders exploded, killing several men and rendering the below-deck guns unusable. Pearson and his crack crew continued flailing away at their antagonist with deadly effect, while Jones repeatedly attempted to lash the vessels together for boarding. His efforts were nearly compromised by Captain Landais, who mistakenly fired three broadsides into *Bonhomme Richard*. Nearly half the American crew were casualties before Jones succeeded in ensnaring the *Serapis*, after which he fired grapeshot and swept the gun deck clean of British crewmen. Pearson then dropped his anchor, hoping that the tide would tear his ship free. As the struggle intensified, several Americans on the top decks began working their way across the yardarm, dropping grenades.

At this juncture Pearson, observing the battered condition of *Bonhomme Richard*, hailed Jones through his megaphone and inquired, "Do you ask for quarter?" Jones shot back fabulously, "I have not yet begun to fight" and exhorted his men to fight on. Suddenly a basket of grenades was tossed down an open hatch of *Serapis* by Nathaniel FANNING, which ignited powder charges below deck. A lucky cannon shot also toppled the British mainmast overboard and Pearson, concerned for the safety of his crew, finally struck his colors. A boarding crew under Lieutenant Richard DALE arrived to secure the quarry while Jones cordially invited the vanquished into his cabin for a glass of wine. *Bonhomme Richard*, critically damaged, sank the following day, and Jones sailed his prize in triumph to Holland. Pearson and his crew were eventually exchanged there.

Pearson's defeat proved honorable, for he unflinchingly engaged superior enemy forces in the finest tradition of the Royal Navy. He was subsequently cleared by court-martial for the loss of his vessel and lauded for mounting such a stout defense. King GEORGE III knighted him, and he also obtained monetary awards from the convoy's insurers. Pearson resumed active duty in 1780 aboard HMS *Arethusa* and retired to command the Greenwich Hospital a decade later. He died there still serving in that capacity in January 1806, having conducted one of the most legendary ship-to-ship encounters in naval history.

Further Reading

Ireland, Bernard. *Naval Warfare in the Age of Sail.* New York: Norton, 2000.

Lambert, Andrew. *War at Sea in the Age of Sail, 1650–1850.* London: Cassell, 2000.

Miller, Nathan. *The Age of Fighting Sail.* New York: Wiley, 2000.

Schaeper, Thomas J. *John Paul Jones and the Battle of Flamborough Head: A Reconsideration.* New York: P. Lang, 1989.

Sweetman, Jack, ed. *Great American Naval Battles.* Annapolis, Md.: Naval Institute Press, 1998.

Percy, Hugh (1743–1817)
English military officer

Hugh Percy was born on August 28, 1742, a son of Hugh, first earl of Northumberland. Despite a sickly childhood that left him predisposed toward painful maladies like gout, he was attracted to a military life and joined the army in 1759 as an ensign in the 24th Regiment. Percy, like many aristocrats, used family connections to advance his career, and in 1762 he was a lieutenant colonel of the 111th Regiment and aide-de-camp to Prince Ferdinand of Brunswick during the Seven Years' War. However, he proved himself an accomplished soldier and, after good service at the Battles of Bergen and Minden, Percy rose to lieutenant colonel of the Grenadier Guards in 1762. Two years later he declined appointment as colonel to serve as aide-de-camp to King GEORGE III. In 1763 Percy also successfully stood for a seat in the House of Commons, where his Whig beliefs sometimes placed him at odds with his sovereign, especially over the hard-line policies adopted toward the colonies. Still, he circulated comfortably among the inner circles of power, and in 1764 he married the daughter of Lord Bute, the king's personal tutor. In November 1768 Percy also purchased his colonelcy of the 5th Regiment, or Northumberland Fusiliers, and distinguished himself for kindness and altruism toward his men. In an age of draconian discipline—and punishment—Percy abolished flogging and established the rule of leadership by example. He also attentively saw to the needs of soldiers' families and provided funding and free transportation where necessary. Consequently the Northumberland Fusiliers became a crack unit, highly disciplined and fiercely devoted to its colonel.

In May 1774 Percy was dispatched to Boston to reinforce the garrison under General Thomas GAGE. He then assumed duties as camp commander with a local rank of brigadier general. By this time lingering resentment toward British imperial policy was on the cusp of erupting into full-scale violence, so Gage enacted a policy of preemptive strikes against colonial military supplies to forestall any possible outbreak of violence. During the night of April 18, 1775, Gage dispatched a column of 800 handpicked regulars under Lieutenant Colonel Francis SMITH and Major John PITCAIRN to seize military arms known to be housed at CONCORD. On the fateful morning of April 19, Pitcairn's men violently brushed aside a MINUTEMAN company under Captain John PARKER, an act precipitating the Revolutionary War. Before noon swarms of angry militiamen began sniping at Smith's column as it withdrew to Boston, reducing it to the point of collapse. Fortunately for the British, Percy had been ordered out that morning with 1,400 soldiers as reinforcements, and he linked up with Smith outside of Lexington. Disaster seemed imminent, but he kept the Americans at bay with volley and cannon fire, hastily reorganized Smith's survivors, and commenced a highly disciplined withdrawal under excruciating circumstances. Percy then led his force back over the last 15 miles, taking heavy

Colonel Hugh Percy's quick thinking saved the British from disaster at the Battle of Concord. *(Courtauld Institute of Art, London)*

losses but maintaining the iron discipline for which the vaunted redcoats were famous. After reaching Menotomy he elected not to retrace his route directly back to Cambridge, which he correctly assumed swarmed with militia, and veered instead toward Charlestown. The decision to suddenly take this less-contested route probably spared the British from disaster, and Percy's men finally trudged into camp by noon, exhausted but intact. General Gage waxed effusively over his stirring performance under fire, and he gained promotion to major general as of July 11, 1775.

Percy was ill and unable to partake in the bloody Battle of BUNKER HILL on June 17, 1775, where the Northumberland Fusiliers sustained heavy losses under the direction of General William HOWE. Typically, he paid all transportation costs to ship the widows home and granted each a small cash endowment for resettlement back in England. He accompanied Howe to Halifax once Boston was evacuated in March 1776 and subsequently fought in the campaign around New York. On August 27, 1776, Percy and General Henry CLINTON commanded the flanking action at LONG ISLAND that routed American forces under General Israel PUTNAM. On November 16, 1775, he assisted HESSIANS under General Wilhelm von KNYPHAUSEN during the storming of Fort Washington, again at great cost to the Americans. Percy received promotion to lieutenant general in consequence, but he began waxing critical over Howe's conduct of the war. Not surprisingly, he was exiled with the unpopular General Clinton on an expedition against Newport, Rhode Island, in December 1776. Percy served as garrison commander once Clinton returned to England, and he continued criticizing Howe for not capturing the capital of Providence. Percy's mounting disillusionment with the war, along with poor health, finally induced him to ask for a leave of absence. Howe, eager to rid himself of a difficult subordinate, readily assented, and he sailed home in May 1777, never to return. Considering Percy's obvious military ability, his premature departure represented a serious loss to the British war effort.

Percy became the new duke of Northumberland following his father's death in 1784, and he began dabbling in national politics again. He also accepted a succession of military appointments, which crested in 1793 with his promotion to lieutenant general, but he saw no serious campaigning. Percy apparently preferred the role of a benevolent landowner who treated his renters kindly and enjoyed great popularity among them. The gout-ridden duke died at his estate on July 10, 1817, greatly lamented by those who knew him. He was the British hero of Concord and possibly their most underrated field commander of this conflict.

Further Reading
Babinski, Mark. *Notes on C. J. Sauthier and Lord Percy.* Garwood, N.J.: Krinder Peak, 1997.
Bolton, Charles K., ed. *Letters of Hugh, Earl Percy, from Boston to New York, 1774–1776.* Boston: Gregg Press, 1972.
Cumming, William P., and Elizabeth Cumming. "The Treasures of Alnwick Castle," *American Heritage* 20, no. 5 (1969): 27–33.
Murdock, Harold. *Earl Percy Dines Abroad: A Boswellian Episode.* Port Washington, N.Y.: Kennikat Press, 1970.
———. *Earl Percy's Dinner Table.* Boston: Houghton, Mifflin, 1907.
———. "Earl Percy's Return to Boston on the 19th of April, 1775," *Colonial Society of Massachusetts Transactions* 24 (1920–22): 257–292.
Percy, Hugh. "Original Letters of Hugh, Earl Percy and Afterwards Duke of Northumberland, between April 17, 1774, and July 11, 1778," *Boston Public Library Bulletin* 10 (January 1892): 317–327.

Petty, William (1737–1805)
English politician
William Petty was born in Dublin, Ireland, on May 2, 1737, a son of John, first earl of Shelburne. Well educated by tutors and at Christchurch, Oxford, he joined the army in 1757 and distinguished himself in combat as an aide-de-camp. Petty then successfully stood for a seat in the House of Commons in 1760 and joined the House of Lords the following

year after inheriting his father's title. Petty quickly exhibited intelligence and somewhat progressive views, particularly toward colonial administration, and he soon became a protege of William PITT, earl of Chatham. In this capacity he served as secretary of state for the Southern Department, 1766–68, and conferred with Massachusetts agent Benjamin FRANKLIN on a variety of issues affecting colonial relations. He resigned in 1768 in a dispute over the responsibility of his office and remained out of politics for the next 15 years. Petty, despite a reputation for scheming and political intrigue, then succeeded Pitt as leader of the Chathamite Whigs, and he functioned as a counterweight to Charles WATSON-WENTWORTH, Lord Rockingham. His steadfast opposition to Rockingham did not go unnoticed by King GEORGE III, who, following the departure of Lord Frederick NORTH in March 1782, sought to play both Whig leaders off against each other. Therefore, when he asked Rockingham to form a government, he also selected Petty to serve within his ministry as home secretary. As both leaders clearly detested each other, the king hoped that this mutual antipathy would hold their policies in check. The labyrinthine and backbiting nature of Hanoverian politics was seldom more pronounced.

It fell upon Petty, as home secretary, to fulfill Rockingham's desire for a speedy conclusion to the war with the former colonies. He did so cannily, using his own set of negotiators in Paris to undercut the prime minister's policy of unconditionally recognizing American independence. His machinations also brought him into conflict with Charles James FOX, the foreign secretary of state, who regarded him as little more than a court puppet. The situation was further complicated by Rockingham's death in July 1782, whereupon the king appointed Petty first lord of the treasury and de facto prime minister. Fox resigned in protest but peace negotiations continued without him. At this juncture Petty reluctantly acknowledged American independence as inevitable and, in his uniquely far-sighted way, sought to cut as good a deal as possible with a view toward promoting future relations. He then generously agreed to the Mississippi River as the western boundary, granted free access to the Old Northwest, and fishing rights off the Canadian Grand Banks in exchange for abstract promises to return LOYALIST property and resume payment of prewar debts. Preliminaries to the TREATY OF PARIS were then signed on November 30, 1782, and debated in Parliament the following spring. Despite Petty's good intentions the peace terms were highly unpopular and Fox and North, eager to embarrass the government, managed to defeat its passage twice in February 1783. His ministry consequently ended after holding power for only eight months. When a new Fox-North coalition government was formed, they readily reversed themselves and endorsed the treaty that fall, finally ending the war.

Afterward Petty was created First marquis of Lansdowne, but he never again held public office. He was a capable, if ambiguous, politician and too intensely disliked by enemies—and sometimes friends—to govern effectively. His sole claim to fame was ending the eight-year-old colonial struggle. Petty died on May 7, 1805, a capable politician but one of the more contentious personalities of his age.

Further Reading
Merwin, Mile M. "Lord Shelburne and America, 1763–1783: Personality for Failure." Unpublished Ph.D. diss., University of North Carolina, 1971.
Norris, John M. *Shelburne and Reform.* New York: Macmillan, 1963.
Ritcheson, C. R. "The Earl of Shelburne and Peace with America, 1782–1783: Vision and Reality," *International History Review* 5, no. 3 (1983): 322–345.
Simpson, W. O. "Lord Shelburne and North America," *History Today* 10, no. 1 (1960): 52–62.
Skaggs, David C. "Lord Shelburne's Gift: The Old Northwest," *Military Review* 56, no. 9 (1976): 56–57.
Stockley, Andrew. *Britain and France at the Birth of America: The European Powers at the Peace Negotiations, 1782–1783.* Exeter, U.K.: University of Exeter Press, 2001.
Walsh-Atkins, P. C. "Shelburne and America, 1763–1783." Unpublished Ph.D. diss., Oxford University, 1971.

Phillips, William (1731–1781)
English military officer

William Phillips was born in England in 1731, the son of a career soldier. Lacking money and influence to purchase a commission, he enrolled at the Woolwich Military Academy in 1746 as a gentleman cadet, where he excelled at mathematics and artillery practice. Phillips graduated in April 1750 to become quartermaster of the Royal Artillery Regiment. He rose in this capacity to first lieutenant in 1756 before transferring to the staff of Sir John Ligonier, lieutenant general of ordnance. He then fought in the Seven Years' War as a captain, highly distinguishing himself as an artillerist in the Battles of Minden and Warburg, 1759–60. In this last engagement Phillips made history by rapidly relocating his cannon in mid-battle, and even the marquis de Ternay, his French opponent, commended his performance. Afterward he proved instrumental in establishing the Royal Artillery Band to enhance esprit de corps and gained promotion to colonel in May 1772. He also functioned as inspector general of artillery and commander of the artillery school at Woolwich for several years. Once the Revolutionary War commenced he was attached to the staff of General John BURGOYNE and arrived at Montreal in the fall of 1776, commanding all artillery forces in Canada. He also became nominal second-in-command of Burgoyne's army, numbering 7,000 strong and intending to deal a decisive blow to the rebels by capturing Albany, New York.

During the summer of 1777 Burgoyne's army advanced down the Lake Champlain corridor until it confronted rebel-held Fort Ticonderoga under General Arthur ST. CLAIR. Preparations were made for an assault but Phillips, assisted by General Simon FRASER, personally reconnoitered nearby Mount Independence, which had been viewed as too steep for artillery emplacements. Undeterred by this assessment, Phillips drove his gun crews up the slopes on the night of July 4, 1777, placed his cannon, and by daybreak had completely compromised St. Clair's position. The Americans quickly retreated without firing a shot, thereby justifying Phillips's personal dictum: "Where a goat can go a man can go, and where a man can go he can drag a gun." Unfortunately, by the early fall Burgoyne's offensive stalled in the heavily wooded terrain of Saratoga, and he launched two costly reconnaissances in force at FREEMAN'S FARM and BEMIS HEIGHTS to gather intelligence. Phillips commanded the British left wing on both occasions and employed numerous cannon to negate superior rebel numbers. Burgoyne could not forestall the inevitable, however, and he surrendered his entire army to General Horatio GATES on October 17, 1777. He was then paroled, sent to Boston, and returned to England while Phillips commanded his so-called Convention Army on its march to Cambridge, Massachusetts, for eventual shipment home.

General William Phillips was the most accomplished British artillerist of the war. *(National Army Museum, Chelsea, England)*

Ultimately, the Continental CONGRESS refused to honor the terms of Burgoyne's convention, and his soldiers passed into captivity. Phillips, who frequented the home of Thomas JEFFERSON, complained so constantly about the shoddy treatment they received that he was eventually arrested and detained. He was finally exchanged for General Benjamin LINCOLN in November 1779 and reported for duty at New York. There General Henry CLINTON ordered him to Virginia in April 1781, where he was to assume command of British forces there under General Benedict ARNOLD, his former adversary at Saratoga. From Portsmouth their united forces quickly marched overland and captured Williamsburg on April 20, 1781. Phillips, now commanding 3,500 veteran troops, marched south to rendezvous with General Charles CORNWALLIS, then pressing upward from North Carolina. En route he paused to burn the Chickahominy shipyard before moving on to Petersburg and dispersing militia forces under General John P. G. MUHLENBERG on April 25, 1781. Two days later he scored an even bigger success when his artillery met and drove off a large American flotilla on the James River. Phillips had nearly finished his highly successful and destructive raid when he contracted typhoid fever shortly after returning to Petersburg. He died there suddenly on May 13, 1781, the most accomplished British artillerist of the war. His talents would be sorely missed at the siege of YORKTOWN.

Further Reading
Bailey, James H. *Petersburg in the Revolution.* Petersburg, Va.: Petersburg Bicentennial Commission, 1976.
Davis, Robert P. *Where a Man Can Go: Major General William Phillips, British Royal Artillery, 1731–1781.* Westport, Conn.: Greenwood Press, 1999.
Fleming, Thomas. "Burgoyne's Wandering Army," *American Heritage* 24, no. 1 (1972): 10–15, 89–93.
Ketchum, Richard M. *Saratoga: Turning Point in America's Revolutionary War.* New York: Henry Holt, 1997.
May, Robin. *The British Army in North America, 1775–1783.* London: Osprey, 1997.

Morrissey, Brendan. *Saratoga, 1777.* Oxford: Osprey, 2000.

Pickens, Andrew (1737–1817)
American militia officer

Andrew Pickens was born in Paxton Township, Pennsylvania, on September 19, 1739, and he relocated with his family to the Waxhaw District of South Carolina as a boy. After serving in the Cherokee War of 1761 as a militia captain, he resettled at Long Cane Creek to farm and trade with the Indians. In the period leading up to the Revolutionary War, the South Carolina polity became sharply divided between Patriots and LOYALISTS. Pickens sided with the former, and when hostilities commenced in 1775 he rejoined the militia as a captain. He first saw service in the western reaches of the state by helping fight off a larger Loyalist contingent at Fort Ninety Six. The two groups subsequently agreed to a truce and withdrew, then Pickens participated in a punitive campaign against the Cherokee. The Indians sustained a serious defeat, but Pickens was ambushed and his company nearly annihilated on August 12, 1776. Two years later he accompanied General Andrew Williamson on an unsuccessful foray into British-held East Florida. Patriot fortunes plummeted following the December 1778 capture of Savannah, Georgia, by Lieutenant Colonel Archibald CAMPBELL, which sparked a regional Loyalist resurgence. Pickens, now colonel of the Upper Ninety Six Regiment, decided to intercept a large body of Loyalists under Colonel John Boyd before they could unite with the British. Assisted by Colonel Elijah CLARKE, Pickens's 300 militia stealthily surrounded Boyd's 700 men at Kettle Creek on February 14, 1779, then attacked and totally defeated them. He next fought at the unsuccessful action at Stono Ferry on June 20, 1779, which spelled the end of General Benjamin LINCOLN's invasion of Georgia, but worse news was yet to come.

In February 1780, British forces under General Henry CLINTON commenced the siege of CHARLESTON, South Carolina, and the city fell the following May. Organized American resistance all but collapsed following another severe defeat at CAMDEN in August 1780, at which point Pickens and his band surrendered at Fort Ninety Six and accepted parole. He remained neutral until December 1780, when a marauding band of Loyalists plundered his plantation, and he rejoined light forces under General Daniel MORGAN. Aware of Pickens's reputation as a fighter, Morgan entrusted him with command of his second line at the decisive victory at COWPENS on January 17, 1781. As British forces under Lieutenant Colonel Banastre TARLETON impetuously advanced, Pickens expertly fired two accurate volleys and withdrew behind a hill, there to rally and charge in concert with cavalry under Colonel William WASHINGTON. For his role at Cowpens, Pickens received a sword from the Continental CONGRESS and promotion to brigadier general of militia.

At length British forces under General Charles CORNWALLIS abandoned the Carolinas, and an intense, backwoods partisan war erupted. Pickens, now tied to the main American army under General Nathanael GREENE, began a concerted campaign to reduce British and Loyalist strong points dotting the interior of the state. The war at this point had degenerated into savage, no-quarter fighting between former neighbors. Between May and June of 1781 Pickens operated with Colonel Henry LEE in a difficult siege of Augusta, Georgia. He next commanded at the unsuccessful attempt to storm Fort Ninety Six and bore a prominent role at the hard-fought encounter at Eutaw Springs against Colonel Alexander STEWART in October 1781. By this time the war in the south had been all but won, and Pickens fought well in a difficult campaign against the Cherokee in 1782 before finally laying down his musket.

Pickens's wartime activities rendered him a state hero, and he was elected to the state legislature six times between 1781 and 1793, and also held a seat in the U.S. House of Representatives, 1793–95. Afterward he performed useful services as a surveyor working the Indian boundary, and his former adversaries came to regard him as an honest broker. His popularity had scarcely waned in 1812, when he was invited to run for the governorship, but he declined in favor of another term with the legislature. Pickens died at Tomassee, South Carolina, on August 11, 1819; owning to his stern, upright Presbyterian demeanor, he was popularly known as the Fighting Elder.

Further Reading
Buchanan, John. *The Road to Guilford Courthouse: The American Revolution in the Carolinas.* New York: Wiley, 1997.
Edgar, Walter. *Partisans and Redcoats: The Southern Conflict That Turned the Tide of the American Revolution.* New York: William Morrow, 2001.
Gordon, John W. *South Carolina and the American Revolution: A Battlefield History.* Columbia: University of South Carolina Press, 2003.
Helsley, Alexia. *South Carolinians in the War for American Independence.* Columbia: South Carolina Department of History and Archives, 2000.
Pickens, Andrew. *General Andrew Pickens: An Autobiography.* Clemson, S.C.: Pendleton District Historical and Recreational Commission, 1976.
Waring, Alice W. *The Fightin' Elder, Andrew Pickens, 1739–1817.* Columbia: University of South Carolina Press, 1962.

Pickering, Timothy (1745–1829)
American military officer

Timothy Pickering was born in Salem, Massachusetts, on July 17, 1745, the son of a prosperous farmer. He passed through Harvard College in 1763, read law, and gained admittance to the bar, but he declined practicing law in favor of minor civil offices. During events leading up to the break with Great Britain he emerged as one of Salem's most prominent Whigs, and he also joined the local militia in 1766 as a lieutenant. By 1775 Pickering functioned as colonel of Essex County militia, and in February of that year his men stood off a British column sent there under Colonel Alexander LESLIE. After hostilities commenced he served in the siege of Boston and also published *An Easy Plan of Discipline for a Militia,* which served as a standard American drill manual until General

Friedrich von STEUBEN's *Blue Book*. Pickering was eventually drawn into the Continental ARMY and fought in the campaigns at New York and New Jersey throughout 1776. His good conduct and performance brought him to the attention of General George WASHINGTON, who appointed him adjutant general on May 24, 1777, to replace Horatio GATES. Pickering performed well as a staff officer and, during the Battle of GERMANTOWN in October 1778, he prevailed upon Washington to bypass the fortified Clivedon House. Shortly after, the Continental CONGRESS tapped him to serve on the newly created Board of War, while he simultaneously discharged his duties as adjutant general.

Pickering served capably on the Board of War, although he gradually distanced himself from Washington and briefly flirted with the cabal of Colonel Thomas CONWAY. In the summer of 1780 he accepted his most arduous task of the war by replacing General Nathanael GREENE as quartermaster general while still part of the Board of War. This was easily the most unpopular appointment in the military establishment and perpetually lacked funds to purchase food, equipment, and supplies for the main army. Pickering nevertheless shouldered his impossible responsibilities as well as possible, and pioneered the use of "specie certificates" to obtain badly needed commodities. In the summer of 1781 his efforts proved particularly useful in victualing and relocating Washington's main army on its march from New York to YORKTOWN, Virginia, the decisive campaign of the war. Afterward Pickering remained on as quartermaster general and he also prompted Congress to consider establishing a formal military academy at West Point, New York, to train future generations of officers. He finally mustered out on July 25, 1785, and returned to civilian life.

Pickering turned out to have one of the most active—and controversial—political careers of the young republic. President Washington successively appointed him postmaster general, secretary of war, and secretary of state, in each of which he performed capably. In 1790 he was asked to negotiate a treaty with the New York Iroquois under CORNPLANTER, and a treaty was successfully concluded. Pickering remained with the State Department under President John ADAMS, although he became a warm partisan of Federalist Alexander HAMILTON and gradually conspired behind the president's back. Adams dismissed him in May 1800, and Pickering took his unique brand of Federalist obstructionism to Congress to oppose the administrations of Thomas JEFFERSON and James MADISON. He adamantly opposed the War of 1812 and went as far as to suggest the secession of New England to preserve its economic advantages. Pickering retired from public life in 1817 to pursue farming, where he helped pioneer agricultural improvements. He died at Salem on January 29, 1829, a highly contentious and querulous personality of early U.S. history, yet an effective military administrator when his country needed him most.

Further Reading

Clarfield, Gerard H. *Timothy Pickering and the American Republic.* Pittsburgh: University of Pittsburgh Press, 1980.

Fitzpatrick, Michael G. "The Canandaigua Treaty: A Saga of War and Peace on the Old Frontier, 1775–1795." Unpublished master's thesis, St. Bonaventure University, 2000.

McLean, David. *Timothy Pickering and the Age of the American Revolution.* New York: Arno Press, 1982.

Phillips, Edward H. "Salem, Timothy Pickering, and the American Revolution," *Essex Institute Historical Collections* 111, no. 1 (1975): 65–78.

Risch, Erna. *Supplying Washington's Army.* Washington, D.C.: Government Printing Office, 1981.

Wilbur, William A. "Crisis in Leadership: Alexander Hamilton, Timothy Pickering, and the Politics of Federalism." Unpublished master's thesis, Syracuse University, 1969.

Pigot, Robert (1720–1796)
English military officer

Robert Pigot (sometimes rendered Pigott) was born at Patshull, Staffordshire, in 1720. He joined the military and in 1745 fought at Fontenoy as a lieutenant with the 31st Regiment. He rose to captain following serval tours of garrison duty at

Minorca and in Scotland and transferred as major to the 70th Regiment in 1758. Pigot became lieutenant colonel of the 38th Infantry in 1764, performing additional useful services in Ireland and southern Europe. He next shipped across the Atlantic to Boston in 1774 as part of the garrison under General Thomas GAGE. Flank companies of the 38th Regiment were present in the fighting at Lexington and CONCORD, but Pigot remained in the city with his center companies. He then marched with Colonel Hugh PERCY on the relief expedition to rescue the British column under Lieutenant Colonel Francis SMITH. General William HOWE, who replaced Gage in the fall of 1775, jokingly referred to Pigot as "the little man" on account of his short stature. Such remarks proved no reflection on his abilities, for just prior to the Battle of BUNKER HILL on June 17, 1775, Howe appointed Pigot his second in command, with a local rank of brigadier general. In this capacity he led the 38th, 43rd, and 47th Regiments against an assortment of American militia ensconced on the heights. Advancing against their left flank, Pigot was blasted back by severe musket fire and reformed his men at the bottom of the hill. Howe then ordered him to assault the main enemy redoubt at the top of the hill, which was also grievously repulsed. With commendable resolve, Howe and Pigot rallied their men for a third charge, ordered their backpacks dropped, and advanced back up the bloody hillside. By now the defenders' ammunition was nearly exhausted, and Pigot was among the first British officers to leap the parapet and flush them out at bayonet point. For such conspicuous displays of bravery he became colonel of the 38th Regiment by special order of King GEORGE III. It was an apt tribute to Pigot, who, at 55 years of age, was also among the most senior officers present.

Howe evacuated Boston in March 1776 and Pigot accompanied him to Halifax to assume command of a brigade consisting of the 5th, 28th, 35th, and 49th Regiments. In this capacity he fought in the New York campaign of 1776 and bore a conspicuous role in the British victory at LONG ISLAND on August 27, 1776. Once the Americans under General George WASHINGTON fled the New York region, Pigot served as the city's garrison commander. He functioned there until July 1777, when Howe placed him in charge of British forces holding Newport, Rhode Island, with a rank of major general. Pigot conducted his usual garrison affairs until July 1778, when a large French expedition arrived in Narragansett Bay under Admiral Charles-Hector-Théodat, comte d'ESTAING. They were shortly after joined by a division under General John SULLIVAN, which brought coalition forces up to 10,000 men. Pigot mustered only 6,000 soldiers but, pugnacious as ever, he determined to fight. His men fought stubborn delaying actions at barricades built around Newport's perimeter, forcing Sullivan to commence formal siege operations. At this juncture help arrived in the form of Admiral Richard HOWE's squadron, and d'Estaing promptly took his forces out to sea to meet them. After a storm badly damaged both squadrons, d'Estaing decided to abandon his allies altogether and sailed to Boston for a refit. This leveled the odds considerably, and Pigot aggressively sortied in strength possibly to trap Sullivan on Aquidneck Island. The ensuing Battle of Rhode Island, fought on August 29, 1778, proved a bloody draw, but Newport remained safely in British hands for another year. Moreover, Pigot's tenacious defense handed the newly enacted FRENCH ALLIANCE a serious rebuff and placed it under considerable strain.

In October 1778, Pigot was replaced by a recently repatriated General Richard Prescott (embarrassingly kidnapped by Colonel William BARTON) and returned to New York. In November 1782 he sailed for England, where he was promoted to lieutenant general. Pigot died at Patshull on August 2, 1796, short in stature, perhaps, but decidedly tall in reputation.

Further Reading

Brooks, Victor. *The Boston Campaign, April 19, 1775–March 17, 1776*. Conshohocken, Pa.: Combined, 1999.

Conley, Patrick T. "The Battle of Rhode Island, 29 August 1778: A Victory for the Patriots." *Rhode Island History* 62, no. 3 (fall 2004): 51–65.
Dearden, Paul. *The Rhode Island Campaign of 1778: Inauspicious Dawn of Alliance.* Providence: Rhode Island Historical Society, 1980.
Hagist, Don N., ed. *General Orders, Rhode Island: December 1776–January 1778.* Bowie, Md.: Heritage Books, 2001.
Ketchum, Richard M. *Decisive Day: The Battle for Bunker Hill.* New York: Henry Holt, 1999.
Morrissey, Brendan. *Boston 1775: The Shot Heard around the World.* Westport, Conn.: Praeger, 2004.

Pinckney, Charles C. (1746–1825)
American military officer

Charles Cotesworth Pinckney was born in Charleston, South Carolina, on February 25, 1746, into one of that colony's most aristocratic families. Well educated by tutors, he passed through Christ Church College, Oxford, in 1764 and subsequently studied law at London's Middle Temple. Pinckney then attended the Caen military academy in France before returning home in 1769. He successfully entered politics that year by winning a seat in the colonial assembly and by 1773 was also acting as attorney general for several towns. In 1775 Pinckney was firmly identified with the Patriot cause, and he sat with the extralegal provincial assembly to draft plans for a new interim government to replace the royal charter. When fighting began in April 1775 Pinckney joined the 1st South Carolina Militia Regiment as a captain, and the following June he led a raid that captured Fort John in Charleston Harbor. He next fought under Colonel William MOULTRIE during the attack on CHARLESTON in June 1776 and rose to colonel that September. Feeling that the South had become a military backwater, Pinckney ventured north to serve as aide-de-camp to General George WASHINGTON. In this capacity he fought well at the Battles of BRANDYWINE and GERMANTOWN in 1777 before returning home the following spring. He then accompanied the ill-fated expedition against St. Augustine, Florida, May–June 1778, and subse-

Charles C. Pinckney served as an aide-de-camp to General Washington at the Battles of Brandywine and Germantown. *(National Archives)*

quently joined the army of General Benjamin LINCOLN. Pinckney fought well during the disastrous siege of SAVANNAH in October 1779 and was captured at the siege of CHARLESTON in May 1780. While a prisoner he refused all British overtures to change sides, and he was not exchanged until 1782. Despite a generally lackluster career, surprising because he was one of few officers in the Continental ARMY with professional military training, Pinckney mustered out of service in November 1783 as a brevet brigadier general.

After the war Pinckney resumed his legal activities in Charleston and also served in both houses of the state legislature. In 1787 he made his influence felt on local politics by attending the state constitutional convention, where he strongly and persuasively argued for more centralized governance. Once the new government was established in 1789, President Washington offered Pinckney several positions within the War Department,

Supreme Court, and State Department, but he consistently declined. In 1796 the government tendered him a position as minister to France to succeed James MONROE, and he accepted. The revolutionary French government, or Directory, initially refused his credentials but, once joined by Elbridge GERRY, he was finally allowed in the country. At that time France and the United States were edging toward war, and he was informed by agents X, Y, and Z that peace could be negotiated only after paying a quarter-million-dollar bribe to Talleyrand, the foreign minister. Pinckney angrily declared, "Not a sixpence!" and withdrew to the United States as an undeclared naval conflict, the Quasi-War of 1798–1800, commenced in the West Indies. President John ADAMS then appointed him major general in the U.S. Army, but his service abruptly terminated once the conflict was successfully negotiated.

In 1800 Pinckney, now a leading Federalist and ally of Alexander HAMILTON, ran for the vice presidency against Thomas JEFFERSON and lost. Eight years later he ran for the presidency itself against James MADISON, losing again. He then returned to Charleston to dabble in law and local politics, gaining considerable renown through his generous philanthropy. He died in Charleston on August 16, 1825, part of an influential political family that produced several national figures of note.

Further Reading

Bell, Cynthia A. "South Carolina Statesmen: Constitutional Problems Facing the Signers after Ratification." Unpublished master's thesis, University of South Carolina, 1994.

Lefkowitz, Arthur S. *George Washington's Indispensable Men: The 32 Aides-de-camp Who Helped American Independence.* Mechanicsburg, Pa.: Stackpole Books, 2003.

Pinckney, Charles C. "The Battles of Brandywine and Germantown," *Historical Magazine* 10 (1866): 202–204.

Ulmer, Shirley S. "The South Carolina Delegates to the Constitutional Convention of 1787: An Analytical Study." Unpublished master's thesis, Duke University, 1956.

Williams, Frances L. *A Founding Family: The Pinckneys of South Carolina.* New York: Harcourt, Brace, Jovanovich, 1978.

Zahniser, Marvin R. *Charles Cotesworth Pinckney, Founding Father.* Chapel Hill: University of North Carolina Press, 1967.

Pitcairn, John (1722–1775)
royal marine officer

John Pitcairn was born in Dysart, Scotland, the son of a parson. He joined Cornwall's Seventh Marines as a lieutenant in 1756 and, after the royal marines were formally established in 1756, he transferred as a captain. Pitcairn had since acquired a reputation as a strict disciplinarian, but one who was attentive to the needs of his men. He rose to major in 1771 and three years later shipped to Boston as part of the garrison under General Thomas GAGE. There he commanded a composite battalion drawn from the Chatham, Portsmouth, and Plymouth divisions. Pitcairn kept his men in a constant state of readiness through repeated drilling and forced marches—accompanying them on foot—and consequently his marines were among the toughest and best-trained units in Boston. In addition to military matters, Pitcairn also displayed a flair for public relations. He was a Scot Tory by nature with little sympathy for colonial unrest and advocated harsh measures to keep them in line. However, Pitcairn was also diplomatic and tactful in his dealing with civilians, becoming one of the most popular officers of the Boston garrison.

Everything changed on the night of April 18, 1775, when Gage ordered a column of 800 hand-picked troops under Lieutenant Colonel Francis SMITH to march from Boston, 16 miles into the countryside, and seize a cache of colonial arms at Concord. The redoubtable Pitcairn was ordered to accompany him as second-in-command. As the British tramped off into the gloom they heard church bells and alarm cannons pealing in the distance as riders like Paul REVERE alerted the countryside of their approach. At dawn Smith dispatched Pitcairn ahead of the column with

Royal marine major John Pitcairn was in charge of the soldiers who responded to the first shot of the war, at Lexington. *(Lexington Museum)*

several light infantry companies; on the morning of April 19, 1775, they encountered the MINUTEMAN company of Captain John PARKER at Lexington. Not wishing to provoke a confrontation, Parker deployed on the green astride the road and was prepared to let the British pass. Pitcairn, however, was not willing to leave a potentially hostile force to his rear, so he paraded on the green, rode up to Parker, and summarily ordered him to disperse. Parker, badly outnumbered, willingly obliged and was in the act of departing when a musket suddenly barked from out of nowhere. The British, wet, fatigued, and angry, now perceived themselves as under attack. They fired several volleys into the milling Americans and followed up with bayonets before Pitcairn restored order. Eight militiamen lay dead, with an additional 10 wounded; one British soldier was slightly injured, and Pitcairn's horse had been grazed by a bullet. Smith arrived shortly after with the main column, and both officers pushed on to their objective.

After securing Concord and failing to find any supplies, Smith ordered his men to retrace their steps back to Boston. En route they were greeted by swarms of angry militiamen who pelted his column with accurate sniper fire. Order had nearly collapsed by the time the British reached Lexington, where they were reinforced and rescued by a relief column under Colonel Hugh PERCY. At this juncture Pitcairn's horse threw him, and he ended up walking the rest of the day; his brace of pistols was subsequently captured, and they are still displayed at the Lexington Historical Society. Having sustained heavy losses, the British remained cooped up in Boston over the next two months. The impasse broke on the evening of June 16, 1775, when the rebels seized the high ground near Charleston Harbor, and Gage ordered them pushed off. On June 17, 1775, General William HOWE attacked at BUNKER HILL and was grievously repulsed two times. On his third attempt the marine battalion was ordered up under Pitcairn, who charged at the head of his troops. The British succeeded in breaching American defenses, but as soon as Pitcairn mounted the parapet he was fatally wounded, as tradition asserts, by Salem Prince, a free AFRICAN AMERICAN. Pitcairn was subsequently borne away by his son, Lieutenant Thomas Pitcairn, where he was attended to by Dr. Thomas Kast, Gage's personal physician. He died the following day, swearing to his last moments that he did not order the shots that precipitated a war. Pitcairn was buried at the Old North Church, but in 1791 his remains were shipped back to London for reinterment.

Further Reading

Boaz, Thomas. *"For the Glory of the Marines": The Organization, Training, Uniforms, and Combat Role of the British Marines during the American Revolution.* Devon, Pa.: Dockside Press, 1993.

Brooks, Victor. *The Boston Campaign, April 19, 1775–March 17, 1776.* Conshohocken, Pa.: Combined, 1999.

Hallahan, William H. *The Day the Revolution Began, 19 April 1775.* New York: Avon Books, 1999.

Hudson, Charles. "The Character of Major John Pitcairn," *Massachusetts Historical Society Proceedings* 17 (1879–80): 315–326.

Kehoe, Vincent J-R. *The British Story of the Battle of Lexington and Concord on the Nineteenth of April 1775.* Los Angeles, Calif.: Hale & Co., 2000.

Murphy, J. F. "We Have All Lost a Father," *Naval History* 16, no. 5 (2002): 20–23.

Pitt, William (1708–1778)
English politician

William Pitt was born in London, England, on November 15, 1708, the son of a parliamentarian from Cornwall. Educated at Eton and Oxford, he won a seat in the House of Commons in 1735 and maintained a formidable presence in politics over the next four decades. Pitt initially distinguished himself as an opponent of Sir Robert Walpole's ministry and his stridency cost him the friendship of King George II. However, once the Seven Years' War erupted in 1755, he seized the opportunity to catapult himself to power. A gifted orator endowed with rapier wit and a commanding demeanor, Pitt maneuvered his way to power in 1757 by crafting a coalition between himself and Lord Newcastle. Now de facto prime minister, he artfully marshaled the entire military might of England to defeat France in the New World, not simply in Europe. He by and large succeeded by 1760, but a new monarch, King GEORGE III, disliked his overbearing policies intensely and sought to replace him. The following year the king prevailed upon his mentor, Lord Bute, to become secretary of state over Pitt's objections and with the compliance of Newcastle. Pitt then resigned over proposed changes in the conduct of the war, although he remained a pivotal figure in the House of Commons. After the war was concluded by what he considered an unsatisfactory peace, he remained a strident opposition figure, better known to throngs of public supporters as "The Great Commoner."

Following passage of the STAMP ACT in 1765, Pitt brought his anger to bear on the policies of his brother-in-law, George GRENVILLE. He argued stridently and forcefully that Parliament lacked the right to tax the colonies in the absence of representation, although he acknowledged the supremacy of that body in administrative matters. Such posturing won him accolades in the colonies, and he further endeared himself, following the Stamp Act's repeal, by opposing the Declaratory Act passed the next day. In July 1766, the first administration of Charles WATSON-WENTWORTH, Lord Rockingham, collapsed, and Pitt managed to have himself appointed prime minister. In this capacity he also accepted the peerage title of earl of Chatham, which disillusioned many of his former supporters. Moreover, he was continually undermined by bouts of poor health and backbiting by various ministers, so his ministry collapsed by the spring of 1767. Thereafter Pitt took successively declining roles in national affairs as his mental state vacillated between fits of lethargy and his former brilliance. For this reason he could do little to forestall passage of the TOWNSHEND DUTIES in 1767, which reignited turmoil between Parliament and its colonies. By 1774 he mustered the acumen to oppose the COERCIVE ACTS, even while condemning the BOSTON TEA PARTY. But on the whole Pitt's ability to influence events waned to insignificance. A confirmed imperialist, he sought better treatment for the colonies but only in as much as it facilitated continuation of the empire. In March 1778 the king reversed his longtime opposition to Pitt and invited him to join the ministry of Lord Frederick NORTH, but he refused to serve an administration responsible, in his opinion, for bringing on the war with America. One month later Pitt collapsed on the floor of Parliament while voicing opposition to American independence. Pitt, England's dominant political personality for 30 years and among its most sagacious wartime leaders, died in London on May 11, 1778.

Further Reading

Black, Jeremy. *Pitt the Elder.* New York: Cambridge University Press, 1992.

Derry, John W. *Politics in the Age of Fox, Pitt, and Liverpool.* New York: Palgrave, 2001.

Peters, Marie. *The Elder Pitt.* New York: Longman, 1998.

Schweitzer, Karl W. *William Pitt, Earl of Chatham, 1708–1778: A Bibliography.* Westport, Conn.: Greenwood Press, 1993.

Thomas, Peter D. G. "The Great Commoner: The Elder William Pitt as Parliamentarian," *Parliamentary History* 22, no. 2 (2003): 145–163.

Ward, Lee. *The Politics of Liberty in England and Revolutionary America.* New York: Cambridge University Press, 2004.

Pomeroy, Seth (1706–1777)
American militia officer

Seth Pomeroy was born in Northampton, Massachusetts, on May 20, 1706, the son of a gunsmith. He pursued his father's profession with great skill until 1743, when he enlisted in the local militia as an ensign. Two years later Pomeroy was a captain in the 4th Massachusetts Regiment and he accompanied General William Pepperell on his expedition against Louisbourg on Cape Breton Island. He performed useful service there by repairing several captured French cannon, which were then promptly turned upon their former owners. By 1755 Pomeroy had risen to lieutenant colonel, and he fought under Sir William Johnson in the campaign against Crown Point. On September 8 he succeeded Colonel Ephraim Williams, who died in an ambush at Lake George, and fought capably until he received the surrender of the French commander, Baron Jean-Hermant de Dieskau. After the French and Indian War, Pomeroy returned to Northampton to resume his gunsmithing activities and took little interest in politics. It was not until 1774 that he became reliably identified with the Patriot faction by serving on the local committee of safety. Pomeroy subsequently represented his town in two provincial congresses, and in February 1775 he joined Artemas WARD and Jedidiah Preble as the colony's three senior militia leaders. His principle activity was in actively recruiting and drilling raw troops throughout western Massachusetts.

The 69-year-old Pomeroy was present during the siege of Boston, and on June 17, 1775, he fought as a volunteer at the Battle of BUNKER HILL. He did so by borrowing a horse in western Massachusetts and arriving at the battle scene after a hectic ride. Consequently, on June 22, 1775, the Continental CONGRESS made him one of eight new brigadier generals in the Continental ARMY. However, Pomeroy declined the distinction in favor of remaining a major general of Massachusetts militia. He then returned home to continue training and recruiting new troops. He died of illness at Peekskill, New York, on February 19, 1777, en route to reinforce the main army under General George WASHINGTON in New Jersey. For the time that he lived, Pomeroy enjoyed one of the most celebrated military reputations among his fellow militiamen.

Further Reading

De Forest, Louis E., ed. *The Journal and Papers of Seth Pomeroy, Sometime General in the Colonial Service.* New York: Society of Colonial Wars in the State of New York, 1926.

Pomeroy, Albert A. *History and Genealogy of the Pomeroy Family,* 2 vols. Toledo, Ohio: Franklin Printing and Engraving Co., 1912–23.

Pomeroy, George E. *An Address of the Character of General Seth Pomeroy, Delivered on the Two Hundredth Anniversary of His Birth.* Toledo, Ohio: The Franklin, 1906.

Sutton, Frank. "Neglected Grave of Seth Pomeroy," *Magazine of American History* 23 (March 1890): 247–248.

Trumbull, James R. *History of Northampton, Massachusetts, from Its Settlement in 1654,* 2 vols. Northampton, Mass.: Press of Gazette Printing Co., 1898–1902.

Poor, Enoch (1736–1780)
American military officer

Enoch Poor was born in Andover, Massachusetts, on June 21, 1736, and he apprenticed as a cabinet maker. In 1760 he relocated to Exeter, New Hampshire, where he served as a local politician. Poor, while personally opposed to the STAMP ACT of

1765, also served with several deputations created to enforce laws against violent protest. However, as the Revolutionary War approached, he enforced strictures against importing British goods and held seats in the provincial congresses. On May 24, 1775, Poor became colonel of the 2nd New Hampshire Regiment, and he spent several months improving the coastal defenses of Exeter. He participated in the siege of Boston until March 1776, then accompanied General George WASHINGTON on his march to New York. From there he joined General William THOMPSON's brigade and transferred north to reinforce Colonel Benedict ARNOLD in Canada. That fall he became one of several senior officers objecting to General Philip SCHUYLER's intention to abandon Crown Point, New York, without a fight. Poor then marched to join Washington in New Jersey, where he fought well in the Battles of TRENTON and PRINCETON. Consequently, on February 21, 1777, he gained promotion to brigadier general, a move prompting Colonel John STARK, who regarded Poor as his junior, to resign.

By the summer of 1777, Poor was commanding a New Hampshire brigade as part of the army under General Horatio GATES within the Northern Department. In this capacity he distinguished himself in fighting against the army of General John BURGOYNE. Poor's command formed the center of Gates's line at FREEMAN's FARM in September and fought veteran British troops to a draw. At BEMIS HEIGHTS the following month, he formed up on the right wing under General Arnold and spearheaded the successful charge against the Balcarres and Breymann redoubts. The Americans drove British and HESSIAN forces from their works, and Poor's command sustained 60 percent of the casualties but performed well. He next rejoined Washington at Valley Forge and was assigned to forces commanded by the marquis de LAFAYETTE. Poor's exemplary leadership helped extract American forces from the trap laid for them at Barren Hill on May 20, 1778, and three months later he was again conspicuously engaged in hard fighting at MONMOUTH as part of General Charles LEE's advance guard.

In the summer of 1779 Poor was reassigned to a division under General John SULLIVAN, then massing in southern New York for a punitive raid into Iroquois territory. He fought well at the decisive battle of Newtown on August 29, 1779, detecting an elaborate ambush set by Chief Joseph BRANT and driving off numerous warriors and LOYALISTS. After several months of garrison duty at West Point under Arnold, Poor then returned to New Jersey, where he and General Edward HAND assumed command of Lafayette's light infantry brigades. While in camp at Paramus, New Jersey, he apparently contracted a severe fever and died on September 8, 1780. Considering his reputation as a fighter and an iron disciplinarian, Poor's passing was lamented by Washington and other ranking officers. He accordingly received the largest funeral service given to any fallen officer in the Continental ARMY.

Further Reading
Akerman, Amos T. *Sketches of the Military Career of Enoch Poor, Brigadier in the Revolutionary War.* Manchester, N.H.: T. H. Tuson Book, Card, and Job Printer, 1878.
Baker, Henry M. "General Enoch Poor," *Journal of American History* 15 (April 1921): 117–132.
Beane, Samuel C. "General Enoch Poor," *New Hampshire Historical Society Proceedings* 3 (1895/1899): 435–473.
Heathcote, Charles W. "General Enoch Poor—Loyal Patriot and Devoted Friend of Washington," *Picket Post* no. 56 (May 1957): 4–10.
McMahon, Reginald. *The Death and Burial of General Enoch Poor.* River Edge, N.J.: Bergen County Historical Society, 1992.
Randall, Peter E. *New Hampshire: Years of Revolution, 1774–1783.* Hanover, N.H.: Profiles Pub. Corp., 1976.

Prescott, William (1726–1795)
American militia officer

William Prescott was born in Groton, Massachusetts, on February 20, 1726, the son of a judge. He joined the colonial militia as a lieutenant in 1745 and performed service throughout the siege of

Louisbourg on Cape Breton Island. Prescott conducted himself so well that he was proffered a regular British army commission, but declined. He then settled in the town of Pepperell to pursue farming while remaining active in militia affairs. In the run up to war with Great Britain, Prescott opposed the COERCIVE ACTS and shipped food and other supplies to the inhabitants of Boston. In 1774 he became colonel of a regiment of MINUTEMEN, and on April 19, 1775, he led them into combat after CONCORD but arrived too late to participate. Thereafter he settled into the siege of Boston with the provincial army and gained appointment to the council of war under General Artemas WARD. In this capacity he bore a conspicuous role in events leading to the battle of BUNKER HILL. When American intelligence was apprised of British intentions to attack their lines through Charlestown, Ward decided to preempt them by seizing the heights overlooking the harbor. On the evening of June 16, 1775, Prescott was ordered to take 1,200 men to Bunker Hill and cover Colonel Richard GRIDLEY's engineers as they constructed breastworks. He marched as ordered but, in concert with General Israel PUTNAM, Prescott disregarded his orders and fortified Breed's Hill instead, as it was closer to the water. This proved an unfortunate decision, tactically, for it placed the Americans beyond the ready reach of reinforcements, who declined to cross the peninsula under fire. But the next day British military leaders were astounded to observe the intricate network of entrenchments that had suddenly appeared overnight, as if by magic. General Thomas GAGE ordered General William HOWE to land a force on the peninsula and drive them off.

Prescott's regiment manned the main fortification on the crest of Bunker Hill, with his left wing covered by additional forces under Colonel John STARK. When ships of the Royal Navy began a heavy bombardment of his works in an attempt to drive the defenders off, he simply mounted the parapet and calmly paced about in his broad-brimmed hat to inspire the men. At length Howe made two determined attempts to attack Prescott's position head on and was bloodily repulsed by point-blank musketry. By the time Howe had reformed his soldiers for a third and final charge, the Americans had expended their ammunition and the British gained a lodgment in their works. The defenders wilted before this onslaught of cold steel, and Prescott fought back desperately with his sword, being one of the last officers to quit his post. He then returned to headquarters and offered to take back the hill with three fresh regiments, but Ward declined. Prescott's heroic stance, combined with the heavy casualties his men inflicted on the heretofore invincible redcoats, indelibly impressed Howe with the power of American defense works. He never again attacked them frontally.

On January 1, 1776, Prescott was inducted into the Continental ARMY as colonel of the 7th Massachusetts Continental Infantry. In this capacity he marched with General George WASHINGTON to New York and fought in several battles around the city. Thereafter the effects of an old farm injury persuaded him to abandon active field service, although he fought at Saratoga as a volunteer aide under General Horatio GATES. Prescott resumed his farming activities in Pepperell and also dabbled in local politics. In 1786 he denounced Shays's Rebellion and tendered his services to the state to help suppress it. Prescott died at Pepperell on October 13, 1795, hailed as the commander of American forces at Bunker Hill and among the Revolutionary War's earliest heroes.

Further Reading
Cray, Robert. "Bunker Hill Refought: Memory and Partisan Conflicts, 1775–1825," *Historical Journal of Massachusetts* 29, no. 1 (2001): 22–52.
Edgar, Gregory T. *Reluctant Break with Britain: From Stamp Act to Bunker Hill.* Bowie, Md.: Heritage Books, 1997.
Morrissey, Brendan. *Boston, 1775: The Shot Heard Round the World.* Westport, Conn.: Praeger, 2004.
Parker, Francis J. *Colonel William Prescott: The Commander in the Battle of Bunker Hill.* Boston: A. Williams & Co., 1875.

Schwartz, F. D. "The Battle of Bunker Hill," *American Heritage* 51, no. 3 (2000): 109–111.

Prevost, Augustin (1723–1786)
English military officer

Augustin Prevost was born in Geneva, Switzerland, on August 22, 1723, one of five brothers active in the long tradition of mercenary soldiering. After serving several years with the Dutch army, he transferred to the English in 1756 as part of the 60th Regiment, the Royal Americans, a unit specializing in light infantry tactics. In this capacity Prevost distinguished himself as a regimental officer and was severely wounded at Quebec on September 13, 1759, where a bullet heavily grazed his skull. Thereafter he became popularly known as Old Bullethead. In 1761 Prevost advanced to lieutenant colonel and fought in the sieges of Martinique and Havana. He then returned to England in 1763 to demobilize, but upon the outbreak of the Revolutionary War 12 years later, he raised a new battalion and shipped overseas as a full colonel to help defend East Florida. From his headquarters at St. Augustine, Prevost cobbled together scattered redcoats, LOYALISTS, and Native Americans in this military backwater and fought off numerous American incursions from Georgia. The fall of Savannah to Lieutenant Colonel Archibald CAMPBELL in December 1778 greatly improved his military options, and he marched north to join him. After capturing Fort Morris in January 1779, he learned that strong American forces under General Benjamin LINCOLN were gathering at Purysburg. Prevost then landed part of his forces behind the Americans to deflect their impending advance on Augusta and grant Campbell additional time to recruit Loyalists. At length stronger forces under General William MOULTRIE forced him to embark at Beaufort on February 3, 1779.

On that same day, Prevost became both major general and commander in chief of British forces in the south. Campbell, meanwhile, abandoned Augusta and was closely pursued by American forces under General John ASHE. Prevost decided to strike at Ashe before he could be reinforced by the main body under Lincoln, and on March 3, 1779, British forces directed by his son, Lieutenant Colonel Mark Prevost, attacked and completely routed the defenders at Briar Creek. He then followed up this success by marching north to threaten Charleston, South Carolina, and almost forced Governor John RUTLEDGE into signing a neutrality pact, but on May 3, 1779, superior forces under Lincoln and Count Kazimierz PULASKI forced him back into Georgia. The impasse continued several months until the appearance of Admiral Charles-Hector-Théodat, comte d'ESTAING, off the coast in September 1779. He promptly landed 5,000 soldiers and commenced a siege of SAVANNAH while awaiting 1,500 reinforcements under Lincoln. When d'Estaing demanded Prevost's surrender, the general requested a customary 24-hour truce to consider the proposal, then managed to slip in 800 additional soldiers under Lieutenant Colonel John Maitland

Major General Augustin Prevost led the British to victory at the Battle of Savannah. (*Bridgeman Art Library*)

for a total garrison of 3,000. The allies then closely invested Savannah and were making good progress when d'Estaing's mounting concerns about the onset of hurricane season prompted a direct assault. On October 9, 1779, French and American columns battered their way toward British fortifications at Spring Hill—exactly as Prevost had predicted—and were bloodily repulsed, losing over 750 men to a British loss of 155. D'Estaing then sailed away with his army while Lincoln, now heavily outnumbered, fell back to Charleston. Coming on the heels of the Franco-American defeat at Newport in August 1778, Prevost's seemingly easy success placed the young alliance under additional considerable strain. It also prompted General Henry CLINTON to begin organizing a bigger amphibious expedition against Charleston for the spring; Georgia remained firmly in British hands until nearly the end of the war.

Prevost's victory at Savannah marked the end of his military career, for he returned to England shortly thereafter and died in Hertfordshire on May 5, 1786. Like Frederick HALDIMAND, he was one of several professional Swiss mercenaries to fight with distinction in this war. His son, General George Prevost, was commander in chief of British forces in Canada during the War of 1812.

Further Reading
Freeman, H. Ronald. *Savannah under Siege: The Bloodiest Hour of the Revolution*. Savannah, Ga.: Freeport Pub., 2002.
Prevost, Augustin. "Journal of the Siege of Savannah in 1779, by General Prevost, Commanding the Town," *Southern Historical Association Publications* 1 (October 1897): 259–268.
Schafer, Daniel L. *St. Augustine's British Years, 1763–1784*. St. Augustine, Fla.: St. Augustine Historical Society, 2002.
Searcy, Martha C. *The Georgia-Florida Contest in the American Revolution, 1776–1778*. Tuscaloosa: University of Alabama Press, 1985.
Wainwright, Nicholas B. "Turmoil at Pittsburgh: Diary of Augustin Prevost, 1774," *Pennsylvania Magazine of History and Biography* 85, no. 2 (1961): 111–1162.

Wilson, David K. *The Southern Strategy: Britain's Conquest of South Carolina and Georgia, 1775–1780*. Columbia: University of South Carolina Press, 2005.

Princeton, Battle of (January 3, 1777)

British reaction to the American victory at TRENTON on December 26, 1776, was swift and strong. General Charles CORNWALLIS canceled plans to sail home and rode furiously from New York for 50 miles until reaching the main British encampment at Princeton, New Jersey. There he called in various detachments that boosted his strength to upward of 8,000 men and marched south to confront the impudent rebels. Prior to departing he detached 1,700 men of the 4th Brigade under Lieutenant Charles Mawhood to guard Princeton while General Alexander LESLIE marched another 1,200 to Maidenhead. Meanwhile, the victorious Americans under General George WASHINGTON had since recrossed the Delaware River back into New Jersey. They then began entrenching themselves along a series of low ridges behind Assumpink Creek near Trenton to await developments. Washington possessed 5,100 men and 40 cannon but, in so much as the bulk of his force was poorly trained militia, he felt unequal to confronting the British head on. To buy as much time as possible he dispatched light troops and riflemen under French volunteer General Alexis-Roche de Fermoy to harass and delay Cornwallis's approach. Fermoy soon abandoned the troops, but they were ably led by Colonel Edward HAND, who tied down the British at Shabbakonk Creek for nearly three hours. When they finally arrived before Assumpink Creek on January 2, 1777, Cornwallis made a few halfhearted attempts to cross in the fading daylight but called off the attack. With 5,000 veteran troops and Washington apparently backed against the Delaware River, he intended to attack and eliminate the Americans on the following day.

Cornwallis never had the chance to strike as planned. Washington, eager to maintain the strategic initiative, decided upon the bold expedient of tip-toeing around the British right flank at night and rapidly marching upon Princeton and New Brunswick, then lightly guarded. He summarized that quick raids here would net several hundred prisoners along with many valuable supplies. On the evening of January 2, 1777, he detailed 400 New Jersey militiamen to remain in camp, maintain the campfires, and give all appearances that the main army was still present. That evening he led his troops quietly westward, assisted by newly frozen roads that made marching much easier. Cornwallis was taken in by the facade and never stirred. By dawn on January 3, 1777, the Americans had made excellent progress and crossed Stony Creek to within two miles of their objective. At this juncture Washington dispatched an advance force of 350 men under General Hugh MERCER to guard the approaches to the Stony Creek bridge, thereby severing the British retreat. But while deploying his men, Mercer suddenly collided with Mawhood's brigade of three crack British regiments, simultaneously marching down the same road to join Cornwallis. A fierce engagement erupted in the woods surrounding Stony Creek bridge until Mawhood, realizing that the bulk of his opponents were riflemen lacking bayonets, ordered a charge with cold steel. The 17th Regiment quickly overturned Mercer's force, fatally wounding him, and also routed the newly arriving militia under Colonel Lambert Cadwalader. Suddenly, Washington galloped onto the scene leading Colonel Daniel Hitchcock's Continental brigade. Rallying his men, he led them in a concerted charge against Mawhood and emerged unscathed from a British volley delivered at 30 yards. This new influx of manpower stunned the redcoats and, while the 17th Regiment cut itself free at bayonet point, the remainder of his force fell back in confusion to Princeton. As Washington's entire force flooded into the town they were confronted by 200 British who had barricaded themselves in Nassau Hall on the Princeton College campus. A section of cannon under Captain Alexander HAMILTON was then brought up to flush the defenders out; it fired two rounds, and they surrendered en masse.

Washington had won another small but improbable victory in the face of seemingly insurmountable odds. Knowing that Cornwallis was probably fast approaching, he quickly gathered up his men and prisoners and marched immediately for the safety of Morristown in the highlands. The Americans departed Princeton just as the British advance guard approached the southern end of town. Anticipating that Washington intended to hit thinly guarded New Brunswick, Cornwallis then drove his men on a forced march all night and arrived there exhausted. The equally tired but victorious Americans then established their winter quarters for a well-deserved respite. The affair at Princeton, though relatively small, was also a clear-cut tactical triumph for the perpetually ragtag Americans. For a loss of 23 killed and 20 wounded, they inflicted 28 killed, 58 wounded, and 323 taken captive. The American Revolution, perilously close to extinction only two weeks before, had recovered a healthy beat at Princeton. The battle also further enhanced Washington's reputation for decisive, unexpected strokes.

Further Reading
Dwyer, William M. *The Day Is Ours! November 1776–January 1777: An Inside View of the Battles of Trenton and Princeton.* New York: Viking, 1983.
Fischer, David H. *Washington's Crossing.* New York: Oxford University Press, 2004.
Ketchum, Richard M. *The Winter Soldiers: The Battles for Trenton and Princeton.* New York: Henry Holt, 1999.
Lefkowitz, Arthur S. *The Long Retreat: The Calamitous American Defense of New Jersey, 1776.* Metuchen, N.J.: Upland Press, 1998.
Mitnick, Barbara J. *New Jersey in the American Revolution.* New Brunswick, N.J.: Rutgers University Press, 2005.
Shea, Patrick. " 'A Providential Change of Weather': The Princeton Campaign, 1777." Unpublished master's thesis, East Stroudsburg University, 2001.

privateering

At the time of the Revolutionary War the Royal Navy was the world's preeminent naval force, and the United States, with its handful of frigates, could not seriously contest Britain's control of the sea lanes. For this reason the Americans resorted to the time-honored practice of privateering, namely, the licensing of private armed vessels to serve as commerce raiders. This was envisioned as a cheap and readily available alternative to raising, training, and outfitting a conventional navy in wartime. On March 19, 1776, the Continental CONGRESS began formally issuing letters of marque and reprisal to commence privateering operations formally. The response in many port cities was overwhelmingly enthusiastic.

Privateers were basically reconditioned merchant vessels sporting up to 20 cannon for armament. Though armed, they were not designed to engage regular warships and usually depended on speed alone to escape dangerous predicaments. However, they were usually more than enough to capture unarmed or lightly defended vessels of the British merchant marine. Once a prize was taken, it was manned by members of the victorious crew and sailed to a friendly port. There the captured vessel was legally declared an enemy combatant by the Admiralty Court, and, along with its cargo, put up for auction and sold. The money accrued from such sales was then distributed among crew members according to rank. In practice, the enterprising and individualistic Americans were highly successful in privateering, although their motivation for going to sea was more skewed toward profit, not patriotism. But the lure of lucre frequently militated against other services as both the Continental ARMY and Continental NAVY, which offered much lower wages, competed for the pool of trained and willing manpower. Scores of individuals in port cities like Boston, Philadelphia, Baltimore, and Charleston made personal fortunes through privateering, which can also be seen as an agent for social advancement.

Ultimately, the Americans fielded around 1,700 privateers, representing an aggregate of 15,000 cannon and 55,000 crewmen. This was in addition to scores of vessels allotted to various state navies, which performed an identical service. The highest concentration of privateers was found in New England ports, which also enjoyed the longest traditions of maritime service. These daring mariners usually plied the waters of the West Indies and Gulf of St. Lawrence, which were favorite hunting grounds for American privateers and the source of lucrative prizes. Between 1775 and 1783 they accounted for around 2,200 British prizes worth an estimated £66 million. While not crippling to British maritime interests, this represented a considerable loss of property and, consequently, helped drive up the insurance rates by 30 percent and sometimes as much as 50 percent. Such increases, in turn, fostered a great deal of unhappiness among England's politically influential shipping and mercantile classes, and they applied pressure on Parliament for a peaceful termination of the conflict. In a strictly military sense, privateering had little influence on the overall conduct of the war, but it did force the Royal Navy to spread its resources thinly to guard against commerce raiding. It also complicated the British army's attempt to feed and equip itself at the end of a 3,000-mile supply line, especially after 1778, when the large and efficient French navy became a factor. So, compared to the celebrated but generally lackluster endeavors of the Continental navy, privateering constituted America's sole success at sea.

Privateering was also openly conducted by the British and especially LOYALISTS, usually out of New York or Jamaica. In New York the letters of marque and reprisal were issued by Governor William TRYON. Enemy privateers ultimately seized some 1,135 American vessels, which infringed upon the American ability to shuttle supplies along the coastline and conduct trade with Europe. And, in identical fashion, many Royal Navy sailors and British army deserters found their way onto privateers seeking better pay and living conditions unavailable to them elsewhere.

Further Reading
Crawford, Michael J., ed. *Autobiography of a Yankee Mariner: Christopher Prince and the American Revolution.* Washington, D.C.: Brassey's, 2002.

Dougher, Richard D. "Averse... to Remaining Idle Spectators: The Emergence of Loyalist Privateering in the American Revolution, 1775–1778." Unpublished Ph.D. diss., University of Maine, 2002.

Gilje, Paul A. *Liberty on the Waterfront: American Maritime Culture in the Age of Revolution.* Philadelphia: University of Pennsylvania, 2003.

Kelly, M. Ruth. *The Olmstead Case: Privateers, Property, and Politics in Pennsylvania, 1778–1810.* Selinsgrove, Pa.: Susquehanna University Press, 2005.

Macy, Thomas. *Hannah and the Nautilus: The Beginning of the American Revolution at Sea.* Beverly, Mass.: Beverly Historical Society, 2002.

Rodenberg, Frank. "The Richard Smith Affair and the Case of the Polly: Loyalty, Privateering, and Jurisdiction in the American Revolution." Unpublished master's thesis, Trinity College, 2002.

Proclamation of 1763

The English victory in North America after the French and Indian War, 1755–63, resulted in the acquisition of Canada, Florida, and a huge tract of land extending from the Appalachian Mountains to the Mississippi River. Traditionally, the English government had invoked a laissez-faire approach to western migration by allowing individual colonial governments to regulate such matters. But after 1763 the ministry of George GRENVILLE began contemplating a complete overhaul of imperial procedures to promote greater oversight and control. The bloody uprising by Chief Pontiac of the Ottawa in 1763 underscored the need for greater regulation of white encroachment to placate Native Americans and forestall the outbreak of future violence. It fell upon William PETTY, earl of Shelburne then secretary of state for the Southern Department, to draft and refine what became known as the Proclamation of 1763. This royal decree, issued by King GEORGE III on October 7, 1763, entailed a reorganization of lands recently acquired. New colonies were established in Quebec and in East and West Florida, while the boundaries of Georgia were extended to the St. Marys River. Henceforth British law and the right to political representation in local assemblies would be established. However, the proclamation also forbade further settlement over a line drawn down the Appalachian Mountains to preserve the integrity of Indian land. Furthermore, settlers already ensconced there were required to abandon their plots and relocate to the eastern side of the boundary. The British felt this was the quickest and most cost-effective way to preclude frontier violence—and the concommitant expense of large military garrisons. But from a colonial standpoint, it now became illegal to either purchase or speculate in Indian lands without the consent of the royal government. Many frontiersmen thus began resenting British interference in their affairs.

The Proclamation of 1763, for all its sweep, did not contain a mandatory enforcement mechanism and, consequently, was all but ignored by settlers who continued flooding the frontier to obtain Indian land, specially in Tennessee and Kentucky. Its stated intent was widely resented by rich and poor colonials alike, for the frontier represented both an opportunity to make money and an ability to escape creditors and debt. Colonial governments also viewed it as an infringement upon their internal affairs, especially for those who already possessed extensive claims to western lands. Statutes of the Proclamation of 1763 remained in effect until the passage of the QUEBEC ACT in 1774, which transferred most of the western lands to Canada. Whatever their original intent, such actions only reinforced popular and mounting perceptions that the British government was conspiring against its North American subjects.

Further Reading

Cook, Don. *The Long Fuse: How England Lost the American Colonies, 1760–1785.* New York: Atlantic Monthly Press, 1995.

Del Papa, Eugene M. "The Royal Proclamation of 1763: Its Effect upon Virginia and Companies," *Virginia Magazine of History and Biography* 83, no. 4 (1975): 405–411.

Fierst, John T. "The Struggle to Defend Indian Authority in the Ohio Valley–Great Lakes Region, 1763–1794." Unpublished master's thesis, University of Manitoba, 2001.

Hurd, Margaret J. "A Study of the Causes of the American Revolution and Their Origins." Unpublished master's thesis, California State University, Dominguez Hills, 2002.

Hutton, Woody. "The Ohio Indians and the Coming of the American Revolution in Virginia," *Journal of Southern History* 60, no. 3 (1994): 453–479.

Pulaski, Kazimierz (Casimir Pulaski) (1747–1779)
Polish military officer

Kazimierz Pulaski was born in Podolia, Poland, on March 4, 1747, son of Count Jozef Pulaski, a member of the minor gentry. Poland at that time was falling under the sway of its more powerful neighbors, Austria, Prussia, and Russia, who managed to manipulate the weak king Stanislaw II. Pulaski was well educated, and in 1768 he joined the Confederation of the Bars, established by his father to fight the Russians. He fought several successful actions, including a famous defense of the monastery of Czestochowa in 1771, but was eventually defeated and exiled to Turkey. Poland then suffered its first partitioning, and Pulaski spent several years among the Turks, inciting them to fight Russia. When this failed he subsequently sailed to France, penniless and broken, until he heard of the American Revolution. Fired by its idealism, he approached American agents Benjamin FRANKLIN and Silas DEANE in Paris about a possible military commission. Franklin supplied him with a letter of introduction, and Pulaski sailed to Boston in July 1777. After conferring with members of the Continental CONGRESS, he volunteered his services to General George WASHINGTON as an aide. In this capacity Pulaski fought well in the defeat of BRANDYWINE on September 11, 1777, and Washington recommended to Congress that it accept his services. Accordingly he was made a brigadier general and the first chief of the Continental cavalry.

Nobody questioned Pulaski's heroism under fire, nor his commitment to the revolution, but as an officer he was quarrelsome, headstrong, and overly sensitive to matters of rank. The difficulties arising from a hot temper were further compounded by his complete unfamiliarity with English. In the spring of 1778 he bickered with General Anthony WAYNE throughout a foraging expedition and threatened to resign. Washington persuaded him to remain and urged Congress to create his own fighting unit, the Pulaski Legion. This was largely recruited from HESSIAN deserters at Baltimore and numbered 200 infantry and 68 cavalry armed with lances. In its first battle at Little Egg Harbor on October 4, 1778, the Legion was surprised in camp by Major Patrick FERGUSON and lost heavily. The British had been alerted by one of Pulaski's own troopers, who deserted. Pulaski was then reassigned to a quiet sector along the upper Delaware River to prevent Indian raids, but he waxed indignant over garrison duty. He also court-martialed his subordinate Major Stephan MOYLAN over an alleged slight and threatened to resign again. Washington again interceded on his

Polish soldier Kazimierz Pulaski volunteered his services to the Continental army and was made brigadier general and first chief of the cavalry. *(Independence National Historical Park)*

behalf and transferred the troublesome leader and his legion to the south, where the locus of combat operations had shifted.

In the spring of 1779 Pulaski joined the army of General Benjamin LINCOLN in the vicinity of Charleston, South Carolina. At that time the city was being threatened by British forces under General Augustin PREVOST, but Pulaski bravely and foolishly attacked them while outnumbered on May 11, 1779, and was badly repulsed. Returning to the city, he encouraged the inhabitants not to surrender tamely and they held out until reinforcements under Lincoln arrived. Pulaski then joined the combined Franco-American army during the siege of SAVANNAH, Georgia. The French commander, Admiral Charles-Hector-Théodat, comte d'ESTAING, concerned by approaching hurricane season, decided to stake everything on a sudden attack launched October 9, 1779, and was heavily defeated. Pulaski, impetuous as ever, launched a full-scale cavalry charge against the British fortifications and was mortally wounded. Evacuated to the ship *Wasp*, he died two days later, on February 11, 1779, and was buried at sea. The remainder of his men subsequently transferred to the legion of Colonel Charles ARMAND for the rest of the war. Despite his haughty and querulous disposition, Pulaski was a fierce fighter who willingly sacrificed himself in battle. Consequently the U.S. Cavalry adopted guidons, or swallow-tailed flags, in red and white—the national colors of Poland. His name also adorns numerous towns and counties across the nation for which he died.

Further Reading

Holst, Donald. "Dress and Equipment of Pulaski's Independent Legion," *Military Collector and Historian* 16, no. 4 (1964): 97–103.

Kajencki, Francis C. *Casimir Pulaski: Cavalry Commander of the American Revolution.* El Paso, Tex.: Polonia, 2001.

Kemp, Franklin W. *A Nest of Rebel Pirates: The Account of an Attack by the British Forces on the Privateer Stronghold at Little Egg Harbor.* Batsto, N.J.: Batsto Citizens Committee, 1993.

Loescher, Burt G. *Washington's Eyes: The Continental Light Dragoons.* Fort Collins, Colo.: Old Army Press, 1977.

Obst, Peter J. "Myth and the Elusive Truth in the Story of Casimir Pulaski." Unpublished master's thesis, La Salle University, 2004.

Szymanski, Leszek. *Casimir Pulaski: A Hero of the American Revolution.* New York: Hippocrene Books, 1994.

Putnam, Israel (1718–1790)
American military officer

Israel Putnam was born in Salem, Massachusetts, on January 7, 1718, where he obtained little formal education. He relocated to Brooklyn, Connecticut, in 1740 and successfully pursued farming until the advent of the French and Indian War in 1755. Putnam initially joined the militia and performed scouting missions for Sir William Johnson at Crown Point, but he subsequently volunteered for service in Major Robert ROGERS's elite ranger battalion. He rendered valuable services throughout the ill-fated Ticonderoga campaign of General James Abercromby and was later caught by Indians. Faced with imminent torture, he was spared at the last moment by a generous French officer. Putnam was then exchanged and sailed with a relief expedition to Havana only to be shipwrecked on the Cuban coast. He was among the few survivors, returned in 1764, and marched with Colonel John Bradstreet to Detroit during Pontiac's rebellion. Back home Putnam became increasingly identified with the Patriot faction as tensions with Great Britain increased, and in 1766 he joined the local SONS OF LIBERTY. He then embarked on numerous exploring expeditions in West Florida and the Mississippi River to seek bounty land for military veterans. He resumed his revolutionary activities by serving on the local COMMITTEE OF CORRESPONDENCE and by 1775 also functioned as lieutenant colonel of the 11th Connecticut Regiment. According to folklore, Putnam, upon hearing of fighting at Lexington and CONCORD, mounted his horse and rode straight to Cambridge, Massachusetts, covering the 100 miles in 24 hours. While encamped there he was promoted to brigadier general of Connecticut troops under General Artemas WARD. In light of his age and military reputation, the burly leader was popularly regarded as Old Put.

On June 16, 1775, Ward instructed troops under Colonels John STARK and Samuel PRESCOTT to seize the high ground on BUNKER HILL overlooking Charlestown Harbor. Putnam then intervened and convinced Prescott to fortify nearby Breed's Hill instead, which was closer to the harbor. This act brought a sharp response from the British garrison of Boston, which attacked the Americans on June 17, 1775, and defeated them after a sanguine struggle. Just before the onslaught Putnam issued his most famous command, "Men, you are all marksmen— don't one of you fire until you see the whites of their eyes." He conducted himself with characteristic bravery during the affair and consequently became one of four new major generals in the Continental ARMY. Putnam's elevation to high command was warmly greeted by his fellow New Englanders, for he enjoyed a reputation as utterly fearless in battle, but proved incapable of high command. He followed General George WASHINGTON back to New York, where he assumed command of General John SULLIVAN's division. Unfortunately, Putnam did not have sufficient time to familiarize himself thoroughly with the terrain he defended. On August 27, 1776, General William HOWE noticed a gap in the American line and completely outflanked Putnam, driving his men back to Brooklyn Heights. After this defeat Washington entrusted him with the defense of Philadelphia but became disillusioned by his tardy response for troops during the PRINCETON campaign. Putnam was diplomatically removed from active field service and sent to the Hudson Highlands of New York, a relatively quiet sector, in May 1777. That October he failed to reinforce General James CLINTON and George CLINTON in time to prevent the capture of Forts Montgomery and Clinton by British forces under General Henry CLINTON. A court-martial exonerated him of any misconduct, but Washington again assigned him to a secondary sector.

For the next two years Putnam fulfilled recruiting service in Connecticut from his headquarters at West Greenwich. This region was subject to persistent LOYALIST raids conducted by Governor William TRYON of New York, and on one occasion Putnam courageously spurred his horse straight down a precipice to escape capture. He suffered a stroke in December 1777 that effectively ended his military career. Putnam, by dint of his military activities—and perhaps in spite of them—remained a popular icon and folk hero throughout Connecticut. He died at Pomfret on May 29, 1790.

Further Reading

Callahan, North. *Connecticut's Revolutionary War Leaders*. Chester, Conn.: Pequot Press, 1973.

Cody, Robert M. "The Special Defense and Safety of This Colony: Revolutionary War Actions in Connecticut, 1777–1781." Unpublished master's thesis, Southern Connecticut State University, 2000.

Gallagher, John. *The Battle of Brooklyn, 1776*. New York: Sarpedon, 1995.

Morrissey, Brendan. *New York, 1776: The Continentals' First Battles*. Oxford: Osprey, 2004.

Niven, John. *Connecticut Hero? Israel Putnam*. Hartford: American Revolutionary Bicentennial Commission of Connecticut, 1977.

Putnam, Hamilton S. *Country on Fire: Israel Putnam and the Colonial Struggle for Survival, 1755–1765*. Concord, N.H.: H. S. Putnam, 1974.

Putnam, Rufus (1738–1824)
American military officer

Rufus Putnam was born in Sutton, Massachusetts, on April 9, 1738, a younger cousin of Israel PUTNAM. He received a rudimentary education and was apprenticed to a millwright until he joined the militia in 1757 as an ensign. Putnam performed useful services in the Lake Champlain region and he gradually developed an interest in military engineering. He resettled in Brookline in 1765 to take up farming and surveying. In 1773 he accompanied his cousin on an extensive trip to examine

Rufus Putnam was responsible for engineering the fortifications on Dorchester Heights in Boston that protected the Continental army from British fire and forced them to evacuate the city. *(Independence National Historic Park)*

lands in Florida and along the Mississippi River granted to veterans of the last war. Putnam rejoined the militia as part of Colonel David Brewster's Massachusetts Regiment after Lexington and CONCORD, where he functioned as lieutenant colonel. In March 1776 he was responsible for erecting fortifications upon Dorchester Heights in Boston. Due to the frozen ground, he resorted to the use of chandeliers, or movable wooden curtains, to shield the work crews from British fire. His good work forced General William HOWE to evacuate the city as of March 17, 1776, and Putnam subsequently accompanied General George WASHINGTON to New York City. There Putnam erected numerous fortifications upon Brooklyn Heights that stymied General Howe after his significant victory on LONG ISLAND in August 1776.

The Continental CONGRESS appointed Putnam chief engineer with the rank of colonel in the Continental ARMY, but he found his department too unorganized and pressed the legislators for a separate corps. When they failed to comply he resigned from his position that December.

Putnam subsequently served as colonel of the 5th Massachusetts Continental Infantry and was assigned to the brigade of General John NIXON. In this capacity he was actively engaged in military affairs at Saratoga throughout 1777. The following year Putnam was ordered to survey and construct fortifications near West Point, New York, and on July 16, 1779, he assisted General Anthony WAYNE during the storming of Stony Point. In 1782 he served as a commissioner tasked with settling claims for the inhabitants of New York City. Putnam finished his wartime service in the Hudson Highlands, and in March 1783 he framed the infamous address at the NEWBURGH CONSPIRACY to protest congressional neglect of the army. That same year he gained promotion to brigadier general before mustering out in November.

After the war Putnam farmed near Rutland, Massachusetts, and in 1786 he joined the staff of General Benjamin LINCOLN during the suppression of Shays's Rebellion. He also accepted a congressional appointment to survey lands in the newly acquired Ohio valley for the purposes of distributing it to veterans. In March 1786 Putnam helped to found the Ohio Company, and two years later he led the first group of colonists to the settlement of Adelphia (Marietta) on the north bank of the Ohio River. In March 1790 President Washington made Putnam a judge in the Northwest Territory, and two years later he became a brigadier general to assist General Wayne in peace negotiations with the Indians. Washington then named him the nation's first surveyor general as of October 1796, in spite of his deficiency in mathematics. President Thomas JEFFERSON removed him from that post in September 1803, after which he bore an increasingly important political role in the new state of Ohio. During the constitutional convention of the year previous, his influence proved essential for keeping slavery out of that territory. More competent than distinguished, Putnam died at Marietta on May 4, 1824. At the time he was the only surviving Revolutionary War general next to the marquis de LAFAYETTE.

Further Reading

Buell, Rowena, ed. *The Memoirs of Rufus Putnam and Certain Official Papers and Correspondence.* Boston: Houghton, Mifflin, 1903.

Buzzaird, Raleigh B. "Washington's Favorite Engineer," *Military Engineer* 40, (March 1948): 115–118.

Cayton, Andrew R. "The Contours of Power in a Frontier Town: Marietta, Ohio," *Journal of the Early Republic* 6, no. 2 (1986): 103–126.

Hutslar, Donald A. "Campus Martius," *Timeline* 18, no. 1 (2001): 2–13.

Walker, Paul K. *Engineers of Independence: A Documentary History of the Army Engineers in the American Revolution, 1775–1783.* Washington, D.C.: Historical Division, Office of the Chief of Engineers, 1981.

Walton, Frank L. "The Ride of Colonel Rufus Putnam," *Yonkers Historical Bulletin* 14, no. 1 (1967):10–13.

Quartering Act (1765, 1774)

To help maintain large numbers of military troops in North America, Parliament passed the Quartering Act on May 3, 1765, to ensure adequate housing and supplies for its forces. This was done at the behest of General Thomas GAGE, then commander in chief of North America, who was simply expanding upon the earlier Mutiny Act to improve the living conditions of British soldiers. The act stipulated that his majesty's forces were to be billeted in either barracks or vacated public buildings but restricted them from private residences. However, Americans became somewhat annoyed by new obligations for funding through local legislatures. Most colonies willingly complied with the law but in January 1766 the New York assembly staunchly refused to raise the money. Such recalcitrance roiled many in Parliament, still smarting over repeal of the STAMP ACT, so they passed the New York Suspending Act on July 2, 1767, which dismissed the assembly until it complied with the Quartering Act. Upon further reflection, New York politicians agreed to provide limited funding to house various garrisons in December 1769 and were allowed to reconvene.

Because the Quartering Act was slated to expire in two years it was periodically renewed over the next decade with little fanfare. In 1766 its provisions were modified slightly by including public houses and any unoccupied homes for billeting. All told, most colonials were far more incensed by new revenue measures approved by Parliament than by the money necessary to house his majesty's forces. The only outbreak of violence associated with the Quartering Act occurred on January 19, 1770, in the so-called Battle of GOLDEN HILL, when the New York assembly voted funds necessary to sustain the troops.

By 1774 the political atmosphere was highly charged; when the Quartering Act was again renewed, Americans viewed it as part and parcel of the ongoing COERCIVE ACTS. This time it allowed a local commander to choose the location where his men were to be billeted in order to prevent colonial assemblies from quartering troops far from where they were actually needed. Furthermore, if barracks and vacated buildings were not available, the soldiers could now legally seek shelter and accommodations in private homes. The Quartering Act was originally intended to reassert royal authority in Massachusetts, but on June 2, 1774, its provisions were extended to include all thirteen colonies. Resistance to the Quartering Act and the three Coercive Acts gave greater impetus for the Continental CONGRESS finally to convene in Philadelphia that September and address all its grievances.

Further Reading

Cook, Don. *The Long Fuse: How England Lost the American Colonies, 1760–1785.* New York: Atlantic Monthly Press, 1995.

Edgar, Gregory T. *Reluctant Break with Britain: From Stamp Act to Bunker Hill.* Bowie, Md.: Heritage Books, 1997.
Gerlach, Don R. "A Note on the Quartering Act of 1774," *New England Quarterly* 39, no. 1 (1966): 80–88.
Shy, John. *Toward Lexington: The Role of the British Army in the Coming of the American Revolution.* Princeton, N.J.: Princeton University Press, 1965.
Thomas, Peter D. *Revolution in America: Britain in the Colonies, 1763–1776.* Cardiff, U.K.: University of Wales Press, 1992.
Zimmerman, John J. "Governor Denny and the Quartering Act of 1756," *Pennsylvania Magazine of History and Biography* 91, no. 3 (1967): 266–281.

Quebec, attack on (December 31, 1775)

In June 1775 the Continental CONGRESS authorized an invasion of Quebec (Canada), with a view toward possibly assimilating it as the 14th state. To facilitate this General Philip J. SCHUYLER began assembling an army at Fort Ticonderoga, New York, for a rapid march up the Lake Champlain corridor. His health failed en route, so command devolved upon General Richard MONTGOMERY, a popular and effective officer. The Americans, poorly trained, wretchedly equipped, and badly supplied, managed to capture Fort Chambly on October 19, 1775, before pushing on to the stone fortress at Fort Saint Johns, 20 miles south of Montreal. Dogged defenders kept Montgomery occupied until November 12, 1775, when artillery brought up from Fort Chambly induced the garrison to surrender. The British under Governor-General Guy CARLETON then fell back to the mighty bastion of Quebec City to entrench and await reinforcements. Concurrently, a second American offensive, spearheaded by the highly capable colonel Benedict ARNOLD, was fulfilling an epic trek through the Maine wilderness. Enduring incredible hardships, Arnold browbeat his command northward until they emerged opposite Quebec City on November 9, 1775. At that time the Americans mustered only 700 ragged, half-starved soldiers, while Carleton commanded over 1,200 regulars, sailors, and militia. On November 19, 1775, Arnold ferried his men across the St. Lawrence River and tried unsuccessfully to bluff the defenders into submission before establishing a loose siege of the city. On December 1 he was reinforced by Montgomery, who arrived with another 375 soldiers. Both men faced the threat of expiring enlistments on January 1, 1776, which would eviscerate their already puny forces, so they elected to take Quebec by a coup de main beforehand. Because the Upper Town was strongly defended by a massive stone citadel, they chose to storm the less fortified Lower Town.

Quebec City, by dint of its high elevation, stone walls, and 200 heavy cannon, was the strongest fortified city in North America. The Americans eventually settled upon a two-pronged strategy to overcome their scanty numbers: Arnold was to attack from the north while Montgomery advanced from the south. The night of December 31, 1775, bore down freezing cold but American movements were conveniently masked by a howling blizzard. At approximately 4 A.M. a signal rocket indicated that both Arnold and Montgomery were in position, and they pushed forward into the snow. Unfortunately, the British were also alerted and made ready to receive them. Montgomery's column, the smaller of the two, groped along the darkness to Point Diamond, where it encountered barricaded streets and other obstacles. The Americans overcame the first barricade and entered the town with Montgomery at their head. While approaching a fortified house, the British defenders unleashed a torrent of musketry and cannon shot into the oncoming throng, killing Montgomery and several followers. The loss of the advance party took the starch out of the Americans, and they unceremoniously fell back, abandoning their commander's body in the snow.

Meanwhile, Arnold led a strong column down from the north and attacked the palace gate. The Americans were fortunate enough to drag along two cannon in support, but both were eventually abandoned. They nonetheless clawed through the heavily barricaded streets until being fired upon. Arnold received a serious leg wound and was borne to the rear as command reverted to Colonel

Daniel MORGAN. He led his ragtag ensemble in hand-to-hand fighting that overcame two barricades and was preparing to storm a third when subordinates urged him to pause and allow reinforcements to come up. Carleton used this interval to throw his own column of 200 men and strike at Morgan's rear, and the attackers collapsed. For a loss of five killed and 13 wounded, the British handily repelled this desperate assault, killing 30 and capturing 426, including Morgan. The surviving Americans had no recourse but to resume their shivering blockade of the city, while Carleton remained warmly ensconced, awaiting reinforcements destined to arrive that spring. Despite impressive marches and performances by two very determined leaders, Canada had been preserved for the British Empire.

Further Reading

Gabriel, Michael P., ed. *Quebec during the American Invasion, 1775–1776: The Journal of Francois Baby, Gabriel Taschereau, and Jenkin Williams.* East Lansing: Michigan State University Press, 2005.

Hatch, Robert M. *Thrust for Canada: The American Attempt on Quebec, 1775–1776.* Boston: Houghton Mifflin, 1979.

Lawson, Philip. *The Imperial Challenge: Quebec and Britain in the Age of the American Revolution.* Cheektowaga, N.Y.: McGill-Queen's University Press, 1989.

Morrissey, Brendan. *Quebec, 1775: The American Invasion of Canada.* Oxford: Osprey, 2003.

Pearson, Michael. "The Siege of Quebec, 1775–1776," *American Heritage* 23, no. 2 (1972): 8–15, 104–108.

Stanley, George F. G. *Canada Invaded, 1775–1776.* Toronto: Hakkert, 1973.

Quebec Act (1774)

England's victory in the French and Indian War, 1754–63, resulted in the acquisition of Quebec (Canada), along with 65,000 French-speaking inhabitants. Nearly a decade lapsed before the government under Lord Frederick NORTH could enact legislation to bring that region politically in line with other parts of the empire. In many respects the unique circumstances surrounding the province required a highly nuanced approach not applied elsewhere. Quebec acquired its initial English governance through provisions of the PROCLAMATION OF 1763, which allowed for the imposition of English law and a representative assembly. But a decade later, because English-speaking inhabitants of Quebec constituted only 1 percent of the population, Governor-General Guy CARLETON prevailed on the North ministry to adopt legislation more responsive to political and social realties there. Hence the Quebec Act, when it passed on June 22, 1763, was a sober, realistic compromise in light of that province's competing interests. First, it established a formal regime consisting of a government-appointed governor-general and an appointed—not elected—assembly. Second, it split the difference on legal aspects, preserving English law for criminal cases but also restoring French law and tradition in civil matters. Third, it granted complete religious freedom to Quebec's preponderantly Roman Catholic population. Fourth, and most important from an American perspective, it extended the physical boundaries of Quebec down through the Ohio River valley and west to the Mississippi River. This had the net effect of sealing off Britain's 13 North American colonies behind the Appalachian Mountains—something the Proclamation Act of 1763 had attempted earlier and failed.

Given the spiraling political hostility of colonial Americans in 1774, the Quebec Act was construed as simply the latest installment of the punitive COERCIVE ACTS and further proof that the royal government warred against their rights and liberties. Colonies such as Massachusetts, Connecticut, Pennsylvania, and Virginia, which had extensive and abiding land claims in the Trans-Appalachian region, resented this intrusion of royal authority on the frontier, for it precluded their ability to purchase and speculate in Indian land. Moreover, the indelibly Protestant majorities in the colonies recoiled at this newfound tolerance toward Catholicism, and many feared that the British were resurrecting the defunct French province. In concert with the Boston Port Act and the QUARTERING ACT, the Quebec Act provided greater impetus for the Continental CONGRESS to convene in Philadelphia that fall. In October 1774 this body ratcheted up tensions by adopted the Suffolk Resolves, which formally condemned the Quebec Act and urged the colonies to resist British tyranny by force, if necessary.

Further Reading
Cook, Don. *The Long Fuse: How England Lost its American Colonies, 1760–1785.* New York: Atlantic Monthly Press, 1995.
Lawson, Philip. *The Imperial Challenge: Quebec and Britain in the Age of the American Revolution.* Cheektowaga, N.Y.: McGill-Queen's University Press, 1989.
Neatby, Hilda. *The Quebec Act: Protest and Policy.* Toronto: Prentice Hall, 1972.
Stanbridge, Karen A. "British Catholic Policy in Eighteenth-Century Ireland and Quebec." Unpublished Ph.D. diss., University of Western Ontario, 1998.
Thomas, Peter D. *Revolution in America: Britain in the Colonies, 1763–1776.* Cardiff: University of Wales Press, 1992.

Quincy, Josiah (1744–1775)
American politician

Josiah Quincy was born in Boston, Massachusetts, on February 23, 1744, the son of a wealthy merchant. Raised in Braintree, his wealth afforded an excellent education, and he attended Harvard College. After receiving his bachelor's in 1763 and master's in 1766, Quincy studied law under noted jurist Oxenbridge Thacher and, following Thacher's death two years later, he assumed his practice at the age of 21. In short order he established himself as one of Boston's leading attorneys and was gradually drawn into the radical coterie of Samuel ADAMS and John HANCOCK. A gifted writer, Quincy composed erudite essays, newspaper articles, and pamphlets on behalf of his associates against the regime of Governor Thomas HUTCHINSON, winning plaudits for lucidity and persuasiveness. His followers were therefore somewhat dismayed when he joined John ADAMS in defending Captain Thomas Preston and eight British troops accused of murder in the BOSTON MASSACRE of March 5, 1770. Quincy, however, entertained no such qualms and felt that the rights of all individuals, no matter how unpalatable to public opinion, must be protected. When Quincy and Adams managed to acquit most of the soldiers, fellow Bostonians celebrated their victory in upholding the rule of law.

As relations with Great Britain gradually deteriorated, Quincy became commensurately more active in Patriot politics. In 1772 he served on the Boston COMMITTEE OF CORRESPONDENCE and also worked with James OTIS on writing, publishing, and distributing political literature throughout the countryside. The following year he traveled extensively throughout the colonies as a Massachusetts emissary to explain and clarify their resistance. Quincy lauded the BOSTON TEA PARTY of December 1773 and reacted very strongly against the COERCIVE ACTS with his polemic *Observations on the Act of Parliament Commonly Called the Boston Port-Bill; with Thoughts on Civil Society and Standing Armies* (1774). In it he attacked Parliament's punishment of an entire colony for the handiwork of a few individuals and held that armed soldiers were a potential threat to personal liberties. His standing among fellow Patriot thinkers was such that in September 1774 they dispatched him to England to confer with high British officials. Quincy arrived in London in September 1774 and met with Lord Frederick NORTH and William PETTY, Lord Shelburne, among others, but he failed to win any concessions. He departed for Boston on March 16, 1775, and sailed 41 days before dying of tuberculosis on April 26, 1775, aged 30 years. Quincy never lived to see the revolution he so passionately sought to foment, but he nonetheless made indelible contributions to its legal and intellectual underpinnings.

Further Reading
Coquillette, Daniel R. "First Flower—The Earliest Law Reports and the Extraordinary Josiah Quincy, Jr. (1744–1775)," *Suffolk University Law Review* 30, no. 1 (1996): 1–34.

———, and Neil York, eds. *The Josiah Quincy Papers,* 4 vols. Charlottesville: Published for the Colonial Society of Massachusetts by the University Press of Virginia, 2005.

McFarland, Philip J. *The Brave Bostonians: Hutchinson, Quincy, Franklin, and the Coming of the American Revolution.* Boulder, Colo.: Westview Press, 1998.

Nash, George H. "From Radicalism to Revolution: The Political Career of Josiah Quincy, Jr.," *American Antiquarian Society Proceedings* 79, no. 2 (1979): 253–290.

Quincy, Josiah. "Journal of Josiah Quincy, Jun., during his Voyage and Residence in England from September 28th, 1774, to March 3rd, 1775," *Massachusetts Historical Society Proceedings* 50 (1916/1917): 433–470.

Shaw, Peter. *American Patriots and the Rituals of Revolution.* Cambridge, Mass.: Harvard University Press, 1981.

Rall, Johann (ca. 1720–1776)
Hessian military officer

Johann Rall was born in the German principality of Hessen-Kassel around 1720 and joined the army at an early age. He fought well throughout the Seven Years' War, 1756–1763, and thereafter tendered his services to the Russian Crown for additional combat against the Turks from 1768 to 1774. In 1775 his monarch offered to rent several thousand soldiers to Great Britain for use in the Revolutionary War, and Rall, now colonel of a grenadier battalion bearing his name, accompanied the Second Division under General Wilhelm von KNYPHAUSEN to America. There he formed part of the army under General William HOWE and performed well under fire at the Battles of LONG ISLAND and Fort Washington. The raw, badly equipped Americans seemed incapable of withstanding the toughly disciplined HESSIANS in the field, and Rall became utterly contemptuous of them. As General George WASHINGTON led his defeated army across snowbound New Jersey in December 1776, it appeared to all purposes that the revolution had reached its terminus. Howe then called off his pursuit for the winter and established a chain of strongpoints across the state while the bulk of the army withdrew into winter quarters. It fell upon Rall to command at TRENTON with 1,600 veterans, his being the outpost closest to American forces in Pennsylvania. Howe's choice of leaders here was peculiar, for he was known to hold the hard-drinking Hessian's leadership in low regard. Nonetheless, as his men settled in for the winter, several of Rall's officers suggested that they fortify Trenton to guard against any possible surprise attack. He responded by daring the Americans to make the attempt and focused his attention toward traditional holiday celebrations.

Shortly before Christmas day, General James GRANT sent a messenger to Rall that the Americans were possibly preparing a strike upon Trenton and that he should be on the alert. The Hessian scoffed at the notion and dismissed such intelligence as alarmist, trusting in his iron men and their steel bayonets to resolve any crisis. But on the morning of December 26, 1777, freezing Hessian sentries were startled to observe Washington's army of 2,400 men bearing down on them in the predawn darkness. The alarm went out, and the soldiers mustered, but Rall, apparently still reeling from the previous night's revelries, could scarcely mount his horse. The defenders were then hit by concentrated artillery fire as the massed Americans charged down the streets of Trenton. Rall attempted to rally his flagging command in an orchard but was shot down and mortally wounded. Within two hours Washington had clinched an impressive victory, capturing 918 Hessians, hundreds of muskets, and valuable supplies for a handful of casualties. The victorious leader also paid Rall a bedside visit before he died on December 27, 1776. He was not the only professional, European-trained soldier to underestimate his adversaries; within 10 days General Charles CORNWALLIS would endure a similar humiliation from this same ragtag ensemble at PRINCETON.

Further Reading
Burgoyne, Bruce E. *The Trenton Commanders: Johann Gottlieb Rall and George Washington as Noted in Hessian Diaries.* Bowie, Md.: Heritage Books, 1996.
Cunningham, John T. *With Him All Is Over.* Trenton: New Jersey Tercentenary Commission, 1962.
Fisher, David H. *Washington's Crossing.* New York: Oxford University Press, 2004.
Miller, William P. "Victory by a Precise Plan," *Military History* 8, no. 6 (1991): 42–49.
Stephens, Thomas R. " 'In Deepest Submission': The Hessian Mercenary Troops of the American Revolution." Unpublished Ph.D. diss., Texas A & M University, 1998.
Wiederhold, Andreas. "Colonel Rall at Trenton," *Pennsylvania Magazine of History and Biography* 22 (1898): 462–467.

Rathbun, John P. (1746–1782)
American naval officer

John Peck Rathbun was born in Exeter, Rhode Island, in 1746 and went to sea at an early age. He was among the first lieutenants commissioned in the Continental NAVY and was initially assigned to the 12-gun sloop *Providence*. Rathbun sailed with Commodore Esek HOPKINS on his raid upon the Bahamas in the spring of 1776 and remained onboard when command shifted to Captain John Paul JONES. After briefly serving with Jones aboard the brig *Alfred*, he was promoted to captain as of February 15, 1777, and returned to take charge of the *Providence*. On the night of January 27, 1778, Rathbun made a daring second raid on the Bahamas, capturing Forts Nassau and Montagu without a shot and making off with valuable gunpowder and supplies. On the morning of January 30, he also seized three unsuspecting British brigs in the harbor, along with numerous American prisoners. In 1779 Rathbun assumed control of the frigate *Queen of France* and accompanied *Providence* and *Ranger* as part of Commodore Abraham WHIPPLE's squadron. On July 18, 1779, while off Newfoundland, they encountered a heavily escorted convoy of merchantmen headed for Britain. As a dense fog settled, *Queen of France* worked its way into the midst of the formation and next to a transport, which assumed it was a British warship. He quickly captured that vessel while *Ranger* and *Providence* followed suit: In all, 10 prizes were seized worth over $1 million—one of the largest hauls of the entire war. In the spring of 1780 Rathbun followed Whipple south to partake in the siege of CHARLESTON. Positioned in the Ashley River, he was tasked with preventing British infantry from crossing and storming the city. As the siege tightened, Rathbun sank the *Queen of France* in order to block a river crossing while transferring its armament ashore. He was taken prisoner when Charleston surrendered on May 12, 1780.

Rathbun was quickly paroled and dispatched to New England in search of another command. However, at this juncture the Continental navy had been all but driven from the sea, so he transferred to the Massachusetts state privateer *Wexford* on August 4, 1781. In this capacity he sailed for the English Channel and was captured by the 32-gun frigate HMS *Recovery* on September 29, 1781. Rathbun was interned at Kinsale Prison, Ireland, for a brief period before transferring to Mill Prison, Plymouth. He died there of illness on June 20, 1782, at the age of 36, one of the more talented sailors in the American service. His has since been commemorated by two U.S. Navy destroyers.

Further Reading
Atkinson, Amalia I. "Captain Rathbun's Last Voyage," *New England Historical and Genealogical Register* 105 (July 1961): 164–169.
Cook, Fred J. *What Manner of Men: Forgotten Heroes of the American Revolution.* New York: William Morrow, 1959.
Morgan, William J. *Captains to the Northward: The New England Captains in the Continental Navy.* Barre, Mass.: Barre Gazette, 1959.

Rathbun, Frank H. "Rathbun's Raid on Nassau," *U.S. Naval Institute Proceedings* 96 (November 1970): 40–47.

Rider, Hope S. *Valour Fore & Aft: Being the Adventures of America's First Naval Vessel.* Annapolis, Md.: Naval Institute Press, 1975.

Trevett, John. "Journal of John Trevett, U.S.N., 1774–1782," *Rhode Island Historical Magazine* 6, nos. 1–4 (1885): 72–74, 106–110, 194–199, 271–278; 7, nos. 3–5 (1887): 38–45, 151–160, 205–208.

Rawdon, Francis (1754–1826)
English military officer

Francis Rawdon was born in County Down, Ireland, on December 9, 1754, a son of the earl of Moira. While passing through Oxford he joined the army in 1771 as a lieutenant of the 5th Regiment and interrupted his studies four years later to become part of the Boston garrison. On June 17, 1775, Rawdon fought conspicuously at the Battle of BUNKER HILL, commanding a company after his captain had been wounded. He then gained appointment as aide to General Henry CLINTON and fought in various battles around New York, rising there to lieutenant colonel. In 1778 Clinton authorized Rawdon to raise a battalion of LOYALISTS in Philadelphia, and he subsequently became colonel of the Volunteers of Ireland. This highly disciplined unit, containing a high number of deserters from the Continental ARMY, was one of the best provincial units in British service. In June 1778 Rawdon won additional laurels for leading his men into action at MONMOUTH, and Clinton granted him further distinction by making him adjutant general of the army at 25. However, Clinton's oftentimes irascible disposition grated upon Rawdon, and in 1779 he transferred from the general's staff and was replaced by Major John ANDRE. He therefore remained behind in New York during Clinton's expedition to South Carolina in December 1779.

Rawdon was eventually summoned south during the siege of CHARLESTON and later joined the army of General Charles CORNWALLIS once Clinton returned to New York. In this capacity he bore a conspicuous role at the victory of CAMDEN on August 16, 1780, and capably led the British left flank against veteran Continental infantry. Over the next nine months he commanded a series of strongpoints throughout the Carolinas, and in the spring of 1781, after Cornwallis elected to invade Virginia, Rawdon received the local rank of brigadier general and authority as commander of the Carolinas and Georgia; he was only 27 at the time. The American army under General Nathanael GREENE was then overrunning the interior of South Carolina, and on April 25, 1781, he

British general Francis Rawdon was popularly regarded as the "boy general" of the Revolutionary War because of his youth. *(The Royal Collection Picture Library)*

brought 1,500 battle-hardened veterans to within a few miles of Rawdon's main base near the old Camden battle site. Rawdon no sooner learned of this development than he rustled up 900 soldiers and marched to engage them. On April 25, 1781, he audaciously attacked Greene at Hobkirk's Hill, marching first along a narrow front and then swinging his flanks outward to engulf the Americans. Greene's veterans fought back gamely until the 1st Maryland Continental Infantry Regiment suddenly bolted, precipitating a retreat. Rawdon pursued the Americans sharply and Greene, who intervened personally to save his cannon, was fortunate to have escaped disaster. Casualties in this stout action were nearly even, with the British losing 38 killed and 220 wounded to an American tally of 25 killed, 108 wounded, and 136 missing. But, because Rawdon could not readily replace his losses, he abandoned the field and withdrew to Charleston. In June 1781 he sortied briefly to the relief of Fort Ninety Six, forcing Greene to lift his costly siege, but later abandoned that post as too exposed.

In July 1781 Rawdon engendered considerable controversy and antipathy for the British cause by ordering the execution of Colonel Isaac HAYNE for allegedly violating his parole. Greene angrily threatened to hang a British officer of equal rank in retaliation, and Rawdon's rashness only promoted a greater resistance to British rule throughout South Carolina. Ill and worn out after seven years of continuous campaigning, Rawdon sailed for England that month only to be captured by a French privateer. From the deck of this vessel he observed the defeat of Admiral Thomas GRAVES at the Battle of the Virginia Capes, September 10, 1781, which sealed the fate of Cornwallis's army at YORKTOWN. Rawdon remained a prisoner at Brest until his exchange in 1782. Upon returning to England he was appointed aide to King GEORGE III and joined the peerage as Lord Rawdon. Over the next 40 years he continued on in the British army, rising to general. In 1813 he became governor-general of India and capably administered his charge for 13 years. In 1824 Rawdon became governor-general of Malta, where he died on November 28, 1826. This distinguished battle captain was interred within the ancient stone walls of his command. Because of his youth and the various high commands he fulfilled in America, Rawdon was popularly regarded as the "boy general" of the Revolutionary War.

Further Reading
Gordon, John W. *South Carolina and the American Revolution: A Battlefield History.* Columbia: University of South Carolina Press, 2003.
Historical Manuscripts Commission. *Report on the Manuscripts of the Late Reginald Rawdon Hastings*, 4 vols. London: H. M. Stationary Office, 1928–47.
Nelson, Paul D. *Francis Rawdon-Hastings, Marquess of Hastings: Soldier, Peer of the Realm, Governor-general of India.* Madison, N.J.: Fairleigh Dickinson University Press, 2005.
Ross-of-Bladensburg, John F. G. *The Marquess of Hastings.* Oxford: Clarendon Press, 1900.
Snoddy, Oliver. "The Volunteers of Ireland," *Irish Sword* 7 (Winter 1965): 147–159.
Troxler, Carole W. "Origins of the Rawdon Loyalist Settlement," *Nova Scotia Historical Review* 8, no. 1 (1988): 62–76.

Red Jacket (ca. 1756–1830)
Seneca chief

Red Jacket was born Otetiani ("Always Prepared") to the Wolf clan of the Seneca nation, then the largest tribe within the Iroquois Confederacy. Nothing is known of his early life, but, by 1777 he had adopted the name Sagoyewatha ("He Causes Them to Be Awake") and gained prominence as a civil chief. At that time the Revolutionary War had been raging for two years, and up until that time Governor-general Guy CARLETON had striven assiduously to keep the Indians neutral. Sagoyewatha had been employed by the British as a courier and received numerous red jackets as a reward. Conspicuously adorned, he became more popularly known among whites as Red Jacket. In the spring of 1777 the British orchestrated a tribal council at Oswego, New York, and now urged the Iroquois to fight as Britain's allies against the Americans. Their posi-

Gifted orator and Seneca chief Red Jacket was known for his diplomacy in dealing with the whites at the end of the Revolutionary War. *(Albright-Knox Art Gallery)*

tion was strongly endorsed by Chief Joseph BRANT of the Mohawk, but Red Jacket, fearing disaster, demanded neutrality. Although Brant accused him of cowardice, he was seconded by Seneca war chief CORNPLANTER, who also urged circumspection. Nonetheless, the Six Nations opted for war and Red Jacket was obliged to take to the field. Never known for military prowess, he apparently fled the Battle of ORISKANY and subsequently refused to accompany raiding parties in the Cherry Valley throughout 1778. In August 1779 Red Jacket strongly urged his people to flee before the advance of General John SULLIVAN's punitive expedition, which culminated in the Indian defeat at Newtown. Despite taunts from Brant and others, he continued his fine oratory in pursuit of moderation until the Revolution concluded.

The end of the war found a young and restless United States astride a greatly weakened Iroquois Confederation. Red Jacket now came to the fore as an eloquent tribal spokesman who ceaselessly opposed land sales to the whites and strove to maintain traditional Seneca mores and religion. Between 1790 and 1794 he attended no less than seven major conferences with American officials, where he clashed with Cornplanter and other moderates who were willing to trade land for peace. Red Jacket's renown was such that in 1792 he visited Philadelphia to confer with President George WASHINGTON and received an ornate silver medal, which he conspicuously wore for the remainder of his life. Despite his opposition to land sales, in 1797 he accepted Cornplanter's advice and surrendered the title to thousands of acres while the offer was still favorable. This transfer reduced the once mighty Seneca holdings to a few stretches along the Niagara River, where Red Jacket established himself and his core supporters.

Red Jacket's grasp on power was further complicated by the rise of Handsome Lake, Cornplanter's brother, who was a visionary mystic. He shared Red Jacket's desire to preserve nativistic culture and religion, but Handsome Lake's popularity was castigated as a threat to tribal leadership. Handsome Lake countered by having Red Jacket brought up on charges of witchcraft in 1801, which could have incurred the death penalty, but he eloquently and forcefully defended himself before his peers and won acquittal. Ever mindful of his proximity to the United States, Red Jacket rejected the overtures of Shawnee leader Tecumseh in 1810 and refused to join a pan-Indian confederation. He was initially neutral when the War of 1812 commenced two years later but afterward committed his warriors to fight on behalf of the United States. Red Jacket himself took to the field in 1814 and was present at the Battle of Chippewa that July. After the war ended, he was again at the height of his influence and redoubled efforts to reject Christianity and its missionaries. In 1827 several younger chiefs finally deposed the elderly sachem, and he gradually sank into alcohol-induced debauchery. Red Jacket died near Buffalo on January 20, 1830, and ironically received a Christian burial given by his wife. Never a noted military figure, he was a great Indian orator and a leading Seneca spokesperson for nearly four decades. His grandson, Ely S. Parker, fought as a Union general in the Civil War.

Further Reading
Abler, Thomas S., ed., *Chainbreaker: The Revolutionary War Memoirs of Governor Blacksnake as told to Benjamin Williams.* Lincoln: University of Nebraska Press, 2005.
Clarke, James B. "Red Jacket and the Political Disintegration of the Six Nations Confederacy in the Late Eighteenth Century." Unpublished master's thesis, University of Houston, 1993.
Densmore, Christopher. *Red Jacket: Iroquois Diplomat and Orator.* Syracuse, N.Y.: University of Syracuse Press, 1999.
Klees, Emerson. *The Iroquois Confederacy: History and Legends.* Rochester, N.Y.: Cameo Press, 2003.
Mintz, Max M. *Seeds of Empire: The American Revolutionary Conquest of the Seneca.* New York: New York University Press, 1999.
Taylor, Alan. "The Divided Ground: Upper Canada, New York, and the Iroquois Six Nations, 1783–1815," *Journal of the Early Republic* 22, no. 1 (2002): 55–75.

Reed, James (1723–1807)
American military officer

James Reed was born in Woburn, Massachusetts, on January 8, 1722, and he apprenticed as a tailor. During the French and Indian War he held the rank of captain in the militia and served variously at Crown Point and Ticonderoga. After the war he eventually relocated to Fitzwilliam, New Hampshire, being among that town's first inhabitants, and he operated a tavern. During the period leading to the Revolutionary War, Reed maintained his militia connections and was a senior military leader by the time hostilities erupted. In April 1775 he was appointed colonel of the 3rd New Hampshire Regiment, and Reed marched his command south to Boston to partake of the siege there. On June 17 he assumed positions at BUNKER HILL somewhat to the left of troops under Captain Thomas KNOWLTON and behind a flimsy rail fence. In this capacity Reed assisted in repelling two determined British attacks upon his position and gradually fell back upon Charlestown when American defenses finally collapsed. After additional service at Boston his regiment was inducted into the Continental ARMY as the 2nd New Hampshire Continental Infantry and ordered north into Canada. However, Reed proceeded only as far as Fort Ticonderoga when he was struck by smallpox, which nearly destroyed his sight and hearing. As senior colonel from New Hampshire, the Continental CONGRESS nevertheless appointed him brigadier general on August 9, 1776, but his disabilities precluded any further service. Reed resigned from the army the following September. He lived 30 more years before dying at Fitchburg, Massachusetts, on February 13, 1807. Reed's tenure in military affairs was brief but eventful.

Further Reading
Blake, Amos J. "Gen. James Reed," *New Hampshire Historical Society Proceedings* 1 (1875): 109–115.
Garfield, James F. D. *General James Reed.* Fitchburg, Mass.: Sentinel Printing Co., 1908.
Norton, John F. *The History of Fitzwilliam, New Hampshire, from 1752–1887.* New York: Burr Printing House, 1888.
Randall, Peter E., ed. *New Hampshire: Years of Revolution, 1774–1783.* Hanover, N.H.: New Hampshire Revolution Bicentennial Commission, 1976.
Reed, Sylvanus, Amos J. Blake, and Francis R. Parker. *Addresses at the Dedication of the Memorial Bronze Tablet and Granite Boulder to Brig. Gen. James Reed.* Winchendon, Mass.: Courier Press, 1924.

Reed, Joseph (1741–1785)
American military officer

Joseph Reed was born in Trenton, New Jersey, on August 27, 1741, the son of a merchant and minor civil servant. After attending the Academy of Philadelphia, he passed through the College of New Jersey (now Princeton University) in 1757 before obtaining a law degree three years later. Reed then packed off to London for additional studies at Middle Temple before commencing his legal practice at Trenton in 1765. Five years later he had reestablished himself at Philadelphia and was among the city's most promising young attorneys. In this capacity he also engaged in a lengthy correspondence with Lord Dartmouth, secretary of state for the American colonies, and strongly advised against the use of force. As the tempo of revolutionary activity increased, Reed served on the Philadelphia COMMITTEE OF CORRESPONDENCE and also functioned as president of the Pennsylvania provincial congress. Officially, he posited himself as a moderate, but, following the outbreak of violence, he committed himself to the Patriot cause and served as a lieutenant colonel of militia. In June 1775 he was appointed personal secretary to General George WASHINGTON and was part of his immediate military family. Reed functioned well at headquarters, and in the spring of 1776 he was made adjutant general with the rank of colonel, in effect, Washington's chief of staff. Despite oftentimes chaotic conditions in the Continental ARMY, he managed to keep the paperwork flowing smoothly and greatly facilitated administrative matters. Reed was so trusted that Washington selected him to attend the peace conference on Staten Island held by Admiral Richard HOWE. Afterward, he fought capably at the Battles of LONG ISLAND, WHITE PLAINS, TRENTON, and PRINCETON. In the last two engagements, fought in his hometown and former school, Reed's intimate knowledge of local geography proved essential to American success there.

For all his close rapport with the commander in chief, Reed was unhappy with Washington and privately discounted his military abilities. He strongly urged his commander to abandon Fort Washington before it was captured and felt his advice was being ignored. Worse, when Washington happened upon a letter written by General Charles LEE to Reed, which castigated his leadership, Reed denied any knowledge of the subject, but the two men never healed the rift. He subsequently resigned his commission in January 1777 and served as an unpaid volunteer for over a year. In May 1777 he was tendered the rank of brigadier general, but declined. Reed next fought bravely at BRANDYWINE, GERMANTOWN, and especially MONMOUTH, where his horse was shot from beneath him. That fall he was also elected a delegate to the Continental CONGRESS in Philadelphia, where he signed the ARTICLES OF CONFEDERATION. He also functioned as part of the peace commission that met with Lord George Carlisle in 1778 and reported the latter's attempted bribery. This revelation completely discredited the effort and the British went home. At this time delegate Arthur LEE openly accused Reed of disloyalty in his dealings with the British, especially for his earlier correspondence with Lord Dartmouth, but the accusation never gained legitimacy.

In December 1778 Reed was elected head of the Pennsylvania Supreme Executive Council—in effect, governor. The war-ravaged economy floundered and he proved unable to bolster the currency and bring rampant inflation under control. Reed did manage to abolish slavery in the state and also served as prosecutor in General Benedict ARNOLD's trial for misusing military authority. He then lent his skills as a negotiator while helping to defuse a mutiny by Pennsylvania troops in January 1781. Reed left office later that year and resumed his private law practice. He died in Philadelphia on March 5, 1785.

Further Reading
Eliot, Ellsworth. *The Patriotism of Joseph Reed*. New Haven, Conn.: Yale University Press, 1943.
Heathcote, Charles W. "General Joseph Reed—a Devoted Patriot and Loyal Supporter of General Washington," *Picket Post* no. 73 (July 1961): 12–18.
Ketchum, Richard M. "Men of the Revolution," *American Heritage* 27, no. 4 (1976): 64–65, 93.
Lefkowitz, Arthur S. *George Washington's Indispensable Men: The 32 Aides-de-camp Who Helped Win American Independence*. Mechanicsburg, Pa.: Stackpole Books, 2003.
Reed, Joseph. "General Joseph Reed's Narrative of the Movements of the American Army in the Neighborhood of Trenton in the Winter of 1776–77," *Pennsylvania Magazine of History and Biography* 7 (1884): 391–402.

Roche, John F. *Joseph Reed, a Moderate in the American Revolution.* New York: Columbia University Press, 1957.

Revere, Paul (1735–1818)
American militia officer

Paul Revere was born in Boston on January 1, 1735, the son of a silversmith. After acquiring a common education he followed into his father's profession and exhibited genuine skill as an engraver, metalsmith, and artisan. Revere also joined the artillery company of Colonel Richard GRIDLEY in 1756 and participated in the unsuccessful expedition against Crown Point, New York, that year. He resumed his successful career back in Boston and became increasingly radicalized through friendship with James OTIS and Dr. Joseph WARREN and his membership in the local SONS OF LIBERTY. In this capacity he drew and printed numerous propaganda plates for the radical Whigs, which crested with his famous—if inaccurate—depiction of the BOSTON MASSACRE of March 5, 1770. This famous print was circulated throughout the colonies and did much to harden attitudes toward the British. Tensions increased throughout Boston following passage of the TEA ACT of 1773, and Revere assumed leadership roles in the anti-British movement and helped orchestrate the BOSTON TEA PARTY of December 16, 1773. When Parliament retaliated against Boston with passage of the COERCIVE ACTS, Revere functioned as a messenger for the extralegal provincial congress. Galloping hard, he brought word of the tea party to New York and subsequently carried copies of the recently adopted "Suffolk Resolves," advocating armed resistance, to the Continental CONGRESS in Philadelphia. In December 1774 Revere performed similar work by riding ahead to Portsmouth, New Hampshire, with intelligence that General Thomas GAGE had ordered the confiscation of gunpowder at Fort William and Mary.

On the evening of April 18, 1775, Revere performed his most celebrated deed by galloping out to Lexington and warning Samuel ADAMS and John HANCOCK that British troops under Colonel Francis SMITH were en route to capture them. Revere and two other riders, William Dawes and Dr. Samuel Prescott, were all apprehended by a British patrol that night and only Prescott managed to escape and warn Concord that the regulars were out. Revere was eventually released without his horse, made his way to Lexington on foot to secure Hancock's papers, and witnessed British troops firing on the MINUTEMAN company of Captain John PARKER. Afterward he served on the Massachusetts COMMITTEE OF CORRESPONDENCE and was authorized by the provincial congress to established a powder mill in Canton to manufacture ammunition. Revere also held the rank of major in the local militia, and throughout 1778 and 1779 he commanded the garrison at Castle William in Boston Harbor.

Revere's subsequent military career proved somewhat less than salubrious. He led an artillery company without distinction during General John SULLIVAN's invasion of Rhode Island in August 1778, yet gained promotion to lieutenant colonel. He next commanded three artillery companies under General Solomon LOVELL during the ill-fated Penobscot campaign, July–August 1779. Throughout most of the fighting on land, Revere apparently elected to remain on board a warship while his cannon lacked the appropriate leadership to be of much use. After the entire expedition was captured and destroyed by Commodore George COLLIER, General Peleg WADSWORTH accused Revere of cowardice and incompetence, so he was relieved of command and placed under house arrest. He angrily demanded a court of inquiry, which met in February 1782 and acquitted him of all charges, but his reputation suffered.

After hostilities ceased in 1783, Revere resumed his successful career in his silversmith business, gaining renown as one of America's most gifted artisans. He also dabbled in the manufacture of copper bells, naval wares, cannon, and even contributed parts to inventor Robert Fulton's steam engines. Revere was a common sight on the streets of Boston, still decked out in his revolutionary uniforms, until he died on May 10, 1818.

Among the earliest heroes of the Revolutionary War, he has been immortalized in national memory by Robert Wadsworth Longfellow's famous poem *The Ride of Paul Revere*.

Further Reading
Caes, Charles J. "Midnight Riders," *American History* 39, no. 5 (2004): 34–41.
Fischer, David H. *Paul Revere's Ride*. New York: Oxford University Press, 1994.
Martello, Robert. "Paul Revere's Last Ride: The Road to Rolling Copper," *Journal of the Early Republic* 20, no. 2 (2000): 219–239.
———. "Paul Revere's Metallurgical Ride: Craft and Proto-Industry in Early America." Unpublished Ph.D. diss., Massachusetts Institute of Technology, 2001.
Revere, Paul. *Paul Revere's Three Accounts of His Famous Ride*. Boston: Massachusetts Historical Society, 2000.
Triber, Jayne E. *A True Republican: The Life of Paul Revere*. Amherst: University of Massachusetts Press, 1998.

Riedesel, Fredericke von (1746–1808)
Prussian baroness

Fredericke Charlotte Louise von Massow was born in Brandenburg, Prussia, in 1746, daughter of General Hans Jurgen Detloff von Masow, then commissary in chief to King Frederick the Great. She was raised in a military environment and matured into an attractive, young aristocrat. In 1762 she met and married Friedrich von RIEDESEL, a dashing light cavalry officer from Brunswick. The couple had two children and were expecting their third when Ferdinand, duke of Brunswick, contracted out part of his army to Great Britain for service in North America. General Riedesel was then appointed to lead a large contingent of Brunswick troops—known collectively to the Americans as HESSIANS—and the baroness insisted that she accompany him with their children. He capitulated and Riedesel arrived at Quebec in June 1777, three daughters and several maids in tow. Thereafter she popularized herself among General John BURGOYNE's staff through her polished bearing, graciousness, and good humor. She also became something of a camp celebrity for dashing about in her expensive silk and satin wardrobe. Riedesel accompanied her husband down the Lake Champlain corridor and toward Albany, New York. She was present at the defeat of FREEMAN'S FARM on September 19, 1777, and worked side by side with the nurses tending the wounded. During the Battle of BEMIS HEIGHTS on October 7, 1777, she sought refuge with her daughters in a nearby cellar to escape American cannonading. The following day the baroness had the melancholy chore of attending the funeral of her friend, General Simon FRASER. Riedesel became a prisoner following Burgoyne's surrender at Saratoga on October 17, 1777, and accompanied the now captive "convention army" to Cambridge, Massachusetts, for eventual repatriation. Before departing the baroness secretly managed to stuff a

Fredericke Riedesel wrote and published a memoir of her time in America during the Revolutionary War. *(National Archives)*

regimental flag into her bedding and presented it to the men later.

Riedesel was contemptuously received in Boston by American women, who spit on her for being a mercenary. Worse, when the Continental CONGRESS eventually reneged on Burgoyne's convention, his army formally passed into captivity. For Riedesel, this meant relocation to Virginia until her husband could be exchanged for an officer of equal rank. En route, the couple was entertained by a gracious marquis de LAFAYETTE and were eventually settled in Richmond. There they befriended Governor Thomas JEFFERSON and were his frequent guests before a parole was arranged in October 1780. The baroness also had her fourth daughter, whom she christened America. Riedesel subsequently ventured to New York, where her husband reported to General Henry CLINTON, and the couple gradually worked their way up toward Quebec. They sailed back to England in 1783 and were cordially received by King GEORGE III and his retinue.

Riedesel returned to Brunswick and settled down in a castle at Lauterbach to raise their five daughters, including the newest addition, Canada. She eventually wrote and published her memoirs of what she deemed a "Tour of Duty" in America, consistent with her military upbringing. Baroness Riedesel died in Berlin on March 29, 1808, a witness to monumental events of the Revolutionary War.

Further Reading

Brown, Marvin, ed. *Baroness von Riedesel and the American Revolution: Journal and Correspondence of a Tour of Duty, 1776–1783.* Chapel Hill: University of North Carolina Press, 1976.

Ellet, Elizabeth F., ed. *The Women of the American Revolution,* 3 vols. New York: Haskell House, 1969.

Matthies, Katharine. "Baroness von Riedesel," *Daughters of the American Revolution Magazine* 109, no. 9 (1975): 984–986.

Parker, Amelia C. "Baroness Riedesel and Other Women in Burgoyne's Army," *Quarterly Journal of the New York State Historical Association* 9 (April 1928): 109–118.

Rhoden, Nancy L., and Ian K. Steele, eds. *The Human Tradition in the American Revolution.* Wilmington, Del.: Scholarly Resources, 2000.

Tharp, Louise. *The Baroness and the General.* Boston: Little, Brown, 1962.

Riedesel, Friedrich von (1738–1800)
Hessian military officer

Friedrich Adolphus von Riedesel was born in Lauterback, Hesse-Kassel, in 1738. He joined the city battalion in 1738 while studying at the University of Marburg and was commissioned an ensign. In 1756 he accompanied his regiment to England to serve as part of the British military establishment under King George II, himself a German. Riedesel subsequently fought in the Seven Years' War, 1755–63, as aide-de-camp to the duke of Brunswick and afterward formally transferred his services to that principality. In 1762 he met and married Fredericke von RIEDESEL, daughter of a Prussian general, and the duke threw them a lavish wedding ceremony. Riedesel was serving as garrison commander at Wolfenbüttel when the Revolutionary War commenced in 1775, and the duke contracted out a large part of his army to fight as mercenaries for King GEORGE III. Accordingly, he sailed for Quebec in April 1776 at the head of the Brunswick contingent of 4,000 men and 336 dismounted dragoons under Colonel Friedrich BAUM. He then reported for duty to Governor-General Guy CARLETON and spent nearly a year in garrison before accompanying offensive operations.

In the spring of 1777 General John BURGOYNE amassed a large force of 7,000 veteran troops, including Riedesel's Brunswickers, British troops under General Simon FRASER, and artillery forces under General William PHILLIPS. That June he led the whole down the Lake Champlain corridor in an ill-fated attempt to capture Albany, New York, and separate New England from the rest of the colonies. American forces under General Arthur ST. CLAIR quickly abandoned Fort Ticonderoga, but Fraser surprised his rear guard at Hubbardton, Vermont, on July 7, 1777. The more numerous Americans gradually gained an

Hessian officer Friedrich Riedesel and his soldiers distinguished themselves at the Battles of Freeman's Farm and Bemis Heights. *(National Archives)*

advantage on Fraser and were pressing him back when Riedesel's men suddenly appeared on the field of battle, singing psalms and military bands blaring to give the impression of a much greater force. The British prevailed in this stiff encounter, and Burgoyne continued pressing southward into heavily wooded, inhospitable terrain. Running short of supplies by August, he dispatched Baum's dragoons on a foraging expedition into nearby Vermont. Riedesel, however, strongly remonstrated against this move, which came to grief at BENNINGTON on August 16, 1777. Considering the intractable geography and pervasive supply shortages, Riedesel strongly recommended that Burgoyne cancel his offensive and return to Canada, but his sage advice was ignored and they pressed on.

At length the British confronted superior American forces under General Horatio GATES at Saratoga, New York. Burgoyne then launched two desperate attacks at FREEMAN's FARM and BEMIS HEIGHTS, in both of which Riedesel and his Germans distinguished themselves. Lacking the strength to cut his way out, Burgoyne finally capitulated to Gates on October 17, 1777, and Riedesel became a prisoner. He and his wife marched to Cambridge, Massachusetts, as part of the neutralized "convention army" until the Continental CONGRESS discarded the agreement. Riedesel then passed into formal captivity in Virginia, where he met and befriended Governor Thomas JEFFERSON. It was not until October 1780 that he was finally exchanged for General Benjamin LINCOLN and released in New York. There General Henry CLINTON assigned him command of Long Island with a local rank of lieutenant general until poor health necessitated a transfer back to Quebec. Riedesel completed his final North American duties under Governor-General Frederick HALDIMAND by drawing up elaborate plans for a renewed offensive from Canada. He and his wife finally departed the New World in August 1783 and sailed home.

Back in Brunswick, Riedesel received a hero's welcome and was allowed to parade his surviving 2,400 soldiers before their monarch. He eventually rose to lieutenant general before retiring at Lauterback in 1793, where he also served as commandant of the city of Braunschweig. Riedesel died there still serving in that capacity on December 7, 1800, one of the most accomplished HESSIAN officers to see service in the war.

Further Reading
Andrews, Melodie. "'Myrmidons from Abroad': The Role of the German Mercenary in the Coming of Independence." Unpublished Ph.D. diss., University of Houston, 1986.
Eelking, Max von, ed. *Memoirs, Letters, and Journals of Major General Riedesel during His Residency in America*, 2 vols. New York: Arno Press, 1969.
Hoffman, Elliott W. "The German Soldiers of the American Revolution." Unpublished Ph.D. diss., University of New Hampshire, 1982.

Ketchum, Richard M. *Saratoga: Turning Point in America's Revolutionary War*. New York: Henry Holt, 1997.
Stephens, Thomas R. "In Deepest Submission: The Hessian Mercenary Troops of the American Revolution." Unpublished Ph.D. diss., Texas A & M University, 1998.
Tharp, Louise. *The Baroness and the General*. Boston: Little, Brown, 1962.

Rochambeau, Jean-Baptiste-Donatien de Vimeur, comte de (1725–1807)

French military officer

Jean-Baptiste-Donatien de Vimeur was born in Vendôme, France, on July 1, 1725, the son of a French marshal. Originally intended for service with the church, he received permission to join the army following the death of his elder brother and was commissioned an ensign in the Saint-Simon Cavalry Regiment in 1742. Over the next 38 years, Rochambeau conducted himself with distinction as a combat officer. By the end of the War of the Austrian Succession in 1748 he was a colonel at the age of 22. Rochambeau then campaigned well throughout the Seven Years' War, in which France was badly defeated. Thereafter he became an outspoken proponent of military modernization, and went to great lengths improving discipline and living conditions of common soldiers. His success culminated in promotion to major general in 1761 and by 1776 he also functioned as governor of Villefranche. The FRENCH ALLIANCE in the spring of 1778 actively committed French combat forces to the Revolutionary War, although their initial efforts under Admiral Charles-Hector-Théodat, comte d'ESTAING, proved both futile and frustrating to the new allies. In 1780 King Louis XVI sought to dispatch even larger forces, and that March he appointed Rochambeau head of the *"Expedition Particuliere"* with a rank of lieutenant general. The calm, affable, and systematic general was also under direct orders to subordinate himself to General George WASHINGTON for purposes of greater harmony and unity of action. Fortunately for both sides, this consummate professional officer fulfilled his mandate to the letter.

Rochambeau sailed from Brest in May 1780 with 5,500 veteran troops and some of the best regiments in the French army. They landed at Newport, Rhode Island, on July 11, 1780, and spent nearly a year in garrison there awaiting naval support that never arrived. Meanwhile, Rochambeau worked hard at improving relations between his army and the local population, and successfully deflated a hundred years of hatred and mistrust between the two peoples. The American war effort had reached its nadir, as the nation was broke, British forces were overrunning the South, and the perpetually ragged, understrength Continental ARMY reeled from the first of several mutinies. It was against this backdrop that Rochambeau cheer-

General Rochambeau was dispatched to America by King Louis XVI as head of the *"Expedition Particuliere."* (*The Society of the Cincinnati*)

fully submitted to the orders and priorities of Washington, who was embarrassingly too weak to initiate a major offensive of his own. Gradually the two leaders struck up a personable relationship based upon respect and genuine friendship. However, Rochambeau rejected the marquis de LAFAYETTE as their official liaison, finding him too youthful and impulsive. Instead, he assigned the more seasoned François-Jean, marquis de CHASTELLUX, to the delicate task of go-between.

In May 1781, Washington and Rochambeau conferred at Wethersfield, Connecticut, to hammer out a viable strategy, and his American counterpart prevailed upon him to leave Newport and rendezvous outside New York. There they would mount a combined attack upon the city, guarded by strong British forces under General Henry CLINTON. Rochambeau waxed warily but diplomatically over the proposed attack, but eventually reached an agreement with Washington. Then, in August 1781, a letter suddenly arrived from Admiral de GRASSE, who informed Rochambeau that he was transporting 3,000 troops from Saint-Domingue (Haiti) to Chesapeake Bay, and his fleet would remain in that vicinity through October. Fortuitously, British forces under General Charles CORNWALLIS had ensconced themselves at YORKTOWN, Virginia, and were awaiting reinforcements. In one of military history's masterstrokes, Washington peremptorily abandoned his New York strategy and urged a sudden descent upon Yorktown to trap the British there. Rochambeau concurred and on August 18, 1781, their combined armies began a fateful march southward while General William HEATH kept Clinton distracted in New York. On October 2, 1781, the veteran Rochambeau demonstrated his mastery of 18th-century siege warfare by initiating trenches and parallels around the British position. Once de Grasse had defeated the fleet of Admiral Thomas GRAVES off the Virginia Capes on September 5, 1781, precluding any chance for seaborne reinforcements, Cornwallis's army was doomed. He capitulated on October 19, 1781, and directed his aide, General Charles O'HARA, to surrender in his place. But when O'Hara tendered his commander's sword to Rochambeau, he was curtly directed by Captain Mathieu DUMAS to hand it to General Washington. Success at Yorktown ended major land operations, and Rochambeau spent the winter in Virginia. Congress then voted him its thanks before he marched back to Boston with his army and embarked for France In January 1783.

Back home Rochambeau received a hero's welcome and commanded a succession of districts. He initially supported the French Revolution and served in the Assembly of Notables. In 1791 he became the last French marshal appointed by the Bourbon dynasty and fought against the Austrians while leading the Army of the North. Unfortunately, the revolution's escalating violence induced him to resign from the military in July 1792, and two years later he was arrested. Only the death of Robespierre spared him from the guillotine, and he retired to his estates in Vendôme. In 1804 Emperor Napoleon Bonaparte inducted him into the Legion of Honor with a pension. Rochambeau, the efficient, tactful soldier-diplomat of the Revolutionary War, died at Thoré, France, on May 10, 1807. Considering the delicacies of coalition warfare and the military obstacles to be surmounted, he was an ideal choice to lead coalition forces in America. In 1902 a statue of Rochambeau was unveiled in Washington, D.C., a gift from the French government.

Further Reading
Rice, Howard C. *The American Campaign of Rochambeau's Army, 1780, 1781, 1782, 1783*. Princeton, N.J.: Princeton University Press, 1972.
Scott, Samuel F. *From Yorktown to Valmy: The Transformation of the French Army in an Age of Revolution*. Niwot: University Press of Colorado, 1999.
Simpson, Alan, and Mary Simpson. "A New Look at How Rochambeau Quartered His Army in Newport (1780–1781)," *Newport History* 56, no. 2 (1983): 30–67.
Ultan, Lloyd. "The Grand Reconnaissance," *Bronx County Historical Society* 39, no. 1 (2002): 14–37.
Whitridge, Donald. *Rochambeau*. New York: Macmillan, 1965.

Woodbridge, George. "Rochambeau Two Hundred Years Later," *Newport History* 53, no. 1 (1980): 5–21.

Wright, M. W. E., ed. *Memoirs of the Marshal Count de Rochambeau, Relative to the War of Independence of the United States.* New York: Arno Press, 1971.

Rodney, George (first baron Rodney)
(1718–1792)

English naval officer

George Brydges Rodney was born in England in January 1718, part of an impeccably aristocratic family whose lineage produced several distinguished soldiers and statesmen. He joined the Royal Navy at the age of 11 and, by dint of exceptional service, rose to captain in 1743 at the age of 23. As a commander, Rodney demonstrated a flair for aggressive tactics that set him apart from other naval commanders in the War of the Austrian Succession and the Seven Years' War. In 1759 he distinguished himself by destroying a fleet of flat-bottomed boats at Le Havre intended for an invasion of England. He then successively captured the French Carribean islands of Martinique, St. Lucia, and Grenada, which resulted in promotion to rear admiral in 1764. Rodney capped his prerevolutionary career by a stint as commander of the Jamaica station and reveled in his two major infatuations: women and wealth. He also sat in Parliament, deliberately remaining aloof from party factions and allegiances. Consequently he was forced to defend his nominally safe seat in 1768 and spent £30,000—nearly his entire holdings—to maintain it. He thereafter endured a spate of financial problems and fled to Paris in 1774 to escape creditors. Apparently his rapacious nature irked the Lord of the Admiralty, John MONTAGU, earl of Sandwich, who refused to assist him with a sinecure. Rodney thus remained in France until a local aristocrat agreed to lend money, and he came home in 1778. At that time France had entered the Revolutionary War on behalf of the United States, and England needed competent naval commanders. The situation proved so grave that Lord Sandwich even tendered him a position as commander of the Leeward Islands, seeing no other qualified commander was available. In December 1780 the aged, gout-wracked Rodney was tasked with leading a relief expedition to the besieged peninsula of Gibraltar. En route he captured a Spanish convoy at the "Moonlight" battle of January 6, 1780, and then destroyed a strong Spanish squadron off Cape St. Vincent on January 16, 1780. After successfully reaching Gibraltar he sailed westward to take command of British naval forces in the Caribbean. In light of his financial difficulties—and a little-concealed lust for cash—Rodney appeared to be more concerned with prize money than naval victories.

Rodney cruised the West Indies for several weeks searching for the French fleet commanded by Admiral Luc-Urbain de Bouexic, comte de Guichen. On April 17, 1780, he skirmished indecisively off Martinique, having previously—and without authorization—instructed his captains to ignore the traditional "Fighting Instructions" and seek ship-to ship combat. Rodney then angrily, and perhaps unfairly, castigated his subordinates for losing the battle, when the real problem lay more with faulty signaling. After two more indecisive skirmishes, he removed part of his fleet to New York for the hurricane season and argued with Admiral Marriot ARBUTHNOT over the division of prize money. Rodney then learned of England's declaration of war against the Netherlands, and he was teamed with General John VAUGHAN. On February 3, 1781, they stormed ashore at the Dutch-held island of St. Eustatius, an important staging area for supplies en route to America. Both then disgraced themselves by thoroughly plundering all available warehouses, most of which were owned by English merchants, then absconding with the loot. The ensuing lawsuits kept Rodney entangled in the courts for years, especially after the French captured his treasure-laden convoy. The admiral then took a much-needed sick leave in England; while absent, de GRASSE successfully sortied from Haiti to Chesapeake Bay and trapped the army of General Charles CORNWALLIS at YORKTOWN.

Rodney returned to the West Indies in the spring of 1782, assisted by his able if cantankerous subordinate Admiral Samuel HOOD. The two cruised the Caribbean for several weeks trying to flush out de Grasse before he launched a much-anticipated invasion of Jamaica. Rodney briefly tangled with the French between Guadelupe and Dominica on April 9, 1782, and finally cornered de Grasse off the Saintes on April 12. The ensuing scrape was a clear-cut British triumph, simply because Rodney again ordered his captains to disregard traditional tactics and break the French battle line. The British sank one French warship and captured five more—including de Grasse and his mammoth flagship, *Ville de Paris*. However, when Rodney failed to pursue the defeated foe more vigorously, Hood and others accused him of being concerned more with securing prize money than total victory. But news of the startling triumph was joyously received back at home and Rodney received a baronetcy. It also improved Britain's bargaining position with the Americans at the TREATY OF PARIS. Ironically, the admiral's politically inspired replacement arrived in the West Indies before word of the Saintes was received. He nonetheless gladly retired after five decades of conscientious service and spent the last years of his life basking in wealth and celebrity. Rodney died in London on May 24, 1792, one of England's most controversial naval leaders. The novel tactics he pioneered would again be employed by Admiral Horatio Nelson at the victory of Trafalgar in 1805.

Further Reading

Breen, Kenneth. "Sir George Rodney and St. Eustatius in the American War: A Commercial and Naval Distraction," *Mariner's Mirror* 84, no. 2 (1998): 193–203.

Conway, Stephen. " 'A Joy Unknown for Years Past': The American War, Britishness, and the Celebration of Rodney's Victory at the Saintes," *History* 86, no. 282 (2001): 180–199.

Hurst, Ronald. *The Golden Rock: An Episode of the American Revolutionary War of Independence, 1775–1783*. Annapolis, Md.: Naval Institute Press, 1996.

O'Shaughnessy, Amber J. "The Other Road to Yorktown: The St. Eustatius Affair and the American Revolution," *Maryland Historical Magazine* 97, no. 1 (2002): 33–59.

Synett, David, ed. *The Rodney Papers: Selections from the Correspondence of Admiral Lord Rodney*. Burlington, Vt.: Ashgate, 2005.

Syrett, David. "Admiral Rodney, Patronage, and the Leeward Squadron, 1780–2," *Mariner's Mirror* 85, no. 4 (1999): 411–420.

Rogers, Robert (1731–1795)
English military officer

Robert Rogers was born in Methuen, Massachusetts, on November 7, 1731. Barely educated, he matured on the New Hampshire frontier, becoming adept at such woodland skills as hunting and scouting. In 1755 he joined the militia to avoid charges of counterfeiting and finally found his niche. Rogers performed so well as a scout for Sir William Johnson at Crown Point that he advanced to captain and authorized to recruit an independent light infantry company, better known as rangers. In this capacity Rogers gained considerable renown by winning innumerable skirmishes and pitched battles with French and Indian forces. Promoted to major in 1758, he raised and commanded nine additional ranger companies and spearheaded the drive toward Montreal for victorious British forces. Rogers acquired a reputation as a fearless, wily commander, thorough in planning and ruthless in execution. But afterward he slunk back to drinking, sloppy administration, and petty theft. To escape debts and creditors he fled to England in October 1765, published his memoirs, and was widely hailed as a hero. He then received command of Fort Michilimackinac as a regularly commissioned British officer. Three years later Rogers was accused of embezzlement, hauled before a court-martial, and acquitted. In 1769 he returned to England seeking a sinecure and remained in debtor's prison for 22 months until his brother agreed to settle his accounts.

Rogers returned to America in 1775 just as the Revolutionary War was breaking out, but he was idle and listless, with few remaining friends in America. In February 1776 General Henry CLINTON offered him a new commission, but he remained aloof. Rogers then tendered his services to the Continental CONGRESS in Philadelphia, but, as a British officer on half-pay, he was viewed with suspicion. General George WASHINGTON ordered him arrested as a spy in June 1776, but he escaped. Rogers then received permission to raise a new ranger formation of two companies, the Queen's American Rangers. Under his now debauched leadership this formation turned out to be a mere shadow of his former rangers. On October 28, 1776, it was surprised at Mamaroneck, New York, by Colonel John Haslet and suffered 58 casualties. Rogers was finally relieved of command in February 1777 and the following October his unit, renamed the Queen's Rangers, fell under the highly effective leadership of Captain John Graves SIMCOE. Rogers spent the remainder of the war in New York and did not return to London until 1782. There he lived the rest of his life in poverty and dissipation. Rogers died in a London boarding house on May 18, 1795, a pivotal figure in colonial military history but perpetually smitten by greed and dissipation.

Further Reading
Brumwell, Stephen. *White Devil: Revenge and Survival in Colonial America.* London: Cassell Military, 2004.
Glover, Susan. "Battling the Elements: Reconstructing the Heroic in Robert Rogers," *Journal of American Culture* 26, no. 2 (2003): 180–187.
Loescher, Burt G. *Genesis: Roger's Rangers, the First Green Berets.* Bowie, Md.: Heritage Books, 2000.
McConnell, Michael N. *Army and Empire: British Soldiers on the American Frontier, 1758–1775.* Lincoln: University of Nebraska Press, 2004.
McCulloch, Ian. "Buckskin Soldier: The Rise and Fall of Major Robert Rogers," *Beaver* 73, no. 2 (1993): 17–26.
Rogers, Robert. *The Annotated and Illustrated Journals of Major Robert Rogers.* Fleischmanns, N.Y.: Purple Mountain Press, 2002.

Ross, Betsy (1752–1836)
American seamstress

Elizabeth (Betsy) Griscom was born in Philadelphia, Pennsylvania, on January 1, 1752, into a Quaker household. Early on she developed an interest in sewing and honed her skills as a seamstress. In 1773 she was disowned from the Quakers for marrying John Ross, an Episcopalian, and temporarily relocated to Gloucester, New Jersey. The couple eventually returned to Philadelphia, where they operated a successful sewing and upholstery shop. John, a member of the city militia, died in a gunpowder explosion in January 1776, and Betsy remarried, this time to Joseph Ashburn, a sailor. Ashburn's vessel was caught by the British, and he died at Old Mill prison, Plymouth, in 1782. Ross then married a third time to John Claypoole, a prison mate of Ashburn's, in May 1783. They both continued in the upholstery business and also joined the non-pacifistic Society of Free Quakers. The couple lived happily in Philadelphia until John's death in 1817, whereupon Betsy moved in with one of her daughters. She died in Philadelphia on January 30, 1836.

Ross's national fame rests upon folklore surrounding her alleged creation of the United States flag. According to legend, in June 1776 she was approached by a deputation sent by the Continental CONGRESS consisting of George WASHINGTON and Robert MORRIS, just as the nation verged on declaring independence. She was asked to sew a new, national standard based upon a sketch provided to her by Washington. Ross went on to construct a design sporting a blue field in the upper left corner with 13 stars in a circle, and fleshed out by alternating rows of 13 red and white stripes. The story has it that she modified Washington's suggestion to use six-pointed stars in favor of the now-familiar five-pointed ones. Thus she is traditionally considered the creative force behind the "Stars and Stripes" of lore. In 1777 Ross was also called on to make flags for the Pennsylvania state navy, and her work here is documented. But the polite fiction surrounding Ross's relationship to the national flag stems from an 1870 meeting at the Historical Society of Pennsylvania, wherein her grandson, William Canby, presented a paper. There he stated that his grandmother declared on her deathbed her meeting with Washington and her part in designing the standard. These circumstances have never been documented and, in so much as Canby was only 11 years old at the time of the incident, his veracity remains suspect. But Ross is so indelibly associated with the flag that she remains a national icon.

Further Reading
Harker, John B. *Betsy Ross's Five Pointed Star.* Melbourne Beach, Fla.: Canmore Press, 2005.
Kashatus, William C. "Seamstress for a Revolution," *American History* 37, no. 3 (2002): 20–22, 24, 26.
Mock, Sanford J. "Our Lady of the Flag," *Financial History* 68 (2000): 30–33, 36, 39.
Morris, Robert. *The Truth about the Betsy Ross Story.* Beach Haven, N.J.: Wynnehaven Pub. Co., 1982.
Peterson, Allan E. "Cherished and Ignored: A Cultural History of Betsy Ross." Unpublished master's thesis, San Diego State University, 2001.

Rouerie, Armand-Charles Tuffin, marquis de la.

See Armand, Charles

Rush, Benjamin (1746–1813)

American physician and Patriot

Benjamin Rush was born in Byberry, Pennsylvania, on January 4, 1746, the son of a gunsmith. He graduated from the College of New Jersey (now Princeton University) in 1760 and subsequently studied medicine at the College of Philadelphia (today's University of Pennsylvania). In 1766 Rush attended Edinburgh University, Scotland, then considered one of the best medical schools of the time. He graduated two years later and moved to London, where he met and befriended Benjamin FRANKLIN. At this time Rush became increasingly drawn into revolutionary politics and began espousing the Patriot cause. He returned to Philadelphia in July 1769 and—as one of the best-educated physicians in the colonies—established a successful medical practice. He also gained appointment as the first professor of chemistry at the College of Philadelphia. Rush then began dabbling in local politics, where he was an outspoken opponent of slavery, and also gained a measure of renown for treating the poor, gratis. He made himself readily available when the Continental CONGRESS convened in town twice, and in this capacity befriended such political luminaries as Patrick HENRY, John ADAMS, and Thomas JEFFERSON. Apparently he did this less out of patriotism than for his appetite for politics and intrigue.

In June 1776 Rush won a seat in Congress, where he signed the DECLARATION OF INDEPENDENCE. After serving on several committees, he next accompanied a militia regiment to New Jersey and was present in the Battles of TRENTON and PRINCETON. After the first engagement he visited the British camp to treat the mortally wounded General Hugh MERCER. Rush was generally dissatisfied with the slipshod medical arrangements in the Continental ARMY's Medical Department and made his complaints known to Congress. Consequently, in April 1777 he was appointed surgeon general of the Middle Department and composed his most famous tract, *Directions for Preserving the Health of Soldiers,* a common-sense compilation of field sanitation. This became a standard military text and was widely used until the War of 1812. The following July he advanced to physician general of the Middle Department and used his high office to advance his political agenda. Specifically, he was unimpressed by the leadership abilities of General George WASHINGTON, while admiring those of fellow schemers Colonel Thomas CONWAY and General Horatio GATES. In January 1778 he wrote an anonymous letter highly critical of Washington to Patrick Henry, who then turned it over to the general. When Washington recognized the handwriting, he complained to Congress, and Rush was required to resign his office on January 30, 1778.

Out of service, Rush resumed his medical practice with continued success. In the 1790s he broke new ground by pioneering the use of psychiatry and advocated humane treatment for the mentally ill. Rush also became a staunch advocate of bleeding patients, a practice that was then under attack and was eventually discredited. Rush died of typhus in Philadelphia on April 13, 1813, celebrated as one of the foremost medical teachers of his generation. But during the Revolutionary War he functioned as a talented but marginal and somewhat disreputable figure.

Further Reading

Barton, David. *Benjamin Rush: Signer of the Declaration of Independence.* Aledo, Tex.: Wallbuilder Press, 1999.

Brodsky, Alya. *Benjamin Rush: Patriot and Physician.* New York: Truman Talley Books/St. Martin's Press, 2004.

Fox, Claire G. *Benjamin Rush, M.D.: A Bibliographic Guide.* Westport, Conn.: Greenwood Press, 1996.

Gillett, Mary C. *The Army Medical Department, 1775–1818.* Washington, D.C.: Center of Military History, 1981.

Kloos, John M. *A Sense of Deity: The Republican Spirituality of Dr. Benjamin Rush.* Brooklyn, N.Y.: Carlson Pub., 1991.

Strozier, Charles B. "Benjamin Rush, Revolutionary," *American Scholar* 64, no. 3 (1995): 415–421.

Rutherford, Griffith (ca. 1721–1805)
American militia officer

Griffith Rutherford was born in Ireland around 1721 and was raised in Pennsylvania. Orphaned as a child, he eventually made his way to Rowan County, North Carolina, sometime in the 1750s. Rutherford worked as a surveyor for many years, amassed a small fortune, and also served as a captain in the local militia. In 1766 he held a seat in the colonial assembly, where he sympathized with —but did not endorse—the activities of the so-called regulators. In 1771 he fought briefly in the regulator war and persuaded General Hugh WADDELL not to engage the superior forces of the enemy. As tensions increased with Great Britain, Rutherford waxed increasingly active on behalf of Patriot causes, and in 1775 he served in the provincial congress. That September he became colonel of Rowan County militia and helped quell a backwoods uprising by LOYALIST forces. Rutherford's good conduct and his ruthlessness toward Loyalists endeared him to many politicians, so in April 1776 he became brigadier general of state militia. At that time the Cherokee Indians began raiding white frontier settlements, so Rutherford spent several months raising and training a force of 2,500 men for a punitive campaign. Crossing the Swannanoa Gap on September 1, 1776, he advanced directly against the Middle Towns Cherokee, burning 36 villages en route. However, the Americans went to some length to spare the settlement of Chota, home of Cherokee woman and peace advocate Nancy WARD. He concluded his successful and destructive campaign by September 26, having lost only three men. Consequently, in May 1777 Cherokees under OCONOSTOTA signed the Treaty of Long Island, which ceded all their land east of the Blue Ridge Mountains.

In between field activities, Rutherford served in the legislature and advocated the interests of planters and the lower classes, including majority rule, social equality, and elimination of privilege. He resumed military activities in 1779 by assisting General Benjamin LINCOLN in his failed attempt to reconquer Georgia. Thereafter he redoubled his efforts against a periodic Loyalist resurgence. On June 20, 1780, his men attacked and defeated a larger force at Ramsour's Mills, although Rutherford was not personally present to command. This victory greatly dampened British attempts to recruit Loyalist sympathizers to their standard. Two months later Rutherford commanded a North Carolina brigade at the disastrous engagement of CAMDEN, August 16, 1780, and was captured during the ensuing rout. Initially detained at Charleston, he was eventually imprisoned at St. Augustine, Florida, until being exchanged on June 22, 1781. Once back home, he gathered together 1,000 vengeful militia and conducted another harsh campaign against the Loyalists of eastern North Carolina, routing them at Raft Swamp. His final action of the war was to lay siege to Wilmington, which was abandoned by the British as of November 14, 1781. His men apparently pillaged the town after occupying it.

Afterward, Rutherford resumed his political career in the state senate, denouncing any leniency toward former Loyalists. His incessant vitriol reflected the raw feelings inherent from the internecine backwoods struggle of the war. In 1788 he attended the Constitutional Convention and voted with the anti-Federalists to oppose the new Constitution. Because of this stance he lost his seat and in 1792 relocated to Sumner County, in what became the state of Tennessee. There Rutherford served in the territorial legislature, and in 1794 President George WASHINGTON appointed him to a five-man legislative council, pending statehood. Rutherford died in Sumner County on August 10, 1805, an important leader in North Carolina's bloody struggle against Indians and Loyalists.

Further Reading
Badders, Hurley E. *Broken Path: The Cherokee Campaign of 1776.* Pendleton, S.C.: Pendleton District Historical and Recreational Commission, 1976.
Carpenter, Robert C. "Griffith Rutherford: North Carolina Frontier Military and Political Leader." Unpublished master's thesis, Wake Forest University, 1974.
Dickens, Roy S. "The Route of Rutherford's Expedition against the North Carolina Cherokees," *Southern Indian Studies* 19 (1967): 3–24.
Ganyard, Robert. "Threat from the West: North Carolina and the Cherokees, 1776–1778," *North Carolina Historical Review* 45 (January 1968): 47–66.
O'Donnell, James H. *Southern Indians in the American Revolution.* Knoxville: University of Tennessee Press, 1973.
Ward, H. Trawick. "Fiction and Fact at the Townson Site in Swiern, North Carolina," *Southwestern Archaeology. Special Publication* 7 (2002): 84–91.

Rutledge, John (1739–1800)
American politician

John Rutledge was born in Charleston, South Carolina, in 1739, the son of a wealthy physician. He was well educated locally and subsequently read law at London's Middle Temple. Rutledge returned home in 1760 and established a successful legal practice but felt a calling in politics. In 1761 he gained a seat in the local legislature, where he worked on behalf of large planters and generally looked askance at the lower orders. In 1765 he sided with anti-British factions to oppose the STAMP ACT and represented his colony in the Stamp Act Congress in New York later that year. However, Rutledge maintained a conservative mind-set; he never advocated breaking with Great Britain and invariably sought constitutional solutions to the crisis. Nonetheless, he was elected to the First Continental CONGRESS in 1774 and the second one in 1775, again distinguishing himself by advocating moderation. However, Rutledge grew more concerned with affairs at home, so after two terms in Philadelphia he returned to Charleston in 1775, where the state assembly appointed him president—in effect, governor. In this capacity he energetically threw himself into wartime preparations and helped organize the city's defenses in time to repulse the British attack on CHARLESTON in June 1776. Afterward radical politicians drafted a new state constitution that disestablished the Anglican Church and provided for a popularly elected upper house, but Rutledge, decidedly undemocratic, vetoed it and resigned from office. His successor, Rawlins Lowndes, subsequently approved the new document, and Rutledge was surprisingly reelected governor in January 1779.

The British began turning their attention back toward South Carolina in 1779, and Rutledge obtained near-dictatorial powers to oppose them. But when General Augustin PREVOST marched up from Georgia on May 11, 1779, Rutledge offered to declare his neutrality if the British withdrew. This stance cost him some popularity, but the city was rescued by the approach of General Benjamin LINCOLN's army. However, in the spring of 1780 General Henry CLINTON appeared again off the coast and initiated the siege of CHARLESTON. When General Lincoln intended to evacuate the city to save his army, Rutledge remonstrated strongly against him, threatening civil unrest. Consequently, the Americans lost heavily when Charleston surrendered on May 12, 1780. Rutledge managed to flee the city, then endured a heart-pounding pursuit by Lieutenant Colonel Banastre TARLETON. Having narrowly escaped, he was further downtrodden by the annihilation of General Horatio GATES at CAMDEN in August 1780, when all organized resistance collapsed. But Rutledge demonstrated surprising resolve during his state's darkest hour by encouraging guerrilla forces under Francis MARION, Thomas SUMTER, and Andrew PICKENS to fight back. He then lent valuable assistance to the resurgent forces of General Nathanael GREENE and by 1782 was able to partially reconstitute state authority. The war ended in 1783, and Rutledge left the governorship, returning to Congress for another term.

Afterward Rutledge resumed his interest in local politics. In 1788 he attended the state constitutional convention, offering tepid endorsement of the document. In 1791 President George WASHINGTON tendered him the position of associate justice of the U.S. Supreme Court, but he resigned to occupy the same position on the state court. Four years later he accepted Washington's offer to serve on the national court, where he replaced John JAY as chief justice. However, Rutledge outspokenly denounced the Jay Treaty of 1795, so the Federalist-dominated U.S. Senate refused his confirmation. Rutledge was by then suffering from periodic bouts of insanity, so he resigned from public office altogether and went home. He died in Charleston on July 18, 1800, an effective wartime administrator.

Further Reading

Bledsoe, Julia G. "The Failure of Colonial Government and the American Revolution in South Carolina: A Long View." Unpublished master's thesis, College of William and Mary, 1996.

Griffiths, John W. " 'To Receive Them Properly': Charlestown Prepares for War, 1775–1776." Unpublished master's thesis, University of South Carolina, 1992.

Haw, James. *John and Edward Rutledge of South Carolina.* Athens: University of Georgia Press, 1997.

Horne, Paul A. "Forgotten Leaders: South Carolina's Delegation to the Continental Congress, 1774–1789." Unpublished Ph.D. diss., University of South Carolina, 1988.

Peoples, Cora M. "What One Lawyer Did." *Daughters of the American Revolution Magazine* 118, no. 3 (1984): 156–180.

Ratzlaff, Robert K. "The Evolution of a Gentleman-Politician: John Rutledge, Jr., of South Carolina," *Midwestern Quarterly* 27, no. 1 (1985): 77–95.

St. Clair, Arthur (1736–1818)
American military officer

Arthur St. Clair was born in Thurso, Scotland, on March 23, 1736. He purchased his ensign's commission in the 60th Regiment of Foot, or Royal Americans, in 1757 and subsequently served in the colonies. St. Clair performed well at the capture of Louisbourg in 1758 and Quebec in 1759, rising to lieutenant. After the war he initially settled in Boston before relocating to the frontier wilds of western Pennsylvania at Ligonier. St. Clair was active and industrious as a farmer/fur trader, and he also held several local offices. In 1773 he functioned as justice of the peace for Westmoreland County, where his fair dealings with the Indians kept Pennsylvania out of Lord Dunmore's War. As hostilities with Great Britain approached, he also became colonel of the local militia regiment, and on January 3, 1776, the Continental CONGRESS appointed him colonel of the 2nd Pennsylvania Continental Infantry. In this capacity he marched north into Canada and helped cover the retreat of Colonel Benedict ARNOLD. On June 8, 1776, St. Clair fought in the disastrous affair of Trois-Rivières and succeeded to command after General William THOMPSON was wounded. He then skillfully managed a retreat to northern New York where, on August 9, 1776, St. Clair gained promotion to brigadier general.

In November 1776 St. Clair's brigade was ordered to join the main army under General George WASHINGTON in New Jersey. He fought capably at the Battles of TRENTON and PRINCETON and is credited by some sources with originating the famous flanking movement at the latter. In light of his distinguished service, St. Clair was promoted to major general the following February—the only Pennsylvania officer so honored. He then reported back to the Northern Department under General Philip J. SCHUYLER, who placed him in charge of Fort Ticonderoga. He assumed command on June 12, 1777, and found it in a poor state of repair and, with barely 2,220 men, under-garrisoned. The following month the British army of General John BURGOYNE, 7,000 strong, approached the fort with the intention of storming it. Worse, General Wiliam PHILLIPS seized nearby Mount Defiance, which had been judged too steep for artillery by the defenders, and mounted a battery of 12-pounders. Badly outnumbered and now subject to plunging artillery fire, St. Clair took the bold step of evacuating Fort Ticonderoga on the night of July 5–6. His plans were carefully laid and executed, although the rear guard under General Seth WARNER disobeyed orders and was surprised at Hubbardton two days later.

St. Clair's skillful evacuation left his brigade intact, and it subsequently formed the core of a new

Arthur St. Clair was appointed colonel of the 2nd Pennsylvania Continental Infantry in 1776 and castigated for abandoning Fort Ticonderoga. *(Independence National Historical Park)*

army under General Horatio GATES, which captured Burgoyne's army the following October. However, the general was highly criticized for his decision to abandon Fort Ticonderoga, so he was stripped of command and investigated by a congressional committee. Meanwhile, he served as an aide-de-camp to General Washington at the Battle of BRANDYWINE, having a horse shot from under him. In September 1778 a court-martial cleared St. Clair of any wrongdoing in the loss of the fort, but he never again held an independent command. In 1781 he led troops to YORKTOWN just prior to the British surrender on October 19 and then marched additional forces south to General Nathanael GREENE in South Carolina. His final act of the war came in June 1783 when he helped to dissuade mutinous Pennsylvania soldiers from marching on Congress; he mustered out of the service the following November.

St. Clair enjoyed a very active postwar career in both political and military realms. After serving as a delegate to Congress he served as president of that body in February 1787. That same year he gained appointment as governor of the Northwest Territory and helped establish the settlement of Cincinnati, Ohio. When a major Indian war erupted in 1791, St. Clair was called back into service as a major general, but his army was disastrously defeated by Chief Little Turtle on November 4. Exonerated by a second court-martial, he served as territorial governor until 1802, when President Thomas JEFFERSON sacked him for opposing Ohio statehood. St. Clair spent the rest of his days at home in Ligonier, Pennsylvania, where he died in poverty on August 31, 1818. He was a solid and dependable staff officer but lacked the dash and imagination necessary for higher command.

Further Reading
Edel, Wilbur. *Kekionga! The Worse Defeat in the History of the U. S. Army.* Westport, Conn.: Praeger, 1997.
Murphy, John A. *Shattered Glory.* Pataskala, Ohio: Brockston Pub. Co., 2000.
Phifer, Mike. "Campaign to Saratoga," *Military Heritage* 2, no. 1 (2000): 40–51, 94.
Ranzan, David. " 'Thus a War Has Begun': The Capture of Fort Ticonderoga and Its Influence on the American Revolution." Unpublished master's thesis, East Stroudsburg University, 2002.
Smith, William H. *The St. Clair Papers.* New York: Da Capo Press, 1971.
Willson, John. *Arthur St. Clair and the Northwest Ordinance.* Hillsdale, Mich.: Hillsdale College Press, 1993.

St. Leger, Barry (1737–1789)
English military officer
Barrimore Matthew St. Leger was born around May 1737 in County Kildare, Ireland, a nephew of the Fourth Viscount Doneraille. After passing through Eton and Cambridge he joined the army as an ensign with the 26th Regiment in April 1756

and shipped out to North America to fight in the French and Indian War. He performed well for General James Abercromby in 1757 and also rendered meritorious service at the captures of Louisbourg and Quebec. St. Leger won promotion to brigade major during General James Murray's advance upon Montreal in 1760 and afterward rose to major, 95th Regiment. When the Revolutionary War commenced in April 1775, St. Leger operated with the 34th Regiment as lieutenant colonel. In this capacity he assisted Governor-general Guy CARLETON by driving American forces out of Canada throughout the summer and fall of 1776. The following spring General John BURGOYNE arrived from England with reinforcements—and an audacious, three-pronged strategy for capturing Albany, New York, to separate New England from the rest of the colonies. An essential component of this plan was an ancillary offensive up the Mohawk River valley by forces that would ultimately unite with the main column at Albany. Burgoyne specifically requested St. Leger to conduct this part of the offensive, based on his reputation as a skilled and knowledgeable frontier fighter.

On June 23, 1777, St. Leger departed Montreal with an army of 2,000 men. Roughly half its number were Native Americans under Chiefs Joseph BRANT and CORNPLANTER, with the remainder equally divided between LOYALISTS under Colonel John JOHNSON and Major Walter BUTLER, and some British and HESSIAN regulars. He also took along several light artillery pieces but elected to leave heavier ordnance behind so as not to impede his wilderness march. The British landed at Oswego, New York, on July 25, then pushed steadily up the Mohawk River valley as planned. St. Leger's immediate objective was strategic Fort Stanwix (Rome, New York), positioned directly in his path. This recently repaired fortification was garrisoned by 750 men under Colonel Peter GANSEVOORT and ably seconded by Lieutenant Colonel Marinus WILLETT. Once St. Leger arrived outside and conducted a personal reconnaissance it was apparent that he had seriously underestimated both the size of the fort and its garrison. Concluding Fort Stanwix was beyond his capacity to storm, he threw a cordon of Indians around the post and established a loose siege. St. Leger then paraded his entire force in an attempt to awe the garrison into submission, but the sheer number of Indians convinced Gansevoort and others that they would be massacred if taken. The Americans consequently rejected all surrender summons and St. Leger commenced an ineffectual bombardment with his small cannon.

Lieutenant Colonel Barry St. Leger led a failed British attempt to capture Fort Stanwix in Rome, New York. *(Courtauld Institute of Art)*

Word of the British arrival promoted a relief column under Colonel Nicholas HERKIMER to march with 800 men from Fort Dayton. St. Leger was alerted of his impending arrival by Molly BRANT, the chief's sister, and he dispatched his Indians and Loyalists to interdict them. On August 6, 1777, a blood ambush was sprung at ORISKANY, which occasioned heavy losses to both sides, and the Americans withdrew. Meanwhile, the energetic Willett successfully sortied from Fort Stanwix and overran St. Leger's weakly defended camp, thoroughly plundering it. At this juncture, the Native Americans grew disheartened and began deserting St. Leger. He once more threatened the garrison with massacre if they did not surrender, but Gansevoort refused and the two men agreed upon a short truce. Willett was then dispatched to ride through British lines to Stillwater, where he conferred with General Philip J. SCHUYLER. The result was a new relief expedition under General Benedict ARNOLD, who sent a deranged man, Hon Yost, into the British camp. Yost's ravings about Arnold's force being "more numerous than the leaves on the trees" thoroughly unnerved the remaining Indians, and they abandoned the siege in droves. St. Leger, now badly outnumbered, had little recourse but to abandon Fort Stanwix on August 25, 1777, and he retraced his steps back into Canada. Defeat here denied Burgoyne badly needed reinforcements during his fateful campaign at Saratoga and directly contributed to ultimate capitulation.

Back at Montreal, St. Leger made a halting attempt to reinforce Burgoyne but proceeded no farther than Fort Ticonderoga when word of his surrender arrived. Thereafter he commanded several ranger companies and conducted several raids against the Americans, including a failed attempt to kidnap General Schuyler. In 1781 General Frederick HALDIMAND dispatched him back to Ticonderoga to confer with the dissident Ethan ALLEN, but their scheme came to naught. After the war St. Leger remained in Canada, and in 1784 he rose to brigadier general. He briefly succeeded Haldimand as commander in chief but poor health necessitated his retirement the following year, and he was dropped from the army list. St. Leger died in Canada in 1789, a solid regimental grade officer but decidedly less capable with an independent command.

Further Reading

Edgar, Gregory T. *Liberty or Death: The Northern Campaigns of the War for Independence.* Bowie, Md.: Heritage Books, 1993.

Luzader, John F., et al. *Fort Stanwix.* Washington, D.C.: National Park Service, 1975.

May, Robin. *The British Army in North America, 1775–1783.* New York: Hippocrene Books, 1997.

Scott, John A. *Fort Stanwix and Oriskany.* Rome, N.Y.: Rome Sentinel, 1927.

Venables, Robert W. "The Valley of Nettles: The Revolutionary War in the Mohawk Valley, Summer, 1777." Unpublished master's thesis, Vanderbilt University, 1965.

Watt, Gavin K. *Rebellion in the Mohawk Valley: The St. Leger Expedition of 1777.* Toronto: Dundurn Press, 2002.

Salomon, Haym (ca. 1740–1785)

American merchant, Patriot

Haym Salomon was born in Lissa, Poland, around 1740, into an observant Jewish family. His early life is not well known but he apparently migrated to New York sometime before the Revolutionary War erupted in 1775. Salomon was a unique individual through dint of extensive traveling in Europe and his skill at linguistics. Apparently he was fluent in German, Spanish, and French and became conversant in English. After arriving in New York City he established himself as a broker and merchant, making several important contacts among the local business elite. Salomon requested to serve the Patriot cause directly and gained appointment as sutler to the army of General Philip J. SCHUYLER. After the fall of New York to British forces under General William HOWE in September 1776, Salomon elected to remain behind as an intelligence operative. He was arrested and detained by British authorities for being a Patriot sympathizer, then released into the service of General Leopold von HEISTER, commanding general of HESSIAN forces, who valued his skills as a linguist. Salomon functioned in this capacity for several months while simultaneously gathering useful military intelligence and encouraging Germans to desert. He also aided innumerable American prisoners with money and facilitated their escape. When the British finally uncovered his clandestine activities, he was arrested again in August 1778 and condemned to death. Salomon then managed to bribe a prison guard and escaped to Philadelphia, abandoning his wife and child. Within two years they joined him in his new abode.

For three years Salomon made repeated requests for employment from the Continental CONGRESS but received no offers. He then set himself up as a commission merchant, specializing in foreign bills of exchange, and his command of French and Spanish proved most useful. In 1780 he worked closely with General Jean-Baptiste, comte de ROCHAMBEAU, and served as the treasurer of French expeditionary forces. Success attended his efforts, and his activities brought him to the attention of Robert MORRIS, newly appointed superintendent of the Office of Finance. Morris hired Salomon as a bill broker to help market foreign bills and raise money for the tottering American government. By the fall of 1781 his work proved instrumental in providing funds to underwrite the decisive YORKTOWN campaign that ended the war. As the economy gradually worsened by 1782, Salomon became the government's official broker and was authorized to market government bills. Having acquired great wealth and a generous reputation, he help fund Philadelphia's first synagogue and the Travelers Aid Society, America's first Jewish charity. More important, his ultimate cash investment in the government was estimated at $600,000—a tremendous sum for the time.

Salomon's unflinching and continued investments in rapidly depreciating government bills left him nearly destitute by war's end. In 1784 he purchased a house in New York, intending to move back, but then died of illness in Philadelphia on January 6, 1785. Reputedly, Salomon was so impoverished at the time that his family could not afford a headstone, hence his grave remains unmarked. But his skill as a financier, coupled with a willingness to invest his personal fortune in the American cause, marks him as one of the nation's earliest Jewish Patriots. Along with Morris, he was a bulwark of public credit and kept the American Revolution fiscally solvent.

Further Reading
American Jewish Historical Society. *Haym Salomon: A Gentleman of Precision and Integrity*. Waltham, Mass.: American Jewish Historical Society, 1976.
Andrews, Joseph L. "To Bigotry No Sanction: The Role of American Jews in the Revolution," *Midstream* 48, no. 4 (2002): 25–29.
Hirschfeld, Fritz. *George Washington of the Jews*. Newark: University of Delaware Press, 2005.
Rezneck, Samuel. *Unrecognized Patriots: The Jews in the American Revolution*. Westport, Conn.: Greenwood Press, 1995.
Sarna, Jonathan D., and Benny Kraut. *Jews and the Founding of the Republic*. New York: M. Wiener, 1985.
Schwartz, Laurens R. *Jews and the American Revolution: Haym Salomon and Others*. Jefferson, N.C.: McFarland, 1987.

Saltonstall, Dudley (1738–1796)
American naval officer
Dudley Saltonstall was born in New London, Connecticut, on September 8, 1738, the son of a militia general. He joined the merchant marine as a youth, displayed competency as a sailor, and served on a privateer during the French and Indian War. At the onset of the Revolutionary War, Saltonstall commanded the fort at New London and used family connections to acquire high military rank. His sister was married to Silas DEANE, a member of the Continental CONGRESS, who sat with the naval committee. Deane then arranged for his brother-in-law to be commissioned one of the first captains of the Continental NAVY on November 27, 1775. Saltonstall then assumed command of the converted merchantman *Alfred*

of 24 guns, which also served as the flagship for Commodore Esek HOPKINS. In February 1776 he accompanied Hopkins and his squadron on a successful foray against Nassau, capturing it on March 3, along with many valuable supplies. On the return leg of the voyage, he managed to seize the British brig *Bolton* but was then roughly handled by the frigate HMS *Glasgow* off Block Island. A congressional investigation cleared him of any misconduct but, when the captain's list was published that October, Saltonstall was rated fourth.

Shortly after returning to New London, Saltonstall obtained command of the brand-new frigate *Trumbull*. This deep-draft vessel took nearly two years to make its way over the sandbars in the Connecticut River, however, and Saltonstall was forced to accept another *Trumbull* operated by the Connecticut state navy. In April 1777 he made several small captures off the Virginia Capes, but it was not until the summer of 1779 that Saltonstall returned to a Continental warship. In June of that year British general Francis McLean occupied the Bagaduce peninsula of Penobscot, Maine, then administered by Massachusetts. State officials were eager to evict him, so they appealed to Congress for help, and Saltonstall arrived as commander of a large combined expedition. His force consisted of the frigate *Warren,* the brig *Diligent,* and the sloop *Providence,* along with 16 smaller armed vessels, 24 transports, and 900 militiamen under General Solomon LOVELL. This impressive armada dropped anchor off Penobscot on July 25, 1779, but no sooner had preparations been made to storm British-held Fort George than combined operations floundered upon cross-purposes. Lovell argued that the fort could not be taken until the navy first eliminated three small British warships in Penobscot Bay, while Saltonstall, leery of committing his vessels to confined waters, refused cooperation until the fort fell first. The embarrassing impasse continued for days until August 13, 1779, when a powerful British squadron under Commodore George COLLIER appeared off Penobscot Bay and sealed the Americans inside. Saltonstall ordered his ships withdrawn upstream where they were all burned to prevent capture. This action represented a tremendous loss to Massachusetts, both in terms of shipping and finances. After enduring a long walk back to Boston, Saltonstall was subjected to an immediate court-martial. Found guilty, he was unceremoniously dismissed from the Continental service on December 27, 1779.

Saltonstall eventually drifted back to New London, where he took charge of the privateer *Minerva*. He apparently enjoyed some minor successes before the war ended and then resumed his career in the merchant marine before dying at Mole Saint Nicolas, Hispaniola (Haiti) in 1796. Saltonstall was a marginally capable, if utterly recalcitrant, individual; his sole claim to fame rests with presiding over one of the largest disasters in U.S. naval history.

Further Reading

Buker, George E. *The Penobscot Expedition: Commander Saltonstall and the Massachusetts Conspiracy of 1779.* Annapolis, Md.: Naval Institute Press, 2002.

Corbin, Gary. "Disaster at Penobscot Bay." Unpublished master's thesis, State University of New York, Brockport, 1992.

Fay, John H. "Disaster on the Penobscot," *Naval History* 14, no. 6 (2000): 31–33.

Moody, Robert E., comp. *The Saltonstall Papers, 1607–1815.* Boston: Massachusetts Historical Society, 1972.

Norton, Louis A. "Dudley Saltonstall and the Penobscot Expedition, 1779," *Connecticut History* 42, no. 1 (2003): 19–39.

Sharp, Arthur G. "The Penobscot Expedition: An Exercise in Folly," *Military History* 20, no. 5 (2003): 50–57.

Sampson, Deborah (1760–1827)
American soldier

Deborah Sampson was born in Plympton, Massachusetts, on December 17, 1760, one of eight children born to a poor farming family. Her father died in her infancy so at the age of 10 she became indentured to farmer Jeremiah Thomas and spent several years toiling in his fields for freedom.

Already tall for her age, this employment rendered Sampson exceptionally strong and physically fit for a young woman. She was also quite adept at loading and shooting a musket. Once released from her indenture, Sampson taught school briefly but gradually became caught up in the patriotic ardor of the Revolutionary War. Tiring of domestic roles, in 1782 she disguised herself as a man and unsuccessfully attempted to enlist in the Continental ARMY. Sampson's perseverance finally paid off on May 20, 1782, when she managed to join the 4th Massachusetts Continental Infantry under the pseudonym Robert Schurtleff. She then marched off to New York to join her regiment at West Point. The war at that time was winding down, but LOYALISTS maintained a *petite guerre* throughout Hudson Valley. Sampson was involved in several skirmishes around Tarrytown, and in one exchange she received a ball in the thigh. Rather than risk being uncovered, she apparently extracted the ball by herself, dressed the wound, and maintained her secret identity.

Sampson endured the pain from her unhealed injury stoically and subsequently accompanied a surveying expedition to the Ohio Valley. She was regarded as an excellent soldier, and in 1783 General John PATERSON appointed her his aide in Philadelphia. Sampson apparently discharged her duties well until contracting a malignant fever. The doctor attending her subsequently discovered her gender and so informed Paterson. The general, rather pleasantly surprised, ordered Sampson paraded in front of her regiment in a dress, and so artfully had she conducted her ruse that nobody recognized her. In October 1783 Sampson was formally discharged by General Henry KNOX, who congratulated her for 18 months of devoted service to the country. She married Benjamin Gannett in 1784, settled at Sharon, Massachusetts, and had three children. However, Sampson suffered continually as a result of her wounds, and in 1790 she petitioned and received a pension from the state government. In 1797 Gannett printed a highly embellished edition of her memoirs entitled *The Female Review: or, Memoirs of an American Young Lady,* reigniting her celebrity. In 1802 she began touring New England bedecked in her old revolutionary uniform and lecturing about her experiences. Two years later noted Patriot Paul REVERE assisted her in securing a pension from CONGRESS, and she was also placed on the Massachusetts Invalid Pension Roll at $4.00 per year. Gannett (née Sampson) died in Sharon on April 29, 1827, at the age of 63, and was survived by her husband, Benjamin. He then applied to Congress for a military pension based on his wife's prior service but died himself before it materialized. But in 1838 Congress mandated payment of $466.00 to Gannett's children in light of their mother's contributions to national independence. In 1944 her memory was further perpetuated through christening of the Liberty ship *Deborah Gannett.*

Further Reading

Bohrer, Melissa L. *Glory, Passion, Principle: The Story of Eight Remarkable Women at the Core of the American Revolution.* New York: Atria Books, 2003.

Hiltner, Judith. " 'The Example of the Heroine': Deborah Sampson and the Legacy of Herman Mann's The Female Review," *American Studies* 41, no. 12 (2000): 93–113.

Keiter, James. *Deborah Sampson, Continental Soldier; the Westchester Connection.* Elmsford, N.Y.: Westchester County Historical Society, 2000.

Leonard, Patrick J. "As Private Robert Shurtliff, Deborah Sampson Served 18 Months in the Continental Army," *Military History* 18, no. 1 (2001): 16–20.

Swan, Jon. "Never Before a Case Like This," *MHQ* 10, no. 4 (1998): 98–101.

Young, Alfred F. *Masquerade: The Life and Times of Deborah Sampson, Continental Soldier.* New York: Alfred A. Knopf, 2004.

Savannah, siege of (September–October 1779)

In September 1778, Admiral Charles-Hector-Théodat, comte d'ESTAING, responded to the urging of his American allies and sailed from Haiti to the Georgia coast. On September 8 he dropped anchor off the Savannah River with 22 warships, 10 frigates, and numerous transports carrying

4,500 troops. Four days later the French landed men and equipment at Beaulieu's Plantation, eight miles south of Savannah, and began marching northward. At that time the city was defended by approximately 2,400 British, HESSIAN, and LOYALIST soldiers under General Augustin PREVOST. He availed himself of d'Estaing's leisurely approach to summon 800 additional regulars under Lieutenant Colonel John Maitland from Port Royal on the South Carolina coast. On September 16, 1779, the French were reinforced by the army of General Benjamin LINCOLN, who added another 1,600 Continentals and militia to the allied camp. D'Estaing then rather arrogantly issued a formal surrender summons to Savannah in the name of the French king, completely ignoring American sensitivities. Prevost requested and received 24 hours to consider the request and used the interval to further strengthen his works and allow Maitland's command, by dint of a heroic forced march through the swamp, to join his garrison. Thus augmented, Prevost flatly refused to surrender, and d'Estaing commenced formal siege operations on September 23. Over the next two weeks the British, aided by over 500 AFRICAN-AMERICAN slaves, fortified Savannah and thoroughly entrenched themselves for the inevitable onslaught.

The allies commenced digging a series of intricate trenches and parallels, and on October 4 their siege batteries commenced an ineffectual cannonade. After a five-day bombardment d'Estaing was pressured by his captains to abandon the siege and depart before the onset of hurricane season. He agreed to attack over Lincoln's objections, and the allies made preparations to carry the city by a *coup de main*. The plan called for a major diversion launched by 500 militia under General Isaac HUGER on the southwest corner of the city, while the main effort would be concentrated at the southeast corner, centered upon the Spring Hill redoubt. Unfortunately, Prevost was alerted to allied intentions by a deserter, and he redeployed all his best troops at the intended object. Early in the morning of October 9, 1779, Huger led his militia column out but became mired in a swamp and failed to carry out his feint effectively. Another major column under General Lachlan MCINTOSH also failed to make its rendezvous and, after receiving artillery fire, failed to press home. It thus fell upon a combined force of 1,200 French and Continental infantry under Colonel Francis MARION to storm the alerted British works.

The French and Americans bravely surged out of the swamps toward their objective, severely cut up by enemy fire. The French were repulsed, but a section of South Carolina Continentals under Marion gained a toehold on the parapet and a fierce hand-to-hand struggle erupted. The attackers were driven back and returned several times while Sergeant William JASPER managed to plant the regimental colors on the works before being killed. The allies made several determined efforts to storm the Spring Hill redoubt, and d'Estaing was wounded twice rallying his men but to no avail. In a heroic but foolish endeavor, General Kazimierz PULASKI also launched a headlong cavalry charge upon the British works and was heavily repulsed. Pulaski himself fell mortally wounded by canister fire. At daybreak French and American troops recoiled from the vicinity and retreated back to their lines. It had been a brief but bloody morning.

The siege of Savannah cost the allies 244 killed and 584 wounded, a very high proportion considering the number of troops involved. Prevost's men suffered an estimated 155 killed and wounded. Lincoln was willing to renew the contest on another day, but d'Estaing made preparations to embark, and on October 20, 1779, his fleet sailed from sight. Lincoln, now seriously outnumbered by Prevost, likewise withdrew back to Charleston, leaving Savannah under total British domination for three more years. This defeat, coupled with the unsuccessful affair at Newport in August 1778, placed the FRENCH ALLIANCE under tremendous strain. Furthermore, it induced General Henry CLINTON in New York to cobble together a new expedition of his own for his successful siege of CHARLESTON.

Further Reading

Cole, Richard C. "The Siege of Savannah and the British Press," *Georgia Historical Quarterly* 65, no. 3 (1981): 189–202.

Freeman, H. Ronald. *Savannah under Siege: The Bloodiest Battle of the Revolution.* Savannah, Ga.: Freeport Pub., 2002.

Kennedy, Benjamin, ed. *Muskets, Cannonballs, and Bombs: Nine Narratives of the Siege of Savannah in 1779.* Savannah, Ga.: Beehive Press, 1974.

Wilson, David K. *The Southern Strategy: Britain's Conquest of South Carolina and Georgia, 1775–1780.* Columbia: University of South Carolina Press, 2005.

Scammell, Alexander (1747–1781)
American military officer

Alexander Scammell was born in Milford, Massachusetts, on March 27, 1747, the son of a physician. He attended Harvard College, acquiring his master's in 1772, and briefly taught school thereafter. He relocated to Durham, New Hampshire, the following year and studied law in the office of John SULLIVAN. Scammell had also committed himself to the Patriot cause, and on December 15, 1774, he accompanied Sullivan on a raid to seize arms and ammunition from Fort William and Mary. Following the onset of hostilities with Great Britain, Scammell became a major in the New Hampshire militia and subsequently served in the siege of Boston as brigade major to state troops. General George WASHINGTON was impressed by the young man's demeanor and upon his recommendation the Continental CONGRESS elevated him to brigade major in the Continental ARMY. In this capacity Scammell accompanied Sullivan to Canada and helped cover the American retreat during the spring of 1776. He performed so well that he became colonel of the 3rd New Hampshire Continental Infantry and aide-de-camp to General Washington. Scammell next fought at LONG ISLAND, TRENTON, and PRINCETON, winning applause for coolness under fire. By the summer of 1777 his regiment formed part of General Enoch POOR's brigade and fought at FREEMAN's FARM and BEMIS HEIGHTS. Scammell was wounded in the last engagement, but Washington, in dire need of competent staff officers, appointed him adjutant general of the army on January 15, 1778, to replace outgoing Timothy PICKERING.

In a military establishment renowned for chaotic paperwork, Scammell functioned capably within Washington's staff and also worked closely with General Friedrich von STEUBEN to help systematize and standardize administrative procedures. His other routine duties included the arrest of General Charles LEE for insubordination at MONMOUTH and arranging the execution of Major John ANDRE. Despite these contributions, Scammell yearned for action, and on September 30, 1780, he resigned from headquarters to resume duties with his regiment and was replaced by Colonel Edward HAND. In the spring of 1781 he accepted command of a newly raised corps of light infantry as part of the marquis de LAFAYETTE's division. As such he bore a full measure in the operations at YORKTOWN and found himself deployed at Gloucester on the opposite side of the York River. On September 30, 1781, Scammell was reconnoitering British lines when he was surprised by cavalry belonging to Lieutenant Colonel Banastre TARLETON's British Legion and taken prisoner. He was then either accidentally or deliberately shot in the back while a captive. Scammell was returned to American forces the following day and died of his injuries at Williamsburg on October 6, 1781. The nature of his demise angered the rank and file of his command, and on October 14, 1781, following the storming of British Redoubt No. 10, Colonel Alexander HAMILTON physically restrained them from killing their captives. Scammell, for the time that he served, was among the best-functioning staff officers in the Continental army.

Further Reading

Clough, William O. "Colonel Alexander Scammell," *Granite Monthly* 14 (September 1892): 262–275.

Coffin, Charles. *The Lives and Services of Major General John Thomas, Colonel Thomas Knowlton, Colonel Alexander Scammell, and Major General Henry Dearborn.* New York: Egbert, Havey, & King, 1845.

Lefkowitz, Arthur S. *George Washington's Indispensable Men: The 32 Aides-de-camp Who Helped Win American Independence.* Mechanicsburg, Pa.: Stackpole Books, 2003.

Randall, Peter. *New Hampshire: Years of Revolution, 1774–1783.* Hanover, N.H.: Profiles Pub. Co., 1976.

Scammell, Alexander. "Two Letters of Col. Alexander Scammell," *Magazine of American History* 10 (August 1883): 151–155.

———. "Colonel Alexander Scammell and His Letters from 1768 to 1781," *Historical Magazine* 8 (September 1870): 129–146.

Schuyler, Philip J. (1733–1804)
American military officer

Philip John Schuyler was born in Albany, New York, on November 20, 1733, into a wealthy family of Dutch ancestry. As an aristocrat he was well educated, and he also developed an affinity for the nearby Mohawk Indians, becoming fluent in their language. During the French and Indian War Schuyler served as a militia captain, specializing in logistics and performing well. Afterward he settled into the role of a wealthy patroon, or landowner, eventually becoming one of New York's wealthiest citizens. In 1768 he commenced his political career by winning a seat in the colonial legislature, where he modestly criticized British imperial policy but distanced himself from radical elements within the SONS OF LIBERTY. He also served on a commission tasked with resolving a territorial dispute between New York and New Hampshire and made powerful enemies throughout New England for siding with his colony. After the Revolutionary War commenced in April 1775, Schuyler was elected a delegate to the Second Continental CONGRESS in Philadelphia and sat on a commission drawing up rules and regulations for the nascent Continental ARMY. In this capacity he met and befriended General George WASHINGTON, who prevailed on Congress to make him one of four new major generals on June 15, 1775. Schuyler clearly possessed military potential, but his appointment reflected more the need to solidify New York's support for the war.

Schuyler thus became commander of the Northern Department, centered upon Albany, and was tasked with preparing an invasion of Quebec. Beforehand, he urgently conferred with leaders of the Six Nations, many of whom he knew personally, and secured Iroquois neutrality over the next two years. During this interval, command devolved upon General Richard MONTGOMERY, who impatiently launched the Canadian invasion without authorization. Schuyler, debilitated by gout, approved of his advance and remained behind to orchestrate the flow of supplies and reinforcements. However, when the attack on Quebec City disastrously failed that December, Schuyler's New England enemies blamed him for the debacle and demanded his resignation. Subsequent affairs in Canada fell upon General John SULLIVAN, who was gradually forced back onto New York territory by Governor-General Guy CARLETON. Schuyler, anticipating a Patriot defeat, speedily rushed boats and transportation up Lake Champlain to spare Sullivan's force from impending capture. Fort Ticonderoga was then hastily garrisoned and strengthened to obstruct Carleton's advance. Schuyler also authorized General Benedict ARNOLD to commence building a fleet of gunboats, which was ultimately defeated by the British at Valcour Island in October 1776. But such tactical ploys convinced Carleton not to advance upon Ticonderoga that winter, and he returned to Canada, granting the Americans time to recuperate.

Schuyler was incensed by his critics in Congress, and he engaged in a disrespectful diatribe that resulted in his dismissal and replacement by General Horatio GATES by March 1777. An uproar ensued from the New York delegation, however, and he was restored to command shortly after. By summer Schuyler had made strenuous preparations to contest a large British invasion down the Lake Champlain corridor under General John BURGOYNE. The Americans had high hopes that Fort Ticonderoga was unassailable, but on July 6 General Arthur ST. CLAIR, outgunned and outnumbered, evacuated it without a struggle. Schuyler approved the withdrawal and ordered a move southward, taking great pains to fell trees and erect other obstacles to impede Burgoyne's advance. This strategy successfully allowed the Americans to consolidate their defenses at Saratoga, but congressional critics howled over Schuyler's perceived ineptitude. In August 1777 he was again relieved of command and replaced by the ever-ambitious Gates. The general angrily demanded and received a court-martial, which convened in 1778 and cleared him of improprieties, but thereafter he remained without a command. Schuyler resigned his commission in April 1779, returned to Congress, and saw no further military service. Washington still valued his friendship highly and called upon him for advice throughout Sullivan's punitive Indian expedition of 1779. Schuyler, despite a real grasp for strategy and logistics, remains the only senior American commander who never fought a major battle. But his Fabian tactics, however unpopular politically, laid the groundwork for an eventual American victory at Saratoga in October.

After the war Schuyler resumed his political activities at home by serving in the state senate. In 1787 he attended the state constitutional convention and lobbied on behalf of its passage. Consequently, he became one of two U.S. senators appointed to the new federal Congress in 1789. There Schuyler functioned as a staunch Federalist and fully embraced the economic and fiscal policies of his son-in-law, Alexander HAMILTON. He lost a bid for reelection in 1792, won his seat back in 1797, then resigned a year later owing to poor health. Schuyler died in Albany on November 18, 1804, a senior military leader of the Revolutionary War—and among its most controversial.

Further Reading

Billias, George A., ed. *George Washington's Generals*. New York: Morrow, 1964.

Bush, Martin H. *Revolutionary Enigma: A Re-Appraisal of General Philip Schuyler of New York*. Port Washington, N.Y.: Ira J. Friedman, 1969.

Gerlach, Don R. *Proud Patriot: Philip Schuyler and the War of Independence, 1775–1783*. Syracuse, N.Y.: Syracuse University Press, 1987.

Nelson, Paul D. "Legacy of Controversy: Gates, Schuyler, and Arnold at Saratoga," *Military Affairs* 37, no. 2 (1973): 41–47.

Phifer, Mike. "Campaign to Saratoga," *Military Heritage* 2, no. 1 (2000): 40–51, 94.

Rossie, Jonathan G. *The Politics of Command in the American Revolution*. Syracuse, N.Y.: Syracuse University Press, 1975.

Scott, Charles (ca. 1739–1813)
American military officer

Charles Scott was born in Powhatan County, Virginia, around 1739. Orphaned while young, he fled an apprenticeship program and joined Colonel George WASHINGTON's Virginia Regiment in 1755. Scott fought well during the ill-fated expedition of General James Braddock, served in the Cherokee War of 1759–60, and departed militia service a captain. He sided with the Patriots after the onset of the Revolutionary War and raised an independent militia company in April 1775. Shortly thereafter he was voted commander in chief of all state forces but eventually lost that position to General Andrew LEWIS. Scott next became lieutenant colonel of the 2nd Virginia Regiment the following August. He performed conspicuously at the Battle of Great Bridge on December 9, 1775, and helped defeat LOYALIST forces of Governor John MURRAY, Lord Dunmore. In light of good service, Scott rose to colonel of the 2nd Virginia Continental Infantry in February 1776, although he subsequently transferred to the 5th Infantry. He won praise for hard fighting at the December 26, 1776, Battle at TRENTON and then for skirmishing along Assumpink Creek on January 3, 1777. The following month he drove off superior British and HESSIAN foraging parties at Drake's Farm. Such good conduct resulted in his promotion to brigadier general on April 2, 1777, and, along with William WOODFORD, he helped comprise General Adam Stephen's Virginia division.

Scott was closely engaged at the Battle of BRANDYWINE in September 1777, where his stubborn delaying tactics slowed a determined flank attack by General Charles CORNWALLIS. The following month he attacked zestfully at GERMANTOWN but, like other formations, became lost in a fog and ultimately withdrew. In August 1778 he fought as part of General Charles LEE's division and inexplicably retreated from the battlefield. However, he did so only at the behest of Lee and later testified against him at his court-martial. Afterward Washington placed Scott in charge of his intelligence apparatus until he went on leave in the spring of 1779. That May the government of Virginia recalled him to active service to help repel the raid of Commodore George COLLIER and, while he saw no fighting, he received an elegant steed for organizing local defenses. In December 1779 Scott was ordered to take recruits down to South Carolina and join the army of General Benjamin LINCOLN. He unfortunately arrived just as General Henry CLINTON commenced the siege of CHARLESTON and fell captive when the city surrendered on May 12, 1780. Scott was paroled soon after and ultimately exchanged for Colonel Francis RAWDON in July 1782. He was breveted major general in September 1782 just prior to being discharged.

After the war Scott relocated to the frontier wilds of Kentucky, where he became embroiled in a decadelong war against hostile tribesmen. He accompanied the failed expedition of Colonel Josiah Harmar and witnessed his son brutally scalped before his own eyes in November 1791. Promoted to major general of Kentucky militia, he then led two organized raids by 1,500 mounted riflemen against villages in Ohio and Indiana before supporting General Anthony WAYNE's victory at Fallen Timbers in August 1794. Back home, Scott delved into local politics as a Jeffersonian Democratic-Republican, and in 1808 he was elected governor of Kentucky. He energetically upheld the public interest and also helped mobilize state resources and manpower in the War of 1812. One of his final acts was appointing future president William Henry Harrison a major general of militia in August 1812, and he prevailed upon President James MADISON to employ Harrison in the Old Northwest. Scott, a celebrated frontier figure like his great contemporary Daniel BOONE, died at his home in Clark County on October 22, 1813. At the time he was one of the last surviving Revolutionary War generals.

Further Reading

Harrison, Lowell H., ed. *Governor of Kentucky.* Lexington: University Press of Kentucky, 2004.

Heathcote, Charles W. "General Charles Scott—an Able Officer on Whom Much Depended," *Picket Post* no. 57 (July 1957): 4–16.

Lobdell, Jared C. "Two Forgotten Battles in the Revolution," *New Jersey History* 85, nos. 3–4 (1967): 225–234.

Sellers, John R. "The Virginia Continental Line, 1775–1780." Unpublished Ph.D. diss., Tulane University, 1968.

Smucker, Isaac. "General Charles Scott," *Historical Magazine* 3 (February 1874): 88–90.

Ward, Harry M. *Charles Scott and the "Spirit of 76."* Charlottesville: University Press of Virginia, 1988.

Sevier, John (1745–1815)
American militia officer

John Sevier was born near New Market, Virginia, on September 23, 1745, the son of a farmer. Well educated locally by contemporary standards, he labored as a farmer and land speculator for many years before migrating to the Watauga River settlement (present-day Tennessee) in 1772. The following year he moved again to the Holston River region and joined the militia as a captain. Sevier fought in the Battle of Point Pleasant under Colonel Andrew LEWIS on October 10, 1774. Afterward he severed all political ties to Virginia by winning a seat in the North Carolina provincial legislature. There Sevier represented the so-called Washington District and prevailed upon the assembly to annex it as a western county of North Carolina. This done, he also served as a county clerk and as a lieutenant colonel of militia commencing in 1777. Sevier was continually active in frontier defense matters and waged a long and bloody partisan conflict against Cherokee bands under DRAGGING CANOE. While defending Fort Watauga from an Indian attack on July 21, 1776, Sevier rescued a girl who leapt into his arms and ultimately married him four years later. Significantly, he had been warned of the attack in advance by the Cherokee woman Nancy WARD.

By 1780 the tempo of war had increased throughout the south once British forces overrode South Carolina and pressed northward under General Charles CORNWALLIS. The left flank of his army consisted of LOYALISTS under Major Patrick FERGUSON, a noted light infantry specialist. During the summer of 1780, Ferguson dispatched messengers to the Overmountain districts in Tennessee, threatening them with "fire and sword" if they failed to renew their allegiance to the Crown. Sevier, accompanied by Colonel Isaac SHELBY, eagerly took up the challenge and organized 240 gruff frontiersmen at Sycamore Shoals before leading them into North Carolina to confront Ferguson. There they joined Majors Joseph McDOWELL and Joseph WINSTON, while Colonel William CAMPBELL of Virginia was elected nominal commander of the ad hoc force. The 1,200-man militia finally cornered the British at KING'S MOUNTAIN on October 7, 1780, where Sevier bore a conspicuous role in leading his men up the "heel" of Ferguson's position, crushing the enemy and winning great renown. He then briefly operated with the partisans of General Francis MARION in South Carolina before returning to Tennessee and continuing his *petite guerre* against the Cherokee. Sevier defeated Dragging Canoe's band at Boyd's Creek on December 16, 1780, and, almost two years later, defeated him again at Lookout Mountain on September 20, 1782. This, one of the last pitched engagements of the Revolutionary War, finally convinced Dragging Canoe to surrender and resulted in additional land concessions from the Indians.

Afterward Sevier's career and reputation became increasingly entwined in frontier politics. He was a driving force behind creation of the new state of "Franklin" in March 1785, in which he served as governor, but it collapsed in 1788 once the Confederation CONGRESS refused recognition. He then lived several months as an outlaw, but Sevier was ultimately paroled and began cavorting with the Spanish possibly to detach the southwest from the United States. This scheme also collapsed, and by 1789 he regained his respectability by winning a seat in the North Carolina senate. After serving in the state constitutional convention Sevier successfully stood for a seat in the new U.S. House of Representatives in 1789. However, once Tennessee was formally admitted into the Union as a state, he came home and became its first governor. Sevier won three consecutive terms, generally acquitting himself well and upholding the public trust. In 1798 President John ADAMS also appointed him a brigadier general in the U.S. Army during the crisis with France. Sevier again served as governor of Tennessee, 1803–09, and

American militiaman John Sevier became the first governor of Tennessee. *(Tennessee State Museum, Tennessee Historical Society Collection)*

from 1810 to 1815 he retained his old seat in the national Congress. In 1812 he spoke out strongly in favor of renewed war against Great Britain, and three years later President James MADISON appointed him to a commission to establish new boundaries for the Creek Nation. Sevier, a legendary frontier figure, died at Fort Decatur, Alabama, on September 24, 1815.

Further Reading
Bradley, Michael R. "John Sevier, 1745–1815," *Franklin County Historical Review* 23, no. 1 (1992): 7–10.
Driver, Carl S. *John Sevier, Pioneer of the Old Southwest.* Chapel Hill: University of North Carolina Press, 1932.
Evans, E. Raymond. "Was the Last Battle of the American Revolution Fought on Lookout Mountain?" *Journal of Cherokee Studies* 5, no. 1 (1980): 30–40.
Hildreth, Howard P. "John Sevier and Isaac Shelby," *Virginia Cavalcade* 14, no. 3 (1964): 10–15.
Hindraker, Eric, and Peter C. Mancall. *At the Edge of Empire: The Backcountry of British North America.* Baltimore: Johns Hopkins University Press, 2003.
Turner, Francis M. *Life of General John Sevier.* Johnson City, Tenn.: Overmountain Press, 1997.

Shelby, Evan (1719–1794)
American militia officer

Evan Shelby was born in Tregaron, Wales, in October 1719, and he migrated with his family to Pennsylvania by 1735. Four years later he ended up in Hagerstown, Maryland, and in 1758 he became a lieutenant for service in the French and Indian War. Shelby was promoted to captain and commanded a ranger company for General John Forbes during the Fort Duquesne expedition and is attributed with slaying a noted Indian chief in personal combat. Afterward he moved to the Virginia frontier near present-day Bristol, Tennessee, to speculate in land and trade with the Indians. In 1772 he also established Fort Shelby, which served as a major defensive post for the Holston Valley. Shelby resumed his military activities in 1774 as a captain commanding the Fincastle County militia; his son, Isaac SHELBY, served as his lieutenant. In this capacity he participated in Lord Dunmore's war and fought conspicuously under Colonel Andrew LEWIS at the Battle of Point Pleasant, October 10, 1774.

In the period leading up to the Revolutionary War, Shelby served with the Fincastle Committee of Safety and rose in rank to major. He then accompanied the Overhill Cherokee expedition of Colonel William Christian in August 1776. Promoted to colonel for good performance, Shelby next helped negotiate the Treaty of Long Island with the Cherokee on July 20, 1777. He then served as justice of the peace in newly created Washington County. Two years later Governor Patrick HENRY chose Shelby to lead a new expedition against the Chickamauga faction of the Cherokee Nation under DRAGGING CANOE. Concluding a successful campaign, he rose to brigadier general of militia and received the Thanks of CONGRESS. Shelby then resumed his surveying activities during a lull in the fighting, at which time his home at Sapling Grove was discovered to be in North Carolina territory. In March 1781 General Nathanael GREENE tapped him to renegotiate the Treaty of Long Island with the Cherokee, and he subsequently won a seat in the North Carolina senate.

After the war Shelby functioned as a brigadier general of North Carolina militia at the behest of Governor Richard CASWELL and, after 1787, he worked with John SEVIER, governor of the renegade state of Franklin, to circumvent outbreaks of frontier violence. He performed honestly in that role and was nominated to succeed Sevier as governor of Franklin but declined to serve. Shelby resigned from the militia soon after, and he died at his home in Sapling Grove on December 4, 1794.

Further Reading
Barnes, Arthur G. "The Virginia-North Carolina Frontier in 1776: William Preston, William Christian, and the Military Expedition against the Overhill Cherokee Towns." Unpublished master's thesis, College of William and Mary, 1969.
Burton, Patricia. *Virginia Begins to Remember: Her Men Who Went to "The Point" in 1774: Opening of the American Revolution.* Birmingham, Mich.: Burton, 1980.

Hammond, Neal O., and Richard Taylor. *Virginia's Western War, 1775–1786.* Mechanicsburg, Pa.: Stackpole Books, 2002.
Hindracker, Eric., and Peter C. Mancall. *At the Edge of Empire: The Backcountry of British North America.* Baltimore: Johns Hopkins University Press, 2003.
Nester, William R. *The Frontier War for American Independence.* Mechanicsburg, Pa.: Stackpole Books, 2004.
Powell, Allan. *Forgotten Heroes of the Maryland Frontier.* Baltimore: Gateway Press, 2001.

Shelby, Isaac (1750–1826)
American militia officer

Isaac Shelby was born near Hagerstown, Maryland, on December 11, 1750, the son of Evan SHELBY. He relocated with his family to the Holston River region of modern-day Tennessee and grew up steeped in the nuances of frontier living and fighting. When Virginia governor John MURRAY, Lord Dunmore, provoked a conflict with the Shawnee under Chief CORNSTALK, Shelby joined the local militia as a lieutenant and served under his father. On October 10, 1774, he fought conspicuously at the Battle of Point Pleasant, storming high ground on the Indian flank and forcing them to retreat. Afterward he helped command a garrison maintained on the site of the engagement. In 1776 Shelby rejoined the militia as a captain and was appointed by Governor Patrick HENRY to fulfill commissary duties along the western frontier. In this capacity he materially aided Colonel George Rogers CLARK's effort in the Illinois territory and his own father's defeat of DRAGGING CANOE along the Tennessee River in 1779. When it was discovered that his home actually lay within the confines of North Carolina, he became colonel of militia and was also elected to a session in the state assembly.

Shelby was visiting Kentucky when the British concluded the siege of CHARLESTOWN and began pressing northward against feeble resistance. He hurried home, raised 200 men on a 30-day enlistment period, and joined forces with Colonel Joseph MCDOWELL to contest the advance of General Charles CORNWALLIS and his LOYALIST allies. On July 31, 1780, Shelby and his cohorts managed to surround Thickety Fort on the Pacolet River and bluffed its commander into surrendering 94 prisoners without a shot. He then operated with a roving band of partisans under Lieutenant Colonel Elijah CLARKE and, taking 200 men, they moved against a Loyalist outpost at Musgrove Mills. Though outnumbered two to one he helped repulse a determined attack and drove them from the field. Such activities threatened Cornwallis's rear area security so he dispatched a large Loyalist force under Major Patrick FERGUSON to dispense with the guerrillas. But these efforts were completely overshadowed on August 16, 1780, after the British victory at CAMDEN, whereupon all organized resistance in South Carolina collapsed. Consequently, McDowell, Clarke, and Shelby took

Isaac Shelby, hero of King's Mountain and a future governor of Kentucky *(Filson Historical Society, Louisville, Kentucky)*

their forces westward and melted away into the frontier hinterlands, awaiting developments.

At length, as Cornwallis pushed into North Carolina, Ferguson felt sufficiently emboldened to send messages to "Over the Mountain Men" and threatened their homes with destruction if they did not submit. His missive had an unexpectedly galvanizing effect on the frontiersmen, for Shelby, in concert with John SEVIER, quickly raised a force of 200 volunteers at Sycamore Shoals and headed back into North Carolina. There they accepted the leadership of Colonel William CAMPBELL and marched to intercept Ferguson before he reached the main British column. On October 7, 1780, the Americans cornered him at KING'S MOUNTAIN, just over the South Carolina border, and attacked. The sharpshooting frontiersmen wiped out Ferguson and his entire command, the first of many reverses Cornwallis would suffer. Shelby conspicuously distinguished himself in both planning and executing the battle, and he emerged as a regional hero. He then campaigned several weeks under General Francis MARION and assisted in the capture of Monk's Corner, South Carolina, before returning home.

After the war Shelby parlayed his wartime popularity into a viable political career. He relocated to Kentucky and helped organize the defenses and political infrastructure of that region, being elected the first governor in 1792. Throughout his term in office he criticized President George WASHINGTON's foreign policy as too cautious and gave unstinting support to the Indian campaigns of General Anthony WAYNE in 1794. Shelby spent many years as one of the state's leading citizens until 1812, when he succeeded Charles SCOTT for a second term as governor. In this capacity he forcefully mobilized Kentucky for the War of 1812, and in 1813 he personally took to the field at the head of 3,500 mounted riflemen to assist General William Henry Harrison at the Thames, Ontario. Congress awarded him a gold medal and Shelby retired to private life. In 1817 he declined President James MONROE's offer to serve as secretary of war. Shelby died near Danville, Kentucky on July 18, 1826, one of the most celebrated frontiersmen of his generation and an effective partisan leader.

Further Reading
Hamilton, J. G. De Roulhac, ed. "King's Mountain: Letters of Colonel Isaac Shelby," *Journal of Southern History* 4 (1938): 367–377.
Hildreth, Howard P. "John Sevier and Isaac Shelby," *Virginia Cavalcade* 14, no. 3 (1964): 10–15.
Hindraker, Eric, and Peter C. Mancall. *At the Edge of Empire: The Backcountry of British North America*. Baltimore: Johns Hopkins University Press, 2003.
Keller, S. Roger. *Isaac Shelby: A Driving Force in America's Struggle for Independence*. Shippensburg, Pa.: Burd Street Press, 2000.
Riley, Agnes. "The Shelby-Campbell King's Mountain Controversy and the Gubernatorial Campaign of 1812," *Filson Club History Quarterly* 66, no. 2 (1992): 220–231.
Wrobel, Sylvia, and George Grider. *Isaac Shelby*. Danville, Ky.: Cumberland Press, 1974.

Sheldon, Elisha (1740–?)
American military officer

Elisha Sheldon was born in Lyme, Connecticut, in 1740, and he settled in nearby Salisbury to farm. Brash and somewhat rakish by nature, he also served in the local cavalry troop as a captain. When the Revolutionary War began in April 1775, Sheldon transferred his allegiance to the Patriots and in 1776 became a major in the Connecticut Light Horse Regiment. He campaigned in New York under General George WASHINGTON, who found little use for the mounted arm beyond scouting and skirmishing. Nonetheless, Sheldon performed competently and in December 1776 he was installed as colonel of the newly created 2nd Continental Light Dragoons. This unit consisted of four troops raised in Connecticut, with one each from Massachusetts and New Jersey. They performed the usual reconnaissance duties throughout the Philadelphia campaign of 1777, whereupon Sheldon was transferred to the Hudson River region. There his units served as the eyes and ears of Major Benjamin TALLMADGE's intelligence apparatus. On August 13, 1777, while battling a LOYALIST uprising at Flockey, New York, a troop of Sheldon's unit made military history in the first American cavalry charge.

Sheldon's main action in the war occurred on July 2, 1779, at Poundridge, New York. On that day Lieutenant Colonel Banastre TARLETON advanced out of White Plains attempting to capture Major Ebenezer Lockwood, a noted partisan. Tarleton headed his own British Legion, some of the Queen's Rangers under Major John Graves SIMCOE, and 70 troopers from the 17th Light Dragoons, for a total of 360 men. Sheldon, whose command consisted of only 70 dragoons, attempted to stand at Poundridge but was surprised and driven back by sheer numbers. Lockwood managed to escape but the raiders burned several buildings before withdrawing. They also captured Sheldon's regimental colors, which had been stored with some officer's baggage. The Americans lost eight missing and 10 wounded to a British total of one dead and one injured. Despite this setback, Sheldon was promoted to brigadier general on September 30, 1780, and continued waging his little war of outposts. On July 3, 1781, Sheldon was part of an unsuccessful American raid to seize noted Loyalist Oliver De Lancey near Morrisania, New York, one of several moves intended as cover for the Franco-American march to Virginia. Sheldon and his unit were not discharged but rather furloughed from government service in November 1783 and returned to the service of Connecticut. A gallant trooper, it is not known when or where he died.

Further Reading
Hays, John T. *Connecticut's Revolutionary Cavalry, Sheldon's Horse.* Chester, Conn.: Pequot Press, 1975.
———. *Elisha Sheldon: Washington's First Choice to Command Continental Cavalry.* Fort Lauderdale, Fla.: Saddlebag Press, 1994.
———. *The Poundridge Raid: Banastre Tarleton versus Elisha Sheldon, July 2, 1779.* Fort Lauderdale, Fla.: Saddlebag Press, 1987.
———. *A Substantial Yeomanry: The Connecticut Light Horse, 1776–1783.* Fort Lauderdale, Fla.: Saddlebag Press, 1994.

Lockey, Donald V. "Cavalry of the Continental Army during the War of the American Revolution, 1775–1783." Unpublished master's thesis, Duke University, 1971.
Loescher, Burt G. *Washington's Eyes: The Continental Light Dragoons.* Fort Collins, Colo.: Old Army Press, 1977.

Sherman, Roger (1721–1793)
American politician

Roger Sherman was born in Milford, Massachusetts, on April 19, 1721, the son of a cobbler. He trained as a shoemaker but also took an interest in surveying and eventually relocated to New Haven, Connecticut, to work there. Sherman gradually developed a taste for law and was admitted to the bar in 1754; he subsequently functioned as a successful merchant, a justice of the peace, and a judge on the superior court. He also found time to hold seats in both the upper and lower chambers of the colonial legislature, while also serving as treasurer of Yale College. In 1768 that esteemed institution awarded the former shoemaker an honorary master's degree. Politically, Sherman generally sided with the Patriots in the run-up to war with Great Britain, and he strongly denounced Parliament's ability to tax the colonies. But Sherman was no radical and he decried violence, hoping for a peaceful solution to the crisis. When this outcome proved untenable, he served with the New Haven COMMITTEE OF CORRESPONDENCE and also endorsed the nonimportation of British goods.

In 1774 Sherman became a delegate to the First Continental CONGRESS, where he signed the Declaration of Association to enforce the boycott. The following year he sat with the Second Congress and served on the committee drafting the DECLARATION OF INDEPENDENCE. Sherman, though low-key and somewhat undramatic by nature, proved himself a surprisingly artful legislator and was possibly the most influential delegate at Philadelphia. He helped draft the ARTICLES OF CONFEDERATION while also serving on the committee of ways and means, the Board of War and Ordnance, and the committee on Indian affairs. Furthermore Sherman, drawing upon his own experience as a successful businessman, argued that the war should be financed by higher taxes instead of the ruinous practices of constantly borrowing and issuing paper money. Calm, impeccably honest, and methodical, he was deemed "the Old Puritan" by fellow New Englander John ADAMS.

After the war Sherman returned home to resume his political career. He was elected mayor of New Haven in 1784 and also helped codify the state's statutory laws. Sherman had always felt that the Articles of Confederation needed strengthening but now recognized that an entirely new scheme of governance was necessary. Thus in 1787 he represented Connecticut at the Constitutional Convention in Philadelphia and performed his most useful work by championing the so-called Great Compromise. This plan broke the deadlock between large and small states by proposing a bicameral congress consisting of a lower house based on population and an upper house (senate) where all states enjoyed equal representation. His proposal paved the ground for the constitution's approval by fellow delegates, and he later proved instrumental in securing Connecticut's ratification. Afterward, Sherman resumed his national career by winning a seat in the U.S. House of Representatives from 1789 to 1791, and then the U.S. Senate from 1791 to 1793 as a Federalist. Here he supported Alexander HAMILTON's policy of assuming state debts and also opposed relocating the national capital to the Potomac. Sherman died in New Haven on July 23, 1791; like Robert MORRIS, he is the only other individual to sign all three seminal documents of American political history: the Declaration of Independence, the Articles of Confederation, and the U.S. Constitution. He is the only person to have also signed the Articles of Association in 1774, for a total of four.

Further Reading

Boardman, Roger S. *Roger Sherman, Signer and Statesman.* Philadelphia: University of Pennsylvania Press, 1938.

Callahan, North. *Connecticut's Revolutionary War Leaders.* Chester, Conn.: Pequot Press, 1973.

Collier, Christopher. *Roger Sherman's Connecticut: Yankee Politics and the American Revolution.* Middletown, Conn.: Wesleyan University Press, 1971.

Gerber, Scott D. "Roger Sherman and the Bill of Rights," *Polity* 28, no. 4 (1996): 521–540.

Grossbart, Stephen R. "The Revolutionary Transition: Politics, Religion, and Economy in Eastern Connecticut, 1765–1800." Unpublished Ph.D. diss., University of Michigan, 1989.

Rommel, John G. *Connecticut Yankee Patriot: Roger Sherman.* Hartford: American Revolution Bicentennial Commission of Connecticut, 1980.

Shippen, Margaret (1760–1804)
Loyalist spy

Margaret Shippen was born in Philadelphia, Pennsylvania, on June 11, 1760, into one of the colony's foremost families. Her father, in addition to being a leading merchant, also served as chief justice of Pennsylvania. "Peggy" Shippen matured into a bright young lady, excelling in mathematics and adept at bookeeping, accounting, and real estate. And, despite her reputation as a beguiling belle, she inherited her father's strict LOYALIST sensibilities. By the advent of British occupation of Philadelphia in the fall of 1777, the 18-year-old Shippen began attracting the attention of several British officers, most notably the dashing captain John ANDRE. The two maintained a romantic relationship for several months until General William HOWE was ordered to transfer his troops back to New York. Before parting, Shippen acquired a lock of Andre's hair as a memento and maintained—at great personal risk—a steady and secret correspondence.

Once American forces reoccupied Philadelphia in May 1778, General Benedict ARNOLD gained appointment as military governor of the city. In this capacity he encountered the alluring 19-year-old Shippen at a social function and was gradually smitten with her. The two then courted and were married on April 8, 1779, just as Arnold was buffeted by allegations of misappropriating funds and misusing his authority. He also resented what he

Margaret Shippen Arnold was instrumental in persuading her already disgruntled husband, Benedict Arnold, to betray the Patriots and become a spy for the British. *(National Archives)*

deemed—perhaps justly—lack of recognition from the Continental CONGRESS and began questioning his relationship to the Patriot side. His anger intensified after he was found guilty of misappropriating funds and received a mild rebuke from his erstwhile friend and superior, General George WASHINGTON. It was precisely at this juncture that the highly intelligent, well-placed Mrs. Benedict Arnold prevailed on her husband to switch sides. Eventually, he began clandestine contacts with General Henry CLINTON in New York and offered to surrender highly sensitive military intelligence about West Point—for a price. When Clinton declined to turn over the money, their correspondence ceased. It was only in the following year that Andre, now head of British intelligence and still in contact with Shippen, persuaded Clinton to meet Arnold's price of £10,000 and a general's commission in the British army. Once Clinton agreed, Arnold and his wife began enacting their devious stratagem. Arnold asked Washington for a transfer to West Point, which was granted. Then, on September 22, 1780, he met with Major Andre behind American lines. The plot quickly unraveled once Andre was caught while returning, and Arnold had to flee for his life. Shippen, for her part, hysterically feigned ignorance of the matter and eventually rejoined her husband in New York.

After the war Arnold and his wife arrived in London, England, where they were introduced to King GEORGE III. At that time Shippen was also rewarded for her intelligence activities and received an annual stipend of £1,000 a month for life—making her the highest paid spy of the Revolutionary War. But Arnold's reputation as a pariah preceded him, and he made few, if any, English friends. After failing at many business ventures he died in 1801, leaving his family staddled with debts. Shippen, however, used her business acumen to pay off her late husband's accounts while also raising their five children. She died of cancer in London on August 24, 1804, a devoted Loyalist and a highly successfully spymistress.

Further Reading

Ethier, Eric. "The Making of a Traitor," *American History* 36, no. 3 (2001): 22–27, 29–30.

Goodfriend, Joyce D. "The Widowhood of Margaret Shippen Arnold, Letters from England, 1801–1803," *Pennsylvania Magazine of History and Biography* 115, no. 2 (1991): 221–255.

Mahoney, Harry T., and Marjorie L. Mahoney. *Gallantry in Action: A Biographical Dictionary of Espionage in the American Revolutionary War.* Lanham, Md.: University Press of America, 1999.

Randall, Willard S. "Mrs. Benedict Arnold," *MHQ* 4, no. 2 (1992): 89–91.

Thomas, Cynthia S. "Margaret Shippen Arnold: The Life of an Eighteenth-Century Upper Class American Woman." Unpublished master's thesis, University of Houston, 1962.

Tillotson, Harry S. *The Exquisite Exile: The Life and Fortunes of Mrs. Benedict Arnold.* Boston: Lothrop, Lee, and Sheppard, 1932.

Shuldham, Molyneux (ca. 1717–1790)
English naval officer

Molyneux Shuldham was probably born in Ireland around 1717, the son of a clergyman. He entered the Royal Navy as a cabin boy in 1732 and subsequently lied about his age to take and pass the lieutenant's exam seven years later. In service Shuldham proved himself a competent, if lackluster, commander, and he rose to captain by 1746. He fought in several actions throughout King George's War, and on March 11, 1756, his ship was captured by a French squadron before the Seven Years' War officially commenced. He was exchanged two years later, cleared by a court-martial for the loss of his vessel, and subsequently rendered useful service in the seizure of several West Indian islands. Shuldham then served under Admiral George RODNEY at the reduction of Martinique on January 8, 1762, when his vessel struck a reef and sank. Exonerated again, Shuldham fulfilled a succession of commands over the next decade, and in February 1772 he replaced Admiral John BYRON as commander in chief of Newfoundland, Canada, with a rank of commodore. He functioned in this capacity for three years and generally upheld the rule of law with the slimmest of resources. Shuldham also sponsored several expeditions to map and chart the waters around Labrador for the first time. He returned to England in the spring of 1775 to hold his seat in Parliament and also gained promotion to rear admiral. On September 29, 1775, Lord John MONTAGU, earl of Sandwich and head of the Admiralty, appointed him commander in chief of the North American station to replace the ineffective admiral Samuel GRAVES. While en route to his destination he gained further promotion to vice admiral as of December 7, 1775.

Shuldham arrived in Boston on December 30, 1775, to find the Revolutionary War well under way and the city besieged. After March 4–5, when Patriot forces seized Dorchester Heights overlooking the harbor and brought up cannon, it was Shuldham who prevailed upon General William HOWE either to storm the position or evacuate the city. The Royal Navy subsequently and efficiently evacuated thousands of British troops and LOYALISTS to Halifax, Nova Scotia. Shuldham then spent several months preparing to lift Howe's heavily reinforced army to New York when he was suddenly succeeded by Admiral Richard HOWE in July 1776. Rather than return home, Shuldham agreed to act as Howe's second in command, and he accompanied the massive expedition to Staten Island two months later. As a sop to any ruffled feathers, Shuldham was made a baron in the Irish peerage, becoming the only senior navy leader of this war to obtain a title.

After several months of chafing under Howe, Shuldham returned to England in 1777, where he served as port admiral at Portsmouth. He was then successively promoted admiral of the blue in September 1787 and admiral of the white in February 1793. Shuldham, who performed adequately yet lacked a chance for distinction in America, died at Lisbon, Portugal, on September 30, 1798.

Further Reading

Gardiner, Robert, ed. *Navies and the American Revolution, 1775–1783.* Annapolis, Md.: Naval Institute Press, 1996.

Nesser, Robert W., ed. *The Dispatches of Molyneux Shuldham, Vice-Admiral of the Blue and Commander in Chief of His Britannic Majesty's Ships in North America, January–July, 1776.* New York: Naval Historical Society, 1913.

Syrett, David. *The Royal Navy in American Waters during the Revolutionary War.* Columbia: University of South Carolina Press, 1998.

Tilly, John A. *The British Navy and the American Revolution.* Columbia: University of South Carolina, 1987.

Tracy, Nicholas. *Navies, Deterrence, and American Independence: Britain and Seapower in the 1760s and 1770s.* Vancouver: University of British Columbia Press, 1988.

Silliman, Gold S. (1732–1790)
American militia officer

Gold Selleck Silliman was born in Fairfield, Connecticut, on May 7, 1732, the son of a noted judge. He passed through Yale College in 1752, studied law, and eventually became Crown attorney for Fairfield County. As tensions increased between Great Britain and its colonies, Silliman joined the local militia as a colonel of cavalry. He functioned in this capacity once the Revolutionary War broke out in April 1775 and the following year rendered useful service at the Battles of LONG ISLAND and WHITE PLAINS. Silliman then gained promotion to brigadier general of Connecticut militia and was tasked with defending the southwestern corner of his state. This region, given its proximity to British-occupied New York City, was a frequent target of destructive LOYALIST raids.

Silliman's most important service occurred in the spring of 1777. On April 25, Governor William TRYON of New York landed several thousand soldiers at Compo Point and proceeded overland to sack Danbury. Silliman, assisted by Generals Benedict ARNOLD and David WOOSTER, gathered as many local militia as possible and harried the British back to the coast. On April 27, 1777, the three attacked Tryon at Ridgefield as he tried to embark and were repulsed after a hard fight. Silliman then resumed his usual militia service until May 1779, when he was surprised and captured at his house by Loyalists dispatched for that purpose by General Henry CLINTON. He remained in captivity on Long Island for a year until being exchanged. Silliman died at Fairfield on July 21, 1790.

Further Reading
Callahan, North. *Connecticut's Revolutionary Leaders.* Chester, Conn.: Pequot Press, 1973.
Cody, Robert M. "The Special Defense and Safety of This Colony: Revolutionary War Actions in Connecticut, 1777–1781." Unpublished master's thesis, Southern Connecticut State University, 2000.
Cummin, Katharine H. *Connecticut Militia General: Gold Selleck Silliman.* Hartford: American Revolutionary Bicentennial Commission of Connecticut, 1980.
Jones, Keith M. *Farmers against the Crown: A Comprehensive Account of the Revolutionary War Battle in Ridgefield, Connecticut, on April 27, 1777.* Ridgefield: Connecticut Colonel Pub. Co., 2003.

McDevitt, Robert F. *Connecticut Attacked, a British View Point: Tryon's Raid on Danbury.* Chester, Conn.: Pequot Press, 1974.

Simcoe, John G. (1752–1806)
English military officer

John Graves Simcoe was born in Cotterstock, England, on February 25, 1752, the son of a Royal Navy officer. He graduated from Eton and Oxford before obtaining an ensign's commission with the 35th Regiment in 1771. As a young officer he maintained a literary bent and was well versed in the classic military texts of Xenophon and Tacitus. Simcoe arrived in Boston two days after the Battle of BUNKER HILL and transferred to the 40th Regiment. He then fought under General William HOWE in several major engagements over the next two years and was seriously wounded at BRANDYWINE in September 1777. Previously, Simcoe opined to superiors his belief that the British military required effective light infantry to counter the vaunted skirmishing tactics of American riflemen. That October Howe acted upon such sagacious advice by promoting him to major in charge of the Queen's Rangers, a LOYALIST force previously commanded by the famous Robert ROGERS. Under Simcoe's tutelage the rangers emerged as possibly the best light infantry formation of the entire war. Clad in green uniforms and systematically drilled for forest and ambush warfare, they proved the bane of American outposts.

Simcoe's unit acquired its baptism under fire in March 1778, when it mauled two American militia detachments at Quintan's and Hancock's Bridges, New Jersey. On May 1, 1778, it also roughly handled another force under General John LACEY at Crooked Billet, Pennsylvania. Later that month Simcoe accompanied the lethargic General James GRANT to Barren Hill, where they tried to trap a scouting force under the marquis de LAFAYETTE but failed. He then performed useful service covering the withdrawal of General Henry CLINTON's army from Philadelphia on its march back to New York. In recognition of excellent service, Simcoe rose to lieutenant colonel in June 1778

British major John Simcoe commanded the Queen's Rangers, possibly the best light-infantry formation of the entire war. *(Toronto Public Library)*

and thereafter distinguished himself during the incessant *petite guerre* north of New York. In June 1779 his rangers successfully spearheaded the captures of Stony Point and Verplanck's Point on the Hudson, and the following month he accompanied Lieutenant Colonel Banastre TARLETON's British Legion on a successful raid against Poundridge. However, following a series of small actions in New Jersey, Simcoe was himself ambushed and captured by American militia on October 17, 1779. He was briefly interred and finally exchanged on December 31, 1779, just in time to accompany General Clinton's amphibious expedition against South Carolina.

In the spring of 1780 Simcoe shipped south along with Lieutenant Colonel Francis RAWDON to partake of the siege of CHARLESTON. After the city surrendered that May, he accompanied Clinton back to New York and subsequently joined General Wilhelm von KNYPHAUSEN on large-scale raids into New Jersey. In December 1780 Simcoe was assigned to the staff of turncoat general Benedict ARNOLD during a large and destructive raid through Virginia. He was actually posted with Arnold to keep a close eye upon him, but the two men—both talented leaders—worked well together. Simcoe, usually brigaded with HESSIAN jaegers under Major Johann EWALD, defeated the Virginia militia in a number of well-executed attacks around Richmond, and he also hoodwinked General Friedrich von STEUBEN at Point of Forks and captured many valuable supplies. After General Charles CORNWALLIS arrived in Virginia, Simcoe joined his army as part of the advance guard. On June 26, 1781, the Queen's Rangers were hotly engaged at Spencer's Ordinary by Pennsylvania riflemen under Colonel Richard BUTLER and abandoned their wounded on the field. Afterward they marched to YORKTOWN with the main army and occupied Gloucester Point on the other bank of the York River. Simcoe ultimately surrendered alongside Cornwallis on October 17, 1781, and he was paroled and sent to New York. His unit gradually made its way to New Brunswick, Canada, where it finally disbanded in October 1783.

Simcoe sailed back to England late in 1781, where he was granted an audience with King GEORGE III, and briefly withdrew from public life. He reemerged in July 1792 to become lieutenant general of newly created Upper Canada (now Ontario) under Governor-General Guy CARLETON. Here he took an active interest in promoting agriculture, as well as the settlement of the new province. He also reestablished the old Queen's Rangers, with himself as colonel, as the nucleus of its defense. Simcoe was virulently anti-American, and he took great pains in fortifying his charge for what he feared would be an eventual invasion from the south. One of his last acts in Canada was relocating the provincial capital from Newark to York (present-day Toronto) for that reason. In 1794 Simcoe became governor-general of the Caribbean island of Santo Domingo, where he remained for three years. He then returned to England a lieutenant general and prepared the defenses of Plymouth against a possible French invasion. In 1806 he sailed to Portugal as part of a military mission there but fell ill and was forced to return home, where he learned of his appointment as commander in chief of British forces in India—before dying in Devonshire on October 26, 1806, at the age of 54. Simcoe proved himself to be a learned and scholarly warrior and an aggressive leader of partisan forces, among the best serving in the Revolutionary War.

Further Reading
Bull, Stewart H. *The Queen's York Rangers: An Historic Regiment.* Toronto: Boston Mills Press, 1993.
Cruikshank, Ernest A., ed. *Correspondence of John Graves Simcoe,* 5 vols. Toronto: Ontario Historical Society, 1921–31.
Fryer, Mary B., and Christopher Dracott. *John Graves Simcoe, 1752–1806: A Biography.* Tonawanda, N.Y.: Dundurn Press, 1998.
Hayes, John T. *Prelude to Glory: Early Operations of Britain's Two Most Famed Cavalrymen of the American Revolution.* Fort Lauderdale, Fla.: Saddlebag Press, 1996.
Simcoe, John G. A *Journal of Operations of the Queen's Rangers.* North Stratford, N.H.: Ayer, 2002.
Van Steen, Marcus. *Governor Simcoe and His Lady.* Toronto: Hodder and Stoughton, 1968.

Smallwood, William (1732–1792)
American military officer

William Smallwood was born in Charles County, Maryland, in 1732, the son of a successful planter and politician. Well educated in England, he came home to serve as a militia lieutenant during the French and Indian War, then commenced his political career by winning a seat in the general assembly in 1761. Smallwood sided with the radical Whigs on issues pertaining to Great Britain and in 1767 he opposed the TOWNSHEND DUTIES by upholding nonimportation. In 1774 he attended several extralegal provincial congresses, and in June 1776 state officials appointed him colonel of the 1st Maryland Regiment. Smallwood demonstrated real ability as a recruiter and drillmaster; consequently, Maryland Continentals under his command acquired well-deserved reputations for excellence. In June 1776 Smallwood marched nine companies of his regiment to New York City as part of the main army under General George WASHINGTON and was posted with the division of General William ALEXANDER, Lord Stirling. However, he missed the Battle of LONG ISLAND on August 28, 1776, being absent on court-martial duty, although his men distinguished themselves under Major Mordecai GIST. On October 28, 1776, Smallwood found himself arrayed against Colonel Johann RALL's HESSIANS at WHITE PLAINS and was wounded twice at Chatterton's Hill, acquitting himself well. His well-trained troops subsequently fought well at Fort Washington, TRENTON, and

William Smallwood was promoted to brigadier general by the Continental Congress after his exceptional service in the Battles of Trenton and Princeton. *(Independence National Historical Park)*

PRINCETON. The Continental CONGRESS thought highly enough of Smallwood to make him a brigadier general that month, although he remained in Maryland for several months to convalesce. While at Baltimore, Smallwood briefly resumed active service to help suppress a LOYALIST insurrection along Maryland's eastern shore.

Smallwood, now assigned to a large body of militia, returned north to Pennsylvania to take part in the Philadelphia campaign. In September 1777 he was ordered to reinforce General Anthony WAYNE just prior to the heavy defeat at Paoli, but he failed to arrive in time. Smallwood's next engagement was at GERMANTOWN in October 1777, where his poorly trained levies failed to reach their assigned positions. Thereafter Washington returned him to command of the Maryland regulars and he spent the winter in garrison at Wilmington, Delaware. Smallwood performed reconnaissance duty along Chesapeake Bay over the next two years until the spring of 1780, when he was transferred to the southern division of General Johann de KALB. In this capacity he commanded a brigade of four regiments under General Horatio GATES during the disaster of CAMDEN on August 16, 1780. He was swept from the field by fleeing militia, but his Maryland Continentals again performed heroically under Major John E. HOWARD. Once Gates had been relieved, command of the Southern Army devolved upon Smallwood, who received the Thanks of Congress and promotion to major general—making him the highest-ranking Marylander of the war. However, he was eventually superseded by General Friedrich von STEUBEN and complained bitterly to Congress and Washington about taking orders from a foreigner. The new army commander, General Nathanael GREENE, defused the crisis by dispatching Smallwood back to Maryland for recruiting and training purposes. He performed well in these tasks, as usual, and finally resigned from the service in November 1783.

Afterward, Smallwood resumed his interest in politics by being elected to Congress in 1784, but he declined to serve. The following year the general assembly appointed him governor of Maryland, where he served three consecutive, one-year terms. In 1791 he won a seat in the upper house of the assembly and was also elected its president. Smallwood died on his plantation in Charles County on February 14, 1792, a good regimental-grade officer but prone to self-promotion and incessant complaining.

Further Reading
Batt, Richard J. "The Maryland Continentals, 1780–1781." Unpublished master's thesis, Tulane University, 1974.
Keith, Arthur L. "General William Smallwood," *Maryland Historical Magazine* 19 (1924): 304–306.
Kilbourn, John D. *A Short History of the Maryland Line in the Continental Army.* Baltimore: Society of the Cincinnati of Maryland, 1992.
Kimmel, Ross M., and Gail A. Crews. *In Perspective: William Smallwood.* Annapolis: Maryland Park Service, 1976.
Papenfuse, Edward C., and Gregory A. Stiverson. "General Smallwood's Recruits: The Peacetime Career of the Revolutionary War Private," *William and Mary Quarterly* 30, no. 1 (1973): 117–132.
Tacyn, Mark A. " 'To the End': The First Maryland Regiment and the American Revolution." Unpublished Ph.D. diss., University of Maryland, College Park, 1999.

Smith, Francis (ca. 1723–1791)
English military officer

Francis Smith was born in Scotland around 1723, and he purchased his ensign's commission in the Royal Fusiliers in April 1741. Six years later he transferred to the 10th Regiment as a captain and remained with that unit over the next 16 years. Smith rose to lieutenant colonel in January 1762, and five years later he accompanied his men to Boston as part of the garrison. He then became brevet colonel as of September 8, 1774, despite his reputation as an overweight, gregarious individual of modest military talent. By 1775 the colony of Massachusetts was ripe for rebellion, and Governor Thomas GAGE enacted decisive measures to forestall a possible outbreak of violence. That April he received positive instructions from London to arrest agitators Samuel ADAMS and John HANCOCK, who were known to be residing at the hamlet of Lexington. On the evening of April 18, 1775, he therefore selected Smith, his most senior commander, to march secretly with 800 picked men into the countryside, arrest the wanted agitators, then proceed to seize a cache of arms at Concord. This was a crucial mission and conducted under the strictest security, but the usually vigilant colonial intelligence apparatus divined its purpose before it was launched. Several riders, including Paul REVERE, were therefore posted at strategic intervals throughout Boston to alert Lexington and Concord once the regulars turned out.

Late that evening Smith, ably seconded by Major John PITCAIRN of the royal marines, were ferried from Boston to Lechmere Point in the dark and commenced their 16-mile sojourn in the dark. Throughout the night church bells and alarm guns pealed in the distance, indicating that Smith's mission had been compromised and that the countryside was alerted. At dawn on April 19, 1775, Smith dispatched Pitcairn and the light infantry to scour and secure the bridges at Concord and hold them until he arrived. En route the British encountered the MINUTEMAN company of Captain John PARKER and, inexplicably, shots were exchanged and blood spilled. Smith then came up as planned and pushed on to Concord, which he found deserted and all its military supplies long removed. After granting his weary men an hour to repose, he led them back down the road to Boston. Almost immediately British troops guarding the North Bridge were confronted by throngs of angry militia, who drove them off in an exchange of musketry. By the time Smith's column had reached Meriam's Corner, the woods were lined with sharpshooting militia who commenced a desultory fire upon the tightly pressed ranks.

The British lost heavily as they proceeded down the main road, and at one point Smith was wounded and Pitcairn unhorsed. Disaster seemed imminent save for the timely arrival of Colonel Hugh PERCY, who brought up 1,000 men as reinforcements. The exhausted remnants of Smith's command were fortunate to reach Charlestown intact as the fighting died down. His clumsy handling of a preemptive strike precipitated a war that would cost the empire dearly. But Gage saw fit to praise him in official dispatches and proffer him the local rank of brigadier general. Smith missed the bloody Battle of BUNKER HILL due to wounds but eventually resumed active service. In March 1776 he failed to alert superiors as to the American seizure of Dorchester Heights, which ultimately led to the British evacuation of Boston. Smith then commanded a brigade as part of General William HOWE's army and fought against General George WASHINGTON at the Battle of LONG ISLAND on August 27, 1776. He later served under General Robert PIGOT in Rhode Island and campaigned

British colonel Francis Smith's preemptive strike mission to Lexington and Concord led to the first shots of the Revolutionary War. *(Lexington Museum)*

indifferently during the Battle of Newport on August 29, 1779. Here he attacked the entrenched forces of General John SULLIVAN at Turkey Hill, was abruptly repulsed, and failed to threaten materially the American left for the rest of the day.

In 1779 Smith was finally recalled to England, having little to show for his five years in the colonies. His seniority held him in good stead when he was promoted to major general that year and to lieutenant general in 1787. But Smith, despite his high rank, never again held an active field command. He died in England on November 17, 1791, a generally ineffectual leader of the Revolutionary War—and the soldier responsible for starting it.

Further Reading

Brooks, Victor. *The Boston Campaign, April 19, 1775–March 17, 1776.* Conshohocken, Pa.: Combined Pub., 1999.

Dearden, Paul. *The Rhode Island Campaign of 1778: Inauspicious Dawn of Alliance.* Providence: Rhode Island Historical Society, 1980.

Fischer, David H. *Paul Revere's Ride.* New York: Oxford University Press, 1994.

Hallahan, William H. *The Day the Revolution Began, 19 April 1775.* New York: Avon Books, 1999.

Kehoe, Vincent J-R. *The British Story of the Battle of Lexington and Concord on the Nineteenth of April, 1775.* Los Angeles: Hale & Co., 2000.

Lee, Albert. *History of the 10th Foot (The Lincolnshire Regiment).* Aldershot, U.K.: Gale and Polden, 1911.

Smith, Samuel (1752–1839)

American military officer

Samuel Smith was born in Carlisle, Pennsylvania, on July 27, 1752, the son of a wealthy merchant. He relocated with his family to Baltimore, Maryland, where he pursued mercantile activities. After the Revolutionary War broke out in April 1775, Smith received a captain's commission in Colonel William SMALLWOOD's 1st Maryland Regiment, and over the next two years he fought conspicuously at WHITE PLAINS and BRANDYWINE. In 1777 he rose to lieutenant colonel and was tasked with the defense of Fort Mifflin, on an island in the Delaware River. This post, in concert with Fort Mercer on the nearby New Jersey shore, was part of an American defense scheme to deny Admiral Richard HOWE's fleet free access to the waterway. Smith, however, commanded only 450 men while Fort Mifflin was little more than a muddy embankment in places. Nonetheless, the British were determined to clear their path and on October 23, 1777, Howe dispatched a squadron of warships upstream. Smith, aided by the armed galleys under Commodore John HAZELWOOD of the Pennsylvania state navy, resisted tenaciously and severely pummeled the British. The 64-gun ship of the line HMS *Augusta* and the 16-gun sloop *Merlin* were both run aground and set afire. Howe then pulled his ships back and over the next two weeks redoubled his preparations to clear the river.

The British returned in strength on November 23, 1777, with a large floating battery of 22 heavy cannon, several frigates, and five additional land batteries on nearby Province Island. Smith's men then endured a horrific bombardment at near point-blank range, returning fire as fast as possible, but their batteries were all eventually silenced. Smith was seriously wounded in the exchange and evacuated while command devolved upon Major Simeon Thayer. The valiant American stand ended on November 15, when Thayer evacuated Fort Mifflin, having sustained 250 casualties. Considering the odds, Smith's performance was commendable and he received both the Thanks of the Continental CONGRESS and an elegant sword from his native state. After recovering, Smith fought well at MONMOUTH in 1778, then resigned his commission, returned to Baltimore, and spent the remainder of the war managing a fleet of privateers.

Afterward Smith resumed his commercial career, becoming one of Maryland's wealthiest citizens. In 1791 he was appointed major general commanding state militia to assist in suppressing the whiskey rebels of western Pennsylvania. Smith also parlayed his burgeoning popularity into politics, gaining a seat in the U.S. House of Representatives in 1792 and serving four consecutive terms. In 1794 he grew disillusioned with the terms of the Jay Treaty and left the Federalists for the Democratic-Republicans of Thomas JEFFERSON. In 1800 he supported Jefferson's successful candidacy for the presidency and then served as acting secretary of the navy until 1803. That year he successfully stood for a seat in the U.S. Senate, where he entered into a long-standing feud with Secretary of State James MADISON. Their antipathy only increased following the onset of the War of 1812, where Smith delighted in his role as an obstructionist. In 1814, however, he donned his uniform again and served as commander in chief of Maryland militia during the British invasion of September 1814. His able leadership resulted in the death of General Robert Ross and a British repulse, for which he became a national hero. Smith then resumed his political career by winning several more terms in the U.S. House and Senate. His final service came in 1836, when he became major of Baltimore. Smith died there on April 22, 1839, a popular and capable military figure of the young republic.

Further Reading

Browne, Gregory M. "Fort Mercer and Fort Mifflin: The Battle for the Delaware River and the Importance of American Riverine Defense during Washington's Siege of Philadelphia." Unpublished master's thesis, Western Illinois University, 1996.

Cassell, Frank A. *Merchant Congressman in the Young Republic: Samuel Smith of Maryland, 1752–1839.* Madison: University of Wisconsin Press, 1971.

Dowart, Jeffrey M. *Fort Mifflin of Philadelphia: An Illustrated History.* Philadelphia: University of Pennsylvania Press, 1998.

MacDonald, James M. "A Tale of Two Soldiers: John Eager Howard, Samuel Smith, and the New Nation." Unpublished master's thesis, Appalachian State University, 1997.

Pancake, John S. *Samuel Smith and the Politics of Business: 1752–1839.* Tuscaloosa: University of Alabama Press, 1972.

Tacyn, Mark A. " 'To the End': The First Maryland Regiment and the American Revolution." Unpublished Ph.D. diss., University of Maryland, College Park, 1999.

Smith, William S. (1755–1816)
American military officer

William Stephens Smith was born in New York City, New York, on November 8, 1755, the son of a wealthy merchant. He attended the College of New Jersey (now Princeton University) before returning home to read law. The onset of war with Great Britain interrupted his studies and on August 15, 1776, he joined the Continental ARMY as a major and aide to General John SULLIVAN. In this capacity he fought conspicuously at LONG ISLAND and was captured with Sullivan before escaping. Reputedly he evacuated Brooklyn on the last boat available, which he shared with General George WASHINGTON. Smith next served as an aide to General Nathanael GREENE and was closely engaged at Harlem Heights, being wounded. He then distinguished himself by almost singlehandedly destroying a bridge at Throg's Neck and preventing General William HOWE from outflanking the Americans. After additional good conduct at WHITE PLAINS and TRENTON, Smith gained promotion to lieutenant colonel in Colonel William Lee's regiment as of January 1, 1777. He was in the thick of the fighting at MONMOUTH in June 1778 and reunited with Sullivan for additional campaigning at Newport, Rhode Island, the following August, and during an extended raid into Iroquois territory, May–November 1779. After fighting at Springfield, New Jersey, in June 1780, Smith transferred south to join the light division of the marquis de LAFAYETTE as inspector and adjutant. In recognition of his military talents, he became aide-de-camp to Washington from July 1781 to December 1783. In this capacity Smith participated at YORKTOWN and was ultimately tasked with orchestrating the British evacuation of New York in November 1783.

Out of the army, Smith pursued an extremely checkered career. In 1785 he served as secretary to the American legation in London, where he met and married the daughter of U.S. minister John ADAMS. He also befriended Francisco Miranda, the Venezuelan revolutionary, and toured the Continent with him. Smith returned home three years later to engage in land speculation and also worked as New York's supervisor of revenue. During the Quasi-War with France in 1798 his father-in-law, by now President Adams, tried having Smith appointed brigadier general and adjutant general of the U.S. Army, but his nomination died in the Senate due to strenuous objections by Timothy PICKERING. Smith then served as lieutenant colonel in the infantry before the crisis passed in 1800. In 1806 Smith became embroiled in a quixotic plot of Miranda's to overthrow the Spanish government; he was arrested, tried, and acquitted. During the War of 1812, Abigail ADAMS tried to secure him a military appointment, but he was prevented from serving by James MONROE, then secretary of war. Smith successfully ran for Congress as a Federalist in December 1812, where he served one term. He was reelected again in 1814, but his opponent legally challenged the outcome, and his old nemesis Pickering, now heading the U.S. House of Representatives election committee, prevented him from being seated. Smith retired from public life in December 1815 to his farm in Lebanon, New York. He died there on June 10, 1816, something of an embarrassment to the prestigious Adams family.

Further Reading
Greene, Joseph W. "Mount Vernon on the East River and Colonel William Stephens Smith," *New York Historical Society Bulletin* 10 (January 1927): 115–130.
Lefkowitz, Arthur S. *George Washington's Indispensable Men: The 32 Aides-de-camp Who Helped Win American Independence.* Mechanicsburg, Pa.: Stackpole Books, 2003.
Nagel, Paul C. *Descent from Glory: Four Generations of the John Adams Family.* Cambridge, Mass.: Harvard University Press, 1983.
Raymond, Marcus D. "Colonel William Stephens Smith," *New York Genealogical and Biographical Record* 25 (October 1894): 154–160.
Roof, Katharine M. *Colonel William Smith and Lady.* Boston: Houghton, Mifflin, 1929.

Sons of Liberty

Colonial reaction against the STAMP ACT of 1765 encouraged the rise of various secret societies known collectively as the Sons of Liberty. These varied in nature and composition, colony to colony, but all were united in their resistance to the evolving imperial policy. They derived their name from English parliamentarian Isaac Barre, who once referred to dissenting colonists as "these sons of liberty." The first recognizable chapter of the Sons of Liberty arose in New York City through the machinations of men like John LAMB, Alexander MCDOUGALL, and Marinus WILLETT, who could be frequently and violently disposed toward English authority. Their efforts crested on January 19, 1770, when the mob, incensed over funding of the QUARTERING ACT, rioted against troops in the Battle of GOLDEN HILL. As a group they also employed street-front muscle to enforce nonimportation among otherwise reluctant or uncooperative merchants. Boston proved another hotbed of political agitation by the Sons of Liberty under the aegis of Samuel ADAMS, Paul REVERE, John HANCOCK, and Joseph WARREN. Their group was likewise responsible for acts of violence against Crown officials, including instances of tarring and feathering. On August 14, 1765, the Sons of Liberty emphasized their displeasure with the new levy by sacking the home of stamp distributor Andrew Oliver. When this failed to elicit a contrite response form British authorities, on August 26, 1765, they then also burned the records of the Vice-Admiralty Court, sacked the home of Lieutenant Governor Thomas HUTCHINSON, and drove Governor Bernard FRANCIS to seek refuge in Boston Harbor. Their skill at intimidation can be gauged by the fact that all authorized stamp agents resigned from office even before the Stamp Act became law on November 1, 1765. In December 1773 the Sons of Liberty wielded their greatest impact on British/colonial relations by orchestrating the BOSTON TEA PARTY in protest—and defiance—of parliamentary rule. When not resorting to acts of violence, the Sons of Liberty used their members to print and distribute anti-British pamphlets and broadsides around town. Having discovered their newfound sense of political power, they remained a force in local affairs long after the Stamp Act was repealed in 1766.

The greatest efficacy of the Sons of Liberty was not in empowering the lower orders with political influence but rather, in giving rise to numerous and semiautonomous bodies such as COMMITTEES OF CORRESPONDENCE and committees of safety. Committees of correspondence were established to improve lines of communication with organized dissenters in other colonies and included such luminaries as Thomas JEFFERSON and Patrick HENRY. The committees of safety, on the other hand, wielded real authority and enjoyed the power to mobilize the militia and confiscate military supplies. Beyond serving useful functions at the local level, they granted members administrative experience in self-governance. Consequently, with the collapse of British authority across the colonies, the committees were in place and functioning to give order and direction to Patriot affairs. In effect the most significant outgrowth of the Sons of Liberty was the rise of de facto state governments until new state constitutions were adopted and in play. By transcending street violence they bequeathed to the colonies experience at self-rule—itself an important precursor to independence.

Further Reading
Bridenbaugh, Carl. *Silas Downer, Forgotten Patriot: His Life and Writings.* Providence: Rhode Island Bicentennial Commission, 1974.
Cashin, Edward J. "Thomas Brown and the Sons of Liberty," *Richmond County History* 28, no. 12 (1997): 4–10.
Champagne, Roger J. "Liberty Boys and Mechanics of New York City, 1764–1774," *Labor History* 8, no. 2 (1967): 115–135.
Churchill, Robert H. " 'The Highest and Holiest Duty of a Freeman': Revolutionary Libertarianism in American History." Unpublished Ph.D. diss., Rutgers State University, 2001.
Nail, Lillian S. "The Role of the Sons of Liberty in the Pre-American Revolutionary Era." Unpublished master's thesis, Arkansas State College, 1956.
Talen, Timothy L. "The Role of the Sons of Liberty in Savannah, Georgia, 1765–1776." Unpublished master's thesis, California State University, Chico, 1972.

Spain

Spain approached the prospect of American independence with some ambivalence, based upon overriding prerogatives in the New World. It was naturally concerned with its own holdings in Central and South America and apprehensive that the contagion of liberty might stir up unrest there. But, weighed against these factors was a deep-seated antipathy for Great Britain, Spain's chief imperial competitor since the 17th century. Unready for war and unwilling to tangle with England without powerful allies like France, Spanish diplomacy initially centered upon maintaining peace in Europe while clandestinely encouraging the American revolt. In this manner King Charles III aspired to weaken seriously the British empire while preserving and possibly enlarging his own. By 1776 the monarchy had allowed France to create the bogus company of Roderigue, Hortalez et Cie through which French and Spanish weapons and funding secretly flowed. Otherwise, the government distanced itself from the Americans and their first unofficial envoy, Arthur LEE, following his arrival in February 1777; while some loans were granted, they basically snubbed him. But following General John BURGOYNE's surrender at Saratoga the following October, the tempo and tenor of Spanish involvement intensified. Negotiations were conducted with France's foreign minister, Charles Gravier, comte de VERGENNES, over a Franco-Spanish coalition to supplement the ongoing FRENCH ALLIANCE with America. The Spanish extracted pledges of military assistance to regain the strategic peninsula of Gibraltar, lost to England in 1713, along with guarantees not to sign a separate treaty until the peninsula was taken. Secondary considerations, but equally important to events in North America, were the reacquisition of East and West Florida from England, along with recognition of Spanish claims to the Mississippi River valley. Once these conditions were met, Spain's ambassador notified England of its willingness to arbitrate England's war with France—once Gibraltar had been handed back. When this failed to materialize, Spain declared war on June 21, 1779.

The onset of Spanish intervention meant that the usual flow of weapons and credit was now above board, but the government stipulated such support only as an ally of France. Therefore, it politely and persistently declined, for the time being, extending diplomatic recognition to the United States. A new American minister, John JAY, arrived in Madrid in January 1780, remaining there two years in a fruitless quest for recognition. Instead, all he managed to obtain was a $170,000 loan and diplomatic circumspection from the court. In a military sense, however, Spain's contribution was pronounced and elicited concrete results. The governor-general of Louisiana, Bernardo de GÁLVEZ, who proved himself a first-rate general, embarked on a systematic campaign to eradicate British holdings along the Mississippi River and Gulf of Mexico. He did so patiently and methodically, capping a brilliant, small-scale campaign by capturing Pensacola from the British on May 9, 1781. Furthermore, ancillary operations ranged from the defense of St. Louis against a British attack to the capture of St. Joseph, near Detroit, in January 1781. And, equally vital from a strategic standpoint, was the addition of 25 Spanish ships of the line to an already powerful French fleet. This forced an already widely dispersed Royal Navy to withhold naval assets in Europe rather than commit them to fighting in America. By forcing the British to spread their resources ever thinner, France was enabled to contest seriously the Royal Navy in the West Indies and, above all, during the YORKTOWN campaign. Indirectly, Spain's contributions were partially decisive.

Ironically, the largest and most protracted engagement of the Revolutionary War was not waged in America but rather over the peninsular fortress of Gibraltar. Franco-Spanish forces commenced a siege on June 21, 1779, and sustained it for four years. Both sides endured considerable losses in a series of floating artillery duels, but the garrison was reinforced by fleets under Admirals George RODNEY in January 1780 and Richard HOWE in October 1782, thwarting Spain's goal. Diplomatic objectives were further undercut by the TREATY OF PARIS, negotiated behind the backs of France and Spain, whereby England recognized American claims to lands west of the Appalachian Mountains up through the Mississippi River. All told, Spain received little compensation for its involvement in the Revolutionary War beyond Florida and parts of Central America. It was not until 1785 that an ambassador was finally dispatched to the United States, motivated primarily by negotiations to preserve the new Spanish acquisitions and protect the existing ones in North America. Such a status quo could not be realistically maintained alongside a vigorous, expansion-minded young republic, and by 1819 the Floridas, New Orleans, and the Mississippi River valley were predictably in American hands.

Further Reading
Broughton, William H. "Francisco Rendon: Spanish Agent in Philadelphia, 1779–1786, Intendant of Spanish Louisiana, 1793–1796." Unpublished Ph.D. diss., University of New Mexico, 1997.
Chavez, Thomas E. *Spain and the Independence of the United States: An Intrinsic Gift.* Albuquerque: University of New Mexico Press, 2002.
Cummins, Light T. *Spanish Observers and the American Revolution, 1775–1783.* Baton Rouge: Louisiana State University Press, 1991.
Devine, Michael J. "Territorial Madness: Spain, Geopolitics, and the American Revolution." Unpublished master's thesis, College of William and Mary, 1994.
Lolianette, Emmanuelli. "Spanish Diplomacy and Contribution to the United States Independence, 1775–1783." Unpublished Ph.D. diss., University of Massachusetts, 1990.
Thomson, Buchanan P. *Spain, Forgotten Ally of the American Revolution.* North Quincy, Mass.: Christopher Pub. House., 1976.

Spencer, Joseph (1714–1789)
American military officer
Joseph Spencer was born in East Haddam, Connecticut, on October 3, 1714, the son of a well-to-do farmer/merchant. He studied law and became a probate judge in 1753 and also occasionally served as a deputy to the Connecticut assembly. Spencer

joined the militia in 1744 to fight in King George's War, and he rose to captain by 1752. When the French and Indian War broke out in 1755 Spencer was serving in the 12th Connecticut Regiment as a major, and he was successively promoted to lieutenant colonel and colonel in 1759 and 1766, respectively. In such capacities he saw extensive service at Louisbourg, Ticonderoga, Crown Point, and Quebec, generally acquitting himself well. In the period leading up to the break with Great Britain Spencer sided with the Patriots and, following word of the fighting at Lexington and CONCORD in April 1775, he marched the 2nd Connecticut Regiment to Roxbury, Massachusetts, as its colonel. Shortly after, the state assembly elevated him to brigadier general of state forces and on June 2, 1775, he was absorbed into the Continental ARMY with the same rank. However, Spencer became rankled by the fact that Israel PUTNAM, an officer with less seniority, had been promoted to major general over him. He left the army in a huff and returned to Connecticut without informing his superior, General George WASHINGTON. Silas DEANE, a congressional delegate and former ally, was outraged by his behavior and demanded his immediate resignation. At length a deputation from the assembly met with Spencer, assuaged his hurt feelings, and convinced to rejoin the army at Boston. He spent the remainder of the year in Massachusetts before accompanying Washington and the main army to New York. There, on August 9, 1776, the Continental CONGRESS finally elevated him to the rank of major general.

The 60-year-old Spencer was present through the ill-fated defense of New York, where he commanded a large body of troops until General Nathanael GREENE recovered from illness. In September 1776 he joined General William HEATH and George CLINTON in urging Washington not to abandon New York and rather hold the north end of the island above Harlem Heights. The British under General William HOWE eventually drove the Americans out of Manhattan and WHITE PLAINS, at which point Spencer was reassigned the relatively quiet post at Providence, Rhode Island. For several months he prepared an amphibious assault upon enemy positions in nearby Tiverton, but in September 1777, while his men were waiting in boats, he canceled the operation after learning that his secrecy had been compromised. Spencer was therefore enraged when Congress began investigating the incident, and he demanded a court of inquiry. He was subsequently cleared of any wrongdoing, but when Congress insisted on reopening the matter he tendered his resignation on January 13, 1778. Few in the army regretted his departure.

Once home, Spencer renewed contacts with his political base and was elected back to the Connecticut assembly as a deputy. There he also functioned on the council of safety before becoming a delegate to the Congress in October 1779. He served one term in Philadelphia without distinction, then resigned and returned to the council of safety at home. Spencer died in East Haddam on January 13, 1789, a rather touchy and ineffectual senior military leader on the American side.

Further Reading
Callahan, North. *Connecticut's Revolutionary War Leaders.* Chester, Conn.: Pequot Press, 1973.
Heathcote, Charles W. "General Joseph Spencer of New England—an Associate of Washington," *Picket Post* no. 80 (May 1963): 4–8.
Shipton, Nathaniel. "General Joseph Palmer: Scapegoat for the Rhode Island Fiasco of October 1777," *New England Quarterly* 39, no. 4 (1966): 498–512.
Whittlesey, Charles B. *Historical Sketch of Joseph Spencer: Major General of Continental Troops, Member of the Council of Safety, Congressman, Judge, Deputy Deacon, and Farmer.* Hartford, Conn.: Hartford Press, 1904.

Stamp Act (1765)
Victory in the French and Indian War saddled Great Britain with enormous wartime debts, and the government of Prime Minister George GRENVILLE, quite sensibly, began casting about for new sources of revenue to retire them. The American colonies, heretofore untaxed and the greatest

recipient of recent military expenditures, seemed like a logical place to start. After persuading Parliament to authorize the SUGAR ACT in 1764, which basically tightened imperial restrictions upon smuggling, Grenville convinced them to pass the Stamp Act in 1765. This law mandated that all paper products and documents—including mortgages, certificates, newspapers, playing cards, and even dice—were required to be affixed with an official stamp that was to be purchased from a designated stamp authority. Through such an expedient Grenville and others felt that upward of £66,000 sterling could be raised annually partially to offset the enormous outlay of maintaining military garrisons to protect colonists from Indian hostilities. However, several colonial agents in London, including Benjamin FRANKLIN, warned the government that, given their long traditions of self-taxation, the colonies would inevitably view such measures as unconstitutional and arbitrary. Leading British politicians, such as John WILKES and William PITT, also gradually sided with colonial dissenters. Casting such concerns aside, Parliament passed the Stamp Act on March 22, 1765, with enactment slated for the following November. Nothing could have prepared it for what followed.

The imposition of the new tax, however reasoned or well-intended, ignited a firestorm of protest and indignation across the American colonies. Local political leaders viewed it as a threat to their own ability to raise taxes while legal scholars waxed that for Parliament—or any body—to tax individuals without representation was manifestly illegal. Resistance to the act transpired at several levels of society. In Virginia, Patrick HENRY rose in the House of Burgesses to denounce the act and subsequently shepherded through the Virginia Resolves, which reaffirmed the stance that only colonial assemblies had the right to raise revenues. Massachusetts, however, proved a vortex of resistance. In June 1765 members of the General Court appealed for an extralegal, intercolonial gathering now known as the Stamp Act Congress, which would convene in New York that fall. Delegates from nine colonies ultimately attended and debated the issue, which culminated in the modest and respectful "Declaration of Rights and Grievances" addressed to King GEORGE III and Parliament. In it they pledged their support of the monarchy, but reiterated their deeply held belief that taxes could be levied only by their own representatives. This cordial and thoughtful resistance marked the intellectual underpinnings for what culminated in the American Revolution.

At the street level, resistance to the Stamp Act proved much more direct. Throngs of angry dissenters coalesced into bodies collectively known as SONS OF LIBERTY to harass stamp agents. Backed by street muscle, legislatures were now free to adopt retaliatory nonimportation of British goods—with local enforcers free to impose compliance upon balky merchants. At one point the Boston Sons of Liberty trashed the Admiralty Court, burned the home of Lieutenant Governor Thomas HUTCHINSON, and virtually ensured a boycott of British merchandise to underscore their discontent. Grenville and his ministers failed to comprehend the depth of colonial resistance to the Stamp Act, for its measures cut across all class lines and especially antagonized legal and commercial classes who were hardest hit. Faced with spiraling street violence abroad, along with mounting protests from Britain's influential merchant community at home, it fell upon Grenville's successor, Charles WATSON-WENTWORTH, marquis of Rockingham, to declare the Stamp Act as unenforceable and repeal it as of March 17, 1766. News of the cancellation engendered wild celebrations throughout the colonies, where a newfound sense of unity and collective defiance thwarted a hated tax. Few revelers heeded the fact that Parliament, on the day after the Stamp Act's repeal, also passed the Declaratory Act reasserting all legal and political prerogatives over all colonies, including that of taxation. Colonial unrest and boycotts basically petered out and subsided in 1766, but the Stamp Act, an earnest attempt to make colonists subsidize the troops protecting them, became a defining moment in British-colonial relations. Hereafter the imposition of greater control over colonial affairs, and the concomitant resistance it occasioned, fostered lingering resentment on both sides of the Atlantic. Over the next eight years, commencing with the TOWNSHEND DUTIES of 1767, Briton and American inexorably squared off over the seminal issue of taxation without representation—with fatal consequences to the empire.

Further Reading
Akmens, Robert. "The Stamp Act Congress: Herald of American Union." Unpublished master's thesis, California State University, Dominguez Hills, 1994.
Bullion, John L. *A Great and Necessary Measure: George Grenville and the Stamp Act, 1763–1765.* Columbia: University of Missouri Press, 1982.
Cook, Don. *The Long Fuse: How England Lost the American Colonies, 1760–1785.* New York: Atlantic Monthly Press, 1995.
Edgar, Gregory T. *Reluctant Break with Britain: From Stamp Act to Bunker Hill.* Bowie, Md.: Heritage Books, 1997.
Shonk, John P. "The Stamp Act of 1765: An Interpretation of Reaction in Massachusetts and Pennsylvania." Unpublished master's thesis, New Mexico State University, 1987.
York, Neil L. "Thomas Crowley's Proposal to Seat Americans in Parliament, 1765–1775," *Quaker History* 91, no. 1 (2002): 1–19.

Stark, John (1728–1822)
American military officer

John Stark was born in Londonderry, New Hampshire, on August 28, 1728, the son of Scottish immigrants. He matured in the wilderness regions of his colony, becoming adept at hunting, trapping, and—after being kidnaped by Abenaki Indians and held for ransom—at bush fighting. When the French and Indian War commenced in 1755, Stark joined Major Robert ROGERS's rangers and distinguished himself in many hard-fought skirmishes. He ended the war in 1763 as a captain and settled down as a farmer to raise his 11 children. Once news of fighting at Lexington and CONCORD arrived in April 1775, Stark immediately departed for Boston and was subsequently joined by 2,000 militia designated to serve under him. His first action was a well-executed raid against British foragers on Noddle's Island, Boston Harbor, on May 27, 1775. Stark next fought at the June 17, 1777, Battle of BUNKER HILL, occupying a flimsy rail fence on the American left flank. When assailed by the crack Welsh Fusiliers, he bellowed "Boys, aim at their waistbands" and repelled three attacks. He managed to extricate safely his men and was then inducted into the Continental ARMY as colonel of the 5th New Hampshire Continental Infantry. In this capacity Stark accompanied General George WASHINGTON to New York and was closely engaged in several battles. His performance at TRENTON in December 1776 and PRINCETON the following month exceeded all expectations and confirmed his reputation as a talented tactician. However, he felt slighted when the Continental CONGRESS promoted Enoch POOR to brigadier

John Stark won the spectacular victory at Bennington in August 1777. *(Collection of the State of New Hampshire, Division of Historical Resources)*

general over him, and Stark withdrew from the army in a huff. After resigning his commission in March 1777, he vowed never to obey orders from either Congress or army officers.

As Stark fumed in New Hampshire a large British army under General John BURGOYNE began its fateful march down the Lake Champlain corridor toward Albany, New York. In August 1777 the New Hampshire General Court implored Stark to return to the colors and he agreed, but only after assurances of an independent command free of military or political control. Stark quickly raised a force of 1,700 militia as a defensive force—and flatly disobeyed General Benjamin LINCOLN's orders to cross the Hudson River and join the forces in New York. Fate intervened when Burgoyne, eager to gather supplies and solicit LOYALIST support, dispatched a large HESSIAN column under Lieutenant Colonel Friedrich BAUM into Vermont. Stark reacted quickly by secretly marching to attack him near BENNINGTON August 17, 1777. Repeatedly feinting and falling back to get the Germans to exhaust their ammunition, the Americans suddenly charged and overran several Hessian strongpoints, killing Baum and capturing his whole force. An additional column of 600 soldiers were likewise dispatched under Colonel Seth WARNER. For a cost of 100 casualties, Stark's forces had killed 200 of the enemy and captured 700 more. All told, Bennington proved a tremendous psychological victory for the Americans, and Stark went on to recruit greater numbers of volunteers for the ultimate victory at Saratoga that fall. It was his command that finally cut off Burgoyne's escape route, inducing his surrender.

A contrite Congress finally elevated Stark to brigadier general in October 1777. He subsequently commanded the Northern Department twice and also assisted General John SULLIVAN during the Rhode Island campaign of 1778. Stark later distinguished himself in combat against General Wilhelm von KNYPHAUSEN's Hessians at Springfield, New Jersey, in June 1780, and later served on the court-martial that condemned Major John ANDRE of spying. Stark finally mustered out of the army in September 1783 with a final rank of major general. Then, like Cincinnatus, he returned quietly to his plow, declining all invitations to seek political office. The grim-faced, humorless Stark, in many ways embodying the physical toughness of his native "granite" state, died at Manchester on May 8, 1822—the longest-living Continental army general. Beyond an uncanny ability to appear suddenly where the enemy least expected, his insubordination and belligerence toward authority remain legendary.

Further Reading
Anderson, Leon W. *Major General John Stark, Hero of Bunker Hill and Bennington, 1778–1826.* Concord, N.H.: Evans Printing Co., 1972.
Hatch, Robert M. "New Hampshire at Bunker Hill," *Historical New Hampshire* 30, no. 4 (1975): 215–220.
Moore, Howard P. *A Life of General John Stark of New Hampshire.* New York: Privately Printed, 1949.
Randall, Peter E., ed. *New Hampshire: Years of Revolution, 1774–1783.* Hanover, N.H.: Profiles Pub. Corp., 1976.
Squires, J. Duane. "A Summary of Events which Led to General Stark's March to and Victory at Bennington," *Historical New Hampshire* 32, no. 4 (1977): 165–170.
Tarrant, Isabel H. "John Stark, Man of Granite," *Daughters of the American Revolution Magazine* 104 (1970): 16–24.

Stephen, Adam (ca. 1721–1791)
American military officer

Adam Stephen was born in Rhynie, Scotland, and educated locally. He passed through the University of Aberdeen in 1740 and subsequently studied medicine at the University of Edinburgh. Following a stint in the Royal Navy as a surgeon, Stephen migrated to Fredericksburg, Virginia, in 1748 and established a flourishing practice. He joined the militia as a captain in anticipation of the French and Indian War and served under Lieutenant Colonel George WASHINGTON. Thus began an on-again, off-again lifelong rivalry between two headstrong individuals. Stephen was present at the surrender of Fort Necessity in July 1754 and managed to survive Braddock's defeat a year later. After commanding various detachments Stephen fought and won a battle at Fort Ligonier in July 1759, which finally expelled French forces from the Pennsylvania frontier. In 1761 he was tapped to lead an expedition against the Cherokee Indians, which ended amicably in a peace treaty. Afterward Stephen turned to politics where he unsuccessfully challenged Washington for his seat in the House of Burgesses. He then held various offices throughout Berkeley County as sheriff, justice of the peace, and county lieutenant. After briefly campaigning with Governor John MURRAY, Lord Dunmore, in 1774, Stephen threw his lot in with the Patriot movement and became a delegate to the Third Virginia Convention the following year.

In May 1776 Stephen was inducted into the Continental ARMY as colonel of the 4th Virginia Continental Infantry, and he rose to brigadier general as of September 4, 1776. In this capacity he led an untrained brigade of Virginia troops northward to join Washington's main force in New Jersey. Overly given to initiative, Stephen nearly compromised the successful American attack at TRENTON by pushing patrols forward without orders until they skirmished with HESSIAN sentinels. During the battle, fortunately, he fought bravely and won promotion to major general the following February. After the army encamped at Morristown for the winter, he assumed command of forward forces and conducted foraging operations. On May 10, 1777, he had the misfortune of ordering a full-scale attack upon British detachments defending Piscataway, New Jersey. This brought his men into conflict with the elite regiment of Black Watch Highlanders, which easily repulsed the Americans with few losses to themselves. After being closely pursued nearly three miles into his own camp, Stephens compounded his difficulties by distorting events in his official report, which drew a sharp reprimand from Washington.

Stephen subsequently clashed with Washington over the proposed employment of troops: The former sought to pin down the enemy in small skirmishes while the latter endeavored to preserve his scarce manpower, expending it only in major engagements. Nevertheless, in the summer of 1777 Stephen was posted with forces under General Nathanael GREENE throughout the defense of Philadelphia. He fought bravely enough at BRANDYWINE that September and was also closely engaged at GERMANTOWN the following October. Unfortunately, as he shepherded his men through a dense fog, they strayed across the battlefield and blundered into troops under General Anthony WAYNE. An intense firefight broke out between them and in the ensuing confusion Washington lost what might have been a bigger victory than Trenton. Stephen ordered a withdrawal that nearly degenerated into a rout. Three weeks later charges were preferred against him by his brigadiers Charles SCOTT and William WOODFORD. A court of inquiry found him frequently intoxicated, inexplicably absent from his troops, and guilty of "unofficerlike behavior." When Washington approved the verdict, Stephen became one of the few senior officers drummed out of the service. Command of his division then passed to the marquis de LAFAYETTE.

Back in civilian life, Stephen experienced no difficulty being elected a delegate to the Continental CONGRESS, where he served from 1780 to 1784. He subsequently founded the settlement at Martinsburg (West) Virginia, and in 1788 attended the state constitutional convention, giving two speeches denouncing Patrick HENRY. Stephen died at Martinsburg on July 16, 1791, a capable leader when he chose to be, but otherwise marred by petty dishonesty and intoxication.

Further Reading
Mish, Mary V. "General Adam Stephen: Founder, Martinsburg, West Virginia," *West Virginia History* 22, no. 2 (1961): 63–75.
Nelson, Paul D. "Lee, Gates, Stephen, and Morgan: Revolutionary War Generals of the Lower Shenandoah

Valley," *West Virginia History* 37, no. 3 (1976): 185–200.
Stephen, Adam. "Letters of General Stephen Adam to R. H. Lee," *Historical Magazine* 9 (April 1865): 118–122.
Ward, Harry M. *Major General Adam Stephen and the Cause of American Liberty.* Charlottesville: University Press of Virginia, 1989.

Steuben, Friedrich von (1730–1794)
Prussian military officer

Friedrich Wilhelm Ludolf Gerhard Augustin von Steuben was born in Magdeburg, Prussia, on September 17, 1730, the son of an army officer. As such he was groomed for service in the notoriously militaristic Prussian state and entered the army as a lance corporal at 17. Steuben performed well, rose to captain during the Seven Years' War, and was eventually posted on the staff of King Frederick the Great. After peace arrived in 1763 he was discharged and went to work among several petty German princes as a chamberlain. Although a commoner, around this time he began affixing the noble distinction of "von" to his last name. Steuben tended to live beyond his means so in 1777 he left the principality of Hohenzollern-Hechingen in search of military employment to pay his debts. Finding none available in the armies of France and Austria, he approached American agents Benjamin FRANKLIN and Silas DEANE, known to be recruiting professional soldiers for the Revolutionary War. Steuben, a bluff, imposing man with impeccable manners, passed himself off as a former "lieutenant general" in the employ of the Prussian king and so favorably impressed his hosts that Franklin provided him a letter of introduction to the Continental CONGRESS—this despite the fact that he spoke no English, a severe handicap for any military officer serving in America. Steuben then left France, arrived at Portsmouth, New Hampshire, in December 1777, and presented his credentials to Congress at York, Pennsylvania, shortly thereafter. After pledging to work for expenses incurred he was dispatched to meet with General George WASHINGTON at nearby Valley Forge in February 1778.

Baron von Steuben used Prussian drill systems to train the ragtag and poorly organized Continental army, a tactic that enabled the soldiers to hold their own against the highly trained British. *(National Archives)*

"Baron" von Steuben, his fictitious rank and lineage notwithstanding, favorably impressed Washington with his martial demeanor and became acting inspector general. His arrival could not have been more fortuitous, for the ragtag ensemble known as the Continental ARMY was then freezing in its cantonments, poorly organized, and barely disciplined. But Steuben began remedial measures by adapting the feared Prussian drill system for his scarecrow recruits and distilling it to the very basics. Then, with himself acting as drillmaster—cursing incomprehensibly in French and German—he selected a model company to master the nuances of European-style military drill. Once proficient, he made its members drill sergeants who went on to train model companies of their own.

The result of such systematized instruction proved near miraculous. The Continental army, which heretofore had proved unequal to withstanding the famed British redcoats in an open engagement, began maneuvering with the skill of veterans. Steuben also overhauled quartermaster procedures to improve efficiency and eliminate waste, and provided new and uniform tables of organization for infantry, cavalry, artillery, and engineers. Moreover, the Prussian staff practices he imparted were the world's best and virtually unknown in French and British armies. He also broke precedent by authoring his *Regulations for the Order and Discipline of the Troops of the United States,* the first drill manual in American history. Known more simply as the *Blue Book,* it underwent some 30 editions and remained the standard army text until 1812. Washington was so pleased with Steuben's accomplishments that he recommended him as inspector general of the army with a rank of major general.

The fruits of Steuben's labor manifested readily at MONMOUTH in June 1777, when Continental troops and militia successfully weathered their more veteran British opponents under fire. The baron performed staff functions until November 1780, when, after lobbying hard for a field command, he became aide-de-camp to General Nathanael GREENE in Virginia. Once Greene departed for North Carolina, Steuben succeeded him as commander until his own eventual replacement by the youthful marquis de LAFAYETTE in April 1781. But he failed to flourish in an independent role, however, and saw only minor action in sparring with light troops under General William PHILLIPS at Blandford on April 25, 1781. On June 5, 1781, Lieutenant Colonel John Graves SIMCOE apparently duped him into abandoning his supply dump at Point of Fork. Despite this lackluster display, Steuben commanded one of three divisions present during the successful siege of YORKTOWN, and his troops manned the trenches when General Charles CORNWALLIS asked for a parley that October. After the war ended, Steuben remained a military adviser to Washington until his discharge on March 24, 1784.

Afterward Steuben became an American citizen and took up residence in New York City. There his extravagant lifestyle nearly drove him into bankruptcy, and he prevailed upon Congress to provide an annual pension of $2,800 for services rendered. He then purchased a farm at Remsen, New York, where he spent the rest of his days. Steuben was also active in founding the Society of the Cincinnati, a conservative group of politically connected officers, and served as president of the New York branch. The self-styled "baron" died at Remsen on November 28, 1794. In terms of results this former Prussian captain was the most influential foreigner of the Revolutionary War and indelibly left his stamp on American armies by providing their first brush with military professionalism.

Further Reading
Bodle, Wayne K. *The Valley Forge Winter: Civilians and Soldiers in War.* University Park: Pennsylvania State University, 2002.
Danckert, Stephen L. "Baron von Steuben and the Training of Armies," *Military Review* 74, no. 5 (1994): 29–34.
Eastby, Allen G. "The Baron," *American History Illustrated* 25, no. 5 (1990): 28–35, 66–69.
Jones, Helen E., and Lorena S. Jersen, eds. *Steuben: the Baron and the Town.* Remsen, N.Y.: Remsen-Steuben Historical Society, 1994.
Krewson, Margrit B. *Von Steuben and the German Contribution to the American Revolution: A Selective Bibliography.* Washington, D.C.: Library of Congress, 1987.
Philander, Chase D. "Baron von Steuben in the War of Independence." Unpublished Ph.D. diss., Duke University, 1972.

Stewart, Alexander (ca. 1741–1794)
English military officer
Alexander Stewart was born in England around 1741, although little is known of his early years. He joined the army in 1755 as an ensign in the 37th Regiment and eventually transferred to the famous 3rd Regiment, or Buffs. He was lieutenant colonel by the time his unit shipped to Charleston

in June 1781 as part of the army under General Charles CORNWALLIS. Cornwallis at that time was operating in Virginia, so Stewart initially served under Lieutenant Colonel Francis RAWDON. Pushing inland to Orangeburg, South Carolina, Stewart succeeded Rawdon as commander of field forces in the Carolinas by the fall. At that time Americans under General Nathanael GREENE were invading South Carolina and picking off isolated British and LOYALIST garrisons throughout the back country. In September Greene acquired knowledge that Stewart was positioned along the Santee River at Eutaw Springs and determined to engage him. He gathered up 2,200 men, including two brigades of veteran Continental infantry and detachments of cavalry under noted Colonels William WASHINGTON and Henry LEE. Greene hoped to drive Stewart back to Charleston, thereby freeing the state's interior of all British influence. Covering 90 miles with celerity, the American march was so well conducted that the British remained unaware of their approach until the battle was joined.

On September 8, 1781, Stewart deployed his 2,000 men at Eutaw Springs in a line with the Santee River guarding his right and a deep ravine protecting his left. To his rear stood a stout, two-story brick building that, once barricaded and loopholed, made a formidable strongpoint. In front he drew up his veteran 3rd, 63rd, and 64th Regiments in a line, buttressed by a LOYALIST battalion. From these he culled the grenadier and light companies and posted them behind dense thickets on his right flank under Major John Marjoribanks. Thus disposed, any frontal attack committed by Greene would be subjected to a heavy fire from the front and a raking enfilade from the right. Despite his adroit deployment, the Americans advanced suddenly upon Stewart's outposts and ambushed a detachment of 60 Loyalist cavalry foraging for sweet potatoes. Greene then came up with his main body and threw the partisans of Generals Francis MARION and Andrew PICKENS across his front, followed by three regiments of North Carolina Continentals under General Jethro SUMNER. The British were slightly outnumbered and the veteran American troops—the best army Greene ever commanded—were eager to grapple with them.

The Battle of Eutaw Springs commenced when Greene sent his partisan militia forward with orders to fire a few rounds to soften up the British line and then retire. To his surprise, they loosed no less than 17 volleys before finally yielding to a sharp British bayonet attack. Stewart ordered his men onward until they butted against Sumner's Continentals, who stopped them in their tracks with a crushing, point-blank volley. When these green troops finally gave way, the British next engaged veteran Maryland Continentals under Colonel Otho Holland WILLIAMS. Suddenly the British flinched before cold steel and Stewart's line

Colonel Alexander Stewart led the British to victory at the Battle of Eutaw Springs, the last major engagement fought in the south. *(Bridgeman Art Library)*

collapsed in disorder. Greene had apparently won a resounding victory over the redcoats but then lost control of the battle when part of his force attacked the fortified brick house while the others began looting the British camp. Meanwhile, from his vantage point on the right, Majoribanks kept a hot fire upon his assailants, dropping them in scores. One of his victims was Colonel Washington, who was wounded and captured. As the Americans milled around, Stewart quickly rallied his scattered command near the brick house and led them in a determined counterattack. At this precise moment Majoribanks also emerged from the thickets on the right and charged. This British resurgence proved too much for the disorganized Americans, who lost two cannon before Greene officially sounded the retreat. The thin red line had again been perilously stretched but, under Stewart's capable leadership, it proved resilient once again.

Eutaw Springs is distinct in being the last major engagement fought in the south, and a British victory. Greene was forced back with 139 killed, 375 wounded, and eight missing, nearly a quarter of his command. Stewart's loses, however, proved even heavier: 85 killed, 351 wounded, and 430 missing—a horrific 42 percent of those engaged. Unable to sustain such attrition, Stewart abandoned his hard-won field and withdrew to Charleston in good order. Greene, consistent with his war-winning strategy, had lost another engagement yet forced the British to withdraw to the coast. In May 1782 Stewart was promoted to colonel and placed in charge of the Charleston garrison. He returned to England the following year, rising there to major general in April 1790 before his death in 1794. One of the lesser-known British combatants, Stewart proved himself an adroit tactician, a fearless battle captain, and capable of defeating America's best.

Further Reading
Gordon, John W. *South Carolina and the American Revolution: A Battlefield History.* Columbia: University of South Carolina Press, 2003.

Griffen, Willie L. "The Battle of Eutaw Springs," *South Carolina History Illustrated* 1, no. 3 (1970): 24–27.
Londahl-Smidt, Donald. "After Eutaw Springs: The Last Campaign in the South." Unpublished master's thesis, University of Delaware, 1972.
May, Robin. *The British Army in North America, 1775–1783.* New York: Hippocrene Books, 1999.
Russell, David L. *The American Revolution in the Southern Colonies.* Jefferson, N.C.: McFarland & Company, 2000.
Snow, Richard F. "Eutaw Springs," *American Heritage* 26, no. 5 (1975): 53–56.

Suffren de Saint-Tropez, Pierre de (1729–1788)
French naval officer

Pierre-André de Suffren de Saint-Tropez was born in Aix-en-Provence, France, on July 17, 1729, into an established noble family. In 1743 he entered the navy as a midshipman onboard the *Solide* and fought at the Battle of Toulon and several other engagements before being captured by the English off Cape Finisterre in October 1747. The following year he joined the Knights of Malta and saw action against the Turks and Arabs. Suffren rejoined the French navy in time for the Seven Years' War in 1755, where he fought at Minorca, gained promotion to captain, and fell captive again at the Battle of Lagos in August 1759. He then performed a second tour of duty with the Knights of Malta until 1771, rising to the rank of commander. That year he again rejoined the French service as part of a tactical demonstration squadron, winning high marks for his aggressive ship handling.

In June 1778 de Suffren accompanied the squadron of Admiral Charles-Hector-Théodat, comte d'ESTAING, to America as part of the FRENCH ALLIANCE. On August 5, 1778, he unexpectedly led his own 64-gun ship of the line *Fantasque* and several frigates into Narragansett Bay, which forced the British squadron at Newport to beach and burn several warships. When the combined allied effort in Rhode Island fizzled out, Suffren accompanied d'Estaing to the West Indies, where, on July 6, 1779, he bore a prominent role in fighting the British squadron of Admiral John BYRON to a draw off Grenada. This was an action that the French should have won handily, and de Suffren subsequently criticized his superior's lack of aggressiveness. Nonetheless, d'Estaing was highly complimentary toward his subordinate and recommended him for an independent command. Accordingly, in March 1780 de Suffren received the 80-gun ship of the line *Zèle,* along with a squadron of five warships, and orders to aid Dutch allies at the Cape of Good Hope, South Africa, before proceeding into the Indian Ocean. En route he espied a British squadron under Admiral George Johnstone, which was headed against Capetown, carelessly anchored at neutral Puerto Praya in the Cape Verdes. Suffren suddenly attacked on April 16, 1781, catching the British unprepared, and inflicted such heavy damage that Johnstone's expedition was greatly delayed. He might have captured the entire squadron save for the timidity of his captains, only two of whom eventually engaged at close quarters. De Suffren then reinforced the Dutch as ordered before rounding the Cape of Good Hope and joining the fleet of Admiral d'Orves at Mauritius.

De Suffren reached the Bay of Bengal in December 1781 and assumed command of the 11-ship squadron following the death of d'Orves in February. Over the next 18 months he engaged Admiral Edward Hughes in a series of running battles off the Indian coast, commencing with a slight tactical victory at Madras on February 17. This was followed by another victorious skirmish at Trincomalee on April 12, and a minor defeat at Cuddalore on July 6. Suffren then trumped his opponent by seizing the harbor of Trincomalee on August 22 and fighting Hughes to another draw there on the following September 3. After several months refitting at Sumatra, Suffren returned to India and attacked Hughes again at Cuddalore on June 20, 1783, forcing the British to raise their siege of that town. Both sides were then materially reinforced for a final showdown, which never occurred once news of the TREATY OF PARIS arrived. De Suffren, by dint of aggressive leadership, was by far the most capable French naval leader that the Royal Navy contended with during the Revolutionary War. Had his timid subordinates been equally disposed, the damage wrought might have been incalculable to British interests in India. As it was, on his return voyage several of Suffren's erstwhile adversaries honored him at a banquet in Capetown.

For his exploits de Suffren received a hero's welcome back in France, where he was promoted to rear admiral and *bailli* (senior officer) among the Knights of Malta. King Louis XVI also created the special office of fourth vice admiralty exclusively for him. Unfortunately he died of a stroke on December 8, 1788, before adding additional luster to an already celebrated reputation.

Further Reading
Cavaliero, Roderick. *Admiral Satan: The Life and Campaigns of Suffren.* New York: I. B. Tauris, 1994.
Cockfield, Jamie H. "The Admiral from Hell," *MHQ* 10, no. 1 (1997): 86–96.
Dull, Jonathan R. *The French Navy and American Independence: A Study of Arms and Diplomacy, 1774–1787.* Princeton, N.J.: Princeton University Press, 1975.
Gardiner, Robert, ed. *Navies and the American Revolution, 1775–1783.* Annapolis, Md.: Naval Institute Press, 1996.
Killion, Howard R. "The Suffren Expedition: French Operations in India during the American War of Independence." Unpublished Ph.D. diss., Duke University, 1972.
Moran, Charles. "Suffren, the Apostle of Action," *U.S. Naval Institute Proceedings* 64 (March 1938): 313–320.

Sugar Act (1764)
Victory over France in the Seven Years' War left Great Britain awash in debt and forced it to cultivate new sources of revenue to pay them. Because the North American colonies had been the greatest recipient and benefactor of military expenditures, it was not considered politically or economically untoward to have them partially shoulder the burden of subsidizing imperial defense. In 1764 Prime Minister George GRENVILLE initiated the first

scheme to directly raise taxes from the colonies by passing the so-called Sugar Act. This substantially modified the Molasses Act of 1733 by reducing the duties paid on a gallon of molasses from six pence to three pence per gallon. It was intended to undercut the price of smuggled molasses and, indirectly, grant British West Indian sugar growers a monopoly on the molasses trade. On the surface, the Sugar Act appeared innocuous enough, but it had the net effect of severely disrupting long-established colonial patterns of smuggling, itself an important undercurrent of the local economy. Furthermore, the act placed new tariffs upon coffee, wine, iron, and other enumerated products whose importation to the colonies was now allowed by Britain alone.

Colonials found other provisions of the Sugar Act equally disturbing and unprecedented. Determined to eradicate smugglers, it established an Admiralty Court in Halifax, Nova Scotia, for the purpose of trying all cases pertaining to smuggling. Henceforth, offending parties would have to travel to Halifax to plead their case before a judge—and no jury. This was enacted to negate the long-standing practice of local courts to ignore or leniently punish offenders. Furthermore, all cargo ship captains were now subject to bonding regulations requiring them to post bonds for all cargoes carried. If at any time a customs official uncovered items not strictly covered by the enumerated list, they were subject to immediate confiscation. This resulted in some high-profile seizures, such as John HANCOCK's ship *Liberty* and Henry LAURENS's vessel *Ann,* and the perceived arbitrariness roiled political waters throughout the colonies. In 1766 Parliament tried to make the legislation more palatable by further reducing duties to one pence per gallon of molasses. Protests of the Sugar Act remained muted, especially compared to what followed, but it alerted colonists that Parliament was revising its heretofore benign neglect of the colonies and imposing greater oversight—and restrictions—to raise money. This fact, the systematic measures for enforcement adopted, and quiet but persistent accusations of taxation without representation, foreshadowed the unified colonial response occasioned by the ensuing STAMP ACT.

Further Reading
Cook, Don. *The Long Fuse: How England Lost the American Colonies, 1760–1785.* New York: Atlantic Monthly Press, 1995.
Crowley, John E. *The Privileges of Independence: Neomercantilism and the American Revolution.* Baltimore: Johns Hopkins University, 1993.
Edgar, Gregory T. *Reluctant Break with Britain: From Stamp Act to Bunker Hill.* Bowie, Md.: Heritage Books, 1997.
McCusker, John J., and Russell R. Menard. *The Economy of British America, 1607–1789, with Supplemental Bibliography.* Chapel Hill: Published for the Institute of Early American History and Culture by the University of North Carolina, 1991.

Sullivan, John (1740–1795)
American military officer

John Sullivan was born in Somersworth, New Hampshire, on February 17, 1740, the son of an immigrant Irish schoolteacher. Well educated at home, he read law, was admitted to the bar, and commenced his practice in Durham at the age of 20. A successful attorney, Sullivan also espoused empathy for the Patriot cause, and in 1772 he joined the local militia as a major. He then attended the First Continental CONGRESS as a delegate in 1774 and that December led a raid against Fort William and Mary in Portsmouth Harbor to seize arms and ammunition. The following year Sullivan returned to Congress, where he met and impressed George WASHINGTON with his martial bearing. Accordingly, in June 1775 he became a brigadier general in the Continental ARMY and was ordered to participate in the siege of Boston. After the siege concluded in March 1776 Sullivan was ordered north into Canada with six new regiments. There he succeeded General John THOMAS, who died of illness, and led his raw troops in an unsuccessful attack upon Trois Rivieres, Quebec. Thoroughly bested by forces under Governor-general Guy CARLETON, Sullivan fell back with his survivors to Crown Point, New York, where only

American major general John Sullivan was outflanked and captured at the Battle of Long Island. *(Collection of the State of New Hampshire, Division of Historical Resources)*

the timely arrival of General Philip J. SCHUYLER, with boats and other craft, allowed him to escape capture. Then he learned that Horatio GATES, an officer of less seniority, had been promoted to major general ahead of him. Sullivan angrily took leave of his forces, returned to Congress, and threatened to resign—but was dissuaded from doing so by President John HANCOCK. He reported back to Washington's main army at New York, where, in August, he advanced to major general.

While at New York Sullivan assumed command of the division of General Nathanael GREENE, who was sidelined by illness. In this capacity he fought and lost the Battle of LONG ISLAND on August 27, 1776, being outflanked and captured. Sullivan was next paroled by Admiral Richard HOWE, who dispatched him to Congress with word of his peace commission. This unauthorized act angered many delegates, who clamored for his resignation, but Washington vouched for Sullivan and he was exchanged and rejoined the main army. He performed well at TRENTON and PRINCETON, silencing his critics for the time being. Then, on August 21–22, 1777, Sullivan conducted an ill-advised raid upon Staten Island, New York, which was badly defeated and resulted in a congressional investigation. He was again closely engaged at the defeats of BRANDYWINE and GERMANTOWN, gaining few laurels but remonstrating loudly for his own independent command.

In the summer of 1778 Washington finally acceded to Sullivan's request and made him commander of American forces in Rhode Island. There he was to assist the newly arrived French expedition under Admiral Charles-Hector-Théodat, comte d'ESTAING, for the purpose of capturing Newport that August. Cooperation proved tenuous at best with the haughty admiral, who quickly abandoned his allies after a storm damaged his fleet. Sullivan had few options but to withdraw, and on August 29, 1778, he was attacked in force by the British garrison under General Robert PIGOT. The Americans eventually repulsed their assailants, and a dejected Sullivan spent the winter in Providence awaiting a new assignment. This finally manifested the following summer when Washington, eager to avenge the massacres at Cherry Valley and Wyoming, ordered Sullivan to lead a punitive expedition against the Iroquois heartland in concert with forces under Colonel Daniel BRODHEAD. Sullivan gathered his forces at Tioga, Pennsylvania, was gradually reinforced by additional troops under General James CLINTON, and on August 22 he commenced marching through Indian country. After dispersing the forces of Chief Joseph BRANT and Major William BUTLER at Newtown on August 29, the Americans gradually razed and torched 40 Indian villages, along with stored crops. This was a serious setback to the British Indians, who now faced starvation and deprivation over the winter. However, when Brodhead failed to rendezvous with Sullivan as planned, the latter declined to attack Fort Niagara, a staging area for many Indian and LOYALIST attacks. After the Americans withdrew for the winter, Brant and his tribesmen regrouped and resumed their raids along the New York frontier. Consequently, Congress threatened him with another investigation, and Sullivan, ill and weary of complaints about his leadership, resigned his commission and left the army on November 30, 1779.

In 1780 Sullivan returned to Congress as a delegate, and two years later he commenced a career in public service at home. He proved much better at politics than warfare and served as governor for three consecutive terms, from 1786 to 1789. He also served as chairman of the state constitutional convention in 1788, advocating adoption of the proposed federal constitution. In 1791 President Washington appointed his former comrade in arms to be federal district judge for New Hampshire. He died in this capacity at Durham, on January 23, 1795. Sullivan, despite a tall, imposing mien, proved himself a reliable subordinate but a mediocre and essentially luckless commander.

Further Reading
Conley, Patrick T. "The Battle of Rhode Island, 29 August, 1779: A Victory for the Patriots," *Rhode Island History* 62, no. 3 (2004): 51–65.
Fischer, Joseph R. *A Well-Executed Failure: The Sullivan Campaign against the Iroquois, July–September, 1779*. Columbia: University of South Carolina Press, 1997.
Hammond, Otis G., ed. *Letters and Papers of Major General John Sullivan, Continental Army*, 3 vols. Concord: New Hampshire Historical Society, 1930–39.
McKone, Frank E. *General Sullivan: New Hampshire Patriot*. New York: Vantage Press, 1977.
Morrissey, Brendan. *New York, 1776: The Continentals' First Battles*. Oxford: Osprey, 2004.
Whittmore, Charles P. *A General of the Revolution: John Sullivan of New Hampshire*. New York: Columbia University Press, 1961.

Sumner, Jethro (1733–1785)
American military officer

Jethro Sumner was born in Nansemond County, Virginia, in 1733, and he served in the French and Indian War as a lieutenant. In 1764 he relocated to Granville County, North Carolina, where he ran a tavern and also worked as a planter. Sumner became increasingly active as he accumulated wealth and prestige, being a justice of the peace in 1768 and county sheriff, 1772–77. He did not profess overt sympathies for the Patriot movement until being elected a delegate to the Third Provincial Congress in 1775. There he gained appointment as major of the Halifax District MINUTEMEN and, on April 15, 1776, became colonel of the newly constituted 3rd North Carolina Continental Infantry. He initially served under General Charles LEE during the attack on CHARLESTON, South Carolina, in June 1776, and then marched his command north to join the main army under General George WASHINGTON in New Jersey. He fought well at the Battles of BRANDYWINE and GERMANTOWN in the fall of 1777 and spent the ensuing winter at Valley Forge, Pennsylvania. After obtaining sick leave, Sumner was discharged back to his home state to recuperate and perform recruiting services.

In light of his excellent service, the Continental CONGRESS appointed Sumner a brigadier general in the Continental ARMY on January 9, 1779. He was subsequently entrusted with a brigade of North Carolina troops and ordered to reinforce the army of General Benjamin LINCOLN in South Carolina. On June 20, 1779, he fought bravely but unsuccessfully at Stono Ferry and was sidelined with illness again. For this reason he missed the siege of CHARLESTON in the spring of 1780 and was not captured. That September, North Carolina was invaded by General Charles CORNWALLIS, and Sumner performed near miracles recruiting and training new militia troops for its defense. However, he was angered when command of all state forces was given to General William SMALLWOOD in October 1780 and retired from military service in protest. By February 1781 he had been coaxed back into the field by General Nathanael GREENE, but Governor Richard CASWELL failed to find him a new command. In July Greene finally assigned him three newly recruited North Carolina regiments. With them he bore a conspicuous part in the hard-fought action at Eutaw Springs on September 8, 1781, and his men performed tenaciously like veterans. Sumner then assumed control of all state forces for the remainder of the war. He was discharged from the army in November 1783.

After the war Sumner returned to managing his personal business, although in 1784 he helped organize the state chapter of the Society of the Cincinnati. He died at his home in Warren County, North Carolina, on March 18, 1785, an accomplished regimental and brigade-level officer.

Further Reading
Ashe, Samuel A., ed. *The Biographical History of North Carolina,* 8 vols. Greensboro, N.C.: C. L. Van Noppen, 1905.
Battle, Kemp P. "Career of Brigadier General Jethro Sumner," *Magazine of American History* 26 (December 1891): 415–433.
———. "The Life and Services of Brigadier General Jethro Sumner," *North Carolina Booklet* 8 (October 1908): 111–140.
Clark, Walter M., ed. *The State Records of North Carolina,* 26 vols. Raleigh: P. M. Hale, 1886–1907; vols. 11–24.
Rankin, Hugh F. *The North Carolina Continentals.* Chapel Hill: University of North Carolina Press, 1971.
Snow, Richard F. "Eutaw Springs," *American Heritage* 26, no. 5 (1975): 53–56.

Sumter, Thomas (1734–1832)
American militia officer
Thomas Sumter was born in Hanover County, Virginia, on August 14, 1734, where he was scantily educated. He served in the militia as a sergeant after the French and Indian War erupted in 1754, survived General Edward Braddock's disastrous Fort Duquesne expedition, and subsequently campaigned against the Cherokee Indians. Sumter, now a captain, participated in peace talks and accompanied several chiefs to England, where they met King GEORGE III in 1762. Back in Virginia, Sumter was tossed into debtor's prison, then escaped to the frontiers of South Carolina and established a trading post. Over the next decade he became closely identified with the Patriot cause and, when war with England broke out in 1775, he was commissioned a lieutenant colonel of the 2nd South Carolina Rifle Regiment. In this capacity he assisted General Charles LEE during the attack on CHARLESTON in June 1776 and then accompanied a campaign against the Over Hill Cherokees. Sumter then saw extensive service along the Georgia–East Florida border as a colonel in the Continental ARMY until stricken by malaria and sent home in 1778. At that time he resigned his commission and withdrew from active service.

Two more years lapsed before the British returned to South Carolina and scored a major victory during the siege of CHARLESTON in May 1780. This led to a local LOYALIST resurgence, and at one point a party of renegades burned Sumter's home. He then collected and organized his own guerrilla band, which, after the crushing American defeat at CAMDEN in August 1780, constituted the only organized resistance in South Carolina. Sumter initially won a small action at Williamson's Plantation on July 12 but was repulsed the following month at Rocky Mount on August 1. Six days later he successfully attacked Hanging Rock, taking many prisoners, but his recurring activity brought him to the attention of General Charles CORNWALLIS. Consequently, the mounted British Legion under Lieutenant Colonel Banastre TARLETON was ordered to chase him down and, on August 18, Tarleton surprised Sumter's encampment at Fishing Creek. The Americans sustained 400 casualties and prisoners while Sumter escaped capture by the narrowest of margins. But, displaying a tenacity that garnered him the nickname "Gamecock," he simply regrouped and resumed his "hit and run" warfare. That October he was appointed brigadier general of militia, and on November 7, 1780, Sumter mauled a Loyalist garrison at Fishdam Ford. Two weeks later he bloodily repulsed his nemesis Tarleton at Blackstock's Hill but was severely wounded. Sumter required several months to recuperate, but the South Carolina government in exile voted him a gold medal while the Continental CONGRESS extended him its thanks in January 1781. Cornwallis, whose rear area security suffered from Sumter's relentless attacks, paid him an even higher compliment by proclaiming him "our greatest plague in this country."

Sumter renewed his war upon British lines of communication in the spring of 1781 as commander of all state forces. He impetuously attacked and was repulsed at Fort Watson on February 28 but then managed to overrun the village of Orangeburg on May 11. Perpetually short on pay for his troops, he incurred a degree of notoriety by promulgating "Sumter's Law," whereby troops received enlistment bounties in the form of slaves and other property confiscated from Loyalist estates. The practice was widely condemned by General Nathanael GREENE and Governor John RUTLEDGE as robbery and only intensified the hatreds of an already brutal civil war. Unlike his contemporaries Francis MARION and Andrew PICKENS, Sumter disdained fighting in concert with the Continental army or other bands. Cooperation, where given, proved sullen at best. From May to June 1781 Sumter failed to support Greene's efforts to evict a Loyalist garrison from Fort Ninety Six and, on July 17, 1781, ignoring sound tactical advice from Marion and Major Henry LEE, he badly mismanaged an attack upon Quinby Bridge. The Americans sustained a heavy repulse, and Major Thomas Taylor, incensed by the loss of life, swore he would never to serve under the "Gamecock" again. Sumter then placated his troops by allowing them to plunder the town of Georgetown, which brought a swift retaliatory response. Exhausted by wounds and reprimanded by Greene for insubordination, he was finally removed from command by Governor Rutledge in August 1781.

Despite his obstinate nature, Sumter was a bona fide war hero in South Carolina, and he embarked on a successful political career. After serving several terms in the state legislature, he was elected to the U.S. House of Representatives and Senate repeatedly by a grateful populace. Sumter retired from public life in 1810 but remained dogged by debts until the legislature canceled them in 1827. He died in Statesburg on June 1, 1832, the longest-living general of the Revolutionary War. His heavyhanded tactics and checkered battle record remain controversial, but Sumter served a useful purpose by taking the war to the British and sustaining the Revolution in very dark times. A city, a county, and Fort Sumter in Charleston Harbor, where the Civil War commenced in 1861, were all named in his honor.

American general Thomas Sumter's aggressive tactics and inconsistent battle record made him a controversial figure. *(Independence National Historical Park)*

Further Reading
Bass, Robert D. *Gamecock: The Life and Campaigns of General Thomas Sumter.* New York: Holt, Rinehart, & Winston, 1961.
———. *Ninety-Six: The Struggle for the South Carolina Back Country.* Lexington, S.C.: Sandlapper Store, 1978.

Edgar, Walter. *Partisans and Redcoats: The Southern Conflict That Turned the Tide of the American Revolution.* New York: William Morrow, 2001.

Gordon, John W. *South Carolina and the American Revolution: A Battlefield History.* Columbia: University of South Carolina Press, 2003.

Helsley, Alexia J. *South Carolinians in the War for American Independence.* Columbia: South Carolina Department of History and Archives, 2000.

Russell, David L. *The American Revolution in the Southern Colonies.* Jefferson, N.C.: McFarland & Co., 2000.

Talbot, Silas (1751–1813)
American naval officer

Silas Talbot was born in Dighton, Massachusetts, on January 11, 1751, the son of farmers. Though trained as a stonemason he chose instead to serve with the merchant marine and settled in Providence, Rhode Island, as a ship captain. When the Revolutionary War broke out in April 1775, Talbot was commissioned a captain in the state militia, and he fulfilled a tour of duty in the siege of Boston. After passing into the Continental ARMY the following July, he accompanied General George WASHINGTON's army to New York City. There he unsuccessfully attempted a fireboat attack upon HMS *Asia* off Manhattan and was badly burned in the process. But the attack so unnerved Admiral Richard HOWE that his squadron hoisted anchor and settled below the city for safety. Talbot gained promotion to major as of October 10, 1777, and fought well on Hog Island in defense of Fort Mifflin. Wounded again, he then joined General John SULLIVAN's army in its unsuccessful attempt to capture British-held Newport. His activities constituted one of the few bright spots in an otherwise dismal campaign. That October he outfitted and led the sloop *Hawk* on one of many forays against LOYALIST privateers operating near Narragansett Bay. He had one particular offender, the schooner *Pigot*, in mind. Mindful that his quarry draped high nets over its side as an anti-boarding device, Talbot rigged his own vessel with a large kedging anchor on the bowsprint to rip away the nets as he ran alongside. The ploy succeeded brilliantly, and the *Pigot* was stormed and taken. He cruised the bay for several

Continental army officer Silas Talbot was the only army officer of the Revolutionary War to command naval vessels. *(Naval Historical Center)*

more months in the 12-gun schooner *Argo,* until August 7, 1779, when the larger British privateer *Dragon* hove into view. Badly outmatched, Talbot immediately attacked and was damaged by enemy fire, yet captured his antagonist when a lucky shot brought down a mainmast. That same afternoon, he also attacked and took the privateer brig *Hannah,* which had the misfortune of appearing in his vicinity. Onlookers at Providence wharf were surprised, when the small and badly battered *Argo* limped into port with two armed prizes larger then itself.

Talbot's successes resulted in promotion to lieutenant colonel, but the army at that time lacked a battalion for him to command. He then prevailed upon the Continental CONGRESS for a captain's commission in the Continental NAVY, which materialized in September 1779. However, the navy was also in dire straits with few available vessels, so Talbot requisitioned the privateer *George Washington* in early 1780. After several more captures Talbot ran afoul of HMS *Culloden* off New York and was taken. He spent many difficult weeks crammed into the hold of the prison ship *Jersey* before transferring to Mill Prison at Plymouth, England. Talbot made several failed escape attempts before being exchanged through the efforts of Benjamin FRANKLIN and John JAY in Paris. Talbot then departed on a Rhode Island brig, was briefly detained at sea by another British vessel, and spent several months at Philadelphia litigating his prize claims.

After the war Talbot settled in Fulton County, New York, on property formerly owned by Sir John JOHNSON. In 1792 he held a seat in the state legislature and the following year was elected to Congress as a Federalist. Two years later President Washington appointed him third on the captain's list of the new U.S. Navy, and Talbot spent several months supervising construction of the large frigate USS *President.* He remained without an active command until 1799, when he replaced Samuel NICHOLSON as captain of the new frigate USS *Constitution.* In this capacity he led a small squadron through several sweeps of the Carribean during the so-called Quasi-War with France, netting several privateers. His most dramatic capture occurred on May 11, 1800, when he dispatched Captain Daniel Carmick of the marines and Lieutenant Isaac Hull of the navy to cut out the French vessel *Sandwich* in neutral Puerto Plata, Santo Domingo. The attack succeeded, but the Admiralty Court ruled against Talbot for violating Spanish neutrality and no monetary gains were realized. In September 1801 Talbot became entangled in a seniority dispute with Captain Thomas Truxtun and angrily resigned. He died in New York City on June 30, 1813, the only army officer of the Revolutionary War to command naval vessels.

Further Reading
Fowler, William M. *Silas Talbot: Captain of Old Ironsides.* Mystic, Conn.: Mystic Seaport Museum, 1995.
Leiner, Frederick C. "Anatomy of a Prize Case: Dollars, Side Deals, and Les Deux Anges," *American Journal of Legal History* 39 (April 1995): 214–232.
Miller, Nathan. *Sea of Glory: A Naval History of the American Revolution.* Mount Pleasant, S.C.: Nautical and Aviation Pub. Co., 2000.
Morgan, William J. *Captains to the Northward: The New England Captains in the Continental Navy.* Barre, Mass.: Barre Gazette, 1959.
Norton, Louis A. "The Second Captain: Silas Talbot of the U.S.S. Constitution," *Sea History* no. 81 (spring/summer 1997): 37–39.

Tallmadge, Benjamin (1754–1835)
American military officer

Benjamin Tallmadge was born in Brookhaven, Long Island, New York, on February 25, 1754, the son of a clergyman. He passed through Yale in 1773 and briefly served as superintendent of the Wethersfield school. Tallmadge was a good friend and close associate of fellow classmate Nathan HALE. After the Revolutionary War commenced, he became a lieutenant in Colonel John Chester's regiment and fought capably at LONG ISLAND and WHITE PLAINS. On December 14, 1776, Tallmadge transferred as a captain into Colonel Elisha SHELDON's 2nd Continental Light Dragoons, rising to major there the following April. In this capacity he campaigned at BRANDYWINE and GERMANTOWN in 1777 and MONMOUTH the following year. Tallmadge's good behavior and military bearing caught the attention of General George WASHINGTON, who then appointed him head of army intelligence in November 1778. This was a marked distinction for so young an officer and he became one of the few individuals who reported directly to the commander in chief.

Tallmadge proved himself a legendary intelligence operative. He established and directed the infamous "Culper Spy Ring" on Long Island, recruited primarily from former friends at Yale. They were responsible for keeping an eye on the intentions and activities of General Henry CLINTON at New York, as well as collecting routine military intelligence on enemy troop strength and dispositions. One of his most celebrated coups occurred in 1780, when Tallmadge obtained word of an impending British expedition against the marquis de LAFAYETTE in Rhode Island. This information was immediately relayed to Washington, who then ordered his army into an offensive posture, and Clinton, fearful about being attacked, canceled the offensive. In another celebrated affair, Tallmadge was tipped off to the impending arrival of a British spy called "John Anderson." This turned out to be none other than Major John ANDRE, who was captured by guards and turned over to Tallmadge. Tallmadge, now suspecting General Benedict ARNOLD of treason, deliberately withheld Andre rather than release him to Arnold's headquarters; hence, he did not escape. Tallmadge subsequently befriended the doomed British officer, accompanied him to the gallows, and was the last individual to bid him farewell at his execution in October 1780.

In addition to intelligence gathering, Tallmadge also proved himself to be an enterprising partisan fighter. On the evening of September 9, 1779, Tallmadge loaded 150 dismounted dragoons onto boats at Shippen Point, Connecticut, silently crossed Long Island Sound, and suddenly stormed Lloyd's Neck, taking 500 LOYALIST captives. A year later, on November 21, 1780, he slipped a number of dragoons across the sound again, then stealthily approached and captured Fort St. George at Oyster Bay. The Loyalists lost 200 men captured for one American slightly wounded. For this effort he received the Thanks of the Continental CONGRESS and official commendation from Washington. Afterward, General Jean-Baptiste, comte de ROCHAMBEAU, spoke favorably of intelligence reports obtained from Tallmadge while passing through Connecticut to New York. Tallmadge was advanced to lieutenant colonel on September 30, 1783, just prior to his discharge.

After the war Tallmadge resettled at Litchfield, Connecticut, where he operated a store and later stood for public office. He performed stints as postmaster and president of the Connecticut Society of the Cincinnati before winning a seat in the U.S. House of Representatives in 1801. Over the next decade he functioned as an ardent Federalist and a staunch political adversary of presidents Thomas JEFFERSON and James MADISON. He adamantly opposed the War of 1812, feeling the nation was woefully unprepared, and declined to seek reelection in 1817. Tallmadge died at Litchfield on March 7, 1835, one of the most accomplished spymasters of early American history.

Further Reading

Capron, Dennis C. "The Revolutionary War of Benjamin Tallmadge." Unpublished master's thesis, Midwestern State University, 2005.

Fawcett, Bernadine. *Missing Links to the Culper Spy Ring?* Conshohocken, Pa.: Infinity Publishing, 2005.

Hall, Charles S. *Benjamin Tallmadge, Revolutionary Soldier and American Businessman.* New York: Columbia University Press, 1943.

Mahoney, Harry T., and Marjorie L. Mahoney. *Gallantry in Action: A Biographic Dictionary of Espionage in the American Revolutionary War.* Lanham, Md.: University Press of America, 1999.

Smith, Alvin R. L. *History and Guide to the Major Benjamin Tallmadge Trail: The Capture of Fort St. George at Mastic, N.Y., and the Burning of Forage at Coram, N.Y.* Brookhaven, N.Y.: Town of Brookhaven Bicentennial Commission, 1976.

Tallmadge, Benjamin. *Memoir of Colonel Benjamin Tallmadge.* New York: Arno Press, 1968.

Tarleton, Banastre (1754–1833)
English military officer

Banastre Tarleton was born in Liverpool, England, on August 21, 1754, the son of a wealthy merchant. Educated at Eton and Oxford, he neglected his studies and appeared more interested in drinking and gambling. When his debts threatened to overwhelm him he purchased a cornet's commission in the King's Dragoon Guards; suddenly, this pampered wastrel found his calling. Tarleton volunteered for service in America and crossed the Atlantic with General Charles CORNWALLIS. After witnessing the unsuccessful attack on CHARLESTON in June 1776, he reported to General William HOWE in New York and was posted with the 16th Dragoons, one of two regular cavalry regiments in the theater. Here Tarleton quickly established a near-legendary reputation for dash and daring. On December 13, 1776, he accompanied the force that surprised and captured General Charles LEE at Basking Ridge, New Jersey. After several more successful skirmishes he was promoted to lieutenant colonel of the newly constituted British Legion, a mixed, green-clad cavalry/infantry force recruited from LOYALISTS. With them he launched an audacious raid against Poundridge, New York, on July 2, 1779, driving back American cavalry under Major Elisha SHELDON. He then rendered useful service in the Philadelphia campaign and at MONMOUTH. Tarleton's opportunity for distinction arrived in December 1779, when he shipped south with General Henry CLINTON on the expedition against South Carolina. The fact that all horses died in transit did not dampen the spirit of his troopers, now imbued with their jaunty commander's aggressive spirit.

For several months in 1780 Tarleton fought alongside such unconventional notables as John Graves SIMCOE and Patrick FERGUSON throughout the siege of CHARLESTON. Once Clinton returned to New York in May, he rejoined Cornwallis as cavalry commander and perfected his battlefield routine: accurate reconnaissance and rapid movement, invariably followed by relentless assault. In this manner he quickly smashed two American

British officer Banastre Tarleton was known for his daring and ruthlessness on the battlefield. *(National Gallery, London)*

formations at Monck's Corner (April 14) and Lenud's Ferry (May 6), but it was at Waxhaws on May 29, 1780, that Tarleton and his Legion gained lasting infamy. There, having attacked and overrun the defenses of Colonel Abraham BUFORD, Tarleton's horse was shot under him, and in the chaos that followed his enraged troopers killed some Americans trying to surrender. The "massacre" was unintentional and most likely an unfortunate by-product of the furious fighting, but Tarleton was forever branded as "Bloody Ban." Thereafter his reputation for ruthlessness, deserved or not, terrorized partisan bands throughout the Carolinas.

Tarleton next spearheaded Cornwallis's march from Charleston, and he led a helter-skelter pursuit of defeated Americans at CAMDEN on August 16, 1780. Two days later he suddenly galloped into the midst of General Thomas SUMTER's encampment at Fishing Creek, nearly wiping them out. But he proved considerably less successful at cornering the elusive colonel Francis MARION, who artfully dodged his pursuers in the swamps and acquired a reputation as the "Swamp Fox." Curiously, the fearsome British Legion was roughly handled in two engagements that July and September under Major George HANGER, who commanded while Tarleton was ill. Once recovered, Tarleton pounced on Sumter again at Blackstocks on November 20, 1780, and was rebuffed after a hard-fought action. The turning point in the career of this headstrong dandy came in the spring of 1781, when Cornwallis invaded North Carolina. Tarleton was dispatched on a wide sweep to intercept Americans under General Daniel MORGAN, and the two willful leaders clashed at COWPENS on January 17, 1781. Typically, the impetuous redhead charged headlong into a carefully staged American ambush and was all but annihilated. Tarleton then traded cuts with Colonel William WASHINGTON as his army disintegrated and was lucky to escape. Several British officers rather impolitely gloated over his comeuppance and castigated him for such Custer-like rashness. Tarleton then dejectedly tendered his resignation to Cornwallis, but the general, valuing his talents, refused to accept it. The British Legion was subsequently reconstituted in time to fight at the bloody Battle of GUILFORD COURTHOUSE on March 17, 1781, where Tarleton was in the thick of the fray and lost two fingers. Cornwallis, inundated by heavy casualties, abandoned all hope of conquering the Carolinas and moved northward into Virginia.

Tarleton, though humbled, had lost none of his potency as a strike force. On June 4, 1781, he suddenly dashed to the capital of Charlottesville, capturing Daniel BOONE and forcing Governor Thomas JEFFERSON to flee. He next galloped off on another destructive and unstoppable raid across the length of Virginia, July 9–24, expending many irreplaceable men and horses, before reuniting with the main army at YORKTOWN. As allied armies arrived to encircle Cornwallis, Tarleton was posted on the opposite side of the York River at Gloucester. There, on October 3, 1781, he had a sharp but inconsequential duel with another *beau sabre*, the duc de LAUZUN, and escaped again. After the British surrender of October 19, 1781, Tarleton was paroled but, in light of his unsavory reputation, he complained loudly when American officers refused to dine with him in their tents. He remained the most hated British officer of the Revolutionary War, particularly in the South.

After the war Tarleton returned to England to revel in his heroic reputation and resume his extravagant lifestyle. Between 1786 and 1806 he served intermittently in Parliament while reinforcing his reputation for fast living. Tarleton also remained active in military circles, rising to major general in 1798 and full general in 1812, but he never held another field command. Having married an aristocrat's daughter, he eventually settled into the lifestyle of a respectable country gentleman. "Bloody Ban" died at Leinwardine on January 25, 1833; his once daring exploits were all but forgotten at home but not so in America, where he remained a maligned, reviled figure. Notwithstanding his hard-won celebrity on the battlefield, the ruthlessness with which Tarleton pursued glory occasioned rallying cries of "Tarleton's Quarter" and ultimately stiffened the very resistance he sought so hard to break.

Further Reading

Chenney, J. B. "Bloody Ban," *American History* 17, no. 3 (2000): 16–18.

Eanes, Greg. *Tarleton's Southside Raid: Prelude to Yorktown*. Burkeville, Va.: E. & H. Pub. Co., 2002.

Maass, John. " 'To Disturb the Assembly': Tarleton's Charlottesville Raid and the British Invasion of Virginia, 1781," *Virginia Cavalcade* 49, no. 4 (2000): 148–157.

Rider, Thomas A. "Massacre or Myth? No Quarter at Waxhaws, 29 May 1780." Unpublished master's thesis, University of North Carolina, Chapel Hill, 2002.

Scotti, Anthony J. *Brutal Virtue: The Myths and Realities of Banastre Tarleton.* Bowie, Md.: Heritage Books, 2002.

Swisher, James K. "Duel in the Backwoods," *Military Heritage* 4, no. 3 (2002): 50–57.

Tarleton, Banastre. *A History of the Campaigns of 1780 and 1781, in the Southern Provinces of North America.* North Stratford, N.H.: Ayer Co., 2002.

Tea Act (1773)

Tea was by far the most popular beverage imbibed by colonials, and the demand for it had been traditionally met by a combination of direct importation from England and smuggling from Dutch and French sources. This seemingly innocuous commodity became caught up in the firestorm of protest surrounding the TOWNSHEND DUTIES of 1767, whereby a slight tax was levied. After three years of unrest the administration of Prime Minister Frederick NORTH finally repealed the Townshend levies in 1770, although the tea tax remained in place—solely to underscore Parliament's intrinsic ability to tax the colonies. This retention caused some outpouring of anger toward tea imports, but over the next three years consumption basically returned to normal levels.

The turning point with respect to tea occurred in May 1773 when Lord North prevailed upon Parliament to pass the so-called Tea Act. This was accomplished at the behest of the influential East India Company, which enjoyed a near-monopoly on the growing and distribution of tea throughout the empire. But, hamstrung by debt, mismanagement, and bouts of nonimportation arising from other disputes, the company was nearing bankruptcy and petitioned Parliament for relief. The Tea Act, which became law on May 10, 1773, seemed at first glance a simple and attractive solution. First, it guaranteed the East India Company a total monopoly of trade with the colonies, as only its agents were certified to market the product. Next, in an effort to eliminate revenues lost through smuggling, the tax on tea itself was reduced to a pittance, thus rendering it cheaper than Dutch or French commodities. Finally, even with the lower tax, tea would still generate revenues for the empire, further demonstrating Parliament's ability to regulate colonial matters.

Unfortunately for the British, the Tea Act was construed abroad as an act of political favoritism, aimed squarely at curtailing the colonial economy. Non-registered tea agents—along with merchants deeply involved in smuggling—would suffer from the new pricing scheme. Moreover, to radical elements the continuing importation of British tea, and the revenues it accrued, legitimized taxation without representation. Protests sprang up in port cities across North America and many tea-carrying ships were either turned back or prevented from discharging their cargoes. Events crested in December 1773, when Governor Thomas HUTCHINSON of Massachusetts would not allow tea ships to leave without first paying the tax. The impasse was finally and dramatically broken by the BOSTON TEA PARTY.

Further Reading

Cook, Don. *The Long Fuse: How England Lost the American Colonies, 1760–1785.* New York: Atlantic Monthly Press, 1995.

Crowley, John E. *The Privileges of Independence: Neomercantilism and the American Revolution.* Baltimore: Johns Hopkins University, 1993.

Edgar, Gregory T. *Reluctant Break with Britain: From Stamp Act to Bunker Hill.* Bowie, Md.: Heritage Books, 1997.

McCusker, John J., and Russell R. Menard. *The Economy of British North America, 1607–1789, with Supplemental Bibliography.* Chapel Hill: Published for the Institute of Early American History and Culture by the University of North Carolina Press, 1991.

Thomas, Peter D. G. *Tea Party to Independence: The Third Phase of the American Revolution, 1773–1776.* New York: Oxford University Press, 1991.

Ternant, Charles (1751–1816)

French military officer

Charles-Jean-Baptiste de Ternant was born in Damviliers, France, on December 12, 1751. In 1772 he joined the French army as part of the elite Royal Corps of Engineers, rising there to lieutenant. In 1778, possibly motivated by idealism, he resigned his commission and sailed to the United States seeking to join the Continental ARMY. After being interviewed by the Continental CONGRESS, he introduced himself to General George WASHINGTON at Valley Forge, but, in so much as he lacked letters of introduction or other appropriate references, Ternant was not tendered a military post. He then came to the attention of General Friedrich von STEUBEN, who valued his English fluency and prevailed upon Washington to appoint him divisional sub-inspector, a civilian position. In this capacity Ternant assisted Steuben's famous training routine and acquitted himself well—usually translating Steuben's colorful profanity into English for the soldiers' benefit. Having favorably impressed his superiors, he was commissioned lieutenant colonel on September 24, 1778, and ordered to join General Robert HOWE as an inspector in the Southern Department.

Ternant functioned at Charleston for many months and reported his charge woefully trained, equipped, and undermanned. He was also responsible for transplanting Steuben's training methods onto southern recruits. After detailing Charleston's military weaknesses to authorities he accompanied Howe during the ill-fated defense of Savannah in December 1778, where they were routed by Lieutenant Colonel Archibald CAMPBELL. He then joined the staff of General Benjamin LINCOLN at Purysburg, South Carolina, and fought at the unsuccessful attack upon Stono Ferry on June 20, 1779. Ternant next fought at the siege of CHARLESTON in the spring of 1780 and was dispatched to Havana, Cuba, by Governor John RUTLEDGE to request military assistance from SPAIN. When this failed he returned to Charleston and became a captive when the city surrendered on May 12, 1780. Ternant represented the American military during surrender negotiations and dealt exclusively with Major John ANDRE. But, as a French national, he was quickly paroled by General Henry CLINTON and headed north to Philadelphia awaiting his exchange. There he met and befriended several influential congressmen, who became quite impressed by his cordiality and devotion to the cause. When Ternant was formally released for duty in January 1782, he was assigned to the First Partisan Corps of Colonel Charles ARMAND. He also functioned as inspector general of the Southern Army on the staff of General Nathanael GREENE. Ternant performed these tasks until the end of the war and finally mustered out of service with the rank of colonel in 1783. Before departing for France, Ternant received the thanks of the president of Congress, Thomas MIFFLIN, and he was also commended by General Washington.

Back home Ternant continued in military circles until 1785, when he became French agent in the army of the Dutch Provinces. After campaigning against Prussian forces he returned home in 1788 and three years later arrived back in the United States as minister plenipotentiary. Ternant proved himself a skilled negotiator during the difficult period leading up to the Quasi-War with France, and he was replaced by Citizen Edmond Genet. He then settled at Conches, where, many years later, he declined a general's commission offered by Napoleon. Ternant died in 1816, a gallant and invaluable allied officer.

Further Reading

Adams, Douglas N. "Jean Baptiste Ternant, Inspector General and Advisor to the Commanding Generals of the Southern Forces, 1778–1782," *South Carolina Historical Magazine* 86, no. 1 (1985): 221–240.

Clary, David A., and Joseph W. A. Whitehorne. *The Inspectors General of the United States Army, 1777–1903.* Washington, D.C.: Office of the Inspector General and Center of Military History, U.S. Army, 1987.

Nicolai, Martin L. "Subjects and Citizens: French Officers and the North American Experience, 1755–1783." Unpublished Ph.D. diss., Queen's University, Kingston, 1992.

Turner, Frederick J. *Correspondence of the French Ministers to the United States, 1791–1797,* 2 vols. New York: Da Capo Press, 1972.

Thomas, John (1724–1776)
American military officer

John Thomas was born in Marshfield, Massachusetts, on November 9, 1724, and he studied medicine in the office of a local doctor. After establishing a successful practice in Kingston, he joined the militia as a surgeon in March 1746 and campaigned at Nova Scotia during King George's War. When the French and Indian War commenced in 1755, Thomas was commissioned a lieutenant and a surgeon's mate and saw extensive campaigning throughout Canada. An accomplished leader, he was promoted colonel in 1760 and commanded a regiment until war's end three years later. Afterward he resumed his medical practice in Massachusetts and Governor Thomas HUTCHINSON also appointed him justice of the peace in 1770. Over the ensuing decade Thomas gradually aligned himself with the Patriot movement. He was active in the local SONS OF LIBERTY and in February 1775, before the outbreak of hostilities, he became a brigadier general of colonial militia. At this time Thomas was regarded as the senior military figure in Massachusetts, and on May 19, 1775, he was elevated to lieutenant general commanding all state forces. The following June he was inducted into the Continental ARMY. Thomas, however, was angered that two prior subordinates, William HEATH and Seth POMEROY, received greater seniority, and he threatened to resign until cajoled by General George WASHINGTON into remaining. He subsequently rendered useful service during the siege of Boston by occupying the important post at Roxbury. On March 4, 1776, men from his command occupied strategic Dorchester Heights overlooking Boston Harbor and planted artillery pieces—one of the most remarkable engineering feats of the entire war. This broke the impasse and prompted General William HOWE to evacuate the city two weeks later.

On March 6, 1776, Thomas advanced to major general and was ordered north by the Continental CONGRESS to take command of American troops still in QUEBEC. These were the remnants of forces under Generals Benedict ARNOLD and Richard MONTGOMERY, which had been repulsed at Quebec the previous December and had maintained a loose siege of the city ever since. Thomas arrived in Canada on May 1, 1776, and was dismayed to find his command consisting of 1,700 men, of whom only 1,000 were fit for duty. Faced with an onslaught of British reinforcements under Governor-General Guy CARLETON, Thomas ordered a retreat to Montreal. En route he contracted smallpox and died near Fort Chambly on June 2, 1776, and was briefly superseded by William THOMPSON. Thomas was regarded by contemporaries as a capable leader.

Further Reading
Brooks, Victor. *The Boston Campaign, April 19, 1775–March 17, 1776.* Conshohocken, Pa.: Combined, 1999.

Coffin, Charles. *The Life and Services of Major General John Thomas.* New York: Egbert, Hovey & King, 1844.

Hamilton, Edward P. "General John Thomas," *Massachusetts Historical Society Proceedings* 84 (1972): 44–52.

Lord, Arthur. "General John Thomas," *Massachusetts Historical Society Proceedings* 18 (1903–04): 419–432.

———. "A Soldier of the Revolution: General John Thomas," *Bostonian Society Publications* 12 (1915): 7–35.

Thompson, William (1736–1781)
American military officer

William Thompson was born in Ireland in 1736, and he immigrated to Carlisle, Pennsylvania, as a young man. During the French and Indian War he functioned as a militia cavalry captain and accompanied the expedition of Colonel John ARMSTRONG against Indian settlements at Kittanning in 1756. Afterward he undertook surveying work in western Pennsylvania and Kentucky. As war with Great Britain approached, Thompson sided with the Patriots and served on the Cumberland County COMMITTEE OF CORRESPONDENCE in response to the COERCIVE ACTS. In May 1775 he was elected colonel of a battalion of riflemen authorized by the Continental CONGRESS as the nucleus of a new Continental ARMY, seconded by Lieutenant Colonel Edward HAND. In this capacity he marched nine companies of sharpshooters north, becoming the first troops from the mid-Atlantic states to reach Boston. There his rough-hewed, hard-drinking frontiersmen gained a measure of notoriety for superb marksmanship and blatant insubordination. Thompson first saw action on November 9, 1775, when his riflemen, assisted by troops under Colonel John PATERSON, drove off a British foraging party from Lechmere Point. The British managed to abscond with 10 cows, but General George WASHINGTON publicly thanked the otherwise troublesome riflemen for their assistance. Thompson rose to brigadier general on May 1, 1776, shortly before the siege of Boston successfully concluded.

That summer Thompson marched north to join American forces already in Quebec (Canada). After arriving he briefly replaced General John THOMAS as commander before being succeeded in turn by General John SULLIVAN. In June 1776 Sullivan dispatched Thompson on an ill-advised attack against the Trois-Rivières district. His 2,000-man force, including Arthur ST. CLAIR, Anthony WAYNE, and William IRVINE, executed a night march on June 7, 1776, but was betrayed by their guide and foundered in a swamp by morning. Worse, the approach of several thousand British reinforcements under General Simon FRASER induced him to surrender with 236 of his men. Thompson was paroled soon after and spent the rest of the war awaiting exchange. Anxious to return to combat, he maliciously slandered Congressman Thomas McKean for deliberately delaying the process and was subsequently tried in Congress and fined. Thompson was eventually exchanged for General Friedrich von RIEDESEL on October 25, 1780, but he never received a field command and died at Carlisle on September 3, 1781.

Further Reading

Crist, Allan G. *William Thompson, A Shooting Star: The Colorful, Tragic Life of an Early Citizen Soldier.* Carlisle, Pa.: Cumberland County Historical Society, 1976.

Heathcote, Charles W. "General William Thompson—An Earnest Pennsylvanian Military Officer and Supporter of Washington," *Picket Post* no. 71 (February 1961): 4–10.

Kennedy, William V. *Thompson's Pennsylvania Rifle Battalion: Keystone of the U.S. Army.* Carlisle, Pa.: Stone House Studio, 1985.

Montgomery, Thomas L. *Col. William Thompson's Battalion of Riflemen, June 25, 1775–July 1, 1776.* Harrisburg, Pa.: Harrisburg Pub. Co., 1906.

Stroh, Oscar H. *Thompson's Battalion, and/or, the First Continental Regiment.* Harrisburg, Pa.: Graphic Services, 1976.

Thompson, William, and John Armstrong. "Letters of Two Distinguished Pennsylvania Officers of the Revolution," *Pennsylvania Magazine of History and Biography* 35 (July 1911): 304–307.

Tilghman, Tench (1744–1786)
American military officer

Tench Tilghman was born in Talbot County, Maryland, on December 25, 1744, the son of an attorney. Well educated at the Philadelphia Academy (now University of Pennsylvania), he graduated in 1761 and worked as a successful merchant until the outbreak of war with Britain in 1775. Curiously, Tilghman sided with the Patriots while his father remained a steadfast LOYALIST, but the two corresponded throughout the war. He initially tendered his services as secretary and treasurer of a committee dispatched to the Iroquois League by the Continental CONGRESS. Concurrently, Tilghman also held a captain's commission in a city militia formation, the "Ladies Light Infantry." As such he performed field duties with his unit throughout 1776 when it formed part of the strategic reserve, or "Flying Camp," under General Hugh MERCER. While acting in this capacity Tilghman attracted the attention of General George WASHINGTON at New York and gained appointment as aide-de-camp without pay and the honorary rank of colonel. From the onset the young officer proved a boon to Washington's military family, being responsible for writing, processing, and filing the voluminous correspondence generated at headquarters. He executed his duties punctually over a seven-year period becoming, like Alexander HAMILTON and the youthful marquis de LAFAYETTE, a surrogate son to the childless commander in chief. In time the quiet, capable Tilghman served longer than any of the 31 other aides so appointed.

It was not until May 1781 that Congress saw fit finally to commission Tilghman a lieutenant colonel, with seniority backdated to April 1777. He then accompanied Washington throughout the siege at YORKTOWN and witnessed the surrender of General Charles CORNWALLIS on October 19, 1781. Washington further honored his young charge by tasking him with riding to Philadelphia with news of the final victory. Covering 245 miles in only four days, Tilghman galloped into the city on the night of October 22, 1781, declaring "Cornwallis is taken!" to overjoyed inhabitants and congressional delegates. Tilghman finally left Washington's side in December 1783; he returned to Baltimore to establish a business relationship with Robert MORRIS. Unfortunately he died of illness in that city on April 18, 1786, at the age of 42, widely mourned by his circle of military friends and associates. As an aide he fulfilled a critical niche with the general staff and indelibly contributed to a smoothly performing headquarters within the Continental ARMY.

Further Reading

Bast, Homer. "Tench Tilghman—Maryland Patriot," *Maryland Historical Magazine* 42 (June 1942): 71–94.

Harrison, Samuel A., ed. *Memoir of Lieut. Col. Tench Tilghman.* New York: Arno Press, 1971.

Lefkowitz, Arthur S. *George Washington's Indispensable Men: The 32 Aides-de-camp Who Helped American Independence.* Mechanicsburg, Pa.: Stackpole Books, 2003.

Shreve, L. G. *Tench Tilghman: The Life and Times of Washington's Aide de Camp.* Centerville, Md.: Tidewater Publishers, 1982.

Stenger, W. Jackson. "Tench Tilghman—George Washington's Aide," *Maryland Historical Magazine* 77, no. 2 (1982): 136–153.

Weiss, Ruth T. "Yorktown Victory Ride and Lieutenant Colonel Tench Tilghman," *Daughters of the American Revolution Magazine* 115, no. 8 (1981): 828–831.

Townshend Duties (1767)

The replacement of Lord Charles WATSON-WENTWORTH's administration in July 1766 by a new ministry under William PITT did nothing to alleviate Great Britain's ongoing fiscal crisis. Cancellation of the STAMP ACT that year left the empire still awash in debts accrued by the French and Indian War. When Pitt was sidelined by one his recurring bouts of mental depression, Charles Townshend, minister of the Exchequer, emerged as de facto head of government. Like his predecessor George GRENVILLE, Townshend saw no reason why the relatively prosperous North American colonies should not be tapped as a source of revenue to help subsidize imperial administration. And, mindful of the touchy colonial distinction between internal taxes and external duties, he opted for the latter to avoid provoking an uproar such as accompanied the STAMP ACT. Thus, in June 1767, he prevailed upon Parliament to pass the first of three measures intent upon producing revenue for the treasury and promoting tighter control of colonial affairs. Known collectively as the Townshend Acts, they provoked the latest round in a spiraling escalation of political and economic defiance from the colonies.

The first law was the Suspending Act, passed in response to New York's failure to conform with provisions of the QUARTERING ACT of 1765. It mandated suspension of the colonial assembly until all requisite funding to support British troops was provided. More central to the issue of taxation, however, was the second law, or Revenue Act, which levied import duties on specific products such as glass, lead, paper, and tea, which were imported from Great Britain. Annual income from this act was estimated at only £40,000 sterling, but it would be applied to supplement colonial administration by paying the wages and salaries of customs officials and judges, thereby breaking their dependency upon local legislatures for incomes.

Through such expedients, it was hoped that local officials would be less beholden to local interests and at greater liberty to enforce customs and anti-smuggling regulations. The third of the Townshend Acts created a customs board of commissioners to be located in Boston, long viewed as a center of smuggling and trade violations. Furthermore, it empowered government officials with court-issued writs of assistance enabling customs officials to search any suspected location for smuggled goods or confiscate ships and other private properties involved in clandestine trade. New Admiralty courts were also established in Boston, Philadelphia, and Charleston to try customs violators in juryless trials.

Compared with the outrage accompanying the Stamp Act, American reaction to the Townshend Duties and their ancillary functions was comparatively muted. Few questioned Parliament's right to regulate either commerce or the empire, but thoughtful individuals viewed the manipulation of trade laws to raise money as simply another way of achieving taxation without representation. Moderate John DICKINSON forcefully exposed and decried such practices in his popular pamphlet *Letters from a Farmer in Pennsylvania* (1767–68). Nonimportation was then resurrected with varying results. But, and perhaps not surprisingly, it fell upon the denizens of Boston, Massachusetts, to foment outright dissent over the latest levies—and export that dissent to other colonies. Word of the Townshend Duties led to a resurgence of the local SONS OF LIBERTY and renewed political agitation from Samuel ADAMS and James OTIS. As before, customs officials became the focus of local anger and were harassed out of the city. In the fall of 1768 they returned backed by the bayonets of four British regiments, but resentment seethed below the surface. In 1770 tensions escalated to open confrontation during the BATTLE OF GOLDEN HILL and the BOSTON MASSACRE, which prompted British officials either to remove or severely constrain the movement of British troops in cities. Faced with rising unrest, the new ministry of Lord Frederick NORTH sought to calm the waters by formally revoking the Townshend Duties in April 1770. However, to underscore symbolically Parliament's unalienable right to tax its colonies, the levy on tea remained. The stage was set for a new round of confrontation arising from the TEA TAX in 1773.

Further Reading
Cook, Don. *The Long Fuse: How Britain Lost the American Colonies, 1760–1785.* New York: Atlantic Monthly Press, 1995.
Edgar, Gregory T. *Reluctant Break with Britain: From Stamp Act to Bunker Hill.* Bowie, Md.: Heritage Books, 1997.
Knight, Carol L. *The American Colonial Press and the Townshend Crisis, 1766–1770: A Study in Political Imagery.* Lewiston, N.Y.: Edwin Mellen Press, 1990.
McCusker, John J., and Kenneth Morgan, eds. *The Early Modern Atlantic Economy.* New York: Cambridge University Press, 2000.
Thomas, Peter D.G. *The Townshend Duty Crisis: The Second Phase of the American Revolution, 1767–1773.* New York: Oxford University Press, 1987.

Trenton, Battle of (December 26, 1776)
The forcible ejection of General George WASHINGTON's army from New York by General William HOWE in the autumn of 1776 left the Americans in dire strategic straits. Outnumbered and outperformed by his professional military adversaries, Washington had little recourse but to rapidly withdraw across New Jersey to the perceived safety of Pennsylvania. Once across the Delaware River, he then faced the specter of expiring enlistments on January 1, 1777, when nearly half of his remaining 2,000 soldiers would return home. Compounding these difficulties was the behavior of General Charles LEE, commanding 2,500 soldiers in New York, who consistently ignored Washington's orders to join him in New Jersey. When Lee was captured at Basking Ridge on December 13, his successor, General John SULLIVAN, finally put the troops in motion to join the main body. By December 7 the columns had united with the remnants of General William ALEXANDER, Lord Stirling's divi-

sion, and all proceeded toward the Pennsylvania border, hotly pursued by the aggressive general Charles CORNWALLIS. Their retreat occasioned considerable panic in Philadelphia, seat of the Continental CONGRESS, and Washington was forced to dispatch General Israel PUTNAM to calm nerves and restore order there. At length the Americans barely managed to ferry themselves across the Delaware in time, and Cornwallis reined in his pursuit. In accepted European practice, Howe himself had suspended operations for the winter and returned to New York. Cornwallis had likewise departed for the coast, intent upon returning to England. The British grip on New Jersey thus hinged on a series of strong outposts dotting the state, manned chiefly by HESSIAN professionals.

The Revolutionary War had all but reached its nadir for the Americans, but a glimmer of hope remained. While in Pennsylvania, Washington received 2,000 newly drafted militia under General James Ewing, which temporarily brought his numbers up to 6,000 men. As intelligence arrived as to the winter disposition of enemy forces and the absence of senior leaders, it became apparent that the 1,500-man outpost at Trenton, New Jersey, the closest post to American lines, invited an attack. Eager to revive American fortunes and to restore morale, Washington summoned a council of war and announced his determination to turn and pounce upon Trenton on Christmas Day. Because the Hessian garrison would be materially outnumbered, and quite possibly inebriated from the effects of Christmas revelry, the prospects for success seemed too good to ignore. To a man, Washington's leading officers concurred with this bold strategy, and preparations commenced to implement it. "Victory or death" was selected as the day's password and morale was further buttressed by the reading of Thomas PAINE's *The Crisis* to troops by their firesides. "These are the times that try men's souls," it began.

On the evening on December 25, 1776, three American columns prepared for a concerted river crossing followed by a sudden descent upon the unsuspecting Germans. Their movements would be fortuitously masked by a severe winter storm settling upon the area. But things immediately went awry when the columns under Ewing and Colonel John Cadwalader failed to cross as planned. The main force under Washington fared better; assisted by the Marblehead mariners of Colonel John GLOVER, around 2,500 soldiers and 18 pieces of artillery under General Henry KNOX braved the ice-choked Delaware and assembled on the New Jersey shore around 3 A.M. Washington then led his shivering host 18 miles toward its objective. The American column split in two a few miles from Trenton, with Sullivan passing along the river from the south while General Nathanael GREENE's division attacked from the north. Alert Hessian sentries spotted the attackers en route and alerted Colonel Johann Gottlieb RALL, who sounded the alarm and turned the garrison out. But tactical surprise was complete, and as the Hessians stumbled out of their comfortable lodgings into the cold, the massed Americans greeted them with concentrated musketry and artillery fire. The defenders crumbled under the onslaught and fled to the outskirts of town, rallying in an orchard. There Rall was mortally wounded and his command, outnumbered and nearly surrounded, capitulated. Washington's surgical strike had succeeded brilliantly. The triumph was even more remarkable, considering the essentially raw nature of his troops, the failure of two-thirds of his command to cross the river, and the horrendous weather in which it was accomplished.

Ninety minutes of fighting at Trenton resulted in 22 Hessians killed, 93 wounded, and 918 captured. Only 400 managed to evade the encirclement and escape. Remarkably, the Americans sustained two men frozen to death and five wounded, including Colonel William WASHINGTON and Lieutenant James MONROE, the future president. Rather than face a possible British counterstroke, Washington trundled up all prisoners and captured supplies, and harried his men back over the Delaware as fast as possible. It was a herculean effort from all ranks, marching and fighting for 36 hours in bitter cold and without sleep, but the dividends garnered far outweighed the exertion involved. Washington's brilliant stoke, born of desperation, gained a badly needed respite and kept the Revolution alive.

Further Reading

Dwyer, William H. *The Day Is Ours! November 1776–January 1777: An Inside View of the Battles of Trenton and Princeton.* New York: Viking, 1983.

Edgar, Gregory T. *Campaign of 1776: The Road to Trenton.* Bowie, Md.: Heritage Books, 1995.

Fischer, David H. *Washington's Crossing.* New York: Oxford University Press, 2004.

Lefkowitz, Arthur S. *The Long Retreat: The Calamitous American Defense of New Jersey, 1776.* New Brunswick, N.J.: Rutgers University Press, 1999.

Miller, William P. "Victory by Precise Plan," *Military History* 8, no. 5 (1991): 42–49.

Tunis, Edwin. *The Tavern at the Ferry.* Baltimore: Johns Hopkins University Press, 2002.

Tryon, William (1729–1788)
English politician

William Tryon was born in Surrey, England, on June 8, 1729, a product of the minor aristocracy. He used his family wealth to purchase a lieutenant's commission in the First Foot Guards in 1751, where he rose to lieutenant colonel after six years. In 1764 he consorted with his brother-in-law, Lord Hillsborough, head of the Board of Trade, to secure appointment as royal governor of North Carolina. He arrived the following year and found his charge in disarray owing to the STAMP ACT of 1765 and the periodic regulator disturbances on the western frontier. Tryon sympathized with the colonists over taxation without representation but nonetheless felt honor-bound to enforce the law. When the colonial leadership threatened violence against stamp agents, the governor dropped veiled hints of military force to gain compliance. Fortunately the crisis subsided once the Stamp Act was repealed in 1766. Tryon next tried to address difficulties arising from corrupt officials and excessive taxation in the western counties. He honestly endeavored to curtail such abuses, but when the regulators began seizing courthouses and refused to pay taxes, the governor raised an army and marched to the frontier. On May 16, 1771, his force of 2,000 militia defeated a large force of regulators at the Battle of ALAMANCE, which signally ended the disturbance. Tryon then returned in triumph to New Bern, where an appointment as governor of New York awaited him.

In 1771 Tryon replaced outgoing John MURRAY, Lord Dunmore, and he performed many useful services such as founding King's College (now Columbia University) and modernizing the militia. He also entered into a protracted contretemps with New Hampshire over the tract of land that constitutes present-day Vermont. At one point he issued an arrest warrant against Ethan ALLEN and his gang of ruffians known as the Green Mountain Boys. However, Tryon's good intentions as an administrator were overwhelmed by a new wave of colonial resentment against the TEA ACT of 1773, and the following year he was recalled to England for consultations. There he argued for moderation and restraint on the issue of colonial revenues. But by the time he returned to America in 1775 New York was buffeted by revolutionary violence. Tryon, given his strong British loyalties, was singled out by the SONS OF LIBERTY for harassment, and the governor, fearing for his life, sought refuge on board a Royal Navy vessel in the harbor. Here he maintained a floating government in exile for almost a year. It was not until August 1776 that General William HOWE recaptured New York from the rebels and Tryon stepped ashore.

The energetic Tryon did not wait for the military to restore civilian authority but, instead, sought out a commission as major general of provincial LOYALIST forces. He also dropped any pretense toward moderation and labored to bring fire and sword to nearby rebel strongholds. In April 1777 he led a large amphibious expedition against Danbury, Connecticut, which was burned and sacked, only to endure a lengthy running battle back to his vessels against forces under Generals Benedict ARNOLD, Gold SILLIMAN, and David WOOSTER. On one of his many forays into Connecticut, Tryon surprised and nearly captured General Israel PUTNAM, who escaped only by running his horse over a steep embankment. The regional British commander, General Henry CLINTON, waxed critical over the destruction inflicted by Tryon's punitive measures and feared for the resentment and resistance they generated. Nonetheless, in July 1779 the former governor conducted another lengthy raid along the Connecticut coast, burning and plundering the towns of New Haven, East Haven, Fairfield, and Norwalk. His success made him one of the most hated British officers of the war and did much to turn public opinion against Great Britain. In 1780 illness necessitated Tryon's resignation and he returned to England. He died in London on January 27, 1788, a political moderate and an efficient imperial administrator, transformed by war into an avenging angel of the Crown.

Further Reading
Fingerhut, Eugene R., and Joseph S. Tiedemann. *The Other New York: The American Revolution Beyond New York City.* Albany: State University of New York Press, 2005.
Ketchum, Richard M. *Divided Loyalties: How the American Revolution Came to New York.* New York: Henry Holt, 2002.
Nelson, Paul D. *William Tryon and the Course of Empire: A Life in British Imperial Service.* Chapel Hill: University of North Carolina Press, 1990.
Ranlet, Philip. *The New York Loyalists.* Lanham, Md.: University Press of America, 2002.
Tiederman, Joseph S. *Reluctant Revolutionaries: New York City and the Road to Independence, 1763–1776.* Ithaca, N.Y.: Cornell University Press, 1997.
Tryon, William. *The Correspondence of William Tryon and Other Selected Papers,* 2 vols. Raleigh: North Carolina Department of Cultural Resources, Division of Archives and History, 1981.
Van Buskirk, Judith L. *Generous Enemies: Patriots and Loyalists in Revolutionary New York.* Philadelphia: University of Pennsylvania Press, 2004.

Tucker, Samuel (1747–1833)
American naval officer
Samuel Tucker was born in Marblehead, Massachusetts, on November 1, 1747, the son of a merchant sea captain. Tucker joined the fleet as a cabin boy and served on board the colonial warship *King George* during the French and Indian War. At the age of 21 he mastered his own vessel and was berthed in England when the Revolutionary War broke out. He returned to Marblehead in the fall of 1775 and the following January General George WASHINGTON authorized him to outfit the schooner *Franklin* as a privateer. In this capacity he captured several store-laden transports in Boston Harbor and turned their valuable cargo over to the Continental ARMY outside Boston. Tucker then transferred to the privateer *Hancock* and went on to seize several prizes directly under the guns of British warships. In light of his sterling conduct and naval acumen, the Continental CONGRESS appointed him a captain of the nascent Continental NAVY in March 1777. He received his first official command, the new frigate *Boston,* on December 27, 1777.

In May 1777, Tucker accompanied Captain John MANLEY of the frigate *Hancock* on a cruise of the North Atlantic. On June 7, he assisted in the capture of the British frigate HMS *Fox,* although a month later, on July 8, he was unable to prevent the *Hancock* from being captured. Tucker spent the rest of the year acquiring numerous prizes until February 1778, when he was tasked with transporting John ADAMS and his son John Quincy Adams to France. The voyage proved daring and eventful as Tucker capably weathered storms, skillfully evaded pursuing frigates, and even captured a British privateer before safely delivering both future presidents to Bordeaux on April 1, 1778. Adams subsequently introduced Tucker at the gilded Bourbon court, but his blustery language and behavior resulted in immediate expulsion. After returning home he made several more captures before joining up with Captain Samuel NICHOLSON and his small squadron off the Delaware River. Cruising Chesapeake Bay proved fruitful for Tucker, who seized eight more prizes, including the Royal Navy sloop HMS *Thorn* and the privateer *Pole,* the latter taken in concert with Captain Seth HARDING. In November 1778 he joined Commodore Abraham WHIPPLE's squadron off South Carolina. Tucker fought well during the siege of CHARLESTON, wherein his vessel was anchored in the nearby Cooper River before being stripped of armament and sunk. He fell captive when the city fell on May 12, 1780, and was paroled. Ironically, he was exchanged for Captain Wardlaw, whom he had previously captured on the *Thorn*. Returning north, Tucker failed to procure a Continental navy warship to command, so he assumed control of the *Thorn*, now outfitted as a privateer. After seizing several more prizes, Tucker was himself taken by the frigate HMS *Hind* off the St. Lawrence River and interned on Prince Edward Island. There he was ordered to pilot a small, open vessel to Halifax, but he escaped and sailed back to Boston—then profusely apologized to the British garrison commander for his subterfuge. By the time hostilities ceased Tucker had taken a total of 41 vessels.

Afterward Tucker settled back at Marblehead and resumed activities with the merchant marine for a decade before retiring to a farm in Maine (Massachusetts). Once the War of 1812 commenced, anxious neighbors prevailed upon the old sailor to outfit the schooner *Increase* to protect the coastline, and with it he captured the British privateer *Crown* in 1813. The following year he won a seat in the Massachusetts legislature, where he served four years and also took part in the Maine constitutional convention in 1819. Once Maine had achieved statehood, he sat in the legislature, 1820–21, and also became a presidential elector. In March 1821, Congress voted the now enfeebled Tucker a pension for exemplary services rendered during the Revolutionary War. The old sea dog died on his farm in Bremen, Maine, on March 10, 1833, one of the most enterprising naval officers in the Revolutionary War.

Further Reading

Caldwell, Margaret N. "Samuel Tucker–Revolutionary Patriot," *Nautical Research Journal* 3 (August 1951): 97–102.

Hearn, Chester D. *George Washington's Schooners: The First American Navy*. Annapolis, Md.: Naval Institute Press, 1995.

Lord, Alice F. "Hero of the Early American Navy," *Journal of American History* 3, no. 3 (1909): 435–440.

Morgan, William J. *Captains to the Northward: The New England Captains in the Continental Navy*. Barre, Mass.: Barre Gazette, 1959.

Sheppard, John H. *A Brief Sketch of Commodore Samuel Tucker*. Boston: D. Clapp & Sons, 1872.

Smith, Philip C. F. *Captain Samuel Tucker (1747–1733), Continental Navy*. Salem, Mass.: Essex Institute, 1976.

Varnum, James M. (1748–1789)
American military officer

James Mitchell Varnum was born in Dracut, Massachusetts, on December 17, 1748, the son of prosperous farmers. He briefly attended Harvard College but was expelled for riotous behavior and subsequently graduated from Rhode Island College (now Brown University) in Providence, Rhode Island. Varnum then settled in East Greenwich, where he opened a successful legal practice and also served as colonel of the Kentish Guards, a local militia unit. Among his soldiers was the future general Nathanael GREENE, who was excluded from the officer corps on account of his ungainly limp. Following the outbreak of hostilities with Britain, Varnum was installed as colonel of the 1st Rhode Island Infantry, and he led it throughout the siege of Boston under General John NIXON. In 1776 his regiment mustered into Continental ARMY service, and he marched with General George WASHINGTON to New York City. Varnum fought well in the Battles of LONG ISLAND and WHITE PLAINS before rising to brigadier general of both the Rhode Island militia and of the Continental army in February 1777. That fall Washington assigned him nominal command of the Delaware River defenses outside of Philadelphia. His two subordinates, Colonels Christopher GREENE and Samuel SMITH, fought tenaciously at Forts Mercer and Mifflin, respectively, assisted by gunboats under Commodore John HAZELWOOD of the Pennsylvania state navy. The Americans were eventually defeated that November but had materially delayed the fleet of Admiral Richard HOWE. In 1778 Varnum transferred back to Rhode Island

American colonel James Varnum led the 1st Rhode Island Infantry throughout the siege of Boston. *(Independence National Historical Park)*

as part of General John SULLIVAN's division. He fought at the unsuccessful siege of Newport in August and subsequently served as commander of the Rhode Island district. However, his complaints over pay deficiencies drew a sharp response from Sullivan, and Varnum tendered his resignation on March 15, 1779. He then resumed his legal practice while serving as major general of Rhode Island militia.

In 1780 Varnum was elected to the Continental CONGRESS as a delegate and was reelected three times. While present he argued that the ARTICLES OF CONFEDERATION were deficient and needed strengthening. In August 1787 he became director of the Ohio Company of Associates, and the following October Congress appointed him a judge in the Northwest Territory. He subsequently resigned his commission as major general and resettled in Marietta, Ohio. After helping establish the region's first legal codes Varnum died there of illness on January 10, 1789.

Further Reading
D'Amato, Donald. *General James Mitchell Varnum (1748–1789): The Man and His Mansion.* East Greenwich, R.I.: The Varnum House Museum, 1996.
Damon, S. Foster. "Varnum's 'Ministerial Oppression': A Revolutionary Drama," *American Antiquarian Society Proceedings* 55 (October 1945): 287–298.
Gardner, Asa B. "General James M. Mitchell of the Continental Army," *Magazine of American History* 18 (September 1887): 185–193.
Heathcote, Charles W. "General James M. Varnum and His Services to the Country," *Picket Post* no. 50 (November 1955): 4–10.
Varnum, James M. *A Sketch of the Life and Public Services of James Mitchell Varnum of Rhode Island.* Boston: D. Clapp, 1896.
Walker, Anthony. *So Few the Brave: Rhode Island Continentals, 1775–1783.* Newport, R.I.: Seafield Press, 1981.

Vaughan, John (ca. 1731–1795)
British miliary officer

John Vaughan was probably born in Ireland around 1731, a son of the Third Viscount Lisburne. He joined the army in 1746 as an ensign in the 52nd Regiment, rising steadily through the ranks. After campaigning several years with the 10th Dragoons in Europe, Vaughan transferred back to the infantry as lieutenant colonel of the 94th Regiment and rendered valuable service in the capture of Martinique in February 1762 while operating with Admiral George RODNEY. Vaughan then returned to England, where he became colonel of the 46th Regiment in 1775. The following year he accompanied General Charles CORNWALLIS to America with a local rank of brigadier general and commanded two infantry regiments during the aborted attack on CHARLESTON in June 1776. Vaughan then transferred to the army of General William HOWE at New York, fighting conspicuously at the Battles of LONG ISLAND and WHITE PLAINS. Being severely wounded in the last encounter, he sailed back to England for a lengthy convalescence. Vaughan returned to America in the spring of 1777 as a local major general and a part of the New York garrison under General Henry CLINTON. In this capacity he accompanied Clinton's amphibious expedition up the Hudson River as part of a large-scale diversion in favor of General John BURGOYNE. On October 6, 1777, Vaughan distinguished himself by driving troops under General George CLINTON out from Fort Montgomery, his horse being shot from beneath him. He then boarded the fleet of Commodore James Wallace and sailed farther up the Hudson, burning the town of Esopus (Kingston) on October 16, 1777. This placed him within 46 miles of Burgoyne's main army at Saratoga—the closest any reinforcements approached that beleaguered leader. Clinton subsequently recalled Vaughan's force and the whole returned to New York.

In May 1779 Vaughan accompanied a second expedition up the Hudson River at Clinton's behest. On June 1, 1779, he landed and stormed Fort Lafayette at Verplanck's Point in conjunction with the main assault upon Stony Point. The following December, Vaughan departed New York and returned to England on leave, acquiring there the position of commander of British land forces in the Lesser Antilles islands. He again teamed up with his old consort, Admiral Rodney, and sailed for the Caribbean. The two men reached Barbados on February 11, 1780, and he proceeded to the island of St. Lucia to bolster its defenses. The following month Vaughan helped repulse a marauding French fleet under Admiral Louis-Urbain, comte de Guichen. That December he rejoined Rodney in an ill-fated attempt to storm French-held St. Vincent. The island had been recently ravaged by a hurricane, and Vaughan believed its defenses had been severely weakened but withdrew on December 14, 1780, after learning the garrison was intact. While refitting at St. Lucia, Vaughan and Rodney were apprised of the British declaration of war against the Netherlands and made preparations to storm the Dutch island of nearby St. Eustatius, an important source of money and supplies to the United States. Their quarry fell without a shot on February 3, 1781, and the British seized 130 merchant vessels and nearly 2,000 American prisoners. They also continued flying the Dutch flag over the island and lured additional vessels into the trap. However, Vaughan and Rodney disgraced themselves by thoroughly plundering all warehouses, despite the fact that most of the property seized was British-owned. Vaughan, however, tired of service in the Caribbean, and in May 1781 he obtained another leave. Back in England he took his seat in Parliament, defended his behavior at St. Eustatius, and declared he had not gained "One shilling by the whole business." He also obtained promotion to major general in 1782 and was considered to succeed Clinton as head of British forces in North America. In October 1794 he replaced General Charles GREY as commander in the Caribbean before finally dying of disease at Martinique on June 3, 1795. Vaughan was a highly competent soldier despite his propensity for plunder.

Further Reading

Begnaud, Allen E. "British Operations in the Caribbean and the American Revolution." Unpublished Ph.D. diss., Tulane University, 1966.

Conley, Jan S. *The Battle of Fort Montgomery: A Short History.* Fleischmanns, N.Y.: Purple Mountain Press, 2002.

Diamant, Lincoln. *Chaining the Hudson: The Fight for the River in the American Revolution.* Bronx, N.Y.: Fordham University Press, 2004.

Hurst, Ronald. *The Golden Rock: An Episode in the Revolutionary War of Independence, 1775–1783.* Annapolis, Md.: Naval Institute Press, 1996.

McLarty, Robert N. "The Expedition of Major General John Vaughan to the Lesser Antilles, 1779–1781." Unpublished Ph.D. diss., University of Michigan, 1951.

Mills, Louis V. "Attack in the Highlands: The Battle of Fort Montgomery," *Hudson Valley Regional Review* 17, no. 2 (2000): 37–49.

Vergennes, Charles Gravier, comte de (1717–1787)
French politician

Charles Gravier, comte de Vergennes, was born in Djion, France, on December 20, 1717, into an aristocratic Burgundian family. He commenced his diplomatic career by serving as secretary to his uncle, then ambassador to Portugal, in 1740. Vergennes then proved himself an able diplomat in Germany and fulfilled a succession of important posts as ambassador to Turkey, 1754–68, and Sweden, 1771–74. He returned in 1774 to become French foreign minister at the behest of King Louis XVI. At the outbreak of the Revolutionary War in April 1775, Vergennes divined an opportunity to avenge France's recent defeat in the Seven Years' War by detaching the American colonies from Great Britain. Beyond an obvious motivation for revenge he believed that the ensuing loss of trade would cripple England economically, reducing its military ascendancy throughout Europe. At no time did he display sympathy for the idealistic mores of the American revolutionaries but, as a fine exponent of 18th-century *realpolitik,* sought to use them to gain advantages over France's ancient adversary.

Such a strategy necessitated diplomatic tact and patience, lest France become engaged in a new war with England before her army and navy were adequately prepared. As early as 1775 Vergennes arranged for French agents to visit Philadelphia and assess the revolutionary movement, and on May 2, 1776, he convinced his reluctant monarch to fund money and weapons secretly through Pierre-Augustin Caron de Beaumarchais's bogus company, Roderigue, Hortalez et Cie. The court also allowed professionally trained military officers, such as the marquis de LAFAYETTE, to serve and assist American armies. Concurrently, the French began gently nudging their Bourbon dynastic consorts in SPAIN toward a new military alliance against England. This took considerable persuasiveness because King Charles III was uninterested in supporting an insurrection against a fellow monarch. But by dangling the prospects of French military aid to regain the strategic peninsula of Gibraltar, Vergennes gradually obtained their support. And Spain, while refusing outright diplomatic recognition of the United States, secretly provided money and arms. The Netherlands, by comparison, required much less coaxing to hit back at England, and it also allowed shipments of contraband to the Patriots through its Caribbean entrepot at St. Eustatius. Domestically, Vergennes also urged a complete expansion and modernization of the French army and navy, thereby releasing stocks of older weapons for export while revitalizing the military for the inevitable rematch with England.

As Vergennes solidified European support for the Revolution, he also dealt directly with American representatives in Paris such as Benjamin FRANKLIN. However, it was not until the defeat of General John BURGOYNE at Saratoga in October 1777, which demonstrated that the rebels might actually win the war, that he escalated French aid from covert to overt. On February 6, 1778, Vergennes concluded the FRENCH ALLIANCE by signing two treaties conferring both diplomatic recognition and a promise of direct military intervention. This became a major factor on June 17, 1778, when France declared war on Britain, thereby transforming a regional revolt into a wider conflict of global import. But Vergennes steadfastly kept the interests of France and Spain at heart by refusing American demands to recognize the Mississippi River as its western boundary. Such reticence induced American minister John JAY to violate the alliance with France and seek a separate peace treaty with Great Britain. Vergennes was understandably angered when the TREATY OF PARIS was concluded on September 3, 1783, ignoring prior understandings with France, but he pragmatically used American subterfuge to convince Spain to abandon Gibraltar and end the war. Thus by 1783 Great Britain surrendered its holdings in the New World, just as France had lost its own holdings two decades earlier. In this respect Vergennes's carefully crafted ploy worked brilliantly—although with unforeseen implications for France.

French foreign minister Charles Vergennes orchestrated the monetary and military assistance that made American independence from Britain possible. *(Bridgeman Art Library)*

The United States, in all likelihood, could not have won independence from Great Britain without the massive influx of monetary and military assistance orchestrated by Vergennes, and this occurred over the objections of France's controller-general, Anne-Robert-Jacques Turgot. Consequently, the French obtained revenge for their sacrifice but little else. Staggering debts accrued through such assistance pushed France to the verge of bankruptcy, devastated the national economy, and were a direct cause of the French Revolution of 1789. Vergennes did not live to see the havoc unwittingly sown by his generosity toward the Americans, as he died at Versailles on February 13, 1787. But few individuals played a more important role in helping secure American independence.

Further Reading

Hardeman, John, and Munro Price, eds. *Louis XVI and the Comte de Vergennes: Correspondence, 1774–1787.* Oxford: Voltaire Foundation, 1998.

Morton, Brian N., and Donald C. Spinelli. *Beaumarchais and the American Revolution.* Lanham, Md.: Lexington Books, 2003.

Murphy, Orville T. *Charles Gravier, Comte de Vergennes.* Albany: State University of New York Press, 1982.

Price, Munro. *Preserving the Monarchy: The Comte de Vergennes, 1774–1787.* New York: Cambridge University Press, 1995.

Pritchard, James. "French Strategy and the American Revolution: A Reappraisal," *Naval War College Review* 47, no. 4 (1997): 83–108.

Stockley, Andrew. *Britain and France at the Birth of America: The European Powers and the Peace Negotiations of 1782–1783.* Exeter, U.K.: University of Exeter Press, 2001.

Waddell, Hugh (1734–1773)
American militia officer

Hugh Waddell was born in County Down, Ireland, in 1732. His father fled to Boston, Massachusetts, after killing his opponent in a duel, and Waddell returned to Ireland but finally immigrated to North Carolina in 1754. There he gained a commission in the local militia for service in the French and Indian War. Waddell discharged himself capably in various capacities, and in 1755 he constructed Fort Dobbs near the Yadkin and Catawba Rivers. He then led a ranger company on several punitive raids against hostile Cherokee while also serving as a justice of the peace in Rowan County. In 1758 Waddell rose to major and accompanied General John Forbes on his successful expedition against French-held Fort Duquesne. Returning to North Carolina, he conducted additional forays against the Cherokee, rising to the rank of colonel. After the war Waddell settled in the Cape Fear region, where he married and established a plantation. He also sat four terms in the colonial assembly and was nominated twice to the royal provincial council but declined to serve. In 1765 Waddell struck up cordial relations with the new governor, William TRYON, at a time of increasing tension over British imperial practices. Like many merchants he opposed imposition of the STAMP ACT and commanded Brunswick militia in a raid upon Fort Johnson that prevented stamped paper from being landed. Tryon apparently sympathized with the merchants and held no grudge against Waddell, and he subsequently commanded the governor's armed guard on a diplomatic mission to the Cherokee in 1767. The following year he returned to Ireland on an extended visit and therefore missed the outbreak of regulator violence in the backwoods portions of the colony.

By 1771 the extent of regulator defiance against authority prompted Governor Tryon to raise an army and march against them. Waddell was commissioned a brigadier general of militia and ordered to raise a column of soldiers and march inland and rendezvous with the governor. On May 9 Waddell marched from Hillsboro and encountered a much larger force of regulators at the Yadkin River. These rebels captured his ammunition wagons and forced him to retire without fighting. But, following Tryon's victory at ALAMANCE, Waddell commanded a six-week campaign aimed at pacifying the western counties. He died at Castle Haynes, North Carolina, on April 9, 1773, one of the most respected military leaders of that colony. His death was regarded as a loss to the then-burgeoning Patriot movement.

Further Reading
Clark, Walter J., ed. *The State Records of North Carolina*, 30 vols. Raleigh, N.C.: P. M. Hale, 1886–1914; vols. 19–25.

Kars, Marjoleine. *Breaking Loose Together: The Regulator Rebellion in Pre-Revolutionary North Carolina.* Chapel Hill: University of North Carolina Press, 2002.
Lee, Wayne E. *Crowds and Soldiers in Revolutionary North Carolina: The Culture of Violence in Riot and War.* Gainesville: University Press of Florida, 2001.
Powell, William S., James K. Huhta, and Thomas J. Franham, eds. *The Regulators in North Carolina: A Documentary History.* Raleigh: North Carolina State Department of History and Archives, 1971.
Saunders, William L., ed. *The Colonial Records of North Carolina,* 10 vols. Raleigh, N.C.: P. M. Hale, 1886–1890; vols. 5–9.
Waddell, Alfred M. *A Colonial Officer and His Times, 1754–1773, A Biographical Sketch of General Hugh Waddell.* Raleigh, N.C.: Edwards & Broughton, 1890.

Wadsworth, Peleg (1748–1829)

American militia officer

Peleg Wadsworth was born in Duxbury, Massachusetts, on April 25, 1748, the son of a deacon. He passed through Harvard College in 1772 with a master's degree and shortly afterward opened a private school in Plymouth. By the advent of war with Britain three years later, Wadsworth was a captain commanding a company of MINUTEMEN and was functioning on the local COMMITTEE OF CORRESPONDENCE. After news of fighting at Lexington and CONCORD he marched to Boston as part of Colonel Theophilus Cotton's regiment. In this capacity he was present throughout the ensuing siege and assisted General John THOMAS in constructing fortifications upon strategic Dorchester Heights on March 4, 1776. This move forced General William HOWE to abandon Boston altogether two weeks later. As the locus of warfare shifted westward to New York, Wadsworth remained behind as a militia major and helped fortify Plymouth against attack. Rising to colonel by August 1778, he next commanded the Essex militia during General John SULLIVAN's aborted attack upon Newport, Rhode Island. Concurrently, Wadsworth remained politically active by sitting with the house of representatives and serving as justice of the peace for Plymouth County. After a term with the Board of War, Wadsworth gained appointment as adjutant general of militia as of August 1778 and was responsible for the recruiting, training, and outfitting of state forces.

On July 7, 1779, Wadsworth rose to brigadier general of militia. He then joined General Solomon LOVELL and Commodore Dudley SALTONSTALL on their ill-conceived and poorly executed campaign against Bagaduce (Castine), Massachusetts (Maine). When the invasion collapsed and was completely destroyed by Commodore George COLLIER that August, Wadsworth trekked overland to Boston on foot. Like Lovell, he escaped any culpability for the disaster and retained his rank. In March 1780 Wadsworth gained appointment as commander of Massachusetts's Eastern District with headquarters at Thomaston, Massachusetts (Maine). He served with little fanfare until February 18, 1781, when a raiding party of British and LOYALISTS kidnapped him from his house. Wadsworth remained in captivity until June 18, 1781, when he engineered a daring escape from Fort George in Castine. After the war, he settled at Falmouth (Portsmouth) and held a seat in the new U.S. Congress for 17 years, from 1793 to 1807. Wadsworth died in Portland on November 12, 1829, grandfather of noted poet Henry Wadsworth Longfellow.

Further Reading

Butler, Joyce. "The Wadsworths: A Portland Family," *Maine Historical Society Quarterly* 27, no. 4 (1988): 2–19.
Cohen, Sheldon S. "Escape from Fort George," *New England Galaxy* 20, no. 2 (1978): 12–19.
Dana, Richard H. *Address on General Peleg Wadsworth.* Cambridge, Mass.: N.P., 1908.
Dwight, Timothy. "The Story of General Wadsworth," *Maine Historical Society Quarterly* 15, no. 4-B (1976): 226–256.
Shipton, Clifford K. "Peleg Wadsworth," *Maine Historical Society Quarterly* 15, no. 4-B (1976): 211–226.
Wadsworth, Peleg. *Letters of General Peleg Wadsworth to His Son John, Student at Harvard College,*

1796–1798. Portland: Maine Historical Society, 1961.

Ward, Artemas (1727–1800)
American militia officer

Artemas Ward was born in Shrewsbury, Massachusetts, on November 26, 1727, the son of an attorney. He passed through Harvard College with honors in 1751 before opening up a general store in Shrewsbury, where he also served as tax assessor. When the French and Indian War commenced in 1755 Ward became a captain in the 3rd Massachusetts Regiment and saw considerable fighting in New York. By July 1758 he was promoted lieutenant colonel for good conduct, and by the time the war ended he ranked a full colonel. Ward returned home to pursue politics as part of the governor's council, while maintaining his militia connections. Throughout the decade of increasing friction with England, he also consorted with the likes of John ADAMS, Samuel ADAMS, John HANCOCK, and Joseph WARREN. His oftentimes blatant sympathy for the Patriot cause induced Governor Francis BERNARD to revoke his colonelcy in 1776, but Ward's popularity resulted in his reelection to the governor's council. In 1774 the new governor, Thomas HUTCHINSON, removed him from the council for his activism. That October Ward sat with the First Provincial Congress at Worcester, where he became brigadier general. He was ill with recurring kidney stones at the time of Lexington and CONCORD, yet left his bed, mounted a horse, and painfully rode to Boston to help organize a siege of the city. In light of his popularity with the troops and impressive military credentials, Ward rose to be captain-general of all state militia on April 22, 1775.

Initially, Ward was entrusted with commanding an ill-assortment of 15,000 militiamen drawn from every part of New England. He did so while suffering from military shortages of every description and from free-spirited subordinates like John STARK and Israel PUTNAM, who tended to come and go as they pleased. But by sheer dint of his Congregationalist personality, stern and steady, Ward somehow kept his ad hoc forces assembled and in place. Together they bottled up the army of General Thomas GAGE until Ward learned that the British were planning an offensive against them. He sought to preempt Gage by ordering Colonel William PRESCOTT to seize the high ground overlooking Charlestown Harbor on the evening of January 16. Gage responded the next day with a bloody attack at BUNKER HILL, which the Americans lost while inflicting heavy losses upon the British. Ward was roundly criticized for remaining at headquarters throughout the action. Worse, that July he was promoted to first major general of the Continental ARMY by the Continental CONGRESS but subsequently became second in command to General George WASHINGTON.

Ward and Washington were correct but cool toward each other for the remainder of the siege,

Artemas Ward was instrumental in keeping America's first military force intact. *(Independence National Historical Park)*

and he resented being passed over by a Virginian who knew nothing of the temperament of New Englanders. He nonetheless accepted command of the army's crucial right division—a post of honor, being entrusted with the defense of Roxbury, Boston Neck, and Dorchester Heights. He functioned capably, if grudgingly, and on the evening of March 4, 1776, Ward ordered General John THOMAS to seize the high ground at Dorchester and plant batteries there. This proved a tactical coup for which General William HOWE had no counter, so on March 17, 1776, British forces evacuated Boston altogether. Ward, still feeling slighted, agreed to remain in the service as commander of the Eastern Department at Boston until March 20, 1777, when he resigned in favor of General William HEATH. He then served as president of the state executive council until being elected a delegate to Congress in November 1779. Ward remained in Philadelphia one term, refused reappointment, and preferred holding a seat in the Massachusetts house of representatives where, in 1785, he functioned as speaker. After the war Ward enjoyed a very active and highly varied political career. He strongly opposed and denounced Shays's Rebellion of 1787, and four years later went to the new U.S. Congress as a Federalist. He died at his home in Shrewsbury on October 28, 1800, having briefly served as the nation's highest commander. Though not highly regarded by others, he proved instrumental in keeping the New England army, America's first military force, intact.

Further Reading

Billias, George A. *George Washington's Generals.* New York: William Morrow, 1964.

Brooks, Victor. *The Boston Campaign, April 1775–March 1776.* Conshohocken, Pa.: Combined Publishing, 1999.

Florence, Justin. "Minutemen for Months: The Making of an American Revolutionary Army before Washington, April 20–July 2, 1775," *Proceedings of the American Antiquarian Society* 113, part 1 (2005): 59–102.

Goetz, Rebecca A. "General Artemas Ward: A Forgotten Revolutionary Remembered and Reinvented, 1800–1938," *Proceedings of the American Antiquarian Society* 113, part 1 (2005): 103–134.

Kurtz, Henry I. "Victory on Dorchester heights." *American History Illustrated* 4, no. 8 (1969): 20–34.

Smith, James F. "The Rise of Artemas Ward, 1727–1777: Authority, Politics, and Military Life in the Eighteenth Century." Unpublished Ph.D. diss., University of Colorado, Boulder, 1990.

Ward, Nancy (ca. 1738–ca. 1822)
Cherokee warrior and negotiator

Nanye'hi ("One Who Goes About") was probably born around 1738 in the Overhill Cherokee settlement of Chota (near Fort Loudoun, Tennessee). She apparently married Kingfisher, a warrior, while a teenager, producing several children with him. The turning point in her career occurred in 1755 at the Battle of Taliwa against their ancestral enemies, the Creek. Nanye'hi accompanied Kingfisher into combat and was preparing his bullets when he was killed. The encounter appeared lost, but she suddenly picked up her husband's rifle and rallied the dispirited Cherokee, who went on to decisively repulse their foes. Consequently, Nanye'hi was made War Woman of the Chota establishment with the right to address councils and the power to spare prisoners from the hatchet. She also acquired the title Ghigou, or "Beloved Woman." Sometime in the 1750s Nanye'hi married English trader Bryant Ward and Anglicized her name to Nancy Ward. Recurring frontier conflicts eventually drove the couple apart and Bryant returned to South Carolina to remarry, but Nancy remained kindly disposed toward most whites. Following the onset of the Revolutionary War in 1775, when most Cherokee under DRAGGING CANOE, her cousin, favored war, Ward remained outspoken in advocating peaceful relations.

No sooner had a new Cherokee war begun in July 1776 than Ward dispatched a secret messenger to Colonel John SEVIER about impending Indian moves against the settlements of Watauga and Holston. The attacks were repulsed and a punitive campaign launched in retaliation, but Sevier carefully skirted Ward's hometown of

Chota. Over the next five years she became a common sight at various peace conferences and was even acknowledged by Virginia governor Thomas JEFFERSON for her endeavors. Warfare flared up again in 1781, and this time Ward was unsuccessful in dissuading Americans under Colonel Arthur CAMPBELL from burning her village. After the war ended she figured prominently in peace negotiations, invariably declaring her desire for peaceful relations with whites. Ward continued on as a force with tribal politics for many years, although in 1817, in light of continuous American demands for Cherokee land, she remonstrated against further sales. Two years later she was forced to leave Chota with her people and resettle on land in the southwestern corner of Tennessee. Ward ran an inn for many years, acquiring considerable wealth and enjoying the continued respect of her countrymen. She died on the Ocoee River sometime in 1822.

Further Reading
Adams, Robert G. *Nancy Ward, Beautiful Woman of Two Worlds.* Chattanooga, Tenn.: Hampton House Studios, 1979.
Barker-Benfield, J. G., and Catherine Clinton, eds. *Portraits of American Women: From Settlement to the Present.* New York: Oxford University Press, 1998.
Kidwell, Clara S. "Indian Women as Cultural Mediators," *Ethnohistory* 39, no. 2 (1992): 97–102.
Lillard, Roy G. "The Story of Nancy Ward," *Daughters of the American Revolution Magazine* 110, no. 1 (1976): 42–43, 158.
McClary, Ben H. "Nancy Ward: The Last Beloved Woman of the Cherokees," *Tennessee Historical Quarterly* 21 (December 1962): 352–364.
Tucker, Norma. "Nancy Ward, Ghigham of the Cherokees," *Georgia Historical Quarterly* 53, no. 2 (1969): 192–200.

Warner, Seth (1743–1784)
American militia officer

Seth Warner was born in Woodbury (Roxbury), Connecticut, on May 17, 1743, the son of a physician. He was relatively well educated by the day's standards and in 1765 relocated to Bennington in the region known as the New Hampshire Grants. Possession of this land was hotly disputed by New Hampshire and New York, so New Englanders under Ethan ALLEN formed a group of frontier vigilantes, the Green Mountain Boys, to evict whomever they considered hostile squatters. Warner joined the group with considerable success, and in 1774 New York governor William TRYON ordered arrest warrants and a possible death penalty for any members captured alive. Warner was a captain in the Bennington militia when the Revolutionary War commenced in April 1775, and he joined Allen and Colonel Benedict ARNOLD on a successful raid against Fort Ticonderoga. On May 12, he led an amphibious expedition up Lake Champlain that captured Crown Point and an additional 113 cannon for the Patriots. Shortly after Warner and Allen ventured to Philadelphia, where they prevailed upon the Continental CONGRESS to induct the Green Mountain Boys into the Continental ARMY. This was accomplished on June 25, 1775, and Warner was installed as lieutenant colonel. A month later he was made colonel over the head of the increasingly unpopular Allen. He next marched into Canada to assist the ongoing invasion under General Richard MONTGOMERY. On October 31, 1775, Warner and 300 men defeated a larger relief force under Governor-General Guy CARLETON at Longueuil, which resulted in the capitulation of Fort Saint Johns. He subsequently covered the American withdrawal from Canada in the spring of 1776, until expiring enlistments forced his command to be reconstituted.

By July of 1777 Warner returned to the field as colonel of a newly recruited formation, now part of General Arthur ST. CLAIR's division at Fort Ticonderoga. On July 6, he was ordered to retreat from the fort and march overland toward Skenesborough, New York, but Warner disobeyed and encamped at nearby Hubbardton. The following morning he was surprised by British and HESSIAN forces under Generals Simon FRASER and Friedrich von RIEDESEL and retreated with heavy loss. After rallying his command at Manchester, he next operated in concert with General John STARK at the victory of BENNINGTON, where his timely appearance toward the end of the battle repulsed Hessian reinforcements under Lieutenant Colonel Heinrich Breymann. Afterward Warner served under Stark as part of General Horatio GATES's command in latter phases of the Saratoga campaign that October but saw no more serious fighting. In March 1778 the newly constituted Vermont legislature appointed him brigadier general, but Warner's health had been seriously declining for some time, and he refused any further commands. In 1780, following wounds received in an Indian attack near Lake George, he gradually withdrew from active service.

Warner returned to Woodbury in 1782 and finally resigned his commission on June 1, 1783, terribly afflicted by disease. He died there on December 26, 1784, at the age of 41, a celebrated military figure from the hinterlands of Vermont.

Further Reading
Barrows, June. "Seth Warner and the Battle of Bennington: Solving a Historical Puzzle," *Vermont History* 39, no. 2 (1971): 101–106.
Chipman, Daniel. *The Life of Col. Seth Warner with an Account of the Controversy between New York and New Hampshire from 1763 to 1775.* Burlington, Vt.: Free Press Office, 1849.
Dean, Leon W. *Green Mountain Boy: The Story of Seth Warner.* New York: Farrar & Rinehart, 1944.
Fenton, Walter S. "Seth Warner," *Vermont Historical Society Proceedings* 8 (December 1940): 325–350.
Petersen, James E. *Seth Warner.* Middlebury, Vt.: Dunmore House, 2001.
Williams, John A. *The Battle of Hubbardton: The American Rebels Stem the Tide.* Montpelier: Vermont Division for Historic Preservation, 1988.

Warren, Joseph (1741–1775)
American militia officer

Joseph Warren was born in Roxbury, Massachusetts, on June 11, 1741, the son of farmers. He passed through Harvard College in 1759 before being apprenticed to Dr. James Lloyd and trained as a doctor. Warren quickly established himself as a gifted physician, and in 1764 he was among the earliest of Boston's medical community to embrace immunization as a way of combating smallpox. In this manner he befriended one patient, John ADAMS, and was gradually brought into his political coterie. The STAMP ACT of 1765 inexorably committed Warren to radical Whig politics, and he was soon rubbing elbows with Samuel ADAMS, John HANCOCK, and James OTIS at numerous protests and gatherings. Warren exhibited a flair for incendiary politics and quickly emerged as one of Boston's most vocal opponents of British imperial regulations. He gained prominence throughout the colony for his fiery oration commemorating the second anniversary of the BOSTON MASSACRE and two years later was an original member of the famous Boston COMMITTEE OF CORRESPONDENCE. In 1773 he protested vigorously against the TEA ACT and may have played a role in orchestrating the BOSTON TEA PARTY that December. By 1774 Warren had emerged as the de facto leader of the Patriot movement in Massachusetts, once Adams and Hancock were driven underground, and that fall he sponsored the famous "Suffolk Resolves," which condemned the COERCIVE ACTS and urged military preparations to resist British tyranny. These were then dispatched to the First Continental CONGRESS in Philadelphia through his favorite courier, Paul REVERE. On the evening of April 18, 1775, Warren ordered Revere and Samuel Dawes to warn Adams and Hancock that British troops were heading toward Lexington to arrest them. The next day, after the Battle of CONCORD, he arrived at the scene to treat the American wounded. Warren subsequently functioned as president of the Third Massachusetts Provincial Congress. In the weeks following the outbreak of violence, Warren moved quickly to consolidate the support of the colonial populace for the Revolution. He even dispatched an account of Lexington and Concord to England, which arrived and was read two weeks before the official report of General Thomas GAGE. He also actively assisted General Artemas WARD to collect

Joseph Warren was appointed major general of militia in Boston on June 14, 1775, only a few days before his death in the Battle of Bunker Hill. *(Adams National Historic Park)*

and organize the disparate New England army for a siege of Boston. In light of his stirring contributions, Warren was appointed major general of militia on June 14, 1775. Three days later he showed up at Charlestown in anticipation of major fighting there. Refusing to take command from General Israel PUTNAM, he offered to fight as a volunteer and placed himself under the command of Colonel William PRESCOTT. During the bloody Battle of BUNKER HILL, waged June 17, 1775, Warren fought bravely and helped repulse two determined British attacks, but was killed when they finally overran American defenses. Warren, who died at the age of 34, was subsequently interred in an unmarked grave, but his remains were later identified by Revere, who recognized some artificial teeth he had crafted for the doctor. Warren was officially reburied at Forrest Hills Cemetery in 1855, one of the first and most lamented martyrs of the Revolutionary War.

Further Reading

Angelis, Angelo T. "Pregnant with Future Consequences: Political Culture in Revolutionary Massachusetts, 1774–1787." Unpublished Ph.D. diss., City University of New York, 2002.

Beagle, Jonathan M. "The Cradle of Liberty: Faneuil Hall and the Political Culture of Eighteenth-Century Boston." Unpublished Ph.D. diss., University of New Hampshire, 2003.

Cary, John H. *Joseph Warren; Physician, Politician, Patriot.* Urbana: University of Illinois Press, 1961.

Ketchum, Richard M. "Men of the Revolution," *American Heritage* 22, no. 5 (1971): 20–21.

Truax, Rhoda. *The Doctors Warren of Boston: The First Family of Boston.* Boston: Houghton, Mifflin, 1968.

Ward, Steven E. "Joseph Warren and the Approach of the American Revolution." Unpublished master's thesis, Wesleyan University, 1980.

Warren, Mercy Otis (1728–1814)
American satirist, writer

Mercy Otis was born at Barnstable, Massachusetts, on September 14, 1728, daughter of a leading militia officer and sister of James OTIS. Consistent with prevailing social practice, she received little formal education but was nonetheless allowed to attend private lessons arranged for her brother. Otis, a voracious reader, also enjoyed unlimited access to her uncle's library and immersed herself in the nuances of literature and history. In 1754 she married James Warren, a rising politician, and through him became acquainted with John and Abigail ADAMS, among others, and maintained a lifelong correspondence. The Warren house soon became a central meeting place for leading Whig politicians and thinkers, and she frequently surprised guests by her exacting grasp of politics and history. When brother James, a brilliant legal mind in his own right, was seriously injured during a brawl in 1769, Warren supplanted him as the family devotee of politics. Commencing in 1772 she also made her mark publishing numerous and biting historical satires, aimed principally at Governor Thomas HUTCHINSON. It had been heretofore unprecedented—if not unthinkable—for a woman to venture into politics, let alone compose erudite criticism, but Warren possessed what John Adams described as the best pen of her age. By the end of the Revolutionary War she had authored and published three works of satire and several poems, all of which were well received. Warren's literary activity established her as the earliest female exponent of *belles lettres* and among the foremost literary minds of her day, gender notwithstanding.

After the war the Warren political dynasty fell into disrepute, principally over its suspected sympathy for Shays's Rebellion of 1787. Warren was, in fact, an unapologetic Democratic-Republican and increasingly critical of Federalist policies. In 1788 she waxed against adoption of the Federal constitution, fearing the imposition of tyranny. She also suffered from estranged relations with John Adams following publication of her landmark three-volume *History of the Rise, Progress, and Termination of the American Revolution* (1805), in which she accused Adams of harboring monarchical tendencies. The two leading lights were reconciled only through the intercession of Elbridge GERRY in 1812. Warren died in Plymouth on October 19, 1814, having rarely ventured beyond her town, yet possessing a world view remarkable in scope and complexity. Like her contemporary Phillis WHEATLEY, she was among the first American women writers to publish under her own name.

Further Reading

Anderson, Maureen, and John Shields. "Poetic Resistance: Mercy Otis Warren's Poetry of the American Revolution." Unpublished master's thesis, Illinois State University, 2002.

Berkin, Carol. *America's Revolutionary Mothers: Women in the Struggle for Independence.* New York: Alfred A. Knopf, 2005.

Davies, Kate. *Catharine Macaulay and Mercy Warren Otis: The Revolutionary Atlantic and the Politics of Gender.* New York: Oxford University Press, 2005.

Maney, Jill M. "A Bold Design: The Life of Mercy Otis Warren, 1728–1814." Unpublished Ph.D. diss., University of Rochester, 2002.

Schloesser, Pauline E. *The Fair Sex: White Women and Racial Patriarchy in the Early American Republic.* New York: New York University Press, 2002.

Washington, George (1732–1799)
American military officer, first president of the United States

George Washington was born in Westmoreland County, Virginia, on February 22, 1732, the son of a prosperous planter. Indifferently educated, he proved adept at mathematics and gradually pursued surveying at the age of 16. When his elder stepbrother died in 1752 he inherited a vast estate at Mount Vernon and established himself as part of the landed gentry. However, Washington also developed an interest in military affairs and in 1753 became a major in the Virginia militia. The following year he fired the first shots of the French and Indian War and was then forced to surrender his makeshift encampment, Fort Necessity, to superior numbers. In 1755 he rose to lieutenant colonel and aide-de-camp to General Edward Braddock during the ill-fated expedition against French-held Fort Duquesne (now Pittsburgh), Pennsylvania. He fought bravely during the disastrous ambush of British forces at Monongahela on July 9, 1755, and subsequently took charge of Virginia forces along the frontier. As commander he remained plagued by shortages in manpower, supplies, and money, but the experience taught him how to wage war with limited objectives and slender resources, lessons he absorbed for a future conflict. After the war Washington married Martha Dandridge Custis, overnight becoming one of the wealthiest men in Virginia. Status apparently whetted his appetite for politics, for he also sought and won a seat in the House of Burgesses. Throughout the decade preceding hostilities with Great Britain, Washington embraced the Patriot cause and argued against the STAMP ACT of 1765 and other imperial measures. In 1774 he sat with the First Continental CONGRESS, where he impressed fellow delegates with his soldierly mien and calm, dignified bearing. Simply put, Washington looked good in uniform, great on horseback, and projected an air of command. This is precisely what the jittery revolutionaries needed, and John ADAMS of Massachusetts nominated him as commander in chief of the nascent Continental ARMY on June 15, 1775. Unknown at the time, this singular act proved one of the most fortuitous events of the then unfolding Revolutionary War.

Washington arrived at Cambridge, Massachusetts, on July 3, 1775, and replaced General Artemas WARD as commanding general. He also confronted a daunting task that would have flummoxed any commander: His so-called army was actually an amalgam of loosely organized militias and short-term Continentals, the whole poorly disciplined and supplied. Worse, he was arrayed against a tough and highly professional British army under General William HOWE, himself a distinguished commander. After an impasse of several months, Washington finally availed himself of ordnance taken at Fort Ticonderoga by Colonel Ethan ALLEN and laboriously transported to Boston by General Henry KNOX. These cannon were then masterfully arrayed upon Dorchester Heights on the evening of March 4–5, 1776, which prompted Howe's evacuation of the city 10 days later. Washington had scant time for celebration before divining that the enemy would most likely strike next at New York in an attempt to split New England from the rest of the colonies. Accordingly he marched and met Howe's invigorated army at LONG ISLAND on August 22, 1776, and was disastrously defeated when forces under Generals John SULLIVAN and Isaac PUTNAM were outflanked. The Americans appeared perilously trapped upon Brooklyn Heights, but Washington, assisted by Colonel John GLOVER's maritime regiment, cleverly slipped through Howe's fingers to Manhattan. This was the first of several daring evasions and earned him the moniker Old Fox. Additional skirmishes ensued as the Americans were slowly ejected from New York City; following another hard action at WHITE PLAINS, Washington began a painful retreat across New Jersey. After Howe captured Fort Washington and its 3,000-man garrison on November 16, 1776, the game seemed all but up for the rebels. Nobody knew this better than Washington, whose army had dwindled to 3,000 men, was nearly out of supplies, and, worst of all, faced expiring enlistments on New Year's Day. But the lofty leader had one final card to play and did so masterfully. The moment Howe called off his campaign for the winter and left a string of garrisons across New Jersey, Washington suddenly tuned and pounced on the HESSIANS at TRENTON on December 26, 1776, crushing them. He then cleverly outmaneuvered the aggressive General

George Washington was commander in chief of the Continental army and the first president of the United States under the Constitution. *(Independence National Historical Park)*

Charles CORNWALLIS and mauled another British detachment at PRINCETON on January 2, 1777, before seeking winter refuge in the New Jersey highlands. The nascent revolution had been brought perilously close to the brink, but Washington's daring leadership kept it alive against tremendous odds. The exigencies of war, and his latent abilities, rendered him the fulcrum upon which important events—and the fate of a nation—now hinged.

Throughout the spring and summer of 1777, Washington was preoccupied with rebuilding his exhausted army while fending off legions of critics within Congress. His efforts were assisted by the arrival of professionally trained French volunteers like the marquis de LAFAYETTE and Johann de KALB. Washington was further tasked with protecting Philadelphia, Pennsylvania, the seat of the American government, from British attack. However, once a potentially dangerous offensive was launched from Canada by General John BURGOYNE, which threatened to seize Albany, New York, and isolate New England, he dispatched some of his very best regiments and leaders, like Colonel Daniel MORGAN, to assist General Horatio GATES in New York. Washington was then narrowly bested by Howe in two hard-fought actions at BRANDYWINE and GERMANTOWN, which resulted in the capture of Philadelphia. Worse, in light of these latest failures, Washington's critics coalesced around Gates, now the victor of Saratoga. GATES's ally Colonel Thomas CONWAY then began the shadowy "Conway Cabal" to replace Washington as commander in chief. Fortunately, and despite the less-than-subtle machinations of politicians like Thomas MIFFLIN and Benjamin RUSH, the cabal collapsed and Washington remained in power. Over the winter of 1777–78, the Americans at Valley Forge were further augmented by the arrival of Prussian adventurer Friedrich von STEUBEN, who bestowed on the Continental army its first systematized military drill and instruction. Consequently, when Washington emerged from Valley Forge the following spring, his army proved capable of meeting its veteran adversaries on equal terms. Their newfound abilities were quickly made manifest at the Battle of MONMOUTH on June 27, 1778, when he attacked and fought General Henry CLINTON to a draw, despite the treacherous ineptitude of General Charles LEE. But Washington's unstinting efforts brought the war effort in the north into a stalemate, and the locus of fighting shifted southward where colonial defenses were weakest.

In time the south proved a graveyard of American reputations. British forces under Lieutenant Colonel Archibald CAMPBELL brushed aside General Robert HOWE, who had captured Savannah in December 1778. In October 1779, General Benjamin LINCOLN, assisted by a French expeditionary force under Admiral Charles-Hector-Théodat, comte d'ESTAING, tried and bloodily failed to retrieve it from General Augustin PREVOST. The following spring Clinton embarked on a large amphibious expedition against South Carolina and initiated the successful siege of CHARLESTON. When that city capitulated on May 12, 1780, and General Gates lost the mismanaged Battle of CAMDEN that August, organized resistance collapsed. It appeared that the south might be retained by the British until Washington made another crucial decision by dispatching his greatest general, Nathanael GREENE, to revitalize American fortunes. He did so brilliantly at GUILFORD COURTHOUSE in March 1781, which forced General Cornwallis to abandon his conquest of the Carolinas and move northward into Virginia. He did so against the wishes of Clinton, who then ordered him to establish a fortified point on the coast where he could be reinforced by sea.

This was exactly the moment Washington had been waiting for. Previously, he had been coaxing French forces under General Jean-Baptiste, comte de ROCHAMBEAU, to attack New York City, but once Cornwallis entrenched himself at YORKTOWN, Virginia, this placed him within striking distance of combined allied armies. Leaving 2,000 men to keep Clinton occupied at New York, Washington and Rochambeau quickly marched south and suddenly materialized before the unsuspecting British. By

September Cornwallis was invested by 15,000 French and American troops—twice his number—while a French fleet under Admiral François-Joseph-Paul, comte de GRASSE, defeated the Royal Navy under Admiral Thomas GRAVES, sealing Cornwallis within his works. Unable to withstand this combined onslaught, Cornwallis capitulated on October 17, 1781, becoming the second British field army taken whole. This concluded the major land actions of the Revolutionary War, although it took another two years of negotiations before the TREATY OF PARIS was concluded on September 3, 1783. During this interval Washington masterfully kept a disgruntled military from unleashing its wrath against Congress over the issue of back pay, and he defused a possible coup attempt stemming from the NEWBURGH CONSPIRACY on March 10–12, 1783. He also blasted suggestions from conservatives like Colonel Lewis NICOLA to dispense with Congress and install himself as king. Washington, to the end, remained true to his deeply held republican precepts. On December 23, 1783, he appeared in Congress and formally surrendered his sword to President Thomas Mifflin in deference to civilian authority.

After the war Washington sought to live the remainder of his life in anonymity, but the newly roiled waters of nationhood returned him to the forefront of politics. In 1787 he attended the Constitutional Convention in Philadelphia, convened to overhaul the tottering ARTICLES OF CONFEDERATION, and presided over it as president. After the federal Constitution was finally ratified by the states, he was unanimously elected the first chief executive of the American republic in February 1789 and was reelected again three years later. As president, Washington proved moderately disposed toward national governance and distanced himself from mounting ideological discord between factions under Alexander HAMILTON and Thomas JEFFERSON. A thoroughly popular figure and enshrined as a national hero, he set another precedent by refusing a third term in 1796 and passed the mantle of leadership to John Adams. Washington then resumed life as a private citizen until his death at Mount Vernon on December 14, 1799. He was eulogized by his friend and former comrade in arms Henry LEE as "First in war, first in peace, and first in the hearts of his countrymen," sentiments few would contest. In a very real sense Washington became the indispensable man of the Revolutionary War, possessing both the strategic grasp and the indomitable will necessary to surmount impossible odds.

Further Reading
Buchanan, John. *The Road to Valley Forge: How Washington Built the Army That Won the Revolution.* New York: John Wiley, 2004.
Burns, James R., and Susan Dunn. *George Washington.* New York: Times Books, 2004.
Chadwick, Bruce. *George Washington's War: The Forging of a Revolutionary Leader and the American Presidency.* Naperville, Ill.: Sourcebooks, Inc., 2002.
Ellis, Joseph. *His Excellency, George Washington.* New York: Alfred A. Knopf, 2004.
Fleming, Thomas. *Washington's Secret War: The Hidden History of Valley Forge.* New York: Smithsonian Books; Collins, 2005.
Johnson, Paul. *George Washington.* New York: Atlas Books/HarperCollins Publishers, 2005.
Lengel, Edward G. *General George Washington: A Military Life.* New York: Random House, 2005.
McCullough, David G. *1776.* New York: Simon & Schuster, 2005.
O'Brien, Grey. *George Washington's South.* Gainesville: University Press of Florida, 2004.
Patterson, Benton R. *Washington and Cornwallis: The Battle for America, 1775–1783.* Lanham, Md.: Taylor Trade Pub., 2004.
Vidal, Gore. *Inventing a Nation: Washington, Adams, Jefferson.* New Haven, Conn.: Yale University Press, 2003.
Williams, Glenn F. *Year of the Hangman: George Washington's Campaign against the Iroquois.* Yardley, Pa.: Westholme, 2005.

Washington, William (1752–1810)
American military officer
William Washington was born in Stafford County, Virginia, on February 28, 1752, but little is known of his family or childhood. He was apparently

studying for the clergy when the Revolutionary War erupted, and he joined the 3rd Virginia Continental Infantry as a captain in February 1776. In this capacity Washington campaigned in New York under his noted cousin, General George WASHINGTON, and was wounded at the Battle of LONG ISLAND. After recovering, Washington again distinguished himself at TRENTON on December 26, 1776, when both he and Lieutenant James MONROE captured a HESSIAN artillery battery. He accompanied General Hugh MERCER's force at PRINCETON shortly after and was present when the latter fell mortally wounded. In light of his excellent service, Washington left the infantry in January 1777 by transferring to the 4th Continental Dragoons. A year and a half later he succeeded the mortally wounded Colonel George Baylor of the 3rd Continental Dragoons after they had been roughly handled by General Charles GREY at Old Tappan. In November 1779, Washington was ordered south to bolster the army of General Benjamin LINCOLN and arrived in 1780, just as British forces under General Henry CLINTON initiated their successful siege of CHARLESTON, South Carolina.

Washington's troopers were initially posted outside the city under General Isaac HUGER to secure and maintain American lines of communication. In this capacity he clashed repeatedly with the British Legion under Lieutenant Colonel Banastre TARLETON, besting him at Bee's Plantation and along the Ashley River in March 1780. However, Washington's command suffered from somewhat lax discipline respecting security, and the wily Briton surprised and defeated Washington twice, at Monck's Corner on April 14 and at Lenud's Ferry on May 6. Recovering from his reverses, Washington subsequently joined forces with light troops under General Daniel MORGAN during the American resurgence in North Carolina. On December 4, 1780, he bluffed a large force of LOYALISTS into surrendering Rugeley's Mills by employing a fake cannon, more commonly known as a Quaker gun. Washington followed this up with a sudden and successful descent upon Hammond's Store, South Carolina, on December 27–31, killing 150 and netting 40 captives. General Charles CORNWALLIS could not allow such attacks against his supply lines to continue, so he dispatched light forces under Tarleton to corner and destroy the Americans.

On January 17, 1781, Tarleton attacked Morgan at COWPENS and stumbled headlong into a carefully laid snare. At a given signal, Washington's command suddenly galloped over a hill and attacked the British left, routing them. The rival cavalry commanders then briefly went boot to boot in a spectacular demonstration of swordplay that ended when Tarleton managed to shoot and kill Washington's horse. The Continental CONGRESS subsequently awarded him a silver medal for bravery. On March 15, 1781, Washington performed similar work by crashing into the British line at GUILFORD COURTHOUSE, which nearly clinched the victory for General Nathanael GREENE. He then campaigned well for Greene at

William Washington fought bravely and well at several major battles of the Revolution. *(Independence National Historical Park)*

the hard-fought battles of Hobkirk's Hill on April 25, 1781, and Eutaw Springs, September 8, 1781. In this last engagement, Washington's troopers were shot down by British forces posted in a thicket, and he fell wounded and was captured. He remained a prisoner at Charleston for the remainder of the war. Afterward, Washington settled down in Charleston and married a local belle he encountered there while a prisoner. He thereafter turned to politics, served several terms in the state legislature, and politely declined an invitation to become governor. During the Quasi-War with France, Washington returned to active service as brigadier general in the Provisional Army as of July 1798, serving two years. He died in Charleston on March 6, 1810, one of the most dashing cavalry officers of the American army.

Further Reading

Babits, Lawrence E. *A Devil of a Whipping: The Battle of Cowpens.* Chapel Hill: University of North Carolina Press, 2001.

Cureton, Charles H. "The Virginia Cavalry, 1646–1783: A History of Organizational Development." Unpublished Ph.D. diss., Miami University, 1985.

Haller, Stephen E. *William Washington: Cavalryman of the Revolution.* Bowie, Md.: Heritage Books, 2001.

Lockey, Donald V. "Cavalry of the Continental Army during the War of the American Revolution, 1775–1783." Unpublished master's thesis, Duke University, 1971.

Loescher, Burt G. *Washington's Eyes: The Continental Light Dragoons.* Fort Collins, Colo.: Old Army Press, 1977.

Washington, Ella B. "William Washington, Lieut.-Colonel, Third Light Dragoons, Continental Army," *Magazine of American History* 9 (February 1883): 94–106.

Waterbury, David (1722–1801)

American militia officer

David Waterbury was born in Stamford, Connecticut, on February 12, 1722, and joined the colonial militia for service in the French and Indian War. He accompanied General William Johnson in the campaign against Crown Point in 1755 and three years later fought under General James Abercrombie at Ticonderoga. When the Revolutionary War began in April 1775 he was appointed lieutenant colonel of the 9th Connecticut Militia Regiment. In this capacity Waterbury accompanied the Canadian invasion of General Richard MONTGOMERY the following fall. Retreating back to New York, he was advanced to brigadier general of state forces in June 1776 as part of the Northern Department. From his headquarters at Skenesborough, New York, Waterbury assisted General Benedict ARNOLD in constructing a scratch-built fleet of galleys and gunboats on Lake Champlain to resist the advance of British forces under Governor-General Guy CARLETON. He himself was entrusted with command of the galley *Washington,* armed with 10 cannon, and also served as Arnold's second in command. All told Waterbury helped supervise construction of 25 small vessels of varying description. The British also began building their own fleet of warships to gain control of this strategic waterway, and both sides prepared for the inevitable clash.

Waterbury, like most of Arnold's captains, sought to engage the British head-on. Arnold, however, realized that Carleton's recent addition of the frigate HMS *Inflexible,* which had been dragged overland from the St. Lawrence River in pieces and reassembled, rendered such tactics suicidal. Therefore, on October 11, 1776, he ordered his vessels behind Valcour Island to make the British track and approach him against the wind. The battle commenced that fateful day, and the Americans fought valiantly but futilely against heavier firepower, being soundly defeated. That evening Arnold ordered a retreat up the lake, with Waterbury and his waterlogged *Washington* serving as a rear guard. On October 13 the bulk of Carleton's fleet caught up to the Americans and, after another stiff fight, Waterbury finally struck his colors with 110 prisoners. The bulk of Arnold's fleet was subsequently beached and destroyed. Waterbury remained a prisoner until 1781, when he was exchanged and took command of an infantry brigade under General George WASHINGTON. After the war he returned to Stamford and served several years in the state legislature. Waterbury died in Stamford on June 29, 1801, a soldier forced by military expedience to fight as a sailor.

Further Reading

Bellico, Russell P. *Chronicles of Lake Champlain: Journeys in War and Peace.* Fleischmanns, N.Y.: Purple Mountain Pres, 1999.

Clark, A. H. *A Complete Roster of Colonel David Waterbury, Jr.'s Regiment of Connecticut Volunteers.* New York: A. S. Clarke, 1897.

Huntington, E. B. *History of Stamford, Connecticut, from Its Settlement in 1641 to the Present Time.* Camden, Maine: Picton Press, 1992.

Robbins, Peggy. "The Forgotten Battle of Valcour Island," *Periodical: Journal of America's Military Past* 23, no. 2 (1996): 53–64.

Sweetman, Jack, ed. *Great American Naval Battles.* Annapolis, Md.: Naval Institute Press, 1998.

Waterbury, David, Jr. "Extracts from the Original Order Book of Colonel David Waterbury of Stamford, Connecticut," *Magazine of American History* 12 (December 1884): 552–555; 15 (December 1885): 410–411.

Waters, Daniel (1731–1816)

American naval officer

Daniel Waters was born in Charleston, Massachusetts, on June 20, 1731, and he went to sea at an early age. Successful as a ship captain, he subsequently settled in Malden and joined the local militia. He fought at the Battle of CONCORD on April 19, 1775, and afterward the Malden committee of safety entrusted him with the town's defenses. Waters later commanded a gun boat in the Charles River throughout the siege of Boston. That fall General George WASHINGTON authorized creation of a small fleet of schooners to harass British shipping in and out of Boston Harbor, and Waters became commander of the schooner *Lee.* Over the intervening months he took no less than nine valuable prizes and on June 16, 1776, he assisted Captain Seth HARDING in capturing a Highland regiment commanded by Lieutenant Colonel Archibald CAMPBELL. In light of his success, Waters next ventured to Philadelphia, where he prevailed upon the Continental CONGRESS to commission him captain in the Continental NAVY. He acquired his rank on March 15, 1776, and returned to Boston looking for a ship to command. When none materialized he signed on to the frigate *Hancock* under Captain John MANLEY and assisted in capturing the British frigate HMS *Fox* in June 1777. However, less than a month later Waters was himself taken by HMS *Rainbow,* and he endured several months of imprisonment in New York before being exchanged.

In 1778 Waters assumed control of the sloop *General Gates* and cruised the West Indies in concert with Captain John P. RATHBUN. However, Congress questioned his seemingly exorbitant expenses, so he resigned his commission and joined the Massachusetts state navy. In July 1779 he led the sloop *General Putnam* on the ill-fated Penobscot expedition under Commodore Dudley SALTONSTALL and burned his ship rather than see it captured. Undeterred, Waters left the state service for the infinitely more profitable business of PRIVATEERING and assumed command of the former British warship *Thorn.* With it he boldly engaged the equally large LOYALIST privateers *Sir William Erskine* and *Governor Tryon* on December 25, 1779, defeating both in sterling displays of seamanship. One prize managed to escape, but Waters went on to seize the privateer *Sparlin* before putting back into Boston. After another cruise in the privateer *Friendship,* Waters retired from active service and went home. He died in Malden on March 26, 1816, a coarse, outspoken, and typical sailor of his generation.

Further Reading

Allen, Gardner W. *Massachusetts Privateers of the Revolution.* Boston: Massachusetts Historical Society, 1927.

Faibisy, John D. "Privateering and Piracy: The Effects of New England Raiding upon Nova Scotia du-ring the American Revolution, 1775–1783." Unpublished Ph.D. diss., University of Massachusetts, 1972.

Hearn, Chester G. *George Washington's Schooners: The First American Navy.* Annapolis, Md.: Naval Institute Press, 1995.

McManemin, John A. *Revolution on the High Seas: A History of Maritime Massachusetts during the Revolutionary War.* Spring Lake, N.J.: Ho-Ho-Kus Pub. Co., 1988.

Morgan, William J. *Captains to the Northward: The New England Captains in the Continental Navy.* Barre, Mass.: Barre Gazette, 1959.

Morse, Sidney G. "New England Privateering in the American Revolution." 2 vols. Unpublished Ph.D. diss., Harvard University, 1941.

Watson-Wentworth, Charles (second marquis of Rockingham) (1730–1782)

English politician

Charles Watson-Wentworth was born in London, England, on May 18, 1730, the fifth son of Thomas Watson-Wentworth, marquis of Rockingham. He was well educated at Westminister School before running away to join the duke of Cumberland's army and fighting in the Jacobite Rebellion of 1745. Rockingham then came home, passed through Cambridge University, and inherited his father's title and vast estates in 1750. That year he also commenced his public career by taking a seat in the House of Lords, but Rockingham evinced far more interest in horse racing than politics. Nonetheless, he staked out a position opposing the growth of kingly powers and became closely identified with the opposition, or Whig, faction. Tolerably erudite yet a dull speaker, Rockingham seemed destined for political mediocrity until July 1765, when King GEORGE III appointed him prime minister to replace outgoing George GRENVILLE. This unlikely event transpired only because the king's first choice, William PITT the Elder, refused to serve. Fortunately, Rockingham was ably seconded by his secretary, the brilliant Edmund BURKE, at a time when political discussion was dominated by events in America. He remained unswervingly faithful to Whig principles, preservation of the empire, and parliamentary supremacy over the colonies, but felt only reconciliation could forestall violence and restore British authority. Therefore, in March 1766 he secured repeal of the hated STAMP ACT, which made him a hero in American circles. But to accentuate his loyalty, Rockingham also endorsed the so-called Declaratory Act, which reiterated Parliament's right to regulate the colonies "in all cases whatsoever." The king was livid over what he considered betrayal of monarchical prerogatives and managed to arrange the ministry's collapse by July 1766.

For the next 16 years Rockingham stood in opposition to the Crown as nominal head of what became known as the "Rockingham Whigs." And, while sympathetic to the ability of Parliament to run the empire, he was increasingly alarmed by its apparent arbitrariness respecting America. In 1774 he came out strongly against the COERCIVE ACTS as violations of British constitutional law. He also condemned the QUEBEC ACT and supported Pitt's motion to have all British troops withdrawn. Once fighting erupted and England declared war on its former colonies, Rockingham underscored his discontent by withdrawing from the House of Lords altogether. He did not reoccupy his seat until after the FRENCH ALLIANCE transpired in the spring of 1778, at which point he agitated for immediate recognition of American independence. Rockingham did so less out of altruism than the possibility of restoring the close economic ties essential to Britain's growth and thus keeping its former colonies from entering a French orbit.

The defeat of General Charles CORNWALLIS at YORKTOWN in October 1781, combined with rising discontent over the course of the war, finally caused the collapse of Lord Frederick NORTH's ministry by the spring of 1782. Again, King George was forced to appoint Rockingham prime minister, although he strongly opposed any notion of American independence. To that end he allowed Rockingham to rule only in concert with William PETTY, Lord Shelburne, who also sought to preserve the colonies. Their respective factions squabbled over peace negotiations, but Rockingham finally prevailed in Parliament, and by May 1782 the government voted in favor of recognizing the United States. The peace negotiations he authorized eventually concluded with the TREATY OF PARIS in 1783. Rockingham also remained committed to reducing monarchical powers by granting legislative independence to the Irish parliament and reducing the size of the king's household. The prime minister did not savor his long-sought victories, for on July 1, 1782, he died of illness in London. Thereafter, leadership of the Rockingham Whigs, and their strong emphasis on British constitutional rights, reverted to Charles James FOX.

Further Reading
Elofson, W. M. *The Rockingham Connection and the Second Founding of the Whig Party, 1768–1773.* Buffalo, N.Y.: McGill-Queen's University Press, 1996.
Hoffman, Russ J. S. *The Marquis: A Study of Lord Rockingham, 1730–1782.* New York: Fordham University Press, 1973.
Knee, Stuart. "Rockingham and the American Struggle," *New England Journal of History* 57, no. 2 (2001): 1–26.
O'Gorman, Frank. *The Rise of Party in England: The Rockingham Whigs, 1760–82.* London: Allen & Unwin, 1975.
Ward, Lee. *The Politics of Liberty in England and Revolutionary America.* New York: Cambridge University Press, 2004.
Weintraub, Stanley. *Iron Tears: America's Battle for Freedom, Britain's Quagmire, 1775–1783.* New York: Free Press, 2005.

Wayne, Anthony (1745–1796)
American military leader

Anthony Wayne was born in Waynesboro, Pennsylvania, on January 1, 1745, the son of a tanner. After being educated at the Philadelphia Academy, he worked as a surveyor in Nova Scotia before returning to Pennsylvania in 1766. Friction with Great Britain was growing, and Wayne became active within Patriot circles and served in the colonial legislature in 1774. The following year he raised a militia regiment from surrounding Chester County, and in January 1776 he was commissioned colonel of the 4th Pennsylvania Continental Infantry. In this capacity he marched north into Canada as part of General John SULLIVAN's division and, on June 8, 1776, fought a brave but futile battle against superior numbers at Trois Rivieres, Quebec. He then performed useful work covering the army's retreat from Canada and received command of Fort Ticonderoga for several months. In February 1777 Wayne advanced to brigadier general and joined General George WASHINGTON's main army near Philadelphia. He fought exceptionally well at BRANDYWINE on September 11, 1777, successfully withstanding attacks by HESSIANS under General Wilhelm von KNYPHAUSEN. Once the Americans abandoned Philadelphia, Washington instructed Wayne to shadow closely the British army under General William HOWE and to menace his lines of communication. However, while encamped at Paoli, Pennsylvania, on September 21, 1777, Wayne's encampment was attacked at night by General Charles GREY and badly defeated in a surprise bayonet attack. The Americans lost heavily and he demanded a court-martial, which exonerated him of blame. Wayne subsequently fought well at the defeat of GERMANTOWN the following October, driving British forces back four miles before becoming lost in a fog and mistakenly attacked by General Adam STEPHEN.

After a wintery ordeal at Valley Forge, Wayne next commanded troops at MONMOUTH, New Jersey, in June 1778. His deliberate stand against great odds succeeded in restoring order to General Charles LEE's reckless withdrawal and allowed Washington to bring up reinforcements. He subsequently testified strongly against Lee at his court-martial. Wayne now enjoyed a well-deserved reputation as one of the best American battle captains and received his greatest challenge on June 27, 1779, when Washington ordered him to storm the British fortress at Stony Point, New York. Taking only 1,500 handpicked men from the corps of light infantry, Wayne silently crossed the Hudson River and at midnight took the fort at bayonet point, along with valuable stores and 600 prisoners. This action did much to restore American morale, and the Continental CONGRESS voted Wayne its Thanks of Congress and a gold medal. In September 1780 Wayne acted with typical alacrity when, after learning of General Benedict ARNOLD's defection, he drove his men 16 miles in only four hours to prevent West Point's capture. By January 1781 men of the Pennsylvania line, ragged and unpaid for months, mutinied en masse, but Wayne suppressed the uprising after executing several ringleaders. By now his reputation for daring and rashness had garnered him the unflattering sobriquet of "Mad Anthony."

In the spring of 1781 Wayne's career entered a new phase when he marched south to join the marquis de LAFAYETTE's division in Virginia. On July 6 he mistakenly attacked what he thought was the British rear guard at Green Spring, only to discover the entire army of General Charles CORNWALLIS laying in ambush for him. Ignoring desperate odds, he ordered his 500 men to charge the British immediately, which threw Cornwallis off balance long enough for Wayne to extricate his command. After additional service in the YORKTOWN campaign, Wayne marched farther south to join General Nathanael GREENE in Georgia. Together their united forced liberated Savannah in July 1782 and Charleston the following December. He then campaigned against marauding Creek and Cherokee Indians and personally killed a chief during a night attack on his camp. In light of his excellent service during the war, Wayne was breveted major general before mustering out of service in October 1782.

After the war Wayne was variously employed in farming and political activities, none of which proved particularly successful. However, in 1791 President Washington called him back to the colors as major general commanding the Army of the Old Northwest. Since 1790 a confederation of Miami and Shawnee Indians under Chief Little Turtle had defied American authority in Ohio and in 1791 crushed the army of General Arthur ST. CLAIR. Wayne, a precise, methodical planner, took nearly two years to recruit and train additional soldiers before leading them back into Indian country. On June 30, 1794, he attacked and scattered the Indians at the Battle of Fallen Timbers, which ended frontier hostilities for the next 15 years. Moreover, the ensuing Treaty of Greenville opened up Ohio to white migration, thereby encouraging American settlement of the Old Northwest. Wayne was next slated to take possession of Detroit from the British, per provisions of the Jay Treaty, but he sickened and died at Presque Isle (Erie), Pennsylvania, on December 15, 1796. For his efforts at revitalizing discipline in the early days of the republic, he is regarded as father of the U.S. Army.

Further Reading

Fox, Joseph. *Anthony Wayne: Washington's Reliable General.* Chicago: Adams Press, 1988.

Gaff, Alan D. *Bayonets in the Wilderness: Anthony Wayne's Legion in the Old Northwest.* Norman: University of Oklahoma Press, 2004.

Loprieno, Don. *The Enterprise in Contemplation: The Midnight Assault of Stony Point.* Westminster, Md.: Heritage Books, 2004.

Brigadier General Anthony Wayne led the Americans to success at the Battle of Monmouth and Stony Point. *(Independence National Historical Park)*

McGuire, Thomas J. *Battle of Paoli.* Mechanicsburg, Pa.: Stackpole Books, 2000.
Poirier, Noel B. "Generalship at Jamestown: The Marquis de Lafayette and Anthony Wayne at the Battle of Jamestown Ford, 1781," *Virginia Cavalcade* 48, no. 3 (1999): 134–143.
Trudeau, N. A. "The Fort's Our Own!" *MHQ* 16, no. 1 (2003): 84–93.

Weedon, George (1734–1793)
American military leader

George Weedon was born in Westmoreland County, Virginia, the son of farmers. He first saw military service in the French and Indian War as an ensign in Colonel George WASHINGTON's Virginia regiment. While he saw no combat, Weedon performed capably and rose to captain-lieutenant by war's end. Afterward he settled at Fredericksburg, where his wife was sister-in-law to Hugh MERCER. He ran a successful tavern for prominent Virginia gentlemen and also served as captain in the Spotsylvania County militia. In January 1776 Weedon gained appointment as lieutenant colonel of the 3rd Virginia Regiment and rose to colonel after it was inducted into the Continental ARMY that August. In this capacity he fought under Washington at Harlem Heights in September 1776 and at WHITE PLAINS the following October. In the spring of 1777 he enjoyed the honor of escorting HESSIAN prisoners taken at TRENTON to Philadelphia and also briefly served as army adjutant. That February the Continental CONGRESS elevated him to brigadier general, and he rejoined the main army in Pennsylvania. Weedon was closely engaged at the defeat of BRANDYWINE that September as part of General Nathanael GREENE's division. There his outnumbered troops tenaciously defended the "ploughed field" and partially thwarted a flanking movement by General Charles CORNWALLIS. However, when Congress revised its general's list in 1778 and granted William WOODFORD greater seniority over Weedon, he angrily tendered his resignation. Congress refused to accept his resignation, but he departed anyway and resumed operating his tavern. At length Weedon agreed to return to active duty if his state were threatened.

Weedon remained at Fredericksburg until 1781, when the army under the marquis de LAFAYETTE arrived in Virginia to counter an invasion by Cornwallis. He proved particularly useful raising recruits and supplies, so during the YORKTOWN campaign, Washington assigned him command of a militia brigade. Weedon became tasked with cordoning off Gloucester, across the York River from YORKTOWN, in concert with French light troops and cavalry under the Duc de LAUZUN. The spit and polish Lauzun had little use for Weedon's ragged levies and declined using them in skirmishes with Lieutenant Colonel Banastre TARLETON. After the war Weedon served as mayor of Fredericksburg and president of the state's Society of the Cincinnati. He died there on December 23, 1793, a capable combat leader but overly sensitive to matters of rank.

Further Reading
Balch, Thomas. *Papers Relating Chiefly to the Maryland Line during the Revolution.* Philadelphia: Printed for the Seventy-Six Society, 1857.
King, George H. S. "General George Weedon," *William and Mary Quarterly* 20 (April 1940): 237–252.
Pennypacker, Samuel W., ed. *Valley Forge Orderly Book of George Weedon.* New York: Arno Press, 1971.
Ward, Harry M. *Duty, Honor, Country: General George Weedon and the American Revolution.* Philadelphia: American Philosophical Society, 1979.
Weedon, George. "Calendar of the Correspondence of Brigadier-General George Weedon, U.S.A.," *American Philosophical Society Proceedings* 38 (1899): 81–114.

Wheatley, Phillis (ca. 1754–1784)
African-American poet

Phillis Wheatley was born in present-day Gambia around 1754, and she was kidnapped by slave traders and brought to Boston in 1761. There she was purchased by John Wheatley, a local tailor, as domestic help for his wife, Susanna. Unlike many AFRICAN AMERICANS held in bondage, the Wheatleys treated their youthful charge lovingly and allowed her to be educated. The young Wheatley readily absorbed a steady regimen of history, astronomy, and geography, along with the writings of Alexander Pope, Milton, Virgil, Homer, and Ovid. She was also reared in a strict Congregationalist environment and became intensely religious. In 1767, Wheatley, at the age of 12, demonstrated prowess as a child prodigy by publishing her first poem in the *Newport Mercury*. Thereafter she gained notoriety by composing an elegant elegy for noted revival minister George Whitfield, which was published in Boston in 1770 and reached London the following year. In this manner Wheatley became celebrated in literary circles for being not only a female but also a slave who composed excellent meter and verse. In 1773 Wheatley visited London at the behest of Selna Hastings, countess of Huntington, and was formally introduced to many significant personages, including colonial agent Benjamin FRANKLIN. With the countess's help she went on to compile and publish her first volume, *Poems on Various Subjects, Religious and Moral* (1773), which was critically well received at home and abroad.

Wheatley returned to Boston in 1774 shortly before the death of Susanna Wheatley and was manumitted that same year. When the Revolutionary War commenced in April 1775 she wielded her quill on the Patriots' behalf, penning several elegant lines in honor of General George WASHINGTON. This resulted in a friendly missive from the commander in chief and a personal audience with him at his headquarters in Cambridge, Massachusetts, in March 1776. Two years later Wheatley married a free black, John Peters, with whom she bore three children. Unfortunately, none of her offspring survived infancy and, after her husband abandoned her, she eked out only a marginal existence. Wheatley tried mitigating her circumstances by composing additional volumes of poetry, but no Boston-based publisher would consider the jottings of a black authoress. Wheatley died in poverty on December 5, 1784, at the age of 31 and was soon forgotten. However, by the 1830s her poetry was rediscovered and inspired the rising tide of abolitionism in the very same city that had once so scorned her.

Further Reading

Bohrer, Melissa L. *Glory, Passion, and Principle: The Story of Eight Remarkable Women at the Core of the American Revolution.* New York: Atria Books, 2003.

Clayman, Marjorie J. " 'A Monarch's Smile Can Set His Subject's Free': Uncovering Protest in Phillis Wheatley's Poetry." Unpublished master's thesis, Kent State University, 2003.

Comi, Dana R. " 'In a Shade of Solitude': The Mind of New England Women, 1630–1805." Unpublished Ph.D. diss., Brandeis University, 2003.

Ennis, Daniel J. "Poetry and American Revolutionary Identity: The Case of Phillis Wheatley and John Paul Jones," *Studies in Eighteenth Century Culture* 31 (2002): 85–98.

Gates, Henry L. *The Trials of Phillis Wheatley: America's First Black Poet and Her Encounters with the Founding Fathers.* New York: Basic Civitas Books, 2003.

Wheatley, Phillis. *Complete Writings.* New York: Penguin Books, 2001.

Whipple, Abraham (1733–1819)
American naval officer

Abraham Whipple was born in Providence, Rhode Island, on September 23, 1733, and he joined the merchant marine while a boy. Whipple rose to become a merchant captain in the employ of Nicholas Brown, and during the French and Indian War he commanded the privateer *Gamecock*, taking 23 French prizes. He then resumed plying the West Indies trade until the English government began imposing tighter trade and tax restrictions upon the colonies. In Rhode Island, tensions crested on June 18, 1772, in the noted GASPÉE AFFAIR, when the British revenue cruiser *Gaspée* grounded while chasing the smuggler packet *Hannah* in Narragansett Bay. Whipple, heading a deputation of 80 sailors, piled his men into eight launches, then boarded, seized, and burned the *Gaspée* in a daring raid. After the Revolutionary War commenced in April 1775, the state assembly authorized creation of a tiny, two-ship navy in which Whipple served as com-

Commodore Abraham Whipple tricked British ships by running a Union Jack up his mast. This ruse helped seize 10 vessels worth over $1 million. *(U.S. Naval Academy Museum)*

modore. On June 15, 1775, he departed Providence aboard the armed sloop *Katy* and captured a tender belonging to the frigate HMS *Rose*. This was one of the earliest victories of the nascent American navy in combat. *Katy* was then renamed *Providence*, in which he took additional prizes. That December Whipple was commissioned into the Continental NAVY as a captain, and he led the 28-gun frigate *Columbus* during Commodore Esek HOPKINS's successful descent upon Nassau in February 1776. He subsequently fought in the ill-managed attempt to capture the frigate HMS *Glasgow* off Block Island on April 6, 1776, and was exonerated by a court of inquiry after charges of timidity arose against him.

Whipple made several successful sorties out of Narragansett Bay, making many captures in the *Columbus*. He next received the new frigate *Providence* in the spring of 1778 and successfully ran the blockade of Rhode Island on the evening of March 27, damaging several British vessels en route. He then carried important dispatches to France, taking three additional prizes on the return leg of his voyage. The most celebrated incident of Whipple's career occurred in July 1779 while commanding the frigate *Queen of France* in concert with Captain John P. RATHBUN of the *Ranger*. After navigating through dense fog off the Newfoundland banks, they found themselves in the midst of a large British convoy escorted by a single warship. For several days thereafter, Whipple ran the Union Jack up his mast and posed as an escort vessel by day—while seizing an unsuspecting merchant vessel each night. Before his ruse was uncovered, the Americans took 10 vessels worth over $1 million. It was one of the most audacious naval deeds of the entire war and a tribute to his daring leadership.

In December 1779 Whipple and his squadron of warships, now reinforced by the frigate *Boston* under Captain Samuel TUCKER, were detailed to South Carolina to serve under General Benjamin LINCOLN during the siege of CHARLESTON. His vessels ably defended the adjoining Cooper River from assault until the siege lines of General Henry CLINTON forced the city's surrender on May 12, 1780. Whipple, who had sunk his vessels and taken their armament ashore as land batteries, passed into captivity but was quickly paroled and spent the remainder of the war in Chester, Pennsylvania. Afterward he sailed the merchant ship *George Washington* to England in 1784, becoming the first vessel to fly the American flag on the Thames River. Whipple then briefly pursued farming in Cranston, Rhode Island, before relocating to the frontier town of Marietta, Ohio. There he obtained a congressional pension for his Revolutionary War services and died there on May 27, 1819, an enterprising naval leader.

Further Reading

D'Amato, Donald A. "Audacious Abraham Whipple Causes Grief for the British Navy," *Old Rhode Island* 3, no. 5 (1993): 50–54.

Mazet, Horace S. "The Navy's Forgotten Hero," *U.S. Naval Institute Proceedings* 63 (March 1937): 347–354.

McManemin, John A. *Abraham Whipple, Commodore of the Continental Navy: A Forgotten Hero.* Spring Lake, N.J.: Ho-Ho-Kus Pub. Co., 1999.

Miller, Nathan. *Sea of Glory: A Naval History of the American Revolution.* Mt. Pleasant, S.C.: Nautical & Aviation Pub. Co., 2000.

Morgan, William J. *Captains to the Northward: The New England Captains in the Continental Navy.* Barre, Mass.: Barre Gazette, 1959.

Rider, Hope S. *Valour Fore & Aft, Being the Adventures of the Continental Sloop Providence, 1775–1779, Formerly Flagship Katy of Rhode Island's Navy.* Annapolis, Md.: Naval Institute Press, 1977.

White Plains, Battle of (October 28, 1776)

The successful landing of British troops at Pell's Point on October 18, 1776, despite a splendid rearguard action by Colonel John GLOVER, compromised General George WASHINGTON's army on the northern part of Manhattan Island. General William HOWE was now positioned to cut the Americans off from the mainland as his forces spilled onto Westchester County. To preclude this occurrence, Washington hurriedly crossed back to the mainland and gradually assumed defensive positions along three hills astride White Plains, New York. Howe followed in his accustomed leisurely manner and dallied several days at New Rochelle to receive 5,000 HESSIAN reinforcements under General Wilhelm von KNYPHAUSEN. Both combatants now possessed roughly 14,000 soldiers apiece, making them among the largest field armies of the conflict. It was not until October 28, 1776, that the British finally advanced upon Washington's defensive line in two columns commanded by Generals Henry CLINTON and Leopold von HEISTER. Washington, meanwhile, commanded the center of his three-mile line, with General Isaac PUTNAM leading the right and William HEATH the left. While preparing for Howe's impending assault, it suddenly dawned on Washington that his position was dominated by Chatterton Hill on his right, which lay across the rain-swollen Bronx River. He immediately dispatched light troops, Continentals, and militia under Colonel Joseph REED and General Alexander MCDOUGALL to seize the high ground and keep it out of British hands. Engineering colonel Rufus PUTNAM subsequently arrived to erect some hasty fortifications.

Around mid-morning, contact was established among light troops under General Joseph SPENCER, which Howe brushed aside, gradually deploying a force of eight regiments in full view of the enemy and supported by several artillery pieces. As if conscious of his tactical superiority, Howe paraded his redcoats in full view of the enemy with all the fearful precision and deliberation for which they were renowned. After forming on the bank of the Bronx River, he dispatched three Hessian regiments under Colonel Johann RALL around the American right to flank them. Meanwhile, two additional regiments under General Alexander LESLIE charged the defenders from across a ford and were heavily repulsed. The main British assault on Chatterton Hill then commenced. Howe fully appreciated its position as an artillery platform for raining down enfilade fire on his adversaries, and its acquisition would facilitate a frontal assault. Washington, meanwhile, also ordered reinforcements to the hillside, but gradually the exhausted Continentals under General William SMALLWOOD gave ground. Worse, supporting militia troops on the extreme right fled from a British cavalry charge. The combined British/Hessian force then crowned the heights, and Washington ordered a gradual disengagement. As the Americans withdrew toward defensive positions at nearby North Castle in the waning daylight, they observed the fearful sight of a triumphant British army in full battle array—but Howe inexplicably failed to pursue. Instead, he held his ground and simply returned to camp the following day. A tremendous rainstorm on the 29th kept both sides from further fighting. Howe subsequently concluded that Washington's new position at North Castle was impregnable to assault, and so ordered his men back to Manhattan on November 4 to entrap the 2,800 defenders marooned at Fort Washington—another disaster for the Americans.

White Plains was a significant action whereby Howe tactically outmaneuvered Washington from strong defensive terrain. Had he then and there pinned him frontally, rolled up his right, and engaged the ramshackle American army on open terrain with his professionally trained soldiers, Washington might have been destroyed in detail—and the revolution ended that very day. As it was, the fighting on Chatterton Hill proved intense and bloody: For a loss of 150 casualties the Americans inflicted 336 on their formidable adversaries. More important, although Washington had again lost the field to Howe, both he and his army performed well on balance. They lived to fight another day.

Further Reading
Edgar, Gregory T. *Campaign of 1776: The Road to Trenton.* Bowie, Md.: Heritage Books, 1995.
Merrill, Arthur A. *The Battle of White Plains.* Chappaqua, N.Y.: Analysis Press, 1975.
Sanford, Harry E., and Michael J. Kern, eds. *American Revolutionary History in North Castle.* North Castle, N.Y.: North Castle Bicentennial Committee, 1976.
Schecter, Barnet. *The Battle for New York: The City at the Heart of the American Revolution.* New York: Walker, 2002.
Spear, Moncrieff J. *To End the War at White Plains.* Baltimore: American Literary Press, 2002.

Wickes, Lambert (ca. 1742–1777)
American naval officer

Lambert Wickes was born in Kent City, Maryland, around 1742, the son of planters. Entering the merchant marine as a youth, he rose to captain of his own vessel by 1774. In this capacity he gained notoriety while berthed at London by refusing to take on board a shipment of tea. Returning home after the Revolutionary War commenced, the Continental CONGRESS appointed him a captain in the nascent Continental NAVY in March 1776, and he flew his pennant from the 16-gun sloop *Reprisal*. While cruising Chesapeake Bay for enemy warships on June 28, 1776, Wickes stopped to assist the vessel *Nancy*, which had run aground. There he removed its valuable cargo of gunpowder, set powder charges, and watched them explode the moment pursuing British vessels boarded it. In July he transported congressional agent William Bingham to Martinique, taking several prizes en route. On July 27, 1776, he engaged in a running battle with the larger HMS *Shark* off St. Pierre, which ended after French cannon in a nearby fortress fired on the British vessel. This was the first battle fought by an American vessel in foreign waters and precipitated a diplomatic row between France and Britain. In October 1776 Wickes was tasked with conveying American agent Benjamin FRANKLIN to France; he discharged his passenger at L'Orient the following month after taking two more prizes. Then, with French authorities turning a blind eye, he cruised the English Channel, took additional captives, and returned with them to France. This act established Wickes as one of the earliest American raiders to scour English waters, and Lord Stormont, British ambassador to France, angrily protested what he considered acts of piracy. In this respect Wickes enjoyed the same notoriety as Captain Gustavus CONYNGHAM.

In May 1777 Wickes departed the French port of St. Nazaire in concert with the brig *Lexington* and the cutter *Dolphin* under Captain Samuel NICHOLSON. His squadron then circumnavigated the British Isles, taking 18 prizes in eight days and returning to France. En route he was intercepted by the 74-gun ship of the line HMS *Burford* and jettisoned *Reprisal*'s entire armament overboard in order to reach St. Malo. Further British protests coupled with the threat of war induced the French government to order him finally out of its waters, and Wickes departed Europe for the last time on September 14, 1777. While sailing off the Newfoundland coast on October 1, *Reprisal* floundered in a large storm with the loss of all hands save the cook. In his short career Wickes took no less than 28 vessels and helped establish an American naval presence in the very chops of the English Channel.

Further Reading

Clark, William B. *Lambert Wickes, Sea Raider and Diplomat: The Story of a Naval Captain of the Revolution.* New Haven, Conn.: Yale University Press, 1932.

Bolander, Louis H. "A Forgotten Hero of the Revolutionary War," *Americana* 22 (April 1928): 119–128.

Bowen-Hassell, E. Gordon, Dennis M. Michael, and Mark L. Hayes. *Sea Raiders of the American Revolution: The Continental Navy in English Waters.* Washington, D.C.: Naval History Center, 2003.

Hardy, Henry. *Narrative of Events in the Several Cruises of Captain Lambert Wickes.* Washington, D.C.: H. Hardy, 1877.

Plummer, Norman H. *Lambert Wickes: Patriot or Pirate.* Centerville, Md.: Cornell Maritime Press, 2003.

Thom, DeCourcy W. "Captain Lambert Wickes, C. N.— A Maryland Forerunner of Commodore John Paul Jones," *Maryland Historical Magazine* 27 (March 1932): 1–17.

Wilkes, John (1727–1797)
English politician

John Wilkes was born in Clerkenwell, England, on October 17, 1727, the son of a prosperous distiller. Educated abroad at the University of Leiden, he married a nobleman's daughter in 1747, which enabled him to serve as sheriff of Buckinghamshire County and hold a seat in the House of Commons, as of 1757. Physically disfigured due to a chronic squint, highly intelligent, and possessing both a rapier wit and a rakish, profligate disposition, Wilkes revelled in defying social conventions. While in Parliament he became a supporter of William PITT and publisher of the *North Briton,* an antiadministration newspaper that routinely lambasted King GEORGE III or any other figure unfortunate enough to garner its editorial wrath. However, in 1763 Wilkes overstepped the bounds of political prudence with issue number 45 by strongly suggesting that the monarch and his ministers had lied about the recent peace treaty with France. The king was outraged, charged Wilkes with seditious libel, and had him arrested under a general warrant (which did not name him specifically). After a brief stint in the Tower of London, he fled to France in 1764 to escape further prosecution and was expelled from the House in absentia. Wilkes remained abroad until 1768, when debts forced him home to face prosecution. He was then reelected to Parliament four times while in detention, yet not allowed to hold a seat. His defiance made him the darling of England's poor and radical elements, and they took up subscriptions to pay off his debts. As the decade of the Revolutionary War approached, the cry of "Wilkes and Liberty" became a byword for political discontents on both sides of the Atlantic.

Wilkes was finally allowed to be seated in 1774, and he quickly agitated against the colonial policies of Lord Frederick NORTH, characterizing them as "unjust, felonious, and murderous." In fact, Wilkes had long been a political fixture in North American political circles owing to what was viewed as unjust prosecution by a corrupt government. His fate dovetailed perfectly with rising apprehension over an incipient conspiracy to rob Americans of their rights as Englishmen. So popular a symbol did Wilkes become in prewar years that the government of South Carolina voted money to retire his debts, while Virginia and Maryland sent him gifts of tobacco. During the war years he steadfastly supported the Americans and even defended the DECLARATION OF INDEPENDENCE as the logical outgrowth of British misrule. He also struck up a close liaison with Arthur LEE, then in London as a covert agent of the Continental CONGRESS, and helped channel money raised by English sympathizers to the rebels.

Wilkes reveled in his role as England's most notorious and outspoken radical, although his support for suppressing the anti-Catholic Gordon Riots in 1780 cost him political support among the poor. Three years later he also embraced William PETTY, Lord Shelburne's preliminary peace treaty with the Americans, which proved equally unpopular. By war's end Wilkes had ceased to be the towering symbol of liberty at home, and his public appeal waned. By 1790 his sinking popularity induced him to retire from politics altogether. Wilkes died in London on December 26, 1797, largely dismissed at home but still enshrined and idolized as a champion of freedom abroad. The city of Wilkes-Barre, Pennsylvania, commemorates his memory along with that of Isaac Barre, another sympathetic parliamentarian. He is also considered the father of modern British radicalism.

Further Reading
Byrne, William F. "Moral Imagination and the Problem of Public Order." Unpublished Ph.D. diss., Catholic University of America, 2003.
Cash, Arthur H. *John Wilkes: The Scandalous Father of Civil Liberty*. New Haven, Conn.: Yale University Press, 2006.
Cohen, Sheldon S. *British Supporters of the American Revolution, 1775–1783: The Role of "Middling-Level" Activists*. Rochester, N.Y.: Boydell, 2004.
Colin, Jonathan G. "High Art and Low Politics: A New Perspective on John Wilkes," *Huntington Library Quarterly* 64, nos. 3–4 (2001): 356–381.
Davis, Michael T. *Radicalism and Revolution in Britain, 1775–1848: Essays in Honor of Malcolm I. Thomis*. New York: St. Martin's Press, 2000.
Ward, Lee. *The Politics of Liberty in England and Revolutionary America*. New York: Cambridge University Press, 2004.

Willett, Marinus (1740–1830)
American military/militia officer

Marinus Willett was born at Jamaica, New York, on July 31, 1740, the son of a tavern keeper. He was apprenticed as a cabinetmaker when the French and Indian War commenced in 1754 and joined the New York Regiment under Colonel Oliver De Lancey as a lieutenant. Willett performed admirably during the ill-fated Ticonderoga campaign of General James Abercrombie and fought during the capture of Fort Frontenac with Colonel John Bradstreet. Willett resettled in New York City after the war, joining John LAMB and Alexander MCDOUGALL as a leader of the local SONS OF LIBERTY. Militantly active, Willett was involved at the Battle of GOLDEN HILL in January 1770 and led raids against British arms depots in the city in April 1775. At one point he organized a large street protest that prevented a convoy of British military supplies from leaving the city. When war broke out with England he joined the 1st New York Regiment as a captain and accompanied the Canadian invasion under General Richard MONTGOMERY. He then served as commander of captured Fort Saint Johns in Quebec before expiring enlistments brought him back home for recruitment. He next fought at the Battle of LONG ISLAND in August 1776 and was evac-

Marinus Willett was promoted to lieutenant colonel of the 3rd New York Continental Infantry in 1776, becoming one of the best regimental leaders of the war. *(Metropolitan Museum of Art, Bequest of George Willett Van Nest)*

uated to New York to fight again at Harlem Heights and WHITE PLAINS that fall. Willett's consistently good performance resulted in promotion to lieutenant colonel in Peter GANSEVOORT's 3rd New York Continental Infantry in November 1776; he was posted at Fort Constitution on the Hudson River, opposite West Point, where he energetically repelled a British assault upon Peekskill, New York, on March 24, 1777. That summer he accompanied Gansevoort to Fort Stanwix (Rome, New York) as part of the garrison.

In August 1777 Fort Stanwix was invested by British, LOYALIST, and Indian forces under Lieutenant Colonel Barry ST. LEGER. On August 6, while the bulk of the enemy force was resisting a relief column in the nearby Battle of ORISKANY, Willett led a daring sortie from the fort that routed defenders under Sir John JOHNSON and ransacked St. Leger's camp, thoroughly disheartening his Indian allies. During a three-day truce Willett slipped through enemy lines and rode to Fort Dayton to assist a new relief column under General Benedict ARNOLD. In recognition of his efforts, the Continental CONGRESS voted him an elegant ceremonial sword. In August 1778 Willett fought well at MONMOUTH, and during the following May to November of 1779 he also rendered valuable service under General John SULLIVAN's expedition.

Willett became lieutenant colonel of the 5th New York Continental Infantry in July 1780, rising to colonel that November. However, when his regiment was consolidated under officers with less seniority he resigned from the Continental ARMY and accepted a militia commission from Governor George CLINTON. Willett now was entrusted with defending the Mohawk Valley frontier against numerous incursions by Loyalists and Indians. Aggressive as always, he did not hesitate to attack a larger enemy force at Sharon Spring Swamp on July 9, 1781, driving back the Indians of Major John Doxtader. A few months later he engaged in another major scrape against Major John Ross near Johnston on October 25, 1781, defeating them soundly. Willett then vigorously pursued his foe, overtook their rear guard at West Canada Creek on October 30, 1781, and killed Major Walter BUTLER. This action marked the last attack upon the war-ravaged New York frontier and was a tribute to Willett's energy as a military leader. After the war he returned to New York City and gained election to the state assembly. In 1790 President George WASHINGTON dispatched him as a peace emissary to Chief Alexander MCGILLIVRAY of the Creek Indians and persuaded him to attend a peace conference in New York. Afterward Willett declined a brigadier general's commission in the U.S. Army; he felt that hostilities with Indians in Ohio could be settled peaceably. In 1807 Willett became mayor of New York, and in 1811 he lost a bid to serve as lieutenant governor. The enterprising Willett died in Cedar Grove, New York, on August 22, 1830, an excellent regimental officer.

Further Reading
Cook, Don. *What Manner of Men: Forgotten Heroes of the American Revolution.* New York: William Morrow, 1959.
Horton, William T. "Colonel Marinus Willett saves Peekskill from the British," *Westchester County Historical Society Quarterly Bulletin* 30 (April 1954): 43–48.
Lowenthal, Larry. *Marinus Willett: Defender of the Northern Frontier.* Fleischmann's, N.Y.: Purple Mountain Press, 2000.
Thomas, Howard. *Marinus Willett, Soldier-Patriot, 1740–1830.* Prospect, N.Y.: Prospect Books, 1954.
Watt, Gavin K. *The Burning of the Valleys: Daring Raids from Canada against the New York Frontier in the Fall of 1780.* Buffalo, N.Y.: Dundurn Press, 1997.
Willett, Marinus. *A Narrative of the Military Actions of Colonel Marinus Willett.* New York: Arno Press, 1969.

Williams, John F. (1743–1814)
American naval officer

John Foster Williams was born in Boston, Massachusetts, on October 12, 1743, and he joined the merchant marine as a youth. He was an established sea captain by the advent of the Revolutionary War and tendered his services to the nascent Massachusetts state navy. Williams initially received the 12-

gun sloop *Republic* and a similar vessel, *Massachusetts*, during the spring of 1776 and completed several lackluster cruises. He then switched over to PRIVATEERING and was captured twice before returning to state service in 1778. Now captain of the 16-gun brig *Hazard*, he shepherded his charge through several cruises between Newfoundland and the West Indies. On March 16, 1779, Williams fought his first memorable battle and captured the British privateer *Active* off St. Thomas. The following August he accompanied Commodore Dudley SALTONSTALL on the ill-fated Penobscot expedition, where the *Hazard* was necessarily beached and burned to prevent capture.

No blame was attached to Williams for the disaster, and the following year he received command of the 26-gun frigate *Protector*, the largest warship operated by the Massachusetts naval establishment. He took several prizes, and while patrolling the coast of Newfoundland, he encountered the larger, 32-gun English privateer *Admiral Duff* on June 9, 1780. The two contestants engaged in a close-quarters running fight for 90 minutes before *Admiral Duff* caught fire and exploded; Williams was able to rescue only 55 out of 150 crewmembers. On the return voyage he sustained another close scrape with the frigate HMS *Thames* but safely returned to port. Unfortunately, on May 5, 1781, Williams and the *Protector* ran afoul of British frigates HMS *Roebuck* and *Medea* off Block Island and were taken. Following a stint of imprisonment at Mill Prison in England, he was exchanged and commanded the privateer *Alexander* before hostilities ended. At that time he enjoyed one of the best wartime reputations of any American captain.

Williams resumed his activities with the merchant marine out of Boston until 1790 when President George WASHINGTON appointed him a master in the newly established U.S. Revenue Cutter Service (forerunner of today's Coast Guard). For many years thereafter he commanded the cutter *Massachusetts* while suppressing smuggling, conducting coastal surveys, and even inventing his own system for distilling saltwater into freshwater.

But as an ardent Jeffersonian, Williams was politically out of tune with the Federalist-dominated administration of President John ADAMS and failed to see service during the Quasi-War with France, 1798–1800. He nonetheless remained with the revenue service in various capacities almost until his death in Boston on June 24, 1814.

Further Reading
Gardner, Frank A. "State Ship Protector," *Massachusetts Magazine* 3 (July 1910): 181–183.
Kern, Florence. *John Foster Williams' U.S. Revenue Cutter Massachusetts.* Washington, D.C.: Alised Enterprises, 1976.
King, Irving H. *George Washington's Coast Guard: Origins of the U.S. Revenue Cutter Service, 1789–1801.* Annapolis, Md.: Naval Institute Press, 1978.
McManemin, John A. *Captains of the State Navies during the Revolutionary War.* Ho-Ho-Kus, N.J.: Ho-Ho-Kus Pub. Co., 1984.
Snow, Elliot. "Making Fresh Water by Distilling Salt Water in 1796: Experiments of Captain John Foster Williams," *Journal of the American Society of Naval Engineers* 40, no. 4 (1928): 541–545.
Strobridge, Truman R., and Bernard C. Nalty. "Captain John Foster Williams: Commander of the Coast Guard's First Cutter—A Revolutionary Hero," *The Retired Officer* 32 (February 1976): 34–37.

Williams, Otho H. (1749–1794)
American military officer

Otho Holland Williams was born in Prince Georges County, Maryland, in 1749 and began his civil career by clerking with the county office at the age of 13. He worked as a merchant by the time the Revolutionary War broke out and on June 22, 1775, received a lieutenant's commission in the Frederick City Rifle Corps. Williams participated in the siege of Boston and between January and June gained promotion to captain and major, respectively, within Colonel Hugh Stephenson's regiment. He succeeded to command when Stephenson died of illness the following August and fought with distinction during the fall of Fort Washington, New York, on November 16, 1776. Williams was severely wounded and, being sus-

General Otho H. Williams distinguished himself at the Battle of Guilford Courthouse. *(Independence National Historical Park)*

pected of espionage, imprisoned under harsh conditions from which he never recovered. While incarcerated he shared a cell with Ethan ALLEN and advanced to colonel of the 6th Maryland Continental Infantry although still captive. Williams was released in January 1778, joined his regiment, and fought valorously at the Battle of MONMOUTH that June. He continued serving in the New York–New Jersey theater until April 1780, when General George WASHINGTON ordered his regiment south with forces under General Johann de KALB.

In July 1780 General Horatio GATES replaced Kalb as commander of the Southern Department, and he appointed Williams to his staff as deputy adjutant general. In this capacity he performed exceedingly well at the disastrous defeat at CAMDEN on August 16, 1780, unassisted by Gates, who remained in the rear before fleeing with the militia. Later that month Gates cobbled together his surviving soldiers and appointed Williams colonel of a combined regiment of Maryland and Delaware Continentals. Upon the arrival of General Nathanael GREENE in December 1780, Williams again assumed staff functions as adjutant general while performing as acting colonel of the 1st Maryland Continentals. Greene, cognizant of his talents as a light infantry leader, next ordered him to lead the elite light infantry forces of General Daniel MORGAN, who had retired recently owing to poor health. Williams flourished brilliantly in this role and stiffly resisted invading forces of General Charles CORNWALLIS during the noted "race to the Dan" River. On March 2, 1780, he engaged light forces under Lieutenant Colonel Banastre TARLETON at Clapp's Mills and four days later conducted a successful rearguard action at Wentzel's Mills. In this form of fighting, with quick marches and sudden maneuvers, Williams had few equals.

Williams rose to command a brigade and subsequently distinguished himself in severe fighting at GUILFORD COURTHOUSE in March 1781, then Hobkirk's Hill the following April, and Eutaw Springs that September. At the later engagement he led a successful bayonet charge that temporarily swept the army of Lieutenant Colonel Alexander STEWART from the field. Afterward Greene dispatched Williams to the Continental CONGRESS in Philadelphia, where he received promotion to brigadier general as of May 1782. After the war, Williams returned to Baltimore to work as naval officer for the city and as a merchant. In 1790 President Washington appointed him collector of Baltimore while he also functioned as assistant secretary-general of the Society of the Cincinnati. In 1792 Washington tendered him a position as senior brigadier general in the army of General Anthony WAYNE, then preparing for war against the Ohio tribesmen, but poor health precluded his acceptance. After visiting Barbados to recoup his health, Williams died at Miller's Town, Virginia, on July 15, 1794. He was one of the most capable staff and line officers in the Continental ARMY.

Further Reading

Batt, Richard J. "The Maryland Continentals, 1780–1781." Unpublished Ph.D. diss., Tulane University, 1984.

Gordon, John W. *South Carolina and the American Revolution: A Battlefield History.* Columbia: University of South Carolina Press, 2003.

Kalmanson, Arnold W. "Otho Holland Williams and the Southern Campaigns of 1780–1782." Unpublished master's thesis, Salisbury State University, 1990.

Kilbourn, John D. *A Short History of the Maryland Line in the Continental Army.* Baltimore: Society of the Cincinnati of Maryland, 1992.

Tacyn, Mark A. " 'To the End': The First Maryland Regiment and the American Revolution." Unpublished Ph.D. diss., University of Maryland, College Park, 1999.

Williams, Otho H. *Calendar of the Otho Holland Williams Papers in the Maryland Historical Society.* Baltimore: Historical Records Survey Project, 1940.

Wilson, James (1742–1798)

American politician

James Wilson was born at Carskendo, Scotland, on September 14, 1742, the son of farmers. Intended for the clergy, he was educated at the University of St. Andrews and the divinity school at the University of Glasgow before quitting school in 1765 and immigrating to Pennsylvania. Apparently Wilson developed an obsession for acquiring wealth, and he pursued land speculation and other business investing for the rest of his life. He also studied law in Philadelphia under John DICKINSON, gained admittance to the bar in 1767, and eventually opened a successful practice at Carlisle. In the period leading up to difficulties with Britain, Wilson ardently espoused the Patriot faction and in 1774 he served on the Cumberland County COMMITTEE OF CORRESPONDENCE. He then composed and published a noted legal tract entitled *Considerations on the Nature and Extent of the Legislative Authority of the British Parliament* (1775), which was subsequently distributed to all members of the First Continental CONGRESS. Here he denounced parliamentary authority over the colonies and expressed a belief that all political legitimacy is derived from the people. Such sentiments placed him at the forefront of radical agitation, but Wilson also exhibited a strong conservative streak. He then sat with the Second Continental Congress but in June 1776 postponed a vote on the DECLARATION OF INDEPENDENCE, feeling it premature. On July 2, 1776, he recanted and voted in favor of independence but thereafter waxed cautious over the excesses of mob democracy.

Whatever his reservations about independence, Wilson stood foursquare against the radical politicians of Pennsylvania whose new constitution of 1776 abolished the office of governor and who ruled through a unicameral legislature. His reticence, combined with vocal opposition to price controls—and strong public perceptions that he waged war against the lower orders—precipitated a riot outside his house on October 4, 1779. Wilson had to be rescued by the militia, and the experience intensified his abhorrence of mob rule. For pursuing conservative policies he was also turned out of office. By 1782 a conservative resurgence sent him back to Congress, and he also helped draft a new state constitution with an executive officer in charge. After the war Wilson argued forcefully that the ARTICLES OF CONFEDERATION were inadequate, and in 1787 he sat with the Constitutional Convention in Philadelphia. There he served with the Committee on Detail and pushed unsuccessfully for the direct election of senators, but his plan for an electoral college to choose a president was adopted. Wilson subsequently spearheaded the ratification effort in Pennsylvania, which successfully transpired that December.

In 1789 Wilson became the first lecturer of law at the University of Pennsylvania. But, ambitious as ever, he approached President George WASHINGTON for an appointment as chief justice of the new Supreme Court. That position was eventually awarded to John JAY, but Washington allowed Wilson to serve as an associate justice. In this capacity he rallied behind the practice of judicial review, viewing it as a central function of the new court. His 1793 ruling in *Chisholm vs. Georgia* upheld national authority against states' rights, consistent with his nationalist leanings. However, Wilson pursued the chimera of amassing wealth through speculation and other investments and gradually went bankrupt. In 1797 he fled Pennsylvania to escape creditors and died at Edenton, North Carolina, on August 21, 1798.

Further Reading

Hall, Mark D. *The Political and Legal Philosophy of James Wilson, 1742–1798.* Columbia: University of Missouri Press, 1997.

McCloskey, Robert G., ed. *The Works of James Wilson,* 2 vols. Cambridge, Mass.: Harvard University Press, 1967.

Murphy, Tara A. "A Study of James Madison and James Wilson's Use of Nationalism in Creating the New Republic." Unpublished master's thesis, University of Connecticut, 2001.

Pascal, Jean-Marc. *The Political Ideas of James Wilson, 1742–1798.* New York: Garland Pub., 1991.

Read, James H. *Power versus Liberty: Madison, Hamilton, Wilson, and Jefferson.* Charlottesville: University Press of Virginia, 2000.

Velasquez, Eduardo A. "James Wilson Liberalism." Unpublished Ph.D. diss., University of Chicago, 1994.

Winston, Joseph (1746–1815)

American militia officer

Joseph Winston was born in Louisa County, Virginia, on June 17, 1746, and he joined the militia at 17 to fight in the French and Indian War. He served as a ranger but was ambushed and severely wounded on September 30, 1763, outside Fort Dinwiddie; the ball that hit him was never extracted. In 1769 Winston received a grant of 10,000 acres in Surry County, North Carolina, and relocated there to farm. He supported the Patriots during the period of tensions with Great Britain and in August 1775 sat with the provincial congress at Hillsboro to appoint a new government. The following September Winston became a major in the local militia, and in 1776 he accompanied General Griffith RUTHERFORD on his expedition against the Over Hill Cherokee. He also remained politically active and in 1777 held a seat in the provincial legislature. In this capacity he secured appointment as Indian commissioner and helped negotiate the Treaty of Long Island with the Cherokee in 1777. Over the next few years Winston alternatively served in the assembly or campaigned in the field. In 1780 he joined General William L. DAVIDSON on a punitive campaign against LOYALISTS and fought in skirmishes at New River and ALAMANCE. That fall he performed his most important work by joining Colonels Isaac SHELBY, Benjamin CLEVELAND, William CAMPBELL, John SEVIER, and Joseph McDOWELL to defeat a Loyalist column commanded by Major Patrick FERGUSON. On October 7, 1780, they cornered Ferguson at KING'S MOUNTAIN, South Carolina, and Winston distinguished himself in the victory there by commanding the right wing. He subsequently joined the army of General Nathanael GREENE and fought at GUILFORD COURTHOUSE on March 15, 1781, acquitting himself well. In view of his military contributions the state legislature voted him an elegant ceremonial sword.

Winston returned to Surry County after the war; it was later divided to create the new Stokes County. From there he alternately served several terms in the state legislature and the U.S. Congress from 1790 to 1812. In 1800 Winston was also a presidential elector and cast his vote for Thomas JEFFERSON. When not in session he maintained his military ties by serving as lieutenant colonel of the Stokes County militia. Winston died near Germantown, North Carolina, on April 15, 1815, and several decades later his remains were reinterred at the old Guilford Courthouse battlefield. He was one of the few Revolutionary War figures to succeed simultaneously in both military and political realms.

Further Reading

Dameron, J. David. *King's Mountain: The Defeat of the Loyalists, October 7, 1780.* Cambridge, Mass.: Da Capo Press, 2003.

Dildy, David S. "North Carolina's Revolutionaries in Arms: The Battle of King's Mountain." Unpublished master's thesis, College of William and Mary, 1997.

Downey, Jerry C. "A Soldier of the Revolution: Joseph Winston and the Surry Back Country of North Carolina." Unpublished master's thesis, Wake Forest University, 1989.

Hendricks, James E. "Joseph Winston, North Carolina Jeffersonian," *North Carolina Historical Review* 45 (summer 1968): 284–297.

Johnston, Peter R. *Poorest of the Thirteen: North Carolina and the Southern Department in the American Revolution.* Haverford, Pa.: Infinity Pub., 2001.

Wheeler, Earl M. "The Role of the North Carolina Militia in the Beginning of the American Revolution." Unpublished Ph.D. diss., Tulane University, 1969.

Woodford, William (1734–1780)

American military officer

William Woodford was born in Caroline County, Virginia, on October 6, 1734, the son of a prosperous planter. Well educated by private tutors, he joined Colonel George WASHINGTON's Virginia Regiment during the French and Indian War as an ensign, and subsequently campaigned against the Cherokee in 1761 under Colonel Adam STEPHEN. Afterward Woodford established himself as a country gentleman and something of a dandy. In 1775 he sided with the Patriots and served on the Caroline County COMMITTEE OF CORRESPONDENCE while also holding a seat in the Virginia Convention of that year. On August 5, 1775, Woodford gained appointment as colonel of the 2nd Virginia Regiment, and with it he scored an early victory by repelling an attack by Governor John MURRAY, Lord Dunmore, upon Hampton on October 26–27. Two months later the Virginia Committee of Safety dispatched Woodford to recover Norfolk from British, LOYALIST, and newly freed AFRICAN-AMERICAN forces operating there. This was accomplished over the objections of Colonel Patrick HENRY of the 1st Virginia Regiment, who technically enjoyed seniority over Woodford but lacked military experience. On December 9, 1775, Woodford cleverly lured Lord Dunmore into attacking across Great Bridge on the Elizabeth River, completely defeating him. He next occupied Norfolk in concert with reinforcements under Colonel Robert HOWE on December 14, 1776. After Dunmore's fleet bombarded the town on January 1, 1776, his troops burned known Loyalist residences in retaliation. All told, Woodford's efforts constituted the first American land victory since BUNKER HILL in the previous spring.

In February 1776 the Continental CONGRESS made Woodford colonel of the 2nd Virginia Continental Infantry. When he briefly resigned his commission upon learning that Adam Stephen had been promoted brigadier general ahead of him, General Washington convinced him to rejoin. Consequently, Woodford rose to brigadier general in February 1777, although his earlier departure had left him with less seniority than John P. G. MUHLENBERG, George WEEDON, and Charles SCOTT. On September 11, 1777, Woodford capably handled his brigade at the defeat of BRANDYWINE, artfully defending his position at Birmingham Hill and stalling a British turning movement under General Charles CORNWALLIS. Wounded in the hand, he missed subsequent fighting at GERMANTOWN and spent a harsh winter at Valley Forge with his troops. There he engaged in another struggle over seniority with Muhlenberg, Weedon, and Scott over possible promotion to major general to replace the now disgraced Stephen. Ultimately, Woodford obtained his seniority in March 1778—which prompted Weedon's resignation—but none of the contestants ever rose to major general. In June 1778 Woodford again performed useful service under General Charles LEE at MONMOUTH and later testified against him.

In December 1779, Washington ordered Woodford south to recruit additional men for his brigade and then join the army of General Benjamin LINCOLN in South Carolina. While at Petersburg he engaged in another heated seniority dispute with General Weedon, who refused to serve under him, although Scott volunteered to take his place. He then executed a difficult winter march under trying circumstances and shepherded his young recruits to participate in the siege of CHARLESTON. When the town surrendered to British forces under General Henry CLINTON on

May 12, 1780, Woodford passed into captivity. Taken to New York, he endured squalid conditions in close confinement and died there of disease on November 13, 1780, at the age of 46.

Further Reading

Anderson, D. R., ed. "The Letters of Col. William Woodford, Col. Robert Howe, and Gen. Charles Lee to Edmund Pendleton," *Richmond College Historical Papers* 1, no. 1 (1915): 96–163.

Heathcote, Charles W. "General William Woodford—A Gallant Officer Who Helped Washington," *Picket Post* no. 60 (May 1958): 4–5, 37–41.

Jordan, John W., ed. "Unpublished Letters of General Woodford of the Continental Army, 1776–1779," *Pennsylvania Magazine of History and Biography* 23 (January 1899): 453–463.

Sellers, John R. *The Virginia Continental Line.* Williamsburg: Virginia Independence Bicentennial Commission, 1978.

Stewart, Catesby W. *The Life of Brigadier General William Woodford of the American Revolution,* 2 vols. Richmond, Va.: Whittet & Shepperson, 1973.

Tarter, Brent, ed. "The Orderly Book of the Second Virginia Regiment, September 27, 1775–April 15, 1776," *Virginia Magazine of History and Biography* 85, nos. 2–3 (1977): 56–183, 302–336.

Wooster, David (1711–1777)

American military officer

David Wooster was born in Stratford, Connecticut, on March 2, 1711, the son of a mason. After attending Yale in 1738 he joined the militia during King George's War and served as a lieutenant onboard the armed sloop *Defense*. Wooster then transferred to the infantry as a captain and saw extensive service at Louisbourg under General William Pepperell. After the war he settled in New Haven as a merchant and as master of the local Masonic lodge. In 1756 he returned to the colors as colonel of the 2nd Connecticut Regiment, rendering useful services at Crown Point, Ticonderoga, and in the campaigns of General Jeffrey Amherst. When peace arrived, he resumed his mercantile activities in New Haven, serving as both collector of customs and justice of the peace.

Wooster was 64 and a senior colonial military figure when the Revolutionary War erupted in April 1775, so the Connecticut assembly appointed him both major general of state forces and colonel of the 1st Connecticut Regiment. The Continental CONGRESS also appointed him a brigadier general in the Continental ARMY. Wooster, however, was insulted that his Continental rank was not equivalent to his state rank, and it became a protracted point of contention. After a tour defending New York City he was ordered north as part of General Peter P. SCHUYLER's—with whom he squabbled incessantly—invasion of Canada and subsequently served under General Richard MONTGOMERY. In this capacity he commanded the garrisons at Saint Johns and Montreal in Montgomery's absence; following Montgomery's death during the attack on QUEBEC, he rose to the Canadian command. Wooster, unfortunately, was completely out of his element as a senior leader, and his ham-fisted tactics against the Catholic population of Quebec only alienated them from the American cause. Typically, he remained in comfortable quarters at Montreal and did not visit the shivering remnants of Montgomery's army outside until later that spring. By the time he was replaced by General John THOMAS in May 1776, American forces in Canada were completely wretched and demoralized. Congress consequently summoned him to Philadelphia to answer numerous charges leveled against him. There Connecticut delegate Silas DEANE contemptuously referred to Wooster as an "old woman," but he was eventually exonerated by a court of inquiry. He retained his army rank but returned to Connecticut to function as major general and commander in chief of state forces.

Wooster led a division of Connecticut troops that garrisoned the New York border, a site of frequent raids by LOYALIST forces under Governor William TRYON. In January 1777 he fought under General William HEATH at the badly managed siege of Fort Independence, New York, and returned home without ceremony. On April 26, 1777, Governor Tryon landed 2,000 men at

Compo Hill, marched overland, and burned American supplies gathered at neighboring Danbury. Wooster promptly rallied what few troops remained and harassed the British withdrawal back to the coast. On April 27, 1777, assisted by additional forces under General Benedict ARNOLD and Gold S. SILLIMAN, Wooster engaged a superior enemy force at Ridgefield. He displayed far greater bravery than common sense in the fighting and was mortally wounded by musket fire. Wooster died in Danbury on May 2, 1777, an experienced but basically incompetent senior military leader.

Further Reading

Callahan, North. *Connecticut's Revolutionary War Leaders*. Chester, Conn.: Pequot, 1973.

Cody, Robert M. "The Special Defense and Safety of This Colony: Revolutionary War Actions in Connecticut, 1777–1781." Unpublished master's thesis, Southern Connecticut State University, 2000.

Deming, Henry C. *An Oration upon the Life and Services of General David Wooster*. Hartford, Conn.: Press of Case, Tiffany, 1854.

Douglas, Damon G. *The Bridge Not Taken: Benedict Arnold Outwitted*. Westport, Conn.: Westport Historical Society, 2002.

Jones, Keith M. *Farmers against the Crown: A Comprehensive Account of the Revolutionary War Battle in Ridgefield, Connecticut, April 27, 1777*. Ridgefield: Connecticut Colonel Pub. Co., 2003.

Reed, John I. "Red Tape at Valley Forge," *Manuscripts* 20, no. 2 (1968): 20–27.

Y

Yorktown, siege of (September–October 1781)

General Charles CORNWALLIS, after his failure to conquer the Carolinas, invaded Virginia in May 1781, waxing confident that he could inflict far more damage upon the American war effort there. His 1,500 troops were augmented by the survivors of General William PHILLIPS and Benedict ARNOLD and brought total numbers up to 8,000 veteran combat troops. For several months he engaged in a strategic cat and mouse campaign with forces under the marquis de LAFAYETTE, whom he contemptuously referred to as "the boy," and failed to decisively corner him. But Cornwallis was operating in Virginia contrary to the wishes of the commander in chief, General Henry CLINTON, at New York; in July, Clinton ordered him to cease further operations, repair to the coast, and await reinforcements. Cornwallis expertly disengaged his forces, closely shadowed by Lafayette, and marched them to Yorktown. By August 22, 1781, the British had entrenched themselves and passively awaited succor from the sea. General George WASHINGTON watched these developments from his headquarters outside New York. By discarding Clinton's instructions, Cornwallis had inadvertently placed himself within striking distance of the strongest portion of the Continental ARMY and of sizable French forces under General Jean-Baptiste, comte de ROCHAMBEAU. Washington had previously toyed with mounting an attack upon New York but abandoned the venture after learning that French naval forces under Admiral François-Joseph, comte de GRASSE, would be in the region of Chesapeake Bay through October. Then Washington, in a flash of strategic brilliance, divined an opportunity to hem Cornwallis in by land and sea and catch him. He prevailed upon the very compliant Rochambeau and marched south with the bulk of their forces on August 20, 1781. The curtain thus rose on the final act of an internecine, six-year struggle.

Cornwallis's fate was effectively sealed as early as September 5, 1781, when de Grasse's fleet defeated a relief effort under Admiral Thomas GRAVES off the Chesapeake Capes. Soon afterward, on September 14, 1781, advanced elements of the allied army trickled into Virginia, and within two weeks Washington had deployed the divisions of Lafayette, Benjamin LINCOLN, and Friedrich von STEUBEN across Yorktown's land side. Sizable French contingents from the fleet brought the entire host up to 15,000 men, twice the British muster. The nominally aggressive Cornwallis remained a passive spectator as French and American engineers under Colonel Louis DUPORTAIL began methodically laying out siege lines. He also kept a sharp and somewhat forlorn eye cast toward the sea for promised reinforcements. But the general inadvertently expedited his own demise by consolidating his position and withdrawing men from his outer works. This enabled the allies to move closer to his defenses much sooner than anticipated. On October 1, 1781, the first siege batteries were erected and ready to commence their deadly work in earnest. Washington personally sighted and fired the first piece on October 9, which signaled a general discharge from over 100 cannon. Simultaneously, allied sappers began digging parallel trenches and inched toward the British defenses. When British-held Redoubts Nos. 9 and 10 began firing into the flanks of the oncoming troops, plans unfolded to storm them. The attack transpired on the evening of October 10, 1781, when two columns under Colonels Alexander HAMILTON and Colonel Guillaume de DEUX-PONTS successfully carried the redoubts after a brief but sanguine struggle. Washington and Rochambeau then moved their cannon even closer to Cornwallis's lines and unleashed an incessant bombardment. The British, losing men heavily to concentrated fire, responded with a desperate sortie under Colonel Robert Abercromby on October 16 and spiked a French battery before being repelled. Cornwallis at this juncture had little recourse but to slip across the York River to Gloucester and break out, but he was thwarted at the last moment by boisterous weather. Facing an impending assault that he could not withstand, and with promised reinforcements nowhere in sight, the general reluctantly ordered a solitary drummer boy to beat a parley on October 17.

Intense negotiations followed among British authorities, Colonel John LAURENS, and Louis-Marie NOAILLES, with Laurens insisting that Cornwallis endure the same harsh terms inflicted upon General Lincoln after the siege of CHARLESTON. The general glumly accepted and on the afternoon of October 19, 1781, the British army left its entrenchments, paraded before massed French and American lines, and began sullenly stacking its arms. They marched out to a tune called "The World Turned Upside Down," ironically an effective metaphor for the occasion. Cornwallis, feeling thoroughly disgraced, feigned illness and requested his second in command, General Charles O'HARA, to surrender in his place. However, when that officer tried capitulating to the French, he was curtly directed by Colonel Mathieu DUMAS to the Americans. The dejected British leader then tendered the sword to Washington, who likewise refused it from anybody but its proper owner. Therefore, Washington's own second in command, Benjamin Lincoln, who had himself surrendered to Clinton on May 12, 1780, received O'Hara's charge. Yorktown had been a relatively brief but bloody affair, with British casualties of 156 killed, 326 wounded, and 70 missing. A further 8,081 men passed into captivity, a larger total than had been surrendered by General John BURGOYNE at Saratoga in 1777. French collaboration cost them 60 killed and 197 wounded, while the Americans sustained 23 dead and 56 injured. Washington's consummate grasp of strategy, his ability to facilitate combined operations, and his willingness to entertain great risks, were never more apparent—nor more effective—than here. But the import of Yorktown transcended mere casualties, simply because it finally broke the British resolve to wage war. After the fall of Lord Frederick NORTH's cabinet in February 1782, a new ministry under Charles WATSON-WENTWORTH, marquis of Rockingham, agreed to initiate peace negotiations in Paris with representatives from Britain's former colonies.

Further Reading

Grainger, John D. *The Battle of Yorktown: A Reassessment.* Rochester, N.Y.: Boydell, 2005.

Greene, Jerome A. *The Guns of Independence: The Siege of Yorktown, 1781.* New York: Savas Beatie, 2005.

Hallahan, William H. *The Day the Revolution Ended.* New York: Wiley, 2004.

Ketchum, Richard M. *Victory at Yorktown: The Campaign That Won the Revolution.* New York: Henry Holt, 2004.

Migliacci, Louis W. "The Battle of Yorktown, 1781." Unpublished master's thesis, East Stroudsburg University, 1999.

Morrissey, Brendan. *Yorktown, 1781: The World Turned Upside Down.* Westport, Conn.: Praeger, 2004.

Tinder, Robert W. "Extraordinary Measures: Maryland and the Yorktown Campaign, 1781," *Maryland Historical Magazine* 95, no. 2 (2000): 132–159.

Maps

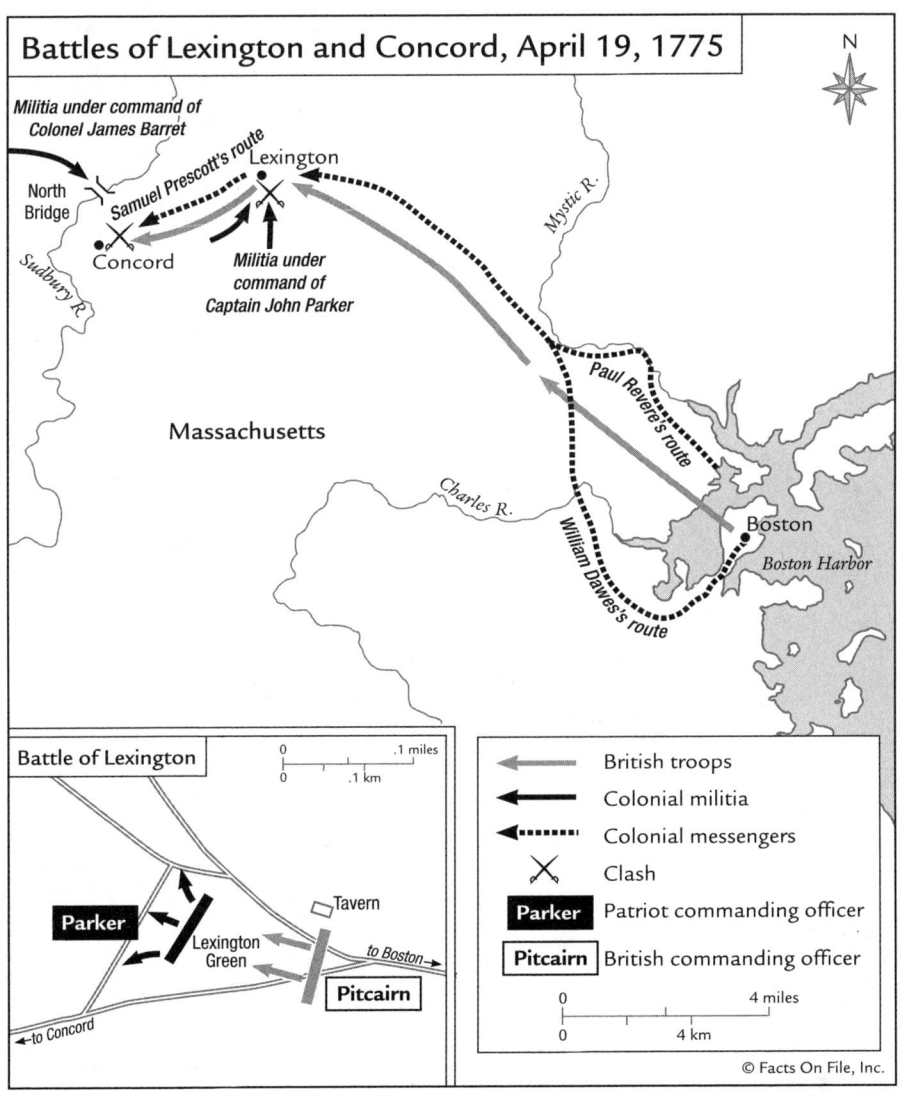

Maps 715

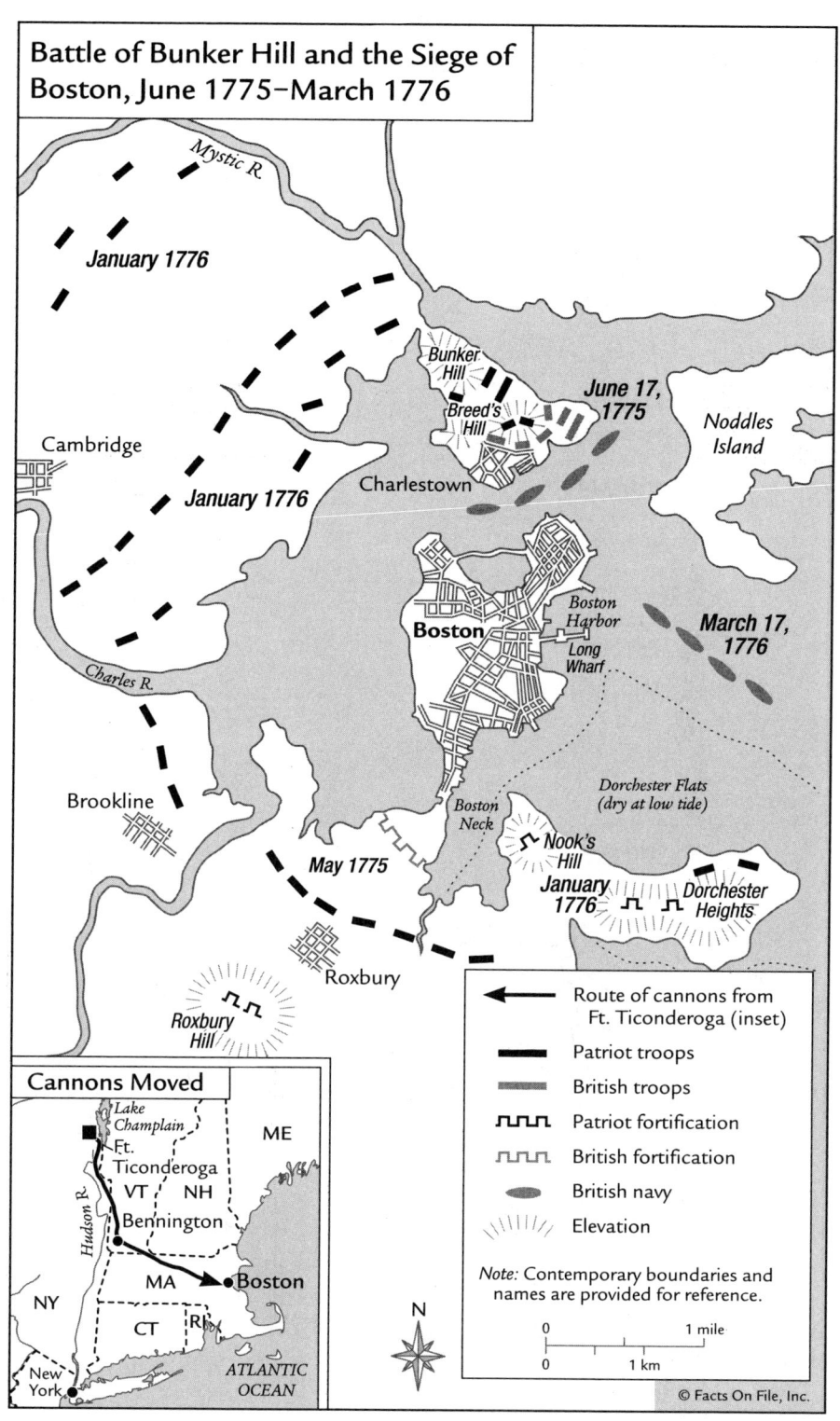

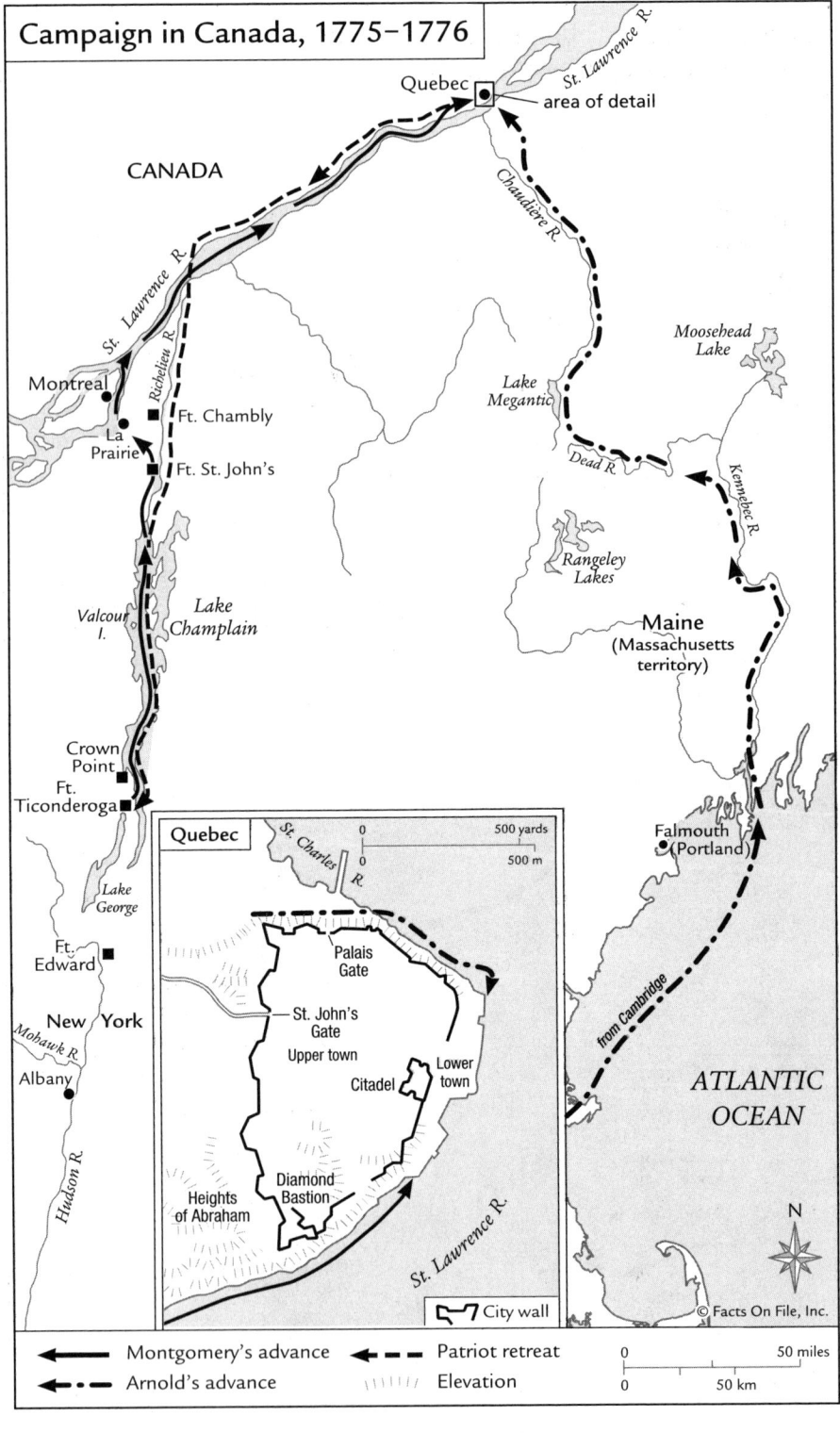

Maps 717

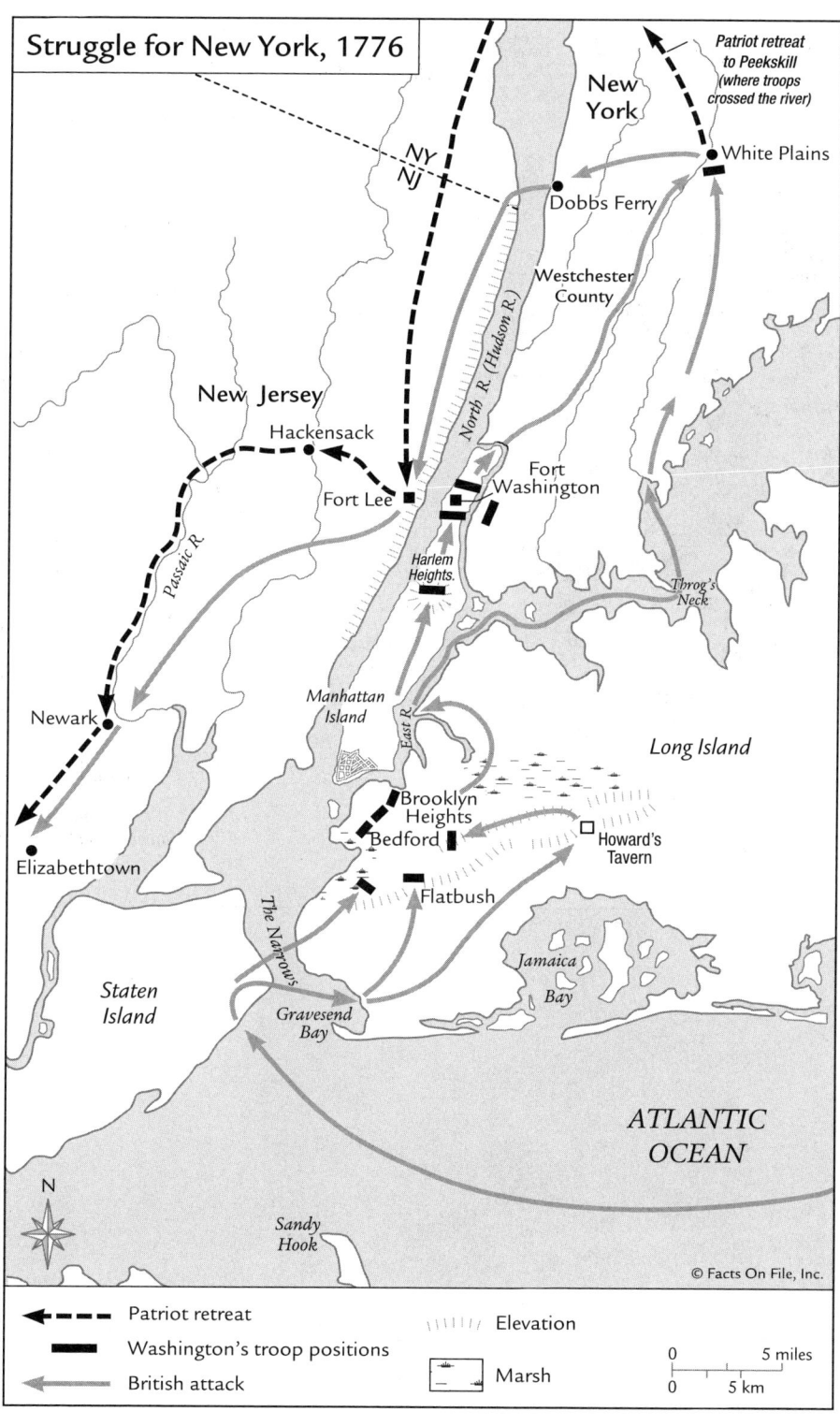

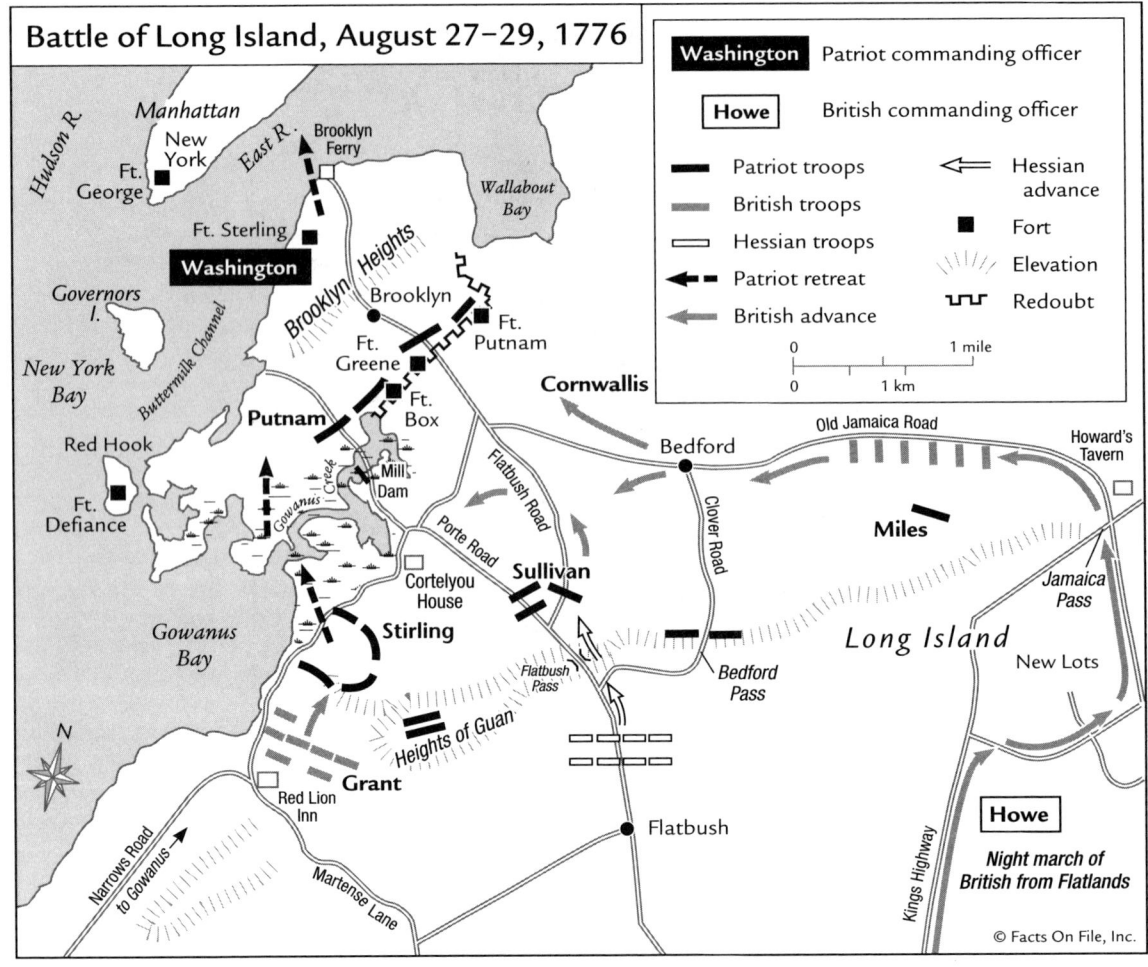

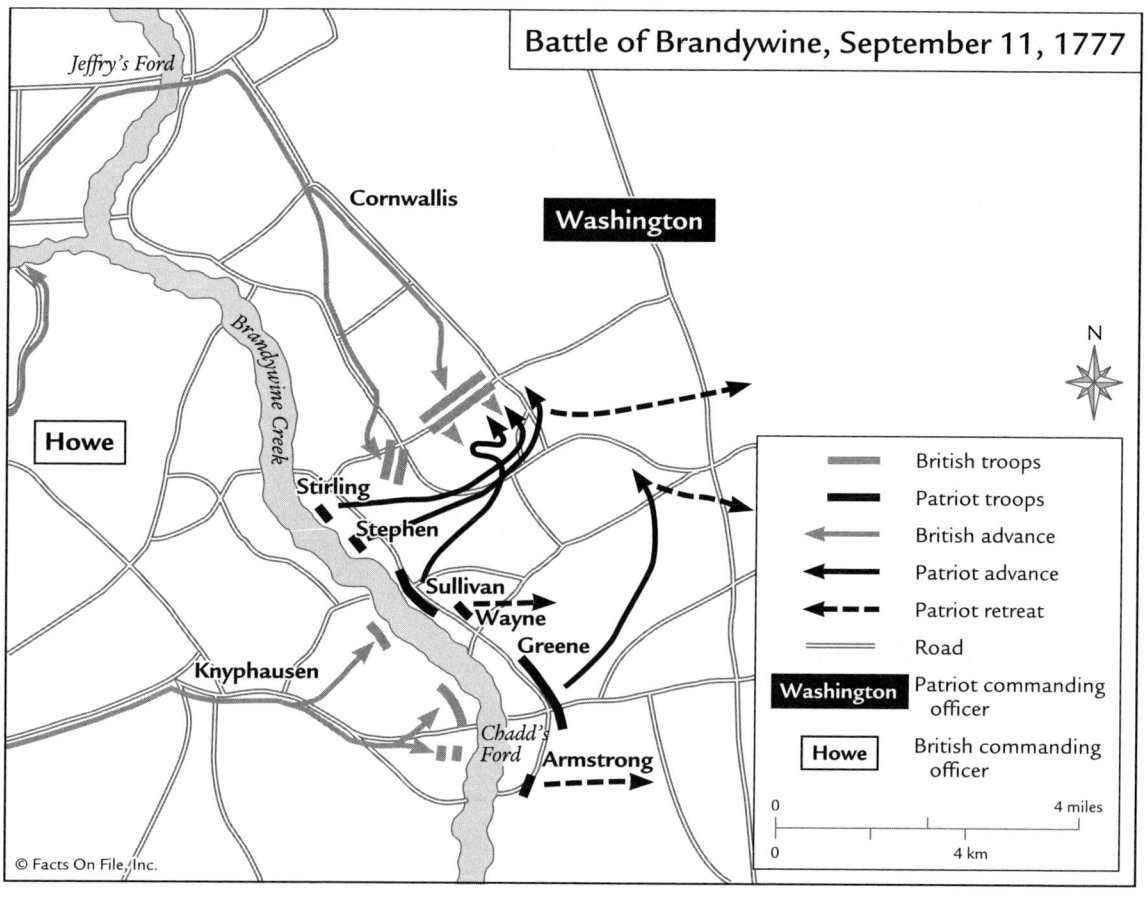

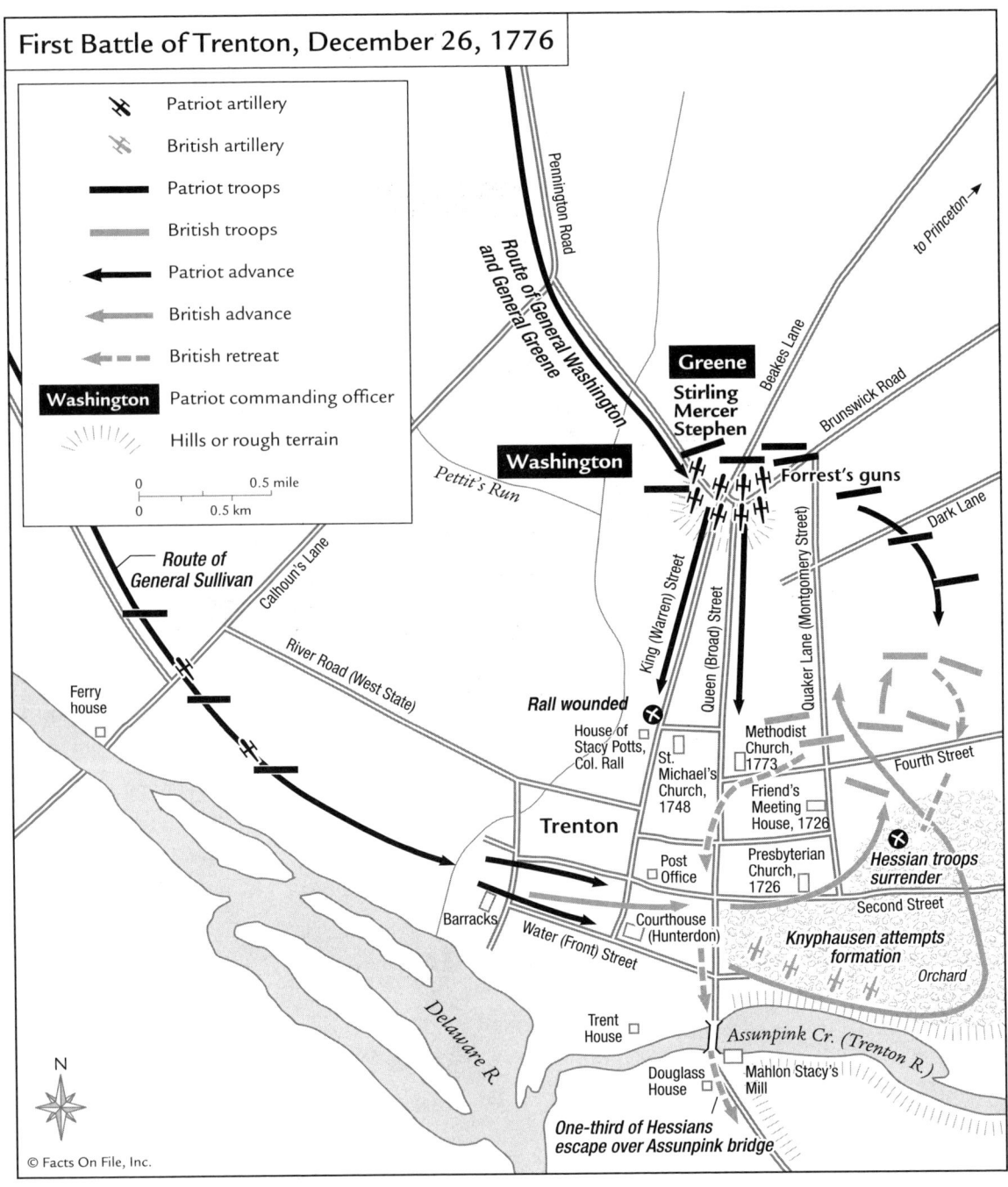

Maps 721

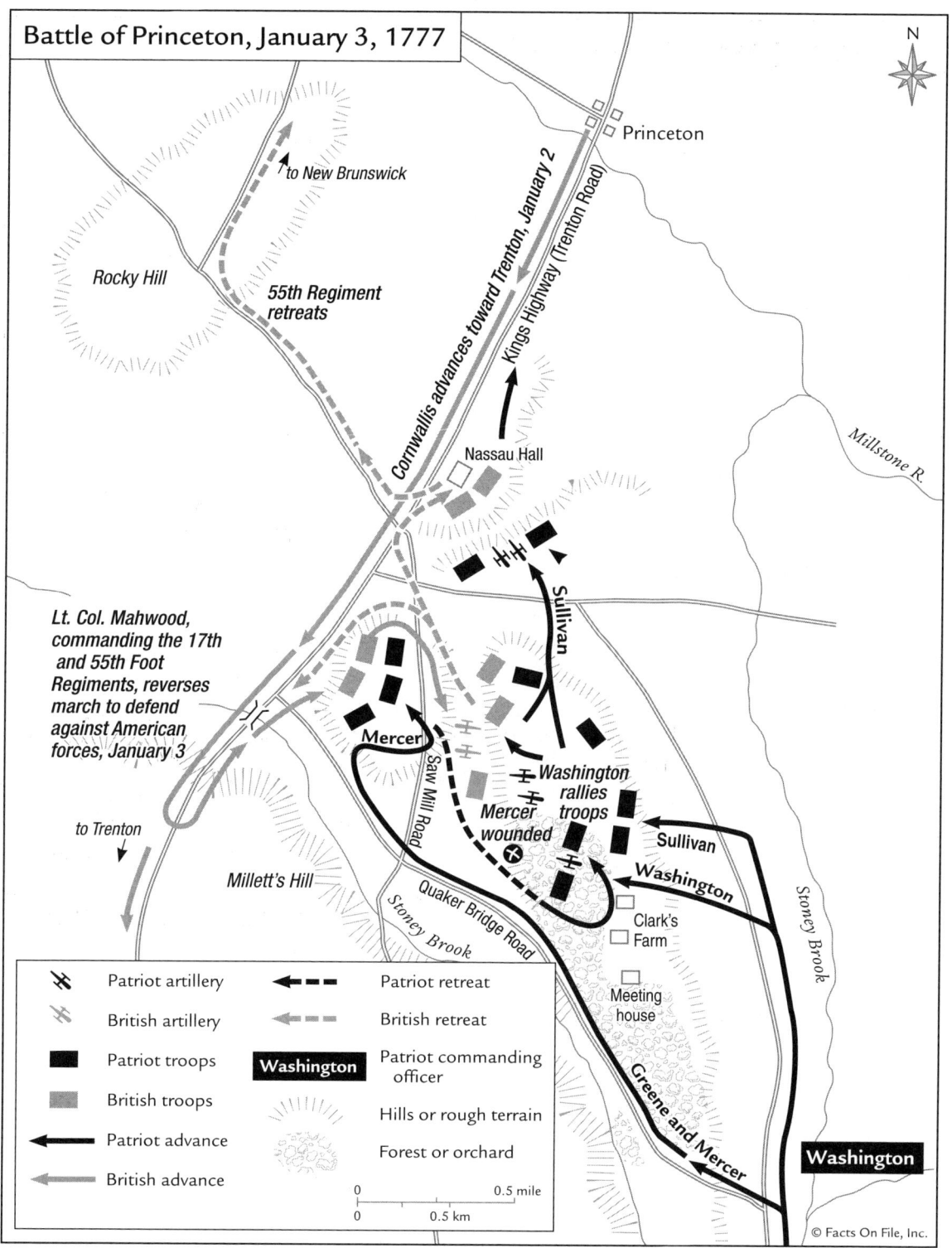

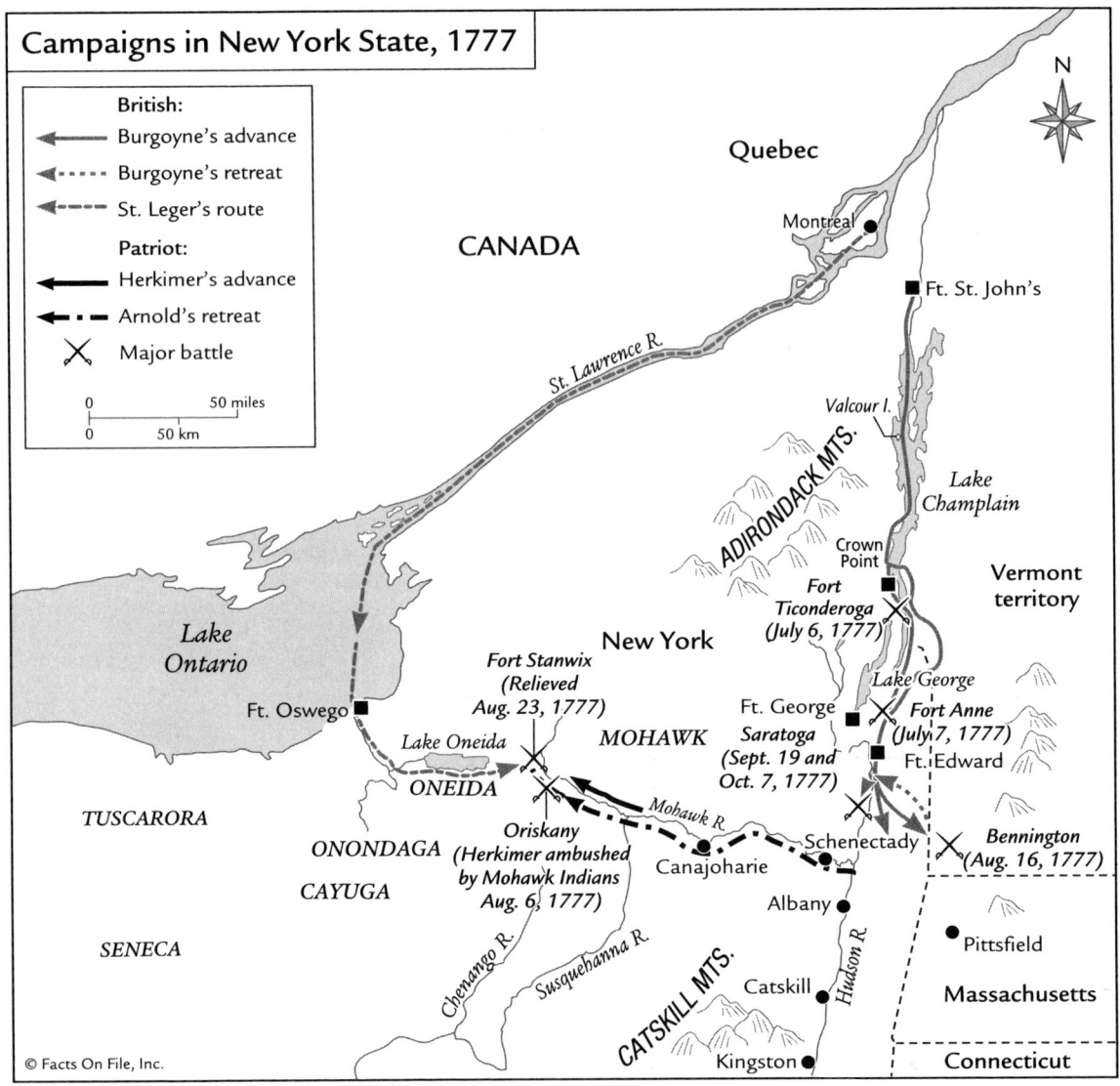

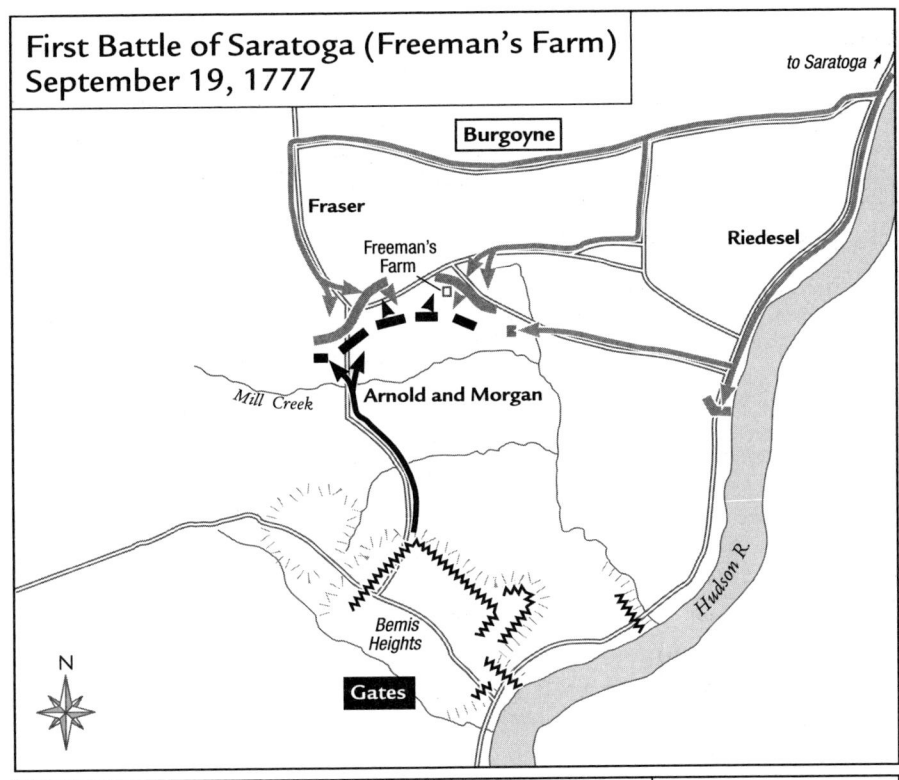
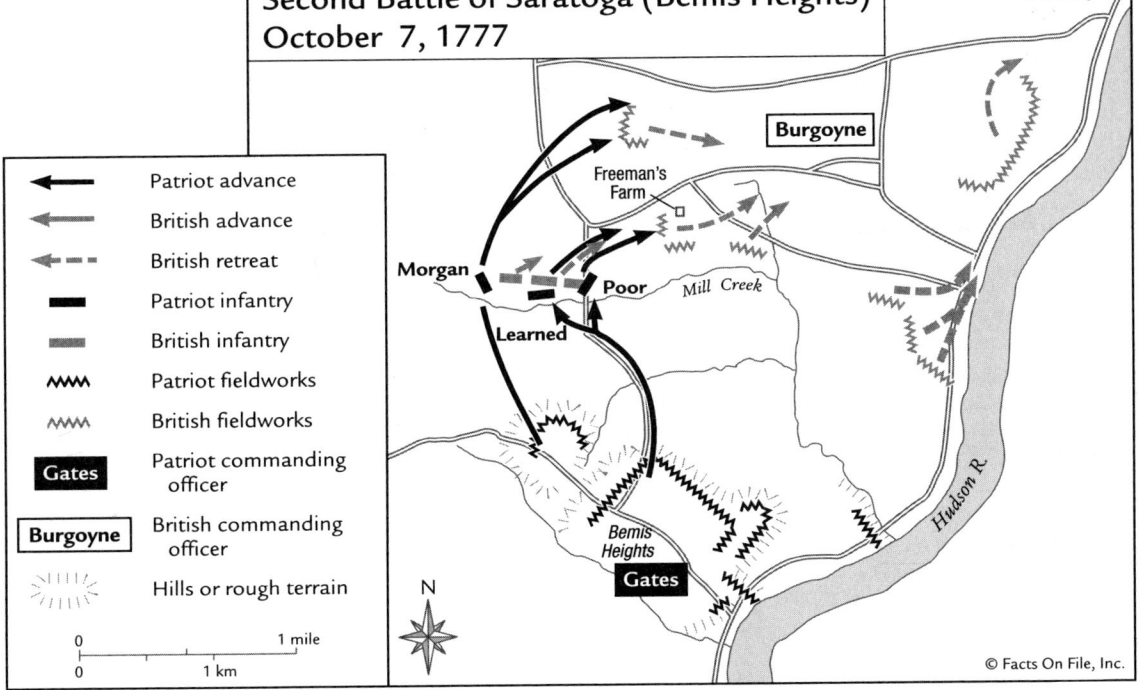

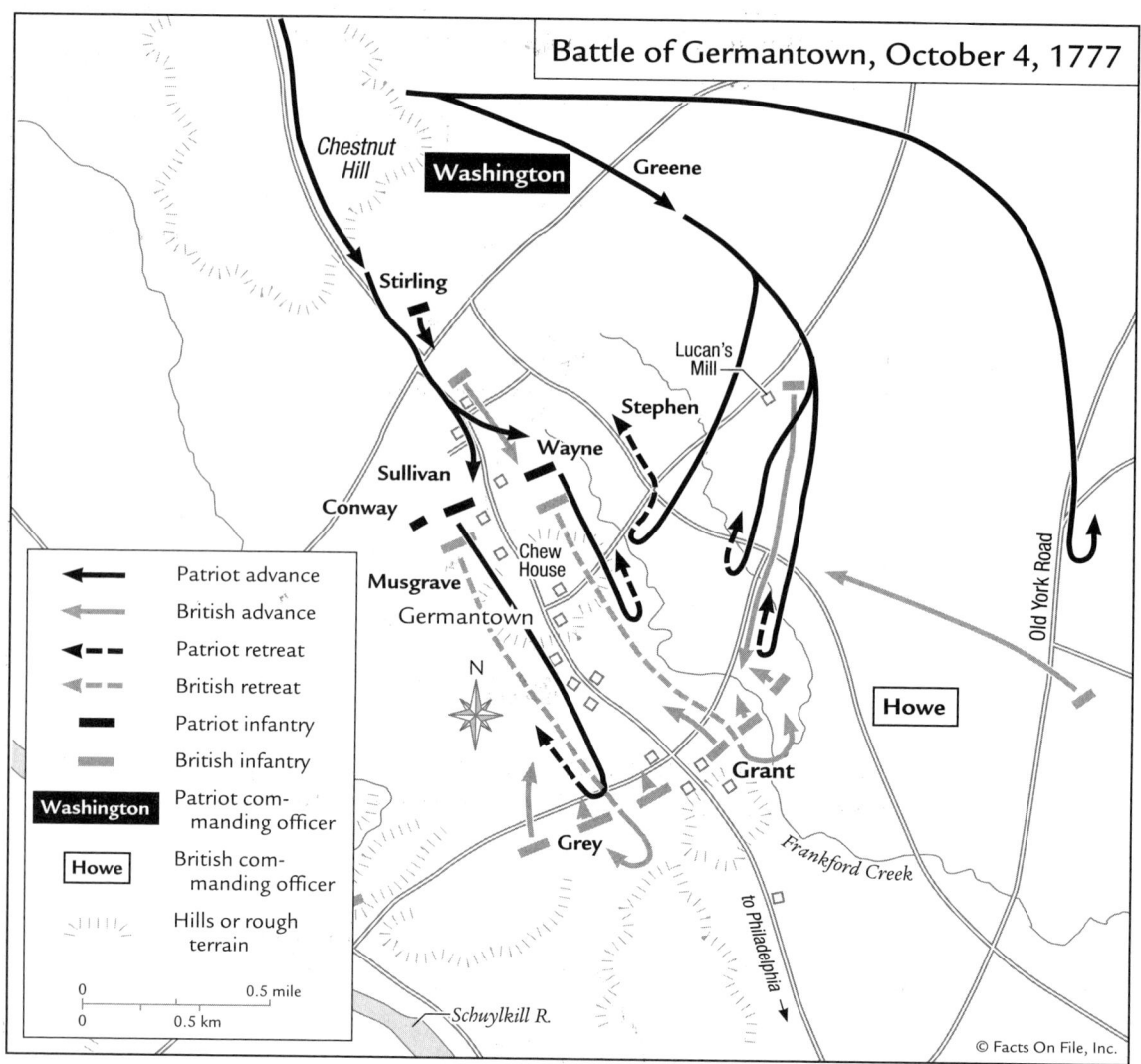

Maps 725

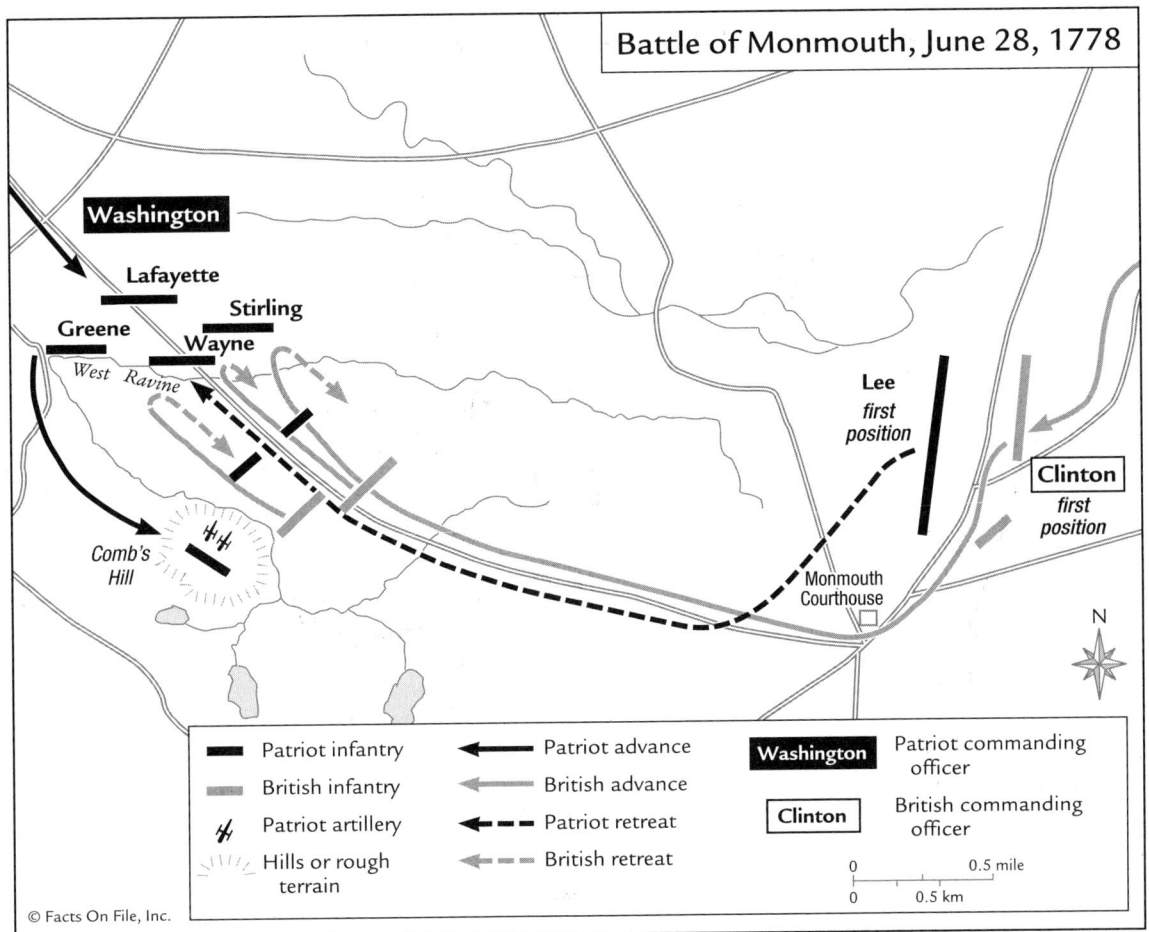

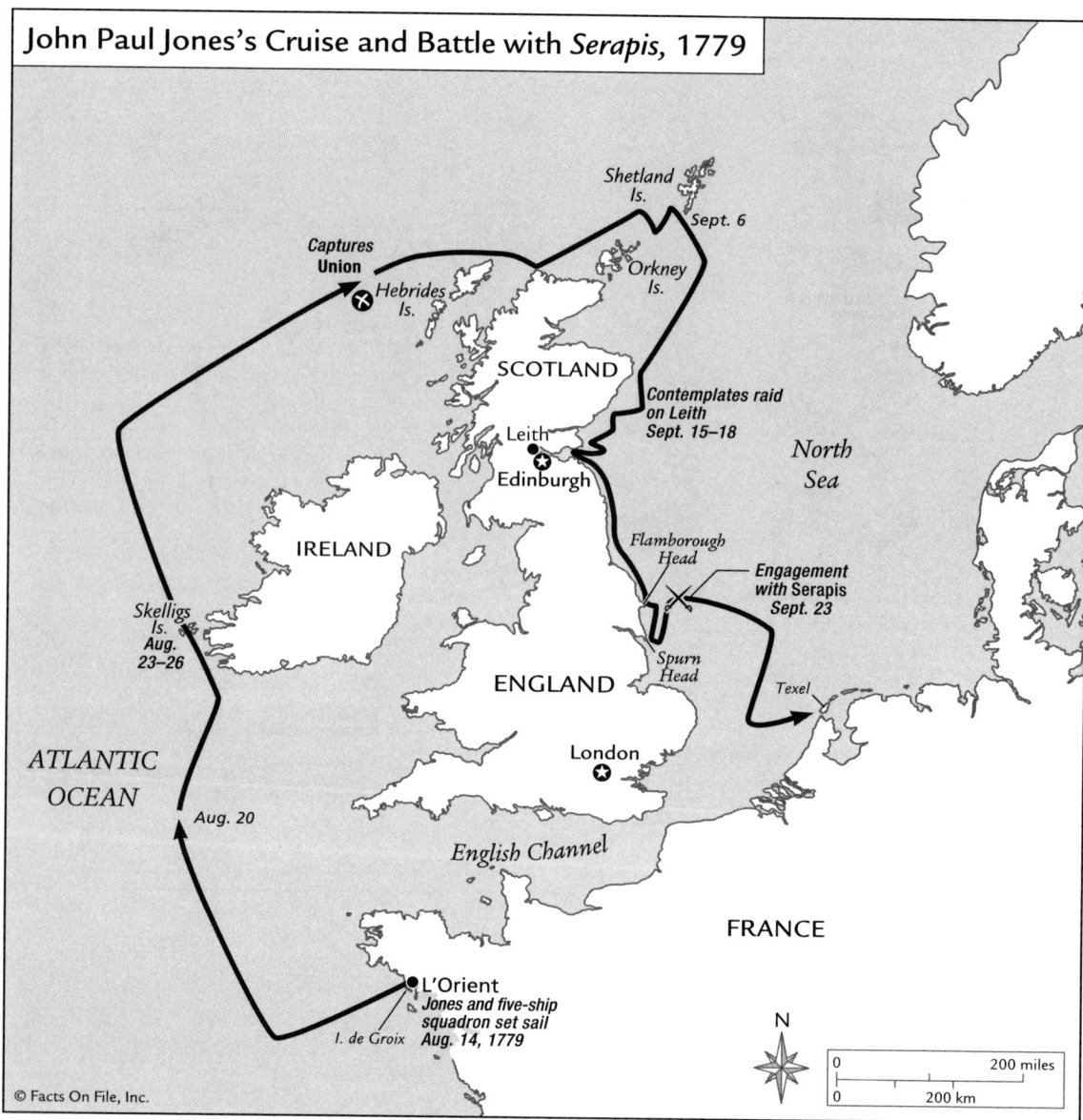

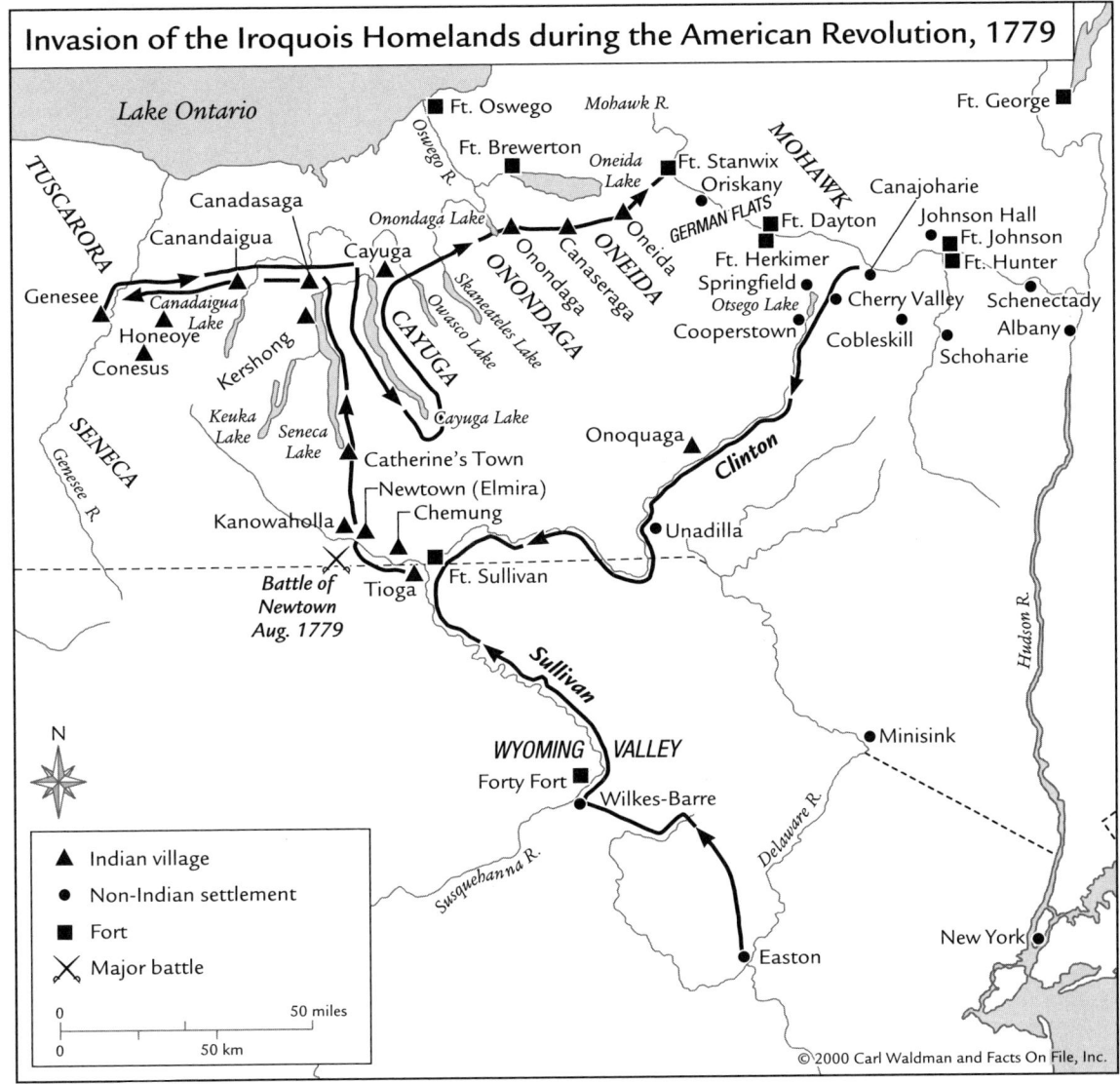

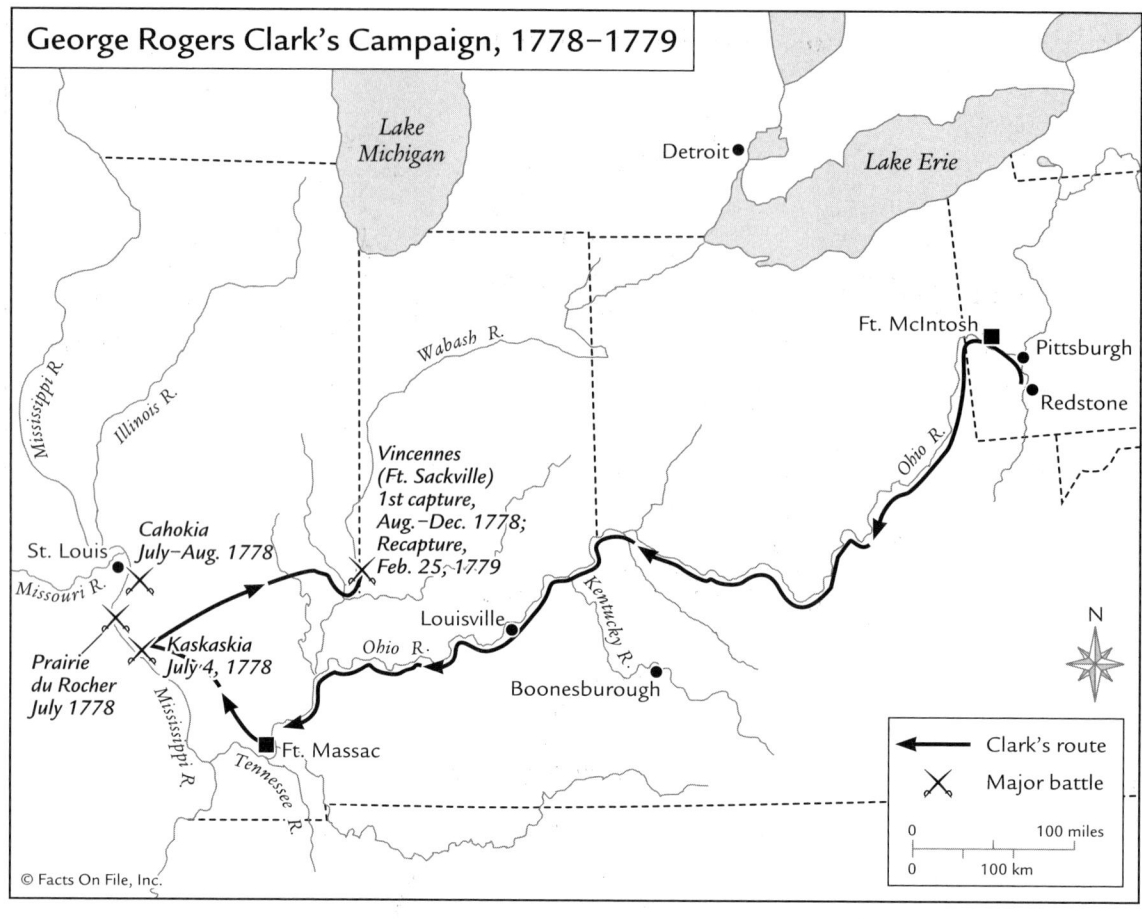

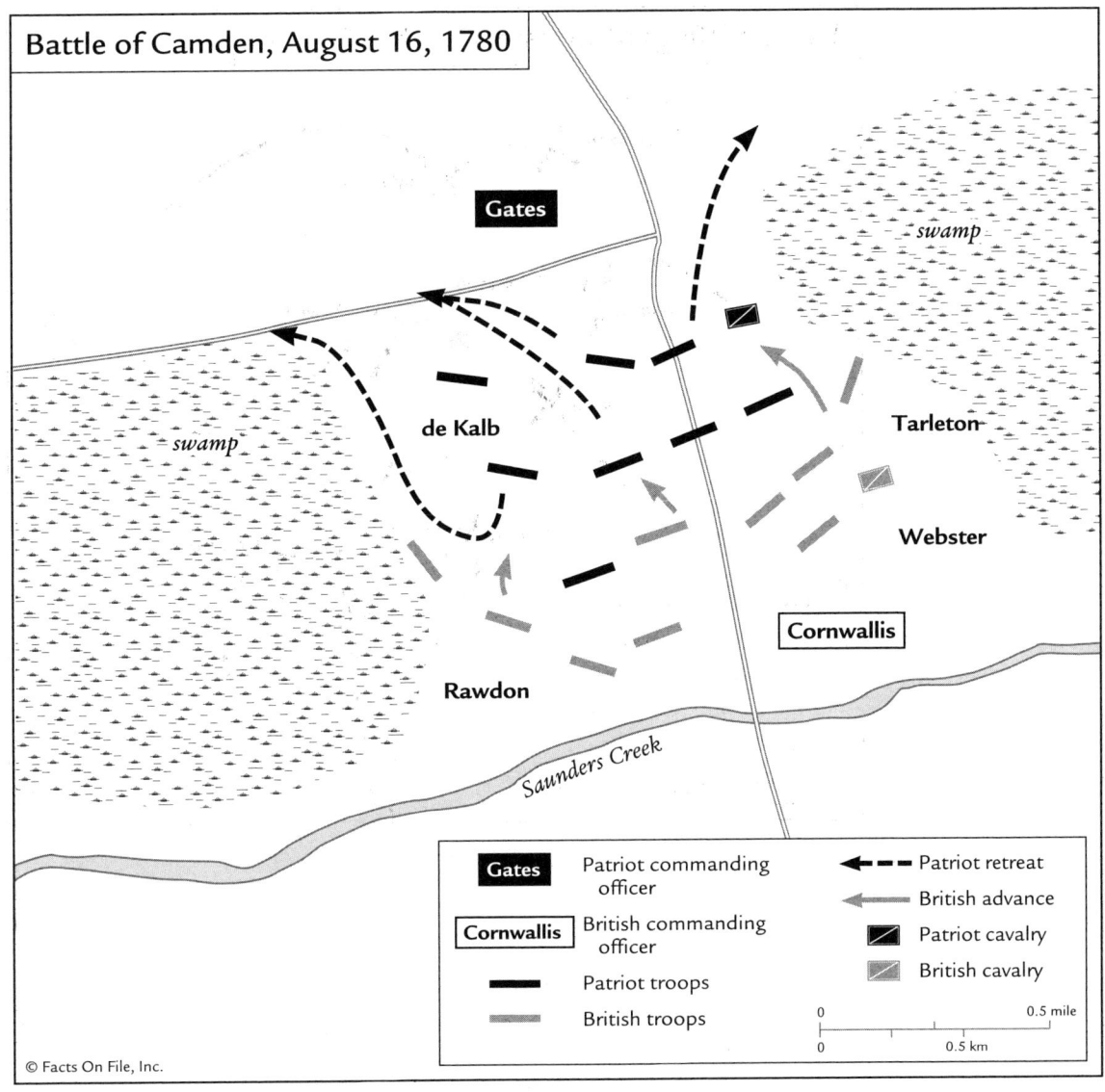

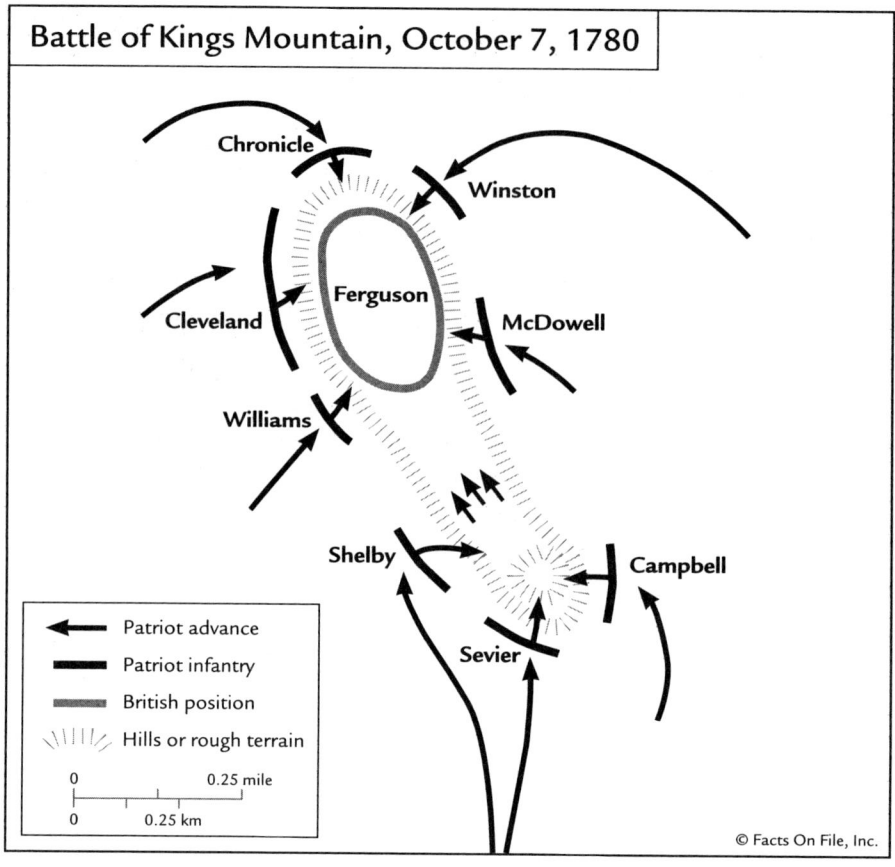

Battle of Cowpens, January 17, 1781
Washington's dragoons
Morgan
Continentals
Militia
Riflemen
Tarleton
Patriot infantry
British infantry
Patriot cavalry
British cavalry
Patriot advance
British advance
Morgan
Patriot commanding officer
Tarleton
British commanding officer
Hills or rough terrain
0
500 feet
0
150 m
© Facts On File, Inc.

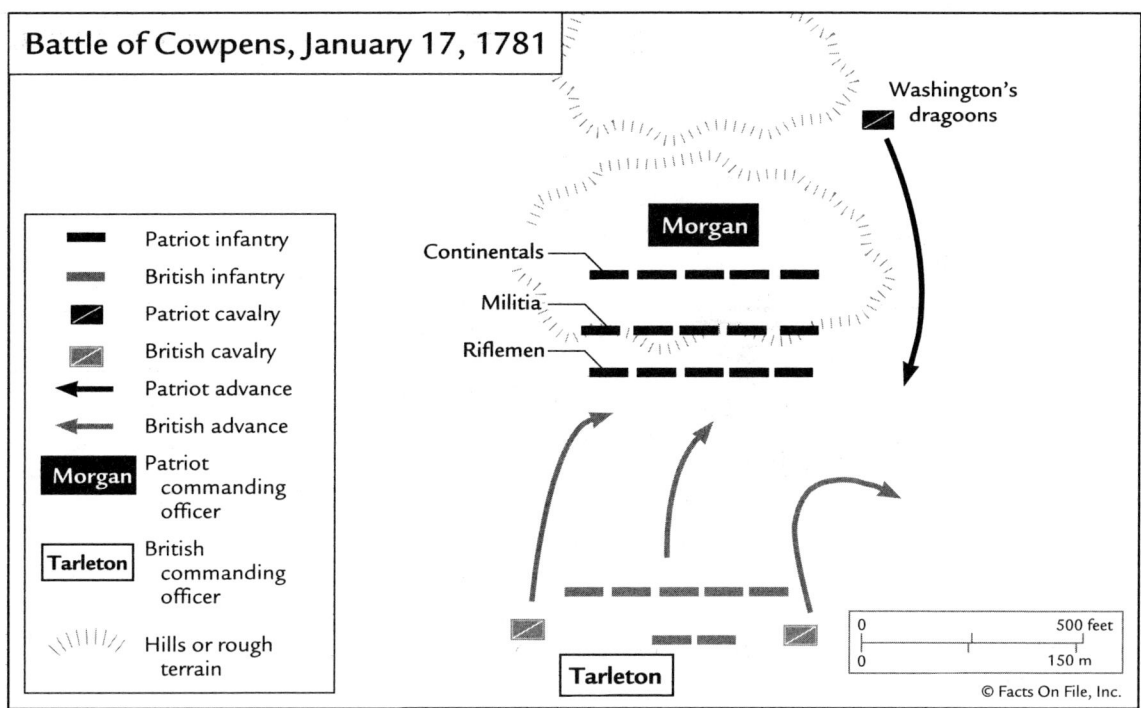

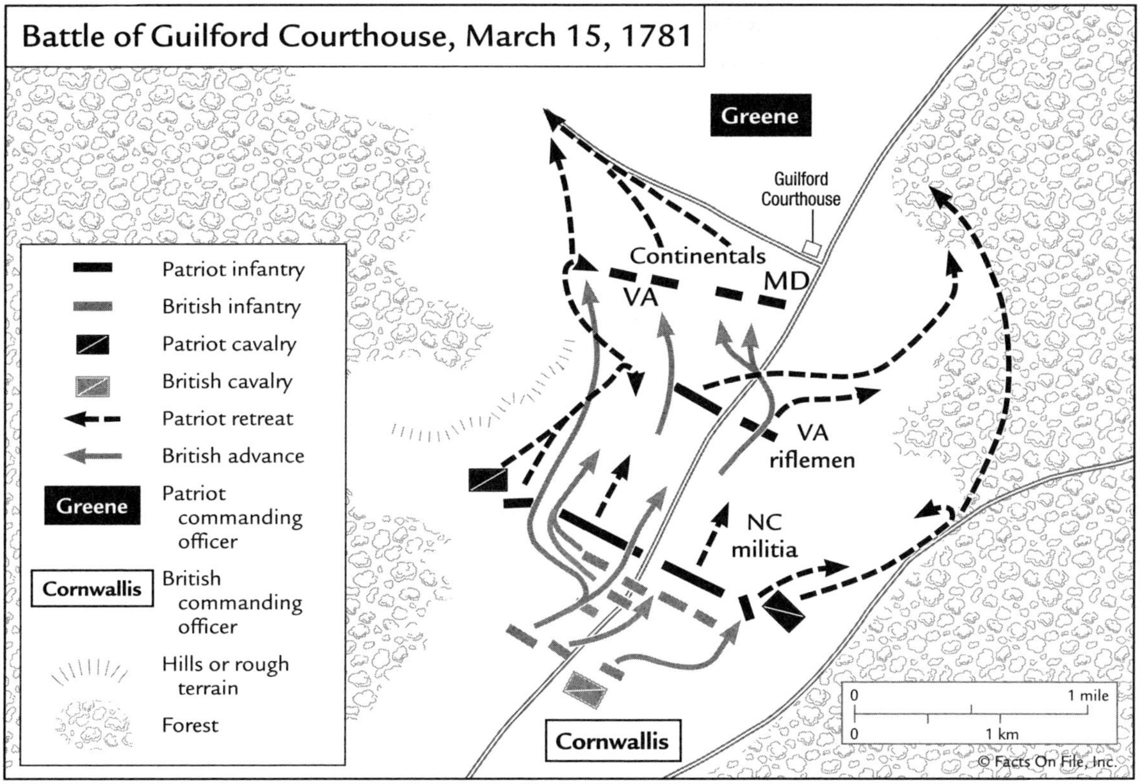
Battle of Guilford Courthouse, March 15, 1781
Greene
Guilford Courthouse
Continentals
VA
MD
VA riflemen
NC militia
Cornwallis
Patriot infantry
British infantry
Patriot cavalry
British cavalry
Patriot retreat
British advance
Greene
Patriot commanding officer
Cornwallis
British commanding officer
Hills or rough terrain
Forest
0
1 mile
0
1 km
© Facts On File, Inc.

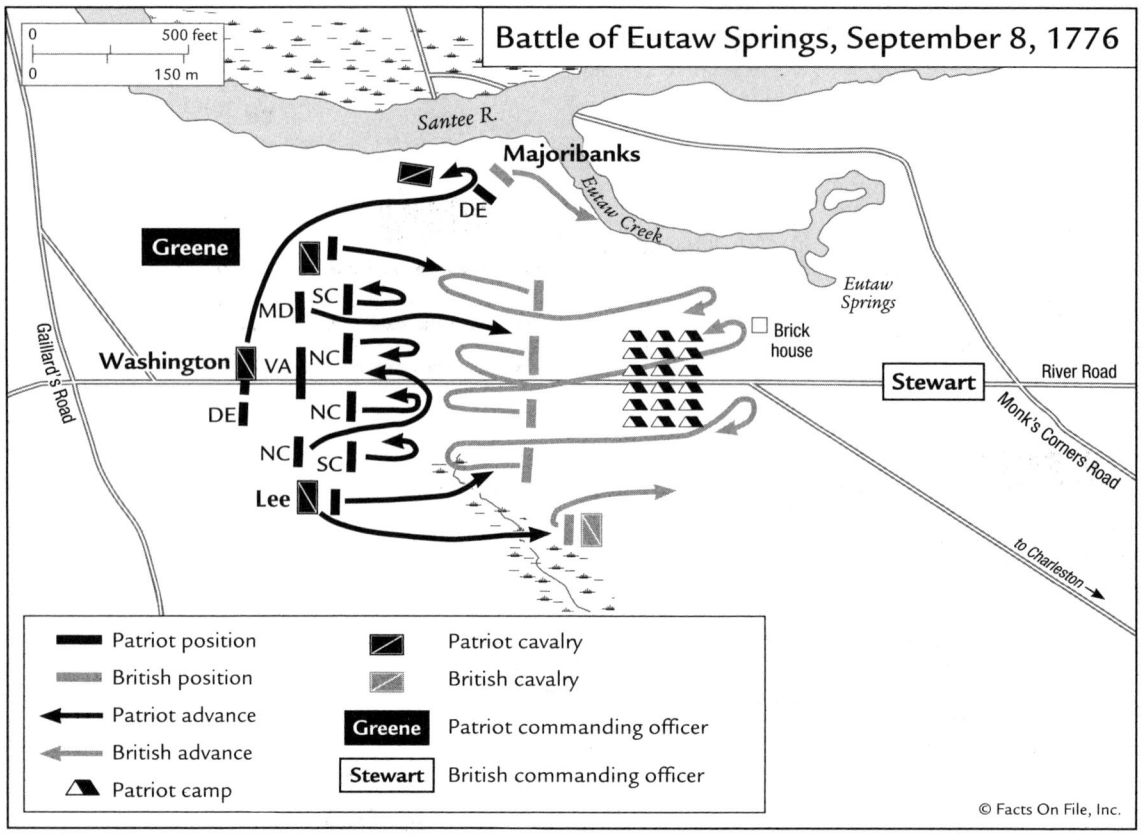

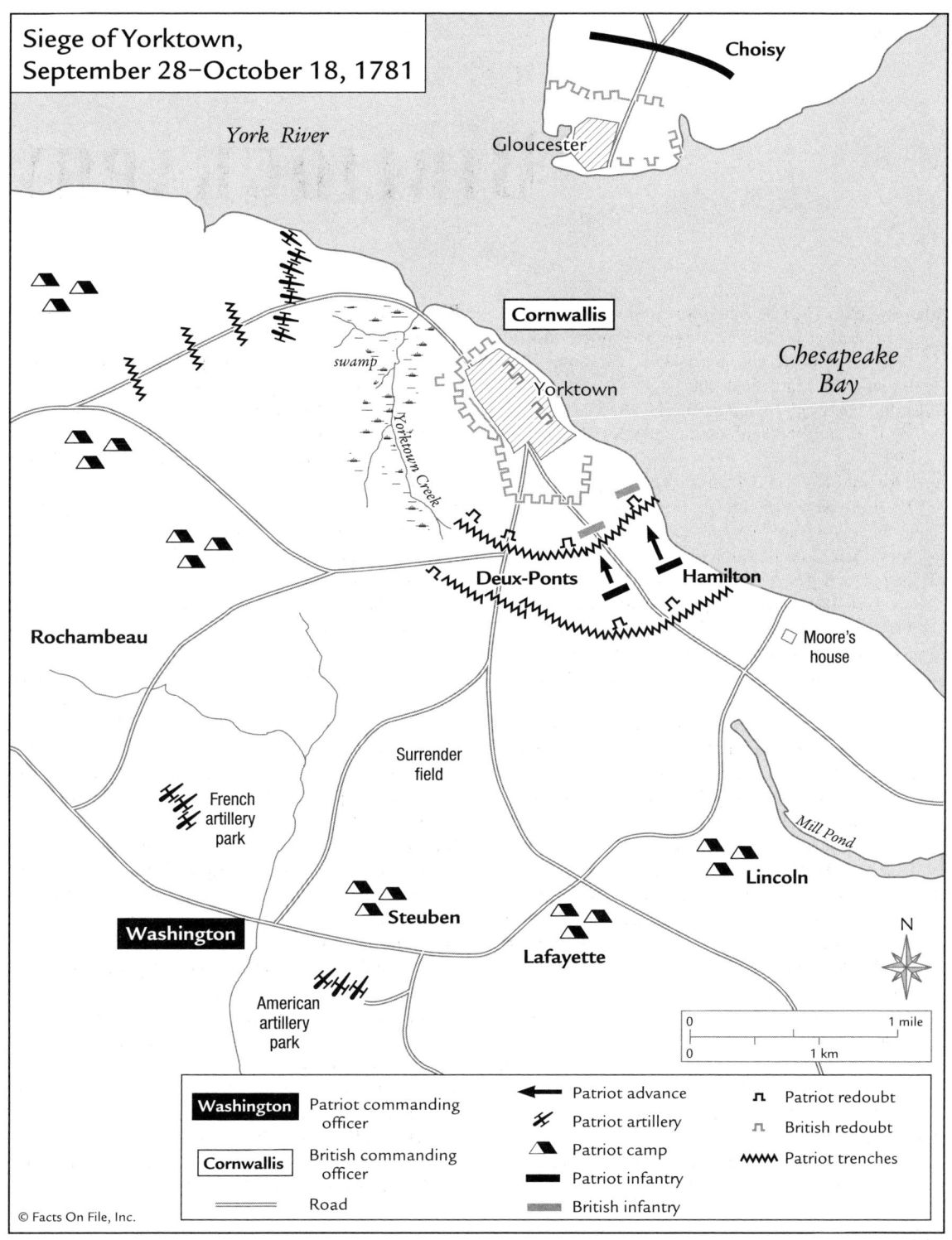

BIBLIOGRAPHY

Adams, Willi P. *The First American Constitutions: Republican Ideology and the Making of the State Constitutions in the Revolutionary Era.* Lanham, Md.: Rowman and Littlefield, 2001.

Adler, Bill. *America's Founding Fathers: Their Uncommon Wisdom and Wit.* Lanham, Md.: Taylor Trade Pub., 2003.

Agel, Jerome. *The U.S. Declaration of Independence for Everyone.* New York: Perigee Book, 2001.

Allen, Steve W. *Founding Fathers: Uncommon Heroes.* Mesa, Ariz.: Legal Awareness Series, Inc., 2002.

Andrews, Dee E. *The Methodists and Revolutionary America, 1760-1800: The Shaping of an Evangelical Culture.* Princeton, N.J.: Princeton University Press, 2000.

Appleby, Joyce O. *Inheriting the Revolution: The First Generation of Americans.* Cambridge, Mass.: Belknap, 2000.

Axelrod, Alan. *The Complete Idiot's Guide to the American Revolution.* Indianapolis, Ind.: Alpha Books, 2000.

Backofen, Walter A. *Local Control and Gun Ownership in Revolutionary New Hampshire.* East Plainfield, N.H.: Lord Timothy Dexter Press, 2003.

Barnes, Ian. *The Historical Atlas of the American Revolution.* New York: Routledge, 2000.

Becker, Ann M. "Smallpox in Washington's Army: Strategic Implications of Disease during the American Revolutionary War," *Journal of Military History* 68, no. 2 (2004): 381–430.

Bell, James B. *The Imperial Origins of the King's Church in Early America, 1607-1783.* New York: Palgrave Macmillan, 2004.

Bendall, S. "The Uniform of Colonel Edmund Fanning (1739-1818)," *Journal of the Society for Army Historical Research* 79, no. 319 (2001): 188-195.

Bezis-Selfa, John. *Forging America: Ironworkers, Adventurers, and the Industrious Revolution.* Ithaca, N.Y.: Cornell University Press, 2004.

Bicheno, Hugh. *Rebels & Redcoats: The American Revolutionary War.* London: HarperCollins, 2004.

Bickhorn, Troy O. "Noble Savages? British Discussions and Representations of Native American Indians, 1754–1783." Unpublished master's Ph.D. diss., University of Oxford, 2000.

Black, Jeremy. *War for America: The War for Independence, 1775-1783.* Stroud, U.K.: Sutton, 2001.

Blanck, Emily V. "Revolutionizing Slavery: The Legal Culture of Slavery in Revolutionary Massachusetts and South Carolina." Unpublished Ph.D. diss, Emory University, 2003.

Bleyer, Bill. "Whaleboat Soldiers Launch America's First Amphibious Assault," *Naval History* 14 (August 2000): 56–59.

Blinka, Daniel D. "Trial by Jury in Revolutionary Virginia: Old-style Trials in the New Republic." Unpublished Ph. D. diss., University of Wisconsin, Madison, 2001.

Blosser, Jacob M. "The Changing Face of America: Historical Conceptions of American Identity, 1778–1808." Unpublished master's thesis, James Madison University, 2001.

Blumrosen, Alfred W., and Ruth G. Blumrosen. *Slave Nation: How Slavery United the Colonies and Sparked the American Revolution.* Napierville, Ill.: Sourcebooks, 2005.

Bly, Antonio. "American Plebian: Ordinary People in the Age of the American Revolution," *Eighteenth-Century Studies* 35, no. 2 (2002): 326–332.

Bolton, Linda. *Facing Each Other: Ethical Disruption and the American Mind.* Baton Rouge: Louisiana State University Press, 2004.

Bonomi, Patricia U. *Under the Cope of Heaven: Religion, Society, and Politics in Colonial America.* New York: Oxford University Press, 2003.

Bonwick, Colin. *The American Revolution.* Basingstoke, U.K.: Palgrave Macmillan, 2005.

Bookchin, Murray. *The Third Revolution. Popular Movements in the Revolutionary Era.* New York: Continuum, 2005.

Boucher, Lisa D. "Re-reading Captivity Narratives and the Captivity Motif as a Cultural Discourse." Unpublished master's thesis, Cleveland State University, 2003.

Bowling, Kenneth R. *Peter Charles L'Enfant: Vision, Honor, and Male Friendship in the Early American Republic.* Washington, D.C.: Friends of George Washington University Libraries, 2002.

Boyle, Joseph. *"Death Seem'd to Stare": The New Hampshire and Rhode Island Regiments at Valley Forge.* Baltimore: Clearfield, 2005.

Bradley, Michael R. *It Happened in the Revolutionary War.* Guilford, Conn.: Globe Pequot Press, 2003.

Breen, T. H. *Tobacco Culture: The Mentality of the Great Tidewater Planters on the Eve of Revolution.* Princeton, N.J.: Princeton University Press, 2001.

Brooks, Joanna. *American Lazarus: Religion and the Rise of African-American and Native American Literatures.* New York: Oxford University Press, 2003.

Brown, Richard D. *Major Problems in the Era of the American Revolution, 1760–1791: Documents and Essays.* Boston: Houghton Mifflin, 2000.

Bruce, Dickson D. *The Origins of African-American Literature, 1680-1865.* Charlottesville: University Press of Virginia, 2001.

Bukovansky, Mlada. *Legitimacy and Power Politics: The American and French Revolutions in International Political Culture.* Princeton, N.J.: Princeton University Press, 2002.

Burg, David F. *The American Revolution: An Eyewitness History.* New York: Facts On File, 2001.

Burkett, Brigitte. *The Journal of Johann Michael Lindenmuth (1737–1812).* Rockport, Maine: Picton Press, 2000.

Burstein, Andrew. *America's Jubilee: How in 1826 a Generation Remembered Fifty Years of Independence.* New York: Knopf, 2001.

Butler, Jon. *Becoming America: The Revolution before 1776.* Cambridge, Mass.: Harvard University Press, 2000.

Caldwell, Lee Ann. "Allegiance in Early Georgia: Revolutionaries, Race, and Class." *Georgia Historical Quarterly* 86, no. 4 (2002): 620–634.

Calhoun, Charles W., ed. *The Human Tradition in America from the Colonial Era through Reconstruction.* Wilmington, Del.: SR Books, 2002.

Carey, Charles W., ed. *The American Revolution.* San Diego, Calif.: Greenhaven Press, 2004.

Carp, Benjamin L. "Nations of American Rebels: Understanding Nationalism in Revolutionary North America and the Civil War South," *Civil War History* 48, no. 1 (2002): 5–33.

_____. "Fire of Liberty: Firefighters, Urban Voluntary Culture, and the Revolutionary Movement," *William and Mary Quarterly* 58, no. 4 (2001): 781–818.

Carr, Jacqueline B. "A Change as 'Remarkable as the Revolution itself': Boston's Demographics, 1780–1800," *New England Quarterly* 73, no. 4 (2000): 583–602.

Cashin, Edward J. *William Bartram and the American Revolution on the Southern Frontier.* Columbia: University of South Carolina Press, 2000.

Chartrand, Rene. *American War for Independence Commanders.* Oxford: Osprey, 2003.

Chew, Richard S. "The Measure of Independence: From the American Revolution to the Market Revolution in the Mid-Atlantic." Unpublished Ph. D. diss., College of William and Mary, 2002.

Chu, Jonathan M. "An Independent Means: The American Revolution and the Rise of a National Economy," *Journal of Interdisciplinary History* 31, no. 1 (2000): 63–71.

Cleary, Patricia. *Elizabeth Murray: A Woman's Pursuit of Independence in Eighteenth-Century America.* Amherst: University of Massachusetts Press, 2000.

Cogliano, Francis D. *Revolutionary America, 1763–1815: A Political History.* New York: Routledge, 2000.

Colley, Linda. *Captives.* New York: Pantheon, 2002.

Conway, Dick. "Roots of Revolution," *American History* 37, no. 5 (2002): 56-58, 60.

Countrymen, Edward. *The American Revolution.* New York: Hill and Wang, 2003.

Crist, Elizabeth B. "'Ye Sons of Harmony': Politics, Masculinity, and the Music of William Billings in Revolutionary America," *William and Mary Quarterly* 60, no. 2 (2003): 333–354.

Crompton, Samuel W. *Pillar to Post: Odysseys in Revolutionary America.* New York: Writer's Showcase, 2000.

Curtis, George M., III, and Harold B. Gill. "A Man Apart: Nicholas Cresswell's American Odyssey, 1774–1777," *Journal of Interdisciplinary History* 96, no. 2 (2000): 169–190.

Dalliston, Robert L. *Hope Restored: The American Revolution and the Founding of New Brunswick.* Fredericton, N.B.: Goose Lane Editions, 203.

Davis, Robert S. "A Georgian and a New Country: Ebenezer Platt's imprisonment in Newgate for Treason in 'The Year of the Hangman,' 1777," *Georgia Historical Quarterly* 84, no. 1 (2000): 106–115.

Dent, Joel M. "A Study of the Pension Programs for Veterans of the American Revolution." Unpublished Ph.D. diss., University of South Carolina, 2001.

Desmarais, Norman. *Battlegrounds of Freedom: A Historical Guide to the Battlefields of the War of American Independence.* Ithaca, N.Y.: Busca, 2005.

Doll, Peter M. *Revolution, Religion, and National Identity: Imperial Anglicanism in British North America, 1745–1795.* Cranbury, N.J.: Fairleigh Dickinson University Press, 2000.

Downes, Paul. *Democracy, Revolution, and Monarchism in Early American Literature.* New York: Cambridge University Press, 2002.

DuFour, Robert L. "'We Shall Know Better': The Impact of Warfare in America on the Development of the British Army." Unpublished master's thesis, California State University, Dominguez Hills, 2002.

Dunkerly, Robert M. *More than Roman Valor: The Revolutionary War Fact Book.* Baltimore: PublishAmerica, 2003.

Dunn, Susan. *Sister Revolutions: French Lightning, American Light.* New York: Faber and Faber, 2000.

Dunn, Walter S. *People of the American Frontier: The Coming of the American Revolution.* Westport, Conn.: Praeger, 2005.

Dussek, Hugh. "Pre-revolutionary History: Socio-Religious Perspectives on the Scots-Irish and Highland Scots in the Backcountry of North Carolina." Unpublished Ph.D. diss., Graduate School of Union Institute, 2002.

Elliott, Emory. *The Cambridge Introduction to Early American Literature.* New York: Cambridge University Press, 2002.

Ellis, Joseph. *Founding Brothers: The Revolutionary Generation.* New York: Knopf, 2000.

Eustace, Nicole E. "'Passion Is the Gale': Emotion and Power on the Eve of the American Revolution." Unpublished Ph.D. diss., University of Pennsylvania, 2001.

Farrelly, Maura J. "Papist Patriots: Catholic Identity and Revolutionary Ideology in Maryland." Unpublished Ph.D. diss., Emory University, 2002.

Fehrenbacher, Don E., and Ward McAfee. *The Slaveholding Republic: An Account of the United States Government's Relations to Slavery.* New York: Oxford University Press, 2001.

Fenn, Elizabeth. *Pox Americana: The Great Smallpox Epidemic of 1775–82.* Stroud, U.K.: Sutton, 2004.

———. "Biological Warfare in Eighteenth-Century North America: Beyond Jeffrey Amherst," *Journal of American History* 86, no. 4 (2000): 1552–1580.

Ferguson, Robert A. *Reading the Early Republic.* Cambridge, Mass.: Harvard University Press, 2004.

Ferris, Robert G., and Richard E. Morris. *The Signers of the Declaration of Independence.* Flagstaff, Ariz.: Interpretive Publications, 2001.

Finkelstein, Lori Beth. "Matrons of the Nation: Old Women, Younger Men, and the Pursuit of Revolutionary War Pensions in Nineteenth-Century America." Unpublished Ph.D. diss., New York University, 2003.

Fishman-Cross, Michelle N. "A Transatlantic War: Staten Island, New York, and Nottingham, England, during the Era of the American Revolution." Unpublished Ph.D. diss., University of Nottingham, 2001.

Fiske, William W. "William Burrows of New Ipswich, New Hampshire," *New England Historical and Genealogical Society* 154 (July 2000): 290–320.

Fitzpatrick, Alan. *Wilderness War on the Ohio: The Untold Story of the Savage Battle for British and Indian Control of the Ohio Country during the American Revolution.* Benwood. W.Va.: Fort Henry Publications, 2003.

Flavel, Julie M. "Government Interception of Letters from America and the Quest for Colonial Opinion in 175," *William and Mary Quarterly* 58, no. 2 (2001): 403–430.

———, and Stephen Conway, eds. *Britain and America Go to War: The Impact of War and Warfare, 1755–1815.* Gainesville: University Press of Florida, 2005.

Foote, Thelma W. *Black and White in Manhattan: The History of Racial Formation in New York City, 1624–1783.* New York: Oxford University Press, 2003.

Foster, A. Kristen. "Moral Visions and Material Ambitions: Republican Culture, the Market Economy, and the Loss of Ideal in Philadelphia, 1776–1836." Unpublished Ph.D. diss., University of Wisconsin, Madison, 2001.

Fox, Francis S. *Sweet Land of Liberty: The Ordeal of the American Revolution in Northampton County, Pennsylvania.* University Park: Pennsylvania State University Press, 2000.

Fredriksen, John C. *America's Military Adversaries: From Colonial Times to the Present.* Santa Barbara, Calif.: ABC-CLIO, 2001.

Frohnen, Bruce. *The American Republic: Primary Sources.* Indianapolis: Liberty Fund, 2002.

Gabarino, William. *Indian Wars along the Upper Ohio: A History of the Indian Wars and Related Events along the Upper Ohio and Its Tributaries*. Midway, Pa.: Midway Pub. Co., 2001.

Geraghty, David A. "Sufferers of the Revolution: The Paper Money Movement in Brunswick County, Virginia." Unpublished master's thesis, University of Richmond, 2003.

Giles, Paul. *Transatlantic Insurrections: British Culture and the Formation of American Literature, 1730–1860*. Philadelphia: University of Pennsylvania Press, 2001.

Gitlin, Jay L. "Negotiating the Course of Empire: The French Bourgeois Frontier and the Emergence of Mid-America, 1763–1863." Unpublished Ph.D. diss., Yale University, 2002.

Godfrey, W. G. "'The Peoples in Between': Phips, Eddy, and Acadie/Nova Scotia," *Acadiensis* 29, no. 2 (2000): 147–155.

Goloboy, Jennifer L. "'Success to Trade': Charleston's Merchants in the Revolutionary Era." Unpublished Ph.D. diss., Harvard University, 2003.

Gould, Dudley C. *Times of Brother Jonathan: What He Ate, Drank, Wore, Believed In & Used for Medicine during the War for Independence*. Middletown, Conn.: Southfarm Press, 2001.

Gould, Eliga H., and Peter S. Onuf, eds. *Empire and Nation: The American Revolution in the Atlantic World*. Baltimore: Johns Hopkins University, 2005.

Grabb, Edward, James Curtis, and Douglas Baer. "Defining Moments and Recurring Myths: Comparing Canadians and Americans after the American Revolution," *Canadian Review of Sociology and Anthropology* 37, no. 4 (2000): 373–419.

Gravil, Richard. *Romantic Dialogues: Anglo-American Continuities, 1776–1862*. New York: St. Martin's, 2000.

Greene, Jack P. "The American Revolution," *American Historical Review* 105, no. 1 (2000): 93–102.

_____, and J. R. Pole, eds. *A Companion to the American Revolution*. Cambridge, Mass.: Blackwell, 2000.

Grenier, John. *The First Way of War: American Warmaking on the Frontier, 1607–1814*. New York: Cambridge University Press, 2005.

Guenther, Karen. "A Crisis of Allegiance: Berks County Pennsylvania Quakers and the War for Independence," *Quaker History* 90, no. 2 (2001): 15–34.

Hack, Timothy. "Shaping a Revolution: The County Committees of Safety in Virginia, 1774–1776," Unpublished master's thesis, James Madison University, 2002.

Haller, Charlotte A. "Taking Liberties: Households, Race, and Black Freedom in Revolutionary North Carolina." Unpublished Ph.D. diss., University of Wisconsin, Madison, 2000.

Hamilton, Phillip. *The Making and Unmaking of a Revolutionary Family: The Tuckers of Virginia, 1752–1830*. Charlottesville: University of Virginia Press, 2003.

Harper, David B. "Ambitious Marylander: Caleb Jones and the American Revolution." Unpublished master's thesis, Utah State University, 2001.

Harris, Christopher. *Public Lives, Private Virtues: Images of American Revolutionary War Heroes, 1782–1832*. New York: Garland, 2000.

Harris, Sharon M., ed. *Women's Early American Historical Narratives*. New York: Penguin, 2003.

Harvey, Robert. *A Few Bloody Noses: The Realities and Mythologies of the American Revolution*. Woodstock, N.Y.: Overlook Press, 2002.

Haulman, Catherine A. "The Empire's New Clothes: The Politics of Fashion in Eighteenth-Century British North America." Unpublished Ph.D. diss., Cornell University, 2002.

Haven, Kendall F. *Voices of the American Revolution: Stories of Men, Women, and Children Who Forged Our Nation*. Englewood, Colo.: Libraries Unlimited, 2000.

Heideking, Jurgen. "The Pattern of American Modernity from the Revolution to the Civil War," *Daedalus* 129, no. 1 (2000): 219–247.

_____, and James A. Henrietta. *Republicanism and Liberalism in America and the German States, 1750–1850*. Washington, D.C.: German Historical Institute, 2001.

Herrick, Arthur R. "In Search of the Fair American," *Nautical Research Journal* 45, no. 3 (2000): 133–140, 213–222; 46, no. 1 (2001): 3–11.

Hester, Tom, and Len Melisurgo. *Center of the Storm: New Jersey and the American Revolution*. Newark, N.J.: Star-Ledger, 2001.

Higginbotham, Don. *Revolution in America: Considerations and Comparisons*. Charlottesville: University of Virginia Press, 2005.

Hoeveler, J. David. *Creating the American Mind: Intellect and Politics in the Colonial Colleges*. Lanham, Md.: Rowman & Littlefield, 2002.

Hough, Granville W., and N. C. Hough. *Spanish, French, Dutch, and American Patriots of the West Indies during the American Revolution*. Midway, Calif.: SHHAR Press, 2001.

Howe, John R. *Language and Political Meaning in Revolutionary America*. Amherst: University of Massachusetts Press, 2004.

Hume, Brad. "The Naturalization of Humanity in America, 1776–1861." Unpublished Ph.D. diss., Indiana University, 2000.

Humphrey, Carol S. *The Revolutionary Era: Primary Documents on Events from 1776 to 1800.* Westport, Conn.: Greenwood Press, 2003.

Hunter, Brooke. "Rage for Grain: Flour Milling in the Mid-Atlantic, 1750–1815." Unpublished Ph.D. diss., University of Delaware, 2002.

Hunter, Phyllis W. *Purchasing Identity in the Atlantic World: Massachusetts Merchants, 1670–1780.* Ithaca, N.Y.: Cornell University Press, 2001.

Hurd, Margaret J. "A Study of the Causes of the American Revolution and Their Origins." Unpublished Ph.D. diss., California State University, Dominguez Hills, 2002.

Irvin, Benjamin H. "The Streets of Philadelphia: Crowds, Congress, and the Political Culture of Revolution, 1774–1783," *Pennsylvania Magazine of History and Biography* 129, no. 1 (2005): 7–44.

———. "Tar, Feathers, and the Enemies of American Liberties, 1768–1776," *New England Historical Quarterly* 76, no. 2 (2003): 197–238.

Isaac, Rhys. *Landon Carter's Uneasy Kingdom: Rebellion and Revolution of a Virginia Plantation.* New York: Oxford University Press, 2004.

Jaffee, David. "The Ebenezers Devotion: Pre- and Post-Revolutionary Consumption in Rural Connecticut," *New England Historical Quarterly* 76, no. 2 (2003): 239–264.

Jennings, Francis. *The Creation of America: Through Revolution to Empire.* New York: Cambridge University Press, 2000.

Johnsen, Heidi Linn. "'Conveyed through This Corrupted Channel': A Transatlantic Study of Five Revolutionary Women Writers." Unpublished Ph.D. diss., State University of New York, Stony Brook, 2000.

Johnson, Ken D. *The Bloodied Mohawk: The American Revolution in the Words of Fort Plank's Defenders and Other Mohawk Valley Partisans.* Rockport, Maine: Picton Press, 2000.

Kafer, Peter. *Charles Brockden Brown's Revolution and the Birth of American Gothic.* Philadelphia: University of Pennsylvania Press, 2004.

Kallen, Stuart A. *The Age of Revolution.* San Diego, Calif: Greenhaven Press, 2002.

Kamrath, Mark, and Sharon M. Harris. *Periodical Literature in Eighteenth-century America.* Knoxville: University of Tennessee Press, 2005.

Keithly, David. "Poor, Nasty, and Brutish: Guerrilla Operations in America's First Civil War," *Civil Wars* 4, no. 3 (2001): 35–69.

Kelly, C. Brian. *Best Little Stories of the American Revolution.* Nashville, Tenn.: Cumberland House, 2001.

Kennedy, Billy. *The Making of America: How the Scots-Irish Shaped a Nation.* Belfast: Causeway Press, 2001.

Kierner, Cynthia A. *Revolutionary America, 1750–1815: Sources and Interpretation.* Upper Saddle River, N.J.: Prentice Hall, 2003.

Knott, Sarah. "Sensibility and the American War for Independence," *American Historical Review* 109, no. 1 (2004): 19–40.

Kormkowski, Charles A. *Recreating the American Republic: Rules of Apportionment, Constitutional Change, and American Political Development, 1700–1870.* New York: Cambridge University Press, 2002.

Kretchnik, Walter E. "Peering through the Mist: Doctrine as a Guide for United States Army Operations, 1775–2000." Unpublished Ph.D. diss., University of Kansas, 2001.

Krug, Andrew. "'Such a Banditti You Never See Collected!' Frederick Town and the American Revolution," *Maryland Historical Magazine* 95, no. 1 (2000): 4–28.

Kulikoff, Allan. "Revolutionary Violence and the Origins of American Democracy," *Journal of the Historical Society* 2, no. 2 (2002): 229–260.

Lambert, Frank. "'Father against Son, Son against Father': The Habershams of Georgia and the American Revolution," *Georgia Historical Quarterly* 84, no. 1 (2000): 1–28.

———. *The Founding Fathers and the Place of Religion in America.* Princeton, N.J.: Princeton University Press, 2003.

Langston, Scott M. "Negotiating the Boundaries of Power: Governor Thomas Burke as Mediator in Revolutionary North Carolina." Unpublished master's thesis, University of Texas, Arlington, 2000.

Larimer, Natasha A. "Step Forth like Men: Negotiating Manhood and Military Service in Revolutionary Pennsylvania, 1775–1790." Unpublished Ph.D. diss., University of Wisconsin, Madison, 2003.

Lee, Wayne E. *Crowds and Soldiers in Revolutionary North Carolina: The Culture of Violence in Riot and War.* Gainesville: University Press of Florida, 2001.

Lenman, Bruce. *Britain's Colonial Wars, 1688–1783.* New York: Longman, 2001.

Levy, Andrew. *The First Emancipator: The Radical Life of Robert Carter III, America's Forgotten Revolutionary*. New York: Random House, 2005.

Lips, Walter. "Hans Heinrich Felder, Jr., Captain in South Carolina's Revolutionary Army, 1778." *Swiss American Historical Society Review* 37, no. 1 (2001): 28–34.

Locante, Joe, and Edwin J. Feulner. *Minister to Freedom: The Legacy of John Witherspoon*. Washington, D.C.: The Heritage Foundation, 2001.

Lohrenz, Otto. "Parson and Vagrant: The Life and Career of Lewis Gwilliam of Revolutionary Pittsylvania, Virginia," *Lamar Journal of the Humanities* 27, no. 2 (2002): 43–57.

Lowance, Mason I. *A House Divided: The Antebellum Slavery Debates in America, 1776–1865*. Princeton, N.J.: Princeton University Press, 2003.

Lucier, Armand F. *Newspaper Datelines of the American Revolution*. Bowie, Md.: Heritage Books, 2001.

Luddington, James N. "One Nation under God: The Influence of Christianity on the American Founding." Unpublished master's thesis, Claremont Graduate University, 2003.

Lurie, Maxine N. "Envisioning a Republic: New Jersey's 1776 Constitution and Oath of Office," *New Jersey History* 119, nos. 3–4 (2001): 2–21.

Maglieri, Cristine E. "The Language of the Clergy: Religious and Political Discourse in Revolutionary America, 1754–1783." Unpublished master's thesis, College of William and Mary, 2000.

Maltz, Leora. *The Founding of America*. San Diego, Calif.: Greenhaven Press, 2002.

Mapp, Alf J. *The Faith of Our Fathers: What America's Founders Really Believed*. Lanham, Md.: Rowman and Littlefield, 2003.

Marlowe, Stephen M. "Colonel William Billy Hill: The Patriot Iron Master Who Turned the Tide." Unpublished master's thesis, Winthrop University, 2002.

Marston, Daniel. *The American Revolution, 1774–1783*. New York: Routledge, 2003.

Mays, Terry M. *Historical Dictionary of Revolutionary America*. Lanham, Md.: Scarecrow Press, 2005.

McCue, Michael W. "The Spy Who Wasn't There," *American History* 36, no. 4 (2001): 56–58, 60, 62–65.

McDonnell, Michael. "National Identity and the American War for Independence Reconsidered," *Australasian Journal of American Studies* 20, no. 1 (2001): 3–17.

———, and Woody Holton. "Patriot vs. Patriot: Social Conflict in Virginia and the Origins of the American Revolution," *Journal of American Studies* 34, no. 2 (2000): 231–256,

McDougall, Walter A. *Freedom Just around the Corner: A New American History, 1585–1828*. New York: HarperCollins, 2004.

McGill, Kathy O. "'A Remote People': British National Identity and America in the Eighteenth Century." Unpublished Ph.D. diss., George Mason University, 2002.

Melton, Buckner F. *The Quotable Founding Fathers: A Treasury of 2,500 Wise and Witty Quotations from the Men and Women Who Created America*. Washington, D.C.: Brassey's, 2004.

Merrill, Herbert L. "The Last Puritan: The Loyalism and Neutrality of Ebenezer Parkman, 1703–1782." Unpublished master's thesis, Gordon-Conwell Theological Seminary, 2002.

Messer, Peter C. "From a Revolutionary History to a History of Revolution: David Ramsay and the American Revolution," *Journal of the Early Republic* 22, no. 2 (2002): 205–234.

———. *Stories of Independence: Identity, Ideology, and History in Eighteenth-Century America*. DeKalb: Northern Illinois University Press, 2005.

Miller, Kerby A., ed. *Irish Immigrants in the Land of Canaan: Letters and Memoirs from Colonial and Revolutionary America, 1675–1815*. New York: Oxford University Press, 2003.

Millward, Jessica. "'A Choice Parcel of Country Born': African-Americans and the Transition to Freedom in Maryland, 1770–1840." Unpublished Ph.D. diss., University of California, Los Angeles, 2003.

Milsop, John. *Continental Infantry of the American War for Independence*. Oxford: Osprey, 2004.

Moody, John W. "British Prisoners of War in the American Revolution." Unpublished master's thesis, State University of Western Georgia, 2002.

Moore, Lucinda. "Capturing America's Fight for Freedom," *Smithsonian* 31, no. 4 (2000): 44–48, 50, 52–53.

Moore, Rogan H. *The Bloodstained Field: A History of the Sugarloaf Massacre, September 11, 1780*. Bowie, Md.: Heritage Books, 2000.

Morgan, Edmund S. *The Genuine Article: A Historian Looks at Early America*. New York: W. W. Norton, 2004.

Morley, Vincent. *Irish Opinion and the American Revolution, 1760–1783*. New York: Cambridge University Press, 2002.

Morris, Richard J. "Redefining the Economic Elite in Salem, Massachusetts, 1759–99: A Tale of Evolution,

Not Revolution," *New England Quarterly* 73, no. 4 (2000): 603–624.

Morrison, Michael A., and James B. Stewart, eds. *Race and the Early Republic: Racial Consciousness and Nation-Building in the Early Republic.* Lanham, Md.: Rowman & Littlefield, 2002.

Morrissey, Brendan. *The American Revolution: The Global Struggle for National Independence.* San Diego: Thunder Bay Press, 2001.

Morrison, Jeffrey H. *John Witherspoon and the Founding of the American Republic.* Notre Dame, Ind.: University of Notre Dame Press, 2005.

Morton, Joseph C. *The American Revolution.* Westport, Conn.: Greenwood Press, 2003.

Mulford, Carla, ed. *Early American Writings.* New York: Oxford University Press, 2002.

Murray, Aaron R., ed. *American Revolution Battles and Leaders.* New York: DK Pub., 2004.

Nash, Gary B. *First City: Philadelphia and the Forging of Historical Memory.* Philadelphia: University of Pennsylvania Press, 2002.

———. *The Forgotten Fifth: African Americans in the Age of Revolution.* Cambridge, Mass.: Harvard University Press, 2006.

———. *Landmarks of the American Revolution.* New York: Oxford University Press, 2003.

———. *The Unknown American Revolution: The Unruly Birth of Democracy and the Struggle to Create America.* New York: Viking, 2005.

Noll, Mark A. *Christians in the American Revolution.* Vancouver, B.C.: Regent College Pub., 2005.

O'Brien, Greg. " 'We Are Behind You': The Choctaw Occupation of Natchez in 1778," *Journal of Mississippi History* 64, no. 2 (2002): 107–124.

———. *Choctaws in a Revolutionary Age, 1750–1830.* Lincoln: University of Nebraska Press, 2002.

O'Connor, Jeff. *Thunder in the Valley: The Story of the Schoharie Valley Loyalist Uprising That Led to the First Cavalry Charge of the United States Army at the Battle of the Flockey, August 13, 1777.* Schoharie, N.Y.: Schoharie County Historical Society, 2002.

O'Rourke, Kevin H. *The Worldwide Economic Impact of the Revolutionary and Napoleonic Wars.* Cambridge, Mass.: National Bureau of Economic Research, 2005.

O'Shaughnessy, Andrew J. *An Empire Divided: The American Revolution and the British Caribbean.* Philadelphia: University of Pennsylvania Press, 2000.

Outwin, Charles P. M. "The 'Pointer Draft' of Falmouth in October 1775," *Maine History* 39, no. 2 (2000): 133–136.

Pauly, Philip J. "Fighting the Hessian Fly: American and British Responses to Insect Invasion, 1776–1789," *Environmental History* 7, no. 3 (2002): 485–507.

Pearsall, Sarah M. "'After all these Revolutions': Epistolary Identities in an Atlantic World, 1760–1815." Unpublished Ph.D. diss., Harvard University, 2001.

Pearson, Matthew. "The Local Origins of Maine Antifederalism: Revolutionary Liberty and Political Change in New Gloucester, Maine, 1774–1788." Unpublished master's thesis, University of Maine, 2000.

Pierce, Lee N. "Fulcrum of Revolution: Continental Army Composition, Evolution, and Performance; Brandywine to Monmouth." Unpublished master's thesis, Eastern Washington University, 2002.

Polzonetti, Pierpaolo. "Opera Buffs and the American Revolution." Unpublished Ph.D. diss., Cornell University, 2003.

Purcell, Sarah J. *Sealed with Blood: War, Sacrifice, and Memory in Revolutionary America.* Philadelphia: University of Pennsylvania Press, 2002.

Railton, Arthur R. "The Story of Martha's Vineyard: How We Got to Where We Are," *Dukes County Intelligencer* 44, no. 2 (2002): 78–106.

Ranlet, Philip. "In the Hands of the British: The Treatment of American POWs during the War of Independence." *Historian* 62, no. 4 (2000): 731–757.

———. "The British, Their Virginian Prisoners, and Prison Ships of the American Revolution," *American Neptune* 60, no. 3 (2000): 253–262.

Raphael, Ray. *A People's History of the American Revolution: How Common People Shaped the Fight for Independence.* New York: New Press, 2001.

Reid, Stuart. *Soldiers of the Revolutionary War.* Oxford: Osprey, 2002.

Resch, John. *Suffering Soldiers: Revolutionary War Veterans, Moral Sentiment, and Political Culture in the Early Republic.* Amherst: University of Massachusetts Press, 2000.

Richardson, Peter J. "'A Clear and Steady Channel': Isaac Backus and the Limits of Liberty," *Journal of Church and State* 43, no. 3 (2001): 447–482.

Risjord, Norman K. *Jefferson's America, 1760–1815.* Lanham, Md.: Rowman & Littlefield, 2001.

Robarge, David. *A Chief Justice's Progress: John Marshall from Revolutionary Virginia to the Supreme Court.* Westport, Conn.: Greenwood Press, 2000.

Rodenbough, Charles D. *Governor Alexander Martin: Biography of a North Carolina Revolutionary War Statesman.* Jefferson, N.C.: McFarland, 2004.

Russell, David L. *The American Revolution in the Southern Colonies.* Jefferson, N.C.: McFarland, 2000.

Sadosky, Leonard J. "Revolutionary Negotiations: A History of American Diplomacy with Europe and Native America in the Age of Jefferson." Unpublished Ph.D. diss., University of Virginia, 2003.

Sanger, Chesley W. "The Impact of the American Revolutionary War on Scottish Northern Whaling: The Dunbar Factor," *Northern Scotland* 20 (2000): 71–86.

Saxton, Thomas R. "'In Reduced Circumstances': Aging and Impoverished Veterans in the Young Republic." Unpublished master's thesis, Lehigh University, 2001.

Schama, Simon. *Britain, the Slaves, and the American Revolution.* London: BBC, 2005.

Schauffler, Robert A., ed. *Independence Day: Its Celebration, Spirit, and Significance as Related in Prose and Verse.* Detroit: Omnigraphics, 2000.

Schloesser, Pauline E. *The Fair Sex: White Women and Racial Patriarchy in the Early American Republic.* New York: New York University Press, 2002.

Schmidt, Klaus H., and Fritz Fleischmann. *Early America Re-explored: New Readings in Colonial, Early National, and Antebellum Culture.* New York: P. Lang, 2000.

Schofield, Norman. "Quandaries of War and of Union in North America: 1763 to 1861," *Politics & Society* 30, no. 1 (2002): 5–49.

Scofield, Telitha. "The American Cause: The Role of Isolation in the Move Toward Independence." Unpublished master's thesis, California State University, Dominguez Hills, 2001.

Scoggins, Michael C. *The Day It Rained Militia: Huck's Defeat of the Revolution in the South Carolina Backcountry, May–July, 1780.* Charleston, S.C.: History Press, 2005.

Scott, James W. "Francis Hopkinson and Philip Freneau: Political Poets of the American Revolution." Unpublished master's thesis, Southwest Texas State University, 2000.

Scott, Jane. *A Gentleman as Well as a Whig: Caesar Rodney and the American Revolution.* Newark: University of Delaware Press, 2000.

Scott, John T. "On God's Side: The Problem of Submission in American Revolutionary Rhetoric," *Fides et Historia* 34, no. 1 (2002): 111–122.

Shalev, Eran. "Ancient Masks, American Fathers: Classical Pseudonyms during the American Revolution and Early Republic," *Journal of the Early Republic* 23, no. 2 (2003): 51–173.

Shenstone, Susan B. *So Obstinately Loyal: James Moody, 1744–1809.* Montreal: McGill-Queen's University Press, 2000.

Shepherd, Elizabeth. "'The Devil's Own Imponderables': Two Smithtown Men in the American Revolution," *Long Island Historical Journal* 14, nos. 1–2 (2001–2002): 102–118.

Smith, John H. "'Sober Dissent' and 'Spirited Conduct': The Sandemanians and the American Revolution," *Historical Journal of Massachusetts* 28, no. 2 (2000): 142–1,966.

Smith, Robert. *Keeping the Republic: Ideology and Early American Diplomacy.* DeKalb: Northern Illinois University Press, 2004.

Sobel, Mechal. *Teach Me Dreams: The Search for Self in the Revolutionary Era.* Princeton, N.J.: Princeton University Press, 2000.

Stacy, Kim R. "Crime and Punishment in the 84th Regiment of Foot," *Journal of the American Society for Army Historical Research* 79, no. 318 (2001): 108–118.

Starr, Rebecca, ed. *Articulating America: Fashioning a National Political Culture in Early America: Essays in Honor of J. R. Pole.* Madison, Wis.: Madison House Publishers, 2000.

Stewart, Cory J. "'You Know I Am a Great Politician': Elizabeth Maxwell Steele and the American Revolution in the South: A Thesis." Unpublished master's thesis, Appalachian State University, 2003.

Stockdale, Eric. *T'is Treason, My Good Man!: Four Revolutionary Presidents and a Picadilly Bookshop.* New Castle, Del.: Oak Knoll Press, 2005.

Stophlet, Carl. "A Comparison and Contrast of the Roles of Religious Leaders of the American Revolutionary War and the Civil War." Unpublished master's thesis, California State University, Dominguez Hills, 2002.

Sword, Kirsten D. "Wayward Wives, Runaway Slaves, and the Limits of Patriarchal Authority in Early America." Unpublished Ph.D. diss., Harvard University, 2002.

Teipe, Emily J. *America's First Veterans and the Revolutionary War Pensions.* Lewiston, N.Y.: Edwin Mellen Press, 2002.

Thompson, Bruce E. R., ed. *The Revolutionary Period, 1750–1783.* San Diego: Greenhaven Press, 2003.

Thompson, John M. *The Revolutionary War.* Washington, D.C.: National Geographic Society, 2004.

Thonhoff, Robert H. *The Texas Connection: With the American Revolution.* Austin, Tex.: Eakin Press, 2000.

Thorpe, Scott. *Revolutionary Strategies of the Founding Fathers: Leadership Lessons from America's Most Successful Patriots.* Naperville, Ill.: Sourcebooks, 2003.

Traister, Bryce. "Criminal Correspondence: Loyalism, Espionage, and Crevecoeur," *Early American Literature* 37, no. 3 (2002): 469–496.

Trees, Andrew. *The Founding Fathers and the Politics of Character*. Princeton, N.J.: Princeton University Press, 2004.

Vaught, Rebecca A. *They Also Served: The Women of Southwestern Virginia during the American Revolution*. Milton, Fla.: Cantadora Press, 2002.

Verhoeven, W. M., ed. *Revolutionary Histories: Transatlantic Cultural Nationalism, 1775–1815*. New York: Palgrave, 2002.

Vollstadt, Elizabeth W. *Understanding Johnny Tremain*. San Diego, Calif.: Lucent Books, 2001.

Volo, James, and Dorothy. *Daily Life during the American Revolution*. Westport, Conn.: Greenwood Press, 2003.

Wahrman, Dror. "The English Problem of Identity in the American Revolution," *American Historical Review* 106 (October 2001): 1236–1262.

Walling, Richard S. "Patriot's Blood: The Indian Company of 1778 and Its Destruction in the Bronx," *Journal of America's Military Past* 27, no. 3 (2001): 15–26.

Walsh, Martin W. "A War Council for the Drawing Room: Arent Schuyler De Peyster's 'Speech to the Western Indians,'" *Michigan Historical Review* 28, no. 1 (2002): 90–106.

Ward, Harry M. *Between the Lines: Banditti of the American Revolution*. Westport, Conn.: Prager, 2002.

Warner, Jessica. *John the Painter: Terrorist of the American Revolution*. London: Profile Books, 2005.

Wasserstrom, Jeffrey N., Lynn Hunt, and Marilyn Young, eds. *Human Rights and Revolutions*. Lanham, Md.: Rowman and Littlefield, 2000.

Watts, Edward, and David Rachels, eds. *The First West: Writing from the American Frontier, 1776–1860*. New York: Oxford University Press, 2002.

Welch, John W., and Stephen Fleming. *Lectures on Religion and the Founding of the American Republic*. Provo, Utah: Brigham Young University, 2003.

Whisker, James B. *Productions of Military Arms in the Commonwealth of Virginia*. Lewiston, N.Y.: Mellen Press, 2004.

Whitehead, Ruth. *The Black Loyalists of Nova Scotia: Tracing the History of the Tracadie Loyalists, 1776–1787*. Halifax: Nova Scotia Museum, 2001.

Williams, Ian R. *Rum: A Social and Sociable History of the Real Spirit of 1776*. New York: Nation Books, 2005.

Williston, George C. "Desperation on the Western Pennsylvania Frontier: a 1781 Petition to Congress for More Effective Defense," *Pennsylvania History* 67, no. 2 (2000): 298–312.

Wood, Gordon S. *The American Revolution: A History*. New York: Modern Library, 2003.

Wood, Timothy L. "'That They May Be Free Indeed': Liberty in the Early Methodist Thought of John Wesley and Francis Asbury," *Methodist History* 38, no. 4 (2000): 231–241.

Wright, Conrad E. *Revolutionary Generation: Harvard Men and the Consequences of Independence*. Amherst: University of Massachusetts Press, 2005.

Wright, Mike. *What They Didn't Teach You about the American Revolution*. Novato, Calif.: Greenhill, 2001.

Yokota, Kariann A. "Post-colonial America: Transatlantic Networks of Exchange in the Early National Period." Unpublished Ph.D. diss., University of California, Los Angeles, 2002.

York, Neil L. *Turning the World Upside Down: The War of American Independence and the Problem of Empire*. Westport, Conn.: Praeger, 2003.

Zamoyski, Adam. *Holy Madness: Romantics, Patriots, and Revolutionaries, 1776–1871*. New York: Viking, 2000.

INDEX

Italic page numbers indicate illustrations; page number followed by *c* denote entries in the chronology.

A

Abercrombie, Robert 221*c*
Adams, Abigail **241–242**
Adams, John **242–243**
    Abigail Adams 241, 242
    Boston Massacre 11*c*, 242, 279
    Continental navy 47*c*, 537
    Declaration of Independence 65*c*, 243
    France 120*c*, 243
    Netherlands treaty 233*c*
    Paris, Treaty of 233*c*
    peace negotiations 168*c*, 227*c*, 233*c*
    preamble resolution 59*c*
    The Rule of Law and the Rule of Men 21*c*
    Samuel Tucker 672
    Mercy Otis Warren 685, 686
Adams, Samuel **244–245**
    Boston Tea Party 15*c*, 280
    circular letter of 7*c*
    committees of correspondence 13*c*, 326
    Continental Congress 18*c*–19*c*
    sedition of 30*c*
    Sons of Liberty 640
    Stamp Act 8*c*
Admiral Duff (ship) 704
Admiralty courts 2*c*–4*c*, 6*c*, 46*c*, 552, 581, 669
African Americans 154*c*, **245–246**. *See also* slaves and slavery
    abolition society 23*c*
    Crispus Attucks 11*c*, 245, 263–264, 279
    and British army 44*c*, 51*c*, 67*c*
    in Continental army 35*c*

    James Lafayette 470–471
    John Laurens and 475
    John Murray and 534
    Savannah, siege of 620
    Phillis Wheatley 54*c*, 696–697
Alamance, Battle of 12*c*, **246–247**, 671
Albany, New York 91*c*
Alexander, William *248*, **248–249**
    arrives in New York state 53*c*
    and Conway letter 117*c*, 118*c*
    Elizabethtown, New Jersey 52*c*
    Long Island, Battle of 71*c*, 248, 491
    Monmouth, Battle of 135*c*
    Paulus Hook, New Jersey 165*c*
    Staten Island 171*c*
Alfred (ship) 432, 457, 617–618
Allen, Ethan 26*c*–28*c*, 40*c*, 41*c*, *41c*, 128*c*, **249–250**, 304, 683
Alliance (ship) 269
American Crisis 84*c*
Andre, John 187*c*–189*c*, **250–252**, 260, 630, 631, 661
Angell, Israel **252**
Annapolis, Maryland 239*c*
Anne, Fort 99*c*, 100*c*
Aranjuez, Convention of 155*c*
Arbuthnot, Marriot 58*c*, 170*c*, 173*c*–175*c*, 203*c*, **252–254**, *253*, 312–313, 520
Armand, Charles (Armand-Charles Tuffin, marquis de la Rouerie) *254*, **254–255**
Armstrong, John 235*c*, **256**
army, Continental **256–258**. *See also* minutemen; *specific headings, e.g.:* Washington, George
    John Adams 242

    African Americans 245–246
    bounty for enlisting in 149*c*
    George Clinton 113*c*, 318–319
    James Clinton 165*c*, 321–322
    Continental Congress 36*c*, 257, 330
    Declaration of Independence 67*c*
    demobilization of 236*c*
    departments for the 54*c*
    disbanding of 239*c*
    draft 125*c*
    foreign officers in 91*c*
    formation of 31*c*
    Horatio Gates. *See* Gates, Horatio
    Nathanael Greene. *See* Greene, Nathanael
    Edward Hand 77*c*, 418–419
    inspector generals for 121*c*
    Charles Lee. *See* Lee, Charles
    Henry Lee. *See* Lee, Henry
    Light Infantry Regiment 106*c*
    Benjamin Lincoln. *See* Lincoln, Benjamin
    Alexander McDougall 10*c*–12*c*, 79*c*, 92*c*, 234*c*, 504–505
    Thomas Mifflin 239*c*, 513–515
    Richard Montgomery. *See* Montgomery, Richard
    Daniel Morgan. *See* Morgan, Daniel
    William Moultrie 60*c*–61*c*, 64*c*, 150*c*, 156*c*, 311, 312, 527–528, 558
    Timothy Murphy 370, 530–531
    Newburgh Conspiracy 539
    Lewis Nicola 543
    occupies Boston 56*c*

pay for 127*c*, 131*c*, 234*c*, 505, 527, 689
Timothy Pickering 569
and power of George Washington 150*c*
Kazimierz Pulaski 128*c*, 144*c*, 169*c*, 529, 583–584
Joseph Reed 599
reorganization of 44*c*, 132*c*
Benjamin Rush 23*c*, 609–610
Arthur St. Clair 95*c*, 96*c*, 98*c*, 566, 613–614
Deborah Sampson 561, 618–619
Alexander Scammel 219*c*, 621–622
Philip J. Schuyler 36*c*, 39*c*, 51*c*, 96*c*, 100*c*, 622–623
Friedrich von Steuben. *See* Steuben, Friedrich von
John Sullivan. *See* Sullivan, John
Silas Talbot 659, 660
Valley Forge, Pennsylvania 122*c*
William Washington. *See* Washington, William
Anthony Wayne. *See* Wayne, Anthony
David Wooster 58*c*, 93*c*, 709–710
army, Convention 122*c*, 124*c*, 128*c*, 148*c*, 544, 566–567, 601–603
Arnold, Benedict **258–260**, *259*
allegations against 150*c*, 172*c*
John Andre 156*c*, 251
Bemis Heights, Battle of 114*c*, 260
betrayal of West Point 187*c*, 188*c*
John Burgoyne 292, 293
Canadian expedition of 42*c*, 43*c*
Guy Carleton 309
Champlain, Lake 70*c*, 75*c*
Henry Clinton 321
as commander of West Point 184*c*
Connecticut 93*c*, 216*c*–217*c*
Dayton, Fort 104*c*
Simon Fraser 370
Freeman's Farm, Battle of 109*c*, 110*c*
as governor of Philadelphia 132*c*, 134*c*
John Lamb 473
William Ledyard 478, 479
marries Margaret Shippen 154*c*

Allan McLane 510
Richard Montgomery 521
Montreal 60*c*, 62*c*
Petersburgh, Virginia 205*c*
promotion of 51*c*, 94*c*
Quebec 28*c*, 39*c*, 45*c*–47*c*, 49*c*, 56*c*, 63*c*, 249, 589
resignation of 90*c*
Barry St. Leger 616
Margaret Shippen 630, 631
John G. Simcoe 634
Stanwix, Fort 105*c*–106*c*
Benjamin Tallmadge 661
Ticonderoga, Fort 26*c*–28*c*, 77*c*, 258
Valcour Island, Battle of 76*c*, 76*c*, 77*c*
Virginia raids 194*c*–196*c*, 203*c*, 204*c*, 206*c*
David Waterbury 691
Articles of Confederation **260–262**
Continental Congress 119*c*, 260–261
John Dickinson 62*c*, 67*c*, 260–261, 350
Benjamin Franklin 36*c*
Alexander Hamilton 414
John Hanson 420
Richard Henry Lee 485
Gouverneur Morris 524
ratification of 134*c*, 145*c*, 146*c*, 150*c*, 200*c*
Roger Sherman 629, 630
and western land claims 138*c*
Asgill, Charles 230*c*
Ashe, John 153*c*, **262–263**
Attucks, Crispus 11*c*, 245, **263–264**, 279
Augusta, Georgia 187*c*, 204*c*

B

back pay 234*c*, 505, 689
Bahamas 236*c*
Bailey, Anne **265–266**
Baker, John 94*c*, 95*c*, 145*c*
Bancroft, Edward **266**, 347
Barney, Joshua 227*c*, **266–268**, *267*
Barren Hill, Pennsylvania 131*c*, 132*c*
Barrington, Fort 126*c*
Barry, John 143*c*, 208*c*–209*c*, 235*c*, 268, **268–269**
Barton, William **269–271**, *270*

Baum, Friedrich 103*c*–104*c*, **271–272**, 273, 274
Bemis Heights, Battle of 113*c*–114*c*, 115*c*, 260, **272–273**, 293, 478, 576, 723*m*
Bemis Heights, New York 108*c*, 109*c*
Bennington, Battle of 103*c*–104*c*, 105*c*, 271–272, **273–274**, 293, 646, 684
Bermuda 179*c*
Bernard, Francis 4*c*, 8*c*–10*c*, **274–276**
Biddle, Nicholas 125*c*, **276**, **276–277**
Bill of Rights 389, 429, 501
Biron, comte de. *See* Lauzun, Armand-Louis de Gontaut, duc de
Biscay, Bay of 422
Black Horse Tavern 121*c*
Blackstock's Plantation, South Carolina 192*c*
Bloody Act 12*c*
"Bloody Ban." *See* Tarleton, Banastre
Blue Book 130*c*
Blue Licks 231*c*, 392
Blue Savannah, South Carolina 187*c*
Board of War 116*c*, 120*c*, 123*c*, 569
Bonhomme Richard (ship) 167*c*, 363, 457–458, 561, 562
Boone, Daniel 22*c*, 87*c*, 124*c*, 230*c*, 231*c*, *277*, **277–278**
Boonesborough, Battle of 278
Boston, Massachusetts. *See also* Bunker Hill, Battle of
Samuel Adams 244
Francis Bernard 275
Dorchester Heights 53*c*–55*c*, 408, 464, 586, 666, 687
Thomas Gage 375
Samuel Graves 399
Richard Gridley 408–409
John Hancock 417
William Heath 426–427
William Howe 28*c*, 442
Thomas Knowlton 463–464
Henry Knox 464
Ebenezer Learned 477
John Paterson 560
Ploughed Hill 38*c*
William Prescott 577
Molyneux Shuldham 632
siege of 715*m*
William Thompson 667
Artemas Ward 681, 682

Boston Massacre **278–279**
   John Adams 11*c*, 242, 279
   African Americans 245
   Crispus Attucks 263
   John Hancock 417
   Josiah Quincy 591
   Paul Revere 11*c*, 600
   Townshend Duties 669
Boston Port Bill 17*c*
Boston Tea Party 16*c*, 18*c*, **279–280**
   Samuel Adams 15*c*, 280
   Edmund Burke 294
   Coercive Acts 280, 323
   committees of correspondence 326
   George III (king of Great Britain) 280, 384
   Thomas Hutchinson 15*c*, 280, 447
   Paul Revere 600
   Sons of Liberty 15*c*, 280, 640
Boudinot, Elias **281**
Bound Brook, New Jersey 92*c*
Bouquet, Henry 1*c*
boycott (of British goods) 5*c*, 7*c*, 10*c*, 11*c*, 324, 483, 576, 644
Boyd, John 151*c*
Brady, Samuel **282**
Brandywine, Battle of 107*c*–108*c*, **282–283**, 337, 443, 694, 696, 719*m*
Brant, Joseph 161*c*, *284*, **284–285**
   Andrustown, New York 138*c*
   attack on settlement of 144*c*
   John Butler 296
   Walter Butler 298, 299
   Canajoharie, New York 183*c*, 184*c*
   Cherry Valley, New York 145*c*
   Cobbleskill, New York 132*c*
   German Flats (Herkimer, New York) 142*c*
   Great Miami River, Ohio raid 215*c*
   Johnstown, New York 178*c*
   Newtown, New York 165*c*
   Oriskany, Battle of 551
   Enoch Poor 576
   Red Jacket 597
   Schoharie Valley 190*c*
   and Fort Stanwix expedition 102*c*
   John Sullivan 654, 655

Brant, Molly 102*c*, **285–286**, 551
Breed's Hill, Massachusetts 33*c*, 577, 585
Briar Creek, Battle of 262–263
British East India Company 14*c*, 15*c*, 664
Brodhead, Daniel **286–287**
Brooklyn Heights, New York 70*c*, 72*c*, 393–394, 491, 492, 586, 687
Brooks, John 234*c*
Brown, John 38*c*, 40*c*, 41*c*, 46*c*, 109*c*, 111*c*
Brown, Thomas 94*c*–95*c*, 126*c*, 135*c*, 137*c*, 149*c*, 187*c*, 204*c*, **287–288**, 316
Brown, William *237c*
Bryan's Station, Kentucky 230*c*
Buford, Abraham 179*c*, **288–289**
Bull's Ferry, New Jersey 183*c*
Bunker Hill, Battle of 31*c*–33*c*, *32c*, **289–291**, *290*, 715*m*
   Thomas Gage 32*c*, 289, 290, 376
   William Howe 32*c*, 33*c*, 290, 291, 442
   Thomas Knowlton 463
   Robert Pigot 570
   Seth Pomeroy 575
   William Prescott 577
   Israel Putnam 33*c*, 585
   James Reed 598
   John Stark 290–291, 645
   Joseph Warren 33*c*, 685
Burgoyne, John **291–293**, *292*
   Albany, New York 91*c*, 92*c*
   Fort Anne 100*c*
   Friedrich Baum 271
   Bemis Heights, Battle of 109*c*, 113*c*–114*c*, 115*c*, 272–273
   Bennington, Battle of 273, 274, 293
   Guy Carleton 309
   Convention army 122*c*, 124*c*, 128*c*
   Edward, Fort 101*c*
   Simon Fraser 370
   Freeman's Farm, Battle of 109*c*, 110*c*, 371, 372
   William Howe 292, 293, 442, 443
   Loyalists 494
   Jane McCrea 503, 504
   New York campaign of 99*c*, 103*c*
   William Phillips 566, 567
   Quebec 59*c*, 95*c*–96*c*, 292

   Friedrich von Riedesel 602, 603
   Arthur St. Clair 613, 614
   Saratoga, New York 108*c*, 112*c*, 115*c*, 293
   surrender of 116*c*, 123*c*
   Ticonderoga, Fort 97*c*
Burke, Edmund 22*c*, 45*c*–46*c*, **293–295**
Bushnell, David 72*c*, 103*c*, 122*c*, **295–296**
Butler, John **296–297**, 551
Butler, Richard **297–298**
Butler, Walter 136*c*, 144*c*, 145*c*, 165*c*, **298–299**
Butler, Zebulon 136*c*, **299–300**
Byron, John 133*c*, 146*c*, 147*c*, **300–301**

C

Caldwell, William 229*c*, 230*c*
Cambray-Digny, Louis **302**
Camden, Battle of 185*c*–186*c*, **302–304**, 729*m*
   Richard Caswell 310
   Charles Cornwallis 185*c*–186*c*, 303, 337
   Peter Francisco 367
   Horatio Gates 185*c*, 186*c*, 302–303
   Mordecai Gist 393
   Johann de Kalb 185*c*, 186*c*, 461
   John Rutledge 611
   Banastre Tarleton 186*c*
   George Washington 688
Camden, South Carolina 183*c*, 206*c*, 207*c*
Campbell, Archibald 146*c*, 148*c*, 150*c*, 151*c*, **304–305**, *305*
Campbell, Arthur **305–306**
Campbell, William 39*c*–40*c*, 189*c*, 201*c*, **306–308**
Canada. *See also* Carleton, Guy; Quebec
   Ethan Allen 250
   Benedict Arnold 258–259
   John Burgoyne 292
   campaign in (1775-1776) 716*m*
   Continental Congress and 123*c*, 126*c*
   expedition into 123*c*
   Benjamin Franklin 56*c*, 58*c*
   Frederick Haldimand 411–412

Henry Hamilton 415, 416
  invited to side with Americans
    29c, 56c, 58c
  John Jay 29c
  Loyalist exodus to 120c, 494
  Montreal 40c, 41c, 521, 709
  Trois-Rivières 61c–63c, 370, 653,
    667
Canajoharie, New York 183c, 184c
Cape Henry, Battle of 203c
Capes, Battle of the. *See* Virginia
  Capes, Second Battle of the
Cape Verde 204c
Carleton, Guy 308, **308–310**
  Ethan Allen 40c, 41c
  appointed governor-general 6c
  Benedict Arnold 259
  assumption of North American
    command 228c
  John Burgoyne 292
  Champlain, Lake 75c
  Crown Point 80c
  escape of 46c
  evacuates 45c
  Quebec 44c, 47c, 49c, 59c,
    308–309, 589, 590
  Quebec Act 30c, 590
  Ticonderoga, Fort 77c
  Trois-Rivières, Canada 62c
  David Waterbury 691
Carlisle Commission 129c, 133c, 143c,
  146c, 599
Carlos, Fort 236c
Carr's Fort, Georgia 151c
Caswell, Richard 310
Catherine II (czarina of Russia) 173c
cavalry 628–629
Ceylon 228c, 229c, 231c
Chambly, Fort 40c, 43c, 62c, 520, 589
Champlain (Lake and region) 70c,
  75c, 91c, 97c, 602, 603. *See also* Valcour Island, Battle of
Charles III (king of Spain) 62c, 158c,
  641, 677
Charleston, attack on 64c, 65c,
  311–312, 527–528
Charleston, siege of 170c, 172c–178c,
  312–313
  Henry Clinton 170c, 172c, 173c,
    175c, 177c, 178c, 312, 313, 321
  Charles Cornwallis 337
  Christopher Gadsden 374

James Hogun 433
Isaac Huger 444
Benjamin Lincoln 172c, 173c,
  175c–178c, 312–313, 488
William Moultrie 528
Charles C. Pinckney 571
Kazimierz Pulaski 584
John Rutledge 611
Samuel Tucker 673
George Washington 688
William Washington 690
Abraham Whipple 698
William Woodford 708–709
Charleston, South Carolina 60c, 156c,
  234c, 423–424, 485, 571, 572, 665
Charlotte, North Carolina 188c, 420
Charlottesville, Virginia 209c, 210c
Chastellux, François-Jean, marquis de
  313–314
Cherokee Indians
  Thomas Brown and 287, 288
  Dragging Canoe 68c, 95c, 154c,
    352–353, 624, 625
  Dewitt's Corner, Treaty of 95c
  Long Island, Treaty of 100c
  Return J. Meigs and 512
  Oconostota 95c, 548–549, *549*
  Andrew Pickens and 567, 568
  Griffith Rutherford and 610
  John Sevier and 624, 625
  Evan Shelby and 626
  Nancy Ward 68c, 682–683
  wars of 64c, 67c, 68c–69c, 72c,
    74c, 548
Cherry Valley, New York 144c, 145c,
  299
Chesapeake Bay 203c, 216c, 398
Churchill, Elijah 237c
Clark, George Rogers **314–316**, *315*
  Henry Hamilton and 416
  Kaskaskia 137c, 147c
  map of 1778-1779 campaign
    728m
  Mississippi–Ohio River Valley
    122c, 131c, 132c, 134c
  raid against Shawnee 184c, 185c,
    233c
  Vincennes 138c, 150c, *152c*,
    152c–153c
Clarke, Elijah 67c, 137c, 187c, 192c,
  204c, 288, **316–317**
Cleveland, Benjamin **317–318**

Clinton, Fort 113c, 320, 322
Clinton, George 113c, **318–319**
Clinton, Henry **319–321**, *320*
  John Andre 251
  Marriot Arbuthnot 253, 254
  Benedict Arnold 260
  Battle of Bunker Hill 33c, 290
  John Burgoyne 110c–111c, 292,
    293
  burns Esopus, New York 116c
  Cape Fear, North Carolina 50c,
    52c, 55c
  capture of South Carolina 180c
  Charleston, attack on 311, 312
  Charleston, siege of 170c, 172c,
    173c, 175c, 177c, 178c, 312,
    313, 321
  Clinton, Fort 113c
  George Collier 325
  Charles Cornwallis 320, 321,
    336–338
  evacuates Philadelphia 133c
  Long Island, Battle of 71c, 320,
    491
  Long Island, New York 63c
  Manhattan Island 78c
  Monmouth, Battle of 134c, 135c,
    320, 516, 517
  Newport, Rhode Island 142c
  Peter Parker 558, 559
  resignation of 228c
  Roxbury, Boston 34c
  Stony Point, New York 157c
  George Washington 688
  West Indies 127c
Clinton, James 165c, **321–322**
Closen, Ludwig von **322–323**
Cobleskill, New York 132c
Coercive Acts 17c, 19c–21c, **323–324**
  Boston Tea Party 280, 323
  Edmund Burke 294
  Thomas Gage 375
  George III 17c, 384
  William Pitt 574
  Quartering Act 588
  Quebec Act 590
  Josiah Quincy 591
  Charles Watson-Wentworth 692
Colbert, James 236c
Collier, George 156c, 157c, 164c, 325,
  325–326, 538
Combahee Ferry, South Carolina 231c

Committee of Secret Correspondence to Conduct Foreign Relations 47c, 49c, 93c
committees of correspondence 13c–15c, 280, **326–327,** 483, 641
Common Sense 51c, **327–328,** 330, 554
Concord, Battle of 23c–25c, 25c, 27c, **328–329,** 713m
    Thomas Gage 24c, 328, 376
    minutemen 24c, 25c, 25c, 328, 329, 516
    John Parker 557
    Hugh Percy 563, 564
    John Pitcairn 21c, 24c, 328, 329, 572–573
    Israel Putnam 25c, 584–585
    Paul Revere 328, 600
    Francis Smith 637
    Peleg Wadsworth 680
    Artemas Ward 681
    Joseph Warren 684
Confederation Congress. *See* Congress, Confederation
Confiscation Act 48c
Congress, Confederation 210c, 234c–237c
Congress, Continental **329–331**
    actions of 28c
    Samuel Adams 18c–19c
    approves articles of war 34c
    approves League of Armed Neutrality 189c
    Articles of Confederation 119c, 260–261
    Canada 123c, 126c
    Continental army 36c, 257, 330
    Continental navy 48c, 49c, 330, 537
    convening of 18c–19c, 27c
    Declaration of Independence 65c–66c, 330, 348, 349
    Declaration of Rights and Grievances 20c
    delegates to the 17c
    Forty to One Act 174c
    French alliance 130c, 149c
    Joseph Galloway 377
    Elbridge Gerry 389
    Alexander Hamilton 414–415
    John Hancock 417
    John Hanson 420
    Patrick Henry 428, 429
    and independence 52c, 59c, 64c
    John Jay 146c, 451
    Thomas Jefferson 452, 453
    Henry Laurens 474
    and military waste 160c
    Model Treaty 75c
    Newburgh Conspiracy 538–539
    Olive Branch Petition 34c–35c, 38c, 47c, 330
    paper currency 33c, 37c, 90c
    and privateering 46c, 56c, 79c
    requests for additional men and money 172c–173c
    William Smallwood 636
    Friedrich von Steuben 152c
    Ticonderoga, Fort 29c
Connecticut
    Benedict Arnold 93c, 216c–217c
    Danbury 93c, 473, 495, 633, 671, 710
    Hartford strategy conference 187c
    Jedediah Huntington 445
    New London 216c–217c
    Samuel H. Parsons 559–560
    Israel Putnam 584–585
    Ridgefield 495, 633, 710
    Elisha Sheldon 628–629
    Roger Sherman 629–630
    Gold S. Silliman 632–633
    Joseph Spencer 642–643
    Stonington 38c, 363
    William Tryon and 93c, 114c, 153c, 159c, 160c, 671–672
Connecticut Farms, New Jersey 180c
Constellation (ship) 532
Constitution, U.S. 497, 501, 502, 526, 630. *See also* Bill of Rights
Constitution, USS (ship) 542, 660
Constitutional Convention 389, 497, 630, 706
Continental army. *See* army, Continental
Continental Congress. *See* Congress, Continental
Convention army. *See* army, Convention
Conway, Thomas 115c, 117c, 118c, 121c–123c, **331,** 688
Conway Cabal 115c, 122c–124c, 383, 514, 688
Conyngham, Gustavus 99c, *332,* **332–333**
Cooch's Bridge, Delaware 106c
Corbin, Margaret 81c, **333–334**
Cornplanter 136c, 296, **334–335,** *335,* 551, 597
Cornstalk 19c–20c, **335–336,** 486, 534
Cornwallis, Charles **336–338,** *337*
    Black Horse Tavern 121c
    Bound Brook, New Jersey 92c
    Brandywine, Battle of 107c, 108c, 337
    Camden, Battle of 185c–186c, 303, 337
    Cape Fear, North Carolina 50c
    Charleston, attack on 311
    Charleston, siege of 337
    Charlotte, North Carolina 188c
    Henry Clinton 320, 321, 336–338
    Couch's Bridge, Delaware 106c
    Cowan's Ford skirmish 198c
    Cowpens, Battle of 196c, 337–339
    William Richardson Davie 345
    Johann Ewald 360
    Nathanael Greene 196c–199c, 337
    Green Spring, Virginia 212c
    Guilford Courthouse, Battle of 199c, 202c, 203c, 337, 409–410
    Harlem Heights, New York City 77c
    Hillsboro, North Carolina 200c
    King's Mountain, Battle of 189c, 190c, 461–463
    Kip's Bay, New York City 74c
    James Lafayette 470
    marquis de Lafayette 472
    John Laurens 475
    Fort Lee 81c–82c
    Liberty Pole, New Jersey 143c
    Long Island, Battle of 491
    Mercer, Fort 119c
    Hugh Mercer 513
    Monmouth, Battle of 134c, 337, 517
    occupies Philadelphia 111c
    Charles O'Hara 550
    Pell's Point, New York 78c
    Petersburg, Virginia 208c

Princeton, Battle of 87c–89c, 579–580
San Domingo 181c
Short Hills, New Jersey 97c
Somerset Courthouse, New Jersey 96c
South Carolina 178c, 179c, 194c
Thomas Sumter 656
Banastre Tarleton 662, 663
Trenton, Battle of 670
Trenton, New Jersey 83c
George Washington 336, 688, 689
Anthony Wayne 695
Williamsburg, Virginia 211c–212c
Wilmington, North Carolina 204c
Yorktown, Virginia 213c, 219c, 221c, 711–712. *See also* Yorktown, siege of
Cornwallis, Fort 209c
Cowan's Ford skirmish 198c
Cowpens, Battle of 196c, 197c, **338–339**, 731m
    Charles Cornwallis 196c, 337–339
    John E. Howard 437–438
    Daniel Morgan 196c, 338, 339, 523, 524
    Andrew Pickens 196c, 568
    Banastre Tarleton 196c, 338, 339, 663
    William Washington 196c, 339, 690
Crawford, William 229c, **339–340**
Creek Indians 506–507, *507*
Crown Point, New York 66c, 80c
Cuddalore, siege of 238c
"Culper Spy Ring" 661
Cumberland, Fort 82c
currency 33c, 37c, 90c, 137c, 340, 341, 526
Currency Act 2c–3c, **340–341**

D

Dale, Richard *342*, **342–343**
Danbury, Connecticut 93c, 473, 495, 633, 671, 710
Darmouth, Lord. *See* Legge, William
Darragh, Lydia 120c, **343–344**, 510
Dartmouth (ship) 15c

Davidson, William Lee **344–345**
Davie, William Richardson 184c, 188c, **345**, 420
Dayton, Elias 52c, 180c, **346**
Deane, Silas **346–348**
    Edward Bancroft 266
    charges against 139c, 149c
    France 54c, 66c, 75c, 85c, 92c, 119c, 124c, 347
    French alliance 124c, 347c, 372
    Arthur Lee 479–480
    recalled from Paris 119c
Declaration of Independence 65c–67c, **348–349**
    John Adams 65c, 243
    committee to explore drafting of 62c
    Continental Congress 65c–66c, 330, 348, 349
    Benjamin Franklin 65c, 368
    George III and 385
    John Hancock 66c, 417
    Hessians 431
    Thomas Jefferson 34c, 63c, 65c, 348, 349, 452
    George Mason 501
    refusal to rescind 73c
    Roger Sherman 629
    signing of 69c, 89c
    James Wilson 706
Declaration of Rights 62c
Declaration of Rights and Grievances 4c, 20c
Declaration on Taking up Arms, A 34c, 35c
Declaratory Act 6c, 692
Delaware 509, 510
Delaware Capes 234c
Delaware Indians 226c
Delaware River 119c, 394
Destouches, Charles-René Sochet, chevalier 203c
Deux-Ponts, Guillaume de 220c–221c, **349–350**, 712
Dickinson, John **350–351**
    Articles of Confederation 62c, 67c, 260–261, 350
    Declaration of Rights and Grievances 4c, 20c
    Joseph Galloway 377
    Letters from a Farmer in Pennsylvania 7c, 8c

Olive Branch Petition 34c–35c, 350
Townshend Duties 669
Dickinson, Philemon 90c, 181c–182c, **351–352**
Dix's Ferry, North Carolina 199c
Dobbs Ferry 78c, 80c
Dolly, Quamino 148c, 304
Dominica 176c, 227c
Donop, Karl von 84c, 117c
Dorchester, Fort 223c, 682
Dorchester, South Carolina 228c
Dorchester Heights 53c–55c, 408, 464, 586, 666, 687
Dragging Canoe 68c, 95c, 154c, **352–353**, 624, 625
Drayton, William Henry 40c, **353–354**
Dudingston, William 12c, 13c, 381–382
Dumas, Mathieu **354–355**
Dunmore, Lord. *See* Murray, John
Duportail, Louis 218c, *355*, **355–356**

E

economy 527
Eddy, Jonathan 80c
Edward, Fort 101c, 103c
Elbert, Samuel 150c, 153c, **357–358**
Eliott, Augustus 232c
English Channel 97c, 332, 700, 701
Erskine, William 93c
espionage. *See* spying (spies)
Estaing, Charles-Hector-Théodat, comte d' 131c, 137c, 138c, 140c, 141c, 145c, 158c, 159c, **358–360**, *359*
    John Byron and 301
    departs for Boston 141c
    French alliance 145c, 358, 372
    Grenada 160c
    Richard Howe 137c, 358, 440
    Newport, Rhode Island 138c–140c, 358
    Robert Pigot 570
    Augustin Prevost 578, 579
    sails for Brest, France 128c–129c
    Savannah, siege of 167c–169c, 619–620
    Pierre-André de Suffren Saint-Tropez 651–652
    George Washington 138c, 145c
    West Indies 145c, 147c, 358, 359

Eutaw Springs, Battle of 217c, 499, 650, 651, 656, 691, 732m
Ewald, Johann 211c, **360–361**

F

Falcon (ship) 26c
Fanning, David **362–363**
Fanning, Nathaniel **363–364**
Federalist Papers, The 415, 497
Ferguson, Patrick 143c, 144c, 364, **364–365**
    William Campbell 307
    Charleston, siege of 175c, 176c
    Benjamin Cleveland 317
    King's Mountain, Battle of 189c, 365, 461–462
    Joseph McDowell 506
    Isaac Shelby 627, 628
Fishdam Ford, South Carolina 191c–192c
Fiske, John **365–366**
flag (American) 47c, 50c, 96c, 98c, 124c, 503, 608–609
Forty, Fort 136c
Forty to One Act 174c
Fox (ship) 511
Fox, Charles James 234c–235c, **366–367**
France
    John Adams 120c, 243
    aid from 58c
    alliance with. *See* French alliance
    Charles Armand 254–255
    Edward Bancroft and 266
    John Barry and 269
    Louis Cambray-Digny 302
    François-Jean, marquis de Chastellux 313–314
    Ludwig von Closen 322–323
    Thomas Conway and 331
    Silas Deane and 54c, 66c, 75c, 85c, 92c, 119c, 124c, 347
    declares war on Great Britain 133c, 139c
    Guillaume de Deux-Ponts 220c–221c, 349–350, 712
    Mathieu Dumas 354–355
    Louis Duportail 218c, 355–356
    emissaries to 75c, 78c–79c, 83c–85c
    Charles-Hector-Théodat, comte d'Estaing. *See* Estaing, Charles-Hector-Théodat, comte d'
    Benjamin Franklin 75c, 78c–79c, 83c–85c, 124c, 127c, 142c, 368–369
    Elbridge Gerry and 389
    François-Joseph-Paul, comte de Grasse. *See* Grasse, François-Joseph-Paul, marquis de Grasetilly, comte de
    John Jay and 451
    Thomas Jefferson and 75c, 453
    John Paul Jones and 118c, 120c, 131c, 150c
    marquis de Lafayette. *See* Lafayette, marquis de
    John Laurens and 475
    Armand-Louis de Gontaut, duc de Lauzun 219c, 476–477
    Arthur Lee and 479–480
    Robert R. Livingston and 490
    Louis XVI 58c, 121c, 127c, 604
    James Monroe and 518
    Louis-Marie, comte de Noailles 221c, 544–545
    Thomas Paine and 555
    Paris, Treaty of 555, 556
    Charles C. Pinckney and 572
    Jean-Baptiste-Donatien de Vimeur, comte de Rochambeau. *See* Rochambeau, Jean-Baptiste-Donatien de Vimeur, comte de
    Seven Years' War 1c
    and Spain 121c, 151c, 154c–155c, 158c, 373, 641, 642
    Pierre André de Suffren de Saint-Tropez 204c, 225c, 228c, 229c, 231c, 238c, 651–652
    Charles Ternant 664–665
    Charles de Vergennes. *See* Vergennes, Charles Gravier, comte de
    Lambert Wickes and 700
Francisco, Peter **367–368**
Franklin, Benjamin **368–369**
    abolition society 23c
    Articles of Confederation 36c
    Canada 56c, 58c
    commits to American cause 26c
    Declaration of Independence 65c, 368
    France 75c, 78c–79c, 83c–85c, 124c, 127c, 142c, 368–369
    French alliance 124c, 127c, 369, 372
    Thomas Hutchinson 14c
    Arthur Lee 479
    new instructions for 144c
    Paris, Treaty of 233c, 369, 555, 556
    peace negotiations 227c, 232c
    postwar negotiations with France 234c
    reaction to secret negotiations 231c
    Stamp Act 3c, 5c
    Friedrich von Steuben 648
Fraser, Simon 96c–98c, 114c, 369, **369–371**, 530–531, 602, 603
Freeman's Farm, Battle of 109c, 110c, 259–260, 293, 370, **371–372**, 723m
French alliance **372–373**
    Continental Congress 130c, 149c
    Continental navy 537
    Silas Deane 124c, 347, 372
    Charles-Hector-Théodat, comte d'Estaing 145c, 358, 372
    Benjamin Franklin and 124c, 127c, 369, 372
    François-Joseph-Paul, comte de Grasse 372
    Arthur Lee and 479–480
    John Montague and 519
    Samuel Nicholson and 541–542
    Frederick North and 124c–126c
    Paris, Treaty of 555, 556
    Augustin Prevost and 579
    Jean-Baptiste-Donatien de Vimeur, comte de Rochambeau 372, 604
    Spain 641
    Charles Vergennes 120c–122c, 124c, 372, 677
    Charles Watson-Wentworth and 692

G

Gadsden, Christopher 177c, **374–375**
Gage, Thomas **375–376**, *376*
    appointed commander in chief 2c
    Bunker Hill, Battle of 32c, 289, 290, 376

Concord, Battle of 24c, 328, 376
as governor of Massachusetts 16c–19c, 21c–24c, 28c, 30c, 375
minutemen 515
Hugh Percy 563
Quartering Act 3c, 5c, 7c, 8c, 375
recall/replacement of 41c, 42c
Galloway, Joseph **377–378**, 493
Gálvez, Bernardo de 164c, 166c–168c, 173c, 174c, 201c, 206c–207c, 378, **378–379**, 642
Gambier, James 142c, **379–380**
"Gamecock." *See* Sumter, Thomas
Ganey, Micajah 187c
Gansevoort, Peter 101c, 102c, 183c, **380–381**, *381*, 615
Gaspée affair 12c–13c, **381–382**, 697
Gates, Horatio 35c, **382–384**, *383*
　Bemis Heights, Battle of 114c
　Bemis Heights, New York 108c
　Camden, Battle of 185c, 186c, 302–303
　Camden, South Carolina 183c
　as commander of northern forces 66c
　Thomas Conway 331
　Conway Cabal 124c
　Freeman's Farm, Battle of 109c, 110c, 371, 372
　Jane McCrea 504
　Newburgh Conspiracy 539
　Saratoga, New York 114c, 115c, 383
　surrender of John Burgoyne 116c
　George Washington 124c, 382–384, 688
　Otho H. Williams 705
George III (king of Great Britain) **384–386**, *385*
　Boston Tea Party 280, 384
　Coercive Acts 17c, 384
　Continental Congress 330
　Leopold von Heister 427
　and independence 133c, 385
　and Massachusetts 21c
　New England Restraining Act 22c–23c
　Frederick North 384, 385, 544–546
　petitions to 10c, 15c, 34c–35c, 47c, 644
　William Pitt 574

Proclamation of 1763 2c, 582
Quebec Act 18c
refusal to end war 223c
Royal Proclamation of Rebellion 38c
Stamp Act 3c
Tea Act 14c
John Wilkes 701
Georgetown, South Carolina 197c
Georgia 187c, 204c, 287–288, 304, 305, 316–317. *See also* Savannah, Georgia; Savannah, siege of
Germain, George 91c, 92c, 130c, **386–387**
Germantown, Battle of 112c, 113c, 337, **387–388**, 407, 443, 536, 647, 724*m*
Germany. *See* Hessians
Gerry, Elbridge **388–390**
Gibraltar 232c–234c, 642, 677
Gillon, Alexander 228c, **390–391**
Girty, Simon 106c, 149c, 215c, 229c–231c, 278, **391–392**
Gist, Mordecai 120c, 143c, 185c, 231c, **392–393**
"give me liberty or give me death" 22c
Glover, John 78c, **393–395**, *394*
Golden Hill, Battle of 10c, **395**, 588, 640, 669
Granby, Fort 199c, 206c, 207c
Grant, James 71c, 87c–88c, 131c, 132c, 147c, **395–397**, *396*
Grasse, François-Joseph-Paul, marquis de Grasetilly, comte de 206c, 214c, 227c, **397–399**, *398*
　arrival at Chesapeake Bay 214c
　arrival at Virginia Capes 215c–216c
　Chesapeake Bay battle 216c
　French alliance 372
　Samuel Hood 434–435
　Jamaica 227c
　Allan McLane 510
　George Rodney 606, 607
　West Indies 224c, 225c
　Yorktown, siege of 218c, 398, 711
Graves, Samuel 40c, 42c, 52c, **399–400**, 711
Graves, Thomas 216c, 218c, **400–402**, *401*
Greene, Christopher 117c, *402*, **402–403**

Greene, Nathanael 33c, **403–405**, *404*
　Charles Cornwallis 196c–199c, 337
　Cowpens, Battle of 338
　William Richardson Davie 345
　Eutaw Springs, Battle of 217c
　Granby, Fort 206c
　Ninety Six, Fort 208c, 210c, 211c
　Germantown, Battle of 112c, 113c
　Guilford Courthouse, Battle of 199c, 201c–203c, 409–410
　Hillsboro, North Carolina 200c, 404
　Hobkirk's Hill 205c
　Isaac Huger 444–445
　Tadeusz Ko_ciuszko 468
　Lee, Fort 82c
　Mercer, Fort 119c
　Monmouth, Battle of 135c
　Charles O'Hara 550
　pursuit of Francis Rawdon 203c–204c
　Francis Rawdon 595, 596
　Rhode Island 141c
　South Carolina 193c, 404–405
　Alexander Stewart 650, 651
　Trenton, Battle of 86c
　Washington, Fort 81c
　George Washington 688
Green Mountain Boys 26c, 27c, 249, 250, 683
Green Spring, Virginia 212c
Grenada 160c, 301
Grenville, George 1c, 3c, 4c, **405–406**, 643, 644
Grenville Acts 405–406
Grey, Charles 111c, 113c, 120c, 142c, 143c, **406–408**, *407*
Gridley, Richard 55c, **408–409**
Griswold, Fort 216c–217c, 478–479
Guadeloupe 227c
Guilford Courthouse, Battle of 199c, 201c–203c, **409–410**, 731*m*
　William Campbell 307
　Charles Cornwallis 199c, 202c, 203c, 337, 409–410
　Peter Francisco 367
　Nathanael Greene 199c, 201c–203c, 409–410
　John E. Howard 438
　Henry Lee 201c, 482

Charles O'Hara 550
George Washington 201*c*, 202*c*, 688
Otho H. Williams 705
Gwynn Island 486, 534

H

Haldimand, Frederick 135*c*, **411–413**, *412*
Hale, Nathan 73*c*, 75*c*, **413–414**
Halifax Resolves 57*c*
Hamilton, Alexander 18*c*, 50*c*, 88*c*, 154*c*, 220*c*, **414–415**, 453, 539
Hamilton, David 229*c*
Hamilton, Henry 147*c*, 152*c*, 152*c*–153*c*, 315, **415–417**, *416*
Hammond's Store, South Carolina 194*c*
Hancock (ship) 498, 511, 672
Hancock, John 8*c*, 27*c*, 30*c*, 66*c*, 330, **417–418**, 640, 653
Hancock's Bridge, New Jersey 127*c*
Hand, Edward 77*c*, **418–419**
Hanger, George **419–420**
Hanging Rock, South Carolina 184*c*
Hannah (ship) 38*c*, 39*c*, 42*c*
Hanson, John **420–421**
Haraden, Jonathan 180*c*, **421–422**
Harding, Seth 63*c*, **422–423**
Harlem Heights, New York 74*c*, 76*c*, 77*c*
Hartford, Connecticut, strategy conference 187*c*
Haw River, North Carolina 200*c*
Hayne, Isaac **423–424**
Hays, Mary 135*c*, **424–425**, 517
Hazard (ship) 704
Hazelwood, John 117*c*, 119*c*, **425–426**
Heath, William 89*c*–90*c*, **426–427**
Heister, Leopold von 68*c*, 71*c*, 97*c*, **427–428**, 616–617
Henry, Fort 106*c*, 232*c*, 644
Henry, Patrick 4*c*, 9*c*, 22*c*, 26*c*, 37*c*, 64*c*, **428–429**
Herkimer, Nicholas 101*c*–102*c*, **429–430**, 551
Hessians **430–431**
  Bemis Heights, Battle of 114*c*, 272, 273
  Brandywine, Battle of 107*c*, 108*c*
  Castleton, New York 99*c*
  Connecticut Farms, New Jersey 180*c*
  Cooch's Bridge, Delaware 106*c*–107*c*
  and Declaration of Independence 431
  Karl von Donop 70*c*, 84*c*
  Johann Ewald 211*c*, 360–361
  Freeman's Farm, Battle of 110*c*
  Gloucester, New Jersey 119*c*
  George Hanger 419
  Harlem Heights, Battle of 74*c*
  Leopold von Heister 68*c*, 71*c*, 97*c*, 427–428, 616–617
  Hubbardton, Vermont 98*c*
  Independence, Fort 90*c*
  Wilhelm von Knyphausen. *See* Knyphausen, Wilhelm von
  Lee, Fort 82*c*
  Mercer, Fort 117*c*
  Monmouth, Battle of 135*c*, 517
  Kazimierz Pulaski and 583
  Johann Rall 593–594, 670, 699
  Rhode Island 141*c*
  Fredericke von Riedesel 601–602
  Friedrich von Riedesel. *See* Riedesel, Friedrich von
  Haym Salomon and 617
  John Stark and 646
  Throg's Neck, New York 77*c*
  Trenton, Battle of 85*c*–86*c*, 86*c*, 670
  Washington, Fort 81*c*
  George Washington and 687
  White Plains, Battle of 699
  White Plains, New York 79*c*
Hillsboro, North Carolina 200*c*
Hinman, Elisha **432**
Hobkirk's Hill, South Carolina 205*c*, 596
Hogun, James **432–433**
Hood, Samuel 225*c*, 227*c*, **433–435**, *434*
Hopkins, Esek 52*c*, **435–436**
  attacks *Diamond* 88*c*
  attacks Nassau 53*c*, 55*c*
  battles off Rhode Island 57*c*
  censure of 77*c*
  Continental Congress 330
  Continental navy 537
  dimissal of 122*c*
  naval appointment of 44*c*, 49*c*
  Samuel Nicholas 539–540
  ordered to clear coast 50*c*
Hopkins, John B. 154*c*, **436–437**
House of Commons, peace resolutions of 225*c*–226*c*
Howard, John E. 196*c*, **437–439**, *438*
Howe, Richard *439*, **439–440**
  Charles-Hector-Théodat, comte d'Estaing 137*c*, 358, 440
  Gibraltar 233*c*
  William Howe 442, 443
  Fort Mifflin 117*c*
  New England coastal raids 125*c*
  Newport, Rhode Island 139*c*, 140*c*
  peace negotiations 69*c*
  returns to England 146*c*
  Savannah, Georgia 148*c*
  Samuel Smith 638
  John Sullivan 654
Howe, Robert 53*c*, 132*c*, **440–441**
Howe, William **442–444**, *443*
  Barren Hill, Pennsylvania 131*c*–132*c*
  Boston, Massachusetts 28*c*, 45*c*
  Brandywine, Battle of 107*c*, 282–283, 443
  Bunker Hill, Battle of 32*c*, 33*c*, 290, 291, 442
  John Burgoyne 292, 293, 442, 443
  Henry Clinton 50*c*, 319, 320
  Charles Cornwallis 336
  Lydia Darragh 343
  departs America 132*c*
  Dobbs Ferry, New York 80*c*
  evacuation of Boston 55*c*–56*c*
  Germantown, Battle of 112*c*, 113*c*, 443
  Harlem Heights, New York 74*c*, 76*c*
  Head of Elk, Maryland 106*c*
  Leopold von Heister 427–428
  Kip's Bay 73*c*–74*c*
  Long Island, Battle of 70*c*, 71*c*, 442, 491, 492
  Manhattan Island 78*c*
  New Jersey 89*c*, 95*c*, 96*c*
  pardon of 82*c*
  Hugh Percy 564
  Philadelphia, Pennsylvania 85*c*, 91*c*, 443
  Robert Pigot 570

William Prescott 577
proclamation by 43c
replaces Gage 41c
resignation of 117c
Staten Island, New York 97c
Washington, Fort 81c
George Washington 55c, 56c, 96c,
 97c, 442, 443, 687–688
Whitemarsh, Pennsylvania 120c,
 121c
White Plains, Battle of 699
wintering of 84c
Hubbardton, Vermont 98c
Hudson River 91c–93c, 113c, 675
Huger, Isaac 168c, 169c, 176c, 201c,
 205c, **444–445**
Hughes, Edward 225c, 228c, 229c,
 231c, 238c
Huntington, Jedediah **445–446**
Huntington, Samuel 200c
Hutchinson, Thomas **446–447**
 Francis Bernard 275
 Boston Massacre 279
 Boston Tea Party 15c, 280, 447
 burning of home of 4c
 as governor-general 10c, 12c–14c,
  16c
 Loyalists 493
Hyder Ally (ship) 267

I

Independence, Fort 90c
Indian Ocean 225c
Iroquois homelands, invasion of
 (1779) 168c, 297, 727m
Irvine, William **448–449**

J

Jamaica 227c
Jasper, William 64c, **450–451**
Jay, John **451–452**
 Canada 29c
 Continental Congress 146c, 451
 discovery of secret negotiations
  231c
 Robert R. Livingston 490
 Paris, Treaty of 233c, 451,
  555–556
 peace negotiations 168c, 227c,
  229c, 232c
 Spain 451, 642
 warns on tyranny 20c

"Jay Treaty" 451–452
Jefferson, Thomas **452–453**
 Charlottesville, Virginia 209c
 Declaration of Independence
  34c, 63c, 65c, 348, 349, 452
 Declaration on Taking up Arms, A
  34c, 35c
 France 75c, 453
 James Madison 496
 James Monroe 518
Johns Island, South Carolina 224c
Johnson, Guy **453–455**, *454*
Johnson, Henry 160c
Johnson, John 51c, 66c, 178c, 190c,
 191c, **455–456**
Johnson, William 6c
Johnstone, George 204c
Johnstown, New York 178c
Johnstown Hall, New York 222c
Jones, Icabod 29c, 30c
Jones, John Paul 167c, **456–458**, *457*
 captures by 70c–72c, 79c, 80c,
  119c
 Continental navy 538
 cruise and battle with *Serapis*
  167c, 726m
 Nathaniel Fanning 363
 flies American flag 47c, 98c, 124c
 France 118c, 120c, 131c, 150c
 mission to English coast 96c,
  128c–130c
 Richard Pearson 561, 562
Jouett, Jack **458–459**

K

Kalb, Johann de *460*, **460–461**
 Camden, Battle of 185c, 186c,
  461
 commission of 109c
 Philadelphia, Pennsylvania 96c,
  100c
 recruitment of 92c, 93c
 George Washington 461, 688
Kentucky 277, 278
Keppel, Augustus 128c, 133c, 135c,
 138c, 141c, 144c
Kilroy, Matthew 11c
King's Mountain, Battle of 189c–190c,
 461–463, 730m
 Benjamin Cleveland 317
 Charles Cornwallis 189c, 190c,
  337

Patrick Ferguson 365
Joseph McDowell 506
John Sevier and 625
Isaac Shelby 628
Joseph Winston 707
Kip's Bay 73c, 74c
Kittanning 256
Knowlton, Thomas 51c, **463–464**
Knox, Henry 52c, 88c, 218c, **464–465**,
 465
Knyphausen, Fort 211c
Knyphausen, Wilhelm von 81c,
 466–467
 Israel Angell 252
 Brandywine, Battle of 107c, 108c,
  283
 Cecil Courthouse, Maryland
  106c
 Connecticut Farms, New Jersey
  180c
 Monmouth, Battle of 134c
 replaces Leopold von Heister 97c
 Springfield, New Jersey
  181c–182c
 White Plains, Battle of 699
Kościuszko, Tadeusz 108c, 208c, *467*,
 467–468

L

Lacey, John 130c, **469–470**
Lafayette, James **470–471**
Lafayette, marquis de *471*, **471–472**
 Barren Hill, Pennsylvania 131c,
  132c
 Brandywine, Battle of 108c
 Canadian expedition 123c, 125c,
  126c
 Cape Henry, Battle of 203c
 Charlottesville, Virginia 210c
 commission of 101c
 Thomas Conway 123c, 331
 departure for Virginia 200c
 and French fleet 141c
 Gloucester, New Jersey 119c
 Green Spring, Virginia 212c
 Johann de Kalb 460, 461
 James Lafayette 470
 Monmouth, Battle of 134c,
  516–517
 Philadelphia, Pennsylvania 96c,
  100c
 recruitment of 92c, 93c

return to France 224c
in Rhode Island 139c
Spencer's Tavern 211c
George Washington 471, 472, 688
Williamsburg, Virginia 212c
Yorktown, siege of 472, 711
Lake Indians 229c
Lamb, John 38c, **472–474**
Laurens, Henry 118c, 123c, 227c, 233c, **474–475**
Laurens, John 141c, 221c, 231c, **475–476**
Lauzun, Armand-Louis de Gontaut, duc de 219c, **476–477**
League of Armed Neutrality 173c, 189c
Learned, Ebenezer **477–478**
Ledyard, William 216c–217c, **478–479**
Lee, Arthur 78c–79c, 85c, 124c, **479–480,** 641
Lee, Charles **480–481**
   Charleston, South Carolina 60c
   court-marital of 136c, 140c, 146c
   Monmouth, Battle of 135c, 481, 516, 517
   New Jersey 83c, 84c
   North Castle, New York 82c
   prisoner exchange of 128c, 129c
   Anthony Wayne 694
Lee, Fort 81c–82c, 265
Lee, Henry 123c, **481–483,** *482*
   Fort Cornwallis 209c
   Fort Granby 207c
   Ninety Six, Fort 210c
   Guilford Courthouse, Battle of 201c, 482
   Haw River, North Carolina 200c
   Paulus Hook, New Jersey 164c–165c
   Springfield, New Jersey 182c
   Fort Watson 204c, 205c
   Wetzel's Mill, North Carolina 201c
Lee, Richard Henry 9c, 61c, 83c, **483–484**
"Lee's Legion" 482
Legge, William 21c, 23c
Leslie, Alexander 22c, 190c, 192c, 202c, 234c, **484–486,** *485*
Letters from a Farmer in Pennsylvania 7c, 8c, 350, 669
Letters of the Federal Farmer to the Republican 484

Lewis, Andrew 19c, 66c, **486–487**
Lexington and Concord, Battles of. *See* Concord, Battle of
Liberty (ship) 8c, 653
Liberty Pole 10c
Light Infantry Regiment 106c
Lincoln, Benjamin **487–489,** *488*
   Bound Brook, New Jersey 92c
   Charleston, siege of 172c, 173c, 175c–178c, 312–313, 488
   as commander of Southern Department 143c
   Savannah, Georgia 148c, 487, 488
   Savannah, siege of 169c, 170c, 620
   Stono Ferry, South Carolina 158c
   George Washington 688
   Yorktown, siege of 221c, 711, 712
Little, George **489**
Little Egg Harbor, New Jersey 144c
Livingston, Robert R. 221c, **489–491**
Livingston, William 281
Locke, Francis 181c
Long Island, Battle of *71c*, 71c, 72c, **491–492,** 718m
   William Alexander 71c, 248, 491
   Henry Clinton 71c, 320, 491
   George Collier 325
   Leopold von Heister 427
   William Howe 70c, 71c, 442, 491, 492
   Peter Parker 558–559
   Hugh Percy 564
   John Sullivan 71c, 491, 654
   George Washington 71c, 72c, 491–492, 687
Long Island, New York 63c, 511–512
Long Island, Treaty of 626
Lookout Mountain, Tennessee 232c
Lord Dunmore's War 16c, 17c, 20c
Louis XVI (king of France) 58c, 121c, 127c, 604
Lovell, Solomon 141c, 161c–163c, **492–493**
Loyalists **493–495**
   Arthur Campbell and 306
   William Campbell and 307
   Cherry Valley, New York 144c, 145c
   confiscation of property of 120c
   disarming of 55c
   evacuation of 133c
   David Fanning 362–363

   Patrick Ferguson and 364, 365
   Great Bridge, Virginia 48c
   Halifax 56c, 58c
   Icabod Jones 29c, 30c
   Josiah Martin and 500, 501
   Jane McCrea 503–504
   John Murray and 534
   New Jersey 84c
   North Carolina 50c, 51c, 53c–54c
   Oriskany, Battle of 551
   Paris, Treaty of 556
   Andrew Pickens and 567, 568
   Francis Rawdon 595
   recruiting of 66c
   Griffith Rutherford and 610, 611
   Margaret Shippen 630–631
   South Carolina 36c, 40c, 46c, 49c, 67c
Ludington, Sybil **495**

M

MacDonald, Donald 53c, 54c
Macleod, Alexander 54c
Madison, James **496–497**
Maitland, John 158c, 159c
Manley, John 46c, 99c, **497–498,** 511, 537, 672
Margaretta (ship) 30c–31c, 547
marines, Continental 539–540
marines, royal 572–573, *573*
Marion, Francis **499–500**
   Blue Savannah, South Carolina 187c
   Eutaw Springs, Battle of 217c
   Parker's Ferry 214c
   Savannah, siege of 620
   South Carolina raids 191c–193c, 197c
   Tearcourt Swamp 191c
   Watson, Fort 204c, 205c
Martin, Josiah 51c, 54c, **500–501**
Martinique 206c
Maryland 420–421, 438, 635, 636
Maryland Convention (Annapolis) 51c, 64c
Mason, George 9c, 62c, **501–502**
Massachusetts. *See also* Boston, Massachusetts; Bunker Hill, Battle of; Concord, Battle of
   abolition in 238c
   Samuel Adams 244
   Francis Bernard 275

Breed's Hill 33c, 577, 585
Thomas Gage. *See* Gage, Thomas
George III and 21c
John Hancock 417–418
Thomas Hutchinson 446–447
Alexander Leslie and 484–485
Solomon Lovell 492–493
minutemen 515–516
North Bridge 22c, 24c, 516, 637
James Otis 552–553
John Parker 556–557
Penobscot Bay 161c–164c, 325–326, 492–493, 600, 618, 692, 704
Seth Pomeroy 575
Josiah Quincy 591
Stamp Act 644
Peleg Wadsworth 680
Artemas Ward 681, *681*, 682
Joseph Warren. *See* Warren, Joseph
Massachusetts Government Act 17c, 324
Mathew, Edward 156c, 157c
Mawhood, Charles 126c–127c, 580
Maxwell, William 106c–107c, 113c, 182c, 206c, **502–503**
McCrea, Jane 100c, **503–504**
McDougall, Alexander 10c–12c, 79c, 92c, 234c, **504–505**, 539
McDowell, Joseph **505–506**
McGary, Hugh 230c, 231c
McGillivray, Alexander **506–508**, *507*
McGowan's Blockhouse 151c
McIntosh, Lachlan 55c, 286, *508*, **508–509**
McLane, Allan 120c, 132c, 133c, 159c, **509–510**
McLean, Francis 158c
McNeill, Hector 498, **510–511**
Mecklenburg Declaration 29c
Meigs, Return J. **511–512**
Mercer, Fort 117c, 119c, 252
Mercer, Hugh 81c, 88c, **512–513**, 580
Michilimackinac, Fort 1c
Middlebrook, New Jersey 146c, 147c, 150c
Mifflin, Fort 116c–119c, 638
Mifflin, Thomas 239c, **513–515**, *514*
militia 12c, 20c, 26c, 36c, 125c, 515–516. *See also* minutemen; *specific individuals; specific states*

mines (weapons) 122c
minutemen **515–516**
 Concord, Battle of 24c, *25c, 25c,* 328, 329, 516
 Hugh Mercer 513
 Francis Smith 637
Model Treaty 68c, 75c
Mohawk Indians. *See* Brant, Joseph; Brant, Molly
Mohawk Valley 298, 703
Mohawk Valley raids 284, 296, 456, 615
Molasses Act 653
"Molly Pitcher." *See* Hays, Mary
Monmouth, Battle of 134c, 135c, 136c, **516–517,** 725m
 Henry Clinton 134c, 135c, 320, 516, 517
 Charles Cornwallis 134c, 337, 517
 James Grant 397
 Mary Hays 424
 Charles Lee 135c, 481, 516, 517
 Friedrich von Steuben 649
 George Washington 135c, 516, 517, 688
 Anthony Wayne 135c, 694
Monroe, James **517–519**
Monroe Doctrine 518
Montagu, John (fourth earl of Sandwich) 131c, 138c, **519–520**
Montgomery, Hugh 11c
Montgomery, Richard **520–521**, *521*
 Guy Carleton 309
 Montreal 44c
 Quebec 44c, 47c, 49c, 50c, 520–521, 589
 Ticonderoga, Fort 38c
 David Wooster 709
Montreal 40c, 41c, 521, 709
"Moonlight Battle" 171c
Moore, Henry 6c
Moore, James 29c–31c, **521–522**
Moore, John 181c
Moore's Creek Bridge (North Carolina) 522
Moravian Indians 226c
Morgan, Daniel **522–524**, *523*
 Bemis Heights, Battle of 114c
 Cambridge, Massachusetts 37c
 Cowpens, Battle of 196c, 338, 339, 523, 524

 Simon Fraser 370
 Freeman's Farm, Battle of 109c, 371
 Quebec, attack on 523, 590
 Saratoga, New York 115c, 523
 Somerset Courthouse, New Jersey 96c
 Banastre Tarleton 523, 524, 663
 William Washington 690
Morris, Gouverneur **524–525**
Morris, Robert 207c, 208c, 216c, 224c, 235c, **525–527**
Morristown, New Jersey 89c, 91c, 94c, 95c, 171c, 178c, 181c
Motte, Fort 206c, 207c
Moultrie, Fort 177c
Moultrie, William 60c–61c, 64c, 150c, 156c, 311, 312, *527*, **527–528**, 558
Mount Kemble, New Jersey mutiny 194c
Mowat, Henry 42c–43c
Moylan, Stephen **528–529**
Mugford, John 59c, 60c
Muhlenberg, John P. G. 205c, **529–530**
Murphy, Timothy 370, **530–531**
Murray, Alexander **531–533**, *532*
Murray, John 486, *533*, **533–535**
 Cornstalk 335, 336
 dissolves House of Burgesses 17c
 Great Bridge, Virginia 48c
 Gywnn Island 66c
 Hampton Creek, Virginia 43c
 Kemp's Landing, Virginia 45c
 martial law 44c
 Norfolk, Virginia 50c
 raids of 67c, 68c
 seeks refuge 30c
 and supplies at Williamsburg 25c
Musgrove Mill, South Carolina 186c
mutiny (1781) 194c–198c

N

Nash, Francis **536–537**
Nassau, Bahamas 53c, 55c, 123c, 435–436, 540, 618
Native Americans. *See also specific tribes, e.g.:* Seneca Indians
 Daniel Boone and 277, 278
 Samuel Brady and 282
 Joseph Brant. *See* Brant, Joseph
 Molly Brant 102c, 285–286, 551
 John Butler and 296–297

Richard Butler and 297, 298
Walter Butler and 298–299
Zebulon Butler and 299–300
Canada 60c
George Rogers Clark and 315
Cornplanter 136c, 296, 334–335, 335, 551, 597
Cornstalk 19c–20c, 335–336, 486, 534
councils with 35c
William Crawford and 340
Dragging Canoe 68c, 95c, 154c, 352–353, 624, 625
Fort Forty 136c
Simon Girty and 391–392
Frederick Haldimand and 412
Henry Hamilton and 415–416
Nicholas Herkimer and 430
Guy Johnson and 454–455
John Johnson and 455–456
Loyalists and 494
Jane McCrea and 504
Return J. Meigs and 512
Timothy Murphy and 531
Narrows, West Virginia 112c
Oconostota 95c, 548–549, *549*
at Onondaga Creek 155c
Oriskany, Battle of 102c, 551–552
and Paris, Treaty of 507
peace conference with 41c
Pontiac 1c–3c, 6c
Proclamation of 1763 and 582
Red Jacket 334, 596–598, *597*
Barry St. Leger and 615, 616
Sons of Liberty disguised as 15c, 16c
John Sullivan and 654, 655
Thomas's Swamp, Florida 94c
Nancy Ward 68c, 682–683
Anthony Wayne and 695
Naval Construction Act of 1777 90c
Navigation Acts 2c
navy, Continental **537–538.** *See also* Hopkins, Esek; Jones, John Paul; privateering
  John Adams 47c, 537
  American galleys 69c
  Joshua Barney 267–268
  John Barry 268–269
  Nicholas Biddle 276–277
  David Bushnell 295–296

Continental Congress 48c–49c, 330, 537
construction for 43c, 48c–49c
Gustavus Conyngham *332*, 332–333
Richard Dale *342*, 342–343
Nathaniel Fanning 363
John Fiske 365–366
formation of 42c, 47c
Alexander Gillon 390–391
Jonathan Haraden 421–422
Seth Harding 422–423
Elisha Hinman 432
John B. Hopkins 154c, 436–437
George Little 489
John Manley 46c, 99c, 497–498, 511, 537, 672
Hector McNeill 510–511
Alexander Murray 531–533
Naval Construction Act of 1777 90c
James Nicholson 540–541
Samuel Nicholson 541–542
Jeremiah O'Brien 547
proposed creation of 38c
purchases for 44c
John P. Rathbun 594
and Royal Navy 537–538, 581
Dudley Saltonstall 161c–164c, 492, 493, 538, 617–618
Silas Talbot 659–660
Samuel Tucker 672–673
Turtle 72c, 76c
Daniel Waters 692
Abraham Whipple. *See* Whipple, Abraham
Lambert Wickes 68c, 97c, 112c, 700–701
John F. Williams 703–704
navy, French. *See* Estaing, Charles-Hector-Théodat, comte d'; Suffren de Saint-Tropez de, Pierre de
Navy, Royal
  Marriot Arbuthnot. *See* Arbuthnot, Marriot
  George Collier 156c, 157c, 164c, 325–326, 538
  James Gambier 142c, 379–380
  Samuel Graves 40c, 42c, 52c, 399–400, 711
  Thomas Graves 216c, 218c, 400–402

Samuel Hood 225c, 227c, 433–435
Richard Howe. *See* Howe, Richard
Hector McNeill 511
Mifflin, Fort 638
John Montague 519–520
Peter Parker. *See* Parker, Peter
Richard Pearson 538, 561–562
privateering and 580–581
George Rodney 171c, 176c, 178c, 198c, 433–435, 606–607
Molyneux Shuldham 52c, 55c, 632
Spain 642
Pierre-André de Suffren de Saint-Tropez and 651–652
Negapatam, Battle of 229c
Netherlands 233c, 474
Newburgh Conspiracy 235c, 414, 505, **538–539,** 586, 689
New England 91c, 125c. *See also* specific states
New England Restraining Act 22c–23c
New Hampshire 239c, 645, 646
New Jersey. *See also* Princeton, Battle of; Trenton, Battle of; *specific headings, e.g.:* Hancock's Bridge, New Jersey
  Francis Bernard 275
  Elias Boudinot 281
  Charles Cornwallis 83c, 92c, 96c, 97c, 143c
  Wilhelm von Knyphausen 180c–182c
  Charles Lee 83c, 84c
  Loyalists in 84c
  William Maxwell 502–503
  privateering 144c
  George Washington 83c, 85c–89c, 91c, 94c, 95c, 146c, 147c, 669–671, 687
  Anthony Wayne 126c, 183c, 194c
New London, Connecticut 216c–217c
New Orleans, Louisiana 378
Newport, Rhode Island
  Henry Clinton 142c
  Charles-Hector-Théodat, comte d'Estaing 138c–140c, 358
  Richard Howe 139c, 140c
  Robert Pigot 570

Jean-Baptiste-Donatien de
  Vimeur, comte de Rochambeau
  183c, 604
Pierre-André de Suffren de Saint-
  Tropez 651
John Sullivan 138c–141c, 654
Silas Talbot 659, 660
James M. Varnum 675
New Providence (on Nassau,
  Bahamas) 53c, 55c, 123c, 540
New York City
  Brooklyn Heights 70c, 72c,
    393–394, 491, 492, 586, 687
  Charles Cornwallis 74c, 77c
  evacuation of 73c–74c
  Golden Hill, Battle of 395
  Harlem Heights 74c, 76c, 77c
  William Heath 426
  Richard Howe 439–440
  Thomas Knowlton 463–464
  Wilhelm von Knyphausen and
    466
  John Lamb 38c
  Robert R. Livingston 489–490
  Joseph Spencer 643
  struggle for (1776) 717m
  George Washington 57c, 146c,
    213c, 687
New York State. *See also* Champlain
  (Lake and region); Mohawk Valley
  raids; Tryon, William; *specific head-
  ings, e.g.:* Long Island, Battle of
  Joseph Brant 284–285
  Walter Butler and 298–299
  George Clinton 318–319
  Loyalists 494
  map of campaigns in (1777)
    722m
  Oriskany, Battle of 102c, 286,
    296, 334, 430, 551–552
  Stony Point 157c, 159c–161c, 694
  Banastre Tarleton 662
  John Vaughan 675
  Marinus Willett 702, *702*, 703
Nicholas, Samuel 45c, **539–540**
Nicholson, James **540–541**
Nicholson, Samuel **541–542**
Nicola, Lewis 228c, **542–543**, 689
Ninety Six, Fort 46c, 208c, 210c, 211c
Nixon, John **543–544**
Noailles, Louis-Marie, comte de 221c,
  544–545

nonimportation movement. *See* boy-
  cott (of British goods)
Nook's Hill 55c
North, Frederick 11c, **545–546**
  Boston Tea Party 279, 280
  Carlisle Commission 129c
  Coercive Acts 323
  Charles James Fox 366, 367
  and French alliance 124c–126c
  George III and 384, 385, 544–546
  resignation of 226c
  Tea Act 664
North Bridge (in Massachusetts) 22c,
  24c, 516, 637
North Carolina. *See also* Camden, Bat-
  tle of
  Alamance, Battle of 12c,
    246–247, 671
  Charles Cornwallis 50c, 188c,
    200c, 204c
  William Lee Davidson 344
  David Fanning 362, 363
  Patrick Ferguson 365
  Nathanael Greene 200c, 404
  Henry Lee 200c, 201c
  Loyalists 50c, 51c, 53c–54c
  Josiah Martin 500, 501
  James Moore 521–522
  Francis Nash 536
  Griffith Rutherford 610–611
  Evan Shelby 626
  Isaac Shelby 627, 628
  Jethro Sumner 655–656
  Banastre Tarleton 201c
  William Tryon 671
  Hugh Waddell 679

O

O'Brien, Jeremiah **547–548**
Oconostota 95c, **548–549**, *549*
Ogden, Matthias 234c
O'Hara, Charles 202c, 221c, 354,
  549–551, 712
Old Tappan, New Jersey 143c
Olive Branch Petition 34c–35c, 38c,
  44c, 47c, 330, 348, 350
Oliver, Andrew 8c
O'Neal, Ferdinand 228c
Oriskany, Battle of 102c, 286, 296,
  334, 430, **551–552**
Orvillers, Louis d' 137c, 138c, 141c
Oswald, Richard 227c

Otis, James 3c, 4c, 7c, 8c, 10c, 13c, 326,
  552–553
Ottawa Indians 1c–3c, 6c

P

Paine, Thomas 51c, 84c, 327–328, 330,
  554, **554–555**
Paoli, Pennsylvania 407, 694
Paris, Treaty of (1763) 1c
Paris, Treaty of (1783) **555–556**
  formal conclusion of 238c
  Benjamin Franklin 233c, 369,
    555, 556
  John Jay 233c, 451, 555–556
  Native Americans 507
  William Petty 565
  ratification 236c
  signing of 233c
  Spain 642
  Charles de Vergennes 677–678
  Charles Watson-Wenworth
    694
Parker, John 24c, **556–557**, 637
Parker, Peter 64c, 68c, 311–312, 491,
  557–559, 558
Parker's Ferry, South Carolina 214c
Parliament 5c, 11c, 14c, 48c, 701
Parsons, Samuel H. **559–560**
Paterson, John **560–561**
Paulus Hook, New Jersey 164c–165c
peace conference 73c
peace negotiations 168c, 227c,
  231c–233c, 451
peace terms 152c
Pearson, Richard 538, **561–562**, *562*
Peekskill, New York 92c
Pennsylvania. *See also specific headings,
  e.g.:* Philadelphia, Pennsylvania
  emancipation ordinance 173c
  William Howe 85c, 91c, 120c,
    121c, 131c–132c, 443
  William Irvine 448–449
  Johann de Kalb 96c, 100c
  John Lacey 469
  marquis de Lafayette 96c, 100c,
    131c, 132c
  Thomas Mifflin 513–515, *514*
  Valley Forge 114c, 121c–123c,
    125c, 130c, 505, 508, 688
  George Washington 101c, 110c,
    114c, 120c–123c, 688
  Anthony Wayne 111c

Penobscot Bay, Massachusetts 161c–164c, 325–326, 492–493, 600, 618, 692, 704
Pensacola, Florida 379
Percy, Hugh 70c, 329, 491, 516, *563*, **563–564**
Petersburgh, Virginia 205c, 208c
Petty, William 232c, **564–565**
Philadelphia, Pennsylvania
    Benedict Arnold 132c, 134c
    Joshua Barney 267
    Henry Clinton 133c
    Charles Cornwallis 111c
    Joseph Galloway 377
    Battle of Germantown 387, 388
    James Grant 396
    John Hancock 417
    John Hazelwood 425
    Richard Howe 440
    William Howe 85c, 91c, 443
    intention to burn 84c
    Johann de Kalb 96c, 100c
    marquis de Lafayette 96c, 100c
    Allan McLane 509–510
    John P. G. Muhlenberg 529, 530
    proposed capture of 85c
    Israel Putnam 83c
    George Washington 101c, 110c, 688
Phillips, William 98c, 203c, 205c, *566*, **566–567**
Pickens, Andrew **567–568**
    Augusta, Georgia 204c
    Carr's Fort, Georgia 151c
    Cherokee War 64c
    Cowpens, Battle of 196c, 568
    Eutaw Springs, Battle of 217c
    Cornwallis, Fort 209c
    Ninety Six, Fort 210c
    South Carolina 68c, 69c
Pickens, Francis 200c
Pickering, Timothy **568–569**
Pigot, Robert 141c, 290, 291, **569–571**
Pinckney, Charles C. *571*, **571–572**
Piscataway, New Jersey 647
Pitcairn, John **572–574**, *573*
    Bunker Hill, Battle of 33c
    Concord, Battle of 21c, 24c, 328, 329, 572–573
    John Parker 557
    Francis Smith 637
Pitcher, Molly. *See* Hays, Mary

Pitt, William 5c, 21c, 131c, **574–575**
poetry 696–697
Poland 583, 584
Pomeroy, Seth **575**
Pontiac (chief of the Ottawa) 1c–3c, 6c
Poor, Enoch 131c, **575–576**
Port Royal Island, South Carolina 150c
Prescott, Richard 270
Prescott, William 289, 290, **576–578**
Preston, Thomas 279
Prevost, Augustin 146c, 149c, 153c, 155c, *578*, **578–579**, 620
Princeton, Battle of 87c–89c, 336, 513, **579–580**, 688, 721m
Princeton, New Jersey 83c, 87c, 237c
privateering 180c, **580–582**
    John Barry 269
    and British shipping 135c
    Continental Congress 46c, 56c, 79c
    Continental navy and 537, 538, 581
    Hancock 69c
    John Paul Jones 130c
    Little Egg Harbor, New Jersey 144c
    John Manley 498
    Alexander McDougall 504
    Hector McNeill 511
    Alexander Murray 532
    James Nicholson and 541
    Jeremiah O'Brien 547
    Parliament 90c
    John P. Rathbun 594
    Dudley Saltonstall 618
    Silas Talbot 660
    Samuel Tucker 672, 673
    George Washington and 537
    Daniel Waters 692
    John F. Williams 704
Proclamation of 1763 2c, **582–583**
Prohibitory Act 48c, 57c
Providence (ship) 594, 618, 698
Providence, Rhode Island 382
Prussian drill system 127c, 135c, 648–649
Pulaski, Kazimierz 128c, 144c, 169c, 529, *583*, **583–584**
Putnam, Israel **584–585**
    Brooklyn Heights, New York 70c

    Bunker Hill, Battle of 33c, 585
    Concord, Battle of 25c, 584–585
    as general 31c
    New York City 73c
    Noodle's Island, Boston Harbor 29c
    Philadelphia, Pennsylvania 83c
    Fort Washington 81c
Putnam, Rufus **585–587**, *586*
Pyle, John 200c

Q

Quartering Act **588–589**
    expiration of 11c
    Thomas Gage 3c, 5c, 7c, 8c, 375
    Golden Hill, Battle of 395
    Alexander McDougall 504
    New York assembly 6c–8c
    revision of 17c
    Sons of Liberty 7c, 640
    Townshend Duties 668
Quebec
    Benedict Arnold 28c, 39c, 45c–47c, 49c, 56c, 63c, 249, 589
    John Burgoyne 59c, 95c–96c, 292
    Guy Carleton 44c, 47c, 49c, 59c, 308–309, 589, 590
    Simon Fraser 370
    Hector McNeill 511
    Richard Montgomery 44c, 47c, 49c, 50c, 520–521, 589
    as new colony 2c
    siege of 47c, 60c, 258–259, 309, 473, 666
    John Sullivan 60c, 63c
    John Thomas 666
    David Wooster 709
Quebec, attack on 49c, 259, 309, 473, 521, 523, **589–590**, 590, 709
Quebec Act 18c, 20c, 308, **590–591**, 692
Queen of France (ship) 594, 698
Queen's Rangers 127c, 633, 634
Quimby's Bridge, South Carolina 212c–213c
Quincy, Josiah 11c, 279, **591–592**
Quintin's Bridge, New Jersey 126c–127c

R

Rall, Johann **593–594**, 670, 699
Ramsour's Mill, North Carolina 181c

Randolph (ship) 276–277
Ranger (ship) 594, 698
Rathbun, John P. 123*c*, 161*c*, **594–595**
Rawdon, Francis 205*c*, 210*c*, 211*c*, 595, **595–596**
Red Jacket 334, **596–598**, *597*
Reed, James **598**
Reed, Joseph **598–600**
regulators 12*c*, 246–247, 671, 679
Reprisal (ship) 700–701
Revenue Act 668–669
Revere, Paul **600–601**
    Boston Massacre 11*c*, 600
    circular letter 16*c*
    Concord, Battle of 328, 600
    Penobscot expedition 161*c*
    Sons of Liberty 640
    Suffolk Resolves 19*c*
    warns of British approach 23*c*, 24*c*
    Joseph Warren 23*c*, 24*c*, 684
Revolutionary War, major battles of 714*m*
Rhode Island. *See also* Newport, Rhode Island
    Israel Angell 252
    William Barton 269, 270
    Gaspée affair 381–382
    Christopher Greene 402, 403
    Nathanael Greene 141*c*
    marquis de Lafayette 139*c*
    Providence 382
    Tiverton 269, 270
    James M. Varnum 674, 675
Richmond, Virginia 194*c*–195*c*
Ridgefield, Connecticut 495, 633, 710
Riedesel, Fredericke von *601*, **601–602**
Riedesel, Friedrich von **602–604**, *603*
    Bemis Heights, Battle of 114*c*
    Bemis Heights, New York 109*c*
    Castleton, New York 99*c*
    Freeman's Farm, Battle of 110*c*
    Hubbardton, Vermont 98*c*
    Fredericke von Riedesel 601, *601*, 602
    St. Lawrence River 58*c*
Rochambeau, Jean-Baptiste-Donatien de Vimeur, comte de 604, **604–606**
    François-Jean, marquis de Chastellux 314
    Ludwig von Closen 322, 323

    French alliance 372, 604
    Hartford strategy conference 187*c*
    Newport, Rhode Island 182*c*, 604
    reconnoitering of New York City 213*c*
    Yorktown, siege of 214*c*–215*c*, 221*c*, 605, 711, 712
Rockingham, Lord (second marquis of Rockingham). *See* Watson-Wentworth, Charles
Rodney, George 171*c*, 176*c*, 178*c*, 198*c*, 433–435, **606–607**
Rogers, Robert 78*c*, **607–608**
Roman Catholics 18*c*, 56*c*, 590
Ross, Betsy 96*c*, **608–609**
Ross, John 222*c*
Rouerie, Armand-Charles Tuffin, marquis de la. *See* Armand, Charles
Rule of Law and the Rule of Men, The 21*c*
Rush, Benjamin 23*c*, **609–610**
Rutherford, Griffith 68*c*, 72*c*, **610–611**
Rutledge, John 56*c*, 73*c*, 174*c*, **611–612**

S

Sag Harbor, Long Island 511–512
St. Clair, Arthur 95*c*, 96*c*, 98*c*, 566, **613–614**, *614*
St. Johns Island, South Carolina 233*c*
St. Kitts, West Indies 224*c*, 225*c*
St. Leger, Barry **614–616**, *615*
    Albany, New York 92*c*
    Joseph Brant 284
    Molly Brant 285, 286
    John Burgoyne 292
    John Butler 296
    Peter Gansevoort and 380–381
    John Johnson and 456
    Battle of Oriskany 551, 552
    Fort Stanwix 97*c*, 100*c*–102*c*, 105*c*–106*c*, 615, 616
Salomon, Haym 207*c*, **616–617**
Saltonstall, Dudley 161*c*–164*c*, 492, 493, 538, **617–618**
Sampson, Deborah 561, **618–619**
San Domingo 181*c*
Sandwich, fourth earl of. *See* Montagu, John
Sandusky, Ohio 229*c*

Saratoga, Battles of 723*m*
    Benedict Arnold 259–260
    Bemis Heights 113*c*–114*c*, 115*c*, 260, 272–273, 293, 478, 576, 723*m*
    John Burgoyne 108*c*, 112*c*, 115*c*, 293
    Freeman's Farm, Battle of 109*c*, 110*c*, 259–260, 293, 370, 371–372, 723*m*
    Horatio Gates 114*c*, 115*c*, 383
    George Germain 386
    Daniel Morgan 115*c*, 523
    John Nixon 543–544
    Philip J. Schuyler 623
Savannah, Georgia
    attack on 55*c*, 146*c*, 148*c*, 304
    Archibald Campbell 146*c*, 148*c*, 304
    Samuel Elbert 357–358
    Robert Howe 441
    Alexander Leslie 485
    Benjamin Lincoln 148*c*, 487, 488
Savannah, siege of 166*c*–170*c*, 359, 488, 509, 578–579, 584, **619–621**
Scammel, Alexander 219*c*, **621–622**
Schaik, Gose Van 155*c*
Schuyler, Philip J. 36*c*, 39*c*, 51*c*, 96*c*, 100*c*, **622–623**
Scott, Charles **623–624**
Seneca Indians 82*c*, 144*c*, 287. *See also* Cornplanter; Red Jacket
Serapis, HMS (ship) 167*c*, 342, 363, 457–458, 538, 561–562
Sevier, John 188*c*, **624–626**, *625*, 682–683
Shawnee Indians 19*c*–20*c*, 229*c*, 278, 282, 298, 335–336, 486, 534
Shelby, Evan **626–627**
Shelby, Isaac 188*c*, 189*c*, 627, **627–628**
Sheldon, Elisha **628–629**
Sherman, Roger 65*c*, **629–630**
Shippen, Margaret 134*c*, 154*c*, 260, **630–631**, *631*
Shuldham, Molyneux 52*c*, 55*c*, **632**
Silliman, Gold S. **632–633**
Simcoe, John G. 127*c*, 130*c*, 142*c*, 205*c*, 209*c*, 211*c*, **633–635**, *634*
Six Nations 161*c*
slaves and slavery 154*c*
    abolishing of 99*c*
    abolition in Massachusetts 238*c*

African Americans 245–246
  emancipation of slaves who fought in Continental army 238c
  Thomas Jefferson 452
  James Lafayette 470
  Richard Henry Lee 484
  George Mason and 502
  John Murray and 534
  Pennsylvania emancipation ordinance 173c
  Savannah, siege of 620
slave trade, abolishment of 20c
Smallwood, William 635, **635–636**
Smith, Francis 24c, 328, 329, 572–573, **636–638**, *637*
Smith, Samuel 118c, **638–639**
Smith, William S. **639–640**
Sons of Liberty **640–641**
  attack customs officials 8c
  Boston Tea Party 15c, 280, 640
  disguised as Native Americans 15c, 16c
  Golden Hill, Battle of 10c, 395
  John Lamb 472–473
  Alexander McDougall 11c
  Quartering Act 7c, 640
  Stamp Act 644
  Townshend Duties 669
  Vice-Admiralty courts 4c
South Carolina. *See also* Charleston, attack on; Charleston, South Carolina; King's Mountain, Battle of; Marion, Francis
  Abraham Buford 288–289
  Charles Cornwallis 178c, 179c, 194c
  William Henry Drayton 353
  Horatio Gates 183c
  Nathanael Greene 193c, 404–405
  Isaac Hayne 423–424
  Isaac Huger 444–445
  Henry Laurens 474–475
  Charles Lee 60c
  Loyalists in 36c, 40c, 46c, 49c, 67c
  William Moultrie 527–528
  Francis Rawdon 595, 596
  John Rutledge 611–612
  Thomas Sumter 656–657
  Banastre Tarleton 177c, 179c, 192c, 194c, 662
  William Washington 179c, 194c

Spain **641–642**
  aid from 58c
  attacks West Florida 167c
  and France 121c, 151c, 154c–155c, 158c, 373, 641, 642
  Bernardo de Gálvez 378–379
  and Great Britain 154c, 157c, 158c
  John Jay 451, 642
  Arthur Lee 479
  Alexander McGillivray 507
  "Moonlight Battle" 171c
  offers to mediate peace 154c
  Paris, Treaty of 556
  Charles de Vergennes 677
Spencer, Joseph 74c, **642–643**
Spencer's Tavern 211c
Springfield, New Jersey 181c–182c, 252
spying (spies)
  Edward Bancroft 266
  Lydia Darragh 120c, 343–344, 510
  Nathan Hale 413–414
  James Lafayette 470
  Margaret Shippen 134c, 154c, 260, 630–631
  Benjamin Tallmadge 661
Stamp Act **643–645**
  Samuel Adams 8c
  authorization of 3c
  Francis Bernard 275
  Edmund Burke 294
  celebrations on anniversary of 8c
  Benjamin Franklin 3c, 5c
  Joseph Galloway 377
  George III 3c
  George Grenville 405, 406
  Patrick Henry 428
  Thomas Hutchinson 446
  James Otis 4c, 8c
  William Pitt 574
  protests against the 4c, 5c
  repeal of 5c, 6c
  William Tryon 671
  Charles Watson-Wentworth 692
Stamp Act Congress 4c–5c, 420
Stanwix, Fort
  Benedict Arnold 105c–106c
  Joseph Brant 102c, 284
  Molly Brant 285–286
  Cornplanter 334

  Peter Gansevoort and 380–381
  John Johnson and 456
  Oriskany, Battle of 551, 552
  Barry St. Leger 97c, 100c–102c, 105c–106c, 615, 616
  Marinus Willett 703
Stark, John *105c*, **645**, **645–646**
  Bennington, Battle of 103c, 273–274, 646
  Bunker Hill, Battle of 290–291, 645
  John Burgoyne 293
  commission of 100c
  Manchester, New Hampshire 101c
  Saratoga, New York 115c
  Staten Island, New York 97c, 104c, 105c, 171c, 172c, 239c
Stephen, Adam 118c, **646–648**
Steuben, Friedrich von *648*, **648–649**
  arrives in Portsmouth 120c
  Continental army 125c, 127c, 135c, 258, 648–649
  Continental Congress 152c
  as inspector general 130c
  Point of Fork 209c
  Charles Ternant 665
  George Washington 648, 649, 688
  Yorktown, siege of 711
Stewart, Alexander 217c, **649–651**, *650*
Stonington, Connecticut 38c, 363
Stono Ferry, South Carolina 158c, 159c
Stony Point, New York 157c, 159c–161c, 694
Suffolk Resolves 19c, 21c, 329
Suffren de Saint-Tropez, Pierre-André de 204c, 225c, 228c, 229c, 231c, 238c, **651–652**
Sugar Act 2c, 3c, **652–653**
Sullivan, Fort 311, 312, 450, 527, 558
Sullivan, John **653–655**, *654*
  James Clinton 322
  Crown Point, New York 66c
  Charles-Hector-Théodat, comte d'Estaing 358
  Germantown, Battle of 112c, 113c
  Iroquois homelands invasion 165c–166c, 168c

Long Island, Battle of 71c, 491, 654
William Maxwell 502, 503
Newport, Rhode Island 138c–141c, 654
Pennsylvania 85c
Robert Pigot 570
Ploughed Hill 38c
Quebec 60c, 63c
Rhode Island 142c
Staten Island, New York 104c, 105c
Trenton, Battle of 86c
Trois-Rivières, Canada 61c, 62c
Sumner, Jethro 217c, **655–656**
Sumter, Thomas 184c–186c, 191c, 192c, 199c, 206c, **656–658,** *657*
Suspending Act 7c, 668
Swallow (ship) 24c
"Swamp Fox." *See* Marion, Francis
Sybil, HMS 423
Sycamore Shoals, Tennessee 188c

T

Talbot, Silas *659,* **659–660**
Tallmadge, Benjamin **660–661**
Tangier Sound 232c
Tarleton, Banastre *662,* **662–664**
    Blackstock's Plantation, South Carolina 192c
    Abraham Buford 288–289
    Camden, Battle of 186c
    Charleston, siege of 173c, 176c
    Charlottesville, Virginia 209c
    Cowan's Ford skirmish 198c
    Cowpens, Battle of 196c, 338, 339, 663
    Hammond's Store, South Carolina 194c
    George Hanger 419, 420
    Isaac Huger 444
    Jack Jouett 458–459
    Armand-Louis de Gontaut Lauzun 476
    Lenud's Ferry, South Carolina 177c
    Francis Marion 499
    Daniel Morgan 523, 524, 663
    South Carolina 177c, 179c, 192c, 194c, 662
    South Carolina raids 179c
    Stony Point 159c
    Thomas Sumter 656
    William Washington 690
    Waxhaws Creek, South Carolina 179c
    Wetzell's Mill, North Carolina 201c
    Yorktown, siege of 219c
"taxation without representation" 3c, 406
Taylor, Daniel 116c
Tea Act 14c, 16c, 279–280, 294, 326, **664.** *See also* Boston Tea Party
Tennessee 625–626
Ternant, Charles **664–665**
Thomas, John 58c–60c, 666
Thomas's Swamp, Florida 94c–95c
Thompson, William 61c, **666–667**
Throg's Neck, New York 639
Ticonderoga, Fort
    Ethan Allen 26c–28c, 249–250
    Benedict Arnold 26c–28c, 77c, 258
    British evacuate 118c
    John Brown 38c, 109c
    John Burgoyne 97c
    Guy Carleton 77c
    Continental Congress 29c
    Simon Fraser 370
    Henry Knox 52c, 464
    Richard Montgomery 38c
    William Phillips 566
    Arthur St. Clair 95c, 98c
    Philip J. Schuyler 36c, 96c, 622–623
Tilghman, Tench 222c, **667–668**
Tiverton, Rhode Island 269, 270
Tom's River, New Jersey 226c
Tories. *See* Loyalists
torpedo 103c
Townshend Duties 6c, 7c, 9c, 11c, 294, 446, 574, **668–669**
Trenton, Battle of 85c–87c, *86c,* **669–671,** 720m
    Charles Cornwallis 336
    Philemon Dickinson 351
    Leopold von Heister 428
    Hessians 85c–86c, *86c,* 670
    Hugh Mercer 513
    James Monroe 518
    Johann Rall 593–594
    Adam Stephen 647
    George Washington 83c, 85c–87c, 669–671, 687
    William Washington 690
Trenton, New Jersey 83c, 88c
Trois-Rivières, Canada 61c–63c, 370, 653, 667
Trumbull (ship) 541, 618
Tryon, William **671–672**
    Battle of Alamance 246–247
    Connecticut raids of 93c, 114c, 153c, 159c, 160c, 671–672
    escapes to New York Harbor 43c
    mobilizes militia 12c
    Gold S. Silliman 633
    Hugh Waddell 679
Tucker, Samuel **672–673**
Turtle (submarine) 72c, 76c, 295

U

Unadilla conference 430

V

Valcour Island, Battle of 76c, *76c,* 77c, 691
Valley Forge, Pennsylvania 114c, 121c–123c, 125c, 130c, 505, 508, 688
Van Rensselaer, Robert 191c
Varnum, James M. *674,* **674–675**
Vaughan, John 198c, **675–676**
Vergennes, Charles Gravier, comte de **676–678,** *677*
    French alliance 120c–122c, 124c, 372, 677
    peace negotiations 229c
    and peace negotiations 234c
    secret negotiations 231c
    Spain 641
Vermont 89c, 292–293, 412
Vermont Convention 99c
Vincennes 147c, 150c, *152c,* 152c–153c, 315, 416
Virginia. *See also* Yorktown, siege of
    Benedict Arnold 194c–196c, 203c–206c
    Arthur Campbell 305–306
    William Campbell 306–307
    Charles Cornwallis 208c, 211c–213c, 219c, 221c, 711–712
    emancipation of slaves who fought in Continental army 238c
    Patrick Henry 428–429
    Thomas Jefferson 452–453
    Jack Jouett 458–459

marquis de Lafayette 200*c*, 210*c*, 212*c*
Loyalists in 48*c*
George Mason 501–502
James Monroe 518
John Murray (Lord Dunmore) 43*c*, 45*c*, 48*c*, 50*c*, 533, *533*, 534
William Phillips and 567
Charles Scott 623–624
John G. Simcoe 205*c*
Banastre Tarleton 209*c*
Williamsburg 211*c*–212*c*
Virginia (ship) 540–541
Virginia Capes, Second Battle of the 215*c*–216*c*, 398, 401, 434
Virginia Declaration of Rights 501
Virginia House of Burgesses 17*c*
Virginia Plan 497
Virginia Resolves 9*c*, 501, 644

W

Waddell, Hugh 247, **679–680**
Wadsworth, Peleg **680–681**
Wahab's Plantation 345
Ward, Artemas 26*c*–28*c*, 31*c*, 289, *681*, **681–682**
Ward, Nancy 68*c*, **682–683**
Warner, Seth 98*c*, 103*c*, 104*c*, 274, **683–684**
Warren, Joseph **684–685**, *685*
    Bunker Hill, Battle of 33*c*, 685
    committees of correspondence 13*c*, 326
    Noodle's Island, Boston Harbor 29*c*
    provincial congress 21*c*
    Paul Revere 23*c*, 24*c*, 684
    Solemn League and Covenant 17*c*
    Sons of Liberty 640
    Suffolk Resolves 19*c*
Warren, Mercy Otis **685–686**
Washington, Fort 63*c*, 80*c*, 81*c*, 442, 466
Washington, George *237c*, **686–689**, *687*
    abandons New York region 82*c*
    appointed commander of Continental army 31*c*
    authority of 84*c*, 150*c*
    Brandywine, Battle of 107*c*–108*c*, 282, 283
    Brooklyn Heights, New York 70*c*, 72*c*
    Canadian expedition 149*c*
    charters first warship 38*c*
    Common Sense 327
    Continental army 257, 258
    Continental Congress 330
    Continental navy 537
    Thomas Conway 115*c*, 117*c*, 118*c*, 122*c*, 331
    Charles Cornwallis 336, 688, 689
    dismissal of suggestion that he be installed as king 228*c*
    Dorchester Heights 53*c*
    Louis Duportail 355
    Charles-Hector-Théodat d'Estaing 138*c*, 145*c*
    farewell to troops 238*c*–239*c*
    Patrick Ferguson 364
    Horatio Gates 124*c*, 382–384, 688
    George III on resignation of 239*c*
    Battle of Germantown 112*c*, 113*c*, 387, 388
    Guilford Courthouse, Battle of 201*c*, 202*c*, 688
    Harlem Heights, New York 74*c*, 77*c*, 78*c*
    Hartford strategy conference 187*c*
    William Howe 55*c*, 56*c*, 96*c*, 97*c*, 442, 443, 687, 688
    intent to remain private citizen 34*c*
    Johann de Kalb 461, 688
    Henry Knox 464–465
    marquis de Lafayette 471, 472, 688
    Charles Lee 480, 481
    Long Island, Battle of 71*c*, 72*c*, 491–492, 687
    Lachlan McIntosh 508, 509
    Hugh Mercer 513
    Middlebrook, New Jersey 146*c*, 147*c*
    Thomas Mifflin 514
    Monmouth, Battle of 135*c*, 516, 517, 688
    Morristown, New Jersey 89*c*, 91*c*, 94*c*, 95*c*, 169*c*, 171*c*, 178*c*
    Stephen Moylan 528–529
    Newburgh Conspiracy 235*c*, 539
    New York City 57*c*, 146*c*, 213*c*, 687
    Lewis Nicola 543
    Charles O'Hara 550
    overhaul of supply procedures 172*c*
    Thomas Paine 554
    Peekskill, New York 211*c*
    Philadelphia, Pennsylvania 101*c*, 110*c*, 688
    Princeton, New Jersey 83*c*, 87*c*–89*c*, 579, 580
    and privateering 537
    Johann Rall 593–594
    Joseph Reed 599
    reprimand of 129*c*
    resignation as commander in chief 239*c*
    Jean-Baptiste-Donatien de Vimeur, comte de Rochambeau 604, 605
    Benjamin Rush 609
    Alexander Scammel 621
    Adam Stephen 646–647
    Friedrich von Steuben 648, 649, 688
    Stony Point 159*c*–161*c*
    Tench Tilghman 667–668
    Battle of Trenton 83*c*, 85*c*–87*c*, 669–671, 687
    Valley Forge, Pennsylvania 114*c*, 122*c*, 123*c*
    Artemas Ward 681, 682
    Fort Washington 80*c*, 81*c*
    Wethersfield strategy conference 208*c*
    Whitemarsh, Pennsylvania 120*c*, 121*c*
    White Plains, Battle of 699, 700
    White Plains, New York 139*c*
    Yorktown, siege of 214*c*–215*c*, 218*c*, 219*c*, 221*c*, 688–689, 711, 712
Washington, Martha 67*c*
Washington, William **689–691**, *690*
    Cowpens, Battle of 196*c*, 339, 690
    Eutaw Springs, Battle of 217*c*
    Guilford Courthouse, Battle of 201*c*, 202*c*, 688
    Hammond's Store, South Carolina 194*c*

Hobkirk's Hill 205*c*
Waxhaws Creek, South Carolina 179*c*
Wetzell's Mill, North Carolina 201*c*
Waterbury, David **691–692**
Waters, Daniel **692–693**
Watson, Fort 204*c*, 205*c*
Watson-Wentworth, Charles 4*c*, 366, 367, 565, **693–694**
Watt (ship) 541
Waxhaws Creek, South Carolina 179*c*, 289
Wayne, Anthony **694–696**, *695*
    Monmouth, Battle of 135*c*, 694
    Bull's Ferry, New Jersey 183*c*
    Richard Butler and 297–298
    Battle of Germantown 112*c*, 113*c*
    Green Spring, Virginia 212*c*
    Monmouth, Battle of 135*c*, 694
    Mount Kemble, New Jersey mutiny 194*c*
    Paoli, Pennsylvania 111*c*
    Quintin's Bridge, New Jersey 126*c*
    Stony Point 159*c*–160*c*
    Trois-Rivières, Canada 61*c*
Webster, James 202*c*
Weedon, George 219*c*, **696**
Wemyss, James 191*c*, 192*c*
West Canada Creek 222*c*
West Florida 379
West Indies
    Nicholas Biddle 276–277
    John Byron and 301
    Henry Clinton 127*c*
    Charles-Hector-Théodat, comte d'Estaing 145*c*, 147*c*, 358, 359
    Rodney George 198*c*
    James Grant 397
    François-Joseph Paul, comte de Grasse 224*c*, 225*c*
    Samuel Nicholson 542
    George Rodney 606–607
    Spain 642
    Pierre-André de Suffren de Saint-Tropez 651–652
    John Vaughan 676
Wetzell's Mill, North Carolina 201*c*
Wheatley, Phillis 54*c*, **696–697**
Whipple, Abraham 56*c*, 128*c*, 161*c*, 170*c*, 174*c*, 312, **697–699**, *698*
White, Hugh 279
White Horse Tavern 108*c*
Whitemarsh, Pennsylvania 343
White Plains, Battle of 79*c*, 442, 505, **699–700**
Wickes, Lambert 68*c*, 97*c*, 112*c*, **700–701**
Wilkes, John 519, **701–702**
Willett, Marinus 102*c*, 103*c*, 222*c*, 615, 616, *702*, **702–703**
William and Mary, Fort 21*c*
Williams, John F. **703–704**
Williams, Otho H. 201*c*, 205*c*, **704–706**, *705*
Williamsburg, Virginia 211*c*–212*c*
Williamson, Andrew 68*c*, 69*c*, 72*c*, 74*c*
Williamson, David 226*c*
Williamson's Plantation, South Carolina 182*c*
Wilson, James 18*c*, 53*c*, **706–707**
Winston, Joseph **707–708**
women
    Abigail Adams 241–242
    Margaret Corbin 81*c*, 333–334
    Lydia Darragh 120*c*, 343–344, 510
    Sybil Ludington 495
    Jane McCrea 100*c*, 503–504
    Betsy Ross 96*c*, 608–609
    Deborah Sampson 561, 618–619
    Margaret Shippen 134*c*, 154*c*, 260, 630–631
    Nancy Ward 68*c*, 682–683
    Mercy Otis Warren 685–686
Woodford, William 46*c*–48*c*, **708–709**
Wooster, David 58*c*, 93*c*, **709–710**
Wyandot Indians 226*c*
Wyoming Valley Massacre 296–297, 299–300

X
XYZ affair 389, 572

Y
Yarmouth, HMS (ship) 276–277
Yorktown, siege of 219*c*–221*c*, **711–712**, 733*m*
    Charles Armand 255
    Henry Clinton 321
    Charles Cornwallis 219*c*, 221*c*, 337, 338, 711–712
    Elias Dayton 346
    Guillaume de Deux-Ponts 349–350
    Mathieu Dumas 354
    events leading to 218*c*
    George Germain 386
    François-Joseph-Paul, comte de Grasse 218*c*, 398, 711
    Thomas Graves 401
    Alexander Hamilton 220*c*, 414
    Henry Knox 464
    James Lafayette 470
    marquis de Lafayette 472, 711
    Benjamin Lincoln 221*c*, 711, 712
    Allan McLane 510
    Louis-Marie, comte de Noailles 544
    Frederick North 546
    Charles O'Hara 550
    Timothy Pickering 569
    Jean-Baptiste-Donatien de Vimeur, comte de Rochambeau 214*c*–215*c*, 221*c*, 605, 711, 712
    Alexander Scammel 621
    John G. Simcoe 634
    Spain 642
    George Washington 214*c*–215*c*, 218*c*, 219*c*, 221*c*, 688–689, 711, 712
    Anthony Wayne 695
    George Weedon 696
Yorktown, Virginia 213*c*